Africa
on a shoestring

Geoff Crowther

Africa on a Shoestring
5th edition

Published by
Lonely Planet Publications
Head Office: PO Box 617, Hawthorn, Victoria 3122, Australia
US Office: PO Box 2001A, Berkeley, CA 94702, USA

Printed by
Singapore National Printers Ltd, Singapore

Cover illustration by
Joanne Ryan

First Published
November 1977 (Africa on the Cheap)

This Edition
August 1989

National Library of Australia Cataloguing in Publication Data

Crowther, Geoff, 1944 –
  Africa on a Shoestring

  5th ed.
  Includes index.
  ISBN 0 86442 053 6.

  1. Africa – Description and travel –
  1977- – Guidebooks. I. Title.

  916'.04328

Geoff Crowther

Born in Yorkshire, England, Geoff took to his heels early on in the search for the miraculous. The lure of the unknown took him to Kabul, Kathmandu and Lamu in the days before the overland bus companies began digging up the dirt along the tracks of Africa. His experiences led him to join the the the now legendary but sadly defunct alternative information centre BIT in the late '60s.

In 1977, he wrote his first guide for Lonely Planet – *Africa on the Cheap*. He has also written *South America on a Shoestring*, travel survival kits to *Korea* and *East Africa* and has co-authored LP's guides to *India*, *Malaysia*, *Singapore & Brunei*, and the new *Morocco*, *Algeria & Tunisia*.

After travelling extensively, Geoff and Hyung Pun have recently discovered the joys of family life with baby Ashley. They expect to move out of a banana shed and into the house that Geoff (et al) built somewhere in the wilds of northern New South Wales. Geoff continues to pursue noxious weeds and brew mango wine.

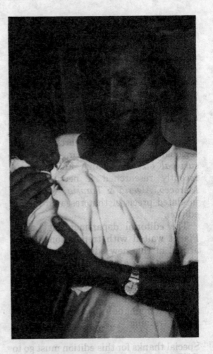

From the Author

The feedback on the last two editions of this book has been nothing short of miraculous and I'm extremely grateful to everyone who took the time and trouble to write. As always the major credit for a new edition of this long-running book must go to those travellers, though there were times when the sheer volume of material threatened to overwhelm not only my capacity to deal with it but also the physical constraints of my workplace.

It's taken a monumental effort to put together this new edition. It would be no exaggeration to say that it has topped the 1000 letter mark! But don't let that dissuade you from writing. All travellers see and experience things differently and it's those differences which allow us to cross-reference and make informed statements on issues of contention.

It's impossible to produce a flawless

guidebook to a continent like Africa. With such a diverse range of peoples, cultures and climate it's a land where nothing stays the same for very long. A coup, a devaluation, a civil war, a drought, even less dramatic events, can render information in any guidebook obsolete overnight; so bear this in mind if you find that things have changed.

Judging from the feedback, those who complained that the last book didn't contain enough information were equally matched by those who groaned about the burden. One of the most amusing comments about the last edition was from the Kenyan resident who spotted the howler on the cover and wrote: '*Mzee*, sitting here in Lamu – one of your favourite spots – reading *Africa on a Shoestring*. Good book, man, but why the fuck did you put an Indian elephant on the back cover? Say *Jambo* to Oz for me.'

Sorry, mate, not guilty. Maybe LP's Art Department need longer holidays!

Well this time, apart from the historical and political reviews at the beginning of each chapter, virtually the entire book has been rewritten, new sections added, a major effort at cross-reference undertaken and some 150 new maps drawn. It's resulted in a very substantial improvement on the 1986 edition.

I spent most of 1986 researching a new regional book *East Africa – a travel survival kit*; and Hugh Finlay and I recently researched a new book on *Morocco, Algeria & Tunisia*. You'll find up-dated précis of that research in this edition.

The editorial department at Lonely Planet waited with trepidation for the arrival of this new edition having been warned it was a mutant monster. It's a fine line to tread, but we have tried to keep things lean. To those weight-conscious travellers who abhor large books all I can say is now might be a good time to take up weight training!

Special thanks for this edition must go to Jes Ford and Alison Lescure (UK), Jan King and Tom Harriman (USA), and Keith Richmond (UK) for their many precise and detailed letters which helped enormously. My old friends, John and Jane Ridge, presently teaching in Botswana, helped a great deal in re-writing and up-dating that country and keeping me informed. LP author Hugh Finlay (Aus), kindly agreed to re-write Algeria and Tunisia and contribute to Morocco despite having other urgent work to complete. I also must thank Marie Jack (Aus) and Choe Hyung Pun (Aus) for helping in the preparation of many of the new maps.

A good deal of the donkey-work and grind of extracting and collating info from travellers' letters and adding it to the text was undertaken by Margaret Moult (Aus) and Nell Steptoe (Aus) and I'm very grateful for their enthusiasm.

On the high-tech side, I'd like to thank Jim Hart and Tony Wheeler of LP for keeping me supplied with working computers – writing this book wore out no less than two computers!

Finally, I'd like to thank George Pavlu (Aus), author of *Diogenes – An Anecdotal Biography of the World's Greatest Cynic*, for his explosively funny and hyper-enthusiastic visits which breathed renewed enthusiasm into the completion of this book.

Special thanks go to all the travellers who wrote in; they are listed at the back of the book.

Lonely Planet Credits

Editors	Sue Mitra
	Tom Smallman
Design &	Trudi Canavan
illustrations	
Typesetting	Ann Jeffree

Thanks also to: Hugh Finlay and Brenda Hannigan for copy editing; and again to Hugh for organising the 25-cm-high printout and 20 disks when they arrived at LP; Tricia Giles and Gaylene Miller for additional typesetting; Laurie Fullerton, Lyn McGaur, Lindy Cameron, Debbie Rossdale, Katie Cody, James Lyon, Debbie Lustig and Michelle de Kretzer for proofreading and corrections; Sharon Wertheim for indexing; Sue Tan for coping with the readers' letters; and to Graham Imeson for monitoring the percentage increase. Gold stars to Tom for surviving the mammoth task of co-editing this, his first book for LP and for ensuring the political histories were as current as possible; and to Trudi who was not only on her first book, but was solely responsible for the design, paste-up, illustrations, map bromiding, and photocopying of the 1150-odd pages that follow.

Contents

For the technically-minded, this is the second edition of *Africa on a Shoestring* to be written on a solar-powered computer using a Kaypro 4 microprocessor, eight Solarex X100GT solar panels, a Santech 1000 watt inverter and 12 ex-Telecom 2v 500AH lead-acid batteries. It all worked perfectly except during four weeks of continuous rain and floods in 1988 when I had to recharge the batteries with a generator and battery charger.

A Warning & a Request

Things change – prices go up, schedules change, good places go bad and bad places go bankrupt – nothing stays the same. So if you find things better or worse, recently opened or long since closed, please write and tell us and help make the next edition better!

Your letters will be used to help update future editions and, where possible, important changes will also be included as a Stop Press section in reprints.

All information is greatly appreciated and the best letters will receive a free copy of the next edition, or any other Lonely Planet book of your choice.

Introduction

This vast and diverse continent of 53 countries stretching from the shores of the Mediterranean to the Cape of Good Hope and encompassing the world's largest desert and one of its most extensive rainforests is the adventurer's last frontier. Whether it's the stunning wastes of the Sahara Desert with its barren mountains, the inspiring beauty of snow-capped Kilimanjaro rising sheer from the East African plateau, the lush, mist-covered volcanoes and lakes of Kenya's Rift Valley, colourful tribal peoples, or the lure of ancient Egypt, this continent has them all.

Perhaps nowhere in the world will you find such a variety of cultures, vistas, contrasts and contradictions, cities ancient and modern, and certainly not the sheer numbers of big game which still roam the plains of this fascinating land.

Now regarded as the 'birthplace of humanity' as a result of the Leakey excavations in East Africa, Africa was also home to one of the cradles of civilisation. Pharaonic Egypt was to wax and wane over 5000 years until finally eclipsed by the rise of the Roman Empire. The monuments that the ancient Egyptians left are among the wonders of the world and the ideas which they developed strongly influenced other civilisations.

Later, Christianity was to take hold of northern Africa until swept aside by the armies of Islam in the 8th century AD. Islam itself was to produce some of its greatest cultural achievements on African soil. Cairo was, for many centuries, the cultural and political centre of the Islamic world.

Elsewhere on the continent, highly skilled and organised civilisations, empires and kingdoms flourished and foundered particularly in West Africa and southern Africa and not even the advent of the European maritime nations and the slave trade to the Americas, has succeeded in destroying completely the legacy of the past. Likewise on the east coast, there remains the fascinating legacy of the Shirazi/Omani coastal trading cities. What traveller to Africa would not want to visit Zanzibar? Yet Lamu is even more exotic and still totally unspoiled.

It would be irresponsible to suggest that all African countries now enjoy political and social stability. There has been a considerable reduction in the endless round of political turmoil despite continuing conflicts in the Western Sahara, Sudan, Chad, Namibia/Angola, Mozambique and South Africa. You need to keep an eye on the newspapers, your wits together, your eyes and ears open and your mouth in check. Do that, and you're in for the adventure of a lifetime. This is no package tour. It requires determination, patience, stamina and a respect for the local custom. There's one thing you can be certain of in Africa there's never a dull moment!

Always remember one thing: respect other peoples' customs and sensibilities and regardless of their politics, religion or whatever else is going down, you'll always have a friend. Hospitality is a synonym for Africa. This continent has a great deal to teach and offer to the other races of the world. Treat it and them with respect.

Africa offers the largest game reserves in the world. Considering the pressures of population expansion, it is nothing short of miraculous that the governments of the countries concerned have chosen to maintain these sanctuaries and to spend scarce resources to pay for the wardens to keep poaching to a minimum.

All things considered, there is no other continent even vaguely comparable to Africa. It offers you everything you could possibly conceive of. Go there and experience it.

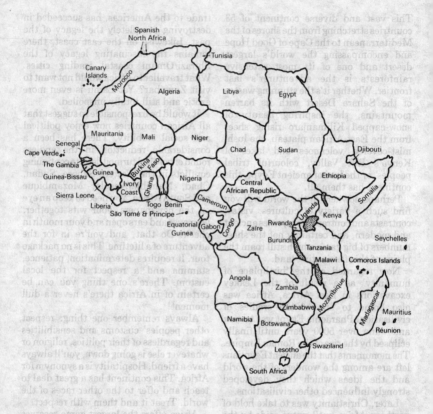

Spanish North Africa
Tunisia
Canary Islands
Morocco
Algeria
Libya
Egypt
Mauritania
Mali
Niger
Chad
Sudan
Djibouti
Senegal
Cape Verde
The Gambia
Guinea-Bissau
Guinea
Burkina Faso
Ghana
Nigeria
Central African Republic
Ethiopia
Somalia
Sierra Leone
Ivory Coast
Togo
Benin
Cameroun
Liberia
São Tomé & Príncipe
Equatorial Guinea
Gabon
Congo
Zaïre
Rwanda
Burundi
Uganda
Kenya
Tanzania
Seychelles
Malawi
Comoros Islands
Angola
Zambia
Mozambique
Madagascar
Mauritius
Réunion
Namibia
Zimbabwe
Botswana
Lesotho
Swaziland
South Africa

Facts for the Visitor

PAPERWORK

The essential documents are a passport and an International Vaccination Card. If you already have a passport, make sure it's valid for a reasonably long period of time and has plenty of blank pages on which stamp-happy immigration officials can do their stuff. If it's only a quarter full and you're thinking of spending a long time in Africa then it might be best to get a new one before you set off. Some countries demand that you register with police or immigration whenever you stay overnight in a town, in which case your passport will get filled rapidly with stamps. Getting a new passport not only takes time but can be expensive since it usually involves a telex to your home country and you'll be paying the charges.

If you're British then get one of the 94-page 'jumbo' passports. USA nationals can have extension pages stapled into otherwise full passports at any of their embassies. This facility is also available to UK and other Commonwealth country passport holders at British embassies in various countries such as the Central African Republic. Extensions cost about US$2.50.

Make a photostat copy of the first few pages of your passport before you leave and keep it in a separate place. It could well speed up replacement in case of loss or theft.

An up-to-date vaccination card is equally essential. They're usually provided by whoever supplies you with your vaccinations. Some countries refuse admission to travellers without a current card or insist that you have the necessary vaccinations there and then.

If you're taking your own transport or thinking of hiring a vehicle to tour certain national parks, get hold of an International Driving Permit before you set off. Any national motoring organisation will fix

you up with this provided you have a valid driving licence for your own country. The cost of these permits is generally about US$5.

An International Student Identity Card or the graduate equivalent is also very useful in many places and can save you a small fortune in some countries. Some of the concessions available include airline tickets, train and river boat fares and free or reduced entry charges to museums and archaeological sites. If you're not strictly entitled to a student card, it's often possible to get one if you book a flight with one of the 'bucket shop' ticket agencies that have proliferated in certain European and North American cities. (The deal usually is that you buy an airline ticket from one of them and they'll provide you with a student card.) Another possibility is to buy a fake card (average price around US$10). There always seems to be someone selling these wherever travellers collect in numbers, but examine them carefully before buying as they vary a great deal in quality. It's also a good idea to have the institution which issues you with the card provide you with a letter on headed paper confirming that you are a student there.

Another useful thing to have is a Youth Hostels membership card, particularly if you're going to Egypt, Kenya, Morocco, Namibia, South Africa, Tunisia or Zimbabwe, all of which have a network of youth hostels.

All the concessions which are possible with an International Student Card or a Youth Hostel membership card are mentioned in the appropriate chapters.

VISAS

Visas are a stamp in your passport permitting you to enter a country and stay there for a specified period of time. They are obtained from the embassy or consulate of the appropriate country either before you set off or along the way. It's best to get them along the way, especially if your travel plans are not fixed, but keep your ear to the ground regarding the best places to get them. Two different consulates of the same country may have completely different requirements before they will issue a visa. The fee may be different; one consulate might want to see how much money you have whereas another won't ask; one might demand an onward ticket while another won't even mention it; one might issue visas while you wait and another insist on referring the application back to the capital (which can take weeks). Whatever you do, don't turn up at a border without a visa (where required) unless you're absolutely sure you can get one at the border. If you do this you'll find yourself tramping back to the nearest consulate and, in some countries, this can be a long way.

You'll occasionally come across some tedious, petty power freak at an embassy or consulate whose sole pleasure in life appears to be making as big a nuisance of himself/herself as possible and causing you the maximum amount of delay. If you bite the carrot and display your anger or frustration, the visa will take twice as long to issue or they'll refuse to issue one at all. There's one of these creeps born every minute, but if you want that visa then keep your cool. Pretend you have all day to waste and that your patience is infinite.

Consular officials sometimes refuse pointblank to stamp a visa on anything other than a completely blank page, so make sure your passport has plenty of them.

Some countries – Zaïre is the main one – demand that you produce a 'letter of recommendation' from your own embassy before they will issue a visa. This is generally no problem as your embassy will be aware of this, but you may sometimes have to pay for it. British embassies make

you pay through the nose for these letters.

If you plan on going to Libya you must have the first few pages of your passport translated into Arabic before you apply for a visa. You can have this done either at your embassy in Tunis or before you leave at the passport office in your own country.

Another important fact to bear in mind about visas is the sheer cost of them. Very few are free and some are outrageously expensive. Regardless of what passport you carry, you're going to need quite a lot of visas, and if you're on a tight budget they can eat into your funds in an alarming way. It's a good idea to make a rough calculation of what the visa fees are going to amount to before you set off, and allow for it.

Make sure you have plenty of passport-size photographs for visa applications. Twenty four should give you a good start. Others can be obtained along the way.

Some countries, it seems, are so suspicious about your motives for wanting to go there that they demand you have a ticket out of the country before they will let you in. So long as you intend to leave from the same place you arrived at, there is no problem, but if you want to enter at one point and leave from another, this can sometimes be a headache. Fortunately, not too many African countries demand that you have an onward ticket. Ex-Portuguese and Spanish colonies, South Africa, Zimbabwe and sometimes Niger are the main exceptions but there are ways of getting round this requirement.

It's generally no great problem so long as officials will accept a return bus or rail ticket since these are usually cheap. Where they won't, your options are limited and you're looking at either an airline ticket or what is known as 'sufficient funds'.

The days when an MCO (Miscellaneous Charges Order) for, say, US$100 from an international airline used to be acceptable in lieu of a specific ticket are over. Most budget travellers have to rely on buying the cheapest ticket available out of the country and then refunding it later on. If you do this, make sure you can get a refund without having to wait months for it. Don't forget to ask specifically where you can get the refund (some airlines will only refund tickets at the office where you bought them; some only at their head office). It isn't a particularly good thing to do for entry into Zimbabwe or South Africa as immigration officials usually stamp the ticket nonrefundable. The only other way to avoid this requirement is to have plenty of money (cash or travellers' cheques or both) and/or a major international credit card. It's assumed that if you have US$500 to US$1000 in your possession (or access to it) then you have enough to pay for your return to your own country and the ticket requirement can be waived.

Most African countries take a strong line against South Africa to the point of refusing entry to South African nationals. They are also not keen on people whose passports show that they have visited South Africa. If that's the case they may refuse entry. As a rule, the only area where you might run into problems is in southern Africa. Zambia and Tanzania are the most prominent examples – the latter exceptionally so. Tanzanian immigration officials will often refuse entry if they even suspect – with or without proof – that you have been to South Africa. A Botswana, Lesotho, Mozambique, Swaziland or Zimbabwe entry stamp obtained on any of these countries' borders with South Africa is sufficient proof that you have been to the latter and will guarantee you refusal. Zambian officials are much less strident about this. There are no such problems entering any of the countries which actually border South Africa.

Likewise the Arab countries of North Africa (except Egypt) refuse entry to Israeli nationals and to anyone with Israeli stamps in their passport. Some countries, like Sudan, have got this down to a fine art and will refuse you a visa even if your passport has no Israeli stamps in it but has Egyptian stamps issued at the Egyptian side of the Egyptian-Israeli border. So if you do visit Israel from Egypt and then want to go through Africa, you may as well throw your passport away and buy a new one. But don't do it in Cairo. The Sudanese Embassy in Cairo won't accept new passports issued in Egypt! One last point to bear in mind about visas is that certain countries take a long time to issue them or impose conditions which make it hardly worth the while. Angola, Libya and São Tomé e Principe are the main ones but Nigeria and Gabon can also be difficult. The usual obstacles to overcome are referral of your application to the capital (which may only be a few days but which can be weeks) or demands for references within the country (often impossible). These sort of obstacles are usually a function of the stability – or lack of it – of the country in question and the situation changes constantly.

In order to balance what has already been said, it should be mentioned that most visas are easily obtained without fuss. You simply fill in the necessary forms, hand over your photographs and the appropriate fee and collect your passport the same day or 24 to 48 hours later. It's just that with a total of 55 countries, visas assume an importance in Africa which they don't elsewhere in the world.

MONEY
Which Currency?
However much money you decide on, take a mixture of UK£ sterling, French francs and US dollars. French francs are the preferred currency in the Francophone countries (mainly West and Central Africa) and you'll get a much better rate of exchange for them than you would if you only had UK£ sterling or US dollars. On the other hand, the UK£ sterling and US dollars are the preferred currencies in Anglophone countries and western-oriented countries such as those on the west coast, southern Africa, Kenya and

Zaïre. If you take currencies other than these three you'll find it difficult, if not impossible, to find out the exact exchange rate on any particular day except in capital cities.

Travellers' Cheques, Cash & Credit Cards

For the maximum flexibility take the bulk of your money as travellers' cheques and the rest in cash – say up to US$500. American Express, Thomas Cook and First National City Bank cheques are the most widely used and they offer – in most cases – instant replacement in the event of loss or theft. Keep a record of the cheque numbers and the original bill of sale for the cheques in a safe place in case you lose them. Replacement is a whole lot quicker if you can produce this information. Even so, if you don't look clean and tidy, or they don't believe your story for some reason or another, replacement can take time because quite a few travellers have been selling their cheques on the street market (black market) or simply pretending to lose them and then demanding a replacement set. This is particularly so with American Express cheques. You should avoid buying cheques from small banks which only have a few overseas branches, as you'll find them very difficult if not impossible to change in many places.

Make sure you buy a good range of denominations when you get the cheques – US$10, US$20 and US$50s (or the equivalent in UK£ or francs). The reason for this is that if you have too many large bills you may find yourself having to change, say, US$50 in a country that you're only going to stay in for a day or two, and end up with a wad of excess local currency which you can only reconvert at a relatively poor rate or not at all.

Having a credit card and a personal chequebook is another way of having secure funds to hand. With these you can generally withdraw up to US$50 in cash and US$500 (sometimes US$1000) in travellers' cheques per week from any

branch of the credit card company. This way you can avoid having to carry large wads of travellers' cheques. If you don't have a personal chequebook but you do have a credit card there's usually no problem. Simply present your card and ask for a counter-cheque.

American Express, Diners Club, Visa and Mastercard are all widely recognised credit cards. Another which has been brought to our attention is the National Westminster card. This is particularly useful in Anglophone countries where they have many branches. Credit cards also have their uses where 'sufficient funds' are demanded by immigration officials before they will allow you to enter a country. It's generally accepted that you have 'sufficient funds' if you have a credit card.

Exchange Rates

You cannot always change travellers' cheques in small places or when the banks are closed. (They can often be changed outside of bank hours at large hotels but the commission charged at such places is often extortionate.) It can also be extortionate at banks in certain countries, especially Rwanda. There's also the time consumed changing travellers' cheques to be taken into account. In some places – Zaïre, in particular – it can take hours. These are two reasons why you should bring some cash with you.

The major reason for bringing cash with you, however, is that it allows you to take advantage of any difference between the street rate of exchange (otherwise known by the racially suspect term of the 'black market') and that offered by the banks. Sometimes you can change travellers' cheques on the black market but this isn't always the case.

There are many countries in Africa where you can get considerably more for your 'hard' currency on the streets or in shops and hotels than you can in the banks. In some cases the difference is little short of spectacular. Algeria, Ghana,

Guinea-Bissau, Mozambique, Tanzania and Uganda fall into this category. Ethiopia, Nigeria, Sudan and Zimbabwe are less spectacular examples. If you don't take advantage of this then you are going to find many countries very expensive. Conversely, if you do, they'll be relatively cheap.

Some people regard the black market as morally reprehensible. It's certainly predatory and it contributes to the corruption which plagues many African countries. It is, however, a fact of life and its bases are many – greed, insecurity, unrealistic economic and/or political policies, unsupportable external debt and civil war, to name a few. Nevertheless, some countries overvalue their currency to such a degree that it is nothing short of Mickey Mouse. Whether you take advantage of it or not is your decision but there is no point in pretending that it does not exist and the fact is that most travellers do take advantage of it.

In some countries the black market is wide open and there appear to be few constraints on it by the authorities. In most, however, caution and discretion are the name of the game. Being caught unofficially changing money in many African countries can be a serious matter.

Wherever a black market exists, there are always plenty of touts offering to do it right there on the street. The conspiratorial half-whisper, 'Change money?' will be one of your most enduring memories of a visit to Africa. The honesty or good intentions of these touts covers a minefield of opinion and everyone has a story to tell. Most of them are 'runners' for someone else and work on a commission basis. The less they can get you to accept, the more they make. But they're not out to totally rip you off. There are others, however, who are definitely out to either rip you off or turn you in to the police (for a price, of course). The trouble is, it's very difficult to decide which category they belong to unless you've been there for a

while or you've met another traveller who changed with them without problems.

Whatever else you do, if you decide to change on the street, make sure you have the exact amount you want to change available. Don't pull out large wads of notes. Be very wary about sleight of hand and envelope tricks. Insist on counting out personally the notes that are handed to you. Don't let anyone do this for you and don't hand over your money until you're satisfied you have the exact amount agreed to. If at any point you hand the notes back to the dealer (because of some discrepancy, for example) count them out again when they're handed back to you. If you don't you'll probably find that all but the smallest notes have been removed. Some operators are so sharp they'd have the shoes off your feet while you were tying up the laces. Don't allow yourself to be distracted by supposed alarms like 'police' and 'danger'. If that happens, give them back their money, keep yours and get moving.

You can avoid this sort of melodrama in most places by approaching shopkeepers selling imported products (TVs, radios, fabrics, motor spares, etc) or expatriates. Not only will you usually get a better rate of exchange than on the street but you can do it in relative safety. They have even less desire than you have to be arrested. And they don't want any fuss so you won't be short changed. It's remarkable how many employees of national tourist organisations offer top rates of exchange in congenial surroundings.

The authorities of countries where this takes place are, naturally, not unaware of what is going on and various schemes have been put into operation to either contain it or even kill it. To kill it, the country concerned has to float the currency – usually against the US dollar. The IMF is usually involved in this sort of operation. But the economic, political and social consequences *can* be hazardous if not disastrous. Zambia and Zaïre are two recent examples of countries which have virtually killed the black market by this means. A safer method has been to have two official exchange rates – a lower one for international transactions (including the purchase of international airline tickets) and a higher one for tourists. The latter is generally a lot nearer to, if not equal to, the black market rate. Egypt is an example. Uganda tried it under Obote but it didn't work. Another way is to force incoming tourists to change a certain amount of money at the official rate of exchange – usually much more than budget travellers would need. Algeria and Uganda are two current examples. Egypt used to do the same but has since abolished this requirement.

Yet another scheme is to have a mixed programme. Tourists are hit for 'hard' currency to pay for entry to national parks and expensive hotels but allowed to pay for meals and transport in local currency. Tanzania is a prime example of this.

Regardless of what schemes are brought in to combat the black market, nothing changes faster in Africa than prices and exchange rates. As far as this book is concerned, you must treat all these things as a guide only. Some countries devalue by 1000% overnight so your best guide to prices and exchange rates are your fellow travellers along the way.

Lastly, if you're setting off from Europe, note that the Credit Suisse bank at Kloten Airport in Zurich, Switzerland, will change all paper money from any country in the world at very reasonable rates and they will also issue paper money in all currencies. Their rate for the Algerian dinar, for example, is about the same as the black market rate inside Algeria.

Currency Declaration Forms

Many African countries issue currency declaration forms on arrival. You must write down how much cash and travellers' cheques you are bringing into the country. Some countries check these very thoroughly when you leave and if there are any discrepancies you're in the soup. Others couldn't care less. Whatever the case, if you intend using the black market inside the country, you must declare less than you are bringing in and hide the excess.

A million schemes have been invented over the years to 'doctor' such forms ranging from children's 'John Bull' printing outfits, to having rubber bank stamp replicas made up, to buying local currency at lower 'black market' rates in exchange for having the currency form stamped so that it looks official. It isn't worth it. Keep it simple. There are easier ways of doing things than messing about with currency forms.

More details about the forms can be found in the appropriate country chapters.

Currency Unions

Currency in Africa is less complicated than 55 different political entities might suggest. Most of the Francophone countries belong to the Communauté Financielle Africaine and use the same unit of currency – the CFA franc. In theory, the CFA francs of one country have the same value as those of another and should be freely interchangeable, but the Communauté seems to have split into two blocks these days. The first block consists of Benin, Burkina Faso, Guinea, Ivory Coast, Mali, Senegal and Togo whose bank notes bear the logo 'Banque Centrale des Etats de l'Afrique de l'Ouest'. The second block consists of Cameroun, Central African Republic, Chad, Congo, Equatorial Guinea, Gabon and Niger whose bank notes bear the logo 'Banque des Etats de l'Afrique Centrale'. When you go from one zone to another, you'll have to change your CFA into those of the other block and there will be a commission to pay.

What hasn't changed is that both types of CFA are pegged to the French franc at the constant rate of CFA 50 equal to one franc. CFAs are, therefore, 'hard' currency and there should be no commission charged for converting French bank notes into CFA bank notes.

In southern Africa, there's a similar situation in operation where the currencies of Botswana, Lesotho and Swaziland are tied to the South African rand. They may have a different name and usually attract an exchange commission in South African banks but they are essentially the same.

Carrying Money

There is no 'safe' way to keep your money whilst you're travelling, but the best place is in contact with your skin where, hopefully, you'll be aware of an alien hand before your money disappears. One method is to wear a leather pouch hung around your neck and kept under cover of a shirt or dress. If you do this, incorporate a length of old guitar string into the thong which goes around your neck (the D string should be thick enough). Many thieves carry scissors but few carry wire cutters. Another method is to sew an invisible pocket onto the inside of your trousers. Others prefer a money-belt. Ideally your passport should be in the same place but this isn't always possible as some are either too thick or too stiff. Wherever you decide to put your money, it's a good idea to enclose it in a plastic bag. Under a hot sun that pouch or pocket will get soaked with sweat – repeatedly – and your cash or cheques will end up looking like they've been through the launderette.

If you run out of money whilst you're abroad and need more, ask your bank back home to send a draft to you (assuming you have money in an account there). Make sure you specify the city and the bank branch. Transferred by cable, money should reach you within a few days. If you correspond by mail the process will take at least two weeks, often longer. Remember that some countries will only give you your money in local currency. Others will let you have it in US dollars or UK£ sterling. Francophone countries will usually let you have it in French francs. Find out what is possible before you request a transfer otherwise you could lose a fair amount of money if

there's an appreciable difference between the official and unofficial exchange rates.

If you have taken your entire worldly assets with you and can't lay your hands on another penny, then you have very few options. It's possible to get a job in some places but don't count on it. The one thing you can do is go to your embassy and get repatriated. If you have to do this, many embassies take your passport away from you and you won't get it back until you repay the debt – and they'll fly you back at full-fare economy rates.

The process can be long and drawn out if you are a USA citizen. First you have to give them a list of all the people in the USA who might be willing to help you get back home but, as soon as you do this, you have to accept accommodation and meals in a 1st class hotel. They pay for the communications with the people you have listed but, if no-one is capable or willing to help you get back home, then you're not only up for that bill but for the flight home plus 9½% interest (or whatever the Federal Reserve Bank is charging at that time) on the whole lot. And you have six months to repay. In other words, it can take a long time. You can't just get a ticket home like that.

COSTS

It's very difficult to make predictions about what a trip to Africa is going to cost since so many factors are involved. How fast do you want to travel? What degree of comfort do you consider to be acceptable, where there's a choice? How much sight-seeing do you want to do? Do you intend to hire a vehicle to explore a game park or rely on other tourists to give you a lift? Are you going to be travelling alone or in a group? Will you be changing money on the street or in banks? And a host of other things. There's only one thing which remains the same in Africa and that's the pace of change. It's fast and things like inflation and devaluations can wreak havoc with your travel plans if you're on a very tight budget.

To generalise, you should budget for at least US$10 per day in the cheaper countries and US$20 in the more expensive ones. This should cover the cost of very basic accommodation, food in local cafés and the cheapest possible transport. It won't include the cost of getting to Africa, safaris in game parks or major purchases in markets. In some countries such as Gabon, Ivory Coast, Nigeria and Rwanda you may well find yourself spending considerably more than US$20 per day. On the other hand, if you stay in one place for a long time and cook your own food you can reduce costs considerably since you won't be paying for transport and you'll get a better deal on the cost of accommodation.

BARGAINING

In many countries bargaining for something that you want is a way of life. This includes hotels, transport, food, cigarettes, etc, but the prices of basic commodities are settled within minutes. Commodities are looked on as being worth what their owners can get for them. The concept of a fixed price would invoke laughter. If you cop out and pay the first price asked, you'll not only be considered a half-wit but you'll be doing your fellow travellers a disservice since this will create the impression that all travellers are willing to pay outrageous prices (and all are equally as stupid). You are expected to bargain. It's part of the fun of going to Africa. All the same, no matter how good you are at it, you'll never get things as cheaply as local people do. To traders, hotel and café owners you represent wealth – whatever your appearance – and it's of little consequence that you consider yourself to be a 'traveller' rather than a 'tourist'. In the eyes of a trader, you're the latter.

Bargaining is conducted in a friendly and, sometimes, spirited, manner though there are occasions when it degenerates into a bleak exchange of numbers and leaden head-shakes. Some sellers will actually start off at a price 350% to 400% higher than what they are prepared to accept though it's usually lower than this. Decide what you want to pay or what others have told you they've paid, and start off at about half of this. The vendor will often laugh heartily or even feign outrage but the price will quickly drop to a more realistic level. When it does, you start making somewhat better offers. Eventually you arrive at a mutually acceptable price. For larger purchases in souks, bazaars and markets, especially in Muslim countries, you may well be served tea as part of the bargaining ritual. Accepting it places you under no obligation to buy. It's just social lubrication.

There will be times when you simply cannot get a shopkeeper to lower the price to anywhere near what you know the product should be selling for. This probably means that a lot of tourists are passing through and if you don't pay those outrageous prices, some mug on an overland tour bus or package tour will. There's no call for losing your temper when bargaining. If you get fed up or it seems a waste of time, politely take your leave. You can always try again the next day. This is one way of getting something at a price which approximates to what local people pay.

TAKING YOUR OWN VEHICLE & CARNETS

A *carnet de passage* (sometimes known as a *triptyque*) is required for the majority of countries in Africa with the exception of Morocco, Algeria and Tunisia. You also don't need to prearrange them for most West African countries. Documentation can be arranged at the Niger or Mali borders. At the Niger border they'll charge you CFA 5500 per month and the documents will cover you for all CFA countries.

The purpose of a carnet is to allow an individual to take a vehicle into a country where duties would normally be payable without the necessity of having to pay those duties. It's a document which guarantees that if a vehicle is taken into a country but not exported, then the organisation which issued it will accept responsibility for payment of import duties. Carnets can only be issued by one of the national motoring organisations (in the UK, this is the AA or RAC; in Australia, the AAA), and before they will issue such a document they have to be absolutely sure that if the need to pay duties ever arises they would be reimbursed by the individual to whom the document is issued.

The amount of import duty can vary considerably but generally speaking, it's between one and 1½ times the new value of the vehicle. There are exceptions to this where duty can be as high as three times the new value.

The motoring organisation will calculate the highest duty payable of all the countries that you intend to visit and arrive at what is known as an 'indemnity figure'. This amount must be guaranteed to the motoring organisation by the individual before carnet documents are issued. The indemnity or guarantee can be of two types:

(i) Banks can provide the indemnity but they require an equal amount of cash or other collateral to be deposited with them.
(ii) An insurance company will put up the necessary bond in return for a nonrefundable premium. In the UK, for AA carnets, the premium required is calculated at 3% of the indemnity figure subject to a minimum premium of UK£25. Indemnity figures in excess of UK£5000 qualify for a slightly lower premium. For RAC carnets, the premium is calculated at 10% of the indemnity figure though half of this is refunded when the carnet is eventually discharged.

If duties ever become payable – for example, if you take the vehicle into a country but don't export it again – the

authorities of that country will demand payment of duties from the motoring organisation. It, in turn, would surrender the indemnity it was holding. If this were a bank indemnity then the bankers would hand over the deposit they were holding. In the case of an insurance company, they would have to settle the claim. In the case of the latter the insurance company has the right of recovery from an individual of the amount it has had to pay out. It is possible to take out a double indemnity with some insurance companies whereby they'll not only make funds available for the issue of the carnet but will also waive the right of recovery from an individual. If you want this kind of cover, the premium is exactly double that normally required.

To get a carnet you first need to make an application to one of the motoring organisations. They will issue you an indemnity form for completion either by a bank or an insurance company. Once this is completed and a bond deposited with a bank or a premium paid to an insurance company, the motoring organisation issues a carnet. The carnets themselves cost approximately UK£20. The whole process takes about a week to complete.

Important Points about Carnets

(a) Insurance companies designate certain countries as 'war zones' and no insurance company will insure against the risks of war. This means that for such countries the only options are to get a carnet with a bank deposit or go without a carnet and make transit arrangements at the border.
(b) If you intend to sell the vehicle at some point, arrangements have to made with the customs people for the carnet entry to be cancelled. This means surrendering the vehicle into a customs compound from which it will not be released until duties have been paid by the prospective buyer. In some places (eg Niamey, Niger) the buyer has to bribe a minister before a vehicle can change hands. It's fairly easy to sell a car in Ouagadougou (Burkina Faso) but you must sell it within three

days of arrival, otherwise you run into complications. It's legal to sell cars in Togo, Benin and the Ivory Coast without going through customs but the price you get for it will be correspondingly lower. Generally, the older a car, the less duty is payable and therefore the easier it is to sell but no-one is going to want a heap of rubbish. In Bamako (Mali) cars under five years old carry prohibitive duty.

(c) Indemnity insurance is issued for a minimum period of one year. You cannot get a reduction in premium or a refund for shorter trips.

(d) Though you don't need a carnet to take a foreign registered vehicle into Algeria, if you have to abandon it in the desert, you'll be up for import duties which are twice the new value of the car. And they won't let you out of the country until you pay. You might think this is unfair since you haven't sold the car. Tough luck! As far as customs is concerned, you've sold it, and they are not prepared to go out into the desert to confirm that it had to be abandoned. Your only option around having to pay the import duties is either to get it going again or have it towed in. The latter would cost a fortune.

The road between Tamanrasset and the Algeria-Niger border is littered with abandoned cars so you won't be the first. The moral of the story is simple. Make sure what you are driving is in top mechanical condition before you set off. Carry spares and be able to fix it if anything goes wrong.

The addresses of various motoring organisations are:

France
Automobile Club de France, 6 Place de la Concorde, Paris 8e (tel 265 3470)
West Germany
ADAC, 11 Konigstrasse, Munchen
ADAC, Bundersalle 9-30, Berlin 31
UK
Automobile Association, Overseas Operations Department, Leicester Square, London WC1

Royal Automobile Club, PO Box 92, Croydon CR9 6HN (tel 01-686 2314)

These organisations can be very fussy if you're a foreign national or have a vehicle with foreign registration plates. Some of them insist that you must first be a member of one of your own national motoring organisations before they'll issue a carnet. In Germany you also need to have good references.

Insurance

Legislation about compulsory third-party insurance varies considerably from one country to another. In some places it isn't even compulsory. Where it is, you generally have to buy the insurance on the border but the liability limits on these policies is often absurdly low by western standards and if you have any bad accidents you could be in deep water. Also, you can only guess whether or not the premium is simply pocketed by the person collecting it or is actually passed on to the company. Perhaps this doesn't concern you, but if you want more realistic cover then you will have to arrange this before you leave.

If you're starting from the UK, the company that everyone recommends for insurance policies and for detailed information on carnets is Campbell Irvine Ltd, (tel 01 937 9407), 48 Earls Court Rd, London, W8 6EJ. The people who work here are not only very friendly and will give you personal attention, but they've been handling these kinds of enquiries for years and they know the business inside out. Most of the overland tour companies use them too. Write to them for a copy of their *Overland Insurance* leaflet or call round there and discuss it with them.

Taking a vehicle around Africa requires thorough preparation and is really outside the scope of this book. An excellent guide which discusses all aspects of this is *Sahara Handbook* by Simon & Jan Glen (Lascelles, London, 1987). Another which has been recently updated and doesn't confine itself to the Sahara is *Overland & Beyond* by Jon & Theresa Hewatt (Lascelles, London). In the German language a very good book is *Durch Afrika* by K & E Darr (Touring Club Suisse, Zurich, 1983).

Selling Cars in West Africa

For years now large numbers of French, German and Swiss travellers and small entrepreneurs have been buying second-hand cars in northern Europe, driving them across the Sahara Desert and selling them in West Africa. For most travellers this is a one-off affair, the object of which is to reduce the costs of an Africa trip, but there are quite a few people who do it full-time for a living by taking several cars at once on the back of a truck. It's still possible to make a reasonable profit on the transaction but don't expect too much by the time you've deleted expenses and the wear and tear which a car inevitably goes through when it's driven through the desert. You'll certainly still cover your costs (including the purchase price of the car).

There's a ready market for certain cars (Peugeot, Renault, Mercedes Benz) in Niger, Burkina Faso, Benin, Togo and the Ivory Coast, but selling a car in Niger involves a lot of paperwork. In Benin and Togo, on the other hand, all you have to do is register your name and that of the buyer in a book kept for the purpose at a local police station. Make sure it is decided before you sell the car, however, who is going to pay the appropriate fees to the police, the local authorities, customs and the commissioner. Generally, the seller only pays the last. The most sought-after cars are the Peugeot 504 (the 404 is somewhat dated) and Mercedes 280S (not the SE), but avoid injection engines. The vehicle should be at least three years old, though up to seven is acceptable. Left-hand drive and a speedometer calibrated in km per hour are necessary.

It's easy for non-German residents to get customs plates for the car (though if you buy a car in France and are a foreign national you may have insurance problems). The cars listed can be driven easily through the Sahara via the Route du Hoggar. Take spare tyres, jerry cans, tools, a couple of radiators, etc. Like the cars, all these accessories are easily sold either with the car or separately.

If you're going to be driving in Morocco, make sure you have a Green Card. The police there can fine you Dr 35 (over US$6) if you can't produce one.

Fuel Costs

These vary widely in West Africa and you can save a small fortune if you plan ahead. As we go to press, Ghana is cheapest, Benin next, then Togo. Ivory Coast is the most expensive. Use the following as a guide:

	regular		super		diesel	
Algeria	AD	2.70	AD	3.20	AD	0.80
Benin	CFA	170	CFA	175	CFA	132
Burkina Faso	CFA	272	CFA	285	CFA	240
Ghana			C	42		
Ivory Coast	CFA	325	CFA	350	CFA	255
Mali	CFA	300				
Morocco	Dr	5.40	Dr	6.12	Dr	3.52
Niger	CFA	255	CFA	280	CFA	190
Togo	CFA	200	CFA	205	CFA	180

SOMEONE TO TRAVEL WITH

Travelling overland is rarely a solo activity unless you want it that way. Even if you set off travelling alone, you'll quickly meet other travellers who are heading in the same direction, as well as others who are returning. This is especially true of the two main north-south routes from the Mediterranean to Central Africa – Algeria to Zaïre via Niger, Nigeria, Cameroun and CAR; and Egypt to Kenya via Sudan and Uganda. Crossroads where travellers congregate are also good places to meet other travellers and team up with someone. The best are Athens, Bangui, Cairo, Dar es Salaam, Harare, Kampala, Lomé, Nairobi, Niamey, Lamu, and any of the Moroccan cities.

If you'd prefer to find someone before you set off, check out the classified advertisements in national newspapers or the notice boards at colleges and universities before the summer holidays come up. If you're in London, UK, very good places to look are *Time Out*, *LAM* (London Alternative Magazine), *TNT* (previously *Australasian Express*) and the notice board at Trailfinders, 48 Earls Court Rd, London, W8. In New York, USA, try the New York Student Centre, (tel 212 695 0291), Hotel Empire, Broadway and 63rd St, or get hold of something like the *Village Voice*.

POST

Have letters sent to you c/o Poste Restante, GPO (PTT in Francophone countries), in whatever city or town you will be passing through. Alternatively, use the mail-holding service operated by American Express offices and their agents if you're a client (ie if you have their cheques or one of their credit cards). Most embassies no longer hold mail and will forward it to the nearest poste restante. Plan ahead. It can take up to two weeks for a letter to arrive even in capital cities, and it sometimes takes much longer in smaller places.

The majority of postes restantes are pretty reliable though there are a few exceptions. Cairo is one of the most notorious. Mail is generally held for four weeks – sometimes more, sometimes less – after which it is returned to the sender. The service is free in most places but in others, particularly Francophone countries there is a small charge for each letter collected. As a rule, you need your passport as proof of identity. In large places where there's a lot of traffic the letters are generally sorted into alphabetical order, but in smaller places they may all be lumped together in the one box. Sometimes you're allowed to sort through them yourself. In others, a post office employee will do the sorting for you.

If you're not receiving expected letters, ask them to check under every conceivable combination of your given name, surname, any other initials and even under 'M' (for Mr, Ms, Miss, Mrs). This sort of confusion isn't as widespread as many people believe, though most travellers have an improbable story to tell about it. If there is confusion, it's generally because of bad handwriting on the envelope or because the sorter's first language is not English, French or another European language. If you want to make absolutely sure that the fault won't be yours, have your friends address letters as follows:

BLOGGS Joe
Poste Restante,
GPO,
Nairobi,
Kenya

Make sure the surname is in block capitals.

Avoid sending bank notes through the post. They'll often be stolen by post office employees no matter how cleverly you disguise the contents. There are all sorts of ways of finding out whether a letter is worth opening up. Still, some people do get cash through the mail in this way.

When sending letters yourself, try to

use aerogrammes (air letters) rather than ordinary letters, but if you do send the latter make sure that the stamps are franked in front of you. If not, there's a fair chance they will be steamed off, re-sold and the letter thrown away.

There's little point in having any letter sent by express delivery (called special delivery in the UK), as they won't get there any quicker on average than an air letter.

HEALTH

Two useful books to read before you set off are *The Traveller's Health Guide* by Dr A C Turner (Lascelles, London) and *Preservation of Personal Health in Warm Climates* put out by the Ross Institute of Tropical Hygiene, Keppel St, London WC1. Another helpful book on health is David Werner's *Where There is No Doctor: a Village Health Care Handbook* published by Macmillan Press Ltd, London.

Equip yourself with as much useful health information as you can. Understand properly the use and dosages of all medications you are carrying. If you have vomiting, diarrhoea or dysentery it is very important to maintain a high level of liquid intake to avoid dehydration.

Vaccinations

Before you're allowed to enter most African countries you must have a valid International Vaccination Card as proof that you're not the carrier of some new and exotic plague. The essential vaccinations are cholera (valid for six months) and yellow fever (valid for 10 years). In addition, you're strongly advised to have vaccinations against typhoid (valid one year), tetanus (valid for five to 10 years), tuberculosis (valid for life) and polio (valid for life). Gamma globulin shots are also available for protection against infectious hepatitis (Type A) but they are ineffective against serum hepatitis (Type B). Depending on how much gamma globulin you receive, protection lasts three to six months. There is a vaccine

available for Type B but it's only recommended for individuals at high risk (medical personnel and people expecting to have sexual contact with local people). It's expensive, and the series of three injections takes six months to complete.

You need to plan ahead for these vaccinations, as they cannot all be given at once and typhoid requires a second injection about two or three weeks after the first. Cholera and typhoid jabs usually leave you with a stiff and sore arm for two days afterwards if you've never had them before. The others generally don't have any effect. Tetanus requires a course of three injections.

If your vaccination card expires whilst you're away, there are a number of medical centres in African cities where you can be re-vaccinated, often free of charge. The centres that we know of are listed in the respective country chapters.

Avoid turning up at borders with expired vaccination cards, as officials may insist on you having the relevant injection before they will let you in. The same needle is often used on a whole host of travellers without any sterilisation between jabs, so you stand a fair chance of contracting serum hepatitis and, perhaps, AIDS.

Your local physician will arrange a course of injections for you if you live outside a city. Most large cities have vaccination centres which you can find in the telephone book. Fees for injections vary from US$4 to US$9 depending on the vaccine.

You can get vaccinations from the following places:

Belgium
Ministère de la Santé Publique et de la Famille, Cité Administrative de l'Etat, Quartier de l'Esplanade, 1000 Brussels
Centre Médical du Ministère des Affaires Etrangères, 9 Rue Brederode, 1000 Brussels

France
Direction Départmentale d'Action Sanitaire et Sociale, 57 Boulevard de Sébastopol, 75001 Paris (tel 45 08 96 90)

Institut Pasteur, 25 Rue du Docteur Roux, 75015 Paris (tel 45 66 58 00)

Holland

Any GGD office or the Academical Medical Centre, Amsterdam.

Switzerland

L'Institut d'Hygiène, 2 Quai du Cheval Blanc, 1200 Geneva (tel 022-43 8075)

UK

Hospital for Tropical Diseases, 4 St Pancras Way, London, NW1 (tel 01-387 4411). Injections are free but they're often booked up about a month ahead.

West London Designated Vaccination Centre, 53 Great Cumberland Place, London W1 (tel 01-262 6456). No appointment is necessary – just turn up. The fees vary depending on the vaccine.

British Airways Immunisation Centre, Victoria Terminal, Buckingham Palace Rd, London, SW1 (tel 01-834 2323). Try to book a few days in advance otherwise you might have to wait around for a few hours before they can fit you in.

British Airways Medical Centre, Speedbird House, Heathrow Airport, Hounslow, Middlesex (tel 01-759 5511)

Medical Insurance

Get some! You may never need it, but if you do you'll be very glad that you have it. Only very rarely will you find a country where medical treatment is free. There are many different travel insurance policies available and any travel agent will be able to recommend one. The best thing to do before you choose one is to collect half a dozen different policies and read through them for an hour or two, as the cost of a policy and the sort of cover required can vary quite considerably. Many pitch themselves at the family package tour market and are not really appropriate for a long spell in Africa under your own steam. Usually medical insurance comes in a package which includes baggage insurance and life insurance, etc. You need to read through the baggage section carefully, as many policies put a ceiling on how much they are prepared to pay for individual items which are lost or stolen.

General Health

Get your teeth checked and treated if necessary before you set off. Dentists are few and far between in Africa, and treatment is expensive.

The main things which are likely to affect your general health whilst abroad are diet and climate. Cheap food bought in cafés and street stands tends to be overcooked, very starchy (mainly maize and millet) and lacking in protein, vitamins and calcium. Over a period of time the latter two, when combined with lack of exercise for your gums, can seriously affect the health of your teeth, so make sure you supplement your diet with milk or yogurt (where available and pasteurised) and fresh fruit or vitamin/mineral tablets. Avoid untreated milk and milk products – in many countries herds are not screened for brucellosis or tuberculosis. Peel all fruit. Read up on dietary requirements before you set off. And watch out for grit in rice and bread: a hard bite on the wrong thing can lead to a cracked tooth.

In hot climates you sweat a great deal and so lose a lot of water and salt. Make sure you drink sufficient liquid and have enough salt in your food to make good the losses (a teaspoon of salt per day is generally sufficient). If you don't make good the losses, you run the risk of suffering from heat exhaustion and cramps. Heat can also make you impatient and irritable. Try to take things at a slower pace. Hot, dry air will make your hair brittle, so oil it often with, say, refined coconut oil. Take great care of cuts, grazes and skin infections otherwise they tend to persist and get worse. If they're weeping, bandage them up. Open sores attract flies and there are plenty of those. Change bandages daily and use an antiseptic cream if necessary.

A temporary but troublesome skin condition which many people from temperate climates suffer from initially is prickly heat. Many tiny blisters form on one or more parts of your body – usually where the skin is thickest, such as your hands. They are sweat droplets which are trapped under your skin because your pores aren't large enough or haven't opened up sufficiently to cope with the greater volume of sweat. Anything which promotes sweating – exercise, tea, coffee, alcohol – makes it worse. Keep your skin aired and dry, reduce clothing to a loose-fitting minimum and keep out of direct sunlight. Calamine lotion or zinc oxide-based talcum powder help soothe the skin. Apart from that, there isn't much else you can do. The problem is one of acclimatisation and will go away in time.

Adjustment to the outlook, habits, social customs, etc, of different people can take a lot out of you too. Many travellers suffer from some degree of culture shock. This is particularly true if you fly direct from your own country to an African city. Under these conditions, heat can aggravate petty irritations which would pass unnoticed in a more temperate climate. Exhausting all-night, all-day bus journeys over bad roads don't help if you're feeling this way. Make sure you get enough sleep.

Drinking Water

Avoid drinking unboiled water anywhere that is not chlorinated unless you're taking it from a mountain spring. Unboiled water is a major source of diarrhoea and hepatitis, as are salads that have been washed in contaminated water and unpeeled fruit that has been handled by someone with one of these infections.

Avoiding contaminated water is easier said than done, especially in the desert and in parts of Zaïre, and it may be that you'll have to drink water no matter what source it comes from. This is part of travelling and there is no way you can eliminate all risks. Carrying a water bottle and a supply of water-purifying tablets is one way around this. Halazone, Potable Aqua and Sterotabs are all good for purifying water, but have little or no effect against amoebas or the hepatitis virus. For this you need a 2% tincture of iodine –

five drops per litre in clear water and 10 drops per litre in cloudy water. Wait 30 minutes and it's safe to drink though it will taste foul.

Malaria

This is caused by a blood parasite which is spread by certain species of night-flying mosquito (*anopheles*). Only the female insects spread the disease but you can contract it through a single bite from an insect carrying the parasite. Start on a course of antimalarial drugs before you set off and keep taking them as you travel. The drugs are fairly cheap in some countries but quite expensive in others (the USA and Scandinavia in particular).

There are basically two types: (i) proguanil (or paludrine) which you take once daily and (ii) chloroquine, which you take once or twice per week (depending on strength). Both are marketed under various trade names. In some areas of Africa the parasite is beginning to acquire immunity against some of the drugs. This is particularly true in East and Central Africa. Here you will need to take maloprim in addition to chloroquine. You would be very unlucky to contract malaria if you are taking one or more of these drugs but they are not a 100% guarantee. Talk to any American Peace Corps volunteer in Africa. Most of them have had at least one bout. Fortunately, pharmacology is one step ahead of the mutational capabilities of the malarial parasite – just – so a cure is available.

If you develop malarial symptoms – high fever, severe headaches, shivering – seek expert medical advice immediately. If you are not within reach of medical attention, the treatment (until you can get to a doctor) is one single dose of four tablets (600 mg) of chloroquine followed by two tablets (300 mg) six hours later and two tablets on each following day. As an alternative (or in chloroquine-resistant areas) take a single dose of three tablets of fansidar, but do not use fansidar as a prophylactic.

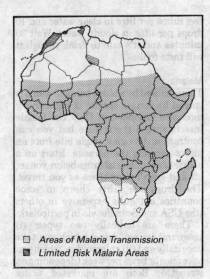

☒ *Areas of Malaria Transmission*
◼ *Limited Risk Malaria Areas*

Other than the malaria hazard, mosquito bites can be troublesome and although it's probably useless to say this, *don't scratch the bites*. If you do, and they don't heal quickly, there's a chance of them being infected with something else. You'll come across people in Africa pock-marked with angry sores which started out as insignificant mosquito bites whose owners couldn't resist the urge to scratch them. Don't join them. Will-power works wonders, as does antihistamine cream. Malaria-carrying mosquitoes only come out in the evening and at night. If you want to keep the mosquitoes away at night, use an insect repellent, mosquito coils or sleep under a mosquito net. Sleeping under a fan is a good idea as mosquitoes don't like swift-moving currents of air and will stay on the walls of the room in these circumstances.

No vaccination is possible against malaria – but work is in progress. Take those pills.

Bilharzia

This is caused by blood flukes (minute worms) which live in the veins of the bladder or the large intestine. The eggs which the adult worms produce are discharged in urine or faeces. If they reach water, they hatch out and enter the bodies of a certain species of freshwater snail where they multiply for four or more weeks and are then discharged into the surrounding water. If they are to live, they must find and invade the body of a human being where they develop, mate and then make their way to the veins of their choice. Here they start to lay eggs and the cycle repeats itself. The snail favours shallow water near the shores of lakes and streams and they are more abundant in water which is polluted by human excrement. Generally speaking, moving water contains less risk than stagnant water but you can never tell.

Bilharzia is quite a common disease in Africa. To avoid catching it, stay out of rivers and lakes. If you drink water from any of these places, boil it or sterilise it with chlorine tablets. The disease is painful and causes persistent and cumulative damage by repeated deposits of eggs. If you suspect you have it, seek medical advice as soon as possible – look for blood in your urine or faeces that isn't associated with diarrhoea. The only body of water in Africa which is largely free of bilharzia is Lake Malawi. Keep out of lakes Victoria, Tanganyika, Mobutu Sese Seko, Edward (Idi Amin) and Kivu and the rivers Congo, Nile and Zambezi. As the intermediate hosts (snails) live only in freshwater, there's no risk of catching bilharzia in the sea.

Trypanosomiasis (Sleeping Sickness)

This is another disease transmitted by biting insects, in this case by the tsetse fly. Like malaria, it's caused by minute parasites which live in the blood. The risk of infection is very small and confined to areas which are only a fraction of the total area inhabited by the tsetse fly. The flies are found only south of the Sahara but the disease is responsible for the absence of horses and cattle from large tracts of central Africa. The fly is about twice the size of a common housefly and recognisable from the scissor-like way it folds its wings while at rest. The disease is characterised by irregular fevers, abscesses, local oedema (puffy swellings caused by excess water retained in body tissues), inflammation of the glands and physical and mental lethargy. It responds well to treatment.

Yellow Fever

Yellow fever is endemic in much of Africa. Get that vaccination before you set off; then you won't have to worry about it.

Hepatitis

This is a liver disease caused by a virus. There are basically two types – infectious hepatitis (known as Type A) and serum hepatitis (known as Type B). The one you're most likely to contract is Type A. It's very contagious and you pick it up by drinking water, eating food or using cutlery or crockery that has been contaminated by an infected person. Foods to avoid are salads (unless you know they have been washed thoroughly in purified water) and unpeeled fruit that may have been handled by someone with dirty hands. It's also possible to pick it up by sharing a towel or toothbrush with an infected person.

An estimated 10% of the population of the third world are healthy carriers of Type B, but the only ways you can contract this form are by having sex with an infected person or by being injected with a needle which has previously been used on an infected person.

Symptoms appear 15 to 50 days after infection (generally around 25 days) and consist of fever, loss of appetite, nausea, depression, complete lack of energy and pains around the base of your rib cage. Your skin will turn progressively yellow and the whites of your eyes yellow to orange. The easiest way to keep an eye on the situation is to watch the colour of your eyes and urine. If you have hepatitis, the

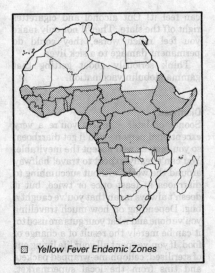

colour of your piss will be deep orange no matter how much liquid you've drunk. If you haven't drunk much liquid and/or you're sweating a lot, don't jump to conclusions. Check it out by drinking a lot of liquid all at once. If the urine is still orange then you'd better start making plans to go somewhere you won't mind convalescing for a few weeks. Sometimes the disease lasts only a few weeks and you only get a few really bad days, but it can last for months. If it does get really bad, cash in that medical insurance you took out and fly back home.

There is no cure as such for hepatitis except rest and good food. Diets high in B vitamins are said to help. Fat-free diets have gone out of medical fashion, but you may find that grease and oil make you feel nauseous for a long time. If that's the case, cut them out of your diet until you can handle them again. Seeking medical attention is probably a waste of time and money. There's nothing doctors can do for you that you can't do for yourself other than run tests that will tell you how bad it is. Most people don't need telling; they can feel it! Cut alcohol and cigarettes right off the slate. They'll not only make you feel much worse, they could do permanent damage to a sick liver.

Think seriously about getting that gamma globulin vaccination.

Diarrhoea

Sooner or later – unless you're a very exceptional person – you'll get diarrhoea, so you may as well accept the inevitable. You can't really expect to travel halfway around the world without succumbing to diarrhoea at least once or twice, but it doesn't always mean that you've caught a bug. Depending on how much travelling you've done and what your guts are used to, it can be merely the result of a change of food. If you've spent all your life living out of sterilised, cellophane-wrapped packets and tins from the local supermarket, you're going to have a hard time at first until you adjust.

There are lots of flies in Africa – flies which live on the various wastes produced by humans and other animals. In most places local people shit fairly indiscriminately wherever the urge takes them. Public toilet facilities are rare or nonexistent and that goes for sewage-treatment systems too. Some places are notorious for their open sewers and in very few of them is the connection ever made between food, flies and shit. This is the source of most gut infections which afflict both travellers and local people alike. The situation is changing – but slowly – and travellers are helping to spread the concept of hygiene in many places.

If and when you get a gut infection, avoid rushing off to the chemist and filling yourself with antibiotics. It's a harsh way to treat your system and you can build up a tolerance to them with overuse. Try to starve the bugs out first. Eat nothing and rest. Avoid travelling. Drink plenty of fluids. Have your tea without milk and add a small amount of sugar and dissolved salt to it. Diarrhoea will dehydrate you

and may result in painful muscular cramps in your guts. The cramps are due to a bad salt balance in your blood, hence the idea of taking a small amount of salt with your tea. Chewing a small pellet of opium or taking a tincture of opium (known as 'paregoric' and often mixed with kaolin – a stronger version of milk of magnesia) will also relieve the pain of cramps. Something else you may come across, called RD Sol, also helps to maintain a correct salt balance and so prevent cramps. It's a mixture of common salt, sodium bicarbonate, potassium chloride and dextrose, and although somewhat unpalatable itself, is OK when mixed with tea. Two days of this regime should clear you out.

If you simply can't hack starving, keep to a *light* diet of dry toast, dry biscuits and black tea. To keep up your liquids drink bottled soda water and flat lemonade – it is most important not to let your body dehydrate. Once you have started to make a recovery try some curd/yogurt. Stay away from butter, milk, cake and fruit.

If starving doesn't work or you really have to move on and can't rest for a couple of days, try Pesulin (or Pesulin-O which is the same but with the addition of a tincture of opium). Dosage is two teaspoons four times daily for five days. Or try Lomotil – the dosage is two tabs three times daily for two days.

If you have no luck with either of these, change to antibiotics or see a doctor. It may be necessary to have a stool test. There are many different varieties of antibiotics and you almost need to be a biochemist to know what the differences between them are. They include tetracycline, chlorostep, typhstrep, sulphatriad, streptomagma and thiazole.

If possible, have a word with the chemist about their differences. Avoid Enterovioform, which used to be sold widely in Europe and is next to useless for treating gut ailments in Africa. Anyway, it is now suspected of causing optic nerve damage. With antibiotics, keep to the correct dosage. Overuse will do you more harm than good.

There are several other treatments for diarrhoea. One is Pepto-Bismol liquid, 60 ml four times a day, it's effective, relatively safe and non-antibiotic but inconvenient to carry. Vibramycin (doxycycline), 200 mg on the first day of travel and 100 mg once per day for three weeks, is also effective but this antibiotic has several potential side effects. Bactrim DS or Septra DS (trimethoprimsulphamethoxazole), one tablet per day for two weeks, is also effective but again, it's an antibiotic.

Dysentery

This is, unfortunately, quite prevalent in some places. It's characterised by diarrhoea containing blood and lots of mucus and painful gut cramps. (Ah, travellers' toilet tales!) There are two types: (i) bacillary dysentery which is short, sharp and nasty but rarely persistent – the most common variety; (ii) amoebic dysentery which, as its name suggests, is caused by amoebic parasites. This variety is much more difficult to treat and often persistent.

Bacillic dysentery comes on suddenly and lays you out with fever, nausea, painful cramps and diarrhoea but, because it's caused by bacteria, responds well to antibiotics. Amoebic dysentery builds up more slowly but is more dangerous. You cannot starve it out and if it's untreated it will get worse and permanently damage your intestines. If you see blood in your faeces persistently over two or three days, seek medical attention as soon as possible.

Flagyl (metronidazole) is the most commonly prescribed drug for amoebic dysentery. The dosage is six tablets per day for five to seven days. Flagyl is both an antibiotic and an antiparasitic. It is also used for the treatment of giardiasis and trichomoniasis. Flagyl should not be taken by pregnant women. If you get bacillic dysentery, the best thing for slowing down intestinal movements is

codeine phosphate (30-mg tablets – take two once every four hours). It's much more effective than Lomotil or Imodium and cheaper. Treatment for bacillic dysentery consists of a course of tetracycline or bactrim (antibiotics).

If you get heavy 'rice-water' diarrhoea without pains (or almost without pains) then you could have caught a type of cholera – the vaccination you get is not totally effective. If this happens, the most important thing is to drink as much liquid as you can and take salt. Your urine should remain clear, not yellow or concentrated.

Giardia

This is prevalent in tropical climates and is characterised by swelling of the stomach, pale-coloured faeces, diarrhoea and, after a while, depression and sometimes nausea. Many doctors recommend Flagyl (a dosage of seven x 250 mg over a three-day period should clear up the symptoms, repeated a week later if not). Flagyl, however, has many side effects and some doctors prefer to treat giardiasis with Tinaba (tinadozole) (two grams taken all at once – this normally knocks it right out but if not you can repeat the dosage for up to three days).

Venereal Disease & AIDS

These diseases are prevalent in Africa to a degree unfamiliar with most western travellers. And, if you don't know how they are contracted, then you shouldn't be travelling. Gonorrhoea, syphilis and urethritis are easily cured these days – but don't delay! Herpes may or may not be curable. It's best to assume that it is not. The thing which causes most *angst* these days is AIDS. AIDS is a death sentence and will continue to be until a cure is found – and that may not be for a long time.

Known colloquially in East Africa as 'Slim', AIDS is prevalent in Burundi, Rwanda, Uganda and Zaïre but less so in Kenya and Tanzania. Nevertheless, it is spreading to many other countries. Most of those who have it are not aware of the fact and hospitals (if these people ever get to them) are likely to diagnose their symptoms as something more mundane. The obvious way to avoid the disease is to be celibate. Not everyone can – or is inclined to be. If you do have sex, cut the risk by using condoms. You are still a long way from 100% safe if you do this.

There are two other ways you can pick up AIDS. The first is if you need a blood transfusion. Blood donors in Africa are rarely, if ever, screened for AIDS. Your options are obviously limited if you get into this sort of strife. It is also possible to pick up the virus if you are injected with an unsterilised needle. If you need an injection in Africa make sure the needle is either new or properly sterilised.

Despite some scare reports in newspapers which depend on such copy to maintain sales, there is no evidence that mosquitoes are capable of transmitting AIDS.

Tropical Ulcers
These are sores which often start from some insignificant scratch or burst blister but they never seem to get better and they often get worse and spread to other areas of the body. They're also quite painful. If you keep clean and look after any sores which you get on your arms and legs (eg from ill-fitting shoes or accidents to your feet or from excessive scratching of insect bites) then it's unlikely you will be troubled by them. However, if you do develop sores which won't clear up then you need to hit the antibiotics quickly. Don't let them spread.

Fellow Travellers – of the insect variety
The main ones you're likely to come across are fleas, lice and bed bugs. There isn't a lot you can do about the first. They vary considerably in numbers from one season to another; some places have a lot, others none at all. The less money you pay for a bed or a meal, the more likely you are to encounter them. You can generally avoid

lice by washing yourself and your clothes frequently. You're most likely to pick them up in crowded places like buses and trains, but you might also get them by staying in very cheap hotels. You'll occasionally meet tribespeople whose hair is so matted and hasn't seen water for so long that it's literally crawling with lice. However, it takes a while for lice to get stuck into you so you should get a companion to have a look through your hair about once a week to see if you've acquired any eggs. They are always laid near the base of the hairs. If you find any you can either pick them out one by one (very laborious) or blitz them with insecticide shampoo like Lorexanne or Suleo. We've had letters from people who have doused their hair in petrol or DDT. You're certainly guaranteed total wipe-out this way but it does seem mildly hysterical and I dread to think what condition it leaves your hair and scalp in!

With luck you won't come across bed bugs too often. These evil little bastards live in the crevices of walls and the framework of beds where they hide during the day. They look like lice but they move like greased lightning once you become aware of their presence and switch on the light to see what's happening. Look for tell-tale bloodstains on the walls near beds in budget hotels. If you see them, find another hotel.

Don't Panic
This section might seem long and full of foreboding. It isn't meant to be. Most travellers arrive healthy and leave even healthier. If you do pick something up, however, it's useful to know what to do about it.

FILM & PHOTOGRAPHY
Many African countries have restrictions on what you can photograph. The main reasons for this are fear of espionage and mercenary-backed coups – all very real threats. Other reasons are more personal – religion, tribal myths, press image, etc.

In general, if you stay clear of taking pictures of anything connected with the armed forces, bridges, railway stations, post offices, radio/TV stations, prisons and port facilities then you will be OK. If in doubt – ask. And do the same before taking shots of people. Respect their right to privacy. Respect them as individuals. Many of these people have customs which totally contravene your own. Most Muslim women strongly resent having their photographs taken by strangers and you could get yourself into a lot of trouble by doing so without permission. The same goes for many tribal people especially the Masai of Kenya and Tanzania. Where people have been exposed to tourism for a long time, however, it's generally a question of negotiating a price.

This might strike you as nonsense or as an example of a people spoiled by tourism. Yet who is exploiting whom? You come through briefly with your expensive camera gear and an (apparently) endless supply of leisure time in search of local colour and then you're gone having contributed nothing to the local economy and, sometimes, not even spoken to anyone. They go back to their mud huts and a bowl of beans; you jump on a 747 and go back to the land of plenty. How would you feel if you were an 'extra' on a film project and didn't get paid?

It's a good idea to take all your film requirements with you including a set of replacement batteries for your camera. Only in Nairobi and South African cities will you find the same sort of choice available in photographic materials and services as you would expect in your own country. You may well be able to pick up colour negative film in many other large cities but it's usually limited to 100 ASA. You'd be very lucky to find 400 ASA. You certainly won't find slide film of any speed and, even in Nairobi, you'd be extremely lucky to find 800 or 1600 ASA (essential for photography in the jungle). Likewise, camera batteries are hard to find.

If you buy film in Africa, check the expiry date carefully and remember that most of it will not have been kept under refrigeration.

Wrap unexposed and exposed film in heavy-duty aluminium foil. It will help to prevent spoilage.

When leaving a country by air, think about those so-called 'film-safe' X-ray machines which you'll have to put your hand baggage through. They probably won't affect 100 or 200 ASA film but 400 and 800 ASA might be a different matter. Most security personnel are aware of this and will consent to personally examining your camera equipment without you having to put it through the X-ray machine. Tell them you have high speed film in your bag.

ACCOMMODATION

There are many different types of places where you can stay cheaply in Africa. They range from youth hostels in such countries as Egypt, Kenya, Morocco, South Africa, Tunisia and Zimbabwe, to religious missions in the Francophone countries, to government rest houses in such places as Malawi and Namibia and bath-houses (*hamman*) in Algeria. *Hamman* are for men only. The religious missions in the more visited places, however, are becoming less and less willing to take travellers unless they have purpose-built accommodation, but in the more remote areas you should still be able to find a welcome there. Where there are no youth hostels there are often youth centres which can offer floor space or a bed in a dormitory. Most of these places shouldn't cost you more than a few dollars a night – if that.

The next option is a cheap hotel. What you get depends largely on what you pay. If you're paying less than US$5 a single then, as likely as not, the hotel will double as a brothel. Even US$10 a single won't guarantee that the hotel isn't used for the same purposes in some places. Things like a fan, a private bathroom or a mosquito net, for example, will all bump up the price of a room. In cities and towns where there are distinct 'African' and so-called 'European' quarters (the latter are generally the parts of a city constructed initially by the colonial authorities), the cheapest hotels will be in the 'African' quarter. Hotels which you find in the 'European' quarter will generally be similar in quality to those you find in most western countries.

More and more African countries are setting up purpose-built camp sites, but where there are no such places you can always find a place to pitch a tent. In some countries you will be obliged (and it's common courtesy to do so) to first seek permission from the village elder or chief. A tent is also extremely useful if you're thinking of doing a lot of walking, climbing mountains or staying in the bush (especially in Zaïre). Never assume, however, that your gear is safe even at a camp site which is supposedly guarded 24 hours a day.

BOOKS
Guide Books
The following books are worth getting hold of if you need more detailed information about specific areas of Africa.

The *Sahara Handbook* by Simon & Jan Glen (Lascelles, London 1987) is the most comprehensive guide you can get for this part of Africa. It's certainly pitched at those taking their own vehicles, but almost half the book is taken up by very detailed descriptions of all the possible current routes through the Sahara. There are plenty of maps, illustrations and sketches. It's an excellent book which I recommend to anyone but, because it assumes you'll be sleeping and eating in your own metal box most of the time, it has little to suggest about where to stay and eat or the cost of transport of trucks and buses.

Durch Afrika by K & E Darr (Touring Club Suisse, Zurich 1983) is in German, and covers many routes through Africa. It concentrates on information for those taking their own vehicles.

Egypt & the Sudan – a travel survival kit by Scott Wayne (Lonely Planet, South Yarra, 1987). This is one of the new series of regional guides to Africa put out by Lonely Planet. I'd recommend it highly to any traveller who is thinking of spending a lot of time in Egypt. It's packed full of detailed information and peppered with excellent maps of all the places discussed.

East Africa – a travel survival kit by Geoff Crowther (Lonely Planet, South Yarra, 1987). This was the first of the new regional guides to Africa put out by Lonely Planet and covers Kenya, Uganda, Burundi, Rwanda, Tanzania, a thin sliver of Eastern Zaïre and the Comoros Islands. It's the book you need if you're going to be spending a long time in this part of Africa or want more detail than you will find in this book.

West Africa – a travel survival kit by Alex Newton (Lonely Planet, South Yarra, 1988). Written by someone who has lived and travelled in West Africa for many years, this book is a comprehensive guide to the area.

Central Africa – a travel survival kit by Alex Newton (Lonely Planet, Hawthorn, 1989). This is a thorough guide to the region.

Morocco, Algeria & Tunisia by Geoff Crowther & Hugh Finlay (Lonely Planet, Hawthorn, 1989). This is the most recent in the Lonely Planet series of regional guides to Africa.

Le Guide du Routard – Afrique Noire (Hachette, Paris, France, 1986). In French, this guide covers the West African countries of Benin, Burkina Faso, Cameroun, The Gambia, Ivory Coast, Mali, Mauritania, Niger, Nigeria, Senegal and Togo. While it may be good on essential information, places to stay and eat, it makes no attempt to price anything and maps are few.

Guide to Mount Kenya & Kilimanjaro ed Iain Allan (Mountain Club of Kenya, Nairobi, 1981). This guide was first published in 1959 and has gone through four editions and is heading for its fifth. As you might expect, being published by the MCK, it has been written and added to continuously over the years by dedicated enthusiasts who spend a large part of their free time doing nothing but exploring these two mountains. What isn't in this book isn't worth knowing. It contains minute descriptions of each trail (as well as sheer rock faces); good maps and photographs; descriptions of the fauna and flora, climate and geology; and even mountain medicine. It's also a very convenient size with a plastic cover. This guide is a must for anyone thinking of spending some time in Kenya or Tanzania. Pick up your copy from their HQ at Wilson Airport, Nairobi, or write to PO Box 45741, Nairobi.

Guide to the Ruwenzori Osmaston & Pasteur (West Col Productions, Reading, UK, 1974). Despite the publication date, this is still the best guide to the Ruwenzori available and should be an essential part of any trekker's baggage. It's a complete guide to routes with maps and sketches as well as details of climate, vegetation and history.

Atlas Mountains – Morocco by Robin G Collomb (West Col Productions, Reading, UK, 1980) is an essential guide for anyone intending to climb mountains in Morocco. It contains complete descriptions of most of the possible routes with maps and photographs.

The Guide to Lesotho David Ambrose (Winchester Press, Johannesburg and Maseru, 1976). David Ambrose is a mountain climber and trekker who has lived and worked in Lesotho since 1965. If the contents of the book are anything to go by, he knows this country like the back of his hand. Although written in the style of an 'official handbook' (and therefore containing a lot of detail of little use to travellers), his descriptions of various treks, climbing possibilities, sights worth seeing, the handicrafts, culture and history of the Basotho are excellent. There are also some stunning colour photographs

which, if you haven't already thought about visiting Lesotho, are certainly going to draw you to this beautiful country. Get hold of a copy as soon as you get to Maseru!

Periodicals

The best periodical for a very detailed political and economic analysis of every African country except Réunion, Spanish North Africa and BIOT, is *The Africa Review* (World of Information, 21 Gold St, Saffron Walden, Essex, UK). This is mainly an annual economic and business review by many different writers but it also covers political developments in considerable detail.

Africa Journal (Kirkman House, 54a Tottenham Court Rd, London W1P 0BT) is a monthly magazine that has been going for years. It covers in well-researched detail political, cultural and economic issues throughout Africa. It's essential reading for anyone with more than a passing interest in the continent. Available from bookshops and newsagents in London or by subscription.

West Africa (Graybourne House, 52-54 Gray's Inn Rd, London WC1X 8LT) is another monthly magazine similar to the *Africa Journal* but concentrates on West Africa. It's available on the same basis.

MAPS

The best maps of Africa are undoubtedly those published by Michelin. Buy these maps before you leave home! You won't find them in Africa. They are much more accurate and far more detailed than those put out by Bartholomew's. The Michelin African series consists of the following:

No 153   North West Africa
No 154   North East Africa
No 155   Southern Africa
No 169   Morocco
No 172   Algeria & Tunisia
No 175   Côte d'Ivoire

The last edition of No 153 was published in 1984 and is in need of revision, but political difficulties have so far prevented research being done. It's particularly inaccurate as regards the roads in Ghana. No 155 is also in need of revision.

If you can't get hold of Michelin maps, then Bartholomew's are adequate for most purposes but they do contain serious errors. Some of the worst errors are the marking of an 'A' class road where none exists or a thin red line where a fully sealed major highway exists. Tracks which they mark through the desert are largely a figment of the imagination. For small countries (especially Burundi, Rwanda, Lesotho and Swaziland) you needn't even bother opening them since the detail is nonexistent. Just don't use them as though they were a road map.

Good suppliers of maps are:

France
　Institut Géographie National, 17 Rue de la Boétie, Paris 16e (off the Champs Elysées)
UK
　Edward Stanford, 12-14 Long Acre, London WC2 (tel 01-836 1321)
　West Col Productions, 1 Meadow Close, Goring, Reading, Berks RG8 9AA. These people cater largely for climbers and they also have a good selection of trekking guides to the mountains of Africa.
　The French Map & Guide Centre, 122 Kings Cross Rd, London WC1 (tel 01-278 0896/7). This place specialises in Institut Géographie National maps of former French and Belgian colonies.

WHAT TO BRING

Take the minimum possible. An overweight bag will become a nightmare. A rucksack is preferable to an overnight bag since it will stand up to rougher treatment and doesn't screw up your posture by putting unequal weight on one side of your body. Choose a pack which will take some rough handling – overland travel destroys packs rapidly. Make sure the straps and buckles are well sewn on and strengthened if necessary before you set off. Whether you take a pack with or without a frame is up to you but there are some excellent packs

on the market with internal frames (eg Berghaus). Probably the best stockists in Britain are the YHA Adventure Centre, (tel 01 836 8541), 14 Southampton St, London WC2. Take a strong plastic bag with you that will completely enclose the pack. Use it on dusty journeys whether your pack is in the luggage compartment of a bus or strapped onto the roof. If you don't, you'll be shaking dust out of your pack for the next week.

A sleeping bag is more or less essential. It gets very cold in the desert at night and, if visiting mountainous areas, you'll need one there as well. You'll also be glad of it on long bus or train journeys as a supplement to the wooden seats or sacks of potatoes. A sheet sleeping bag – similar to the ones used in youth hostels – is also good when it is too hot to use a normal bag. It's cool and keeps the mosquitoes off your body.

Take clothes for both hot and cold climates, including at least one good sweater for use at night in the mountains and the desert. You needn't go overboard, however, and take everything in your wardrobe. Things like T-shirts, cotton shirts and sandals are very cheap in most places and it's usually more interesting and economical to buy these things along the way. In places like Tanzania people are prohibited from wearing clothes that reveal large areas of their body. This includes shorts, short skirts and see-through garments. Even flared trousers are frowned on. Much the same applies in Malawi where men must wear long trousers and women must wear skirts below the knee (except in resort areas).

It's inadvisable for women to wear anything short in Muslim countries, otherwise they'll be hassled endlessly by local men or youths. Most women in these countries are veiled from head to toe so if you go around with little on they will assume you are sexually available. Long skirts and a resilient nature can allay this kind of attention but doesn't guarantee success. On the other hand, being sexually hassled is by no means an exclusively female complaint.

Some people take a small tent and a portable stove. These can be very useful and save you a small fortune but they do add considerably to the weight of your pack. Many local people carry portable stoves around with them. If you take a stove make sure it's leakproof! The 'Gaz' stoves have been highly recommended by many travellers and the gas canisters are widely available throughout West Africa and even in Zaïre.

Don't forget the small essentials: a combination pocket knife or Swiss Army knife; needle and cotton and a small pair of scissors; pair of sunglasses; towel and tooth brushes; oral contraceptives (if used); tampons; a supply of antimalarial pills; and one or two good novels. Most toiletries – toilet paper, toothpaste, shaving cream, shampoo, etc – are available in all the capital cities and large towns. A water bottle (fabric covered) is very useful when it's hot or for walking in the mountains. It also enables you to give those dubious water holes a miss and so cut down your chances of getting hepatitis. The 'Gaz' Isotherm 1000 which comes in half, one and 1½ litre sizes has been recommended and is said to be surprisingly rugged. A torch is also very useful along with a replacement set of batteries.

LANGUAGE

The main languages are English, French, Portuguese, Arabic and Swahili, though there are many areas where other languages are widely spoken. Some of the other important languages include Hausa (parts of Nigeria, Niger, Burkina Faso and Mali), Shona and Ndebele (Zimbabwe), Afrikaans (South Africa and Namibia) and Amharic (Ethiopia). It is essential to have a working knowledge of English and French, and a smattering of Arabic and Swahili would repay over and over again the time spent learning it . Local people will always warm to any attempt you

make to speak their language no matter how botched the effort.

Arabic

Even if you don't have the time or inclination to learn Arabic, you need to be familiar with some of the numerals.

0	sifr
1	wahid
2	zouje (itneen in Egypt/Sudan)
3	talata
4	arba'a
5	hamsa
6	setta
7	seb'a
8	thimanya
9	tesa'a
10	ashara
11	hadashara
12	etnatashara
13	talathashara
14	arba'ashara
15	hamsashara
16	settashara
17	sabashara
18	thamania ashara
19	tisashara
20	ishrun (ishreen in Egypt/Sudan)
30	talat'in
40	arba'in
50	hamsin
60	set'in
70	sab'in
80	thaman'in
90	tis'in
100	mia
200	miat'in
1000	alef
2000	alfain
¼	rub
½	nus

Some Arabic words which you may find useful are:

yes	nam
no	ley

thank you	*shukran*
(response to thank you)	*afwan*
sir (polite form)	*mansour*
sir (very polite form)	*sidi*
madam (polite form)	*lalla*
greetings	*salaam al laikoum*
hello (Algerian form)	*labass*
river bed	*oued/wadi*
sand	*ramia (ramla in Egypt/Sudan)*
mountain	*djebel*
camel	*djemal*
market	*souk*
tea	*atai*
coffee	*kahoua*
bread	*khobz (eesh in Egypt/Sudan)*
water	*mey/ma*
how much?	*kem?*
knife	*mouse (sekan in Egypt/Sudan)*
fork	*mtaka*
spoon	*tobsi*

The pronunciation of Arabic is substantially different in Egypt and Sudan than it is elsewhere. Even between the two there are marked differences – eg camel is *gamal* in Egypt but *jamal* in Sudan.

Somali is the only Arabic-derived language to use Romanised script though Swahili – also Romanised – contains many Arabic words.

Hausa

Further south a knowledge of Hausa numbers would be useful.

1	*daya*
2	*biu*
3	*uku*
4	*hudu*
5	*biyar*
6	*shida*
7	*bakwai*
8	*takwas*
9	*tara*
10	*goma*
11	*gomashadaya*
12	*gomashabiu*
20	*ashirin*
21	*ashirindadaya*
22	*ashirindabiu*
23	*ashirindaoku*
24	*ashirindahudu*
30	*talatin*
100	*dari*

Some useful Hausa words include:

yes/OK	*toh*
no	*babu*
no/don't want it	*uhuh*
thank you	*nagode*
good	*da kyau*
greetings (very polite)	*ranka ya dade (ranki for women)*
greetings (universal)	*sannu (pl sanunku)*
welcome (polite)	*barka da zuwa/ sannu da zuwa*
welcome (colloquial)	*lafia/lafia lau*
reply to the above	*lafia*
expression of surprise	*haba/wallahi!*
expression of surprise or disgust	*khai!*
how much?	*nawa?*
don't want it	*shikenah*
is there tiredness?	*ina gajiya?*
no tiredness	*ba gajiya*
water	*ruwa*
hot	*zafi*
cold	*sanyi*
food	*abinchi*
rice	*shinkafa*
okra	*guro*
onions	*albasa*
cola nut	*goro*
meat	*nama*
eggs	*kwai*
fish	*kifi*
milk	*madara*
chicken	*dantsako*
camel	*rakumi*
salt	*gishiri*

man	*mutum*
woman	*mache*
house	*gida*
market	*kasuwa*
sick	*yi shiwo*
slowly	*sannu sannu*
quickly	*muza muza*
carefully	*hankali*
(come back) tomorrow	*sai gobe*
this/that	*wanne*

The Hausa greetings don't translate strictly into their English equivalents. *Ranka/ranki ya dade* means 'may your life be long' and is said to seniors or those deserving of respect. *Sannu* is the universal greeting and means 'gently'. The word *zuwa* in the 'welcome' phrase means 'arrival'.

Swahili

Swahili has become the lingua franca of Tanzania (though educated people still speak English). Much the same thing is happening in Kenya though the process there will be much slower since English is far more entrenched. Swahili is also useful in parts of Uganda and Eastern Zaïre. This is especially so in the rural areas where the local people may only have had a smattering of education or none at all and so are unlikely to be able to speak any English or French. The Comoran language is also derived from Swahili. Swahili is a composite language and still evolving. There are still no agreed words for many things though this is rapidly changing. An extremely useful pocket-sized phrasebook for travellers is Lonely Planet's *Swahili Phrasebook*.

Pronunciation of vowels is as follows:
a is like the 'a' sound in 'father'
e is like the 'e' sound in 'better'
i is like the 'ee' sound in 'bee'
o is like the 'a' sound in 'law'
u is like the 'oo' sound in 'too'

Double vowels, or any two vowels together, are pronounced as two separate syllables. Thus *saa* (time/hour) is pronounced 'sa-a', and *yai* is pronounced 'ya-i'. There are no diphthongs as in English.

Swahili is a prefixed language: adjectives change prefix according to the number and class of the noun. Thus *mzuri, wazuri, vizuri* and *kizuri* are different forms of the word 'good'. Verbs use a prefix noun:

I	*ni*
you	*u*
he/she	*a*
we	*tu*
you	*m*
they	*wa*

and a tense prefix:

present	*na*
past	*li*
future	*ta*
infinitive	*ku*

giving you:

We will go to Moshi.
   tutakwenda moshi
Can I take a picture?
   ninaweza kupiga picha?
Juma spoke much.
   juma alisema sana

Some useful words in Swahili:

hello*	*jambo* or *salamu*
welcome	*karibu*
thank you	*asante*
thanks very much	*asante sana*
How are you?	*habari?*
I'm fine, thanks.	*mzuri*
What's your name?	*jina lako nani?*
It is	*ninitwa ....*
How was the journey?	*habari ya safari?*
goodbye	*kwaheri*
yes	*ndiyo*
no	*hapana*
how much/ how many?	*ngapi?*

money	*pesa*
where?	*wapi?*
today	*leo*
tomorrow	*kesho*
guesthouse	*nyumba ya wageni*
toilet	*choo*
eat	*kula*
sleep	*lala*
want	*taka*
come from	*toka*
is	*ni*
there is	*kuna*
there isn't	*hakuna*
white people	*wazungu*
food	*chakula*
rice	*mchele*
bananas	*ndizi*
bread	*mkate*
vegetables	*mboga*
water	*maji*
salt	*chumvi*
meat	*nyama*
goat	*mbuzi*
beef	*ng'ombe*
chicken	*kuku*
fish	*samaki*
egg(s)	*(ma)yai*
milk	*maziwa*

*There is also a respectful greeting used for elders – *shikamoo*. The reply is *marahaba*.

Numbers in Swahili are:

1	*moja*
2	*mbili*
3	*tatu*
4	*nne*
5	*tano*
6	*sita*
7	*saba*
8	*nane*
9	*tisa*
10	*kumi*
11	*kumi na moja*
20	*ishirini*
30	*thelathini*
40	*arobaini*
50	*hamsini*
60	*sitini*
70	*sabini*
80	*themanini*
90	*tisini*
100	*mia*
½	*nusu*

Getting There

If you're setting out from Europe you have the choice of either flying to Africa or going overland to one of the Mediterranean ports from which you can get a ferry to North Africa. If you are departing from any other continent, you'll have to either fly first to Europe or fly direct to Africa. In most cases it's often cheaper to fly first to Europe and then make your way to Africa than it is to fly direct.

Trying to find a passage on a ship to Africa these days (except across the Mediterranean Sea) is virtually a waste of time. There are no regular passenger services and you won't get onto a freight ship without a mariner's ticket. And just in case that hoary old rumour about boats between India and Africa is still floating around: there are no passenger ships between India and Africa. They have not existed for years and you are wasting your time trying to find them. There are about four or five Arab dhows which do the journey between Zanzibar-Mombasa and Karachi-Bombay each year via Somalia, South Yemen and Oman, but they are extremely difficult to locate and to get onto to. The days of the dhows were numbered decades ago.

AIR

Before you go out and buy an airline ticket do some homework. There are a bewildering number of possibilities and, unfortunately, there's no magic key which will instantly reveal all about this market. What you end up paying for your ticket depends on many factors – how flexible you can be, your age, whether you want stopovers, how long you want to go for and what travel agents you have access to, to name a few.

Buying an ordinary economy-class ticket is not the most economical way to go, although it does give you maximum flexibility and the ticket is valid for 12 months.

Students and those under 26 years old can often get discounted tickets so it's worth checking first with a student travel bureau to see if there is anything on offer.

Another option is an APEX (advanced purchase excursion ticket) which is usually between 30% and 40% cheaper than the full economy fare although it does have restrictions. You must purchase your ticket at least 21 days in advance (sometimes more) and you must stay away for a minimum period (usually 14 days) and return within 180 days (sometimes less). The main disadvantage is that stopovers are not allowed and if you have to change your dates of travel or destination then there will be extra charges to pay.

Standby fares are another possibility. Some airlines will let you travel at the last minute if there are seats available just before departure. These tickets cost less than the economy fare but are usually not as cheap as APEX fares.

Of all the options, however, the cheapest way to go is via the so-called 'bucket shops'. These are travel agents who sell discounted tickets. Airlines only sell a certain percentage of their tickets through bucket shops so the availability of seats can vary widely, particularly in the high season. You have to be flexible with these tickets although if the agents are sold out for one flight they can generally offer you something similar in the near future.

Most of the bucket shops are reputable organisations but there is always the occasional fly-by-night operator who sets up shop, takes your money for a bargain-basement ticket and then either disappears or issues you with an invalid or unusable ticket. Check carefully what you are buying before you hand over the money. I've used bucket shops for years and been handed the most weird and wonderful tickets yet they've all been sweet.

Bucket shops generally advertise in newspapers and magazines. There's a lot of competition and different routes available so it's best to phone first then rush around if they have what you want. In Europe the market for these tickets to American and Asian destinations has been well developed over many years but little was available to African destinations south of the Sahara. This is changing quite rapidly and fares are becoming more flexible. The options to any destinations south of a line drawn from West Africa to Kenya, however, are still limited and fares are relatively high.

If you have to buy tickets in Africa to Europe, America or Asia then Nairobi is probably your best bet. There are plenty of bucket shops there and competition for business is stiff. Elsewhere, you'll be hard pressed to find such agencies, though a number of cheap charter flights are available from various West African countries such as Burkina Faso and The Gambia.

Between Africa and Australasia there are few options available as not many airlines fly between the two continents. Those that do are at full capacity most of the year so you're looking at full economy fares.

Remember that it is always cheaper to add on places to a long-haul ticket rather than buy a straight A to B ticket and then start all over again at the other end. Likewise, two one-way tickets are always more expensive than one return ticket.

From Europe

You can find bucket shops by the dozen in London, Paris, Amsterdam, Brussels, Frankfurt and a few other places as well. In London there are several magazines with lots of bucket shop ads which will give you a good idea of current fares. The best ones are:

Trailfinder

A magazine put out quarterly by Trailfinders (tel 01-603 1515 from 9 am to 6 pm Monday to Friday), 42-48 Earls Court Rd, London W8 6EJ. It's free if you pick it up in London but if you want it mailed it costs UK£6 for four issues in the UK or Eire and UK£10 or the equivalent for four issues in Europe or elsewhere in the world (airmail). Trailfinders can fix you up with all your ticketing requirements. They've been in business for years, their staff are very friendly and we recommend them highly.

Time Out

Timeout (tel 01-836 4411), Tower House, Southampton St, London WC2E 7HD, is London's weekly entertainment guide and it's available from all bookshops, newsagents and newsstands. Subscription enquiries should be addressed to Time Out Subs, Unit 8, Grove Ash, Bletchley, Milton Keynes MK1 1BZ, UK.

TNT Magazine

At 52 Earls Court Rd, London W8 (tel 01-937 3985), this is a free magazine which you can pick up from most London underground stations. The magazine is oriented towards Australians and New Zealanders living in the UK, but it has pages of travel advertising.

In these magazines you'll find discounted fares to Cairo, Nairobi, Dar es Salaam, Kilimanjaro, Harare, Johannesburg, Lagos, Accra, Banjul and a number of Moroccan cities but usually not to the Francophone countries. Most of them use Aeroflot and other Eastern European and Middle Eastern airlines. London to Nairobi, for example, can come as cheap as UK£190 one-way and UK£330 return. London to Cairo prices vary enormously. There are some great bargains so shop around. Fares to Moroccan destinations can be incredibly cheap if you're lucky enough to track down an agent who has spare seats on a charter flight – less than the cost of a one-way train fare in 2nd class between London and Edinburgh!

Likewise, there are very cheap charter flights between London and The Gambia. These can go for as little as UK£59 (but up to UK£180 depending on availability) for a two-week return ticket if you're willing to go at the last minute. The companies which operate these are Horizon, Blue Sky and Thompson. They run about twice weekly to Banjul. Most travel agents are very unhelpful about getting the tickets since commission is so low. You can discard the return half or sell it, though in the latter case you'll have to check the person who buys it into the airport.

Don't take the advertised fares as gospel truth. To comply with advertising laws in the UK, companies must be able to offer *some* tickets at their cheapest quoted price, but they might only have one or two of them each week. If you're not one of the lucky ones, you may find yourself looking at tickets which cost up to UK£50 or more (one-way or return). The best thing to do, therefore, is to start looking into tickets well before your intended departure date so you have a good idea of what is available.

A charter flight company which is popular with travellers in Europe is Nouvelles Frontières. They charter flights from Paris to various African destinations, but they have offices in various European countries. Their main contact addresses are:

74 Rue de la Fédération, 75015 Paris (tel 273 25 25)

66 Blvd Saint-Michel, 75006 Paris (tel 634 55 30)

83 Rue Sainte, 13007 Marseilles (tel 54 18 48)

21 Rue de la Violette, 1000 Brussels, Belgium (tel 511 80 13)

19 Rue de Berne, 1201 Geneva, Switzerland (tel (22) 32 04 03)

UTA is also worth checking out. It flies Paris/Niamey/Ouagadougou for US$650 return including a student discount for those under 26 years old. Tickets have a maximum validity of 60 days with fixed dates of departure and return.

If you are thinking of flying to Cairo, it's often considerably cheaper to take one of the budget buses advertised in various newspapers and magazines from various northern European cities to Athens and then buy an Athens/Cairo ticket in Athens. A one-way flight from Athens to Cairo with student discount or for those under 26 years old is around US$105.

From North America

In the USA, the best way to find cheap flights is by checking the Sunday travel sections in the major newspapers such as the *Los Angeles Times* or *San Francisco Examiner-Chronicle* on the west coast and the *New York Times* on the east coast. The student travel bureaus are also worth trying – STA or Council Travel.

North America is a relative newcomer to the bucket shop traditions of Europe and Asia, so ticket availability and the restrictions attached to them need to be weighed against what is on offer on the more normal APEX or full economy price tickets.

It may well be cheaper in the long run to fly first to London from the east coast of the USA using Virgin Atlantic (for around US$225 one-way and US$560 return), or standby on the other airlines for a little more, then buy a bucket shop ticket from there to Africa or go overland. But you must do your homework to be sure of this. All the main magazines which specialise in bucket shop advertisements in London will mail you copies so you can study current prices before you decide on a course of action.

From South America

Just about the only convenient flights between South America and Africa are those operated by Varig and South African Airways. These two share the Rio de Janeiro/Cape Town sector on alternate weeks (one flight per week). Tickets cost US$950 plus 25% sales tax if bought in Brazil or 13% tax if bought in Bolivia. The only way of avoiding the sales tax is to pay with a credit card.

From Asia

Flying is the only feasible way of getting between India or Pakistan and Africa. There are bucket shops of a sort in New Delhi, Bombay and Calcutta. In New Delhi, Tripsout Travel, 72/7 Tolstoy Lane behind the Government of India Tourist Office, Janpath, can be warmly recommended. It's very popular with travellers and has been in business for many years. As a guide to prices, a one-way Nairobi/Bombay ticket bought in Nairobi at a bucket shop costs around US$260. The most usual airlines are PIA (Pakistan International Airlines) and Air India.

From Australasia

Although there are no longer rigid constraints on ticket discounting in Australia, Australians and New Zealanders are at a distinct disadvantage as there are very few route options to Africa. Even less now that the Australian government has withdrawn permission for South African Airways to fly between Johannesburg and Perth. The only direct flight between Australia and Africa is Qantas' once-weekly Perth/Harare flight on which there are certainly no discounts as it flies at full capacity all year. For a one-way Sydney/Perth/Harare ticket you are looking at a minimum of A$1200.

It may well be cheaper to buy a ticket which routes you via Singapore since, from here, there are any number of options to Africa including via the islands of the Indian Ocean. Discuss your options with several travel agents before buying because many of them know virtually nothing about the cheapest routes to Africa.

It obviously makes sense for Australasians to think in terms of a round-the-world ticket or, from Australia or New Zealand to Europe a return ticket with stopovers in Asia and Africa. It shouldn't be too much trouble for a travel agent to put together a ticket, which includes various Asian stopovers plus a Nairobi stopover (at the very least). Round-the-world tickets with various stopovers can still be found for as little as A$1800. The best publications for finding good deals are the Saturday editions of the daily newspapers such as the *Sydney Morning Herald* and the Melbourne *Age*. Also, try the student travel agencies (STA), which have branches in all the state capitals.

OVERLAND

Europe is the only continent from which you can get overland to Africa and even this will involve a ferry crossing at some point.

Whether you're hitching, taking a bus or going by train across Europe, you should decide which of the two routes south through Africa you want to take – through the Sahara from Morocco or Algeria to West Africa, or down the Nile from Egypt to Uganda and Kenya. The reason for this is that the Egyptian-Libyan border is closed so you cannot swap routes once you get to North Africa, unless you fly from either Morocco, Algeria or Tunisia to Egypt. You must also bear in mind that if you choose the Nile route then you will only be able to get as far south as Khartoum due to the civil war in Sudan. From Khartoum you will have to fly to Uganda or Kenya. These flights will cost you only slightly less than those from Cairo.

You can of course, hitchhike free all the way through Europe to the Mediterranean (other than the cost of a ferry across the English Channel if starting from the UK) but this isn't necessarily the cheapest way of going because by the time you've paid for accommodation you might as well have bought a ticket on an express bus. There's a wide choice of buses available from places like London and Amsterdam as well as from other northern European cities. The cost of these is, however, creeping up to the point where, for another UK£25 or so, you could fly. Fares on these buses are: London to Athens UK£49/90 one-way/return and London to Madrid UK£52/96 one-way/return.

If all you want to do is hop across the channel and hitch from there, it's well worth taking the bus first to either Brussels (about UK£19.50) or Paris (about UK£21.50). If you are going to take one of these buses and are heading for Egypt then check out whether they also have coach-plane ticket deals to Cairo. If they have, it could be considerably cheaper than taking the bus followed by the ferry from an Italian port or from Athens to Egypt. Those long-haul ferries are no longer cheap.

If you want to make your own way through Europe or don't want to take an express bus and you're starting from London, you must first decide which of the cross-Channel ferries you are going to take. The most popular ones are from Dover to Zeebrugge, Ostend, Dunkirk, Calais and Boulogne; or from Folkestone to Ostend, Calais and Boulogne; or from Ramsgate to Dunkirk. If you're hitching to Athens, then Zeebrugge or Ostend would be the best places to go. If you're heading for southern Spain, one of the French ports would be best. There are several companies which operate the ferries (P&O, Townsend Thoresen, Sealink, Hoverspeed and Sally The Viking Line), and all but the last have many departures daily in either direction so there's no chance of you not being able to get on the day you want to go.

There are any number of different ways you can travel overland through Europe to end up in southern Spain, France, Italy or Greece. The choice is yours. Hitching is good in Belgium, Germany, Holland and northern Italy. In the other countries it tends to be slower, particularly in Spain. London to Athens should take four or five days; London to Marseilles two to three days (one if you're lucky); and London to Algeciras up to a week. The cheapest places to stay en route are the youth hostels but you need a Youth Hostels membership card to use them.

If you decide to hitch through Italy and then take a ferry across to Greece, there

are a number of possibilities. The main ones are:

R Line - Otranto to Corfu & Igoumenitsa Drive-on/drive-off car ferry. Daily departures in either direction between 13 June and 18 September and three times per week in either direction between 3 June and 12 June and between 19 September and 3 October (on Monday, Wednesday and Saturday from Otranto and Tuesday, Friday and Sunday from Igoumenitsa and Corfu). There are no ferries on this line during the rest of the year. The journey takes 8½ hours.

R Line - Brindisi to Corfu to Patras (Pátrai) Drive-on/drive-off car ferry. There are departures on alternate days in either direction. The journey takes 8½ hours and 19½ respectively. A bus meets the ferry on arrival at Patras and gets you to Athens in three hours.

Strintzis Lines SA - Brindisi to Corfu or Igoumenitsa & Patras Drive-on/drive-off car ferry. There are departures on alternate days in either direction.

Libra Maritime - Brindisi to Corfu or Igoumenitsa & Patras Drive-on/drive-off car ferries. There are daily departures in either direction daily except on Tuesdays from Brindisi and Mondays from Patras. Brindisi to Patras take 20 hours. A bus from Patras to Athens is available and takes three hours.

Fragoudakis Line - Brindisi to Corfu or Igoumenitsa & Patras Drive-on/drive-off car ferry. There are departures most days in either direction.

Adriatica Line/Hellenic Mediterranean Lines - Brindisi to Corfu or Igoumenitsa & Patras Drive-on/drive-off car ferry. There are daily departures in either direction throughout the summer months (less in winter).

There is also a ferry from Brindisi to Piraeus operated by Sol Maritime Services Ltd. It departs on Wednesdays from Brindisi and Tuesdays from Piraeus. The journey takes 22 hours. This ferry does not call at Patras.

If you're hitching down through Italy to

Sicily to catch the ferry from Trapani or Palermo to Tunis, there are ferries every 20 minutes in either direction across the Straits of Messina between Italy and Sicily. The ferries run day and night between Messina and Reggio di Calabria and Villa San Giovanni, and cost less than US$1.

Mediterranean Ferries

The last step to Africa is to take a ferry across the Mediterranean. The ferry you take will depend on which way you want to travel through Africa, but in order of cheapness they are: Spain to Morocco; Italy to Tunisia; Greece to Egypt and France to Algeria. A list of these ferries can be found in the next section.

If you're taking a car to either Algeria or Tunisia, the cheapest is the Tunisian Compagnie Tunisie de Navigation boat *Habib Bourguiba*, which goes Tunis, Genoa, Tunis, Marseilles, Tunis. Genoa to Tunis will cost around US$80 for the car plus US$90 per adult. It's cheaper on the Palermo or Trapani to Tunis car ferry, but the cost of driving down through Italy and the freeway fees will just about cancel out the advantages.

MEDITERRANEAN FERRIES

The following list starts from Spain and moves east to finish with Jordan (Red Sea). It's not an exhaustive list but includes all the ferries you are likely to use. Many of the ferries from Greece actually start from Venice but would, of course, be much more expensive from there.

Which ferry you want to take depends largely on where you want to travel and how much you want to pay. Obviously the shorter the route, the cheaper the fare, which makes the Spain to Morocco ferries the cheapest at around US$21 per person, US$90 for a large car or 4WD and around US$20 for a motorcycle.

Next are those from southern Italy to Tunis, the cheapest being from Trapani in Sicily which costs US$55 per person and around US$95 for a vehicle. A more convenient route may be the one from Genoa to Tunis (which costs US$105 per person and US$160 for a vehicle) as you don't have to drive right down through Italy.

There are direct ferries from France to Algeria but these are not that cheap at US$140 per person and US$300 for a vehicle from Marseilles to Algiers.

Another alternative is to go from Italy or Greece to Egypt, although these ferries are very infrequent (and possibly nonexistent) in winter.

Whichever route you want to take, *all* are heavily subscribed in the summer months and if you plan to take a vehicle across, it is imperative that you book well in advance, especially for the Tunisian and Algerian crossings. The situation is not quite as bad for Morocco as there are many more sailings.

Spain to Morocco

There's a whole variety of car ferries operated by Compania Transmediterranea and the Compagnie Marocain de Navigation. The most popular of these is the Algeciras to Tangier route but the others are Algeciras to Ceuta (Spanish North Africa), Almeria to Melilla (Spanish North Africa) and Malaga to Melilla. All ferries are of the drive-on/drive-off type.

There are also hydrofoil services between Tarifa and Tangier operated by Transtour, and a high-speed catamaran from Gibraltar to Tangier.

Algeciras to Tangier On this route there are a minimum of three daily departures in each direction. This rises to six in the peak season from the beginning of July to mid-September.

The crossing takes about 2½ hours and the minimum fares are Ptas 2550 or Dr 170. For a car up to six metres long it costs Ptas 11,200 or Dr 740 and a for a motorcycle it's Ptas 2400 or Dr 160.

Tarifa to Tangier The Transtour hydrofoil service operates daily as long as the weather isn't too rough and at only 30 minutes is by far the quickest way to make the crossing.

It leaves Tarifa at 9 am and returns from Tangier at 4.30 pm. The one-way fare is Ptas 2400, Dr 150 or UK£12.

Algeciras to Ceuta (Spanish North Africa)
This Compania Transmediterranea service operates in summer up to eight times daily, except Sunday when there are only three crossings.

The trip takes 1½ hours and the fare is Ptas 1100 or Dr 76 per person.

Almeria to Melilla (Spanish North Africa)
A three-times-weekly Compania Transmediterranea service, this crossing takes 6½ hours. Ferries leave Almeria on Tuesday, Thursday and Saturday at 2 pm, and from Melilla on Monday, Wednesday and Saturday at 11 pm. The fare is Ptas 2000 per person.

Malaga to Melilla (Spanish North Africa)
Also operated by Compania Transmediterranea, ferries leave Malaga on Monday, Wednesday and Friday at 1 pm, and from Melilla on Tuesday, Thursday and Saturday at 11.30 pm.

The journey time is 7½ hours and the fare is Ptas 2000 per person.

Gibraltar to Morocco
Gibraltar to Tangier The only services between the two places are a hydrofoil and a high-speed catamaran, neither of which take vehicles.

The Transtour hydrofoils operate daily, leaving Gibraltar at 4 pm and Tangier at 9.30 am. The trip takes one hour and costs Ptas 3115, Dr 180 or UK£15 per person.

The catamaran is operated by Gibline and there are up to three departures daily. The trip takes 75 minutes and the fare is UK£16.

Gibraltar to M'Diq This route is also operated by Gibline and at last report it was only on Thursdays, leaving Gibraltar

at 9 am and M'Diq at 4.30 pm. The fare is UK£16.

I've never actually heard of anyone entering Morocco this way but if it's possible, it would be a good way to avoid the touts at Tangier and the chaotic border south of Ceuta.

M'Diq is just north of Tetouan and there are regular buses between the two.

France to Morocco
Sète to Tangier This car ferry service is operated by the Compagnie Marocaine de Navigation and the crossing is made between five and eight times per month, depending on the season.

The trip takes 38 hours and the minimum fare is UK£90 or FFr 720 one-way, and a similar amount for a vehicle.

France to Algeria
The Compagnie Nationale Algerienne de Navigation (CNAN) operates regular services to Marseilles from Oran, Algiers, Bejaia, Skikda and Annaba, and to Sète from Oran.

In summer these services are heavily subscribed and if you intend bringing a vehicle across, make a reservation as far in advance as possible.

These are the most expensive of the Mediterranean ferries. Those to Morocco and Tunisia are cheaper.

Marseilles to Algiers This is the most popular (and therefore most crowded) route. In summer there are departures almost daily, but these drop to about two per week in winter. Fares from Algiers are AD 409/748 (FFr 730/1318) one-way/return per person, and about AD 1250 (FFr 2100) one-way for the average 4WD vehicle.

Marseilles to Oran Six sailings per month in summer dropping to weekly in winter. Fares are AD 461/832 for passengers and AD 1250 for a vehicle.

Marseilles to Bejaia Seven per month in summer, weekly or less in winter. Same fares as previous route.

Marseilles to Annaba Four per month in summer, twice monthly in winter, fares the same.

Marseilles to Skikda Three per month in summer, monthly in winter; same fares.

Sète to Oran One of the less crowded routes, but only three per month in summer, less in winter. Fares are the same as from Oran to Marseilles.

Spain to Algeria

There are regular sailings from the Spanish port of Alicante to Oran and Algiers. The port of Palma on the Balearic island of Majorca is also served by ferries from Algiers.

Alicante to Oran Eight sailings monthly in summer, two in winter. The economy-class fare is AD 270/474 (FFr 428/752) one-way/return per person. For a vehicle you are up for AD 942 (FFr 1600) one-way.

Alicante to Algiers Only two sailings per month in summer, nothing in winter; AD 325/596 one-way/return; AD 1058 for a vehicle.

Palma to Algiers This is another popular route. The boats stop in Palma and continue on to Marseilles. Four per month in summer, one in winter; fares are the same as Oran to Alicante.

Italy to Tunisia

There are frequent crossings throughout the year between Tunis and the Italian port of Trapani in Sicily. Some boats go on to (or start from) Cagliari in Sardinia and Genoa on the Italian riviera.

In summer they are heavily booked and if you are taking a vehicle it is essential that you book well in advance. If you are

on foot you can get on without a booking but it can be torrid.

The Sicilian and Sardinian service are operated by the Tirrenia Line (see Addresses further on).

Trapani to Tunis The service from Trapani is weekly, officially leaving at 9 am on Wednesdays, but you'll be lucky if it goes before midday. It arrives in Tunis at 4.30 pm and costs 65,000 lire (about US$55). In the other direction it departs Tunis at 8 pm on Wednesday and arrives in Trapani at 6 am on Thursday.

Cagliari to Tunis This run is actually a continuation of the Tunis to Trapani service. It leaves Cagliari (Sardinia) at 7 pm on Tuesday, and arrives back at 8 am Friday.

The fare for Cagliari to Tunis is about UK£40 per person.

Genoa to Tunis The Compagnie Tunisienne de Navigation (CTN) operates a boat regularly between Tunis and Genoa. Service varies between four per month in winter up to 11 per month in the height of the summer. The one-way fare is TD 47,000 (FFr 560) and the trip takes about 24 hours.

Catania to Tunis From Catania on the southern coast of Sicily, CTN operate a weekly car ferry service leaving Catania at 9 pm on Saturday, arriving in Tunis at 3 pm on Sunday.

Departure from Tunis is at 6 pm on Thursday, arriving back in Catania at 6 am on Saturday. This service goes via Valletta in Malta on the way back to Italy.

France to Tunisia

Marseilles to Tunis Also operated by CTN, this ferry service is packed in summer so vehicle owners will need to book ahead. They operate nine services per month in summer, four in winter; the trip takes 22 hours and the fare is TD 65,000.

Greece to Egypt

Piraeus to Alexandria Adriatica Line operates weekly services to Alexandria. The trip takes about 48 hours (with stops) and the minimum fare varies from UK£122 to UK£223, depending on the season. This service calls in at Heraklion in Crete en route, from where the trip to Alexandria takes 22 hours and costs from UK£88 to UK£167. The company usually offers discounts to holders of Youth Hostel cards, International Student Cards, Eurail and Eurail Youth Pass, so make sure you ask about these.

The starting point for this route is Venice. The minimum fare from Venice to Alexandria is UK£217 and the trip takes about 60 hours with stops.

Also operating on the Piraeus to Alexandria route is the Louis Cruise Lines Ltd which has a weekly car-ferry service via Rhodes and Cyprus. It leaves Piraeus at 3.30 pm on Wednesday and arrives in Alexandria at 7 am on Saturday; the minimum fare is UK£67 in an aircraft-type chair. From Alexandria the ferry departs at 8 pm on Saturday.

Piraeus to Larnaca, Lattakia & Alexandria The Black Sea Shipping Co operates a ferry in either direction along this route twice per month, but few travellers appear to use it.

Jordan to Egypt

These services between Suez and Nuweiba (Sinai) and Aqaba on the Gulf of Aqaba are an alternative to the Israel-Egypt overland crossing.

Aqaba to Nuweiba There are two sailings daily from Aqaba at 12 noon and 4 pm. The trip takes three hours and costs US$25.

Aqaba to Suez Msir Edco Shipping Company operates a twice-weekly service leaving Aqaba at 4 pm on Monday and Thursday. The trip takes 22 hours and costs UK£95 in deck class.

Addresses

Compania Mediterranea
Spain
  Plaza Manuel Gomez Moreno s/n, Esquina a Orense 4, Madrid 28020 (tel 455 0049)
Morocco
  Intercona, 31 Ave de la Résistance, Tangier (tel 36 745)
France
  Voyages Melia, 31 Ave de l'Opéra, Paris 75001 (tel 42 61 56 56)
UK
  Melia Travel, 12 Dover St, London W1X 4NE (tel 499 6731)
West Germany
  Melia Reisebüro GmbH, 54 Grosse Bockenheimerstr, Frankfurt 6000 (tel (49) 69 295303)
Holland
  Melia Travel Holland, Leiderstraat 27, Amsterdam 1017 (tel (31) 20 252552)
Switzerland
  Voyages Melia Suisse, 13-17 Rue de Chantepoulet, Geneva 1201 (tel (41) 22 319491)

Transtour
Spain
  Tourafrica, Estacion Maritima, Algeciras 11201 (tel 65 3706)
  Tourafrica, Estacion Maritima, Tarifa (tel 68 4751)
Morocco
  4 Rue Jabha al Ouatania, Tangier (tel 34 004)
Gibraltar
  Batmar Ltd, The Arcade, 30-38 Main St, Unit L (tel 77 666)

Compagnie Marocaine de Navigation
Morocco
  Comanav, 43 Ave Abou Alaa El Maari, Tangier (tel 32 652)
  Comanov Voyages, 43 Ave des FAR, Casablanca (tel 31 2050)
France
  SNCM, 12 Rue Godot de Mauroy, Paris 75009 (tel 42 66 60 19)
  SNCM, 4 Quai d'Alger, Sète 34203 (tel 67 74 70 55)
UK
  Continental Shipping & Travel Ltd, 179 Piccadilly, London W1V 9DB (tel 491 4968)
West Germany
  Karl Geuther GmbH, Heinrichstr 9, Frankfurt 6000 (tel (49) 69 730471)

Switzerland
Gondrand Reisen AG, Tastrasse 66, Zürich 8021 (tel (01) 211 5938)

Gibline
Gibraltar
Gibline Ltd, Seagle Travel Ltd, 9B George's Lane, PO Box 480, Gibraltar (tel 71 415)

CNAN
Marseilles
29 Blvd des Dames, Marseilles 13002 (tel 91 90 64 70)
Paris
25 Rue St Augustin, Opéra, Paris (tel 67 42 02 70)
Sète
4 Quai d'Alger; Sète 34203 (tel 67 74 70 55)
Lyon
3 Rue Président Carnot, Lyon 69002 (tel 78 42 22 70)
Palma
Agencia Schembri, Plaza Lonja 2-4, (PO Box 71) (tel 72 7141)
Alicante
Agencia Romeu, Plaza 18 Julio 2, Alicante (tel 20 8333)
Madrid
Romeu Y Cia SA Cristobal Bordiu 19-21 (tel 234 7407)

CTN
Tunisia
122 Rue de Yougoslavie, Tunis (tel 242 801)
Italy
Tirrenia Line, Ufficio Passeggeri, Ponte Colombo, Genoa 16100 (tel 25 8041)
Rione Sirignano 2, 80121 Naples (tel 721 662)
France
SNCM, 61 Blvd des Dames, 13002 Marseilles (tel 91 91 92 20)
UK
Serena Holidays, 40-42 Kenway Rd, London, SW 5 (tel 373 6548)
West Germany
Karl Geuther GmbH, Heinrichstr 9, Frankfurt 6000 (tel (49) 69 730471)

Tirrenia Line
Tunisia
CTN, 122 Rue de Yougoslavie, Tunis (tel 242 801)
Italy
Via Roma 385, Palermo (tel 58 5733)
Corso Italia 52, Trapani

Stazione Marittima, Molo Angiono, Naples (tel 551 2181)
Agenave, Via Campidano 1, Cagliari, Sardinia (tel 66 6065)
France
SNCM, 12 Rue Godot de Mauroy, Paris 75009 (tel 42 66 60 19)
Switzerland
Avimare Ltd, Oerlikonerstr 47, Zürich 8057 (tel 311 7650)
UK
Serena Holidays, 40-42 Kenway Rd, London SW5 0RA (tel 373 6548)
West Germany
Karl Geuther GmbH, Heinrichstr 9, Frankfurt 6000 (tel (49) 69 730471)

Adriatica Line
Egypt
Menatours, 28 El Ghourfa el Togarieh St, PO Box 260, Alexandria (tel 806909)
France
CIT, 3 Blvd des Capucines, Paris 75002 (tel 42 66 00 90)
Greece
Gilnavi Ltd, 97 Akti Liaouli & Favierou St, Piraeus (tel 4524-580)
Italy
Zattere 1411, Palazzo Sociale, Venice 30123 (tel 781 611)
Netherlands
Anthony Veder & Co, BV De Ruyterkade 125, Amsterdam 1011 AC (tel 241677)
UK
Sealink UK Ltd, Victoria Station, PO Box 29, London SWIV IJX (tel 828 1940)
West Germany
Seetours International, Seilerstr 23, Frankfurt 6000 (tel 1333-0)

Black Sea Shipping Co
Egypt
Among Shipping Agency, 71 El Horreya St, PO Box 60764, Alexandria
France
Transtours, 49 Ave de l'Opéra, Paris 75002 (tel 42 61 58 28)
Greece
CTC (Hellas), 25 Akti Miaouli St, 1st floor, Piraeus 18535 (tel 30 411 8740)
UK
CTC Lines, 1-3 Lower Regent St, London SW1Y 4NN (tel 930 5833)

Msir Edco Shipping
Egypt
    Menatours, 28 Chambre de Commerce St,
    Alexandria (tel 808407)
Jordan
    Telstar Travel & Tourism, 3rd Circle, Jebel
    Amman, Riyadh Centre, Amman (tel
    640213)
    Telstar Travel & Tourism, near Jordan-
    Kuwait Bank (behind post office), PO Box
    1077, Aqaba (tel 314724)

Warning

This chapter is particularly vulnerable to change – prices for international travel are volatile, routes are introduced and cancelled, schedules change, rules are amended, special deals come and go, borders open and close. Airlines and governments seem to take a perverse pleasure in making price structures and regulations as complicated as possible and you should check directly with the airline or a travel agent to make sure you understand how a fare (and ticket you may buy) works. In addition, the travel industry is highly competitive and there are many lurks and perks. The upshot of this is that you should get opinions, quotes and advice from as many airlines and travel agents as possible before you part with your hard-earned cash. The details given in this chapter should be regarded as pointers and are not a substitute for doing your own careful, up-to-date research.

STOP PRESS

Since this book went to press the airline company Le Point Air-Mulhouse (popularly known as 'Le Point') is no longer operating flights to Ouagadougou (Burkina Faso) and Bangui (CAR) or any of its other African destinations (Senegal, Ivory Coast and Cameroun). Please remember this when any reference is made to the airline in this guidebook.

In Burkina Faso the office of Le Point at 17 Ave Bassawarga, Ouagadougou, is now occupied by another airline.

Getting Around

Most African countries offer a choice of railways, buses, taxis (shared or private), trucks, river boats and lake ferries.

ROAD

The state of the roads doesn't just reflect the climate but also the political stability of the country. If there's been a long period of instability or rampant corruption then the roads are likely to be in poor shape. In that case, break-downs and getting stuck are a regular feature of the journey. Don't look too closely at the tyres or the springs. When you see the state of many of the roads you'll know why nothing lasts very long. In some places like the Central African Republic, Ghana, Mozambique, Sudan, Tanzania and Zaïre, the roads have to be seen to be believed – potholes which would swallow up a truck, bridges washed away, etc. Desert roads in places like Sudan, Chad, Mali, Niger and Mauritania are just a set of tyre tracks left in the sand or the dust by previous trucks. Don't pay any attention to red lines drawn on maps in places like this. Many roads are impassable in the wet season.

There are trucks, buses and shared taxis to most places on main routes every day, but in the more remote areas they may only run once or twice a week.

Hitching

For many travellers, trucks are the favoured means of transport. They're not only the cheapest way of getting from A to B as a rule, but you can get an excellent view from the top of the load. A few years ago it used to be possible to hitch free on trucks all the way through Africa, assuming you were prepared to wait until the free lifts came along. It's now more difficult to do this and you should expect to pay for lifts. Hitching is a recognised form of public transport in much of Africa. Most of the time you will be on top of the load, though you can sometimes travel in the cab for about twice what it costs on top. For the most regular runs there will be a 'fare' which is more or less fixed. You'll be paying what the locals pay – but check this out before you agree to a price. Sometimes it's possible to get the truck driver to lower the price if there's a group of you (form an impromptu group where possible). Trucks are generally cheaper than buses over the same distance.

Lifts on trucks are usually arranged the night before departure at the 'truck park' – a compound/dust patch that you'll find in almost every African town of any size. Just go there and ask around for a truck which is going the way you want to go. If the journey is going to take more than one night or one day, ask whether the price includes food and/or water.

In the more developed countries where there are plenty of private cars on the road, it's not only possible to hitch free but, in some cases, very easy indeed, and you may well be offered somewhere to stay the night. Countries where this applies are Algeria, Ghana, Kenya, Morocco, South Africa, Tunisia and Zimbabwe. On the other hand, don't expect much in the way of lifts from expatriate workers. They have a tendency to regard travellers as a lesser form of humanity. Much the same seems to be happening to the attitudes of volunteers who work for the American Peace Corps and the British Voluntary Service Overseas (VSO). Perhaps this is because the hospitality given in the past has been abused, so if you are offered help by one of these people, please make sure you don't overstay your welcome and that you pay your way. Many of the volunteers have to get by on next to nothing and they haven't gone there in order to be a convenience for travellers. They're committed people who are there to help local people improve their lot.

Remember that sticking out your thumb in many African countries is the equivalent of an obscene gesture, although allowances are generally made for foreigners. Wave your hand vertically up and down instead.

Warning Just a word of warning about lifts in private cars. Smuggling across borders does go on, and, if whatever is being smuggled is found, you may be arrested even though you knew nothing about it. Most travellers manage to convince police that they were merely hitching a ride and otherwise had nothing to do with the smuggler (passport stamps are a good indication of this), but the convincing can take days. It's unlikely they'll let you ring your embassy during this time, and even if you do you shouldn't count on their ability to help you. If you're worried about this, get out before the border and walk through.

Bus & Taxi

Buses are usually quicker than going by rail or truck but are more expensive. Where there is a good network of sealed roads, you may have the choice of going by 'luxury' air-conditioned bus or by ordinary bus. The former naturally cost more but are not always quicker than the ordinary buses. When there are very few or no sealed roads, the ordinary buses tend to be very crowded and stop frequently to pick up or put down passengers. Book in advance if possible.

Most countries also have shared and private taxis. You can forget about the latter if you're on a budget. Shared taxis, however, should definitely be considered. They can cost up to twice the price of the corresponding bus fare, but in some places they're only slightly more expensive and they're certainly quicker and more comfortable.

The word 'taxi' doesn't necessarily denote quite the same thing as it does in developed countries. In Africa it comes in all shapes and sizes ranging from Toyota minibuses to pick-up trucks (utilities) and Peugeot 505s. They are also known by many different names – bush taxi (*taxi-brousse* in Francophone countries), mammy wagons, *matatu* (East Africa), taxi-be (Madagascar), to name a few. They're all basically 'the people's' transport and they leave when full but 'full' can mean many different things depending on which country you are in. In some, a sardine tin would be an accurate description. In others, it means when all the seats are taken. Standards of driving also vary considerably

You should expect to pay a fee for your baggage in addition to the fare on most buses and taxis in West Africa but usually not elsewhere. Also, in countries where the roads quickly turn into mud baths during the rainy season, the fares on buses and taxis can double and even triple.

TRAIN

Trains are generally slow – sometimes very slow – but 3rd class and sometimes 2nd class are often cheaper than other forms of transport.

BOAT

There are many river boats and lake ferries in Africa. The main river boat of interest to travellers is the one on the Zaïre River from Kinshasa to Kisangani. The Nile steamer from Khartoum to Juba was blown up some time ago and there is no longer a service. The ones on the Niger River in Mali are very erratic and you can't rely on them. All the main lakes – Victoria, Tanganyika, Malawi, Kivu, Volta and Nasser have regular ferries and are very popular with travellers.

Algeria

In 1962, after eight years of guerrilla warfare in which one million Algerians died, Algeria gained independence from France. Algeria had been a French colony since 1830.

A brief struggle for power followed between 'moderates' and 'militants' before Colonel Boumedienne led the Armée de Libération to victory with the 'Front de Libération Nationale' (FLN). Ben Bella was elected prime minister. He pledged allegiance to a 'revolutionary Arab-Islamic state based on the principles of socialism and collective leadership at home and anti-imperialism abroad'.

Landless peasants quickly put these ideals into practice and moved in on the land vacated by the French, setting up cooperative farms to be run by peasant councils. But, with the French common enemy gone, there was rapid polarisation between the advocates of real socialism and those who saw the French expulsion as their chance to become rich. Nationalisation of major industries was carried out, but the redistribution of land was limited to that previously owned by the French, leaving large estates still owned by rich Algerians.

These conservative landowners were particularly frightened by the call for liberation of women. Army revolts, based on the slogan 'Islam is not compatible with socialism', broke out in 1963 and 1964. But, with the people tiring of civil disorder and economic stagnation and impatient for the prosperity and progress for which they'd sacrificed a whole generation, most were relieved when Colonel Boumedienne staged a bloodless coup in 1965.

Boumedienne was a competent, if authoritarian, pragmatist, who made economic reconstruction his first priority. Economic growth was boosted by the exploitation of vast deposits of natural gas in the Sahara Desert. Yet unemployment remained high and large numbers of Algerians were forced to go to France to look for work, despite a vicious climate of racism there. While more than 70% of the workforce was employed on the land in the 1970s, agriculture was neglected in favour of industry and production fell below levels achieved under the French.

Since 1971, approximately 1000 square km have been distributed on the condition they be farmed collectively. Agricultural machinery and expertise have been made available for this, and efforts are being made to improve literacy and the understanding of agricultural technology.

Colonel Boumedienne died in December 1978. At a meeting of the FLN in Algiers, Colonel Chadli Benjedid was elected to succeed him. He held onto the post in elections in 1984.

There has been very little political change since independence. The FLN remains the sole political party and pursues socialist policies. Poor planning by the lumbering centralised bureaucracy is largely responsible for the poor state of the agricultural sector, and over the past few years, President Chadli has undertaken a certain amount of cautious reform aimed at reducing the dependence on imported food, clothing and medical supplies.

In foreign policy, Algeria is often seen as being anti-western. It is, however, an active member of the Non-Aligned Movement and in fields such as gas exports is in direct competition with the Soviet Union.

Algeria is very conscious of its role as a model for less fortunate third world countries. Its regime earns a great deal of respect for its intelligence and integrity. It supports a number of liberation struggles around the world. For several years now, it has been deeply committed to supporting the Polisario guerrilla army of the Western Sahara in its struggle against Morocco, which, after the withdrawal of Mauritania, occupies the whole of what was formerly the Spanish Sahara. This support has brought Algeria and Morocco to the brink of war on several occasions and tension between the neighbours remains high. This explains why there are only two

crossing points between Algeria and Morocco.

In its drive to bring about equality between the sexes, the socialist government encouraged the education of women and tried to change male attitudes in what was essentially an exclusively male-dominated society. It has been relatively successful in the north, especially in the urban areas, but in the south, women remain chattels, locked away at the age of 12 and never appearing in public unless veiled and suitably chaperoned. As a result, there's a popular myth that any female over the age of 12 who isn't locked up or veiled is obviously a whore, or, at least, sexually available. Algeria is not the exclusive holder of this attitude; it is quite common throughout the Arab world.

This, however, must be balanced by an emphatic affirmation that Algerians in general are one of the most generous and hospitable people you are likely to meet anywhere in the world. Hitching in the north, and even further south, is a dream (but only for men and couples). The people who pick you up will often invite you to stay with them for the night, especially if you can speak French, or, even better, Arabic.

Facts

CLIMATE & GEOGRAPHY

Algeria is Africa's second largest country. The mountain range to the north – the Saharan Tell – runs roughly parallel to the coast and is dissected by valleys and plateaus. South of the Saharan Tell is the Saharan Atlas range, which marks the rough divide between arable land to the north and desert to the south.

There are many important Roman ruins in excellent condition in Algeria due to the dryness of the desert. The most important of them are at Djemila, near Sétif; Timgad, near Batna in the Saharan Atlas mountains; and, Tipasa, on the coast about 70 km west of Algiers.

The temperature and rainfall vary considerably. The average coastal temperature in winter is about 12°C, rising to around 25°C in summer. The humidity is very high. Inland, the average temperatures are much higher, ranging from 12°C in winter to 33°C plus in summer, with peak temperatures rising much higher still. Rainfall varies from nothing to 70 to 100 cm. Heavy rains in April, and snow in the Kabylie mountains in winter, make some roads impassable or very hazardous.

PEOPLE

The population of an estimated 22 million lives mostly in the north. One-third live in the cities, with the capital of Algiers having about two million people. The least densely populated area is the Sahara, with less than one person per square km.

The Berbers are the largest of the ethnic groups and most of them are farmers, living in small towns and villages.

In fact, the minority groups within the country are part of the Berber group. The Kabylies in the north speak Kabyle as a first language, French as a second and Arabic third. They have had a long history of popular education and many of them hold important administrative positions within the government. The Chaouias and Mozabites tend to live in the Saharan oases, especially Ghardaia. Most of them are merchants, many owning businesses and land in France. Politically they are strongly conservative. The Tuareg are Berber nomads, travelling throughout the Sahara herding goats and camels. Their way of life, cohesiveness and culture have been severely affected by the continuing drought in the Sahel region (immediately south of the desert proper), and many thousands are now destitute, scratching a bare living on the outskirts of Saharan towns and villages.

VISAS

Visas are required by all, except nationals of Denmark, Finland, Italy, Norway, Sweden, Switzerland and the UK. Nationals of Israel, Malawi, South Africa, South Korea and Taiwan are not admitted, and if you have a stamp in your passport from any of these countries you will probably be refused entry or your visa application rejected.

It is advisable to get your visa before leaving your own country. Dutch and German citizens are in for a hard time if they fail to do this. I came across one German who was refused an Algerian visa in Rabat (Morocco) after several weeks' negotiation even though he was married to an Algerian! Germans without connections get even less consideration.

Dutch people applying for visas outside the Netherlands have had to wait at least six weeks. The Algerian Embassy in Bonn issues visas for West Germans the same day. They cost DM 30, require four photos and are valid for a month from the day of issue. Just why the Dutch and Germans are singled out for this treatment isn't clear. Perhaps someone could enlighten us?

Visas cannot be issued at the border.

Though relations between Algeria and Morocco remain tense, there are Algerian consulates in Rabat (tel 24215, 24287), at 8 Rue d'Azrou; and at Oujda (tel 3740/1), at 11 Rue de Taza.

The embassy in Rabat is friendly and helpful, especially if you speak French or Arabic, but still your application may have to be referred to Algiers. This takes time so plan ahead. In Oujda, the situation varies. Sometimes visas are issued on the spot, but mostly people are sent back to Rabat. Both consulates are open daily from 9 am to noon. Visas cost Dr 33.

Visa extensions can be obtained from the Service des Étrangers, Blvd Zeroud Yousef 19A, Algiers. They take 24 hours to issue and require two photos and proof you have changed AD 1000. They also are available in most provincial cities, including Tamanrasset. They cost AD 60, payable only in fiscal stamps available from the post office.

Other Visas

Chad In Algiers these cost AD 61 and are issued in 24 hours. You need two photos. The embassy (tel 60 5316) is at Cité DNC, Villa No 18, Chemin Ahmed Kara, Hydra, Algiers.

Burkina Faso Visas are obtainable from the French Embassy.

CAR The French Embassy will only issue a 48-hour transit visa, costing AD 37, so it's hardly worth getting one here.

Mali The embassy (tel 60 6118) is at Cité DNC, Villa No 14, Chemin Ahmed Kara, Hydra, Algiers. Visas cost AD 150 for a 30-day visit, require two photos and are issued within 48 hours (sometimes while you wait). There also is a consulate in Tamanrasset, where visas (same price) are issued while you wait.

Niger The embassy (tel 78 8921) is at 54 Rue Vercors, Rostomia, Al-Hamadia, Bouzaréah, Algiers. (It's a long way from the centre. Bus No 59 from Place des Martyrs drops you almost right outside – just ask the driver. A taxi will cost around AD 40 each way.) It's open Tuesday, Thursday and Saturday from 7.30 am to 12 noon. Visas for up to seven days are free: seven to 20 days, AD 20. You must have a vaccination certificate that includes yellow fever, the Algerian currency form, three photos and three forms. Your application will be refused unless you have all of these. Visas are usually issued within 24 hours, but can take as long as two weeks.

Even with a visa, you may be refused entry to Niger at the Assamaka border, south of Tamanrasset, if you don't have an onward ticket. Lately this rule has been relaxed, but things change so make enquiries before you set off.

If your vaccinations are out of date you can get new ones from the Institute Pasteur, just below the Martyrs Monument in Algiers.

MONEY

US$ 1	= AD 5.00	(official rate)
UK£ 1	= AD 6.56	
FFr 1.8	= AD 0.50	

The unit of currency is the Algerian dinar = 100 centimes. You are allowed to import/export up to AD 50.

You must buy AD 1000 (about US$210 or the equivalent in another hard currency) at the official rate of exchange, regardless of how long you intend to stay. This applies to *everyone*. If you are a married couple you must change the equivalent of AD 2000. While you may meet someone who escaped the net, don't count on doing so yourself!

There is a thriving black market both in and outside Algeria. The places to ask about it in Algeria are souvenir and camera shops, but be discreet. Ask the price of something and then ask how much it is in francs or dollars – they usually take the hint.

French francs are the preferred currency. FFr 1 = AD 2 to AD 2.5 or CFA 1000 = AD 50, depending on where you are and who you meet. US$1 = AD 12 to AD 15 and UK£1 = AD 20 to AD 25. While the US and sterling rates are acceptable, it is much harder to find someone willing to take them.

Similar, though usually slightly lower, rates are available in Melilla (Spanish North Africa) and in banks in Germany and Switzerland. The rates in Melilla are better than those in Oujda (Morocco).

The Algerian authorities are well aware of these rates and are very keen to stop you using the black market. As a result, there are heavy baggage searches at the Moroccan-Algerian border posts, especially at Figuig. If you're carrying black market money, hide it very well. It will be confiscated if found.

Currency declaration forms are issued on arrival and must be kept in very good order as the customs officials can be very strict about them when you leave the country. If you're bringing in valuables, such as cameras and jewellery, and intend to take them out of the country, declare them on the currency form if you want to avoid hassles when leaving. We've had letters from travellers whose cameras and Walkmans were confiscated because they didn't declare them on the currency form. Be careful! If driving your own vehicle, declare all large car spares, regardless of what you are told on entry. Some travellers have had problems by not doing this.

There is now a bank at the Algerian customs at Hazoua, on the Tozeur to El Oued road from Tunisia, so there's no way of getting out of the money change requirement.

If you *do* get into Algeria without changing the AD 1000, it is quite likely that when you leave (especially if exiting through In Guezzam to Niger) you'll be fined a similar amount. This fine money may get to the bank, but is more likely to be pocketed by the official. So, the option for those who do get through without having to officially change AD 1000 is change officially and spend, or take the risk of being nabbed at the border.

Most travellers import a bottle of whisky to sell in order to keep their costs down. A litre bottle (bought duty-free in Melilla) sells for up to AD 450, though AD 300 to AD 350 would be average. You need not look for buyers – they'll find you. The best prices are paid in the south. Other items that are good for barter are jeans (in any condition), running shoes, sunglasses (preferably Ray-Bans) and cameras (not listed on your form). If you have your own vehicle, jerry cans fetch good prices. There's also a good market for second-hand clothes, and, one traveller suggested, instant coffee.

ACCOMMODATION

Algerian hotels are expensive when you are paying in dinar bought at the official rate. Remember, however, this is really an artificial rate and bears no relation to the value of the dinar in the country. The true value is something much closer to what you get on the black market. So, although it's no consolation, if you're paying AD 75 for a room, officially it's costing you US$15, but in real prices it's a reasonable US$5.

It's not always easy to find a relatively cheap room in summer, as these places fill very quickly.

Many travellers stay in the bathhouses (*hamman* in Arabic and *bain maure* in French), as they are the cheapest accommodation. But they are for *men only*. There's usually at least one bathhouse even in the smallest place. For

AD 10 to AD 15 you will get a mattress on the floor. As you might expect, they're warm but often damp, and you usually have to be out between 6.30 and 7 am.

The cheaper unclassified hotels cost between AD 50 and AD 80 a double, sometimes including breakfast. Above this, the hotels are graded from one to four stars and the prices are set by the government. For a double room with breakfast you pay AD 120 for one star and AD 159 for two stars.

Algeria has an extensive network of youth hostels, which, at AD 15 a night are handy for budget travellers. They are often difficult to find, open only in summer and have as much atmosphere as a football club changing room. They are in Algiers, Annaba, Batna, Bejaia, Biskra, Blida, Borj Bou Arreridj, Bou Saâda, Constantine, Djelfa, El Oued, Ghardaia, Jijel, Guelma, Laghouat, Lakhdaria, Miliana, Oran, Sidi Bel Abbès, Sidi Fredj, Tamanrasset, Tizi Ouzou, Touggourt and Zéralda.

Algeria is in the process of removing street signs in French and replacing them with signs in Arabic. The streets also have been renamed after well-known Algerians, rather than Frenchmen. This can make finding a place very difficult as the locals probably know the streets by their old French names, or something different again!

LANGUAGE

The main languages are Arabic, French and Berber. Very little English is spoken. Many Algerians mix French with Arabic or French with Berber without a second thought.

Getting There & Around

AIR

Internal flights must be paid for with dinars changed at the official rate, over and above the AD 1000 you changed on entry. (There are some agencies that may let you get away with just showing your receipt from the border.) To buy a ticket you need a special form, called *Attestation de Cession de Devises* and available at the Banque Centrale d'Algérie.

Air Algérie offers substantial discounts for anyone under 22. The price of most flights is only about 20% more than the equivalent fare on a TVE bus, but you need to book a couple of weeks in advance. All flights are heavily subscribed.

ROAD
Hitching

Hitching in Algeria is a dream come true for men and couples. For single women, however, it rates as one of the worst countries in the world because of the sexual hassles involved.

Most Algerians are very hospitable and will go out of their way to help you. They think nothing of packing their cars to the roof. So, when an apparently full car screeches to a halt, don't give it another thought – get in. Whatever you do, get out of the towns before you put your thumb out. You'll be ignored inside towns and cities.

You'd be very unlucky to have to pay for any lifts in the north, but south of the Atlas Mountains you should be prepared to do so. Quite a few travellers, however, are still getting free lifts as far south as Tamanrasset. If you're asked to pay for a lift, it's good to have some idea of what the locals are paying. Most lifts south of the Atlas Mountains will be on the top of trucks and the 'fare' will be about half the cost of the bus.

The drivers of trucks belonging to state-owned companies (which have a large 'D' on the cab) officially are forbidden to take on passengers. Most observe this rule, but may pick you up if they know there are no checkpoints ahead. The government transport company is SNTR and each town has a depot, usually on the outskirts. This is a good place to approach drivers, but be discreet, these guys can get the sack if they are caught with a foreigner in the cab.

If you're travelling on top of trucks there are a few essentials you need. The first is something to cover your head with to avoid getting sunstroke. The second is water – a 10-litre collapsible container is ideal, otherwise take several of the two-litre plastic soft drink bottles that are common in Europe. You also need a sleeping bag, as the desert gets very cold at night, and a jumper is useful once the sun goes down.

Most of the roads in the north are surfaced, so it's easy and quick travelling.

Further south it's a different story, even though the Algerian army is busy surfacing sections of the main roads. The surface is good as far as El Goléa, but after that there are some bad stretches. Sections through the Arak gorge and between In Eker and Tamanrasset are surfaced. Between Tamanrasset and In Guezzam (the Algerian-Niger border) it's rough *piste* and very difficult to follow in places. Anywhere off the main road is *piste*, or simply tracks in the dust or sand.

Bus

There is a good network of long-distance buses run by the national bus company, TVE, which is also known as SNTV or TVSE. These generally are comfortable, reliable, fast where the roads allow and expensive in 'official' dinars. It's unlikely you will use them much in the north as hitching is so easy, but they are useful for getting south.

At times demand exceeds supply, particularly on the less well-serviced routes such as El Goléa to In Salah and In Salah to Tamanrasset, and vice versa. The day before you want to travel, find out what time the tickets go on sale and be in the queue early.

Avoid travelling north from Béchar or Figuig during June, July and August. Not only is it unbearably hot (40°C to 50°C), but it's holiday time for the soldiers along the Moroccan border and the buses will be full. At these times you can often find up to 300 people waiting at the bus station, many of whom have been there for days.

TO/FROM MOROCCO

There are only two crossing points between Algeria and Morocco: Oujda-Tlemcen and Figuig-Beni Ounif. On foot you can cross from Algeria to Morocco at either place without complication. If you're going from Morocco to Algeria, you can only walk across at Figuig-Beni Ounif, though recent reports suggest otherwise. Check it out before you set off from Oujda as the Moroccan officials have been known to let people through knowing they will be turned back by the Algerian officials – a very unfunny Moroccan joke.

If you're hitching a lift through the Oujda-Tlemcen border, the Moroccan entry stamps on your passport must match those on the driver's passport. If they don't, expect to be turned back.

You can cross at either place if you have your own vehicle. You'll have to telephone or telex your own embassy in Rabat to confirm that you intend to re-export your vehicle – you must wait in Oujda or Figuig until this clearance is sent through to the border post. Motor insurance costs AD 130 a month at the border.

There are no buses or trains between the two countries. But there are five buses daily to the border from Tlemcen for AD 12.30. The first one leaves at 7.40 am, the last at 2.10 pm. There is also a daily train to the border from Oran, via Tlemcen.

On the Moroccan side of the border, you can get a taxi to Oujda for Dr 10 per person.

There is no regular transport between Figuig and Beni Ounif. It's a three-km walk from Figuig to the border and a further 1½ km to Beni Ounif. Expect heavy searches at both borders when entering Algeria – they're looking for drugs and Algerian currency. Expect border formalities at Figuig-Beni Ounif to take many hours – six isn't unusual. On leaving they are much slacker, although your currency form gets checked.

TO/FROM TUNISIA

There are two main routes between Tunisia and Algeria, with the southern route being the more interesting.

At the northern Souk Ahras-Ghardomao crossing, you can either hitch between the two places or take the daily train. (This is actually the Trans-Maghreb Express between Tunis and Algiers, but the term 'express' is used fairly loosely.)

If you're hitching and get stuck, it's a 20-km walk between the two border posts. On the train, your currency form is checked thoroughly when leaving Algeria.

If you're on your way to Tunisia and have excess dinar at this border, it will be confiscated in return for a receipt (there is no bank here). If you return within 12 months and show your receipt, your money will be refunded. Well, that's what they tell you. This practice has yet to be confirmed, so get rid of your dinar before arriving at the border.

In the north you can cross the border by taking one of the buses from Constantine to Tunis (every second day), or Annaba to Tunis (daily). The hassle with these is you have to catch them from the point of origin as they don't stop en route to pick up passengers.

The more interesting southern route passes through the oasis towns of Touggourt, El Oued, Nefta and Tozeur. It's very picturesque between El Oued and Tozeur – drifting sand dunes – and there's a good sealed road connecting Nefta with the rest of Tunisia.

Tunisian customs are quick and there's no fuss, but be prepared for very thorough searches on the Algerian side. There is now a bank at the Algerian customs.

There are daily buses from the Algerian-Tunisian border to Tozeur, stopping at Nefta, or you can get a *louage* from the border to Nefta for 550 millimes. If you have to walk, it's four km between the two border posts. There are taxis, but at TD 30 they are very expensive. There are no through buses. From the Algerian side of the border to El Oued there are irregular share taxis.

There is another route along the Mediterranean coast from El Kala (Le Calle) to Tabarka. There is regular transport along this route during the day. No public transport, however, actually crosses the border.

Avoid taking the train direct from Algiers to Tunis. You have to produce bank receipts proving you changed at least AD 1000 before they will sell you a ticket. The 2nd-class fare is AD 149 and the trip takes about 24 hours.

TRANS-SAHARAN ROUTES

There are basically three routes through the Sahara.

The most popular and most reliable as far as transport and facilities are concerned is the Route du Hoggar, running from El Goléa to Agadez (Niger), via In Salah and Tamanrasset. It's an interesting trip through many of the oasis towns south of the Atlas Mountains. If you go this way, it's worth taking time to see the Hoggar Mountains east of Tamanrasset.

The other main route runs south from Adrar to Gao (Mali), via Reggane and Tessalit, and is known as the Route du Tanezrouft. It's more rugged than the Route du Hoggar, takes considerably longer and there's far less transport along the way.

The most westerly route, the Route de la Mauritanie – from Béchar to Nouakchott (Mauritania), via Tindouf, Bir Moghreim, F'Derik and Atar – has not been open for many years because of the war between Polisario front guerrillas and Morocco over the Moroccan occupation of the former Spanish colony.

If you have plenty of time or your own vehicle there is one much more rugged and far more interesting route. It goes from Touggourt, through the Tessili Mountains via In Aménas and Djanet, to Tamanrasset. There are occasional trucks along the way, connecting all three places as well as In Salah and Ouargla, but don't expect free lifts. There used to be a weekly bus from In Aménas to Illizi (420 km north of Djanet), but I haven't heard of it for some time.

Travellers who have gone this way have got stuck here and there. If this happens, there are planes from Illizi to Ouargla (AD 164, six times weekly) and Djanet (AD 108, four times weekly), and from In Aménas to Djanet (AD 144, weekly), and from Djanet to Tamanrasset (AD 108, weekly). These flights are usually booked out well in advance. But you can be lucky and get a seat on the day. It's sometimes possible to pick up free lifts with tourists heading for Niger from Djanet.

If you're either taking your own vehicle across the Sahara, or planning to spend time in the desert, get the *Sahara Handbook* by Simon & Jan Glen (Lascelles, London, 1987, £17.95). It is an excellent book, packed with information about everything you could possibly want to know about crossing the Sahara Desert and the places along the way. While it's oriented toward people with their own vehicles, it has plenty of detailed descriptions and maps of places you wouldn't hear about unless you were part of the archaeology *cognoscenti*. Highly recommended.

Route du Hoggar

This is the most easterly route through the Sahara, running from Ghardaia to Agadez and Zinder (Niger), via El Goléa, In Salah and Tamanrasset. Other than the River Nile, it's the most travelled route between the Mediterranean and southern Africa. The road wears out very quickly because of this. What used to be a very good surfaced road between In Salah and Tamanrasset is now so badly potholed that it takes two full days to complete. It's still very good in the Arak canyon and from In Eker to Tamanrasset, which was resurfaced recently.

The road south of Tam is paved for about 30 km and then reverts to *piste*. You may need a compass as it can be quite hard to follow in places. It's supposed to be marked every five km or so, but many of the markers are missing. There are some bad patches of sand, more towards the In Guezzam end of the road.

The trucks follow a route roughly parallel to the *piste*. It's marked more or less with piles of stones every 100 metres. There are lots of totally stripped car bodies, lying rusting, but don't let them dismay you. If you're lucky, you can get to In Guezzam in one day. It would be wise, however, to allow two.

While In Guezzam is an expanding town, it's nothing special. The border post has been moved 10 km south of the town, so you may as well drive straight through. The post is open daily from 9 am to 12 noon and 5 to 7 pm.

It's best to assume your currency form will be checked thoroughly at the border. Make sure it's in order.

This border post acquired a bad reputation a few years ago. It seems that the guards were hitting the whisky heavily and becoming thoroughly obnoxious, especially with women travellers (sexual harassment, etc). Most travellers say this has changed, but some say not. Try to get through early to avoid hassles.

Assamaka (the Niger border post) is about 35 km from In Guezzam. You can't miss it as it probably has the only shady trees in this part of the Sahara. It also has *cold* beers for CFA 700 a bottle (!), but after coming through the desert you'll probably appreciate one. Don't arrive here after 4 pm or you'll have to spend the night putting up with unruly soldiers whose only hobby is drinking beer – not much else to do really.

Niger customs will want to see valid vaccination cards and may want to check that you have 'sufficient funds'. They no longer require onward tickets.

There are natural water springs here. While the water does contain sulphur, it is palatable if you add a water-purifying tablet. It's sometimes possible to change dinar here – ask around. Photography is forbidden, but possible if you're discreet.

From Assamaka to Arlit (about 200 km) the *piste* is badly marked and you may need a compass. The journey will take you all day.

Buses run between Algiers and Tamanrasset, but they're not all that cheap. Many travellers prefer to hitch. The stretch between In Salah and Tamanrasset is notoriously bad for hitching and you may have to take a bus. It would be the exception rather than the rule to hitch free all the way to Tamanrasset.

Tourists in their own cars and those driving Peugeot 504s and 505s to sell in West Africa are usually very conscious of weight and reluctant to give lifts. People in 4WDs are usually pretty good about picking up hitchers.

You can take the train south from Algiers as far as Djelfa and Touggourt. It, however, is extremely slow and only for die-hard train fanatics.

Following are some examples of transport costs and journey times:

Ghardaia to El Goléa – two buses daily and no problem getting a seat.

El Goléa to In Salah – one bus every two days. Things can get a bit frantic at the booking office so find out in advance about tickets. The bus leaves El Goléa at 4 pm one day and arrives at In Salah around midnight. It then heads back to El Goléa at 4 pm the next day. Tickets cost AD 72.

In Salah to Tamanrasset – buses three times weekly. These are fast bone-shakers, doing the trip nonstop in about 18 hours – 'quick but painful' is the general consensus. Departures from In Salah are on Monday, Wednesday and Friday at 4 am; and from Tamanrasset on Monday, Wednesday and Saturday. The fare is AD 130, and possibly an extra AD 10 or AD 20 for your pack. The only trouble with this service is that demand is sometimes heavy and the ticket office won't sell tickets until late in the afternoon on the day prior to departure. It therefore develops into a free-for-all and you may lose. Also, you have to fight your way on to the bus to get a seat. Make sure you don't end up with a seat behind the rear wheels for your backbone's sake.

SNTR trucks between In Salah and Tamanrasset are very reluctant to take passengers.

There are planes four times a week between the two towns, costing AD 180. They're often booked out two weeks in advance.

Tamanrasset to In Guezzam – one bus weekly in either direction. It leaves Tamanrasset at 5 am on Mondays. The fare is AD 75. This bus isn't particularly useful as you have to wait around in In Guezzam for a lift further south. It's much better while in Tamanrasset to arrange a lift all the way to Arlit or Agadez.

Tamanrasset to Agadez – trucks between these two places cost CFA 10,000 or FFr 300. The first price quoted tends to be high – you must haggle. Dinars, £ sterling and US dollars are not accepted. The price should include food and the journey takes an average two days, but can take up to five if there are problems, such as soft sand, punctures, etc. It's a rugged journey. Petrol and food are available at In Guezzam and Arlit.

One of the best places to find a lift south from Tamanrasset is at the customs post, where all trucks have to stop. The gas station is another good bet, as is Camping Zerib. You shouldn't have to wait too long for a lift as there is a lot of traffic between Algeria and Niger these days.

Tamanrasset to Gao (Mali) – it's possible to find lifts. A few trucks do this route, though they're nowhere near as common as ones going to Agadez.

Route du Tanezrouft

This is the central route, running from Adrar to Gao (Mali). You can get onto it from Ghardaia, via El Goléa and

Timimoun, or from Béchar, via Beni Abbès.

Nowhere near as many trucks use this route as use the Route du Hoggar. In Adrar stock up on essentials – food, water and, if you're driving, petrol. It's virtually impossible to get supplies further south until Borj Mokhtar (the border) and Gao. Even the supplies in Adrar are limited. There is a twice-weekly bus service between Adrar and the border.

Adrar is also the last place you will find a hotel for a long time. Don't forget to report to police and customs here before you head south.

Finding a lift from Adrar to Gao could take you a week or more. Only five or six trucks do the run every week. The road is surfaced as far as Reggane, but after that it's *piste* or bush tracks all the way to Gao. The first 10 to 15 km out of Reggane are very bad, but after that, all the way to Borj Mokhtar, it's OK.

There are solar-powered beacons at regular intervals from Reggane to Borj Mokhtar. But the tracks can stretch for several km on either side of the 'road', so you won't always see them.

Take plenty of water. Poste Weygand is derelict and there's no water there. Poste Maurice Cortier (Bidon Cinq) has been re-opened and is likely to remain open.

The Algerian border post is at Borj Mokhtar, a small oasis. Customs and immigration will occupy several hours of your time. You must leave the border the same day you arrive as it's prohibited to stay overnight.

It is about 160 km from Borj Mokhtar to the Malian border post at Tessalit. Expect to be hassled here for 'gifts' – cigarettes, sleeping bags, jerry cans of petrol, spare parts, etc. If you want to get through quickly, give them cigarettes, lighters, T-shirts and the like. Don't get upset. Stand your ground politely over anything more substantial.

There is one 'hotel' at Tessalit that serves food (and has bucket showers). The next place with any facilities is Bourem.

From Tessalit to Gao the 'road' is so bad that it's advisable to hire a guide – but don't take just anyone. Choose someone who has references written by previous satisfied travellers. If you don't take a guide, for much of the journey you'll have to find an alternative route through the bush. This can be difficult.

Expect a lot of punctures between Bourem and Gao – the track runs through scrub and dunes and is littered with camel thorns. From Gao you can either go to Mopti and Bamako or to Niamey (Niger). Lifts from Gao to Timbuktu are very hard to find.

This route is sometimes closed between May and September. Ask before you set off. There is no Malian consulate in Adrar, so be sure you get your visa in Algiers or Tamanrasset before you set off across the desert. There are regular buses in either direction between Ghardaia and Adrar.

Around the Country

ADRAR

This desert town is the gateway to the Route du Tanezrouft to Gao in Mali. Going south, it's the last chance to have a shower, sleep in a proper bed and get a decent meal for quite a long time. There's very little to see in Adrar, but every building in town has been redwashed and the overall effect is quite pleasing.

If you are heading south, make sure you check in with customs on the southern edge of town. While formalities are supposedly taken care of at Borj Mokhtar, this may have changed and it's a long way to backtrack.

Information

All the main services – banks, post office, Air Algérie, the tourist office and the town's flash hotel – are around the enormous main square, Place des Martyrs.

The bus station is 500 metres north of the centre. Tickets can be booked the day

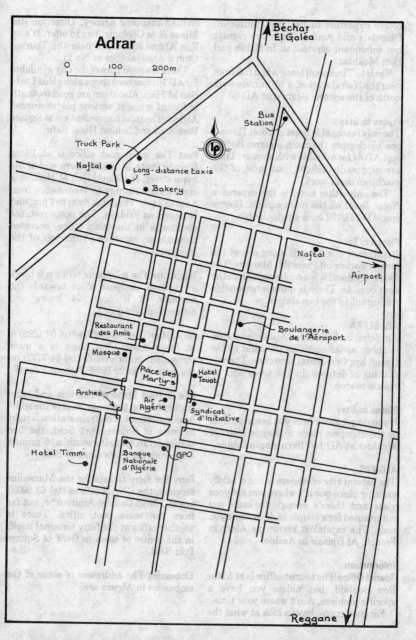

Adrar

0   100   200m

before departure to Béchar, Timimoun, Ghardaia and Aoulef. There are regular but infrequent services to In Salah and Borj Mokhtar.

Taxis to Timimoun leave when full from near the Naftal station, a 10-minute walk north of the square. Seats cost AD 60.

Places to Stay

The only reasonable hotel is *Hotel Timmi*, one block from the main square. Rooms cost AD 87 for a double with shower. They are supposedly air-con, but most of the machines don't work.

The only other hotel is the expensive *Hotel Touat* on the main square. Rooms cost AD 141/192 for a single/double.

Places to Eat

Restaurant des Amis is along one of the streets leading off Place des Martyrs. The food is good and it is a cool escape from the heat outside. There is quite a reasonable restaurant in the bus station.

AIN SEFRA

Ain Sefra, in the Saharan Atlas mountains, is about as far north as the sand of the Grand Erg Occidental stretches. There is nothing of interest in the town and no reason to stop.

Places to Stay

If you do get stuck here you are in trouble as the cheapest place to stay is *Hotel el Mekhter* at AD 140/180 a single/double.

ALGIERS

The capital city of Algiers is not a wildly exciting place but it's where you get your visas and there's enough to keep you entertained for a couple of days while you wait. The capital is known as Alger in French, Al Djazair in Arabic.

Information

Tourist Office The tourist office is at 5 Rue Ben Boulaid, but unless you have a specific problem, don't waste your time.

For good maps, have a look at what the civilian mapping agency, Direction des Mines et la Géologie, has to offer. It's on Rue Abane Ramdane, near the Touring Club d'Algérie office at No 21.

There is a good map of the city available for AD 10 from bookshops along Rue Larbi Ben M'Hidi. Also there are good footpath billboard maps at various places around Algiers. The most convenient are at Square Port Said and behind Hotel Safir.

Post The main post office is at Place Grande Poste, at the southern end of the main street, Rue Larbi Ben M'Hidi. It is open from Saturday to Wednesday from 8 am to 7 pm, Thursday 8 am to 1 pm, and is closed on Fridays. The poste restante counter is in the telex office, accessed through an entrance to the left of the front steps.

Telephone The telephone office is a block away from the post office towards the harbour. It is open 24 hours and connections are quick.

Air Algérie The head office (tel 63 1282) is at Place Audin, but there is a more convenient branch office (tel 64 7722) on the corniche at 29 Blvd Zighout Youcef.

Bus & Train Stations The bus and train stations are on the lower level of the split-level waterfront. The train station is right in front of Square Port Said, the bus station is further to the south, a 15-minute walk from the Place Grande Poste.

Ferry For ferry tickets for the Marseilles services, the CNAN offices (tel 63 8932) are at 7 Blvd Colonel Amirouche, not far from the main post office. There is another office at the ferry terminal itself, in the centre of town in front of Square Port Said.

Embassies The addresses of some of the embassies in Algiers are:

Australia
12 Djenane Mali, Hydra (tel 60 1965)
Benin
16 Lotissement du Stade, Birkhadem (tel 56 627)
Burkina Faso
12 Rue Mouloud Belhouchat, Algiers (tel 61 3897)
Britain
Batiment B, 7 Chemin Capt Hocine Sliman (tel 60 5038)
Cameroun
60 Blvd Colonel M'Hamed Bougara, El Biar (tel 78 8195)
France
6 Ave Larbi Alik, Hydra (tel 60 4488)
Gabon
80 Rue Ali Remli, Al Hamadya, Bouzareah (tel 78 0264)
Ghana
62 Rue des Frères Benali Abdallah, Hydra (tel 56 2332)
Guinea
43 Blvd Said Hamdine, Hydra (tel 60 0059)
Guinea-Bissau
Villa No 17, Cité DNC, Chemin Ahmed Kara, Hydra (tel 60 0151)
Mali
Villa No 15, Cité DNC, Chemin Ahmed Kara, Hydra (tel 60 6118)
Mauritania
107 Lot Baranès, El Hamadya, Bouzareah (tel 79 2044)
Morocco
16 Rue Dr Kaldi Abdelaziz, El Mouradia (tel 56 2752)
Niger
54 Rue du Vercos, Rostomia, Al Hamadya, Bouzareah (tel 78 8921)
Nigeria
27B Rue Ali Boufelgued (tel 60 6050)
Senegal
1 Rue Mahieddine Bacha, El Mouradia (tel 56 9043)
Tunisia
11 Rue du Bois de Boulogne (tel 60 1388)
USA
4 Chemin Cheikh Bachir El Ibrahimi, El Biar (tel 60 1186)
Zaïre
104 Lot Cadat, Djenne Ben Omar, Kouba (tel 580679)

There are also Malian and Niger consulates in Tamanrasset.

Things to See

While most of the buildings in the **medina** are of French origin, there are still some magnificent Turkish palaces to be seen. The main concentration is near the **Ketchaoua Mosque**, in Rue Hadj Omar, the street that runs to the right as you face the mosque.

Off Rue Hadj Omar, to the left after about 100 metres, is Rue Mohammed Akli Malek, which is just a stairway. At No 9 is the **Museum of Popular Arts & Traditions**, housed in one of the finest Turkish palaces in the city. It is open from 10 am to 12 noon and 2 to 5 pm daily, except Saturday.

Up on the hill behind the new city is a group of interesting museums. Take bus No 35 or 40 from Place Grande Poste and get off at the Palais du Peuple stop. The **National Museum of Antiquities** is in the small Parc de la Liberté on the left. One hundred metres up the hill is the **People's Palace**, the former residence of the French governor and Algerian head of state. Today it houses a couple of museums in its luxuriant gardens. The grounds are open Monday to Saturday from 9 am to 9 pm. Entry is AD 10.

A few minutes' walk down the hill is **Bardo Museum**, which houses the prehistory and ethnography displays. It is open from 9 am to 12 noon and 2.30 to 5.30 pm, closed Friday mornings and Saturday.

The concrete monstrosity that dominates the city skyline is the **Martyrs Monument**, opened in 1982 on the 20th anniversary of Algeria's independence. It is regarded as the true heart of this developing country and represents everything the Algerian people have struggled for. It all sounds like good propaganda, but it is hard not to be impressed by the whole thing. In the area beneath the three stylised palm fronds is an eternal flame guarded night and day by two soldiers. The views from the edge of this area out over the city are the best you'll get.

Beneath the monument is **Djihad Museum**. Displays relate to the war of independence and all labels are in Arabic.

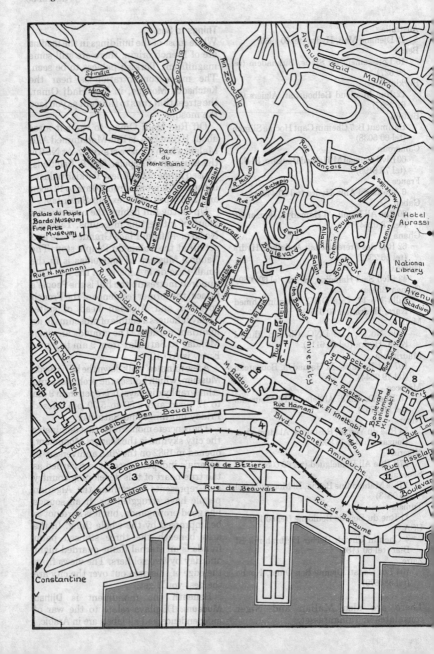

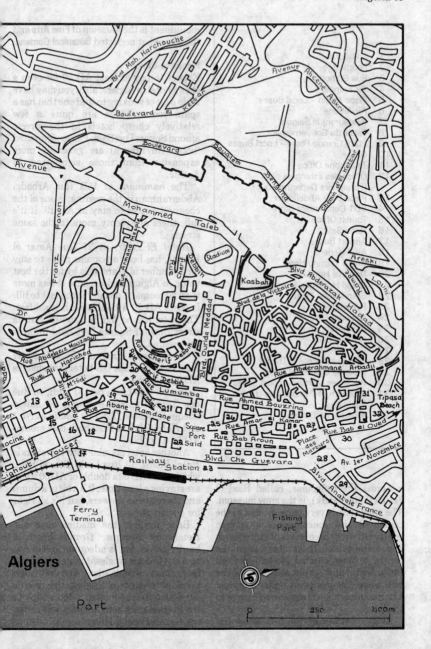

Algiers

Port

1	Cathedral
2	Footbridge
3	Bus Station
4	Air France
5	Place Audin – Local Buses
6	Air Algérie
7	Restaurant le Saigon
8	Palais du Gouvernement
9	Place Grande Poste – Local Buses
10	GPO
11	Telephone Office
12	Office des Etrangers (Foreigners Department)
13	Place Emir Abdelkader
14	501 Department Store
15	Tourist Office
16	Hotel Safir
17	Airport Buses
18	Air Algérie
19	Grand Touring Hotel
20	National Hotel
21	Grand Hotel des Etrangers
22	Grand Hotel Tipaza
23	Passenger Lift
24	National Theatre
25	Restaurant Couscous
26	Hotel el Badr
27	Grand Hotel
28	Mosque Djemaa el Djedid
29	Mosque Djemaa el Kebir
30	Place des Martyrs – Local Buses
31	Museum of Popular Arts & Traditions
32	Mosque Ali Bitchin

Across the concourse, called Riad el Fet'h (Victory Park), is the **army museum**. The whole site is very popular, and in the centre of the concourse is a sunken courtyard with three levels of fancy shops and restaurants. To get here from the centre of town, catch a No 32 bus from Place Audin and get out at the top of the hill, where the bus stops under a bridge. The monument is a few hundred metres to the left.

At the bottom of the hill below the monument is the **Museum of Fine Arts** and the somewhat neglected **Botanical Gardens**.

Places to Stay

Expect to pay at least AD 50 for even a cheap hotel in Algiers; also, you may have to do a lot of walking to find one that has a spare room. There are quite a few relatively cheap hotels in the streets around Square Port Said. Places signposted 'hotel' (in French) are generally more expensive than those signposted in Arabic.

The *hamman*, at 15B Rue Arbadgi Abderrahman in the medina, is one of the cheapest places to stay at AD 13. If it's full, there are plenty more in the same street.

Hotel El Badr, at 31 Rue Amar el Kamar, has been a popular place to stay for a number of years. It is by far the best value in Algiers and because it has more than 80 rooms, it usually is the last to fill. It costs AD 70 a double with breakfast. The hotel has no sign in English, but its street runs off Square Port Said towards the medina.

On the same street at No 38 is *Hotel Tunis* – a small but OK hotel that charges AD 70 a double.

Just off Rue Larbi Ben M'Hidi, on Rue des Tannuers, are a couple of barely adequate places. *Hotel Es Saada* at No 1 and *Hotel Club* at No 2 both cost around AD 60 a double.

Another hotel popular with travellers is *Hotel Bearn*, 13 Rue Larbi Ben M'Hibi, which costs AD 60 a double or AD 50 if you are staying a long time. It's a bit of a dump and there are no showers, but it's all right for a short stay.

Back towards the medina near the Ketchaoua Mosque, *Grand Hotel* is hardly grand, but is adequate and cheap at AD 44/55 for singles/doubles. It is at 4 Rue Aoua Abdelkader, and although there is no sign in English the mosaic nameplate in the footpath dates back to the French era when the hotel was called the Grand Hotel d'Hivers.

The closest youth hostel and camping ground are at Zeralda, 40 km west of the capital and accessible by bus from the main bus station.

Going up in price to the one-star hotels, *Grand Hotel Tipaza* is on the southern side of Square Port Said and is not bad at AD 118 for a double with breakfast. Similar is *Grand Hotel des Etrangers*, on the west side of the square, just up from the National Theatre.

The next step up are the two-star hotels, which give you little more than the one-star hotels. One of the better ones is *Hotel Grand Palais* on Rue Abane Ramdane, not far from Square Port Said. *Hotel Regina* and *Hotel d'Angleterre*, on Rue Ben Boulaid, are staffed by the most surly and unhelpful people you are ever likely to come across in this country.

Places to Eat

The best hunting ground for cheap food is in the pocket of streets between Rue Larbi Ben M'Hidi and Rue Abane Ramdane. There are a number of small places selling all the usual stuff – soup, brochettes, chicken, chips and salads. One place that stands out is the small place at 7 Rue du Coq, a small street running off Rue Larbi Ben M'Hidi at the northern end.

On Square Port Said, near the entrance to Rue Amar el Kamar, *Restaurant Couscous* does reasonable food cheaply.

For something different, *Restaurant Le Saigon*, at 10 Rue Valentin, does excellent Chinese food. The street is the one that runs up beside the Air Algérie head office at Place Audin. This restaurant is popular with expatriates and costs around AD 50 a person.

Around Algiers

The Roman ruins of **Tipasa**, some 65 km west of Algiers on the coast, are well worth a visit. There are buses from the main bus station in Algiers, costing AD 10 and taking about two hours.

You can camp on the beach near the village of Chenoua, a 30-minute walk along the beach to the west of Tipasa through the tourist complex, or see the ruins in a day trip from Algiers.

ANNABA

Annaba is largely an industrial city on a small coastal plain. It has boomed to become the fourth largest city in the country. The city's main claim to fame is that the greatest writer and thinker in the history of Christianity, and bishop here for 34 years, Augustine, wrote his definitive work *City of God* here in the 5th century. The monstrous basilica on the hill to the south of the city is dedicated to him. Apart from that, there is little to do or see, but it is a pleasant enough place to spend a day or so on the way to or from Tunisia.

There are direct buses and trains to Tunis daily.

Information

There is a tourist office behind Grand Hotel d'Orient, on Rue Tarik Ibn Zaid. It is open daily from 8 am to 12 noon and 2 to 6 pm. The guy is helpful and can speak reasonable English.

The railway station is in the town centre on Place 1 Mai, while the bus station is a 15-minute walk from the centre along Ave de l'Armée de Libération Nationale.

There are direct ferry services to Marseilles, and the CNAN office is on Cours de la Révolution, the main street, just up from the old theatre.

The Tunisian Embassy (tel 82 4447) is at 6 Rue Emir Abdelkader.

Things to See

The **Basilica of St Augustine** is a 30-minute walk from the centre of town. It looks no better close up than it does at a distance, but the views from it over the town are excellent. The baptistry is open daily from 8.30 to 11.30 am and 2.30 to 4.30 pm.

The ruins of the Roman town **Hippo Regius**, also known as Hippone, are at the foot of the hill beneath the basilica. Nothing much here, but worth a wander

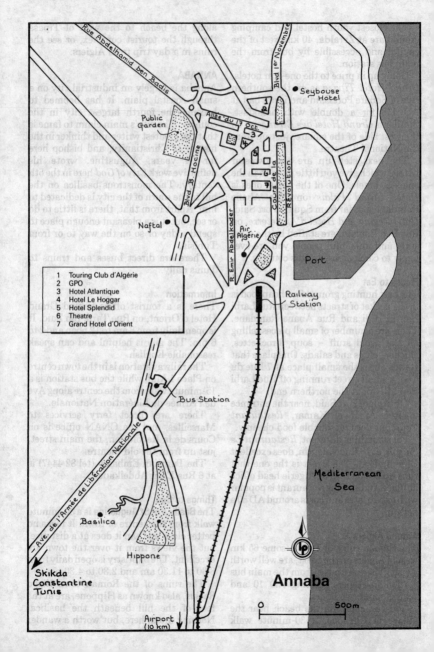

1 Touring Club d'Algérie
2 GPO
3 Hotel Atlantique
4 Hotel Le Hoggar
5 Hotel Splendid
6 Theatre
7 Grand Hotel d'Orient

Annaba

0   500m

Skikda
Constantine
Tunis

Airport
(10 km)

Mediterranean
Sea

around. The site is open on Wednesdays, Thursdays and Fridays.

Places to Stay

One of the cheapest hotels is *Hotel Cirta*; clean rooms for AD 60 a double. *Hotel du Theatre*, costing the same, is one street up from the theatre.

More expensive is *Hotel Atlantique*. It is clean and pleasant and costs AD 118 a double, including breakfast.

Grand Hotel d'Orient on Cours de la Révolution has some great old colonial touches, but at AD 200 for a double with breakfast it has been described as 'not worth the extra'.

Avoid *Hotel Le Hoggar*. Its two-star rating must be some bad Algerian joke: it's the filthiest hotel I have seen in the whole of North Africa, the water rarely works and the cockroaches are taking over. Forget it!

Places to Eat

Try the small restaurant on the small square near Hotel Le Hoggar. It is run by a good-natured character who was a shoe-shine during WW II when Annaba was a base for British and American soldiers. He loves to reminisce and starts singing all the old songs. His food isn't bad either.

ARAK

Arak is a small Tuareg settlement on the road between In Salah and Tamanrasset, about halfway between the two. For that reason, the buses stop here for a meal break.

The settlement itself consists of little more than a café and a fuel station. The gorges around are quite steep. Arak is a hellishly hot and uninviting place in summer, and just plain uninviting in winter.

Places to Stay & Eat

There is a small camp site with *zeribas*, where you can rent mats for AD 20 a night. There's also water available for washing. It's all part of the restaurant, so just ask there.

BATNA

Batna, in the heart of the Aurès Mountains and with an altitude of more than 1000 metres, is blessed with a cool climate. It is a pleasant regional town set in a wide valley.

There is little of interest in the town itself, but it is a useful base from which to visit the exceptional ruins of **Roman Timgad**, 40 km to the east. There is, however, accommodation in the small village of Timgad, so it's possible and preferable to stay there.

The enormous bus station is in the centre of town next to a large roundabout with decorative fountain, which works occasionally. Taxis leave from an area a couple of blocks from the bus station, in the opposite direction to the fountain.

Places to Stay & Eat

Hotel Laverdure is at 3 Ave de l'Indépendence and only a couple of minutes' walk from the bus station. It's not fantastic value at AD 80 for a tiny double, but the choices are limited. From the bus station, go straight past the roundabout and take the first street on the left; the hotel is on the right at the end of a block of shops.

There is another cheapie close by that has triple rooms only: AD 90 for the room, AD 30 for a bed. From the bus station, turn right at the roundabout and the hotel is on the right after 100 metres.

Restaurant El Atik is on the opposite side of the street and on a corner a couple of blocks up from Hotel Laverdure. It does excellent chicken, chips and salad for AD 32. Towards the market from El Atik there are a number of small restaurants that serve rotisseried chickens and sheep heads.

BÉCHAR

Béchar is a modern, sprawling, administrative town. It is the capital of this area of the Sahara, known as the Saoura. While it has nothing to recommend it, you'll probably stop here. It is the last major town on the road south until you get to Adrar, and that is much smaller. It has a couple of banks.

Next to the large mosque on the main street is the well-stocked market, and one block further is the busy bus and taxi station.

Places to Stay

The best place to stay is the friendly *Grand Hotel de la Saoura* at 24 Rue Kada Belahrech, just around the corner from the post office. It does tend to fill up early. Rooms cost AD 60/100 a single/double, which isn't all that cheap but is in line with hotel prices in this town.

There is a nameless cheapie nearby that takes men only. It is as rough as guts, but cheap at AD 30. Ask around.

The other choice is *Hotel de la Paix*, also known as Hotel Salaam, in the same area. While it may appear to be locked, just bash on the side shutter. Double rooms are AD 105.

BEJAIA

Bejaia is a port town beautifully situated on the flank of Jebel Gouraya on the eastern end of the Gulf of Bejaia. It's a very easy-going and relaxed place, if a little polluted from the petrochemical complex at its southern edge. Despite the town's long history, there is very little to see. The beach at **Tichi**, 17 km to the east, however, is one of the best in Algeria. Although there is accommodation at the beach, the best bet is to stay in Bejaia.

Information

The tourist office and CNAN office are one and the same place and are on the small central square, Place Chérif Medjahid, as is the post office and Air Algérie office.

The bus station is at the bottom of the hill south of the centre. Take a local bus from just below Place Chérif Medjahid.

The port is below the centre of town (signposted).

Places to Stay

The best bet is the friendly *Hotel Touring* at 6 Rue Hocine Hihat, just off Place Chérif Medjahid. A double costs AD 60. The rooms at the back are quieter. The other cheapie, *Hotel Saada* is definitely not as good: it's a bit grubby. Also, avoid room No 3. When the hotel is locked at midnight, all those locked out want to come through this room as its window faces the courtyard, which bypasses the main door! It is on Rue Ben M'Hidi, the pedestrian street that joins Place Chérif Medjahid and Place 1 Novembre.

For something a bit better, *Hotel l'Etoile* on Place 1 Novembre has some fine views over the harbour and bay. Rooms cost AD 88/120 a single/double with breakfast.

Places to Eat

Restaurant de la Soummam is next door to Hotel Touring and does a good-value, two-course lunch for AD 22.

BENI ABBÈS

This is another beautiful oasis town on the southern edge of the Grand Erg Occidental. Behind it are some excellent dunes, from the top of which the views out over the Grand Erg Occidental are stunning.

The town has a market, banks, supermarket (of sorts), post office and a couple of expensive hotels. (You can camp in the grounds of one of them.)

The *palmeraie* lies at the foot of the escarpment below the town. Out to the left past Hotel Grand Erg and below the stone water tower, is an excellent **swimming pool** filled with beautiful clear spring water. There are some trees for shade, making it a cool retreat from the blinding desert all around.

There is a small **museum** and **zoo**, both about 100 metres along the track to the left, near the bridge. There is an interesting selection of desert flora and fauna, but the birds and animals in the zoo are kept in poor conditions. Both are open from 7 am to 12 noon and 2 to 5 pm daily, except Friday.

The bus station is up by the market in the same area as the supermarket (the big blue building) and post office.

Places to Stay

Hotel Grand Erg is the cheaper of the two alternatives and costs AD 120 a double. You can camp in its gardens – still expensive at AD 20 a person and AD 5 a shower. The management is extremely unhelpful, but it's this or nothing.

The only other place is the government-run three-star *Hotel Rym* at the foot of the dunes. Rooms cost a hefty AD 140/180 a single/double with breakfast.

Places to Eat

There are only two restaurants in town and both are extremely basic. Lunch is the main meal of the day, so finding anything in the evening can be difficult. The restaurant near the bus station is marginally better and has meat, omelettes and chips. The other restaurant is on the corner of the main street, which leads to the museum, next to the river. If you are putting your own food together be warned that the two town bakeries are closed on Fridays.

BENI-OUNIF

Beni-Ounif is the first Algerian town you will come to if you're crossing the Moroccan-Algerian border on foot. The only hotel is often full, so it's best to cross the border early and move on to Béchar the same day.

There are regular buses both north (Oran, Tlemcen, Algiers) and south (Béchar). They stop outside the hotel. Often, however, there are no seats and buses are not allowed to carry standing passengers. It is an easy hitch from Beni Ounif to Béchar.

Place to Stay & Eat

The only hotel is *Hotel Afrique* on the main road near the turn-off to Figuig. It was redecorated recently and costs AD 60/100 a single/double.

Restaurant El Feth, at the town's main intersection, has good spaghetti and salad for AD 25 or omelette and chips for AD 15.

BISKRA

This town on the southern edge of the Saharan Atlas is the gateway to the Sahara in this part of Algeria. Though it has a *palmeraie*, there is really no reason to stop.

Places to Stay

As well as a *Youth Hostel*, there is a cheap hotel in the bus station building, about 300 metres north of the centre. In the main part of town, *Hotel Gendouz* charges AD 159 a double with breakfast.

CONSTANTINE

If you are crossing north-eastern Algeria, don't bypass Constantine. Perched on the edge of the Rhumel Gorge, it has one of the most spectacular settings in the country.

As Cirta Regia in Punic and Roman times, it was here that the Numidian king Massinissa made his capital in the 2nd century BC, and from here that he launched attacks against the Carthaginians.

Today the gorges are the main attraction. The river at the bottom is little more than a black trickle and the sides of the gorge are littered with garbage tossed down over the years.

Information

There is a helpful local tourist office at 32 Rue Abane Ramdane, the street that runs uphill from Place des Martyrs, one of the two main squares and easily identifiable by the large Air Algérie office.

The other square is Place 1 Novembre and around it are the post office and main banks.

Because of the hilly terrain, the bus station is a few km south of the centre at the bottom of the gorge, where it widens out a bit. To get there catch a No 18 bus

Constantine

1	Suspension Bridge
2	Kantara Bridge
3	Grill Room
4	Restaurant Le Tassili
5	Hotel La Famille
6	Hotel Central
7	Banque Centrale d'Algérie
8	Local Bus station
9	Hotel Grand
10	Banque Nationale d'Algérie
11	Theatre
12	GPO
13	Touring Club d'Algérie
14	Hotel Cirta
15	Air Algérie
16	Museum
17	Tourist Office
19	Footbridge

from the local terminus behind the Palais de Justice between the two squares.

Places to Stay

Hotel Central is at 19 Rue Hamloui, a narrow street just behind Place 1 Novembre. It is clean, secure and friendly and costs AD 44/66 a single/double. Couples can usually take a single room as the beds are large. A little further up the street, *Hotel La Famille* is similar, but not as good.

There also are two extremely basic men-only places in the same street. These have signs in Arabic only.

For something a bit better, *Hotel Grand* is at 2 Rue Larbi Ben M'Hidi, right on the edge of Place 1 Novembre. It's not bad value at AD 80/120 a single/double with breakfast.

Places to Eat

The best area for cheap eating is around the bottom end of Rue Hamloui, where there are a dozen or so snack eateries. All have their food on display, so just take a wander around.

Restaurant El Baraka, at 23 Rue Hamloui, is not bad for a sit-down meal. It has main courses for AD 20 and salads for AD 6. Avoid *Restaurant Dounyazed* at No 29. While it looks good from the outside, you will have to do battle with the dozens of tiny cockroaches for the bread.

DJANET

Djanet is the main town of the Tassili and has a post office, bank, Air Algérie office and a few basic shops. It's a pretty place, built on the edge of the *palmeraie*.

There are no bus services in or out, so it's a matter of hitching. There is very little traffic to Tamanrasset.

Places to Stay

The only place to stay is *Camping Zeribas* in the centre of town. The grass bungalows cost AD 50 a person. There is a restaurant. You are not allowed to camp in the palmerie.

DJEMILA

The old Roman city of Cuicul has a superb mountain setting, and some of its buildings are remarkably well preserved.

Cuicul is served by public transport and because there is no accommodation in the immediate area, it is best seen as a day trip from Sétif, 40 km to the south-west. To get there from Sétif, catch a bus (or hitch) to El Ouelma on the Constantine road, and from there take a share-taxi to Djemila (AD 12 a person).

The small town has a couple of restaurants where you can get a bite to eat and a cold drink.

There are regular taxis to El Ouelma and from there it's easy to bus or hitch back to Sétif.

Things to See

Just inside the entrance to the **ruins** is the **museum**. It is stacked full of interesting finds from the site, and its 10-metre-high walls are covered in mosaics. The main features of the ruins are the baptistry, the enormous grand baths, the new forum, with its highly decorative triumphal arch

Map legend:

1. Restaurant des Amis
2. Supermarket
3. Air Algérie
4. Market
5. Bus Station
6. Police
7. Mosque
8. Café Port Said

El Goléa

and Septimien Temple, the old forum, market and theatre.

There are plenty of would-be guides hanging around who will take you through for a few dinar. The site is open daily in summer from 7 am to 6 pm, 5 pm in winter. The museum is open from 9 am to 12 noon and 2 to 5 pm, closed Saturday.

EL GOLÉA
El Goléa is a beautiful oasis town surrounded by thousands of palm and fruit trees on the eastern edge of the Grand Erg Occidental. The water here is some of the sweetest in the whole of the Sahara. In fact it's so good they bottle it and sell it throughout the country. Fill up if you're driving.

The town has a bank, post office, Air Algérie office, market and a poorly-stocked supermarket.

Places to Stay & Eat
There are two camping grounds. The private one, 500 metres north of the centre on the road out of town, is the better of the

two. It is surrounded by a high fence. The corrugated iron gate has 'Camping' written on it. There's plenty of shade and adequate facilities. It costs AD 20 a person.

The other camping ground is run by the Touring Club d'Algérie and is three km south of the centre. It is neither as shady nor as private as the first.

The only reasonably priced hotel is *Hotel Vieux Ksar* near the southern camping ground, about a 25-minute walk from the centre. It costs AD 90 for a double with breakfast. This is also the closest

place to eat if you are staying at the Touring Club camping ground.

In the centre, *Restaurant des Amis* has very mediocre food. But it does stay open late to cater for the buses on the Ghardaia to Adrar run.

There's a good little restaurant opposite the Naftal fuel station, near the private camping ground.

EL OUED

Tagged the 'Town of a 1000 Cupolas', El Oued is the major town of the Souf region in the Grand Erg Oriental. As the tag

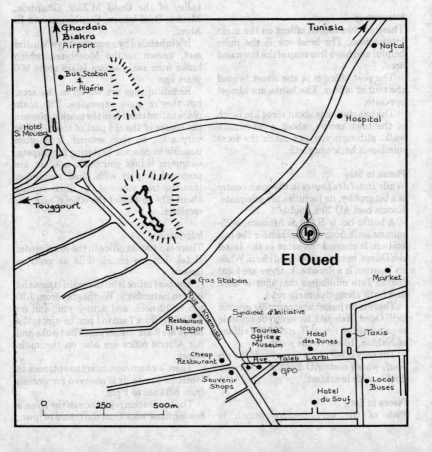

suggests, most of the buildings have domes, built in an effort to alleviate the summer heat, which has been known to climb to 60°C in summer, although a mere 45°C is more usual.

The town is also famous for its carpets, which often bear the traditional Cross of the Souf. The prices are better than in Ghardaia, a major outlet for the Souf product.

The daily **market** in the old part of town is a colourful affair and is at its most animated on Fridays.

The small **museum**, in between the two tourist offices, is worth a quick look.

Information

There are two tourist offices on the main intersection. The local one is the more helpful and has a free map of the town and area.

The post office is in the street behind the tourist offices. The banks are almost opposite.

The bus station is about three km north of the town centre, about a 30-minute walk, although you can catch the local minibuses back and forth.

Places to Stay

While *Hotel des Dunes* in the town centre is a bit grubby, its facilities are adequate. Rooms cost AD 70 a double.

A better bet is *Hotel Si Moussa*, a 25-minute walk from the centre near the bus station. It charges the same as the Hotel des Dunes, but is very new and clean. While its location is a drawback, there are local Indian Tata minibuses that shuttle back and forth along this main road.

There is no longer any camping ground in El Oued. It should, however, be possible to camp at the *Youth Hostel* in the village of Nakhla, 16 km to the south.

The only other place to stay is *Hotel du Souf*, which costs AD 192 for an air-con double with breakfast.

Places to Eat

Pick of the very meagre bunch is

Restaurant El Hoggar, halfway along the main street. It's one of the few places that doesn't close in the middle of the day, and as such is a 'relatively' cool haven. The food isn't bad either.

There's a small restaurant on the corner diagonally opposite the tourist office. It serves quite reasonable food and the shop next door sells cans of *cold* grapefruit or orange juice for AD 7.

GHARDAIA

Ghardaia is one of the most fascinating of the oasis towns and well worth exploring. It's actually a cluster of five towns in the valley of the Oued M'Zab: Ghardaia, Melika, Beni Isguen, Bou Noura and El Ateuf.

It's inhabited by a conservative Muslim sect, known as the Mozabites, which broke from mainstream Islam some 900 years ago.

Beautiful rugs are woven in the area, but they're quite expensive. The main place to find them is in the market place in the centre of the old part of town. Prices vary a lot, so shop around. It is often possible to do some bartering for carpets, swapping things you don't need or are prepared to part with. Just remember that the true value of the dinar is only about 30% to 40% of the official rate you received.

Information

There is a tourist office in the Rostimedes Hotel, but, as usual, it is as good as useless.

The post office is on the main street and is open Saturday to Wednesday from 7.30 am to 12 noon and 4 to 7 pm, and on Thursday from 7 am to 1 pm. In winter the hours are 8 am to 6.30 pm. The banks and Air Algérie office are also on the main street.

There's a *hamman* near the entrance to Hotel Es Saada. It is reserved for women from 8.30 am to 1 pm.

The bus station is just across the river, a few minutes' walk from the centre of town.

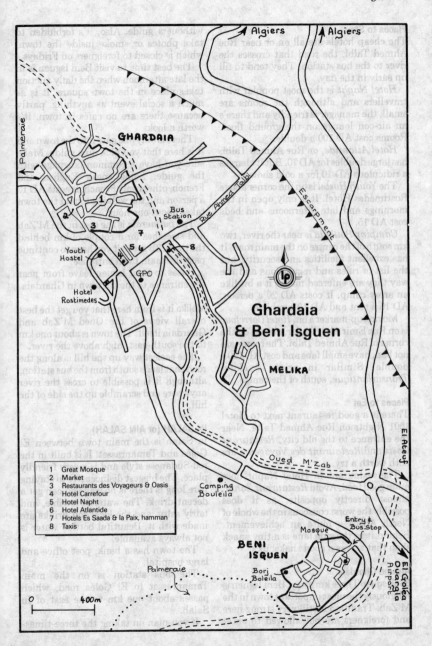

GHARDAIA

Ghardaia & Beni Isguen

MELIKA

BENI ISGUEN

Bus Station

Youth Hostel

GPO

Hotel Rostimedes

Camping Bouleila

Palmeraie

Rue Ahmed Talbi

Escarpment

Oued M'Zab

El Ateuf

Mosque

Entry & Bus Stop

Borj Boleila

El Goléa Ouargla Airport

Algiers

Algiers

1 Great Mosque
2 Market
3 Restaurants des Voyageurs & Oasis
4 Hotel Carrefour
5 Hotel Napht
6 Hotel Atlantide
7 Hotels Es Saada & la Paix, hamman
8 Taxis

400m

Places to Stay

The cheap hotels are all on or near Rue Ahmed Talbi, the road that crosses the river to the bus station. They tend to fill up early in the day.

Hotel Napht is the most popular with travellers and although the rooms are small, the manager is friendly and there's an air-con lounge on the ground floor. Rooms cost AD 100 a double.

Hotel Atlantide, on Rue Ahmed Talbi, has large doubles for AD 70. But it charges a ridiculous AD 10 for a cold shower.

The *Youth Hostel* is on the corner above Rostimedes Hotel. It is only open in the mornings and late afternoons and beds cost AD 15.

Camping Bouleila is near the river, two km south of the centre on the main road. It has excellent facilities and security, but the list of rules and regulations and the way they are enforced makes it a bit like an army camp. It costs AD 20 a person, AD 15 a tent and AD 10 a vehicle.

Moving up-market a bit, *Hotel Carrefour* is on Rue Emir Abdelkader, almost on the corner of Rue Ahmed Talbi. The rooms are not bad, have small fans and cost AD 120 a double. Similar in price is *Hotel Transatlantique*, south of the centre.

Places to Eat

There is a good restaurant next to Hotel 1001 Nights on Rue Ahmed Talbi. Near the entrance to the old city, *Restaurant Oasis* and *Restaurant des Voyageurs* are both worth a try.

The restaurant in Hotel Napht does quite good food. Avoid *Restaurant Zahia*, almost directly opposite, as it does possibly the worst couscous in the whole of North Africa – quite an achievement. Behind it in the side lane is a tiny snack shop that serves a good shakshuka.

Around Ghardaia

Beni Isguen Three km away, Beni Isguen is religiously the most important town in the M'Zab. Tradition is still very strong here and foreigners are not allowed to enter without a guide. Also, it's forbidden to take photos or smoke inside the town, which is closed to foreigners on Fridays.

The best time to visit Beni Isguen is in the late afternoon when the daily auction takes place in the town square. It is as much a social event as anything, partly because there are no cafés in town. It's worth a look.

There is only one gate into the town and it is here that you pick up a guide. Make sure you have a common language with the guide. Some speak English and French, others only French. It costs AD 10 a person and the walking tour of the town takes about one hour.

The *palmeraie* is the best in the M'Zab and stretches for a couple of km behind the town. To get to it you have to continue past the main town entrance.

Buses to Beni Isguen leave from near the entrance to the old town in Ghardaia.

Melika It is from here that you get the best overall views of the Oued M'Zab and Ghardaia itself. The town is about one km to the south-east, high above the river.

The easiest way up the hill is along the road that leads south from the bus station, although it is possible to cross the river anywhere and scramble up the side of the hill.

IN SALAH (or AIN SALAH)

In Salah is the main town between El Goléa and Tamanrasset. It is built in the red Sudanese style and is a very friendly place. The biggest disincentive to staying here long is there is no way you can get a decent drink. The water is terrible, and fairly salty, and the local soft drinks are made with it. Beautiful bottled water is not always available.

The town has a bank, post office and large hospital.

The bus station is on the main Tamanrasset to El Goléa road, which passes about one km to the east of In Salah.

If you plan on taking the three-times-

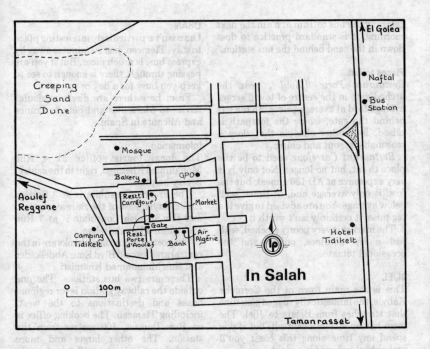

Map labels:
El Goléa
Naftal
Bus Station
Creeping Sand Dune
Mosque
Bakery
GPO
Aoulef Reggane
Restt Carrefour
Market
Gate
Rest Porte d'Aoulef
Bank
Air Algérie
Camping Tidikelt
Hotel Tidikelt
In Salah
0   100 m
Tamanrasset

weekly bus to Tamanrasset, book your ticket the day before as demand sometimes exceeds supply. A ticket does not reserve you a seat, so be at the bus at least 30 minutes before departure at 5 am to be assured of a place in front of the rear wheels. If you sit behind the rear wheels, be prepared to arrive in Tam with a backbone about three inches shorter than when you set out. Yes, it's a rough, bone-jarring, 19-hour ride.

Things to See
The most interesting feature of the town is the **creeping sand dune** on the western edge by the Aoulef road. From behind the mosque you can see how the dune is gradually encroaching on the town, and from the top of the dune it becomes apparent that it has actually cut the town in two. The dune moves at the rate of about one metre every five years. The amount of sand on the move is constant, so while it is swallowing up a building on its leading edge, it is uncovering one behind, which may have been buried for a couple of generations.

Places to Stay
Camping Tidikelt is in the centre of town. It's clean and friendly and there's plenty of shade, although the facilities are hopelessly inadequate. Camping costs AD 20 a person, plus AD 5 a car. You can sleep in one of the tiny *zeribas* if you want. Cold drinks are available. The other camp site, called *Zribat*, is three km south of town on the road to Tamanrasset. Recent reports say that it is closed. Check this out.

The only hotel is the up-market *Hotel Tidikelt*, near the bus station. It costs AD 192 a double.

If you arrive on a bus late at night or are

catching the bus to Tam at 5 am the next morning, it is standard practice to doss down in the sand behind the bus station.

Places to Eat

Restaurant Porte d'Aoulef, near the arched gate in the centre of town, serves average food at average prices. To the left behind the gate, where the footpath is raised, is another cheapie that does a reasonable ragout and chips.

Restaurant Carrefour used to be the place to eat, but no longer. Not only is it very expensive at AD 130 a meal, but the food is only average and, at times, well below average. You are advised to give it a big miss, it certainly isn't worth it.

The market is very poorly stocked, with just a few potatoes, onions and the occasional tomato.

JIJEL

This is the main town of the Corniche Kabyle, the fantastically rugged coastline that stretches from Bejaia to Jijel. The town has no attractions itself, but if you spend any time along this coast you'll probably stay here for a night.

The bus station is about 100 metres from the town hall, along the waterfront road.

Places to Stay

The best place to stay is *Hotel du Littoral* on Rue 1 Novembre 1954, not far from Place de la République, easily recognised as the town hall, with its clocktower, is right in the middle. The hotel is dilapidated but clean. Rooms cost AD 55 a double. There are no showers, but there is a public bathhouse next door.

The other cheapie for men only is *Hotel en Nassre*, a couple of blocks from Hotel du Littoral. It's a bit of a dive, but would do at a pinch.

Places to Eat

The restaurant attached to *Hotel en Nassre* is not too bad, although couples and solo women have to sit in the separate 'salon'.

ORAN

Oran isn't a particularly interesting place to stay. Tlemcen, just 90 minutes away by express bus, is much nicer. But if you are passing through, there is enough to see to keep you busy for a day or so.

From here there are direct vehicular ferries to Marseilles and Sète in France and Alicante in Spain.

Information

The local tourist office at 4 Rue Mohammed Khemisti, right in the centre, is very helpful.

The French Consulate is at 3 Square Émile Cayla, east of the railway station, and the Spanish Consulate is at 7 Rue Mohammed Benabdeslem.

The post office and main banks are in the central area around Blvd Emir Abdelkader and Rue Mohammed Khemisti.

There are two bus stations. The one outside the railway station is for regional buses and destinations to the west, including Tlemcen. The booking office is on Rue Tenazet, 100 metres from the station. The other larger and more crowded station is a long 10-minute walk south of the museum, or 20 minutes' from the centre of town. It serves all other parts of the country.

The train station is on Blvd Mellah Ali, a 10-minute walk up the hill from the centre.

Tickets for the ferries can be bought either from the CNAN office at the ferry terminal or the office at 13 Blvd Abane Ramdane, near the French Consulate.

Things to See

The **Grand Mosque** is just down the hill from the main square, Place 1 Novembre. Built in 1796 and restored in 1900, it is possible to visit the semicircular courtyard.

Towards the waterfront from Place 1 Novembre is **Promenade Ibn Badis**. This is and gives good views over the harbour and Jebel Mudjadjo. It is open daily from 8 am to 12 noon and 2 to 5 pm.

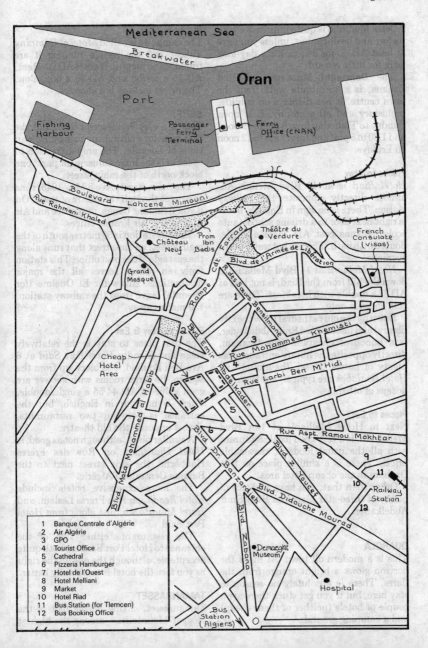

Mediterranean Sea

Breakwater

Oran

Port

Fishing Harbour

Passenger Ferry Terminal

Ferry Office (CNAN)

Boulevard Lahcene Mimouni

Rue Rahmani Khaled

Château Neuf

Prom Ibn Badis

Théâtre du Verdure

French Consulate (visas)

Blvd de l'Armée de Libération

Grand Mosque

Rampe Cdt. Farrad

Rue des Soeurs Bensimone

Blvd Emir Abdelkader

Rue Mohammed Khemisti

Cheap Hotel Area

Rue Larbi Ben M'Hidi

Blvd Mata Mohammed al Habib

Blvd Dr. Benzerdeb

Blvd Nabana

Rue Aspt. Ramou Mokhtar

Blvd Z. Youcef

Blvd Didouche Mourad

Railway Station

Demaeghi Museum

Hospital

Bus Station (for Tlemcen)

Bus Booking Office

Bus Station (Algiers)

1 Banque Centrale d'Algérie
2 Air Algérie
3 GPO
4 Tourist Office
5 Cathedral
6 Pizzeria Hamburger
7 Hotel de l'Ouest
8 Hotel Melliani
9 Market
10 Hotel Riad
11 Bus Station (for Tlemcen)
12 Bus Booking Office

Jebel Mudjadjo is quite impressive with its fort and basilica, but, unless you have at least AD 50 for a taxi, it's a day-long walk for little reward.

The **Demaeght Museum**, on Blvd Zabana, is a 15-minute walk from the town centre. It has displays on wildlife, prehistory and ethnography. It is open Sunday to Thursday from 8 am to 12 noon and 1.30 to 5 pm, and from 8 am to 12 noon on Fridays.

Places to Stay

Hotel Riad is at 46 Blvd Mellah Ali, almost directly opposite the railway station. There is no sign in English, but it is right next door to a driving school (auto école). Rooms cost AD 75/93 a single/double with bath. There is hot water in the evenings.

Hotel Melliani at 14 Blvd Mellah Ali, down the hill from the Riad, is not bad at AD 87 a double with breakfast. There are cold showers only.

Down by the old cathedral (now the city library) and just off Blvd Emir Abdelkader, is a bunch of cheapies. Rue Ozanam, directly opposite the library entrance, has plenty of hotels. *Hotel Takadoum* and *Hotel Baalabek* are typical, but there are dozens of others.

Places to Eat

Next to Hotel Melliani, at 14A Blvd Mellah Ali, is a very good local restaurant with all the usual foods at reasonable prices. There is a similar place on Rue Ozanam in the cheap hotel area.

Other than that, you have a choice of plenty of three-star places on Blvd Emir Abdelkader.

OUARGLA

This is a modern oil town. At night the horizon glows a bright orange from the flares. There is absolutely no reason to stay here, but if you get stuck there are a couple of hotels (neither of them cheap) and a camping ground.

Places to Stay

The camp site is called *Motel et Camping Tahost* and the people running it are friendly and helpful. It costs AD 20 a tent, AD 25 a *zeriba* and AD 95 a bungalow. The prices include hot showers.

SÉTIF

Sétif is a very nondescript town, but the best base for visiting the nearby Roman ruins at Djemila. The only attraction to speak of is the huge amusement park, one block north of the main street.

The main street, Ave 8 May 1945, runs east-west through the centre of town. On it you'll find the banks, post office and Air Algérie and Air France offices.

The bus station is 50 metres south of the main street, on the street that runs along the east side of the post office. This station (only an office) serves all the major destinations. Buses for El Ouelma (for Djemila) leave from the railway station, 150 metres away.

Places to Stay & Eat

The best place to stay is the relatively clean and friendly *Hotel Port Said* at 6 Ave Ben Boulaid, one block up from the square. Its large rooms with shower are good value at AD 44/55 a single/double. There is no sign in English, but the entrance is between two restaurants, almost opposite the old theatre.

A similar place, although not as good, is *Hotel Djurdjura* on Rue des Frères Habbèche, the side street next to the Banque Centrale D'Algérie.

The more expensive hotels include *Hotel Readh*, on Rue Frères Leslem, and *Hotel Mountazeh*, just along from Hotel Port Said.

The restaurants either side of the entrance to Hotel Port Said are both quite acceptable, although the one on the right as you face the hotel is marginally better.

TAMANRASSET

Tamanrasset, sitting at the foot of the Hoggar Mountains – among the highest mountains in the Sahara – is the last major town on the route south to Niger.

At one time supplies and facilities at Tamanrasset were limited, but the place has grown rapidly in recent years and supplies are now plentiful.

Tam is the place to find a lift or rent a vehicle to get to Assekrem, not to be missed.

If you are heading for Niger, be sure to report to the police to get permission to travel south. Your currency form will be scrutinised at customs, but is actually handed in at the border. Passport control is also at the border.

Information

The post office, banks and shops are in the one area in the centre of town. The poste restante counter is in the telephone office next door to the post office. Be warned that it holds mail for 15 days only. The banks are open daily, except Friday.

There are both Malian and Niger consulates in Tamanrasset. They are on the main street, towards the camping ground. To get a Niger visa you need a cholera vaccination certificate (not strictly enforced), three passport photos and AD 64. It takes up to three days to come through. Malian visas are usually issued the same day and paid for in French francs.

There are travel agents dotted around town, where you can rent a 4WD and driver for AD 900 to AD 1100 a day. The vehicles carry up to six people, so if you can get a group together the cost starts to become reasonable. Two of the best agencies are Tarahist, near the post office, and Akar Akar, at the camp site.

The bus station is on the road to the north of town. If you are camping, it is a solid one-hour walk, so if you arrive late or are leaving early the best bet is to sleep out at the bus station along with the locals.

Places to Stay

The camp site where most travellers stay is *Hotel Dassine*, though it's more popularly known as *Camping Zerib* and

there is no hotel on the site. You can camp here for AD 15 a person and AD 10 a vehicle. There are *zeribas* for AD 40 a person, but they are small and claustrophobic. If you don't need the comfort of a bed, camping out is the best idea. There are cold showers and clean toilets, but the water is only on for a couple of hours in the mornings and afternoons. The big *zeriba* is a café and you can get drinks here.

This camp site is crawling with tourists, making it a good place to ask around for lifts. It is also the only place in town to fill up with water. The staff are generally unhelpful.

There's another camp site, known as *La Source*, about 15 km out of town on the road to Assekrem. It costs AD 15 a person and is the place to go if you have a vehicle and want to escape the crowds. However, recent reports suggest it may be closing.

Hotel Ilamane is the cheapest hotel, though it's none too great. Rooms cost AD 50 a person. The only advantage to staying here over camping is that it is close to the centre of town. If it's full, try *Hotel Tinhinane* for AD 120 a double with breakfast. This hotel has the main bar in town.

Hotel Tahat is the most expensive hotel at AD 121/142 a single/double with communal facilities and AD 141/192 a single/double with shower and toilet. Prices include breakfast.

Places to Eat

Restaurant Le Palmier is the best of the group of restaurants on the main street – tasty main courses for AD 20 and soup for AD 10. The other places are cheaper, but less appealing.

Around Tamanrasset

Without your own vehicle visiting **Assekrem**, 75 km north-east of Tamanrasset, is difficult. But, it's worth the effort. The scenery is absolutely incredible, and a sunrise in these mountains is memorable.

Charles de Foucauld, a dedicated Christian who came to the Hoggars early

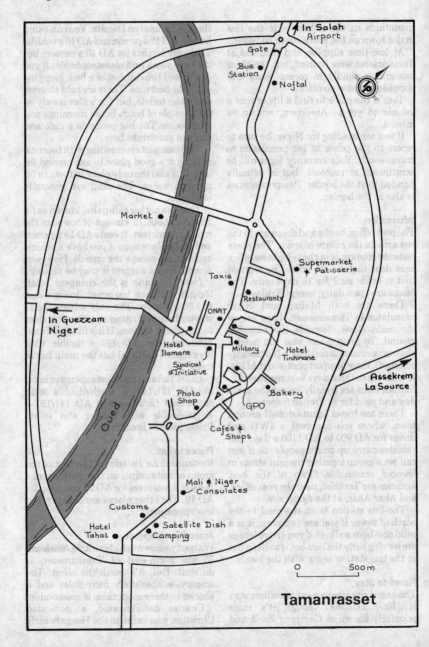

Tamanrasset

this century, built a hermitage on top of the Assekrem plateau in 1910. It is still lived in and maintained by Fathers. It is accessible only by foot, taking about 30 minutes to walk up from the refuge below. This is the place to watch the sun rise. You can either sleep in the refuge or camp nearby.

TIMIMOUN

Timimoun is a beautiful oasis town on the fringe of the Grand Erg Occidental. If you are only able to stop at one oasis, this has to be it. It's an enchanting place, built mostly in the red-mud Sudanese style on the edge of an escarpment. There are fantastic views out over an ancient salt lake to the sand erg in the distance, and on a bright moonlit night the effect is magic. Also, the locals are very friendly.

The Gourara Circuit is a 70-km loop around a number of villages to the north. It is a must if you have your own vehicle. There is a map of the route in the tourist office on the main street.

The post office, bank, market and bus station are on the main street.

Places to Stay & Eat

Camping le Palmeraie is on the edge of the escarpment, to the left as you enter town. It costs AD 20 a person, and there's plenty of shade, hot showers and the staff is friendly and eager to please.

Hotel Ighzer, on the main street past the mosque, has OK rooms for AD 80 a double. You camp in the back yard, but without shade it is a bit bleak.

Hotel Rouge de l'Oasis is a fantastic old place, but unfortunately it is being allowed to deteriorate. Rooms used to cost AD 90 a double, and may still be available. The bar certainly remains open.

There is just one restaurant. It's off the main street, between Hotel Rouge de l'Oasis and the gardens opposite the municipality building. Camel stew with rice is often on the menu.

TIZI-OUZOU

Tizi-Ouzou is the capital of the Kabylie region and home of the Kabyle Berbers, who have retained their own language and are still pushing for some degree of autonomy.

The town itself is nothing special, but the mountains around offer some spectacular scenery, particularly on the road to Azazga and Bejaia.

The bus station is on the main street, 300 metres down the hill from the roundabout towards Algiers. It is a large blue building; the ticket office is upstairs. Taxis leave from here.

Places to Stay & Eat

The only budget place is *Hotel Olympia*. It is up a side street one block from the main street, Rue Larbi Ben M'Hidi, and about a 10-minute walk from the bus station.

The two-star *Hotel Beloua*, just up from the bus station, costs AD 120/160 a single/double with breakfast.

On the same street as Hotel Olympia, and almost directly opposite, is *Restaurant Mediterranean*. It caters more for those who want a beer or wine, but the food is passable if a bit expensive. There are a couple of cheaper places on Rue Larbi Ben M'Hidi.

TLEMCEN

Tlemcen is a beautiful old city and well worth a visit, especially if you are heading for Morocco from the Sahara or touring the east of Algeria as it's not much of a detour. Because of its altitude, the weather at Tlemcen is cooler than on the steamy coast. The locals are friendly and the town is one of the nicest in the country.

Founded by the Almoravide dynasty, Tlemcen was the capital of the central Maghreb and had its heyday under the Zianids in the 13th century. It thrived on the trans-Saharan trade between Black Africa and Europe. The Zianid's Berber cousins, the Merenids, became entrenched

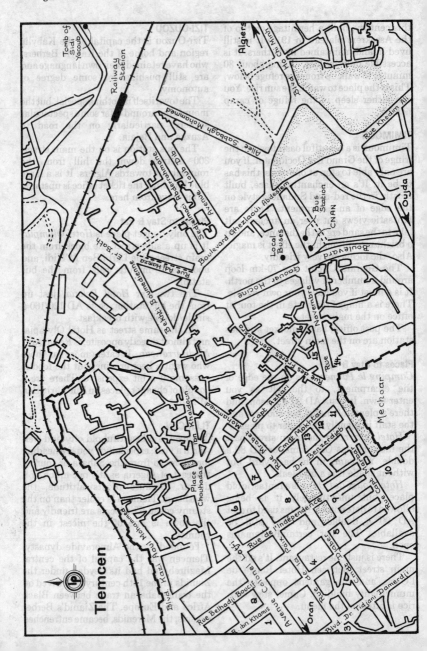

1	GPO
2	Banque Centrale d'Algérie
3	Air France
4	Public Douche
5	Mosque Sidi Bel Hassan
6	Snack Shop
7	Market
8	Great Mosque
9	Banque Nationale d'Algérie
10	Syndicat d'Initiative
11	Hotel Maghreb
12	Hotel Majestic
13	Restaurant
14	Restaurant du Coupole
15	Hotel Restaurant Moderne
16	Hamman

in Morocco and the resulting rivalry between the two groups became the main threat to the town.

Tlemcen became embroiled in the struggle for power between the French and Turks, and in 1842 became part of French Algeria. In the lead up to independence, it was the founding place of the forerunner to the FLN and Emir Abdelkader was active in the area.

If you're coming from Morocco on foot, Tlemcen is going to be well out of your way; at the time of writing, the only border open to walkers was at Figuig-Beni Ounif. People with vehicles face no such restrictions.

Information

The helpful syndicat d'initiative is on Ave Commandant Farradj, opposite the entrance to the Mechouar. It has a good handout map of the city.

The post office and banks are on the main street, Ave Colonel Lotfi.

The excellent produce market is just off the central square, Place Emir Abdelkader.

The bus station is on the basement level of the building on the corner of Rue 1 Novembre and Blvd Gaouer Hocine, about a 10-minute walk from the centre. There are five buses daily to the Moroccan border.

The railway station is a grand white building about a five-minute walk past the bus station. There is a train servicing the border, but the bus is far more convenient.

Things to See

The **Great Mosque** backs onto the main square, Place Emir Abdelkader. It was built by the Almoravide ruler Ali Ben Youssef in 1135, and extended by the Zianid ruler Yaghmoracen, who was responsible for the polychrome-tile minaret. The dome above the mihrab (prayer niche) has some excellent stalactite decoration and the mihrab itself is covered with delicate stucco work. The mosque is one of the few, and certainly the most important, in the Maghreb open to non-Muslims. Visitors are allowed in daily from 8 to 11 am, except Friday. The entrance is down the side lane to the right.

At the eastern end of the main square, the **Mosque Sidi Bel Hassan** dates back to the 13th century. It has been converted to a good little museum.

One block south of the main square is the **Mechouar**, the site of the palace of the early Almohade governors. The present walls date only to the time of the French occupation, and whatever is inside remains hidden from the visitor.

About a km to the west of town are the ruins of ancient **Mansourah**. The four km of walls date to the end of the 13th century and mark the perimeter of the walled Merenid town which covered an area of about 100 hectares. The only ruin left inside the walls is the minaret and mosque. Mansourah was used only during the Merenid invasions. After the last of these, it was deserted and became a handy source of building materials for nearby Tlemcen.

In the opposite direction from the town centre is the mosque and tomb of **Sidi Bou Mediène**. It is an important example of Merenid architecture and one of the finest monuments in the Maghreb. Sidi Bou

Mediène was a mystic who died here on his way from Bejaia to Marrakesh. The present *koubba* was built in 1339, but has suffered from heavy handed 18th-century restoration. The main item of interest is the monumental porch, with bronze-clad cedar doors and stalactite cupola.

Places to Stay

Pick of the very small bunch is *Hotel Majestic*, on the shady Place Cheikh Bahir Ibrahimi, one block south-east of Place Emir Abdelkader. It is the grey building on the corner and the entrance is on the side street – there is no sign in English. Rooms cost AD 80/120 a single/double. Couples can pay just for a single.

Hotel Moderne, at 20 Rue 1 Novembre, is less friendly but cheaper at AD 70 a double.

Up the scale a bit is *Hotel Maghreb*, just along from Hotel Majestic. It is expensive at AD 121/161 a single/double with breakfast and bath. It is possible to change money here outside banking hours.

Camping Municipale is among the olive groves inside the walls of Mansourah, a solid 20-minute walk from the town centre. Facilities are extremely basic, but it is cheap at AD 7.50 a person and AD 10 a vehicle or tent.

Places to Eat

There is one good little place on the corner one block up from Hotel Majestic. A good meal of chicken, chips and salad costs AD 25.

On Rue 1 Novembre, *Restaurant du Coupole* has a reasonable set menu for AD 45, while *Restaurant Moderne*, attached to the hotel of that name, charges AD 35.

TOUGGOURT

A totally unremarkable, and in summer, unbearably hot oasis town. If you do stop for a day, it is worth exploring the small towns of Tamelhat and Temacine, in the oasis directly to the south and easily accessible by bus.

Tamelhat, 12 km south of town, is a mud-brick village on the edge of a *palmeraie*. It has an old mosque with a decorated cupola. Temacine is more picturesque as it is built around a ksar on a small hill. Palm tree trunks have been used extensively in the construction of the fortification.

Buses to the two villages leave from a stop to the right of the municipality building in the centre of town – ask for directions. The bus station is just a small office by the railway station, which is a 10-minute walk from the town centre.

Taxis for El Oued leave from the square near the market place.

Places to Stay & Eat

Hotel Marhaba is next to the taxi station and charges AD 70 a double. The smart thing to do is adopt the local habit and sleep on the roof as the rooms become intolerably hot. The showers are supposedly cold, but the water in the pipes gets so hot that it's hard to stand under it.

The other cheapie is *Hotel de la Paix*, near the market but closer to the main street.

Between the taxi station and the market are a couple of ultra-basic restaurants.

Angola

Angola is still preoccupied with reconstruction after the devastating civil war that engulfed the country when independence was abruptly granted by the Portuguese in 1975. This war, together with continual political and military interference by other countries and their surrogates ever since, has resulted in social dislocation on a vast scale, the neglect or abandonment of agriculture and the ruin of the country's road and rail network. Even today, large parts of the south are out of government control.

The newly independent Angola quickly became a classic case of superpower rivalry. Not only did it face full-scale military invasions by the regular troops of South Africa and Zaïre, but incursions by European mercenaries and the rebel forces of Jonas Savimbi's South African-supported Unita. Added to this, there was a less serious threat from rebel forces in the oil-rich Cabinda enclave for a while.

Despite all this, much headway was made in putting Angola back on its feet, with a lot of help from Cuban and Portuguese advisers and voluntary workers. But it was the presence of an estimated 37,000 Cuban troops, and their real or imagined support of Swapo guerrillas, that was used by the South Africans as a pretext for invading the country's south several times. The Cubans also became central to the continuing saga over independence for Namibia. Nevertheless, towards the end of the 1980s, it became clear that Angolan government troops were capable of containing these threats without resorting to direct Cuban involvement. After much diplomatic manoeuvring, agreement was finally reached on the withdrawal of Cuban and South African troops from Angola and the eventual independence of Namibia.

With security and stability such elusive commodities in Angola, it's hardly surprising that the government has discouraged tourism. Its priorities have been much more basic.

Angola suffered one of the most backward forms of colonialism. Portugal itself was – in European terms – a relatively undeveloped country. It lacked a substantial industrial base and simply had neither the inclination nor the resources to develop its African colonies. While a settlement was established at coastal Luanda as early as 1575, there was no attempt to settle inland until the end of the 19th century. Even then, it was done with convict labour from the prisons of the mother country. Until then, Portugal was content to milk the area for slaves for its far more lucrative colony in Brazil and to capitalise on the occasional discovery of precious metals and gemstones.

By 1900 there were fewer than 10,000 whites in the colony. By 1950, their numbers had grown to around 80,000, largely because of the coffee boom after WW II. The last 25 years of colonial rule saw immigration from Portugal take off on a large scale, but even then, about half the new immigrants were illiterate peasants from the more impoverished parts of Portugal. Not only were the vast majority of them destined to spend only a very short time in the colony, but it seems that few of them were cut out for life in the Angolan bush. Only 1% of the European population was established in the rural settlements prior to independence.

Popular resistance to colonial rule had its roots in the system of forced labour, and after WW II spontaneous clashes

between the various African communities and the colonial administration became increasingly frequent. The first really serious confrontations took place in February and March 1961 and were directed at European and mestizo plantation owners, as well as the jails in Luanda where political prisoners were held.

The protests were organised by supporters of the Popular Movement for the Liberation of Angola (MPLA) and by the Union of the Populations of Northern Angola (UPNA), soon to become part of the National Front for the Liberation of Angola (FNLA). Some three years after the formation of the FNLA, a group of southerners broke away to form the National Union for the Total Independence of Angola (Unita) in protest at what they perceived to be an attempt by tribes of the north to monopolise the movement.

All three groups took to guerrilla warfare shortly after the 1961 uprisings as a consequence of the vicious military and political campaign launched by the colonial authorities. There were few major differences between the three groups as far as objectives were concerned, but there were great differences in the sources from which they drew their support.

The FNLA appealed to tribal allegiances in the country's north and was supported by Zaïre and a number of western countries opposed to a communist takeover of Angola. For this group, the destruction of the MPLA was as important as ousting the Portuguese.

The MPLA emphasised the importance of transcending tribalism and appealed to a broad sense of nationalism. It was linked to the liberation movements in the other Portuguese colonies and was supported by the USSR and its allies. Its popular base of support was concentrated in the south and centre of the country.

Unita also drew the bulk of its support from the south and there was fierce rivalry between it and the MPLA. Unita certainly had the confidence of the Ovimbundu in the early stages, but its leaders soon revealed themselves as opportunists. Not only were they prepared to accommodate the right-wing Portuguese forces and exploit superpower rivalry prior to independence, but, once it was granted, they formed an open alliance with South Africa!

Following the overthrow of the fascist regime in Portugal in 1974 by the armed forces movement, negotiations began on a programme for Angolan independence. A transitional government, consisting of the three nationalist groups and Portugal, was set up. But it broke down and the country was plunged into civil war. It was invaded on the one hand by regular troops from Zaïre in support of the FNLA, and, on the other, by regular South African forces in support of Unita.

A massive airlift was organised to evacuate the bulk of the white population to Portugal and other countries.

The invasions failed and the MPLA, backed by combat troops from Cuba, Guinea and Guinea-Bissau, and equipment from Mozambique, Nigeria and Algeria, was able to seize control of the bulk of the country by early 1976.

Many years were to pass, however, before the FNLA and FLEC (Front for the Liberation of Cabinda) were crushed. Unita continues to wreak havoc in the south and south-east, though its fortunes wax and wane according to the extent of South African involvement at any particular time.

In recent years, the situation in Angola has become a valuable bargaining counter for the South Africans in the protracted negotiations for independence in Namibia. While Cuban troops remain in Angola, South Africa will continue to support Unita and prevaricate over independence for Namibia.

A high-level meeting was held in Luanda in early 1988 between US, Cuban and Angolan government officials in an attempt to hammer out a settlement – the withdrawal of the Cuban troops in return for peace in Angola and the independence of Namibia. It certainly was a step in the right direction, because nothing short of an internationally guaranteed settlement is going to end the civil war in Angola, but its success hinges on whether South Africa will negotiate in good faith.

As soon as the Luanda meeting was mooted, Pretoria began encouraging and directly supporting Unita in a major push north to capture strategic towns. By late March 1988 they were on the brink of taking Cuemba, a town on the Benguela railway line.

Despite having to rely heavily on assistance from its socialist allies, Angola has been re-establishing ties with the USA and other western countries in the past few years. Still, the internal conflict never prevented the US doing business with Angola or exploiting its oil reserves.

The American oil companies Chevron and Gulf have been operating in the Cabinda enclave for many years, more or less unaffected by the turmoil in the rest of the country – well, almost. In 1985, the

Angolan armed forces intercepted and captured a South African commando team in Cabinda, trying to pass themselves off as Unita rebels. Their targets were the American oil companies' installations. It seemed South Africa was acting independently on this occasion, despite US financial support of Unita, and it led to a serious cooling of relations between Washington and Pretoria. Had the operation succeeded, it would have brought the Luanda government to its knees (around 95% of Angola's exports are oil-based) and demanded armed intervention from overseas. This would have been a diplomatic coup for the South Africans since they would then be able to claim that the Luanda government obviously was a communist client state.

Even with its large and powerful backers, Unita alone probably did not represent a serious military threat to the Luanda government. While it appeared to be a very disruptive and destructive force in the south, much of what it was credited with was actually the work of regular South African forces. In 1975, the CIA estimated membership of Unita at 700. Today, it may be 10,000.

Despite recent agreements, as long as the Luanda government feels threatened by South Africa and its surrogates it will be forced to concentrate the bulk of its resources on military expenditure – to the detriment of both development and the provision of essential services (social, educational and medical) for its people.

Facts

WARNING

Should you wittingly or unwittingly come into contact with Angolan authorities, do not give up your passport without obtaining a receipt. Any difficulties should be reported to your country's embassy, or its representative in Angola.

Find out what embassy that is and where it is before arriving in Luanda.

There is a strictly enforced curfew in Luanda from midnight to 5 am.

VISAS

Visas are required by all. In Europe there are embassies in Lisbon, Paris and Rome. All visa applications have to be referred to DEFA (Direção de Emigração e Fronteras de Angola) in Luanda, regardless of where they are received. If you apply direct to DEFA (by registered post or telex 3127 MIREX AN) make sure you have the letter or telex that states your visa reference number when you arrive at Luanda airport.

To get a visa you must supply: your full name; the full names of both your parents; your occupation; your date and place of birth; the purpose of your visit and the proposed length of stay; the number, place and date of issue of your passport; four passport photos; a photostat of the first six pages of your passport (the latter two only if you are applying by mail – if you apply by telex then you must have the last two on arrival); and an International Vaccination Card for cholera and yellow fever (it helps also to prove you have been vaccinated against typhoid and hepatitis). You'll be given a visa authorisation number and on arrival you'll have to pay US$20 for the visa. Visa applications generally take six weeks to process.

It's unlikely your application will be approved unless you have a very good reason for wanting to go there: 'tourism' is not regarded as a good reason. One of the best ruses for getting a visa is the need to spend a few days in Angola between flights from one place to another. There is no way you will get a visa if there is any evidence that you have visited South Africa or Israel.

Despite all this, change is on the way. In 1987, Anghotel was taken over by the Agencia Nacional de Turismo, (Agnatur, tel 372750), Palacio de Vidro, Caixa Postal

1240, Luanda, and, from the beginning of 1988, tourist visas became available on the basis of pre-paid arrangements with Agnatur. Agnatur will also be responsible for improving the services of the Centro de Informação e Turismo de Angola, which shares its offices.

Travel anywhere outside Luanda requires a special permit, known as a *Guía de Marche* and issued by DEFA, and plenty of photographs. Take at least 20 with you!

MONEY
UK£ 1 = Kz 50

The unit of currency is the kwanza = 100 lweis. You can import up to Kz 1000, but export of the local currency is prohibited. On arrival, you must fill in a currency declaration form of all your foreign currency at the Banco Nacional de Angola. All your currency exchanges must be recorded on this form, which is thoroughly checked on departure. Don't try to circumvent the system. The penalties for black market dealings are severe.

There are only two official currency exchange points in Luanda. They are at Hotel Presidente Meridien and the Banco Nacional de Angola, Departamento dos Operações Internacionnais, Rua Rainha Ginga (near the Diamang building). You can only exchange currency between 8 am and 12 noon and 2.30 and 3.30 pm. Any 'hard' currency is accepted.

Several years ago the restrictions were even tighter. Since the loosening up of the system, a black market has developed, particularly for US dollars. The street rate is around US$1 = Kz 1000. But as there is very little on which to spend your kwanza, it's hardly worth it.

When leaving Angola, the airport departure tax is Kz 30.

Getting There & Around

You can only enter Angola by air. In Africa this is possible from Lusaka, Kinshasa or Brazzaville. There are also a number of connections to Europe. Discounted air tickets are sometimes available from Aeroflot or Balkan Air.

To go anywhere outside Luanda you must have authorisation (a *Guía de Marche*) from DEFA.

AIR
Most internal travel in Angola is by air. Almost all flights are heavily booked, especially those to Cabinda. The flights are operated by TAAG. Its office in Luanda is on the 6th floor, Rua da Missão 123.

There are flights from Luanda to Benguela (twice daily in either direction), Cabinda (once daily in either direction), Huambo (once daily in either direction), Lubango (two flights in either direction on Monday, Wednesday, Thursday and Sunday), Luena (on Tuesday, Thursday and Friday in either direction), Malange (once daily in either direction), Menongue (on Tuesday, Thursday, Saturday and Sunday in either direction), Namibe (on Wednesday, Thursday and Sunday in either direction) and Porto Amboini (on Monday, Tuesday, Thursday and Saturday in either direction).

Examples of fares from Luanda are: Benguela Kz 1650; Cabinda Kz 1600; Huambo Kz 1925; Lubango Kz 2190; Luena Kz 2395; Malange Kz 1480; Menongue Kz 2450; Namibe Kz 2210; and Porto Amboini Kz 1095. There are also flights between these major destinations. There is a 30-minute minimum check-in time for all internal flights.

It's very difficult to get from the airport to downtown Luanda as there are no taxis. It's a four-km walk, so probably worth the effort of asking around on the plane for a lift before you touch down.

ROAD

If you can persuade DEFA to let you out of Luanda it might be worth enquiring about road transport. Bus travel to Lobito, Benguela and Huambo can be arranged through Direção Nacional dos Transportes Rodoviários (tel 339390), Rua Rainha Ginga 74, 1° andar, Luanda.

TRAIN

Despite Unita and South African military incursions, the railway system still functions. But the only feasible route to travel is from Lobito and Benguela to Luau and Dilolo (in Zaïre). Getting to travel on it is a *major* hassle, but possible if you are pig-headed and persistent enough.

The first step is to get DEFA to allow you to travel the line. It insists that you pay for an 'escort' and sign documents accepting full responsibility for your personal safety. The *Guia de Marche* will cost you Kz 50 and your escort's expenses will be Kz 1200. Your fare from Lobito to Dilolo is Kz 750. Having achieved this, go to the offices of the Empresa dos Caminhos de Ferro de Luanda (tel 373380), Largo Eng Pedro Folque (Caixa Postal 2077), Luanda, or the Companhia do Caminho de Ferro de Benguela at 3 Rua Praça 11 de Novembro, Lobito.

There are daily trains, with passenger vehicles, leaving Lobito at 1 pm and arriving in Luena two days later at 4 am. From here you travel by box car or guard's van on another train for the 14-hour journey to Luau and Dilolo. You can wait up to two days for this connection.

Food and water for the journey will cost about US$20. You need two or three spare pages in your passport for rubber stamps. If you have a camera, DEFA will place it in a sealed bag which must be presented intact at Luau as photography en route is prohibited.

Around the Country

LUANDA

A useful shop in Luanda is Lojas Francas, (tel 372832), Ave 4 de Fevereiro 35/36, which is the state duty-free shop. Only hard currency is accepted.

There are three hospitals in Luanda and their facilities are free to all. They are, however, very short of drugs and equipment. They are Hospital Americo Boavida, Ave dos Massacres; Hospital Maria Pia, Ave Alvaro Ferreira; and Hospital Do Prenda, Rua do Prenda.

Places to Stay

Hotel accommodation must be prebooked at least 15 days in advance with Anghotel (telex 3492 ANGOTE AN). Anghotel expects all foreign visitors to stay at *Hotel Presidente Meridien*, Largo 4 de Fevereiro, Caixa Postal 5791. Rooms cost US$100/125 a single/double with breakfast. Because food is scarce in Luanda, you will have to pay an additional US$50 a day for lunch and dinner.

There are two other hotels in the capital. *Hotel Tropico* (tel 331593), Rua da Missão, costs Kz 2310/3500 a single/double with full board. *Hotel Panorama* (tel 37841), Ilha de Luanda, costs Kz 1200/1500 a single/double. Meals cost Kz 140/360 for breakfast/lunch and dinner. Unfortunately, it's very difficult to get permission to stay at either of these two cheaper hotels unless you are a guest of the Angolan government.

Anghotel has just completed renovating two other hotels – *Grande Hotel* (tel 333193), Rua Vereador Castelbranco, and *Hotel Continental* (tel 325231), Rua Duarte Lopes, but these are not open to independent travellers.

Places to Eat

Officially there are no restaurants in Luanda except at the hotels. There are a number of *cafés trabalhistas* (workers' cafés), but using them is difficult unless you have ration coupons (which, in effect,

Luanda

Panorama
Hotel

Key:
① Immigration (DEFA)
② British Embassy
③ French Embassy
④ Hotel Tropico
⑤ Hotel Presidente Meridien

Port

⑤

Railway
Station

Post
Office

Banks

U.N. Office

means you know a resident who has them). It's possible to feign incomprehension, in which case they might serve you, but they may also take a note of your passport number. Meals at these places will consist of a sticky ball of stodge (made from pulverised yams) and a spicy meat sauce, accompanied by beer and coffee. If you're very lucky you might get a traditional Portuguese pudim (creme caramel pudding). Meals cost about Kz 20. Don't look too closely at the standards of hygiene in these cafés.

Benin

For 12 years after its independence from France in 1960, Dahomey, as Benin was known until 1975, lurched from one coup to another until power was seized by a group of young army officers led by Major Kerekou. The country then took a sharp turn to the left politically and for many years was known as 'the Cuba of West Africa'. While its policies were based on Marxism-Leninism, in other ways the comparison was inappropriate as Benin was hardly trying to export its revolution. What it was trying to do was make a major effort to break the ties with the colonial era and, in so doing, distance itself from the more 'moderate' states of West Africa. This was by no means easy. Tense relations with neighbouring states led to frequent border closures and the disruption of trade. Togo, in particular, was badly affected by these disruptions and frequently closed its borders in retaliation.

There was an attempted coup in 1977 led by the French mercenary Bob Denard, who landed at Cotonou in the early hours of the morning with 50 other European mercenaries and 30 Africans. They were forced to withdraw, but left behind compromising documents that showed that Morocco and Gabon had financed the operation and that France also was implicated. Subsequently, diplomatic relations with Gabon were broken off, leading to the violent expulsion of some 9000 Beninese from Libreville and a serious curtailment of French aid.

Nevertheless, Kerekou's regime survived and major reforms have been carried out, particularly in education and agriculture. Benin is now considered one of the most stable states in Africa and its frosty relations with neighbouring states have thawed of late.

Like the borders of many African countries, particularly those in West Africa, Benin's are a legacy of 19th-century colonialism and they could not be more inappropriate. They completely disregard the fact that from the 16th century onwards a number of independent kingdoms coexisted along the coast of this part of Africa. These were the Fon kingdoms of Abomey, Allada and Porto Novo, noted for their sacred societies, witchcraft and elaborate rituals. What is more, these kingdoms were powerful enough to withstand a number of invasions by the Yoruba from neighbouring Nigeria. The wealth of these kingdoms was based on the slave trade, which began with the Portuguese in the 16th century but was progressively monopolised by Britain and France during the 17th and 18th centuries. All three European nations established forts on the coast at Ouidah, but their hold was tenuous and in 1727 they were recaptured.

After the abolition of the slave trade, the European interests began to seek concessions for palm oil plantations from the local rulers. The French were the most successful in this and they gradually declared 'protectorates' over certain areas of the coast.

The French creep was accelerated by the bombing of Porto Novo by the British in 1863 and, some 30 years later, French retaliation for an attack on their garrisons at Cotonou and Porto Novo by the king of Abomey. Following the defeat of the king, the French declared a 'protectorate' over the whole region.

Pacification of the rest of the colony was not completed until 1914, and it failed to

Benin

came to most French colonies in 1960, the majority of these workers were forced to return to Benin where they became a distinct group of unemployed and disenchanted intellectuals. Their interests, along with the factionalism associated with the various kingdoms that existed before the French conquest, were largely responsible for the endless power struggles that were the order of the day before Kerekou seized power.

Facts

Benin is a small polyglot nation. A lot of thought has gone into guaranteeing the rights of different nationalities, cultures, languages and traditions. The population of about 3½ million largely follows traditional religions: only 17% are Christian and about 15% Muslim. The major ethnic groups are the Fon, Yoruba (as in western Nigeria), Bariba and Somba.

Benin has a poorer standard of living and higher prices than neighbouring Togo, but a distinct naturalness and vitality. Its markets, too, are lively and vibrant.

Southern Benin has an equatorial climate. Most of the year it is very humid. The dry seasons are from January to April and during August. Northern Benin is less humid, but very hot during March and April. Its dry season is from November to June.

VISAS

Visas are required by all, except nationals of Denmark, France, West Germany, Italy, Sweden and the UK. South Africans are not admitted.

You can get visas in Freetown (Sierra Leone), Abidjan (Ivory Coast), Accra (Ghana), Niamey (Niger) and Lagos (Nigeria).

There are no Benin embassies in either Lomé (Togo) or Ouagadougou (Burkina

quell opposition to French rule. As early as 1923, anticolonial newspapers were in circulation, set up by French-educated Dahomians and former slaves who had returned from Brazil. Education and trade unionism were major formative influences in the making of the nation between WW II and independence.

In addition, large numbers of Dahomians were employed by the French colonial authorities in the administrations of other West African colonies. When independence

Faso), or in Cameroun (leaving Lagos the only place to get a visa en route from the Central African Republic).

You cannot get visas from French embassies in countries where there is no Benin consular representative. Generally you cannot get visas at the borders, the exception being from Togo via Ouidah (it seems Benin has finally woken up to the fact that the lack of a Benin embassy in Lomé makes it difficult for travellers coming from Togo). A one-month visa at this border costs CFA 2000 and is issued while you wait.

A seven-day visa in Niamey costs CFA 1000 and takes 48 hours to issue. In Accra they cost CFA 1800 (cedis not accepted), require two photos and take 24 hours. The staff is friendly and there's no fuss.

If you fly to Benin you can get a visa on arrival if you can convince them that they were not available anywhere else you've been. They'll direct you to immigration where visas cost CFA 5000, require two photos and take 24 hours to issue. Doing this, however, leaves you open to being stung for an entry permit – CFA 10,000. This may be partially negotiable for men; entirely so for women (a few smiles, etc).

Visa extensions are available in Cotonou from immigration (almost opposite the French Embassy) for up to one month and cost CFA 7000. Two photos are required and they are issued in 48 hours – no problems.

Officially you are supposed to get a *permis de circulation* from the police or Chef du District in each town or city you stay in overnight, excepting Cotonou and Porto Novo. Many travellers neglect to do this, risking trouble. Cover yourself by asking the hotel staff to report your presence to the police.

It's only necessary to get an exit visa if you are flying out of Benin. They can be obtained from immigration in Cotonou. They'll issue it while you wait if you make a fuss. These requirements, however, change from time to time so make enquiries beforehand.

Other Visas

Nigeria These cost CFA 950 and take 24 hours to issue. You can have either a 48-hour transit visa or a three to four-day tourist visa. It's hard to get a one-week visa. The embassy, on Blvd de l'Indépendence, next to the American Embassy, is a long way from town on the way to the airport.

Togo These are obtainable at the French Consulate in Cotonou and take 24 hours to issue.

Cameroun There is no Cameroun embassy in Benin.

MONEY
US$1 = CFA 284

The unit of currency is the Central African franc (CFA). There are no restrictions on its import or export. There is no black market.

Foreign currency, other than French francs, can only be changed in Cotonou and Parakou. Elsewhere, carry French francs.

A good place to change money outside banking hours in Cotonou is at Hotel Sheraton, a 15-minute walk from the airport. It's open from 8.30 am to 2.30 pm and from 4.30 to 6.30 pm. There are no hassles, no commission on travellers' cheques and no waiting. The bank at the airport is usually closed.

If coming from Nigeria, change excess naira into CFA at the border. The banks inside Benin won't accept them. If going to Nigeria, Cotonou is a good place to buy naira.

The airport departure tax for international flights is CFA 2500.

POST
The poste restante in Cotonou is reliable, but there's a charge for each letter or telex you receive. If you leave an address, they will forward mail on to you.

PHOTOGRAPHY

The authorities in Benin are very suspicious of cameras. If you have one, whether you intend to use it or not, you must get a tourist card (*carte*) from the Office National du Tourisme et des Hotels (ONTH) in Cotonou. Without a card you are courting trouble. Even with a card, you will invite trouble by taking photographs. Many travellers have been arrested and had their film confiscated. Some have had their cameras confiscated as well. In the north they're more easy-going about photography than in the south.

LANGUAGE

French is the official language. The main African languages are Fon, Yoruba, Bariba and Dendi.

Getting There & Around

AIR

For discounted tickets in Cotonou contact a Frenchman named Maurice at Hotel de la Plage, or go to Cobenham Voyages, behind La Gerbe d'Or coffee shop, which is in front of the market on Ave Clozel. They offer 40% student discounts with Air Afrique to African destinations, and similar deals with Aeroflot to Europe. Air Afrique itself only offers 8% discounts on the same tickets. Don't deal with anyone but Maurice at Hotel de la Plage, even if they claim they work for him.

Many airline companies in Cotonou will only sell return tickets. They're doing this so they don't end up with the responsibility of returning tourists who are refused entry.

If you're flying from Cotonou to Lagos, a reservation means nothing. It's all a question of fighting your way onto the plane before anyone else. Maybe it's better to go by road after all?

ROAD

There are two main routes through Benin. The first is the coast road connecting Lagos with Porto Novo, Cotonou, Lomé and Accra. The other goes through the centre of the country, via Parakou and the Malanville-Gaya border, connecting Cotonou and Niamey. Both roads are in excellent shape. There are buses and shared taxis along both routes, or you can hitch.

A *taxi-brousse* from Cotonou to Lomé costs CFA 1500, plus CFA 1000 for a pack, and takes about three hours. It's an easy border to cross. Cotonou to Lagos by *taxi-brousse* also costs CFA 1500 but you shouldn't have to pay for a pack. Make sure you set off early in the morning to avoid arriving in Lagos during the afternoon rush-hour. It's no joke arriving during rush-hour as the traffic congestion is incredible.

Other routes of interest are:

Cotonou to Abomey – bus or *taxi-brousse* for CFA 1000, including bags. The journey takes two hours.
Cotonou to Porto Novo – bus or minibus for CFA 200.
Parakou to Malanville – state transport bus for CFA 1800, plus CFA 200 for a pack. It's a comfortable journey and takes about five hours.
Malanville to Gaya – pick-ups are available for CFA 400. Expect a search and a check of your vaccination card at the Niger border. They don't ask for onward tickets or to see how much money you have.
Gaya to Niamey (Niger) – daily buses for CFA 1800, plus CFA 300 a pack. The journey should take about four hours but can take up to six as there are many police checkpoints and baggage searches along the way.

TRAIN

Benin has two main railway lines. One follows the coast and links Porto Novo, Cotonou and Lomé (Togo) (though there are no services across the border). The other goes north and links Cotonou with Savé and Parakou.

On the Cotonou to Parakou line there are two trains daily and they are not usually crowded. The day train leaves in either direction at 9.20 am and takes about 10½ hours. The fares are CFA 4965 1st class, and CFA 3025 2nd class (padded seats). Food is available at various places along the way. A bus between the two cities costs about double the 2nd class fare, but takes half the time.

BOAT

There are quite a few cargo boats plying between Cotonou and various ports in Cameroun with limited space for fare-paying passengers. They are not easy to find, however, and you will need patience. It's best to check with the *capitainerie* (port captain) at the harbour. The people are very friendly and helpful. The fares are not cheap, but they are certainly

cheaper than flying (for a discounted Cotonou/Douala flight you are looking at around CFA 38,000 from Cobenham Voyages).

Around the Country

ABOMEY

Abomey was once the capital of a Fon kingdom and is one of the most interesting places to visit in Benin, though the palaces are somewhat neglected and badly in need of maintenance.

Things to See

There's an excellent **museum** that covers the history of the kingdoms and includes human skulls that were once used as musical instruments. Entry costs CFA 1000, or CFA 1500 for a guided tour. Other places worth visiting are the **Fon Palace** and **Fetish Temple**. Next to the museum is the **Centre des Artisans**, which has a good

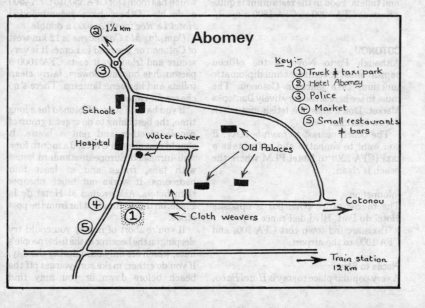

Abomey

Key:-
① Truck & taxi park
② Hotel Abomey
③ Police
④ Market
⑤ Small restaurants & bars

Schools

Water tower

Hospital

Old Palaces

Cloth weavers

Cotonou

Train station 12 Km

collection of crafts for sale at prices as low as you're likely to find anywhere.

There's a large **market** on Tuesdays.

Places to Stay & Eat

One of the cheapest places to stay is *L'Auberge du Roi*, about one km out of town on the road to Cotonou, just past the Office Beninois de Securité Sociale. A small single costs CFA 2000 with shower and fan but communal toilet.

Also outside of town is *Chez Monique*, which costs CFA 2000 for up to three people. It's a very pleasant place but the food is expensive.

Much closer to the centre of town is *Hotel La Lutta*, about 200 metres from the taxi stand. Double rooms with shower cost CFA 1500.

More expensive is *Hotel Abomey*, formerly the Foyer des Militants and before that Le Campement, about two km from the market. It's a pleasant place with large rooms and friendly staff and costs CFA 6000 a double. You also can camp here for CFA 300 a tent, with use of the showers and toilets. Food in the restaurant is quite pricey at CFA 1200 to CFA 1800 a meal.

COTONOU

Although Porto Novo is the official capital, most government and diplomatic functions take place in Cotonou. The must to see here is the very lively **Dantopka Market**. Don't miss the fetish and witch doctor section.

The beach nearest to town is dirty. If you want to sunbathe and swim, take a taxi (CFA 250) to Hotel PLM where the beach is clean.

Information

The tourist office (Onatho) is opposite Hotel du Port, Blvd de France.

Taxis around town cost CFA 100, and CFA 1000 to the airport.

Places to Stay

A very popular place to stay is *Hotel Babo*, well known in the African quarter and near the Blvd St Michel. It's a six-storey building so there's always space. Try to get a room on the top floors as they're cooler. It's a fairly clean place, but avoid room No 33 – it has a smelly shower and lumpy beds. The person in reception can be a little off-hand, but don't let this put you off. Prices are CFA 2500/2800 a single without/with fan and CFA 3200 a double without fan. There are rooms with three, four and five beds. Meals are reasonable at CFA 250 for breakfast and CFA 700 to CFA 1000 for dinner. You can, however, find better elsewhere.

Also good is *Hotel Pacific*, on the other side of the bridge leading to the town centre. This hotel is much quieter than the others and has better facilities, good meals and a baggage storage room. Double rooms cost CFA 4500 with shower and fan.

Next to the railway station is *Pension Le Muguet*, which has doubles with fan for CFA 3000. Also worth trying is *Hotel Atlantique*, formerly Benin Palace Hotel, which has rooms for CFA 3500 to CFA 4500 a double. Others have recommended *Hotel Le Rêe* for CFA 4000 a double.

Camping Ma Campagne is 12 km west of Cotonou on the road to Lomé. It is very secure and friendly. It costs CFA 1000 a person, has bucket showers, fairly clean toilets and kerosene lanterns. There's no charge for cars.

If you have to stay in Cotonou for a long time, the best thing to do is get a group of people together and rent a house. It should cost around UK£200 a month for a well-furnished European-standard house with fans, fridge and at least four bedrooms. It works out much cheaper than hotels. Ask around at Hotel de la Plage, on the seafront not far from the post office.

If you're short of money you could try sleeping on the beach or in the fisherpeople's huts, which are only used during the day. If you do either, make sure you get off the beach before dawn or you may find

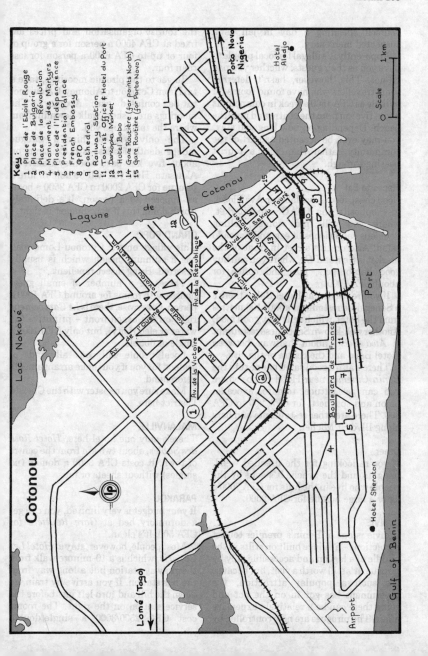

yourself spending a day in jail as a suspected mercenary.

Apparently it's illegal for local people to have you as their guests, whether you pay or not. This, however, hasn't deterred some travellers who have found rooms for as little as CFA 1500 a week in compounds about five km from the centre and near the beach. Depending on how long you stay, you may even be accepted as part of the community rather than just a tourist passing through.

Places to Eat

Good cheap food is available on Ave Clozel, just opposite the CFAO supermarket, where you will find women selling delicious sandwiches of egg and avocado salad. Also on this street in front of the market is Gembe d'Or, where you can buy good hamburgers, pies and coffee for about CFA 1000.

If you're staying at Hotel Babo, there's a Senegalese restaurant about 100 metres from the hotel, which sells very good food. Another well-known Senegalese restaurant is Awa Seck, about halfway between Hotel Babo and the centre of the city.

There's also a good salad bar next to the Benin Cinema, near Hotel Babo, where you can get lettuce, tomato, avocado, onion and spaghetti for CFA 200 to CFA 300. There are other restaurants and bars along Blvd St Michel.

Other

If you're looking for the dreaded weed, hang around the beach. It's sold by the people who live in the huts for CFA 7000 a kg or a large bundle for CFA 2000.

GANVIE

Ganvie is one of Benin's premier tourist attractions – a village built on stilts in the middle of a lagoon and accessible only by pirogue. It's still worth a visit, but because it's such a popular attraction, the government has got in on the act and going there can be a relatively expensive affair. The pirogues are now controlled by the tourist organisation and prices are fixed at CFA 4500 a person for a group of four or up to CFA 6500 a person for less than four.

To get to the pirogue moorings, take a taxi from Cotonou to Abomey-Calavi (not to be confused with Abomey). The moorings are a short walk downhill from where the taxi drops you.

The only way to hire a pirogue independently for less is to continue on about five km past Abomey-Calavi to Akassato. Here you will be able to hire a pirogue for CFA 2000 to CFA 2500 a boat, as opposed to a person. It's definitely worth doing this if your budget is tight.

GRAND POPO

This village on the Cotonou-Lomé road has a stunning beach which is usually deserted. Bring insect repellent.

There are a number of small guest houses with rooms for around CFA 1000 a person. Otherwise, there is Le Campement right on the beach front – primitive (no water or electricity), but only CFA 1000 a single or double.

Local people will cook all kinds of seafood for you if you make arrangements beforehand.

Make sure you register with the Chef du District here.

MALANVILLE

There's only one hotel here, Hotel Rose des Sables, about two km from the centre of town. It costs CFA 3000 a double (no singles) without sheets or fans.

PARAKOU

If your budget is very limited, you can get a dormitory bed at Gare Routière for CFA 500. It's clean.

Most people, however, stay at Hotel Les Canaris, which is a 10-minute walk from the railway station but a long way from the bus station. If you arrive by train, go down the hill and turn left just before the service station on the right. The rooms cost CFA 2500/3000 a single/double

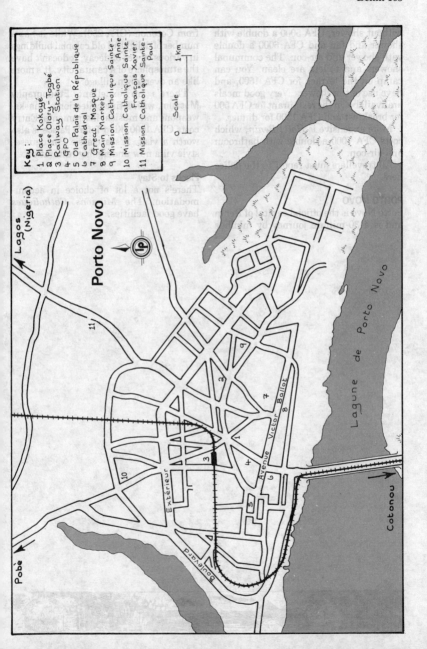

Key:
1 Place Kokoyé
2 Place Olory-Togbé
3 Railway Station
4 GPO
5 Old Palais de la République
6 Cathedral
7 Great Mosque
8 Main Market
9 Mission Catholique Sainte-Anne
10 Mission Catholique Sainte-François Xavier
11 Mission Catholique Sainte-Paul

Porto Novo

Lagos (Nigeria)

Pobé

Cotonou

Lagune de Porto Novo

Avenue Victor Ballot

Boulevard Extérieur

Scale
0   1 km

without shower, CFA 5000 a double with shower and fan and CFA 6000 a double with shower and air-con. The communal showers and toilets are clean. You can camp on the terrace for CFA 1500, and have use of the showers. Very good meals are available in the restaurant for CFA 500 for breakfast and CFA 1300 for dinner.

More expensive is *Hotel Benin*, which costs CFA 7000 a double with bathroom and air-con.

All travellers must report to the police here.

PORTO NOVO

Porto Novo is the official capital of Benin and is a 30-minute journey by minibus from Cotonou (CFA 250). While it has a number of delightful old colonial buildings in various stages of decay, it doesn't have the atmosphere of a capital city. It's more like an overgrown village.

There's an excellent **Ethnography Museum**, with a fine collection of masks, weapons and musical instruments. Entry costs CFA 1000. **King Toffa's Palace** is also worth a visit. It's a classic Portuguese-style villa now undergoing restoration.

Places to Stay

There's not a lot of choice in accommodation. The *Missions Catholiques* have good facilities.

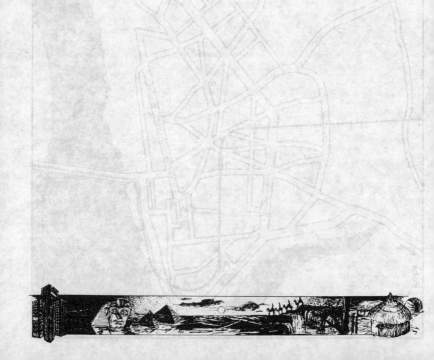

British Indian Ocean Territory

The Chagos Archipelago, just south of the Maldive Islands and Equator, might seem a strange inclusion in a book about Africa. The archipelago, however, has historical connections with Mauritius as it was to here that the inhabitants of the Chagos, the Ilois, were banished by the British when Mauritius attainted independence.

There is evidence that Arab and Malay navigators knew of and occasionally visited the Chagos Archipelago, but the first European visitors were the Portuguese in 1743. An English attempt to establish a settlement some 20 years later failed and it was not until 1776, by which time the islands had been claimed by France, that a successful colony was established.

The islands were leased to a M Lenormand to use as he wished. In return, he was obliged to accept all the lepers sent over from the then French colony of Mauritius. Copra production began and, by the end of the century, the plantations were well established and regular exports were being made to Mauritius. In addition, the population was augmented by slaves from Madagascar and the African mainland.

In 1838, the practice of sending lepers to the Chagos was discontinued. By 1900, the population of some 420 families was a mixture of 60% African/Malagasy and 40% Tamil. Life was based on subsistence agriculture and fishing. The majority of people worked on the plantations and were paid in rations of basic foodstuffs – rice, cooking oil, other essentials – and some cash, which was generally saved for spending trips to Mauritius.

This tranquil existence suddenly came to an end in 1965, when the British Indian Ocean Territory (BIOT) was created primarily for military purposes. At the time, it included the islands of Aldabra, Desroches and Farquhar, now part of the Seychelles.

The USA expressed its desire to lease an uninhabited group of islands from the British to house a communications facility. The British suggested the Chagos islands fitted the bill. The available evidence from the British Foreign Office suggests the Americans were not told of the presence of an 'indigenous population'. With the deal signed and sealed, the British saw these people as temporarily resident contract labourers, despite the fact that many of them were descendants of families who had been on the islands for generations.

A decision was taken to remove them. The methods used would have provoked international outrage had the facts been widely known. Initially, those who visited Mauritius for medical reasons, shopping or to visit relations were simply told they could not return (once they had reached Mauritius, naturally). Later, people were simply told to leave until, finally, the last handful of reluctant and bewildered islanders arrived in Port Louis on 2 May 1973. The British were then conveniently able to hand over an uninhabited island group to the US.

For the Ilois, however, their problems had just begun. On arrival in Mauritius they were left on the dock and those who had no family or friends were forced to fend for themselves. The last boat of people to arrive knew this and refused to disembark until guaranteed accommodation. This was eventually arranged in flats belonging to the sugar industry, though, supposedly, for 'two or three weeks' until something more permanent could be found. They are still there. Jobs were as hard to find as accommodation, and those who could find work were often given only the coins from their wage packets, the notes being kept by intermediaries. Being unfamiliar with a cash economy, they could only express surprise at how little money could buy in Mauritius.

They wised-up quickly. Protests were organised, their claims taken to the UN and hunger strikes staged outside the British High Commission in Port Louis. The Mauritian government, too, got in on the act and still refuses to accept the detachment of the Chagos from its territory (a resolution to this effect was passed in the UN General Assembly). The results of all this, however, have been far from satisfactory for the Ilois. Although the British belatedly agreed to pay compensation, it was a pittance, and subject to the condition that the Ilois renounce all rights to the islands (despite the fact that many of the Ilois are British passport holders). These days the Ilois are a broken people living wretched lives in the slums around Port Louis. They are despised by all those around them.

A fuller account of this disgraceful episode can be found in *Diego Garcia: A Contrast to the Falklands* (The Minority Rights Group, London).

Facts

Strung out between the 5th and 8th parallels south of the equator, the Chagos Archipelago extends over an area some 160 km long by 110 km wide. It consists of three large atolls and several smaller island groups and sandbars. Diego Garcia is the largest island (21 km by 9½ km). The other two large atolls are Peros Banhos (32 islets) and Salomon (six islets). The wet season is December to March. Cyclones are rare. The bulk of the population are

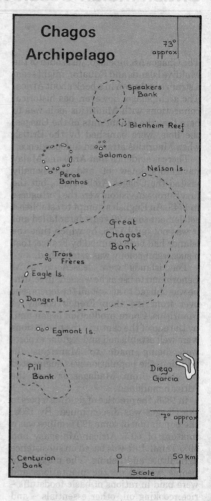

American military personnel, the remainder being some 250 Mauritian and Filipino labourers and a few British civil servants (administrators, police, customs and immigration).

VISAS

In theory, entry requirements ought to be the same as those for the UK. This,

however, is unlikely because of the military installations on Diego Garcia. One thing is certain – citizens of the BIOT are not admitted. Does anyone know of a similar case around the world where citizens are refused entry to their own 'country'!?

MONEY
The unit of currency is the UK£ sterling.

LANGUAGE
English is the official language.

Getting There & Around

Getting to the Chagos is virtually impossible unless you have a job there or a very good reason for visiting. Unofficially, if you have your own transport (ie a boat),

it's no problem. You simply turn up. There's not a lot they can do about it, and, if you stay away from Diego Garcia, you won't be bothered by anything other than the occasional plane.

Diego Garcia has been transformed into a massive base and it was from here that the abortive Iranian hostage rescue attempt was launched in 1979. There is evidence that nuclear weapons are stored on the island, though all parties concerned hotly deny it. Travel to the eastern side of Diego and the other islands by those living on the base is subject to all manner of restrictions. On the other islands, which are beautiful and where most of the settlements are still standing but are now somewhat overgrown, there's plenty of food for the gathering. We have heard of two yachties who spent two months on Salomon and had nothing but praise for the islands.

Botswana

The original inhabitants of Botswana were Bushpeople. The current theory is that they originated somewhere to the north (relics have been found as far as Spain!) and gradually migrated southwards. They were followed by the Hottentots and later by Bantu speakers (about 2000 years ago). Relations between the three groups appear to have been amicable and certainly there was a flourishing trade between them. Northeast Botswana was settled by Shona speakers around the 10th century AD and the first Tswana speakers probably settled in south-east Botswana by the 15th century having migrated there from further south. By the 18th century, the Tswana were well established in the area.

It wasn't until the 1820s that the various clans began to consolidate into a string of nations along what is now the border area between Botswana and South Africa. The change was prompted by the clans' need to defend themselves against the fleeing tide of humanity displaced from the Transvaal and Natal between 1820 and 1840 by Zulu militancy and Boer expansionism.

Tswana society was highly structured. Each nation was ruled by an hereditary monarch and aristocracy whose economic power was based on the ownership of large herds of cattle and the use of tribute labour. In each one of the eight nations, the kings' subjects lived in centralised towns and satellite villages divided into wards under the control of headmen. The latter were responsible for allocating land and recruiting tribute labour for work on the monarchs' fields and pastures. By the second half of the 19th century some of these towns had grown to considerable size. The capital of the Bangwato clan at Shoshong, for example, had a population of about 30,000 by 1960. The orderliness and structure of the town-based society certainly impressed the explorers, Moffat and Livingstone.

In 1885 the country's borders were secured from further encroachment by various colonisers, with the declaration of a British protectorate known as Bechuanaland. The rationale behind this declaration was the rivalry between the British and the Boers and a desire to prevent encroachment by other European powers. However, it also had a lot to do with skilful lobbying by missionaries and various Tswana chiefs. In 1895 the same combination also prevented the area from coming under the control of Cecil Rhodes' British South African Company. Foremost among Tswana chiefs was Tshekedi Khama, the Christian chief of the Bangwato.

By selling cattle, draught oxen and grain to Europeans streaming north in search of farming land and minerals, the protectorate was able to retain some degree of economic independence. This didn't last long. The construction of a railway through Bechuanaland to Rhodesia (built at the rate of a mile a day) and a serious outbreak of rinderpest in the 1890s destroyed the transit trade. By 1920 the commercial maize farmers in South Africa and Rhodesia were producing grain in such quantities that Bechuanaland no longer had a market.

This loss of a market led to the protectorate becoming a labour reserve for South African farms and mines. A series of drought years quickened this trend. Up

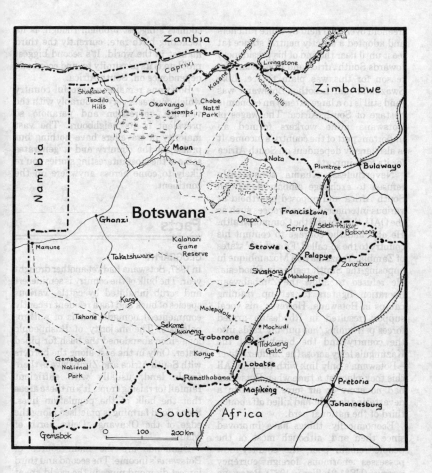

to a quarter of the entire male population could be away at any one time. The drift south in search of work accelerated the breakdown of traditional land usage patterns. The aristocrats and a few rich cattle barons were able to turn this to their advantage by increasing their areas of cultivation and the size of their herds. The result of this change was a widening of the gap between rich and poor. Today the disparity is probably worse with the wealth being generated by diamonds.

Botswana became independent in 1966

though until the late 1970s, the British government paid the wages of all civil servants. The country's first president was Seretse Khama, a nephew of Tshekedi Khama. Seretse Khama was rejected by the Bangwato and exiled by the British government for having the temerity to marry a white woman. The Bangwato later relented and took him back as their chief while the British began grooming him for the presidency.

Seretse Khama was certainly no revolutionary. He guaranteed continued freehold over land held by white ranchers and adopted a strictly neutral stance (at least until near the end of his presidency) towards South Africa and Rhodesia. The reason for this was plain to see. Like Swaziland and Lesotho, Botswana was (and still is to a large extent) an economic hostage of South Africa. The wages of Botswana mine workers formed an important part of the country's income. It is also largely dependent on South Africa for its food imports.

Nevertheless, Khama consistently refused to exchange ambassadors with South Africa and opposed apartheid at various international conferences such as the OAU, the UN and the Commonwealth. He also had the courage to commit his country to the so-called 'Front Line' states of Zambia, Tanzania and Mozambique in opposing the Smith regime in Rhodesia. He refused to allow the Zimbabwean liberation fighters to set up training camps in Botswana. However, his vocal support resulted in Rhodesian armed forces performing 'hot pursuit' raids into the country and the bombing of the Kazungula ferry across the Zambezi River – Botswana's only link with Zambia. All this took place at a time when Botswana had no army or air force and when a devastating drought had killed off about a third of the national herd.

Economically, things have improved since then and, although most of the people remain poor, the country now possesses enormous foreign currency reserves (US$1.2 billion in 1987). Botswana showed the world's second highest rate of economic growth in 1986.

The party formed by Sir Seretse Khama – the Botswana Democratic Party – still commands a substantial and democratically elected majority in the Botswana parliament. It continues with similar pragmatic, cautious and pro-western policies. There are occasional incursions from South Africa and a rise in all the problems produced by increasing urban drift and lack of employment. The country's biggest problem though, is its rocketing birth rate, currently the third highest in the world. It's second biggest problem is its proximity to, and economic dependence on, South Africa.

Botswana remains a peaceful country which contrasts very favourably with the violence, repression and paranoia so prevalent in its neighbours. The vast majority of travellers have nothing but praise for the country and it generates some of the most interesting stories you're likely to come across anywhere on the continent.

Facts

GEOGRAPHY

In 1987, Botswana had yet another drought year. The bulk of the country is semidesert and scrub inhabited by cattle, various species of buck and (as a resident recently commented) nomadic bands of anthropologists. The majority of Bushpeople long since abandoned the bush for piped water. Only in the east along the borders with South Africa and Zimbabwe is there fertile land, usually with sufficient rainfall for raising crops. It's in these areas that the bulk of the population lives. Some flood farming is practised along the edge of the Okavango Delta north of Maun.

Diamonds are the main source of Botswana's income. The second and third largest diamond pipes in the world are at Orapa and Jwaneng. Ranching is the second largest industry and the one that employs most people. In addition, there is a copper and nickel mine at Selebi-Phikwe, a coal mine at Morupule, and it is likely that a soda ash plant will be set up at Sua Pan in the near future. Coal from the Morupule mine provides power for electricity, supplying most of the urban centres and the Selebi-Phikwe mine.

CLIMATE

Partly because of the altitude, the climate is hot and dry during the summer months. During the winter months (May to July) there are occasional overnight frosts. Most of the rain falls between December and April.

VISAS

Visas are required by all except nationals of Commonwealth countries, Western Europe (except Portugal and Spain), South Africa and the USA. Stay permits are issued at the border for 90 days (though some people only get 30 days). If you wish to stay longer you must apply to the Immigration & Passport Control Officer, PO Box 942, Gaborone.

Working in Botswana

The Botswana government is spending some of its diamond wealth on improving services – education, health, roads, etc. If you have professional qualifications, you may be able to find a job in this country although some occupations are reserved for Botswanans (nursing is one of them).

MONEY

US$ 1 = P 2.15
UK£ 1 = P 3.95

The unit of currency is the pula which is made up of 100 thebe. There are no restrictions on the import of local currency, but export is limited to P 200. There is no black market.

In theory, the pula is tied to the South African rand so they should be interchangeable. In practice, this isn't the case and the pula is always valued lower.

There are very few banks outside the Francistown to Gaborone area. Barclays Bank operates a flying banking service to Ghanzi each Thursday which is open for business from 11 am to 1 pm, so if you need to change travellers' cheques that's the only time you can do it. If you're travelling through to Zambia the bank in Kasane won't change pula into kwacha.

Commission on travellers' cheques can be high – about P 7.

TOURIST INFORMATION

You really need a 4WD vehicle to see most of the interesting parts of Botswana.

If you're planning on staying for a while it's worth getting hold of a copy of *Guide to Botswana* by Alec Campbell (Winchester Press).

ACCOMMODATION

Botswana is not as cheap as its northerly neighbours. Most hotels are expensive and you should expect to pay at least P 30 per night. Phuti Travel in Gaborone, Pan African in Francistown and Bonaventures Travel Agents in Maun as well as the tourist offices in the same towns will all provide information about places and prices. Some places simply have nowhere cheap to stay. In this case, a tent comes in useful. You will certainly need one if you plan to visit any of the national parks or game reserves.

There are hotels in Gaborone, Lobatse, Kanye, Tlokweng Gate, Mahalapye, Palapye, Serowe, Selebi-Phikwe, Francistown, Maun, Nata and Kasane. The hotels at Sherwood Ranch and Zanzibar are temporarily closed. There are also many safari lodges around Maun, the Tuli Block, Nata and Shakawe. Some of these are very expensive and only offer 'all-in' packages. Others are more reasonable and will allow camping. Many of the lodges are managed or owned by people who regard the Tswana and travellers as inferior species. Facilities at the public camp sites in the game parks are very limited and primitive.

Outside these areas, you can camp virtually anywhere but you should make the point of going to see the village chief before erecting your tent. There is a good possibility that by doing this you will be offered accommodation under a roof. You can also try asking around among volunteer workers – Peace Corps, German Volunteer Service, etc – if you are willing to help out and pay for your keep. You might be offered accommodation. On the other hand, you should be aware that we've had quite a few letters from irate volunteer workers. They're getting pissed off with the constant stream of travellers who turn up on their doorsteps taking it for granted they will be offered accommodation and even a meal. Remember, especially in Maun and Kasane, that you are probably the umpteenth person this year who would like a floor for the night. So, if you're offered accommodation, please help out and pay your way.

HEALTH

Tsetse flies have all but been eradicated from the Okavango Swamps. The water in these swamps is free from bilharzia and generally safe to drink. So too is the tap water in all urban centres and most villages. Hepatitis is rare. There are clinics in all the larger villages and hospitals in the major centres. In comparison with many countries in Africa, the public health services are competent and well supplied.

LANGUAGE

English is the official language of the country and the medium of instruction in secondary schools. The most common language, however, which is understood by over 90% of the population and which is the medium of instruction in the primary schools, is Setswana. This is the language of the dominant group – the Tswana. It's interesting to note that the majority of Tswana speakers live in South Africa, especially in the so-called homeland of Bophuthatswana. Ikalanga, the second major language, is spoken by the Kalanga, who occupy the land to the north-east of Francistown. They are related to the Shona people of Zimbabwe.

It's extremely impolite not to greet people that you meet. If you fail to do so, people will stop you and teach you the routine. So it's best to learn it straight away and keep those faces smiling.

Some words of Setswana which you will find useful are:

hello father/mother	dumela rra/mma
How are you?	ke tsogile, o tsogile jang?
good evening	o tlhotse jang
stay well (goodbye)	sala sentle
go well (response to 'goodbye')	tsamayang sentle
I am pleased (thank you)	ke itumetse
yes	eeyee
no	nyaa
What do you want?	o batlang?
I want	ke batla
milk	mashi
meat	nama
eggs	mae
bread	borotho
food	dijo
water	metsi
How much?	ke bokai?
I have no money.	ga ke na madi

The language is spelt phonetically except 'g' is sounded as a 'w' and words in which English speakers use 'h' may become a 'g'. For example, Kalahari is pronounced Kalagari. The greeting dumela rra/mma is a compliment so say it to everyone. There is no word for 'thank you' as such. Instead you take hold of something with both hands. If you can't do that, take hold of it with your right hand, using your left hand to hold your right arm. Never accept anything with your left hand – it constitutes an insult.

Getting There & Around

ROAD

There is a sealed road all the way from near Kazungula to Mafikeng via Nata, Francistown, Gaborone and Lobatse (known as the BOTZAM road). Also there are sealed roads to Molepolole, Serowe, Bobonong via Selebi-Phikwe and Jwaneng.

Tarring is taking place on the road to link Serowe with Orapa and it is proposed to extend this to Maun. At present, though, the latter section is still a gravel track. So too is the Kasane to Kazungula road.

Hitching is very easy but beware of pick-ups full of goods – they stop everywhere and take ages. Also beware of drunken drivers because they cause a lot of accidents. Hitching at weekends can be very slow. Lifts with settlers and expatriates are usually free but you should expect to pay black drivers. The usual price is about P 1 per 50 km.

There are buses between most of the major centres and privately run minibuses that cover certain sections of the route. To reach many places, however, requires considerable patience or a 4WD vehicle. One of the best ways to get a ride to the more remote areas is to go to the CTO (Central Transport Organisation) depot and ask if there are vehicles going to the place you wish to reach. Like all government vehicles, CTO trucks have red BX plates. Other government vehicles are not officially allowed to carry passengers but many will, so it's worth asking at health, drought relief and post office departments. Most Botswana government officials are very helpful about finding lifts for you, especially in remote districts. Otherwise, ask around at stores and bars – many of the stores have outlets in the more remote areas or supply the shops there.

It's also worth asking at the Peace Corps office in Gaborone. It's adjacent to the Red Cross building on Independence Ave just north-east of the mall past the cathedral and museum. Two other sources of lifts are drought relief officers who often come into Gaborone from isolated villages, or associate directors who may be planning site visits.

If you're going out west (Kanye to Ghanzi) the Matsha Community College sends a supply truck on the first weekend of every month from Kang to Gaborone. The truck leaves from the Education Ministry building on Government enclave at 9 am sharp.

Lobatse to Ghanzi & Maun

The road from Lobatse to Jwaneng is sealed. After that, up to Ghanzi, it is one of the worst roads in the country, passing through desert and scrub. To find a lift in Lobatse, check out the registration numbers of the trucks or ask at the Botswana Meat Corporation. CTO trucks travel as far as Kang fairly regularly but rarely go further. There is also the very faint possibility of getting a lift with the Standard Bank plane which flies from Lobatse to Ghanzi on Thursday mornings (Thursday is bank day in Ghanzi). In Ghanzi, the best person to ask is the storekeeper near the Kalahari Arms. Trucks leave Ghanzi on Sundays and Mondays.

The road from Ghanzi to Maun is better than the Lobatse to Ghanzi stretch, the scenery slightly more varied and the traffic more regular. The most reliable possibility is the mail truck which leaves Maun on Tuesdays and Ghanzi on Thursdays but there is stiff competition for the five places available. The journey takes about six hours. There are also water trucks on which you might get a lift. Ask at the CTO depot at either place. Hitching to Ghanzi or out again is not easy. If you are lucky enough to get a ride to there, be prepared to wait several days for a lift out again.

Francistown to Nata & Maun

There are buses six days a week in either direction. There is no bus going to Maun from Francistown on Sundays and none in the opposite direction on Mondays. Buses leave Francistown about 10 am and from Maun about 8 am. The journey takes all day. The fare from Francistown to Maun is P 16.50 and from Nata to Maun it is P 11.10. (There are other buses which cover the Francistown to Nata to Kasane route.)

Hitching is usually easy and should take about a day if you get started early, though you might be unlucky and get stuck. If that happens ask at the Sua Pan bar in Francistown. The barman is very helpful and will find you accommodation for the night. Truck drivers usually ask P 10 but are sometimes willing to take you for as little as P 2. They can be slow, however, and they stop often. Have warm clothes handy if you are travelling on the back of a truck at night.

In Maun, the best place to find out about lifts and spare seats on planes to Ghanzi and the Delta is at the Duck Inn restaurant out at the airport.

Maun to Kasane

This is quite a rough road and very difficult to hitch (there are no buses). About the only traffic doing this route are tourists on safari and the occasional government truck. Most government trucks now go to Kasane via Nata as the road is better and the journey faster. The best places to find out about lifts are the CTO depots or the camp sites at the various safari lodges. The chances of getting a lift are small but the sights on the road, especially around Savuti, make the effort worthwhile. If all else fails and you can find a few other interested travellers, it's possible to hire a self-drive 4WD vehicle from Avis in Maun. It is, however, much easier to go via Nata to Kasane or to come west from Kasane to Maun.

Zambian truck drivers all stay overnight in Nata so it is very easy to hitch north. Ask around at the bar.

Maun to Shakawe

There are no buses but there are trucks which make the run regularly. Ask at the same places you would for lifts between other centres. It is possible to enter the Delta from Gomare or Etsha – details are in the Okavango Delta section.

Palapye to Tuli Block

There is a daily bus service, though departure times vary, from Palapye to Lerale, Sherwood Ranch or the border at Martins Drift. There are also various trucks and cars which make the run. Hitching the first stretch isn't particularly difficult but going further north can be problematical because there's so little traffic. Alternatively, the Tuli Block can be reached via Selebi-Phikwe, Bobonong and Zanzibar. Getting to Bobonong is easy as there are regular trucks and buses. Getting beyond there can be a major problem. Ask at the CTO depot, health and drought relief offices in Bobonong.

Lobatse to Tshabong to Mabuasehube or Gemsbok

It's impossible to do this journey without your own 4WD vehicle.

TRAIN

There are both road and rail connections between Botswana and Zimbabwe (Bulawayo to Plumtree and Francistown) and South Africa (Mafikeng to Ramatlhamaba and Gaborone), but the vast majority of travellers take the train.

There is one ordinary train (four classes) in either direction daily. First and 2nd class are reserved sleeping compartments shared with others – four berths in 1st class and six in 2nd class. Third class has soft seats while 4th class has wooden benches. Sexes are separated in the sleeping compartments except for married couples. All classes have access to the buffet car. The trains leave Francistown heading south at about 7 pm and depart northwards from Gaborone about 6 pm. If possible, avoid travelling by train at the end of the month. Miners from Botswana who work in Johannesburg return home on leave at this time and the train is usually chock-a-block. During the rest of the month there is usually plenty of room. You need not be at all apprehensive about travelling in 4th class in Botswana.

Fares between Gaborone and Francistown are P 38.50 (2nd class) and P 10.50 (3rd class).

In addition there is a luxury coach – known as the Chitanda line – that travels between Harare, Bulawayo, Francistown, Gaborone and Mafikeng twice a week. It leaves Harare on Sundays and Mondays, and Mafikeng on Tuesdays and Saturdays very early in the morning. The fare is roughly the same as a 2nd class ticket on the ordinary train. Expect delays at the border.

Tickets are valid for a month so you can make any stops you like in Botswana. However, you must get the ticket endorsed by the station master each time you get off for it to be honoured when you board again. If you're travelling to South Africa on the train via Ramatlhabama, everyone has to dismount and walk through the Bophuthatswana and South African immigration posts. This takes a long time so it is better to get off in Gaborone and hitch via the Tlokweng Gate, 30 km to the east.

TO/FROM NAMIBIA

Going into Namibia from Botswana along the Ghanzi to Gobabis track is considerably more difficult than other points of entry because of the lack of transport. The road is sealed on the Namibian side and in reasonable condition on the Botswana side. On the other hand, if you do want to go direct between these two countries you should seriously consider going via the Caprivi Strip. Much of the road along the strip is paved and, contrary to what you might hear, this is not a prohibited military area. The Ngoma post into Caprivi (54 km west of Kasane) is open seven days a week from 7 am to 6 pm. Refer to the Namibian chapter for details.

Lifts west into Namibia from Ghanzi are not that easy to find. There are a few trucks which do the run every week in the dry season, stopping at Kuke overnight and continuing on to Gobabis the next day. The best place to find them is the Oasis store as they have a petrol truck which goes to Gobabis every two or three days for supplies. The owner of the Oasis also knows who else is going that way

because he has a two-way radio and everybody stops there for petrol. Afrikaner farmers go to Gobabis to shop and will usually give you a lift if you ask. The border officials are very easy-going since few people use the crossing. They don't ask for onward tickets or to see how much money you have. Expect delays due to soft sand. This is the only entry/exit point along the whole western border which is marked by a high barbed wire fence.

TO/FROM SOUTH AFRICA

The usual way into South Africa is to hitch or take public transport from Gaborone to Mafikeng via Ramatlhabama. The trouble with this route is that it's difficult to get lifts out of Mafikeng going south (no problem if you are on public transport, of course). A better way is to go from Gaborone east to Tlokweng Gate (30 km) and from there to Zeerust and Johannesburg. This is positively the best border crossing into South Africa. Immigration is fast, they don't ask for onward tickets and bags are rarely searched. Other travellers have recommended the Zanzibar crossing south-east of Selebi-Phikwe which has been described as 'a breeze'. There is a police post there but no customs. Look clean and hitch a ride with an Afrikaner – no problem at all.

As we go to press, there are no longer any through trains from Botswana to South Africa because of bad relations between Botswana and Bophuthatswana (the Black 'homeland'). You have to get off at the border, walk across and catch another train from Mafikeng. No doubt through services will be restored when relations improve but, until they do, it's easier to get off the train at Gaborone and go through the Tlokweng Gate.

TO/FROM ZAMBIA

Entry from Zambia is via the Kazungula ferry across the Zambezi River. This usually operates on weekdays only, but sometimes runs at weekends too. The customs posts are open from 6 am to 6 pm seven days a week. The ferry is quite an experience when it is working. Heavy trucks have to speed on board and come to a sudden halt to provide the ferry with the momentum to break away from the shore. Occasionally a truck will stop a little short or a little long and the whole ferry will flip. Whenever this happens there's quite a mess and a lengthy delay in crossing. Luckily, it doesn't occur too often.

If you're heading north into Zambia, it's possible to pick up South African trucks at Kasane that are going through to Lusaka, Kabwe and Ndola. Another possibility is with Zambian truck drivers who often stay overnight in Nata, so ask around in the bars. Remember that you cannot change pula into kwacha at the bank in Kasane.

Alternatively, it may be quicker to cross from Kasane into Zimbabwe at Kazungula, travel the 80 km to Victoria Falls then recross the border from there into Livingstone. This way you avoid the ferry altogether. Pula cannot be changed into Zimbabwean dollars at the bank in Kasane.

Around the Country

FRANCISTOWN

One of the cheapest places to stay is the camp site at the *Marang Hotel* about five km out of town. Ask for directions. It costs P 6 per person. The charge includes hot showers and the use of the swimming pool. The hotel itself is very pricey (P 110 a single) but it does have good food. On Sundays you can really gorge yourself at the *braai* (barbeque) for about P 10. A similar *braai* is available at the *Thapama Lodge*.

In the centre of town are the *Tati Hotel*, opposite the train station and the *Grand Hotel*. The cheapest rooms at the Tati are P 25/35 for a single/double. The Grand charges from P 20/30 for a single/double. The Tati is the better of the two but the food has been described as 'terrible'.

Those short of funds could sleep at the railway station – no problems. You could also stay at the police station though the officers there are getting tired of impecunious travellers. So have a good story ready.

The municipal **swimming pool**, behind the post office, is good value at 60 thebe.

If you arrive late with no local currency, there's a shop open until late which will change travellers' cheques at a reasonable rate. It's just round the corner from the Grand Hotel towards the Cave Restaurant. For lifts south, ask at Guys & Gals clothing store. The truck driver who makes the deliveries here does a weekly Francistown, Gaborone, Johannesburg, Maseru run and will usually take passengers free. Otherwise, the best place to wait is at the roundabout next to the Thapama Lodge.

The truck weighbridge a few km out of Francistown is a good place to wait for lifts to Maun and Kasane. You can talk to the drivers while their trucks are being weighed. If you're hitching to Maun you must walk out to the airport turn-off where there is a tree next to which the locals wait for the buses and trucks. Most potential lifts won't stop before they get there. Very few lifts will be free and you'll have to negotiate the price.

GABORONE

Gaborone is the capital of Botswana. It's not a particularly interesting place because it's mainly a modern urban sprawl. Think twice about staying if you are on a strict budget.

Things to See

The **museum** in Gaborone is interesting and worth a visit. It is open Tuesday to Friday from 9 am to 6 pm and on Saturday and Sunday from 9 am to 5 pm. Admission is free. There is an excellent **basket store** (the only one) on the square. The work is nice and the pieces are sold according to size.

The **Lentswe La Udi weavers** live in a

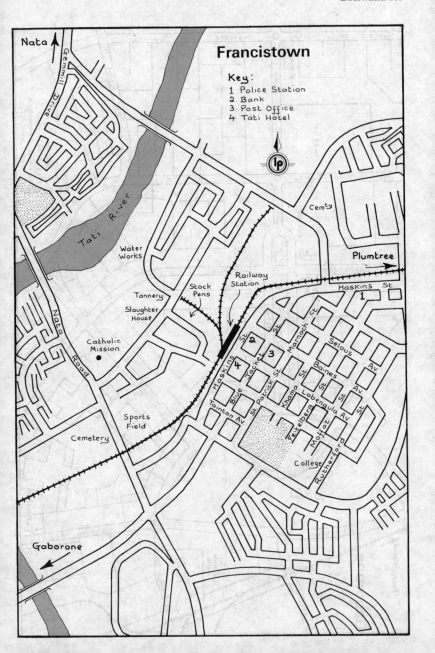

Francistown

Key:
1 Police Station
2 Bank
3 Post Office
4 Tati Hotel

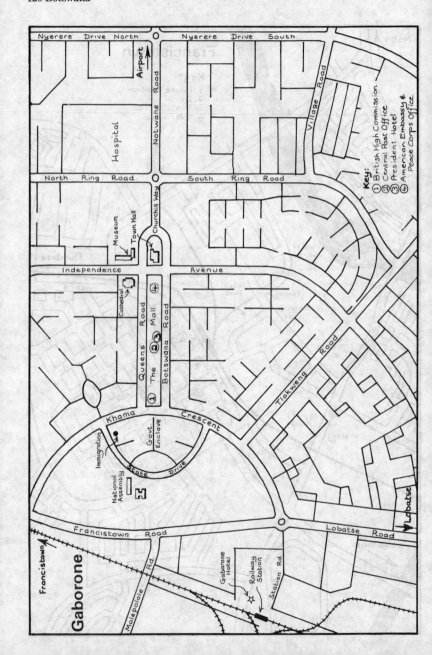

Gaborone

Key:
1. British High Commission
2. Central Post Office
3. President Hotel
4. American Embassy & Peace Corps Office

picturesque village 15 km north of Gaborone. They are open most days, and tea and snacks are available. A Swede taught them to weave and did much of the designing.

The regional capital of the Bakgatla tribe, **Mochudi**, north of Gaborone, is an interesting place to visit and the second largest village in Botswana. It's one of the few places in Botswana where the traveller can feel a sense of history. Buses from Gaborone take about an hour. The excellent **Phuthadikabo Museum** chronicles the history of the Bakgatla people. Chief Linchwe II appears to be keeping up his father's campaign to have the 'dreaded weed' legalised (the colonial administration banned it). The museum is open Monday to Friday from 8 am to 5 pm and on Saturday and Sunday from 2 to 5 pm. Admission is free. There are no hotels in the village.

At **Manyana**, 90 km from Gaborone, there are paintings by Bushpeople on the rocks. *Kgotla* chairs are made here also.

Places to Stay

Most of the hotels cost P 30 to P 40 per night. The cheapest place to stay is the *Gaborone Hotel*, opposite the railway station, which has dormitory beds for P 26, singles for P 42 and more for doubles. The prices include breakfast. If you want to leave before breakfast let them know the night before and they'll give you a huge pile of four sandwiches per person at dinner time (eg fried egg, roast beef, bologna, etc).

The *Mago Hotel* is even cheaper but it has the disadvantage of being 10 km out of town (a taxi there costs P 2 to P 3 but there's also a bus for 25 thebe). This hotel has an excellent nightclub called the *Blue Note*.

There's also the possibility of the *Morning Star Hotel* at Tlokweng Gate, 30 km from Gaborone. They charge P 55 a double (no singles).

If you are short of cash and only staying overnight, you can sleep at the railway station – no problems. There's nowhere to camp in Gaborone.

Several volunteer agencies (Norad, Peace Corps, WUSC, etc) maintain houses in Gaborone for the use of volunteers in town on business. If you have any contacts, it may be possible to stay at one of these. The two best places to meet volunteers and other expatriates are the bars of either the *Gaborone Sun Hotel* or the *President Hotel*. The German Volunteer Service is at 2931 Pudologo Crescent and the Peace Corps is at 133 Legonono Place, just north of the cathedral. There are also hostels for the Dutch, Canadian and Swedish volunteers where you might be offered somewhere to stay. Be warned, however, that both the German Volunteer Service and the US Peace Corps have advised us that they're not taking travellers anymore. Too many have abused the privilege.

It might still be worth checking out the *Botswana Nurses Association Hostel* opposite the Holiday Inn. You can get a double room for P 10 . The *International Volunteer Services House*, off Moremi Rd, is another possibility. They charge P 7 per person per night but they only have three rooms available.

Places to Eat

There is cheap food in the market near the station and for P 1.50 to P 2 you can have a good filling meal. Try mealie meal, pickled spinach, chubuku (sorghum beer), goat, mopani worms ('Don't leave Botswana without trying mopani worms!' said one volunteer worker). The market is only open for breakfast and lunch. There's also the Chinese restaurant at the *Oasis Motel* and *The Sitar* which has Indian food. Both are good value. The *Midnight Grill* (American food) and *Kentucky Fried Chicken* are popular with expatriates.

An expatriate friend of mine has recommended the *President Hotel* for lunch or the *Park Restaurant* at any time for relatively cheap food (but he stressed that it is 'relative').

For a splurge, try *Georgina in the Village* restaurant.

The *Bull & Bush*, an English-style pub, serves draught beer. Around 6 pm every evening they lay on free bar snacks in such quantities that you can virtually eat your fill. It's also a good place to meet expatriates and to ask around for somewhere to stay.

GHANZI

The only place to stay in Ghanzi is the *Kalahari Arms Hotel* which costs P 35 a single and P 70 a double. You can also camp on the grass at the back of the hotel for P 5 per tent. The fee includes the use of hot showers. Good breakfasts are available at the hotel for P 7.

If you don't want to pay P 5 to camp, walk a short distance out of town and erect your tent there. Ghanzi is quite small so this is no problem.

Ghanzicrafts, a cooperative run by Danish volunteers, is thoroughly recommended as the cheapest and best place in Botswana to buy Bushpeople artefacts. Started in 1983 as an outlet and training centre for local craftworkers in the Ghanzi area, it is a non-profit organisation where all the proceeds go to those who bring in crafts for sale. A 10% surcharge on articles under P 20 or a P 2 surcharge on articles over that covers rent and administrative costs. You can pick up traditional craftwork at a third to a half of the selling price of similar articles in Maun or Gaborone. They offer a wide range of crafts including dyed textile work, decorated bags, hunting sets, skirts, bead or ostrich shell necklaces, karosses, mats and headgear. The craftshop is between the Kalahari Arms Hotel and the post office in Ghanzi.

For lifts to Lobatse or into Namibia, ask for David Thomas. he knows every truck which leaves town and may be able to help.

GWETA

Gweta is 100 km from Nata along the Maun road. You can camp at the *Gweta Rest Camp* for P 5 per person including use of facilities. They also have *rondavels* for P 40 to P 60 (depending on the season). The camp is run by Keith Poppleton and his wife and they know a lot about the surrounding area. The food at the camp is excellent.

Gweta is a very convenient base from which to explore the Makgadikgadi Pans – a vast tract of rolling grassland peppered with Mokolwane palms. In the wet season, the pans have plenty of animals including the largest herds of gemsbok you will see anywhere, anytime. In the dry season, the pans are almost deserted but still spectacular. If there are at least two of you and you don't have transport leave the vehicle you are in at the turn-off to the Makgadikgadi Pans (about 150 km from Nata). Then walk into the pans or sit at the roadside and wait for lift into Rakops. After that, get out where you feel like it. Take everything you need including water. This trip isn't recommended for one person as there are lions and leopards and other dangerous animals around. The wildlife is there because there are no boreholes and, so, no cattle.

Vehicles to Rakops are few and far between. They will nearly always stop for you if only because they simply cannot believe you are wandering about there without wheels.

KANG

An Afrikaner couple (George and Turina Joubert) run the general store. If you have rand they may be able to change it into pula and they can also be very helpful about finding lifts out of the village. All the locals hang around here looking for lifts.

KASANE

The *Khubu Lodge* (tel 312) between Kasane and Kazungula (two km from Kazungula), and the *Kasane Game Lodge*, both overlooking the river, have camp sites with all facilities for P 5 per night per person under thatched roofs. Facilities include good showers and toilets, swimming pool, tennis court, restaurant, bar, bottle shop and general store. There are also on-site caravans and self-contained chalets which cost P 24 and P 36 respectively. They both sleep four people. The owner Nick Bornman is very helpful. Both lodges have excellent restaurants where you can dine like a king for around P 11.

Alternatively, you can walk to the gates of the Chobe National Park, about three km from the Game Lodge, and ask drivers if they would mind taking you to the camp site at *Serondella*. The only facilities there are potable water, toilets and broken showers but it's a beautiful site right next to the Chobe River. You must take everything with you and watch out for the vervet monkeys which will steal anything remotely edible.

MAUN

Maun is where every traveller in Botswana goes to since it's on the edge of the Okavango Delta. However, if your time or your funds are limited, think twice about going. Maun itself is little more than a dusty village. Local expatriates are accustomed to meeting travellers who came believing they could see the Delta on a shoestring. Instead they merely spent all week hassling and had to leave after seeing almost nothing.

The Department of Wildlife has a small park on the south side of the river roughly opposite the airport. Entry is free. To visit the park you must enquire at the Wildlife Training Centre next to the park gates. They will organise a guide for you but you may have to wait for a while – you cannot enter without a guide. There are no dangerous animals in the park but a good variety of herbivores. To get to the park when there is water in the river, walk down to the bridge, then take the turn off on the left past Barney's Bar – or simply walk along the river bank. The training centre is about four km from the bridge. If the river is empty, simply cross the bed anywhere between Riley's and the airport.

Take a camera and expect a fairly long, hot walk inside the park.

Places to Stay & Eat

Riley's Hotel is the only hotel in Maun itself. It was recently renovated and offers a variety of rooms. The old rooms cost P 28 a single without bath, P 37.50/52 for a single/double with bath. The new rooms, which are all with air-con, cost P 95/105 for a single/double with bath. All prices include breakfast. The hotel has a restaurant and bar. The latter is a popular expatriate watering hole.

There is nowhere to camp in Maun itself. If you're really stuck they are very helpful at the police station.

A good place to eat is the *Paradise Café* behind the post office. The *Duck Inn* (restaurant and bar) at the airstrip is another popular expatriate hang out. It's a good place to find lifts and glean information about what's available.

Rather than stay in Maun, most people prefer to head out to one of the lodges in the Okavango Swamps (about 13 km from Maun) where you can camp for P 3 to P 5 per night. If you're looking for a lift out there, ask at Bonaventures or Bushman Curio Shop in the centre of Maun. It is possible to get out to camps deep inside the delta very cheaply in supply planes, but it's all a question of luck. Try contacting June Leversedge of Travel Wild opposite the airport or go to the Duck Inn at the airport and ask around. More details about these in the section on the Okavango Delta.

NATA

The *Nata Lodge* is one of the most pleasant sites in Botswana. It is some 10 km south of Nata and about 10 km east of Sua Pan. Camping costs P 5 per person. They also have a permanent tent for slightly more or *rondavel* accommodation for P 60 per per night. Meals are available. The *Nata Bottle Store & Bar*, right on the turn-off to Maun, also offers accommodation but, unless you have transport, it's out of reach of Sua Pan. You can also camp free at the petrol station on the corner of the Maun road. Ask at the police station if you don't have a tent. They're quite friendly.

Sua Pan (an enormous, flat saltpan) is one of the more spectacular sights in Botswana. Go there at dawn or in the evening for the most incredible sunrises and sunsets. When the pan is flooded (usually December to March), it attracts giant flocks of herons, pelicans and other large waders.

SEROWE

This is an interesting village and the largest in Botswana. It was the home village of Sir Seretse Khama. Botswanan politics is still strongly influenced by what happens in the Serowe *kgotla*.

Stay at the *Tshwaragano Hotel* (formerly the Coop Hotel) which is run by the Brigades – a local cooperative organisation. It is a stone building on the hillside overlooking the village. It's basic and clean and *rondavels* cost P 10. Food is available for P 1.50 and is good value. If it's full, go to the *Tshengowe Hotel* though this is a little more expensive.

Game Reserves & National Parks

Entry fees to the National Parks are P 10 per week per person and P 1 per car. The camping fee is P 2 per night. The government is about to substantially increase these fees.

OKAVANGO DELTA

This area north-west of Maun is really beautiful. It abounds with birdlife and other game including elephant, zebra, buffalo, wildebeest, giraffe, hippo and kudu. You haven't seen Botswana until you've been here. The swamps are actually the inland delta of the Okavango River, which originates in the mountains of western Angola and eventually spills out over the northern plateau of Botswana. The cone shaped delta covers an area of over 15,000 square km and is the largest inland delta in the world. The river annually brings more than two million tonnes of sand and silt into the delta, yet less than 3% of the water emerges at the other end to either flood Lake Ngami or cross another 500 km of the Kalahari to enter Lake Xau and the Makgadikgadi Pans.

The flood waters generally reach Shakawe around March and Maun in late June. In recent years, however, precipitation has been very low and the Thamalakane River, which flows through Maun, has been a dried up riverbed by February. No water has reached Lakes Ngami and Xau or the Makgadikgadi Pans for the last three years.

The delta is made up of large areas of papyrus reed beds, low, flat islands covered with trees and water channels. It's believed that the whole delta is moving slowly eastwards. Even apparently insignificant events like a new hippo run can change the water courses over large areas. Attempts to alter the water courses in the early 1970s produced unexpected results and such attempts have now been abandoned.

A part of the eastern side of the delta including Chief's Island is enclosed by the **Moremi Wildlife Reserve**. Entry fees are payable in this part of the delta. They are P 10 per person for a week plus P 1 per vehicle. Camping fees are P 2 per person for a night.

There are plenty of mosquitoes in the delta so take insect repellent with you but the tsetse flies have been largely wiped out.

The best time to visit the swamps to see big game is between October and February (they are marooned on the islands and therefore easier to find). Between May and August is the best time for birdlife. Don't expect to see a lot of wildlife especially if you are only going there for a few days. It's *possible* to see plenty but it's all a question of luck.

Organised Safaris

Other than hiring a *mokoro* and poler either privately or through a company, Botswana does not really cater for budget safaris of the type you can find in, say, Kenya. Going on an organised safari is going to cost you a lot of money. Both mobile and foot safaris are available. What they do more or less guarantee is that you will see much more wildlife than you will in the camps nearer to Maun.

If you're interested contact Island Safaris (tel Maun 300) PO Box 116 Maun, or Delta Camp (tel Maun 220) PO Box 39 Maun, or Bonaventures (tel Maun 205) PO Box 448 Maun, and ask for their brochures. If arriving in Maun without a booking then contact either the Bushman Curio Shop or Bonaventures in the centre of town.

You can sometimes get what amounts to a free safari if one of the lodges is moving its overnight safari stop camps. This sometimes happens when either the water gets too low or the swamps flood. They often appreciate help at these times and will take you along for just the cost of your food.

Flights over the swamps are available from Maun and are said to be worth every dollar. There are two air charter companies – Air Kavango and Northern Air which both have single and twin engine aircraft. The planes cost P 210 per five-seater per hour and P 370 per nine-seater per hour.

Places to Stay

As well as the Moremi Wildlife Reserve there are many different camps and lodges in the delta. The most interesting ones for wildlife, however, are on Chief's Island. The ones nearest Maun, though readily accessible by vehicle, don't offer much in the way of wildlife. They are, however, cheap and good fun. You're likely to meet many other travellers and so find out what alternatives are available

to the expensive safaris which go deeper into the delta.

The three lodges closest to Maun are *Island Safari Lodge* (tel Maun 300) PO Box 116, Maun, *Okavango River Lodge* and *Crocodile Camp*. They're all close to each other, about 13 km northeast of Maun. Further out, some 20 km from Maun, is *Oddball's* (part of Karo Safari Lodge). You shouldn't have any trouble getting out to any of these places as there are Land Rovers to and from Maun every day. They all offer camping with excellent facilities for P 3 to P 5 per person per night depending on the season. They also have more expensive private rooms.

Of the three nearest Maun, Island Safari Lodge is still rated the best. It has a swimming pool, films four times a week, a good bar and restaurant, an excellent amenities block (watch out for greedy monkeys), a free book swap service and a nice friendly atmosphere. The brick and thatch chalets are fairly plush and cost P 70/80 for a single/double with breakfast. (Thanks for the letter folks!). Dinner costs P 14.

Okavango River Lodge and Crocodile Camp are similar though the charges for the chalets differ. At Okavango they are are P 45/56 for a single/double with breakfast. Dinner costs P 14. At Crocodile they are P 70/75 for a single/double with breakfast. Dinner costs P 18.

Island Safaris, Okavango River Lodge and Crocodile Camp have their own smaller camps further into the delta where they take visitors on safari. Like other organised safaris on offer, these are quite expensive. So, if you have limited funds, you'll have to content yourself with hiring a *mokoro* and poler for a few days. You can arrange these at any of the camps or at the bottle shop in the village (next to Island Safaris). If you hire privately, you can be sure that the money you pay goes directly to the local people. Hire them from a company or agency and a substantial part of the fee will go to that company or agency. A fourth camp has recently opened close to Crocodile Camp. It is called *Kubu Camp* and is run by Paul and Ann who are very friendly and easygoing. Our correspondent didn't provide too many details but camping costs just P 2. They provide the usual services – *mokoro*, trips, etc.

Though further from Maun, *Oddball's* is popular. It has a reputation for being the most entertaining of the budget camp sites plus it has 'resident' crocodiles and hippos. It is run by Corrie and Sue who are very friendly and helpful. The camp site costs P 5 per person per night and there are hot showers, clean toilets, laundry facilities, fireplaces, a shop and bar. Lifts into town are no problem and they'll even do your shopping for you. Oddball's is close to *Delta Camp* but the latter is strictly for those on organised safaris and you cannot use the facilities there if staying at Oddball's. *Makoro* trips can be arranged for P 20 a day (two passengers) or P 15 a day for six or more days. This includes the fee for the poler. You provide your own camping equipment and food though equipment can be hired on site.

For those who don't like hitching, Oddball's have their own airstrip. There's a daily flight in either direction to and from Maun for P 80 return. There's also transport from the airstrip to the camp for P 5 (which entitles you to one night's stay at the camp site free of charge). There's a strict baggage limit of 10 kg on these flights.

The camps and lodges deep inside the delta are much more expensive. Visitors usually fly to them though you can get there by *mokoro* from the camps outside Maun in about three days. Air transfers are usually P 80 per person return.

Camp Okavango is a luxury tented camp for P 235 per person all inclusive. *Xaxaba Camp* has luxury reed and thatch chalets at P 80 per person including dinner and breakfast and P 120 per day per person all inclusive (plus you can camp for P 5 per person per night).

Qhaaxwa Fishing Camp is a tented camp in the north-western area of the delta which costs P 45 per person including meals. *Delta Camp* has luxury reed and thatch chalets at P 130 per person all inclusive. *Mombo Camp* provides luxury tented accommodation for P 185 per person all inclusive. The *Xugana Lodge* has luxury tented accommodation at P 160 per person all inclusive. Xugana Lodge also has the houseboat *Sitatunga* which can be hired for P 200 per day all inclusive for groups of four or more.

A relatively new outfit is *Gunn's Camps* run by Mike Gunn who can be contacted at Merlin's Services out at Maun airport. He has set up a lodge on Inchwe Island about 100 km from Maun near to the Moremi Game Reserve. Camping there costs P 5 per night or you can rent a self-help *banda* for P 100 (sleeps up to six people). The cheapest way to get there is by 4WD jeep which costs P 40 one-way. There's usually one every day (no weight restrictions). Otherwise you can fly for P 110 return. *Mokoros* can be hired for P 25 per day. Those who have stayed here say it's an excellent place.

You don't *have* to stay in the luxury accommodation at some of the lodges and camps. Once you've got there (by air) you can, if you wish, take off straight away with a *mokoro* and poler (at normal rates). Xaxaba is one such camp. Confirm these arrangements before you leave Maun to avoid disappointment.

Getting There & Away

Before you leave Maun, it's a good idea to get as much information as possible about the variety of accommodation, safaris and their respective costs in the delta. Budget travellers will find their options severely limited. Many of the camps deep inside the delta are expensive luxury lodges and the only feasible way of getting to them for most of the year is by plane. Make enquiries at either Bonaventures or Bushman Curio Shop in the centre of Maun.

If you fly then you're looking at P 80 to P 120 return and there are strict baggage limits – usually 10 kg.

If you don't want to fly or can't afford to, you'll have to hire a *mokoro* and poler. This is best done at one of the camps near Maun or at Gomare or Etsha. Etsha is the closest to the delta but you will have to pole for two days to get out of cattle country. Go to Etsha 6 and ask around. If you're trying to arrange this privately, be prepared to wait while a *mokoro* and a poler are found and an agreement reached on how your money will be split. This can take time. Don't pay in advance and don't expect to get something substantially cheaper than what you'd pay by going through a safari company.

The usual charge for a *mokoro* and poler is P 18 to P 20 per day including the poler's food. Some companies charge this per person and others per *mokoro* so make sure you know what the deal is. A normal *mokoro* takes three people including the poler. You must carry your own food so stock up at Maun Fresh Produce before you go. Take enough for the poler as well. Such a friendly gesture will pay dividends. His rations are a bag of mealie meal and a tin or two of corned beef per week. The poler will keep a fire burning all night, so this is one of the few wilderness areas in Botswana where you do not need to take a tent unless it's raining.

You won't see too much in the way of wildlife if you don't venture far from Maun or the camps nearest Maun. One traveller who paid for a return flight, *mokoro* and poler for a day saw virtually nothing but 'reeds, reeds and more reeds'. If it's wildlife you want to see then you're going to have to hire a *mokoro* for at least a week or go on an organised safari. You won't see very much if you just go out for a few days. There is sometimes a choice between *mokoros*. Wooden ones take two people in addition to the poler. Fibreglass *mokoros*, which cost the same, will take three people and a poler.

Another option is to drive into the delta.

This can be done from Maun when the Boro River is dry and will take you to Chief's Island. A map of the area will be needed. Take the road north out of Maun, past Tswarango Community Junior School. Keep driving north as best you can until you reach the buffalo fence. Turn left here and drive along the fence until you reach a gate. Tell the person at the gate you are going to Chief's Island. Drive north-west for about 30 km and then try to head north. You should cross the Boro about 60 to 70 km past the gate. Until you cross the Boro, you are in a hunting concession area and, although you have every right to use the road, you have absolutely no right to camp.

There are two vehicle hire companies in Maun including Avis. Prices range from P 90 to P 195 per day. Mileage rates are 60 thebe per km once you've used up your free daily allowance (usually 100 km per day).

MOREMI WILDLIFE RESERVE

Moremi is an eastern extension of the Okavango Delta. Most of it is Mophane woodland but the eastern and northern parts are a mixture of pans, creeks, papyrus and woodland. Herds of game are guaranteed even if you only go for one day.

It is possible at certain times of year to get into this reserve in a 2WD vehicle but you really need a 4WD. You may get a lift in one of the latter if you hang around the lodges near Maun but you may have to wait for quite some time. Otherwise, enquire at Bonaventures in Maun or hire a vehicle. Unless you are going to one of the safari company camps, you will need to take all your own food, drink and fuel.

To get there, drive north-east out of Maun past Crocodile Camp and Okavango River Lodge. The road is terrible since it's almost entirely soft sand. After about 60 km you pass the buffalo fence. A few km later the road forks. The 'main road' continues on to Savuti and Kasane and the signposted left hand fork leads to Moremi. The road improves from here as does the scenery. The park gates are a further

20 km ahead. There is a camp site at South Gate but it's not very pleasant. Most people prefer to push on to either Third Bridge or Xakanaxa.

The camp site at *Third Bridge* is (literally) at the third wooden bridge along the road, about 35 km from South Gate. It will take about an hour's drive though most people spend longer because there's plenty to see en route. Xakanaxa is about 20 km further on and, even with 4WD, only accessible from Third Bridge when the water in the swamps is low.

Otherwise, if approaching from Maun, you must drive directly north from South Gate, turn left at North Gate and drive another 30 km west. Third Bridge has the best scenery. You can swim there and the water is safe to drink. Xakanaxa is the area where you are most likely to see elephant and hippo. Watch out for baboons at both places. Facilities at both of the camp sites are primitive. There are several private safari camps at Xakanaxa and it's possible to hire a boat from them to visit **Xakanaxa Lagoon** or to go further into the swamps.

There are luxury camps in Moremi. *Camp Moremi* on the banks of Xakanaxa Lagoon has tented accommodation for P 235 per person all inclusive. *Xakanaxa Camp* has tented accommodation for P 81.50 per person for dinner, bed and breakfast and P 125 per person all inclusive.

TSODILO HILLS

The hills are about 30 km due east of the Maun-Shakawe road and about 50 km south of Shakawe. They feature heavily in many travelogues and coffee-table books. They're beautiful, visible for miles and have many legends associated with them. The hills have many fascinating rock paintings on them and, once you have found one, you will find many more. The paintings are in Bushpeople and Bantu styles. There are also several Iron Age sites in the area. The whole area is a national monument and you must not remove anything.

There is a guide stationed at the hills who will show you around. He's not keen on walking though and will only show you the more accessible areas. There's also a small village of 'professional' Bushpeople near the largest hill.

You must take all your own supplies with you including water. People have been known to walk there from the road but it is more usual to drive in a 4WD vehicle. The 45 km journey will take about two hours as the road is very sandy. There are no dangerous wild animals in the area. However, recent reports suggest that a (saline) borehole has been opened near the hills so expect to be overrun with cattle and their inevitable camp followers – flies.

The best place to camp is on a small clearing towards the top of the second largest hill.

CHOBE NATIONAL PARK

It's virtually impossible to see this park of 11,700 square km – or the interesting Xau and Makgadikgadi Pans further south near Nata – without your own 4WD vehicle. These are not easy to find and are expensive to hire. You could try Ad Vriend in Francistown, who hire Toyota Land Cruisers. Entry to the Chobe National Park costs P 10 per week plus P 1 per vehicle. Camping fees are P 2 per person per night.

While there's plenty of game everywhere in this park including large herds of elephant, the most interesting part is the 50 km stretch that runs along the river past Kasane. Many animals go down to the river to drink especially in the dry season. You can see a wide variety of animals in just an afternoon's drive. This stretch of road is fairly easy driving in an ordinary car in the dry season. Chobe is the best game park in Botswana to see wild animals.

Many tourists stay at the camp sites and lodges in Kasane and go out into the park for morning or afternoon game drives and don't mind taking others with them.

Ask around or walk the three km to the park gate and try again there. You cannot enter the park without a vehicle. For those with 4WD, the area around Nogatsau, 80 km south of Kasane, is recommended during the wet season.

The *Serondella Campsite* in the park is beautifully situated above the Chobe River. It costs just P 2 per night with hot showers and flush toilets. It's not protected from the wildlife so expect to be woken up by lions roaring around your tent. It's safe so long as you stay in the tent but not if you leave it. The baboons and monkeys are what you need to watch. Don't leave a trace of food anywhere near the tent as baboons can unzip tents and rucksacks without any problem. Don't chase baboons because they'll bite you and they can break an arm. They also carry rabies. Throw rocks at them or pretend to – they know the score.

The *Chobe Game Lodge* is on the banks of the Chobe River, 12 km from Kasane and 80 km from Victoria Falls. It has 45 luxury air-con rooms with bath which costs P 105 each per night including breakfast. Lunch and dinner are available for P 12. The Game Lodge also rents boats with a guide for P 16 each (a maximum of four people). You can also camp for P 3 per person. The *Chobe Safari Lodge* is in the centre of Kasane but also on the banks of the Chobe River. It has double *rondavels* for P 25 per night (bed only) and air-con rooms for P 45/65 for a single/double (bed only). Camping costs P 5 per tent per night. Like the Game Lodge, the Safari Lodge offers boat trips on the Chobe River but for P 7 each (a maximum of 10 people). The trips last three hours.

TULI BLOCK

The Tuli Block is the largest private game reserve in southern Africa. The Block actually consists of three reserves in total. One of them, the *Tuli Lodge*, has camping facilities. The others cater exclusively for the designer safari suit set. You might be able to camp on the edge of one of the villages there or on the opposite bank of the Motlhutse River but you cannot camp anywhere inside the reserves.

The area boasts the largest population of elephant anywhere in southern Africa. The scenery is spectacular – sandstone *kopjes* and rock outcrops with boulders balanced improbably one on top of the other. There are also several archaeological sites along the banks of the Limpopo River.

Camping at Tuli Lodge costs P 10 per tent. Game drives are available in the morning, afternoon or evening for P 10 to P 15 or you can go for a walk with a guide for P 5. The people are very friendly and helpful. They also have an excellent and comfortable hide in the bush where you can stay for the night if you wish.

SHAKAWE

It is possible to enter Botswana from the Caprivi Strip via the ferry at Muhembo, a few km north of Shakawe. The river here is quite spectacular.

There are now two lodges where you can stay. These are the *Shakawe Fishing Camp* and a new lodge further south. You can camp at either for P 5 per person. Both have excellent facilities. The Shakawe Fishing Camp also has luxury rooms for P 150 per person all inclusive. Both lodges can arrange boats for you but they're not cheap. You can also hire a 4WD vehicle from the Shakawe Fishing Camp and drive from there to the Tsodilo Hills and back in a day though these cost P 350 (shared by up to six people) including packed lunch.

Burkina Faso

Burkina Faso (known as Upper Volta until mid-1984) is one of the world's poorest countries and seems locked into a vicious poverty cycle. Not only is much of the land infertile, but 'aid' organisations seem unwilling to finance projects appropriate to basic local needs. Instead, they insist on the cultivation of cash crops – principally cotton – which further impoverishes the soil, reduces the amount of land available for food production and does nothing to lay the basis for a more viable rural economy. Most of the country's basic food needs have to be imported. Added to this, Burkina Faso suffered disastrously from the Sahel droughts of the 1970s when at least a third of the country's livestock perished.

Another factor which contributes to its underdevelopment is a long history of labour migration to Ghana and the Ivory Coast. At any particular time the majority of the country's young men will be away working on the plantations and in the factories of those two countries. While this has greatly benefited the economies of the recipient states, the destructive effects are plainly visible in Burkina Faso.

About half the population belong to the Mossi tribe. Their ancestors set up a number of centralised kingdoms in the area from the 15th century onwards. The most important of these were at Ouagadougou and Ouahigouya, whose kings exercised considerable influence over the course of politics right up to independence. Ouagadougou was taken by the French in 1896 and its king was forced to take refuge in Dagomba country. Only in 1947 were the borders of the country finally defined.

Between WW I and WW II, the French colonial authorities put into operation a system of forced labour recruitment among the Mossi to supply the European-owned plantations in the Ivory Coast. The system was abolished in principle by the late 1940s but continued in practice under another name right up to independence in 1960. In order to escape forced recruitment, many preferred to make their way to Ghana but what awaited them there was in many ways no better than the Ivory Coast. Instead of being exploited by French plantation owners, the Mossi found themselves exploited by the British.

When independence was granted in 1960 the first president was Maurice Yameogo, one of the principal figures in national politics since the end of WW II. Though re-elected with an overwhelming majority in 1965, Yameogo's increasingly autocratic style of government and his mismanagement of the economy resulted in his overthrow in a military coup led by Lieutenant Colonel Sangoule Lamizana in 1966. The military remained in power for four years and was gradually able to put the economy onto a healthier footing. Many of these gains, however, were frittered away by political infighting during the four years of civilian government from 1970 to 1974, so the army once again intervened.

Another attempt at civilian government followed a period of military rule. This in turn, was followed by a mixed civilian and military government. One of the most powerful lobbies in the country is the trade union movement, which has forced the armed services to compromise on more than one occasion.

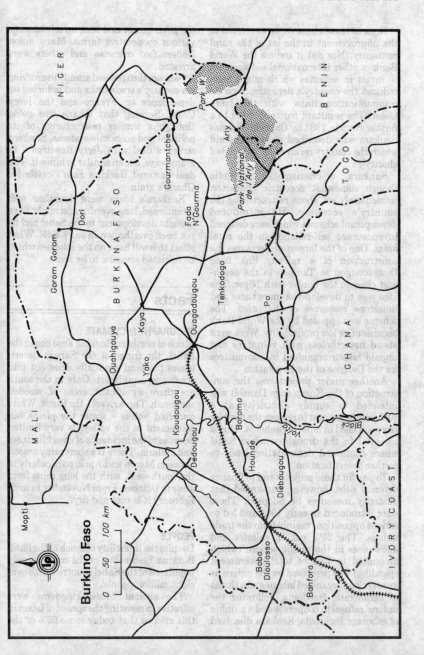

None of these changes, however, led to the improvement in the lot of the rural peasantry. Nor did it induce the World Bank or other international aid agencies to invest in schemes which might have reduced the country's dependence on its communication links with the Ivory Coast. The resultant frustration led to a further coup in 1983 by Captain Thomas Sankara who described most of the aid which the country received as 'calculated charity'.

Sankara, a charismatic, energetic though somewhat eccentric character, immediately set about restructuring the country's economy. He introduced development schemes which were designed to encourage self-reliance in the rural areas. One of the largest projects was the construction of a railway link from Ouagadougou to Tambao in the north-east close to the border with Niger. The idea was to develop the manganese and limestone resources of that area. The scheme was opposed by the World Bank because of its low profitability. Work went ahead nevertheless with voluntary and unpaid labour organised by committees for the Defence of the Revolution.

Another major project was the construction of the Kompienga Dam. It was intended to supply electricity at a sufficiently low cost to replace the need for firewood used in most households. This is essential in the drought-stricken Sahel where continued deforestation leads to further desertification.

To pay for these projects and to finance external debt, however, demanded that austerity measures be adopted. These were introduced in early 1985 and led to serious opposition, mainly from the trade unions. The 25% cut in salaries and allowances in the public service (which amounted to 75% of total government spending) was perceived by the unions as an attack on organised labour and a threat to democratic freedoms. Following the unions' refusal to cooperate and a number of sabotage incidents, Sankara dissolved the government and sent its ministers to various cooperative farms. Many union leaders fled overseas and others were arrested.

Sankara then pressed ahead, diversifying his country's trade links and reducing its dependence on France and the Ivory Coast. Sensing that Ghana was going through a similar restructuring of its political and economic systems, Sankara struck a deal with Jerry Rawlings – in many ways, a man similar to himself. The deal bartered Burkina Faso's cattle for Ghana's grain.

Sankara's ideas were doubtless well intentioned, long overdue and might have brought development to the Sahel had he not been overthrown in early 1988. What effect this will have on the schemes which he initiated remains to be seen.

Facts

GEOGRAPHY & CLIMATE

Much of northern Burkina Faso lies in the Sahel, the fringe of the Sahara desert, where the land gradually dries out into scrub and semidesert. Only in the south are there significant areas of wooded savannah. Three rivers – the Black, White and Red Voltas – water the plains but settlement in the valleys is very limited because of the incidence of river blindness and malaria. There is a short rainy season between March and April, particularly in the south-west, with the long rains from June to October. From November to mid-February it is cool and dry.

PEOPLE

Despite the infertility of much of the land, Burkina Faso is one of the most densely populated of the Sahel countries with over eight million people.

The ancient Mossi kingdoms were effective in resisting the spread of Islam in this area so that today some 65% of the population still follow traditional beliefs. Only some 30% are Muslim.

VISAS

Visas are required by all except nationals of Belgium, West Germany, Italy, Luxemburg, the Netherlands and Sweden. From April 1987, French nationals have also required visas though these are free from the French Consulate in Niamey (Niger). They are issued in 48 hours. Visas for French nationals were introduced in retaliation for French immigration policies.

You may have to name an address when you enter the country. Just choose a hotel – it doesn't affect anything that's stamped in your passport.

There are very few Burkina Faso embassies. In Africa they are in Abidjan (Ivory Coast), Accra (Ghana), Cairo (Egypt) and Lagos (Nigeria). Where there is no embassy, visas can be obtained from the French embassy or consulate. Burkina visas cost twice as much in Bamako (Mali) as they do in other countries (CFA 6000 as opposed to CFA 3000).

Visit visas valid for eight days are available to most nationalities and usually take 24 hours to issue. In some places they can be obtained while you wait.

Exit permits are no longer required.

Other Visas

Algeria These are obtainable in Ouagadougou for the equivalent of AD 92 and four photos. They are issued the same day if you get there early. The visas are for 30 days.

Benin There is no Benin embassy in Ouagadougou and you cannot get a Benin visa at the French Embassy, so plan ahead.

Ghana The embassy in Ouagadougou is on Ave Bassawarga opposite the Le Point office. Visas cost CFA 5000 for Commonwealth citizens and CFA 9000 for other nationals plus five photos. You must leave your passport at the office on Monday

morning and collect your visa on Thursday. The staff can be very unhelpful.

Nigeria Again, these are difficult to get. They cost CFA 9000 for a two-day visa!

Togo Visas are available from the French Embassy for CFA 1000 with two photos and are issued in 24 hours. They are only a two-day transit visa but can be extended in Lomé.

MONEY

US$1 = CFA 284

The unit of currency is the CFA franc. There are no restrictions on the import or export of local currency.

The black market rate for Ghanaian cedis in Ouagadougou is not as good as at the border, and much less than the rate in Ghana itself.

The airport departure tax for international flights is CFA 4000.

LANGUAGE

French is the official language. The main African languages are More (spoken by the Mossi), Dioula, Gourmantche and Peul.

Getting There & Around

AIR

Burkina Faso, like the Central African Republic, is served by the air charter company Point Air Mulhouse, usually known simply as Le Point. This company offers the cheapest flights to and from Europe. There are two flights per week between Paris or Marseilles (France) and Ouagadougou. For further details of flights from France, see the main introductory chapter.

Even if you didn't fly to Africa with Le Point, you can still fly with them to France from Ouagadougou but you need to book and pay for the flight at least one month ahead. Their office (tel 33 41 51) in

Ouagadougou is at 17 Ave Bassawarga, BP 4580. One-way fare to Paris costs CFA 101,000.

Some travellers have commented that it's very easy to hitch flights with the military on internal routes.

Air Burkina flies from Ouagadougou to Niamey (Niger) on Monday mornings. The flight costs CFA 37,000 including a 40% student discount. Bring a photostat of your card with you when buying the ticket. They also fly from Ouagadougou to Bamako (Mali) on Wednesday mornings. The ticket costs CFA 17,600 including 40% student discount.

ROAD

Hitching is slow and many of the roads are poor, though there are a couple of good stretches from Ouagadougou to the Ivory Coast and from Ouagadougou to Togo. The road south to Ghana is also in reasonable shape. The road between Ouagadougou and Niamey is sealed all the way though there are a total of 15 police checkpoints en route. When hitching expect to pay around CFA 1000 per 100 km. Regular buses link all the major towns. There are plenty of Peugeot taxis available but they are not particularly cheap.

Ouagadougou to Bobo Dioulasso – there is a daily bus in either direction except on Monday which departs at 7 am (2 pm on Sundays), costs CFA 2600 and takes about 5½ hours. There's also a deluxe bus which leaves at 7 am, costs CFA 3200 and takes five hours. It leaves from Fasotours, Rue Brunnel, on the left hand side near the market. Book your ticket the day before and get there half an hour before departure. A Peugeot 505 shared taxi costs CFA 3500 plus CFA 300 for a backpack. A Peugeot 404 pick-up costs CFA 2500 over the same route.

Ouagadougou to Fada N'Gourma – a shared taxi costs CFA 3000 plus CFA 500 for a pack and takes about five hours.

Ouagadougou to Ouahigouya – the bus costs CFA 3000.

Bobo Dioulasso to Banfora – a *taxi-brousse* costs CFA 1000 plus CFA 200 for a backpack.

TRAIN

The Ouagadougou to Abidjan railway timetable is in the Ivory Coast chapter.

TO/FROM GHANA

Taxis from Ouagadougou to Paga (Ghanaian border) cost CFA 3000 plus CFA 500 for a backpack.

TO/FROM IVORY COAST

Most travellers take the train between Burkina Faso and Ivory Coast. If you want to go by taxi it costs CFA 14,000 plus a luggage charge (Ouagadougou to Abidjan) or CFA 3500 including baggage (Banfora to Ferkessedougou).

TO/FROM MALI

Taxis from Bobo Dioulasso to Bamako cost CFA 8000 and can take up to 19 hours, though mostly the ride doesn't take more than 12 hours. The delays are due to road blocks, of which there up to 18! It's a rough road.

TO/FROM NIGER

There are buses from Ouagadougou to Niamey which leave on Monday, Wednesday and Friday around 11.30 am (or when full). They cost CFA 6750 and take about 30 hours. You can't book a seat in advance so you need to be there well before the bus is due to leave. A direct *taxi-brousse* will cost CFA 7800 plus CFA 300 for a backpack. Otherwise, go by *taxi-brousse* first to Fada N'Gourma (CFA 3000 plus CFA 500 for a backpack, takes five hours) then by truck to Niamey (CFA 4000 including pack, takes six hours).

TO/FROM TOGO

There is a good paved road all the way from Ouagadougou to Lomé and hitching is easy. A truck will cost CFA 9000 and take about 22 hours. If you decide to take a taxi don't take one direct to Lomé or it will cost CFA 12,500 plus baggage. Instead, take one first to Bitou (the border) for CFA 4000 and from there hitch a ride into Dapaong (plenty of trucks). From Dapaong, take another taxi to Lomé. Taxis in Togo cost much less than in Burkina Faso. Expect heavy searches at the border. The border between the two countries closes at 6 pm.

Around the Country

BANFORA

Banfora is in a particularly beautiful area of Burkina Faso. You shouldn't miss the cascades about 13 km from town. You'll need to hire a taxi to get there or a bicycle (CFA 750 to CFA 1000 per day) or a motorbike (CFA 2500 per day). The cascades are spectacular during the wet season but may not be worth it in the dry season. Swimming is possible.

Places to Stay & Eat

You can sometimes get a room at the Maison des Jeunes. Otherwise, try La Comoe, which has some old but pleasant rooms at the back for CFA 2000 though they're reluctant to rent them out. Bicycles can be rented from this hotel for CFA 1000 per day. If they have no room, try the Hotel Fara behind the gare routière which is clean and costs CFA 3000 a double with shower and fan. You can also camp at the cascades.

The Restaurant Bangui-So is a very popular place to eat, drink and listen to music.

BOROMO

This town is about halfway between Ouagadougou and Bobo Dioulasso. The best place to stay is Le Campement. It's good value at CFA 1500 a room, and includes shower and fan when the generator is running.

BOBO DIOULASSO

This is Burkina Faso's second largest city and considerably more pleasant than Ouagadougou.

Information

The gare routière is on the Ave de la République north-east of the market. You must register with the Sûreté. It's just a formality but don't neglect to do it.

Things to See

The mosque is a beautiful example of Sahelian architecture and the number one sight in town. The old part of town is well worth a visit for its artisans and colourful atmosphere. It's also much cheaper than the Grand Marché. Hire a guide to show you around. The Grand Marché itself (map reference No 5) is good for beadwork and carvings.

The other thing to watch out for is the Fête des Masques which takes place seven times a year. Very few tourists get to see this ceremony. It takes place in the old part of town behind the mosque. Five or six people covered in colourful feathers from head to toe and wearing wooden masks, pursue children through the streets and are provoked by them with sticks and whips. It's quite a violent game! They eventually end up where they started from and dance to the rhythm of rapid, intense drum beats until exhausted. It's a very colourful ceremony and doesn't come to an end until late at night.

Some 40 km from Bobo is the Mar aux Hippopotames, a lake filled with hippos. There's no local transport so you'll have to get a group together and hire a taxi. Once there, hire a local to take you out in a canoe for about CFA 500.

Places to Stay

The Mission Protestante no longer takes travellers but just across the street is a small restaurant called La Carafe. It has rooms for CFA 2000 a double and others for CFA 1000 though the latter are usually full. Good cheap meals are also available.

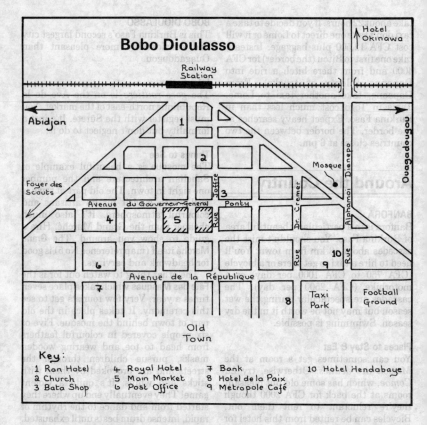

The *Mission Catholique*, on the other hand, still takes guests. A clean, quiet room with shower and mosquito net costs CFA 4000 a double. Meals are available. There's also a lounge and library. Cold drinks and beer can be bought.

One of the cheapest places to stay is the *Hotel de la Paix* at the *gare routière*. It costs CFA 2500 a double and has a good restaurant. Similar, and close by, is the *Hotel Hamdalaye*, Rue Alphamdi Dienego between the Ave de la République and the Ave de la Liberté just round the corner from the *gare routière*. Double rooms cost CFA 3000 with shower and fan or CFA 3500 with shower, toilet and fan. Some travellers

have commented that you need to be a disco lover to stay here. Similar in price is the *Hotel de Renaissance*. A double room with shower costs CFA 2500 while a double with shower, fan and mosquito net is CFA 3500. The hotel does seem to attract its undue share of mosquitoes.

The *Hotel Soba*, near the main post office, offers decent cheap rooms at CFA 2500/3600 for a single/double though you need to haggle to get these prices. Similar is the *Hotel de l'Amitié*, which charges the same but is about a 30-minute walk from the centre of town. The staff are friendly.

Outside the main part of town in the

'African' quarter (Sector 9), many travellers have recommended the *Hotel Okinawa*. Rooms for CFA 2000 without a fan and CFA 2500 with a fan are provided. It also offers very good, reasonably priced food. If it's full, try the nearby *Hotel Bar Liberté*.

The *Foyer des Scouts*, just off the Ave Guimba Oatara, Quartier Coco, used to be very popular with travellers but they've put up their prices considerably. It now costs CFA 5000 per room though they still have much cheaper beds in shared rooms. If you arrive by train it's best to take a taxi as it's a long walk.

The *Hotel du Commerce* costs CFA 5000 per room with air-con.

Places to Eat

Le Makhno, in front of the main post office and run by an urbane Frenchman called Bernard, has been recommended by many travellers. The food is good though a little expensive. The main attraction is the African dances which are put on every Saturday night. Cheaper is *Le Black* where you can get good steak and chips for CFA 650. For a splurge, try *Le Hibou* where excellent meals cost around CFA 2000. It's popular with expatriates.

Others have recommended *L'Auberge* as a good place to meet travellers and enjoy a fruit juice. They have a swimming pool which costs CFA 750 per day.

KOUDOUGOU

The area around Koudougou is worth exploring for its many picturesque villages and friendly people. **Goundi**, eight km from Koudougou, is typical of these villages. There are others between Koudougou and the junction with the main Ouagadougou to Bobo Dioulasso road at Sabu some 27 km from Koudougou. At **Sabu** itself there is a lake inhabited by many crocodiles.

Places to Stay

The cheapest place to stay in Koudougou is the *Hotel Bar Oasis* which has clean rooms for CFA 2000.

OUAGADOUGOU

The capital of Burkina Faso, Ouagadougou has a long history as the centre of one of the Mossi kingdoms which was founded in the 15th century. Apart from the former colonial centre itself, Ouagadougou doesn't have the atmosphere of a capital city. It's more like a collection of overgrown villages and suburbs.

Information

The tourist office is in the foyer of the Hotel de l'Indépendence, Ave Révolution du 17 Mai (formerly the Ave Quezzin Coulibaly) at the junction with Ave de l'Indépendence. Maps of Burkina Faso can be obtained from the Institut du Géographie for CFA 2500.

Le Point (tel 33 41 51) is at 17 Ave Bassawarga. It's open daily, except Sunday, from 8 am to 1 pm. The best rates for changing money are at the BIB bank, Rue Brunnel on the south side of the old market square. Go to the top floor, sign your travellers' cheque and collect your cash. There's no waiting and no commission charged. The poste restante charges CFA 150 per letter collected. The Sûreté is on the Ave de l'Indépendence at Rue Galleni about 100 metres from the Hotel de l'Indépendence.

The main *gare routière* is out past the airport. A taxi there costs CFA 75. The other *gare routière*, eight km south of the centre on the road to Ghana, caters for traffic to Bobo and Ghana. Bus No 9 goes there. Otherwise a taxi costs CFA 500.

The airport is a 20-minute walk from the centre of town.

Warning Be very careful of thieves in Ouagadougou. Keep valuables out of sight.

Things to See

The **Ethnography Museum**, Ave d'Oubritenga opposite the hospital is worth a visit and has a good collection of

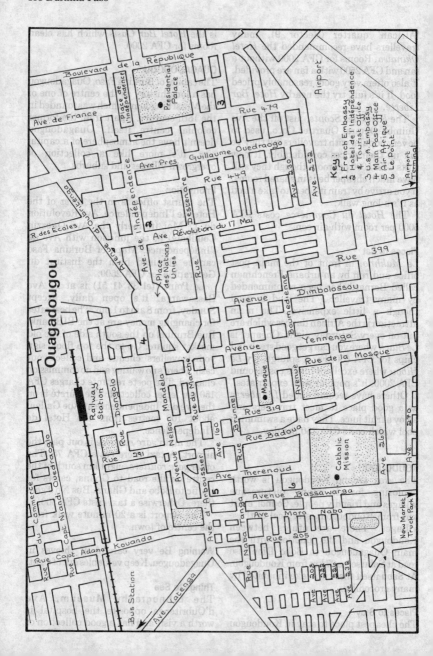

Ouagadougou

Key:
1 French Embassy
2 Hotel de l'Indépendence
3 U.S.A. Embassy
4 Tourist Office
5 Main Post Office
6 Air Afrique
6 Le Point

masks. It's open from 8 am to 12 noon and 3 to 5 pm. Entry costs CFA 100. The **Grand Marché** is out of town. To get there, take bus No 3 to the end of the route (CFA 75). It's very good for basket and leather work.

Avoid the **Sacred Crocodile Lake** tourist trap – a day trip from Ouagadougou. It's a heap of rubbish and you'll be hassled to death. If you want to see wildlife go to the **Parc National de Po** (a *taxi-brousse* from Ouagadougou costs CFA 3000). The park is very pleasant and green, and has elephants among other big game.

Places to Stay

Since Le Point started flying to Ouagadougou many cheap hotels have sprung up to cater for budget travellers so there's a good choice available. One such place is the *Pension Guiaseme*, Ave Yennenga, which is clean and friendly and costs CFA 2000 to CFA 2500 a single and CFA 3000 a double. Another is *Les Lauriers* which is the lodging part of the Mission Catholique. It's very clean, good meals are available and it costs CFA 1000 per person in double or triple rooms with a fan. It is often full.

Somewhat more expensive is the *Hotel Yennenga*, Ave Yennenga, which has clean, airy and pleasant double rooms. They cost CFA 3000 with fan and shower, CFA 4000 with air-con and shower, CFA 4500 with air-con, shower and toilet. Rooms with all these amenities plus twin beds cost CFA 5000. The Yennenga is a meeting place for car dealers and ride seekers.

Similar is the *Hotel Idéal*, Ave Yennenga, which has good rooms for CFA 3000/4500 a single/double. Also on Ave Yennenga is the *Sougri Nôma*, near the large mosque about 1½ km from the railway station. Rooms cost CFA 1500 a single. While this is cheap, the place is grubby and the staff have been described as a 'bunch of yahoos'. If you don't like the look of it try the *Restaurant Rialle* a few blocks past the Sougri Nôma. It has a few

rooms for CFA 1700 per room (sleeps up to six people). You can also buy cheap food.

Worth trying is the *Hotel de la Paix* (previously the Hotel de l'Amitié) at CFA 4000 a double with fan. The *Hotel Belindedé*, near the old market place, has doubles at CFA 3000 with fan or CFA 4000 with air-con. Similar is the *Hotel Delwende*, Rue Brunnel, where doubles cost CFA 3000 with fan or CFA 4000 with air-con. The *Hotel Wendkouni* in the Quartier Kamsaoghin has also been recommended. It is a pleasant, clean and friendly place but a little way from the centre of town. A double with fan costs CFA 3500.

Considerably more expensive is the *Hotel Central*, Rue de la Chance, but large discounts are offered to holders of Le Point tickets.

Campers should head for *Camping Ouaga* (on bus route No 4) which costs CFA 800 per night or CFA 1000 for a pleasant, lockable hut. The swimming pool costs CFA 400 extra. This camp site is nowhere near completion – there's a bar but no toilets. It is quiet and very few people go there. Avoid buying food or drink because prices are twice as expensive as in town.

Avoid the *Palais des Jeunes* opposite the Hotel Idéal. It's a cheap place to stay but filthy.

Places to Eat

For street eating, the stalls opposite the Hotel Yennenga offer good, cheap food. Rice, spaghetti, chicken and vegetables cost CFA 200 to CFA 300. The *Restaurant Le Soir Au Village*, about 100 metres from the Hotel Yennenga, offers a big choice at good prices including substantial breakfasts for CFA 250. Also, opposite this restaurant you can buy some of the best brochettes in Burkina for CFA 150 between 7 and 11 pm any night.

The *Café de la Paix*, Rue Brunnel one block east of the old market, has good cheap food – steak for CFA 300, etc.

For a decent splurge, try the *Restaurant L'Eau de Vie*, Rue de Marché near the Central Hotel, which has a menu for CFA 2000. This is one of the best places to eat in West Africa. It's run by nuns and offers a choice of both African and European dishes.

Other recommended places are *La Fourchette Ombu*, Rue Brunnel; *Roti Volta*, near the market; and *L'Escale*, Ave Yennenga (good food, cold beers).

Entertainment

For an entertaining evening try *Le Maxim* nightclub or one of the cheaper places, but males should think twice about the Ghanaian hookers. Venereal disease is known locally as 'Ghanarrhoea'.

If you want to use a swimming pool go to the RAN Hotel (CFA 700 on weekdays and CFA 1000 at weekends) or the Hotel de l'Indépendence (CFA 800 per day).

OUAHIGOUYA

The *Hotel de l'Amitié* is some way from the centre of town but it's quiet. It costs CFA 3500 per room and lunch is available for CFA 350.

Burundi

Burundi is a small but beautiful mountainous country sandwiched between Tanzania, Rwanda and Zaïre with magnificent views over Lake Tanganyika. It has had a stormy history full of tribal wars and factional struggles between the ruling families. This has been complicated in recent times by colonisation first by the Germans and later by the Belgians. It is one of the most densely populated countries in the world with some 145 persons per square km. Despite this, there are few urban centres. The only towns of any size are the capital, Bujumbura, and Gitega. Most people live in family compounds known as *rugos*.

The original inhabitants of the area were the Twa pygmies who now comprise only 1% of the population. They were gradually displaced from about 1000 AD onwards by migrating Hutu, mostly farmers of Bantu stock who make up some 85% of the populace. In the 16th and 17th centuries, however, the country experienced another wave of migration. This time it was the tall, pastoralist Tutsi from Ethiopia and Uganda, now 14% of the population.

The Tutsi gradually subjugated the Hutu into a kind of feudal system very much like that which operated in mediaeval Europe. The Tutsi became a loosely organised aristocracy with a *mwami*, or king, at the top of each social pyramid. Under this system the Hutu relinquished their land and mortgaged their services to the nobility in return for cattle – the symbol of wealth and status in Burundi.

At the end of the 19th century the country, along with Rwanda, was colonised by the Germans. However, it was so thinly garrisoned that the Belgians were easily able to oust the German forces during WW I. After the war, the League of Nations mandated Burundi (then known as Urundi) and Rwanda to Belgium.

Taking advantage of the feudal structure, the Belgians ruled indirectly through the Tutsi chiefs and princes, granting them wide ranging powers to recruit labour and raise taxes. The Tutsi were not averse to abusing these powers whenever it suited them. They considered themselves to be a superior, intelligent people, born to rule, while the Hutu were merely hard-working but dumb peasants.

The Christian missions encouraged this view by concentrating on educating the Tutsi and virtually ignoring the Hutu. Since the missions had been granted a monopoly on education this policy remained unchallenged. The establishment of coffee plantations and the subsequent concentration of wealth derived from its sale in the hands of the Tutsi urban elite, further exacerbated tensions between the two tribal groups.

In the 1950s a nationalist organisation based on unity between the tribes was founded under the leadership of the mwami's eldest son, Prince Rwagasore. In the run up to independence, however, the prince was assassinated. This was done with the connivance of the colonial authorities who feared their commercial interests would be threatened if he came to power. Despite this setback, when independence was granted in 1962, challenges were raised about the concentration of power in Tutsi hands. It appeared that the country was headed for a majority government. This had already happened in neighbouring Rwanda where a similar tribal imbalance existed.

141

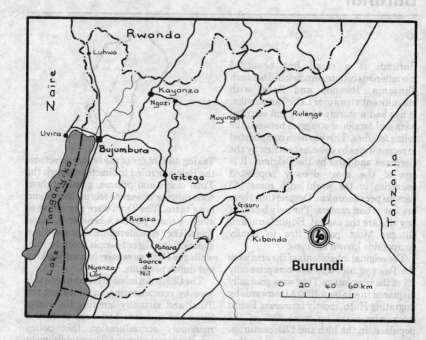

However, following elections in 1964 in which Hutu candidates collected the majority of votes, the mwami refused to appoint a Hutu prime minister. Hutu frustration boiled over a year later in an attempted coup staged by Hutu military officers and political figures. Though it failed, it led to the flight of the mwami into exile in Switzerland. He was replaced by a Tutsi military junta. A wholesale purge of Hutu from the army and the bureaucracy followed but in 1972 there was another large-scale revolt in which over 1000 Tutsi were killed.

The military junta responded to this challenge with what was nothing less than selective genocide. Any Hutu who had received a formal education, had a job in the government or was wealthy was rooted out and murdered, often in the most horrifying way. Certainly few bullets were used. Convoys of army trucks full of the mutilated bodies of Hutu rumbled

through the streets of Bujumbura for days on end, even in broad daylight at the beginning of the campaign. Many of the Hutu were taken from their homes at night while others received summonses to a police station. It is hard to believe how subservient the Hutus had become to their Tutsi overlords. Even the most uninformed peasant was aware of what was going on. After three months some 200,000 had lost their lives and over 100,000 fled to Tanzania, Rwanda and Zaïre. More refugees have poured into Tanzania since.

Neither the Christian missions inside the country nor the international community outside raised any voices of protest about this carnage. Indeed, whilst it was in full swing, an official of the OAU visited Bujumbura to congratulate President Michel Micombero on the orderly way the country was being run! It's quite a contrast to the howls of protest now being raised almost daily over South Africa. Not that two wrongs make a right.

Little changed since those times. The Tutsi continued to rule and the Hutu, despite their numbers, remained a cowed people. Half-hearted attempts were made by the government to remove some of the main causes of intertribal conflict but they're mostly cosmetic. The army and the bureaucracy continued to be totally dominated by the Tutsi with the Hutu confined to menial jobs, agriculture and cattle raising. The government even vetoed international aid when they suspected it might be used to educate or enrich the Hutu and so eventually breed opposition. Religious missions have been regarded with equal suspicion and many missionaries have been told to leave, often at short notice.

Then in mid-August 1988 the conflict between the tribes erupted yet again. Several weeks before, the army had begun a new round-up of educated Hutu in the Marangara region. Fearing a repeat of the 1972 massacre the Hutu panicked and began killing soldiers and other Tutsi civilians with whatever weapons were available – spears and machetes. The army's response was predictable and by the time it had finished its rampage some 5000 Hutu had been slaughtered, tens of thousands made homeless and over 40,000 refugees had fled to neighbouring Rwanda.

The Burundian government blamed the unrest on Hutu activists operating from Rwanda and the president, Major Pierre Buyoya, who took over in a bloodless coup the previous September, told a press conference that he regretted the use of force. Nevertheless, it seems clear that the army would have no hesitation in repeating the slaughter at the slightest provocation. It's a tragic story with no resolution in sight.

As a visitor, it's unlikely that you will be aware of all this. Outwardly the country now appears to be calm and seems destined to stay that way for the foreseeable future. Few travellers stay long in Burundi in any case. Most are only en route to or from Tanzania or Rwanda.

Facts

CLIMATE
The climate is hot and humid especially around Lake Tanganyika, with temperatures varying between 23°C and 30°C. The average temperature in the mountains to the east of the lake is 20°C. The rainy season runs from October to May with a brief dry period during December and January.

VISAS
Visas are required by all. Citizens of South Africa are not admitted. Visas can be obtained from Burundi embassies in Addis Ababa (Ethiopia), Algiers (Algeria), Cairo (Egypt), Dar es Salaam (Tanzania), Kampala (Uganda), Kigali (Rwanda), Kinshasa (Zaïre), Nairobi (Kenya) and Tripoli (Libya). There are Burundi consulates in Bukavu (Zaïre) and Kigoma (Tanzania).

The cost of visas varies depending on where you apply. They are least expensive in Tanzania and Uganda (paying with local shillings exchanged at the street rate) followed by Kenya then Zaïre. Tourist visas allow for a single-entry stay of one month, but there are also cheaper two-day transit visas available. The time it takes to obtain visas also varies. They generally take two days and are only issued on certain days of the week.

At the consulate in Bukavu, SINELAC Building, 184 Ave du Président Mobutu, they cost Z 510 and take 24 hours to issue. You'll need two photographs. The consulate is open Monday to Friday from 7.30 am till 12 noon and 2.30 to 5 pm. Visa applications, however, are only accepted between 3 and 5 pm Monday to Thursday. The consulate is closed on Saturday and Sunday.

At the embassy in Kampala (tel 54584) 2 Katego Rd near the Uganda Museum visas cost USh 3000 and take two days. However, they are only issued on Wednesdays and Fridays so you must apply on a Monday or Wednesday. You'll require two photographs. The embassy is open Monday to Friday from 8.30 am to 12.30 pm and 2.30 to 5 pm.

At the embassy in Kigali, Rue de Ntaruka, visas cost RFr 1500 with two photographs but you need to apply a week in advance. They are only issued on Fridays. The staff are not particularly helpful but it is possible to speed things up if you can enlist the support of your own embassy (some will do this, others won't).

At the consulate in Kigoma they cost TSh 200 with two photographs and take three days. You can only apply on Mondays and Wednesdays between 8 am and 3 pm (pick up on Thursdays and Saturdays respectively). This will present problems if you do not already have a visa and are on the Lake Tanzania ferry coming up from Mpulungu (Zambia).

At the embassy in Nairobi (tel 338735) 14th floor, Development House, Moi Ave, they cost KSh 100 with two photographs and take 24 hours. You can only apply on Mondays and Wednesdays. The embassy is open Monday to Thursday from 8.30 am to 12.30 pm and 2 to 5 pm. The staff are helpful and there's even some tourist literature available.

If you arrive at Bujumbura International Airport without a visa you may be deported on the next available flight. Arriving by ferry on Lake Tanganyika, the authorities are more accommodating. What normally happens is that you pay BFr 1000 for an entry permit and leave your passport with immigration. You pick up your passport 24 hours later and pay a further BFr 1000 for your visa.

Visa extensions can be obtained from immigration in Bujumbura. They cost BFr 1000 per month and take 24 hours.

Other Visas

Rwanda The embassy (tel 26865) is at 24 Ave Zaïre, Bujumbura, next to the Zaïre Embassy. One-month multiple-entry tourist visas cost BFr 1800 with two photographs. They are issued within 24 to 48 hours but only on Tuesdays and Fridays. Try to get there as early as possible on the day before visas are issued and it will probably be given to you the following day. Transit visas cost BFr 900.

Tanzania The embassy is on Blvd Patrice Lumumba opposite the main post office (PTT). Visa prices vary depending on your nationality. They take 24 hours but applications are only accepted in the mornings. The embassy is open Monday to Friday from 8 to 11.30 am and 2 to 4.30 pm. The staff are helpful.

Zaïre The embassy is on Ave Zaïre next to the Rwandan Embassy. The staff are friendly and helpful and you can usually get a visa within 24 hours.

Other Embassies These include Belgium, China (PR), Cuba, Egypt, France, Germany (West), Korea (North), Libya, Romania, USA, USSR and the Vatican City. There are also consulates of Cyprus, Denmark, Greece, Italy, Luxembourg and the Netherlands.

MONEY
US$1 = BFr 104

The unit of currency is the Burundi Franc = 100 centimes (you're very unlikely to see the latter). The exchange value of the Burundi franc fluctuates according to the international currency market, the value of the US dollar and the French franc being the most important factors. Currency declaration forms are not issued on arrival.

Commission rates for changing travellers' cheques at most banks are outright banditry – sometimes up to 7%! The Banque de la République du Burundi and the banks at the international airport do not, according to most travellers, charge commission. Banking hours are Monday to Friday from 8 to 11.30 am. Outside these hours you can change travellers' cheques at one or other of the large hotels in Bujumbura (eg Novotel, Chaussée du Peuple Burundi). Their rates are fractionally below those offered by the banks but they don't charge a commission.

There's a relatively open street market in Bujumbura so you're at a considerable advantage if you bring hard currency with you to Burundi. Dealers generally hang around in front of the petrol station next to the central market on the Chaussée Prince Louis Rwagasore, half a block down from the Banque Commerciale du Burundi. Rates obviously vary according to the official exchange rate and the amount you want to change (large bills are preferred) but you can usually expect 35% above the bank rate. You can also buy Tanzanian shillings at a rate which is usually more than you will get in Kigoma. However, it isn't as good as the rate in Dar es Salaam or Arusha so don't change too much. If you're taking the Lake Tanganyika steamer down as far as Mpulungu (Zambia) or flying internally on Air Tanzania from Kigoma then you need to think about this carefully.

At the border post between Uvira (Zaïre) and Bujumbura you'll run into a lot of moneychangers. They change Zaïres, but not hard currency, to Burundi francs. Their rates are quite reasonable so long as you know the current street rates for the Burundi franc.

POST
The main post office (PTT) in Bujumbura is open Monday to Friday from 8 am till noon and 2 to 4 pm and on Saturday from 8 to 11 am.

TOURIST INFORMATION
The tourist office is on the Blvd de l'Uprona near the Rue de la Mission. Information is limited.

Public holidays are 1 January, 1 May, Ascension Day, 1 July, 15 August, 18 September, 1 November and 25 December.

LANGUAGE
The official languages are Kirundi and French. Swahili is also useful. Hardly anyone speaks English.

Getting There & Around

There are no railways in Burundi. Possible entry points are by air, road and lake ferry.

AIR
The international airport is 11 km from the capital, Bujumbura.

There are no regular internal flights by the national airline, Air Burundi. If you're heading for Tanzania and thinking of flying internally from Kigoma it's worth going to the Air Tanzania office in Bujumbura and making a reservation. You don't have to pay for the ticket until you get to Kigoma but they'll give you written confirmation of the reservation. This way you can pay for the flight in Tanzanian shillings bought on the street market rather than in Burundi francs (a very substantial saving!).

ROAD
Like Rwanda, Burundi used to be a difficult country to travel in especially during the rainy season because of the lack of decent roads and public transport. This has now changed and most of the major routes are sealed. The Bujumbura, Kayanza, Butare, Kigali road; the Bujumbura, Ijenda, Source du Nil, Rutana road; the Bujumbura, Gitega, Rutana; and the Kayanza, Ngozi, Muyinga roads are now sealed all the way. Only a small section of the Bujumbura, Rugombo, Cyangugu road remains to be sealed.

Bus

There are plenty of modern, Japanese-supplied minibuses which are fairly frequent, not overcrowded and cheaper than shared taxis. Destinations are displayed in the front window and the buses go when full. You can usually find one going in the direction you are heading any day between early morning and early afternoon from the *gare routière* (bus stand) in any town or city.

There's also the OTRACO Bus Co which operates normal buses and has a ticket office on the bottom side of the *gare routière* in Bujumbura. In the window of this office there is a detailed map of the country and a timetable of all the routes they cover. Their buses are not as frequent as the minibuses and generally only go several days a week. Sample fares and journey times are:

Bujumbura to Banda (Burundi-Tanzanian border) – BFr 500, about three to four hours (these minibuses stop at Nyanza Lac for immigration formalities)
Bujumbura to Kayanza – BFr 350, about 2½ hours
Kayanza to Rwanda border – minibuses for BFr 150 on Tuesday, Friday and Sunday only; the rest of the week you will have to hire a taxi or hitch (you may have to pay for the latter)

BOAT

The Lake Tanganyika steamer, MV *Liembe*, connects Burundi with Tanzania and Zambia. It used to operate in conjunction with a sister ship, the MV *Mwongozo*, so that there were two ferries in either direction every week. The MV *Mwongozo* now only services ports on the Tanzanian part of the lake. Like everything else in Africa, this may change so it's worth making enquiries.

The schedule for the MV *Liembe* is more or less regular but it can be delayed for up to 24 hours at either end depending on how much cargo there is to load on or off. Engine trouble can also delay it at any point though not usually for more than a few hours. Officially, it departs once a week from Bujumbura on Mondays at about 4 pm, arriving in Kigoma (Tanzania) on Tuesday at 8 am and Mpulungu (Zambia) on Thursday at 8 am. It calls at many small Tanzanian ports en route between Kigoma and Mpulungu but rarely for more than half an hour. In the opposite direction it departs Mpulungu on Friday at about 5 pm, arrives in Kigoma on Sunday at 10 am and Bujumbura on Monday at 7.30 am.

Fares

The fares from Bujumbura to Kigoma are BFr 6740 1st class (two-bunk cabin), BFr 5160 2nd class (four-bunk cabin) and about BFr 2200 3rd class (seats only). In the opposite direction the fares are TSh 257 (1st class), TSh 203 (2nd class) and TSh 92 (3rd class). In addition there are port fees (at the port of embarkation only) of BFr 200 (in Bujumbura) and TSh 40 (in Kigoma).

If you are going all the way from Bujumbura to Mpulungu it is possible to buy a ticket for the whole journey in Bujumbura in local currency but the trip will be very expensive. You can save some money by buying a ticket first to Kigoma. Then, once the boat sails, buy a ticket for the rest of the journey to Mpulungu from the purser. This now has to be paid for in hard currency. Do it as soon as possible if you want a cabin between Kigoma and Mpulungu.

Tickets on the boat coming up the lake from Mpulungu to either Kigoma or Bujumbura have to be paid for in hard currency. You must buy the ticket from the agency in town – not on the boat. They won't accept Zambian kwacha or Tanzanian shillings. This makes the boat very expensive – US$69 from Mpulungu to Bujumbura in 1st class. There is a way to (partially) get around this. Instead of buying a ticket to Kigoma or Bujumbura, ask for one to Kipilli, the third Tanzanian port. This will cost about US$12. Once on board the ship, buy a ticket from the purser for the rest of the journey in Tanzanian shillings. Don't try to buy a ticket from Mpulungu to the first Tanzanian port – you'll be refused as they're wise to this ruse.

In Bujumbura, tickets for the ferry can be bought from SONACO, Rue des Usines off the Ave du Port, (signposted). This can be done on Monday, Tuesday, Wednesday and Saturday from 7.30 am till noon and on Thursday and Friday from 2 to 5 pm. In Kigoma you buy tickets from the railway station. In Mpulungu you buy tickets on the boat.

Third class is not usually crowded between Bujumbura and Kigoma so, if you want to save money, this is a reasonable possibility. Between Kigoma and Mpulungu, however, it is very crowded. The choice is yours.

Meals and drinks are available on board and have to be paid for in Tanzanian shillings. The meals are good value. Bring sufficient shillings with you to cover this – exchange rates on board are naturally poor. The boat from Bujumbura arrives at Kigoma about 6 am but you can't get off until customs and immigration officials arrive at 8 am. So instead of packing your bags and hanging around it's a good idea to have breakfast.

Bujumbura to Kigoma via Gombe Stream

Over the last few years another route into Tanzania has become very popular with travellers since it takes in the Gombe Stream National Park (primarily a chimpanzee sanctuary) half way between Bujumbura and Kigoma. Going this way you first take a minibus from Bujumbura to either Nyanza Lac (Burundi customs and immigration) or Banda (the Burundi border village). There are daily minibuses which cost BFr 500 and take about three to four hours to either place. Make sure you get a stamp from immigration at Nyanza Lac otherwise you'll be sent back from the police checkpoint about half way between Nyanza Lac and Banda.

It used to be possible to get a boat from Nyanza Lac direct to Gombe Stream or Kigoma but, according to the latest reports, this is now prohibited. You'll have to cross the border into Tanzania and take one from there. The first Tanzanian town is Kagunga, about three km from Banda. You'll probably have to walk. Here you clear Tanzanian customs and immigration and wait for a boat. If you bought Tanzanian shillings in Burundi then hide them well. You may have to empty your pockets. If you miss this office then go through formalities when you get to Kigoma (though this involves a lot of walking).

There are daily boats around 7 am to Kalangaabu (two to three hours' walk from Kigoma) or Ujiji via Gombe Stream. The fare to Gombe Stream is TSh 100 and to Ujiji TSh 150. The journey takes about six hours.

These boats are small, partially covered, wooden affairs, often overcrowded not only with people but their produce and they offer no creature comforts whatsoever. They're good fun when the weather is fine. If there's a squall on the lake you may be in for a rough time but it's no worse than being on a dhow in the Indian Ocean.

If you get stuck in Banda there are a couple of restaurants which take both Burundi francs and Tanzanian shillings and will probably let you sleep there for the night.

TO/FROM RWANDA

There is a choice of two routes. The one you take will depend on whether you want to go direct to Kigali or via Lake Kivu. If going direct to Kigali, first take a minibus to Kayanza from Bujumbura (BFr 350, about 2½ hours). Then a minibus to the border for BFr 150 (these only go on Tuesday, Friday and Sunday, the rest of the week you will have to hitch or hire a taxi). From the border a Peugeot shared taxi will take you to Butare (RFr 500), then a minibus from Butare to Kigali

(RFr 400, frequent). To Cyangugu on Lake Kivu you first take a minibus from Bujumbura to Rugombo (BFr 200, about 1½ hours). The next 12 km to the Burundi border post at Luhwa and the following eight km to the Rwandan border post at Bugarama you will probably have to hitch (trucks and cars). From the Rwandan border post to Cyangugu there are shared taxis but it's also fairly easy to hitch.

TO/FROM TANZANIA

There are two routes available both of them using Lake Tanganyika at different points. For more details see the Boat section. You'll be extremely lucky to find road transport from the Burundi border into Tanzania and it's not recommended that you try. You could be stuck for weeks.

TO/FROM ZAÏRE

There are two possible routes. The first goes from Bujumbura to Cyangugu in Rwanda and from there to Bukavu. The direct route into Zaïre is from Bujumbura to Uvira across the top of Lake Tanganyika. You may be able to find a minibus going from Bujumbura to the Burundi border post but usually you will have to get a shared taxi. This will cost BFr 50, and take 10 to 15 minutes. From the Burundi border post to the Zaïre border post it's about one km and you will probably have to walk. From the Zaïre border post to Uvira there are shared taxis until late in the afternoon which cost Z 50 (local people pay Z 25) and take about 10 to 15 minutes. Before you take this route, read what is said about getting from Uvira to Bukavu in the Rwanda chapter.

Around the Country

BUJUMBURA

Sprawling up the mountainside on the north-eastern tip of Lake Tanganyika, Bujumbura overlooks the vast wall of mountains in Zaïre on the other side of the

1	Sonaco (Lake Tanganyika boats)
2	Tourist Hotel
3	Hotel Central
4	Air Tanzania
5	Novotel
6	Hotel Burundi Palace
7	Restaurant Oasis
8	Aux Délices
9	Air Zaïre
10	Au Beau Lilas Restaurant
11	Tanzanian Embassy
12	GPO (PTT)
13	Banque du Crédit du Burundi
14	Banque de la République du Burundi
15	Bus Station & Market
16	American Embassy & American Club
17	Banque Commercial du Burundi
18	Zaïre & Rwandan embassies
19	Hotel Le Résidence & Restaurant Stavros

lake. The capital of Burundi is a mixture of grandiose colonial-style town planning with wide boulevards, imposing public buildings and dusty crowded suburbs of the type which surround many an African city. It's also one of the most important ports on Lake Tanganyika.

Like Kigali in neighbouring Rwanda, it has a sizeable expatriate population. Even Colonel Gaddafi has made his mark here in the form of a large and beautifully conceived Islamic Cultural Centre and mosque. You will also be in for a pleasant botanical surprise. Like many other places along Lake Tanganyika, Bujumbura sports coconut palms! There are not many places in the world where you will find these well over 1000 km from the sea.

Things to See

There are three museums all within a block of each other on the Ave du 13 Octobre which leads down to the Cercle Nautique on the lake front. The first is the **Musée Vivant**, a reconstructed traditional Burundian village with basket, pottery, drum and photographic displays. There

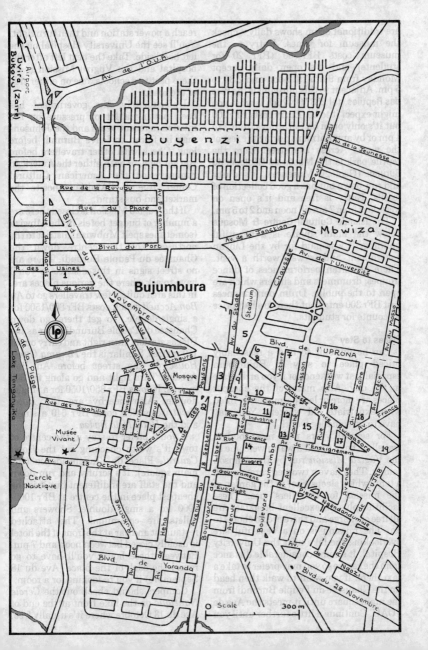

are traditional drum shows daily – check the museum for times. Entry to the museum costs BFr 50 (BFr 20 for students) and it's open daily except Monday from 9 am till noon and 2.30 to 5 pm. Adjacent to this museum is the **Parc des Reptiles** (tel 25374) which is what you might expect it to be. Entry costs BFr 200 but it's only open on Saturdays from 2 to 4 pm or by appointment during the rest of the week. Across the street from the reptile park is the **Musée du Géologie du Burundi** (Geology Museum). It's dusty and run-down but has a good collection of fossils. Entry is free and it's open on weekdays from 7 am till noon and 2 to 5 pm.

The **Islamic Cultural Centre & Mosque** below the main square is a beautiful building. It was paid for by the Libyan government and is well worth a visit. There are often performances of dance troupes, drummers and singers which are open to the public. Drum performances cost BFr 300 entry but there are half price discounts for students.

Places to Stay

It can be difficult to find a reasonably priced place to stay in Bujumbura especially at weekends or if you arrive late in the day. Also many of the cheaper places are more or less permanently filled with expatriate aid workers. You may have to do some leg work!

For several years now most budget travellers have found a warm welcome at the *Vugizu Mission* run by the Johnson family. They have a two-bed caravan and a tent (which sleeps two) in the garden of the mission for travellers' use. These facilities plus an excellent breakfast are all free of charge and there are no chores to do. The mission is on a beautiful site overlooking the lake near the University Hospital. It's some considerable distance from the centre so you may prefer to take a taxi there. If you want to walk then head up the Chaussée du Peuple Burundi from the main square until it meets the Ave de l'OAU. Continue a little further until you reach a power station and then turn right. You'll see the University Hospital on the left hand side. Take the next left after the hospital and the Vugizu Mission is up there past two schools, one on either side of the road.

Unfortunately, the government has been putting a lot of pressure on the mission in recent years and the Johnsons may be forced to leave Burundi before long. Check with other travellers before you get here, or with either the American Embassy or the American Cultural Center, Rue de l'Amitié opposite the market and bus stand.

If the Vugizu Mission is closed there are a number of budget hotels in the Mbwiza (sometimes spelt Mubwiza) district to the north-east of the centre down the Chaussée du Peuple Burundi. There are no street signs in this district so you'll have to ask where the various places are. In this area quite a few travellers go to *Au Bon Accueil* which costs BFr 800/1500 for a single/double. To get there, go down Chaussée du Peuple Burundi as far as the BP gas station, turn right and carry on for 150 metres. Similar is the *Panama Guest House* on the street before Au Bon Accueil. Turn right and go along for 300 metres. It costs BFr 850/1050 for a single/double. Also nearby are the *Hotel Escottise*, which costs BFr 640 a single and the *Hotel New Bwiza*.

If you'd prefer to stay in the centre of town it's worth checking out the *Hotel Central*, Place de l'Indépendence (the main square). It's scruffy and run-down and the staff are indifferent but it is the cheapest place in the centre at BFr 1000/2000 for a single/double. Showers and toilets are communal. The attached restaurant and bar at the front of the hotel is usually closed between noon and 7 pm. Between these hours you'll have to go round the back of the place (Ave du 18 Septembre) if you're looking for a room.

Campers should check out the *Cercle Nautique* on the lake front at the end of Ave du 13 Octobre where it's usually free.

Watch out for the hippos! Otherwise you can camp at the *Club du Lac Tanganyika* for BFr 500 including use of the swimming pool.

Other hotels in Bujumbura are very pricey. Try either the *Hotel Burundi Palace* (tel 2920), on the corner of Blvd de l'Uprona and Chaussée du Peuple Burundi, or the *Tourist Hotel*, Ave des Paysans, facing the Islamic Cultural Centre. The former costs BFr 1570/2610 for a single/double with bath. Air-con rooms with bath cost BFr 2320/3480 for a single/double. Checkout time is 11 am. The Tourist Hotel costs BFr 2320/2900 for a single/double with bathroom (hot and cold water) and fan. The beds are huge and very comfortable but checkout time is 9 am! You're more likely to get a room here than at the Burundi Palace.

Similar are the *Hotel Grillon* (tel 2519), Ave du Zaïre, and the *Hotel Le Résidence* (tel 2773), Ave de Stanley close to the Chaussée Prince Rwagasore.

Places to Eat

Best value for money is the *Restaurant Au Beau Lilas*, Ave du Commerce about half way between the Rue de la Poste and Blvd Patrice Lumumba. It's easy to miss this place as there's no indication outside but look for a red and white sign saying 'Foto'. The food here is excellent and attractively served, the atmosphere pleasant and the staff are friendly. Beer is only for sale during licensing hours. Also very popular is *Aux Délices* opposite the roundabout on the Place de l'Indépendence where the soups and yogurt are recommended. It's a good place to meet local people too. Others have recommended the *Patisserie Snack à la Chez Michel* which offers very reasonably priced meals – excellent garnished sandwiches, omelettes, soups, salads and cold beers. It's closed on Sundays.

If you want to splurge there are a couple of good places to go though they are relatively expensive. The first is the *Cercle Nautique* (tel 2559) on the lake front at the end of Ave du 13 Octobre. It is very popular with expatriates especially at the weekends when it can be full to overflowing. You can eat alfresco and enjoy the views and the antics of the hippos (which are said to occasionally *eat* boats). It's a great place to sip a cold beer even if you don't want to eat. The Cercle Nautique is open daily (except Tuesdays) from 5 pm and all day on Sundays from 11 am. Memorise the number of the waiter here if you require change when paying the bill (otherwise you may not get it).

The other place for a splurge is the *Restaurant Oasis* (tel 2944), on the corner of Blvd de l'Uprona and Ave de la Victoire. It's a popular place and offers excellent multicourse lunches and dinners. It's open daily except Sundays (though I've seen it open on Sunday, too).

Other restaurants in a similar price bracket include the *Restaurant Stavros*, Ave Prince Rwagasore, the *Restaurant Olympia*, Ave de la Victoire, and the restaurant at the Hotel Burundi Palace. The latter two specialise in Greek and Continental dishes.

Entertainment

Both the American Cultural Center and the Centre Culturel Français, opposite each other on Chaussée Prince Rwagasore, have videos, films and other activities. The former shows videos of the ABC news on Mondays and Wednesdays at 5.30 pm and on Saturdays at 2.30 pm. They also have a reading room. The American Club next to the US Embassy, Rue de l'Amitié, used to have two film and two separate chilli and hamburger nights a week but it may no longer be open to nonmembers. The Bureau de Tourisme, Ave de l'Uprona, often puts on a disco in the evenings but the drinks are expensive.

The swimming pool at the Novotel is open to nonresidents for BFr 300 per day. There's no charge for using the poolside bar.

GITEGA

Gitega is the second largest town in

Burundi and it's here that you find the **National Museum**. Though small, it's worth a visit and very educational. Entry is free. There may also be a folklore performance – ask if the *tambourinaires* are playing.

Places to Stay
The *Mission Catholique* is probably the best place to enquire for budget accommodation as they have a huge guesthouse. Some travellers have been able to stay here free in the past but don't count on it.

KAYANZA
Kayanza is on the road north to Kigali and not far from the Rwanda border. There's a good market here on Monday, Wednesday and Saturday.

The missions here won't take guests so stay at the *Auberge de Kayanza* which costs BFr 960 a double.

KILEMBA
The principal attraction is the **Kibabi Hot Springs** about 16 km from town. There are several pools of differing temperature, the main one hovering around 100°C. A little further uphill is a waterfall and another deep pool where it's safe to swim.

Most people stay at the *Swedish Pentecostal Mission* which has a very good guesthouse. A bed in the dormitory costs BFr 150. They also have private rooms with a shower and toilet, and use of a fully equipped kitchen for BFr 600 per person.

SOURCE DU NIL
Source du Nil is the southernmost source of the Nile. If you decide to visit it's possible to stay at the *Mission Catholique* in Rutana seven km away.

Cameroun

If Zambia is Africa's most geographically artificial country, then Cameroun is its most socially artificial. Never at any time were its diverse tribal and linguistic groups united, and the history of Cameroun since independence has been dominated by the intense and often brutal drive towards unification.

Before the area was colonised, the south and east of the country were inhabited by Bantu peoples organised along patrilinear or matrilinear lines. On the central Bamileke plateau there existed a number of well organised and independent chiefdoms. The northern part of the country was peopled by a complex mix of Negroid, Hamitic and Arab-related societies which formed the border areas of the empires of first Bornu, then Mandara and finally Sokoto. By the late 19th century, the whole of the north was ruled by the Emir of Yola, who was himself a vassal of Sokoto.

These different areas developed more or less independently of one another largely due to the different trade links which they enjoyed with places further afield. The coastal peoples, for instance, like the rest of coastal West and Central Africa, were strongly influenced by the slave trade to the Americas until well into the 19th century. At that time local products began to replace slaves as the main export.

Though the Portuguese first made contact at the end of the 15th century, no attempt was made to colonise the area until the 19th century.

A commercial treaty was signed between one of the chiefs of Douala and the British in 1856. When the latter showed no interest in a subsequent request by the chiefs to declare a protectorate over the area, the chiefs turned to Germany. The Germans set up their protectorate in 1884. By WW I, most of the country had been 'pacified' and the Muslim chiefs of the north brought into subjection. Railways were constructed and the beginnings of the school system were established. After WW I the area was divided between the British and French under League of Nations mandates. This arrangement was reconfirmed by the United Nations after WW II.

Nationalism began to take root firmly in the 1950s and elections for a legislative assembly in the French part of the country took place in 1956. They were contested by four parties, only two of which could claim support from all areas of the country. It was the Union Camerounaise led by Ahmadou Ahidjo, representative of the north, however, which picked up the bulk of the seats. Domination by the north naturally was resented by the peoples of the centre and south, and rebellion was a constant feature of the late 1950s. Even as independence was granted to the French part in 1960, a full-scale rebellion was raging on the Bamileke plateau. It was suppressed with extreme ruthlessness over an eight-month period by French troops and a squadron of fighter bombers. Thousands lost their lives and only in 1975 did the government lift the ban on visits to the Bamileke and Sanaga Maritime areas of the country without a special pass.

The British-administered part of the country was granted independence in 1961 and the two halves united by referendum the same year. The president from independence until late 1982 was Ahmadou Ahidjo. This made him one of

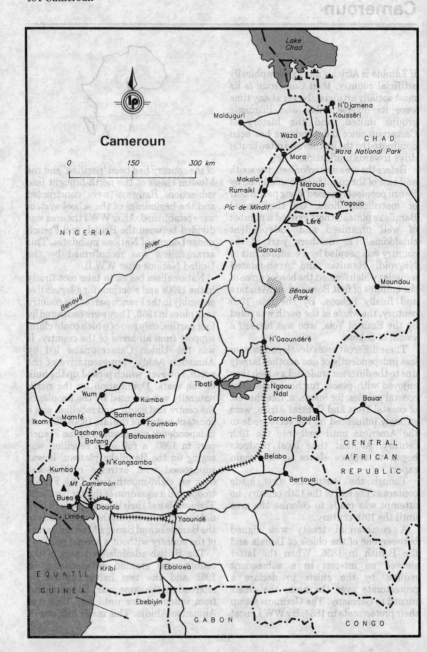

Cameroun

0   150   300 km

Lake Chad

N'Djamena
Kousséri
Maiduguri
Waza
CHAD
Waza National Park
Mora
Mokolo
Rumsiki
Maroua
Yagoua
Pic de Mindif
Léré
Moundou
Garoua
Bénoué Park
NIGERIA
River
Benoué
N'Gaoundéré
Tibati
Ngaou Ndal
Garoua-Boulai
Bouar
Wum
Kumbo
Ikom
Mamfé
Bamenda
Foumban
Dschang
Bafoussam
Bafang
N'Kongsamba
CENTRAL
AFRICAN
REPUBLIC
Belabo
Kumba
Mt Cameroun
Buea
Limbe
Douala
Yaoundé
Bertoua
EQUATORIAL
GUINEA
Kribi
Ebolowa
Ebebiyin
GABON
CONGO

Africa's longest serving elected leaders. Despite Ahidjo's moderating influence and the great strides that had been made towards unification, the early years of rebellion had left their mark on the country. The government armed itself with all manner of legislation which could be used to suppress dissidence. Strikes were banned and the press rendered totally effete. Journalists were constantly harassed and, according to Amnesty International, hundreds of people languished in jail without trial though the government naturally denied this. The abuse of power was commonplace and corruption rife. In spite of this, the country still managed to project an image of stability - something which could not be denied when comparisons were made with its neighbours.

Despite Ahidjo's origins as a Muslim from the north, his hand-picked successor was the 49-year-old prime minister, Paul Biya, a Christian from the south. Biya soon proved to be no puppet of Ahidjo despite the latter's retention of the key post of convener of the ruling party. The new president set about distancing himself from Ahidjo and weeding out many of the old guard from their entrenched positions of power within the government and administration. Tensions rose between the two men and in August 1983, Ahidjo was accused of masterminding a coup plot. He fled to the south of France in disgrace and was sentenced to death in absentia.

This wasn't the end of the affair, however. In April 1984, a group of dissidents led by Issa Adoum attempted to regain their past privileges and favours by inciting the president's own Republican Guard to stage a revolt. They came within a hair's breadth of success but were eventually overcome by the army who remained loyal to Biya. There was heavy loss of life on both sides as well as among the civilian population.

The revolt shook the government severely and Biya in particular. Further purges of former Ahidjo protégés were ordered. While the trials of those implicated in the revolt (which included prominent business executives and government officials) were going on, Biya maintained a low profile. Allegations of French complicity in the revolt were taken very seriously in Cameroun. Not until Biya had undertaken an official visit to that country in early 1985 did relations between the two countries improve.

The alleged French involvement led to a renewed suspicion of foreigners and, until recently, travellers could expect a lot of hassle from the police and army whilst going through Cameroun. Things have cooled down a lot since those days and we're getting very few reports of harassment but people are not generally friendly towards foreigners. It would be wise to keep a low profile if you don't want to run into trouble.

There has been much improvement in the agricultural sector in recent years, but the bulk of the population is still engaged in growing subsistence crops. Much of the little surplus produced is bought by entrepreneurs in Douala and transported to Gabon, where high prices are fetched. This practice continued even when near-famine conditions hit the north in the early 1980s. The famine was only averted by massive imports of grain from America. Efforts are being made to encourage greater self-sufficiency. Large areas of irrigated and nonirrigated land in Yagoua, Mbo and Ndop have been planted with rice - a staple food of most Camerounians. There is some heavy industry - mostly concerned with aluminium - and factories are being set up to manufacture consumer goods. Foreign investment in industry is being encouraged, and the government has used overseas aid to begin the construction of a modern communications network.

Facts

GEOGRAPHY & CLIMATE

There are great differences in geography and climate in this long, wedge-shaped country ranging from the near desert of the north to the dense tropical forests of the south. The centre is largely upland savannah. A chain of volcanic mountains runs from the coast along the border area with Nigeria until it peters out on the plain of Maroua. Some of the most beautiful country is to be found north and north-west of Douala, where there are mountains rising to 2000 metres and more. The cool freshness of the atmosphere, the fine waterfalls and attractive villages make it one of the most popular areas of the country to visit. There are also some spectacular waterfalls along the Sanaga and Nyong rivers.

Travel in the north is best from November to February. Many roads become impassable during July and August because of flooding. Muslim traditions in this area are still very much alive and the people, on the whole, are very friendly. The western part of the country is also a major draw, being the centre of Bamoun culture with its many festivals and feast days which are celebrated with music and dancing. Foumban is an excellent place to see these.

POPULATION

The population stands at a little over 10 million.

VISAS

Visas are required by all. You cannot get a visa at an airport if you arrive by plane. You will be asked for an onward ticket though you may be able to get out of this if you can show them plenty of money. If you have to buy one, the cheapest ticket available is Douala to Malabo (Equatorial Guinea). Make sure your vaccination certificates are up to date – they check them.

Entering overland, you may be asked to show sufficient funds, but otherwise there is no fuss. The only place you can get a visa on the border is at Kousseri across the river from N'Djamena (Chad). You must have an onward ticket or a visa for the country you are going to after Cameroun. They're very strict about this – no begging, pleading or greasing palms makes any difference.

In Africa there are Cameroun embassies in Addis Ababa (Ethiopia), Algiers (Algeria), Bangui (CAR), Brazzaville (Congo), Cairo (Egypt), Kinshasa (Zaïre), Lagos (Nigeria), Libreville (Gabon), Luanda (Angola) and Monrovia (Liberia).

If you're coming from Nigeria you can get a Cameroun visa either in Lagos (4 Elsi Fermi Pearse St, Victoria Island) or Calabar (21 Marian St). Visa prices vary from N 25 to N 90 for a two-week visa, and you need two photos. A visa takes 24 hours to issue though you can sometimes get it the same day if you apply early. Quite a few travellers have had problems getting Cameroun visas even in Lagos and Calabar. The embassies further afield are certainly very unhelpful and will usually tell you to apply in Nigeria unless you are flying. This is probably a legacy of the days when Biya was almost overthrown. If you run into problems, persevere.

Visas can be extended in any provincial capital for a maximum of 10 days for CFA 2000. To get the extension in Yaoundé you must write a letter in French starting 'Monsieur le Commissaire de l'Emi-Immigration', stating your passport details, how long you want and why you need the extension. You also need to buy timbres fiscaux CFA 1500 for the extension, CFA 300 for the letter. In smaller regional capitals it's generally much easier and there's little fuss. If possible, try to take along someone who has been living in Cameroun for a while. Most expatriates know the ropes and can be helpful.

You need an exit visa before leaving the country. The prices for these vary depending on your nationality but are between CFA 3000 and CFA 4500. Stamps (*timbres fiscaux*) for this visa must be bought from the Ministry of the Interior not from the post office. The visas are issued the same day.

Other Visas

Benin There is no longer an embassy in Yaoundé so if you're heading up from the Central African Republic, Lagos is the only possible place where you can get a visa.

Central African Republic The embassy in Yaoundé is in the Bastos district close to the Greek cathedral. Visas cost CFA 2500, and you'll require two photos. They are issued in 24 hours. The visa is for a stay of 15 or 30 days.

Chad In Yaoundé a 15-day visa costs CFA 4000 and takes one hour to issue. The staff are friendly.

Congo In Yaoundé they cost CFA 2500 and are issued in 24 hours without fuss.

Equatorial Guinea These cost CFA 5000 in Douala and CFA 3000 in Yaoundé for a 15-day visa and are issued in 24 hours. The consulate in Douala may demand an onward ticket but the embassy in Yaoundé doesn't normally ask for one.

Gabon These cost CFA 30,000 including the cost of a telex to Libreville, and you'll need two photos. Visas are issued in two weeks if you are lucky. If you're unlucky they can take months or simply not come through at all.

Nigeria These are available from Yaoundé and Buea (but no longer from Douala). Prices vary considerably depending on your nationality but are between CFA 500 and CFA 9700! You need three photos and

they take 24 hours to issue. The visa is usually for a stay of 15 days.

Togo These can be obtained from the French Consulate in Douala. They cost CFA 3000, with two photos and are issued in 24 hours.

Zaïre The embassy is in the Bastos district (Bus No 20). Visas cost CFA 15,000 for a one-month single-entry visa and CFA 20,000 for a one-month multiple-entry visa. You'll need three photos and a letter of introduction from your own embassy. You must be able to show an onward ticket when applying for the visa.

MONEY

US$1 = CFA 284

The unit of currency is the CFA franc. The import and export of local currency up to CFA 75,000 is allowed.

The Société Camerounaise de Banque is recommended for money changing but banks won't accept Nigerian naira. If you have any of these you may be able to change them with traders but the exchange rate won't be anything to write home about. West African CFA can be changed on a one-for-one basis with Central African CFA at banks.

If you're having money sent to you, you need permission from customs to receive it in foreign currency otherwise you'll be paid in CFA. The BICIC is the best place to have money sent to, but it will still take about two weeks to come through. American Express in Douala cashes cheques into any currency requested. No permission is needed from customs if you're doing this.

There are no banks in Banyo, Tibati, Kalaldi or Lokiti. The bank nearest these places is in N'Gaoundéré. There is a bank at Garoua-Boulai (on the Cameroun-CAR border) in the main street, but they won't change travellers' cheques. (The first place you can do this is at N'Gaoundéré.) They are even reluctant to change French francs. The bank is closed on Saturdays and Sundays.

POST

Douala is a better post office to use than Yaoundé if you're having letters sent to you, but they only keep letters for two weeks.

PHOTOGRAPHY

If you have a camera, get hold of a photography permit as soon as possible from the Ministry of Information & Culture in any regional capital. They usually take one day to issue.

Even with one of these permits you may find it difficult to take photographs as cameras invite suspicion and you can expect hassles from the police. Don't be too surprised if you have your film confiscated. This is particularly true in the south. Whatever else you do, don't take photographs of anything vaguely connected with the military, railway stations, post offices, bridges or government buildings.

LANGUAGE

French and English are the official languages but there is also a wide diversity of African languages spoken.

Getting There & Around

ROAD

Despite a lot of investment in roads over the last few years, most roads in Cameroun are either gravel or dirt. There are a few sealed roads: Bafoussam to Yaoundé; Kousseri to N'Gaoundéré; N'Gaoundéré to Waza; Belabo to Bertoua; Douala to Bamenda; and Douala to Yaoundé. Expect uncomfortable journeys. The driving standards are poor and accidents are frequent.

Whatever form of transport you take, journey times can be long because of the numerous police checkpoints where they look for illegal immigrants and people evading taxes. Carry your passport with you at all times. Expect hassles.

Hitching

Hitching can be slow and involve long waits, especially in the wet season when roads and bridges get washed out or damaged. During this season a system of rain barriers are erected in an attempt to protect the surface of the roads. It makes a lot of sense to arrange lifts the night before at the truck park – this applies particularly in the north. Most lifts have to be paid for.

Bus & Taxi

There are buses on some routes but most public transport takes the form of shared taxis or trucks. In theory, taxi and bus fares are fixed at around CFA 10 to CFA 15 per km for long-distance rides plus extra luggage charges which are based on weight. Up to 10 kg should be free but this isn't always the case. Ten to 20 kg should cost CFA 200 but can cost up to CFA 700 on some runs. Backpacks are often free in the north but rarely in the south. The prices are fixed by a society called Setracaucam (PB 4222, Yaoundé). It publishes a list of current fares which you can buy for CFA 3000 but it doesn't really count for much – you still have to ask others what they are paying. Also, in the wet season prices double and triple depending on the state of the road. In this season too, you can expect to get out and push in waist-high mud when your car gets stuck.

Some examples of transport costs around the country are:

Bamenda to Kumbo – taxi costs CFA 1000 and takes three hours
Kumbo to Ndu – taxi costs CFA 500 and takes three hours
Ndu to Nkambe – taxi costs CFA 500 and takes 1½ hours
Kumbo to Foumban – taxi costs CFA 1000 and takes three hours

Garoua to Maroua – bush taxi costs CFA 2000 plus CFA 300 for a backpack and takes 2½ to three hours along a good sealed road

N'Gaoundéré to Garoua – bush taxi costs CFA 2275 plus CFA 225 for each piece of luggage depending on the weight. The trip takes four to five hours. These bush taxis resemble 'bread trucks' and are packed full of people, making them very uncomfortable. If you want to wait as short a time as possible at the *gare routière*, be there between 6.30 and 7 am

Buea to Limbe – bush taxi will cost CFA 400 including baggage

Douala to Kumba – bush taxi costs CFA 1200 including baggage

Limbe to Douala – bush taxi costs CFA 900 including baggage and takes about one hour

Kumba to Bamenda – bush taxi costs CFA 3500 including baggage.

Bamenda to Yaoundé – bush taxi will cost CFA 4000 including baggage

Bertoua to Garoua-Boulai – bush taxi will cost CFA 2300 including baggage

Yaoundé to Douala – taxi costs CFA 3000 including baggage and takes 2½ hours along an excellent sealed road

TRAIN

The main line runs from Douala to N'Gaoundéré via Yaoundé, with a branch line from Douala to N'Kongsamba. There's also a short track between Limbe and Ekona via Buea. Unless you're travelling in 2nd class, get to the station well before departure time otherwise you won't get a seat. The schedule is as follows:

Route & Train No	Departure Station	Time
Ligne Ouest		
Douala-N'Kongsamba (No 161)	Douala	7.30 am
Douala-Kumba (No 165)	Douala	3.00 pm
M'Banga-Douala (No 162)	M'Banga	7.55 am
N'Kongsamba-Douala (No 166)	N'Kongsamba	8.24 am
Ligne Transcam 1		
Douala-Yaoundé (Omnibus 3)	Douala	8.30 am
Douala-Yaoundé (Autorail 1)	Douala	12.00 noon
Douala-Yaoundé (Express 101)	Douala	8.30 pm
Yaoundé-Douala (Omnibus 4)	Yaoundé	7.30 am
Yaoundé-Douala (Autorail 2)	Yaoundé	12.00 noon
Yaoundé-Douala (Express 102)	Yaoundé	9.00 pm
Douala-Edea (Express 103)	Douala	4.00 pm
Ligne Transcam 2		
Yaoundé-N'Gaoundéré (No 11)	Yaoundé	7.40 am
Yaoundé-Belabo (Autorail 13)	Yaoundé	3.50 pm
Yaoundé-Belabo [Express 111)	Yaoundé	7.10 pm
Belabo-Yaoundé (Autorail 12)	Belabo	6.00 am
N'Gaoundéré-Yaoundé (No 1)	N'Gaoundéré	7.40 am
N'Gaoundéré-Yaoundé (No 112)	N'Gaoundéré	6.00 pm

From Douala to Yaoundé the fares are CFA 7000 (1st class sleeper); CFA 6000 (1st class express); CFA 4950 (1st class ordinary); CFA 3485 (2nd class express); and CFA 3075 (2nd class ordinary). First class is very comfortable with linen, blankets and pillows provided. If you take 2nd class, beware of thieves. Reservations can be made at 9 am on the day of departure. The journey takes eight to nine hours.

From Yaoundé to N'Gaoundéré the fares are CFA 12,050 (1st class couchette, a two-bed cabin); CFA 11,845 (1st class couchette, a four-bed cabin); CFA 10,340 (1st class, seats only); and CFA 6700 (2nd class, seats only). Reservations for the couchettes must be made in the morning on the day of departure. Reservations for the day train are not necessary; get your ticket on arrival at the station. Don't count on there being a 1st class car on the day train. Second class is 'colourful' – hot, noisy, crowded, smelly and uncomfortable. The journey should take about 11 hours but can take up to 15 hours. There are plenty of vendors selling food through the train windows at each stop but you should bring your own water.

If you're coming into Cameroun from the Central African Republic via Garoua-Boulai and want to catch the night train to Yaoundé, you should, after crossing the border, take a bus to N'Gaoundal (not N'Gaoundéré). Pick up the train from there. This is much more convenient than going all the way to Belabo to catch the train, but you must arrive at Garoua-Boulai early in the day to do this.

TO/FROM CENTRAL AFRICAN REPUBLIC

The main crossing point is at Garoua-Boulai (not to be confused with Garoua on the Bertoua to Bouar road). You have the choice of going by train from Yaoundé to Belabo (CFA 3815 in 2nd class – three trains daily), then on to Garoua-Boulai by road, or doing the entire journey by road. There is a bus from Yaoundé to Garoua-

Boulai for CFA 4500 which takes 15 to 18 hours.

Alternatively, you can go first to Bertoua on the same bus for CFA 2600, after which you take trucks, buses or taxis to the border (a bus costs CFA 2000). If you prefer, you can arrange a lift on a truck the whole way to the border for around CFA 4200. If taking the bus it's worth paying an extra CFA 1000 to have a seat up with the driver, as the lengthwise benches in the rear are absolute torture. It's a dirt road so allow two days to get from Yaoundé to the border if you go by truck. From Garoua-Boulai there are daily buses to Bangui stopping overnight in Bouar for CFA 7700, and buses to Bouar for CFA 2300. There are many police checkpoints en route so expect delays, but it's a good road from Bouar to Bangui. In the wet season the journey from Yaoundé to Bangui can take at least a week.

TO/FROM CHAD

The pirogues across the Chari River from Kousseri to N'Djamena are CFA 100 but entry is now usually done by means of two bridges.

TO/FROM CONGO

It is possible to go direct between Cameroun and Congo via Ouesso on the Oubangui River. The route is from Bertoua to Moloundou via Batouri and Yokadouma – minibuses available either direct or in stages. The roads are bad. At Moloundou you must obtain an exit permit from the police which is free. There's no hotel in this small town but there is a friendly mission where you can stay. From Moloundou you must backtrack to the crossroads 15 km from town and wait there for a lift to Mongokélé. This village is not on the maps and has been created by French logging companies which are busy raping the rainforests in this part of Cameroun.

You may have to wait a long time for a lift (up to two days) and pay up to CFA 2000 for it when it comes but there are huts at the crossroads where you can stay for the night.

Mongokélé is on the opposite side of the river from Ouesso. A pirogue across costs CFA 1000 and takes 40 minutes but you can wait all day for it. You should report to the police immediately on arrival in Ouesso as they're suspicious of non-Africans using this border crossing. Hotels are available in Ouesso and there is road transport and flights available going south.

TO/FROM EQUATORIAL GUINEA & GABON

If you're going to Bioko (Fernando Póo) you must fly. There are flights at least once a week and sometimes three times per week with Air Cameroun from Douala to Malabo.

If you're going to the mainland half of Equatorial Guinea (Rio Muni) or to Gabon you can go overland. Head south from Yaoundé to Ambam. Taxis from M'Balmayo to Ebolowa and from Ebolowa to Ambam cost CFA 1000 each but baggage charges can be as much again. You'll have to haggle like crazy. There are also direct taxis from Yaoundé to Ambam for CFA 3000 plus baggage charges. At Ambam the road branches, one branch going to Rio Muni and the other to Gabon. You must register with the police in Ambam. For a place to stay for the night, try the Hotel Sejam next to the market and taxi station for CFA 1500 a double.

For Rio Muni you head to Ntem, cross the river by ferry or canoe then take a pick-up to Key-Ossi. From there to Ebebeyin, the first town in Equatorial Guinea, is a walk of one km. If heading for Gabon, take the Ambam to Oyem road which will eventually take you to Ndjole and Libreville. You can't cross into Equatorial Guinea on the coast road south of Kribi.

Likewise, for Gabon, take a taxi from Ambam to Ntem (CFA 1000) then cross the river by pirogue (CFA 50 to CFA 200 but fix the price first). On the other side of the river take a taxi to Bitam (CFA 750). The Gabonese customs are pleasant.

TO/FROM NIGERIA

The most usual overland crossing point between Nigeria and Cameroun is via Ikom and Mamfe. However, as the Nigerians have only recently opened their land borders again, we have no current details of transport costs.

An alternative route between the two countries is by boat from Idua Oron, south of Calabar, to a small port in Cameroun not marked on the maps. Details of these boats can be found in the Nigeria chapter.

Around the Country

BAFANG

The *Auberge du Haut Nkam* offers accommodation at CFA 1500 a double. The showers are none too clean. Simple but comfortable rooms have also been available in the past at Michel Djimai's place opposite the BICIC bank (Michel is a tailor).

BAFOUSSAM

The cheapest place to stay is the *Foyer Evangelique*, 100 metres from the taxi park, which costs CFA 1500 per person including use of shower. If it's full, try the *Hotel Frederick* at CFA 2500, or the *Auberge de la Mifi*, which has a variety of rooms for CFA 3000/3800/5000. Two places recommended for food are the *Restaurant Familiare* at the top of the hill, and the *Riz Restaurant* near the market and taxi park.

BAMENDA

Bamenda is a beautiful and popular resort town in the highlands north of N'Kongsamba with friendly people and a good market. It also has an excellent, though very small, museum and an artisans' co-op where you can find bargains in craftwork – you must bargain hard.

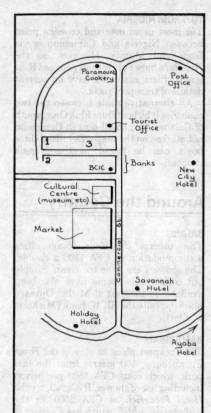

Bamenda

Key:
1 Bamenda Ringway Hotel
2 Bamenda Bakery
3 International Hotel

Information

The bus station/taxi rank is about two to three km from the centre of town. Taxis around Bamenda cost CFA 100.

It's not advisable to walk at night as some of the locals can be quite hostile.

Things to See

Twenty km north is a beautiful village called **Bafut**, which has an interesting **palace** built in the early 20th century for the 75 wives of the Fon (a local ruler). People still walk around this area with flintlock rifles. On 18 December there is a huge feast and festival when all the Fon's masks and costumes are brought out. Make sure you see it if you're in the area when it occurs. Good ebony and other woodcarvings can be found if you look around.

A similar festival takes place at **Bali** around 20 to 22 December and goes on for several days. At this time the nobles, princes, princesses and palace staff dress in traditional costume and honour the Fon.

Places to Stay

Probably the best place to stay in terms of location and price is the *Presbyterian Church Centre*. It is on top of a hill just outside town (ask for the 'church centre', not the main church, as they're a long way apart) and offers dormitory accommodation for CFA 2000 per person. Clean sheets, showers and toilets are provided. You can also camp for CFA 1000 per person including use of facilities. If there are enough people staying they will cook meals for you. Lockers are available for gear.

The *Baptist Mission* is also a popular place to stay and costs CFA 3000 per person (CFA 2000 for Peace Corps volunteers) for a clean room with hot showers.

If you want your own room then one of the cheapest places is the *Savannah* which is clean and adequate but can be very noisy at night. It costs CFA 2500 to

CFA 4500 with the more expensive rooms having a bathroom and air-con. Similar in price is the *New City Hotel* which is older but adequate and costs CFA 3300 to CFA 5000 per room.

Somewhat more expensive are the *Sky Line Hotel* (tel 361289) which costs CFA 5850 per room and the *Bamenda Ringway Hotel* which costs CFA 5000/6500 for a single/double and has deluxe rooms for much more. If you need comfort try the *International Hotel* which is new, very clean but noisy and costs CFA 5000 to CFA 7000. The more expensive rooms have twin beds and a TV.

Places to Eat

The *Paramount Cookery* – a blue coloured hut across from Sentimental Auto Parts (!) near the Ringway Hotel – offers the best omelettes in town for CFA 100. It's clean. Similar is the *Commercial Eating House* on the main street near the market. Another place which has good cheap food is the *Ideal Park Hotel & Restaurant* which is close to the market and has good views over the town.

Entertainment

Try the *Peoples Palace, Monte Cristo, Queens Valley,* or the *Ideal Park,* where people go dancing.

BANGANGTE

You may be able to find accommodation in the *Protestant Mission* in this small village east of Bafang. If they won't let you in try the *Centre Touristique,* two km out of town. It has doubles for CFA 2000, but the staff are not very friendly.

BANSO (also known as KUMBO, NSU & KINBO)

The **Banso** tribes who live in this area are worth a visit. Nso means the tribe and the prefix Ba means 'people of'. The Nso are ruled by the Fon of Nso, with subrulers called Shuu-Fai, and Fais, who are leaders of family units with up to 150 members. Fais are recognisable by their colourful

necklaces, carved walking sticks and a hat which they must always wear except when mourning. Don't shake hands with these people but do shake hands with the more ordinary folk or it will be regarded as an insult.

Places to Stay & Eat

The *Presbyterian Mission* has one room which they'll let out free of charge. Otherwise try the *Baptist Mission Rest House* which has very comfortable rooms with cooking facilities (and can provide meals by arrangement); the *Tobin Tourist Home*; or *Kilo's Rest House*. All offer relatively cheap accommodation.

BELABO

This is a small town on the railway line between Yaoundé and N'Gaoundéré. It can be used as an overnight stop either on the way to N'Gaoundéré or to the border crossing point of Garoua-Boulai (there are buses from Belabo to Bertoua and others from there to Garoua-Boulai).

A good place to stay is the *Auberge Maria Bassa,* also known as Mama Maria's. The woman who runs it is the sister of the stationmaster. The hotel is straight down the street leading from the station to the village, on the right-hand side after you go through the shopping area. You can eat here but there's no electricity or showers – you're given a pail of water to slosh over yourself. It costs CFA 2000 per night (less if you bargain hard).

BERTOUA

The *Mission Catholique* doesn't like backpackers but there are several cheap hotels in town. One of these is the *Auberge Central* hotel near the *gare routière* which costs CFA 1500 to CFA 2000 for a room. The *Jenyf Hotel,* also at the *gare routière,* is clean and friendly and costs CFA 3000 for a double.

BUEA

Buea is on the lower slopes of Mt Cameroun (4070 metres) and is a good base for climbing the mountain. You don't need any special equipment to climb to the top and there is a series of huts that you can stay in en route. A guide is compulsory and will cost CFA 3500 per day but there is no charge for climbing the mountain as such. Porters are available for CFA 3000 per day. Guides must be booked at the tourist office in Buea.

It will take about half a day to the first hut after which the trail emerges from cloud forest onto open mountainside. Upwards from here it's often very misty, with the track poorly marked and very steep. It takes a full day to climb to the third hut, then another day to the top and back down again. Warm clothes are essential because it is extremely cold at the top. You need to carry water after the second hut as there is none above here. Watch out for rats at the second hut. Mt Cameroun is the highest mountain in West Africa but it's a much less strenuous climb than either Mt Kilimanjaro or Mt Kenya.

If you decide to climb this mountain, remember to register with the police and wear the right clothes – sturdy boots and waterproof clothing. Bring a change of dry, warm clothes, camping gear, food and water. The dry season is from November to March.

Places to Stay & Eat

Perhaps the cheapest place to stay is the *Presbyterian Mission* which is clean and has beds for CFA 1500 plus CFA 600 if you need bedding. Otherwise try the *Hotel Mermoz* which costs CFA 4000/6000 for a single/double with shower and toilet. There are conflicting reports on the cleanliness and reliability of the services but the water supply is certainly erratic. The manager, Jean-Claude, is an entertaining man who will charm you with lots of stories. Meals can be bought for CFA 1200. There is also the *Parliamentarian Flats Hotel*, which looks as pretentious as it sounds but is not too expensive with prices starting at CFA 5000 a double. It's

clean, quiet and comfortable. The restaurant serves delicious food but it's expensive.

If you'd like to stay in the area for a while, enquire about renting a house in the country nearby – there are quite a few of them.

DOUALA

Douala is the largest city and the industrial centre of Cameroun. It isn't a very pleasant place with lots of mosquitoes and a bad reputation for muggings. It's particularly dangerous to walk about at night. Even during the day you may find suspicious-looking people following you around waiting for the right opportunity. The worst area is between the railway station and the cathedral.

The **Artisanat National** – a craft and souvenir market – is worth a visit if you're interested in ivory, ebony, malachite jewellery and carvings, musical instruments or leatherwork. Bargain hard! It's across from the cathedral.

Information

A taxi from the airport to the centre of town will cost CFA 2000 but bus No 11 from just outside the terminal will take you there for CFA 100. Taxis around town cost CFA 100 to CFA 200. A shared taxi to the airport costs CFA 1000 per journey. Buses around the centre cost CFA 45 per journey. If you want to get to the airport cheaply, take bus No 1 from the Central Post Office to the market then bus No 11 from there to the airport.

All the airlines are on the Ave de la Liberté and the Blvd de la Liberté. A recommended travel agency is L'Hirondelle Voyages. They're very helpful and can arrange 40% student discounts for airline tickets. It's two blocks back from the Blvd de la Liberté.

American Express (tel 42 31 88) is at Cam Voyages, 15 Blvd de la Liberté, PO Box 4070. Thomas Cook is at Transcap Voyages, 8 Rue Ivy off the Blvd de la Liberté.

Places to Stay

The *Mission Catholique* known as the Procure Générale, Rue Franqueville, is recommended. It's very clean, has hot water, a swimming pool, air-con, a beer machine and meals. It costs CFA 3000 to CFA 4000 per night. You can leave baggage safely. Also cheap is the *Eglise Centenaire* which has rooms for CFA 2500 to CFA 4500 and has been described by some travellers as the 'best deal in town'.

Another good deal is the *Foyer Protestante*, one block from the Foyer des Marines. It has accommodation at CFA 3000 a double and excellent three course lunches from CFA 1500. There are cheaper rooms (only two of them) for CFA 2000 but they're always full. Breakfast is served for CFA 400 but evening meals are not available. Beware of theft.

The *Centre Baba Simon*, Blvd de la Liberté, opposite the cathedral and not far from the railway station, has been recommended by many travellers. It's very friendly and clean and has hundreds of dormitory beds at CFA 3000 per person. Rooms range from CFA 4000 to CFA 8000 – some rooms have air-con. Good meals are available.

Also very popular is the *Foyer des Marines* (Seafarer's Mission), 2 Rue Gallieni, though it's getting expensive these days. Rooms cost CFA 7000/8500 for a single/double with air-con and private bathroom. The atmosphere is friendly and lively. The food is quite expensive at around CFA 3000 for a meal but they do have cheap brochettes. It can sometimes be difficult to get into unless you can convince the management that a member of your family is a seafarer. There is a swimming pool.

Of the hotels, the *Hotel du Wouri* at CFA 5500 a double is one of the cheapest. Similar is the *Hotel du Littoral* which is adequate at CFA 6000 a double with air-con. Going further up-market, there is the *Hotel Joss*, Rue Luy, which costs from CFA 7250 per room.

Two other hotels have been recommended in the past. One is the *Hotel Beauséjour*, on the corner of Rue Joffre and Rue Pau. The second is the *Hotel Kontchupe*, Rue Alfred Saher just off the Blvd du Président Ahmadou Ahidjo.

Places to Eat

The *Restaurant N'Tchango*, Ave de 27 Août, is a good inexpensive place to eat. Also good and cheap is *The Circuit* where you can eat for CFA 1200. The *Moritz Café*, three blocks up from the Foyer des Marines, has relatively cheap steak and salad.

If you want to have a splurge try *La Porte Jaune*. A meal of crocodile and vegetables costs CFA 4250 though they have other delicacies on the menu.

FOUMBAN

Foumban is an interesting place with many old, traditional houses in the surrounding countryside and the German-built **Fon's Palace**. There's also an excellent **museum** (CFA 200 entry) and a good **market**.

Places to Stay

It's no longer possible to stay at the *Mission Catholique* in Foumban. The cheapest hotels are at the southern end of town and you can expect to pay around CFA 4000 per night.

GAROUA

This is the commercial centre of the north and has many foreign residents living here. There is a lively market on Saturday.

Places to Stay & Eat

There are plenty of cheap *auberges* across from the bus station. In the past the *Chambres de Passage* has been recommended but rooms now cost CFA 2500 and they're described as dirty and not worth the money. There's no sign for this place so ask at Restaurant de la Benoue. The *Mission Catholique* sometimes takes guests but isn't very keen to do so. It costs

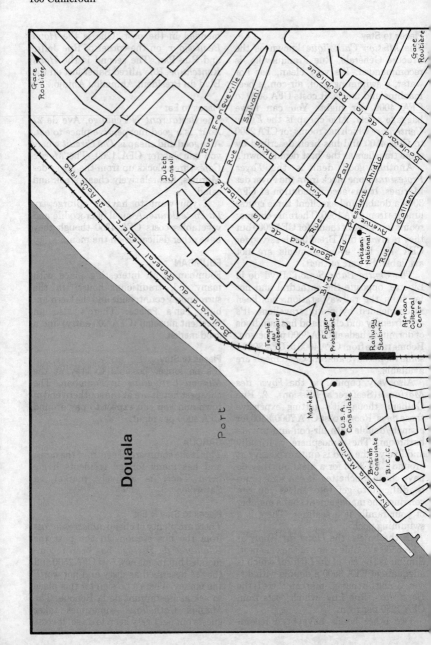

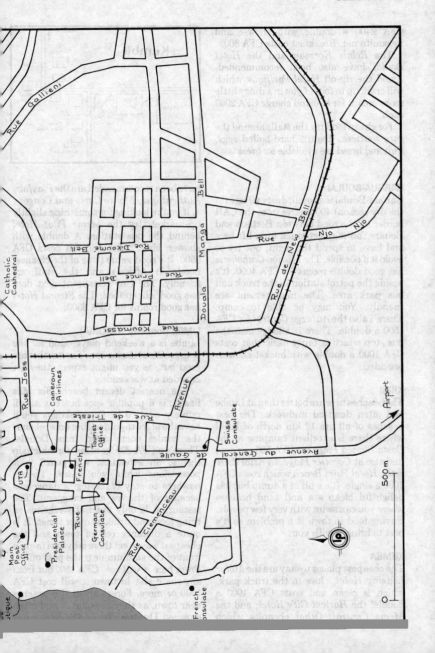

CFA 2400 a double with shower and mosquito net. Breakfast costs CFA 800.

The *Relais Korman* and the *Hotel Boulai* have also been recommended. Avoid the rip-off *Hotel Pacifique* which will cram up to four of you in a dingy little room meant for two and charge CFA 2000 each.

For cheap food try the stalls around the *gare routière*. Yogurt, hard-boiled eggs, fruit and bread are available for breakfast.

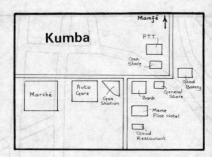

GAROUA-BOULAI
Garoua-Boulai is a small, dusty village (in the dry season) 400 metres from the CAR border on the road between Bertoua and Bouar. You may get stuck for a lift here and have to spend the night, but try to avoid it if possible. The *Mission Catholique* has good double rooms for CFA 4000. It's beside the petrol station in the truck and bus park area. The management are friendly. You may be able to camp. There's also the *Auberge Central* for CFA 1500 a double. There is a lodge near the bus stop which is fairly basic that costs CFA 1000 a double with bucket showers provided.

KRIBI
The beaches here are better than at Limbe and often deserted midweek. The best beaches of all are 12 km north of Kribi where there is excellent camping at the *Costa Blanca Plage* for CFA 500 per day, and also at *Cocotier Plage*. In Kribi there is the *Hotel Palm Beach* which costs CFA 7000 a single. It's a bit of a dump but has delightful clean sea and sand beaches where you can swim with very few people. Buying food in town is a problem so it's best to bring it with you.

KUMBA
The cheapest places to stay are the *Motor Lodging Hotel*, close to the truck park, which is clean and costs CFA 1000 a double; the *Harlem City Hotel*; and the *Meme Central*. Other cheapies which

have been recommended are the *Playfair, Authentique, Monte Carlo* and *Congo*.

If you're looking for something slightly up-market, try the *Meme Pilot Hotel* behind the bus station. A double with shower, sink, toilet and fan costs CFA 3500. It's good value ('one of the cleanest hotels in Africa') and the staff are friendly. The tiny restaurant next door has good, cheap food. The *Strand Hotel* has good rooms for CFA 6300.

LIMBE (formerly VICTORIA)
Limbe is a weekend playground for the bourgeoisie of Cameroun. The beaches are good but, as you might expect, they get crowded at weekends.

The nearest decent beach, **Six Mile Beach**, is a popular spot but has an oil refinery next to it. On weekdays you'll have the place to yourself but on weekends the hordes come down from Douala. There's a CFA 200 'gate fee' for which, in theory, an attendant will guard your possessions while you swim. There's nowhere to stay (camping is dangerous because of thieves and muggers). The restaurant is only open at weekends so bring food and drink at other times. It is quite a distance out of town and the cheapest way to get there is by taxi from in front of the stadium near the post office. From here it will cost CFA 150, but from anywhere else in town it will cost CFA 1000 or more. Forget about the beaches near town, as they're polluted and often crowded. One traveller said he came out of the sea at Limbe 'feeling like a Torrey Canyon seagull'.

For craftwork go to Pres-Craft – they have an unusual and interesting collection of things at very reasonable prices.

Places to Stay

You can camp free in the *Botanical Gardens* near the Tabai Park Hotel and Atlantic Beach Hotels, but beware of thieves. It is dangerous, however, to camp on the beach – you'll be mugged.

Two of the cheapest places to stay are the *Mansion Hotel* and the *City Hotel*. At the former you pay CFA 3000 a double. The rooms are clean and have fans but the toilets outside are dirty. If you get a room near the bar then you can forget about sleep. The rooms upstairs are quieter and have better showers and toilets. One of the

managers, Pierre, is friendly, helpful and can provide a lot of useful information. The hotel has a restaurant but the menu is generally a figment of the imagination. The City Hotel has rooms for the same price.

Another cheapie which has been recommended is the *Konimbo National Hotel* where you can get a room for CFA 2480 a double with fan, shower and toilet. It's sometimes possible to get a bed at the *Presbyterian Youth Centre* for CFA 1000 a night but they only have two beds. It's a great place and the people there are friendly. To get there from the taxi park, turn right when you reach the main road. It's only 150 metres from there.

Somewhat more expensive is the *Victoria Guest House* which has double rooms for CFA 4000. It's clean and

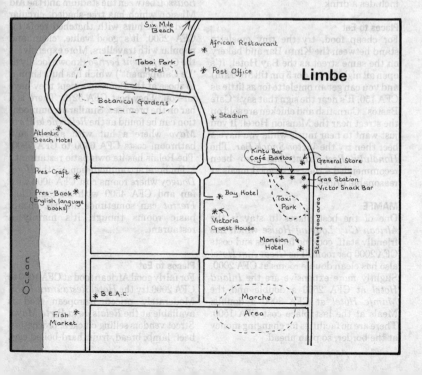

friendly. Further up-market, there is the *Bay Hotel*, next to the Victoria Guest House. The hotel is on a hill with a view and sea breezes. Rooms cost CFA 6500 a double and the restaurant is good. Guests are allowed to use the swimming pool at the Atlantic Hotel.

More expensive are the *Tabai Park Hotel* (previously the Miramar Hotel) and the *Atlantic Beach Hotel* both on the oceanfront. Prices at these hotels range from CFA 7000 to CFA 7500 for non-aircon bungalows to more expensive rooms. There are no discounts even during the week when they're empty. Both these hotels have good *bôites*. The one at the Tabai has no admission fee on weekdays if you just come to dance, but if you sit down at a table you must buy a drink – CFA 1000 for Cokes, CFA 600 for beer. At weekends the admission charge is CFA 1000 but this includes a drink.

Places to Eat

For cheap food, try the tiny omelette stand between the Kintu Bar and bakery on the same street as the Bay Hotel. It's open all night (from 4 or 5 pm till 8 or 9 am) and you can get an omelette for as little as CFA 150. It's near the sign that says 'Café Bastos'. Corn, fish and chicken are sold on the street near the Mansion Hotel. If you just want to hear music while you have a beer then try the *Victor Snack Bar*. The *Honolulu Restaurant* has also been recommended – they serve good meals at reasonable prices.

MAMFE

One of the best places to stay is the *African City Lodging House* which has friendly staff, cooking facilities and costs CFA 2000 per room. The *Great Aim Hotel* also has clean double rooms at CFA 2000. Slightly more expensive are the *Inland Hotel* at CFA 2500 a double and the *Mamfe Hotel* at CFA 3000 a double. Meals at the last place cost CFA 1500. There are no facilities for changing money at the border, so plan ahead.

MAROUA

This region rich in tribal culture and architecture, natural wonders and beautiful scenery, is well worth exploring.

The **market** on Sundays at Mora, on the way to the Waza National Park should be visited if you're going through at that time. Many people come down from the hills to barter goods here.

Places to Stay

The *Mission Baptiste* next to the SGBC bank has a number of small basic rooms for rent at just CFA 600 per night! The *Mission Catholique* also has rooms but the people are not friendly so it may be a waste of time to go there.

Other than the missions, there are a number of *campements* and hotels where you can find accommodation. The cheapest of these is the *Campement Boussou* between the stadium and the Aid Mission which has tree-shaded, circular mud-brick huts with thatched roofs for CFA 2500. It's good value, clean and popular with travellers. More expensive is the *Campement Ferngo* (known locally as 'Le Campement') which has huts similar to those at the Boussou except they have air-con. They cost CFA 5270. There is a bar on the premises. Similar accommodation can be found at the *Relais de la Porte Mayo* where a hut with air-con and bathroom costs CFA 6600 to CFA 7900. The Relais has its own patio restaurant.

For hotel accommodation, try the *Hotel Dougoy* where rooms cost CFA 4000 with fan and CFA 4500 with air-con. *Chez Pierrot* can sometimes arrange cheap, basic rooms though it's mainly a restaurant.

Places to Eat

For fairly good African food at CFA 1000 to CFA 2000 try the *Hotel Restaurant Kohi*. Moderately priced European food is available at the *Relais de la Porte Mayo*. Street vendors selling chicken, brochettes, beef, lamb, bread, fruit, hard-boiled eggs

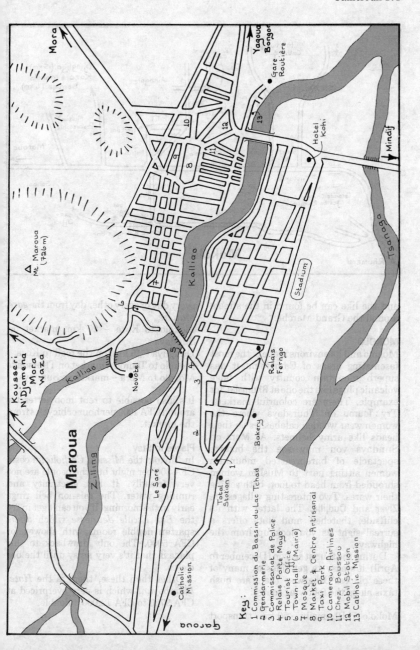

Maroua

Key:
1 Commission du Bassin du Lac Tchad
2 Gendarmerie
3 Commissariat de Police
4 Relais Porte Mayo
5 Tourist Office
6 Town Hall (Mairie)
7 Mosque
8 Market & Centre Artisanal
9 Taxi Park
10 Cameroun Airlines
11 Chez Boussou
12 Mobil Station
13 Catholic Mission

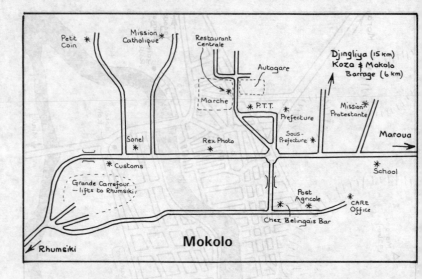

Mokolo

and the like can be found in the streets around the Grand Marché.

MOKOLO

Mokolo and its environs is one of the most fascinating areas of Cameroun. It has superb mountain country with huge volcanic plugs like the one at **Rhumsiki**, for example. There are colourful markets. Try **Tourou** on Thursdays where the women wear wooden calabashes on their heads like army helmets. At **Mora** on Sundays you may see the bizarre spectacle of barebreasted mountain women sitting next to Muslim women shrouded from head to foot, both selling their wares. Two interesting villages are **Ziver** and **Oudjilla**. The latter with its cliffside, thatched mud huts offers a surreal sight as you look up from the highway.

During the tourist season (December to April) it's easy to get rides to many of these places. Otherwise there are bush taxis along the following routes:

Mokolo to Rhumsiki – 50 km, transport every day or every other day from the *gare routière*
Mokolo to Koza – 20 km, market on Sundays
Djingliya – 15 km, on the road to Koza
Mokolo to Tourou – market on Thursdays
Mokolo to Mora – market on Sundays

It's also possible to rent mobylettes for around CFA 1000 per hour or bicycles from the market.

Places to Stay

In Mokolo the *Mission Catholique* costs CFA 800 per night but the people are not very friendly. It has electricity and running water. The mission bell rings early in the morning. If you can't get in try the *Bar Escale Jeunesse* which offers spartan double rooms with shower for CFA 5000. The only drawback to this place is that it's very noisy until the bar closes.

Other than these, there is the *Hotel Flamboyant* which is very overpriced at CFA 9750 to CFA 12,000 a double.

Places to Stay - Around Mokolo At Rhumsiki there is the *Campement* but the huts cost CFA 9750 to CFA 12,000! Instead, ask around for a room to rent with local people – expect to pay around CFA 3000 per person per night. Many tourists visit Rhumsiki so anticipate paying through the nose for just about everything.

At Djingliya there is the *Casse de Passage* which costs CFA 3000 for a room with two beds and enough space on the floor for another two people. There are no problems with the management if you want to do this.

At Waza there's the superexpensive *Campement* for CFA 12,500 to CFA 14,600, though you can find accommodation with local people for much less. There are also a lot of Peace Corps volunteers in the area so you might get lucky and be offered accommodation.

N'GAOUNDÉRÉ

The cheapest place to stay is at the *College Protestante*, Quartier Norvegieu, which has two rooms for rent to travellers. Speak to the principal and, if you're lucky, you'll get one of them for CFA 750 per person per night. Don't be late getting back in the evening as they go to bed early. The *Restaurant Salah* opposite the *gare routière* is also cheap at CFA 1500/2000 for a single/double. If you can't get a bed at these try the *Relais Chateaux de l'Amadoua* which is run by friendly people and costs CFA 3000/3500 for a single/double. Cheap meals are available.

Avoid the *Hotel Transcom* if possible as it charges CFA 12,000. However, it has a branch hotel, *Hotel le Relais*, by the cinema in the centre of town which has rooms for CFA 6970 a double. During school holidays it's worth trying the *College Mazenot*.

Cheap food is available from the stalls at the *gare routière* – bread, hard-boiled eggs, avocados, etc.

N'KONGSAMBA

The *Mission Protestante* may be able to provide you with a cheap bed for the night. If you're unsuccessful, try the *Central Hotel* which has relatively cheap rooms.

YAOUNDÉ

This is the capital of Cameroun. It's a clean, modern city, hilly and picturesque, with a refreshingly cool climate. It has a huge indoor market, two museums, seven cinemas, several large bookshops and lots of other interesting shops.

Information

Public buses cost CFA 50 or CFA 75 depending on the route but are incredibly crowded in the rush hours. Bus No 2 is the one to take for the CAR and Zaïre embassies. Bus No 9 goes to the airport every half hour or so. Taxis within town are CFA 100 but if you have a backpack they charge CFA 500 and won't take a cent less. If you're willing to pay, they'll drive you directly to where you want to go. Taxis leave from behind the main post office.

The Bank of Credit & Commerce (Cameroun), Ave J F Kennedy, charges no commission for changing travellers' cheques.

Useful Addresses
Some addresses which might be handy are:

Canadian Embassy
  Immeuble N Stamatides, Ave de l'Indépendence near the City Hall and Chase Bank
French Embassy
  Ave des Cocotiers Douala, PO Box 1071
Ivory Coast Embassy
  The embassy is in Nlongkak near Bastos at the traffic circle (bus No 4 terminus). From here take the Route du Bastos then the first left. This becomes a dirt road strewn with abandoned cars, but right at the end is the embassy.
Nigerian Embassy
  To get there head up Ave Vogt to the Cameroun Airlines office and then down the side street to the Renault and Mercedes dealers.

UK Embassy
    Winston Churchill Ave (near the Hotel
    Indépendence)
USA Embassy
    Rue Nachtigal, PO Box 817
British Council
    Les Galeries, Ave J F Kennedy
American Cultural Center
    Boston Bank Building near City Hall on
    Ave de l'Indépendence

Things to See

The **Artisanat** at the Place Kennedy is similar to Douala's and has ivory and malachite for sale.

The 9.30 am Sunday service at the **Catholic Church** in N'Djang-Melen is worth attending. It lasts for two hours and involves singing and dancing to the rhythm of tom-toms. The church is on the north-west corner of Rue Nguele Mendouga at the junction with Rue de Melen.

Places to Stay

The place where most travellers stay and one of the cheapest in the city is the *Mission Presbytérienne* (also known as the *Foyer International* and the *Mission Protestante*). It's some distance from the centre of town in the Djongola district between the city centre and the embassy district of Bastos. To get there take bus No 4 from the centre or take a taxi. A dormitory bed costs CFA 2000. Camping costs CFA 1000 though the police sometimes prohibit camping at this place. There are no tents for hire – you must bring your own. It's clean, friendly and has hot showers. Breakfast is available for CFA 300 and they allow use of the cooking facilities (but don't abuse their goodwill so pay for gas, etc). Watch out for thieves and muggers in this area.

Near to the Presbyterian Mission is the *Hotel des Nations* which has rooms for CFA 3000 a double with communal facilities or CFA 3500 a double with shower, toilet and fan. There are problems with the water supply and it's usually only available in the late evening. Another traveller suggested the *Benedictine Monastery* where he was offered a bed and breakfast for CFA 2500.

More expensive is the *Hotel Aurore*, at the junction of Rue Essomba Sebastien and the Rue Fouda Ngomo. Rooms cost CFA 5275 a double, with breakfast available for CFA 400 (omelette and French bread). Other hotels recommended are the *Hotel Flamenco* and the *Hotel Le Progrès* near the Mokolo taxi park across from the market. Both are reasonably priced.

Accommodation can sometimes be found at the *Faculté de Théologie*, but you can give the unfriendly *Mission Catholique* a miss. American nationals are allowed to camp in the grounds of the *International School* – ask for permission at the school.

Places to Eat

If you're staying at the Presbyterian Mission try the *Western Café* which is a little African kiosk on the same road as the Mission. It offers omelettes, bread and coffee and is very cheap. Close to the Hotel Aurore is the *Restaurant Extra Moderne* which is very good. The *Pizzeria* three doors down from the Capitole Theatre, Ave du Marechal Foch, is also good (CFA 1800 for a rather small pizza). So is the *Marseillaise* on the 2nd floor across the road from the theatre. At the latter, you can get chicken & chips, green beans and a Coke for CFA 1750. The large menu includes Chinese food as well. There are also the usual street stalls.

If you get to the African quarter try the *Club l'Année 2000*. It's a long way from the centre of town and you'll have to take a taxi, but the food is excellent. The *American Recreation Camp Club* has good, but expensive, hamburgers and salads.

The *Anerouge Restaurant & Snack Bar*, Place Kennedy, is a meeting place and cheap watering hole for travellers and overland tour trucks.

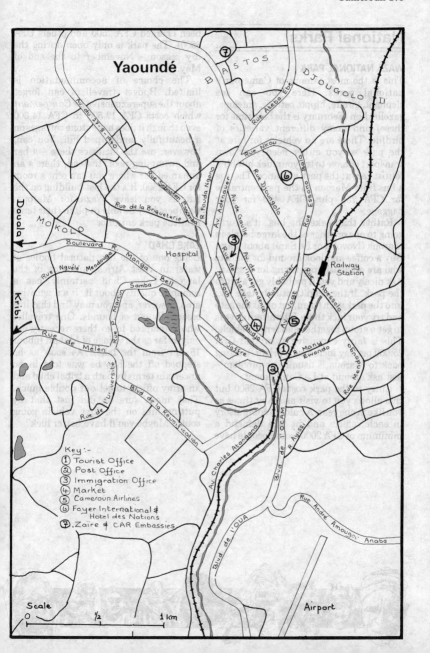

Yaoundé

Key :-
1. Tourist Office
2. Post Office
3. Immigration Office
4. Market
5. Cameroun Airlines
6. Foyer International & Hotel des Nations
7. Zaire & CAR Embassies

Scale
0   ½   1 km

Airport

Douala

Kribi

MOKOLO

B A S T O S

DJOUGOLO D

Hospital

Railway Station

Av. du 27-8-57

Av. Ateba Ebe

Rue Nkou

Rue Bilanga

Av. Aденаuer

Av. de Gaulle

Av. de l'Indépendance

Av. Foch

Av. Narvick

Av. Vogt

Rue Gocker

Rue Abessolo

Av. Jaffre

Av. Ahidji

R. Many Ewondo

Blvd de la Réunification

Av. Charles Atangana

Blvd de I'OCAM

Blvd de IQUA

R. Ayissi

Rue André Amougou

Anaba

Rue de l'Université

Rue de Mélen

Rue P. Martin Samba

Rue Nguélé Mendouga

Boulevard R. Manga Bell

Rue Sebastien Essomba

Rue de la Briqueterie

R. Fouda Ngono

Rue Essessa Bilanga

Rue Ateba Ebe

Rue Djoungolo

Rue Mbougou

National Parks

WAZA NATIONAL PARK

This is the most famous of Cameroun's national parks. Here you can see elephant, giraffe, hippo, ostrich, antelope, gazelle, lion (February is the best time for these) and many different varieties of birdlife. There are no vehicles for hire at the park so you either need your own transport or have to try your luck hitching tourist cars at the park entrance. There is a bus from Maroua to the park entrance for CFA 750 plus CFA 400 for your baggage.

Rather than take the bus, it's worth going to one or other of the large hotels in Maroua (Novotel or Le Saré) about 7 am. Buy a coffee and look around for tourists who are obviously preparing for a safari. Ask nicely and you'll probably get a lift to the park. If they can't actually take you into the park with them, get off at the gate and try your luck there. The alternative is to get a group together and rent a vehicle. This is fairly expensive at around CFA 25,000 per day including a driver. Getting back to Maroua is usually no problem – just ask around at Le Campement.

Entry to the park costs CFA 2500 but this allows you to visit as many times as you like in one year. A guide is compulsory in each vehicle and he will demand a minimum of CFA 2000 (some people have been charged CFA 2500 and others CFA 3500). The park is only open during the dry season – November to the end of May.

The choice of accommodation is limited. Budget travellers can forget about the superexpensive *Le Campement* which costs CFA 12,500 to CFA 14,600 even though it does have stone cottages on a beautifully landscaped hill. You can, however, use the facilities there – a bar and swimming pool. Instead, there's an unnamed bar where you can rent a room for CFA 2500. It's the last building on the left as you leave Waza for Maroua. Campers may be able to pitch their tents near the park entrance.

LAKE CHAD

Being one of the few natural bodies of water in West Africa, and one of the largest, Lake Chad certainly has a romantic quality about it. It's a sensitive area, however, and you may find that it is essentially out of bounds. One traveller who attempted to go there recently got only as far as the village of Makari (about 15 km from the lake). As soon as he stepped off the bus he was told in no uncertain terms by both a tribal chief and an army officer to get out double quick. They made sure he did just that by putting him on the first vehicle going south. Maybe you'll have better luck?

Cape Verde

The Cape Verde Islands lie some 645 km off the coast of Senegal and are one of the smallest and poorest of the African nations. Earlier uninhabited, the islands were colonised by the Portuguese in 1462, the labour and the majority of the population being slaves taken from the West African coast. The racial mixture which developed – mainly mulattos, some blacks and a few whites – remains much the same today. The language – a Cape Verde Creole – is the result of an intermingling of Portuguese and various West African languages.

Even though there is evidence of an earlier, richer vegetation, much of the land is now barren and, like most of West Africa south of the Sahara, the islands have borne the brunt of the Sahel drought throughout the '70s and '80s. The local staple food, maize, grows under very precarious conditions and is correspondingly unreliable. Fruit and vegetables (bananas, manioc, beans, sweet potatoes) are only available in small quantities. All the same, a start has been made in many places to counteract the effects of the drought under the 'green barrier' scheme. Most of the food supplies and the largest contribution to the national wealth continue to come from the sea – there are rich fishing grounds around the islands. Also of some significance is salt mining on the islands of Sal and Maio.

The importance of the islands for the Portuguese lay not so much in any inherent wealth they may have possessed, but in their strategic placement between Africa, America and Europe. Cape Verde was long one of the most important slaving stations of the region. Even when the Portuguese were forced to curtail drastically their slaving activities as a result of British navy intervention in the 19th century, the islands continued to flourish as the centre of the slave trade between West Africa and the Spanish Antilles.

With the advent of the ocean liner, the harbour of Mindelo on São Vicente became an important victualling station where ships took on supplies of coal, water and livestock. Those who made the most of this were not so much the Portuguese colonial authorities as the emerging northern European economic powers – chiefly Britain.

The Portuguese, despite the fact that they were incapable and unwilling to care much for the welfare of the Cape Verdeans, clung on stubbornly to their

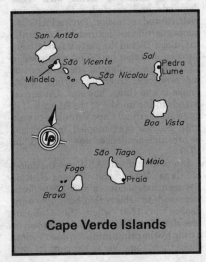

Cape Verde Islands

control of the islands though they did make certain concessions, particularly in the cultural realm. While Portugal continued to neglect the economic and political development of its mainland African colonies, Cape Verde, with its light-skinned population, was regarded as a special case and efforts were made to keep it bound more closely to Portugal and separate from Africa. It was the first Portuguese colony to have a school for higher education, and though education was available only to a small minority, this led to the growth of a rich indigenous literature which found expression in the magazines *Claridade*, *Certeza* and *Suplemento Cultural*, among others.

The ideas expressed in these magazines, however, gave evidence of a growing sense of identity with the African nations. This was accelerated after WW II and eventually led to the formation of the African Party for the Independence of Guinea and Cape Verde (PAIGC).

Under the leadership of Amilcar Cabral, PAIGC began to pressure the colonial authorities to grant independence. The fascist regime in Lisbon was in no mood to come to terms with these demands and reacted with increasing violence and repression, forcing PAIGC to adopt guerrilla tactics from 1961 onwards. In Guinea-Bissau the party was relatively successful so that by 1973 it was possible to make a unilateral declaration of independence. Guerrilla warfare in the jungle is one thing, however. On barren islands in the middle of the Atlantic it is quite another, and Cape Verde had to wait until Salazar was toppled in Portugal before independence was granted in 1975.

One of the aims of PAIGC was the union of Cape Verde and Guinea-Bissau. Between independence and 1980 efforts were made to achieve this, but hopes were dashed in 1980 when the Guinean president, Luiz Cabral, was overthrown in a coup by the prime minister, João Vieira. Since then, Cape Verde has gone its own way under the African Independence Party of Cape Verde (PAICV).

Though Marxist in orientation, PAICV follows a very pragmatic course, and with the generous assistance of international welfare agencies and corporations, life on the islands has improved considerably. Being only too familiar with the harshness of the climate and the need to make the most of the limited resources available, the government is doing its best to see that all is divided equally. The threat of starvation has been removed, illiteracy is being eradicated (a sixth of the population now attend school) and health facilities have been improved considerably.

Nevertheless, independence has brought no immediate prosperity to the islanders and every time the east wind blows many look abroad for their future. In the last 100 years over half a million Cape Verdeans have emigrated, nearly half of them to the USA. Those on the east coast of the USA are well organised socially and culturally and there's a newspaper you can subscribe to if you are interested – the *Cape Verdean News* (tel 617 997 2300), 417 Purchase St, PO Box H-3063, New Bedford, Mass 02741.

Few travellers visit the islands. We have only received two detailed letters in about three years. Cape Verde isn't an exotic tropical paradise. It's a small country, which makes its impression subtly through its cultural independence, pleasant atmosphere and friendly people.

Facts

GEOGRAPHY

The islands cover some 4000 square km, are of volcanic origin and consist of 10 islands and eight smaller islets, nine of which have been settled in the course of time. They fall into two groups depending on their relation to the wind: Barlavento (the windward islands), comprising Santo Antão, São Vicente, Santa Lucia,

São Nicolau, Sal and Boa Vista; and Sotavento (the leeward islands), comprising Maio, São Tiago, Fogo and Brava.

The main towns are the capital, Praia (São Tiago) and Mindelo (São Vicente).

PEOPLE
The population is around 340,000 of whom 50,000 live in the capital.

VISAS
Cape Verde has embassies in the following countries: Angola, Algeria, Argentina, Guinea, Italy, Netherlands, Portugal, São Tomé & Principe, Senegal, USSR and USA. Portuguese speakers can apply direct to the Ministerio de Negocias Estrangeiros, Direccão de Immigracão, Cape Verde. If you can't speak Portuguese, most Portuguese embassies will assist you in filling out the necessary forms and will process your application if there is no Cape Verde embassy in the country where you apply. You need two photos, an onward ticket and an International Vaccination Card for cholera and yellow fever. The embassy in Senegal is at Rue du Relais, off Ave Ponty, Dakar. Visas there cost CFA 2000 and take about three weeks to come through.

MONEY
US$1 = Es 80

The unit of currency is the escudo = 100 centavos. There are no restrictions on the import of local currency but export is limited to Es 6000.

Currency declaration forms are issued on arrival and strictly checked on leaving to make sure that all transactions have gone through a bank (receipts must be shown).

TOURIST INFORMATION
If you'd like more information about Cape Verde, contact the Secretario de Estado de Comercio Turismo e Artesanato, CP105, Praia, São Tiago, Cape Verde.

There are no duty-free allowances of anything (tobacco, alcohol, perfume, etc).

ACCOMMODATION & FOOD
There are a few fairly good hotels in the middle price range at Praia, Mindelo, Sal and São Filipe. Other than these, cheap *pensão* can be found in most places. Average prices are Es 300/450 a single/double.

In Praia, try the unnamed *pensão* on the corner of the Café Portugal, or the *Hotel Felicidade* which costs around US$7 per night. The *Hotel Praia-Mar* has rooms for Es 2500. In Mindelo, try the *Chave d'Ouro*. The *Hotel Porto Grande* has rooms for Es 1000. On Sal try the *Pensão Dona Angela* in the small village near the international airport (within walking distance even with a rucksack). It's cheap, interesting and has great food and drink. The *Hotel Morabeza* has rooms from Es 2000.

Food is available in most hotels and *pensão*. The local dish, cachupa (maize and beans), is generally available in small bars and the like. There's a wide variety of alcoholic drinks – beer, wine, local spirits, punch – but nonalcoholic drinks tend to be quite expensive.

LANGUAGE
Portuguese is the official language but Cape Verde Creole is the everyday language of virtually everyone.

Getting There & Around

Probably the most useful flight for travellers is the direct Dakar/Praia flight which goes on Tuesday (by TACU – the Cape Verde airline) and Saturday (by Air Senegal). All other international flights land at Amilcar Cabral Airport on the island of Sal.

There is a network of internal flights to the islands. Praia to Mindelo (São Vicente) costs US$23. There's also a boat

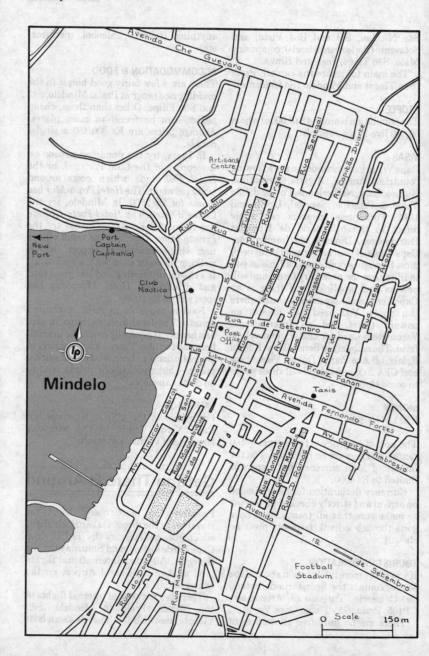

Mindelo

which costs US$8 but the schedule is irregular. Brava can be reached from São Filipe (Fogo) by boat. Travel on the islands themselves is by bus or truck. Taxis are generally very expensive.

Around the Islands

Every island has something of interest, but by and large the pace of life is slow. São Tiago, for instance, is very African and is where the majority of black people live. The markets are very colourful and it's worth making enquiries about the dates of local festivals in honour of various deities. Music is an integral part of these festivities.

The town of Mindelo (São Vicente) is very reminiscent of a deserted Portuguese provincial town. The small bars in and around the harbour have their own special atmosphere and are worth a visit. Because of the rocky coastline, there are only a few beaches. The most beautiful is at Tarrafal (São Tiago), reached by bus from Praia (about 80 km). There's a small, cheap house for rent there. Another is the black volcanic sand beach on the west coast of Fogo south of São Filipe, the main town on the island. The volcano on this island also offers spectacular views. The beaches are anything but overrun and the water is warm all the year round (between 20°C and 27°C). During the cooler months, however, strong north winds make bathing unpleasant.

Central African Republic

This area of Africa has been raped for centuries and the process is still going on. As a result, the CAR is an underdeveloped, fragmented and poverty-stricken country, but with an enlightened government it could be relatively prosperous. Unfortunately, that isn't likely to occur for quite some time, not only because of the rapaciousness of its rulers but also because of the influence of foreign interests. Despite the fact that the country has important deposits of uranium, copper, tin, iron, chromium and diamonds, and could export significant amounts of cotton, timber and textiles, precious little of the wealth which is – and could be – generated ever seeps down to the population at large. Most of it is frittered away by a tiny elite on luxury items. Even the country's independence, which supposedly dates from 1960, is a charade. The Central African Republic remains, to all intents and purposes, a French colony. No president lasts without substantial backing from France. The nation's economy, likewise, is heavily dependent on French aid.

The area's undoing came with the slave trade to the Americas. Archaeological remains indicate extensive settlement in the region long before the rise of ancient Egypt and, later, an advanced culture whose artisans were coveted from far afield. However, organised society gradually collapsed when not only hundreds of thousands of people were dragged in chains to the west coast for transportation to the Americas but when Islamic conquerors swept down from the north to institute their own trade in human flesh. As recently as the 19th century about 20,000 slaves from this part of Africa were sold every year on the Egyptian market.

Into this scene of devastation came the French (bent on rivalry with the British in the Sudan) and Belgians in the 1880s. The territory passed to France, which quickly parcelled it out to private enterprise. The concession agents and managers brought in to exploit the country, proved to be nothing less than murderous psychopaths, and the French colonial authorities were little better in their treatment of the indigenous population. Thousands lost their lives doing forced labour or as a result of torture and execution for supposed misdemeanours and desertion. This kind of treatment naturally generated resentment. Although the Africans resisted the onslaught on their freedom, the backbone of the resistance movement had been broken by the 1930s as a result of French military action, famine and epidemics.

The first signs of nationalism sprang up after WW II in the form of Boganda's Mouvement d'Evolution Sociale de l'Afrique Noire. The party was to be instrumental in forcing the French to grant independence, but before it did so Boganda died in a mysterious plane crash in 1959. The leadership was taken over by David Dacko, who became the country's first president at independence in 1960. Dacko's rule quickly became highly repressive and dictatorial, and in 1966, amid an atmosphere of political rivalry, impending national bankruptcy and a threatened national strike, he was overthrown by the army commander, Jean-Bedel Bokassa (a close relative of Dacko).

So began 13 years of one of the most sordid and brutal regimes Africa has ever

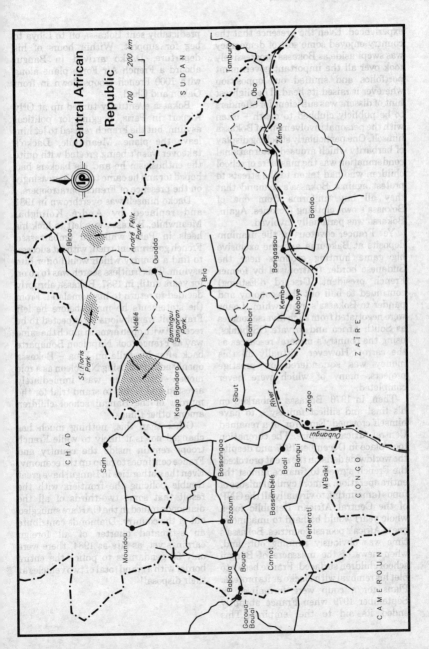

experienced. Even the pretence that the country enjoyed some sort of democracy was swept aside as Bokassa progressively took over all the important government portfolios and snuffed out opposition wherever it raised its head. The slightest hint of dissent was sufficient for offenders to be publicly clubbed to death – often with the personal involvement of Bokassa himself. One particularly shocking display of barbarity which aroused international condemnation was the massacre of school children who had taken to the streets to protest against Bokassa's demand that they all buy uniforms from one of Bokassa's own clothing factories. Again, Bokassa was personally involved.

Yet France, covetous of the uranium deposits at Bakouma and the exclusive big game hunting grounds near the Sudanese border (patronised by former French president, Giscard d'Estaing) continued to bail out the economy and pander to Bokassa's every whim. Loans were negotiated from such diverse sources as South Africa and private US banks, using the country's mineral resources as the carrot. However, virtually all this money was squandered on prestige projects, many of which were never completed.

Then, in 1976, Bokassa embarked on his final and silliest fantasy – to have himself crowned 'Emperor' of a renamed Central African Empire. The coronation took place in December 1977 and despite the worldwide derision the event provoked, the French agreed to finance almost the entire operation. A more cynical misuse of funds (amounting to virtually all the GNP of the Central African Republic for a whole year) would be hard to imagine in one of Africa's poorest countries. Bokassa's time was obviously running out, and, when news of the massacre of Bangui school children surfaced, France began to plot his removal with Dacko as its protégé. Plans for a coup were formalised in September 1979 when France abruptly ended its aid to the 'empire'. This

predictably sent Bokassa off to Libya to beg for support. Within hours of his departure, Dacko arrived in Bangui aboard a French Air Force plane along with 1000 French troops flown in from Gabon and Chad.

Bokassa eventually turned up at Orly Airport in Paris, begging for political asylum, but the French refused to let him leave the plane. Meanwhile, Dacko's takeover wasn't being greeted with quite the enthusiasm he and his backers had hoped for and he came to rely increasingly on the presence of French paratroopers.

Dacko himself was overthrown in 1981 and replaced by André Kolingba. Meanwhile, Bokassa was left to kick his heels in Paris while an embarrassed French government tried, without success, to find a country which would offer him asylum. This fruitless search was to go on for years until, in 1987, Bokassa abruptly decided to return to his homeland. From the statements he made before he left France, it was obvious he expected to be received with open arms in much the same way as France took Napoleon Bonaparte back after his exile on Elba – Bokassa openly admitted using Napoleon as a role model. Instead he was immediately arrested and is due to stand trial for the murder of the Bangui school children among other things.

Other than this, nothing much has changed nor is it likely to while French troops remain inside the country and France continues to prop up the economy. Even the authorities in Bangui have great trouble policing the frontiers with the result that some two-thirds of all the diamonds mined in the CAR are smuggled out of the country. Diamonds contribute an estimated quarter of all foreign earnings yet, as late as 1984, there were only 30 gendarmes to police the entire border with a grand total of two vehicles at their disposal!

Facts

Very few travellers seem to take time to explore this country, particularly east of Bangui, the capital, but those who have, suggest that it's worth the effort.

GEOGRAPHY & CLIMATE
The country is one immense plateau varying in height between 600 and 700 metres with three distinct climatic zones. The south is tropical, with high humidity and temperatures gradually changing to a 'Sudan-Guinea' type of climate in the centre with abundant rainfall. The north is dry scrub and forms part of the Sahel. The main rainy season is from May to November.

PEOPLE
The Central African Republic has a population of around three million. Many still lived a traditional lifestyle in villages in the bush until Bokassa forcibly relocated them near the main roads.

VISAS
Visas are required by all except nationals of France, Germany (West), Israel, Romania, Switzerland and the USA. We've also had reports that British nationals no longer require visas. They should check this out before arriving at the border.

In Africa, there are CAR embassies in Abidjan (Ivory Coast), Algiers (Algeria), Brazzaville (Congo), Cairo (Egypt), Khartoum (Sudan), Kinshasa (Zaïre), Lagos (Nigeria), Libreville (Gabon), N'Djamena (Chad), Rabat (Morocco) and Yaoundé (Cameroun). Elsewhere, visas can be obtained from French embassies and consulates.

Separate entry and exit permits are necessary for Bangui. If you're on your way to Bangui from Cameroun, the entry permits are issued at PK 12 (a police checkpoint 12 km from the centre of Bangui). Before leaving Bangui for Zaïre

you have to get an exit permit which costs CFA 2500 in *timbres fiscaux* at the Domaine office then take it to immigration with your passport. This can take 45 minutes or 24 hours depending on how busy they are. This is also where you must get an entry permit if you're arriving from Zaïre. (If you're coming from Zaïre the entry and exit stamps for Bangui can be obtained at the same time.)

Visa extensions cost CFA 4000 for 20 days with two photos and are sometimes issued while you wait, or within 24 hours.

You must report to the police in each town you stay overnight but this is just a formality and there's usually no fuss.

Other Visas
Cameroun A 10-day visa costs CFA 3000 and a 15-day visa CFA 4800 with two photos, and a letter of recommendation from your embassy (CFA 1800 from British embassies). They take 24 hours to issue.

Chad The embassy in Bangui is on Rue de Bongada. Visas cost CFA 3000 for a stay of less than 30 days and CFA 4500 for a stay of 30 days. They are issued while you wait, and although a lot of questions are asked, the ambassador is very friendly.

Congo A 15-day visa costs CFA 4000 with two photos and takes 24 to 48 hours to issue.

Zaïre The embassy in Bangui is on Ave de l'Indépendence. Visas cost CFA 5000 (one-month, single-entry), CFA 9500 (two-months, single-entry) and CFA 12,000 (three-months, multiple-entry) with two photos. They are issued in 24 hours or sometimes while you wait. No letter of introduction from your embassy is necessary.

Working in CAR
If you're skilled or professionally qualified it's fairly easy to get a job in the Central

African Republic. One man from Australia even got himself a job as a park warden because he'd spent time shovelling shit in a zoo in Australia.

MONEY
US$1 = CFA 260

The unit of currency is the CFA franc. The import and export of local currency is allowed up to CFA 75,000.

The black market rates for Zaïrois currency in Bangui is usually good but check first with travellers coming from Zaïre about current rates inside the country. It may be better to change in Zongo.

The bank in Zongo won't accept travellers' cheques and may demand that you change a certain minimum of cash – usually US$50. The moneychangers know this and lower their rates correspondingly. Hide any zaïres which you buy in the CAR well before crossing the river from Bangui as there's usually a thorough search at the Zaïre customs and immigration.

There are no banks between N'Gaoundéré and Bangui. If you are stuck for money in Bouar try the Maison Murat, which will usually take both cash and travellers' cheques.

The UBAC bank, on the road from the main roundabout in the town centre to the presidential palace in Bangui, will change US$ travellers' cheques for US$ cash at 5% commission. To avoid the commission go to BIAO bank on the roundabout. This bank has the busiest foreign exchange counter in Bangui. Wait until someone comes in wanting to change US$ cash into CFA, then change your US$ travellers' cheques into CFA (no commission) and sell your CFAs for their US$. Banking hours are Monday to Friday from 7 to 11 am.

The airport departure tax for international flights is CFA 2000.

POST
The poste restante in Bangui charges CFA 125 per letter and they are reasonably well organised. If sending mail from here try to get them to frank it in front of you.

Very few travellers seem to take time to explore this country, particularly

HEALTH
Cholera, yellow fever and other vaccinations are available from the Institut Pasteur in Bangui (next to the General Hospital). It is run by westerners and has new needles, etc. Cholera vaccinations are given on Tuesday and Friday at 10.30 am and cost CFA 2000 (plus CFA 250 for a vaccination card if you haven't got one).

LANGUAGE
French is the official language and Sango is the national language. Very little English is spoken.

Getting There & Around

AIR
Since Point Air Mulhouse began flying to Bangui, the CAR has become a starting/returning point in Africa for many travellers, especially those from France. If you want to return to Europe from here, it's worth checking if they have spare seats available. There are two flights per month, always on a Friday, to Marseilles and Paris. The fares are CFA 97,500 (to Marseilles) and CFA 106,000 one-way. The Le Point office in Bangui is on the Ave de la Résistance in the same building as the US Peace Corps and is open from 8 am.

ROAD
There are no railways in the Central African Republic but, at least in the western part of the country, there is a well-maintained network of roads. East of Bangui as far as the border with Sudan the roads are terrible as there has been no maintenance since 1973. Abandoned road graders litter the sides of the road and the jungle is beginning to take over again.

Hitching is easy in the west and lifts

may occasionally be free. Garoua-Boulai (Cameroun border) to Bangui shouldn't take more than two days, and in the right vehicle can take only a day. Where lifts have to be paid for, they will cost about CFA 10 per km. Buses cost CFA 15 to CFA 20 per km. Most of these are minibuses which are supposed to take 18 people, though 24 are often squeezed in.

Some examples of the local transport and costs are as follows:

Boali (from main road turn-off) to Bangui

You can hitch in pick-ups which will cost CFA 1200. At PK 12 you have to get off your ride and walk through the barrier, fill in two forms and get an entry stamp to Bangui. Your taxi may pick you up again on the other side and take you to PK 5 (market) but this would be exceptional. If not there are buses to the centre via PK 5. A taxi from PK 5 to the centre costs CFA 90 with no baggage charge.

Bangui to Bouar

A minibus leaves daily between 6 and 7 am from the *gare routière*, though it's generally 9 am before it finally leaves because of paperwork and cruising around for more passengers. The fare is CFA 5500 and the journey takes 10 to 15 hours.

Bouar to Garoua-Boulai

A minibus leaves daily at 6 am, costs CFA 2300 and takes about six hours. In the opposite direction there is a daily minibus which leaves at 8 am and costs CFA 2300 with no baggage charge. At the border and customs check there are two forms to fill in. There is another cursory baggage check by customs at Baboua, 58 km from the border.

Bouar to Bossembélé

A minibus costs CFA 3500 with no baggage charge. The first leaves at 6.30 to 7 am and later ones may pass through and stop about 12 noon en route from Garoua-Boulai to Bangui.

Bossembélé to Boali Chutes

There are pick-ups early in the morning from the market which cost CFA 800. They leave when full and take 2½ hours with stops at mushroom sellers who are friends of the driver. You will be dropped at the turn-off and from there it's a four km walk.

Birao to Bangui

In the rainy season there is no overland transport of any kind. Regular commercial flights costs CFA 4500 but the French military regularly fly in and out with supplies to Birao and return empty to Bangui so you may be able to get a free flight if you can talk your way into it – not difficult. If you have to take a commercial flight don't change money in Birao. They will let you change at the official rate on arrival in Bangui.

TO/FROM CAMEROUN

The crossing point which most people use is Garoua-Boulai on the road between Bouar and Bertoua. There are direct buses, usually daily, between Bangui and Garoua-Boulai for CFA 7800 as well as buses from Bangui to Bouar for CFA 5500 which take 15 to 20 hours. From Bouar to Garoua-Boulai costs CFA 2300 and takes about six hours. This stretch is easy to hitch and it's often possible to get a free lift. If hitching from Bangui, take a bus or taxi first to checkpoint PK 12, then hitch from there. There are trucks all day and lifts cost about CFA 7000.

If you intend to catch the train once you get into Cameroun, instead of heading for Belabo, which is where many people pick it up, get a bus from Garoua-Boulai to N'Gaoundal (not N'Gaoundéré) and pick up the overnight train to Yaoundé from there. Arrive at Garoua-Boulai early in the day to do this.

TO/FROM CHAD

An interesting route to take into Chad is from Bangui to Sarh via Damara, Sibut, Dekoa, Kaga Barboro and Kabo (640 km in total). Get a taxi from the centre of Bangui and start hitching from PK 12. You may get a direct lift to Sarh from there, but it's more likely you will have to village-hop as there's not much traffic. Expect to pay CFA 7000 to CFA 10,000 for the journey. If offered a lift to Batangafo, get off at Kaga Barboro as the former is off the main road and you could be stuck for days. The Chad customs are at Maro and you can expect a very heavy search. They turn out *everything*! And the process is repeated five times before you reach Sarh!

TO/FROM CONGO

The only feasible way of getting directly into Congo is to buy a pirogue and sail down the Oubangui River. This is not as crazy as it sounds though you do need to do some planning and take food along as there's little for sale except fruit and vegetables in the villages en route.

The best places for buying a pirogue are Mpoko Bac, south of Bangui (take a shared taxi from in front of the US Embassy for CFA 90), or Ouango, north of Bangui (take a minibus from next to the market in town for CFA 70). Expect to pay around CFA 17,000.

On average a pirogue could cover 25 to 30 km daily. The border crossing is at Mongoumba but you also need to get a stamp from the police in Zinga (you can camp next to the police station). Congo customs and immigration are at Betou further down the river. The immigration officer is very friendly and will let you camp in his garden. At Impfondo you need to get both entry and exit stamps. Don't forget to do this otherwise you'll be in for a hard time.

At Impfondo you have three choices: continue down river by pirogue; take a regular steamer to Brazzaville (CFA 15,000 in 2nd class and CFA 8000 in 3rd class, takes seven days), or fly to Brazzaville (CFA 25,000 on a regular flight or CFA 10,000 in a military plane).

TO/FROM SUDAN

In the dry season there are trucks which ply the route between Bangui and Nyala. Few travellers take this route so details are sparse but a truck from Bangui to Am Dafok (the border) costs about US$60 and takes about six days. From Ndélé to the border the road is diabolical, but there is a lot of game to be seen. A truck from Ndélé to Nyala costs about US$100 and takes about seven days.

In the wet season (August to December) you will have to go by camel train or hire donkeys and a guide. If you make use of the camel trains you're in for a very interesting journey. Travellers who have done this have all spoken enthusiastically about it, saying it was one of the highlights of their trip. Further details are in the Sudan chapter.

TO/FROM ZAÏRE

To get to Zaïre simply take the ferry across the Oubangui River from Bangui to Zongo. It costs CFA 100 plus CFA 50 to CFA 100 for a backpack. Don't cross the river at weekends, as the Zaïre customs don't work then and you'll have to hang around in Zongo until Monday morning. If the ferry isn't working – it breaks down occasionally – take a motorboat or pirogue. If you're taking a vehicle across this river the ferry will cost CFA 8000.

If you have travellers' cheques there is now a bank at Zongo (Banque du Peuple).

The main route used by overland travellers from CAR to Zaïre is Bangui/Mobaye/Gbadolite/Lisala. This route is preferred to the Bangui/Zongo/Lisala and the Bangui/Bangassou/Bita routes. The reason for this is because the road from Mobaye to Lisala is in good repair due to the hydroelectric station being built across the Oubangui at Mobaye and the new city being built at Gbadolite. The road from Bangui to Sibut is sealed and from Sibut to Kongbo (the turn-off to Mobaye) it's a well-maintained dirt road. From Kongbo to Mobaye the road becomes rougher. The ferry from Mobaye across the Oubangui costs CFA 25,000.

The Zongo route isn't used much due to the Zaïrois officials in Zongo and the low load carrying capacity of the ferry there. The ferry at Bangassou has been out of commission so if you want to cross here you will have to make enquiries first. (Thanks Rodney from Melbourne for your letter.)

Around the Country

BANGASSOU
The customs on the CAR side of the river are closed on Sundays but you can go into town and report to customs on Monday morning. Camping is free at the *Mission Protestante* or on the grounds of the *Tourist Hotel* for a small charge. Forget about the Mission Catholique as they are very hostile. Apart from these two places there is the exclusive *Hunting Hotel-Restaurant* where you may get to rub shoulders with French cabinet ministers and even Giscard d'Estaing out there on shooting holidays. Watch out for thieves if you are camping.

BANGUI
The capital of the Central African Republic, Bangui is a pleasant, shady town but it does have more than its fair share of thieves so watch out. Many travellers get ripped off.

Information
The immigration office is two blocks west of the market at Rue Joseph Degrain and Ave du Président Senghor, in a dilapidated old house with no sign. It's easy to walk right past it unless you ask.

The BIAO bank, Place de la République, is efficient and makes no charge for changing travellers' cheques. It's open from 7 to 11.30 am. The agent for Thomas Cook is Bangui Tourisme. The post office is open Monday to Friday from 6.30 am to 1.30 pm, and on Saturday from 7 am to 12 noon.

The Martin Luther King Centre next to the US Embassy has an air-con library with magazines and newspapers, and shows movies every Friday at 4 pm (no charge).

There are service taxis along all the main routes which cost CFA 100 (before 9 pm) and CFA 125 (after 9 pm) per journey. To the airport they cost CFA 150 (before 9 pm) or CFA 200 (after 9 pm). All these are shared taxis. The best time for taking taxis is between 9 and 11 am and 2 and 4 pm as it is very busy from 6 to 9 am, lunchtime and 4 to 6 pm. Minibuses are even cheaper and there are also infrequent buses.

The minibuses to Bouar (for Cameroun) leave from the *gare routière* about four km out along the Ave de l'Indépendence early in the mornings between 6 and 7 am. They first cruise along the Ave du Lt Koudoukou to the Km 5 market and back to the Ave de l'Indépendence looking for more passengers before leaving. They can also be caught at PK 12, where the paperwork usually delays them until 9 am.

Warning Bangui is a city of thieves and pickpockets so watch out! Don't wear jewellery, watches or carrier bags. Avoid groups on pavements and stay in at night as many travellers report that gangs roam the streets. Take taxis and don't walk around the streets.

Embassies There are embassies in Bangui for the following countries:

Belgium
    MOCAF, Ave du 1er Janvier
Cameroun
    Off Ave Boganda near the Boganda Museum
Chad
    Ave Boganda about two to three km from the centre
Congo
    Ave Boganda close to the city centre

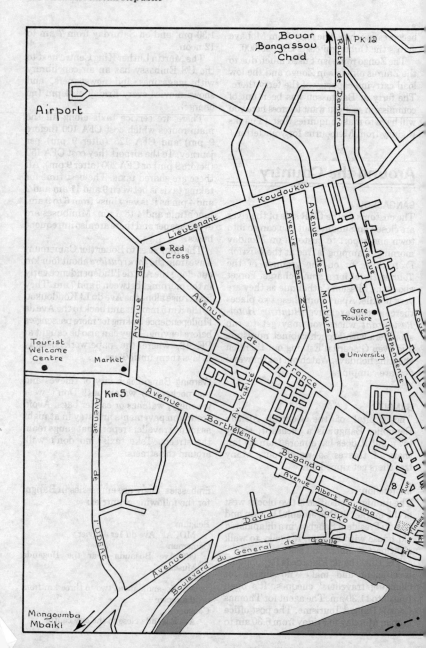

Airport

Koudoukou

Lieutenant

Red
Cross

Tourist
Welcome
Centre

Market

Km 5

Avenue

Avenue de l'UDEAC

Avenue de

Avenue des Martyrs

Avenue ben Zvi

Gare
Routière

University

Avenue de l'Indépendence

Av Yakité

France

Barthélemy

Boganda

Avenue Albert Fayama

David

Dacko

Rue de l'Industrie

8

Boulevard du General de Gaulle

Mongoumba
Mbaiki

Bouar
Bangassou
Chad

PK 12

Route de Damara

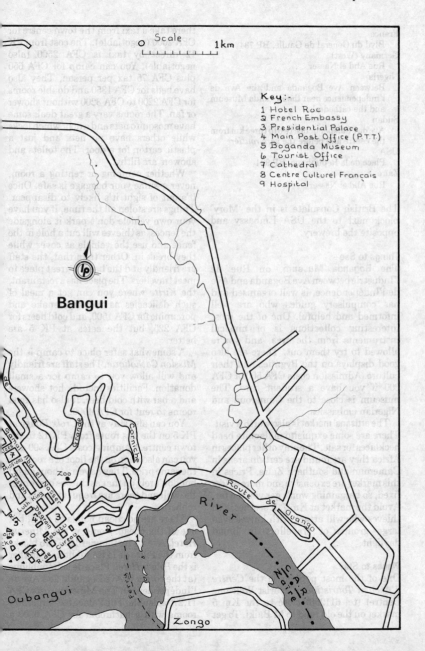

Key:-
1 Hotel Roc
2 French Embassy
3 Presidential Palace
4 Main Post Office (P.T.T.)
5 Boganda Museum
6 Tourist Office
7 Cathedral
8 Centre Culturel Français
9 Hospital

France
Blvd du General de Gaulle, BP 784
Germany (West)
Rue Abd el Nasser
Nigeria
Between Ave Boganda and the Ave de l'Indépendence near the Boganda Museum and the cathedral
Sudan
Ave de l'Indépendence two to three km from the centre and before the *gare routière*
USA
Place de la République, BP 924
Zaïre
Rue Abd el Nasser

The British Consulate is in the 'Mory' block next to the USA Embassy and opposite the brewery.

Things to See

The **Boganda Museum**, on Rue de l'Industrie between Ave Boganda and Ave de l'Indépendence, is well organised and has compulsory guides who are well informed and helpful. One of the most interesting collections is of musical instruments from the area, and you're allowed to try them out. There are also good displays on the Pygmies and their culture. Admission costs CFA 500 or CFA 300 if you have a student card. The museum is close to the Cameroun and Nigerian embassies.

The **artisans' market** is also worth a visit. There are some exquisite malachite bead necklaces for sale. The only other places in Africa they are found are certain areas in Cameroun and southern Zaïre. Prices in this market are expensive and more or less fixed, so bargaining won't get you too far. Avoid the market at Km 7. It seethes with thieves who will attack with knives even large groups of travellers in broad daylight.

Places to Stay

One of the most popular is the *Centre d'Accueil Touristique* (Tourist Welcome Centre) (tel 611256) close to the Km 5 market on the old road to M'Baiki. To get

there take a taxi from the town centre for CFA 2000 (negotiable). The cost from PK 12 direct by taxi is CFA 2500 (also negotiable). You can camp for CFA 650 plus CFA 75 tax per person. They also have beds for CFA 1350 and double rooms for CFA 2200 to CFA 3200 without shower or fan. The rooms vary a great deal: some have mosquito nets and a door which locks while others have no nets and just a plastic carton for a door. The toilets and showers are filthy.

Whether camping or renting a room, never assume your baggage is safe. Once it's out of sight it's likely to disappear. Things are stolen all the time. If you have your own vehicle don't park it alongside the fences, as thieves will cut a hole in the fence and use the vehicle as cover while they break in. Other than that, the staff are friendly and the bar is a great place to meet travellers. The place has a restaurant, the *Kirite* where you can get a meal of such delicacies as monkey, snake and porcupine for CFA 1500, and cold beers for CFA 225, but the cafés at PK 5 are better.

A somewhat safer place to camp is the *Mission Catholique*. The staff are friendly and will allow you to camp for a small donation. Facilities include hot showers and a bar with cold beer. It also has good rooms to rent for CFA 4000.

You can also stay at the *Croix Rouge* at PK 5 on the bus route from PK 12 to the town centre. Camping costs CFA 500 and you can also sleep on the floor of a room for the same price. They have a 24 hour guard but don't rely on that as thieves come over the wall and there are frequent thefts and robberies.

There are no cheap hotels as such, but one of the cheaper ones is the *Minerva Hotel*, Ave du 1er Janvier 1966 two blocks from the Place de la République. Another is the *Palace Hotel*, Place de la République (at the corner of Ave Boganda and Ave de l'Indépendence). The Minerva costs CFA 11,270 a double. The Palace has large, airy rooms with a bathroom for CFA 9500 a double, and also has a bar and restaurant. At the same price as the Minerva is the *Hotel de l'Indépendence*, Ave David Dacko two blocks from the Place de la République.

The *Hotel Roc* is well up-market at a minimum of CFA 12,000 a double. All the rooms have air-con and bathrooms. There is a bar, restaurant, swimming pool, dancing room and even a bowling green.

Entertainment

For something to do in the evening, try the bar of the *Hotel Safari* – once the most expensive hotel in Bangui but now derelict. It has a superb location on an isthmus which juts out about halfway across the river. With luck you might see hippos here. Beers are sold at normal prices – CFA 200 for a large chilled bottle.

At the *Novotel* you can use the swimming pool for CFA 1000 a day.

BIRAO

Birao is a small town near the Sudanese border in the far north-east of the CAR. You can stay free at the *Mission Catholique*, but the volunteers are not very friendly and the mosquitoes are ferocious. The water is in short supply and often dirty. Avoid using the village well or you'll make yourself very unpopular. There are no cafés and it is a very restricted market. Ask coffee shop owners to put meals together for you (meat and spaghetti dishes for CFA 200).

You'll probably find yourself at the mercy of the town's only moneychanger. Unless you bring in CFAs, it's going to be an expensive place to pass through. If you have your own vehicle this can be a serious problem – head on for Ndélé and try the Mission Catholique there.

BOSSEMBÉLÉ

For a place to stay there is an unnamed hotel on the main road, 200 metres towards Bouai from the market on the same side. Look for a block with four doors

and windows numbered one to four (there are many more rooms at the rear). All the rooms are singles but will sleep two and cost CFA 500 a room. They are clean and adequate, with paraffin lamps and bucket showers.

BOUAR

Bouar is an interesting small town on the road from the Cameroun border to Bangui and the area around it is dotted with megalithic stone monuments. It is the country's largest French military base. Keep a low profile especially at night as the locals can be hostile especially when drunk. You can change money at the pharmacy in the main square.

Places to Stay & Eat

The auberge *Chez Pauline*, next to the bus station, offers accommodation at CFA 2000 a double with haggling. Pauline is a big mamma who sits on a mat outside all day so your luggage is safe. If it's full, try the *Hotel des Relais* at CFA 2500 a double or the *Auberge Municipal* at CFA 1500 per person. There's also an unnamed auberge which has three very clean rooms for CFA 1500 each. It has bucket showers and electricity from 6 to 9 pm and the staff are reasonably friendly. They also have meals – 'offal and rice' – for CFA 600, and coffee with milk for CFA 50. Another hotel recommended in the past is the *Hotel Moura* which has four comfortable clean rooms.

There is a barbeque nightly in the market place but watch the prices.

NDÉLÉ

Ndélé is a small, interesting town near the Chad border in north-central CAR with an excellent market. You can stay free at the *Mission Catholique* which also happens to have the only shower in town.

National Parks

A start has been made to train rangers for a number of projected national parks to the east of the country. However, according to expatriates working on the scheme, by the time the areas are eventually opened to tourists all the game will be wiped out. The amount of poaching is incredible. It includes gangs from Chad and the Sudan as well as local entrepreneurs and CAR officials – in fact just about everybody. It's so bad in the east that a Sudanese gang gunned down a local mayor and several other people over a dispute about shooting game. It appears that the Sudanese are highly organised, use automatic weapons and shoot down virtually everything that moves. Sounds just like the Australian outback!

BOALI CHUTES

A few people have written in to recommend a visit to these waterfalls about 80 km north-west of Bangui. These can be impressive in the rainy season but the nearby hydroelectric station takes a lot of the flow. On Sundays though, the intake is turned off to give tourists an opportunity to see them as they originally were. In the dry season the flow is often reduced to 'a dirty dribble'.

There are many walks around the falls through mixed jungle and manioc fields with some traditional bridges (Y-shaped branches lashed together with wire and wood) in the area.

Places to Stay & Eat

The *Hotel de Chutes de Boali* costs CFA 3500 each normally but if it's not busy it is possible to negotiate the price to CFA 1500 for two people in a single room or CFA 2000 for three people in a double. There are also a number of unfinished *campement* huts at CFA 1500 but they are not lockable. Camping is at the discretion of the management.

There is a good variety of cooked food available but it is expensive. There is a small market in the upper village near the disused textile factory that has dough, bread, vegetables and rotisseried meat periodically available. Don't buy too much or you'll leave the villagers with nothing. Instead, stock up at the market in Boali before coming out here.

KEMBE

Equally impressive if not more so are the falls at Kembe, west of Bangassou on the Bangui to Bangassou road. There is an area cleared for campers which is free but there's no bar.

Chad

Ever since independence from the French in 1960, Chad has been torn apart by violent conflicts in which thousands have lost their lives. Far from bringing a resolution nearer, independence has brought the exact opposite. At various times Christians have been pitted against Muslims, northerners against southerners, tribe against tribe and one political faction against another. Arms, cash, training camps and headquarters-in-exile have been provided at various times by France, Libya, Egypt, Gabon and the Sudan to one group or another depending on their political colour or military fortunes. Both France and Libya have intervened directly with their own regular troops on more than one occasion. Alliances between various factions have been formed and broken with bewildering regularity, and all attempts at mediation by neighbouring countries, the OAU and the UN have failed miserably. N'Djamena, the capital, has been besieged by fierce fighting on several occasions despite agreements to demilitarise the area around it.

The latest round of conflict began as a result of the Libyan invasion of the Tibesti – the mountainous area of northern Chad – in late 1980. At that time, 3000 Libyan troops backed by tanks, artillery and war planes gradually fought their way south to N'Djamena where they defeated the troops of Hissene Habré, the leader of one of the strongest factions. The remnants of Habré's forces fled east towards the Sudan after destroying their headquarters and ammunition dumps, while Habré took refuge in Cameroun. Shortly after this, President Goukouni Oueddei made an official visit to Libya where it was announced that the two countries would work towards full unity. The announcement was greeted with consternation not only by the French but by many other Black African countries which viewed it as an annexation of Chad by Libya.

Their fears were probably genuine. Gaddafi is renowned for his abortive attempts at 'union' with other countries – Egypt, Syria, Tunisia and, most recently, Morocco – but Chad was in a different league, being politically, economically and militarily weak. Not only that, but it was no secret that Chad had important deposits of uranium, wolfram and cassiterite in the Tibesti, gold in Mayo Kebbi, and gold, uranium, iron and bauxite in the eastern part of the country as well as oil reserves in the Lake Chad region. Chad is also Africa's second largest grower of cotton.

To understand the factionalism that has split this country, it's necessary to appreciate that the imposition of French colonial rule on this area reversed the traditional balance of power. Before the arrival of the French, the Muslim kingdoms of Kanem and Baguirmi dominated the area and based their economies on the slave trade. The slaves were procured by raiding the Black peoples of the south who could offer little resistance because of their decentralised political structure based on the lineage system. The French likewise found it relatively easy to conquer the south, but the northern kingdoms fought long and hard and it wasn't until 1916 that the French brought this area largely under their control. Even then, fighting continued until 1930.

Having taken over the southern part of

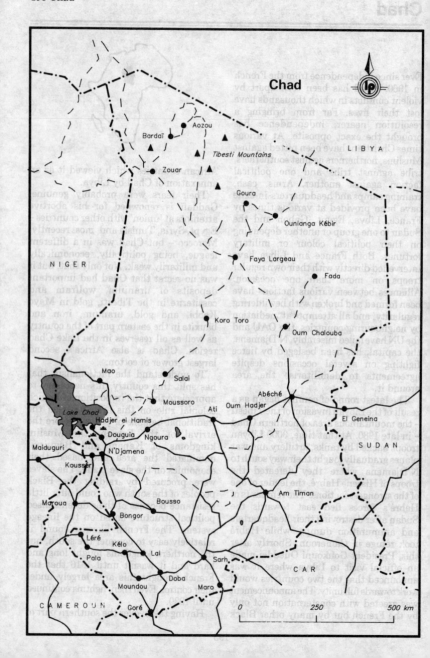

Chad

the country, the French introduced cotton and encouraged the development of a market economy which led to the breakdown of the old social order. The cultivation of cotton brought modest investments, the building of schools and the training of the local population. Nothing of this nature took place in the north until the 1950s. As a result, the educated people of the south were in a much better position to assume leadership of the nationalist movement after WW II.

The first nationalist movement, the Parti Progressiste Tchadien (PPT), set up in 1947, based its struggle around the slogan, 'No more cotton, no more chiefs, no more taxes'. Since this struck at the heart of the colonial system, France switched allegiance to the feudal Muslim forces of the north. After the PPT abandoned its stance in 1950 and integrated itself into the colonial structure, the French were able to install a compliant territorial assembly, known as the Loi Cadre. This body assumed responsibility for the country's internal autonomy, granted in 1956. All this took place in the era of Charles de Gaulle and his attempts to turn all French colonies into overseas departments of metropolitan France.

The Loi Cadre only had limited support and in 1958 the Union Nationale Tchadienne (UNT) was formed by trade unionists, students and intellectuals. It demanded complete independence, the ousting of the French-installed regime and the withdrawal of all foreign troops. When independence was granted in 1960, François Tombalbaye became the first head of state. Intent on making himself a dictator, Tombalbaye purged the government of supporters of its previous leader (Gabriel Lisette), declared a one-party state (the PPT), and arrested the leaders of the UNT. The arrests provoked a series of conspiracies which Tombalbaye conveniently used to bolster his own personal power.

Opposition to Tombalbaye's rule and the exorbitant taxes he imposed was met with violent repression. Against this background the Chad National Liberation Front (Frolinat) was formed at Nyala in Sudan in 1966. Frolinat was an alliance between UNT and the Chad Liberation Front (FLT). The FLT was a regional, conservative Muslim movement which already controlled resistance forces in the east of the country. The resistance movement spread quickly, especially in the north and centre, because of the harassment and contempt shown towards traditional leaders by the central government. The Derde, father of one of Frolinat's leaders, went into exile in Libya in 1966.

By mid-1968 the situation was serious and Tombalbaye was saved only by the intervention of France, which dropped paratroopers into the northern provinces and deployed a further 2500 troops in the country the following year. Tombalbaye was unable, however, to undermine Frolinat, which began to receive substantial aid from Libya after 1971 until power struggles within the Front and the effects of thousands of arrests began to split the movement. Sudan cut off aid to Frolinat early in 1972. At the end of the year Libya did likewise, following a secret deal with Tombalbaye in which Libya was allowed to occupy a part of northern Chad (the 114,000-square-km Aouzou Strip) in return for CFA 23,000 million in aid.

Tombalbaye managed to alienate even further the support he had left by seeking to erase the memory of French colonialism. All French street and place names were changed in favour of traditional names. Christian names were banned and all government officials, civil servants and ranking military officers were forced to undergo the *yondo* initiation rites of Tombalbaye's tribe. He was assassinated in a coup in 1975 and the government was taken over by General Malloum, whom Tombalbaye had imprisoned two years earlier on charges of plotting against him.

Frolinat, however, was suspicious of a man who had once led Tombalbaye's troops against it and refused to lay down arms. Libya resumed its support of the Front in 1976 and after successful offensives in 1977 and 1978 a fragile truce was put together with Goukouni Oueddei assuming the leadership. The truce didn't last long and was complicated by intensified French military involvement, which led to the setting up of a so-called Government of National Unity with key posts distributed equally between the supporters of Malloum and Hissene Habré. (Habré had been dismissed from the leadership of Frolinat in 1976 for his opposition to the Libyan occupation of the Aouzou Strip and had gone on to form his own army.)

A power struggle between Malloum and Habré was inevitable and broke out in 1979. Thousands of civilians were massacred in N'Djamena and the south of the country. The conflict quickly took on a decidedly regional and religious colour with the north pitted against the south and the Muslims against the Christians.

In the meantime, Frolinat was having its own problems with power struggles, so that by the time another truce was arranged in late 1979 there were at least five armies in existence: FAN (Habré), FAP (Oueddei), FAT (Abdelkader Kamougue), FACP (Abba Said), and FAO (Moussa Medela). Again the truce didn't last, and renewed fighting broke out in 1980 in which Habré's FAN, well supplied with arms from Egypt, was pitted against the rest, who in turn were supported by Libya. Habré's forces held their ground for quite some time but when they lost control of N'Djamena, France intervened on their behalf. Oueddei's Libyan-backed forces were quickly pushed back north of a line between Lake Chad and Abéché, and Habré was installed as president.

For several years after that a stalemate ensued with the country effectively divided in half. Neither the French nor the Libyans seemed willing to risk an all-

out confrontation and neither were willing to payroll their respective protégés to do the same thing, though there were constant probing raids by both parties.

In 1987, an attempt was made to resolve the conflict when Mitterand and Gaddafi announced their intentions to withdraw their respective forces from the country. The French duly withdrew theirs but Gaddafi reneged on the agreement. Relations between the two countries plummeted to an all-time low and, when Libya made a renewed attempt to push back Habré's forces shortly afterwards, French forces returned with a vengeance.

The Libyan ruse might have possibly worked had it taken place at a time when President Mitterand was not fighting for his own and his party's political survival in France. It was too provocative and demanded a strong response and in the end, proved to be Libya's undoing. Habré's forces, re-equipped by French and American arms, and supported by regular units of the French army, gradually pushed the Libyans back into the extreme north of the country. The *coup de grâce* came in late 1987 when the Libyans were routed and pushed back over the border leaving vast amounts of military hardware strewn across the desert.

It's unlikely that this military victory will immediately change the situation in Chad though it may seriously discourage Libya from further interference in the country's affairs.

Facts

GEOGRAPHY & CLIMATE

Landlocked Chad is one of the world's poorest countries and development is hampered by insufficient and primitive communications as well as by political turmoil. The Sahel drought which continued more or less through the 1970s and early 1980s probably affected Chad more than any other country by destroying centuries-old patterns of existence and cultivation.

The country has three distinct climatic zones. The south is tropical, with as much as 1000 mm of rain per year. The centre is a mixture of scrub and desert, and is the location of Lake Chad. The north forms part of the Sahara desert and includes the Tibesti mountains, which are some of the highest in North Africa (the highest peak is nearly 3500 metres). The dry season runs from November to May in the south, and while temperatures usually range from 20°C to 25°C, they can rise to 40°C just before the rains arrive.

PEOPLE

Chad, like the Sudan, stands at an ethnic crossroads where Arab Africa meets Black Africa. Unlike the Sudan, however, Black Africans are in the majority here and dominate the government and civil service. The north is populated by people of Arab descent as well as nomadic Tuareg and Toubou.

The population is about 5½ million.

VISAS

Visas are required by all except nationals of Andorra, France, Monaco and West Germany.

In Africa, there are Chadian embassies in Algiers (Algeria), Bangui (CAR), Brazzaville (Congo), Cairo (Egypt), Khartoum (Sudan), Kinshasa (Zaïre), Lagos (Nigeria), Tripoli (Libya) and Yaoundé (Cameroun). There are also consulates in Garoua and Kousseri (Cameroun). In places where there is no Chadian embassy, visas can be obtained from the French embassy.

In Bangui (CAR) a visa costs CFA 3000 for a stay of less than one month, or CFA 4500 for a stay of over one month, and is issued while you wait. A lot of questions are asked but the ambassador is very friendly. The embassy is on Rue de Boganda. In Yaoundé (Cameroun) a visa costs CFA 4000 for 15 days and is issued in

one hour. The official who deals with visa applications is one of the friendliest people you're likely to meet in Africa.

If arriving in N'Djamena by ferry across the Chari River from Cameroun you must visit both police and immigration (in the same compound) to go through entry formalities. The police may tell you that you don't need a stamp in your passport but it is a good idea to confirm this as the situation is liable to change.

An exit stamp must be obtained before leaving. If you're taking the ferry across the Chari River from N'Djamena to Cameroun, you can get the exit stamp at the boat terminal.

Until recently any travel east or north of the capital was forbidden except for the journey around the north of Lake Chad from Zinder-N'Guigmi (Niger) to N'Djamena because of the closure of the Nigerian land borders but these are now open again. Travel anywhere south of N'Djamena is possible without a special permit. The political and military situation in the country north of N'Djamena is, however, very fluid.

It's relatively safe to travel to Abéché but first obtain an *Autorisation Circulaire*. You get this by collecting a letter from the Ministry of Tourism near the Hotel Tchadienne, then taking it to the Ministry of the Interior about 400 metres down the road behind the PTT. ('It's like an American Express Gold Card – you don't even have to produce your passport with this letter!') To get the letter you have to specify your itinerary and the licence number of your vehicle. If travelling by public transport write 'en camion particulière'. The Minister of the Interior himself signs the paper you get, and he's a friendly fellow, who is always keen to meet travellers. The whole process may take a day or two (but can take weeks – it depends on your connections and why you are in Chad) so move quickly when you arrive in N'Djamena if you want to travel north.

There are very heavy searches on the

CAR-Chad border at Maro. They turn out *everything* and even leaf through books, etc. This is repeated no less than five times before you reach Sarh.

Other Visas
Central African Republic A 30-day visa costs CFA 5000 with two photos and is issued the same day.

Zaïre A one-month transit visa costs CFA 6000; a three-month, single-entry visa costs CFA 8000; and a three-month, multiple-entry visa costs CFA 10,000. Visas are issued in three days with no fuss. Don't worry about the list of requirements they show you (onward ticket, entry via Kinshasa, precise itinerary) as they are not enforced. No letter of recommendation from your embassy is necessary.

Other embassies in N'Djamena include those of Egypt, France, Nigeria, Sudan, USA and Zaïre. The British Honorary Consul is a Frenchman (Mr Roc of Socopao – near the airport), so when he is in France you just have to wait or go to the US Embassy.

MONEY
US$1 = CFA 284

The unit of currency is the CFA franc. There are no restrictions on the import of local currency but export is limited to CFA 10,000.

The airport departure tax for international flights is CFA 1200 on one-way tickets and CFA 2400 on return tickets to West Africa, Sudan and Zaïre. It is CFA 3500 on one-way tickets and CFA 7000 on return tickets to all other destinations.

PHOTOGRAPHY
To take photographs in Chad you will need a permit. Some travellers have been able to get these at the roadblock coming into N'Djamena. They cost CFA 5000 (though it's possible to haggle down to CFA 1000 if there's a large group of you).

Otherwise, get them from the Ministry of Information on the 2nd floor of a new building next to the museum and opposite the cathedral. Complete the relevant forms then take them with two photos to be stamped at Sûreté. After this go to the Treasury to pay a fee of CFA 10,000 (no student reductions). The Treasury (*Tresore*) is next to the cathedral opposite the Ministry of Information. When you've done all this, you return to the Ministry of Information and show your receipt. Collect your permit 24 hours later.

LANGUAGE
French is the official language but there are more than 50 local languages.

Getting There & Around

The most usual overland points of entry are by bridge or pirogue across the Chari River to N'Djamena from Kousseri in northern Cameroun (costs CFA 200 and CFA 2000 for a Land Rover); or by road from Bangui (CAR) to Sarh via Maro. It's also possible to enter from Cameroun at Lere and go by road to Sarh via Pala, Kelo, Moundou and Koumba. This road carries much more traffic than the Sarh to N'Djamena road and is an important route to northern Nigeria. There's also a new route opened up between Chad and Niger across the top of Lake Chad, but there's very little traffic along it.

AIR
Air Tchad is now operating again with flights to both Abéché and Sarh. There are also military DC4s and the light planes of Sonasut (sugar industry) and Cotonchad (cotton industry). In Sarh it's worth asking Sonasut pilots for a lift to Bangui (CAR) – said to be easy – or to Yaoundé, Garoua and N'Djamena. Most of the flights are free.

ROAD

The best time to travel by road is between November and May. During the rest of the year roads are often impassable because of flooding and deep mud. There are almost no sealed roads and there is no public transport system (buses, etc). From Sarh to N'Djamena there is at least one truck daily (ask in the market). The journey takes a day and a half and costs CFA 7500. The road is appalling with the exception of a 40-km stretch north of Sarh. You must get a stamp in your passport at Guelengdenl en route. A truck from Sarh to Lai costs CFA 5500.

Overland travel in Chad can be quite an adventure. One white traveller sent in this account of the journey from the CAR to Sarh:

This road's great! Babies burst into tears at your horrible, deformed face (it's white). Crowds of kids gather when you arrive and run away when the terrible white apparition speaks, saying, 'Ca va!' Gradually they all return. I beckon them to come and shake hands. They approach then run away again, four times in all. Finally one plucks up the courage to shake hands and runs away again as soon as he touches. After that, one by one, they come up to shake hands, beaming with pleasure. The younger ones are lifted up to shake hands by their sisters – just incredible. In another village I produced a camera and 50 kids ran into the picture wanting to be photographed. As you leave they all cheer. Totally undeveloped, there are no shops, not even the wooden suitcase sardines, bubble gum and cigarettes you get anywhere else in Africa. Just little round thatched huts with huge piles of cotton everywhere. Very picturesque.

Because of the long closure of the Nigerian land borders throughout much of 1984, a new route opened up across the top of Lake Chad direct to Niger. All you need in order to take this route is a *laissez-passer* from N'Djamena (see the Visa section). You first take a Land Rover from the Parc Mao in N'Djamena to Mao for CFA 10,000. From there take another vehicle to the small village of Baga Sola for CFA 5000. (Since Lake Chad hasn't filled up since 1975, there is an alternative route via Massagnet, Massakory and Bol to Baga Sola.)

Baga Sola is full of friendly people and the police are very likely to provide you with accommodation until transport arrives to take you to Liwa. From Liwa take another Land Rover to N'Guigmi (Niger) for a further CFA 5000. This journey involves driving across the dry bed of Lake Chad, which consists of thick sand. A 4WD vehicle with high clearance is necessary. Expect heavy but civil searches on the Niger side of the border. From N'Guigmi there are minibuses to Zinder for CFA 6000 along an excellent road.

Petrol is expensive in Chad. Expect to pay CFA 350 per litre in N'Djamena, and up to CFA 700 per litre north of Lake Chad. Don't attempt the journey without sufficient fuel, and remember that fuel consumption can be double what it normally is in this area.

Around the Country

N'DJAMENA

With all the fighting that's been going on for years in Chad, the capital has a kind of frontier mentality to it, though it remains good natured. Also, as one never knows when the next army is due to sweep through the place, there's plenty of music, whores and beer flowing.

Although literally every building outside the African quarter is riddled with machine-gun fire and shell holes, with many buildings totally destroyed, a lot of reconstruction is taking place. Despite this, the people are very friendly and the town, especially the African quarter, is active and bustling, with a good lively market.

Information

The poste restante appears to be

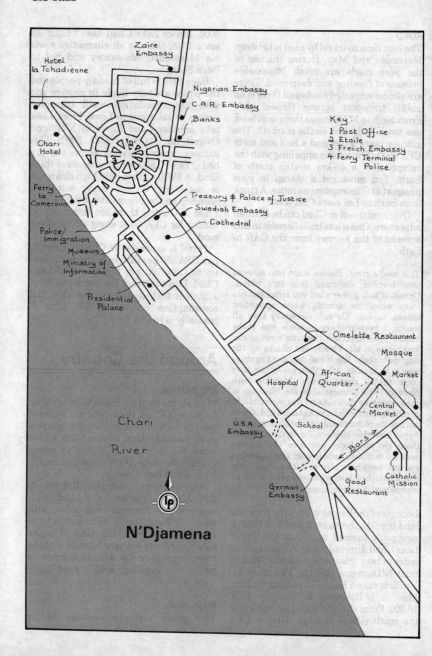

Key:
1 Post Office
2 Etoile
3 French Embassy
4 Ferry Terminal Police

Zaire Embassy

Hotel la Tchadienne

Nigerian Embassy

C.A.R. Embassy

Banks

Chari Hotel

Ferry to Cameroun

Treasury & Palace of Justice

Swedish Embassy

Cathedral

Police/Immigration

Museum

Ministry of Information

Presidential Palace

Omelette Restaurant

Mosque

Market

African Quarter

Hospital

Central Market

U.S.A. Embassy

School

Bars

Catholic Mission

Chari River

Good Restaurant

German Embassy

N'Djamena

competent and charges CFA 60 for each letter. The post from Europe arrives on Mondays and Fridays.

Taxis cost CFA 100 per journey. Bicycles can be hired for CFA 100 per hour.

Things to See

The **Museum** has reopened again with what exhibits remain after being looted. There are Tchadien musical instruments, weapons, initiation masks, plus a section on rock drawings and some reconstructed skeletons of elephants, giraffes and hippos.

Places to Stay

The *Mission Catholique* at Kabalaye in the African quarter costs CFA 3000 per person with breakfast. Mosquito nets are provided. There are showers, washing facilities, running water and a fridge with drinks for sale. On arrival ask to speak to Frère Michel at the Centre d'Accueil, the building to the right of the church. The only cheap hotel in town is the *Hotel l'Hirondelle*, very close to the market and the large modern mosque. It has a selection of rooms available for CFA 2500/3000/3500.

Camping is possible at the *Hotel La Tchadienne* for CFA 1000 per person per night. Beware of thieves. Forget about swimming in the hotel's pool: the pump broke down some time ago and it's now almost a wildlife reserve with toads and algae predominating. The food at the restaurant is reasonably priced (steak with beer for CFA 2000) and there is a bar.

Places to Eat

An excellent place to eat is the *Etoile du Tchad*, Ave Charles de Gaulle, which serves excellent steak & chips for CFA 1250 as well as luxurious fruit milkshakes for CFA 250 each. The staff are friendly too. It's near the mosque. There is plenty of food available in the African quarter. On the road in front of the Mission Catholique are many teastalls, rotisseries and restaurants/bars offering a variety of food and drinks. In the market fruit juices (lemon, banana, melon, mango, orange, etc) are liquidised with sugar, ice, water and milk powder. These can also be found at the *Hotel La Tchadienne*.

The coldest beers are reportedly available at the *Armana Bar*, Ave Charles de Gaulle.

There is exceptionally expensive imported food available at three supermarkets in the European quarter.

SARH

There is a free **museum** near the Mission Catholique which is small but of interest. Also, there's an excellent **workshop** run by artisans which is very interesting. It's on the road to the airport and has some of the best crafts in this part of Africa.

Places to Stay & Eat

The *Mission Catholique* will take you for CFA 600 per night plus CFA 100 to eat, but the pastor will probably only let you stay for one night. Other private accommodation is available. There's also an American couple about seven km from town who run a *Baptist Mission*. They apparently welcome travellers.

LAKE CHAD

With the Sahel drought still going strong, much of Lake Chad has dried up. Of the 250,000 square km of surface which it previously covered, only one third remains, and even if there are good rains, it will be years before it returns to its former size.

Chad has a long-running border dispute with Nigeria over this area and the drying up of the lake will not make resolution of it any easier. One of the main reasons for the dispute is that the area is known to hold oil reserves, and Habré has set great store by its potential to improve the country's economy. Drilling has been resumed.

It's possible to visit this area, but beware of guides who offer their services for what appears to be a song (CFA 5000, say). What they'll do is get you lost or stuck and when you arrive in Bol, they'll insist that you agreed to pay them CFA 100,000. If you don't pay, they'll take you to the police (or bring them to you) and you'll have your passport confiscated until you agree to pay.

Comoros

The Comoros consist of four main islands – Grande Comore, Moheli, Anjouan and Mayotte – as well as a number of islets. They lie between the northern tip of Madagascar and the African mainland. Like Madagascar, they were originally settled by people of Malay-Polynesian origin around the 6th century AD. Since then the population has become much more radically mixed as a result of successive waves of immigration by Africans, Arabs and Shirazis. The Shirazis were Persians from the Gulf area who came between the 10th and 15th centuries and who were responsible for setting up a number of rival sultanates on the islands. Their wealth was based on the slave trade and spices grown on the islands.

The Portuguese largely ignored the islands in their 16th and 17th century rampages up and down the coast of East Africa except for the occasional revictualling stop. They were scooped up by the French in the late 19th century during the European scramble for African colonies. The French conquest was made considerably easier because of the rivalry between the sultans and particularly after the Sultan of Mayotte sold his island to the French for a guaranteed annual payment. The rest succumbed quickly following naval bombardments.

Despite numerous peasant revolts, the French maintained an iron grip over the islands for well over a century. Political organisations and newspapers were banned and revolts suppressed with unrestrained military efficiency. No-one was allowed into or out of the islands without the approval of the colonial authorities. In the early days of the colonial period the islands were administered from Madagascar but they became a separate territory in 1947 with a form of internal autonomy granted in 1961.

Seven years later, however, a strike by local students led to mass demonstrations and the French were forced to allow the formation of political parties. Numerous parties were formed representing various factional interests ranging over the whole spectrum, from those demanding immediate and unconditional independence to those who vigorously opposed independence.

Tensions between the various political parties grew steadily over the next few years and, in an attempt to contain it, the French staged a referendum in late 1974. Overall, 94% of the population was in favour of independence though in Mayotte some 64% were against it. Less than one year later Ahmed Abdallah announced a unilateral declaration of independence while Mayotte's deputies cabled France requesting French intervention. The Federal Islamic Republic of the Comoros – minus Mayotte – was admitted to membership of the UN and the OAU barely two weeks later.

The French retaliated by withdrawing their US$18 million subsidy and 500 technicians. Economic collapse and political turmoil were virtually inevitable. Even before the French withdrew, the islands were barely ticking over on a subsistence economy and a threadbare administration. There were few auspicious signs to suggest optimism. The crunch came just one month later when Abdallah was overthrown in a coup by Ali Solih.

When he first came to power, Solih, an atheist despite his Muslim upbringing

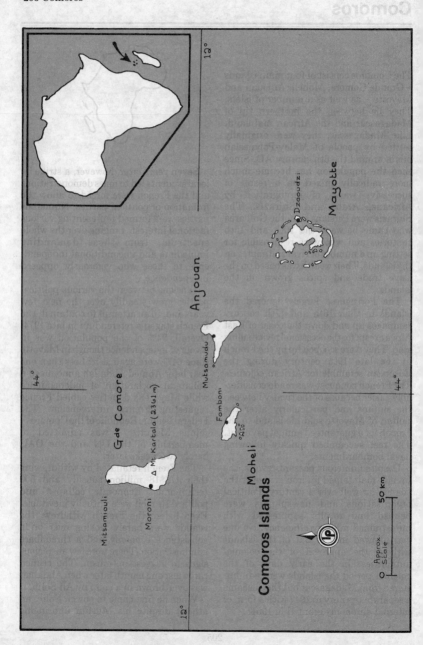

Comoros Islands

12°

Mayotte

Dzaoudzi

Anjouan

Mutsamudu

44°

44°

Gde Comore

Mitsamiouli

Moroni

△ Mt. Kartala (2361 m)

Fomboni

Moheli

12°

0   50 km

Approx.
Scale

and something of an idealist, appeared to be quite normal, and perhaps just what the Comoros needed. Determined to drag the islands screaming into the 20th century and away from colonial-induced attitudes, Solih set about his task with gusto. French citizens were expelled and their property nationalised, feudal institutions were attacked, women were unveiled, the traditionally elaborate and costly arrangements which were part of marriages and funerals were abolished, and the privileges of ancestry based on dubious claims of direct descent from the Prophet's family were likewise attacked.

Revolution was in the air and Solih seemed determined to outdo both Kemal Atatürk and Mao Tse Tung. The trouble was he brooked no opposition and used a rabble of illiterate youths graced with the euphemistic title of 'Jeunesse Revolutionnaire' to enforce his ideas. He dismissed the 3500 members of the civil service and turned it over to the youth brigade and jailed or murdered anyone with the intelligence or courage to speak out against his excesses. Petty criminals and anyone who could be labelled (rightly or wrongly) as 'counter-revolutionary' were dressed in rough sacking, had their heads shaved and were beaten through the narrow streets along with megaphone announcements of their alleged crimes. Even old people were not immune from this kind of brutality. Any ideology that might have been defensible in the early days quickly turned into nothing more than the power of the guns wielded by his teenage thugs.

Solih quickly turned into the living embodiment of the adage that 'Power corrupts; absolute power corrupts absolutely'. He had himself declared a prophet and was heard to tell his people at one rally, 'I am your god and teacher. I am the divine way, the torch that lights the dark. There is no god but Ali Solih'. He was clearly demented and, towards the end, refused to leave his palace for lengthy periods of time during which he went on whisky drinking binges and watched movies in the company of young girls drawn from the youth brigade.

Though the Comoran people took it all with remarkable passivity, something had to give soon. It came in the form of 29 white mercenaries led by Bob Denard. They were recruited by Ahmed Abdallah, the former president, and Mohammed Ahmed, a wealthy Comoran businessman, both of whom were living in exile in Paris. The mercenaries struck at dawn on 13 May 1978 whilst most of the 2000-man army were in Anjouan. Within a few hours it was all over. The army surrendered and people took to the streets to celebrate.

Abdallah returned to the islands two weeks later to a rousing welcome and Ali Solih was shot to death by the mercenaries allegedly for trying to escape. His body was dumped in his mother's back yard on the slopes of Mt Kartala.

The OAU reacted with outrage and refused to accept the new Comoran delegation to its summit conference that year. Meanwhile, Denard's mercenaries took over control of key ministries like defence and communications, and began to get the country back on the rails. The economy was denationalised, relations with France re-established and children sent back to school. The country quickly returned to some semblance of normality. Denard himself hung up his gun, took a Comoran wife and settled down to what he thought would become his home for the rest of his life. His dreams didn't last long. Though Abdallah had agreed to allow him to stay in the Comoros, Denard's presence was creating many problems of recognition for the new government among mainland African states and he was finally persuaded to leave following a lavish state banquet for him. Many of his fellow mercenaries, however, remain and this has not gone unnoticed in places like Madagascar, the Seychelles and Tanzania.

French aid to the island republic has resumed but, despite all the changes, Mayotte still refuses to join the republic and remains to this day a French overseas territory. How long it will continue to tread this path is anyone's guess, though it clearly benefitted from being outside Ali Solih's nightmare and is visibly more prosperous than the other three islands.

Despite the crazy years, the violence and the xenophobia, life has returned to normal and the islands are safe to visit. The people are polite, friendly and honest. The islands themselves are some of the most beautiful in the world and quite different from each other. There are coral reefs, sandy beaches, picturesque old Arab towns, luxuriant vegetation and even an active volcano (Mt Kartala). And not a tourist in sight. Do visit them if you have the chance.

Facts

CLIMATE
The dry season runs from May to October when the average temperature is 24°C. The rainy season runs from November to April and the temperature can range from 27°C to 35°C. Sea breezes make the climate very pleasant for most of the year.

PEOPLE
The population is about 500,000 the vast majority of whom are Muslim.

VISAS
Visas are required by all except French nationals arriving in Mayotte (since Mayotte is still a French overseas territory) but all travellers arriving by air are admitted with or without a visa. If you arrive without a visa, however, you must go to immigration in either Moroni (Grande Comore) or Mutsamudu (Anjouan) as soon as possible in order to get a visa. These cost CFr 2000 for four weeks. Those visiting Mayotte must be in possession of a French visa where necessary. Travellers must have an onward ticket before they will be allowed to enter the Comoros.

There are hardly any Comoros Islands embassies around the world (Paris and Brussels are the only two but you can probably get one from their representative at the UN in New York) even in neighbouring countries. Where there isn't one, the French embassy generally deals with their affairs.

The embassies of Belgium, France and Senegal are in Moroni.

Working in the Comoros
If you have any sort of degree or diploma there are excellent possibilities of getting a job. Wages are about US$300 to US$350 per month which might not be much, but then living is cheap.

MONEY
US$1 = CFr 450

The unit of currency is the Franc Comorien which is linked to the French franc on the basis of CFr 50 = FFr 1. This is exactly the same as the West and Central African CFA. There are no limits on the import or export of local currency and there is no black market.

There is only one international bank on the independent islands (BIC) and this is in Moroni on Grande Comore. Banking hours are Monday to Thursday from 7 am to 12 noon and on Friday from 7 to 11.30 am. They are closed on Saturday and Sunday.

The airport tax for international flights is CFr 5000.

TOURIST INFORMATION
The tourist agency Comores Tours, Services & Safaris (tel 2336), BP 974, Moroni, Grande Comore, puts out free information booklets on the Comoros in both French and English. These include a good map of the four islands and of the capital, Moroni. If you write (in French) they'll send a copy to your home address. Otherwise pick them up when

you get there. The agency offers various tours around the islands.

HEALTH

Cholera and yellow fever vaccinations are mandatory. You are also strongly advised to be vaccinated against typhoid and tetanus. As elsewhere in Africa, you must take precautions against malaria.

Tap water is not safe to drink.

LANGUAGE

The official languages are French and Arabic though most people speak Comoran, a variant of Swahili. Comoran is pronounced very much like Swahili except that 'ou' is pronounced as in French. There are local variants of Comoran on each of the islands but the following phrases will be understood everywhere:

good morning	*bariza soubouni*
good afternoon	*bariza djioni*
good evening	*bariza massihou*
goodbye	*namlala ounono*
How are you?	*habar?*
(response to this question)	*salama* or *njema*
How much is this?	*riyali gapvi?*
I don't speak Comoran	*mimi tsidji ourogowa shi gazidja*
Are you going to Moroni?	*gowedo moroni?*
I'm looking for a place to sleep	*gamtsaho pvahanou nilale*
I'm looking for a place to eat	*gamtsaho pvahanou nililye*
Have you anything to eat?	*kamtsina bahidrou ya houla?*
yes we have	*gassina*
no we haven't	*karitsina*
do you have rice?	*gagnina sohole?*
meat	*gnama*
water	*madji*
bananas	*zikoudou*
coconut (fresh)	*idjavou*
coconut (dried)	*nazi*

1	*motsi*
2	*mbili*
3	*drarou*
4	*nne*
5	*tsanou*
6	*dradarou*
7	*mfoukaré*
8	*nané*
9	*sheda*
10	*koumé*
11	*koumé na motsi*
20	*shirini*
30	*megomirarou*
40	*megominne*
50	*megomitsanou*
100	*ojana*
200	*madjanamayli*
300	*madjanadrarou*
1000	*shihwi*
2000	*shihwizyli*
3000	*shihwidrarou*

Getting There & Around

AIR

Airlines servicing the Comoros are Air France, Air Madagascar and Air Mauritius. There are twice-weekly flights by Air Madagascar and Air Mauritius which take the following route: Kenya (Nairobi)/ Grande Comore/Madagascar/Réunion/ Mauritius. Air France flies once weekly in either direction from Paris to Grande Comore via Jeddah and Dar es Salaam. The best place to buy a ticket on Air Madagascar or Air Mauritius is in Nairobi where a number of relatively cheap deals are available (see the Getting There & Around section in the Kenya chapter).

Air Comores services the internal routes and Mayotte. Their office in Moroni is in the terminal building at the old airstrip opposite the Hotel Karthala.

The international airport in Moroni is at Hahaya about 20 km from the capital. A *taxi-brousse* between the two should cost CFr 250 to CFr 500 though the drivers often ask considerably more from foreigners.

There may be an Air Comores minibus between the airport and Moroni so it's worth enquiring about this before taking a taxi. Taxi drivers will naturally hotly deny there is any such bus. True, it's mainly for staff but passengers can also use it if there is space.

ROAD

Land transport on each island is by *taxi-brousse* (Renault cars or Peugeot 404 or 505). You must bargain over the fares. From the centre of Moroni to the Itsandra Hotel should be about CFr 150 (five km). These taxis are fairly frequent but there are very few sealed roads on the islands.

BOAT

There are no regular boats from the African mainland at present. If you are interested in sailing to the Comoros the only place you'll find a boat is in Dar es Salaam. Enquire at the Tanzanian Coastal Shipping Line (tel 26192), PO Box 9461, Sokoine Drive, Dar es Salaam. The office is at the junction of Sokoine Drive and Mission St. They only do this run once a month at the most.

There are small boats which ply between the islands for very reasonable prices though they are often crowded. They usually sail at night. One of them is the *M'fano* operated by a man named Jeanot who is a really friendly person. He sails from Moroni on Grande Comore to Moheli and Anjouan regularly; sometimes to Mayotte and once in a while to Majunga on Madagascar island. Information about these boats can be obtained down at the harbour in Moroni and at a small office on the 1st floor on the main square between the post office and the 'supermarket' in Mutsamudu (Anjouan).

Around the Islands

GRANDE COMORE - NJAZIDJA

Njazidja is the Comoran name for this island. It's quite pretty being 65 km long with the islands' highest mountain, roughly in the centre of the island. This is Mt Kartala (2461 metres), a dormant volcano. The crater of this volcano is one of the largest in Africa. There are several other volcanic cones over 1000 metres high at the northern end of the island. Most of the coast is raw black lava with semi-submerged coral on the outer edge of that.

At the northern tip of the island the coral reef is more extensive and there is a beach. There are also regular stretches of coral down the eastern side of the island. The vegetation is an interesting mixture of coconut and pandanus palm, bananas and baobab trees. Further up the slopes of Mt Kartala there are plantations of ylang-ylang whose trunks resemble overgrown grape vines. Further up still there is rainforest nourished by almost constant cloud. There's surprisingly little bird life but many bats and spiders. The bats – with wing spans up to a metre across – often fly around even during the day. Mongoose may occasionally be sighted.

The villages outside Moroni are very down-to-earth and services are limited. There are few hotels outside the capital but you may be invited to stay with people.

Moroni is a very small capital city with a population of just 15,000. The main part is the old Arab town clustered around the harbour with its tortuous alleyways and tiny courtyards. Ali Soiih had the whole place whitewashed during his days in power but mildew is again returning. It's still very pretty. The waterfront itself is more Mediterranean than African with solid rock jetties enclosing a small harbour where wooden boats are tied up in parallel. All these boats are hand-built and they serve as dories to the ships which call at the island – larger boats cannot get through the coral reefs.

Things to See

Apart from a walk around the old **Arab**

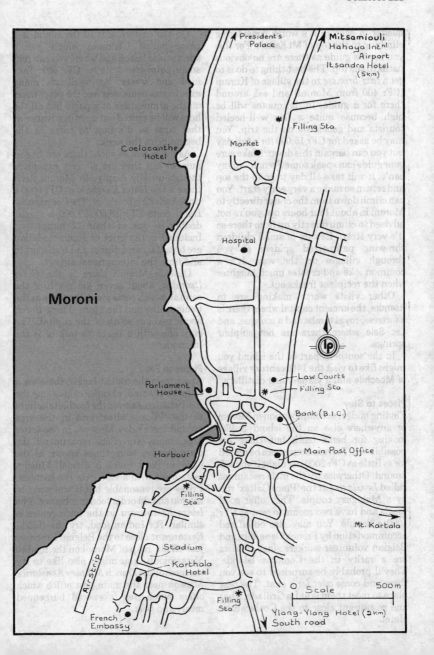

Moroni

President's Palace

Mitsamiouli
Intl
Hahaya Intl
Airport
Itsandra Hotel
(5km)

Filling Sta.

Market

Coelacanthe Hotel

Hospital

Parliament House

Law Courts
Filling Sta.

Bank (B.I.C.)

Main Post Office

Harbour

Filling Sta.

Mt. Kartala

Stadium

Karthala Hotel

0   Scale   500m

French Embassy

Airstrip

Filling Sta.

Ylang-Ylang Hotel (2km)
South road

quarter in Moroni it's worth considering climbing to the top of **Mt Kartala**. For this you need a guide as there are no obvious paths to the top. The best thing to do is to get a *taxi-brousse* to the village of Kurani (CFr 400 from Moroni) and ask around there for a guide. Initial quotes will be high because quite a few well-heeled tourists and geologists do the trip. You may be asked for CFr 15,000 for a full day but you can bargain this down. Make sure your guide can speak some French – many can't. It will take all day to go to the top and return so make a very early start. You can climb down from the crater directly to Moroni in about four hours but you're not advised to climb directly up from there as it's very steep. Beware of small children throwing palm-sized spiders at you through villages on the way. It's a common joke and creates much laughter when the recipient freaks out.

Other visits worth making are to **Itsandra**, the ancient capital where there is a fortress, royal tombs and a mosque, and **Lac Sale** where there are hot sulphur springs.

In the southern part of the island you might like to visit the 14th century village of **Mbachile** and a ylang-ylang distillery.

Places to Stay

Finding budget accommodation in Moroni or anywhere else on the island is like looking for hen's teeth but there are possibilities. Private houses can be rented for as little as CFr 2000 per night if you ask around. Otherwise try the little restaurant called *Le Glacier* at the 'Place Caltex' run by a Malagasy couple. They offer good meals and have two rooms to rent at CFr 4000 a double. You may also be offered accommodation by French Canadian and Belgian volunteer workers since tourists are a rarity in the Comoros Islands. They'll probably be surprised to see you there and come over for a chat. The best place to meet them is at La Grillade, a bar and restaurant close to the Coelacanthe Hotel.

On the eastern side of the island is a place called Chomoni which has a spectacular beach and where you can rent small palm-tree huts for CFr 500. Take food and water. At weekends many expatriates come over and the place takes on the atmosphere of a party but all the huts will be rented out days in advance at that time so it's best to come at the beginning of the week.

As for hotels as such, there are five in number but they are all very expensive though usually empty. In Moroni itself there is the *Hotel Karthala* at CFr 9000 a single including breakfast. The *Coelacanthe Hotel* costs CFr 18,500/27,000 a single/double in one of their 12 bungalows. Included in the price of accommodation are breakfast and dinner and transport to and from the international airport.

Outside Moroni there is the *Hotel Itsandra*, about seven km north of the capital, which costs much the same as the Coelacanthe and the *Ylang-Ylang Hotel*, about two km south of the capital. The only one with a beach to talk of is the Itsandra.

Places to Eat

Apart from the tourist hotels, there are a number of small, cheaper cafés along the road which runs from the football stadium to the 'Place Caltex' and in the area around the Friday Mosque. In the latter area, many travellers recommend the *Café Ikodjou* (sometimes known as the Café du Port) which is a small Muslim restaurant with a view over the harbour. Prices are reasonable but if you want to eat you should order food in advance. The *Islam Restaurant* in the town centre is similar. For Indian food, try the *Babou Restaurant* close to the Belgian Embassy just off our map of Moroni on the road to Mitsamiouli. You might also like to try the mess of the *French Military Assistance Mission* near the main post office which offers brochettes (skewered barbequed meat) and beer.

Entertainment

Movies are shown everyday at *Al Camar* cinema. The *Alliance Franco-Comorienne*, near the Coelacanthe Hotel, shows movies five days a week. You can hear Comoran music every Wednesday at 7 pm at the Ylang-Ylang Hotel.

MOHELI - MWALI

Mwali is the Comoran name for Moheli. This is the least populated of the islands with only some 20,000 inhabitants. The chief town is Fomboni with 3000 inhabitants.

For somewhere to stay ask for M Legrand by the airstrip. He has one or two rooms to rent at a reasonable price. Apart from this there is only the *Relais de Moroni* but it's expensive at around U\$25 per room.

Off the south coast of this island are a number of smaller islands with beautiful beaches and many sea turtles. You can camp on the beaches. Fisherpeople will take you over there and bring you back at a prearranged time or day. 'Fares' are negotiable.

ANJOUAN - NDZUANI

Ndzuani is the Comoran name for Anjouan. The population of the island is about 150,000 and the highest point is 1575 metres. The chief town is **Mutsamudu** (10,000 population) and the second is **Domoni** where the president of the island republic was born. Mutsamudu is notable for its beautiful Arab architecture. Domoni was formerly the capital of the islands and has a colourful market.

One of the few places to stay in Mutsamudu is the *Hotel Al Amal* which has a restaurant, bar and swimming pool but costs about US\$25 per room.

For a cheap place to eat, try *La Paillotte*, a small café just behind the Al Quitar cinema. There's also another cheap restaurant at the port end of the main alley.

At the south end of the island just next to a village called Moya is a very pleasant hotel of sorts with a number of 'bungalows' for rent at CFr 1500 a double. There's a restaurant too, and a very beautiful deserted beach. Except at weekends when foreign volunteer workers come here, you'll be on your own.

MAYOTTE - MAORE

Maore is the Comoran name for Mayotte. Mayotte is, of course, still a French overseas territory and therefore not part of the independent island republic. It voted to stay this way in a referendum after the other islands unilaterally declared independence in 1975. The island, though largely surrounded by coral reefs has the only deep-water harbour in the archipelago.

The main point of interest on Mayotte is the island's capital of **Dzaoudzi** built on a small islet off the coast. It's very similar to Moroni in that it has an old labyrinthine Arab quarter which is worth exploring.

Congo

After independence from France in 1960, the People's Republic of the Congo was for a long time the only unreservedly Marxist state in Africa, with its closest neighbours all more or less ideologically opposed to it. Since then, of course, it has been joined by all the former Portuguese colonies, plus Ethiopia and Zimbabwe. Most of the time it has maintained a nonaligned foreign policy while supporting African struggles for national self-determination, apart from a brief period in the early years of independence when the Youlon regime effectively supported Tshombe's attempted Katangan secession in return for promises of economic aid.

The radicalisation of its people goes back a long way and is rooted in the exploitation it was subjected to first with the slave trade and later by the French colonial authorities. The slave trade resulted in the establishment of a number of small independent kingdoms along the coast, the capital of each being a trading post. For the slavers, this was a very convenient arrangement since milking the interior for a regular supply of slaves was done by these local rulers. All the slavers had to do was turn up at one of these trading posts and take the slaves on board. The loss of population to which the present-day countries of Congo, Zaïre and Angola were subjected is nothing short of staggering and has been estimated at 13,500,000 over the course of three centuries.

When the slave trade was finally abolished, the coastal kingdoms gradually collapsed and the stage was set for the next attempt to milk the area for everything. In the 1880s the French explorer Savorgnan de Brazza floated a plan to divide up the whole of the Congo territory (which then included Gabon and the Central African Republic) between concessionary companies which would exploit the area. By expropriating the land from the local people, Brazza intended to force them into becoming wage labourers for the companies he had in mind. The scheme was only partially successful but resulted in dislocation of a large part of the population, followed shortly by famines brought on as a result of the neglect of food production.

The most accessible areas taken over by the French were bled white and it's estimated that the population was reduced by a factor of two-thirds between 1914 and 1924. As though that were not enough, what remained of the population was subjected to yet another form of exploitation by the construction of the railway to Pointe Noire between 1924 and 1930. In order to secure sufficient labour for the project, the French authorities mounted what were virtually press gangs. Since even the most elementary safety precautions were ignored during the railway's construction, thousands lost their lives.

Because of such conditions, anti-colonialism quickly took root. In the early years it manifested in the form of Matswanism, a quasi-religious movement named after Matswa, one of the first resistance leaders. By the end of WW II, however, Congolese youth, student and trade union movements had become closely connected with developments in the communist world, and resistance to the French took on a more stridently political colour.

By the time independence was granted

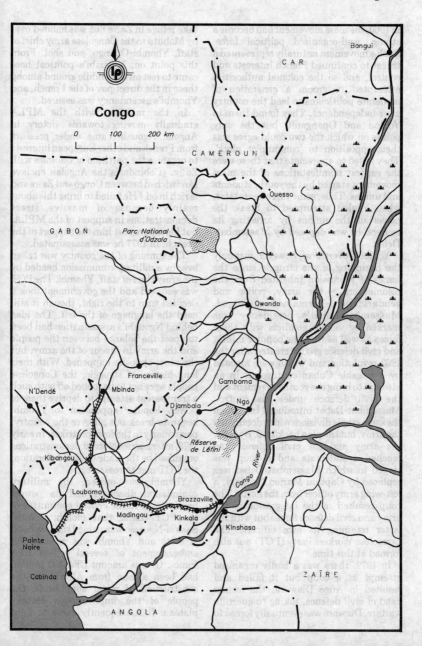

Congo

0   100   200 km

in 1960, the mass movement had become a strong, well-organised political force. Such a movement naturally represented a threat to continued French interests and control, and so the colonial authorities attempted to groom a generation of moderate politicians to lead the country after independence. They found them in Youlou and Opangault, but the only points on which the two could agree was their opposition to 'communist plots'. They failed to appreciate that these were the earliest manifestations of the mass movement started by the youth, students and unions. Thus, some three years later, when Youlou attempted to break the power of the unions by arresting its leaders, he was deposed by Massembat-Debat.

Youlou's overthrow, however, was only the beginning of the struggle since the forces of repression inherited from the colonial era – the army, police and gendarmerie – remained unpurged. Massembat-Debat's presidency was marked by violent conflicts with these forces as well as with the popular militia and civil defence groups created after the 1963 revolution and which were assisted by a sizeable Cuban contingent. In an attempt to bring the youth movement and the civil defence under his control, Massembat-Debat introduced into them the same ethnic divisions which dominated the army, but the plan backfired. By 1968, the army and the civil defence had reached a stalemate and a coup was staged in which Massembat-Debat was replaced by Captain Marien Ngouabi, a left-wing army officer from the north. The coup resulted in the integration of the army and civil defence forces but with the latter retaining its own officers. The Congolese Workers Party (PCT) was also formed at this time.

In 1972, there was a badly organised attempt at a coup but it failed and resulted in Ange Diawara, the former head of civil defence, taking to guerrilla warfare. Diawara was eventually forced to take refuge in Zaïre but was handed over by Mobutu to the Congolese army chief of staff, Yhombi-Opango, and shot. From this point on, Ngouabi's political base came to rest on the middle ground among those in the direct pay of the French, and Yhombi's ascendancy was assured.

In the mid-70s, with the MPLA gradually moving towards victory in Angola, Ngouabi came under pressure from French and other European interests to organise the partition of Cabinda with Zaïre. (Cabinda is the Angolan enclave sandwiched between Congo and Zaïre and is rich in oil.) He failed to bring this about mainly because of massive street demonstrations in support of the MPLA, but his failure cost him the support of the French. In 1977 he was assassinated.

The running of the country was taken over by a military commission headed by the army chief of staff, Yhombi. The PCT was eclipsed and the government took a decided turn to the right, though it still used the language of the left. The idea behind Ngouabi's assassination had been to upset the balance between the people and the army in favour of the army, but the exact opposite happened. With their long history of struggle, the Congolese people were not to be fobbed off with such a transparent attempt to deprive them of power. Popular opposition to Yhombi began to break out all over the country, particularly in the form of strikes. In early 1979, after a series of street demonstrations organised by the trade unions' federation, the PCT met to reassert itself.

Yhombi was ousted, the military commission dissolved and its powers handed over to the central committee of the PCT. Later that month, Colonel Sassou-Nguesso was named the new head of state and Yhombi was arrested for embezzlement of several billion CFA francs. Of this amount CFA 400 million had been a loan from Algeria for the construction of water supplies to the people of the impoverished Batéké plateau. It subsequently came to light that in the matter of corruption Yhombi had surpassed even the excesses of Youlou.

With the removal from power of Yhombi and his group, the army had finally been purged and power centred firmly in the popular movement. The new government included, for the first time, a number of younger ministers who were untainted by the corruption and opportunism of the previous generation of politicians. Some of these ministers were known to have close links with the USSR but the country was not about to become a Russian puppet. A French delegation attending the centenary celebrations in Brazzaville in late 1980 was given the red-carpet treatment, much to the displeasure of the Soviet delegation.

Though Congo is not about to abandon socialism, it has been forced to adopt more pragmatic policies in a bid to attract investment and loans from western countries. Foreign debt stands at almost US$2 billion and servicing the debt soaks up almost 40% of the country's annual income. Part privatisation of certain state companies is being considered in an attempt to make them more efficient and competitive, and Nguesso has successfully out-manoeuvred many of his Marxist hardline critics. François Xavier Kitali, the pro-Soviet minister of defence, was removed in 1984. The Soviet Union, on the other hand, still supplies the bulk of the country's military hardware, and the advisers it sends are essential to Congo's internal security.

Facts

GEOGRAPHY & CLIMATE
The narrow coastal plain is low-lying and dry, with grassland vegetation. Further inland the Mayombe and Chailou highlands and plateaus are forested and deeply dissected with gorges and valleys. The northern part of the country has equatorial rainforests with an average rainfall of 1100 mm. The rainy season lasts from October to May, with a brief dry spell around the end of December. Temperatures average between 21°C and 27°C. Road conditions are pretty poor. There are no sealed roads outside Brazzaville, the capital. Roads are frequently closed during the rainy season to protect the surface.

PEOPLE
The main tribal groups are the Vili, Kongo, Teke, M'Bochi and Sanga. There are sizeable minorities of Gabonese and Europeans (mainly French). The population is about two million.

VISAS
Visas are required by all except nationals of France. Even if you are French, however, it's best to make enquiries at a Congolese embassy before arriving at the border because the regulations change from time to time. In Africa, there are Congolese embassies in Bangui (CAR), Conakry (Guinea), Kinshasa (Zaïre), Libreville (Gabon), Luanda (Angola), Maputo (Mozambique) and Yaoundé (Cameroun).

Depending on your nationality and where you apply for your visa, you may be given only five days, though 15 days is the usual with a fixed date of entry. It will be hard going to get through the country in that time but make sure you do. You'll be in deep water if your visa expires. Visas in Libreville, Gabon, cost CFA 5000, require one photo and can be got in 24 hours, though it's best to allow 48 hours. Officially an onward ticket is required but no-one has mentioned having to produce one.

Visas cannot be extended.

There are police checkpoints every 25 to 30 km in the countryside, where you will be stopped and asked for your passport and vaccination certificates. These stops will take up to half an hour while they study all the stamps. By the time you get through the country, several pages of your passport will have been taken up with various stamps and half-page essays in ballpoint pen. Sometimes these stamps can attract a 'fee'. At Kibangou, for instance, expect to pay CFA 600 to get your passport back, plus CFA 2000 if you have your own vehicle.

Don't miss any of these police posts, or you could find yourself spending half a day explaining why you did. Communications between the posts are rudimentary to say the least, so you can always say they didn't give you a stamp though you checked in there.

You must register with immigration at Loubomo, fill in a form and hand across two photos.

You must obtain a *laissez-passer* (a sort of exit visa) from immigration in Brazzaville before you can leave the country. The office is next to City Hall. Take a letter from the hotel manager (or people you are staying with) stating where you are staying and why you have come to Congo. Get there at 8 am and your passport will be handed back at 2 pm. The cost is CFA 1000 or CFA 300 for students.

Avoid discussing politics with strangers in this country. There are many plainclothes police officers in the towns and cities. You'll find anyone who doesn't belong to the police or the military, however, to be very friendly.

Other Visas

Zaïre You can certainly get these in Brazzaville, but you're advised to get them elsewhere. The reason for this is that in order to take the ferry between Brazzaville and Kinshasa you may need, in addition to your visa, a *laissez-passer* issued by the Zaïre Embassy. In the past they would only issue this if you obtained your visa elsewhere. A lot of travellers were caught out on this one and had to take the flight. Recent reports, however, suggest this no longer applies (see the

Zaïre chapter for further details) and that there are no hassles at all.

MONEY
US$1 = CFA 260

The unit of currency is the CFA franc. The import of local currency is unrestricted but export is limited to CFA 10,000. Inflation is high.

Zaïres can be exchanged for CFA in the dock area.

Getting There & Around

The three points of entry are from the CAR, Gabon and Zaïre. The normal route from Gabon is by road from N'Dendé to Kibangou and from there to Loubomo, where there is a choice of road or rail to Pointe Noire (on the coast) or Brazzaville.

ROAD
There are occasional trucks and jeeps south from N'Dendé to the border, but most of them don't cross. However, there is usually a beer truck from N'Dendé to Loubomo on Tuesday and Friday which stops at every bar en route and takes one or two days. It costs CFA 6500. If you get dumped at the border it's a two-km walk from there to the first Congolese village – Moussogo – where you can stay in a room behind the general store for CFA 500 per person (bed and mosquito net).

From Moussogo there is a twice-weekly beer truck which goes as far south as Kibangou, stopping at every village en route and taking two days. Every stop involves a celebration and you'll be too drunk to notice the passage of time! Once in Kibangou there are plenty of trucks and taxis available to take you further south (the journey from Kibangou to Loubomo is particularly beautiful and the people friendly and unassuming). Many people find they have to do a lot of walking between N'Dendé and Kibangou.

TRAIN

The railway runs between Brazzaville and Pointe Noire. There are daily trains in either direction. The trains which have 1st and 2nd class are faster if there are no complications, and take between 12 and 24 hours. The trains which have only 3rd class take between 20 and 24 hours. Student reductions of 50% are available on the fares. Derailments are frequent and can often put the system out of action for weeks at a time, so don't rely on it. The fares from Brazzaville to Pointe Noire are CFA 12,000 (1st class), CFA 6325 (2nd class) and CFA 3160 (3rd class). Loubomo to Pointe Noire costs CFA 3200 (2nd class). These are full fares.

The day train between Loubomo and Brazzaville costs CFA 2500 (2nd class) or CFA 1700 (2nd class) for students. The fast night train, *L'Eclair*, offers 1st class couchettes on Tuesday, Friday and Sunday from Brazzaville; on Monday, Thursday and Saturday from Pointe Noire. There is a CFA 1000 supplement for this. Buy your tickets a day in advance and pay the extra CFA 250 to book a seat or you will be standing the whole way. When the gates are opened to allow people to board, all hell breaks out.

BOAT

Apart from flying, the only way to get to or from Zaïre is by ferry between Brazzaville and Kinshasa. It goes hourly in either direction between 8 am and noon and 2 and 5 pm. The journey itself takes about 20 minutes, but allow three hours, for the bureaucracy at each end. The fare is CFA 2500 or Z 100 (one-way or return). A 50% reduction is available to student card holders. Before buying your ticket you have to fill in a paper called a *fiche* but you can get this at the harbour.

If you encounter any hassles with the ferry, there is a flight between the capital cities but it's expensive. There is also a weekly ferry between Brazzaville and Bangui which costs CFA 85,000.

It's also possible to get into Congo from the CAR by pirogue but this is not for complete beginners. Details about this can be found in the CAR chapter.

Around the Country

BRAZZAVILLE

This is an interesting place, very green and sprawling with a **cathedral, mosque, markets** and the **National Museum**, all of which are worth visiting. The city was, for a time, the capital of Free France during WW II. The most interesting part of Brazzaville is the suburb of **Poto Poto**. The **Arts & Crafts Centre** is also very good. Ten km from Brazzaville are the **Congo rapids** – a worthwhile excursion.

Information

The tourist office (tel 810953) is in the Plateau district. The Zaïre Embassy is on 130 Ave de l'Indépendence and the French Embassy is opposite the main post office. Taxis around Brazzaville cost CFA 500 per journey (flat rate).

Places to Stay & Eat

Brazzaville is an expensive city for accommodation. Try the *Hotel Petit Logis* which is grubby but costs about CFA 8000 a double. If it's full, the *Hotel M'Foa*, Ave du 28 Août 1940, offers rooms for CFA 8500 a double. The *Olympic Palace Hotel* charges CFA 12,000 a double.

Other travellers have suggested that the *Eglise Kimbanguiste* has accommodation for travellers but we have no details. Two of the cheapest restaurants are *Chez Charton* (Vietnamese) and *Les Caimans*. The *Safari Snack* has also been recommended. In addition there is cheap food available in the markets.

One of the best things about Brazzaville is the nightlife and the local music dives.

POINTE NOIRE

It's hard to find accommodation because

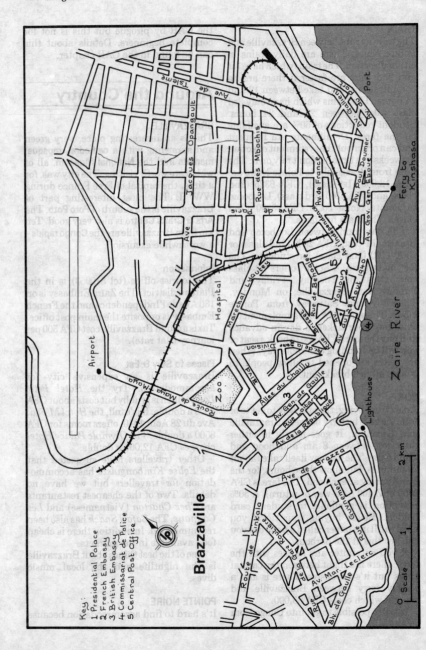

Key:
1 Presidential Palace
2 French Embassy
3 British Embassy
4 Commissariat of Police
5 Central Post Office

Brazzaville

Scale

0   1   2 km

Airport

Zoo

Hospital

Route de Mana Wong

Ave du 28 Aout 1940

Ave de la Base Division

Blvd

Allée du Chaillu

Av. Gen. de Gaulle

Rue Foteké

Av. de la République

Ave de Brazza

Route de Kinkala

Rue Guvremer

Av. Mar Leclerc

Blv. de Gaulle

Route de Gaulle

Rue de Kinkala

Ave Jacques Opangault

Ave de Tsleme

Rue des Mbochis

Ave de France

Ave de Paris

Av. de l'Indépendance

Av. Gen. Eboue

Av. Paul Doumer

Av. Galleni

Port de Port

Port

Ferry to Kinshasa

Zaire River

Lighthouse

Av. Youlou 1

Av. du 28

Rue de Behagle

Marechal Lyoutey

Rue Bassir

Av. de la Base Division

the town simply hasn't got enough hotels to house all the expatriates connected with the oil business. The cheapest hotels are in the Cité (African quarter) and cost around CFA 7500 a double.

Try either the *Atlantic Palace Hotel* at CFA 9000 a double or the *Victory Palace Hotel* which costs CFA 7500 a double. The *Mission Catholique* may also have room but it will still cost CFA 7000 for bed and breakfast. On the other hand, you might meet someone who will offer you a cheaper room if you ask around, especially in the bars. One group of travellers was offered free accommodation for a week here.

If you want to catch some local colour in the evenings, go down to the market. There's heaps going on – music and dancing in the bars seven days a week. Try *Parafifi*, a well-known bar in the Cité.

Djibouti

Previously known as the French Territory of the Afars and Issas, Djibouti was the last French colony on the African mainland to gain its independence (in 1977). It consists of little more than the port of Djibouti and a sliver of semidesert hinterland. The population of just over 300,000 is made up largely of Afars – ethnically a part of Ethiopia – and Issas whose links are with Somalia. There are also sizeable minorities of Somalis, French and Yemenis as well as about 30,000 refugees who fled there as a result of the Ogaden war.

The country's income comes almost entirely from port dues and the Addis Ababa to Djibouti railway – Ethiopia's most important outlet to the sea – but these are totally inadequate to finance the trappings of a modern state. Djibouti remains heavily dependent on French aid to the tune of US$200 million a year. France also retains a strong presence in the form of 10,000 resident nationals, 4000 of whom are military personnel.

The French moved into this area in the middle of the 19th century to counter the British presence in Aden on the other side of the Babel-Mandeb Straits. Agreements were made with the Sultans of Obock and Tadjourah giving the French the right to settle in the area, and in 1888 construction of Djibouti was begun. At the end of the 19th century another treaty was signed with the Emperor of Ethiopia which designated Djibouti as the 'official outlet of Ethiopian commerce'. This led to the construction of the Addis Ababa to Djibouti railway. The railway has been of vital strategic and commercial importance to Ethiopia ever since, and is one of the reasons why that country has refused to compromise over the question of sovereignty of the Ogaden with Somalia. It also explains why Ethiopia is hostile to a merger between Djibouti and Somalia.

The country's borders were established without any consideration given to ethnic links, language, trading patterns or even traditional grazing rights, and these issues continue to dominate politics. As early as 1949 there were anticolonial demonstrations by the Somalis and Issas who were in favour of the British attempt to reunite the territories of Italian, British and French Somalia. Hostility toward the French continued to grow and induced the colonial authorities to switch their allegiance to the Afars in 1958 in an attempt to hang onto the territory.

As a result of this switch, the French placed Ali Aref and his friends in control of the local government council. This didn't stifle opposition, however. There were serious riots in 1966 during the visit of General de Gaulle and again after the 1967 referendum which produced a 60.4% vote in favour of continued rule by France. The vote in favour of France was achieved partly as a result of the arrest of opposition leaders and the massive expulsion of Somalis. Many of those who were expelled went to join the Somali Coast Liberation Front, which increased its terrorist activities within the colony during the early 1970s.

In the end, Ali Aref's position became increasingly untenable. After huge demonstrations in support of the opposition African People's League for Independence (a moderate inter-ethnic party led by Hassan Gouled and Ahmed Dini), and pressure by both the Arab League and the

OAU on France, Aref was forced to resign in 1976. The French again switched allegiances, but tried to retain some control through setting up a government which would remain on favourable terms with them and by reluctantly conceding that granting independence was the only remaining option.

Independence has not bought tribal harmony to the former colony. Hassan Gouled seized on the initial Somali successes in the Ogaden war as an opportunity to remove Afars from key posts in the administration and security forces. When Ethiopia struck back with Russian and Cuban support, he was forced to reinstate many of them as well as readdress himself seriously to Afar grievances. Since then the government has signed new trade and commercial agreements with both Somalia and Ethiopia, and Gouled has added his voice to those attempting to get the two warring countries to agree to a truce and negotiated settlement.

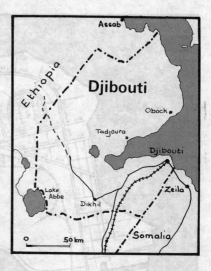

Facts

VISAS
Visas are required by all except nationals of France. A transit visa (*visa d'escale*) or a 10-day entry visa can be granted on arrival to nationals of Belgium, Denmark, Finland, Germany (West), Italy, Japan, Luxemburg, Netherlands, Norway, Sweden, UK and USA. There are very few Djibouti embassies – Addis Ababa, Jeddah, Mogadishu and Tunis are the nearest but, where there are none, visas can be obtained from French embassies.

In Sana'a (North Yemen) a visa from the French Embassy costs 40 Yemeni rial (about US$6), takes 24 hours to issue and is valid for 10 days. No extensions of the 10-day visa are possible.

Nationals of Israel and South Africa are not admitted.

If you arrive without a visa, you have to buy a transit visa on arrival. This costs US$12 for a three-day stay. You must have an onward ticket to get into Djibouti. If you don't they'll force you to buy one before issuing a transit visa. The cheapest is Djibouti to Hargeisa (Somalia) for US$70. Customs will stamp it 'non-refundable'. You can buy the ticket at the airport. No onward ticket is asked for if you arrive by dhow from North Yemen.

Other Visas
Somalia Tourist visas are easy to get and are valid for one month, cost US$10 and take 24 hours to issue.

MONEY
US$1 = DFr 175

The unit of currency is the Djibouti franc. There are no restrictions on the import or export of local currency. You cannot buy Somali shillings in Djibouti at the banks, but moneychangers on the street will do it. Know what the current rate is before you change. There are no moneychanging facilities at the airport.

Djibouti

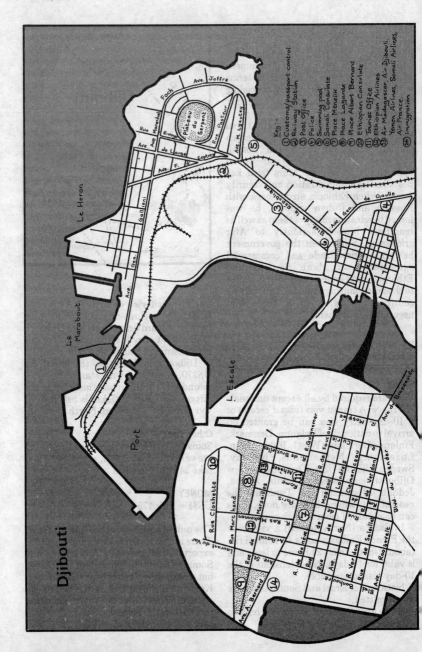

Key:-
1. Customs/passport control
2. Railway Station
3. Post Office
4. Police
5. Swimming pool
6. Somali Consulate
7. Place Menelik
8. Place Lagarde
9. Place Albert Bernard
10. Ethiopian Consulate
11. Tourist Office
12. Ethiopian Airlines
13. Air Madagascar, Air Djibouti, Yemen Airlines, Somali Airlines, Air France
14. Immigration

The airport departure tax for international flights is DFr 2000.

ACCOMMODATION
The only relatively cheap places to stay are the bar/hotels in the African quarter. They are about as rough as you can get and invariably double as brothels. Sleeping on the beach near the tennis courts in the French quarter might still be possible.

If you're only staying overnight try the *Djibouti Palace Hotel* which has rooms for DFr 5250 with shower. The *Hotel Relais* has also been recommended – it's somewhat more expensive, though it is the closest to the airport. There is good cheap food available near the market. Just walk along Place Mahamoud Harbi past the souvenir stalls and you'll find a series of cafés with good meals for around DFr 800.

TOURIST INFORMATION
There is a tourist office in the Place Menelik.

LANGUAGE
Arabic is the official language but French is widely used. Afar and Somali are also spoken.

Getting There & Around

These days, Djibouti is just a glorified truckstop for tourists and travellers en route to somewhere else by air or sea. Because of this, everything is geared to taking as much money from visitors as possible. It's a very expensive place and you're advised to give it a miss unless you are heading for northern Somalia or want to drop a heap of cash for nothing in particular. Ethiopia is virtually a closed country still, and tourists are prohibited from travelling on the Djibouti to Addis Ababa railway. Also, you cannot go overland to Somalia unless you have a visa for that country.

If you're heading into Somalia there are minibuses from Djibouti to the border at Loyoda which cost DFr 600 and take one hour. Cross the border on foot. From the Somali side of the border there are trucks to Hargeisa which take two days and cost SSh 300 (the actual price is SSh 500 but truck drivers are quite accommodating if you bargain). It's a dirt road and in pretty poor shape. There are no problems crossing the border and it's unlikely your baggage will be searched on either side. The Somalis are unlikely to want to see how much money you have and won't issue a currency declaration form unless you ask for one. It's a good idea to ask for one, however, because, although banks in Hargeisa and Mogadishu will probably cash travellers' cheques without one, they certainly won't do so in Kisimayo.

Djibouti has many dhows and you can get rides to Berbera, Sudan, Karachi, Aden, and the Persian Gulf. Also if you're coming from North Yemen and are prepared to wait, you can get dhows from Al Mokha to Djibouti for about 150 Yemeni rial (about US$27). They will even take cars and motorcycles. It takes about 16 hours and is a 'unique adventure'.

Egypt

Egypt, along with Mesopotamia, the Indus Valley and China, was one of the first centres of civilisation in the world. Its recorded history stretches back at least 6000 years to the time of the Pharaohs. Many of its kingdoms showed remarkable vitality, and the ruined cities and monuments which they left – Memphis, Karnak, Thebes, the pyramids, the funerary temples and tombs in the Valley of the Kings and Queens, Abu Simbel, Philae and others – are lasting testaments to their skills and inventiveness. Thanks to the dry desert climate, these remains are well preserved, though many of them bear the scars of vandalism which occurred at various times over the centuries. The Romans were some of the worst perpetrators of this.

Certainly the kingdoms fell apart from time to time as a result of decadence, religious conflicts and invasion – the Assyrians, Persians and Macedonians all conquered Egypt in their time – but it's a measure of the strength of the Egyptian culture that it was able to revitalise and absorb conquerors. Even after conquest by the Romans, who finally eclipsed the Egyptian dynasties, the Ptolemies were more Egyptian than Roman.

Until fairly recently, the Egyptian civilisation was regarded as part of the Middle East cultural genesis rather than of African origin, but this view is gradually changing. Though Middle East influences were absorbed as a result of trade and conquest, it's now known that the early Egyptian kingdoms had far more contact with Africa than was previously supposed. There is evidence that they frequently sent trading missions and expeditions to West Africa and as far south as the rainforests of the Congo basin, and influenced civilisations which were to spring up there later.

A fascinating study of the Dogon people

of Mali, for example, has revealed that they preserve intact certain aspects of ancient Egyptian religious rites and observances, notably reverence of the Dog Star, Sirius. A detailed description of ancient Egyptian history is outside the scope of this book, so before you set off it's a good idea to browse through some books on archaeology, particularly if you want to deepen the experience you get from the world-famous monuments to be found in this country.

Egypt lapsed into relative obscurity following its conquest by the Romans, and was to remain that way until taken by the armies of Islam following the death of the Prophet. Shortly after this event Cairo became one of the greatest centres of Islamic culture ever to arise, and scholars from all over the known world as well as West and Central Africa, came here to study. It's the legacy of this period which today makes Cairo such a fascinating city to explore.

Later on Egypt became a part of the Turkish empire which, at its height, included the whole of North Africa, Saudi Arabia, the Middle East, Greece and a large part of Eastern Europe. As the vitality of this empire waned, however, and the sultans took to being virtual recluses inside the Topkapi Palace at Istanbul, Egypt became autonomous under the rule of the Janissaries – eunuch mercenary troops of the Turks. Corruption, misgovernment and cultural decline set in shortly after this and continued until the government was effectively taken over by the British in the late 19th century, following Egypt's inability to finance its foreign debt.

The 19th century was a time of rivalry between the British and French for political control and trading concessions in the country, and it was during this century that de Lesseps conceived of and built the Suez Canal. The canal has been one of the country's biggest money-spinners ever since, though until it was nationalised in the 1950s, the British and French shareholders in the company creamed off a large percentage of the income.

The founder of the modern nation was Colonel Abdel Nasser, who overthrew the corrupt and effete monarchy in a military coup in 1952. A fervent nationalist and a tough negotiator, Nasser became one of the most prominent politicians of the third world. By making skilful use of the rivalry between the Americans and Russians, he was able to attract the aid he needed for the construction of the Aswan Dam as well as to acquire the military hardware required for the various wars against Israel. During his time there were numerous attempts at federation or unification with other Arab states – notably with Syria and Iraq – but these fell through and for many years the name, United Arab Republic, survived as the official name of Egypt. Similar mergers have been proposed with Libya and Sudan since then but nothing has come of them. Indeed, relations with Libya have deteriorated so far at times that war has seemed inevitable. Relations have remained tense since the 1978 Camp David peace treaty with Israel, and Libya misses no opportunity to pour vitriol on the Egyptian regime.

The wars with Israel have had a devastating effect on the country's economy, diverting much-needed funds for development into military hardware. They also resulted in the closure of the Suez Canal for many years and the consequent loss of income as well as the occupation of Sinai (where Egypt's only oil wells are situated) by the Israelis.

It was Sadat, Nasser's successor, who was instrumental in getting together the peace treaty with Israel despite condemnation by every other Arab state. Though opposition has abated since the accord was signed, Egypt is now in the unusual position of having an open border and trade links with Israel and a closed border and no trade links with Libya. In order to bring about the treaty, Sadat expelled all Russian military advisors and technical experts and accepted an American aid-and-arms package. There have certainly been disputes and delays in the implementation of the accords reached in the peace treaty with Israel – there are still a few outstanding problems – but Egypt has regained the Sinai and is now in a position to concentrate on sorting out its internal economic problems.

Sadat's vision and willingness to compromise, however, eventually cost him his life. He was assassinated during a military parade by members of the Muslim Brotherhood – radical Islamic fundamentalists who have quite a following in Egypt and are dedicated to the overthrow of the secular state and its replacement by an Islamic fundamentalist state along the lines of Khomeini's in Iran. If they were to have their way, they would tear up the peace treaty with Israel tomorrow.

Leadership of the country since Sadat's assassination has been taken over by Murbarak, and though his policies differ in some ways from Sadat's, he seems determined to maintain a pragmatic attitude towards regional politics. He has also clamped down heavily on the Muslim Brotherhood. It seems too that relations with Jordan will soon be normalised and that Egypt may even be readmitted to the Arab League.

Ever since the Nile Valley was inhabited, people have been dependent on the annual flood and the rich silt which this brought in order to grow their crops.

As a result, the population is heavily concentrated along the banks of the Nile and in the delta region. The rest of the country – some 95% of the total – is an almost completely barren, flat plateau broken only by a few scattered but very substantial oases. The building of the Aswan Dam has stopped this annual flood and it may be, in time, that the fertility of the lower Nile Valley will deteriorate since the soil is no longer enriched by deposits of silt. On the other hand, the dam now allows irrigation of a far larger area of land than was previously possible. With a population of 48 million, Egypt desperately needs the extra food which the dam has made possible to grow as well as the hydroelectric power which it generates, but it has proved to be a mixed blessing.

The rich sardine shoals which used to be plentiful off the Mediterranean coast have disappeared and the Egyptian fishing industry with them. There has been an alarming increase in the incidence of bilharzia both in Lake Nasser – the 400-km-long lake created by the dam – and in the lower Nile Valley. It remains to be seen whether the dam will prove to be the panacea it was once hailed as.

Facts

VISAS

Visas are required by all except nationals of the Arab countries (apart from Libya) and Malta. Visas are available on arrival by air for most nationalities but you pay through the nose at E£18 (US$14 at the bank rate) plus the US$150 compulsory change so you're advised to get one beforehand. Nationals of South Africa are not admitted unless they hold a student card proving that they are studying at an Egyptian university.

There are Egyptian embassies in virtually all African capital cities and most other major capital cities around the world.

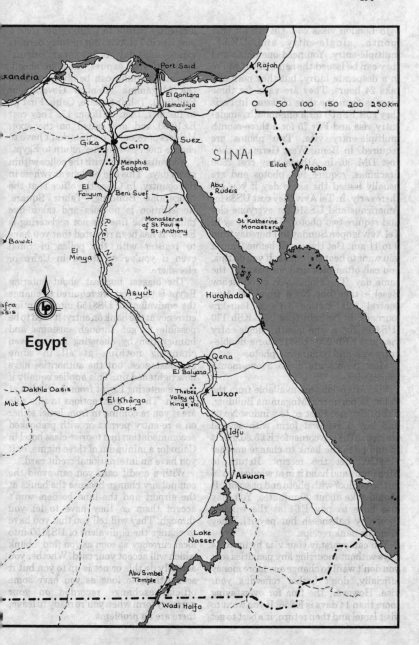

In London visas cost UK£16 for one-month, single-entry and UK£17 multiple-entry. You need one photo and they can be issued the same day if you're in a desperate hurry, but they normally take 24 hours. They are valid for three months from the date of issue. In Paris they cost FFr 60 for a one-month, single-entry visa and FFr 75 for a three-month multiple-entry visa. Two photos are required. In Bonn, West Germany they cost DM 30. In Athens they cost 2650 drachmas, require two photos and are usually issued the same day if you get there early. In Tel Aviv they cost US$8 for Americans and US$16 for everyone else and require two photos. The embassy in Tel Aviv is open Sunday to Thursday from 9 to 11 am. Get there well before 9 am if you want to beat the queue. If you do this, you can often pick up your passport the same day. The embassy is at 50 Rehov Basel – take bus No 5 from Tel Aviv central bus station (it's a four-km journey). In Nairobi they cost KSh 170 (US$10) for a one-month, single-entry visa and KSh 200 (US$12) for a double-entry visa and require one photo.

Most people are given a one-month tourist visa.

Visa extensions are available from the Police Department, Mugamma Building, Tahrir Square. First go to window No 35 and buy a renewal form with several stamps in the top corner for E£5.80. Fill it in and go to the bank to change another US$150. Get the receipt. Return to Mugamma and hand it in at window No 26 on the 1st floor with photo and passport. It should take about 20 minutes. You may also have to pay E£1 at the window (probably baksheesh but pay it). They keep the bank receipt.

You can overstay your visa by up to 14 days without incurring any penalties so if you don't want to change any more money officially, don't bother renewing your visa. However, the fine for overstaying more than 14 days is E£56. If you want to visit Israel and then return, it's best to get a re-entry permit in Cairo rather than a new visa in Tel Aviv, but re-entry permits expire one day before your original Egyptian visa expires, so plan ahead. Re-entry permits can be obtained from the Mugamma (Central Government Building), Tahrir Square, Cairo. First go to Room 1, then to Room 17. They cost E£10.50 and are issued on the spot. Holders of re-entry permits don't have to change money when they return to Egypt.

You must register with the police within seven days. This can be done anywhere in the country. In Cairo the office is at the Mugamma Building, Tahrir Square. Registration is no fuss and takes five minutes. The fine for not registering is E£26. It has been reported that you have to register with the police in Sinai even if you've registered in Cairo or elsewhere.

The biggest bugbear about entering Egypt is that you are required to change the equivalent of US$150 into Egyptian currency at the bank on entry. It used to be possible to get through customs and immigration by changing less or even changing nothing at all in some circumstances, but the authorities have now tightened up. This applies equally if you're entering Egypt from the Sudan at Aswan. The only exceptions to this rule are if you're coming in from Israel either on a re-entry permit or with prebooked accommodation in a tourist-class hotel in Cairo for a minimum of three nights, or if you have an international credit card.

With a credit card you can avoid the compulsory change because the banks at the airport and the land borders won't accept them so they have to let you through. They will tell you that you have to change the equivalent of US$150 into local currency as soon as you find a bank which will accept your card. Whether you actually do this or not is up to you but it seems that, so long as you have some official exchange recorded on your currency form when you're ready to leave, there are no problems.

If you stay in Egypt for fewer than five days you are allowed to reconvert any excess local currency less US$30 per day of your stay. However, it's usually a big hassle to try and do so. Other ruses which have been used include going back to the airport the day after arrival and telling them you're about to fly out – you may have to produce a dated ticket to satisfy them, but you can always change this again after you have reconverted. You'll naturally lose the commissions involved in the various transactions. If you're going to Sudan, you cannot reconvert local currency at Aswan though you can exchange it for Sudanese pounds.

You do not have to produce bank receipts at the border or the airport when leaving. The only time you have to produce receipts is if you apply for a re-entry permit or a visa extension or if you want to buy an airline ticket. You cannot buy the latter without bank receipts to the full amount of what the ticket costs.

Forget about false bank receipts – you're playing a dangerous game and it's not worth the risks. There are several travellers in jail as a result of getting involved in this.

Warning

If you want to visit Israel and then intend to go to Sudan or any other Arab country, you'll have to buy a new passport in Cairo. The Israeli authorities will willingly put entry and exit stamps on a separate piece of paper which can be thrown away on return to Egypt, but you'll still have the Egyptian exit and entry stamps in your passport. Any careful Arab official who

notices these will know that you've been to Israel – and many of them are very astute about this.

The Sudanese Embassy in Cairo is well aware of the situation and will reject your application for a visa. Furthermore, they are now rejecting applications for visas from travellers with new passports issued in Cairo.

Most embassies in Cairo are aware or these problems and are helpful about issuing second passports but it isn't going to help you get a Sudanese visa.

Other Visas

Since Egypt has extensive diplomatic relations with the rest of the world, there are embassies of most countries in Cairo.

CAR The embassy is at 15A Corniche el Nil, Ma'adi. Visas cost E£10, require two photos and take 24 hours to issue. The staff are very friendly.

Ethiopia The embassy (tel 705133) is at 12 Midan Bahlawi, Dokki. A 30-day tourist visa costs E£6, requires two photos and an onward ticket and is issued in 24 hours. Overland entry into Ethiopia is not permitted. The only way you can get in is to fly into Addis Ababa. If you're only stopping overnight you don't need a visa.

Kenya The embassy (tel 704455) is at 8 El Medina el Monawara, Mohandiseen. Visas cost E£8, require two photos and take 24 hours to issue.

Sudan The embassy is at 3 Al Ibrahimi St, Garden City, and the consulate (tel 25043) is round the corner at 1 Mohammed Fahmy el Said St. Visa applications are only accepted on Saturdays. A visa costs E£10.10 plus three photos, and a letter of introduction from your embassy (the British Embassy charges E£13 for these; the American Embassy issues them free of charge). Visas are for a stay of one month and are issued in 24 hours. Your application will be refused if you have either a new passport issued in Cairo or your passport contains evidence that you have visited Israel.

Rwanda The embassy (tel 815651) is at 13 Midan Aswan, Agouza.

The border with Libya is closed so you cannot go overland from Egypt to Libya.

Working in Egypt

There are possibilities of teaching English in Cairo; many Kenyan, Ugandan, Filipino and Americans are doing this. One institute which is always looking for staff either part-time or full-time is the ILLI (tel 720431) Borg el Giza, El Kebly, Giza which has three branches and is run by a Mr Yakhe. The pay is good by Egyptian standards and you can earn up to E£120 a week. If you want to stay longer than a month, Mr Yakhe can probably arrange a work permit for you. Other jobs are advertised in the English-language daily *Egyptian Gazette*.

MONEY

US$1 = E£1.75 (official bank rate)
US$1 = E£2.19 (official tourist rate)

The unit of currency is the Egyptian pound = 100 piastres. Import and export of local currency is allowed up to E£20. There is a thriving black market on which you can get US$1 = E£2.25 for large bills (less for travellers' cheques) and UK£1 = E£3 (approximately) – less for travellers' cheques. It's very open and you shouldn't experience any problems, but beware of sleight-of-hand tricks and having the cash handed to you in an envelope. Insist on counting out the money yourself before handing over your dollars or whatever. The preferred currency is the US dollar, which earns about 2% more than the other acceptable hard currencies (pound sterling, French francs, Swiss francs, Deutschmarks). Cash gets you 2% to 4% more than travellers' cheques.

Don't bring in any other currencies.

Though they may be perfectly respectable in other countries, the black market rates are likely to be even lower than the banks' rates. Don't bring Eurocheques or Dutch Postal Money Orders as the exchange rates are lousy. The same goes for Australian dollar travellers' cheques – you won't find a bank in Egypt which will accept them. The best black market rates are in Cairo. The rates in Hurghada are lousy.

Make sure that you declare all foreign currency (including travellers' cheques) in excess of US$2000 on entry otherwise it may be confiscated on departure.

American Express will change US dollar travellers' cheques into US dollars cash for a 2% commission. Also, if you have an international credit card you can use this to draw US dollars at the Bank of America.

Currency declaration forms are issued on arrival. It's advisable to change some money officially at a bank and have it recorded on your currency form. There's usually no fuss about these when leaving.

International airline tickets bought in Egypt have to be paid for with Egyptian pounds bought at the official bank rate (not the official tourist rate) and bank receipts must be produced.

In the past, there was a lively market in false bank receipts which were used mainly to buy air tickets. You're advised to stay away from this market. Violation of currency regulations can result in court charges and jail and you wouldn't be the first person to be caught. And you can forget about altering genuine bank receipts. Most banks use indelible ink so you cannot alter them.

Twenty-four-hour banking facilities are available at the Nile Hilton, the Sheraton and other large hotels.

The departure tax for international flights is E£10.

Other Currencies

If you're heading further south, you may

well be able to pick up the currencies of the countries you intend to visit fairly cheaply in Cairo. One place that handles a lot of different currencies is Ragab's Bazaar next to the Café Riche, in the pedestrian alley on Talaat Harb St between the Golden Hotel and Tahrir Square. Another good place to buy them is in the small alleys around the Abu Simbel Hotel near Ataba Square. You could also pick up these currencies from travellers returning north – ask around in the budget hotels.

The best place for buying Sudanese pounds at present is at the Aswan boat jetty where you can expect E£1 = S£3. Anywhere else – including with shopkeepers in Aswan and at Wadi Halfa you can expect only E£1 = S£2 to S£2.50.

Transferring Money

Try not to have money sent to you in Egypt but, if you can't avoid it, have it sent either to American Express or Thomas Cook. The Bank of Alexandria has also been recommended. Don't have money sent in the mail.

Selling Things

It's a good idea to bring a bottle of duty-free whisky (you're allowed up to one litre). You'll have no problems selling a good brand for about E£37 to E£40 per litre (Johnny Walker Black Label, Chivas Regal or White Horse) and a cheapo for less. Cognac is also worth bringing in, but duty-free cigarettes are a waste of time.

POST

The poste restante in Cairo is notorious for its inefficiency and it takes on average 28 days for a letter to leave Cairo. Incoming letters can take weeks to get to the stage where you can claim them. There's also a fee for each letter collected. Use American Express clients' mail instead if you have their cheques or a credit card. Whatever else you do, don't have parcels sent to you here. One resident reports that parcels from the USA can take five months. All parcels are intercepted by the censors,

opened, inspected, closed after a fashion, billed and sent to the central parcel office in Ataba Square. You learn – if you're lucky! – of the parcel's arrival by an unintelligible and illegible piece of coloured cardboard that you notice kicking about on the floor of your hotel room or wherever you happen to live. If you know how the system works, or if someone tells you, then you make a time-wasting trek to the dingy parcel office with this piece of card. Someone will duly sift through the shelves of violated and decidedly derelict parcels and, with luck, pick out your parcel. Out will come the *daftar* and you'll be told how much you have to pay. You won't be told what the contents are, nor whether they've been destroyed, censored, thieved or just disappeared. You just have to pay up and take pot luck. Tell your friends to restrain their mailing activities.

GUIDEBOOKS

If you are planning to spend a long time in Egypt and want more in-depth information – particularly on the antiquities and other places to visit – then get hold of *Egypt & the Sudan – a travel survival kit* by Scott Wayne (Lonely Planet, South Yarra, 1987).

STUDENT CARDS & CONCESSIONS

An international student card is very useful in Egypt. You can get a 50% reduction on train fares (all classes). Cards can be obtained at the Histology Lab of the Medical University on Roda Island. Otherwise go to the 'SSS' and ask for a card. If you don't have a student card but you do have a Youth Hostels membership card, you can still get the discount on the trains – just show the ticket office your YHA card.

Antiquities Permit

This permit gets you into all ruins, museums, the Coptic Museum and the Egyptian Museum free. It is available from the Antiquities Building opposite the Police Sports Centre a few blocks from Abbasia Square. Go to the 1st floor between 9 am and 3 pm on Sunday to Thursday with your passport, two photos, student card and/or letter from your university saying you are an archaeology student and 20 pt of fiscal stamps (which are not available at the Antiquities Office). They will demand to see your passport to see when your visa expires as that is also when your permit will expire. Leave your papers and come back next day (though others have got it within 30 minutes).

LANGUAGE

Arabic is the official language but English and French are widely understood. There's also a large Greek minority in the cities.

Getting There & Around

INTERNATIONAL CONNECTIONS
Air

Many travellers fly into Cairo from Athens because there are usually cheap ticket deals available from one or another of the many travel agents around Syntagma Square. A one-way flight costs around US$105 depending on whether you have a student card or are under 26 years old. A recommended travel agent is Fantasy Travel (tel 3228410) 10 Xenofontas St (near Syntagma Square), 10557 Athens. It's run by a friendly and helpful bunch who will give you the under-26 discount regardless of your age as a rule. Speedy Ways Travel Agency on Aristotelous St have also been recommended.

Cairo/Athens with EgyptAir presently costs E£142 with 50% student discount. Bank receipts must be produced.

Student discounts of 25% to 30% may be available on Sudan Air and Kenya Airways, but it can take a considerable degree of persistence to get them. Take a photostat of your student card when you go to buy a ticket. Cairo/Nairobi with

Kenya Airways costs US$340 with a student card.

If you intend flying from Khartoum to Nairobi then buy your ticket in Cairo as the chances of getting the student discount there are far greater than in Khartoum.

Though not a discount in the strict sense, you can fly Cairo/Nairobi via Addis Ababa with Ethiopian Airways and stopover for one night in Addis with all expenses paid by the airline. You don't need a visa for this – they'll give you one on arrival. If you stay more than one night you will need a visa and the free night of luxury will not apply.

Flights to India cost about US$450 and it's difficult to find a discounted ticket. You wouldn't save anything either by flying back to Athens and buying a discounted ticket there.

If you're thinking of flying to northern Europe from Egypt, it's worth enquiring about charter flights from Eilat (Israel) to London. Some travellers have written to say this can cost as little as US$85.

Boat

For information on passenger ferries from Egypt to Greece, go to Minatours, Talaat Harb St, Cairo, behind the American Express office, or to Amon Shipping Agency, 71 Gamal Abdel Nasser Ave, Alexandria. These ferries have become quite expensive in recent years and you may find that they cost more than the air fare if you are entitled to a student discount.

There are no scheduled passenger boats between Egypt and Kenya or Egypt and India. There is a slight possibility of being able to find a free or work-your-passage lift to those places on yachts. Go to Port Said and take the ferry across the canal to the Yacht Club. Don't listen to anyone who tells you that you need a pass to get into the Yacht Club. All you need is your passport. With luck you may meet someone who is going where you want to go.

INTERNAL TRANSPORT
Road

In Cairo, all buses except those to Alexandria, the Western Desert oases and Sinai depart from the Ramses Station terminal. To Alexandria they leave from Tahrir Square. To the Western Desert oases they depart from the Al Azhar terminal. To Sinai they depart from the Sinai terminal which is about four km from Ramses Station and just less than a km from Abassiya Square. Bus No 69 from Ramses Square will take you to the Sinai terminal – about 20 minutes. Otherwise catch any bus to Midan Abassiya from where it's a 15-minute walk to the terminal. Details about bus services to the Sinai and the Western Desert Oases can be found under those respective headings. Try to reserve bus tickets in advance.

The main bus routes of interest to travellers are:

Cairo to Alexandria There are daily buses every hour in either direction which take about three hours. The fare depends on the type of bus you take. Ordinary buses cost E£2.50, air-con buses cost E£4 and luxury air-con buses cost E£7. They depart from Tahrir Square in Cairo. Reserve your seat at least a few hours in advance.

Cairo to Luxor There's a daily air-con bus at 5.30 am which costs E£6.50 and takes about 12½ hours. The bus stops for lunch. Try to book in advance otherwise you may find that it's full.

Cairo to El Minya There is a daily air-con bus at 6.30 am and ordinary buses at 7.30 and 8.30 am. The journey takes 4½ hours. The air-con bus costs E£3.

Cairo to Hurghada There are daily buses in either direction at 4 am (ordinary) and 9 am (air-con) from Cairo, and 6 am (ordinary) and 5.30 am (air-con) from Hurghada. The air-con buses cost E£10 and the others E£8. The journey takes about eight hours. You're advised to book at least one day in advance.

It can be frustrating trying to find the bus terminal in Cairo, so follow these directions: face the railway station in Ramses Square and take the one and only road bridge on the left-hand side that goes over the railway tracks. Once you're over the tracks, take the first set of steps on the right. When you get to the bottom, continue straight ahead for a few hundred metres – through the noise and confusion (stores and buses) – until you get to a green kiosk on the left (no sign). It has a sliding window facing Ramses Station and a slanting roof. Be there at 5.30 am or earlier. Wait in line, and when the man comes between 5.30 and 6 am, make your reservation. He'll give you a piece of paper with the date and your seat number on it. Near this kiosk is a tea shop next to a single tree. The bus will arrive at about 6.30 am. You pay your fare on the bus. Remember to call Hurghada by its Egyptian name of Ghardaka otherwise no one will understand you.

Luxor to Hurghada There are two buses daily in either direction (at 6 am and noon from Luxor). The bus stand is opposite the Horus Hotel. The fare is E£4 and the journey takes five hours. The buses are air-conditioned. Since the buses go via Qena, you can also pick them up here if there are spare seats. If not, there are three ordinary buses daily in either direction between Qena and Hurghada (at 4.30, 8.30 and 11.30 am from Hurghada). The fare is E£3 and the journey takes four hours.

If you'd prefer a service taxi, these are available all day at either Qena or Hurghada and cost E£2 per person (seven passengers to a taxi). They take about 3½ hours. A service taxi from Luxor to

Qena will cost about E£1. Going by service taxi instead of the bus will save you about an hour.

Alexandria to Mersa Matruh There are daily buses at 5 am which take nine hours and cost E£6. They leave from opposite the train station in Alexandria.

Train

Trains are the most popular form of transport in the Nile Valley because they are so cheap. Discounts of about 40% are available in all classes to those with student cards or Youth Hostel membership cards. Only 1st and 2nd air-con classes can be booked in advance. Ordinary 2nd and 3rd class tickets can only be bought on the day of departure, usually one hour before the train is due to leave. You can get onto any train without a ticket but if you do this in the air-con classes you'll be charged a supplement of E£1.50 in addition to the price of the ticket. Since there are rarely any spare seats on the main Cairo to Aswan line you'll be paying that supplement for the privilege of the floor so it pays to book a seat in advance. Booking three to four days in advance is usually necessary for the air-con classes on the Cairo to Aswan line. Two days is usually sufficient on the Cairo, Alexandria, Mersa Matruh line. You cannot book more than six days in advance.

First class is quite plush with three seats across and an off-centre aisle. The seats recline. It's always air-con but is twice the price of 2nd class air-con. Second class air-con is four seats across and almost as comfortable as 1st class. The seats recline. Ordinary 2nd class has padded bench seats back to back onto which six people are usually squeezed. It's comfortable enough for short distances and interesting because of the people and the vendors who get on at each stop. It's cool enough when the train is moving but gets hot when you stop because there's no

glass in the windows. Third class has wooden bench seats and is alright for short journeys but not for long ones. It's usually very crowded except on the Alexandria to Mersa Matruh sector.

On the main Alexandria, Cairo, Aswan line you get two tickets for each journey in either of the air-con classes - one for the journey itself and another for the air-con. On the reverse of the latter ticket is the seat, car and train number as well as the date. All these numbers are in Arabic so make sure you learn those numerals. If the air-con fails (and it sometimes does) you can reclaim the 45 pt which you pay for that ticket at your end destination. It gets incredibly hot in these classes when the air-con fails because the windows are sealed. On the Alexandria to Mersa Matruh line you just get one main ticket which has all seat, car and train information on the reverse side.

When you're buying a train ticket on the Cairo, Luxor, Aswan sector be prepared for it to take about an hour. All the ticket windows are labelled in Arabic and there's no information desk (except on the Cairo to Alexandria line). You'll have to ask others in the line if you're in the right queue for where you want to go and in what class. Above all, know what you want or others will try and push in. Queue jumpers generally relent if you remonstrate. Men and women queue separately. On the Alexandria line the newer layout and information office make booking a relatively quick affair depending on the size of the queues.

Cairo to Luxor & Aswan There are three daily trains in either direction at 7.30 am, 8 and 8.30 pm. The journey from Cairo to Luxor takes between 12½ and 15 hours. From Cairo to Aswan it takes about 20 hours.

In the opposite direction there's a morning train from Luxor to Cairo at 5.15 am. In the opposite direction there's a morning train from Aswan to Luxor at 9 am.

Fares on this sector are:

	1st class	1st class student	2nd class air-con	2nd class air-con student
Cairo to Luxor	E£12	E£8	E£6	E£4.10
Cairo to Aswan		E£9.85		E£5.20
Luxor to Aswan				E£2.20

Cairo to Alexandria There are frequent daily services on the Cairo to Alexandria sector. The journey time is three hours and the fare is E£1.80 (2nd class air-con).

Alexandria to Mersa Matruh On the Alexandria to Mersa Matruh sector, the trains depart Alexandria at 6 am (3rd class) and Mersa Matruh at 7 am (3rd class) and 11 am (2nd and 3rd class) daily. If you prefer to travel in air-con there is a train daily from Cairo to Mersa Matruh at 7.30 am.

In the opposite direction this train departs Mersa Matruh at 1.30 pm. Alexandria to Mersa Matruh takes seven hours. Cairo to Mersa Matruh takes nine hours. The student fare is E£3.50 (2nd class with air-con).

Boat

River Nile One of the things you must do when you're in Egypt is take a felucca (Egyptian sailboat) up or down the Nile between Luxor and Aswan. It's a very relaxing and memorable trip through beautiful countryside. Get a small group together and find a boat. The journey from Luxor to Aswan takes three to five days including stops at villages and antiquities en route. You sleep on the boat at night. In the off-season (summer) you could get one for as little as E£100 with haggling, though the first price quoted is likely to be around E£150. In the high season (winter) it will cost around E£200. If this is too expensive you could hire a felucca from Aswan to Idfu for about E£90 excluding food for a two-day trip. Food for the trip shouldn't cost more than E£4 per person per day. The captain will cook for you. Add to your costs E£5 per person registration fee which you must pay to the

police before setting off. Make sure you pay this. The Nile is well patrolled and there is a fine to pay as well as the fee if you set off without paying.

Feluccas are not luxury boats – there are no cabins and no toilets but they're great fun. Bring a sleeping bag if you go in winter otherwise you'll freeze to death at night and take plenty of water/bottled drinks unless you want to drink the water from the Nile. Make sure you stop off at Idfu, Isna and Kom Ombo en route to see the temples and the towns. Don't swim in the Nile – bilharzia is rife. Most feluccas take eight to 10 passengers.

TO/FROM ISRAEL

There are two ways of getting to Israel. The first is the road direct from Cairo to Tel Aviv or Jerusalem via Rafah on the Mediterranean coast. The second is from Sharm el Sheikh, Dahab or Nuweiba (all on the east coast of Sinai) to Eilat at the head of the Gulf of Aqaba via Taba.

The first is the route used by most travellers but it has the disadvantage that an exit tax for Egypt and an entry tax for Israel are payable at Rafah (the border). These are not payable at the Taba crossing. Returning from Israel to Egypt, however, everyone has to pay the Israeli exit tax regardless of where they cross the border. If you don't have an Egyptian visa or re-entry visa you will be admitted at the Taba border crossing (but not at Rafah) for E£6 for a one-week visa but it will be endorsed 'Sinai visa only'. On such a visa you won't have to change the usually obligatory US$150 into Egyptian currency at the bank but you won't be able to go anywhere other than Sinai – even if the visa allowed time for this.

On the Cairo to Tel Aviv route, the

cheapest method is to take a combination of local shared taxis and buses. This shouldn't cost more than E£11 and you should be able to do it in a day. On the other hand, the quickest way of getting to Israel is to take one of the direct tourist buses from Cairo to Tel Aviv. Depending on which company you go with (Galilee, Isis, Egged, Emeco, etc), this can cost up to US$35 or as little as US$22 but is usually US$25. Student discounts of 10% are available as well as youth and weekend fares which usually bring the price down to about US$20 one-way. The journey takes about nine hours. We've had occasional reports of bank receipts being demanded for these tickets, but this is usually only for round-trip tickets. Some of the services which these companies operate involve a change of bus at the border (eg ISSTA – a student travel agency).

There are also cheaper direct daily buses from Cairo to Tel Aviv which leave at 7.30 am from the Sinai terminal. They cost E£20 and take nine hours. There are also buses from this terminal to Rafah which leave at 7 am daily and cost E£7.

Whichever form of transport you take, you'll have to pay a departure tax of E£10.50 and an entry tax of E£2.50 when you return. Have some Egyptian currency handy or else pay in hard currency.

Details of the cheap way to Israel are as follows: go to Ulali Square (Midan al Ulali) near Ramses Square, Cairo, in the early morning anytime between 4.30 and 6 am. There you will find service taxis to El Qantara on the west bank of the Suez Canal. Let the taxi driver know you are aware that the fare is E£2 and get in. When it's full (seven passengers) it will leave. The journey takes about two hours. When you get to El Qantara, take the ferry across the canal (free and takes a few minutes). On the east bank you'll find more service taxis which will take you to Rafah (the border). These cost E£3 and take about 2½ hours. On the Egyptian side of the border you go through customs,

pay the E£10.50 departure tax then buy a ticket for the bus (50 pt) which runs between the two border posts – you are not allowed to walk. On the other side you go through Israeli customs. The time taken to get through both customs varies between 15 minutes and four hours but is usually around two hours. Once through customs you have a choice of shared taxi (US$5 to US$7) or public bus (US$3 to US$4, depart at 12.30 and 3 pm) to Ashkelon, where you change for Tel Aviv or Jerusalem. The journey between the border and Tel Aviv is usually about three hours.

Don't take a single taxi between Cairo and Rafah. This is usually more expensive and takes longer than the two-taxi trip because the taxis have to wait (sometimes for hours) for a special vehicle ferry to take them across the Suez Canal. You don't have this problem on the passenger ferry.

There are banks on both sides of the border at Rafah.

If you don't want to go through the US$150 compulsory money change a second time on return to Egypt make sure that you have prebooked accommodation in Cairo for at least three nights. All the tourist bus companies mentioned will arrange this. The cheapest is Masada Tours (tel 03 464517), 141 Ibn Gvirol St, Tel Aviv, opposite the Egyptian Embassy, and 20 Slomzion Hamalka, Jerusalem (tel 02 249889). They offer the Tel Aviv to Cairo bus for US$22 one-way or US$35 return plus US$25 for three nights bed and breakfast in a Cairo hotel. Buses depart Tel Aviv on Tuesday, Thursday and Sunday at 9 am and arrive in Cairo between 6 and 7 pm. Their offices are open Sunday to Thursday from 9 am to 6 pm and on Fridays from 9 am to 1 pm.

Very similar to Masada Tours is ISSTA (tel 02 225258), 5 Eliashar St off Jaffna Rd near Zion Square, Jerusalem. Their parallel agency in Egypt is Isis. The package deal they offer is a one-way bus fare and three nights in a one-star hotel in

Cairo for US$51 (US$59 if you want a return bus trip). Their buses leave Jerusalem on Tuesday, Thursday and Sunday at 7 am and involve a change at Rafah. In the opposite direction they leave the Marwa Palace Hotel in Cairo on the same days at 5 am.

If you are not buying one of the combination bus-and-accommodation tickets, then, before going to Israel, make sure you get a re-entry visa for Egypt in Cairo otherwise you'll be up for another US$150 compulsory money change.

There is a 20.60 sheckels departure tax to pay when leaving Israel.

You cannot go to Jordan from Israel unless your journey started in Jordan.

The route via Taba starts at Sharm el Sheikh and goes via Dahab and Nuweiba. There are buses at 9 am daily which cost E£4 and take four hours to Taba. On the Israeli side of the border there are city buses to the centre for US$0.25. In the opposite direction, the buses depart Taba daily at 3 pm (Egyptian time) and arrive Sharm el Sheikh at 7 pm. There's an Egyptian bank at the Taba border. No Egyptian exit or entry fees are payable at Taba but if you are coming from Israel you'll have to pay the usual departure tax.

TO/FROM JORDAN

There are many shipping lines which operate boats between Suez and Aqaba, some of them Saudi, some Jordanian and others Egyptian. The Jordanian boats are the *Farah* and *Caravan*. The *Farah* departs every three days leaving Suez about 12 noon and arriving at Aqaba about 8 am the next day. The fares are E£49 (deck class), E£53.50 (Pullman chair) and E£73.60 (1st class) plus E£9.15 port tax. Book tickets at De Castro & Co, Talaat Harb opposite Felfela's Restaurant. The *Caravan* departs Suez every three days and costs a little more – E£53.85 (deck class), E£57.85 (Pullman seat) and E£76.30 (1st class). Book tickets at Eastmar on the passageway between De Castro & Co and American Express.

Jordanian visas are available on the boats. Egyptian Shipping & Navigation Company also have boats on this route which are popular with Egyptian workers going to and returning from Jordan and Iraq where work is available.

There are also ferries from Nuweiba on the eastern Sinai coast to Aqaba operated by Egyptian Navigation Co. They usually sail twice daily except on Muslim holidays at 9 am and 4 pm, take about three hours and cost US$25.

If you need somewhere to stay in Aqaba, try the *Corniche Hotel* which costs JD 3 a double (about US$9). It's clean and has fans.

For travellers these boats present an alternative way of getting from the Middle East to Egypt without having to go through Israel (and the attendant visa hassles you will experience if you do this).

TO/FROM SAUDI ARABIA

There are three car ferries which ply between Suez and Saudi Arabia. The ships are the MV *Sharazad*, MV *Sindibad* and the MV *Saudi Moon*. There are at least two per week and they cost US$73 one-way. Book tickets at Misr Travel in either Cairo or Suez.

TO/FROM THE SUDAN

The most popular way of getting from Egypt to Sudan is to take the Aswan to Wadi Halfa boat down Lake Nasser. There are supposedly three ferries per week which depart Aswan on Monday, Thursday and Saturday but fairly regular breakdowns reduce the frequency of the service. The journey normally takes 24 hours. The fares are E£26 (2nd class) and E£56 (1st class). A bicycle costs E£6. The cabins are stuffy and uncomfortable and the air-con rarely works. There is no deck class any more.

Second class can be booked up weeks in advance so you need to plan ahead, though there appears to be a little-known 'tourist quota' of 10 tickets per boat. Try to buy tickets in advance in Cairo.

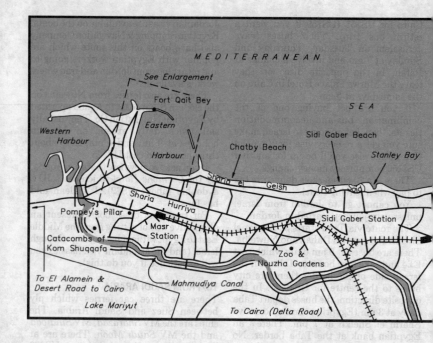

Otherwise you can buy them from Nile Navigation Co near the Marwa Hotel in Aswan. The queue for tickets at Aswan is long and slow but, as a tourist, you get preferential treatment so you can pick them up almost as soon as you arrive.

If you want to have any chance of claiming some deck space in 2nd class (better views, cool breeze and you can stretch out) then you need to get on board at the latest by 12 noon on the day of departure but preferably much earlier. Meals are available on board at E£3.50 (chicken and fuul) but water is taken from the lake so bring your own if you don't want to drink it or buy tea on board. Stoves are not allowed on deck since a fire started by one of these in 1983 was responsible for sinking one of the ferries.

There's no fuss about currency forms at Egyptian customs and Sudanese passport control is done on the boat. Make sure

your vaccination certificates are in order, as they'll be checked. If they have lapsed you'll be given a shot on the boat – the same needle does everyone.

Currency declaration forms are issued at Wadi Halfa (Sudan customs) and cameras are recorded in your passport. Make sure you get rid of any Egyptian currency before you get on the boat, but only buy enough Sudanese pounds to get you as far as Khartoum because the rates for hard currency are much better there. In Aswan you can expect E£1 = S£3 whereas at the boat jetty in Wadi Halfa you will only get E£1 = S£2 to S£2.50.

The Land Rover ride from the boat dock to Wadi Halfa costs S£5. Alternatively, the walk will take you about 1½ hours.

The boats often don't connect with the trains from Wadi Halfa to Khartoum so you may be in for a one to two day wait at Wadi Halfa.

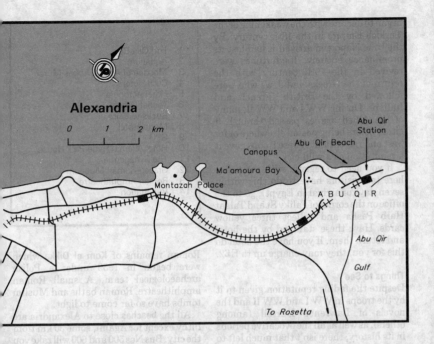

Alexandria

0   1   2 km

Montazah Palace

Canopus

Ma'amoura Bay

Abu Qir Beach

Abu Qir Station

A B U   Q I R

Abu Qir Gulf

To Rosetta

There's also a Port Suez to Port Sudan passenger ferry which departs every 10 days. It's a three-day journey and costs E£139 (tourist class) and E£46 (3rd class) including food. The boat calls at Jeddah but visas for Saudi Arabia are hard to get. Buy the ticket for the boat at Egyptian Shipping & Navigation Co, Talaat Harb, Cairo (next door to the cinema Radio) or in Port Suez at the junction of Sharif and Kasr el Nil Sts.

Those who have taken this ship down the Red Sea say it's quite an exciting trip.

Around the Country

ALEXANDRIA

Alexandria has had a long history as one of the most culturally important cities on the Mediterranean littoral. It was founded by Alexander the Great in 331 BC and was where his embalmed body was laid to rest eight years later after his conquest of Asia. It subsequently became the capital of Egypt under the Ptolemaic dynasty until the last of the line, Cleopatra, committed suicide and the city was taken over by the Romans. During the Roman period the city became the most important centre of Christianity in the Middle East and believers of that faith suffered heavily during the reign of Diocletian (early 4th century AD). Even after the Roman Empire had been split in half and Christian Byzantine emperors ruled Alexandria, the earlier persecutions were not forgotten so that when the Arabs swept into Egypt in 641 AD they were almost welcomed as liberators.

The city thrived on the cultural cross-fertilisation which resulted and only began to decline with the weakening of the Turkish Empire in the 18th century. By the time Napoleon arrived it had lost its prominence entirely. Its fortunes were revived in the 19th century with the return of the Greeks and Jews who were followed by the British, French and Italians. During WW I and WW II, many of the Allied armies passed through it either before being posted elsewhere or for 'rest and recreation'. These troops gave it a reputation as a wild city.

If you need to register with the police here (all visitors have to do this within seven days of arrival in Egypt), go to the office on the corner of Faliky St and Talaat Harb Pasha and collect three yellow cards. Have these stamped by the hotel and return them. If you have the hotel do this for you, they may charge up to E£2.

1	Fort Qait Bey
2	Aquarium
3	Mosque of Abu el Abbas Mursi
4	Cecil Hotel
5	Hotel Acropole
6	Tourist Office
7	Buses to Cairo
8	Metro Hotel
9	GPO
10	Hotel Ailema/Hyde Park House
11	The Synagogue
12	Graeco-Roman Museum
13	Roman Amphitheatre
14	Bus Station

Things to See

Despite the fading reputation given to it by the troops in WW I and WW II and the novels of Lawrence Durrell (among others), as well as all the evocative periods in its history, there isn't that much left to see in Alexandria. Much has disappeared completely.

Probably the most interesting place to visit is the Catacombs of Kom el Shogafa in the south-western part of the city near Pompey's Pillar. They date from the 2nd century AD and are on three levels though the deepest level may be inaccessible. Entry costs 25 pt with a student card. The charge for visiting Pompey's Pillar is the same, though hardly worth it. The Graeco-Roman Museum, off Sharia Horreya, is worth a visit if you like museums though the displays have been neglected and the whole place needs revamping and re-organising. It does, however, cover the historical period between ancient Egypt and the Arab conquest (there's no museum in Cairo which does this). Entry to the museum costs 50 pt for student card holders.

Not far from the museum, to the south, are the excavations of the Ptolemaic and Roman remains of Kom el Dikka which were begun in 1959 under a Polish archaeological team. A small Roman amphitheatre, Roman baths and Muslim tombs have so far come to light.

All the beaches close to Alexandria are filthy except for Agami, some 30 km from the city. Bus Nos 500 and 600 will take you there.

Places to Stay

Hotels with spare rooms can be hard to find in Alexandria during the high season – June to September.

The cheapest place to stay is the Youth Hostel, Port Said St, which costs 90 pt per person. It has basic meals but there is nowhere to leave a pack safely, so it may be better to stay somewhere else. To get there, take tram No 2 from Ramli Station to Chatby Beach. It's open from 7 to 10 am and 2 to 11 pm.

Two relatively cheap hotels to try where many travellers stay are the Hyde Park Hotel (tel 35666/7), 8th floor, 21 Sharia Amin Fikry, near the bus station, and the Hotel Acropole (tel 805980), 4th floor, 1 Sharia Gamal al Din Yassin, opposite the bus station. The Hyde Park is clean and comfortable and offers rooms at E£4.10/6 for a single/double without breakfast,

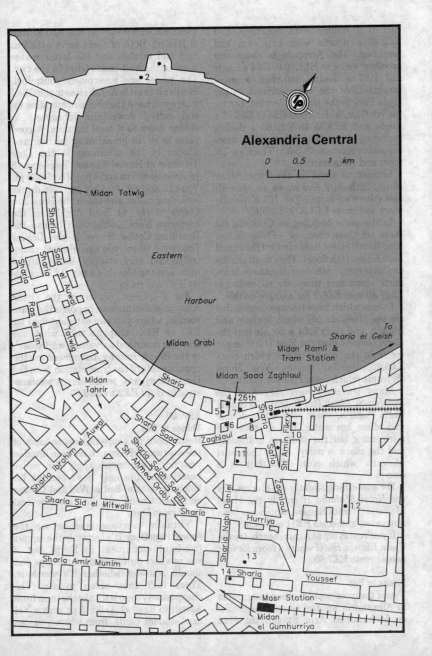

Alexandria Central

0   0.5   1 km

- 1
- 2
- 3
- Midan Tatwig
- Sharia Said el Auwal
- Sharia Ras el Tin
- Sharia Tatwig
- Eastern
- Harbour
- Midan Orabi
- Midan Tahrir
- Sharia
- Midan Saad Zaghloul
- Midan Ramli & Tram Station
- Midan Sharia Saad
- Sharia Salah Salem
- Sh Ahmed Orabi
- Zaghloul
- Sharia Saad
- 26th
- 4
- 5   7
- 6   8
- 9
- Sh Amin Fikry
- 10
- Sharia 26th July
- To Sharia el Geish
- Sharia Ibrahim el Auwal
- Sharia Sid el Mitwalli
- Sharia Amir Munim
- Sharia Zaghloul
- Sharia Nabi Daniel
- 11
- Sharia Hurriya
- 12
- 13
- 14   Sharia
- Sharia Youssef
- Masr Station
- Midan el Gumhurriya

E£7.70 a double with breakfast and E£9.40 a double with bathroom and breakfast. The Acropole is clean and excellent value at E£2.50 to E£4 a single and E£7 a double including a small breakfast. At the same address as the Hyde Park is the *Hotel Ailemma*, but on the 7th floor, which costs E£4 to E£6.65 a single and E£5.75 to E£9.60 a double including breakfast. There are more expensive rooms with bath. There's a TV room and restaurant.

Similar to these is the *New Savoy Hotel*, 26th July Ave above an open-air café (there's a large sign). It's a friendly place and costs E£4.30 a double.

In the same building on Corniche Rd there are three cheapies – *Philip House* (2nd floor), *Hotel Bahrain* (3rd floor) and *Lido House* (4th floor). They're all grubby and have dirty bathrooms but the beds are fairly clean and there are no bedbugs. They all cost E£5/8 for a single/double.

Others which have been recommended are the *Hotel du Nil* which is clean and friendly and costs E£4 a double and the *Hotel Gambil* near the East Harbour not far from the tourist office which costs E£5.20. Similar is the *New Hotel Welcome* which costs E£4 per night.

Many travellers have stayed at the *Pension St Mark* (tel 806923), 26 Sharia Gorfa Fugaria, which costs E£6 a double and offers hot water, use of stove and refrigerator but the staff are unfriendly and the place is noisy. Avoid the *Hotel Minerva* which costs E£4 but is a dump.

For something slightly up-market, try the *Hotel Mahaba* (formerly the Hotel Majestic), Orabi Square, which has been renovated and costs E£11 a double.

If you're staying at Agami beach, try the *Costa Blanca Hotel* where a room for four people costs E£7.60.

Places to Eat

Two of the most popular cheap restaurants in Alexandria are the *Ghad Restaurant* on Mohammed Azni St and the *Foul Mohammed Achmed* on Rue Abd Elfttah el Hadari. Both of them serve excellent fuul and falafels and the latter makes some of the best sandwiches in the city. The prices are government-controlled. Similar is the *Ala Kefak* close to the Ghad where you have the choice of standing up and eating downstairs (cheapest) or sitting down to a meal upstairs. A good place to go for breakfast or for beer and snacks in the afternoon is the *Café Triamon* at Ramel Station. Eggs cost 45 pt, croissants 8 pt and a pot of coffee 25 pt. You can also get good hot and cold drinks including coffee and tea at the *Brazilian Coffee Stores*, 44 Saad Zaghlul on the corner of Nabi Daniel St. Close to the Brazilian Coffee Stores is the *Delices Patisserie* where you can also get cheap coffee and very stodgey, sweet, sticky buns and the like. It's a big old colonial-style dining room.

For a splurge, try either the *Omar Khayyam Restaurant*, opposite the tram station, where you can eat good food for E£3 to E£4 complete with what one traveller described as 'vulture waitresses', or the *Broast Bamby Restaurant*, on the opposite side of the tram station from the Omar Khayyam, which serves western-style food for E£2 to E£2.50.

ASWAN
Things to See

Restrictions on tourist access to most of the sites around Aswan have been lifted so you no longer need apply for police permission. You only need permits for **Kalabsha Temple, Beit el Wali** and **Qartass** on the east bank of Lake Nasser beyond the Aswan Dam.

Virtually everyone goes to see the **Aswan High Dam**. It's certainly the largest (modern) monument in Egypt but if you're short on funds then perhaps you should consider whether it's worth it. There isn't that much to see. The cheapest way to go is to take the train from Aswan to Saad el Aali (15 pt with a YH card/student card), from where you can

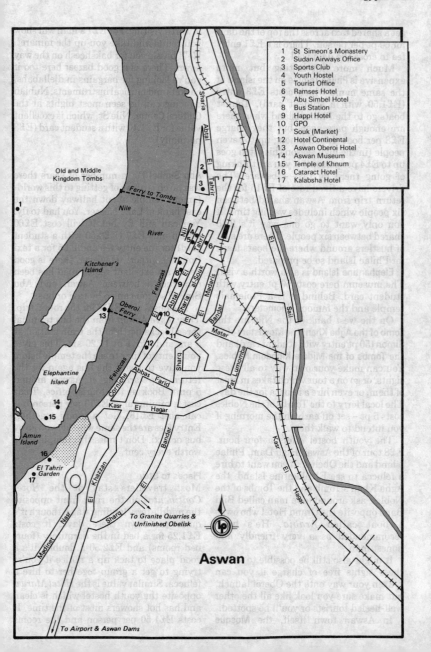

Aswan

To Granite Quarries &
Unfinished Obelisk

To Airport & Aswan Dams

1 St Simeon's Monastery
2 Sudan Airways Office
3 Sports Club
4 Youth Hostel
5 Tourist Office
6 Ramses Hotel
7 Abu Simbel Hotel
8 Bus Station
9 Happi Hotel
10 GPO
11 Souk (Market)
12 Hotel Continental
13 Aswan Oberoi Hotel
14 Aswan Museum
15 Temple of Khnum
16 Cataract Hotel
17 Kalabsha Hotel

get a shared taxi across the top of the dam for 60 pt per person. There is a E£1 entry fee to cross the dam wall.

Much more interesting but more expensive is **Philae Temple** on the island of the same name which costs E£3 entry (E£1.50 with a student card). Tourist boats go to the Philae Island when there are enough passengers but they charge E£8 per boat shared among up to seven people (in the high season this often goes up to E£4 per person!) If you are thinking of going there by taxi - beware! The drivers have a fixed rate of E£15 for the return trip from Aswan shared between six people which includes waiting time. If you only want to go one way it's E£5 shared between six people. There are a lot of hustlers around where the boats leave for Philae Island so be prepared.

Elephantine Island is also worth a visit. The museum here costs 50 pt entry with student card. Behind it is a Ptolemaic temple and the famous **Nilometer**.

On the west bank of the Nile are the **Tomb of the Agha Khan**, the **Monastery of St Simon** (50 pt entry with student card) and the **Tombs of the Middle Kingdom Nobles**. You can make your own way to all these sights, or go on a tour which takes in most of them, or even hire a felucca for the day. The local ferry to the Tombs of the Nobles costs 5 pt - set off early in the morning if you intend to walk there.

The youth hostel offers a four-hour, E£8 tour of the Aswan High Dam, Philae Island and the Obelisk. If you want to hire a felucca to see Elephantine Island, the Agha Khan's Tomb and the Tombs of the Nobles, ask around for a man called Bibi Bana opposite the Grand Hotel who owns a boat called *Arabia*. He's been recommended as a very friendly and honest man.

It might also still be possible to see all these sights free of charge if you can brazen your way onto the Oberoi launch, but make sure you look like all the other well-heeled tourists or you'll be spotted.

In Aswan town itself, the **Mosque** is worth visiting. For E£1 a man will show you round and take you up the minaret. He'll hassle you for baksheesh on the way down. There is a good **bazaar** here too if you're looking for bargains in djellabahs, baskets and musical instruments. Nubian dancing can be seen most nights at the **Cultural Centre**, Nile St, which is excellent value for E£1.10 with a student card (E£3 normally).

Abu Simbel For a number of years there was no cheap way of getting to this world-famous temple about halfway down the east bank of Lake Nasser. You had to fly. You can still fly but it will cost E£60 return plus E£7 (E£3.50 with a student card) for the entry fee and E£5 for a taxi from the airport. However, there is good news! An excellent sealed road has been constructed between Aswan and Abu Simbel so you can go by taxi or bus.

The buses cost E£16 for the round trip. They leave Aswan from the bus terminal three blocks north of the train station at 8 am and arrive at 11.20 am. This gives you plenty of time to see the temple before you have to board the bus again for the return trip (arriving at Aswan around 5 pm). Book at the tourist office. Taxis cost a minimum of E£13 per person but can cost E£16. Get a group together. Entry fees are the same whether you go by bus or taxi. Don't miss this temple - it's worth every cent.

Places to Stay

Most travellers stay at the *Hotel Continental* on the river front opposite the middle ferry landing stage, though it's quite run-down these days. It costs E£1.25 for a bed in the dormitory (four-bed rooms) and E£2.50 a double. It's a good place to tack up a notice if you're trying to get a group together to hire a felucca. Similar value is the *Hotel Marwa* opposite the youth hostel which is clean and has hot showers most of the time. It costs E£1.50 per person and the rooms have fans. It's good value and the manager is very friendly. Your gear is safe here. Don't, however, go to bed too early as it backs onto an open-air cinema.

The *Youth Hostel*, Abtal el Tahrir St (a three-minute walk from the railway station and opposite the Hotel Marwa), was, at one time, a popular place to stay but it's an absolute dump these days. It's filthy, the showers are a mess and the rooms are like an oven in summer. The staff are also reported to be unfriendly. Still, it only costs 60 pt with a YH card and E£1 for nonmembers. The hostel used to be open all day but now closes between 10 am and 2 pm and after 11 pm at night. There are no cooking facilities or meals available.

Also popular is the *Hotel Palace* which costs E£2 a single but is hard to find as it's hidden in the centre of town.

The *Hotel Minar* (in an alley opposite the youth hostel) at E£1.30 a bed has also been recommended. It has occasional hot water and the manager is very friendly and helpful.

More expensive is the *Hotel el Saffa* which is reasonably good value at E£2.90 a double with hot showers. Similar, but more expensive is the *Rosewan Hotel* which costs E£5/8.50 for a single/double. These two hotels are next to each other near the railway station. To get there, turn right coming out of the railway station and take the first left. You could also try the *Hotel el Amin* which is pleasant and clean and costs E£3 per person including breakfast.

Campers can pitch their tents at *Hotel Continental* for a small fee and there's a 24-hour armed guard on the site.

Places to Eat
For a good meal, try the small café opposite the youth hostel where, for 85 pt, you can have a two-egg omelette, yogurt, honey, bread, butter and either orange or banana juice. The *El Shati Terrace* opposite the Continental Hotel also offers good breakfasts and set menu meals for E£1.50 to E£2.

It costs E£2 to use the swimming pools at either the New Cataract Hotel or the Oberoi.

ASYUT
Visit the **Coptic Monastery** here.

A good place to stay is the *Hotel Zam Zam* which is clean, has hot water and costs E£4 a double. The *Youth Hostel* is very pleasant and friendly but a long way out of town. You can also camp at the *Police Officers Club* by the dam for E£2 per night. The showers are grubby, there are no lights and you're not allowed to have an open fire, but otherwise it's OK.

CAIRO
There can be few cities in the world with a history as rich as Cairo's. Where else could you see 6000-year-old pyramids (some of the world's largest constructions) and the Sphinx, Roman ruins, Byzantine Coptic churches, exquisitely carved and brilliantly conceived mosques and fortresses from the days when Cairo was the cultural centre of the Islamic world, traditional lateen-sailed boats on the river, a camel market and even catacombs!? All this plus a vibrant modern political and social culture which is second to none. Whatever the other Arab states might think of Egypt and its peace treaty with Israel, there is no way they can ignore events in Cairo and the influence which Egypt exerts. Despite the country's expulsion from the Arab League, the latter will remain an organisation in need of dental treatment until it takes Egypt back into the fold.

Here is the essence of Islamic culture! And Africa's largest city. The only one which comes close to it in size is Johannesburg though the comparison would probably not be appreciated.

There's an endless variety of things to see and do – noisy, bustling bazaars packed into narrow winding streets and those 1001 aromas (delicious, evocative and

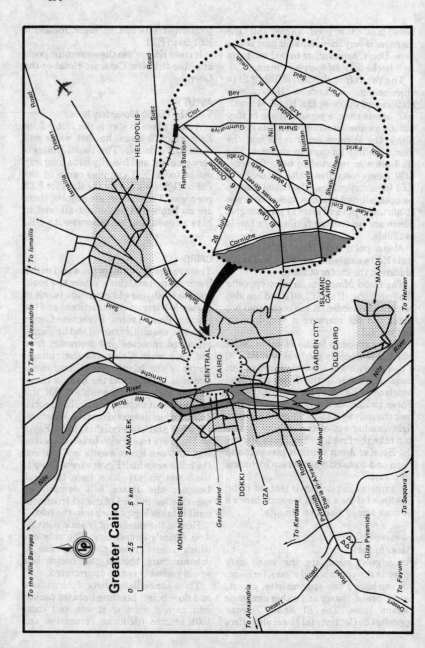

Greater Cairo

occasionally repulsive) which characterise so much of the east.

Though one of the capitals of ancient Egypt – Memphis – is only 20 km to the south and the pyramids are only across the other side of the Nile at Giza, most of Cairo dates from the Islamic period. The Nile, too, has gradually shifted westwards. Since the Arab conquest the city has seen the rise and fall of many dynasties. The Abbasids, Fatimids, Ayyubids and their successors the Mamelukes and Ottomans are just part of picture. Brief occupation by the French under Napoleon and partial incorporation into the British Empire is another aspect. Yet, Cairo remains the most important centre of Sunni Muslim scholarship in the world though for some 200 years from the mid-10th century until the mid-12th century under the Fatimids, Shi'ite doctrines were imposed by the rulers.

Information

The tourist office (tel 923000) is at 5 Adli St, near Opera Square. The office has plenty of information on what's worth seeing in Cairo, though this may not be in a language you can read. Others have said it's about as useful as a glass eye. It may not have maps of the city (take a copy of the *Oxford Map of Egypt* with you if you want to be sure). The staff are, however, very helpful. It's open from 8.30 am to 7 pm.

The tourist police office is down a small alley immediately to the left of the tourist office. If you have to go there for anything (eg reporting a theft from your hotel room) be prepared for a long haul and to pay for even the most trivial tasks.

The American Express office (tel 753142) is at 15 Sharia Kasr el Nil, PO Box 2160. It's open from 8 am to 4.30 pm except during Ramadan when the hours are 9 am to 3.30 pm. There are branch offices at the Nile Hilton (tel 744400), the Meridien Hotel (tel 844017), the Cairo Marriott (tel 698840), the Sheraton Hotel (tel 988000) and Cairo International Airport.

A good place to pick new and second-hand books in several languages is at 21 Sherif St. Another bookshop is Lennert & Landrock, 44 Sherif St.

You can get vaccinations on the ground floor of the Ministry of the Interior, Tahrir Square for 70 pt each or at the Continental Hotel, Opera Square, in the mornings. At the latter they cost about E£1. Bring your passport and health card with you.

Things to See

The Pyramids of Giza & the Sphinx One of
the Seven Wonders of the World, the Giza Pyramids and the Sphinx lie on the west bank of the Nile about nine km from the centre of Cairo. They were built between 2600 and 2520 BC by Cheops, Chephron and Mycerinus, kings of the 4th Dynasty, and are surrounded by smaller pyramids, temples and tombs of the nobles and other court officials. The largest is the Pyramid of Cheops and you're allowed to climb up inside this pyramid to the funerary chamber in the middle. Entry to the site is free, but if you want to climb up inside the Cheops Pyramid this will cost E£3 (E£1.50 with a student card).

It's worth going to a performance of the *son et lumière* one evening. There are separate performances in English, French, German and Arabic. There are two performances each night at 6.30 and 9.30 pm, one of them in English. Entry costs E£10 (no reductions), but if you go beyond the pavilion and sit on the wall there, you'll be able to see almost as much as you would by paying for a seat and you'll probably find yourself in the company of many other travellers. Watch out for guards who patrol the area.

Memphis & the Pyramids of Saqqara About
20 km south of Cairo, Memphis was once the capital of ancient Egypt and there's plenty to see. The pyramids here are much older than those at Giza but smaller. The cheapest way of getting there is to take the train to Badrashayn. There's one every half hour which costs 3½ pt with student card. You can also get there by a taxi-bus

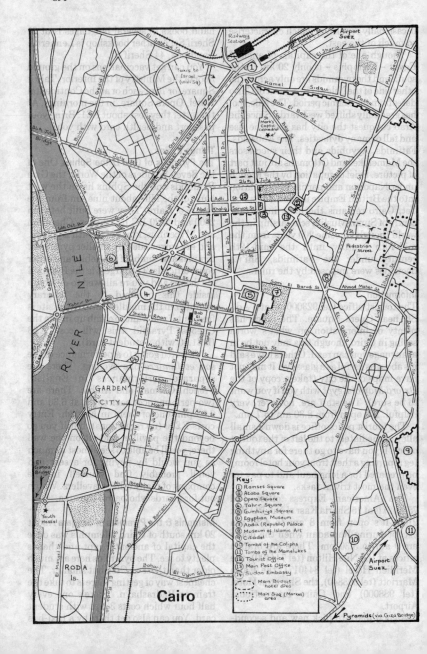

Key:
1. Ramses Square
2. Ataba Square
3. Opera Square
4. Tahrir Square
5. Gumhuriya Square
6. Egyptian Museum
7. Abdin (Republic) Palace
8. Museum of Islamic Art
9. Citadel
10. Tombs of the Caliphs
11. Tombs of the Mamelukes
12. Tourist Office
13. Main Post Office
14. Sudan Embassy

- - - Main Budget hotel area
..... Main Suq (Market) area

Cairo

Pyramids (via Giza Bridge)

combination. First take a bus from Tahrir Square to Giza Square (Nos 900, 904, 108, 124, 8 and others). There are also service taxis for 20 pt to 25 pt. When you get there, continue on foot for a little further in the same direction and ask for the service taxis for Badrashayn. It should cost about 15 pt and take about half an hour. Memphis is close to Badrashayn. From Badrashayn to Saqqara take a service taxi or microbus which will cost around 15 pt and take about 20 minutes. It will drop you about two km from Saqqara, after which you walk along the canal to the pyramids – very picturesque countryside. If this sounds complicated, there are also minibuses and shared taxis which go direct from Giza Square to Saqqara for E£1 per person one-way. Arrange a time for the driver to come and collect you (you'll need about four hours to see the main structures). You can also go by camel from Giza for E£6. Most people explore the area by foot but you can also hire camels and horses to do this. Entry to Saqqara costs E£3 (E£1.50 with student card). There are no hotels at Badrashayn in case you're thinking of staying there overnight.

Egyptian Museum This contains one of the world's best collections of ancient Egyptian artefacts, including the famous mummies and the sarcophagus of Tutankhamen. Don't miss it! The museum is open daily from 9 am to 4 pm except between 11.15 and 11.30 am for prayers and costs E£3 (E£1.50 with student card) excluding the Mummy Room, plus E£10 if you want to take a camera. Unfortunately the Mummy Room is now permanently closed. This was done by Sadat in 1981 as it was felt that having corpses on display offended the Islamic sense of propriety.

Islamic Museum This is also excellent and has displays of artefacts dating from the period when Cairo was the cultural capital of the Islamic world. It is open

daily from 9 am to 4 pm and costs E£2 (E£1 with a student card).

Other sights worth seeing in Cairo are the **Coptic Museum** (E£1 entry with student card), the **Abdin Palace**, the **Tombs of the Caliphs & Mamelukes** and the **Citadel** (E£1 with student card and you no longer need to show your passport to get in) which is used partially as a barracks. The most interesting of the mosques are the **Ibn Tulun Mosque** (50 pt entry – no discounts), **El Ibn el Asn Mosque** (50 pt entry – no discounts), **Sultan Hassan Mosque** and, perhaps best of all, the **Rifali Mosque** (50 pt entry). Inside the Ibn Tulun Mosque is the **Gayer Anderson Museum** which provides a fascinating look into a wealthy traditional Muslim home including secret galleries for the women and art work from the Far East. Entry costs 50 pt.

The oldest bazaar – and the one most visited by tourists – is **Khan el Khalily**. It's worth spending a whole day wandering around. Don't forget the side streets and the level above the street where you'll more than likely be welcomed as a friend instead of a brainless tourist throwing money around. One traveller who lived here for a while suggested walking from this bazaar through Old Cairo to the Citadel around late afternoon, in order to see the sun setting over Cairo and its mosques. It's an unforgettable sight.

Muezni-din-Allah, which runs perpendicular to Al-Azhar St just before Al-Azhar itself, was one of the widest boulevards in the mediaeval world (four laden horses wide) and still retains much of its traditional character. It offers interesting sights at either end – Bab Zuweila in the south where the heads of those who were executed were hung, and the old city walls in the north, once patrolled by Napoleon's graffiti-carving troops.

Another sight worth catching is the **Camel Market** which takes place every Friday morning and sometimes on other days too. Take bus No 99 from Tahrir Square to Suq al Gimaal (the name of the camel market) in Imbaba. You'll see more camels here than you ever dreamed could be brought together in one place, as well as donkeys and all the accessories which go with them. It's very entertaining though, these days, you may be hassled for an 'entry fee' of 50 pt!. Don't confuse this market with the camel meat market in Al Sayyida where the camels are sold for slaughter.

Another great way to spend a few hours is to take a **Cairo water bus** on the Nile. They're cheap – just 5 pt to 10 pt depending on the distance – and you can board them at the Radio & TV building on the Corniche (near the Hilton) or at the southern tip of Roda Island and at other points. You can go all the way to Old Cairo on these water buses, or north to the Barrages (Al-Qanatir) where Sadat had a residence. Here you can spend a pleasant day enjoying the gardens (bicycles and horses for hire).

The **Cairo Tower** has also been recommended for a magnificent view over Cairo. The entrance fee is E£3 and is probably worth it if you go in clear weather. If you are tempted to order a beer up there in the cafeteria it will cost E£2.65. Suppress your thirst until you get down, then have the best karkade in town at the open-air refreshment place at the foot of the tower. They cost 60 pt but are so good and strong that you'll have to buy a bottle of mineral water to mix with them. Other travellers have written to say that the view from the Sky Lair at the top of the **Ramses Hilton** is just as good and the only 'entry fee' is the price of a drink.

Places to Stay

There is a wide choice of cheap and moderately priced accommodation in Cairo, most of it on or off Talaat Harb and between there and Opera Square. Accommodation at any of these generally comes with a level of noise which you might not be used to. Learn to live with it.

One of the cheapest places to stay, but a half-hour walk from Tahrir Square, is the

1	Shepheard's Hotel
2	Garden City House
3	Minibuses to Pyramids
4	Buses & Kiosks for Alexandria & the Mediterranean Coast
5	Nile Hilton
6	Egyptian Museum
7	Ramses Hilton
8	Anglo–Swiss Hotel
9	Viennoise (Hotel/Pension)
10	Pension Suisse
11	Groppi's
12	TWA
13	Sudan Airways
14	Telephone Office & Bus Ticket Office for Buses to Mersa Matruh
15	Wimpy's
16	Lotus Hotel
17	American Express
18	Golden Hotel
19	Felfela's Sandwich Stand & Restaurant
20	Café Riche
21	Tulip Hotel
22	Fataran (Fiteer) Restaurant
23	American University
24	24-hour Sandwich Shop & Bakery
25	Local Food & Juice Stand
26	El Doumyati Restaurant
27	Telecommunications Building & Minibuses to Maadi & Helwan
28	Cosmopolitan Hotel
29	Pension Oxford
30	Zeina Restaurant
31	Pension Beausite
32	Hotel des Roses
33	Claridge Hotel
34	Grand Hotel & the Brazilian Coffee Shop
35	Casablanca
36	Pension Roma
37	Hotel Select
38	Plaza Hotel
39	Tourist Office
40	GPO
41	Islamic Art Museum

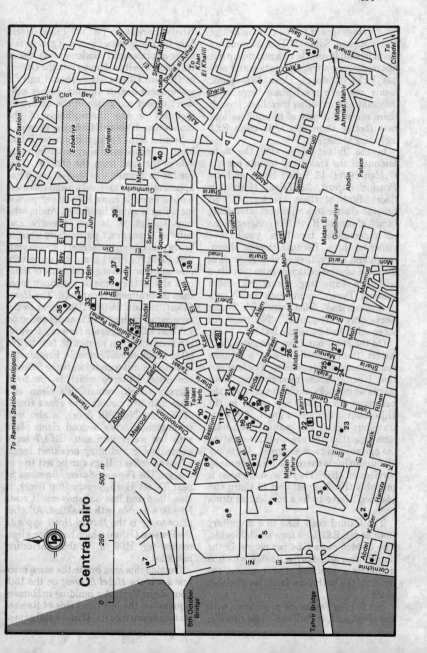

Central Cairo

Youth Hostel, near the El Gamaa Bridge and opposite Salah el Din Mosque on Roda Island. It used to be a real dump but has undergone a transformation and now has locks on doors, clean bathrooms, meals and is a good place to pick up information from other travellers, though there are still plenty of mosquitoes and cats (better than rats!). It costs E£4 including breakfast.

In the Talaat Harb area the most famous of the travellers' haunts are the *Golden Hotel*, 13 Talaat Harb, and the *Pension Oxford*, 32 Talaat Harb (top floor). Both of these are legends and provide shelter to a wild and interesting bunch of people. If you like congregations of impecunious travellers, you'll love either of them. Because they're cheap, rough and ready, they obviously come in for some adverse criticism from travellers who are expecting something more genteel. Typical comments are: 'Dirty and overpriced', 'Bed bugs rife', 'Water works only infrequently', 'Notorious for its squalor, bed bugs, the lot'.

On the other hand, we also get a lot of letters from travellers who are more sympathetic and less fussy. The best one that I came across recently was, 'Your sterile white socks won't stay clean on the bathroom floor like they would in the Hilton but it remains a great, if grubby, travellers' hotel. The manager is a total lunatic, all the staff are really nice and the tea and room service are great.' Certainly all human life is there and there are many services on offer. They also serve what is probably the cheapest beer in Cairo and you don't have to be a resident to drink there.

The Oxford costs E£2 in a dormitory (four beds), E£2.50/5 for a single/double. The Golden costs E£4 per person in the dormitories and E£7 a double which is definitely overpriced. Don't expect too much of the bathroom facilities at either place.

Similar, as far as its popularity with travellers goes, is the *Pension de Famille*, Khaliq Sarwat St just off Talaat Harb. Like the previous two hotels, it gets its fair share of praise and condemnation. Some travellers like it and prefer it to the Oxford or Golden. Others say it should carry a government health warning. Either way, don't expect too much of the bathroom facilities or the thoroughness of the laundering. It costs E£2.50 per person.

Similar is the *Pension Beausite*, Talaat Harb (entrance in an alley on the opposite side of the road from the Oxford). This used to be as grubby as the rest but it has apparently been cleaned up and there are no bed bugs. It costs E£3.50 per person including a small breakfast. Andy, who runs the place, is very friendly and helpful. If you don't particularly want to brave the bed-bug palaces of Cairo on your first night (or ever) there are some very pleasant places to stay and many of them cost almost the same or not much more than those already mentioned. The *Hotel Select*, 19 Adli St (8th floor) next to the synagogue, is clean and friendly and good value at E£4 per person for a mattress on the floor sharing a room with four to five other people or E£7 a double. Breakfast is included. Similar and close to the Select is the *Hotel Minerva* which is run by a friendly Greek woman. It's clean and costs E£5.50 a double. The *Plaza Hotel*, 37 Kasr el Nil (8th floor), is also well recommended. It's a good clean place with hot water and costs E£4/7 for a single/double including breakfast (eggs, rolls and coffee). Bags can be left free of charge. The *Pension Suisse*, Bassiuni St near Talaat Harb Square (top floor), is also clean and has hot showers. It costs E£8.80 a double with breakfast. Another place to try is the *Bussid Hotel* opposite the Pension Oxford which has large, clean rooms for E£6 a double including breakfast.

Outside this area but in the same price bracket is the *Hotel Everest* on the 15th floor of the EgyptAir building in Ramses Square (on the left hand side of Ramses station as you face it). This is a real gem of a place to stay and has been enthusiastically recommended by many travellers for several years. The rooms are bug-free and the bathrooms are so clean you could eat your dinner off them. The staff are very friendly and conscientious, there's a laundry service and a rooftop restaurant from which there are excellent views over Cairo. As you might expect, the rooms are fairly quiet. Singles/doubles cost E£5.25/ 10.50 including breakfast. There are also triple rooms which generally have their own balconies. It can be difficult to get a room at weekends.

Back to the Talaat Harb area and somewhat more expensive are the *Grand Hotel*, on the corner of Talaat Harb and Sharia 26th July, and the *Pension Roma*, Adli St (top floor). The latter has an entrance via an alley opposite the El Walid clothing store (there's a green sign high up). It's very pleasant and has a variety of rooms at different prices though E£11 a double would be average including breakfast. The Grand is clean and semi-luxurious and costs E£17 to E£23 a double including breakfast. It also offers fixed-price lunches and dinners. Quite a few travellers stay here. Similar in price to the Roma are the *Hotel Tulip*, Talaat Harb Square, which is clean, comfortable and has hot water and the *Hotel des Roses* which is very clean, has hot water and costs E£7/15.60 for a single/triple including breakfast.

Others to check out in this area include the *Hotel Hamburg*, 18 El Borsa Tawfikia, where prices include hot showers and a substantial breakfast, and the *Hotel Viennoise*, Bassiuni St (2nd floor) just off Talaat Harb Square. The *Hotel Panorama* opposite the Select is clean and friendly and costs E£12 a double including breakfast. There are hot showers.

Out of the main area but excellent value is the *Tiba House Hotel*, 6 Aly Mohammed St, King Faisal Rd, Giza. It's about 10 minutes' walk from the pyramids and nine km from Tahrir Square. This is a new

place with 40 rooms (singles and doubles) and each floor has toilets and showers. The rooms are all very clean and some have views of the pyramids. The staff are very friendly and there's a small attached restaurant where you can get a sandwich at any time of the day or night. It costs E£12 a double or E£15 with breakfast. If you stay longer than one week, you can renegotiate the price.

Also at Giza there's a camp site very close to the pyramids known as *Camping Saharamar*. Watch for the signpost indicating a left turn on Pyramids Ave just before the pyramids. Follow the sign, then turn right down a lane past what must once have been an abattoir or tannery judging from the smell. It costs E£3 per person. The gate is always kept locked and your gear is watched. The camp site offers pleasant gardens, a new, clean shower block and a kitchen with fridge and stoves. It's good for those with their own vehicles but otherwise hard to get to.

In the unlikely event that all of these hotels are full, or if you can't find a place you like, there are others marked on the map of central Cairo.

Places to Eat

There are literally thousands of fuul and felafal cafés and teahouses in central Cairo where you can get a meal for less than E£1, so long as you don't order meat. There are also a lot of fast food pasta places where you can get a small helping of pasta, rice, lentils, tomato sauce and fried onions for very little. A good hunting ground for these cheap cafés is along the market street between Tahrir St and Mohammed Mahmud St east of Tahrir Square – turn right by the blue footbridge down Tahrir St. One good *kosharia* which has been recommended is on 26th July St diagonally opposite the Grand Hotel towards Opera Square with a sign in the window saying 'Popular Egyptian Food'. It costs 25 pt per plate.

The Khan el Khalily bazaar is also a good place to spend the evening eating and drinking tea in the old fashioned teahouses.

Popular named restaurants include *Felfela's*, Talaat Harb on Talaat Harb Square, where everyone goes to at some time or another. Their meals are quite pricey at around E£4 to E£5 but they have opened up a sandwich bar just around the corner from the main place which sells sandwiches for 50 pt to 60 pt depending on the filling. The *Zeina Cafeteria*, Talaat Harb near Abdel el Khaliq Sarwat St, offers vegetarian meals for less than E£1 but it's not cheap and the food isn't very interesting. Meat meals are more expensive. The café is open until midnight and has English menus. *Roy's Bar & Restaurant*, 42 Talaat Harb, offers very filling meals for between E£2 and E£3. The *Damietta*, Falaki Square (no sign in English), has very cheap meals of fuul, taamiya, lentil soup and yogurt for 20 pt to 40 pt.

Other than the local restaurants, it's worth considering the all-you-can-eat breakfasts offered by the large hotels like the *Hilton*, *Sheraton* and the *Meridien*. Although they're no longer the bargain they used to be, they're still fairly good. The cheapest at present is the Meridien, which costs E£3.85 – the dining room overlooks the Nile. The breakfasts at the Hilton cost E£4.50. There is a minimum charge of E£1.50 in the Hilton coffee shop.

A good place in which to hang around and have a beer is the *Café Riche* on Talaat Harb Square. It's very popular but avoid eating here if you're on a budget. A beer will cost E£2 including service.

If you want a splurge, *El Hatti's* at Midan Halim between the Windsor Hotel on Alfi St and 26th July St has been recommended. It serves great lamb dishes, has heaps of mirrors and chandeliers and is frequented by Arabs from far and near. There is also a new *El Hatti's* beside the Horus Hotel just round the corner, but it doesn't have the atmosphere of the old one.

Getting Around

To/From the Airport There are two terminals so make sure you know which one you are arriving at or leaving from. A taxi between the airport and Tahrir Square will cost E£5 to E£8. Otherwise take bus No 400 from terminal 1 to Ramses Square/Tahrir Square or bus No 410 to Opera Square. They both operate 24 hours a day and cost 10 pt. The journey takes about half an hour during the night but up to an hour during the day. From terminal 2 (the new terminal) take bus No 422 to Tahrir Square but remember that it only operates during the day. There are minibuses several times every hour between the two terminals.

Allow four to five hours between setting off from your hotel and boarding your flight.

In the City Bus numbers are usually in Arabic so make sure you are familiar with Arabic numerals.

The ordinary buses are often very crowded and slow so it's worth considering the microbuses (converted VWs and Toyota vans) for getting around Cairo. They operate on all the main routes and will stop wherever you want them to. The passengers themselves collect the fares as a rule, so you don't need to haggle like you do with the taxi drivers. Some of the buses of interest to travellers are:

No 8 or 900: Tahrir Square to Giza/Pyramids

No 70 or 95: Tahrir Square to Ramses Square

No 65 or 80: Ramses Square to Ataba Square

No 24 or 25: Ataba Square to Ramses Square

No 160 or 163: Tahrir Square to the Citadel

No 92: Tahrir Square to Old Cairo

No 99: Tahrir Square to the Camel Market

No 64: Ataba Square to Abbasiya Square (Sinai bus terminal)

EL BALYANA

This town south of Qena is the site of the **Temples of Abydos**. To get there, go to the bus station and take a taxi to Abydos, which should cost 25 pt per person. Entry to the temples costs E£1 with a student card. It is possible to walk there if time and sweat are no object.

Stay at the *Youth Hostel* at Sohaq further downriver (one hour by train). It's a small, very friendly and pleasant place and costs 60 pt per night (45 pt if you're under 21).

EL MINYA

The main attraction of El Minya is the **Hatshepsut Temple** and the nobles tombs at **Beni Hasan** further south opposite Abu Qirqus. To get there take a local bus from El Minya to Abu Qirqus or a shared taxi (20 pt). From there you'll have to take a shared taxi to the ferry landing stage (5 pt), then the ferry across the Nile. The ferry for locals costs 5 pt but there's also a tourist ferry which costs E£3 shared between six people plus 50 pt extra for each person over six. There are a total of 39 tombs at Beni Hasan of which four are open to the public. Entry costs E£1.25 (75 pt with a student card). The Rest House near the tombs is expensive if you get thirsty (about double normal prices).

Places to Stay

The best place to stay in El Minya is the *Palace Hotel* which is a remarkable French colonial-style hotel with large rooms. It's very clean and good value. Not all the rooms have showers but there is hot water in the communal shower rooms. It costs E£5.50 a double without bathroom and E£6.50 a double with bathroom. Breakfast costs E£1 and is very filling but it can take a while to arrive. If this place is full try the *Hotel Savoy*.

HURGHADA

Hurghada is on the Red Sea coast more or less due west of the tip of Sinai and became a popular travellers resort during

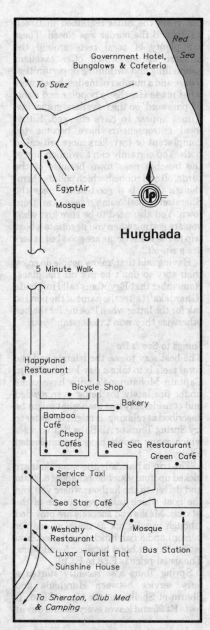

Red Sea

Government Hotel, Bungalows & Cafeteria

To Suez

EgyptAir

Mosque

Hurghada

5 Minute Walk

Happyland Restaurant

Bicycle Shop

Bakery

Bamboo Café

Cheap Cafés

Red Sea Restaurant

Green Café

Service Taxi Depot

Sea Star Café

Weshahy Restaurant

Mosque

Luxor Tourist Flat

Bus Station

Sunshine House

To Sheraton, Club Med & Camping

the years the Sinai remained in Israeli hands and the border was closed. There are plenty of coral reefs around the offshore islands which offer excellent snorkelling and swimming opportunities. These and a number of mellow hotels were what made Hurghada popular and a sort of 'password' on the travellers' grapevine. Times appear to have changed. Either local entrepreneurs have become too complacent or travellers more critical or both. You certainly can't swim on any of the beaches near town because of the turds, oil and rubbish which pollute them, though there is a good beach near the Sheraton Hotel some seven km from town. You also need to be sure just what you are getting when you negotiate a boat trip to the reefs. Some are good but others are a rip-off.

Having said that, many people do enjoy their stay so don't be put off the place. Remember that Egyptians call Hurghada 'Ghardaka', (after the name of the port) so ask for the latter when looking for the bus otherwise they won't understand you.

Things to See & Do

The best way to see the islands and the coral reefs is to take a day-long boat trip. Captain Mohammed's trips have come under fire lately for being overcrowded and considerably less than what might be described as relaxing. It might be better to try Spring Tours or Ali Baba Sea Voyages which many people have recommended lately.

The trip is basically the same. You are picked up from your hotel at about 8.30 am and driven to the harbour where you join the boat which takes you to one of the islands. Masks and snorkels are provided (though usually not as many as one per person) and a fish lunch is included. You return to your hotel between 5 and 6 pm. The usual price is E£8 to E£10.

Spring Tours also recently started a ferry service between Hurghada and Sharm el Sheikh on the tip of Sinai. It costs E£25 and leaves every second day at 10 am. The journey takes about four hours. Book two days in advance at Spring Tours next to EgyptAir or in the Hurghada Hotel further down the road towards the sea.

Places to Stay

Almost everyone who comes here tries to get a room at the *Happy House* on El Dhar Mosque Square. Captain Mohammed, who owns the place, is a popular man, friendly and very helpful. He also speaks excellent English. His place is clean and pleasant and costs E£2 per person. Cooking facilities are provided. If it's full his brother also rents out rooms for E£3 a double. Another good place is the *Luxor Palace*, run by Mohammed Unis, which is clean, friendly and about as popular as the Happy House. It costs E£2 per person plus E£1 if you want breakfast. The toilets often don't work and there are a lot of flies. Two other places are the *Moon Valley Hotel* between the Sheraton and town which costs E£3 for bed and breakfast and the *Sunshine House Hotel* which costs the same.

If these places are full there are plenty of other *locandas* and rooms in private houses available which cost between E£1.50 and E£3 per night. Many of the people who have places to rent will meet you at the bus from Cairo.

There are two good beaches for camping. The one near the government bungalows is free. The other, more picturesque and isolated, is also free, but you'll need to take a bus or taxi to get there as it's seven km from town near the Sheraton Hotel. The buses are fairly regular and cost 25 pt. A taxi will cost E£3 shared by up to seven people, or you can rent a bicycle for E£1 per day. There are no facilities at this beach so you need to bring your own food and water.

Places to Eat

The two best places to eat in the centre of town are the *Happy House Restaurant* (owned by Captain Mohammed) and the

Red Sea Restaurant. The former offers fish & chips (ah! nostalgia!) for E£1.50 pt and eggs, bread, butter, jam and tea for 60 pt. The food at the Red Sea Restaurant is excellent but pricey at around E£3 per meal. Go there for a splurge. Opposite is a restaurant where you can get macaroni and a meat dish with sauce, salad and bread for E£1.75. There's another cheap restaurant in the centre (marked on the map) where you can eat for E£1.10.

Around Hurghada

The two Coptic Christian monasteries of **St Anthony** and **St Paul**, in the mountains overlooking the Gulf of Suez near Zafarana (about a third of the way from Cairo to Hurghada), can be conveniently visited from Hurghada. You don't need permission to visit either of them, but if you intend to stay overnight then you do need permission from the Coptic Cathedral in Cairo. Women can only stay overnight if they remain fully clothed at all times. St Paul's won't take visitors during Lent.

To get to St Paul's, take the coastal road north from Hurghada and get down at the turn-off for the monastery south of the Zafarana lighthouse. From there it's a 13-km walk on a dirt track across baking desert with very little traffic. Bring water with you and don't rely on being able to pick up a lift. The monastery has a guest house where you can stay overnight, or you can camp in the dry riverbed nearby. Bring your own food.

St Anthony's is more modernised. It's about 45 km from the Red Sea coast, but the monks offer a similar welcome to those at St Paul's. To get there take the road which goes inland to the Nile Valley from Zafarana and get down at the monastery turn-off. From there it's a 10-km walk. As with St Paul's, you may have to walk this stretch since there is very little traffic. The visiting hours at St Anthony's are 9 am to 5 pm. If you have the time and the inclination, it's worth climbing the 500 metres up the mountain behind the

monastery to see St Anthony's Cave. Take a torch with you.

About 150 km south of Hurghada is the small town of **Quesir** which sees very few tourists but has an excellent beach five km north of town. The snorkelling here is about as good as at Hurghada. There are buses every day from Qena, Cairo and Hurghada.

The best place to stay is *Samia's* for E£1.50 per night. Samia, a helpful and friendly man, is building a few bungalows with cooking facilities.

IDFU

The attraction at Idfu is the nearby **Temple of Horus**, which is well worth seeing. Entry costs E£2 (E£1 with a student card).

The *Samin Amis Hotel* on the main road into town is where most people stay for the night, but beware of theft. One traveller had his room broken into recently. It costs E£3 per night. The bathrooms are said to be worse than those at the Youth Hostel in Aswan.

ISMAILIYA

If you have to stay here for the night, there is a kind of *Youth Hostel* in the Sea Rangers' Building about one km from the bus station on the shores of Lake Timsah. There are also a number of good, cheap hotels in the town centre.

LUXOR

Luxor stands on the site of Thebes, the southern capital of the Pharaohs and one of the richest areas in the country for ancient Egyptian ruins and monuments. These include the world-famous Valley of the Kings (where the tomb of Tutankhamen was found) and the Temple of Karnak.

Things to See

There are so many different archaeological sites in and around Luxor that you're going to wish you had a student card if you haven't got one. There are 11 separate tickets in all for the sites on the West Bank

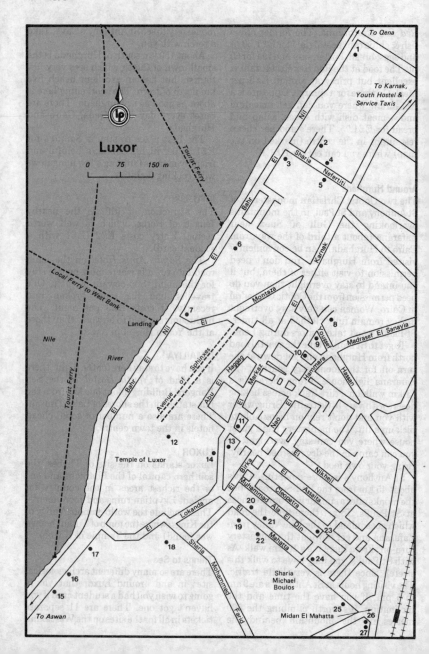

Luxor

0   75   150 m

To Qena

To Karnak,
Youth Hostel &
Service Taxis

Tourist Ferry

Local Ferry to West Bank

Landing

Nile

River

Tourist Ferry

Avenue of Sphinxes

Temple of Luxor

To Aswan

Midan El Mahatta

El Bahr El Nil

Sharia Nefertiti

El Bahr El Nil

El Montaza

Karnak

El Youssef Hassen

Madraset El Sanayia

Abu El Haggag

El Markaz

El Hammara

El Neo

El Nikheil

El Birka

El Lokanda

Muhammad Ala El Din

Cleopatra

Assalta

El Mehatta

Sharia Mohammed Ferid

Sharia Michael Boulos

1
2
3
4
5
6
7
8
9
10
11
12
13
14
15
16
17
18
19
20
21
22
23
24
25
26
27

1	Museum
2	Windsor Hotel
3	ETAP Hotel
4	Hotel Philippe
5	Bicycle Shop
6	Hotel Savoy
7	Mina Palace
8	Bicycle Shop
9	Hotel Dina
10	Pyramids Hotel
11	The Four Seasons Hotel
12	Mosque of Abu El Haggag
13	Horus Hotel
14	Bus Station
15	Winter Palace, American Express & Telephone Office
16	New Winter Palace
17	Tourist & State Information Office / Tourist Bazaar
18	Luxor Hotel (and Camping)
19	GPO
20	Juice Stand
21	Mensa Restaurant
22	Bicycle Shop
23	St Mark's Pension
24	Ramoza Hotel
25	Amoun Hotel
26	New Karnak Hotel
27	Salad & Bread Café

– eight at E£1 plus E£5 for the Valley of the Kings, E£2 for Deir el Bahani and 50 pt for Medinet Habu. On the East Bank there are the Luxor Temple for E£2 and the Temple of Karnak for E£3. (These are full-price tickets.) Without a student card you should buy your tickets for the antiquities on the West Bank from the tourist ferry stop. Student tickets have to be bought from the 'Inspectorate for Students' near the Colossi of Memnon. You should allow several days to see all the main sites. It is a good idea to work out carefully what you are going to see each day as it gets very hot and you're not going to be able to rush around.

There is a *son et lumière* at the Karnak Temple which costs E£5 in any European language but only E£1 in Arabic (Thursdays only). As one traveller commented, 'The *son* is bullshit anyway so catch the *lumière* for E£1'. If money is no object then the English version is at 6 pm on Monday and Wednesday and at 8 pm on Tuesday. There are no student discounts.

The new **museum** in Luxor is worth visiting (E£2 entry) for its striking design and imaginative layout.

Some determined souls walk all the way from Luxor to the Valley of the Kings and the other sites on the West Bank, but you needn't do this as there is a choice of taxi, bicycle or donkey. A taxi to the Valley of the Kings shouldn't cost more than E£1.50 per person (seven passengers). You have to bargain hard for this price if there are a lot of well-heeled tourists around as they tend to pay virtually whatever the taxi driver quotes. Others have hired a cab for the whole morning (7 am to 12 noon) for E£10 shared between five people but you have to haggle hard for this and it's only possible in the low season. Bicycles can be hired from quite a few hotels for E£1.50 (sometimes E£2) per day and, in many ways, they offer the greatest flexibility.

Donkeys generally cost E£5 but you have to hire a guide with them so expect to pay baksheesh in addition to the hire charge. They can be picked up on the West Bank or you can arrange a tour by donkey at one or two of the hotels in Luxor. The Salah el Din Hotel offers an eight-hour donkey tour to the Valley of the Kings, Deir el Bahani and the Ramesseum for E£15 all included. Of this tour one traveller commented, 'I thought it was too much considering that bikes could be rented for E£1 per day and the guide barely spoke English and was essentially there just to lead you from one site to the next.'

There are two ferries across the Nile – a 'tourist ferry' and the local people's ferry.

Take the latter, as it's only 25 pt and bicycles are free (at least they are for the locals though, as a foreigner, you'll probably have to pay 10 pt). The operators of the tourist ferry don't like bicycles.

Maps of the Valley of the Kings, Karnak and Luxor can be bought from Aboudis tourist shop near the Luxor Temple for 40 pt. If you already have a copy of the *Oxford Map of Egypt* then that is adequate.

If you come to Luxor in summer (the off season) it's a good idea to make enquiries about which sites on the West Bank are open. Some are closed at this time of year though there are usually enough open to satisfy the average traveller. Cameras are banned in all of the tombs but you are free to photograph the temples and other monuments.

Places to Stay

One of the cheapest places to stay is the *Youth Hostel*. The staff are not particularly friendly but it's clean, cool and open all day despite notices to the contrary. It costs 80 pt for a bed. Many travellers prefer to stay in one of the hotels in town.

One of the most popular places is the *New Karnak Hotel* near the railway station. It's clean, has hot showers and costs E£2 for a dormitory bed, E£3 a single and E£4 to E£5.50 a double including breakfast. The rooms have fans but none have a bathroom. It's also a very popular place to eat (good food) as it has a balcony overlooking the railway station. The hotel rents out bicycles for E£1 per day.

Also popular is the *Horus Hotel* which has doubles from E£4 to E£6 depending on the size of the room and huge triple rooms with fan and bathroom for E£7. They sell the cheapest beers in town (E£1.60) and because of the proximity of the silicon chip *muezzins* at full volume between 3.45 and 4.15 am you'll never miss that train connection. No alarm clocks needed here! Breakfasts cost 95 pt.

The *Thebes Hotel* is clean and secure and costs E£2 per person on the roof and E£2.50 for a bed plus E£1 for breakfast. The *New Palace Hotel* costs E£1.50 for a bed. The *New Home Pension* is 10 minutes' walk from the railway station – go down between the New Karnak and the Limpy after which take the first left then first right. It has clean rooms with fans and hot showers plus free use of a washing machine. Beds cost E£2 per person and a good breakfast costs E£1. The owner, Kamahl, organises many sightseeing trips but they're relatively expensive. Bicycles can be rented for E£2 per day.

In the same price bracket and equally popular are several other hotels. The *Khan el Khalily*, by the Luxor Temple, costs E£2.50 a single with washbasin and balcony. It's noisy being in a market area and somewhat decrepit, but the beds are clean and comfortable. The staff are very hospitable and entertaining. 'I spent a lazy afternoon in the lobby watching the goings-on – talk about a Le Carré novel co-written by John Cleese!' commented one traveller. Near to the New Karnak is the *Salah el Din Hotel* which is clean, and costs E£2 for a bed in a four-bed room or E£3 a double. There is hot water and a rooftop restaurant (breakfast of two eggs, bread, butter, jam, cheese and tea or coffee costs 70 pt). The *Seti Gordon Hotel* is clean, has hot showers, costs E£1.50 per person including breakfast, and offers bicycle rentals at E£1 per day. Another which has been recommended is the *El Salam Hotel* which costs E£2 per bed and E£4 a double. Breakfast is available for E£1.

Similar is the *Grand Hotel*, which is clean and good value at E£2/4 for a single/double. There are hot showers and a washing machine for guests' use. Bicycles can be rented for E£1 per day.

Somewhat more expensive is the *Titi Home* (!) at E£3.50 per person including a good breakfast. Many people have recommended this place. Similar in price is the *Hotel Atlas* at E£3/6 for a single/double with bathroom, toilet, hot water and breakfast. The manager speaks excellent English and very good evening meals are available for E£2.50. There is the *Hotel Pyramids* which is owned by a very friendly man who speaks English. It costs E£5 a double with bathroom, hot water and breakfast.

If you need relatively cheap comfort, try the two-star *Ramoza Hotel*. All the rooms have air-con and bathroom. In the high season they cost E£12 a double but in the low season you may be able to get the price down to E£8 a double which is excellent value.

There's a popular camp site opposite the Luxor Hotel. A man called Babu Hassan will guard your gear for an agreed price, though he lays on the theatricals for more baksheesh when you leave.

If you don't want to stay in Luxor, there is the possibility of staying on the West Bank. Quite a few travellers have recommended the *Habu Hotel* which is somewhat run-down but has a great

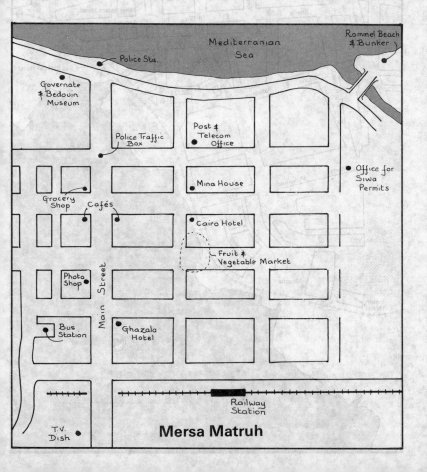

Mersa Matruh

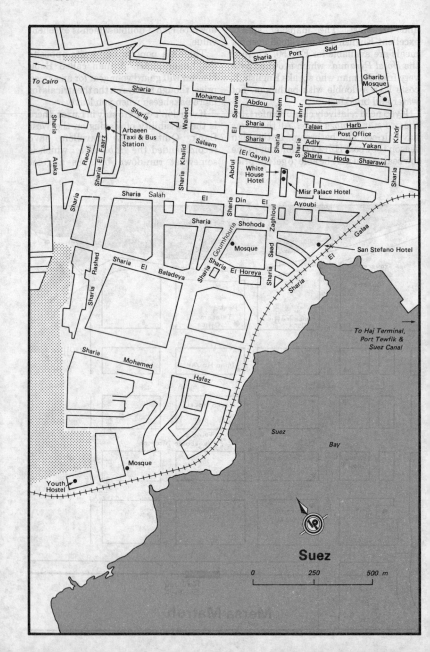

Suez

0   250   500 m

location near the Colossi of Memnon. It costs E£5 per person including breakfast and other meals are available for E£3. Another is the *Abul Kasem Hotel*, four km from the river (E£1 by private taxi or 15 pt by shared taxi). The hotel is on top of an alabaster factory where you can watch the workers make their sculptures. The owner fixes his prices according to demand, so sort it out before taking a room. If the place is empty you pay E£1.50. If it's getting full you pay E£3 per person. It's very clean, hot water is available in the shared bathrooms, the rooms have a fan, and meals and cold drinks are available on request. There is also the *Memnon Hotel* opposite the Colossi of Memnon which costs E£3 per person.

Places to Eat

The *New Karnak Hotel* is a popular place to eat (80 pt for omelette, bread and orange juice), but you can also try *Mensa* on the main street to the right as you leave the station. Many travellers rate this place highly. Huge bowls of spinach, tomato sauce and rice cost 30 pt. Yogurt is 40 pt. For a splurge have a whole roast chicken with bread sauce and pickles for E£3.25. Another place worth trying is *Limpy*, opposite the railway station where you can get a three-course meal for E£1.50. It's unbeatable value at the price. Set menu meals at the *Nile Terrace* cost E£1.50 and are good value.

A good place for a beer in the afternoon is the *Winter Palace*, an old colonial-style building with a lot of atmosphere. In the evenings, try the bar at the *Nile Casino* on the banks of the Nile opposite the Luxor Temple. Here you can often listen to superb Egyptian folk music played live on traditional instruments, though the drinks will be slightly more expensive on such nights (beers are rarely less than E£2).

If you don't want to risk swimming in the Nile to cool off, the cheapest of the swimming pools at the posh hotels is the one at the Winter Palace which costs E£2.50. Towels are provided.

MERSA MATRUH

Mersa Matruh is a small, lively town on the Mediterranean coast about half way between Alexandria and the Libyan border. The main attractions are the beautiful beaches of which there are quite a few and the Siwa Oasis south of here close to the Libyan border. Before visiting Siwa Oasis you must obtain special permission in Mersa. Details for the Siwa Oasis are in the Western Desert Oases section.

Rommel Beach is nearest to the town on the eastern side but it's often crowded. If you prefer more deserted beaches there are some which can be reached by local bus to the west of town. **Ubbayid Beach** is probably the best and although it costs 10 pt entry this entitles you to the use of a shower. Further west is **Ageeba Beach** where there are interesting cliff formations undercut by the sea, but you can't swim there.

Transport to Rommel Beach is by small donkey carts for which you shouldn't pay more than E£1 shared between however many of you there are. To Ubbayid and Ageeba beaches there are local buses from the bus station which cost 10 pt and take about half an hour. The last bus back to town from Ubbayid Beach is at 4 pm.

There is a **Bedouin Museum** in Mersa which is worth visiting. Entry costs 10 pt.

Places to Stay & Eat

The *Ghazala Hotel* is probably the best place to stay. It's very clean and costs E£3 a double. If it's full try the *Cairo Hotel*.

QENA

El Salam Hotel behind the school opposite the post office has been recommended. It has hot and cold water showers on each floor and costs E£2.60 a double. Take precautions against mosquitoes.

SUEZ

Avoid staying here overnight if possible as the town has little to recommend it. Hotels around the bus station are usually very expensive – around E£4 for a grotty bed – and often full. There is a *Youth Hostel* about 3½ km from town on Sharia Tariq al Horia which is very friendly and clean and costs the usual price (E£1 for members and E£1.50 for nonmembers), plus they have group leaders' rooms (very pleasant) for E£1.50 per bed. They are, however, very strict about curfews and segregation of sexes. You can also camp cheaply for 50 pt per night.

The cheapest place in town is the *St Stephen's Hotel* (sometimes called San Stefarno) which is OK, clean and costs E£2 per person. It's on the waterfront. Also good is the *Misr Hotel* which has pleasant, quiet, clean rooms with hot communal showers. It costs E£6.15 including breakfast but those who have eaten the breakfasts say the cook should be assigned to other duties. To get to the Misr, turn right as you come out of the bus station and continue until you come to a major intersection with traffic lights. Turn right here and go down the main street for about three blocks. The Misr is on the right. The *Hotel Bel Air* has also been recommended. It's an old colonial-style place, clean and has excellent food at reasonable prices. Rooms cost E£8 a double.

Buses to St Katherine's leave at 10.30 am from the bus station (E£5.50 with a change at Wadi Feran Oasis).

If you need to change money there are quite a few official moneychangers (no black market) but their rates are excellent so shop around. Avoid using the banks for changing money.

THE WESTERN DESERT OASES

Most travellers who come to Egypt don't venture outside the Nile Valley, which is understandable given that most of the antiquities and the cities are there. If you want to see most of them at a leisurely pace, this will take up virtually all of the month that you get on a normal tourist visa. However, you are allowed to overstay your visa by two weeks without incurring

any penalty so, if you have the time, it's worth experiencing a different dimension of Egypt. This can be found in the oases of the Western Desert or in Sinai. Travellers who have spent time there have raved about it. Very few tourists get this far, so you'll find people genuinely friendly, curious and hospitable.

It's worth considering making the loop through these oases if you have the time. Please remember, however, that in common with all Arab countries, this hospitality is meant to be reciprocated. If you just take without giving, then pretty soon travellers who come after you will find they're being treated with disdain and even contempt. A small gift is all that is necessary. Its material worth is inconsequential so long as it is thoughtful. Of equal importance is your manner of dress – make sure it conforms as closely as possible with what local people would regard as modest and respectable. Don't wear shorts or singlets. This goes for the whole of Egypt, but it's doubly important in the oases.

The most accessible of the oases are west of a line stretching from El Minya to Luxor – Bahariya, Farafra, Dakhla and El Kharga.

The most remote of the oases is Siwa south of Mersa Matruh close to the Libyan border. You're very unlikely to see another traveller here. There's no transport connecting Siwa with the other oases so you have to make a separate trip going via Mersa.

Getting There & Away

Bahariya, Farafra, Dakhla & El Kharga There is a choice of shared taxis and buses to the oases. The buses run from Cairo and Asyut.

The buses from Cairo leave from 45 Al Azhar St and can be difficult to find since it's in a back yard and the sign is entirely in Arabic. The route is Cairo to Bahariya, Farafra and Dakhla then return. There are express buses on Monday, Wednesday and Saturday at 9 am. There are also ordinary buses on Tuesday, Thursday and Sunday at 9 am. All these buses return the following day. The fares are E£4.10 (Cairo to Bahariya), E£3 (Bahariya to Farafra), E£5 (Farafra to Dakhla) and E£10 (Dakhla to Cairo). From Cairo to Bahariya takes about seven hours. In Cairo you should try to reserve your seat two days in advance. The price for a shared taxi will have to be negotiated. Get a group together.

Between Cairo and Kharga there is a daily air-con bus at 10 am – reserve seats at least two days in advance. There are also daily buses from Asyut to Kharga which cost E£2 (air-con) and E£1.60 (ordinary) and take four hours.

Mersa Matruh to Siwa There is a daily bus at 3 pm and usually another at 7 am (but make enquiries about this one the day before because it doesn't always go). In the opposite direction the bus departs Siwa daily at 10 am. The fare is E£3 and the journey takes about five hours.

Siwa to Alexandria There is a daily bus from Siwa to Alexandria at 5 am which usually spends two hours circling the oases before it leaves. The fare is E£6 and the journey takes about 10 hours.

Bahariya Oasis

This oasis is quite a large one and consists of four villages. The administrative centre is Bawiti. People who live in this oasis are very friendly, so just take off, wander through the date and citrus orchards and see who you meet. Have warm clothes for the night as it gets very cold.

Things to See Apart from the **hot springs** in Bawiti, there are others further afield. Any of the mentioned places to stay will arrange an overnight trip to these for around E£1.50 including food. They can also arrange trips to the **White Desert**, about 40 km from Farafra Oasis, for around E£10 per person including food. Even though E£10 is a bit steep for this

trip, the area is spectacular and, under a full moon, it's unforgettable. We have had a few complaints about the trips organised by the Alpenblick so watch out. Some people said it was a litany of disasters and they were left stranded at Farafra. Perhaps it was an isolated event?

Places to Stay & Eat There are a number of places in Bawiti but the most popular is the *Hotel Alpenblick* (previously known as Laconda Salah) which costs E£3 per double including a good breakfast. It is run by a German woman called Gabbi. There's a small store at the hotel (rarely open) and cooking facilities. If you don't want to cook yourself meals can be arranged. It's very basic, friendly and easy going – eat and drink what you like, write it down in the book and pay when leaving. The owner, Salah, is a great guy and will take you to the hot springs where you can wash in the evenings for E£1.25 (there's very little water available for this is Bawiti). Bring mosquito repellent with you.

Other places to stay are the *Hotel d'Alice* which costs 50 pt per person per day (no cooking facilities) and the *Hotel/Café Casino* which costs E£1 per person per day. The latter has a café of sorts and the owner is willing to take groups of people out to the hot springs. He lays a very good hot lunch on for these trips. The Casino also sells beers and you can find a game of chess or dominoes there.

There are several cafés where you can buy basic meals, but if you want to put your own food together you can get fresh vegetables from street sellers and canned goods from the many stores.

Farafra Oasis

You must register with the police on arrival. There is electricity from dusk to 10 pm only. Have warm clothing for the night. Avoid washing your clothes in the hot springs as the iron content of the water will leave them looking decidedly rusty.

Things to See The **Roman Spring** is an iron-free spring in a garden in the village which bubbles up from a very deep well. There are several hot springs and they're quite hot – around 36°C. The one in the village has been piped into a concrete tank and is usually full of children, but there is another about six km north-west (called Bir 6) where you can swim undisturbed.

There are also many small oases just a few km away, so spend a day wandering between them. The experience was described by one traveller as 'more rewarding than all the temples and tombs of Egypt put together'.

Places to Stay & Eat There are two places to stay. The *Rest House* is clean and has a stove which you can use. It costs E£2.15 per bed. There are plenty of mosquitoes in this rest house, so bring repellent. If you're coming from Bahariya it's the first building you see. There is a café of sorts but it only serves sandwiches, tea and cold drinks. Otherwise, make your own arrangements with local people. There are two tiny shops which are closed most of the time and have a very limited range of stock. The best thing to do is make friends with the army, the police, the school teachers or the doctor. They'll be only too pleased to have your company and to offer you a meal.

If you walk around the citrus and date groves, take a bag with you to carry home all the dates, oranges and sweet lemons which will be thrust into your arms.

Dakhla Oasis

Both Dakhla and Kharga are much larger oases than Bahariya and Farafra and are nothing like the palm-fringed pools that movie-goers expect. Mut is the administrative centre of Dakhla. There is now a government tax of E£4.35 to visit Dakhla.

There are regular buses between Dakhla and Kharga.

Ancient **Egyptian ruins & Roman ruins** can be found here and they're open to the public. There are plenty of cafés and even a cinema. However, the oasis is perhaps not as interesting as the more remote ones. There are a lot of squalid tenement blocks going up and new factories are being built. No doubt this is good news for the local people in terms of employment possibilities, but most travellers don't go thousands of km to look at factories.

Places to Stay There's only one place in Mut and it costs E£2.30 per bed and E£4.60 a double. It's clean but there are no cooking facilities. Don't expect washing left on the line unguarded to be there when you return. About four km out of town there is another *Rest House* near the hot springs which costs E£3.30 per person.

Kharga Oasis

While here, make sure you see the **Temple of Hibis** just outside town on the Asyut road. Entry is free. Near the temple is a fascinating **Coptic cemetery** known as Badr el Wait. There are also hot springs in the vicinity.

There is nowhere cheap to stay. The *New Valley Tourist Home* (known locally as the *Hotel Metallco*) costs E£3.20/4.60 for a single/double. The other hotel costs E£7 per night.

Siwa Oasis

This is a beautiful jewel of an oasis about 300 km south-west of Mersa Matruh in a depression to the west of the Qattara Depression. It has some interesting historical relics and the landscape is stunning. Cambysses lost an army trying to get here in 525 BC and Alexander the Great paid a mysterious but peaceful visit to the Temple of Amun here in 331 BC where he was crowned. Part of his coronation hall still stands and a watchtower affords panoramic views over the old town, the nearby hills, desert dunes and salt flats as well as the flat-topped hills bordering Libya.

Information Special permission must be obtained before visiting Siwa but this is just a formality. It costs nothing and takes about half an hour in Mersa Matruh. You must photocopy the page of your passport which has your personal details and photograph (photocopies can be made in Mersa Matruh) and take this to the permit office in the evening before you want to leave between 7 and 10 pm. Ask for as many days permission as you require.

Make sure you dress very modestly in Siwa. It's a very traditional oasis and all the women still cover themselves completely. The Siwis speak a Bedouin-type language but are being slowly Egyptianised. TV has made its appearance and a new road is being built to connect Siwa with Bahariya Oasis. Electricity is available from 7 pm to 1 am only, so bring candles if you want light after that.

On arrival in Siwa you must check in with police – provided it's before 10 pm (the 3 pm bus from Mersa can be very *inshallah* as it comes direct from Alexandria. The police will take your passport and tell you to report back at 9 am the following morning. When you do this they'll take you to the military police who will provide a guide to walk with you round the 11 km of Siwa's main sights.

The day prior to leaving report to the police station between 7 and 10 pm to get your permit stamped. Don't neglect to do this or you'll be sent back from one or other of the police checkpoints between Siwa and Mersa. You'll get your passport back at this time too.

Things to See With the guide you'll view **Alexander's Coronation Hall**, climb the watchtower, and visit the Amun Temple (only a few stones left), **Cleopatra's Bath** where spring water bubbles up from rocks some six metres down (men can swim here – there's a women's bath nearby) and the nearby hills. Despite the heat, the tour isn't that exhausting but you will need to drink a lot. Your guide will present you with wild pomegranates, dates and grapes as you amble along the palm frond-hedged tracks. The guide will also find clean refreshing spring water when you need a drink. It's possible to visit the nearby salt flats too.

In the evening climb up the hill behind the old town and watch the sun set over Libya.

Places to Stay The cheapest places in Siwa are the *Hotel Medina* and the *Hotel Siwa* both of which cost E£1 per night. There's also another hotel near the police station which is very good and costs E£2 per night. A tourist hotel is being built.

SINAI

The big draws of the Sinai Peninsula are the old **St Catherine's Monastery** near the southern tip of the Sinai Desert, **Mt Sinai**, and the resorts of the east coast – **Namaa Bay**, **Dahab**, **Nuweiba** and **Taba**.

Getting There

You can get to all these places by public bus from either Cairo or Suez. There's now a tunnel under the Suez Canal about 18 km north of Suez so there's no need to go to El Shatt across the other side of the canal any longer.

There are usually three buses daily from Cairo to Sharm el Sheikh. Two of the departure times are 7.30 and 10.30 am. In the opposite direction they depart from the diving club at Namaa Bay at 6.30, 9.30 am and 1.30 pm or from Sharm el Sheikh itself at 7, 10.30 am and 2 pm. There is also a bus at 12 midnight from Sharm el Sheikh to Cairo but it's expensive at E£14. All the daytime buses cost E£9.25 (E£9.75 to Namaa Bay) and take seven hours. The buses depart from the Sinai terminal, which is about one km from Abassiya Square past the army barracks. There's a huge sign in English so you can't miss it.

The buses from Suez to Sharm el Sheikh depart daily at 7.30 am and cost E£7. In the opposite direction they depart Sharm el Sheikh daily at 9 am and 7 pm.

There are two direct buses per day leaving Cairo (Sinai terminal) for St Catherine's Monastery at 7 am (air-con, E£10) and 10.30 am (E£8). The 10 am bus makes one stop en route and drops you off at the crossroads about three km from the monastery by 4.30 pm. In the opposite direction the buses leave St Catherine's daily at 6 am and 1 pm except on Saturdays when there is only one bus at 6 am. There are also buses from Suez to St Catherine's daily at 9.30 am which cost E£5. You can also get to St Catherine's from Sharm el Sheikh by bus which departs daily at 11 am (in the opposite direction at 8 am). It costs E£4 and takes about five hours. Other alternatives are to go by taxi, minibus or bus between St Catherine's and Nuweiba along the 100 km of dirt track. Taxis cost E£4.50 per person, minibuses E£4 and buses E£3.

There is at least one daily bus in either direction between Sharm el Sheikh and Taba (the Egyptian-Israeli border) via Nuweiba and Dahab. The most predictable is the one which leaves Sharm el Sheikh between 8 and 9 am and reaches Taba about 1 pm via Dahab (around 10.30 am) and Nuweiba (around 12 noon). In the opposite direction the bus leaves Taba daily at 3 pm and arrives at Sharm el Sheikh approximately 7 pm. The journey time varies between four and 5½ hours and the fare is E£4.

There are also several other buses running daily which connect Sharm el Sheikh, Dahab and Nuweiba but don't go all the way to Taba. Their departure and arrival times are less predictable than the Sharm el Sheikh to Taba buses.

St Catherine's Monastery

Although St Catherine's is becoming something of a tourist trap these days, it's worth making the effort to see this ancient monastery either for its own sake or en route to the east coast resorts. There are still some 17 Greek Orthodox monks in residence so please remember that it's not just a museum. There is no entry charge but you are only allowed to see the 'skull room' (full of the bones of deceased monks) and the beautiful chapel. The monastery is only open to visitors between 9.30 am and 12.30 pm. It's closed on Friday, Sunday and all Orthodox Christian holidays.

Things to See From St Catherine's you can climb **Mt Sinai** (2228 metres). There are two well-defined routes, one via a series of steps and the other by path. The latter starts from the back of the monastery but ask one of the monks for directions if you're not sure where to start. If you go by the path it will take about 2½ hours for the ascent and 1½ hours for the descent. It's best to take the path going up and the steps coming down. There is a tiny mosque on the top and a small chapel containing beautiful paintings and ornaments but they are both usually locked. Even if the mosque is unlocked it's suggested you don't sleep in there otherwise you may well be flung out on your ear at 4 am by irate Muslims going there to pray. If you're fairly robust and have plenty of warm clothing, it's suggested you climb up there for the sunset, camp overnight, then return as the sun rises. The views are magnificent! It's unlikely you will be rewarded with a burning bush and it's also very unlikely you will be able to find any fuel for a fire. There is a well near the summit but it's best to take water with you. There's also a Bedouin who sells tea and biscuits at normal prices!

Places to Stay It used to be possible to stay overnight in the actual monastery with prior permission from the Coptic Cathedral in Cairo, but the monks found many of their visitors disturbing so now you can only stay in the hostel next door. This isn't a very friendly place and costs E£5 per night. However, it's clean and comfortable with cooking facilities and cold water showers. You must bring your own food. To pay and to get the key you have to go inside the monastery and contact one of the monks. The hostel is only open between 5 and 7 pm and it's often full.

If the hostel is full or you can't handle the curfew stay at the Bedouin 'hotel' about two km from the monastery. Accommodation is on foam mattresses in large tents and costs E£1. There's fresh water and toilets but meals are not available so bring your own food. There's one restaurant in St Catherine's village, two basic shops and a bakery. Bread from the bakery costs 2 pt. The hotel which used to be in the village has been closed down.

The only other accommodation possibility is the very expensive tourist resort hotel about 20 km away near the airstrip which costs E£47 a double!

THE EAST COAST RESORTS

Since the Israelis handed the Sinai back to Egypt a number of resorts have sprung up on the east coast which are attracting more and more travellers each year. They are **Sharm el Sheikh**, **Namaa Bay** (five km north of Sharm el Sheikh), **Dahab**, **Nuweiba** and **Taba** (on the Egyptian-Israeli border). All these resorts have similar set-ups – expensive chalet-type accommodation, bars, restaurants and diving clubs with equipment for hire. A few hundred metres up the beach are colonies of budget travellers living in some form of makeshift accommodation or simply on the beach. This type of accommodation is fairly commercialised in Nuweiba and Namaa Bay as local entrepreneurs have moved in, but Dahab is much quieter. Here there are huts scattered along the beach which were built by the Bedouin and then abandoned when they moved to the present village a few km up the coast. Snorkelling is excellent, though some people say it's not as good as at Namaa Bay or Sharm el Sheikh.

Sharm el Sheikh

Sharm el Sheikh has a good beach with coral reefs about two km east of town – on the way there you pass through a police checkpoint where you will be told you cannot sleep on the beach.

It also has two supermarkets with a limited selection of food, a bakery, a small vegetable market, a gas station, bank and tourist police office.

Places to Stay & Eat In town directly above the bus station there is a *Youth Hostel* which costs E£3 per night but you must have a membership card. It's clean and has cold water showers, cooking facilities and a small shop for tea, biscuits, chocolate, etc. The breakfast here (E£1) has been described as 'revolting'.

Just behind the youth hostel is the *Cliff Top Hotel* where you can pitch your own tent for E£4 or rent a bed in an already erected tent for E£9.50 per person (!). Campers can use the cold showers and the very clean toilets. The staff are friendly.

The *Fishermen's Café* at the bottom of the hill past the service station offers good filling meals of fish, chicken, chips and bread for E£3 to E£4 per meal. Portions are large.

Dahab

Dahab is a kind of Egyptian equivalent to India's Goa and attracts hundreds of young travellers. The beach is excellent and snorkelling is just as good as at Sharm el Sheikh though the coral isn't as extensive.

Information You need to register with the police after two days. It's also a good idea to keep a clean house as the police are making regular checks on travellers' haunts these days. The cafés are also obliged to close by 10 pm.

There are actually two villages at Dahab – the Bedouin village and Dahab village itself. On arrival, ask the taxi drivers to take you to the Bedouin village otherwise you'll end up at the mega-dollar tourist resort.

There are buses to Sharm el Sheikh at 8.30 am, 12.30, 2.30, 5.30 and 8.30 pm (E£2); to Cairo at 8 am and 4.30 pm, and to Nuweiba and Taba at 10.30 am and 4.30 pm.

Places to Stay & Eat Accommodation at the Bedouin village is in thatched huts on or near the beach. They come in all shapes and sizes but cost E£2 each. None of them have showers and there are toilets for only one group of huts. If you're not in that block, you'll have to make your own arrangements.

There's also a camp site near the bus station where you can hire a tent for E£6. Facilities include showers and ice.

Excellent cheap seafood can be bought at all the beach restaurants. *Totas* and *Dahab Stars* have been recommended as among the best. A good meal at either would cost E£2 to E£3.

In Dahab village there is a good grocery store and a bakery (a green building on the hill) and you can also buy a limited range of other food (including vegetables). Pitta bread at the bakery costs just 1 pt! The water is brackish but you can buy bottled water for 60 pt per bottle. The village is about three km from the beach where most people stay (about 50 pt by shared taxi).

Namaa Bay

Namaa Bay is, in effect, a R&R place for American GIs and other soldiers from the multinational Sinai force on weekends when they descend with portable coolers full of beer and ice. At this time the beach is lit up and cassette players blare away till midnight. As you might expect, with a clientele like that, it's not a particularly cheap place.

Snorkelling gear (E£5 per day) and scuba diving equipment are available for hire but the latter is expensive – around E£50 for a boat and two tanks to take you to Ras Mohammed. Windsurfing is also available (around E£6 per hour).

Places to Stay There are two camp sites next to one another and there's not a lot to choose between them. Probably the most popular is *Gaffy Camp* (sometimes called Family Garf's Camping) which costs E£8.50 per person for a large tent and E£3 per person for a very small tent. The price for the large tents includes breakfast. If you take a small tent, breakfast is E£1.60 extra. The staff are friendly and there are hot showers. The restaurant here is very overpriced (E£6 for a macaroni meal).

The other camp site is operated by Sinai Hotel & Diving Co and charges E£6.25 per person or E£1.50 if you have your own tent. Electricity is provided and there is water in the showers and toilets for half an hour in the mornings only.

The *El Sharm Hotel* will cost you E£25 per night minimum.

Places to Eat Although there is a well-stocked supermarket in Namaa, it's expensive. Those wanting to conserve funds will have to hitch into Sharm el Sheikh and buy bread and other food at normal prices. Sharm el Sheikh is some eight km south and the best time to hitch is around 8 am when there's plenty of traffic.

Most travellers spend the evenings at the *Snack Bar* since they play a lot of western music. Breakfast costs E£2 to E£3 but you can buy spaghetti for E£1.50.

Nuweiba

As at Namaa Bay, the Sinai Hotel & Diving Co offer three-bed tents for hire but they cost E£10.80 per night. If you can't afford this, sleep under the pointed roof shelters on the protected beach for E£1 per night (something of a rip-off since you're not getting very much for your money). Officially you are not allowed to sleep on the open beach – the police do patrol it – but in practice if you sleep (free) close to the dividing fence and near the tents and cars you shouldn't have any problems.

The protected beach has an expensive restaurant and a shower/toilet block with water all day which costs 25 pt to get in and allows up to three visits per day.

There are restaurants scattered along

the beach. Most of them offer freshly grilled fish, chips and salad for around E£2. There's also a small village nearby where you can buy fruit, vegetables, bread and cheese from the small store.

There are two daily boats to Aqaba (Jordan) which take about four hours and cost E£38. Book a day in advance.

Equatorial Guinea

One of Africa's smallest nations, this former Spanish colony is made up of the islands of Bioko (formerly Fernando Póo) and Pagalu (formerly Annabón), and the mainland enclave of Mbini (formerly Rio Muni).

It attained independence in October 1968 under the presidency of Macias Nguema and for a little while enjoyed a period of relatively free democracy. Several months after independence, however, relations with Spain deteriorated rapidly when it was discovered that the country had almost no foreign currency reserves. Nguema accused Spanish entrepreneurs of neocolonialism in their attempts to renegotiate timber contracts, and encouraged his supporters to intimidate the 7000 Spanish citizens still living in the country. Following a stormy meeting with the Spanish ambassador, Nguema all but ordered the ambassador to leave. Spain reacted by mobilising units of its army stationed in Equatorial Guinea and Nguema responded by declaring a state of emergency. The stage was set for a 10-year dictatorship whose brutality was on a par with that perpetrated by Amin in Uganda and Bokassa in the Central African Republic.

Macias Nguema began his reign of terror by arresting and summarily executing his foreign minister, Atanasio Ndongo, and Equatorial Guinea's ambassador to the UN, Saturnino Ibongo, along with a number of other prominent politicians who had attempted to defuse the political crisis and stop the attacks on the Spanish citizens. They were accused of plotting against Nguema with the connivance of the Spanish.

Over the next 10 years 'plots' and 'conspiracies' were discovered round every corner. Many thousands of people were tortured and executed in the jails of Malabo and Bata, or beaten to death in the forced-labour camps of the mainland. At the height of this butcher's madness there were over 28,000 political prisoners in these camps. Almost all the prominent politicians from the independence period were eliminated and replaced by members of Nguema's family. Intellectuals were personally hunted down by Nguema and either executed or forced to flee into exile. By the time Nguema's regime was toppled in 1979 only one third of the 300,000 Guineans who lived there at independence remained.

Halfway through his reign, Nguema, unable to command either the loyalty or support of his people, was forced to bring in expatriate labour, mainly from Nigeria. However, poor conditions and low wages led to riots and strikes which were crushed with much bloodshed by the army and police. The shooting of these Nigerian workers led to a crisis with Nigeria and demands by politicians in Nigeria for the annexation of Equatorial Guinea. Finally, after diplomats at the Nigerian Embassy in Malabo had been badly beaten by members of Nguema's youth movement, the remaining 20,000 Nigerians were repatriated. The following year, 1977, Spain broke off diplomatic relations and only a handful of Spanish citizens remained in the country.

It wasn't just political figures, intellectuals and expatriates who were persecuted. The Catholic Church, too, was dragged into the net. Priests were arrested and expelled for plots real or imaginary, and in 1975 all mission-run

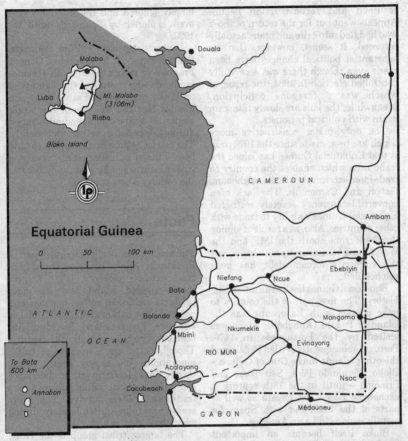

Equatorial Guinea

0   50   100 km

ATLANTIC

OCEAN

To Bata
600 km

Annobon

RIO MUNI

schools were closed, effectively putting an end to formal education in the country. This was followed in 1978 by the forced closure of all churches.

With the country in shambles, bankrupt and all economic activity at a standstill, even Nguema's closest colleagues began to suspect that he was insane, and he was toppled by a coup in August 1979. Along with his bodyguards he fled to his home town of Mongomo on the mainland with every asset he could lay his hands on from the national bank vaults. He was finally brought to heel at Ebebiyin on the

Gabonese border. Nguema, the former chiefs of Malabo and Bata jails, Nguema's chief bodyguard and several others of Nguema's clique were executed in September 1979.

The new government was headed by Colonel Teodoro Nguema, Macias Nguema's nephew, and it seemed for a while that order and some degree of political freedom might be restored. Nguema ordered the release of all political prisoners and the lifting of restrictions on the Catholic Church. Relations with Spain and other western countries were resumed and reconstruction begun. Appeals went out for the return of those who had fled into exile and many actually returned. It seems, however, that no substantial political changes have been made even though there was a carefully controlled election in 1984, the result of which was a foregone conclusion. Meanwhile, the jails are slowly filling up again with political prisoners.

The only major constructive move which has been made since the 1979 coup is that Equatorial Guinea has joined the franc zone which enables the country to trade more extensively with its neighbours, Gabon and Cameroun. The lack of a convertible currency severely restricted Equatorial Guinea's ability to trade with other countries. Also, as a result of joining the franc zone, both the IMF and the World Bank have come up with loans, and the country's foreign debt has been rescheduled.

Equatorial Guinea has had an interesting history. The first part of the country to have contact with Europeans was the island of Pagalu (Annabón), which was visited by the Portuguese in 1470. Portugal subsequently settled Pagalu and the other islands in the Gulf of Guinea – Bioko (Fernando Póo), São Tomé and Principe – until in the 18th century it exchanged Bioko and Pagalu as well as parts of the mainland with Spain for certain regions in Latin America.

Bioko itself became an important staging post and slaving base for several European nations during the 19th century when the rest of West Africa was being colonised. Malabo was founded as a naval base by Britain in 1827 – the first governor of the island appointed by Spain some 20 years later was an Englishman. Britain's interest in the island waned as naval bases were set up on the mainland and control passed to Spain. Cocoa plantations were started on the island in the late 19th century, making Malabo Spain's most important possession in equatorial Africa. The mainland enclave of Rio Muni was largely ignored and the interior wasn't even explored by Spaniards until the 1920s.

During the Spanish Civil War, Equatorial Guinea came out in support of General Franco – or rather the Spanish absentee landlords who controlled the plantations on Bioko came out in Franco's support. Macias Nguema was one of the people employed by the colonial administration during this period as well as subsequently. The fascist regime would appear to have been a major influence on his concept of government when he eventually became the country's first president.

Facts

The most economically important part of Equatorial Guinea, Bioko, is formed from three extinct volcanoes. It's a rugged, jungle-covered island and its main products are cocoa, coffee, bananas and palm oil. The nation's capital, Malabo, is also here. The mainland, Rio Muni, has been largely bypassed in the 20th century. Though there are a number of coffee plantations, it's mostly gently rising, thickly forested country with an abundance of wildlife and interesting villages where traditional beliefs survive. The rainy season runs from April to January, during which humidity is high.

The largest tribal group is the Fang, who make up about 80% of the population of Rio Muni (240,000). Minor tribal groups include the Kombe, Balengue and Bujeba. Macias Nguema was a Fang and so is his successor. On Bioko the most numerous group was formerly the Bubi, but with the economy in dire straits many Fang have been forced to migrate to the island and they now outnumber the others.

VISAS
Visas are required by everyone. There are embassies in Addis Ababa (Ethiopia), Lagos (Nigeria), Libreville (Gabon),

Madrid, Paris, Rabat (Morocco) and Yaoundé (Cameroun) and consulates in Las Palmas (Canary Islands) and Douala (Cameroun).

The price of visas and the length of stay given vary widely and are subject to change. In Douala they cost CFA 5000, are valid for a stay of 15 days and an onward ticket is required. In Yaoundé they cost CFA 3000, take 24 hours to issue and are valid for a stay of 15 days. In Madrid (Alonso Cano 27) they cost Ptas 1000 for a seven-day visa and are issued in 24 hours. No onward ticket is required and no questions asked. In Paris (Rue Alfred de Vigny 6, 75008 Paris) they cost FFr 75, take 24 hours to issue and are valid for a stay of 30 days.

If you have to buy an onward ticket for Equatorial Guinea, probably the cheapest is a Malabo to Douala Air Cameroun ticket.

Visa extensions are virtually impossible to get. Expect customs clearance to take a long time as there are very heavy searches both entering and leaving.

Other Visas

The main foreign embassies in Malabo are France, Gabon, Nigeria, Spain and the USA. Malabo has been suggested as a good place to get a visa for Gabon since there's no fuss, showing of money or onward ticket required.

Cameroun The embassy in Malabo may refuse to issue tourist visas. They will issue transit visas but you must have a return ticket.

Togo These can be obtained from the French Embassy while you wait. The consul is a very friendly and helpful man.

MONEY

US$1 = CFA 284

The unit of currency is the CFA franc.

Equatorial Guinea is a very expensive

place to visit and shortages of goods are frequent.

Many old banknotes from when the unit of currency was the ekuele are still in circulation and can be bought as collectors' items. Coins are much more scarce and in great demand by coin dealers in the west.

Airport tax for international flights is CFA 1000.

POST

Try to avoid having mail sent to Malabo as most things never arrive. If you must have mail sent, make sure letters are addressed to Lista de Correos, Malabo (that's the Spanish for poste restante). On the other hand, mail from Malabo apparently gets to its destination quickly and postage rates are cheap.

LANGUAGE

The official language is Spanish though Fang is the native tongue of most people on the mainland.

Getting There & Around

AIR

Air Cameroun and Iberia fly Douala to Malabo on Wednesday and Saturday and vice versa for CFA 18,500 one-way. If you get stuck it may be possible to get lifts in private planes chartered by businesspeople from Malabo to Douala but expect to pay CFA 25,000 to CFA 30,000 – though occasionally it is free. Also, private flights are occasionally available from Libreville, Gabon. Lage, the local airline, also operates charter flights to Libreville.

An internal flight which may be of interest is the daily Malabo to Bata flight which costs about US$15. It may take two or three days to get on the flight, as overbooking is common. At the airport, it's first come, first served so be there at least two hours before departure.

On your arrival in Bata from Malabo,

immigration officials can act as if you've flown into a different country and may tell you that your visa isn't valid. Just hang on patiently – they'll let you through in the end.

ROAD

There are good sealed roads on Bioko, but on the mainland most of the roads are unsealed. Hitching is very good. There are few cars but everyone stops (foreigners are still a novelty after Macias Nguema's regime). Police roadblocks dot the island's roads. Have foreign cigarettes handy to ensure a smooth passage.

A service taxi from Malabo to Luba costs CFA 1000. From Bata to Ebebiyin (Cameroun border) by truck costs CFA 3600.

If you're heading south for Gabon, there's a truck every two to three days from Bata to Acalayong (Gabon border). From Acalayong there are motorised dugouts to Coco Beach – the cost should be around CFA 3000. It takes about 2½ hours depending on the tides. If you're only willing to pay CFA 2000, the boat owner will probably take you one hour downstream to a place where you'll have to a pay a CFA 2000 'exit permit'. Watch out for corrupt army personnel in Acalayong as they have been known to confiscate items of gear in an attempt to extract bribes. They especially like knives.

BOAT

There is a boat which plies between Malabo and Bata about once a month. It's very overcrowded and the journey takes two days. Small boats, operated by Nigerians, also do the Limbe to Malabo trip and you'll find yourself with a lot of Africans from different countries but there won't be any white people. The name of the boat owner is 'Fine Face' who will quote the fare at CFA 6000, though the guy who collects the money may only take CFA 5000. Before you pay ask if they have handed in their manifest to the police because only then can they sail. If

you can't find anything out ask around for Stanislaus Ndikum, a boarding officer for the National Ports Authority who is pleasant and helpful. Buy him a couple of beers and tell him Paul from Switzerland sends his greetings.

There are no flights to Pagalu and a boat only goes there once every three months so it's difficult to get there.

Around the Country

BATA

This is the principal town on the mainland. There are two cheap hotels, the *Hotel Central* (dirty) and the *Hotel Finisterre* (clean) which both cost the same. The one expensive hotel, the *Hotel Panafricaine* faces the sea and has rooms for CFA 11,000. The *Club de Tenis* has expensive meals for CFA 4000.

EBEBIYIN

Ebebiyin is the first village of any size in Rio Muni as you come across the border from Cameroun. There's no running water and electricity is only available between 7 and 10 pm. The only hotel is the *Hotel Mbengono*. It's dirty and you have to wash in the river. Cheaper but more basic accommodation is available in the bar on the main street.

LUBA

Luba is the island's second city and has some very good, quiet, deserted beaches nearby. It was supposedly a Russian base when Macias Nguema was in power and the local children still speak a few words of Russian.

Places to Stay

The *Hotel Jones* is pleasantly situated near mineral water springs and costs CFA 7000/11,000 for a single/double. It is owned by an eccentric German and his Madagascan wife who argue incessantly but it is renowned for the best meals in

Equatorial Guinea at CFA 2500 a plate for antelope, fish, etc. The German man speaks French, Spanish and English. It is also possible to stay at the *Mission*, 12 km north of town. There are daily taxi trucks from Malabo to Luba which cost CFA 1000.

Some seven km before Luba coming from Malabo is the small fishing village of **Arena Blanca** where you can camp on the beach. From the main road where you will be dropped, it's a 15-minute walk. Make sure you register with the police in Luba first before camping or you could be in trouble.

If you find Luba too hot take a 20-km trip (along bad roads) to **Moka** at an altitude of 1600 metres. They grow vegetables in the cooler climate.

MALABO

The capital, Malabo, is a beautiful town full of Spanish colonial buildings and open plazas with cloud-capped Mt Malabo as a backdrop which, incidentally, is a military area and out of bounds. There are no beaches worth mentioning – if you're looking for these go to Luba.

If arriving by air you will have to take a taxi from the airport to town (about 7½ km). It costs CFA 1500 to CFA 3000 but you'll have to haggle for that. There are no buses.

The water supply in Malabo is erratic. It's generally only available in the mornings and evenings and not for long at that.

Places to Stay

It's more than likely you'll be offered a place to stay by local people before you ever set foot in a hotel, but if an invitation isn't forthcoming one of the cheapest places to stay is the *Hotel Flores* close to the GPO. It is very clean and costs CFA 5000/7000 for a single/double. Most of the other hotels are on the expensive side. They include the *Hotel Bahia*, which is beautifully situated on the Malabo Bay but is somewhat run down and costs CFA 7000/11,000 for a single/double; the *Hotel Eureka*, and the *Hotel Impala*. There's also the *Impala Apartments Hotel* which costs CFA 12,000 a double with air-con (when it works) and cooking facilities.

Places to Eat

The cheapest place to eat is in the market. Restaurants are generally expensive though *El Cachirulo* has snacks for CFA 500. Other than this there are two other restaurants: the *Miramare*, near the harbour, with meals for CFA 5500; and the *Beiruthi* which is a Lebanese restaurant offering good meals for CFA 3000 and up. All food is scarce and even fruit is expensive.

TOURIST VISA NO 001

Equatorial Guinea was virtually closed for years during Macias Nguema's time as president and, even these days, few travellers visit the country. It should, however, be put firmly back on the map. So, to give you some idea of what to expect we're reprinting the popular account of a visit to this country sent in by David Bennett of Canada:

I knew that Equatorial Guinea was off the beaten track, but I didn't fully realise the remoteness of the place until I looked down at my freshly stamped passport. I had just been issued Tourist Visa No 001.

Actually, my presence in the country was quite accidental. My original intention was to travel overland from Cameroun to Gabon, bypassing Equatorial Guinea. Upon my arrival in Cameroun, however, the authorities insisted that I purchase an onward air ticket. Financial considerations and my southward destination made me decide to take the weekly flight to the Guinean town of Bata. My map showed it to be a mere 125 km by road from the Gabonese border.

My outdated guidebook described Bata as a thriving commercial centre with a population of some 30,000 people. I knew, of course, that things had probably changed. Six months earlier, a coup had deposed President Macias Nguema, one of Africa's most tyrannical dictators. During his 10-year rule, many people disappeared, the country's economy collapsed,

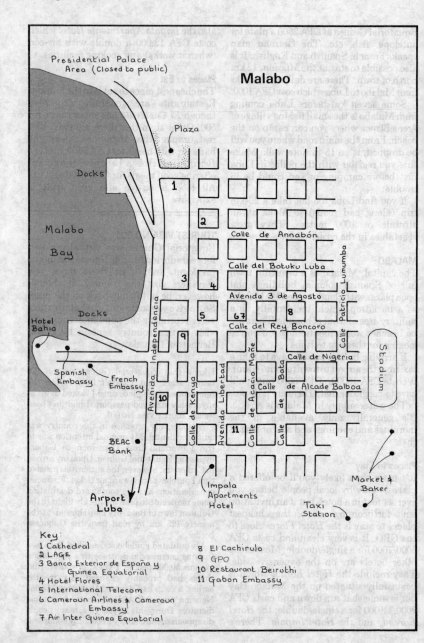

Malabo

Presidential Palace Area (Closed to public)

Plaza

Docks

Malabo Bay

Docks

Hotel Bahia

Spanish Embassy

French Embassy

Calle de Annabón

Calle del Botuku Luba

Avenida 3 de Agosto

Calle del Rey Boncoro

Calle de Nigeria

Calle de Alcade Balboa

Avenida Independencia

Avenida Libertad

Calle de Kenya

Calle de Acacio Mañe

Calle de Bata

Patricio Lumumba

Stadium

BEAC Bank

Impala Apartments Hotel

Market & Baker

Taxi Station

Airport Luba

Key:
1 Cathedral
2 LAGE
3 Banco Exterior de España y
   Guinea Equatorial
4 Hotel Flores
5 International Telecom
6 Cameroun Airlines & Cameroun
   Embassy
7 Air Inter Guinea Equatorial

8 El Cachirulo
9 GPO
10 Restaurant Beiruthi
11 Gabon Embassy

and half the population was forced to flee. This information didn't fully prepare me for what I found. The centre of Bata was a virtual ghost town. The handsome Spanish colonial buildings were boarded up, and the well-maintained streets were empty of both people and vehicles. I surmised that the refugees had little reason to return here from the relative prosperity of Cameroun or Gabon.

This conclusion did nothing to alleviate my present predicament, however. Knowing there to be no flights, I resigned myself to the possibility of having to walk to Gabon. After about half an hour, I was surprised to come upon an apparently well-populated thatched suburb. I say surprised, but after travelling in Africa for a while, nothing seems that surprising. I therefore did not find it strange to hear the sound of a 15-year-old Beatles' record blaring from a large thatched building. Nor did I find it that strange to enter the building and find a well-stocked bar and about 100 dancing patrons, 80 of whom were young women. I am sure the most bizarre event to occur that day was the entrance of a lone white man, with a bag strapped to his back.

In any case, I settled down to enjoy a few beers, answer curious questions and gather more information. Amidst many offers of overnight accommodation, I was able to ascertain that a vehicle would be making its weekly journey to Acalayong, the southernmost town, the very next day.

The next morning, a decrepit pick-up truck did, indeed, turn up. I thankfully scrambled into the back with sacks of grain, baskets of live chickens and about 15 other passengers. Apart from one small village, there was very little to see during the eight-hour journey. The road was in deplorable condition, practically swallowed up by the dense jungle which closed in tightly on both sides. By the time the truck wheezed into Acalayong, I was alone, my fellow passengers having disappeared into the bush along the way.

Acalayong consisted of 30 huts huddled on the shore of a broad estuary. At the shallow water's edge was beached a flotilla of hollowed-out log canoes, some sporting outboard motors. After intense bargaining, one of the owners agreed to take me across the estuary to Gabon. Soon we were underway, skimming over the water which occasionally surged over the prow of the low-sitting canoe.

We must have travelled a good three hours before the engine sputtered to a halt. The estuary had widened considerably at this point and the change in water colour indicated that we were geographically in the Atlantic Ocean. Apart from a few nearby islets, land appeared to be very far away indeed. I was, therefore, greatly relieved when the current carried us to one of these islets, rather than out to sea.

To be truthful, when we landed I really was surprised. There was a village on this half-square-km dot of land, and I was surely the first traveller to ever visit it. Not only that, but the friendly villagers considered me to be an honoured guest who had obviously come there to settle. By nightfall, a reed hut had been constructed for me to live in. Then I, and the entire village, sat down to a feast of grilled fish, manioc and copious quantities of palm wine. This was followed by dancing, drumming, and drinking long into the night.

It was very late when I finally staggered to my hut, and I did not have the inclination to reflect on my onward journey. Were I feeling romantic, I may have conjured up a multitude of exotic, Robinson Crusoe-style scenarios. But sleep intervened and I awoke to the reality of a buzzing outboard motor. And so it was, with the entire village enthusiastically waving farewell, that the possessor of Tourist Visa No 001 finally departed Equatorial Guinea.

Ethiopia

Among African countries Ethiopia is unique in that it largely avoided colonisation except for a brief Italian occupation shortly before and during part of WW II. It also has a home-grown Christian Church dating back to the 4th century AD which has successfully resisted the onslaughts of Islam right up to the present day. Whether it will resist the attacks of doctrinal Marxism-Leninism remains to be seen. The prospects don't look bright at present as the country has become, to all intents and purposes, a Russian satellite state.

Despite the presence of thousands of Russian and Cuban soldiers, the country is wracked by internal revolt, the most serious conflict being in Eritrea, which has been going on for decades. The only way of getting in is by air to Addis Ababa. Overland entry is not permitted. Going anywhere other than Addis and a few other places is hedged with all sorts of bureaucratic restrictions but things are opening up a little so it's worth persevering. It's a beautiful country with a fascinating culture and history.

If the stories in the Christian bible are to be believed, Ethiopia's first entry onto the stage of history began with the Queen of Sheba's visit to King Solomon around 1000 BC. Whether this is fact or fantasy is anyone's guess but the first recorded kingdom in Ethiopia grew up around Axum in the northern highlands during the 3rd century BC, at a time when the Egyptian-influenced state of Meroe was flourishing near what is today Shendi in Sudan. Axum was an offshoot of the Semitic Sabean kingdoms of southern Arabia and soon became the greatest ivory market in north-east Africa. Its king traded with Egyptians and Greeks and even spoke their languages.

Over the next few centuries Axum gradually encroached on Meroe until, in

the 4th century AD when Christianity became the state religion, it finally conquered that declining kingdom and forced its rulers to flee to western Sudan. Christianity was adopted when a Syrian youth and his brother were taken to Axum after being stranded in Adulis, Axum's main port on the Red Sea coast. The remains of Adulis lie buried some 40 km south of present-day Massawa. The youth, Frumentius, grew up in Axum and succeeded in converting the king of Axum to Christianity. He was later consecrated as the first bishop at Axum in 330 AD.

Axum went on to conquer parts of the Yemen and southern Arabia and was to remain the dominant power in the area until after the death of the Prophet Mohammed. During this period, the Axumite and Byzantine emperors collaborated to promote trade in silk and spices from India to Europe via the Red Sea. Even when the armies of Islam began to sweep out in all directions from Mecca and were able to take advantage of a temporary weakness in the kingdom to capture Massawa and the neighbouring Dahlak Islands, Axum remained in control of the western Red Sea coast down to Zeila in Somalia.

As Islam expanded, however, Ethiopia was cut off from direct access to its former Mediterranean trading partners and allies, and Muslim merchants gradually replaced the Egyptians, Greeks and Jews in the Red Sea ports. Surprisingly, this didn't result in hostilities between Ethiopia and the Arab armies.

Historians believe that part of the reason for this remarkable coexistence, compared with European relations with Islam, is the fact that Ethiopia adopted the so-called Monophysite heresy (condemned by orthodox Christianity in 451 AD). This allowed for a 'live and let live' arrangement between the two religions, similar to that enjoyed by the Egyptian Copts. Under the pact, the Ethiopians were allowed to continue to consecrate their bishops in Cairo and thousands of Christian pilgrims were able to make the journey to Jerusalem

in safety without any restrictions on their religious rites and ceremonies. Even Saladin, one of the greatest opponents of the Crusaders, allowed the Ethiopians to maintain their own church in Jerusalem.

The Ethiopians did not, however, have the same relationship with the pagan tribes to the south, and it was from this area that the first major challenge came to their highland empire. Pressure from these tribes eventually forced the Ethiopian emperors to adopt the life of nomadic military commanders living in temporary tented cities and its priests to become monks and hermits in order to keep the religion alive. In time the tribes were pacified and the kingdom recovered sufficiently to take in the provinces of Amhara, Lasta, Gojam and Damot. At the same time the capital was moved south to Amhara province.

Muslim expansion into Ethiopia began in the 12th century as a number of independent trading kingdoms grew up along the Red Sea coast and gradually began to expand down the Awash Valley following the line of the present-day railway between Djibouti and Addis Ababa. Their wealth was based principally on trade in slaves, ivory and gold acquired from the pagan tribes and kingdoms south of the highlands down into the area of the great lakes. They were not to remain independent for long and became Ethiopian vassal states during the 13th and 14th centuries. The largest of these Muslim states – Ifat – was finally eclipsed in 1415 and its people forced to flee to the Yemen after the king was killed in battle at the capital, Zeila.

Ethiopian fortunes were reversed in the 16th century with the expansion of the Ottoman Empire. The Turks, who succeeded the Mamelukes in Egypt, began to support the various Muslim kingdoms in their struggles with the Ethiopians by providing firearms and artillery, and it was only the intervention of the Portuguese in 1542 which saved the Christian empire from collapse. For 100 years thereafter, Portuguese missionaries tried unsuccessfully to persuade the Ethiopians to accept the Pope in Rome as head of the Church.

After what was truly a remarkable life span the empire broke down into its constituent provinces in the 18th century, and 100 years of constant warfare between one warlord and another followed. The shattered empire was eventually put together again by Ras Kassa, who managed to have himself crowned emperor at Axum under the name of Theodore in 1855. He went on to build something approaching a modern army which he used to unite the provinces of Tigre, Amhara and Shoa.

His arrogant treatment of British envoys, however, led to his downfall. A military expedition was mounted by the British under the command of Napier in 1867. After much hardship, the expedition reached the fortress of Magdala and blockaded it for several months. Abandoned by many of his vassals, Theodore shot himself.

His successor, John IV, fought his way to the throne using British arms acquired in exchange for help at Magdala. His success was short-lived and he was forced to accept Menelik, a powerful young vassal king of Shoa, as his heir. While waiting for the throne, Menelik occupied himself building up stocks of European arms, which he used in 1896 to defeat the Italians at Adowa. He expanded his empire at the expense of the Afars, the Somalis of Harrar and the Ogaden, and the Gallas of the south-west. The Italians did, however, manage to hang on to the province of Eritrea which they first occupied in 1889.

After WW I, Ethiopia became a member of the League of Nations, but this didn't prevent the country from being overrun by Mussolini's Italy in 1936. Though the other western nations condemned the invasion (somewhat hypocritically in view of their own activities in Africa) and although the young emperor, Haile Selassie, made many impassioned speeches pleading for assistance, no help was forthcoming. The Italians remained there until 1941, when they were thrown out during WW II.

Ethiopia resumed its course as an independent nation after the war, though the province of Eritrea bordering the Red Sea remained under British administration until 1952 when it was federated with Ethiopia. The federation was a result of a plebiscite organised by the UN the previous year in which more than half the population voted in favour. This reflected the religious and linguistic composition of Eritrea at the time when a large proportion of the people were Christian Tigrinya speakers.

Though the Muslims were unhappy about federation, the real trouble started in 1962 when the federation was dissolved and the province annexed by Haile Selassie. This led to the outbreak of guerrilla warfare, the Muslims supporting one liberation front and the Christians another. The Eritreans had not been a part of Ethiopia for several hundred years and they regarded the annexation as tantamount to being colonised by another African nation. Many years of inconclusive fighting over this issue under extreme hardship and in remote areas sapped the morale of the Ethiopian soldiers, led to mutinies and increased their awareness of the revolutionary current which was beginning to sweep through Ethiopian society. It was one of the principal factors leading to Haile Selassie's downfall.

Although he had established himself as a national hero during the campaigns against the Italians and had become a respected African statesman instrumental in the creation of the Organisation of African Unity (OAU), Haile Selassie appeared to be unaware of the inappropriateness of mediaeval feudalism in the 20th century.

The constant accumulation of wealth by the nobility and the Church, the hardships experienced by millions of landless peasants, student protests and serious famines in the southern half of the country in which hundreds of thousands of people died, combined with the effects of the war in Eritrea, produced a mass feeling of resentment. The break came in 1974 amid a background of strikes, student demonstrations, army mutinies and peasant uprisings against landlords. Haile Selassie was deposed and held under armed guard in his palace until his death several months later.

Overnight, Ethiopia was plunged into a social revolution it was largely ill-prepared to deal with. A clique of junior army officers seized the initiative and imposed a military dictatorship on the country against opposition from trade unionists and intellectuals. Mengistu Haile Miriam emerged as the leader of the army officers. He threw out the Americans who were associated too closely with the imperial regime, instituted a number of radical reforms designed to change the face of Ethiopian society overnight, jailed trade union leaders who were demanding civilian participation in the new government, and appealed to the USSR for economic aid.

Months of chaos and excess followed. Thousands of people – many of them sympathetic to the revolution – were massacred in the streets or in their homes by self-appointed vigilante groups. Opposition sprang up everywhere ranging from pro-imperialist groups to ultra-left revolutionary cells. The prisons were full to overflowing and summary executions were the order of the day.

As the country slipped further and further into anarchy the Eritreans stepped up their guerrilla campaign and the Somalis, who had waited a long time for such an opportunity, decided to press their claims over the Ogaden Desert and invaded in force. By the beginning of 1978, the Somalis had overrun Jijiga, an important Ethiopian military base, and were threatening to take Harrar and Dire Dawa through which the vital rail link to Djibouti runs. The military regime in Addis was on the point of collapse, and probably would have, had it not been for the massive intervention of Russian and Cuban troops.

With help from Moscow and Havana, Mengistu was able to throw the Somalis back across the border and recoup some of the losses sustained in Eritrea. Yet even the Russians and Cubans have been unable to break the back of the Eritrean liberation fighters, so the conflict continues. Meanwhile, Russian support for Somalia's archenemy resulted in the expulsion of all Russian personnel from Somalia and that country's *rapprochement* with the west.

The irony of Cuban troops being committed to fight a war against Eritrean guerrillas whose ideology is essentially identical to that of the Cuban regime has not, however, been lost on Castro. He openly refused to follow Moscow's lead in committing more troops to the Eritrean conflict. Nevertheless, Cuban troop strength in Ethiopia remains at around 12,000.

Fighting is still going on in many provinces of Ethiopia and is likely to do so for a long time, especially with the consolidation of Mengistu's dictatorship and the endless purges conducted to eliminate rivals, real or imagined.

On the other hand, Mengistu has not been allowed to have everything his way. The horrific and widespread famine which swept through the northern provinces of Eritrea, Tigre and Wollo during 1984-5 and beamed onto television screens around the world, has forced a reassessment of the revolution. The glare of publicity about a country which had virtually closed itself off from the rest of the world since Haile Selassie's reign has resulted in the regime's acceptance of a degree of criticism and a questioning of its internal policies. This may lead to a liberalisation of the economic system and a cautious opening up of the country to noncommunist influences.

One of the most important effects of the famine in terms of politics was the setting up of the long-awaited Workers' Party of Ethiopia, though this is still headed by Mengistu as its secretary-general. So far it has failed to win widespread support and is run on a day-to-day basis by four civilian ideologues who enjoy Mengistu's confidence.

It's too early to say with confidence what changes might occur. What is clear is that the regime is none too popular. Neither is the Russian military presence. Almost every province has its guerrilla army and some have several. Famine still stalks the country. Many international relief organisations are working hard to alleviate it though their operations are frequently hampered by military engagements. There have been many allegations, too, that the government is using the relief supplies intended for starving refugees to feed its troops.

Every town has its *kabele* – a sort of people's committee. These committees control the more important aspects of people's lives – where they work, go to school, where and with whom they associate, whether they are allowed to move or even go abroad – but also a lot of minutiae. The committees help enforce the nightly curfew and hold regular political meetings which everyone must attend unless they want problems. The committees also press people to support major political rallies. As a result, much of what the Ethiopian regime claims as 'mass spontaneous demonstrations of public support' at these rallies is pure eyewash. Conscription is in force for all 18 to 30-year-old males. Failure to turn up when called for army service results in the imprisonment of parents, or if you're an orphan, your school teacher. It's no fun being Ethiopian at present.

It also seems that the Eritrean People's Liberation Front has once again intensified its military activities. In late March 1988, it was reported that a three-day battle between them and the government troops near the garrison town of Afabet resulted in the death or capture of 18,000 Ethiopian soldiers, four Soviet advisers and the seizure of some 50 tanks. The rebels now control most of Eritrea outside the main cities. The escalation of the war comes at a critical time in the famine relief operation in Ethiopia especially as the rebels regard food convoys with great suspicion. It's claimed that the Ethiopian army is using them to carry military equipment. Such claims are going to make delivery difficult and hazardous.

Facts

GEOGRAPHY & CLIMATE

The dominant feature of Ethiopia's topography is the high central plateau varying from 2000 to 3000 metres with a number of mountains rising to over 4000 metres. It is dissected by numerous rivers, the most important of which is the Blue Nile (the Abbai) which rises from Lake Tana. The plateau is split diagonally by the Rift Valley which runs from the River Jordan Valley, down the Red Sea coast to Mozambique. Although the country is relatively close to the equator, the central plateau enjoys a temperate climate. Only in the border regions with Djibouti, Somalia, Kenya and Sudan does it get very hot.

The main rainy season occurs between mid-June and mid-September. Light rain also falls during March.

Coffee, sugar cane and cotton are grown in the hotter regions and maize, wheat, barley, tef (a local grain), tobacco, potatoes and oil seeds are grown on the high plateau. Erosion, soil deterioration and drought are serious agricultural problems, which contributed to the famines of the 1980s. Industrialisation is in its infancy.

PEOPLE

The population stands at about 44 million with a growth rate of around 2.5% per annum. Almost 90% of the people work on the land.

VISAS

Visas are required for all visitors except nationals of Kenya. White nationals of South Africa and Zimbabwe are not admitted. You must have an onward ticket and at least US$500 to show on arrival.

Transit visas for Ethiopia (maximum of 72 hours – no extensions possible) are available on arrival by air, but to stay longer requires a tourist visa valid for 30 days. This used to be a long and involved process, but the visas are now much easier to obtain. In Khartoum they cost S£15, require two photos and are issued while you wait, so long as you have a letter of introduction from your embassy (the UK Embassy charges S£6.75 for these) and an onward ticket. In Nairobi they cost KSh 80 and are issued in 48 hours. You must have an onward ticket and sufficient funds.

Since Ethiopia was the founding member of the Organisation of African Unity (OAU), there are Ethiopian embassies in virtually all of the capital cities of Africa and many others in countries outside Africa.

Yellow fever and cholera vaccination certificates are mandatory and checked thoroughly.

Visa extensions up to six months can be obtained from Immigration, Revolution Square, Addis Ababa. They cost Birr 5 with three photos. They'll issue you with a tourist card. When you want to leave you must get an exit visa – this is not necessary if your initial visa has not been extended.

MONEY

US$ 1 = Birr 2.07
UK£ 1 = Birr 3.20

The unit of currency is the birr = 100 cents. The import of local currency is allowed up to Birr 50 but export is prohibited. There is a black market but it's very hard to find, and hazardous unless you know someone well. Expect about Birr 4 for US$1. It's a good idea to keep receipts for everything (even meals) to avoid any hassles when leaving. Cash and travellers' cheques are carefully counted both on arrival and departure. Don't depend on your hotel being willing to change money even if you're staying there. Some travellers have gone hungry for the night because they haven't had birr on arrival.

Currency declaration forms are issued when you enter the country. It's not a good idea to attempt to conceal anything, because there are thorough baggage and personal searches on leaving (though we have had letters saying the check on exit was slack).

Officially excess birr can be reconverted on leaving, less US$30 per day of your stay. In practice, it's difficult and you're only allowed to reconvert up to a maximum of Birr 105 against your currency form and receipts.

The airport tax is Birr 8.

POST

Both outgoing and incoming mail is subject to police scrutiny and censorship so, if you want letters to arrive at their destinations, don't write about politics or mention the black market. Other than this, the mail is very reliable.

TOURIST INFORMATION

Ethiopia uses the pre-Julian solar calendar which has its roots in ancient Egypt and is made up of 12 equal months of 30 days each and a 13th month consisting of five or six days. Because of this, you need to check dates inside the country carefully. The Ethiopian year begins on 11 September. Dates in the two systems are quite different, for example in the Ethiopian calendar, 1 January 1975 corresponds to 11 September 1982 in the Gregorian calendar.

ACCOMMODATION

Officially, you can only stay in government-approved hotels and may be arrested if you stay anywhere else. These approved hotels are always more expensive than ones you would find by yourself. Even if you try to get accommodation in a cheap local hotel, the managers may refuse for fear of trouble with the police.

FOOD

In the countryside and most small Ethiopian towns the only thing to eat as a rule is wat (sometimes called zegeni) and injera. Wat is a fiery hot sauce sometimes containing bits of meat, beans and lentils.

Injera is the national foam-rubber bread made with millet flour (tef) mixed with yeast and left to go sour for about three days before being cooked on a clay board heated by a log fire. It's supposedly rich in iron and vitamin B. Once you get used to this delicacy and the unbearable feeling of your lips unquenchably on fire, it's quite tasty, though of limited nutritional value. Nevertheless, it's cheap.

In the cities and larger towns you'll come across a variety of wat – doro wat (chicken, sometimes with boiled eggs), kai wat (beef), bug wat (lamb), assa wat (fish), atkilt wat (vegetables), kuk wat (chick peas), missur wat (lentils) and minchitavish wat (diced meat – usually beef or mutton). You'll also come across zil zil tibs and karia (fried slices of beef cut in zigzags with hot pepper sauce) and kufto (raw or fried minced beef).

Stay clear of salads as there's a good chance of picking up liver fluke, and DDT is used like water in some areas.

Eating raw meat (even liver) is a national custom among those who can afford it. Avoid this too – tapeworms are common. Local markets are good for fruit, but peel before eating. In the larger towns there is a variety of food available – Italian (common), Indian and Chinese in Addis, Italian in Asmara and Massawa.

The traditional drinks are t'ella (beer), t'ej (mead) and arakie (spirits). T'ella is made from barley in the highlands and maize in the lowlands. It's tasty but not quite the same as western beer. T'ej is, of course, made from honey. Arakie is the local firewater and should be treated with caution.

Ethiopian coffee is excellent and the country is supposedly the original home of the bean.

LANGUAGE

Amharic is the official language though there are large areas of the north and north-west where Tigrinya is the predominant tongue. In the south, Oromigna (previously known as Galligna) is the predominant language. Both Amharic and Tigrinya are derived from Ge'ez, an ancient Semitic language now used only in the Orthodox Church of Ethiopia and they are totally dissimilar to Orominya which is a Hamitic language. All three languages, however, use the same script (which is related to ancient Phoenician) made up of 33 consonants.

Arabic, Italian, English and French are also widely spoken among educated people, but not outside the cities. There are significant numbers of Italian speakers in and around Addis and Asmara. Old people and civil servants can often speak academic French. Arabic speakers live mostly along the Red Sea coast and in the north of the country (Eritrea).

In words with 'gn' it is always pronounced 'ny' as in the Spanish 'ñ'.

Amharic

Some Amharic words and phrases that you may find useful include:

please	*ibakih*
thank you	*amesegunalhu*
yes	*ow* (very breathy)
no	*yelem/aydelem*
OK	*ishi*
hello	*tenaystelegn*
water	*wuha*
tea	*shai*
milk	*wa'tat*
coffee	*buna*
bread	*dabo*
sour bread	*injera*
banana	*mooz*
sauce	*wat*
mincemeat and onion	*kitfo*
egg	*encular*
expensive	*wud*
cheap	*rekash*
road	*mengad*
right	*kagn*
left	*graa/carmachina*
tomorrow	*nega*
tomorrow morning	*nega twat*

Which is the road to . . . ?	*ye . . . mengad yet no?*
Where are you going?	*wadyet te-hedaluh?*
How much does it cost?	*sint no wagaw?*
Where is (Wondo Genet)?	*(wondo genet) yetno?*
What is it?	*minduno?*
one tea please	*ante shai ebakah* (to men)
	ante shai ebakish (to women)
How are you?	*denaneh* (to men)
	denanesh (to women)
(response)	*dena* (to men or women)
I want	*afellegallo*
I don't want	*alfellegum*
(hailing a taxi)	*koi bakah*

The Amharic numerals are:

1	*and*
2	*hulet*
3	*sost*
4	*arat*
5	*amist*
6	*sidist*
7	*sabat*
8	*simint*
9	*zetegn*
10	*assr*
20	*haya*
25	*haya amist*
30	*salassa*
40	*arba*
50	*hamsa*
60	*silsa*
70	*saba*
80	*samagna*
90	*zetana*
100	*moto*
1000	*shi*

Getting There & Around

INTERNATIONAL CONNECTIONS

The only way into and out of Ethiopia is by air to Addis Ababa. Overland entry is not permitted. The country's national airline is Ethiopian Airlines; other major airlines include Aeroflot, Air India, Alitalia, CAAC and Lufthansa.

If flying Ethiopian Airlines from Cairo to Nairobi via Addis Ababa (or vice versa) and there's no immediate connecting flight, you can choose to stop overnight in Addis at Ethiopian Airlines' expense in a luxury hotel with food included. You don't need a visa for this one-night stopover. Stopovers for longer periods are possible but you do need a visa for more than 72 hours.

Avoid buying international airline tickets in Ethiopia. They're very expensive. Similarly, avoid having to change your airline tickets in the country. This will be expensive too. It's a good idea to have a visa for the next country you are going to before arriving in Ethiopia. Some travellers have experienced difficulties and delays getting visas in Addis Ababa.

INTERNAL TRANSPORT

Officially you are not allowed to travel independently outside Addis Ababa (except to Debre Zebit and Sodere) without special permits which must be applied for at the Ethiopian Tourism Commission on Desta Damtew Ave, Addis Ababa. Depending on where you want to go, it can take a lot of persuasion to get these permits. The best way to get them is to enlist the help of your embassy or that of an international organisation (famine relief, for example).

At least, that's the official line. In practice things have eased up considerably over the last two years so that most travellers with initiative manage to see much more than this without going through the hassle of applying for permits. Anywhere in Shoa province seems to be acceptable at present but you'll get turned back at the borders of neighbouring provinces. Debre Libanos is alright to visit but it's a seven-km walk from where the bus drops you. Others have managed to visit Wondo Genet, Lake Langaro, Arba Minch and Shashemene in the Rift Valley south of Addis without encountering problems, but always be prepared to be sent back to Addis if it's discovered you have no permit. No-one has yet been deported for going places without a permit.

If you don't have the courage to set off without permits the National Tourist Organisation (NTO) arranges a number of moderate to expensive tours from Addis to Debre Zebit, Lake Langano, the Blue Nile Gorge, Bahir Dar, Gondar and treks in the Semien Mountains. A six-day trek including everything except flights to and from Gondar would cost about US$230.

Air

There are internal flights from Addis to most towns of any size but most are off-limits to tourists. You'd certainly only get as far as the airport in Addis if you tried to go without the necessary permits. Addis to Gondar costs Birr 88 one-way and takes 1½ hours.

Road

The bus network is fairly extensive and it's much easier to use without a permit. There's always the possibility though, that a police officer will ask to see one as you board the bus and refuse to let you get on if you don't have it.

The bus from Addis to Gondar costs Birr 23.60 and takes 1½ days with an overnight stop. You can only do this if you have a permit, take a 'guide' and pay his expenses.

Train

The Addis Ababa to Djibouti railway is off-limits to foreigners and if you board the train you'll be turned back at the border. However, one traveller said they will accept foreigners as 1st class passengers on overnight trains between Addis and Dire Dawa. There are two trains per day, one in the morning and the other at 7.30 pm, which take 13 hours to Dire Dawa and cost Birr 67 (1st class sleeper) and Birr 30 (2nd class).

Around the Country

Despite the fact that many travellers have been able to successfully circumvent the permit system to travel outside Addis Ababa – particularly down to the lakes of the Rift Valley – many of Ethiopia's most fascinating areas are definitely off limits to foreigners without permits or those who haven't booked a tour with the National Tourist Organisation. They include Axum, Lalibela and Gondar. To visit any of these places you will simply have to book a tour, which is usually too expensive for most budget travellers. Permits for independent travel to these places are extremely difficult to obtain.

Lalibela is currently closed to foreigners because of rebel activities, though the National Tourist Organisation will deny this right till the last minute.

ADDIS ABABA
Founded in 1887 by Menelik II, Addis became the new capital of Ethiopia in 1896. Standing 2440 metres above sea level it is one of the largest inland cities of Africa with a population of some 1.6 million. Shortly after its founding it was almost abandoned entirely in favour of Addis Alem, 55 km to the west, because of the shortage of firewood in the area. It was saved from this predicament by the introduction of eucalyptus trees from Australia. These tough, fast growing trees are now all over Ethiopia.

Addis has been growing apace since the establishment of the United Nations Economic Commission for Africa (UNECA) in 1958 and particularly since the establishment of the Organisation of African Unity (OAU) in 1963. Haile Selassie, for all his faults, was one of the principal motivating forces behind the establishment of the OAU. The huge Africa Hall with its stained glass windows portraying the suffering of the people of Africa has been one of the principal meeting places for African leaders ever since.

Information
A curfew is in force from 12 midnight until 5 am.

Going to and from Bole International Airport, tourists are officially required to use the yellow Mercedes taxis which cost Birr 16 per person. In practice you can get one of the blue taxis instead which cost 60 cents as far as Revolution Square and another 50 cents to the Piazza. Ethiopian Airlines minibuses meet all their incoming flights and some travellers have managed to get a free ride with them as far as the Hilton or Harambee Hotels. For all other taxi rides, fares should be negotiated before starting out. Fares are multiples of 25 cents.

Cholera shots can be obtained from the Black Lion Hospital for Birr 2. If flying to Nairobi from Addis you will need a current vaccination certificate.

Things to See
Addis has several churches and palaces worth visiting. The most famous of the churches is **St George's Cathedral** (Giorgis Cathedral), built in 1896 to commemorate the victory over the Italians at the Battle of Adowa. It's a beautiful building and houses works by Afewerk Teklé, the award-winning Ethiopian artist who specialises in stained glass. Nearby are the **Menelik Mausoleum**, built in 1911, and **Trinity Cathedral**, built in 1941. Also take in Haile Selassie's **Grand Palace** whilst you are in this area. The **National Museum**, Entoto St in the grounds of Addis Ababa University (next to the College of Pharmacy), is definitely worth a visit and

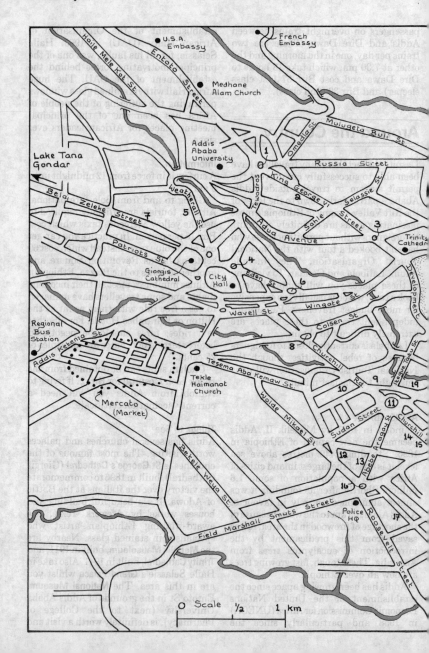

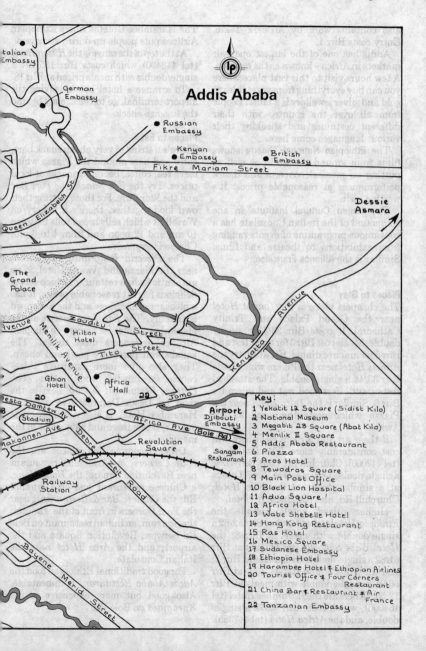

also contains work by Afewerk Teklé. Entry costs Birr 1.

Addis has one of the largest open-air markets in Africa – known as the mercato. A few hours visit to this vast place where you can buy everything from vegetables to gold and silver jewellery is a must. People from all over the country with their different costumes and speaking their various languages come here.

The **Ethiopian National Theatre** shows films from around the world as well as putting on musical concerts and dance performances at reasonable prices. It's worth a visit.

The **Italian Cultural Institute** in the compound of the Italian Consulate has a continuous programme of events ranging from exhibitions to theatre and films. Similar is the **Alliance Française**.

Places to Stay

The cheapest place is the *Tourist Hotel* near the Grand Palace and Trinity Cathedral. It costs Birr 23/33 a single/double. Meals cost Birr 3 for breakfast and Birr 5 for lunch or dinner. If it's full, try the *Awaris Hotel* near the Piazza which costs Birr 33/44 a single/double. The attached restaurant offers good wat and injera for Birr 6. Similar is the *Taitu Hotel* near the Piazza which costs the same as the Awaris.

If these are full a room elsewhere will cost considerably more. The *Ras Hotel* (tel 447060), Churchill Rd, costs Birr 41/62 a single/double with meals at Birr 7. Others at a similar price are the *Nile Hotel*, Churchill Rd, and the *Guenett Hotel*.

Higher priced hotels include the *Ethiopia Hotel* (tel 447400) at Birr 52/62 a single/double with meals at Birr 8; the *Hotel Wabe Shebelle* (tel 447187) at Birr 61/82 a single/double with meals at Birr 7; and the *Hotel Ghion* (tel 447130) at Birr 66/91 a single/double with meals at Birr 12.50. Others are the *Harambee Hotel* (tel 154000), which costs Birr 52/72 a single/double, and the *Africa Hotel* (tel 447385).

The Harambee Hotel is where Ethiopian Airlines puts people up during stopovers.

At the top of the range is the *Hilton Hotel* (tel 448400) which costs Birr 155/194 a single/double with meals priced at Birr 18.

To arrange a hotel before leaving the airport terminal, go to the agency behind the luggage check.

Places to Eat

There's a string of very cheap snack bars, cafés and bars around the Piazza which serve tea, coffee, beer and snacks at local prices. Try the *Kili Snack*, the *Port Bar* and the *Star Café*. For those putting their own food together, there's a bakery on Wavell St which sells bread rolls between 10 am and 12 noon and from 4 to 6 pm. Cheese is expensive.

The *Pizzeria Ristorante da Goiton*, near the Piazza and Awaris Hotel, is an authentic Italian restaurant which serves delicious food at reasonable prices. It has a pleasant atmosphere and the bar crowd is friendly. The *Fan Fan Tavern* at the Harambee Hotel is where Ethiopian Airlines passengers meet to eat. The kebabs and pasta are good and cheap. They also offer more expensive three-course set lunches and dinners. The *Cottage Restaurant & Pub*, next to the river on Desta Damtew Ave near the Harambee Hotel, is also worth checking out. Try a beer there and have a look at the menu.

Other recommended places are the *Four Corners*, an Armenian restaurant near Revolution Square; the *Hong Kong*, a Chinese restaurant just off Churchill Rd; the *Chinese Bar & Restaurant*, near the Four Corners in front of the stadium; the *Sangam*, an Indian restaurant on Bole Rd between Revolution Square and the airport; and the *Aros Hotel* near the Italian Consulate.

For good traditional Ethiopian food the *Addis Ababa Restaurant* is unbeatable. Also good but more expensive is the *Karamara* on Bole Rd.

AXUM

Axum is the holy city of Ethiopia and dates back some 2000 years to the time when it was the capital of the empire which gave rise to what is now Ethiopia. Between the 1st and 6th centuries AD it was linked by caravan routes to southern Arabia through its ancient port of Adulis which lies buried south of Massawa. It maintained regular contacts with Nubia, Egypt, Greece and Rome.

Though Axum is still a living town, all that now remains of its ancient grandeur are the huge granite **monoliths**, some of them fallen, others still standing. One of these, sadly broken, measures an incredible 30 metres long, making it the largest monolith in the world.

There are two churches in Axum, the oldest being **St Mary of Zion**, the holiest shrine in Ethiopia. It was built in the 17th century on the site of a previous Axumite church, which was destroyed in the 16th century when the Muslims invaded the country. There's also a modern **church** of the same name built by Haile Selassie in 1965.

Unfortunately, being close to Eritrea, Axum is definitely off limits to foreigners except those on government tours.

DIRE DAWA

Just about the only choice of hotels for foreigners is the *Olympic Hotel* at Birr 40. A shared taxi to **Harrar** costs Birr 3.

GONDAR

About 400 km north of Addis, Gondar was the capital of Ethiopia from the rise of Fasilidas (1632-1665) to the fall of Theodore (1855-1868). The people are mainly Christian.

Things to See

The city has a number of **castles** and **palaces** built by various emperors during that time. Entry to the main castle costs Birr 15. At first sight, many of these castles seem to bear a resemblance to those found in Morocco and Europe and,

indeed, it may be that the Portuguese, who were allies of the Ethiopians in the late 16th century, did influence the design of the fortresses. Closer inspection, however, reveals a continuity with the Axumite tradition and strong affinities with building styles in vogue at the time in southern Arabia.

Other than the castles, there is the palace of **Ras Beit**, built in the 18th century and in continuous use ever since, the **Bath of Fasilidas**, the so-called **House of Chickens** and the ruined palace of **Kusquam**. There's also a nearby **monastery** and the church of **Debre Birhan Selassie** with its famous murals. Debre Birhan is two to three km from Gondar and costs Birr 1 entry plus extra to take photographs and a tip for the guide.

Ethiopian Jews are known as Falashas and it's possible to visit a **Falasha village** on the outskirts of Gondar.

Places to Stay

There are three government approved tourist-class hotels and one luxury-class hotel. The cheapest hotels are the *Ethiopia Hotel* and the *Fasil Hotel*. The *Fogera Hotel* costs Birr 33/44 a single/double but it's not good value.

LALIBELA

The famous 11 rock-hewn churches built in the 12th and 13th centuries are one of the unrecognised wonders of the world. Certainly you can see other such churches around the world (as in Petra, Jordan) but what sets the Lalibela churches apart is that they are carved completely free from the surrounding stone.

Lalibela was built as the capital of a local king of the same name following the decline and fall of Axum. Little of the capital remains but the churches have been kept alive by generations of priests who guard their precious religious and artistic treasures. All the churches contain beautiful murals, ornamented crosses and illustrated manuscripts.

The churches are only open from 1

October to 30 June because the grass airstrip is unsafe in the rainy season. The tourist office also runs a road tour but it's very expensive and doesn't operate in the rainy season. The only government-approved hotel is the *Seven Olives*.

Lalibela is closed to foreigners at present because of the activities of the rebels.

MASSAWA

Also called Mitsiwa, this is the main Red Sea port of the province of Eritrea.

One of the cheapest places to stay is the *Dahlak Hotel* which costs Birr 33 a double and has a restaurant. The *Red Sea Hotel* is more expensive at Birr 44 a double but has a swimming pool and restaurant.

There are daily buses in either direction between Massawa and Asmara which cost Birr 8 and take five to six hours. It's a beautiful journey down a steep escarpment.

THE RIFT VALLEY LAKES

It's certainly worth getting down to some of these lakes if possible. The area is beautiful, lush and many of the lakes are national parks. It's also in this area that travellers have had most success with circumventing the permit system. Few people have had problems going down to Wondo Genet, Lake Langaro, Arba Minch and Shashemene. Here is one intrepid traveller's description of how to get to this area (without permits):

Go to the bus station at Aitdous Tara in Addis Ababa. Ask a policeman where the ticket office is and he'll probably push you to the front of the queue. Get there early – 6 am for Arba Minch and up to 8 am for Shashemene and Lake Langaro. Addis to Lake Langaro costs Birr 8.40. Buses leave when full and there's no standing. If you want to camp, head for the second *Bekele Moja Hotel* on Lake Langaro (there's another of the same name north of Lake Zway). The bus drops you in the middle of nowhere and you have to walk four km to the lake. Camping costs Birr 5 but they only collect on Sundays and are very slack. There's a restaurant which sells spaghetti for Birr 4.50 and other meals for Birr 5.50. There's also a small shop further on from the restaurant which sells bread, a few canned goods, tea and honey. The beach at the lake is excellent and there's no bilharzia in the water.

Wondo Genet is a hot springs resort about 13 km from Shashemene further down the lake. You have to catch a bus from Shashemene to Wondo Genet then walk up the hill about four km to the *Wabe Shabelle Hotel*. You can camp by the church outside the hotel or inside the hotel grounds for a small fee. The people running the hotel are a very friendly bunch from all over Ethiopia and they may invite you in for the evening. They may even feed you. There's also a commune of Rastafarians from Jamaica in Shashemene who came here just after the revolution. They often go to the hot springs.

To get back to Addis from Wondo Genet first take a bus from Shashemene to Mojo then another to Debre Zebit, followed by a third to Addis. Get moving quickly when buses arrive as it's a rugby scrum getting onto them.

Gabon

Gabon was once regarded as the economic miracle of equatorial Africa. The nation, which attained independence from the French in 1960, got off to an extravagant start. With the money rolling in from the sale of oil, manganese ore (an estimated 25% of the world's known deposits), iron ore, chrome, gold and diamonds, the country sported a per capita income higher than that of South Africa and only slightly lower than that of Libya.

That was before the oil glut, the downturn in the steel industry (the major consumer of manganese) and the recession of the early 1980s. All these wreaked havoc with the Gabonese economy. But external factors were not the only reason for the change of fortunes.

In 1976, an ambitious four-year plan was announced with a budget of US$32 billion intended to create a modern transport system, encourage local industry and develop mineral deposits. Most of the money was squandered on misguided projects. Corruption ran rife and Libreville became a magnet for unscrupulous contractors. The railway which was intended to connect the mineral deposits of the interior with the coast, due for completion in 1980, is still only one-third complete. Agriculture, the occupation of some 80% of the population, was completely ignored, with the result that local food production accounts for only 15% of the country's needs. Neglect of the agricultural sector has also resulted in a drift of the population to the urban centres.

The downturn in the country's earnings, however, did not prevent the completion of the CFA 36,000 million presidential palace, or the staging of one of the most extravagant OAU summits ever held or ever likely to be held again. On the other hand, from a budget deficit of nearly CFA 600 billion in 1977, Gabon's economy appears to be on the mend.

Gabon has been ruled since 1967 by President El Hadj Omar Bongo (who adopted Islam in 1974). With a personal bodyguard composed of European mercenaries (including the notorious Bob Denard) and Moroccan troops and the presence of 400 crack French airborne troops as well as numerous French political and military advisers, Bongo has been able to project a remarkable image of stability for the country. Since 1968 the country has been a one-party state with lucrative ministerial posts frequently shuffled between a small number of political faithfuls.

Despite the obvious nepotism of the political set-up, Bongo has so far been able to find convenient scapegoats whenever his government has been faced with social unrest. In 1976 Bongo took to making speeches about avaricious foreign companies which expatriated profits, yet almost nothing was done to stop the flow. (In 1978 French firms controlled 90% of the vital oil sector and the remittances of expatriate workers to foreign banks turned a Gabonese trade surplus into a deficit!)

In mid-1978, with the oil industry on the downturn, 10,000 Beninese workers were expelled after President Kerebou renewed his allegations that Gabon had been used as the staging post for the 1977 attempt to invade Benin by airborne mercenaries. Again, in 1979, an atmosphere of xenophobia was created towards refugees from Equatorial Guinea.

Political freedom walks a tightrope in

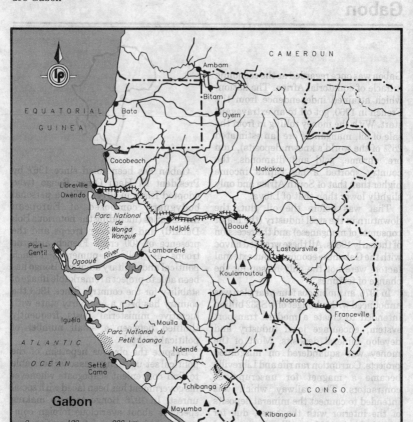

Gabon

this country. Bongo's attitude to government is dictated by what he once called 'political realism with economic affairs overshadowing political matters'. It's interesting to speculate how these two priorities might be reversed in the event of a threat to Bongo's political survival.

Gabon appears to have been populated originally by Pygmies who lived in small family units along riverbanks, but they survive today only in the more remote parts of the country. They were displaced by migrating peoples from the north between the 16th and 18th centuries,

principal among whom were the Fang from what is now Cameroun and Equatorial Guinea.

Contact with Europeans, starting with the arrival of the Portuguese in 1472, set in motion a train of events which had a profound effect on tribal social structures. The Portuguese largely ignored the area, preferring to base their activities on the nearby islands of São Tomé & Principe. However, British, Dutch and French ships called in to trade along the coast regularly for slaves, ivory and precious tropical woods. The slave trade resulted in a staggering loss of population from the interior as well as enhancement of the coastal chiefs' authority.

The capital, Libreville, was established as a settlement for freed slaves in 1849 on the site of a French fort constructed in 1843. French interests became paramount in 1886 with the appointment of a governor whose jurisdiction extended over the whole of the French Congo. The capital of the region was transferred to Brazzaville in 1904 and six years later Gabon became a French colony in French Equatorial Africa. The country became independent in 1960 under the presidency of M'Ba, who died in a French hospital in 1967.

Facts

GEOGRAPHY & CLIMATE

Gabon consists of a narrow, low-lying coastal strip which rises to a series of plateaus with peaks over 1500 metres. Tropical rainforests cover three-quarters of the country and deep river valleys dissect the country into small, relatively isolated units. The climate is hot (average temperature is 27°C) and humid. The dry season extends from May to September with a short dry spell in mid-December. The population numbers about 1.2 million, most of whom are of Bantu origin with the Fang making up about one-third of these. Europeans number around 50,000. Communications outside the coastal area are undeveloped.

VISAS

These are required by all visitors except nationals of France and West Germany. Gabonese visas are not easy to get and all visa applications have to be referred to Libreville. (The government doesn't exactly encourage tourism, especially by shoestring travellers.)

There are Gabonese embassies in Abidjan (Ivory Coast), Algiers (Algeria), Bangui (CAR), Brazzaville (Congo),

Cairo (Egypt), Dakar (Senegal), Kinshasa (Zaïre), Lagos (Nigeria), Lomé (Togo), Malabo (Equatorial Guinea), Rabat (Morocco) and Yaoundé (Cameroun). There is also a consulate in Douala (Cameroun).

Visas for Gabon are outrageously expensive at CFA 30,000 (or the equivalent), require two photos and can take two weeks or more to come through. It helps a great deal if you have a prearranged job here. Even if you get a visa you will be refused entry if your passport reflects previous visits to South Africa. Most travellers apply for their visas in Lomé, Lagos and Douala, where they are reported to be not too difficult to obtain. Gabon refuses admission to nationals of Angola, Benin, Cape Verde Islands, Cuba, Ghana, Guinea-Bissau, Haiti, and São Tomé & Principe. No 'home from home' for those dubious individuals here.

If intending to go overland from Gabon to Congo, make sure you get an exit stamp at N'Dendé, about 40 km from the border.

Other Visas

In the capital, Libreville, there are embassies of Cameroun, CAR, Congo, Egypt, Equatorial Guinea, France, Guinea, Ivory Coast, Morocco, Nigeria, Senegal, Togo and Zaïre among others.

Congo These cost CFA 5000, require one photo and take 24 hours to issue though they're sometimes issued while you wait. The visas are for a stay of 15 days and you must specify your intended date of entry.

Zaïre These cost CFA 4500 for one month, CFA 8500 for two months and CFA 11,000

for three months, with two photos and a letter of recommendation from your embassy. They're issued in 24 hours.

If heading overland through the Congo to Zaïre, make sure you get your visa here and not in Brazzaville. You can certainly get Zaïre visas in Brazzaville, but may encounter problems taking the ferry across the Zaïre River to Kinshasa unless your visa was issued elsewhere. For more details, see the Congo chapter.

Warning

On entry and at all times inside the country, make sure you have your papers handy. The gendarmes frequently hassle foreigners, especially whites. This is usually mild and they're only looking for beer money. They will often continue asking for various papers until they find one that you don't have. Generally, this involves a CFA 3000 'fine'. This mild harassment applies equally to expatriates with legitimate jobs here. One correspondent was threatened with jail for not having a WHO card even though he had a permanent visitor's ID card (carte de séjour). This resulted in a CFA 15,000 'fine'. Tolerance and patience are invaluable in these situations.

MONEY

US$1 = CFA 284

The unit of currency is the CFA franc. The import of local currency is unlimited; export is limited to CFA 75,000.

Changing money at banks is easy but you're advised to stay away from Gabonese banks especially if you are having money transferred from overseas. Use Citibank or Barclays in preference. Their services are better, they offer better rates and there's less fuss. Recommended is Citibank in Trois Quartiers up the hill from the Hotel Dialogue in Libreville (bus No 5 from the gare routière which costs CFA 100). Exchange is difficult elsewhere and in some places impossible. Don't change money at hotels unless you have to.

Inflation is high (around 20%) and most services such as accommodation and transport are outrageously expensive. If you're on a tight budget give serious consideration to skipping this country.

Airport tax for domestic flights is CFA 400.

PHOTOGRAPHY

Photography is a touchy subject in Gabon. Never take a photograph at the airport, nor of any government building, military installation, vehicle or personnel. If you do, your film and camera will be subject to confiscation. Generally, it's best to ask individuals first if you can take their picture. Be prepared to pay a small amount.

LANGUAGE

French is the official language though, in the interior, there are many local languages.

Getting There & Around

ROAD

Roads are generally quite good and many are surfaced, but be careful of local drivers. More people are killed on the roads in a month than are killed by assorted beasts in those legendary ferocious forests in a year.

There are frequent buses and taxi-brousses between the larger cities but they're expensive. Some sample fares are:

Libreville to Lambaréné – CFA 7500
Franceville to Moanda – CFA 1000
Okondja to Franceville – CFA 5000

TRAIN

The Trans-Gabonese Railway runs from Owendo (a few km south of Libreville) to Booué. Spurs are being built from there to Franceville in the south-east and Belinga in the north-east. So far, only the spur to Franceville has progressed very far and is now open to traffic as far as Lastoursville. The schedule is as follows:

Owendo to Booué										
	Mon	Tues	Wed	Thur	Fri	Sat			Sun	
train No	11	11	19	11	11	21	13	17	15	21
Owendo	0700	0700	1830	0700	0700	1830	0700	1545	0920	1830
Ndjolé	0940	0940	2115	0940	0940	2130	0950	1840	1210	2130
Booué			2355			0010	1230	2120	1450	0010

Booué to Owendo										
	Mon	Tues	Wed	Thur	Fri	Sat			Sun	
train No	18	18	10	18	16	14	16	12	16	
Booué			0445		1550		1550	0840	1550	
Ndjolé	1820	1820	0725	1820	1820	1325	1820	1115	1820	
Owendo	2110	2110	1015	2110	2110	1625	2110	1405	2110	

This is a partial schedule only. Between Owendo and Ndjolé the trains call at Ntoum, Andem, Mbel, Oyan and Abanga. Between Ndjolé and Booué they call at Alembé, Otoumbi, Bissouma, Ayem, Lopé and Offoué.

Train Nos 11, 13, 15 and 17 have both 1st and 2nd class. The remainder have only 2nd class carriages.

Train Nos 12, 16 and 18 have both 1st and 2nd class. The remainder have only 2nd class carriages. The fares are as follows:

Owendo to Ndjolé – CFA 8300 (1st class); CFA 6050 (2nd class)
Owendo to Booué – CFA 15,500 (1st class); CFA 10,300 (2nd class)
Ndjolé to Booué – CFA 6950 (1st class); CFA 4650 (2nd class)

Rail fares are cheaper than taking *taxis-brousses*. Second class is quite comfortable but there's no guarantee of a seat. First class has a buffet and bar. Trains usually depart on time and tickets should be bought at the station prior to departure as there's a surcharge for buying them on board. There are no student discounts. Since the Owendo station is about one hour's drive from Libreville, you will have to take a taxi there. This should cost about CFA 2000. Similarly, at Ndjolé, the station is eight km from the town so take a *taxi-brousse* for CFA 300.

BOAT

The boats are far more interesting and the people are very friendly. Sample fares are:

Lambaréné to Port-Gentil – CFA 10,000
Port-Gentil to Omboué – CFA 3000
Port-Gentil to Libreville – CFA 10,000

The Port-Gentil to Libreville boat is a modern ferry which runs three times a week. The others are river barges which take both passengers and produce. At Ndjolé, a 'truck-stop' town on the Ogooué River, there is an oil depot for Mobil. Oil barges run from there to Lambaréné and Port-Gentil on a semiregular basis. There are eight to 10 of them and there's generally one each day or so. Enquire at the depot in Quartier Bingoma about getting onto them, though it's generally best to speak directly with the captains. The office may give you the wrong time and price.

The fare to Lambaréné should be about CFA 3000 with no baggage charge. The barges make several stops at small villages en route, but Ndjolé to Lambaréné should take about seven hours. There's plenty to photograph along the way. Take your own food and drink. (There are two stores near the dock in Ndjolé where you can buy bread, cheese and groceries of all kinds.) Take a mat to sit on as the barges are somewhat dirty and there are no cabins.

TO/FROM CAMEROUN

From Cameroun the route is normally from Ntem to either Libreville or Lambaréné via Oyem.

There are taxis from Bitam (the first town over the border in Gabon) to Oyem for CFA 3000. From there you can get taxis direct to Libreville for CFA 12,000 or a taxi to Ndjolé for CFA 9000. We've had reports from some travellers that if you're planning on going from Gabon to Cameroun you must have special authorisation which will detail the car you are travelling in and the driver's identification number but everyone tells a different story. The standard 'fine' for any infraction is CFA 3000 but it can be up to CFA 15,000.

This might be an isolated incident but we had a letter from a woman traveller who was sent back to Cameroun from Bitam. Here she met a police officer who demanded to see her visa, an onward ticket, a letter from her bank proving she had sufficient funds and a 'lodging certificate' (either a reservation in a hotel in Libreville or a letter from a Gabonese national certifying they would provide accommodation). She didn't have the last of these and was sent back to the border! The moral of the story is to keep moving until you reach Libreville.

TO/FROM CONGO

There are two possible ways to go to Congo. The first is via Lambaréné, Mouila and Ndendé and the other is via Booué and Moanda.

On the first route there are taxis-brousses from Libreville to Mouila via Lambaréné for CFA 14,000 and others from there to Ndendé for CFA 2000. From Ndendé you can either continue by a series of taxis-brousses or hitch lifts on trucks as far as Loubomo where you can pick up the train to Brazzaville. Alternatively, there is now a twice weekly bus from Ndendé to Loubomo which costs CFA 9000 (35% student discounts are available on this bus). They leave Ndendé usually on Tuesday and Friday and Loubomo on Wednesday and Friday but the departure day depends on the demand. The journey takes about 11½ hours.

Ndendé to Loubomo generally takes about two days if you are hitching on trucks because of the frequent stops at bars along the way. Otherwise it usually takes less.

There are a few checkpoints on the road between the border and Loubomo where officials may try to squeeze CFA 1000 out of you.

On the other route, first take a train from Libreville to Booué. From here there are taxis to Bonda for CFA 5000 and others from there to Moanda for CFA 5000. Moanda to Bakoumba by taxi costs CFA 3000 followed by CFA 3000 to Mayoko. From Mayoko you can get a train to Brazzaville. Since the Gabonese railway now goes as far as Lastoursville, it may be possible to go that far by train then take a taxi from there further south.

TO/FROM EQUATORIAL GUINEA

To enter from Equatorial Guinea, head south from Bata to Acalayong on the Equatorial Guinea-Gabon border. From there you need to find a motorised dugout to Coco Beach (the first village in Gabon across the estuary). Insist that the boat owner take you direct to Coco Beach. He'll charge CFA 3000 for this and the journey should take about 2½ hours depending on the tides. You may be offered this journey for CFA 2000, but avoid accepting it as the boat owner will first take you to a place down river where you will have to pay a CFA 2000 'exit tax'. From Coco Beach you can get a taxi-brousse to Libreville.

Around the Country

COCO BEACH

Local people are very friendly, and it's quite likely you'll be offered a place to stay. If not, you can sleep on the beach or find free floor space at the police/customs office. There's also a *Rest House* for CFA 1500 and the *Hotel Restaurant* for CFA 2000 a double. There's an interesting **fishing village** just outside town populated by Nigerians who were originally refugees from the Biafran war.

LAMBARÉNÉ

This town has an interesting setting on an island in the middle of the Ogooué River.

Things to See

The big attraction of Lambaréné is the **Schweitzer Hospital** about eight km from town. A taxi there will cost CFA 200 per person or a pirogue CFA 500 per person. The hospital is still fully functioning and a large new annexe was built in 1981. It's one of Gabon's finest hospitals. Schweitzer's office, home, library, lab and treatment centre are still there although deteriorating. Tours are available (some in English).

The **museums** are now run by a foundation based in Geneva, but they receive 10% support from the government of Gabon. There's also a **gift shop** with local crafts for sale made largely by people from the leper colony. The selection is excellent. Prices are high and fixed. Better bargains can be found by dealing with individual craftspeople or bargaining with dealers in Libreville. However, all proceeds from the craft shop at the Schweitzer Hospital go to the hospital and most of the stuff sold in Libreville actually comes from West Africa. Although the hospital is not keen on putting up travellers, it is possible to get a room and meals there in exchange for a reasonable donation.

Also available in Lambaréné are pirogues into the lake region where hippos and other wildlife can be seen (especially during the dry season). This can be expensive since it takes most of the day to go far enough in order to see much. A one-hour trip is reasonably priced but you won't see a great deal.

Soapstone sculptures and masks are often for sale in the villages north of

Lambaréné. If you're interested, ask the pirogues to stop here (they usually do anyway).

Places to Stay

Probably the cheapest place to stay is the grubby *Collective Rurale de Lambaréné* at CFA 1000 a double. Much better are the *Mission de l'Immaculée Conception* or the other *Mission Catholique*. Both are north of the the town centre (a taxi from the centre or the market costs CFA 100). They're both comfortable, quiet places and the sisters are very pleasant and cooperative. The beds in the dormitory cost CFA 1500 per person including the use of showers, and you'll probably have the place to yourself. There are also small private rooms available for CFA 2000. You can have your laundry done for CFA 1000.

In addition there's a small Peace Corps hostel (known as *Casse de Passage*) near the market for CFA 1500 per person. They have no running water but will give you a bucket of water. Electricity and a bed are about all you get.

Restaurants stay open until about 8 pm. The oil barge dock is near the market, across the river from the town. The area is full of bars and kebab stalls.

LIBREVILLE

Libreville can be an interesting city if you take the time to get to know it. Each *quartier* has its own character and is peppered with bars and boutiques.

Information

There is a local bus system which is pretty good though it's a little difficult to work out. Tickets can be bought in advance from most large bus stops or on the bus. Buses to the airport are also available. There are taxis around the city and to the airport – negotiation is often necessary.

The poste restante charges CFA 225 per letter collected.

Things to See

Don't miss the **St Michel Church** in

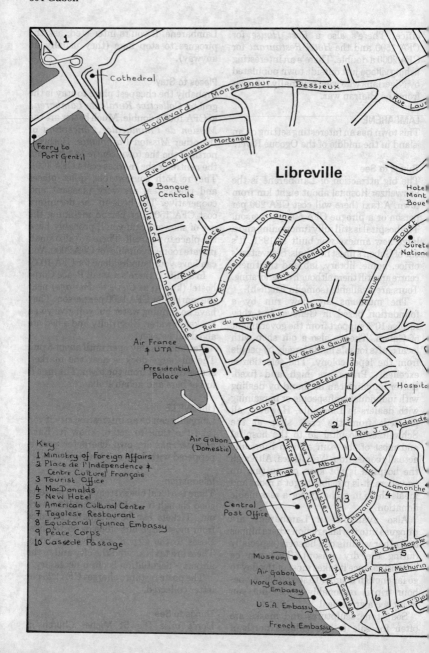

Key:
1 Ministry of Foreign Affairs
2 Place de l'Indépendence & Centre Culturel Français
3 Tourist Office
4 MacDonalds
5 New Hotel
6 American Cultural Center
7 Togolese Restaurant
8 Equatorial Guinea Embassy
9 Peace Corps
10 Cassede Passage

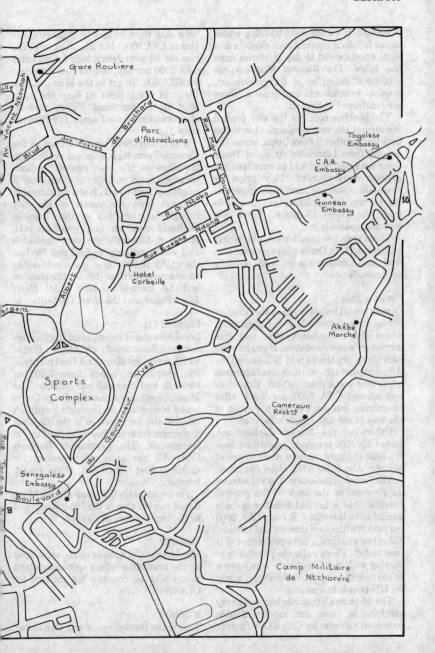

Gare Routière

Av. Vincent Nkounah

Blvd des Frères

Parc d'Attractions

Rue Marc N'Doume

Rue de Bruchard

Togolese Embassy

C.A.R. Embassy

Guinean Embassy

R. G. Ntoko

Ndong

Rue Ewène

Hotel Corbeille

Albert

Sergent

10

Sports Complex

du Gouverneur Yves

Akébé Marché

Cameroun Restnt

Senegalese Embassy

Boulevard

8

Camp Militaire de Ntchorérè

N'Kembo. It's a beautiful building whose entire façade is covered with mosaics and local wood carved to depict stories from the Bible. The **National Museum** has numerous examples of indigenous art, musical instruments and masks. Tours are conducted in French.

The beaches north of the city toward the airport are very pleasant. One is **Cap Estérias**. Another is **Point Denis**, across the estuary from Libreville. At Point Denis there is a small hotel and an excellent but expensive restaurant. Day trips or overnight camping are both possible. Round-trip ferry tickets are available from the Hotel Dialogue. There are several trips daily.

There are a few local bars in the fishing villages on Point Denis where you can also find food, entertainment and possibly accommodation.

Places to Stay

During school holidays ask at the *Mission School* across from the Maison Liebermann, where they'll probably offer you free dormitory accommodation. If you have no luck there, try the bars in N'Kembo (the African Quarter) – you may meet someone who offers you a place to stay. Expect to pay around CFA 8000 per week after bargaining, but don't expect too much in the way of services (electricity, etc).

Otherwise, the *Maison Liebermann* costs CFA 7000 per room, sometimes less. It's near the *gare routière* and the *grand marché*. Also there is the *Hotel Panadou*.

The French organisation, *Les Volontaires du Progrès*, at the back of the general hospital, has a limited number of beds available to travellers. It costs CFA 2000 per person with use of showers and kitchen. Volunteers naturally have preference so it may be full. There's also the possibility of staying with the UN people who have a house near the airport. Officially, it's only for UN people in transit.

The *Mission Catholique* has some very comfortable, clean and modern double rooms with shower for CFA 4000 (if you're on a very tight budget they may reduce this to CFA 2000) but it's often full. You can eat all your meals here for an extra CFA 2500 per day, or take just breakfast for CFA 500. To get to the Mission, take the road which forks off from the coast road at the cathedral. Follow this for about two km then ask again. It's off to the right.

The Peace Corps hostel (known as the *Casse de Passage*) is no longer available to travellers as it's been abused by both travellers and volunteers alike, but it might not hurt to ask. It is a considerable distance from the centre of the city though, at the back of the Togolese Embassy near an old, wrecked taxi. Hotels in Libreville are very expensive and you're unlikely to find one for less than CFA 10,000. Most are considerably more expensive than this. At the cheaper end they include the *New Hotel, Hotel Mont Bouet* and the *Hotel Corbeille*.

Places to Eat

Local volunteers recommend the *Camerounian Restaurant* at Akébé Plaine which serves excellent food (and plenty of it). They're only open from 7.30 pm onwards and they sell out quickly. The Muslim restaurant near the Peace Corps hostel is excellent. *McDonald's Sandwich Shop* is also very good as is the Togolese restaurant (near the Peace Corps office) in Nombakélé. The *Restaurant Baghera Chez Ali* has been recommended for excellent food – fried fish, chips, bread, beer, etc.

For a splurge try *L'Estuaire* in the Mont Bouet market area or the *Piperment* next to the large church in Akébé.

MOANDA

The *Mission Catholique* on the same road as the post office offers spotlessly clean rooms with air-con and hot showers for CFA 4500.

N'DENDÉ

This is the last village of any size before

the Congolese border. If heading for the Congo, remember that you must get an exit stamp before going on to the border.

There are rooms behind the general store at CFA 500 per person (bed and mosquito net). The *Mission Catholique* previously didn't welcome travellers but there are different people there now so you might find a bed for the night. Otherwise, ask around for Luc d'Haveloose who is a Belgian teacher in N'Dendé. He welcomes travellers. It might be best to drop him a line before you get there (BP 3, N'Dendé).

There is a restaurant in town and several stores though the latter have a limited range of food for sale (bread and tinned goods).

NDJOLÉ

Hotel de la Barrière is good value at CFA 3500 a double.

National Parks

Because Gabon has so few people, wildlife is still quite abundant in many areas. Elephants, gorillas, chimpanzees, leopards, mandrills, assorted monkeys and antelope are fairly common. Along the coast and in the lagoons there are still a few crocodiles, hippos, manatees and, offshore in season, humpback whales. There are three national parks – the Parc National de l'Okanda in the centre of the country; the Parc National de Wonga-Wongué, and the Parc National du Petit Loango. You can reach the first of these easily by rail – get off two stops before Booué. This is the best place in the country to see wildlife. You do, however, need your own vehicle to explore the park as you're not allowed in on foot. Camping is not allowed inside the park.

IN THE FOOTSTEPS OF JURGEN SCHULTZ

Since so few people venture this way, we'd like to offer an idea of what it's like. Here is a traveller's tale by David Bennett of Canada:

'But you must know Mr Jurgen, he is your brother', said the immigration officer excitedly. I was led into a thatched hut where a large ledger was opened in front of me. 'Voilà', said the officer, pointing to an entry on one of the pages.

It was true. Jurgen Schultz, nationality – German; mode of transport – foot, had indeed crossed the border between Gabon and the People's Republic of the Congo on 8 November 1977. But what connection did this have to me, standing in the same place, nearly three years later?

I looked down at the ledger again. It was a list of all non-African border crossers. There were no entries between Jurgen's name and my own which was now being inscribed. 'Ah, yes,' I nodded, 'Mr Jurgen'.

This wasn't the first indication I had received of the remoteness of my location. Traffic had become increasingly scarce since my departure from Libreville, the Gabonese capital, four days earlier. Although I was on the main international route between West and Equatorial Africa, I had waited all day for the vehicle which brought me to the border. Now, I faced a 20-km walk to the first Congolese town.

Fortunately, a local who was making the same journey agreed to take me with him. He knew a shortcut that would cut the distance by half. After fording a couple of streams and hacking our way through some dense jungle growth, we finally reached Ngongo, Congo. Ngongo was an almost fairytale village consisting of 100 well-made reed huts set in the midst of a hardwood rainforest. My guide took me directly to the village chief and soon I was shown to a hut. It was mine, for as long as I wanted. I was told the last occupant, a Mr Schultz, had stayed there for more than two weeks.

Later, I was taken to the only stone building in the village, a combination store and bar. As bottles of beer were produced, I reasoned that they must have been delivered by some sort of vehicle. 'It is true', said the chief. 'The beer truck will come tomorrow.' Reflecting on Jurgen's two-week stay, I realised that the word 'tomorrow' simply meant some time in the future.

I spent two days in Ngongo, where, as an honoured guest, I was treated with warmth and friendliness. On the third day, a dilapidated truck, stocked with cases of beer, wheezed into the village.

'No problem', said Pierre, the large, jovial driver, 'I can take you 140 km to Makabana. From there you can take a bus to Loubomo in time for the night train to Brazzaville.'

An hour later we set off, myself, Pierre, two helpers and several passengers. After a bone-wrenching 10-km ride we reached another village very similar to Ngongo. The arrival of the beer truck was the cause of much festivity. I was an honoured guest in this village also, and two hours and two bottles of beer later, we were under way again.

This scene was to be repeated five times before nightfall. We covered no more than 50 km and the beer had taken its toll. But what else could I do? An honoured guest can hardly refuse hospitality.

Finally, we stopped for the night. 'This is my village', said Pierre. 'You must meet my wife and children. Come, we'll take some food and drink.'

I awoke the next morning with a crushing headache. It eased as the day became a repeat of the day before. We visited several villages and covered 100 km by nightfall. Unfortunately, I was still not at my destination, as 50 of those km had been side-trips to villages off the main road.

Once again, Pierre took me to visit his wife and children. 'I suppose you have a wife in Makabana, too.' I said jokingly. 'How did you know that?' said Pierre, surprised. Than a glint of recognition came to his face. 'You've been talking to Jurgen, haven't you? He must have told you.'

Now that I understood Pierre's timetable, I awoke the next morning confident of reaching my destination. We travelled quickly until, outside a large town called Kibangou, we were stopped at a police checkpoint. A stern-faced officer perused my passport. 'You didn't get your passport stamped in Lobo', he said, referring to a forgettable village 80 km back down the road. 'You will have to return there to get it stamped.'

My heart sank. Ten minutes of persistent argument proved fruitless. I would have to return to Lobo and God knows how many days that would take. Then I had a sudden inspiration. 'The reason I didn't get my passport stamped', I blurted out, 'is because Jurgen Schultz told me it was not necessary'. The officer's face lit up and he began to shake my hand vigorously.

After 15 minutes of reminiscences about our nonmutual friend, I was allowed to continue my journey. At the other side of Kibangou, we came to a crossroads. 'Just a quick trip down this side road, and then we can continue on', said Pierre. Well aware of Pierre's quick trips, I diplomatically suggested I wait at the crossroads in the hope of securing a ride to Loubomo.

Half an hour later, a dusty pick-up truck screeched to a halt beside me. The driver, a middle-aged civil servant, was going directly to Loubomo. 'It's 140 km, so we'll be there in two hours', he said. As I reflected on my good fortune and the 140 km I had just travelled, the man looked over at me. 'A couple of years ago, I picked up another traveller quite like yourself . . .'

The Gambia

Consisting of a narrow strip of territory only 24 km to 48 km wide on either side of the Gambia River but nearly 500 km long and surrounded by Senegal, The Gambia is a legacy of the rivalry between the British and French for control of trade in West Africa. Small it may be, but it's one of West Africa's most colourful and interesting countries and would still be worth a visit even if it hadn't been made famous by Alex Haley (of *Roots*) tracing his ancestors back to Juffure. Not only are there numerous tribal groups, all with their own customs, but history has left this country with a treasure chest of relics and ruins ranging from the 12th-century stone circles of Wassu to the forts which dot the mouth of the river. There are unspoilt traditional villages, superb beaches and an endless variety of birdlife.

The Gambia's first contact with Europeans came with the arrival of the Portuguese in 1456. They landed on James Island about 30 km up river from the sea, and although they did not establish a settlement they continued to monopolise trade along the West African coast throughout the 16th century. In those days salt, iron, pots, pans, firearms and gunpowder were exchanged for ivory, ebony, beeswax, gold and slaves.

The first settlement was made by Baltic Germans in the service of the Duke of Courland (now Latvia), who built a fort on James Island in 1651. They were displaced by the British in 1661, after which trade and the defence of the island became the responsibility of a Royal Chartered Company with headquarters in London. The settlement was constantly under threat from pirates, the French and the mainland African kings, who would cut off supplies from time to time. Sickness and mutiny also took their toll. The fort was finally taken by the French

in 1779 while the British were occupied with fighting the war of independence in their American colonies. Though largely destroyed by the French, the fort was recaptured shortly afterwards. It was soon to lose its strategic importance with the construction of new forts at Barra and Bathurst (now Banjul) at the mouth of the river. These were better placed to control the movement of ships. Nevertheless, Fort James continued to be one of the most important collection points for slaves bound for the Americas until the trade was abolished in 1807.

During the early 19th century the British continued to increase their influence further and further upstream until in the 1820s a protectorate was declared over the area. The new colony was ruled for many years from Sierra Leone, but in 1888 The Gambia became a Crown Colony in its own right. Only in 1889 was the boundary between The Gambia and Senegal settled following a treaty between the British and French.

The colony became self-governing in 1963, but the British considered independence to be impractical both economically and politically and there was a period of intense activity over the question of whether The Gambia should be merged with Senegal. Although a Treaty of Association was signed, a United Nations team appointed to look into the possibility decided that it was unrealistic at that stage and the country became an independent nation in 1965. Since independence it has been ruled by

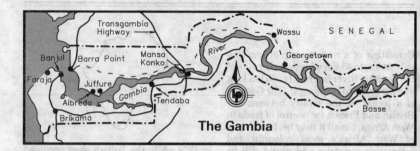

The Gambia

the People's Progressive Party led by Dawda K Jawara.

The Gambia suffers from a lack of natural resources and its only major export is groundnuts, so since independence it's been an uphill struggle to make ends meet. The country is still heavily dependent on foreign aid – mainly from Libya, West Germany, the People's Republic of China and Britain – and even this has been slow in coming at times. Libya virtually suspended aid when transport (in which they had a 40% stake) was nationalised in 1979. When it was discovered that a Senegalese dissident had persuaded several groups of young Gambians to go to Libya for training as part of his plan to takeover The Gambia and make it into an Islamic fundamentalist state, diplomatic relations with Libya were broken off and Libyan nationals were expelled from the country.

Tourism has also failed to become the money-spinner it was hoped it would be. Most of the tourists who come to The Gambia go on package tours, paying for their trip before they arrive. The attempted coup in 1981 led to a serious decline in the tourist industry though this appears to have recovered.

Perhaps sensing the inevitable, The Gambia entered into a confederal arrangement with Senegal in 1982 following the attempted overthrow of the Jawara government the previous year which was only aborted by the intervention of Senegalese troops. Those troops still

remain on Gambian soil and they have become a sensitive issue in the Senegambian confederation. Gambians are not keen to become just another region of Senegal and wish to preserve their identity, but this is viewed in Senegal as a reluctance to implement the agreements which were signed in 1982. Another issue which caused disillusionment in Senegal regarding the confederation was the invitation of the Nigerian president to The Gambia's 20th anniversary of independence and the signing of a number of cooperation agreements with that country. The resumption of Gambian diplomatic relations with Libya also caused some degree of irritation in Dakar.

The population, continues to expand but the number of jobs remains static (The Gambia is one of Africa's most densely populated countries), so many young Gambians have been forced to leave in search of jobs elsewhere – mainly to Britain and France.

Facts

GEOGRAPHY & CLIMATE
Life revolves around the river and there are almost no significant variations in the altitude or the vegetation, which consists largely of savannah and saline marshes. Overgrazing, deforestation and drought have combined to create serious problems in the agricultural sector. The dry season

stretches from November to April with the main rains between July and October. Temperature variations from one season to another are slight, averaging about 24°C in January and 29°C in June. The population numbers around 800,000, 90% of whom are Muslims.

VISAS

Visas are required by all except nationals of Commonwealth countries, Belgium, Denmark, Finland, Germany (West), Iceland, the Irish Republic, Italy, Luxemburg, Netherlands, Norway, Spain and Sweden. If arriving by air you may be asked for an onward ticket. This doesn't apply if you're coming overland. If you're coming in on the Koalack to Barra road, immigration officials will give you a seven-day stay permit. This can be extended in Banjul for up to three months. If you have problems getting the extension from the inspector, go straight to his superior upstairs. He's much friendlier and will help you out.

There are Gambian embassies in Brussels, Dakar, Freetown, Lagos, London, Tripoli and Washington. Visas in Dakar cost CFA 4000 and are issued the same day. The embassy is on Rue Thiong.

Other Visas

Banjul is generally a good place to get visas for other West African countries since it's a small city and very easy to get around on foot. There are embassies/high commissions in Banjul for Guinea-Bissau, Mauritania, Nigeria, Senegal and Sierra Leone and a Mali Consulate. There is no longer a Guinean embassy – get your visa in Bissau or elsewhere.

Guinea-Bissau The embassy is on Wellington St by the CUSO (Canadian University Services Overseas) office. Visas cost Da 25 and are issued in 24 hours or sometimes while you wait. Visas are for a 30-day stay. Photos or a letter of introduction are not needed and there are no questions asked.

Liberia The embassy is on Cameron St. Visas are free for Americans. All visa applications (except from Americans!) have to be accompanied by a letter proving you don't have AIDS!

Mali The honorary consulate is on the corner of Lasoo Wharf and Grant St. The consul is called Girigary Njie and is the head of the Banjul night soil collectors! He's often not at the consulate in which case go to his office at 47 Buckle St. One-week visas cost CFA 5000 with three photos and are generally issued while you wait.

Mauritania Visas cost Da 35 and are issued the same day if you can find any three members of the mission there at one particular time. A letter of recommendation is needed from your embassy.

Senegal The embassy is on Buckle St at the junction with Cameron St. Visas cost Da 22.25 or CFA 1000, with three photos and generally take 48 hours to issue. They're triple entry and allow for three stays of 10 days each.

Sierra Leone These cost Da 25 for a 30-day visa and are issued in 24 hours.

MONEY

US$ 1	=	Da 7.5
UK£ 1	=	Da 11
CFA 100	=	Da 24

The unit of currency is the dalasi = 100 bututs. There are no restrictions on its import or export. You can change dalasi back to hard currency before leaving. The currencies of Algeria, Ghana, Guinea, Mali, Morocco, Nigeria, Sierra Leone and Tunisia aren't accepted and can't be changed in banks. CFA francs are accepted.

A black market does exist, but the difference is so small that it simply isn't worth the trouble. Don't change money at hotels as the rates are very poor – usually around US$1 = Da 6.02. Change your money at the bank instead. The Standard

Bank will give US dollars or UK£ sterling cash in exchange for travellers' cheques – no problem.

The departure tax for international flights is Da 20.

TOURIST INFORMATION

If you're going to be spending much time here it's worth buying a copy of the excellent *Gambia: A Holiday Guide* by Michael Tomkinson.

Warning

If you like a smoke of the dreaded weed, there are minimal hassles in The Gambia and it's very easy to find, but avoid buying it immediately on arrival. There are a lot of tourist touts in Banjul playing at being Mr Ultra-Cool who spout Rastafarian cliches and attach themselves like leaches to starry-eyed new arrivals. Be streetwise or you'll pay five times the going rate. It should cost about Da 1 a foil, though if you buy Da 20 worth you'll get twice as much for your money.

LANGUAGE

English is the official language. The African languages of Wolof, Mandinka and Fula are also spoken.

Getting There & Around

AIR

The Atlantic coast of The Gambia is a package tour destination for British and French groups between November and April and there are many charter flights. These are much cheaper than standard-fare flights so there's the possibility of getting from Europe to West Africa or from West Africa back to Europe for much less than you would normally have to pay. For tickets you should contact Uniclam, Rue Monsieur Le Prince 63, Paris 6, France; or Unigam Travel Service, on the corner of Junction Rd and Kairaba Ave, Bakau, The Gambia; or ask around at

Uncle Joe's in Banjul. Paris to Banjul costs UK£140 one-way (as opposed to UK£400 one-way with British Caledonia). Bought in The Gambia, the tickets cost Da 1330 from Banjul to Paris. There's a flight every Sunday but you may have to go on the waiting list in the high season.

Charter flight tickets from London to Banjul with Calavi can be as low as UK£59 return if you're prepared to wait until the day of departure!

Otherwise, in Bakau, try Columbus Bus Travel at Kotu Strand Village or the same in Banjul on Hagen St. They sell tickets to Germany, Netherlands, the UK and USA. The fare from Banjul to Frankfurt costs DM 1300.

ROAD

In The Gambia itself, there's a good, paved road all the way from Banjul to Basse on the south side of the river. On the north side of the river the gravel road peters out about two-thirds of the way. So, for destinations more than 125 km on the north bank, it's better to travel first along the south bank then cross by ferry. There are ferries at Farafeni, Georgetown, Bansang, Basse and Fatoto.

Bus

There's a regular schedule of government (GPTC) buses. They are always crowded so, to get a seat, you must be there well before the buses depart. The depot for the government buses out of Banjul is actually at Serrekunda, so this is where you must board if you want to be sure of getting a seat. If boarding at Banjul itself, they will already be full and you'll be standing the whole way. The trouble with getting to Serekunda before 6.30 am is that there are no minibuses at that hour of the morning and the taxi fare from Banjul will be more than the bus fare for the whole journey!

There are three government buses daily except on Sunday in either direction along the road south of the river, the first at 7 am from Banjul. In Banjul, the buses leave from the terminus opposite the PWD (Public Works Department) on Bund Rd. The fares are Da 16 to Georgetown and Da 32 to Basse. The journey to Georgetown takes eight hours.

There are also buses operated by private companies which do the run but check out the state of their vehicles as many break down and end up taking far longer. They are somewhat cheaper than the government buses. Private buses leave from the junction of Independence Drive and MacCarthy Square.

All these buses stop at Soma about half way. Get off here if heading for Ziguinchor or Dakar (via the Farafeni ferry across the Gambia River). Don't take photographs of this ferry or you'll probably be arrested by Senegalese troops (even though you're in The Gambia)!

Shared taxis are also available and cost more than the buses, though you are assured of a seat.

BOAT

The ferry across the Gambia River between Banjul and Barra departs once every two hours in either direction, takes about 20 minutes and costs Da 1.75. The first ferry leaves at 8.30 am and the last at 5.30 pm. There are also 'pack 'em in' pirogues which will take you across in the meantime. They cost Da 1, plus 50 bututs if you want to be carried to the pirogue from further west along Wellington St. They go when full.

If you're looking for a passage on a ship to another country, it's worth contacting Mr Dick Parkins, the harbour master. He's friendly and will try to help. His office is near the GPA entrance.

TO/FROM GUINEA-BISSAU

From Banjul, first go to Ziguinchor. From here there are bush taxis to São Domingo (on the Guinea-Bissau frontier) for CFA 600. From there take a ferry (or pirogue if the ferry has broken down – P 50) to Cacheu and from there a series of bush taxis and ferries to Bissau.

TO/FROM SENEGAL

There are two ways of crossing The Gambia from the northern Senegalese town of Kaolack and the southern Senegalese town of Ziguinchor.

The most westerly route will take you from Kaolack to Barra, followed by a ferry across the Gambia River to Banjul. There are two Gambian (GPTC) government buses between Barra and Kaolack and Dakar in either direction every day at 9 and 11 am. If there is enough demand for the second bus by the time the first one has left then the later bus will set off straight away rather than wait until the normal departure time so get there early. From Banjul, take the first ferry of the day to Barra at 8 am. The bus costs CFA 2500 plus CFA 350 to CFA 900 for a backpack or Da 60 and takes about five hours to Dakar. In the opposite direction the buses depart from the Place Leclerc in Dakar.

The more easterly route follows the Trans-Gambia highway which connects Kaolack and Ziguinchor. There is no bridge over the Gambia River on the Trans-Gambia highway, so a ferry crossing is necessary at Mansa Konko.

You can also enter from Tambacounda via Velingara to Basse Santa Su at the eastern extremity of The Gambia. Tambacounda to Velingara will cost CFA 1000 by truck or CFA 1200 by bush taxi and take about two hours along a very good sealed road. Velingara to Basse by pick-up will cost CFA 300 or Da 7 plus Da 3 for a backpack and take about one hour. It's a very rough dirt road. You can change CFA into dalasi either in Velingara or Basse. There is no border control post at this point so you must check in with the police at some point. Some travellers have said there are no problems about this, but others have said they'll stamp you in only for a limited stay and send you to Banjul to get the full period allowed on your visa/stay permit. If you're on a visa and don't check in with the police, however, this allows you to overstay without anyone knowing about it.

Alternatively, take a minibus or truck from the taxi park in Banjul to Brikama (costs Da 1.50 plus 50 bututfor a pack) or a GPTC bus from Banjul to Brikama (Da 1 plus 50 bututs for a pack) followed by a pick-up truck or *taxi-brousse* from there to Ziguinchor (CFA 1550 or Da 16 plus Da 2 for a pack). The road is sealed most of the way and the journey takes about four hours.

If time is no object and you don't mind walking you might like to repeat the following adventure which was described in one traveller's letter:

If you're crossing the border at Brikama you'll probably have to walk the 15 km to the Senegalese side since there's very little traffic. Do the walk in the evening or at night – it's safe and a night walk is an incredible experience. Sometimes the path is only two metres wide and covered by a canopy of forest. The only animals you'll meet are the occasional Mandingo cattle. Arriving at night on the Senegalese side will assure you a free meal and wine from one of the customs officers and a clean room. The mosquitoes are heavy so have a coil handy to burn or repellent. The customs people are very friendly and if you're heading for Ziguinchor they'll stop any car with a spare seat and tell them to take you. You'll *always* get in the first car with a spare seat.

Around the Country

BANJUL

Banjul is virtually an island separated by large areas of swamp from the mainland, or, at least, land suitable for building on. The main population centres are therefore around Serrekunda (about twice the size of Banjul) and Bakau.

Information

A taxi from Yundum International Airport to Banjul costs Da 80. There are no buses between the airport and Banjul, but the Banjul to Brikama bus passes outside the main airport gate. Take a taxi only to the first bus stop on the main road (about a third of the distance) or to Serrekunda (about half of the distance), and take the Banjul bus from there.

Apart from the main bus terminals there is a truck park outside the new mosque on Mosque Rd where there are occasional trucks to Conakry (Guinea) and to Guinea-Bissau.

If you're thinking of staying in Banjul for more than a few days it's much better to look for accommodation in either Bakau or Faraja on the Atlantic coast. For details see Bakau.

Useful Addresses Some useful addresses in Banjul are:

Immigration
    Dobson St (1st floor) at the junction with
    Anglesea St
Post Office
    On the corner of Wellington St and Russell
    St (charges 24 bututs per letter collected
    from poste restante)
Senegal Embassy
    On the corner of Buckle St and Cameron St
Guinea-Bissau Embassy
    Wellington St (1st floor), next to the African
    Heritage Gallery

Things to See

It's worth making a trip to **Fort James** (James Island) while you're in Banjul as well as to **Albreda** and **Juffure** in Banjul organises these trips but it's also possible to make your own arrangements and it works out cheaper this way. Get the first ferry from Banjul to Barra at 8 am then a truck to Albreda for Da 2. From Albreda take a canoe to James Island for Da 30 return. The canoe owners wait for you while you have a look around the island. Juffure is a short walk from Albreda and accommodation is available if you want to stay the night. Beware of tourist touts around Juffure, however, who will offer to take you back to Banjul for Da 30 or more.

The **National Museum of The Gambia**,

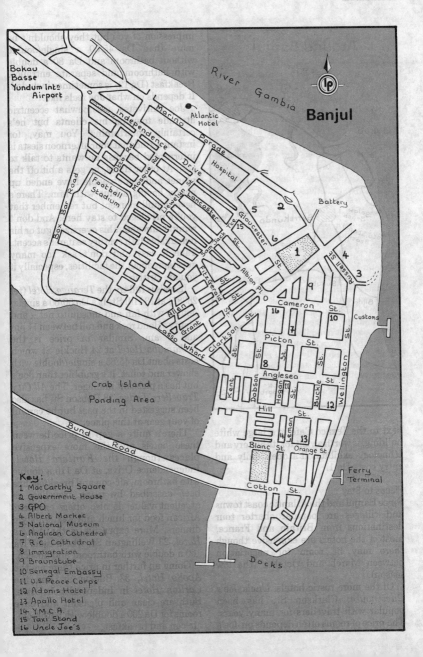

Bakau
Basse
Yundum Intⁿ
Airport

River Gambia

Banjul

Independence Drive

Marine Parade

Atlantic
Hotel

Hospital

Football
Stadium

Box Bar Road

Ma Carthy Square

Gloucester St

Battery

Dobson St

Russell St

Lancaster St

Llewelyn St

Fitzgerald St

Goan Jack St

Albion Pl.

1

5

2

6

15

4

3

Cameron St.

9

Allen St.

Grant St.

Clarkson St.

Lasso Wharf

16

7

10

Customs

Picton St.

Kent St.

Dobson St.

Hagan St.

8

Anglesea St.

Buckle St.

Wellington St.

Crab Island
Ponding Area

Hill St.

Leman St.

12

Bund Road

Blanc St.

13

Orange St.

Cotton St.

Ferry
Terminal

Docks

Key:
1 MacCarthy Square
2 Government House
3 GPO
4 Albert Market
5 National Museum
6 Anglican Cathedral
7 R.C. Cathedral
8 Immigration
9 Braunstube
10 Senegal Embassy
11 U.S. Peace Corps
12 Adonis Hotel
13 Apollo Hotel
14 Y.M.C.A.
15 Taxi Stand
16 Uncle Joe's

Around Banjul

next to the Texaco Café in a large white building, is worth a visit for its history and ethnology exhibits. It's open daily and entry costs Da 1.

Places to Stay

Since Banjul and the Atlantic coast towns and villages are popular charter tour destinations from Britain and France, most of the hotels are expensive though there may be room for negotiation between March and October (the low season).

Of the more rustic hotels, *Uncle Joe's Guesthouse*, Clarkson St, has been popular with travellers for many years. The price of rooms often depends on Joe's

impression of you but they shouldn't be more than Da 45/60 a single/double without bathroom and Da 80 a double with bathroom and separate entrance. Breakfast (Da 12) is sometimes included. It depends on what Joe feels like.

Joe cultivates a somewhat eccentric attitude towards his clients but he's certainly entertaining. You may, for instance, find that your afternoon siesta is interrupted because he wants to talk to you. At other times, he gets a bit off the planet and some people have ended up nearly having a blue with him. There's never a dull moment but remember that you're privileged to stay here. And don't remind him about his oversized gut or his remarkable 19th century seafarer's accent. Take it easy and don't ask too many questions about the facilities, especially if you are British.

If Joe's is full try the *Teranga Hotel* (tel 28387) at 13 Hill St. It's Da 50/60 a single/double with fan and mosquito net – and plenty of loud rock and roll between 11 pm and 3 am. Similar in price is the *Brikamaba Hotel* at 24 Buckle St which costs about Da 45/65 a single/double with shower and toilet. It's grubbier than Joe's but has a pleasant manager. The *All City Travellers' Lodge*, 18 Dobson St, has also been suggested in the past but be careful of your gear at this place.

There's quite a gap in price between these hotels and the more expensive places though the *Kantora Hotel*, Independence Drive, at Da 110 a double with bathroom, air-con and breakfast has been described by many travellers as excellent value. It also offers excellent African food for lunch and western-style dinners. More expensive is the *Adonis Hotel*, 23 Wellington St, which costs Da 160 a double with bathroom and air-con.

Going up further in price there are the *Apollo Hotel*, 33 Buckle St, and the *Carlton Hotel* in Independence Drive. Both are clean and pleasant and have rooms for Da 200 a double with bathroom, air-con and breakfast.

It's very unlikely you will be offered accommodation by VSO or Peace Corps volunteers. They have taken a distinct dislike to travellers over the last few years.

Places to Eat

The *African Heritage Centre*, Wellington St, is a great place to enjoy a steak, sandwich or a beer out on the airy balcony. Excellent African food can be found at 2 Grant St opposite the barber's shop. For fish & chips, try the *Fish & Chips Express*, Leman St. Another very popular place is the *Texaco Café* which has good Gambian food such as brochettes in pitta bread.

The *Apollo Hotel* is recommended for English-style breakfasts and for business lunches. Other restaurants which have been recommended include the *Restaurant Jobet*, Picton St, and the *Milky Way*, Wellington St, which offers great meat and fish pies. Similar is the tea shop at the MacCarthy Square end of Hagen St offering cheap tea and meat pies.

For a light splurge, try the *Barnstable Restaurant*. If putting your own food together, remember that the Albert market is closed on Sundays.

BASSE

One traveller described The Gambia's most easterly town as:

... a nice town with *Uncle Peacock's Bar* behind the taxi park. He's an old Nigerian sailor and boasts the coldest beer in The Gambia. Opposite is the palm wine bar which sometimes has barbequed bush pig. *Finche's Nightclub* hots up once the cinemas have closed around 12 midnight.

One of the cheapest places to stay is the *Government Rest House* which costs Da 20 per person. Enquire at the commissioner's office. There's also the *Hotel Apolo* (that's how it's spelt) on the main street which costs Da 25/35 a single and Da 40/50 a double. There's also a *Hotel Teranga* below the market.

Eat at either the *Basse Restaurant* or *Jobot's Restaurant*. Steak and salad at both will cost Da 5.

GEORGETOWN (Makhati)

Georgetown is a good place from which to visit the **stone circles** at Wassu. There are buses direct from Georgetown to Wassu for a few dalasi. The first one departs at about 9 am. You can camp anywhere around Wassu.

You'll more than likely be offered a place to stay in Georgetown, but if not there is a *Government Rest House* for Da 80 per room. It's clean, has hot and cold water and a lounge. It has been described as 'luxury left over from the 1940s' though other travellers have disputed this description. Apply at the police station. There's also the *Educational Centre Rest House* at the eastern edge of town which costs Da 10 per person. It's clean but there's no electricity or running water.

The Atlantic Coast Resorts

Bakau and Faraja are the main resort towns of the Atlantic coast though there's also Kotu Strand Beach further south.

BAKAU

To get to Bakau from Banjul, take a shared taxi from opposite the Texaco station on Independence Drive (75 bututs).

Places to Stay & Eat

Cape Point Restaurant is very clean and friendly and costs Da 35 a double including shower (hot water) and toilet. They have their own generator when the mains electricity goes off. It's very quiet and only 100 metres from the beach. Breakfast costs Da 5 – bread, butter, cheese, marmalade and tea. Another

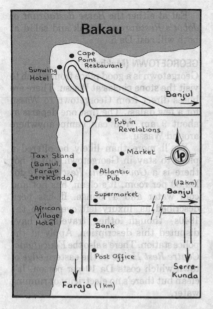

Bakau

snacks for Da 3 to Da 6. *Bakadaji's*, is in Serrekunda off Pipeline Rd and offers excellent Gambian food such as peanut stews with meat and vegetables.

Entertainment

All the hotels have a 'happy hour' from 5 to 6 pm and sometimes 5 to 7 pm when drinks are half price. Otherwise, the *Atlantic Pub* is a good place to hang out with draught Jul-Brew at Da 2. The *Le Mas Lebanese Restaurant* has the cheapest beers at Da 2.75 per pint during happy hours. Many expatriate workers frequent the *Faraja Club*. There's no entrance fee and the beers are cold. *Francisco's Restaurant*, near the Faraja Club, has also been recommended.

FARAJA

This is where the bulk of the tourist-class hotels are, mainly because the beach is superb.

National Parks

ABUKO NATURE RESERVE

This small park, 19 km south of Banjul is worth a visit and is home to vervet monkeys, baboon, bush buck, crocodiles and countless varieties of birds. The park has been in existence for many years and is managed by a Mr Brewer who has been the leading conservationist in The Gambia for at least 30 years. There is a walking circuit of about three km through untouched tropical riverine forest. Entry costs Da 10.

To get there, take a bus from Banjul to Brikama and ask to be let off at Abonko – everyone knows it. If you sit on the right hand side of the bus you'll see a signboard for the park. This marks the exit. The entry is the next stop.

place which has been suggested is *Sambou's Bar & Restaurant* which offers good food and rooms at the back for Da 80 including breakfast. It's a good place to rest up. Other than these, ask for Alpha at the *Pub in Revelations*. He can generally come up with somewhere to stay right on the beach at Bakau for around Da 12 to Da 15 per person.

The *Friendship Hostel* at Independence Stadium near Bakau has pleasant rooms with private bathroom for Da 110.

The *Atlantic Hotel* has discounted accommodation available in the low season for between 40% and 70%. With the larger discount a double with bathroom and breakfast costs about Da 360.

A good place to eat is the *Bomba Dirka* next to the CFAO supermarket. Meals cost Da 7 and up. The *Atlantic Pub* offers

Ghana

The area stretching from present-day Guinea to Nigeria has had a long history of civilisation. As early as the 13th century a number of kingdoms arose which were strongly influenced by the Sahelian trading empires such as those of ancient Ghana (present-day Senegal and western Mali), Songhai, Kanem-Bornu and Hausa. The first of these in Ghana itself were the states of Bono and Banda in the northern orchard bush. They gradually expanded south following the course of the Volta River to the coastal grasslands. Penetration of the rainforests didn't take place until the 15th century.

The most well-known and powerful of the kingdoms of Ghana was the Ashanti who, by the late 17th century, had conquered most of the earlier states and had begun to turn their attention to controlling the trade routes to the coast. Their capital, Kumasi, was highly organised with facilities and services the equal of most European cities at that time. The ruler, known as the Asantehene, employed literate Muslim secretaries from the north to manage trade with the Sahelian kingdoms and to govern distant provinces. As the Europeans became more and more involved on the west coast some of them found employment as advisers to the Asantehene. When the British invaded in the 1870s, for example, a German was engaged to raise and train an army of Hausa troops. Other adventurers involved included a Frenchman who became governor of a province and a Scots-American who was employed as an economic adviser.

For centuries the focus of trade in West Africa had been away from the coast inland towards the kingdoms which held sway along the Niger River and the edge of the Sahara. Gold, ivory, slaves and salt were the principal elements of this trade. The dues which cities like Gao, Timbuktu and Djenné extracted from the trans-Saharan caravans carrying these commodities north made them rich and powerful until the 17th century.

The event which changed all that and led to the decline of these cities was the slave trade to the Americas. Although slaves had been traded along the trans-Saharan routes for centuries, the numbers involved were small in comparison with the vast scale on which the European nations carried it out. In just a short space of time the focus of trade was to be completely reversed so that it centred on the coast, and the coastal kingdoms were to grow rich on the proceeds.

Until the 19th century there was very little penetration of the interior by Europeans, who relied on the rulers of the coastal kingdoms to deliver their human cargoes to a number of coastal forts which were the collection points. The first of these forts were constructed by the Portuguese in the 15th century and it was soon followed by others built by the British, French, Dutch and Danes. Most were held on a very tenuous basis and depended on the maintenance of good relations with the local rulers. The forts were frequently overrun and the slavers thrown out or massacred.

When slavery was abolished in the early 19th century, however, the Europeans were forced to seek other ways of making profits. This led them to become more and more involved in the interior. British interest in the Gold Coast (as Ghana was then known) became paramount after the

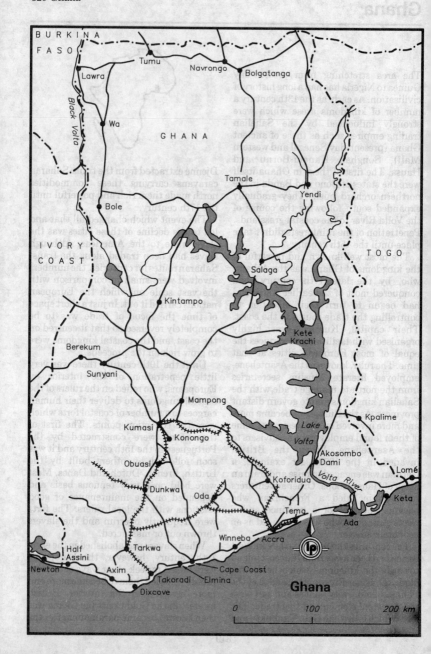

Ghana

Ghana

transfer of the Dutch possessions to the British in 1868.

The British conquest of the Gold Coast was strongly resisted, particularly by the Fante Confederation (an alliance of coastal kingdoms) and the Ashanti and, although Kumasi was sacked in 1874, warfare with that kingdom lasted until 1900. Military conquest didn't, however, extinguish African determination to regain independence, and a number of political parties dedicated to achieving this sprang up in the 1920s and 1930s. Neither these nor the United Gold Coast Convention (UGCC) formed in 1947 were nationally based. They ignored the aspirations of the large numbers of workers attracted to the cities during the boom in public works throughout the 1920s and 1930s. Aware of this, the then Secretary-General of the UGCC, Kwame Nkrumah, broke away in 1948 to found his own party – the Convention People's Party (CPP), which quickly became the voice of the masses and, for the first time, drew the north into national politics. The slogan of the CPP was 'self-government now'.

The CPP was an overnight success and Nkrumah's fiery speeches captured the mood of the nation perfectly. Yet rhetoric alone brought no tangible results and Nkrumah, exasperated by the slow progress towards self-government, called for a national strike in 1949. Seeking to contain the situation, the British hauled Nkrumah before the courts and sentenced him to jail. While he was serving his sentence the CPP won the general elections of 1951 and he was released to become leader of the government. Ghana was granted independence in March 1957, the first African country to achieve it from the European colonisers.

Much remained to be done, however, to consolidate the new government's control over the country. Many factional and regional interests surfaced and there was powerful opposition from a number of traditional chiefs and big farmers.

Repressive laws were passed in an attempt to contain this opposition and the CPP gradually changed from being a mass party into one which dispensed patronage. Individual and group corruption began to grow. Meanwhile Nkrumah skilfully kept himself out of the fray and became one of the most powerful leaders ever to emerge from the African continent. His espousal of pan-Africanism and his denunciations of imperialism and neo-colonialism provided inspiration for other nationalist movements far and wide.

Laudable though his achievements were, unbridled corruption, intrigue, reckless spending on prestige projects inappropriate to the country's needs, unpaid debts to western creditors, and the expansion of his personal guard into a regiment, were his undoing. In February 1966, while on his way to Beijing, Nkrumah was toppled in a coup led by the army and the police.

Describing their coup as essential to save Ghana from a communist dictatorship, the new regime was quickly accorded diplomatic recognition, debts were rescheduled, emergency aid and supplies were flown into the country and western 'experts' were engaged by the thousand. Three years later the military handed over the leadership to a conservative civilian government headed by Dr Busia. From the start his administration was crippled by an empty treasury, debts which Nkrumah had left and continuing widespread corruption. It was overthrown in 1972 in another military coup headed by Colonel Achaempong.

The 1972 coup changed nothing. Corruption and mismanagement continued to plague any progress toward economic stability, and continuing civilian exclusion from power began to generate widespread resentment. Instead of going through normal commercial channels, most of the country's cash crops (particularly cocoa) were smuggled across the border into Burkina Faso (then Upper Volta) and Togo. As food shortages became more and more desperate and the affluence of the army greater and greater, widespread demonstrations against continued military rule began to break out all over the country. The top brass reacted with all the brutality at their disposal but the reckoning was at hand. Even junior military officers were becoming disillusioned by then, and in May 1979 Flight Lieutenant Jerry Rawlings called for a confrontation between officers and men in order to root out those responsible for the corruption.

Rawlings was court martialled but his denunciation of the military elite at his trial received widespread publicity and caught the imagination of the country. A week or so later there was a spontaneous uprising of the junior ranks against their superiors. Rawlings was released from his cell and taken to Broadcasting House where he announced that the junior ranks were to take over the government of the country and bring to trial those responsible for its bankruptcy.

Rawling's Armed Forces Revolutionary Council was handed over to a civilian government several months later after general elections, and a major 'house cleaning' operation began. Eight senior officers, including Generals Achaempong, Akuffo and Afrifa, were executed by firing squad and hundreds of other officers and civilian businesspeople were tried by impromptu 'people's courts' and sentenced to long periods of imprisonment.

The new president, Hilla Limann, was not happy, however, with Rawlings' continued popularity and embarked on a programme of harassing his friends as well as attempting to meddle with the constitution and the composition of the High Court. Detecting a slide back into the old familiar mould, Rawlings began to make speeches warning the population to remain vigilant and not allow the gains of 1979 to be lost. Limann countered by accusing Rawlings of an attempt to subvert constitutional rule and this provoked a second takeover by the Armed Forces Revolutionary Council.

Rawlings remains as popular as ever, but many of the policies adopted by the Revolutionary Council have come in for widespread criticism from radicals both within and without the government. They were particularly aggrieved at the government's willingness to adopt strict austerity measures along lines suggested by the IMF and the World Bank in order to get the economy back on its feet. These measures, however, drew support from the traditional Ashanti chiefs who had been suspicious of the radical speeches made in the early days of the revolution.

Some of the measures adopted included a devaluation of the cedi by 90% in April 1983 (followed by further devaluations since then), the abolition of most price controls (resulting in increased prices particularly in fuel), improving tax collection and limiting the growth of the money supply. Priority has been given to rehabilitating the cocoa, mining and timber industries and to improving the transport network which had almost fallen apart by the early 1980s.

Things are improving and this is being reflected by increased investment from abroad, but it's going to be a long uphill climb. At least the chronic food and fuel shortages of the early 1980s are now a thing of the past but the programme could be set back by unforeseen circumstances. For example in 1983 an estimated one million Ghanaians were expelled from Nigeria contrary to the conventions of ECOWAS (the Economic Community of West African States). The influx created chaos and chronic food shortages.

The situation was made worse by a drought in the same year which seriously affected cocoa and agricultural production and led to a foreign exchange crisis. The drought resulted in an alarming drop in the level of Lake Volta which, in turn, led to the shutting down of four of the six generators at the huge Akosombo power station. The subsequent power cuts saw Accra plunged into darkness every second night, the shutting down of the aluminium smelter at Tema (a major foreign exchange earner) and a drastic cut in electricity exports to neighbouring Togo and Benin.

Nigeria again expelled some 300,000 illegal immigrants, 150,000 of them Ghanaian, in May 1985 but this time they were absorbed without precipitating a crisis. The year 1984 had been one of good rains enabling agriculture and industry to get back onto the road to recovery.

Despite criticism of the government's austerity measures from both sides of the political fence, Jerry Rawlings remains in tight control and indeed personifies the new generation of African leaders. It is unlikely that he will be toppled in the near future though there are usually several attempts to do so every year. Meanwhile, Ghana will continue to be heavily dependent on foreign aid for some time if it is to regain the prosperity it enjoyed at independence.

Facts

GEOGRAPHY & CLIMATE
Most of Ghana consists of wooded hill ranges and wide valleys with a low-lying coastal plain. The damming of the Volta River has created one of the largest lakes in Africa. Humidity is high in the coastal region while the north is hotter and drier. The rainy season stretches from April to September.

PEOPLE
The population is around 14 million, most of whom are Christian. There are, however, large minorities of Muslims and others following traditional beliefs.

VISAS
Visas are required by all except nationals of ECOWAS countries. You cannot get visas or entry permits on arrival at the border. Holders of South African passports are prohibited entry.

Until a year or two ago, visas for Ghana were sometimes difficult to get because of the continuing political and economic problems in the country. This has now changed and there should be no difficulties.

There are Ghanaian embassies in Abidjan (Ivory Coast), Addis Ababa (Ethiopia), Algiers (Algeria), Cairo (Egypt), Conakry (Guinea), Cotonou (Benin), Lagos (Nigeria), Lomé (Togo), Monrovia (Liberia), Ouagadougou (Burkina Faso) and Tunis (Tunisia) among others.

Visas cost CFA 6000 (or the equivalent) for Commonwealth citizens and CFA 9000 (or the equivalent) for non-Commonwealth citizens and are usually issued in 24 to 48 hours, though, for some reason or another, they can take up to one week if you get them in Burkina Faso.

Visa renewals up to one month can be obtained from the Ministry of the Interior, Redemption Circle for C 500 (Commonwealth) and C 800 (non-Commonwealth). Two black and white photos are required plus a *typed* letter saying why you want to stay longer and where you are staying. Typewriters for hire are plentiful outside the GPO. You may also need to show an onward ticket. The extensions take five to 10 days to come through but can take longer. Only a 'chat' with the boss will speed things up though you may have to cross his palm with silver.

You can no longer get extensions anywhere other than Accra though this may change as the country gets back on its feet. If you overstay your visa there is a fine of C 3000 on departure. Exit permits are no longer required.

Other Visas
There are embassies for Algeria, Benin, Burkina Faso, Egypt, Ethiopia, France, Germany (West), Guinea, Ivory Coast, Liberia, Mali, Netherlands, Niger, Nigeria, Switzerland, Togo, UK and the USA among others in Accra.

Burkina Faso These cost CFA 6000 or US$20 with two photos, and are issued in 24 hours. There's no fuss and the visa allows for a stay of three months.

Guinea The embassy in Accra is in the Djorwulu district – take a bus and get off at the Meat Marketing Board and follow the signs from there. They cost C 2500 or US$30.

Ivory Coast These cost C 750 with two photos and are usually issued within 24 hours but can take two to three weeks if they have to telex Abidjan (eg for Australians).

Liberia These cost C 1800 with two photos and take 48 hours to issue. You may also have to pay C 50 for the forms.

Nigeria Visa applications are only accepted on Tuesday. The cost depends on your nationality (C 2500 for British, C 1680 for Dutch, etc) and are usually issued the same day. Visas are for a stay of 15 days and there's no fuss.

MONEY

US$ 1   = C 188
UK£ 1   = C 352
CFA 1000 = C 600

The unit of currency is the cedi = 100 pesewas. The import and export of local currency is allowed up to C 20. Currency declaration forms are usually issued on arrival. If you don't get one ask or you may have problems when leaving. Sometimes, they are not collected on exit but you can't depend on this so keep all bank receipts.

The devaluations of the cedi since 1983 were designed to close the gap between the official and black market rates of exchange. It's been relatively successful so the black market rates are no longer spectacular but still worth it. Expect to get C 240 to C 250 for US$1 and C 660 for CFA 1000.

Be very careful when changing money

on the black market, as people are paid to inform and if you're caught they'll throw away the key! Try around Opera Square, the Arts Centre and Makola market. They'll find you. If bringing cedis into Ghana hide them well. It's best to assume that you will be thoroughly searched at customs on entry though this isn't always the case. You may also be searched at police checkpoints on the highways so hide any undeclared currency.

Petrol costs C 42 per litre for super – much cheaper than the Ivory Coast.

Airline tickets have to be paid for in hard currency. Cedis are not accepted.

The airport tax for international flights is C 200.

PHOTOGRAPHY

In the early days of the revolution, anyone seen taking photographs was viewed as a spy or with suspicion. Things have eased up now, but near The Castle in Accra (Rawlings' work place) and at the Akosombo Dam keep cameras in your bag. Don't take photographs of anything military. On the beach in Accra be careful of people passing themselves off as military in order to 'confiscate' your camera.

LANGUAGE

English is the official language. The main African languages are Akan, Twi, Fante, Ga, Ewe, Dagbeni, Hausa and Nzima. Some of the local languages have no sound for 'r' and instead they use 'l' hence you might hear Accra pronounced as 'Accla'. Bear this in mind.

Getting There & Around

AIR

Since you can still pay for internal flights in cedi, it's worth considering flying if the buses and trains are full or your time is limited. If you're paying with cedi obtained on the black market this makes the flights relatively cheap. Tamale to Accra costs

C 7900 plus C 50 tax. Kumasi to Tamale costs C 4400 one-way and C 6500 return.

Tickets for international flights, on the other hand, must be paid for in foreign currency. The cheapest flights to Europe from Accra are from Secaps Travel, Farrar Rd, Accra, which is the Balkan Airlines agent. Accra/Sofia/London costs US$390. To other European capitals the cost is US$420. Ghana Airways charges US$450 from Accra to London. British Caledonian and KLM are much more expensive.

ROAD

Because of bankruptcy, corruption and mismanagement, Ghana's transport system had virtually ground to a halt by 1981. Around 70% of the bus and truck fleet had been immobilised due to lack of spares and tyres. The railways were in a similarly sorry state. Even the vital line used to transport bauxite to the smelter at Tema was inoperable. Things are gradually improving but there's a long way to go yet.

There are numerous police and army checkpoints on the roads of Ghana. Sometimes they just want to look at your passport. Other times they'll search you. They often ask for a bribe for some real or imagined infraction of the law. If you don't want to be there arguing all day, pay up.

Bus

The good news is that the State Transport Corporation (STC) have acquired a new fleet of comfortable German-built buses which run on a regular schedule between the main towns. As you might expect, they're very popular and faster than private transport. Most private 'buses' are trucks modified to take passengers and they are usually pretty rough and ready.

Depending on where you are, where you want to go, when and what the demand is like, you'll have to put up with a lot of hassle to get tickets. Queues can be incredible and you'll often find that tickets are sold out before they even go on sale – meaning you'll have to buy them from touts at double the price. The only redeeming feature about travel by bus in Ghana at present is that distances are short so the overcrowding doesn't get excessively traumatic.

STC buses are generally waved through police checkpoints on the highways. Some sample bus fares and journey times are as follows:

Accra to Kumasi There are STC buses every hour from 5 am to 2 pm which cost C 400 and take about four hours along a good road. If unable to get tickets (queues rival those for welfare in New York during the Depression) go to the Neoplon station where you will be able to find frequent private services though these are more expensive. In Accra this station is on the Ring Rd a few hundred metres from Nkrumah Circle.

Accra to Akosombo A pick-up will cost C 140 plus half as much again for a backpack, no protests accepted!

Accra to Tamale One STC bus leaves daily at about 8 am and costs C 900 plus C 200 for a backpack. The journey takes 12 hours. To have any chance of getting a ticket on this bus you need to be at the depot by 4 am! This is when the gates open.

Accra to Takoradi There is a daily STC bus at 6 am which costs C 300.

Accra to Cape Coast The daily STC bus costs C 190 plus C 60 for a backpack and takes 2½ hours.

Kumasi to Tamale One STC bus leaves daily at 8 am, costs C 550 and takes eight hours. Tickets are in heavy demand and it's a fairly rough road. You can also get there by truck for C 650 plus C 100 for a backpack but they take around 12 hours.

TRAIN

Like the road transport system, the railways

are gradually being rehabilitated. Most of the trains now have brand new carriages but they are still being pulled by the old locomotives and breakdowns are frequent.

Between Accra and Kumasi there is a daily train which costs C 450. Between Kumasi and Takoradi the fare is C 600 (1st class) and C 350 (2nd class) and the journey takes seven to 11 hours depending on whether there are breakdowns.

BOAT
On Lake Volta, the passenger boat, *Akosombo Queen*, departs Akosombo at 8 am on Mondays, arrives at Kpandu at 2 pm and at Kete Krachi at 9 pm the same day. It then spends Tuesday, Wednesday and Thursday sailing between Kete Krachi and Kpandu and returns from Kete Krachi to Akosombo on Friday. The fare between Akosombo and Kpandu is C 500 and between Akosombo and Kete Krachi it is C 800.

In addition to the passenger boat, there is a cargo boat, the *Yapei Queen* which leaves Akosombo at 1 pm on Tuesdays and arrives at Yeji the next day at 8 am.

There are small boats between Kete Krachi and Yapei (the port for Tamale).

You can stay on the floor of the boat company's offices at Akosombo if you're waiting for a boat.

TO/FROM BURKINA FASO
The usual route to this country is from Bolgatanga to Ouagadougou. A shared taxi will cost CFA 3500 plus CFA 500 (or the equivalent at a sensible rate of exchange in cedi) for a backpack and the journey will take about 10 hours along a good road. The customs are relatively easy-going.

TO/FROM IVORY COAST
In the past, the most popular route between Ghana and Ivory Coast was along the coast road via Half Assini, Frambo and Newtown. It's still a hassle and should be avoided.

A new road has been completed between Takoradi and Abidjan via Elubo and Aboisso and this is the best route to take between the two countries. There are direct buses from Takoradi to Abidjan for CFA 5000.

It is also possible to cross into Ivory Coast from Kumasi to Abidjan via Agnibilekrou. There are direct STC buses three times a week which cost C 5600 and take 12 to 15 hours. If doing this journey in the opposite direction, choose the day you travel carefully. One of the three buses is an 'express' (usually leaving on Saturday from Abidjan). The other two are ordinary buses (departing usually on Monday and Tuesday from Abidjan). They can take 2½ days to do the journey – they have to spend a whole day and a night as a rule at the border because a truck accompanies the buses with goods which have to be declared. As a result, there are protracted negotiations over the amount of bribes which have to be paid.

There's a hotel at the border which charges CFA 1000 per bed and will change CFA into cedi at a reasonable rate. Take advantage of this as there are no banks and every passenger has to pay the driver C 400 to cover bribes to the Ghanaian police en route. The 'express' buses cost CFA 11,000 and the ordinary buses CFA 9000. Bribes have to be paid to Ivorian police, too, so allow another CFA 1000 for this.

TO/FROM TOGO
You have a choice of taking a direct shared taxi or a bus to the border followed by a bus or taxi from the border to Lomé. STC have a daily bus at 10.30 am from Accra to Afflao (the border) which costs C 140 and takes about three hours along a good road. There are also private buses for C 200 to C 250 and shared taxis for C 300 to C 400.

The direct shared taxis charge C 300 or CFA 1200 and take between two and three hours. They leave in the mornings.

Be careful at this border. Men are liable to be searched right down to their short and curlies – and there are female police who mete out the same treatment to women. Togolese customs will search you, too, but they're no problem.

Around the Country

ACCRA
Information
There is a tourist office on Kojo Thompson Rd but it's very short of material. The woman (Comfort Okopu) who runs it, however, is extremely helpful. The best map of Accra available is the one handed out by KLM, Republic House, Nkrumah Ave opposite the Kingsway department store. It's free. Look like you're one of their passengers. American Express is at Scantravel Ltd (tel 63134, 64204), High St, PO Box 1705, Accra. You cannot buy travellers' cheques here with one of their cards.

Taxis around town cost a minimum of C 10 from one circle to the next on the Ring Rd. Elsewhere they cost C 30 along fixed routes. Along other routes you will have to negotiate the fare. If arriving by air don't take a taxi directly outside the arrivals hall otherwise you'll be charged C 300. Instead, walk down to the main road and pick up a shared taxi for C 30.

The British Council on Liberia Rd has a good reading room and library with current British newspapers and magazines.

Things to See
A visit to the **Aburi Botanical Gardens** on Akwapim Ridge about 35 km north of Accra is worthwhile. They were laid out by the British about 100 years ago. It's a beautiful area and the perfect place for a break when you've had enough of the noise and traffic in Accra. There's a fine old colonial-style rest house which costs C 440 a double with mosquito nets and well water. It is booked out at the weekends so it's best to go between Monday and Thursday. There's an excellent restaurant next to the guesthouse where you can get chicken, rice and salad for C 350.

About two km from here on the way back to Accra is the *Restaurant May* where you can get a meal and stay for C 450 a double.

Nearby on the same road is **Larteh** which is the Ghanaian centre of traditional religion – witch doctors, fetish priests, etc. The **Akonedi Shrine** is here, too. Buy a bottle of schnapps at a local bar and someone will show you around. You can take as many photographs as you like. No-one objects. You might also like to pay a visit to Nana Agyemfra, the local chief, who often dons his traditional regalia and gold crown and welcomes you as a long lost friend. There are magnificent views over the Accra plain in daylight from **Akwapim Ridge**.

A little over to the west near Koforidua are the **Begora Falls**. To get there take a local bus from Koforidua to Begora village from where it's one hour's walk. Also on the same plateau are the beautiful **Boti Falls** which support vast numbers of butterflies.

Places to Stay
Probably the cheapest place is the *YMCA* (tel 24700), Castle Rd, where space is set aside for travellers in addition to the inevitable 'permanent' student residents but it's only dormitory accommodation. It costs C 250 per bed and meals are available. Likewise, the *YWCA* sets aside dormitory accommodation for travellers at the same price.

Also very cheap but even better value is the *Methodist Guest House* opposite Mobil House which offers double rooms for C 300.

In the centre of town (Jamestown) is the *Take Care Lodge*, in the square right behind the GPO. It offers very pleasant rooms for C 440/550 a single/double with fans but they only have seven rooms so it's often full. The *Asona Lodge* about 200 metres further down the road has rooms for C 440 a double including fan. In this same area the *Hotel Wato*, next to the GPO, is cheap, noisy and sometimes the

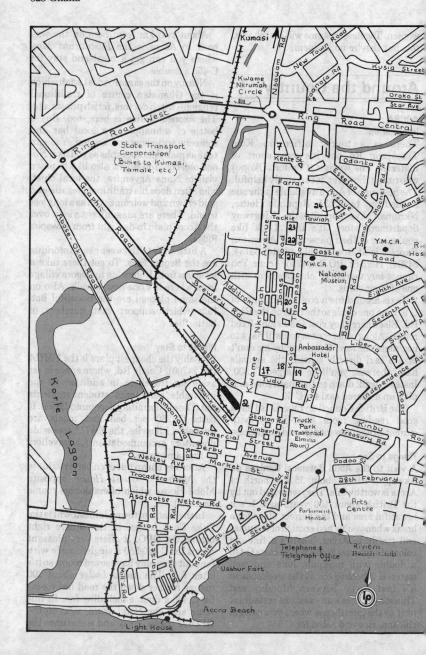

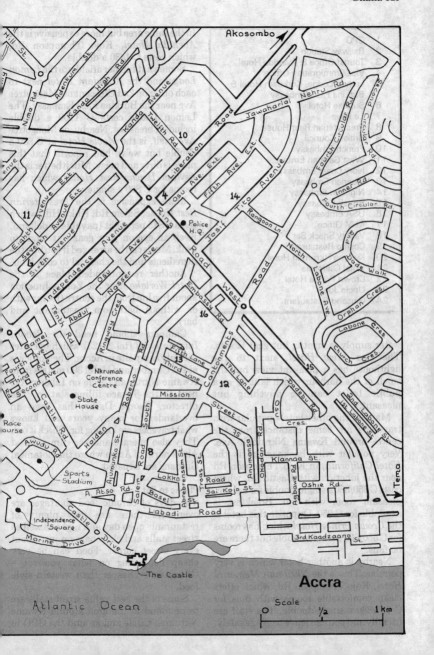

Akosombo

Police H.Q.

Nkrumah
Conference
Centre

State House

Race
Course

Sports
Stadium

Independence
Square

The Castle

Atlantic Ocean

Accra

Scale

0   ½   1 km

Tema

1	GPO
2	Railway Station
3	Tourist Office & Avenida Hotel
4	Visa/Immigration Office
5	Lemon Lodge, Korkdam Hotel & Burkina Faso Embassy
6	Sunrise Hotel
7	Le Rêve
8	Presbyterian Rest House
9	British Council
10	French Embassy
11	West German Embassy
12	Ivory Coast Embassy
13	Liberian Embassy
14	Nigerian Embassy
15	British Embassy
16	USA Embassy
17	KLM Office
18	Variety Snack Bar
19	Cosmo Restaurant
20	Kwame Nkrumah Hotel
21	Hotel California
22	Crown Prince Hotel
23	Uncle Joe's
24	Ginseng Restaurant

water supply is erratic, but gear is safe. The *Sea View Hotel*, next to the lighthouse has a pleasant view but the smell of the harbour which is used as a public toilet can be anything but pleasant.

Many of the other hotels popular with travellers are some distance from the centre around Kwame Nkrumah Ave. Very popular with backpackers is the *Hotel California*, in Kojo Thompson Rd near the junction with Castle Rd, which costs C 650/880 a single/double for a clean, pleasant room with fan. Breakfast is available for C 250. Opposite this hotel is the *Crown Prince Hotel* which has rooms for C 550/660 a single/double but there are no fans.

Nearby is another hotel which is very popular. This is the *Nkrumah Memorial Hotel*, Kojo Thompson Rd, which offers clean comfortable rooms with fans for C 750/880 a single/double. The staff are friendly and you can leave baggage safely.

In the same area but more expensive is the *Avenida Hotel*, Kojo Thompson Rd, which costs C 1430 a double.

Somewhat further afield are the *Lemon Lodge* and the *Korkdam Hotel* next to each other on 2nd Crescent off Mangotree Ave near the Burkina Faso Embassy. The Lemon Lodge costs C 1100 a double including breakfast. Nearby, on Mangotree Ave itself, is the *Mavis Hotel* at C 880 a double but we've had reports that this place is dirty and noisy. Much better is the *Asylum Downs Rest House* which has rooms for C 800 a single.

More expensive is the *Presbyterian Rest House*, Salem Rd, Kuku Hill, which costs US$5 per night (payable in dollars). Keep an eye on your gear – it tends to walk. Meals can be arranged if you buy the ingredients and the charcoal to cook it on.

Another recommended place is the *Hotel Worlako* near the Zongo Junction about five km from the centre (rooms with or without bathroom, restaurant and bar).

Campers should head for *Reborn International* (tel 29123) which operates the only camp site in Accra. Their office is at the Cumberland Hotel 300 metres from Kwame Nkrumah Circle on Liberty Ave next to the Texaco filling station. The director, George Darko, has been an overlander for many years and knows what travellers are looking for. Check it out. They also operate another camp site at Aburi north of Accra where the Botanical Gardens are situated.

Places to Eat

The days of chronic food shortages are over and there are now plenty of restaurants open day and night as well as street stalls and chop bars on just about every street corner. Food can be very cheap depending on what you eat – Ghanaian is cheaper than western-style food.

Some of the best value street stalls are to be found in the area around Kwame Nkrumah Circle and around the GPO in

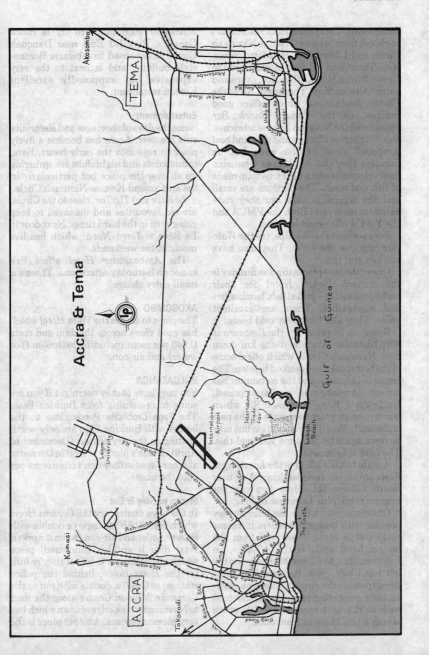

Accra & Tema

Jamestown. There are a lot of restaurants to choose from between Kwame Nkrumah Circle and Liberia Rd. *Henrietta Sams*, Kojo Thompson Rd four blocks from the Crown Prince Hotel, offers rice, sauce and yams. Also on Kojo Thompson Rd is the *Cosmo Restaurant* which offers good lunches, or the *Variety Snack Bar* opposite which has good kofta sandwiches. *Bus Stop* serves chicken and rice, and beef stroganoff most of the week but on Sundays they put on cheaper Ghanaian food – rice balls and a delicious soup made of fish and meat. The portions are small and the service is slow but they have excellent ice cream. Both the *YMCA* and the *YWCA* offer good lunches.

For excellent fish & chips, try the *Wato Bar* opposite the GPO. They also have chicken and rice.

One of the best places to go on Sunday is the *Riviera Beach Hotel* for their barbeque lunches – grilled fish, hamburgers and sandwiches. These are excellent value. They also have very cold beers.

Going up in price, try the *Restaurant 400*, Nkrumah Ave about one km down from Nkrumah Circle, which offers some of the best steaks and seafood in town. The owner is Lebanese and the restaurant has air-con. *Annabels* is similarly priced. *Uncle Joe's*, Kojo Thompson Rd, which was a popular place to splurge in the past is presently closed for renovation but may be open again by the time you read this. The food is Lebanese.

A little further afield is the *Los Amigos Restaurant*, on Independence Ave near South Liberia Rd. Here you can get mignon steak plus Lebanese dishes.

One restaurant which has become very popular with budget travellers in recent years but is quite some way from the budget hotel area, is the *Afrikiko*, on Independence Ave some 200 metres on the left hand side, past Redemption Circle going towards the airport. This is an open-air restaurant offering cheap African food such as rice with meat sauce. It's worth taking a taxi there at least once.

Another good place to try is *Black Caesar's*, Ring Rd East near Danquah Circle. It is housed in a bizarre Roman-style building and is next to the very expensive but supposedly excellent Korean restaurant.

Entertainment

Since the days of shortages and electricity cuts are over, Accra has become a lively place to rage into the early hours. Bars, music joints and nightclubs are springing up all over the place but particularly in the area around Kwame Nkrumah Circle.

Le Rêve and *Tip Toe*, close to the Circle, are old favourites and managed to keep going even in the hard times. Next door to Le Rêve is *Terra Nova*, which has live music at the weekends.

The *Ambassador Hotel* offers live music on Saturday afternoons. There's a small entry charge.

AKOSOMBO

The place to stay is the *Volta Hotel* which has good views across the dam and costs C 840 per room including bathroom (hot water) and air-con.

BOLGATANGA

You may have to stay overnight if you are going to or coming from Burkina Faso. The **Paga Crocodile Ponds** close to the border with Burkina Faso are only worth visiting in the dry season (December to April). There's plenty of food in the water at other times so they don't often come out onto the banks.

Places to Stay & Eat

In the town centre, try the *Central Hotel* which costs C 880 a single or double with shower, toilet and air-con (when it works). Next door is another (unnamed) place which has rooms for C 500. If they're full, try the *Hotel Bolco*, behind the police station, at C 600 a double with fan or the *Christian Mission Centre* along the road to Navrongo at the edge of town which has very pleasant rooms. Another place is the

Hotel Royal on the Tamale road about 10 minutes' walk from the State Transport depot.

The women on Kula St south of the new but incomplete mosque can be depended upon for good cheap food.

KOFORIDUA

The *Partners May Hotel* is highly recommended and cheaper than the *Catering Rest House*. It's very clean, the staff are friendly and it costs C 440 a single with attached bathroom and small sitting room. The beds in these singles will easily accommodate two people. The hotel is surrounded by a beautiful garden.

KPANDU

Kpandu (pronounced without the 'k') is on Lake Volta. A good place to stay is the *Lucky Hotel* which is reasonably clean and costs C 250 a double. Videos are sometimes shown in the courtyard.

KUMASI

Kumasi is the old Ashanti capital and a major cultural and economic centre of Ghana. Even Jerry Rawlings has to negotiate with Ashanti leaders on important issues. It was sacked by the British in the late 19th century so don't expect to see it in all its glory. The Ashanti king, Ashantene II and the Queen Mother still live here.

The **Ashanti Museum** is worth a visit as is the **market** which is one of the largest in West Africa. To visit the **King's Palace** you must be properly dressed (no shorts or revealing tops). Don't expect too much pageantry, however, as the king now lives in a modern palace.

Places to Stay

Many of the hotels are outside the city centre on the Accra Rd. Right in the centre of town about 150 metres from the State Transport depot is the excellent *Hotel Kingsway* which is an old British hotel but it costs C 1200 a double with bathroom and air-con. Also in the centre

on Kingsway Rd is the *Montana Hotel* which costs C 750 a double.

Many travellers, however, stay at the *Menka Memorial Hotel* about two km south-east of the city centre which has a mellow olde worlde atmosphere and friendly staff. It's a bargain at C 350/550 a single/double with fan and C 660 a double with bathroom. The water supply is erratic. Avoid the rooms on the ground floor as they're dark. The ones on the upper floor are much better.

Some 80 metres up the hill opposite the Menka is the *Kusibo Lodging House* run by a friendly family. They have rooms for C 330/660 a single/double with fan. The double rooms have a balcony. The *Cottage Hotel* near the stadium offers double rooms with shower, toilet and fan for C 900. A good breakfast is available for C 350.

Other hotels which have been recommended are the *Stadium Hotel, the Akuanaba Rest House*, Accra Rd, and the *Ayigya Rest House*, Accra Rd near the University Hotel. The *YMCA* is usually not worth trying because it's full of students.

If you've got time to spare it might be worth visiting the campus of the University of Science & Technology. You could strike up a friendship with someone who might invite you back – if this should happen, please pay for your keep, as times are very hard for Ghanaian people at present.

Places to Eat

Lots of market mammas set up street stalls alongside the walls of the stadium and offer excellent kebabs, beans, salad, rice and noodles. You can eat well and cheaply there. *Zart's* is a good place to eat and has been recommended by several travellers. The manager is friendly and will cater for vegetarians. Otherwise, try the *Family Restaurant* (good value) or *Lord's Restaurant*.

Entertainment

A good place to sit and have a beer with local people is the *A1 Bar* outside the stadium. For night life, try *The Dim Light*, *Foxtrot* or *City Hotel*.

NAVRONGO

Navrongo is close to the Burkina Faso border on the main road between Tamale and Ouagadougou. The best place to stay if you can find transport is the *Guesthouse* at the Tono Irrigation Project about five km west of town. It costs C 1500 per night and is one of the cleanest places in Ghana with running water and electricity 24 hours a day.

Tiko's at the STC bus stand has been recommended for food.

TAKORADI

There's very little of interest to travellers in this large city but if you find yourself having to spend a night, try the *Hotel Arvo*. The hotel has been recently refurbished and costs C 770/880 a single/double with bathroom and fan. If it's full, try the *Embassy Hotel*.

TAMALE

North-west of Tamale is the **Mole National Park**, home to elephants, antelopes, monkeys and many other species. Lions are occasionally seen. The best time to visit is the dry season (December to April). Land Rovers are sometimes available to drive you around the park but otherwise hire a guide to take you walking for several hours. The guides charge C 150 but if you want any enthusiasm you're going to have to add a tip.

Stay at the hotel which costs C 550 per person, with breakfast for C 150 and other meals for C 250. The hotel is set dramatically overlooking a water hole where animals come to drink at sunrise and sunset.

There is a daily STC bus from Tamale to Mole which leaves at 2 pm and arrives at the hotel in the park at about 7 pm. The bus returns to Tamale the next day at 6 am. The fare is C 200 plus C 100 for a backpack. Otherwise, take a bus to Bole and get off at Larabanga just after

Damongo. From there it's a six to seven-km walk. Hitching is difficult as there's very little traffic.

If you have time, it might be worth taking a look at the **mosque** in Larabanga. It's the oldest in Ghana.

Places to Stay

A good, clean place to stay is the *Al Hassan Hotel* in the centre of town close to the State Transport depot and the market. It costs C 330/440 a single/double without fan and C 550 a double with fan. The hotel has a good restaurant and bar where meals are available for about C 400. It's a centre of sorts for African music so it's an interesting and lively place to stay. The *Las Hotel* also has good, clean rooms at a reasonable price. There are two other hotels on the road to the hospital.

The *Catering Rest House* is more expensive and there's often no running water. Food is also expensive.

Nightlife

For something to do in the evening, try one or other of the discos/nightclubs (*Los Discos, Royals*, etc) or the pito bars such as *Biafra 1* and *Biafra 2*, *Moustache*, etc. Pito is an alcoholic drink made from corn.

The Coast

All the old colonial forts along the coast – Dixcove, Elmina and Pampam – were converted into rest houses in the 1970s and were very popular with travellers. When Ghana hit hard times in the early 1980s, the rest houses fell into disuse and the only ones you can stay at these days are Dixcove and Elmina. You can, however, still visit the forts, and restoration has been done on some of them.

DIXCOVE

The old Portuguese **fort** is very picturesque but the palm trees are dying of some disease so it's just a question of time before the beach will look like Vietnam after the war. You can stay at the fort for C 170 per person including breakfast. The beds are filthy and there's no toilet. The water is drawn from a well. If you ask around you'll be able to find local people who will cook for you for about C 200 a meal. Otherwise, buy rice and fish on the street at night and cook yourself.

Busua Beach

This beach is a half-hour walk through the bush from Dixcove. It's long, clean and beautiful but getting steadily more popular. There are fairly pleasant bungalows to rent at the *Pleasure Beach Hotel* for C 440 a double but there's usually no water supply or electricity so you'll have to make your own arrangements. Local people will cook for you and, if you find the right person, the food can be excellent (lobster, fish, chicken, etc for around C 200 to C 300).

The camp site is a disgrace – no water, expensive drinks and a lot of thieving. It costs C 110 per person. As at Dixcove, the palm trees are dying here.

ELMINA

There are two **old forts**. You can not stay at the larger one but guided tours are available for C 200. To take photographs costs an extra C 300. The smaller castle on the adjacent hill (known as Coenraadsburg) is the one where you can stay. The charges are the same as at Dixcove. If you don't want to stay at the fort get a room at the *Hotel Hollywood* in town. This is a spotlessly clean place run by friendly people and excellent value at C 650 per room. Room No 1 is the best as it gets sea breezes.

The other two hotels are very expensive and cater for well-heeled tourists. The *Elmina Motel* has chalets for rent at C 2400 a double with bathroom and fan.

There's a good restaurant too, with a live band in the evening. The *Oyster Bay Hotel* is even more luxurious and charges C 3300 a double.

CAPE COAST

Despite the fact that the **castle** here is a prison, you can still visit. Entry costs C 50 and includes a guide.

Places to Stay & Eat

The two cheapest places to stay are the *Savoy Hotel* and the *Palace Hotel* but the Savoy is the better of the two as it's cooler. They're both basic but clean and cost C 550/990 a single/double. The Savoy also has rooms with air-con for C 1650 a double. Running water may not be available all day at either place.

More expensive is *Dan's Paradise* which has air-con rooms with shower and toilet and large beds for C 1100 a double. There are no singles. It's probably the best place in town. Lastly, there is the *Bakado Aprotek* which has chalets for C 1000 a double. This place is an experiment in appropriate technology and everything is made from concrete, including the tables and chairs at the restaurant.

There is a German restaurant at Biriwa Beach some way from Cape Coast on the road to Accra which has been recommended. It serves excellent food.

WINNEBA

Winneba is a small town between Cape Coast and Accra with a very pleasant beach. The cheapest place to stay is the *Flamingo Hotel* which costs C 350 a double with fan. Meals can be arranged on request. There is live music in the garden every Monday. More expensive is the *Tourist Centre* where the cheapest rooms are C 1000.

Guinea

Guinea became a French colony in 1891 and was granted independence in 1958 under the leadership of Sekou Touré and his Parti Démocratique de Guinée. For many years, it was one of Africa's most reclusive states and only recently has it begun to open up to the outside world.

The reasons for its isolation are largely the result of Sekou Touré's principled stand against French colonialism. Never a man to surrender political objectives for economic considerations, Sekou Touré rejected General de Gaulle's offer of membership in a French commonwealth as an alternative to total independence, declaring that 'We prefer poverty in liberty to riches in slavery'. He certainly gained the admiration of many other African countries as a result of this stand, but French reaction was swift and vicious. French financial and technical aid was cut off completely, investment in the mining industry ceased, civil archives were destroyed and massive amounts of capital were withdrawn from the country. It's remarkable that the country survived without becoming a Soviet satellite. Yet it did, though the cost was heavy.

After the heady days of independence had worn off, Sekou Touré became more and more obsessed with what he perceived to be opposition to his rule. So-called conspiracies were detected in one group after another, show trials were held, and dissidents and suspects were imprisoned or executed, until by the end of the 1960s there were some 250,000 Guineans living in exile abroad. At various times he accused both African and other countries around the world of plotting to overthrow him. Among those he accused were the USA, France, the USSR, West Germany and Rhodesia. At least no-one could accuse him of undue bias toward any particular power bloc. All the same, while some of the conspiracies were genuine, the

majority were merely fantasies, though very useful politically in giving him an excuse to eliminate rivals. The event which probably had most effect on him was the Portuguese-backed invasion of Conakry by Guinean dissidents in 1970. While the attempt failed, it led to a series of executions and the expulsion of the 100-person West German technical mission – Bonn was accused of amassing a 500-strong group for yet another invasion.

Towards the end of his presidency, however, Sekou Touré was forced to soft pedal in order to attract the capital and technical aid which the country needed to get moving economically and raise its standard of living. His support among the population was also seriously eroded as a result of the witch-hunts of opponents since independence. Relations with France improved considerably following the visit of Giscard d'Estaing in late 1978 after which French aid began flowing back into the country.

Sekou Touré died in March 1984. Just one month later a military coup was staged by a group of colonels bent on liberalising the political structure, getting the economy back on its feet and sweeping the government and administration clean of all pro-Touré elements.

The coup certainly opened up Guinea and returned it to the western fold but the leaders dithered about what to do next. This was due mainly to a conflict of personalities amongst the soldiers who had seized power, and between President Lansana Conté and Prime Minister

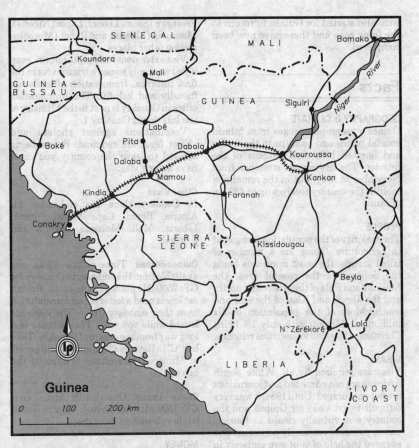

Guinea

0   100   200 km

Diarra Traoré. The showdown came in July 1985 when Traoré attempted to stage a coup whilst Conté was away in Lomé for a summit meeting of ECOWAS (Economic Community of West African States). The coup failed since Traoré did not enjoy sufficient support in either the army or the civilian population and the conspirators were arrested.

The event allowed Conté to consolidate his power but it didn't result in any decisions being taken to bring to trial those arrested for corruption and embezzlement in the Touré administration nor those

involved in the attempted coup. It did, however, enable Conté to face the urgent question of what was to be done about the economy. As a result of the rigid ideological stance adopted by the Touré dictatorship, the country's currency, the syli, was effectively worthless and inconvertible thus making trade with neighbouring countries and the outside world extremely difficult.

Despite the hazardous political repercussions, Conté was eventually forced to adopt austerity measures in order to secure an IMF standby loan. Negotiations were also started for Guinea to return to the franc zone and these have now been completed.

Facts

GEOGRAPHY & CLIMATE

Guinea's geography ranges from humid coastal plains and swamps to the fertile and forested hills and plateaus of the interior. The dry season stretches from November to May, but in the remaining months the country receives up to 430 cm of rain.

PEOPLE

The majority of the population is engaged in agriculture. There are a number of tribal groups, the most numerous being the Soussou of the coastal area, the Malinke and Fula of the centre and north, and the Tenda and Kissi of the east and south. Most of the population of six million are Muslim with only 1% being Christian, while 39% follow tribal religions.

VISAS

Visas are required by all. White South Africans are not admitted and journalists are not encouraged. Until 1984, it was very difficult to get visas for Guinea and the country was virtually closed to tourists unless you were extremely persistent and engaged the help of your own embassy in securing a visa. However, the country is now open normally and visas are easy to obtain, though it helps if you already have a visa for either Mali or Sierra Leone.

Visas are generally for a one-month stay, cost the equivalent of FFr 100, with two photographs and are usually issued while you wait. It is important to look clean and tidy when applying for one. There are Guinean embassies in Abidjan (Ivory Coast), Accra (Ghana), Bamako (Mali), Banjul (The Gambia), Bissau (Guinea-Bissau), Dakar (Senegal), Freetown (Sierra Leone), Lagos (Nigeria), Monrovia (Liberia) and Rabat (Morocco) among other places.

Visa extensions are easy to obtain, even if you were only issued a transit visa in the first instance. Immigration officials are friendly and helpful. The immigration office in Conakry is next to the Ministry of the Interior in Conakry 1.

Vaccinations against cholera and yellow fever are required. Before being allowed to leave the country you must have an exit visa.

Other Visas

In Conakry there are embassies for Algeria, Benin, Cape Verde, Ghana, Liberia, Mali, Morocco, Nigeria and Senegal.

Guinea-Bissau Three-month visas are available from the embassy in Conakry for GFr 2500. No photos are required. British nationals need a letter of recommendation from their embassy (free). The visas are issued while you wait. The embassy is a long way from the centre of Conakry. Take bus 'C' to Ratoma (30 minutes) and get off at Minière. The embassy is opposite the bus stop.

Sierra Leone One-month visas cost GFr 1500 with two photos. They're issued while you wait in most cases.

MONEY

US$ 1 = GFr 280
UK£ 1 = GFr 550

Guinea rejoined the Franc Zone in 1985 replacing the curiously named former unit of currency, the syli, with the Guinean franc (GFr). The new unit of currency is equivalent to the CFA but, although the CFA is a stable currency linked to the French franc, there appears to be a black market for the Guinean franc with rates fluctuating according to the demand by merchants in the major cities for foreign currency. It can be as much as 30%.

Currency declaration forms are not issued on arrival but all the foreign currency in your possession must be declared. You must pay for international airline tickets in either foreign currency or GFr backed up with bank receipts.

Banks are very few and far between outside Conakry.

TOURIST INFORMATION

The best country map of Guinea is that produced by the Institut Géographique National (Paris, France). The scale is 1:1,000,000 and the map costs about US$10. The same organisation also publishes a 1:10,000 street map of Conakry which is very useful if you are going to spend any time there. The price is about US$8.

PHOTOGRAPHY

To use a camera you will have to get a photography permit from the Office du Tourisme, Place des Martyrs in Conakry. Keep cameras out of sight if you don't have a permit.

LANGUAGE

French is the official language, but the majority of the population also speaks a variety of African languages.

Getting There & Around

AIR

Airlines serving Guinea include Aeroflot, Air Afrique, Air Algérie, Air Zaïre, Ghana Airways, Linhas Aéreas da Guiné-Bissau, Nigeria Airways, Royal Air Maroc, Sabena, Sierra Leone Airways and UTA. The Linhas Aéreas da Guiné-Bissau flight from Bissau to Conakry is very cheap if bought with pesos obtained on the black market.

The national airline, Air Guinée, operates an internal service between Conakry, Boké, Kankan, Kissidougou, Labé, Macenta, N'zérékoré and Siguiri.

You should treat internal schedules with a pinch of salt. Flights are often cancelled.

ROAD

Guinea has very few sealed roads and these are mostly in bad shape. There are good sections here and there, mainly around Conakry and Boké.

The Conakry, Kindia, Mamou, Labé road was once paved but is now riddled with potholes and takes around eight hours to traverse. Conakry to Pamélap (on the Sierra Leone border) is mostly good but there's a very bad 10 km section close to the border. The total journey should take three to four hours. Elsewhere in the country the roads are all *piste* and their condition depends on the season – bad in the wet, passable in the dry. Many bridges over seasonal watercourses are washed out but those over permanent rivers are mostly intact.

There are buses or minibuses over the main routes but elsewhere you'll have to rely on shared taxis, pick-ups and trucks. Pick-ups are generally decrepit old wrecks, slow and packed with up to 24 adults not to mention baggage. Shared taxis, which take up to 13 passengers are more expensive but more comfortable and certainly quicker where the road surface allows. Rides on trucks, particularly in the hills, can be a bad deal. As one traveller commented: 'You have to push them up the hills, walk down the other side and pay for the privilege!'

TRAIN

There is a railway line between Conakry and Kankan via Kindia, Mamou, Dabola and Kouroussa which offers a passenger service. The trains usually depart Conakry on Wednesdays and Saturdays between 9 and 10 am and take about 24 hours to reach Kankan. The trains are all 2nd class railcars with a buffet service. The journey can be extremely uncomfortable.

There is no passenger service on the Conakry to Fria line.

TO/FROM GUINEA-BISSAU

The most direct route is from Conakry to Bissau via Boffa, Boké and Cacine but it's very difficult to find transport and you could be stuck for several days in many places. The roads, too, are very poor. A much better route, along which there are regular pick-ups and trucks, is between Conakry and Gabú (sometimes spelt Cabú) via Kindia, Mamou, Labé, Koundara and Saréboido. It's a longer route but far more predictable. In addition, stretches of the road from Gabú (Guinea-Bissau) to Bissau are surfaced.

Conakry to Mamou costs GFr 2000 by bus and takes about six to seven hours. Conakry to Labé by Peugeot 504 costs GFr 3000. The longest part of this trip is the ride from Labé to Koundara over the mountains. A truck will cost GFr 2000 and take about 12 hours in the dry season though it might be better to take a pick-up for GFr 2500 as they only take seven to eight hours assuming there are no breakdowns. There is usually only one pick-up a day between the two places. However long it takes, it's a beautiful trip through the Fouta Djalon Mountains. Getting from Koundara to Saréboido (border) is a question of luck and you may have to wait a while for transport. It should cost around GFr 250. From Saréboido to Gabú there are trucks which cost GFr 1000.

TO/FROM IVORY COAST

The usual route at present is from Kankan to Odienné via Mandiana. There are taxis between Kankan and Mandiana and occasional trucks between Mandiana and the border. From there take a bus to Mininian followed by a taxi to Odienné. The road near the border on the Guinean side is in bad shape and a river crossing is necessary. The journey time between Kankan and Odienné can take up to 30 hours though it's usually less.

There's also another route in the south between N'Zérékoré and Danané via Lola

but we haven't heard of anyone using that route for several years now.

TO/FROM MALI

The usual route is from Kankan to Bamako via Siguiri and Kourémalé. Pick-ups are available as far as Kourémalé but they're decrepit and the road between Siguiri and Kourémalé is very bad indeed.

TO/FROM SENEGAL

The best route is from Koundara to either Kolda or Tambacounda but the road is extremely bad between Koundara and Kaliforou, the first Senegalese town. In the wet season it is often flooded and may be impassable. It took one party six hours to cover 17 km in July and they were in a sturdy 4WD jeep. What makes it so bad is that there are many large Mercedes trucks which go through here carrying groundnut harvesters from Senegal to Guinea and they're loaded to the brim with goods. The effect on already muddy roads can well be imagined. To reach Kaliforou from Koundara before the border closes for the night, set off as soon as the Guinean border opens in the morning. There are few villages on the way so take water with you.

If starting off from Labé, trucks and pick-ups generally stop overnight in Sambailo north of Koundara. There are no hotels, though women are generally accommodated in one or other of the many small coffee houses. The journey from Labé to Dakar, Banjul or Ziguinchor will take 40 to 50 hours but some travellers have been stuck waiting for transport in either Koundara or Sambailo for up to three days.

TO/FROM SIERRA LEONE

There are direct buses between Conakry and Freetown (from the Madina in Conakry around 6 am daily or when full). If you miss this bus take a minibus from Conakry to Pamélap followed by another minibus or taxi from there to Freetown. The latter minibus costs Le 40 plus Le 4 for your baggage and takes about four hours. The charge for the taxi is the same but it can take up to eight hours because of all the stops en route. There's a badly potholed section of road about 10 km in length between Fourécariah and Pamélap. Expect delays on the Sierra Leone side of the border because of many police checkpoints where body and baggage searches are the norm.

Around the Country

CONAKRY

Conakry is a very large, spread-out city and it's going to take some time to familiarise yourself with the layout. It doesn't help that most of the streets are not signposted.

Information

There is a tourist office in the Hotel de l'Unité but it's not open very often. They have a map of Conakry available for GFr 4000.

Essentially there are three parts to the city. The downtown area is at the extreme end of the peninsula and is known as Conakry I. Next comes Conakry II which is where the main *gare routière* – known as the Madina – is found and, lastly, Conakry III where the international airport is. There is a network of red-coloured buses between the three areas as well as taxis, though fuel and spare parts are often scarce. The electricity supply is erratic so be prepared for power cuts in the evenings.

Conakry is a very dirty town with garbage lying all over the place, but the market is interesting and the fruit there is quite cheap. Beware of taking photographs of anything which might be construed as showing Guinea in a bad light (mud, garbage, dirty markets, people labouring in the fields, etc). There are plenty of police and army personnel around and they may confiscate your film. A midnight

to dawn curfew may still be in force though this affects only walkers, not those in vehicles.

Things to See

The **main market** is a very rewarding experience. Local crafts for sale are more genuinely ethnic than those found in The Gambia and Senegal. The leather rugs are amazing.

Places to Stay

Many of the cheap hotels are scattered between the market and the main post office (PTT) but finding a room in any of them can be problematical. Most are full of semipermanent residents. If this proves to be the case ask the taxi driver if he can help out (assuming you're in a taxi). He may be able to fix you up with a room in a private house. The more expensive hotels demand either that foreigners show bank receipts if paying in local currency or that they pay in hard currency. You will also have to report to the police the morning after checking into a hotel. They can ask a lot of irritating questions but otherwise there's no hassle. Don't take a camera otherwise they'll demand that you buy a photography permit.

One of the cheapest hotels is the *Hotel de l'Amitié* behind the post office, which has a restaurant and coffee shop but is next to a noisy disco which rages until midnight most nights. It costs from GFr 2500 to GFr 3000 a double. A meal (steak, bread and salad) in the restaurant costs around GFr 600. The hotel has water problems. Similar in price is the *Hotel Delphine*, just behind the market towards the post office, which costs GFr 3500 a double. More expensive is the *Hotel du Niger*, close to the market, which costs GFr 5000 a double. The *Hotel Restaurant Grillon*, also has some rooms for GFr 3500 with shower and sink as well as more expensive rooms with air-con.

Others which have been suggested are the *El Dorado*; the *Hotel Restaurant Sankaran*; the *Hotel Kalum*; and the

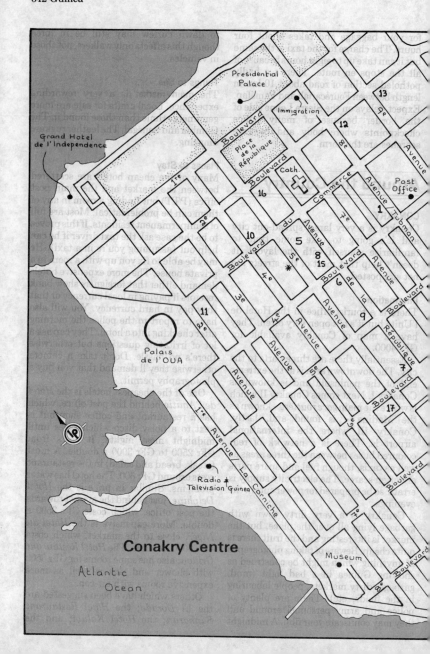

Conakry Centre

Presidential Palace

Immigration

Place de la République

Cath.

Commerce

Post Office

Grand Hotel de l'Independence

Palais de l'OUA

Radio & Television Guinea

Museum

Atlantic Ocean

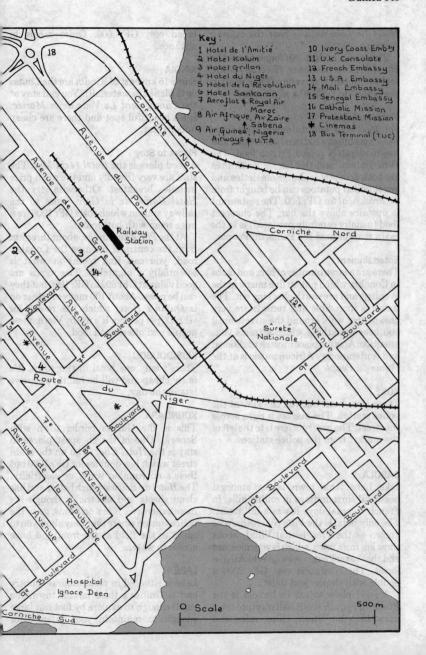

Key:
1 Hotel de l'Amitié
2 Hotel Kalum
3 Hotel Grillon
4 Hotel du Niger
5 Hotel de la Révolution
6 Hotel Sankaran
7 Aeroflot & Royal Air Maroc
8 Air Afrique, Air Zaïre & Sabena
9 Air Guinée, Nigeria Airways & U.T.A.
10 Ivory Coast Emb^{sy}
11 U.K. Consulate
12 French Embassy
13 U.S.A. Embassy
14 Mali Embassy
15 Senegal Embassy
16 Catholic Mission
17 Protestant Mission
∗ Cinemas
18 Bus Terminal (TUC)

Railway Station

Corniche Nord

Corniche Nord

Avenue du Port

Avenue de la Gare

Boulevard

Avenue

Avenue

Boulevard

Avenue

Route du Niger

Sûreté Nationale

12e Avenue

9e Avenue

Boulevard

Avenue de la République

Avenue

Boulevard

10e Boulevard

11e Boulevard

Hospital Ignace Deen

Corniche Sud

0   Scale   500 m

Hotel Le Lokomotive, near the railway station.

Those on a budget can forget about the *Hotel de l'Indépendence, Hotel de l'Unité* and the *Hotel Camayenne*. They're all in the US$60 to US$140 a night range.

Places to Eat
For food and entertainment, *Madame Diop's* is almost a national institution and has moderately priced French food. The *Petit Bateau* and the *Escale de Guinée* are both acceptable. Large omelettes and sweet boiled potatoes can be bought from *Le Provençal* for GFr 500. The restaurant is upstairs above the bar. The cheapest food (usually carefully prepared) is in the main market near the Palais du Peuple.

Entertainment
There are a large number of bars and clubs in Conakry which put on live music in the evenings and are worth checking out. The music is incredible and records are very cheap. Just walk around the streets until you hear something which attracts your attention. Another place to catch traditional and contemporary African music is at the *Palais du Peuple*.

BOKÉ
There is no hotel but you can stay at the police station. The market is right across the street. The *gare routière* is to the left of the market from the police station.

DABOLA
Like Labé, this town is set amongst beautiful surroundings in rolling hills. In French colonial days it was a hill resort. The only hotel is the *Villa Syli* (otherwise known as the Presidential Villa), about three km from town, which is very pleasant and has excellent views overlooking a forest. The *rondavels* cost GFr 2000 a double with shower and toilet.

A good place to eat in Dabola is the *Etoile du Foutah* about half way into town from the Villa. Steak, chips, salad and

bread cost GFr 600. Order meals in advance.

KINDIA
Some 15 km east of Kindia are the **Chutes de la Mariée** (a waterfall). You can stay at the *Campement La Voile de la Mariée*. It's a beautiful spot and there are cheap huts to rent.

Places to Stay
A good place is the *Hotel 14 du Mai*. The staff are very friendly and the room price includes breakfast. Otherwise, try the *Hotel Buffet de la Gare*, close to the railway station which costs GFr 1200 for a huge room with bathroom.

At the *Place de Guinée*, about three km from the centre of town on the Conakry road, you can find rooms at what is essentially a nightclub. The rooms are good value at GFr 800 to GFr 1000 but they can be noisy. About 100 metres further on is *Quinn's Hotel* which has rooms for GFr 500 per person. It's run by Vietnamese people and offers good food.

KISSIDOUGOU
There's only one hotel in this town. It's fairly cheap and will be full if you arrive late in the day.

KOUNDARA
This is the Guinea border town with Senegal. One of the cheapest places to stay is the *Hotel Chez Adja* on the main street which has doubles for GFr 1000 but there's no running water or electricity. The *Hotel de Boiro* is much better and has clean sheets and electricity though it's more expensive. If low on funds, go to the police station where they may allow you to camp in the field at the front and have access to water.

LABÉ
Labé is situated in mountainous country and is Guinea's third largest town. It's small enough to explore by foot but large enough to maintain your interest for

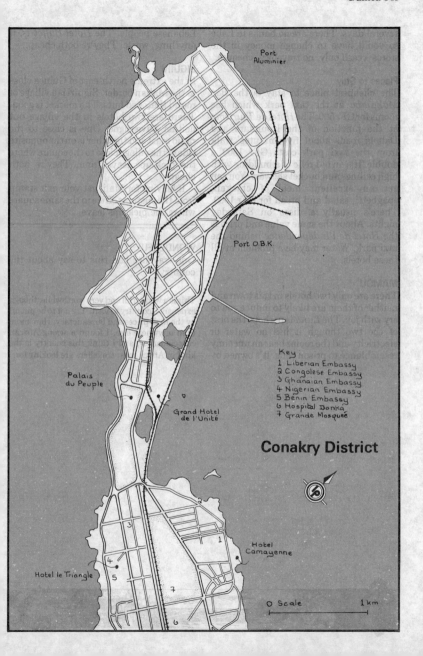

Port
Aluminier

Port O.B.K.

Palais
du Peuple

Grand Hotel
de l'Unité

Conakry District

Key
1 Liberian Embassy
2 Congolese Embassy
3 Ghanaian Embassy
4 Nigerian Embassy
5 Benin Embassy
6 Hospital Donka
7 Grande Mosquée

Hotel
Camayenne

Hotel le Triangle

0 Scale   1 km

several days. There are no banks in Labé so you'll have to change money in the stores – cash only, no travellers' cheques.

Places to Stay

The cheapest place to stay is the *Bar Makumba* at the taxi park which has rooms for GFr 500. The *Hotel de Tourisme* at the junction of the Koundara and Dabola roads about five minutes' walk from the taxi park costs GFr 1500 a double. It's an old relic of a building with high ceilings and bucket showers. You can get an excellent meal of chicken, spaghetti, salad and bread for GFr 1000. There's usually a disco on Saturday nights. About the same value and price is the *Hotel de l'Indépendence* behind the taxi park. Water may be a problem at all these hotels.

MAMOU

There are only two hotels in this town and neither of them are likely to induce you to cry with joy. The *Luna* is perhaps the best of the two though it has no water or electricity and the rooms bear an uncanny resemblance to prison cells. It's owned by Lebanese people. The *Hotel Buffet* is, if anything, worse. They're both cheap.

SIGUIRI

In the extreme north-east of Guinea close to the Malian border, Siguiri is a village of round thatched huts. The market is good. There are two hotels in the village but neither have signs. One is close to the radio mast and the other is on the opposite side of the village close to the square where the pick-ups leave from. They're both cheap.

If leaving for Mali, get your exit stamp from the customs office in the same square where the pick-ups leave.

WONDERFUL

One traveller had this to say about the country:

This is a wonderful and very worthwhile, though expensive, country to visit. Try not to be put off by the high prices and bureaucracy. Here more than anywhere else, I found a strong African consciousness, and I think this country is the kind of Africa most travellers are looking for.

Guinea-Bissau

Guinea-Bissau was a tributary realm of the Mali empire when Europeans first made contact. The Portuguese arrived on the coast as early as the 1440s with trading and raiding parties in search of slaves. As in other parts of its empire, Portugal was content for centuries to control just the coastal area. It was only prompted into laying claim to the interior in the latter part of the 19th century when Africa was being carved up between the industrialised nations of northern Europe. Indeed, both the British and French established trading posts on the Guinea-Bissau coast at this time and Portuguese claims were not recognised until 1884. Actual control of the interior was not established until 1915 and even then pockets of resistance held out until as late as 1936.

Throughout much of the early 1970s Guinea-Bissau's long struggle for liberation from the Portuguese was front-page news. Also, the political organisation, the African Party for the Independence of Guinea and Cape Verde (PAIGC), provided a model for liberation movements in other parts of the world.

PAIGC had its inception in 1956 but it wasn't until 1961 that it resorted to guerrilla warfare in the face of mounting repression by the colonial authorities. Portugal, itself an underdeveloped nation in comparison with most other European countries, was unable to contain the struggle. By the early 1970s about three-quarters of the country had been liberated and the Portuguese armed forces confined to the capital, Bissau, together with a handful of smaller towns and military posts.

A network of material and political support was set up for the peasants in the liberated areas and efforts were made to revive the war-ravaged agricultural sector. Thus by the time independence was unilaterally declared in 1973 virtually all the necessary preparations had been made for post-independence administration. Although the new government was recognised by most countries around the world, it wasn't until Salazar was toppled several months later that the Portuguese finally withdrew from the country.

The leader of the revolutionary struggle was Amilcar Cabral. Unfortunately, he didn't live long enough to see his country liberated as he was murdered by Portuguese agents about half a year before independence. The Portuguese had hoped that by killing him they would be able to force a split in the nationalist movement but in this they were unsuccessful. He was succeeded by his half-brother, Luiz Cabral.

Many of PAIGC's leaders actually came from the Cape Verde Islands and the party was committed not only to the liberation of Guinea-Bissau and Cape Verde but to unification between the two. Efforts were being made to bring this about in 1980 when President Luiz Cabral was overthrown in a coup by Prime Minister Bernardo Vieira while senior army commanders were away in Praia, the capital of Cape Verde.

The coup resulted in a rift between the mainland and Cape Verde and brought to an end the unified political party which the two had shared. Only later were they brought together again as allies through the intervention of Presidents Machel of Mozambique and Santos of Angola, but the idea of political unity is now dead.

Since the coup, the country has been

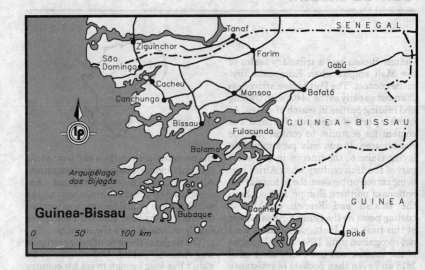

ruled by Vieira. Despite earlier doubts about his commitment to the ideals of the revolution, he has turned out to be a remarkably independent and determined president willing to tackle the country's enormous problems with a high degree of intelligence and sensitivity. Gone are the expensive and largely prestigious projects favoured by his predecessor. The emphasis now is on small but numerous schemes appropriate to the country's needs. Agriculture has a high priority. Vieira has also maintained a nonaligned foreign policy despite the fact that the bulk of the military hardware for PAIGC's war of liberation was provided by the USSR, China and Cuba.

Many countries have helped out with loans – notably Portugal, France and the Nordic countries – though it's generally recognised that these will probably never be repaid since exports (even in a good year) only ever just cover the costs of imports. There is the vague possibility that the country might one day repay them if sufficient oil is discovered offshore. Drilling is already going on but, as yet, little has come of it.

It seems that Guinea-Bissau is destined to remain one of the world's poorest nations. Despite all the effort which is going into agriculture, the country still cannot produce enough food for its one million people. All manufactured goods have to be imported and electricity will remain a scarce commodity since the country is too flat for viable hydroelectricity production. Outside Bissau, roads are poor or simply nonexistent and the only public facilities are schools and health clinics. The fact is that since slavery was abolished, Guinea-Bissau has had little it can export to the outside world.

Guinea-Bissau was almost impossible to visit for many years following independence unless you were a member of a volunteer organisation. Tourism was not encouraged. This has now changed and visas are easy to obtain since tourism provides a small but welcome influx of foreign exchange. You should not, however, expect too much. Life for most people is a hard slog to make ends meet and to have enough to eat.

Facts

GEOGRAPHY & CLIMATE

Much of the country is low-lying with numerous rivers, mangrove swamps and rainforest giving way to savannah further inland. Only on the border with Guinea does the land begin to rise. The rest of the country consists of numerous offshore islands. Rainfall is heavy, especially on the coast, and it's generally hot and humid. The coolest months are December and January, and the hottest are April and May. The average temperature is around 20°C.

PEOPLE

There are numerous tribal groups including the Balante, Fulani, Manjaco and Mandika. Most of the people are engaged in subsistence farming and animal husbandry. About 65% of the people follow tribal religions while 30% are Muslim and the remainder Christian. The population stands at around 900,000.

VISAS

Visas are required by all except nationals of Cape Verde and Nigeria. There are very few Guinea-Bissau embassies around the world – Abidjan, Algiers, Banjul, Brussels, Conakry, Dakar, Lisbon, Moscow, Stockholm and Washington. The most convenient place to get them is in either Dakar (Senegal) or Banjul (The Gambia). In Dakar visas cost CFA 2000 and are issued in 24 hours. In Banjul they cost Da 25 and are issued while you wait or within 24 hours. No photos are required and the ambassador there is very friendly.

It's advisable to have current vaccinations for cholera and yellow fever on entry.

Three-month residence permits are fairly easy to obtain from immigration. You need to say that you've found a job but are waiting for papers. They take three to six days to come through, require three photos and cost P 250.

Exit visas are not necessary for tourists. You only need one of these if you have been working in the country. If that's the case, you can get one at the central police station next to the market place (*mercado*) in central Bissau. You usually have to wait four or five days for it to come through.

Visa extensions can also be obtained from the central police station in Bissau.

Other Visas

There are embassies for Algeria, Cape Verde, Egypt, France, Guinea, Portugal, Senegal and the USA among others in Bissau.

Guinea The embassy is on Rua 12 off Avenida Amilcar Cabral and is open Monday to Thursday from 8.30 am to 3 pm, on Friday from 8.30 am to 1 pm and on Saturday from 9.30 am to 12 noon. One-month visas cost CFA 5000, require three photos and are issued while you wait. 'Tourism' is no longer a problem as a reason given for wanting to go there. It's important to look clean and tidy when applying and it helps a great deal if you already have a visa for either Mali or Sierra Leone.

MONEY

US$ 1 = P 668
UK£ 1 = P 1073
CFA 1000 = 2100

The unit of currency is the Peso da Guiné-Bissau = 100 centavos. The import and export of local currency is prohibited. There is a black market on which you can get US$1 = P 900 to P 950 and CFA 5000 = P 14,000 to P 15,000. Ask around in the *mercado* opposite the USA Embassy or approach Senegalese people, but avoid Mauritanian shopkeepers. The rate for pesos in Ziguinchor (Senegal) is poor.

You may have to change a small amount of hard currency into pesos on arrival by overland bus but this doesn't always happen. If you arrive by air, you will probably have to change CFA 20,000 or the equivalent. Whatever the currency form may say, there is no way this money will be re-exchanged on departure. It's a one-way system. Thorough searches of baggage are made on entry but body searches are very rare. Any pesos found on you when leaving the country will be confiscated.

Travellers' cheques can be cashed in all banks, but personal cheques have to be cashed in the National Bank in Bissau. A commission of P 25 is charged for changing travellers' cheques regardless of the amount you change.

International airline tickets can only be bought with hard currency or with local currency backed up by bank receipts showing that you have exchanged the money legally.

The airport departure tax for domestic flights is P 85. For international flights it is US$8 or CFA 2500 or the equivalent.

PHOTOGRAPHY

Photograph permits are no longer required but it's forbidden to take shots of public buildings, bridges, ports or anything connected with the military.

LANGUAGE

Portuguese is the official language but African languages are also spoken as well as Crioulo. If you want to make a good impression on people, it helps to speak a modicum of Wolof.

Getting There & Around

AIR

The airlines which fly to Guinea-Bissau are Aeroflot, Air Algerie, Air Guinée, Air Senegal, TAP (Air Portugal) and TAAG (Air Angola). The national airline is Linhas Aéreas da Guiné-Bissau (LIA) but recent reports suggest that it has been wound up. Certainly there are no more flights to the offshore islands.

Probably the only flight of interest to budget travellers is the Tuesday Air Guinée flight to Conakry which costs about US$60. Air Senegal has flights to Ziguinchor (US$30) and Dakar (US$102) on Monday and Friday.

ROAD

Guinea-Bissau is a desperately poor country and simply cannot afford the luxury of paved roads. In addition, there are so few export commodities to transport to Bissau that it's hardly necessary to have all-weather roads. This means that the roads are generally in poor shape – passable in the dry season, and difficult to impassable in the wet season. There are, however, sufficient trucks, shared taxis and buses to enable you to get around the country.

In Bissau, long-distance taxis and buses leave from the market. The taxis service most of the smaller towns all over the country, depart several times a day and are inexpensive. The buses, which are Volvos manufactured in Norway in 1977 and given to the country by Sweden's SIDA and Norway's NORAD, service the larger towns and are also inexpensive. They usually have only one departure per day and if you want to be sure of getting on, be at the market by 7 am.

BOAT

In addition to the ferries on the road from Ziguinchor to Bissau, there is a twice weekly ferry from Bissau to Bolama, the old capital, which takes three hours and leaves at high tide. It's liable to be cancelled without notice if the tide isn't right as the ferry has to cross a sandbar on the way to the island. From Bissau to Bubaque there is a ferry once a week, which leaves on Saturdays at high tide and costs P 3050. There's also a once weekly ferry to Catio in the south.

Ferry schedules change quite a lot so check them out at the Rodofluvial on Rua Guerra Mendes down by the dock. The ferry schedules are posted up. You can also buy tickets for the ferries here.

TO/FROM GUINEA

The southern route into Guinea via Cacine and Boké can be problematical, as transport in southern Guinea-Bissau isn't so well developed. The northern route via Bafatá and Gabú (sometimes spelt Cabú) is much easier and there are service taxis from Bafatá to Gabú and the Guinea-Bissau border. Alternatively, there are minibuses from Bissau to Gabú for P 1800 which take 3½ hours. From the border there are shared taxis to Saréboïdo, the first Guinean town.

Another possibility is to arrange a lift on a truck from Bissau or Gabú to Boké, Koundara, Labé, Gaoual or even Conakry (all in Guinea). These trucks only go on Saturdays – there's nothing similar during the week. The price varies a lot and drivers don't like taking pesos. Expect to pay CFA 1500 from Gabú to Koundara or CFA 7600 from Gabú to Labé.

From Saréboïdo you have a choice of routes to Conakry. It's possible to take the western route via Koumbia, Boké and Boffa but this can take up to six days, though the average is four days. There are occasional minibuses from Gabú to Koumbia for around CFA 2000 and trucks from there to Boké and Boké to Conakry. There is a ferry crossing at Boffa over the Fatala River.

The more predictable route to Conakry, however, goes via Koundara, Labé, Mamou and Kindia. There are more trucks, pick-ups and shared taxis along this route than there are via Koumbia and Boké though the road between Koundara and Labé is in poor shape and serpentine once it gets into the mountains. It is, however, an incredibly beautiful route. For details of transport, refer to the Guinea chapter.

You should allow four days from Bissau to Labé and six days from Bissau to Conakry. During the wet season it can be impassable and you'll have to fly.

TO/FROM SENEGAL

There are two ways of entering the country from Senegal. The first is from Ziguinchor to Bissau via São Domingos, Cacheu and Canchungo in the west. The other is from Sedhiou to Bissau via Farim further east. The first route can be impassable at times during the wet season. The second route tends to have the more reliable transport.

From Ziguinchor to São Domingos there are service taxis for CFA 600 plus a baggage charge. At São Domingos there is a daily ferry across the river to Cacheu around 11 am which costs P 1200 and takes two hours. From Cacheu you may be lucky and find a truck all the way to Bissau. The usual 'fare' is P 1200. If you don't find one you'll have to do the journey in stages, first to Canchungo, then to Safim and finally to Bissau. There is a ferry across the River Mansôa at Safim. If it's out of fuel – something which happens quite regularly – you get across the river by canoe. The fare is the same. The ferry doesn't operate between 12.30 and 2.30 pm.

On the second route first take a minibus from Ziguinchor to Tanaf (on the Ziguinchor to Kolda road). There is a daily truck from Tanaf to Farim around midday or when there are enough people. At Farim there is a ferry across the Rio Cacheau which runs every hour and from the other side there are trucks and taxis to Bissau. Farim to Bissau takes about two hours.

Around the Country

BAFATÁ

Accommodation at the *Apartamentos* next to the Pensão Transmontana is available for P 300 per day. The rooms are good and clean. You can buy meals at the *Pensão* for P 120 otherwise bread and breakfast food are available cheaply in the market. However, beer is often in very short supply.

BISSAU

Bissau, the capital, is a small town of

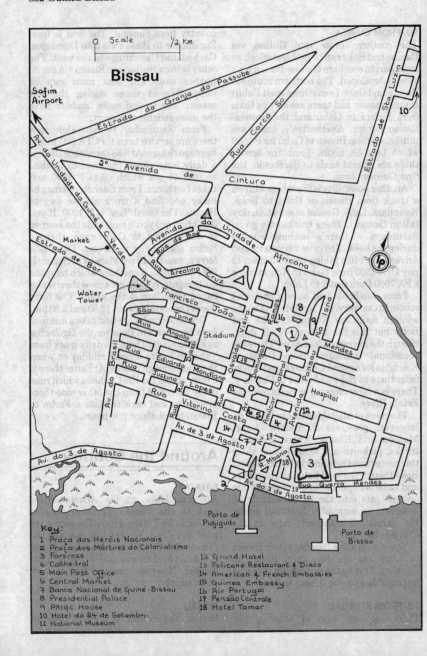

Bissau

O Scale ½ km

Safim Airport

Estrada da Granja do Passube

Rua Corca So

Estrada de Sca Luzia

Av. da Unidade da Guiné e C. Verde

2º Avenida de

Rua Cintura

Estrada de Bor

Market

Avenida da Unidade Africana

Rua de Boé

Rua Areolino Cruz

Water Tower

Av. Francisco João Vieira

São Tomé

Rua Angola

Stadium

Rua Eduardo Mondlane

Rua Justino Lopes

Rua Vitorino Costa

Av. do Brasil

Rua Cassa

Av. Osvaldo Vieira

Av. Domingos Ramos

Av. Na Isna Mendes

Av. Amilcar Cabral

Av. Pansau Na Isna

Hospital

Av. 3 de Agosto

Av. 3 de Agosto

R. Mbana

Rua Guerra Mendes

Porto de Pidjiguiti

Porto de Bissau

Key:
1 Praça dos Heróis Nacionais
2 Praça dos Mártires do Colonialismo
3 Fortress
4 Cathedral
5 Main Post Office
6 Central Market
7 Banco Nacional de Guiné-Bissau
8 Presidential Palace
9 PAIGC House
10 Hotel do 24 de Setembro
11 National Museum

12 Grand Hotel
13 Pelicano Restaurant & Disco
14 American & French Embassies
15 Guinea Embassy
16 Air Portugal
17 Pensão Centrale
18 Hotel Tamar

about 110,000 inhabitants. The simplest way to get around is on foot. The main street is Avenida Amilcar Cabral, which also leads to the marketplace. There's almost no traffic and, because of this, it's one of the most pleasant of all African capitals. There are also no beggars, no thieves, no souvenir sellers and it's safe at night. Make sure you stop what you're doing and stand to attention when the flag is lowered daily to the sound of the bugle.

Information

If you want to work voluntarily in Guinea-Bissau, ask at the Ministerio da Educação near the only high school in town. They'll find you a place to live free of charge. If you want to work in Bissau itself you'll probably get an excellent room at the former hotel (*Estabelecimentos Ancar*), 200 metres from the cathedral and 100 metres from the US Embassy.

There's a city bus service in Bissau which consists of two old buses – one French and the other Belgian. There are taxis which cost P 40 each or P 2000 to the airport (13 km). There are also blue Citroens which act as pick-ups and are cheap. You won't have to haggle about the price.

Things to See

At one time, there were two museums – the **Museum of African Artefacts** in PAIGC House and the **National Museum**, at the junction of Rua Eduardo Mondlane and Rua Osvaldo Vieira – but they are both currently closed. It's worth checking them out, however, as they may reopen.

Places to Stay

If you're planning on staying in Bissau for a while (a week or more), your best bet is to visit the Centro de Informação e Turismo near the Ministry of Education. They have a list of private houses where you can get board and lodging and this will work out considerably cheaper than staying in a hotel. Doing it this way, you will have no problems finding food. The tourist office

which arranges these rooms is one of the friendliest in Africa. Don't be surprised if you get coffee and cakes when calling in (all on the house).

All the better class hotels demand payment in hard currency but at the budget hotels you can pay in local currency. Many hotels have an additional 'service charge' of 5% to 10% which is not mentioned until you leave. Meals can always be paid for in local currency. Electricity cuts are frequent so don't expect fans or air-con to work at these times.

One of the cheapest places to stay is the *Pensão Centrale*, Avenida Amilcar Cabral near the bank which costs P 7000 for a room including three meals and is run by the smiling Dona Berta. The rooms are clean but there are many mosquitoes. This is where many volunteers stay until they find a house to rent. Similar is the *Hotel Tamar*, Avenida 12 de Setembro at Rua 3, which costs US$8 or CFA 2500 (pesos not accepted) a double. It's grubby but there are fans (which naturally only work when the electricity is on). Some of the rooms have balconies. Don't expect the showers to work.

The *Hotel Ronda*, Avenida Amilcar Cabral opposite the church, also has reasonably priced rooms with showers that work and fans, but the toilets are in a miserable state. Many travellers have commented very negatively about the family which runs this place. There may also still be an unmarked pensão at 23A Avenida Amilcar Cabral which is cheap.

More expensive is the *Grand Hotel*, Avenida Amilcar Cabral behind the cathedral, which costs US$22 a double with air-con. It's a little bit old fashioned but still good. Breakfast costs another P 1000 and consists only of coffee and black, dry bread.

The *Hotel 24 de Setembro* costs CFA 11,000/22,000 a single/double with meals for CFA 5000. There's no water in the swimming pool but there is a 24-hour electricity supply. This hotel is also the best place to change money – no queues and good rates.

There are a lot of volunteer workers in Bissau as well as in the countryside and, since travellers are few and far between, one of them may offer you accommodation if you're willing to contribute towards your keep.

Places to Eat

Shortages are still the order of the day but are not as chronic as they used to be. To be sure of getting a meal order it in advance or be there early – things run out quickly.

There are a number of cheap restaurants but few of them have a name so you'll have to search them out. The café on the Praça dos Herois offers spicy sausages with bread and pastries with coffee in the mornings. There's also a bar round the corner from the post office which does meat and rice dishes at exceptionally low prices. The *mercado* is also a good hunting ground for cheap food.

For a main meal, give the *Pensão Centrale* a try. It offers four course meals (small portions) at incredible speed for P 1850 including beer. The restaurant opens at 7.45 pm. The *Casa Santos*, Rua 12 de Setembro next door to the Hotel 24 de Setembro, is popular with expatriates. It has fish, potatoes and beans or beef and spaghetti.

Another place worth trying is *Manuel's Restaurant*, down the street from the Grand Hotel on the left hand side where there's a sign saying 'CICER'. It's a pleasant place to eat but nothing special. The waiters and the owner can be very entertaining. The *Lebanese Restaurant* in between the Grand Hotel and the Hotel 24 de Setembro offers excellent food but you must order in advance.

There are four bakeries in Bissau – the *Padaria Cashew* near the Hotel Portugal (sales at 5 am); the *Padaria Africana* near the stadium (sales at 5 pm); another on the Praça dos Herois (which also sells sandwiches, shrimps, beer and coffee); and

another close to the cathedral on the right hand side coming from the Grand Hotel.

Entertainment

The *Pelicano Night Club* is one of the few places in Bissau where you can find food after 9.30 pm. It's also the liveliest spot in town.

Apart from the Pelicano, the *Grand Hotel* is the best place to meet people. There's a friendly atmosphere and you can relax with a beer under the mango trees. There's also another nightclub, the *Cora Club*, where you can eat and dance though the music has been the same for the last five years. Entry costs P 350 for women and P 700 for men but includes two beers. Good food is available.

Beer can be in short supply especially at the small (unmarked) bars which local people and expatriates use. It was said that at one of these bars the Russian expatriate workers used to regularly reserve six of the 6½ crates which was the bar's daily ration.

BOLAMA

Bolama was the original capital of Guinea-Bissau in colonial days. It's now a crumbling, overgrown ruin which will delight those who like such places. There's no accommodation on the island, but you can camp on the beach across the other side of the island from the town (about five km). Your gear is safe, but beware of the deadly green mamba dropsnakes which live in the trees. (Recent reports say the government is carrying out a culling programme so that tourists don't get put off.) For food, ask the locals if they know anyone willing to cook you a meal – someone will help you out.

BUBAQUE

One of the outer offshore islands, Bubaque is being developed as the 'tourist island' of Guinea-Bissau. To get there take the ferry from Bissau which usually goes once a week on Saturdays and returns the following day. If you decide to go straight back to the mainland on the same ferry, it's free as there's nowhere to buy a ticket.

There is only one hotel on the island, the *Hotel Estancia* which is being renovated – slowly. It costs US$12.50 including breakfast for the cheapest rooms – payable in hard currency. The restaurant has only one dish – fish and rice – and the only thing to drink is water. Meals can be paid for in pesos. Otherwise try the *Swedish Mission*. There are no shops or bakery so you'll have to eat at the hotel.

The beach closest to the hotel isn't very pleasant. There's a better beach elsewhere and a bus goes there from the hotel when demand warrants it.

The offshore islands are definitely worth visiting if you have the time. Outside Bolama and Bubaque, the islands are more or less untouched and life is very close to nature. Watch out for the mamba as well as the tree version of the cobra (white with a black motif on the head).

CACHEU

There is no accommodation in Cacheu. Although it is easy to get from Ziguinchor to Bissau in one day, it's difficult to do this in the opposite direction as the ferry leaves Cacheu early in the day, so the chances are you'll miss it. If you get stuck you can stay with the friendly US AID workers or camp in the old Portuguese fort.

CANCHUNGO

If you get stuck here, the large restaurant in the main square has a few beds but there's no running water.

GABÚ (or CABÚ)

There are no hotels as such but you can find accommodation at the *Apartamentos*

opposite the truck park and taxi park. It's also a bar and restaurant. Rooms cost P 1000 a double but the place is often full.

FRIENDLY

Should you be wondering what Guinea-Bissau is like, this extract from a letter by Tony Nagypal (Norway) who spent two months there may interest you:

To me Guinea-Bissau seems to be something quite different from 'French' West Africa (so far I've been to all West African countries). It's much more friendly. It's very poor, but very well organised. There is absolutely no corruption, and hardly any begging (very few people are as poor as the beggars of Bamako or Ouagadougou). The streets within Bissau are always clean. It's 100% safe to travel in the country and when I was in Bissau and had nowhere to sleep I simply slept on the pavement in the harbour district. There is no dope, prostitution or Coca-Cola. There are no police or military road blocks (except for one small post in Safim near the ferry).

Another, more recent letter confirmed that the people were very friendly but suggested that Tony had got a few things wrong:

It's bullshit to say there's no dope or prostitutes in Bissau. I spent many a long night watching thunderstorms from the roof of *X* completely blown to the very marrow of my bones and brains. Though I admit it's difficult to find and *very risky* – there's a 25-year jail sentence which makes it very unwise to try unless you know the place and the people very well. Bissau is a big knocking shop contrary to what friend Nagypal stated. Take a P 50 cab and ask for the *putas* and they'll take you to a whole street full of whores.

Ivory Coast

Ivory Coast lives and breathes in the image of Felix Houphouet-Boigny, a doctor and wealthy planter who has been the country's president since independence from France in 1960. Along with a few colleagues, Houphouet-Boigny founded the Syndicat Agricole Africain in 1944 to protest against the colonial authorities' preferential treatment of French planters in the allocation of farm labour.

The pressure group soon acquired a broader appeal, leading to mass demonstrations in Abidjan during 1948 to 1949 in favour of greater African participation in the colony's administration. Fifty-two people were killed and over 3000 arrested during those years, but in the face of continued repression by the French authorities, and having gained the commodity price increase his group had campaigned for, Houphouet-Boigny adopted a more conciliatory approach. The change of tack certainly paid off as far as his political career was concerned, but it also led to Ivory Coast becoming a classic case of neocolonialism.

There were few contacts between the peoples of Ivory Coast and Europe before the early 19th century. Most of the trading and slaving took place east of the area. In the 1840s, however, the French embarked on a systematic plan to give French traders a commercial monopoly in the region and a number of treaties were signed with local chiefs. These treaties formed the basis for the French claim to the area in the 1890s when Africa was being carved up by the West European nations. French colonial policy in Ivory Coast was based on stimulating the production of cash crops – cocoa, palm oil, timber and bananas – and to make sure there would be a sufficient supply of labour on the plantations established by French expatriates.

To implement this a 'head tax' was imposed on the indigenous population in 1903. This measure together with large-scale forced labour used for the construction of roads, railways and public buildings not only led to considerable suffering and social dislocation, but also to a mass exodus from the Agni region to Ghana. Despite this early setback, indigenous planters had begun to play an important part in cocoa and coffee cultivation by the late 1930s, though a third of the land under these crops and all of the land under bananas as well as the timber operations remained in French hands.

Concessions have been made to African aspirations since then – or at least to certain sections of the African population – but precious little else has changed. After a brief flirtation with Marxism, Houphouet-Boigny rejected the ideas of 'revolution' and the 'class struggle' on the grounds that classes did not exist in Ivory Coast. That may have been true at the time but it certainly is no longer the case. Unrestricted reliance on foreign and local private enterprise and the large-scale repatriation of profits has resulted in affluence for a minority but also in a wide gap between the haves and have nots. The country has had to face a labour crisis too, brought on by the government's refusal to subsidise workers migrating from Burkina Faso and a very serious balance of payments deficit.

Ivory Coast still continues to support trade and 'dialogue' with South Africa and, until Robert Mugabe took over in

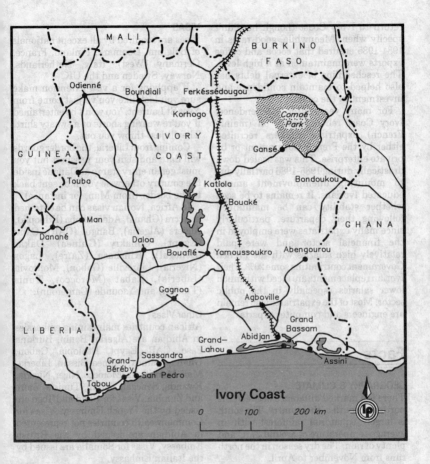

Ivory Coast

0   100   200 km

Zimbabwe, it maintained quiet trade links with Ian Smith's Rhodesia.

While Ivory Coast remained one of Africa's most politically stable countries during the 1970s it appeared for a while that it was headed for an upheaval since there was no obvious successor to the elderly Houphouet-Boigny. Phillipe Yace, who was groomed for this position, was dumped in the early 1980s, having become very unpopular as a result of underhand methods he used to maintain his own and the president's position. This situation

seems to have been resolved with the recent election of a vice-president.

Ivory Coast was rocked by a debt and embezzlement scandal in 1985 involving the former mayor of Abidjan, Emmanuel Dioulo. Dioulo was a leading politician and head of the wholly Ivorian-owned cocoa and coffee exporting company, Cogexim. Dioulo fled to Belgium claiming he'd never get a fair trial since the issue had been politicised. An understanding was reached some time later between the president and Dioulo who pledged to return to Ivory Coast though he didn't specify when. Meanwhile, good rains in 1984-1985 ensured that cocoa and coffee exports were maintained at a high level. The rescheduling of external debts has also helped to maintain confidence and investment in the country.

For many years after independence, Ivory Coast relied heavily on (mainly French) expatriate workers recruited either by the French Government or by private enterprise. This was scaled down drastically during 1985-1986 partially due to mounting unemployment among educated Ivorians. It remains to be seen whether stability can be maintained following their departure, particularly since many expatriates were employed in the financial sector and were paid relatively high salaries with the French Government contributing some 20%. Their Ivorian replacements are faced with much lower salaries especially in the public sector. Most of the expatriates who remain are engineers and computer experts.

Facts

GEOGRAPHY & CLIMATE

There is a marked difference between the north and south of the country. The south is largely equatorial rainforest with an average temperature of around 27°C and plenty of rain. The dry season in the north runs from November to April.

PEOPLE

The population stands at about 10.5 million and consists of more than 60 different tribes, the largest being the Baoule to which Houphouet-Boigny belongs. In addition to the indigenous population there are large numbers of expatriate workers from Burkina Faso, Mali, Guinea, Benin, Togo and Senegal as well as some 50,000 each of French and Lebanese nationals.

VISAS

Visas are required by all except nationals of Belgium, Denmark, Finland, France, Germany (West), Italy, Netherlands, Norway, Sweden and the UK.

If applying for a visa extension make sure you look like you've just come from Yves St Laurent. You won't be entertained if you're wearing shorts or a sweaty shirt. They'll just throw you out.

Coming from Liberia, the border guards will date and sign your passport but you must get an entry stamp at Danané inside the country otherwise you'll be sent back to the border (from Man, for instance).

In Africa, Ivorian visas can be obtained in Accra (Ghana), Addis Ababa (Ethiopia), Algiers (Algeria), Bangui (CAR), Cairo (Egypt), Conakry (Guinea), Dakar (Senegal), Kinshasa (Zaïre), Lagos (Nigeria), Libreville (Gabon), Monrovia (Liberia), Rabat (Morocco), Tunis (Tunisia) and Yaoundé (Cameroun).

Other Visas

African countries maintaining embassies in Abidjan are Algeria, Benin, Burkina Faso, CAR, Egypt, Ethiopia, Gabon, Ghana, Guinea, Guinea-Bissau, Liberia, Mali, Mauritania, Morocco, Niger, Nigeria, Rwanda, Senegal, Sudan, Tunisia, Zaïre and Zambia. Visas for Chad and Togo are issued by the French Embassy. Visas for Commonwealth countries not represented in Abidjan are issued by the British Embassy. Visas for Somalia are issued by the Italian Embassy.

Benin Seven-day visas cost CFA 1000 with two photos, and take 48 hours. The embassy (tel 414414) is a long way from the centre. Take bus No 21 (Treichville Hospital to Plateau to Cocody) to the Cité des Arts which is past the university in Cocody. Then take bus No 35 (signed Adjamé-Agoble). The embassy is on Rue Jasmin two stops before the end of the second bus route so it doesn't matter too much if you miss it.

Burkina Faso The embassy is on Ave Terrasson des Fougeres at the corner of Blvd Carde. Don't be put off by the appearance of the embassy in Abidjan. It might look like a chicken farm/wood yard/car-breakers yard but it *is* the embassy. Visas cost CFA 9000, require two photos and take 48 hours to issue.

Cameroun The embassy is on the 3rd floor, Immeuble General, Blvd Botreau Roussel. A 20-day visa costs CFA 9000 with two photos, and takes 48 hours. It must be used within one month of issue.

Gabon The embassy is in the SOGEFI Building, Blvd Carde, but they're unhelpful and will tell you to get the visa from Cameroun.

Ghana The embassy is in the same building as the tourist office on the 5th floor, Blvd du General de Gaulle. Two-week visas cost CFA 6000 for Commonwealth citizens and CFA 9000 for others with two photos, and take three days to issue (though some people have obtained them in 24 hours). There's no fuss.

Guinea-Bissau These cost CFA 2000, with two photos and take 24 hours. The embassy (tel 415436) is in Cocody.

Liberia One-month visas cost CFA 4000, require two photos and are issued within two hours. The embassy is at Immeuble Le General, Blvd Bertrand Russell at the junction with Ave General de Gaulle.

Mali These cost CFA 5000, require two photos and are issued the same day. The embassy is at Maison du Mali, Ave General de Gaulle on the corner with Rue 1, and is closed on Friday, Saturday and Sunday.

Niger Visas cost CFA 3000 and can take up to six days to come through. The embassy is in Marcory on the Ave Achalme (take

bus No 00 east on Ave 16 in Treichville and get off at the first stop after the bridge).

Senegal Three-month, multiple-entry visas cost CFA 20,000.

Sierra Leone These, and entry permits (for Commonwealth nationals), are issued by the British Embassy. They cost CFA 3600 and take 48 hours. No photos are required. There is sometimes a fuss about onward tickets if it's a visa you're applying for.

MONEY

US$ 1 = CFA 284
UK£ 1 = CFA 537

The unit of currency is the CFA franc. There is no restriction on the import of local currency, but export is limited to CFA 20,000.

Barclays Bank in Abidjan won't accept American Express travellers' cheques. There is an 8% commission on all money transactions.

LANGUAGE

French is the official language. The main African languages are Dioula, Baoulé and Bete.

Getting There & Around

AIR

Abidjan is one of the worst airports in Africa for bribe-seeking agents. Be sure to have your confirmed airline ticket stamped in Abidjan and arrive at the airport at least two hours before your flight takes off. The check-in procedure can be confusing and your evident confusion will mark you out from the rest to the patrolling con merchants. Don't be surprised if you have been wait-listed or that you're not even listed despite having a confirmed seat. If this happens make it very clear, very quickly, that you must leave Abidjan because you have no more

station	rapide		express		omnibus	
	1st	2nd	1st	2nd	1st	2nd
Treichville to Agboville	1800	1200	1200	700	1300	800
Treichville to Bouaké	4000	2500	3500	2200	3900	2600
Treichville to Ferkéssédougou	9100	6300	7300	4800		
Treichville to Banfora	12,500	8500	10,000	6600		
Treichville to Bobo-Dioulasso	14,000	9600	11,300	7600		
Treichville to Ouagadougou	19,600	13,800	15,700	10,600		
Ferkéssédougou to Banfora	3000	2000	2300	1500		
Ferkéssédougou to Bobo-Dioulasso	5600	5400	3600	2600		
Ferkéssédougou to Ouagadougou	14,400	8100	11,600	6600		
Bobo-Dioulasso to Ouagadougou	4700	3000	3700	2400	4200	2800

money or demand to speak to the airport manager. You'll naturally have to do all this in French.

ROAD

Hitching for free is usually only possible with expatriate whites and you can wait all day. In the end you may give up and pay like everyone else! Most of Ivory Coast's roads are in good shape and many are surfaced but, if they're not, a 30-km ride can cost as much as a 150-km ride on a good road. This is fair as far as wear and tear goes.

There is a good network of buses and taxis between the major centres of population as well as to the borders of Mali and Ghana. Going to or from Burkina Faso most people take the train which connects Abidjan with Ouagadougou. On the other hand, the new luxury buses are fast, clean and only nominally more expensive than the trains.

There are daily luxury buses from the *gare routière* in the Adjamé district of Abidjan. Some examples of fares and journey times are:

Abidjan to Ferkéssédougou – there are two buses daily, one in the morning and the other in the evening. They cost CFA 3500 and take about 10 hours.

Abidjan to Man – there are several buses daily, the first at 7.30 am, which costs CFA 3500 and takes nine to 10 hours. Buy your ticket the previous day.

Abidjan to Odienné– one bus leaves daily, costs CFA 4500 and takes about 10 hours.

Abidjan to Aboisso – a Peugeot 504 taxi will cost CFA 1700.

Odienné to Ferkéssédougou – one daily luxury bus leaves at 10 am and costs CFA 3500.

TRAIN

The railway connects Abidjan with Ouagadougou (Burkina Faso) via Bouaké, Katiola, Ferkéssédougou and Bobo Dioulasso. Fares in CFA from Abidjan (Treichville) are above.

Two-bunk couchettes on the Rapide cost an extra CFA 4500 in 1st class and are available regardless of how far you are going.

On the Express, two-bunk couchettes are available for CFA 3500. Four-bunk couchettes are available for CFA 3000 in 1st class.

A couchette in 2nd class can only be booked 24 hours before departure and is subject to availability – 1st class passengers have priority. These couchettes cost CFA 4500. Student reductions are available on these fares.

The table on the opposite page is a precis of the train schedule. The trains from Treichville to Ouagadougou also stop at Abidjan, Agban, Anyama, Yapo, Dimbokro, Latiola, Tafire, Ouangolodougou, Niangoloko, Banfora, Siby and Koudougou.

Abidjan to Ouagadougou: Rapide – 'La Gazelle'			
Treichville 8.30 am	Bouaké 2.30 pm	Bobo 1.15 am	Ouagadougou 7.10 am
Ouagadougou 4.10 pm	Bobo 10.25 pm	Bouaké 8.20 am	Treichville 2.05 pm
Abidjan to Ouagadougou: Express			
Treichville 4.45 pm	Bouaké 12 midnight	Bobo 12.05 pm	Ouagadougou 7.15 am
Ouagadougou 7.20 am	Bobo 2.25 pm	Bouaké 2.55 am	Treichville 9.45 am
Abidjan to Bouaké: Omnibus			
Treichville 6.00 am	Agboville 8.23 am	Bouaké 1.10 pm	
Bouaké 3:00 pm	Agboville 5.35 pm	Treichville 10.00 pm	
Ouagadougou to Bobo-Dioulasso: Omnibus			
Ouagadougou 2.40 pm	Koudougou 4.21 pm	Bobo 9.25 pm	
Bobo 6.00 am	Koudougou 10.50 am	Ouagadougou 12.30 pm	

TO/FROM BURKINA FASO

The easiest way to get to Burkina Faso is to take the train between Abidjan and Ouagadougou.

TO/FROM GHANA

Until fairly recently the usual route to Ghana followed the coast road via Grand Bassam, Assini, Newtown (border), Half Assini and Jewi Wharf.

It is still possible to go this way, but it involves a lot of messing about and takes longer. If you do it, however, you'll be rewarded by a 14-km walk along a beautiful stretch of beach to Newtown (Ghanaian border).

Most travellers, however, take the new sealed road from Aboisso (east of Abidjan) to Sekondi Takoradi via Elubo. There is a daily Ghanaian STC bus from Abidjan to Accra at 6 am which costs CFA 7000 plus

CFA 1000 (for police checkpoint bribes) and takes 24 hours on average. The reason it takes this long is because of delays on the border. Ivorian police and immigration officials don't like Ghanaians or their buses so they spend a lot of time searching bags and the bus.

You can also go direct from Abidjan to Kumasi via Agnibilekrou. There are Ghanaian STC buses three times per week in either direction which cost CFA 9000 (ordinary) and CFA 11,000 (express). Only one of the three buses is an express (usually on Saturday from Abidjan) and you're advised to take it because it's only a 12 to 15 hour journey. The ordinary buses have been known to take 2½ days because you have to spend a whole day and a night at the border as a rule. The main reason for this is that a truck accompanies the ordinary buses containing goods which have to be declared. There are always protracted negotiations over the amount of bribes which have to be paid.

You can avoid most of these hassles by doing the journey in stages. A taxi from Abidjan to Abengourou will cost CFA 1500 including baggage charge. From there take another taxi to the border for CFA 700 including baggage. Don't forget to call in for an exit stamp from police/immigration at Agnibilekrou otherwise you'll be sent back from one of the police checkpoints. From the Ghanaian border there are buses and taxis available to Kumasi. Cedis are available at Ghanaian customs from – guess who! – and it doesn't appear on your currency form.

There's also another route from Ferkéssédougou to Bole. First take a taxi from Ferkéssédougou to Bouna for CFA 4000 which takes 12 hours including surprise visits to local villages en route. Another taxi from there to the Ghanaian border costs CFA 500. From here take a canoe across the river for CFA 200 and on the other side there is transport to Bole for around CFA 500.

TO/FROM GUINEA

The route to Guinea follows the same route as that to Liberia as far as Danané. From Danané to the Guinea border there are taxis which cost CFA 700. From there take taxis to Lola and N'Zerékoré.

TO/FROM LIBERIA

The main crossing point into Liberia is west of Man via Danané. Man to Danané by *taxi-brousse* costs CFA 1200 plus CFA 200 for baggage and takes 2½ to three hours. There are several police checkpoints en route. It's a very bad road. Make sure you get an exit stamp in Danané. From Danané to the Liberian border a taxi will cost CFA 1000 and take about 1½ hours, or there are minibuses for CFA 700 plus CFA 250 for a backpack. Transport to the border only goes in the mornings. The taxis will set you down at the bridge which

forms the border between the two countries. From the border first take a taxi to Kahnplé and from there a truck to Sanniquellie. You may also be able to pick up shared taxis between the border and Sanniquellie for US$1.50 to US$2.

Make sure your papers are in order on this border. The officials go through them minutely looking for anything that's wrong or out of date. If they find something, it's going to cost money.

There's also another route into Liberia via Toulépleu. Take the normal buses or taxis which go to Man and get down at Duékoué. From there pick up transport to Guiglo (CFA 400) and then to Toulépleu (CFA 1700). This way you end up at Ganta.

TO/FROM MALI

There are two road routes to Mali, one via Man, Odienné and Bougouni, and the other via Ferkéssédougou and Sikasso. The first generally takes longer as there is very little traffic and no buses between Odienné and Bougouni, though there are minibuses between Odienné and Manankoro for CFA 2500. The bridge at Manankoro in Mali is usually under water throughout August. If you take the latter route, it's probably better to take the train from Abidjan to Ferkéssédougou first, then go by road from there. There is also a once-weekly bus between Bouaké and Bamako. Coming from Bamako, this bus leaves on Tuesdays when full, costs CFA 13,925 and usually takes 24 to 36 hours but has been known to take 50 hours. Buses between Ferkéssédougou and Sikasso cost CFA 7000 and take about 11 hours. There are no problems at the border. If hitching along this stretch, there are a number of police checkpoints where you can enlist help in finding a lift.

Around the Country

ABIDJAN

The commercial capital of Ivory Coast

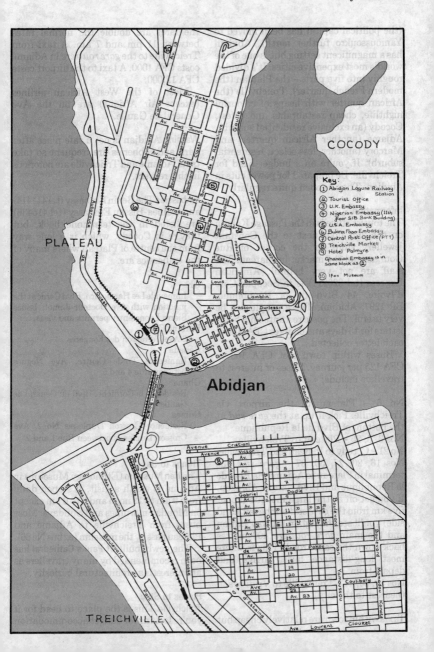

COCODY

PLATEAU

Abidjan

TREICHVILLE

Key:
1. Abidjan Lagune Railway Station
2. Tourist Office
3. U.K. Embassy
4. Nigerian Embassy (11th Floor SIB Bank Building)
5. U.S.A. Embassy
6. Burkina Faso Embassy
7. Central Post Office (PTT)
8. Treichville Market
9. Hotel Palmyre
   Ghanaian Embassy is in same block as 2
10. Ifan Museum

(the political capital has been moved to Yamoussoukro further north), Abidjan has a magnificent setting but is one of the world's most expensive cities. It's divided roughly into five parts – the Plateau (the modern French quarter), Treichville (the African quarter with heaps of colourful nightlife, cheap restaurants and cafés), Cocody (an exclusive residential suburb), Adjamé (another African quarter) and Marcory (another, less select, residential suburb). If you're on a budget head for Treichville. Be prepared for power cuts in Abidjan. They happen quite regularly.

Information

The tourist office is in the Passage Kaladji on the 2nd floor next to the Constant jewellery store on the corner of Rue Gourgas and the market in Plateau. The staff are not very helpful. American Express (tel 320211) is in Socopao-Côte d'Ivoire, 14 Blvd de la République, BP 1297, Abidjan. These people can be very useful. The poste restante only holds letters for 15 days and charges CFA 200 for each letter collected.

Buses within town cost CFA 100 to CFA 125 per journey. Buses of interest to travellers include:

No 6 – Plateau to the airport via Treichville. Pick it up at the *gare sud* at the bottom of Blvd de la République.
Nos 3, 5, 25 – Plateau to Treichville.
No 21 – Cocody to Plateau and Treichville.
Nos 16, 20, 27, 30, 37 – *gare sud* bus terminal in Plateau to Adjamé via Blvd de la République and Blvd Nangui Abragou. If you get off at the large mosque (about five km from the *gare sud* on the left hand side) you'll see the Agban railway station and the main *gare routière* 400 metres back down the same road. This is where most long-distance buses arrive and depart from.
Nos 19, 23, 41 – Treichville to Vridi beach (nearest to the city).

Taxis within town are relatively cheap but the fares are double the normal rates between 11 pm and 7 am. A taxi from Treichville to the *gare routière* in Adjamé costs CFA 1000. A taxi to the airport costs CFA 12,000.

Most of the West African airlines (except Air Afrique) are on the Ave General de Gaulle.

Warning Abidjan is not a safe place after dark and robberies are frequent so take taxis. Adjamé and Treichville are notorious in this respect.

Embassies The Benin Embassy (tel 414414) and Guinea-Bissau Embassy (tel 415436) are listed in the telephone book, but they're in Cocody, which is a long way from the centre of Plateau where many of the embassies are.

UK
Immeuble Les Harmonica, Blvd Carde at the junction with Ave Docteur Jamot. Issues Sierra Leone entry permits and visas.
Burkino Faso
2 Ave Terrasson des Fougères
Canada
Immeuble Trade Centre, Ave Nogues between Rue 4 and 5
Ghana
Résidence la Corniche, Blvd du General de Gaulle
Guinea
Résidence Crosson Duplessis No 2, Ave Crosson Duplessis between Rue 1 and 2

Things to See

The **Ifan Museum** (Ethnology Museum) in Adjamé is worth a visit. It's open daily from 9 am to 12 noon and 3 to 6 pm except on Monday mornings and Sundays. Most buses from Treichville to Adjamé and Plateau pass by the museum (eg bus No 86).

The newly built **St Paul's Cathedral** has been recommended by many travellers as an interesting architectural curiosity.

Places to Stay

Treichville This is the place to head for if you're looking for budget accommodation but you will still pay more than in other Francophone West African countries.

The *Hotel Toulouroux*, Ave 13 between Rue 7 and 9, has large double rooms with shower and fan for CFA 2000. It's fairly clean but the toilets leave a lot to be desired. Rooms at the same price are also available at the *Hotel Zannik*, Ave 12 between Rue 9 and 10. Similar is the *Hotel du Succès*, Ave 14 at Rue 25 (opposite the Mission Catholique). It doubles as a brothel but is reasonable value at CFA 2500 for a room on the 1st floor and CFA 3000 for a room on the higher floors with shower but no fan. The staff are friendly, there's a good roof area and, if you stay for a week, there's a discount of CFA 2000.

The *Hotel Le Prince*, Ave 20, was renovated in 1983. Double rooms with shower cost CFA 4400 to CFA 6000. Close by this hotel is the *Hotel de l'Amitié*, which has rooms for CFA 3000 and air-con rooms for CFA 4500.

In this bracket the *Hotel Liberté* has some rooms for CFA 4000 and others for CFA 4500 a double with fan and shower. The *Hotel Le Perroquet*, Rue 25 between Ave 14 and 15 has rooms for CFA 3500 a double and CFA 4500 a double with air-con and shower. Similar is the *Hotel Maidani*, on the corner of Ave Gabriel Dadie and the Blvd Nanan Yamausstu, which has air-con rooms with shower for CFA 3000.

There is also the *Hotel du Port*, Blvd Marseille 80 close to Treichville railway station, which costs CFA 6000 a double with shower and toilet. The bus to the airport (No 6) leaves from nearby.

The *Hotel Treichville* (formerly the Hotel Palmyre and sometimes called the Treichotel), Ave de la Reine Pokou, used to be an old favourite of budget travellers. It has hiked up its prices considerably and now costs CFA 8000 to CFA 10,000 a double with shower and toilet. Close to it is the *Hotel Atlanta*, Ave 15 near Rue 13, which has rooms for CFA 4300. The rooms have showers and air-con.

Also recommended in this area the

Hotel Fraternité, opposite the railway station in Treichville and next to the Cinema Entente, is quiet and the management are friendly. The *Restaurant du Peuple*, Rue 9 near Ave 12 (next to Jannicks Snack Bar/Disco), has good clean rooms with attached shower and toilet, and fans.

Plateau Try the *Grand Hotel* which overlooks the bridge to Treichville. The cheapest rooms with attached bathroom, balcony and air-con cost CFA 7500. More expensive rooms facing the lagoon cost CFA 8400.

Cocody Try either the *Maison Protestante Etudiante*, behind the Catholic hospital, or the *Mission Biblique*, near the Institut des Arts. They only have rooms during student vacations and cost CFA 2000 per person with kitchen, lounge and bathroom facilities. Fans and mosquito nets are provided. You can camp in the beautiful grounds of the Mission Biblique at anytime for CFA 500 including use of clean showers and toilets. Women might try the *Foyer des Jeunes Filles*, Ave Bachalmé. Bus No 21 will take you to any of these three places.

Adjamé Try the *Hotel Silva* near the cemetery which is good value and has clean, airy rooms for CFA 3000 a double including shower. The *Hotel Liberté*, Ave 13 just north of the *gare routière* and about 400 metres south of the Blvd du General de Gaulle has rooms which range in price from CFA 3000 to CFA 6000 with air-con. Another place worth trying is the *Hotel la Rocade* on the roundabout from which traffic heads towards Plateau. They have double rooms for CFA 2500 with shower.

Somewhat up-market is the very pleasant *Hotel Le Mont Niangbo*, 25 Blvd William Jacob about 400 metres from the large mosque, which costs CFA 7000/7800 a single/double with private bath, air-con and balcony. You can sometimes bargain them down. Similar is the *Hotel Banfor*, Ave 13 just south of the *gare routière* (if coming up Blvd Nangui Abragou turn right at the dispensary – about 400 metres), which costs CFA 6000/6500 a single/double with private bath, air-con and a balcony.

Avoid the *Relais d'Adjamé* next to the truck park if possible, unless you're fond of open sewers, bus horns and the nocturnal habits of cockroaches.

Places to Eat

There are plenty of food stalls all over Abidjan – even in Plateau – where you can get rice with sauce.

In Treichville one of the best restaurants is the *Restaurant Senegalais*, Ave 21, one block from the Hotel Le Prince. Another recommended place in this area is the *Café des Arts* which is good for food and music. For fast food in Treichville, try the *Super Chicken*, Rue 13 near Ave 20, which sells food of the 'finger lickin' good' variety. The Arab bakery on the corner of Ave 9 and Rue 17 also serves good pitta bread with sesame sauce.

Street stalls at the Adjamé truck park sell riz gras.

In the Plateau area *Le Mekong*, 48 Ave General de Gaulle, offers delicious Vietnamese food but it's not cheap. Others which have been recommended are the *Café Central*, Rue Franchal d'Esperey, and the *Brasserie Regent*, notable for its ice cream.

In Marcory, *Le Vatican*, a small African restaurant, has established a noteworthy reputation among expatriates and is very popular. It offers cheap, first rate food and the service is excellent. All the taxi drivers know the place so there's no problem about getting there.

ABOISSO

You may have to stay overnight if going to or from Ghana. Try the *Hotel Bemosso*, which is clean and costs CFA 1500 for a room and CFA 3000 for air-con and bathroom.

There's also the *Hotel Bassagnini* which has doubles for CFA 2500 with fan.

BONDOUKOU

Bondoukou is famous for its old tombs which are decorated with figurative sculptures. The closest is five km west of town. There are two others en route to Soffre about 15 km south-east of town. There's also a good market on Sundays. Try *La Baya*, which has rooms for CFA 1500; or the *Alban*, which costs CFA 2000.

BOUAFLÉ

This is a dusty little town in the middle of the country with little of interest, but it is close by the **Maraoué National Park** so you may need to stay for the night. The *Hotel Aklomiombla* has doubles for CFA 2500 with fan or CFA 3500 with air-con.

BOUAKÉ

Bouakés **market** is large and interesting but it has a bad reputation for crime so be careful when visiting. The **mosque** is also interesting. Lively African nightlife can be found in the Quartier Koko.

The *Auberge de la Jeunesse* behind the stadium is the cheapest place to stay. It has very pleasant bungalows for CFA 2000 per person. Another cheapie is the *Hotel Bakary* (cross the railway tracks at the station and walk up about 100 metres) which has pleasant rooms for CFA 1800 a double or CFA 2500 a double with fan. The *Hotel Ahe N'Gouet* is a European-style hotel with good clean rooms for CFA 3000. Camping is free in the grounds of the *Mission Protestante* or rent a room there with washing and cooking facilities for CFA 1600 per person per night.

The cheapest hotel in the European quarter is the *Central Hotel* which costs CFA 6000 per room.

DANANÉ

Danané stands in a magnificently forested region of Ivory Coast and, not far from town, you can visit one of the last remaining vine bridges in the country. The **bridge** is about 22 km from Danané and about two km from the village of Lieupleu. There are a few *taxi-brousses* from Danané which will drop you off about five km from the village at the turn-off for CFA 500, otherwise you'll have to pay CFA 3000 one-way to the village itself. There's an 'entry fee' to the bridge of CFA 500!

You must get your passport stamped at immigration in Danané if you have come in from Liberia otherwise you'll be sent back to Man. The office is in the centre of town.

The bus terminals for Man and the one for Liberia and Guinea are at opposite ends of the town. It's a long walk between the two so take a taxi (CFA 100).

Places to Stay & Eat

A good place to stay is *Hotel Tia Etienne*, which costs CFA 2500 for a room without a fan, CFA 3000 with a fan, and CFA 5000 with air-con. Others are the *Bar de la Frontière* which costs CFA 2500 a double; and the *Hotel Lianes* at CFA 4000 a double. There are also several hotels outside town. One of the cheapest is the *Hotel Deba* at CFA 2000 to CFA 2500 for a clean room.

FERKÉSSÉDOUGOU

There's not a great deal to see or do in this town but it's fairly small and everything is within walking distance. One of the cheapest places to stay is *Le Campement* beside the railway station which has rooms with a shower for CFA 2500 but it's a grubby place. The *Ikuru Bar* close to the market behind the church which costs CFA 2000 has also been suggested.

Korhogo

While in Ferkéssédougou it's worth going to Korhogo, a half-hour taxi ride to the west, to visit the **Centre d'Artisanats** where the well-known *toiles* of Korhogo are designed. There are also many carvers making Fon masks on the road from the central mosque which is high up on the hill.

Places to Stay & Eat You can stay at the *Mission Catholique* for CFA 1500 per person for a spotless room. Otherwise, one of the cheapest hotels is the *Hotel Gon* which has small grubby rooms with fan for CFA 2000. The *Hotel de la Gare* offers single rooms for CFA 3000. There's a nightclub and a restaurant which serves pizza.

One place to eat is the *Restaurant la Bonne Cuisine* which offers good African meals. It is close to the Hotel Gon.

GRAND BASSAM

Forty-three km from Abidjan and set among coconut palms is Grand Bassam, the capital of Ivory Coast during the colonial era. It's a place for dreamers and full of dilapidated colonial buildings, museums and old churches which almost give it the air of a ghost town but worth a visit. It's also the nearest place to the capital for beaches. They're virtually deserted during the day but don't sleep on them as the chances are you'll be robbed.

The bus terminal is quite some distance from town so it's best to take a taxi (CFA 100 per person).

Places to Stay & Eat

If you spruce yourself up and ask around, you may find the owner of a beach hut who is willing to let you stay in one free (having someone stay in them helps reduce burglaries).

One of the cheapest places to stay is the *Restaurant Tonton Léon* at CFA 3000 (negotiable) a double with shower and toilet. The rooms are very hot, damp and full of mosquitoes. If you can't hack this go to the *Restaurant Long Phung*, which has basic but pleasant double rooms for CFA 3000/4000 a single/double (negotiable). The rooms have fans.

Hotel Restaurant la Taverne, on the

seashore, has the cheapest swimming pool. Entry costs CFA 1000 daily.

JACQUEVILLE

Jacqueville, west of Abidjan, is a pleasant town with an excellent **beach** and friendly people. *Le Campement* has bungalows for CFA 7000 or you can camp there for CFA 3000 per tent.

MAN

Taxis around town cost CFA 100 for locals but at least double that for tourists. There are three road stations in Man: one for the express buses to Abidjan (and other places), another for the taxis to Abidjan, and a third for the trucks and taxis to Danané.

Places to Stay & Eat

One of the cheapest is the *Hotel Mont Dent* near the hospital. Depending on what you want, it has rooms for CFA 1000/2000/2500. Slightly better is the *Hotel Les Montagnes*, which has a range of rooms from CFA 2500 to CFA 4000 – all with attached shower. Some have fans and others have air-con. Other hotels which have been recommended are the *Hotel Virginia* on the eastern edge of town, CFA 2500 per room; *Hotel Miva*, CFA 3000 a double with fan and shower; and *Hotel Fraternité*, 200 metres from the taxi park, CFA 2000 to CFA 2500 a double with private bath and CFA 3000 with private bath and fan.

A good place to eat is the *Restaurant Marie Therese* behind the market. Three km outside the town there's the excellent *Mission Catholique* guesthouse. It's beautifully located and costs CFA 4500 a double including breakfast or you can rent a bungalow for CFA 6000 with four beds. Take a taxi (CFA 250 to CFA 400 from the town centre), as it's a long walk.

ODIENNÉ

If you're heading for Bamako (Mali) this is where the tarmac ends.

Places to Stay & Eat

Le Campement was renovated some time ago and is very clean. A double room with shower, flush toilet and fan costs CFA 3000 and air-con costs CFA 4000. Recent reports, however, suggest that it has been taken over by athletes.

If it's not available, try *La Savanne* which is in easy reach of the town centre, has friendly staff and costs CFA 3000 per room without a fan, CFA 3500 with a fan and CFA 4000 with air-con. All the rooms have attached showers. There's a bar and restaurant as well. If you don't want to eat at La Savanne try the *La Bon Auberge*. The *Marquis Bar* opposite Le Campement is not as expensive as it looks and serves very good food.

SASSANDRA

West of Abidjan, this beach is popular with French expatriate workers. There are two cheap and dirty hotels to stay at as well as an expensive one.

TABOU

West of Abidjan, Tabou is a small, pleasant town with a beautiful **beach** and strong waves. There's one hotel next to the beach which has rooms for CFA 3000 to CFA 5000. It's possible to get into Liberia from here, too. The police will issue you with an exit stamp. To get there, take a taxi or bus down to the river (which forms the border between the two countries) then go on foot and by ferry to Liberia.

YAMOUSSOUKRO

This former village, 2½ hours by bus north of Abidjan, is the birthplace of the president and has been named as the new capital of Ivory Coast. It has been the political capital of the country since 1986 but Abidjan remains the commercial capital. Construction is still going on though there are already vast, wide boulevards and a presidential palace with its own crocodile lake (they get fed at 5 pm daily).

Just how much of a wank this will be

remains to be seen. Brasilia hasn't fared too well and Abuja, the new capital of Nigeria, has proved to be a financial millstone around the neck of the government there.

If you'd like to visit, you can stay at the *Confidences de Ciel* which is a small hotel on the same street as the Etoile cinema (CFA 100 by taxi from the bus station). It has rooms for CFA 2500 with fan and shower. It's very clean and has been recommended by quite a few travellers.

There are many cheap cafés around the bus station.

Kenya

Unlike pre-colonial Uganda, which saw the rise of several large kingdoms, Kenya was populated by a number of small, dispersed tribal groups, principal among whom were the Kikuyu, Kamba, Luo and Masai. These groups, though they shared the same area, had different origins so that, for instance, the Masai are a Hamitic tribe, the Kikuyu are Bantu and the Luo are Nilotic. There was little penetration of the interior by outsiders until the 19th century, and as a result what was to become Kenya escaped the worst depredations of the Arab slavers, who concentrated their attentions further south. The coastal area, however, formed an important part of the chain of Omani Arab trading posts which stretched from the Horn of Africa all the way down to Mozambique. Lamu, Malindi and Mombasa all had their origins as Arab trading cities. This string of trading posts dealt principally in ivory and slaves and was under the control of the Sultan of Zanzibar.

The gradual eclipse of the Sultan's power began in the late 19th century when both the British and the Germans obtained trading concessions along the coast, the former being allotted what is now Uganda and Kenya and the latter what is now mainland Tanzania. Administration of these areas quickly became the prerogative of the British and German governments respectively, so that in 1893 Uganda had become a protectorate followed by Kenya in 1895. In the early years, the British were primarily interested in tapping the rich resources of Uganda, and in order to facilitate this a railway was built between Mombasa and Kampala using indentured labourers from India, many of whom subsequently remained to eventually become the substantial merchant class of today. The arrival of the 20th century, however, saw the British direct their attention to settling Kenya with white farmers who set up plantations producing crops substantially for export.

In the process of establishing these, many Africans lost the lands they had previously cultivated and were either forced into new – and often inferior – land or into the labour market as a result of hut taxes imposed by the colonial administration. By 1915, the racial segregation of land effectively excluded Africans and Asians from holding properties in the fertile highlands. Other Africans, though not actually dispossessed, lost access to the surrounding uncultivated land which in a sense was their fallow ground. When they moved in the course of shifting cultivation they found themselves rent-paying 'squatters' on expropriated land.

The present government is still trying to sort out the legacy of all this, and since independence around 60,000 families have been resettled on land formerly owned by expatriates. Nevertheless, a large proportion of the most important agricultural properties is still owned by expatriates or politicians and much still needs to be done in this direction. Most of the country's employment problems stem from the fact that there is little access to land and that, in any case, only about 7% of the total area receives sufficient rainfall to support viable agriculture.

The reconciliation between Black and White since independence has undoubtedly been a major political feat (Kenya is one of Africa's most stable and prosperous

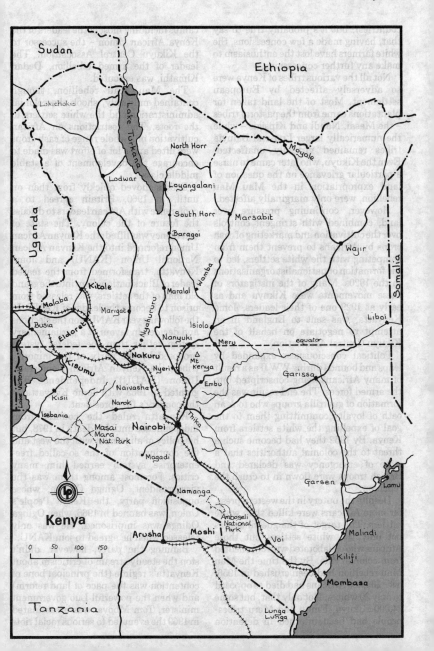

countries), but it's probably true to say that, having made a few concessions, the white farmers have lost the enthusiasm to make any further concessions.

Not all the various tribes of Kenya were so adversely affected by European settlement. Most of the land taken for plantations came from the pastoral tribes – the Masai, Nandi and Kipsigis – while the numerically larger Luo and Baluyia tribes remained virtually unaffected. Even the Kikuyu, who later came to nurse a particular grievance on the question of land expropriation in the Mau Mau rebellion, were only marginally affected.

However, continuing pressure over land, combined with stringent controls over the cultivation and marketing of cash crops by Africans to prevent them from competing with the white settlers, led to the formation of nationalist organisations in the 1920s. Many of the instigators of these movements were Kikuyu and as early as 1929 one of their leaders, Jomo Kenyatta, was sent to England in an attempt to negotiate on behalf of the Kikuyu Central Association.

Political consciousness expanded by leaps and bounds during WW II as a result of many Africans being conscripted into the armed forces. The end result was the formation of guerrilla groups who took an oath of loyalty committing them to the goal of expelling the white settlers from Kenya. By 1952 they had become such a threat to the colonial authorities that a state of emergency was declared and British troops were flown in to crush the rebellion.

Despite the outcry in the western press, far more Africans were killed than white settlers. The target of the guerrillas was not only the white settlers but those Africans who collaborated with or benefited from colonial rule. By the time the Mau Mau rebellion had been crushed in 1956, over 100,000 Africans had died as opposed to only 30 whites. Not only that, but some 24,000 Kikuyu, Embu and Meru tribespeople had been interned in detention camps including most of the leaders of the Kenya African Union – the successor to the Kikuyu Central Association. The leader of the armed rebellion, Dedan Kimathi, was executed.

The Mau Mau rebellion, though contained militarily, shook the colonial administration and the white settlers to the roots. The restrictions on African cultivation of a whole range of cash crops were lifted and a lot of effort was made to encourage the development of a stable middle class.

Events moved quickly from then on until, in 1960, Britain agreed to a conference with African leaders to discuss the future of the colony. The state of emergency was lifted; the Kenyan African Union reformed into the Kenyan African National Union (KANU) and Jomo Kenyatta, transformed from the feared leader of Black nationalism into the grand old man of the settlers, was released from prison to become the leader of KANU. In the following year KANU won the elections and decided in favour of a parliamentary system rather than the federal system proposed by the party of the minority tribes, the Kenyan African Democratic Union (KADU). Independence was granted in 1963 with Jomo Kenyatta as the country's first president.

Kenyatta ruled the country from independence until his death in 1978, but his policy of alignment with the west and the continuation of the so-called free-enterprise system earned him many critics. Foremost among them was the vice-president, Oginga Odinga, whose opposition party, the Kenya People's Union, was banned in 1966, when Oginga Odinga was imprisoned. He was only released when he agreed to join KANU.

Banning the party, however, didn't stop the steady stream of criticism about Kenyatta's regime (the principal bone of contention was the pace of land reform) and when the powerful Luo government minister, Tom Mboya, was assassinated in 1969 the event led to serious racial riots between the Kikuyu and Luo. In the early 1970s, Kariuki became the main opposition leader until he was assassinated in 1975 during a wave of bomb explosions in Nairobi. This time the government acted quickly to restore order using the army and paramilitary police.

With the death of Kenyatta, Daniel Arap Moi took over as president and has managed to keep the country on a fairly even keel though there is opposition to his increasingly autocratic style. Repression has noticeably increased. Much of it is undoubtedly overreaction by the government to innocuous opposition publications which Moi ought to be able to handle with more panache. Other developments, such as withdrawing the independence of the judiciary and making it subservient to the politicians are more ominous.

Nevertheless, Moi has had a number of successes such as the settlement of the border dispute with Somalia (Somalia has relinquished its claims to parts of eastern Kenya) and the normalisation of relations with Tanzania. Kenya, Tanzania and Uganda previously belonged to an economic union which covered railways, the Lake Victoria steamers, airlines, post and telecommunications. It was shattered by Kenya's unilateral seizure of the union's assets. In response Tanzania closed its land border with Kenya and prohibited flights between the two nations. The closure seriously affected Kenya's trading relationships with neighbouring countries and it was only lifted in 1983.

Moi has also begun to diversify the tribal composition of the government and bureaucracy but he still has a long way to go before the Kikuyu stranglehold is broken.

Facts

GEOGRAPHY & CLIMATE
Although Kenya lies astride the equator,

much of the country consists of a high plateau and mountains so the weather is generally warm and pleasant. March to May (the long rains) and October to November (the short rains) are generally wet periods throughout the country but downpours occur mostly in the late afternoons, the earlier part of the day being warm and sunny. Violent storms may be encountered during the wet seasons in the Lake Turkana region especially around Mt Kulal.

On the coast, the hottest months are September, October and between December and April but cool monsoon breezes make these months very pleasant. At other times it is hot and humid but not unbearably so. Kisumu on Lake Victoria has a similar climate because of the influence of the lake. The northern area which is semidesert remains hot and dry throughout the year apart from the occasional downpour. Temperatures in Nairobi range from 11°C to 23°C in July and 13°C to 28°C in February. Nairobi and the highlands can get cold especially in the evenings during July and August.

PEOPLE
Kenya's population is over 21 million and increasing rapidly. The overwhelming majority are African but there are also Arab, Asian and European groups.

VISAS
Visas are required by all except nationals of Commonwealth countries (except Australia, Sri Lanka and British passport holders of Indian, Pakistani and Bangladeshi origin), Denmark, Ethiopia, Germany (West), the Irish Republic, Italy, Norway, Spain, Sweden, Turkey and Uruguay. Those who don't need visas are issued with a visitor's pass valid for a stay of up to three months on entry.

In Africa, visas can be obtained from Kenyan embassies or high commissions in:

Egypt
8 Medina Munawara St, PO Box 362,
Dokki, Cairo
Ethiopia
Fikre Miriam Rd, PO Box 3301, Addis
Ababa
Nigeria
53 Queens Drive, Ikoyi, PO Box 6464,
Lagos
Rwanda
Blvd de Nyabugogo just off the Place de
l'Unité Nationale, Kigali
Somalia
Km IV Via Mecca, PO Box 618, Mogadishu
Tanzania
NIC Investment House, Samora Machel
Ave, Dar es Salaam
Uganda
Plot No 60, Kira Rd, Kampala
Zaïre
Plot No 5002, Ave de l'Onganda, BP 9667,
Gombe, Kinshasa
Zambia
Harambee House, 5207 United Nations
Ave, Lusaka
Zimbabwe
95 Park Lane, Harare

Where there is no Kenyan embassy or high
commission, visas can be obtained from
the British embassy or high commission.

If you apply for your Kenyan visa
outside Africa you may be asked to show
an onward ticket. This generally isn't the
case at embassies in Africa. Other than
this, Kenyan visas are no fuss to get and
are issued either the same day or within
24 hours.

If you enter Kenya through a land
border no-one will ever ask you for an
onward ticket or 'sufficient funds'. This
isn't always the case if you enter by air.
A lot depends on what you look like,
whether you're male or female, what you
write on your immigration card and which
immigration officer you deal with. Most
people are not asked for an onward ticket
or 'sufficient funds' but it's best to assume
that you will be, so look clean and tidy and
write the name of an expensive hotel on
your immigration card in the appropriate
section. Single women have been told at

times that sufficient funds in the absence
of an onward ticket were suspect 'because
women lose money easily'! All the same,
we've never heard of anyone being refused
entry to Kenya although some, as a last
resort, have had to buy (refundable)
onward tickets.

Visas can be renewed in Nairobi at
immigration (tel 332110), Nyayo House
(ground floor), on the corner of Kenyatta
Ave and Uhuru Highway, or at the office
(tel 311745) in Mombasa during normal
office hours. A single re-entry permit costs
US$8 and a multiple-entry permit US$40.
You must pay in foreign currency. No
onward ticket or 'sufficient funds' are
demanded. The staff are friendly and
helpful.

As long as you have a valid visa you can
visit either Tanzania or Uganda and
return without having to apply for
another visa – you don't need a re-entry
permit. This does not apply to visiting any
other countries. There is, however, a
charge at the border for doing this –
usually US$4.

Other Visas
Since Nairobi is a gateway city to East
Africa and the city centre is easy to get
around, many travellers arrange visas
here for other countries which they intend
to visit. If you are going to do this plan
ahead because some embassies only
accept visa applications in the mornings
and others only on certain days of the
week. Some take 24 hours to issue, others
48 hours. Some visa applications (Sudan,
for instance) may have to be referred to
the capital city but this is rare.

The French Embassy (tel 339783)
Embassy House, Harambee Ave issues
visas for Francophone countries which
don't have embassies in Nairobi (Chad and
Central African Republic, for instance).

In addition to the ones listed there are
embassies/high commissions for Algeria,
Australia, Austria, Bangladesh, Belgium,
Canada, Cyprus, Denmark, Finland,
Germany (West), Ghana, Greece, India,

Indonesia, Irish Republic, Italy, Japan, Kuwait, Lesotho, Liberia, Libya, Malawi, Netherlands, Nigeria, Norway, Oman, Pakistan, Saudi Arabia, Spain, Sri Lanka, Swaziland, Sweden, Switzerland, Turkey, UK, USA, USSR, Yemen and Zimbabwe among others.

There are also consulates of Austria, Belgium, Denmark, France, India, Italy, Netherlands and Sweden in Mombasa.

Burundi The embassy (tel 3387350) is on the 14th floor, Development House, Moi Ave. It's open Monday to Thursday from 8.30 am to 12.30 pm and 2 to 5 pm. Single-entry visas cost KSh 50 (two-day transit) and KSh 100 (30-day tourist), with two photographs. Visas take 24 hours to issue but the embassy will only issue them on Tuesdays and Thursdays so you must put in your application on either Monday or Wednesday. The staff are friendly and there are tourist leaflets available.

Egypt The embassy is on Harambee Plaza, on the corner of Uhuru Highway and Haile Selassie Ave. It's open Monday to Friday from 9 am to 12.30 pm and 3 to 3.30 pm. One-month, single-entry visas cost KSh 180 and double-entry visas cost KSh 200 and take 24 hours to issue. You need one photograph and may be asked to show an onward ticket.

Ethiopia The embassy (tel 72 3035) is on State House Ave. It's open Monday to Friday from 8.30 am to 12.30 pm and 2.30 to 5 pm. No visa is necessary if you are going to stay less than 72 hours. A one-month tourist visa costs KSh 80 and is issued in 48 hours. Entry is by air only and you must have an onward ticket.

Madagascar There is no Malagasy embassy or consulate as such in Nairobi. However, there is a consular official who comes into Nairobi every Monday who will accept visa applications at the Air Madagascar office in the Hilton Hotel block (City Hall Way). Visas cost KSh 170. You need four photographs plus an onward ticket. They are issued on Thursdays. (The official takes the application forms to Antananarivo on Mondays and returns on Thursdays.)

Rwanda The embassy (tel 334341) is on the 12th floor, International House, Mama Ngina St. It's open Monday to Friday from 8.30 am to 12.30 pm and 2 to 5 pm. One-month visas cost KSh 200, with two photographs and take 24 hours to issue. On the application form it will ask you the date that you want to enter Rwanda. Think carefully about this as the visa will run from then.

Somalia The embassy (tel 24301) is in International House, Mama Ngina St. Visa applications are only accepted on Mondays. One-month visas cost KSh 200, with two photographs and are issued in 24 hours. You may be asked which country you come from before they will give you the application forms and if there is a Somali embassy in the country you name they may refuse to give you the forms saying you have to apply in your own country. If this happens, tell them you are a permanent resident in a different country. This works like a treat. No problems.

Sudan The embassy (tel 720853) is on the 7th floor, Minet ICDC House, Mamlaka Rd. A one-month visa costs KSh 100, with one photograph and takes between 24 hours and three weeks to issue (more likely the latter if they have to refer the application to Khartoum). An onward ticket is necessary.

Tanzania The high commission (tel 331056/7) is on the 4th floor, Continental House, on the corner of Harambee Ave and Uhuru Highway. It's open Monday to Thursday from 9 am to 12.30 pm and 2 to 5 pm but visa applications are only accepted in the mornings. Only single-entry visas are available. The cost depends on your nationality and varies considerably, but they are issued in

48 hours as a rule. Be very careful when filling in the application form since there is a US$80 per day minimum 'sufficient funds' rule which is enforced here. So if you want one month you must write down at least US$2400. No-one actually wants to see it and if they do, well, it's in the hotel safe.

Uganda The high commission is on the 5th floor, Baring Arcade, Phoenix House, Kenyatta Ave. A two-week visa costs an incredible KSh 330 with two photographs but they are issued in one hour. You may be asked where you are going to stay so have the name of a hotel in Kampala handy.

Zambia The high commission (tel 724799) is on Nyerere Rd next door to the YWCA. One-month, single-entry visas cost KSh 35, with three photographs and take 48 hours to issue.

Zaïre The embassy (tel 29771) is in Electricity House, Harambee Ave. It's open Monday to Friday from 10 am to 12 noon. One-month, single-entry visas cost KSh 160, two-month, multiple-entry visas cost KSh 280 and three-month, multiple-entry visas cost KSh 360. Plus you need four photographs, a letter of recommendation from your own embassy, an 'onward ticket' (which doesn't have to start from Zaïre) and vaccination certificates. They're issued in 24 hours and the staff are helpful. Letters of recommendation are issued free by some embassies but at others there is a charge.

MONEY

US$ 1	=	KSh	18.50
UK£ 1	=	KSh	34.00
FFr 1	=	KSh	3.10
A$ 1	=	KSh	16.00

The unit of currency is the Kenyan shilling = 100 cents. Official bank rates fluctuate according to the international currency markets but not by a great deal. The Kenyan shilling is virtually a hard currency especially in surrounding countries. The import and export of local currency is not permitted and, when you leave the country, customs officials will ask you if you are carrying any. If you say you are not that's generally the end of the matter. If you're only leaving the country for a short while intending to return, and don't want to convert all your Kenyan shillings into another currency you can leave any excess at a border post against a receipt and pick it up again when you get back.

You will probably meet people (especially in Nairobi) who offer to buy US dollars and UK£ sterling but it's more than likely you are being set up for a rip-off. There is no way *anyone* is going to give you KSh 25 to the US dollar. You can, by changing on the street market, get one or two more shillings to the dollar than the banks offer but that's the extent of it.

Travellers' cheques attract a 1% commission at some banks but none at all at others (at Barclays there's generally no commission). Barclays is probably the best bank to change cheques at since there's hardly any red tape and the transaction takes just a few minutes. Avoid Standard Chartered banks where possible as there is a lot of form-filling and it can take more than half an hour to change a cheque. Banking hours are Monday to Friday from 8 or 9 am to 2 pm and on the first and last Saturdays of the month from 9 to 11 am.

At Kenyatta International Airport, Nairobi, the Bureau de Change is open 24 hours a day, seven days a week. The Kenyatta Ave branch of Barclays in Nairobi is open Monday to Saturday from 9 am to 4.30 pm. The Moi Ave branch of Barclays in Mombasa is open Monday to Saturday from 8.30 am to 5 pm. The Malindi branch of Barclays is open Monday to Saturday from 8.30 am to 1 pm and 2.30 to 5 pm.

Currency declaration forms are usually issued on arrival although you may have to ask for one at Namanga on the border with Tanzania. These are collected when you leave but not scrutinised. You cannot change travellers' cheques without a currency form so make sure you get one. If, for any reason, you don't get one, they can be obtained from the Central Bank of Kenya, Kencom House (7th floor), City Hall Way, Nairobi, without any fuss (takes about 10 minutes).

Currency forms and bank receipts have to be produced when buying international flight tickets in Kenya. If you are intending to do this at some point plan ahead because if you leave the country then return you will no longer have your original currency form. So you will have lost credit for the money which you changed on your first visit. See the Getting There & Around section for further details on how this affects you.

If you have money transferred from your home country for collection in Kenya you can pick it up entirely in US dollar travellers' cheques but these may be stamped 'Non-negotiable in the Republic of South Africa'. If you intend to go there, this is going to cause problems. It is, after all, your money and not the bank's. Some travellers regard this sort of interference as totally unacceptable and have spent the best part of a day arguing with bank officials. Some have been successful. Barclays does this but then it's nonsense since they have scores of branches in South Africa.

It used to be possible, and still may be, to cash US dollar travellers' cheques at banks in Kenya and get US dollars cash for them but it's getting harder. At most banks you'll be met with a flat 'no' but some people are successful. Certainly you have to prove that you are leaving the country within 48 hours (using an air ticket or dated visa) and you generally need a convincing story about why you need cash dollars. On the other hand, you can get cash dollars with no problems if you make a withdrawal against your home account using a Visa card at a Barclays bank (no other cards can be used at Barclays). So long as you don't want more

than US$150 to US$200 per day, it takes about 20 minutes. One traveller reported that she was able to get US$1000 in cash though that required a telex to the bank in her home country. Asked why she wanted that amount, she told them she was going to Tanzania where hotel bills and national park entry fees had to be paid for in hard currency. Several other travellers have used the same explanation with success.

At the Bank of Kenya's Bureau de Change at Kenyatta Airport, Nairobi, you can exchange shillings for cash dollars up to any amount so long as you have bank receipts to cover the transaction. They offer a very poor rate of exchange and charge KSh 100 commission. The facility is obviously meant for those who are leaving the country and have excess shillings (which you can't legally export) but they don't ask to see your air ticket.

The airport departure tax for international flights is US$20. You must pay this in foreign currency. Kenyan shillings are not accepted.

POST

Kenyan post offices are usually very reliable. Poste restante is likewise well-organised and reliable. There is no charge for collecting letters and they give you the whole pile to sort through (according to which letter of the alphabet your name falls under). If expected letters are not arriving in the appropriate pigeon hole they're more than willing to let you look through others.

TOURIST INFORMATION

There is no national tourist organisation in Kenya but there is a free fortnightly publication called *Tourist's Kenya* which can be picked up at any of the large hotels in Nairobi or at the Thorn Tree Café at the New Stanley Hotel. It contains most of what you'll need to know - hotels, restaurants, airlines, tour and safari operators, etc. However, beware of relying too heavily on it for addresses (the Zambian High Commission was still listed as being in Kampus Towers at least a year after it had moved to new premises).

National Holidays

The national holidays in Kenya are: 1 January, Maundy Thursday (pm only), Good Friday, Easter Monday, 1 May, 1 June, Id el Fitr (end of Ramadan), 20 October, 15 December, 25 December, 26 December.

HEALTH

If you need to renew vaccinations (for the purposes of your International Vaccination Certificate) you can do this at the City Hall Clinic, Mama Ngina St, Nairobi. You'll get a clean needle each time. They do cholera Monday to Friday from 8.30 am to 12 noon and yellow fever, tetanus and typhoid on the same days from 8.30 to 11 am. Yellow fever costs KSh 25 and cholera KSh 20. The others are free of charge.

FILM & PHOTOGRAPHY

It makes a lot of sense to bring film with you to Kenya especially if you can get a good deal on it, but if you don't or you need more, Kenya is one of the best places in Africa to buy it. There's a wide range of film available in Nairobi and Mombasa and it's not that expensive. If you don't have enough film for your projected needs, buy it in a large city. Don't wait until you get to a game lodge. Most of them carry film for sale but the range is limited and their prices are often up to 50% higher than in Nairobi.

LANGUAGE

Swahili and English are the official languages though there is a movement afoot to make Swahili the sole official language. It will be a long time, however, before most urban Kenyans stop using English in their normal, everyday conversations. On the other hand, it is extremely useful to have a working knowledge of Swahili for outside the urban areas and especially if you are going on safari to remote areas. You won't meet many tribals in the bush who can speak English, particularly those who have had little exposure to tourism. But most of them can speak *some* Swahili whatever their first language might be. Other major languages are Kikuyu, Luo and Kikamba.

Newspapers and magazines are published mainly in English and Swahili.

Getting There & Around

You can get into Kenya by air, road, lake ferry and possibly dhow. There are railways in Kenya but, although the tracks are continuous with the Tanzanian and Ugandan systems, there are no through services.

AIR

International

Kenyatta International Airport in Nairobi is the main gateway to East Africa and is served by airlines from all over the world. Nairobi is the best city in East Africa (and perhaps in the whole of Africa) to pick up cheap air tickets for international flights. There is a lot of competition between travel agents so most of them lean over backwards to give you whatever discounts they can manage. They are the equivalent of 'bucket shops' in Europe. You will not find these discounts at the airline offices themselves. Only a few of the airlines offer discounted tickets to agents for sale to the public. The most common of these are Aeroflot, Ethiopian Airlines, Olympic Airways and Sudan Airways and most of the cheap tickets available are for flights to Europe though there are others to India/Pakistan and to Madagascar/Mauritius/Réunion.

Tickets are paid for in local currency. However, to comply with government regulations it's usually necessary to produce your currency declaration form and bank receipts for the full amount of what a ticket would cost if you bought it direct from the airline concerned. It's important to bear this in mind if you are going to leave Kenya for a while and return later to buy your ticket as your currency form will be collected at the border and you will lose the exchange credits recorded on it. The best thing to do in these circumstances is to buy your ticket just before you leave Kenya for the first time. You can also pay for your ticket in foreign currency in which case you don't need bank receipts.

To find the best deals at any particular time you need to get quotations from several agents since what they offer and the conditions attached vary. One of the most popular agents is Hanzuwan el Kindly Tours & Travel (tel 26810, 338729), Rajab Manzil Building (4th floor, room 3), Tom Mboya St. It's run by a man called Fehed A S H el-Kindly though he's known to everyone as Eddie. Budget travellers have been going through him for years. He's very friendly and helpful and offers some of the best deals in Nairobi. Equally well recommended are Prince Travel, Kenyatta Conference Centre (especially for flights to Cairo), Crocodile Travel, Tom Mboya St in the same block as the Ambassador Hotel, and Falcon Travel, International House, Mama Ngina St. Banko Travel, Latema Rd, are also very friendly and offer similar deals. Others worth checking out are Let's Go Travel, Standard St close to the junction with Koinange St, Appel Travel, Tamana Tours and Kambo Travel.

A Nairobi/London ticket (on Aeroflot or Sudan Air) goes for KSh 4600 to KSh 4800 but you may have to produce bank receipts for KSh 11,600 to KSh 13,600. Olympic Airways on the same route generally costs more – expect KSh 6200. A Nairobi/Bombay ticket (on PIA) goes for KSh 4200 and you have to produce bank receipts for KSh 5830 to KSh 6110. If you're lucky you may find an agency which only wants to see bank receipts for the price of the ticket.

Similarly, there are deals on Air Madagascar and Air Mauritius. Bought from an agent, it's possible to have a 21-day excursion fare 'doctored' to give you up to eight to 10 weeks for the same price. On this basis a Nairobi/Antananarivo/Nairobi ticket would cost about KSh 4250 and a Nairobi/Comoros Islands/Mauritius/Réunion/Madagascar/Nairobi ticket with stopovers in each place would be around KSh 6320.

Internal

There is a departure tax of KSh 50 for internal flights.

Kenya Airways, the national carrier, connects the main cities of Nairobi, Mombasa, Kisumu and Malindi. There is usually no problem in booking a seat with them. There are 47 flights per week in either direction between Nairobi and Mombasa; about 10 or 11 flights per week in either direction between Nairobi and Malindi and Mombasa and Malindi; and nine flights per week in either direction between Nairobi and Kisumu. All flights between Kisumu and Mombasa or Malindi go via Nairobi.

In addition to Kenya Airways there are a number of private airlines which connect the main cities with smaller towns and certain national parks. The main ones are Cooper Skybird and Equator Airlines which connect Mombasa with Malindi and Lamu. Equator Airlines also flies to Garissa, Hulugho, Kunga, Liboi, Masai Mara, Mandera, Marsabit, Moyale, Ukunda and Wajir. It's worth thinking about flying with these companies if your time is limited and/or the roads are bad.

Cooper Skybird flies from Mombasa and Malindi to Lamu at least twice daily. Mombasa/Lamu takes just over an hour and costs KSh 1200 one-way while Malindi/Lamu takes about half an hour and costs KSh 750. There are now a number of other operators on this route including Equator Airlines, Eagle Aviation, African Express Airways and Skyways. Fares vary slightly between the airlines.

Cooper Skybird booking offices are at

Bunsons Travel Services (tel 21992/3/4) and Executive Air Services (tel 500607) in Nairobi; Ambali House (tel 21443, 21456), Nkrumah Rd, Mombasa; and in Malindi on Government Rd (tel 20860/1) near Lawford's Hotel. Equator Airlines' main office (tel 21177, 339557) is in Nairobi in the Baring Arcade (2nd floor), Kenyatta Ave. Their other contact numbers are Mombasa (tel 432355), Malindi (tel 20585) and Lamu (tel 139).

ROAD

Kenyan roads in the south-western part of the country (west of a line drawn through Malindi, Isiolo and Kitale) are excellent and some of the best in Africa. North and north-east of this line and in the national parks they are all gravel roads usually in a reasonable state of repair if you consider *piste* (corrugated gravel) to be a reasonable state of repair. Driving on these at a speed necessary to avoid wrecking a vehicle completely can be agony on your kidneys after several hours and especially on a bus which has had a double set of unyielding springs fitted to it. Naturally, there are washouts on some of these during the rainy seasons and, under such circumstances, journey times can be considerably longer.

Right up in the north, on the eastern side of Lake Turkana especially in the Kaisut and Chalbi deserts, you can make good headway in the dry season. The roads (which would be better described as tracks) are often surprisingly smooth and in good condition. This is certainly true of the road from Wamba to North Horr via Parsaloi, Baragoi, South Horr and Loiyangalani. After rain, however, it's another story particularly on the flat parts of the deserts. They turn into treacherous seas of mud often several feet deep in places. Under these circumstances, only a complete fool would attempt to drive on the tracks without a 4WD, sand ladders, adequate jacking equipment, shovels, a towrope or wire, drinking water and spare (metal) jerrycans of fuel. This is especially true of the stretches of track between North Horr and Maikona and between any of the tracks leading off the Marsabit to Isiolo road to South Horr.

To get out of the mud, if you're really stuck, you're going to be entirely dependent on the small number of vehicles which may pass by and *may* stop to help (they don't want to get stuck either), or a herd of camels to haul you out. It's going to cost money either way.

Fuel is very difficult to find in this region and is usually only available at religious mission stations but at up to three times what you would pay in Nairobi – and they'll only sell you a limited amount. Make adequate preparations if you are taking your own transport.

If you are driving your own vehicle there are certain routes in north-east Kenya where you must obtain police permission before setting out (there will be a roadblock to enforce this). It's usually just a formality. The main stretch is between Isiolo and Marsabit where all transport must travel in convoy at a certain time of day.

Hitching

Hitching is usually good on the main roads and may be preferable to travelling by *matatu* but if you are picked up by an African driver and are expecting a free lift make this clear from the outset. Most will expect a contribution at least. Hitching to the national parks, on the other hand, can be very difficult since most people either go on a tour or hire their own transport. Apart from that, once you get to the park lodges or camping areas, you will be entirely dependent on persuading tourists with their own vehicles to take you with them to view game since walking in the parks is forbidden.

Bus & Matatu

Over the rest of the country there are regular buses, *matatus* (normally minibuses or saloon cars which you share with others) and private taxis. The cheapest form of transport are the buses, next *matatus* and lastly private taxis (expensive). There's not a lot to choose in terms of journey times between normal buses and *matatus* but there is a lot in terms of safety. Most *matatu* drivers are under a lot of pressure from their owners to maximise profits so they tend to drive recklessly and overload their vehicles. They also put in long working days. Stories about *matatu* smashes and overturnings in which a few people are killed and many injured can be found almost daily in the newspapers. Of course, many travellers use them and, in some cases, there is no alternative but if there is (such as a bus or train) take that in preference. The Mombasa to Nairobi road is notorious for smashes.

As in most East African countries, you can always find a *matatu* which is going to the next town or further afield so long as it's not too late in the day. Simply ask around among the drivers at the park. Sometimes it's shared with the bus station. They leave when full and the fares are fixed. It's unlikely you will be asked a higher fare than the other passengers.

Bus fares are generally about half way between what you would pay on the railways in 2nd and 3rd classes and the journey times are quicker. A lot of buses travel during the day whereas most train journeys are at night so you may prefer to take a bus if you want to see the countryside. All the bus companies are privately owned and naturally some of them run better buses than others. Coastline Safari, Goldline and Tana River Bus Co are about the best of the bunch. Mawingo Bus Service and Akamba Bus Service are cheaper but their buses are older (on a long journey you're only looking at about US$1 difference in the fare).

Some Kenyan towns (Bungoma, Eldoret, Malindi, Naivasha) have bus stations, usually nothing more than a dirt patch. In most places each bus company will have its own terminus though these are often close to each other. *Matatu* and taxi lines sometimes share the same stations as

buses but this isn't always the case (especially in Nairobi).

Most of the larger lines such as Coastline Safari and Goldline offer services from Nairobi and Mombasa to Dar es Salaam (Tanzania). Some examples of fares and journey times are:

Nairobi to Mombasa There are many departures daily in either direction (mostly in the early morning and late evening) by, among others, Akamba, Coastline Safari, Goldline and Mawingo. The fare is KSh 100 and it takes seven to eight hours including a lunch break about half way. In Nairobi, most of the bus stations are on Accra Rd close to River Rd except for Akamba which is on Lagos Rd between Latema Rd and Tom Mboya St. In Mombasa the bus stations are all along Jomo Kenyatta and Mwembe Tayari Rd.

Mombasa to Malindi There are many departures daily in either direction from early morning until late afternoon by several bus companies and *matatus*. A bus costs KSh 25 and takes up to three hours. A *matatu* costs KSh 40 and takes about two hours. In Mombasa they all depart from outside the New People's Hotel, Abdel Nasser Rd, and in Malindi they depart from the bus station. There are also share taxis (usually Peugeot 504 station wagons) on this route. They depart as soon as they have seven passengers and cost KSh 50 per person. They take you door-to-door in about 1½ hours. There is a ferry crossing at Kilifi where you will have to disembark but a bridge was nearing completion in early 1989.

Malindi to Lamu If you don't want to see Malindi, you can get a bus or *matatu* all the way from Mombasa to Lamu but very few people do this.

The best company to travel with from Malindi to Lamu is the Tana River Bus Co which has its terminus on Sir Ali Rd opposite the Habib bank. They go to Lamu on Monday, Wednesday and

Friday and return the following day. Other companies making this trip are Lamy Bus and Tawakal. Assuming you go by Tana River Bus Co, make sure you get on one of their Isuzu buses. If possible don't get on a Leyland bus if you have any respect for your kidneys. The road is rough but you won't notice it too much on the Isuzu buses. On the Leyland buses – forget it!

The fare is KSh 85 and the journey takes about six hours. There are two ferry crossings on this route and, like everyone else, you'll have to get down and haul away on the ropes. The buses stop on the mainland and you board a ferry to Lamu (for which you must pay another KSh 5). It's advisable to book in advance for these buses though you can often find seats if you turn up early enough on the morning of departure. In Lamu, all the companies have offices where you can book seats in advance.

Nairobi to Namanga Many bus companies cover this route daily in either direction charging KSh 30 and taking about four hours. The best way of doing it, however, is to take a shared taxi with East African Rd Services (on Ronald Ngala St near the junction with River Rd in Nairobi) since they do the journey in not much more than two hours and the cost is only KSh 50 per person. The taxis leave when full (five passengers). If you do the journey this way you can be in Arusha (Tanzania) in about 4½ hours from Nairobi including crossing the border. *Matatus* leave Namanga (at the border) throughout the day. The fare is TSh 150 and they take between 1½ and two hours. Customs on either side of the border are very easy-going.

Nairobi to Malaba There are daily buses in either direction by several companies. They depart in the evening between 7 and 7.30 pm and arrive the next morning between 5.30 and 6 am. They cost KSh 110. This is the alternative to taking the train. If you don't want to travel at night do the

journey in stages by bus staying at places en route overnight (Nakuru, Eldoret, etc).

In the opposite direction from Malaba to Nairobi, you can do the journey by day if you first take a *matatu* from Malaba to Bungoma (KSh 15, about 45 minutes), stay the night in Bungoma (plenty of budget hotels) then take one of the many buses to Nairobi the following morning at about 8 am. They arrive in Nairobi about 5 pm and cost KSh 90.

There are also daily buses in either direction between Nairobi and Busia if you don't want to go through Malaba.

Nairobi to Garissa There is a direct daily bus to Garissa which leaves from outside the Munawar Hotel opposite the Kenya bus depot in Eastleigh, Nairobi at 6 am. The depot is a 10-minute *matatu* ride from Ronald Ngala St (Route No 9). The fare is KSh 90 and the journey takes about seven hours. All transport along this road has to go in convoy since there has been trouble with *shifta* (bandits) in the past though their activities have been dramatically curtailed due to the provision of military escorts for the convoys.

Marsabit to Isiolo & Moyale There are buses from Marsabit to both Isiolo and Moyale (the latter is on the Kenya-Ethiopia border) at 10 am on Wednesday, Friday and Sunday which cost KSh 100 and take about six hours. As on the Nairobi to Garissa route, all vehicles including buses must travel in convoy and for the same reasons. Only Kenyans and Ethiopians are allowed to cross the border into Ethiopia. Entry into this country by other nationals is by air only.

Nairobi to Kitale There are daily departures in either direction by several bus companies. An ordinary bus will cost as little as KSh 75 whereas a luxury bus will cost KSh 120. The journey takes about 5½ hours. Buses to Kitale go via Eldoret.

Kitale to Lodwar There are two or three daily buses in either direction by different companies which leave at about 8 am (but they often drive around town for another hour picking up passengers). The fare varies between KSh 70 and KSh 90 and the journey takes about eight hours some of it over rough roads. It's also possible to hitch trucks for about KSh 60.

Driving

If you bring your own vehicle to Kenya you should get a free three-month permit at the border on entry so long as you have a valid carnet de passage for it. If you don't have a carnet you should be able to get a free one-week permit at the border on entry after which you must get an 'authorisation permit for a foreign private vehicle' which costs KSh 3900 (about US$244). Before you do this, however, get in touch with the Automobile Association in Nairobi.

Hiring a car in Kenya is expensive but it does give you freedom of movement and the ability to go places which tours don't get to. For visiting the most popular of the national parks (Amboseli, Masai Mara, Tsavo East and West and Lake Nakuru) it's probably cheaper and you will see more, all things taken into account, to go on an organised camping tour. Two of the main reasons for this are that the tour company organises the catering and their guides who take you out on game viewing trips generally have a good idea where to find the animals. In your own vehicle you might drive round all day and not see anywhere near as much as you would on a tour. However, it's probably worth considering hiring a car to explore northern Kenya and particularly the Lake Turkana area.

It's obviously cheaper to hire 2WD cars rather than 4WD vehicles but the whole point about hiring a vehicle is that it will enable you to get off the beaten track. So it's not worth hiring anything that isn't 4WD.

A four-seater Suzuki Safari 4WD will cost around KSh 400 to KSh 500 per day plus KSh 5.50 to KSh 7 per km plus KSh 130 to KSh 230 per day insurance. Unlimited distance weekly rates will be about KSh 8000 to KSh 9000. A larger 4WD like an Isuzu Trooper will cost about KSh 700 to KSh 1000 per day plus KSh 10 to KSh 13 per km plus KSh 200 to KSh 250 for insurance. Unlimited distance weekly rates will be around KSh 15,000. You will also have to pay a (returnable) deposit of between KSh 3000 and KSh 5000 and the estimated cost of the rental in advance if you do not have a suitable credit card. Petrol costs about KSh 9 per litre on average but it can cost up to three times as much in remote areas – if you can find any at all. Take lots of jerrycans with you.

Before you hire a car, go to as many companies as you can find and ask what their rates are. The daily and weekly fixed charges generally only vary by up to KSh 50 but the km charges can vary by much more. This is usually only important if you are hiring for less than one week. Don't forget to ask what the insurance covers – a smashed windscreen? burst tyres? theft? accident damage? Some companies have minimum age limits which can be 23 or 25 years old with a minimum of two years' experience. As far as driving licences go, you only need a licence from your own country or an international driving permit. Some firms offer special rates between the beginning of March and the end of May (the low season).

Companies which travellers have used over the years and found to be consistently reliable and cost competitive are:

Market Service Station
    on the corner of Koinange St and Banda St, Nairobi (the Mobil station) (tel 25797, 335735)
Habib's Cars Ltd
    Agip House, Haile Selassie Ave, Nairobi (tel 20463, 23816)
Polay's Car Hire
    NCM House, 1st floor, Tom Mboya St, Nairobi (tel 334207, 331681)

Let's Go Travel
   Caxton House, Standard St, Nairobi (tel 29539, 29540)
Oddjobs
   on the corner of Koinange St and Monrovia St, Nairobi (tel 21375, 23110)
Central Car Rental
   Fedha Towers, Standard St, Nairobi

TRAIN

Kenyan Railways are excellent, generally punctual and a very popular way of travelling. It's also considerably safer than travelling by bus or *matatu* since the drivers of the latter often take risks, especially on the Nairobi to Mombasa run. The main railway line runs from Mombasa to Malaba on the Kenya-Uganda border via Voi, Nairobi, Nakuru and Eldoret with branch lines from Nakuru to Kisumu, Nairobi to Nanyuki, Voi to Taveta and Eldoret to Kitale. There are no passenger services on the Nairobi to Nanyuki or Eldoret to Kitale branches. Likewise, although the tracks are continuous with both the Tanzanian and Ugandan systems, there are no through services at present.

First class consists of two-berth compartments with a wash basin, drinking water supply, a wardrobe and drinks service. There's a lockable door between one compartment and the adjacent one so, if there are four of you travelling together, you can make one compartment out of two. They're spotlessly clean. Second class consists of four-berth compartments with hand basin and drinking water supply. Third class is seats only. All the compartments have fans. Sexes are separated in 1st and 2nd class unless you book the whole compartment or (in 2nd class) unless you are two couples. Third class can get a little wearing on the nerves on long journeys especially if they are overnight (which most are). Second class is more than adequate in this respect and 1st class is definitely a touch of luxury as far as budget travel goes.

You must book in advance for both 1st and 2nd class – two to three days is usually sufficient – otherwise you'll probably find that there are no berths available and you will have to go 3rd class. If you're in Malindi and planning on taking the Mombasa to Nairobi train you can book in Malindi at a certain travel agent (see Malindi for details). Compartment and berth numbers are posted up about half an hour prior to departure. Bedding (clean sheets, pillow and blanket) is available for KSh 25 if you don't have a sleeping bag – attendants will come round to ask you if you want bedding before the train departs.

There is a dining car on most trains offering dinner and breakfast (two sittings). Dinner on the Nairobi to Mombasa or Mombasa to Nairobi runs is an East African experience you should not miss at any price but try to get into the second sitting as you can hang around afterwards and continue your conversation. The food is excellent, plentiful and goes through four courses on starched white linen with silver-plated cutlery and served by immaculately dressed waiters. Dinner costs just KSh 60 and breakfast KSh 35.

Nairobi to Mombasa
Trains run daily in either direction at 5 pm and 7 pm. The journey takes about 13 hours. The fares are: 1st class – KSh 340; 2nd class – KSh 145; 3rd class – KSh 62.

Nairobi to Malaba
There are trains on Tuesday, Friday and Saturday at 3 pm arriving at 8.30 am the next day. In the opposite direction they depart Malaba on Wednesday, Saturday and Sunday at 4 pm and arrive at 9.30 am the next day. The fares are: 1st class – KSh 356; 2nd class – KSh 152; 3rd class – KSh 65.

Nairobi to Kisumu
Trains leave daily at 6 pm arriving in Kisumu at 8 am the next day. In the opposite direction it is daily at 6.30 pm

arriving at Nairobi at 7.35 am the next day. Depending on demand there is usually an additional train ('express') at 5.30 pm from Nairobi daily for the first week of every month (and sometimes for the second week too) which arrives at Kisumu at 6 am the next day. The fares are: 1st class – KSh 254; 2nd class – KSh 108; 3rd class – KSh 47. As a rule, the carriages used on the Kisumu run are older than those used on the Nairobi to Mombasa run and so not such good value.

Voi to Taveta

There are passenger services on Wednesday and Saturday only. They depart Voi at 5 am and arrive Taveta at 9.50 am. In the opposite direction they depart Taveta at 2.30 pm and arrive Voi at 7.10 pm.

BOAT
Lake Victoria Ferries

Ferries service ports on the small Kenyan part of the lake and others connect Kisumu with the Tanzanian ports of Musoma, Mwanza and Bukoba.

Kisumu to Kendu Bay & Homa Bay These boats depart Kisumu daily except Thursday at 9 am and take four hours to get to Homa Bay via Kendu Bay. The ferries do not always return to Kisumu the same day so you may have to stay in Homa Bay overnight. Make enquiries before setting off. The fares are KSh 19 to Kendu Bay and KSh 24 to Homa Bay.

Kisumu to Musoma, Mwanza & Bukoba The MV *Bukoba* connects all these ports on Lake Victoria. It's operated by Tanzanian Railways Corporation so all on-board services have to be paid for in Tanzanian shillings. It may also be possible to pay for the fare in Tanzanian shillings (rather than Kenyan shillings) by paying on the boat. (It would work out much cheaper this way assuming you bought your Tanzanian shillings on the street market (US$1 buys TSh 160 as opposed to the official rate of about TSh 85.) There's no need to book in advance as there are few passengers between Kisumu and Musoma. The boat schedule is given below and the fares are: Kisumu to Mwanza – TSh 571 (1st class); TSh 453 (2nd class); TSh 206 (3rd class). First class is a cabin with four bunks on the top deck; 2nd class is a cabin with four bunks on the lower deck, and 3rd class is wooden benches only.

There are usually few passengers between Kisumu and Musoma, so 3rd class would be adequate if you have your own bedding since by the time you reach Musoma it will be daylight. Meals are available on the boat for TSh 80 (main course only) and TSh 150 (three course meal). They're not exactly cordon bleu but they're not bad either.

In the past, it used to be necessary to visit Kenyan immigration in Kisumu (Alpha House, Oginga Odinga Rd) before boarding the boat. This may have changed now with all formalities completed in the

day	port	arrive	depart
Monday	Mwanza		9.00 am
Tuesday	Musoma	6.00 am	9.00 pm
Wednesday	Mwanza	6.00 am	-
Thursday	Mwanza		9.00 am
Thursday	Musoma	7.00 pm	9.00 pm
Friday	Kisumu	6.00 am	9.00 pm
Saturday	Musoma	6.00 am	9.00 am
Saturday	Mwanza	6.00 pm	9.00 pm
Sunday	Bukoba	7.00 am	9.00 pm
Monday	Mwanza	7.00 am	

customs building just inside the port entry gate.

Dhows

Sailing on a dhow along the East African coast is one of Kenya's most worthwhile and memorable experiences. There's nothing quite like drifting over the ocean in the middle of the night with the moon up high, the only sounds being the lapping of the waves against the side of the boat and the occasional subdued conversation. But it's enjoyable at any time of day even when the breeze drops and the boat virtually comes to a standstill. There are no creature comforts aboard these dhows so when night comes you simply bed down wherever there is space and you won't be in the way of the crew when they have to turn the sail around. You'll probably get off these boats smelling, to a greater or lesser degree, of fish since fish oil is used to condition the timbers of the boat – nothing that a shower won't remove! Take drinking water and some food with you, though fish is usually caught on the way and cooked up on deck over charcoal.

Lamu is one of the best places to pick up a dhow and many people take them down to Mombasa – a journey of one night and two days on average. Prices vary according to your negotiating powers but should be around KSh 140 to KSh 150 including fish meals. Before you set off you need to get permission from the District Commissioner (on the harbour front close to the post office and opposite the main quay). It's best if you can persuade the captain of the dhow to take you along and guide you through the formalities. It shouldn't take more than 1½ hours in that case. Usually they will do this without charging but be prepared to pay if the captain is unwilling.

It's also possible to find dhows in Lamu going up the coast to Kiunga (about 18 km from the Somali border) and even to Chiamboni (just over the border – you'd need a Somali visa for this). There are very few onward connections going north from Chiamboni, however. Dhows to Kisimayo and Mogadishu are very infrequent and you would have to wait a long time before finding one. If this is where you'd like to go, ask Mr Mwanjala at the customs office in Lamu if he knows of anyone going that way.

There is also a fairly regular schooner, the *El Mansur*, captained by Omar Baqshweni, which sails to Kisimayo. It's a three-day trip and costs KSh 600 including food. The return trip costs SSh 600 (making it much cheaper). You sleep on deck.

TO/FROM SOMALIA

By air, there are flights twice a week in either direction between Nairobi and Mogadishu, one by Somali Airlines and the other by Kenya Airways. The fare is KSh 1638 one-way and KSh 2839 return. Don't put anything of value into your hold luggage as it will probably have disappeared by the time you get your luggage in Mogadishu. The baggage handlers there are notorious for their light fingers.

At least two light planes fly into Liboi daily from Nairobi, drop their load and return – always empty. It's relatively easy to hitch a ride with them and it's usually free but you must be at the airstrip because they don't hang around very long. Picking up these planes in Nairobi to fly to Liboi is much more difficult.

By road, the first part of the journey involves taking a bus from Nairobi to Garissa (details in the Road section). The best place to stay overnight in Garissa is the *Garissa Highlife Lodging*, Mosque St, which costs KSh 50 a double and has a good restaurant. There are other hotels if this one is full. There are buses from Garissa to Liboi (the border village) from the Mobil station on the road out of town to the north at 9 am on Tuesday, Thursday and Saturday. In the opposite direction it is Wednesday, Friday and Sunday. The actual departure time depends on when the military escort is ready. The bus costs KSh 70 and takes about six hours. It's also fairly easy to hitch since a lot of government vehicles cover this route and they frequently have spare seats. Lifts are often free. When you get to Liboi you must report to the police. The immigration official here can be tiring.

The only place to stay in Liboi is the *Cairo Hotel*. Somali shillings can be bought at this hotel. The next morning, very early, a bus will take you to the Somali Liboi (about 20 km) and from there to Kisimayo there is usually one bus per day in either direction. The fare is SSh 300 (plus a small baggage charge) and the trip takes about 10 hours. The 'road' is just a sand track through the scrub and there are numerous security checks which involve baggage searches and document checks. They're mainly concerned with Somalis smuggling goods in from Kenya and don't normally hassle western travellers. Make sure you ask for a currency declaration form at the Somali border. Banks won't change money without one so you'll have to go chasing around town to get one.

Don't forget the possibility of the schooner from Lamu to Kisimayo mentioned in the Dhow section.

TO/FROM SUDAN

The civil war in Sudan is now in full swing again and this has put the whole southern part of the country virtually off-limits to overland travel. Moreover, you'd be very foolish to attempt it even with official permission from the Sudanese authorities (which you won't get). The only way to get to Sudan from either Kenya or Uganda at present is to fly either to Juba or Khartoum. If you fly into Juba you'll have to fly out again as it's virtually the only enclave in the south still controlled by the central government.

TO/FROM TANZANIA

There are several points of entry into Tanzania but the main overland routes are from Nairobi to Arusha via Namanga and from Mombasa to Tanga or Dar es Salaam via Lunga Lunga. Other lesser used routes are from Kisii to Musoma via Isebania in the north-west and Voi to Moshi via Taveta.

There are international buses by several different companies from Nairobi to Arusha and Dar es Salaam, and from Mombasa to Tanga and Dar es Salaam. Companies covering these routes include Goldline, Rombo Investments and Hood from Nairobi, and Goldline and Hood from Mombasa. Rombo and Hood share both routes on alternate days and both have offices in Nairobi on Accra Rd. Hood is sometimes known as the Cat Bus. The buses depart Nairobi at 9 am, arrive Moshi at 6 pm and Dar es Salaam the following morning. Nairobi to Dar costs KSh 345. To Arusha costs between KSh 100 and KSh 120 depending on the company.

Taking an international bus, however, is an expensive way of getting to Tanzania. You can save quite a lot of money by doing the journey in stages and changing at the border. It won't take much longer either if you are only going as far as Arusha (from Nairobi) or Tanga (from Mombasa). Both Namanga and Lunga Lunga are easy-going borders which you can get through in less than half an hour. You might be subjected to a cursory baggage search on the Tanzanian side but currency declaration forms are treated as waste paper.

From Nairobi there are frequent buses, *matatus* and shared taxis to Namanga. Buses cost KSh 30 but they take up to four hours. It's much more convenient to take a shared taxi from East African Road Services at the bottom of Ronald Ngala St. They cost KSh 50 but take only two hours (five passengers per car). From the Tanzanian side of the border there are frequent buses (TSh 60), *matatus* (TSh 150) and shared taxis to Arusha which take less than two hours.

The two border posts are right next to each other at Namanga so, assuming there are no delays at the border, you can be in Arusha about 4½ hours after leaving Nairobi.

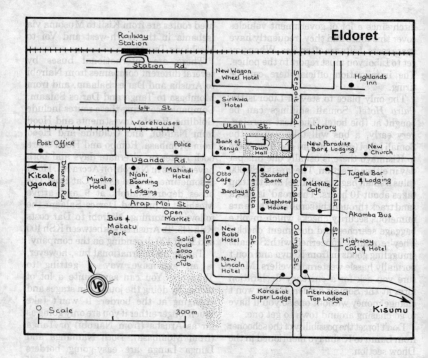

Similarly, there are frequent buses (KSh 30), *matatus* and shared taxis from the southern side of the Likoni ferry in Mombasa to Lunga Lunga which take about 1½ hours. From there you can pick up *matatus* or shared taxis to Tanga for TSh 100 which take about one hour. There is a six km gap between the Kenyan and Tanzanian border posts at Lunga Lunga. If you get there early enough in the day there will be pick-ups available to transport you between the two posts. Later on in the day you may have to hitch.

Likewise, there's usually plenty of transport if you're crossing the border between Voi and Moshi but up in the north between Kisii and Musoma you may get stuck and have to do a considerable amount of walking.

TO/FROM UGANDA

The two crossing points into Uganda are Malaba and Busia. The former is the most popular but it's just as easy to cross the border at Busia. There is a choice of train (three times per week) or bus/*matatu* (daily) from Nairobi, Nakuru, Eldoret to Malaba. From the Kenyan border post it is about one km to the Ugandan post and you will have to walk (no transport). Both border posts are very easy-going though there may be a very cursory baggage search at Ugandan customs. You also have to visit the currency declaration office (see the Money section in the Uganda chapter for details). There are frequent daily *matatus* from the border to Tororo (KSh 600, less than one hour) and to Jinja and Kampala (KSh 900, about 3½ hours).

If your starting point in Kenya is Kisumu then Busia is your nearest border post. There are frequent *matatus* to Busia and others from there to Jinja and Kampala (bypassing Tororo).

Around the Country

ELDORET

Eldoret is a small railway junction town on the main road between Nairobi and the Ugandan border, set among fertile rolling hills north of Lake Victoria. Numerous different crops are produced in this area and are brought here for distribution. If heading for Lodwar on the western side of Lake Turkana, you may have to spend a night here.

Places to Stay

Probably the cheapest place to stay is the *African Inland Church Training & Conference Centre* but it's about half an hour's walk out of town on the Kisumu Rd. You can get a single room for KSh 30. There are no double rooms but they will usually allow two people to share a single room. Hot showers are available.

In town itself, there isn't a great choice of decent budget hotels. The *New Paradise Bar & Lodging, Mayfair Board & Lodging* and the *International Top Lodge* are really just brothels and are very basic, scruffy and noisy. The *Highway Cafe & Hotel* and the *Korosiot Super Lodge* aren't much better either though tolerable as is the *Keringet Hotel* at KSh 50 a double.

If you can't handle these places try the *Miyako Hotel*, close to the bus and *matatu* park. Rooms cost KSh 80 a single without a bathroom, KSh 100/120 for a single/double with bathroom. It's a clean place and the hotel has a bar and restaurant. Slightly better but often full is the *New Lincoln Hotel*, Oloo St, where the rooms surround a shady courtyard and beer garden. Rooms cost KSh 97/171 for a single/double both with bathroom and breakfast. The hotel has a bar and

restaurant. Also very good value in this range is the *Mahindi Hotel*, Uganda Rd, which costs KSh 80 a single without bathroom and KSh 100/140 for a single/ double with bathroom. It's a large place so there is usually room. The hotel has its own restaurant.

A delightful place to stay if you have the money is the *New Wagon Wheel Hotel*, Oloo St. It's a huge, old, rambling, colonial-style wooden building with a large verandah and beer garden and is popular with African travellers. The rooms are in a separate wing to the bar so there are no problems about noise. It costs KSh 98/171 for a single/double without bathroom and KSh 116/195 for a single/ double with bathroom. The beds are comfortable, the rooms secure and the staff friendly. There's hot water 24 hours a day, with soap and towels provided. The prices include a substantial cooked breakfast. Lunch and dinner are available at very reasonable prices (large, tasty portions of keema curry, rice and salad cost KSh 36). The hotel has one of the liveliest bars in town.

Places to Eat

If you're not eating at one of the hotels there are two good restaurants in Eldoret. Very popular at lunch times is the *Remember Otto Café*, Uganda Rd opposite the Bank of Kenya. It offers good, cheap, western-style meals such as steak, chicken, sausages, eggs, chips and other snacks. Also very popular is the *Mid-Nite Café/Mid-Nite Cave*, Oginga Odinga St. It offers good, cheap food and has tables outside as well as inside. It's a popular bar outside meal times.

ISIOLO

Isiolo is north of Mt Kenya on the road to Marsabit and Moyale and is close to both the Buffalo Springs and Shaba National Game Reserves. This is where the tarmac ends and the gravel begins if you are heading north. There are buses to Marsabit three times per week but none to

Loyangalani or the small towns en route. If you're taking the latter route you will have to hitch. There's a colourful **market** and you will come across many Samburu and Turkana tribespeople. Good quality copper and steel items, as well as copper, steel and brass bracelets can be bought. There is a bank (Barclays) and two petrol stations.

Places to Stay & Eat

The *Jamhuri Guest House* is one of the best places to stay and has been recommended by many travellers. It's at the back of Barclays Bank on the street parallel to the main street. It costs KSh 50 a double, mosquito nets, soap and towels are provided, there are hot showers and it's very clean.

Two other good hotels are the *Highway Lodge* and the *Al Hilal Hotel* which both cost KSh 30 a single. They are on the main street as are the *National Hotel* (where the Akamba buses stop), the *Frontier Lodge*, the *Tawakal Hotel Boarding & Lodging*, the *Isiolo Hotel* and the very small *Coffee Tree Hotel*.

KISUMU

Kisumu is Kenya's main port on Lake Victoria and a rail head which is connected to the rest of the Kenyan system via Nakuru. It's a hot, steamy town but pleasant all the same. It is strongly Asian-influenced especially by those Muslims who are followers of the Aga Khan – there are schools, a hospital, a community centre and a mosque all bearing his name.

Information

The immigration office is in Alpha House, Oginga Odinga Rd. It may be necessary to visit it if you are taking the Lake Victoria ferry to Tanzania.

The British Council, Oginga Odinga Rd close to the junction with Jomo Kenyatta Highway, has a good library with current magazines and periodicals.

The train reservations office is open daily from 8 am to 12 noon and 2 to 4 pm.

Things to See

The **Kisumu Museum**, about 15 minutes' walk up Jomo Kenyatta Highway on the way to Eldoret, is one of the best in Kenya and worth a visit. It has the usual natural history displays plus a life-size recreation of a tribal homestead with six mud and grass huts, an aquarium, a snake pit and the inevitable compound of copulating tortoises. Entry is KSh 20.

Places to Stay

There's a very good choice of pleasant budget hotels in Kisumu. The *Sikh Temple* on Mosque Rd will still take travellers for the night. Leave a donation. Otherwise, one of the cheapest is the *YWCA*, on the corner of Omolo Agar Rd and Nairobi Rd. It takes both men and women and costs KSh 35 per person in triple-bedded rooms plus KSh 20 per day temporary membership. Breakfast is available.

If you want your own room the *New Rozy Lodge*, Ogada St, is excellent value at KSh 55/75 a single/double. It's small, very pleasant, clean, the staff are friendly and it has hot water. If it's full, try the *Kisumu Lodge* next door. Another place worth checking in this price range is the *Mirukas Lodge*, Apindi St, which costs KSh 52/65/98 a single/double/triple but it's not as good as the two previous places.

At the very bottom end of the market, mostly along Accra St, are the usual collection of brothels and noisy bars where you can find a room for less (though not always), but the facilities are very primitive and no-one is in a hurry to clean them. They include the rough *Sam's Hotel* at KSh 50/60 for a single/double. Others are the *New Clean PVU Hotel* (!), the *Farid Hotel*, the *Mazamil Lodge* and the *Tivoli Boarding & Lodging*. You'd have to be desperate or of a particular proclivity to want to stay in most of them.

Going up slightly in price the *Razbi Guest House*, on the corner of Kondu Lane and Oginga Odinga Rd, is popular with Peace Corps volunteers and costs KSh 60/100 for a single/double and KSh 200 for a room with four beds. It's very clean, secure, friendly and there's hot water. A towel and soap are provided in each room. Breakfast is available if you want it. The very similar *Mona Lisa Boarding & Lodging*, Oginga Odinga Rd is also very clean, pleasant and friendly and has hot water. Rooms are KSh 75/105 for a single/double.

If you're looking for a mid-range hotel try the very pleasant *Lake View Hotel*, Kondu Lane, where rooms in the front wing have views over Lake Victoria. It costs KSh 100/187 for a single/double including breakfast. There is a bar and restaurant on the ground floor. The *New Victoria Hotel* costs KSh 220/285 for a double/triple including a substantial breakfast. All the rooms have a bathroom and most have a balcony. The hotel has a restaurant but no bar since it's Muslim-owned.

The *Black & Black Boarding & Lodging*, Accra Rd, is slightly cheaper at KSh 92/138 for a single/double with breakfast and is relatively good value.

Places to Eat
There are several restaurants which have good food at reasonable prices. Most are open for both lunch and dinner but others for only one or the other. They include the *Mona Lisa Restaurant* and the *New Victoria Hotel*. The New Victoria offers fruit juice, fruit, two eggs and sausage, toast and butter, tea or coffee for breakfast and also serves lunch and dinner. The food is good and tasty though the atmosphere is subdued.

Much livelier is the *Octopus Club*, Ogada St, where you can eat and drink either on the verandah overlooking the street or inside. Those suffering withdrawal symptoms from fast food, hamburgers and the like should get along to *Wimpy*, on the corner of Jomo Kenyatta Highway and Anaawa Ave. It's a fairly pleasant place to have a snack or meal and you can sit either inside or outside. For a splurge, give Kisumu's only Chinese restaurant a go. This is the *Katai Restaurant* next to the Flamingo Casino & Disco, Jomo Kenyatta Highway. It's only open in the evenings.

KITALE
Kitale, like Eldoret, is set in fertile, rolling hills and the area around it is intensively cultivated. It's a jumping-off point for a visit to the west side of Lake Turkana and Mt Elgon (4321 metres) which is visible to the west of town straddling the border between Kenya and Uganda.

Things to See
The **Museum of Western Kenya** is worth a visit and is open daily from 9.30 am to 6 pm. Entry costs KSh 10. There are displays of stuffed animals' heads and skulls and an ethnology section (Pokot, Turkana and Nandi). Perhaps the most enjoyable parts of the museum are the nature trail through a remnant of rainforest at the rear, and the compound full of copulating tortoises. There's also a craft shop.

To explore the **Mt Elgon** region you first need to get to Endebess, west of Kitale. There was, at one time, a lodge and camping site in the Mt Elgon National Reserve but it has apparently been closed for a number of years so make enquiries before you set off. The best place to do this is at the Youth Hostel in Kitale (the police in Kitale know very little about what is going on there).

Places to Stay
Blue Skies Farm (or Blue Skies Shamba) used to be a youth hostel and you can still camp there for KSh 15 per person per night. There are hardly any facilities and you need to bring your own food. It's about 10 km outside Kitale on the Eldoret road.

Sirikwa Campsite & Safaris is a better

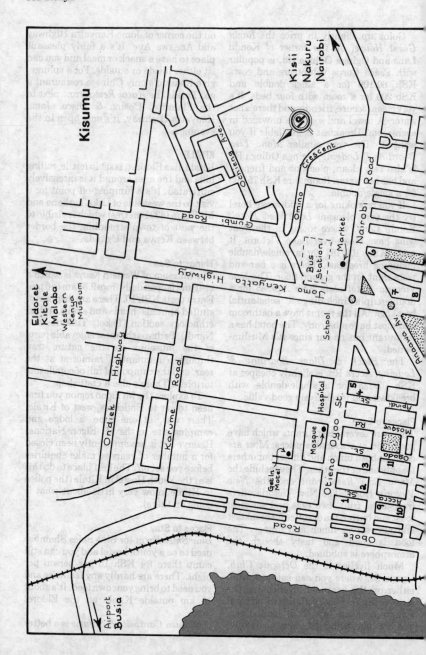

Kisumu

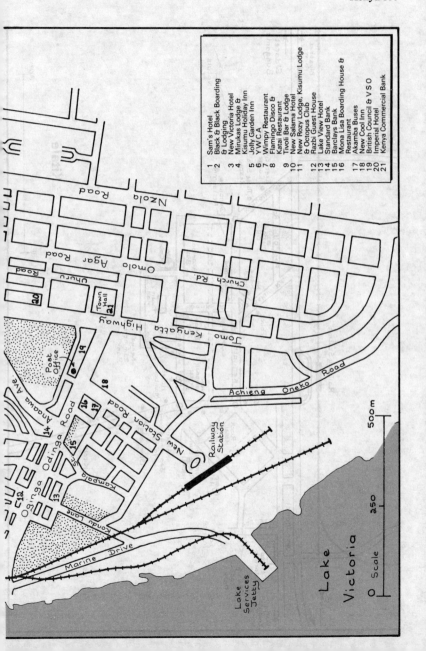

1 Sam's Hotel
2 Black & Black Boarding
   & Lodging
3 New Victoria Hotel
4 Mirukas Lodge &
   Kisumu Holiday Inn
5 Jolly Garden Inn
6 YWCA
7 Wimpy Restaurant
8 Flamingo Disco &
   Katai Restaurant
9 Tivoli Bar & Lodge
10 New Salama Hotel
11 New Rozy Lodge, Kisumu Lodge
   & Octopus Club
12 Razbi Guest House
13 Lake View Hotel
14 Standard Bank
15 Barclays Bank
16 Mona Lisa Boarding House &
   Restaurant
17 Akamba Buses
18 New Cool Inn
19 British Council & VSO
20 Imperial Hotel
21 Kenya Commercial Bank

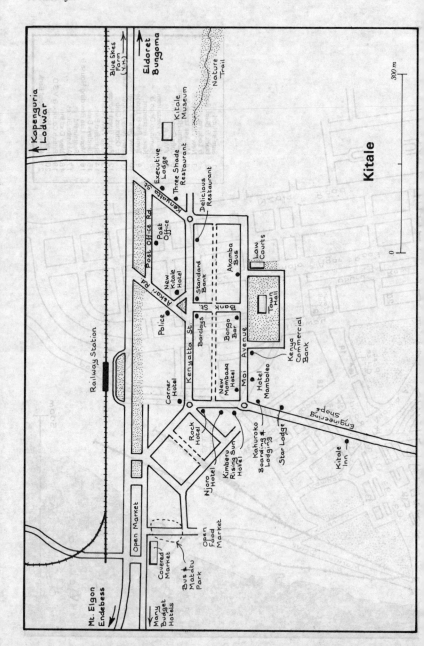

Kitale

place to camp. Camping with your own tent costs KSh 35 per person per night plus they have tents for hire at KSh 60 per person. There are hot showers, flush toilets, food is available and it's a beautiful site. The Barnsley family who run it are friendly and hospitable. Take a *matatu* there, it's several km out of town on the road to Lodwar.

In Kitale itself the pleasant *Star Lodge* has hot water and costs KSh 35/51 for a single/double without a bathroom. The *Rock Hotel* has hot water in the mornings only and costs KSh 35/70 for a single/double without a bathroom. It's pretty scruffy and the bar can be noisy. The *Njoro Hotel* and the *Kimberu Rising Sun Hotel* are similar in quality.

There are plenty of other budget hotels up the rise past the bus station and covered market, including the *Balima Boarding & Lodging*, the *Salama Boarding & Lodging*, the *Bismaliha Hotel*, the *Safari Hotel* and the *Wananchi Hotel*. They're all rock-bottom establishments and there's not much to choose between them.

Excellent value is the *Kahuroko Boarding & Lodging* which offers very pleasant rooms with bathrooms (shower and toilet) on the 1st floor at KSh 65 for a room with one bed (one or two people) and KSh 120 for a room with two beds. The bed in the cheaper rooms is large enough for two people. It's very clean and your gear is safe. There's a bar and restaurant downstairs with traditional African fare.

Two mid-range hotels to try if the Kahuroko is full are the *Hotel Mamboleo*, Moi Ave, and the *Executive Lodge*, Kenyatta St.

Places to Eat

The most popular place to eat is the *Bongo Bar* at the junction of Moi Ave and Bank St which does both lunches and dinners (Indian and western-style dishes). You have to get there early if you want a reasonable choice of dishes in the evening as there'll be very little left by 8 pm. This restaurant actually consists of three parts – a restaurant, a takeaway counter for chips (French fries) and a bar. The food isn't bad but it's not exceptional.

Two other places you might like to try for a reasonably priced meal are the *Delicious Restaurant* and the *Three Shade Restaurant*, both on Kenyatta St. For a splurge, try a lunch or dinner at the *New Kitale Hotel*, a colonial-style watering hole.

LAMU

In the early 1970s Lamu acquired a reputation as the Kathmandu of Africa – a place of fantasy, mystery and otherworldliness. It inevitably drew all self-respecting seekers of the miraculous, globe-trotters and that now much maligned and supposedly drug, sex and rock'n'roll-crazed bunch of people called hippies. The attraction was obvious. Both Kathmandu and Lamu were remote, unique and fascinating self-contained societies which had somehow escaped the depredations of the 20th century with their culture, their centuries-old way of life and architecture intact.

Though Kathmandu is now over-run with well-heeled tourists, Lamu remains much the same as it has always been. Access is either by diesel-powered launch from the mainland or from the airport on Manda Island and the only motor vehicle is the district commissioner's Land Rover. In Lamu you either sail a dhow, walk or ride a donkey. The streets are far too narrow and winding in any case, to accommodate anything other than pedestrians or donkeys.

Swahili Islamic culture is still alive and well. Local festivals take place as though nothing has ever changed. The beach at Shela is still magnificent and uncluttered, and little happens in a hurry. Lamu is one of the most relaxing places you will ever have the pleasure to visit. No other Swahili town can offer you such an uninterrupted tradition and an undisturbed traditional style of architecture (though the old stone town of Zanzibar might come close).

The town dates back to at least the late 14th century when the Pwani Mosque was built. Most of the other buildings date from the 18th century but the lower parts and basements are often considerably older. The streets are narrow, cool and quiet, and there are many small 'squares' and intimate spaces enclosed by tall coral rag walls.

One of the most outstanding features of the houses, as in old Zanzibar, are the intricately carved doors and lintels which have kept generations of carpenters busy. Sadly, many of them have disappeared in recent years but there is now an active conservation movement which should prevent further losses. In any case, the skill has not been lost. Walk down to the far end of the harbour front in Lamu in the opposite direction to Shela and you'll see them being made.

If you want more information on the history and culture of Lamu there are some excellent books available. The best general account is to be found in *The Portuguese Period in East Africa*, Justus Strandes (East African Literature Bureau, Nairobi, 1971). This is a translation of a book originally published in German in 1899 with up-to-date notes and appendices detailing recent archaeological findings.

Lamu: A Study of the Swahili Town, Usam Ghaidan (East African Literature Bureau, Nairobi, 1975), is a very detailed study of Lamu itself by an Iraqi who was formerly a lecturer in architecture at the University of Nairobi. Both of them can be found in most good bookshops in Nairobi or Mombasa. The second is also available at the museum in Lamu.

Information

Bank The Standard Chartered Bank on the harbour front is the only bank in Lamu. It's open Monday to Friday from 8.30 am to 1 pm and Saturday from 8.30 to 11 am. In the low season, cashing a cheque can take as little as half an hour but in the high season it can take considerably longer.

Buses The bus companies (Tana River Bus Co, Lamy Bus and Tawakal Bus Co) which service the Lamu, Malindi, Mombasa route all have offices in Lamu so you can book tickets in advance.

Ferries There are frequent ferries between Lamu and the bus terminus on the mainland (Mokowe). The fare is KSh 5. Likewise there are ferries between Lamu and Manda Island which connect with flights to and from the airstrip there.

Things to See & Do

For an excellent introduction to the culture and history of Lamu you should put aside two hours or so for the **Lamu Museum** on the waterfront next to Petley's Inn. It's one of the most interesting small museums in Kenya. There's a reconstruction of a traditional Swahili house, charts, maps, ethnology displays, model dhows and two examples of the remarkable and ornately-carved ivory *siwa* – a wind instrument peculiar to the coastal region which is often used as a fanfare at weddings. Entry costs KSh 30. There's also a good bookshop.

If you find the museum interesting you should also visit their **Swahili House** (see map) which was restored by the National Museum of Kenya. It provides visitors with a rare opportunity to see inside a traditional home.

You'll see many dhows anchored off the harbour front at the south end of town but to see them being built or repaired visit the **Shela** or **Matondoni** villages. The latter is perhaps the best place to see this and you have a choice of walking (about two hours) or hiring a dhow to sail there. If you choose the dhow it will cost KSh 150 to KSh 200 for the boat (so you need a small group together to share the cost) but it usually includes a barbequed fish lunch.

If you want to walk, leave the main

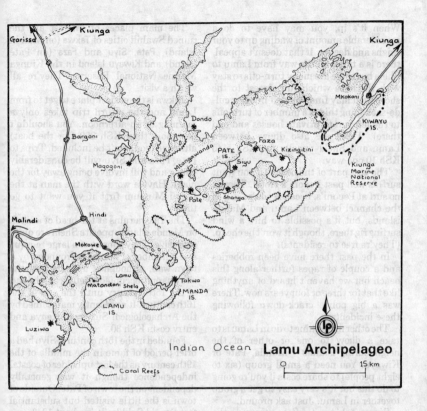

Lamu Archipelago

0   15 km

street of Lamu up the alleyway by the side of Kenya Cold Drinks and continue in as straight a line as possible to the back end of town. From here a well-defined track leads out into the country. You pass a football pitch on the right hand side after 100 metres. Follow the touch line of the pitch and continue in the same direction past the paddock/garden on the left hand side then turn left onto another track. This is the one to Matondoni. The football pitch has telephone wires running above it. These go to Matondoni and they're almost always visible from the track so if you follow them you can't go wrong. If you don't cut across the football pitch you'll head off into the middle of nowhere and probably get lost – although this can be interesting (old houses, wells, goats, etc).

Set off early if you are walking. It gets very hot later in the day. There are no cafés in Matondoni but if you ask around tea and mandazi usually turn up. There's also nowhere to stay unless you can arrange bed or floor space in a private house.

The **beach** is just past Shela village, a 40-minute walk from Lamu. To get there, follow the harbour front road till it ends then follow the shore line. You will pass a new hospital built by the Saudi Arabian government and a ginning factory before you get to Shela. If the tide is out, you can walk along the beach most of the way.

When it's in, you may have to do a considerable amount of wading up to your thighs and deeper. If that doesn't appeal, there is a track all the way from Lamu to Shela but there are many turn-offs so stay with the ones which run closest to the shore (you may find yourself in a few cul-de-sacs doing this as a number of turn-offs to the left run to private houses and end there). There are also dhows between Lamu and Shela usually for KSh 5 to KSh 10 one-way.

The best part of the beach (if you want surf) is well past Peponi's Hotel. There's no surf at Peponi's, because you're still in the channel between Lamu and Manda islands, but it's possible to hire a wind surfing rig there, though it won't be cheap. (They're free to residents).

In the past there have been robberies and a couple of rapes further along this beach but we haven't heard of anything like that for three or four years now. There was a big police crack-down following these incidents.

The other main thing to do in Lamu is to take a **dhow** to one or other of the neighbouring islands – Manda, Paté or Kiwayu. You need a small group (six to eight people) to share costs if you're going to do this but it's very easy to get a group together in Lamu. Just ask around.

Since taking tourists around the archipelago is one of the easiest ways of making money for dhow owners in Lamu, there's a lot of competition and you'll be asked constantly by different people if you want to go on a trip. You'll also see many notices in the cafés to the same effect. You must bargain hard since many people will try to charge you as much as they think you will pay. You'll come across people who paid KSh 200 and others who paid KSh 400 for the same trip. Don't take the first offer unless it's a particularly good one and check if food is included. Dhow trips are usually superb whoever you go with so it's impossible to make specific recommendations about boats or boatpeople.

The main places of interest are the ruined Swahili cities of **Takwa** (on Manda Island), **Paté**, **Siyu** and **Faza** (on Paté Island) and **Kiwayu Island** in the Kiunga Marine National Reserve. They're all worth a visit.

Takwa is the easiest place to get to from Lamu and the return trip takes only a morning or an afternoon. You shouldn't pay more than KSh 200 (for the boat) although food won't be included. Trips to Paté, Faza and Siyu will be considerably longer and will involve being away for the night. Have a word with the man at the Lamu Museum first if you want to go there.

The Takwa ruins at the head of a creek on Manda island opposite Shela are quite extensive. They consist of a large mosque and a number of houses surrounded by a town wall, although it appears that the site was only occupied briefly from the end of the 15th century until the end of the 16th century. It's presently maintained by the Archaeological Survey of Kenya and entry costs KSh 30.

Founded in the 15th century, Siyu had a brief period of fame in the middle of the 19th century as the last upholder of coastal independence though it was generally dependent on the town of Paté. Outside of town is the little visited but substantial fort Seyyid Said built in about 1843.

Faza has had a chequered history. It dates back to at least the 13th century although it has been destroyed and refounded several times since then.

The origins of Paté are disputed. There are claims that it was founded in the 8th century by refugees from Oman, but recent excavations have produced nothing earlier than the 15th century. It's decline set in after the ruling family were driven out by Seyyid Majid in 1865 to set up the short-lived Sultanate of Witu on the mainland. A number of interesting buildings remain, including the gate through the former city wall, the palace and several mosques.

The other place of interest, Kiwayu

Island in the Marine National Reserve, is a two-day, one-night trip which will cost about KSh 200 per person including food. Contact a man called Saidi at the Hapahapa Restaurant after 8 pm any day. The coral reefs off the island are one of the best places to go snorkelling on the whole Kenyan coast. The variety of marine life is incredible but few people get to see it.

Places to Stay

Lamu has been catering for budget travellers for well over a decade and there's a good choice of simple, rustic lodges, rooftops and private houses to rent. Don't believe a word anyone tells you about there being running water 24 hours a day at any of these places. There isn't. Water is not an abundant commodity on Lamu and restrictions are in force most of the year. It's usually only available early in the morning and early in the evening which, in most cases, means bucket showers only and somewhat smelly toilets. The prices are all very similar – KSh 25 to KSh 35 a single and KSh 50 to KSh 70 a double – though they may go up a little in the high season (August and September). If a lodge is full when you arrive but you like it a lot and want to be first in line for a room, they'll usually let you sleep on the roof or elsewhere for about KSh 15 per person.

Where you stay will probably depend largely on what sort of room you are offered and who meets you getting off the ferry from the mainland. Most of the young men who meet the ferries have no connection with any of the lodges other than the hope of a tip (from travellers) or a small commission (from the hotel management). Some of them can be very insistent.

Some of the popular lodges include the *Dhow Lodge*, *Pole Pole Guest House* and *Kisiwani Lodge* all of which are owned by Ali who was once a DJ in Mombasa. He has a good collection of contemporary music. All his lodges have a fridge, cooker for the use of residents, showers (when available) and toilet paper. The Dhow Lodge has a small library. However, one traveller warns of Ali's overcharging for rooms, and of problems arising from booking boat trips or flights through him.

Also popular are the *Castle Lodge* which overlooks the main 'square' and the fortress and picks up sea breezes since it's fairly high up. The *Bahati Lodge* is similar. The *Full Moon Guest House* is right on the harbour front and a great place to stay if you can get one of the better rooms overlooking the harbour. It has an upstairs balcony which is an excellent place to relax and watch the activity below and the guest house has a restaurant (the Hapahapa). The *Beautiful House* likewise has rooms which overlook the harbour. *Kirundoni Lodge*, *Salama Lodge*, *Rainbow Guest House* and *Kodaro's Lodge* are also very popular. Other lodges – not necessarily second best – include the *Aroi Lodge*, *Mnazi Lodge* (but only if you can get a room on the top floor) and the *Masri Hotel*.

If you want slightly better accommodation than the bare essentials which those already mentioned offer try the *Lamu Guest House*. It's good value, clean and the water supply tends to be a little more reliable. It costs KSh 50/100 for a single/double although in the low season you can get a room for less if you negotiate.

The *New Maharus Hotel* (tel 1, 125) on the main 'square' overlooking the fortress has a range of rooms starting from KSh 179/250 for a single/double and going up to KSh 400/500. All prices include breakfast. There is a discount in the low season (April to the beginning of August). The water supply is fairly reliable since they store it in tanks during the times when it is turned on.

Other places in this price category include the very pleasant *Mlangilangi House* behind the fort with rooms at KSh 200 or the *Pool House*, which does indeed have a swimming pool and rooms at KSh 200 to KSh 300. *Yumbe House*

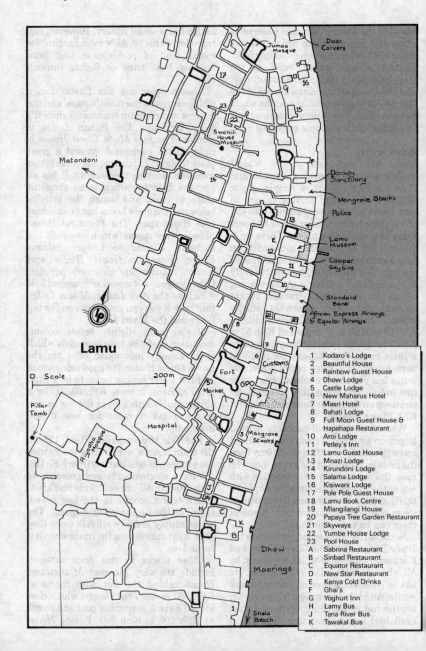

Matondoni

Jumaa Mosque

Door Carvers

Swahili House Museum

Donkey Sanctuary

Mangrove Stacks

Police

Lamu Museum

Cooper Skybird

Standard Bank

African Express Airways & Equator Airways

Lamu

Scale
0   200m

Pillar Tomb

Riyadha Mosque

Hospital

Fort

Market

Customs

GPO

Mangrove Stacks

Dhow Moorings

Shela Beach

1	Kodaro's Lodge
2	Beautiful House
3	Rainbow Guest House
4	Dhow Lodge
5	Castle Lodge
6	New Maharus Hotel
7	Masri Hotel
8	Bahati Lodge
9	Full Moon Guest House & Hapahapa Restaurant
10	Aroi Lodge
11	Petley's Inn
12	Lamu Guest House
13	Mnazi Lodge
14	Kirundoni Lodge
15	Salama Lodge
16	Kisiwani Lodge
17	Pole Pole Guest House
18	Lamu Book Centre
19	Mlangilangi House
20	Papaya Tree Garden Restaurant
21	Skyways
22	Yumbe House Lodge
23	Pool House
A	Sabrina Restaurant
B	Sinbad Restaurant
C	Equator Restaurant
D	New Star Restaurant
E	Kenya Cold Drinks
F	Ghai's
G	Yoghurt Inn
H	Lamy Bus
J	Tana River Bus
K	Tawakal Bus

Lodge, near the Swahili House Museum, costs KSh 280 to KSh 550 including breakfast.

The only top-range hotel in Lamu is Petley's Inn (tel 48) right on the harbour front next to the Lamu Museum. It has the sole bar in Lamu and it is open to nonresidents.

If you plan on staying in Lamu for a while it's worth making enquiries about renting a house. On a daily basis it won't be much cheaper (if at all) than staying at a lodge but on a monthly basis you are looking from KSh 5000 a month in the low season to twice that in the high season. You can share this with as many people as you feel comfortable with or have space for. They're available in Lamu town itself but also at Shela and between Lamu and Shela. Some of them can be excellent value and very spacious. You need to ask around and see what is available. It's possible to find some remarkably luxurious places especially around Shela.

Outside the town at Shela there are also lodges. They include the Samahane which costs KSh 50 a double (more in the high season) and has a good water supply and the Shela Guest House which will quote up to KSh 200 a double (bargain down from there). Both of these lodges will often quote whatever they think you might pay so you need to do some hard bargaining. They're no better than the lodges in Lamu itself but if the beach is your main draw it obviously makes sense to stay if you can get a room at a reasonable price.

Just beyond Shela, right on the beach, is Peponi's (tel 29). It's a three-star hotel with a grill and bar open to nonresidents.

Places to Eat

One of the cheapest places to eat in Lamu is the New Star Restaurant. You certainly won't beat the prices. Some people recommend it highly but others visit once never to return. Service is slow (depending on what you order and the time of day) and the menu is often an unbridled act of creativity. They have fried fish, fish & chips and salads (tomato salad with beans, cabbage and onion). They also have good yogurt. Similar in price is the Sabrina Restaurant which serves mainly Indian food for main courses and western breakfasts but they do offer very reasonably priced lobster, prawn and crab dishes. The staff are very friendly.

For consistently reliable good food at a reasonable price there are three very popular restaurants. The first is the Sindbad Restaurant (formerly the Olympic Restaurant) on the waterfront overlooking the dhow moorings. Here you can get pancakes with various fillings, grilled fish, salad and daily 'specials' which consist of soup, main course and fruit juice.

Another which has been famous for years is the Yoghurt Inn consisting of individual outside tables each with a grass roof and set in an attractive garden. It offers dishes like crab with cheese and chips, prawns or kebabs, grilled fish, barbequed lobster plus there are daily 'specials'. They also have (as you might expect) yogurt, lassi and banana pancakes with wild honey. The food is excellent and well-presented. It's open daily from 7 am to 9.30 pm except on Fridays when it's 7 am to 12 noon and 4 to 9.30 pm.

The Hapahapa Restaurant on the ground floor of the Full Moon Guest House is also very good and offers a similar range of dishes. You may also come across a man popularly called 'Ali Hippy' who, for several years now, has been offering travellers meals at his house. Quite a few people have recommended him.

For a splurge there are several places you can try. Ghai's on the waterfront next to the Donkey Sanctuary office is very well known. Ghai may be somewhat eccentric but he considers himself to be the best seafood cook on the island. He may well be right. The food is excellent and the service is impeccable. The price varies according to what you order.

Also excellent is the Equator Restaurant

which is usually only open in the evenings. It's run by a 'quaint English gentleman' (as one traveller described him) called Ron Partridge. The set-up is very relaxing (classical music and oldies) but it's *very* popular so book a table in advance if possible. It can be more expensive than Ghai's but it's well worth the little extra.

Lastly, there is, of course, the restaurant at *Petley's Inn*. There are actually two restaurants – the barbeque/ice cream garden across the alley from the main building and the restaurant proper which has both inside tables and others on the verandah overlooking the harbour. The prices of food ordered from the main menu are, as you might expect, high (although the cuisine is excellent) but you can also order much less expensive dishes from the barbeque across the alley (such as grilled lobster). If you eat in this restaurant you can drink as much ice-cold beer as you like (not the case in the bar).

For fruit juices and other cold drinks and snacks (such as samosas) make sure you pay at least one visit to *Kenya Cold Drinks* at the back of the Lamu Museum. It's been deservedly popular for years.

There are only two places (unless you get an invitation to the police canteen) where you can drink beer on Lamu island. One is *Petley's Inn* and the other is *Peponi's* at Shela. Petley's sports an English-style pub, the entrance to which is in the alley between the hotel and the barbeque garden opposite. It's a popular watering hole and open to nonresidents. The beer is often lukewarm (usually because of demand) and often 'runs out' around 9 pm. It doesn't actually 'run out' – it's just the hotel's way of rationing the supply so that they always have enough for their guests and those who eat in the restaurant.

Peponi's is a mandatory watering hole en route to or from Shela beach. The bar is on the verandah overlooking the channel and beach. Unlike Petley's, they don't seem to have problems of supply and you

can be guaranteed an ice-cold beer anytime of day.

For a meal outside of Lamu try the *Shela Guest House* at Shela right on the beach. They have fruit juices, yogurt and snacks as well as simple meals. For a splurge try the *BBQ Grill* at Peponi's which is open to nonresidents and offers delicious food. There's a choice of menu but the fish is superb.

MALINDI

Malindi is for sybarites, bacchanalians and beach lovers and rivals the coast north and south of Mombasa as Kenya's premier tourist resort. In many ways it's superior to the latter since it has developed from a town which existed before the tourist boom and so has a recognisable centre where commerce, business and everyday activities which aren't necessarily connected with the tourist trade still continue. Cotton growing and processing, sisal and fishing are still major income earners.

The beach at Malindi, too, is superior if you prefer surf with your ocean since there's a break in the coral reef at this point along the coast (sharks are not a problem). The absence of a coral reef also prevents the build up of seaweed which sometimes almost chokes the beaches north of Mombasa and Shelly beach just south of the city.

Information
Tourist Office There is a tourist office in Malindi past the Stardust Club but they don't have a lot of material.

Bank There are a number of banks. Barclays is open Monday to Friday from 8.30 am to 1 pm and 2.30 to 5 pm and on Saturday from 8.30 am to 12 noon.

Immigration There is an office next to the Juma Mosque and Pillar Tombs on the waterfront (see map).

Bicycle Rental You can rent bicycles from the Silversands booking agency on the top side of Uhuru Park. They cost KSh 10 for the first hour and KSh 6 for each subsequent hour or KSh 45 per day.

Train Bookings You can make advance reservations for Kenyan Railways at the travel agent in the shopping centre along the Lamu road (see map).

Warning Don't walk back to your hotel along the beach at night. Many people have been mugged at knife point. Go back along the main road (which has street lighting) or take a taxi. You also need to exercise caution if returning from the Baobab Café to the Youth Hostel late at night – people have even been mugged along that short stretch of road although you're probably safe if you're part of a group.

Things to See
The most popular excursion is to the **Malindi Marine National Park** to the south of town past Silversands. Here you can rent a glass-bottomed boat to take you out to the coral reef. Snorkelling gear is provided though there generally aren't enough sets for everyone all at the same time. The variety and colours of the coral and the fish are simply amazing and you'll be surprised how close you can get to the fish without alarming them.

The best time to go is at low tide when the water will be clear. It's advisable to wear a pair of canvas shoes or thongs for wading across the coral to where the boats are moored in case you step on a sea urchin or a stone fish. These are extremely well camouflaged and can inflict a very painful sting. The boat trips generally last an hour.

You can arrange these trips in Malindi – people come round the hotels to ask if you are interested in going. The usual price is KSh 90 to KSh 120 per person which includes a taxi to take you there and back from your hotel, hire of the boat and the

park entry fee. You may be able to get it for a little less if you bargain hard.

If you'd like to go scuba diving there's a dive shop at the Driftwood Club at Silversands. It costs KSh 400 per dive or KSh 450 if you go to Watamu, south of Malindi.

It's perhaps worth a visit to the **Vasco da Gama Cross** on the promontory at the end of the bay and on the way you can drop into the **Portuguese Church** just past the Baobab Café. On the south-east corner of the church a painting of a crucifixion is still faintly visible.

There are many **craft shops** which line both sides of the road between Uhuru Park and the post office. Prices are reasonable (though you must bargain) and the quality is high. They offer *makonde* carvings, wooden animal carvings, stone and wooden chess sets, basketware and the like. If you have unwanted or excess gear (T-shirts, jeans, cameras, etc) you can often do a part exchange deal with these people. Apart from Nairobi, it's probably the best collection of such shops in Kenya.

Places to Stay
There are a number of cheap basic lodges in the centre of Malindi but they're usually fairly noisy at night and you don't get the benefit of sea breezes or instant access to the beach. Most travellers prefer to stay in one of the hotels on the beach.

If you do have to stay in the centre of town the *New Safari Hotel* has rooms for KSh 50/70 a single/double without bathroom and KSh 100 a double with bathroom. The *Lamu Hotel* is clean and basic and has doubles at KSh 70, but no singles. Others include the *Malindi Rest House*, *New Kenya Hotel*, *Salama Lodge* and *Wananchi Boarding & Lodging*.

There's a cool and very clean *Youth Hostel* (tel 20531) in Malindi next to the hospital. Mosquito nets are provided and there's a fridge for use by residents. Each room has six beds at a cost of KSh 35 per

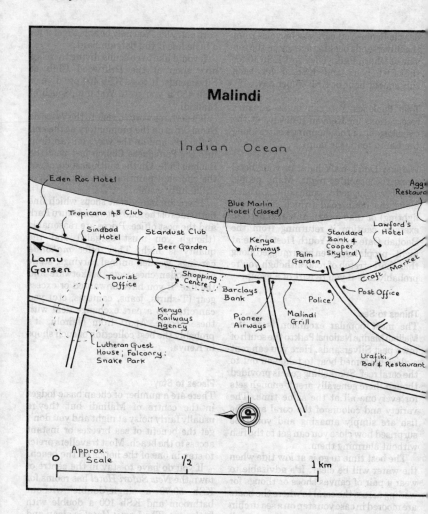

Malindi

Indian Ocean

Eden Roc Hotel

Aggi Restaura

Tropicana 48 Club

Blue Marlin Hotel (closed)

Lawford's Hotel

Sindbad Hotel

Stardust Club

Beer Garden

Kenya Airways

Standard Bank & Cooper Skybird

Palm Garden

Lamu Garsen

Tourist Office

Shopping Centre

Barclays Bank

Craft Market

Police

Post Office

Kenya Railways Agency

Pioneer Airways

Malindi Grill

Lutheran Guest House; Falconry; Snake Park

Urafiki Bar & Restaurant

Approx. Scale

0   ½   1 km

person. No membership card is required and it's quite a popular place to stay.

The *Travellers' Inn* is the best value for money of the beach hotels. It's a fairly new place, very clean with pleasant rooms, excellent showers and mosquito netting on the windows. It costs KSh 100/150 a single/double between September and April, less for the rest of the year. The staff

are very friendly and soft drinks and food are available. It's very popular so you may find it's full during the high season.

If you can't find a room at these places try either *Gilani's* or the *Lucky Lodge* which are priced about the same as the Metro.

Ozi's Bed & Breakfast is a mid-range hotel. It's very clean, fairly new and costs

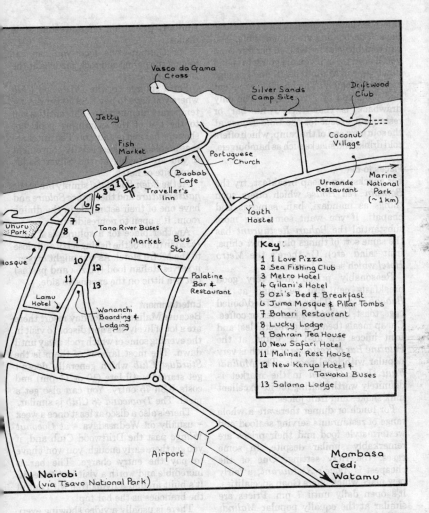

Key:
1. I Love Pizza
2. Sea Fishing Club
3. Metro Hotel
4. Gilani's Hotel
5. Ozi's Bed & Breakfast
6. Juma Mosque & Pillar Tombs
7. Bahari Restaurant
8. Lucky Lodge
9. Bahrain Tea House
10. New Safari Hotel
11. Malindi Rest House
12. New Kenya Hotel & Tawakal Buses
13. Salama Lodge

KSh 150/240 a single/double including breakfast with separate showers and toilets.

About 1½ km south of the hotels along the coast road is the very popular *Silver Sands Camp Site* (and the *Hotel Silver Sands*) which is used by long-distance overland safari trucks whenever they come through. It costs KSh 30 per person

to camp and there are good toilets and showers but very little shade. If you haven't got a tent you can rent a large double room with shower, toilet and kitchen sink at the hotel for just KSh 50 (cheaper than two beds at the Youth Hostel).

They also have *bandas* available for rent at KSh 120/140/220 per night. The prices are lower if you stay for two or three days. The *bandas* are comfortable. You can rent bicycles for KSh 45 per day (and you'll need them if you are going to spend much time in Malindi itself) and baggage can be left safely. The beach is excellent and protected by a coral reef. The only drawback is that there's no bar or restaurant except for the *Cold House* at the southern end of the camp, which offers cold drinks and snacks such as hamburgers.

Places to Eat

For snacks or a cheap breakfast, try the *Bahrain Tea House* which offers such things as mandazi, baji, samosas and chapati. If you want something more substantial the *Bahari Restaurant* has the same sort of things plus fish & chips, fruit salad, etc). Or there's the *Metro Hotel* which serves breakfasts.

Reasonably priced and very good breakfasts can also be found at the *Baobab Café*. They have fried/boiled eggs, toast, butter and jam, tea or coffee. Cheap meals (beans and vegetables) and fruit juices can also be found at the *Palatine Bar & Restaurant* which is very popular with local people. The *Malindi Fruit Juice Garden* in the market is definitely worth visiting for its excellent milk shakes and fruit juices.

For lunch or dinner there are a whole range of restaurants serving seafood and western-style food and their prices are remarkably similar despite, in some cases, the ritzy setting. One of the cheapest is *Aggie's Restaurant*, a fairly new place which offers Goan specialities. It's open daily until 7 pm. Prices are similar at the equally popular *Malindi Grill*.

For cheaper African food, try the *Urafiki Bar & Restaurant* which has ugali and meat stew. The bar gets very lively later in the evening.

For Indian curries you can't beat the *Metro Hotel* which offers a range of good-sized dishes. They also do the best lime juice in town. The Baobab Café is

similarly priced but offers western-style dishes.

For German-style food you can eat among the palms and rock gardens at the *Beer Garden*.

For a splurge try the *Driftwood Club* where you have to pay KSh 10 per day for temporary membership. This entitles you to the use of the swimming pool, hot showers, bar and restaurant. The prices are reasonable and it's especially convenient if you are staying at the Silver Sands camp site or hotel.

At the *Eden Roc Hotel* simply brave the *haute couture* and the *Ambre Solaire* and have one of their set meals in the dining room. It's open to nonresidents.

Another place for a splurge is *I Love Pizza* in front of the fishing jetty and close to the Metro Hotel. As you might expect, it serves Italian food (pizzas and pastas) but is a little on the expensive side.

Entertainment

Because Malindi is a holiday resort there are a lot of lively bars and discos to visit in the evening some of which rock away until dawn. The most famous of them is the *Stardust Club* which generally doesn't get started until late (10 or 11 pm) and costs KSh 75 entry. You can also get a meal. The *Tropicana 48 Club* is similar.

There's also a disco at least once a week – usually on Wednesdays – at *Coconut Village* past the Driftwood Club and, if you get there early enough, you won't have to pay the entry charge. The bar is incredible and worth a visit just to see it. It's built around a living tree with one of the branches as the bar top!

There is usually a video showing every evening in the bar of the *Sindbad Hotel* which is open to nonresidents. Another place which is worth checking out if you want to pick up a film is the *Malindi Fishing Club*, right next to the Metro Hotel. It's a very attractive, traditionally-constructed building with a grass roof. There's a bar and snacks are available.

The three liveliest bars are the *Beer*

Garden, the *Metro Hotel* and the *Baobab Café* which is popular with people who stay at the Youth Hostel. The beers are ice-cold at all of them. The liveliest African bar is the *Urafiki* with its deafening jukebox but it closes by 11.30 pm and the beers are often lukewarm.

MOMBASA

Mombasa is the largest port on the coast of East Africa. It has a population of nearly half a million of which about 70% are African and the rest are mainly Asian with a small minority of Europeans. Its docks service not only Kenya but also Uganda, Rwanda and Burundi. The bulk of the town sprawls over Mombasa Island which is connected to the mainland by an artificial causeway carrying the rail and road links. In recent years, Mombasa has spread onto the mainland both north and south of the island.

Large Mombasa may be but, like Dar es Salaam, it has retained its low-level traditional character and there are few high-rise buildings. Despite the addition of electricity, asphalt streets and a number of craft shops, the old town between the massive, Portuguese-built Fort Jesus and the old dhow careening dock remains much the same as it was in the mid-19th century. It's a hot, steamy town but an interesting place to visit, and it has a long and fascinating history revolving around the struggle for control between the Portuguese and the Omani Arabs.

Information

Tourist Office The office is just past the famous tusks on Moi Ave and is open Monday to Friday from 8 am to 12 noon and 2 to 4.30 pm, and on Saturdays from 8 am to 12 noon. They may have a good map of Mombasa but otherwise they're geared to high spenders – mainly those who want to stay at a beach resort hotel – so they're of little help to budget travellers.

Banks There are many banks in the city centre. Barclays Bank on Moi Ave, just up the road from the Castle Hotel, is open Monday to Saturday from 8.30 am to 5 pm. Outside these hours you can change travellers' cheques at the Castle Hotel (or any of the beach resort hotels north and south of Mombasa) although a commission will be charged.

Maps The best map of Mombasa is the Survey of Kenya *Mombasa Island & Environs* which costs KSh 54 and was last published in 1977. Many of the street names have changed, but little else.

Vaccinations You can get vaccinations from the Public Health Department (tel 26791), Msanifu Kombo St. For yellow fever the times are Wednesday and Friday from 8 to 9 am. Cholera is done on the same days between 2 and 3.30 pm. All shots cost KSh 20. Free bilharzia tests are done at the Control Centre for Communicable Diseases, Mnazi Moja Rd.

Likoni Ferry This ferry connects Mombasa Island with the southern mainland and runs at frequent intervals throughout the night and day. There's a crossing every 20 minutes on average between 5 am one morning and 12.30 am the next; less frequently between 12.30 and 5 am. It's free to pedestrians.

Boat If you're interested in yachts or boats to India or the Seychelles it's worth getting out to Kilibi Creek. Most people moor there because mooring berths at the Mombasa Yacht Club are very expensive. If you want to make enquiries you can get to Kilibi by going to Tom's Beach, about 1½ km from the city centre, near the Seahorse Hotel.

Things to See

Before you set off on a tour of the old town of Mombasa get a copy of the booklet *The Old Town Mombasa: A Historical Guide* by Judy Aldrick & Rosemary Macdonald published by the Friends of Fort Jesus

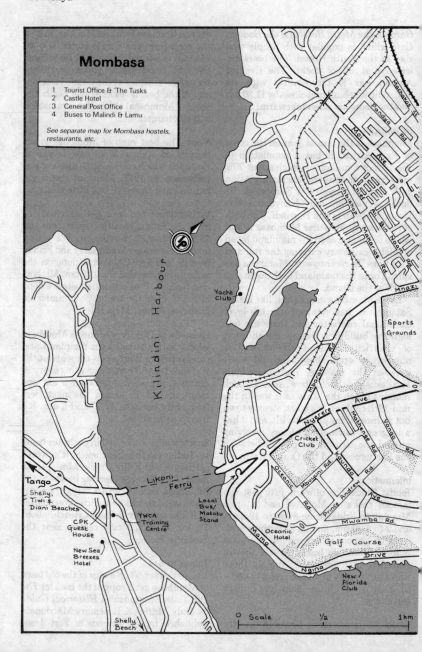

Mombasa

1 Tourist Office & The Tusks
2 Castle Hotel
3 General Post Office
4 Buses to Malindi & Lamu

See separate map for Mombasa hostels, restaurants, etc.

Kilindini Harbour

Yacht Club

Sports Grounds

Cricket Club

Golf Course

New Florida Club

Oceanic Hotel

Local Bus/Matatu Stand

Likoni Ferry

YWCA Training Centre

CPK Guest House

New Sea Breezes Hotel

Tanga

Shelly, Tiwi & Diani Beaches

Shelly Beach

Madaraka Rd

Pandya Rd

Mei Ave

Archbishop

Chief

Mekarice Rd

Bin Nazer

Mnazi

Mbaraki Rd

Nyerere Rd

Mathenge Rd

Vasco Rd

Oceanic Rd

Mbuyuni Rd

Prince Andrew Ave

Kaunda Rd

Mwamba Rd.

Mama

Naina

Drive

0   Scale   ½   1 km

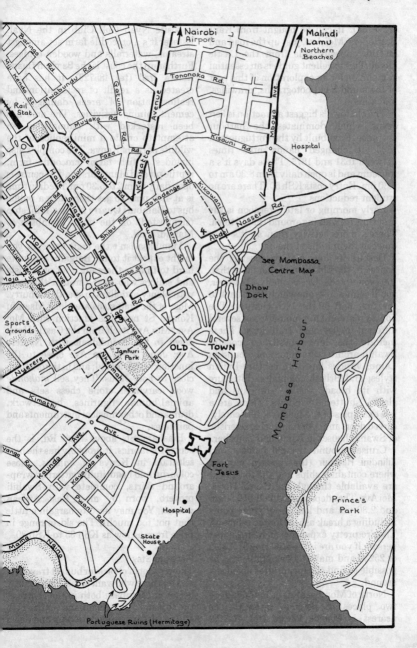

(KSh 50). It can be bought from Kant Stationers, Moi Ave, just up the road and on the opposite side from the Castle Hotel. This excellent guide is an essential companion for an exploration of this part of town and has photographs, drawings, and a map.

The old town's biggest attraction is **Fort Jesus** which dominates the harbour entrance. First built by the Portuguese in 1593, it changed hands nine times between 1631 and 1875. These days it's a museum and is open daily from 8.30 am to 6.30 pm. Entry costs KSh 50. There are no student reductions.

Early morning or late afternoon is the best time for walking around the old town. There's more activity then as it's very quiet in the middle of the day.

Despite its long history, most of the houses in the old town are no more than 100 years old. Occasionally, however, you'll come across one which dates back to the first half of the 19th century. The houses represent a combination of several different styles and traditions. These include the long-established coastal Swahili architecture commonly found in Lamu; various late 19th century Indian styles; and British colonial architecture with its broad, shady verandahs and glazed, shuttered windows. There are a few examples of the massive, intricately-carved doors and door frames characteristic of Swahili houses in Lamu and Zanzibar.

Cruises around the **old harbour** and **Kilindini Harbour** (the modern harbour where container ships and the like dock) are available through the Castle Hotel, Moi Ave. They depart twice daily at 9.30 am and 2.30 pm and last about three hours including a break ashore for refreshment. They're pretty expensive at KSh 250 per person. If you are interested ring 316391/2 or 25230 and make a booking. It may be possible to find cheaper cruises if you ask around.

North of Mombasa on the mainland are two places of possible interest. The nearest is **Mamba Village** (tel 472709)

opposite Nyali Golf Club in the Nyali Estate. It's a crocodile farm set amongst streams, waterfalls and wooden bridges. Further up the coast is the **Bamburi Quarry Nature Trail** (tel 485729). It has been created as a result of reclamation and reafforestation of areas damaged by cement mining activities. The area has been restocked with animals in an attempt to create a mini-replica of the wildlife parks of Kenya. The complex also includes a fish farm, crocodile farm, reptile pit and plant nursery. The centre is open daily from 2 to 5.30 pm. Feeding time is at 4.30 pm. To get there take a public bus to Bamburi Quarry Nature Trail stop (signposted) on the main Mombasa to Malindi road.

Mombasa isn't the craft entrepôt you might expect it to be. Bargains are quite hard to find as there are a lot of tourists and sailors who pass through this port with plenty of dollars to spend in a hurry. Most of the **craft stalls** are along Msanifu Kombo St near the junction with Moi Ave; Moi Ave itself from the Castle Hotel down to the roundabout with Nyerere Ave; Jomo Kenyatta Ave close to the junction with Digo Rd; and in the old town close to Fort Jesus. They sell *makonde* wood carvings, stone chess sets and animal/human figurines, basketwork, drums and other musical instruments and paintings.

Biashara St, above Digo Rd, is the centre for fabrics. It probably has the best selection in Kenya of *kangas*, those colourful and beautifully patterned wraparound skirts, complete with Swahili proverb, worn by most East African women. You may need to bargain a little (but not too much). The skirts range in price from as low as KSh 35 to KSh 80.

Places to Stay

There's a lot of choice for budget travellers and for those who want something slightly better in Mombasa both in the centre of the city and on the mainland to the north and south. Accommodation up and down the coast from Mombasa Island itself is dealt with separately.

By far the best value for money is the *Mvita Hotel*, on the corner of Hospital St and Turkana Rd. The entrance is in the first alley on the left hand side of Turkana Rd or in Hospital St through the bar on the ground floor. It's Indian-run, very clean, quiet, secure and friendly. All the rooms have fans, a hand basin, comfortable beds and even toilet paper. The showers and toilets are scrubbed out daily. All this for KSh 90 a double. There's a lively bar downstairs (which you can't hear in the rooms upstairs) while at lunch and dinner times barbequed meat and other snacks are available in the back yard.

Equally good value and popular with travellers is the *Cosy Guest House*, Haile Selassie Rd. Rooms are KSh 70/90 a single/double and KSh 110 a triple. It's a clean place and all the rooms have fans. It will most likely be full if you get there late in the day. On the opposite side of the road from the Cozy Guest House is the *Midnight Guest House* which is a reasonable alternative at KSh 60/70 a single/double with a common shower and toilet, or KSh 100 for a double with a bathroom.

If these are full try the *Balgis Lodge*, Digo Rd, which is very friendly and good value for KSh 55/70 a single/double. Also worth trying is the *New Britannia Board & Lodging* in Gusii St. It's very clean and tidy, has pleasant rooms with fans and hand basins, and costs KSh 60 a double. The staff are friendly.

Another budget hotel which has been popular for years is the *New People's Hotel*, Abdel Nasser Rd right next to where the buses leave for Malindi and Lamu. Some travellers rate this place very highly and it certainly compares very well in price with the others. Nonetheless, it's a little tatty and the rooms which face onto the main road can be very noisy. The management are friendly though and gear left in the rooms is safe. It costs KSh 37/62 a single/double and KSh 75 a triple with

common shower and toilet; and KSh 60/119 a single/double and KSh 179 a triple with bathroom. All the rooms have fans, the sheets are clean and the water in the showers is generally lukewarm. It's a large place and rarely full. There's a good, cheap restaurant downstairs.

Close to the Mvita and Balgis are two other places worth checking out if you can't find a room. The first is the *Downtown Hotel*, Hospital St, opposite the Mvita. It costs KSh 25 per person in a room with four beds, KSh 60/70 a single/double with common shower and toilet. It's scruffy and some of the back rooms are dingy. The second is the *Hydro Hotel*, Digo Rd at the junction with Kenyatta Ave. This place has been a popular budget hotel for years but it's very run-down these days. It costs KSh 25 per person in the dormitory, or KSh 50/75 a single/double with common shower and toilet. There's a reasonable restaurant on the 1st floor. Both the Downtown and the Hydro are relatively poor value in comparison to the Mvita and Balgis.

Somewhat more expensive (but not necessarily better value) is the *Hotel Fortuna*, Haile Selassie Rd, which costs KSh 125/150 a single/double both with shower and toilet.

In the middle range, one of the cheapest hotels is the *Hotel Relax*, Meru Rd. It's clean and good value at about KSh 175/215 a single/double with private shower, toilet and breakfast. All the rooms have fans. Next door is the *Hotel Splendid*, a huge place which is rarely full. It costs about KSh 200/325 a single/double with private bathroom and breakfast. It's very clean, modern and there's a popular rooftop restaurant which collects the sea breezes in the evenings.

Close to these two hotels is the *Hotel Hermes*, in Msanifu Kombo St. Rooms cost KSh 235/280 a single/double with bathroom and breakfast.

Perhaps the best place to stay in this range is the beautiful *New Palm Tree Hotel*, Nkrumah Rd, which is similar in

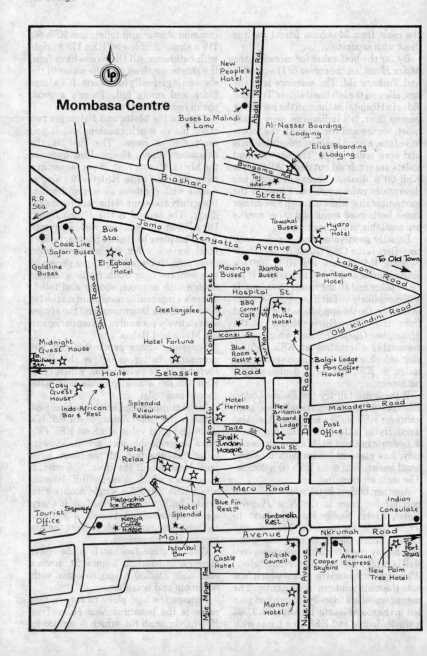

Mombasa Centre

New People's Hotel

Abdel Nasser Rd

Buses to Malindi & Lamu

Al-Nasser Boarding & Lodging

Elias Boarding & Lodging

Bungoma Rd

Taj Hotel

Biashara Street

R.R. Sta.

Jomo Kenyatta Avenue

Tawakal Buses

Hyaro Hotel

Bus Sta.

Coast Line Safari Buses

Goldline Buses

Shibu Road

El-Egbaal Hotel

Mawingo Buses

Akamba Buses

Langoni Road

To Old Town

Downtown Hotel

Hospital St.

Kombo Street

Geetanjalee

BBQ Corner Cafe

Konzi St.

Mvita Hotel

Turkana St

Old Kilindini Road

Hotel Fortuna

Blue Room Restat

Balgis Lodge & Pan Coffee House

Midnight Guest House

To Railway Stn.

Haile   Selassie   Road

Aigo Road

Cosy Guest House

Indo-African Bar & Rest

Splendid View Restaurant

Msanifu St

Hotel Hermes

Makadera Road

New Britania Board & Lodge

Post Office

Taita St

Sheikh Jundani Masque

Hotel Relax

Gusii St

Meru Road

Pistacchio Ice Cream

Hotel Splendid

Blue Fin Restat

Fontanella Rest.

Indian Consulate

Tourist Office

Skyways

Kenya Coffee House

Moi   Avenue

Nkrumah   Road

Istanbul Bar

Castle Hotel

British Council

Cooper Skybird

American Express

New Palm Tree Hotel

Fort Jesus

Mile Mpe Rd

Manor Hotel

Nyerere Avenue

quality to the much more expensive Castle Hotel. A very comfortable room costs between KSh 163 and KSh 234 for a single and from KSh 245 to KSh 292 for a double with shower, toilet and breakfast. The hotel has a bar and restaurant.

The *Taj Hotel*, Bungoma Rd, is priced as a mid-range hotel but the quality is no better than some of the better budget hotels. It's quiet and clean but costs KSh 150/200 a single/double and KSh 250 a double with bathroom. On the other hand, the restaurant serves some of the best Indian food in Mombasa.

Places to Eat

Since many of the restaurants in Mombasa are Indian-owned you can find excellent curries and thalis. At lunch times (12.30 to around 3 pm) there is often cheap, substantial set meals available.

One which you'll hear nothing but praise for is the *Geetanjalee*, Msanifu Kombo St, which offers a 'deluxe' thali for KSh 45. Both the food and service are excellent. Similar is the *New Chetna Restaurant*, Haile Selassie Rd directly under the Cozy Guest House. It has South Indian vegetarian food (masala dosa, etc) and sweets, plus an all-you-can-eat set vegetarian lunch for KSh 45. It's a very popular restaurant.

Also reasonable is the *Taj Hotel*, Bungoma St, which offers curries, biryanis and fresh fruit juices. Like the other places it offers specials of the day. For coastal Swahili dishes (made with coconut and coconut milk), the *Swahili Curry Bowl*, Tangana Rd, is recommended. Prices are reasonable. It's also one of *the* places for coffee and ice cream.

For seafood or western food one of the cheapest is the *Blue Fin Restaurant*, on the corner of Meru Rd and Msanifu Kombo St. There's a fairly extensive menu and it's good value considering the prices and the quality of the food but it has come in for adverse criticism in the past from some travellers. *Roshne's Café*, Meru Rd, is similar and they also offer

breakfast. Good, self-service breakfasts can also be found at the *Blue Room Restaurant*, Haile Selassie Rd at the junction with Turkana St.

Going up slightly in price, try the *Indo-Africa Bar & Restaurant*, Haile Selassie Rd next to the Cozy Guest House, for excellent Indian Mughlai dishes at reasonable prices. The *Masumin*, Digo Rd on the opposite side from the post office, is very good for dishes like prawn masala, chicken curry, meat curries, fish & chips, fruit juices and lassi.

Excellent tandoori specialities can be found at the very popular *Splendid View Café*, opposite the Hotel Splendid but not part of the same hotel. They have things like chicken, lamb, fruit juices and lassi and you can eat well for around KSh 35. There are tables outside and inside. Similar is the *Barbeque Corner Café*, Konzi St near the Mvita Hotel. This is a new place and the food is very good.

For a splurge try a dinner one evening at the rooftop restaurant at the *Hotel Splendid*. There are good views over the city and the restaurant catches the evening sea breezes. For a more expensive splurge try either the *New Palm Tree Hotel* or the *Castle Hotel* but check prices first and take note of hidden extras such as tax and service charges which can increase the bill by up to 25%.

Entertainment

For an ice-cold beer in the heat of the day many people go to the terrace of the *Castle Hotel* which overlooks Moi Ave. It's the nearest thing you'll find to the Thorn Tree Café in Nairobi but the comparison isn't really valid. If you prefer more local colour and a livelier place there's the *Istanbul Bar* just down from the Castle Hotel where you can also get cheap snacks. The bar at the Mvita Hotel is pretty lively most nights and it may surprise you to see Swahili women dressed in *bui bui* sucking on the end of a bottle of White Cap beer. Where else but East Africa would you see this!

The *Rainbow Hotel* is a popular disco/African reggae club always filled with local ragers, sailors, whores and travellers. There are plenty of other excellent reggae clubs in the suburbs which are very cheap and good fun – ask around.

SOUTH OF MOMBASA

The south coast is perhaps the most highly developed of the mainland beaches which stretch both north and south of Mombasa and there is very little cheap accommodation available. From the Likoni ferry going south the beaches are **Shelly, Tiwi** and **Diani**. Another beach is at **Shimoni** much further down the coast near the border with Tanzania. There is also a **National Marine Reserve** there.

All the beaches are white coral sand and are protected by a coral reef so there is no danger from sharks when you go swimming. For most of the way, the beaches are fringed with coconut palms so you can always find shade if you want to get out of the sun. The only trouble with Shelly Beach and, to a lesser extent, Tiwi Beach is the accumulation of seaweed between the reef and the shore. It gets so bad at times that there's no way you would want to go swimming in the sea. Diani is the longest and best of the beaches and doesn't suffer from the seaweed problem but it is the most developed. Virtually the whole of the ocean frontage is taken up by expensive beach resorts.

To get to Shelly Beach you need to turn left at the first major turn-off after getting off the Likoni ferry. This is near the top of the rise past where the buses and *matatus* park. There are no public buses to Shelly Beach so you will either have to hire a *matatu* (about KSh 30 per person), hitch (easy depending on the time of day) or walk (about 30 minutes).

Almost as soon as you have turned off the main road after the Likoni ferry you will come to one of the few relatively cheap places to stay. This is the *CPK Guest House* on the right hand side. It's beautiful and a comfortable room costs about KSh 160 per day with full board. The food is excellent and there's a very large swimming pool for use by residents. Closer to the beach itself you will have to ask around for rooms to rent. There are quite a few (some of them in private houses) but expect to pay around KSh 200 a double per day without food. Try the *Rocking Boat Inn* about one km past the Shelly Beach Hotel.

To get to Tiwi or Diani beaches from the Likoni ferry take either a KRS bus with the sign 'Diani Beach' ('Likoni' in the opposite direction) or a *matatu* with the sign 'Ukunda'. Both cost KSh 6. If going to Tiwi it doesn't matter which you take since you will have to get off about half way.

The only relatively cheap accommodation on Tiwi is the very popular *Twiga Lodge* which costs KSh 20 per person to camp plus KSh 10 if you want to hire a tent. You'll meet a lot of travellers and it's a very beautiful place to stay. The restaurant is quite expensive but the shop nearby sells most of the basics and people will come round everyday offering fish and fruit which you can cook yourself. Whatever you do when you get off the bus, *do not* walk from the main road to Tiwi (about three km). Many people have been mugged doing this. Wait on the main road until you get a lift. The Twiga Lodge is signposted on the main road to Ukunda.

If you are going to Diani Beach it's much more convenient to take the KRS bus from the Likoni ferry rather than a *matatu*. The bus serves all the beach resort hotels along Diani. It heads north first then doubles back and goes to the south end of the beach – just tell the driver where you want to go and he'll make sure you get off at the right stop. The buses leave every 40 minutes throughout the day – the first from Likoni at 5 am and 6 am from Diani. The last bus from Diani to Likoni is at 7.20 pm. If you take a *matatu* from Likoni you'll be dropped at the village of Ukunda and will have to take the bus from there to any of the beach hotels (KSh 2). Don't walk from Ukunda to the beach hotels. The chances are you will be mugged.

The only cheap place to stay on Diani Beach is the well-known and popular *Dan's Trench* which shares the same access road as the Trade Winds Hotel. You won't see any signs for Dan's on the beach road so look out for the Trade Winds Hotel. Walk down the access road to the hotel for about 100 metres and you'll see a blue and white sign with 'Dan's' written on it. You're there.

It's basically a camp site (KSh 15 per person) and a collection of rustic, two-storey, concrete *bandas* with palm thatch-roofs (KSh 50 per bed) and simple cooking facilities. People are friendly and it's a mellow place to stay. It can get a little crowded though, when long-haul overland trucks turn up, as they do from time to time. You can hire bicycles (KSh 20 per hour or KSh 80 per day), tents (KSh 20 per day) and catamarans (KSh 100 per hour). Bring your own food.

If you are prepared to eat at the Trade Winds Hotel you'll probably be able to use their facilities (swimming pool, etc) without having to pay a fee but don't count on it. Depending on how many people are staying at the hotel, you may be charged for using them.

There are also a number of independent restaurants along this beach (usually expensive since they appeal to those staying at the resort hotels). They include *Ali Barbours* which specialises in seafood and is only open in the evenings.

NORTH OF MOMBASA

The north coast like the south coast is well developed with much of the ocean frontage taken up by hotel resort complexes. Again, there are very few cheap places to stay. The only one which is within range of budget travellers is the *Kanamai Youth Hostel* which costs KSh 20 per bed in the dormitory and KSh 60/120 a double (depending on what you take) for a self-contained chalet with bedroom, shower, living room, kitchen and verandah.

Cooking gas is provided if you want to put your own food together. Otherwise you can buy meals at the canteen.

To get there first take a *matatu* (KSh 5) to Majengo on the Mombasa to Kilifi road. Get off when you see a yellow sign saying 'Camping Kanamai'. Go down the dirt track by this sign for about 300 metres then turn left at the fork. Continue for about three km and you'll find it on the left hand side. It's a long, hot walk and lifts are few and far between so think twice about going unless you have your own vehicle. Also the beach is a seaweed disaster. It's completely choked with the stuff and the sea is extremely shallow between the beach and the reef.

NAIROBI

Until the late 1800s, the area where Nairobi stands today was just a watering hole for the Masai. Then came the Mombasa to Uganda railway complete with its 32,000 indentured labourers from Gujarat and Punjab, along with their British colonial overlords intent on beating the Germans to the Ugandan heartland. Within weeks it became tent city. Much of the area was still a foul-smelling swamp and game roamed freely over the adjoining plains. Yet, by 1900 it had become a town of substantial buildings and five years later succeeded Mombasa as the capital of the British East Africa Protectorate. Since then it has gone from strength to strength and is now one of the largest cities between Cairo and Johannesburg (population about one million). Nevertheless, you can still walk from one end of the central business district to the other in 15 minutes. And where else in the world would you be able to see lion, cheetah, rhino and giraffe roaming free with the tower blocks of a city as a backdrop?

It's a very cosmopolitan place, lively, interesting, pleasantly landscaped and a good place to get essential business and bureaucratic matters sewn up. Like most African cities, Nairobi has its crowded

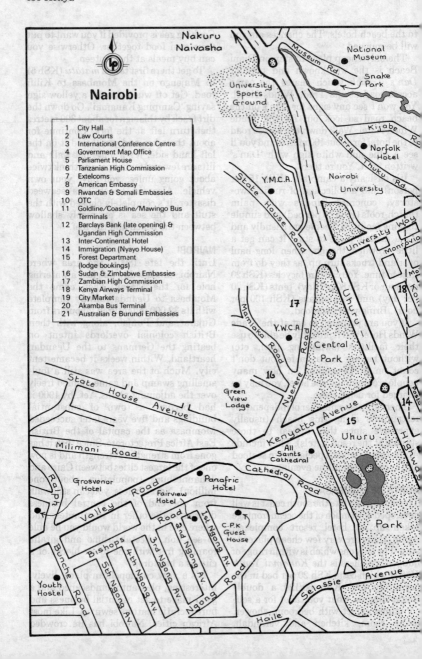

Nairobi

1 City Hall
2 Law Courts
3 International Conference Centre
4 Government Map Office
5 Parliament House
6 Tanzanian High Commission
7 Extelcoms
8 American Embassy
9 Rwandan & Somali Embassies
10 OTC
11 Goldline/Coastline/Mawingo Bus Terminals
12 Barclays Bank (late opening) & Ugandan High Commission
13 Inter-Continental Hotel
14 Immigration (Nyayo House)
15 Forest Departmant (lodge bookings)
16 Sudan & Zimbabwe Embassies
17 Zambian High Commission
18 Kenya Airways Terminal
19 City Market
20 Akamba Bus Terminal
21 Australian & Burundi Embassies

Mrs Roche's Guest House

Juncu Rd

Muranga Rd

Ngara Rd

Desai Rd

Nyeri
Nanyuki

Ngara Rd

Chanan Singh Rd

Park Road

Chambers Rd

Ngara Rd

Ngara
Rd

Pande Rd

Road

Quarry Rd

see Nairobi
Centre map

Nairobi River

Kirinyaga Rd

Racecourse Rd

Keekorok Rd

River Rd.

Lagos Rd

20

Haddoh St

Biashara St.

Tubman Rd.

Tom Mboya St.

Latema Rd.

Accra Rd

River Rd

Mungu Rd

Duruma Rd

Kirkasi Rd

Cross Rd

Road

11

Racecourse Rd

Moi Avenue

Kimathi St.

Luthuli Ave

Tom Mboya St

Karume St

Ronald Ngala St.

Road

10

Mangu St

Banda St

Wabera St.

Standard St

Kaunda St

Ngina St.

Mama Ngina Way

Taifa Rd

Moi Avenue

Mfangano St

Mfangano St

Country
Bus Station

Kenyatta Avenue

12

1

City Hall

2

3

4

Harambee Avenue

Haile Selassie Avenue

Le Tausa Rd

7

8

9

Landhies Rd

Parliament Rd

6

Post
Office

Workshops Rd

Railway
Museum

Station Rd

Station Rd

Railway
Station

Airport
Mombasa

Scale   0   ½   1 km

working class areas and shanty towns, its middle class/office worker suburbs and its spacious mansions and beautiful flower-decked gardens for the rich and powerful. The former is an area full of local colour, energy, aspirations and opportunism where manual workers, exhausted *matatu* drivers, the unemployed, the devious, the down-and-out and the disorientated mingle with budget travellers, whores, shopkeepers, high school students, food stall vendors, drowsy security guards and those with life's little illicit goodies for sale. It's called River Rd – though, of course, it spans more than just this road itself. Even if you are not staying in this area you should make a point of getting down there one evening just to see how the other half lives on the wrong side of Tom Mboya St.

You may hear rumours about Nairobi being a dangerous city at night for robberies. We do get letters from travellers who have been robbed but it's probably no worse than any other city in the world. Keep your wits about you at night and don't walk across Uhuru Park after dark, get too drunk on River Rd, or pull out a wallet when someone asks for a few shillings down a dark alley. Act as though you know where you're going.

Information

Tourist Office There is no national tourist organisation in Kenya. There is a place in the small park in front of the Nairobi Hilton which might pass for a tourist office but it only has information on expensive hotels, safaris and Kenya Airways or charter flights. It has nothing of interest for budget travellers. There is, however, a privately-owned organisation which puts out a leaflet called *Tourist's Kenya*, every two weeks which is free of charge and available from most large hotels. The Thorn Tree Café is the most convenient place to find it.

Maps There are many maps of Nairobi in the bookshops but probably the best is the

City of Nairobi: Map & Guide (KSh 45) published in English, French and German by the Survey of Kenya. It has a red front cover with partially coloured photographs on the back. It covers the suburbs as well as having a detailed map of the central area. If you're staying for a long time, however, the *A to Z: Guide to Nairobi* (KSh 40) is worth buying.

Bookshops The best selection of bookshops are along Kimathi St (Select Bookshop and New Stanley Bookshop) and Mama Ngina St (Prestige Books). For second-hand books, there is a used paperback bookshop on Market St just down from the American Snack Bar and Khima Chapatti Corner. They have a good selection of novels, a fairly fast turnover and will take back their own books and refund you half what you paid for them. The US Peace Corps also have a library in town which has a good selection of books.

Vaccinations You can get these at City Hall Clinic, Mama Ngina St. Yellow fever is done from 8.30 to 11 am Monday to Friday (KSh 25), cholera from 8.30 am to 12 noon Monday to Friday (KSh 20) and tetanus and typhoid from 8.30 to 11 am Monday to Friday (free). If you want a gamma globulin shot (for hepatitis) go to Dr Meyerhold, 3rd floor, Bruce House, Standard St. It costs KSh 150. This doctor has his own pathology laboratory if you need blood or stool tests. It will cost KSh 120 per consultation plus laboratory fees. Otherwise go to the Nairobi Hospital (but not, according to local residents, Kenyatta Hospital).

Photography For passport size photographs, the cheapest place to go is the machine under the yellow and black sign 'Photo Me' a few doors up Kenyatta Ave from the New Stanley Bookshop. It costs KSh 15 for four prints and takes about three minutes. You can also get them from the photography shop in Kimathi House opposite the New Stanley Hotel but they cost KSh 35 for three prints.

For camera repairs or equipment rental try either Camera Maintenance Centre Ltd (tel 26920) in the Hilton Arcade or Camera Experts (tel 337750), KCS House, Mama Ngina St. If you use the first one, make sure you get a quote beforehand. He's definitely not cheap. Camera Experts can also process film overnight (they've got all the equipment).

Embassies Apart from embassies in neighbouring countries mentioned in the Visas section others include:

Australia
    Development House, Moi Ave (tel 334666, 334670)
Belgium
    Silopark House, Mama Ngina St (tel 20501)
Canada
    Comcraft House, Haile Selassie Ave (tel 334033)
Denmark
    HFCK Building, Koinange St (tel 331088)
Finland
    International House, Mama Ngina St (tel 334777/8)
Germany (West)
    Embassy House, Harambee Ave (tel 26661/2/3)
India
    Jeevan Bharati Building, Harambee Ave (tel 22566)
Irish Republic
    Maendeleo Building, Monrovia St (tel 26771/4)
Italy
    Prudential Assurance Building, Wabera St (tel 21615)
Japan
    ICEA Building, Kenyatta Ave (tel 332955)
Malawi
    Bruce House, Standard St (tel 21174)
Netherlands
    Uchumi House, Nkrumah Lane (tel 27111)
Norway
    Rehani House, Kenyatta Ave (tel 337121)
Pakistan
    St Michael's Rd, Westlands (tel 61666/7/8/9)
Saudi Arabia
    IPS Building, Kimathi St (tel 29501/2)

Sweden
    International House, Mama Ngina St (tel 29042)
Switzerland
    International House, Mama Ngina St (tel 28735)
UK
    Bruce House, Standard St (tel 335944)
USA
    On the corner of Haile Selassie Ave and Moi Ave (tel 334141)

Foreign Cultural Organisations There are a number of foreign cultural organisations with offices in Nairobi. Some of these include:

American Cultural Center
    National Bank Building, Harambee Ave (tel 337877). Open Monday to Friday from 10 am to 5 pm and on Saturday from 10 am to 1 pm
British Council
    ICEA Building, mezzanine floor, Kenyatta Ave (tel 334855). Open Monday to Friday from 10 am to 5 pm and on Saturday from 9 am to 12 noon
French Cultural Centre
    Maison Française, on the corner of Monrovia and Loita Sts (tel 336263). Open Monday to Friday from 10 am to 5 pm and on Saturday from 10 am to 1 pm

Things to See
The **National Museum** and **Snake Park**, next to each other on Museum Hill, off Uhuru Highway, are both worth a visit. The Museum has a good exhibition on prehistoric people, an incredible collection of native birds, mammals and tribal crafts as well as a new section on the culture, history and crafts of the coastal Swahili people. Across the road, the Snake Park has living examples of most of the snake species found in East Africa as well as tortoises and crocodiles. Both places are open daily from 9.30 am to 6 pm. Entry to either costs KSh 50 or KSh 10 for students. The local bird-watching club meets at the museum every Wednesday at 9 am. Visitors are welcome.

Another museum worth a visit is the **Railway Museum**, Station Rd (follow the railway tracks until you are almost at the bridge under Uhuru Highway). The curator is very friendly if there's anything you want to ask him about the exhibits. It's open the same hours as the National Museum and costs KSh 10 entry (KSh 3 for students).

The most accessible of all Kenya's game parks is **Nairobi National Park** only a few km from the city centre. You should set aside half a day to see it. As in all the game parks, you must visit them in a vehicle. Walking is prohibited. This means you will either have to arrange a lift at the entrance gate with other tourists or go on a tour.

There are many companies offering tours of Nairobi National Park and there's probably not much to choose between them. They usually depart twice a day at 9.30 am and 2 pm for a four-hour tour and cost KSh 250. Entry to the park costs KSh 80 per person. Most of the tour companies also offer a day-long combined tour of the national park with a visit to the Bomas of Kenya including a gargantuan lunch at the Carnivore for KSh 450. Most of the wild animals found in Kenya except elephants can be seen in the park.

The **Bomas of Kenya** at Langata – a short way past the entrance to the national park on the right hand side – is a cultural centre and worth visiting if you are interested in seeing traditional dances and hearing songs from the country's 16 ethnic groups. There are daily performances at 2 and 4.30 pm. Entry costs KSh 60 or KSh 30 for students. If you are not on a tour, bus No 24 from outside Development House, Moi Ave, will get you there in about half an hour.

The farmhouse which was formerly the residence of Karen Blixen (the author of *Out of Africa*) has been converted into a **museum** and can be visited. The entrance fee is KSh 50 (KSh 10 for students). It's right next door to the Karen College on Karen Rd just before you get to Karen township (what could be easier!). To get there, take public bus No 27 from the central bus station in Nairobi.

1	Garden Guest House & Park View Hotel
2	Terminal Hotel
3	Embassy Hotel
4	Excelsior Hotel
5	680 Hotel
6	New Stanley Hotel & Thorn Tree Café
7	Kambirwa Boarding & Lodging
8	Mombasa Rest House
9	New Kenya Lodge
10	New Safe Life Lodging
11	Bujumbura Lodge & Africana Hotel
12	Sunrise Lodge & Modern Green Bar
13	Iqbal Hotel
14	Al Mansura Hotel
15	Hotel Salama
16	Hotel Solace
17	Gloria Hotel
18	Dolat Hotel
19	Ambassadeur Hotel
20	Hilton Hotel
21	Blukat Restaurant
22	African Heritage Café
23	The Pub & Akasaka Japanese Restaurant
24	Trattoria
25	Satkar Vegetarian Restaurant
26	Grower's Café & Lobster Pot
27	Supreme Restaurant & Mayur Restaurant
28	Mandarin Restaurant
29	Malindi Dishes
30	Supermac

There is a viewing level on the 23rd floor of the **Kenyetta Conference Centre**. Whoever takes you up in the lift may expect a tip. You can take photographs from the top – no restrictions.

Places to Stay

Bottom End The majority of budget hotels, except for two popular places outside the centre, are between Tom Mboya St and River Rd. So if you find one is full, it's only a short walk to another.

The *New Kenya Lodge* (tel 22202), River Rd at the junction with Latema Rd,

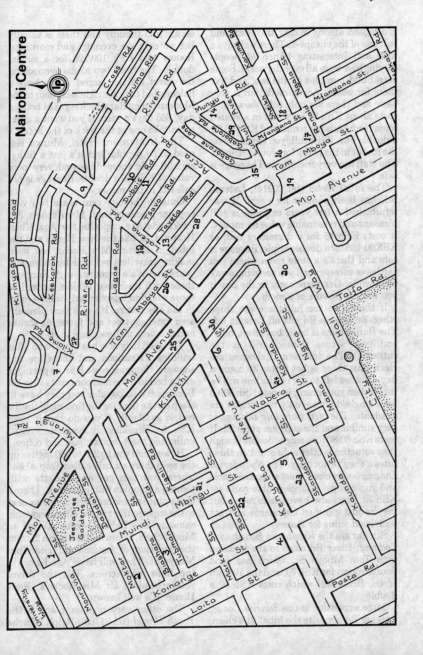

Nairobi Centre

is a legend among budget travellers and still one of the cheapest. There's always a wild and interesting bunch of people staying here from all over the world. Some even build humpies on the roof and live there for weeks. Accommodation is very basic and there are only cold showers. It costs about KSh 50 for a bed in a shared room (four beds per room) and KSh 90 for a double but, if it's full, you can sleep on the roof or in the lobby for around KSh 20. The staff are very friendly and baggage is safe.

The *Iqbal Hotel* (tel 20914), Latema Rd, has been popular for years. It was refurbished a few years ago and is still pleasant and reasonable value for money. It costs KSh 45 for a dormitory bed, or KSh 90/135 for a double/triple. Baggage is safe and there's a store room where you can leave excess gear if you are going away for a while. Get there early in the day if you want to be sure of a room.

If these two are full there are three others on Dubois Rd just off Latema Rd. The *Bujumbura* is basic but clean, quiet and very secure (locked grill at the entrance). The toilets and showers are clean plus there is hot water 24 hours a day. Clothes left to dry on the line will be there when you return. It costs KSh 50/60 for a single/double – only two singles are available. The *New Safe Life Lodging* is very similar and the staff are cheerful. It costs KSh 60/80 for a single/double though they sometimes offer a discount on these rates if they're not busy. The *Nyandarwa Lodging* is very clean, quiet and comfortable and you can get a large double room for KSh 70. They also have single rooms but they're just glorified cupboards and not such good value for money.

Similar are the *Kambirwa Boarding & Lodging*, River Rd close to the junction with Tom Mboya St, which has good double rooms for KSh 70, and the *Yasmin Hotel*, River Rd, which costs KSh 69 a double.

More expensive is the *Sunrise Lodge*, Latema Rd opposite the Iqbal. It's clean,

secure and friendly and there is usually hot water in the evenings and mornings. Rooms cost KSh 100/120 for a single/double. The front two rooms overlooking the street are the largest. They have a balcony but they are right next door to the Modern Green Bar which rages 24 hours a day, 365 days a year. If you want a quiet room take one at the back of the hotel.

The *Al Mansura Hotel*, Munyu Rd, used to be popular but it's just a filthy, squalid hole these days and very poor value at KSh 58 a double. Baggage is not safe left in the rooms.

Outside the city centre are two very popular places to stay. *Mrs Roche's*, 3rd Parklands Ave opposite the Aga Khan Hospital, is, like the New Kenya and the Iqbal, a legend. Mrs Roche has been making travellers welcome for at least 15 years and it's a favourite with campers, those with their own vehicle, as well as those who don't particularly want a room in the city centre. It's in a very pleasant area amongst trees and flowering shrubs and is a very mellow place to stay.

The good lady now has more room after building extensions and there are hot showers. Camping costs KSh 40 per night and a bed in a shared room costs KSh 50. Because it's so popular you may have to sleep on the floor for the first night until a bed is available. If you do this it costs KSh 40. Breakfast is available – eggs, unlimited toast, butter, jam and coffee.

However, if you go 200 to 300 metres up the road there's a café called *Stop n' Eat* where you can get an omelette with tomato and onion filling and tea. There's also a place across 3rd Parklands Ave next to the supermarket which offers vegetable samosas and Indian sweets. To get to Mrs Roche's, take a *matatu* (KSh 2) from the junction of Latema Rd and Tom Mboya St. They will have 'Aga Khan' in the front windscreen. Tell the driver you're heading for Mrs Roche's Guest House. It's well known.

The other very popular place is the *Youth Hostel* (tel 21789), Ralph Bunche

Rd between Valley Rd and Ngong Rd. It's often very crowded so it's a good place to meet other travellers. It's very clean, well-run, stays open all day and there's always hot water in the showers. Dave, the warden is very friendly and will lock up gear safely for you for up to two weeks. On a day-to-day basis there are lockers to keep your gear in when you go out. The notice board (for messages, things for sale, etc) is one of the best in Africa. A bed in a shared room costs KSh 45 but you must have a YHA membership card to stay. If not, you'll have to join the association for KSh 180 plus a photograph.

Any *matatu* or bus which goes down either Valley Rd or Ngong Rd will drop you at Ralph Bunche Rd. The No 8 *matatu* (which goes down Ngong Rd) is probably the most convenient. You can pick it up either outside the Hilton Hotel or the main post office on Kenyatta Ave. If you're returning to the Youth Hostel after dark don't be tempted to walk back from the centre of the city. Many people have been robbed. Always take a *matatu* or taxi.

There are three *YMCAs* (tel 337468) on State House Rd, and one *YWCA* (tel 338689) on Mamlaka Rd off Nyerere Rd. The YMCAs all cost KSh 100 per person for bed and breakfast in a dormitory or shared room plus they have more expensive private rooms (around KSh 240 with bathroom). Baggage left in the rooms is definitely not safe and the prime culprits are fellow travellers. Meals at the YMCAs are excellent value. The YWCA is reluctant to take short-term visitors. It prefers to take people who are going to stay at least one month and the room rates are geared towards this. It does, however, take couples as well as single women.

Some travellers have recommended the *Danish Volunteer Service Guest House*, Ngong Rd just past Kenyatta Hospital, which is a large old house surrounded by a garden. A bed costs KSh 50 and there are cooking facilities. Whether this place is for volunteers alone isn't clear so it would

be best to stay somewhere else initially until you can check it out.

Mid-range Hotels There are several mid-range hotels in the same area as the bulk of the budget hotels.

One of the cheapest is the *Dolat Hotel*, Mfangano St, which is very clean and quiet and costs KSh 94/140 for a single/double both with shower and toilet. Quite a few travellers stay here. Another is the *Gloria Hotel*, Tom Mboya St at Ronald Ngala St, which costs about KSh 135/150/220 for a single/double/triple with bathroom and breakfast. There are hot showers and they store luggage at no extra charge. In the same block is the *Hotel Solace* (tel 331277), Tom Mboya St, which costs KSh 165/215/330 for a single/double/triple.

More expensive is the *Hotel Salama* (tel 25898), Tom Mboya St at Luthuli Ave. It's fairly good value at KSh 195 to KSh 292 for a single and KSh 260 to KSh 339 for a double with breakfast. The rooms are self-contained. Tom Mboya St is a very busy road so, depending on which room you are given, both the Gloria and the Salama can be noisy.

Outside this area, try the *Hotel Terminal* (tel 28817), Moktar Daddah St between Koinange St and Muindi Mbingu St, close to the Kenya Airways city terminus. It's very clean, quiet and the rooms are pleasant and airy. It costs KSh 175/224 for a single/double with shower and toilet. There's always hot water available and there's an overnight laundry service at reasonable rates.

Not such good value but reasonable all the same is the *Embassy Hotel* (tel 24087), on Biashara St and Tubman Rd between Koinange St and Muindi Mbingu St. Rooms there cost from KSh 152 to KSh 175 for a single and KSh 237 for a double with shower and toilet. Hot water is available 24 hours a day. If the Embassy is full try either the *Garden Guest House* or the *Parkview Hotel* both next to each other on Monrovia St at Muindi Mbingu

St overlooking Jeevanjee Gardens. They're clean and quiet and cost KSh 240 a single including breakfast.

Similar to these is the *Hotel Pigale*, Moktar Daddah St, which is popular with Peace Corps volunteers and costs KSh 165/200 for a single/double.

Outside the city centre, one of the cheapest is the *Green View Lodge* (tel 720908), off Nyerere Rd. (It's at the top of the gravel road which runs at the back of the Minet ICDC House and other high-rise offices and there's a sign for the hotel on Nyerere Rd.) It's an older style lodge surrounded by a garden and fairly quiet. Rooms cost KSh 130/240 for a single/double including breakfast. The lodge has a bar and restaurant.

Another place worth trying in this price range is the *CPK Guest House*, Bishops Rd between Valley Rd and Ngong Rd. This is an Anglican guesthouse and they're not too keen on taking travellers. If you're accepted, it's very good value at KSh 160 per day including three meals, morning and afternoon tea. The food is very good. The missionaries who stay here can tell you a lot about what's happening out in the sticks.

Places to Eat

For the majority of people with limited means, lunch is the main meal of the day and this is what the cheaper restaurants cater for. That doesn't mean they're all closed in the evening (though quite a few are). What it does mean is that food available in the early evening is often what is left over from lunch time. If you want a full evening meal it generally involves a splurge.

There are a lot of very cheap cafés and restaurants in the Latema Rd and River Rd area where you can pick up a traditional African breakfast of mandazi and tea or coffee. Most of these places would also be able to fix you up with eggs and the like. Since many of them are Indian-run, they also have traditional Indian breakfast foods like samosa and idli.

If you'd like something more substantial (or don't like Indian food) then the *Grower's Café*, Tom Mboya St, is worth going to and popular with both local people and travellers. They have such things as eggs (boiled or fried), sausages and other hot foods, fruit salads with or without yogurt and good coffee. Prices are reasonable.

The *Bull Café*, round the corner from the New Kenya Lodge on Ngariama Rd, is also popular with people staying on Latema Rd and is a pleasant place to eat. The *Munchberger*, Accra Rd, offers a good sized breakfast for KSh 16. If you're staying at the Hotel Terminal the attached restaurant on the ground floor is a good place to pick up breakfast.

For a breakfast splurge, try the restaurant on the ground floor of the *Ambassadeur Hotel*, Moi Ave, which offers the full range of western breakfast dishes. It's not cheap. Similar is the breakfast buffet at the other international hotels like the *Hilton* or the *New Stanley Hotel*.

Kenya is the home of all-you-can-eat lunches at a set price and Nairobi has a wide choice of them, most offering Indian food. One of the best is the *Supreme Restaurant* at the junction of Tom Mboya St and River Rd. It offers excellent Indian vegetarian food and you can choose either the ordinary lunch or the 'deluxe' lunch and superb fruit juices.

The *Blukat Restaurant*, Muindi Mbingu St between Banda St and Kigali Rd offers both vegetarian and meat set lunches. The day's specials are chalked up on a blackboard outside the restaurant. You'll see quite a few travellers eating here.

The *New Flora Restaurant*, Tsavo Rd just off Latema Rd, is said by some travellers to have the best barbequed chicken in Africa and prices are very reasonable. They also offer other dishes. The *Kamana Restaurant Co* at the back of the Good Hope Hotel, River Rd just before Accra St, has excellent mixed grill lunches which you'll be hard pressed to finish and they do pots of tea. Similar is the *Njogu ini Rwathia Hotel*, Mfangano St near the Dolat Hotel. The servings are enormous.

Don't forget the restaurant on the ground floor of the Iqbal Hotel which offers Indian curries. For traditional coastal Swahili dishes (made with coconut or coconut milk) try one of the restaurants on Gaborone Rd off Luthuli Ave.

If you're staying at Mrs Roche's you can get good, cheap food at *Tom's Shack* which is up the road to the first junction then turn left. His place is on the right hand side. Good Indian food can also be found at *Bimpy's*, 5th Parklands Ave – a short walk from Mrs Roche's.

That well-known British staple, fish & chips, has caught on in a big way in Nairobi and there are scores of places offering it. They're all cheap but the quality varies from instant nausea to excellent. Avoid like the plague the one on the corner of Moktar Daddah St and Muindi Mbingu St on the opposite side of the road from Jeevanjee Gardens.

Instead, try *Supermac*, Kimathi St directly opposite the Thorn Tree Café on the mezzanine floor of the high-rise there. It's very popular at lunch times and deservedly so. It not only does some of the best fish & chips in Nairobi but also offers sausages, salads and fruit juices. Get there early if you don't want to queue.

Other travellers have recommended *Monty's Fish & Chips*, Tubman Rd at Muindi Mbingu St. Like Supermac, they offer fish, chips and sausages to takeaway or eat there.

Going up-market, you can get an excellent western-style lunch in the restaurant section of *The Pub*, Standard St between Koinange St and Muindi Mbingu St directly opposite the British High Commission. It's open daily from 12 noon to 2 pm and 6 to 11 pm. They do such things as grilled steaks, chops, goulash and chicken all served with salad and

chips. Soup and sweets are extra. It's also open for dinner (same prices).

You should also try a set lunch (choice of menu) at the *African Heritage Café*, Banda St between Koinange St and Muindi Mbingu St. The best time to go is on Saturdays when a live band plays for most of the afternoon.

Nairobi is replete with restaurants offering cuisines from all over the world – Italian, Spanish, Japanese, Chinese, Indian, Lebanese, steak houses, seafood specialists, etc – and at many of them the prices are surprisingly reasonable. For US$5 per person you could eat well at quite a few of them. For US$10 per person you could eat very well at almost all of them.

For south Indian vegetarian food you probably can't beat the *Satkar Restaurant* (tel 337197), Moi Ave. The entrance is in the first alleyway on the left hand side past Kenyatta Ave walking towards Jeevanjee Gardens. If you have eaten lunch and you order a full dinner you probably won't be able to finish it.

Similar is the *Mayur Restaurant* (tel 25241) on the 1st floor of the Supreme Restaurant. It's self-serve and open daily for lunch and dinner but closed on Tuesdays.

The *Mandarin Restaurant*, Tom Mboya St, is supposedly the best Chinese restaurant in Nairobi. The *Hong Kong Restaurant* (tel 28612), Koinange St, is also good.

For Italian food there is really only one place to go and that is the very popular *Trattoria* (tel 340855), on the corner of Wabera St and Kaunda St, which is open daily from 8.30 am to 11.30 pm. Both the atmosphere and the food are excellent and there's a wide choice on the menu. As you might expect, the ice cream is superb. It's worth it!

For seafood, try the *Lobster Pot* (tel 20491), on the corner of Tom Mboya St and Cabral St, which offers fish, prawn and lobster dishes as well as charcoal-grilled meats. The only Spanish restaurant in town is the *El Patio* (tel 340114), Reinsurance Plaza Building, mezzanine floor, Nkrumah Lane. Similarly, there's only one Japanese restaurant, the *Akasaka*, which you'll find next to The Pub on Standard St between Koinange and Muindi Mbingu St. It's definitely on the expensive end of a splurge.

For steak eaters looking for a gut-busting extravaganza there's no better place than *The Carnivore* out at Langata just past Wilson Airport (bus Nos 14, 24 and 124). Tell the conductor where you are going and it's a km walk from where you are dropped off (signposted). It's easy to hitch back into the centre when you're ready to go. Whether it's lunch or dinner there's always beef, pork, lamb, ham, chicken, sausages and at least one game meat (often wildebeest or zebra). The roasts are barbequed on Masai spears and the waiters carve off hunks onto your plate until you tell them it's enough. Prices include salads, bread, desserts and coffee.

Many of the large hotels in Nairobi offer all-you-can-eat smorgasbord lunches and dinners often with barbequed steaks and the like for a set price at the weekends. Sunday lunches are popular.

Entertainment

Nairobi is a good place to take in a few films and at prices considerably lower than in the west. There are cinemas on Moi Ave, Nkrumah Lane, Mama Ngina St, Latema Rd and Kenyatta Ave. Check with local papers to see what's on.

There are three main discos in the centre of Nairobi. They are the *New Florida Bar*, Koinange and Banda Sts (a most unusual shaped building), the *Starlight Disco* next to the Panafric Hotel, junction of Milimani Rd and Valley Rd, and *Visions*, Kimathi St. Visions is owned by the same people who run the Trattoria Italian restaurant. They all cost KSh 100 entrance fee unless you get hold of a discount card entitling you (usually) to a 50% discount. If you eat at the Trattoria you'll get one automatically. Otherwise, these cards get handed out on the street when business is slack. With drinks, they're all a pretty expensive night out.

For live music, visit the *African Heritage Café*, Banda St, any Saturday afternoon. It's a popular place to go.

The most popular bar among travellers is probably the *Thorn Tree Café*, part of the New Stanley Hotel on Kimathi St. This is an outdoor bar and café with tables, chairs and Martini umbrellas. If you are arranging to meet someone in Nairobi this is the place to do it. Everyone knows where the Thorn Tree is and there's a notice board where you can leave personal messages (but not advertisements of any kind – things for sale, looking for people to join a safari, etc). The Thorn Tree does breakfasts, lunches and dinners but it's relatively expensive and you don't get much for your money. Between around 11.30 am and 2 pm they won't serve you a beer unless you are also eating.

Another very popular bar (where you don't have to buy a meal in order to have a beer) is *The Pub*, on Standard St between Koinange and Muindi Mbingu Sts. It's open daily from 12 noon to 2 pm and 6 to 11 pm and attracts a remarkable cross-section of the population. The Pub is part of the Six Eighty Hotel which also has the open-air *Terrace Bar* on the 1st floor above the entrance lobby. This bar is open all day unlike The Pub. Another similar place which has been recommended is *Buffalo Bill's Night Club* at the Harrington Hotel – take a taxi from the centre.

For an unparalleled spit-and-sawdust binge put aside a whole evening to join the beer-swilling, garrulous hordes at the *Modern Green Bar*, Latema Rd next to the Sunrise Lodge. This place rages 24 hours a day, 365 days a year and the front door has never been closed since 1968. All human life is here – *miraa*-chewing teenage girls, hustlers, whores, dope dealers and what one traveller once described as 'lowlife whites'. The juke box is always on full blast with screaming Indian vocalists or African reggae. The bar is completely encased in heavy-duty wire mesh with a tiny hole through which money goes first and beer comes out afterwards. It's a great night out if you have the stamina but is definitely not for the squeamish.

Those looking for more genteel surroundings in which to sip their beer should try either the *Grosvenor Hotel*, Ralph Bunche Rd at the junction with Lenana Rd and close to the Youth Hostel, or the lawn of the *Fairview Hotel*, Bishops Rd close to 3rd Ngong Ave.

For something with more intellectual and less alcoholic content there are a lot of specialist clubs and societies in Nairobi, many of which welcome visitors. Most of the foreign cultural organisations have film and lecture evenings (usually free of charge) at least once or twice a week. Give them a ring and see what they have organised. The addresses and telephone numbers of all these can be found in *Tourist's Kenya*.

Getting Around

Bus To Jomo Kenyatta International Airport the Kenya Airways bus leaves the airlines terminal, Koinange St, daily at 8, 9, 10 and 11.30 am, 12.45, 2.30, 4.45, 6.45 and 8 pm. The fare is KSh 40 and the journey takes about half an hour. You can also take public bus No 34 from outside the Ambassadeur Hotel. It costs just KSh 5 but takes considerably longer. To Wilson Airport (for small planes to Malindi, Lamu, etc) take bus Nos 14, 24 or 124 from in front of Development House, Moi Ave, and elsewhere. The fare is KSh 2 off-peak.

To get to the entrance of the Nairobi National Park take bus No 24 or 25 from Moi Ave. Arrange a lift through the park at the entrance gate.

Taxi A taxi to the International Airport will cost KSh 250 and can be shared by up to four people.

Hitching For Mombasa, take bus No 13 or 109 as far as the airport turn-off and hitch from there. For Nakuru or Kisumu, take bus No 23 from the Hilton to the end of its route and hitch from there. Otherwise start from the junction of Waiyaki Rd and Chiromo Rd (the extension of Uhuru Highway) in Westlands. For Nanyuki or Nyeri, take bus No 45 or 145 from the central bus station up Thika Rd to the entrance to Kenyatta College and hitch from there. Make sure you get off the bus at the college entrance not the exit from where it's very difficult to hitch. Otherwise, start from the roundabout where Thika Rd meets Forest Rd and Muranga Rd.

WATAMU

About 24 km south of Malindi is another smaller beach resort called Watamu with its own **National Marine Park** – part of the Marine National Reserve which stretches south from Malindi. The coral reef life here is even more spectacular than at Malindi since it has been much less exploited and poached by shell hunters. It is not, however, as easy to get to and you will probably have to utilise the boats laid on by the large hotels and they're usually more expensive than at Malindi. The beach is excellent and not as crowded as Malindi. There are plenty of *matatus* from the bus station in Malindi to Watamu throughout the day which cost KSh 5 and take 20 to 30 minutes.

Some three to four km from Watamu just off the main road from Malindi are the famous **Gedi** ruins, one of the principal historical monuments on the coast. Though the ruins are extensive, this Arab-Swahili town is something of a mystery since it's not mentioned in any of the Portuguese or Arab chronicles of the time.

Excavations, which have uncovered such things as Chinese porcelain and Persian artefacts, have indicated the 13th century as the time of its foundation but it was inexplicably abandoned in the 17th or 18th century. If you're interested in archaeology it's worth a visit. Entry costs KSh 50 (KSh 20 for student card holders).

To get there you take the same *matatus* as you would to Watamu but get off at Gedi village which is where the *matatus* turn off from the main Malindi to Mombasa road. From there it's about a km walk to the monument along a gravel road (signposted).

Places to Stay

The only trouble with Watamu is the lack of budget accommodation. About the cheapest is the *Seventh Day Adventist Youth Camp* where you can get a bed in one of the three rooms (each with two or three beds) or camp. The camp site is pretty basic and the facilities aren't up to much but there's a kitchen with a gas cooker (which works) and it's close to the beach, about 10 minutes' walk from the village. The beds cost KSh 45 each though you may initially be quoted up to KSh 80.

Otherwise, try the *Mushroom Club* which is a weird but very friendly place and costs KSh 150 a triple with bathroom.

You can use the facilities at the large hotels even if you're not a resident – most of them have a bar, restaurant, swimming pool, disco and water sports facilities but scuba diving (at the Seafarer Hotel) is expensive.

Nakuru & the Rift Valley Lakes

All the Rift Valley lakes with the exception of Naivasha and Baringo are highly saline soda lakes and most are very shallow. Their alkaline waters support high concentrations of microscopic blue-green algae and diatoms which, in turn, provide an ideal environment for tiny crustaceans and insect larvae to thrive in.

They in their turn are eaten by certain species of soda-resistant fish.

These soda lakes are a perfect environment for many species of water bird which flock to them in their millions. Foremost among these birds are the deep pink Lesser Flamingo (*Phoenicopterus minor*), which feed on the blue-green algae, and the pale pink Greater Flamingo (*Phoenicopterus ruber*), which feed on the tiny crustaceans and insect larvae. Also numerous are various species of duck, pelican and stork. The highest concentrations of these birds are naturally found where food is most abundant and this can vary from lake to lake.

Naivasha and Baringo are, by contrast, freshwater lakes. No-one really knows why this should be when all the others are highly saline and none have any outlets. The ecology of these two freshwater lakes is naturally very different from the soda lakes.

Lakes Naivasha, Nakuru, Elmenteita and, to a lesser extent, Baringo are readily accessible to independent travellers without their own vehicle. There are plenty of buses and *matatus* and a rail link between Nairobi, Naivasha and Nakuru and less frequent buses and *matatus* between Nakuru and Marigat (for Lake Baringo). The other lakes, however, are more remote and there's no public transport. Hitching is very difficult and can be impossible. There's also the problem that both Lakes Nakuru and Bogoria are national parks so you are not allowed to walk around. You must tour them in a vehicle.

Tours are available from Nairobi and, to a lesser extent, Nakuru but they're not cheap. It's often cheaper to get a group together and hire a vehicle to visit these lakes.

NAIVASHA

The town of Naivasha is of little interest in itself. Most travellers simply use it as a base or pass through it on the way to **Lake**

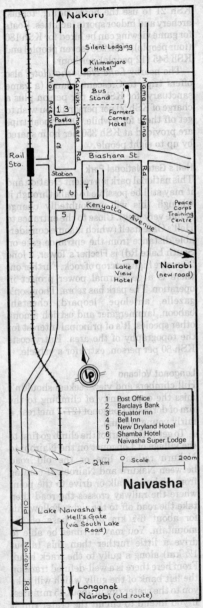

1 Post Office
2 Barclays Bank
3 Equator Inn
4 Bell Inn
5 New Dryland Hotel
6 Shamba Hotel
7 Naivasha Super Lodge

Naivasha

Scale 0   200m

Lake Naivasha & Hell's Gate (via South Lake Road)

Longonot → Nairobi (old route)

Naivasha, Longonot volcano and Hell's Gate National Park.

Places to Stay

There are several reasonable budget hotels in Naivasha town where you can stay. They include the *Lake View Hotel* (KSh 35/60 a single/double, friendly); *Naivasha Super Lodge* (KSh 25/45 for a single/double, very clean); *New Dryland Hotel* and the *Silent Lodging*. Somewhat more expensive are the *Kilimanjaro Hotel* and the *Equator Inn*. Top of the range is the *Bell Inn*.

Places to Eat

Most of the cheapies have their own restaurants where you can get a good, simple meal. For breakfast you probably can't beat the ones offered at the *Bell Inn*. Sit out on the verandah and enjoy a substantial breakfast of juice, croissants, eggs, bacon, sausage, toast and marmalade and tea or coffee. They also serve excellent lunches and dinners.

Getting Around

The usual access to Lake Naivasha is along South Lake Rd. This also goes past the entrance to Hells' Gate National Park. There are fairly frequent *matatus* between Naivasha town and Kongoni for a few shillings. This road has to be one of the worst in Kenya! It is also extremely dusty in the dry season.

Lake Naivasha

The best overall views of Lake Naivasha are to be had from the top of the escarpment which you crest about half way between Nairobi and Naivasha town. There are excellent views of Longonot volcano from here, too.

Naivasha is one of the Rift Valley's freshwater lakes and its ecology is quite different from that of the soda lakes but it's home to an incredible number of different bird species.

With budget accommodation on the lake shore there are several possibilities.

For those without camping equipment, the *YMCA* is probably the best place to stay. You can rent a bed in a *banda* for KSh 35 per night plus KSh 5 for temporary membership of the YMCA. Camping is also possible for KSh 20 but it's not the best site. The *bandas* have kitchens but no firewood or charcoal – this can be bought for KSh 5. Cooking utensils are provided free of charge. The office has a limited supply of canned and packaged foods (corned beef, biscuits, sodas and the like). Look out for the sign on the right hand side after you pass the entrance gate for Hells' Gate. It's also possible to camp or rent an old boat anchored close to the shore for KSh 50 per boat per night (the boats sleep two people) at *Burch's Farm* which is about four km down South Lake Rd from the old Nairobi road turn-off (signposted on the right hand side). The Burches are very friendly and hospitable people. Hot showers are available and you can buy vegetables from their garden.

The most popular place to stay, however, is *Fisherman's Camp* some distance past the YMCA. You can camp for KSh 20 with your own tent or rent a tent for KSh 30 per person. Free rowing boats are available (included in the camping fee).

Near Fisherman's Camp is *Top Camp* where you can rent a *banda* for KSh 60 per person including cooking facilities. It's a very pleasant site and there's a tiny wooden shack nearby called the *Kanjiraini Hotel* which offers simple cooked meals and tea. If you are buying your own supplies, there's a small village about 1½ km away where you can get basic supplies and fresh meat.

Another place worth considering if you have your own camping equipment (no tents for hire) is the *Safariland Lodge* (tel 0311 20241). Camping costs KSh 42 per person per night (children half price). The Lodge itself is a top range hotel with all the facilities you might expect. Facilities are free to residents but campers and nonresidents must pay a daily fee of KSh 21 to use the horse riding, tennis, archery and indoor sports facilities. Boats for game viewing can be hired for KSh 180 (four people), KSh 250 (seven people) and KSh 545 (12 people) per hour.

The nearby *Lake Naivasha Hotel* also offers trips to Crescent Island (a game sanctuary) for KSh 80 per person plus a charge of KSh 50 per person if you wish to get off there for a while. Other boat trips are provided at KSh 350 per hour shared by up to eight people.

Hell's Gate National Park

This national park is a recent creation and it may still be possible to walk through it (though this will undoubtedly change before very long). Close to the entrance to Hell's Gate itself (which is some considerable distance from the entrance gate on South Lake Rd) is **Fischer's Tower**, a lone 25-metre high outcrop of rock. Further on, there is a geothermal power project in operation. The park has zebra, Thomson's gazelle, antelope, leopard, cheetah, baboon, lammergaier and ostrich among other species. It's of principal interest for the topography of the area. Entry costs KSh 80 per person, extra for a vehicle.

Longonot Volcano

Hill climbers and view seekers shouldn't miss the opportunity of climbing to the rim of dormant Longonot (2777 metres), a fairly young volcano.

To get to the start of the climb go first to the village of Longonot on the Nairobi to Nakuru railway line or the old road between Nakuru and Nairobi. If coming from Nakuru, walk or drive to the point where the railway crosses the road then take the road off to the right. Follow this for about 6½ km to the base of the mountain. You may at times be able to drive a little further than this (about 1½ km) along a gully to the track head. From here there is a well-defined track on the left bank of the gully which will take you to the crater rim in about 45 minutes. If you intend to circuit the crater rim it will take a further 2½ to three hours. The views from the top are magnificent.

If you are driving to the track head try to find someone who is willing (for a negotiable price) to look after your vehicle whilst you are away. Cars left unattended may be broken into.

NAKURU

Nakuru is the centre of a rich farming area about half way between Nairobi and Kisumu on the main road and railway line to Uganda. It's here that the railway forks, one branch going to Kisumu on Lake Victoria and the other to Malaba on the Ugandan border. It's Kenya's third largest city with a population of 75,000. The big draw for travellers is the nearby **Lake Nakuru National Park** with its prolific bird life.

Things to See

Rising up on the north side of Nakuru is the **Menengai Crater**, an extinct 2490-metre-high volcano. The crater itself descends to a maximum depth of 483 metres below the rim. You can drive up most of the way if you have a vehicle and walk the last stretch to the rim. Otherwise it shouldn't take you more than half a day to walk all the way there and back from Nakuru. The views from the crater rim are worth all the sweat and hard work!

Another nearby place which is worth visiting is the **Hyrax Prehistoric Site** just off to the left on the main road south from Nakuru. There's a small museum with displays explaining the significance of the site.

Places to Stay

The *Sikh Temple* is reluctant to take travellers any more but some people do manage to get in. If you are offered a place for the night don't forget to leave a reasonable donation in the morning.

Amigos Guest House on Gusil Rd can definitely be recommended. It's friendly, clean, has hot water (only in the morning) and costs KSh 50/80/115 for a single/double/triple with common showers and toilets. Don't confuse this place with the other Amigos at the junction of Kenyatta Ave and Bondoni Rd which isn't anywhere near as good and can be very noisy because of the upstairs bar.

Also recommended is the *Tropical Valley Lodge* on Moi Rd. It's very good value, clean, spacious, friendly and has hot showers. It costs KSh 45/70 for a single/double.

The *Nakuru Inn*, Bondoni Rd, is also reasonable value. It's comfortable, centrally located and has hot showers. The rooms cost KSh 60 a double.

If these three places are full try the *Nakuru Central Hotel* just off Gusil Rd which is basic but has hot showers and costs KSh 50/60 for a single/double. There's only one single. Avoid the *Nakuru 3-Ways Bar & Hotel*, Gusil Rd, if possible. It's a dump and only has cold showers but they'll still charge you KSh 47/70 for a single/double.

Going up in price, the *Mukoh Hotel*, Gusil Rd, is very clean, quiet and comfortable. It costs KSh 60/120 for a single/double without bathroom and KSh 85/170 for a single/double with bathroom. There are hot showers. There's also the *Shirikisho High Life Hotel* (tel 45330) which is good value at KSh 60/120 for a single/double with hot showers.

If you want to camp, the cheapest place is the *Agricultural Showground*, off Showground Rd, which costs KSh 7.50 per night. There are no lights at night so make sure you know where your tent is if walking back from town at that time. There's another very good camp site just inside the entrance to Lake Nakuru National Park which costs KSh 30 per person per night. Because it's inside the national park boundary you will also, however, have to pay the park entrance fee. Fresh water is available.

Places to Eat

For price and quality, the best place to eat is the *Tipsy Restaurant*, Gusil Rd. It's

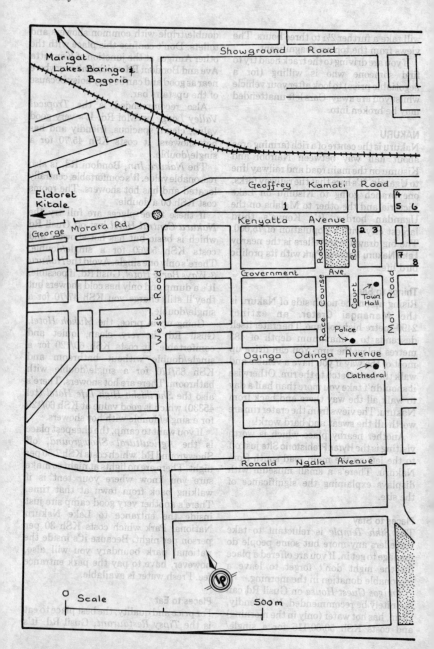

Showground Road

Marigat
Lakes Baringo &
Bogoria

Eldoret
Kitale

George Morara Rd.

West Road

Geoffrey Kamati Road

Kenyatta Avenue

Government Ave.

Race Course Road

Court Road

Moi Road

Oginga Odinga Avenue

Ronald Ngala Avenue

Town Hall

Police

Cathedral

1
4
5 6
2 3
7
8

0   Scale   500 m

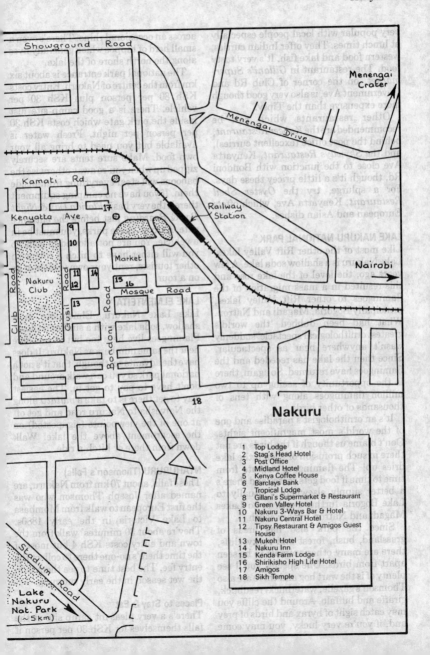

very popular with local people especially at lunch times. They offer Indian curries, western food and lake fish. It's very tasty food. The restaurant in *Gillani's Supermarket*, on the corner of Club Rd and Government Ave, is also very good though more expensive than the Tipsy.

Other restaurants which can be recommended are the *Kabeer Restaurant*, behind the post office (excellent curries), and the *Skyways Restaurant*, Kenyatta Ave close to the junction with Bondoni Rd, though it's a little pricey these days. For a splurge, try the *Oyster Shell Restaurant*, Kenyatta Ave, which offers European and Asian dishes.

LAKE NAKURU NATIONAL PARK

Like most of the other Rift Valley lakes, Lake Nakuru is a shallow soda lake. A few years ago, the level of the lake rose and this resulted in a mass migration of the flamingoes to other Rift Valley lakes, principally Bogoria, Magadi and Natron. What had been dubbed 'the world's greatest ornithological spectacle' suddenly wasn't anywhere near as spectacular. Since then the lake has receded and the flamingoes have returned. So again, there is the opportunity of seeing up to two million flamingoes along with tens of thousands of other birds.

It's an ornithologist's paradise and one of the world's most magnificent sights. Don't blame us though if the birds are not there in such profusion or even if the lake dries up! The flamingoes migrate from time to time if food gets scarce and there's a better supply elsewhere – usually to Lake Bogoria further north or to Lakes Magadi and Natron further south.

Since the park also has areas of grassland, bush, forest and rocky cliffs, there are many other animals to be seen apart from birds. One species you'll see plenty of is the wart hog and there are also Thomson's gazelle, waterbuck, reedbuck, giraffe and buffalo. Around the cliffs you may catch sight of hyrax and birds of prey and, if you're very lucky, you may come across an occasional rhino. There's even a small herd of hippos which generally lives along the north shore of the lake.

The national park entrance is about six km from the centre of Nakuru. Entry costs KSh 80 per person plus KSh 30 per vehicle. There is a good camp site just inside the park gate which costs KSh 30 per person per night. Fresh water is available but you need to bring all your own food. Make sure tents are securely zipped up when you're away otherwise the baboons will steal everything from inside them. If you have no camping equipment there's the very basic *Florida Day & Night Bar & Boarding* just before the entrance gate. As in all game parks, you must be in a vehicle. You are not allowed to walk so you will either have to hitch a ride with other tourists, rent your own vehicle or go on a tour.

LAKE ELMENTEITA

Like Lake Nakuru, Elmenteita is a shallow, soda lake with a similar ecology. Flamingoes live here too but in nowhere near the same numbers as Nakuru. It does have the advantage, though, that it's not a national park so you can walk around and don't have to pay to get in. The easiest way to get there is to take a *matatu* along the Naivasha to Nakuru road and get off at one of the viewpoints (signposted) on the escarpment above the lake. Walk down from there or hitch a ride.

NYAHURURU (Thomson's Falls)

These falls, about 70 km from Nakuru, are named after Joseph Thomson who was the first European to walk from Mombasa to Lake Victoria in the early 1880s. They're about 30 minutes' walk from the town and entry costs KSh 4 but most of the time there's no-one there to collect the entry fee. The best time to see them is in the wet season in the early morning.

Places to Stay & Eat

There's a very pleasant camp site at the falls themselves for KSh 30 per person if you have your own equipment. Bring food and drink with you. There's also a camp site at the *Thomson's Falls Lodge* (tel 22006).

For those without camping equipment there are several budget hotels available. Very popular is the *Muthengera Farmers' Lodge* which costs KSh 50 a single with bathroom. Good food at reasonable prices is available. Also highly recommended is the *Good Shepherd's Lodge* which at KSh 45 per room (one or two people) with shower and toilet, clean towels and soap is a bargain. It's on the left hand side of the road on the way to the falls.

Two recommended places include the *Nyahururu Hotel Boarding & Lodging* at the north end of town which has clean, comfortable rooms with hot showers, and the *Nyandarwa County Council Hostel* next to the post office. Both have their own restaurants and prices are reasonable.

If you're not eating at your hotel try a meal at the *Thomson's Falls Lodge* (tel 22006) which is open to nonresidents. An English-style breakfast costs KSh 40 and lunch or dinner KSh 90 (four courses). They have a very rustic dining room.

LAKE BOGORIA

Lake Bogoria is a shallow soda lake, north of Nakuru off the B4 highway to Marigat and Lodwar. The B4 is a superb, sealed highway all the way.

Bogoria is now a national park so there's an entry fee of KSh 80 per person plus KSh 30 per vehicle. The best entry point to Bogoria is from the 'Loboi Gate' a few km south of Marigat. The gravel road from here to the park is excellent. It's a very peaceful area but it doesn't compare with the ornithological spectacle of Nakuru. There are also the **Hot Springs** and geysers, about three-quarters of the way down the lake going south, which are worth a visit.

Places to Stay

There are two camp sites at the southern end of the lake – *Acacia* and *Riverside* – but there are no facilities whatsoever and

the lake water is totally unpalatable. Bring all water and food with you if you are intending to stay at either site. Otherwise, the camp sites are very pleasant. There's another camp site just outside the northern entrance gate which costs KSh 30 per person per night and where drinking water is available. There's a small shop nearby which sells basic supplies.

LAKE BARINGO

Some 15 km north of the town of Marigat you will come to the village of Kampi ya Samaki which is the centre for exploring Lake Baringo. This lake, like Naivasha, is a freshwater one with a very different ecology from Lake Bogoria. It supports many different species of aquatic and bird life as well as herds of hippos which invade the grassy shore every evening to browse. You'll hear their characteristic grunt as you walk back to your tent or *banda* after dark or settle down for the night. They might even decide to crop the grass right next to your tent. You'll also see the occassional crocodile.

Places to Stay

There's a superb place to stay just before the village called *Roberts' Camp* where you can camp for KSh 40 per person per night or rent a *banda* for KSh 75 per person. The *bandas* are highly recommended if there is one available (there are only a few and demand is heavy). You won't get better value in the whole of Kenya. They are beautiful, circular, grass-thatched traditionally-styled houses which are clean as a new pin and furnished with comfortable beds, table and chairs and mosquito netting at the windows. Showers and toilets are separate and cooking facilities are available for a small extra charge. If you can, book in advance through David Roberts Wildlife Ltd, PO Box 1051, Nakuru. The people are very friendly.

If this place is full and you have no camping equipment try the *Bahari Lodge* in Kampi ya Samaki which costs KSh 30/50 for a single/double. It's basic. This is also the only place where you will find beer apart from the club next door to the Roberts' place. There's a lively bar at the end of the road facing you as you enter the village.

Right next door to the Roberts' is the *Lake Baringo Club* which is a top-range establishment. Nonresidents can use the facilities for KSh 20 per day on weekdays and KSh 50 at weekends except for the swimming pool which is a standard KSh 50 per day. It's the only place on the 'mainland' at Lake Baringo where you will find ice-cold beers. It's also the only place where you will be able to buy petrol (there is no petrol pump in Marigat). Prices are normal and the pumps are open to the public.

There are also places to stay in Marigat. At the crossroads of the B4 and the village is the *Wananchi Lodge* which costs KSh 50 a double and is basic but provides towels, soap and mosquito nets. More expensive is the *Marigat Inn* about 1½ km from the main road turn-off (no signs so you must ask). It costs KSh 70 a double, is very pleasant and has a bar and restaurant.

Mt Kenya & Around

MT KENYA

Climbing to the top of Mt Kenya (5199 metres), Africa's second highest mountain, is high on most travellers' priority list of things to see and do whilst in Kenya. However, many people hurry the ascent ending up with a thumping headache and very little appreciation of what the mountain has to offer. Before rushing off, get hold of a copy of the Mountain Club of Kenya's *Guide to Mount Kenya & Kilimanjaro* edited by Iain Allan. The last edition was published in 1981 but not too much has changed since then especially regarding the main routes which trekkers, as opposed to climbers,

will follow. Look for it in bookshops in Nairobi or direct from the Mountain Club of Kenya, PO Box 45741, Nairobi. It's also a good idea to buy a copy of the Survey of Kenya's map, *Mount Kenya* (1:125,000), for an overall view. It's available from the Map Office in Nairobi or from bookshops for KSh 35.

The entry fee to Mt Kenya is KSh 80 per person plus KSh 30 per person for every night you spend on the mountain.

All the huts on the mountain where people spend the night, except the National Park Rangers Station in Teleki Valley and the Meteorological Station lodge, belong to the Mountain Club of Kenya. Some of them though, are reserved exclusively for use by members. The club's agent on the mountain is the Naro Moru River Lodge (tel 23), PO Box 18, Naro Moru, which is about two km from the town of Naro Moru on the west side of the main road to Nanyuki.

In theory, you are supposed to book and pay for the use of these huts beforehand. This is surely fair since the club has to pay for maintenance and repairs – or, at least, it would be if the overnight fees were reasonable. Many hikers, however, consider the KSh 75 per person per night fee to be a rip-off. Since most of the huts are unlocked and don't have a caretaker, you are presented with a moral choice. A lot of people don't even see it that way and consider the decision to be an entirely practical one.

Mackinder's hut, owned exclusively by the Naro Moru River Lodge, costs even more – KSh 160 per night. The alternative is to take your own tent and, on some routes, this would be almost essential. Camping fees, where they are charged, are usually only KSh 15.

Preparations

The summits of Mt Kenya are covered in glaciers and snow so you are going to need a good sleeping bag, lots of warm clothes including a hat and gloves and preferably waterproof clothing. The need for the latter mainly depends on the time of year but it can rain at any time. The best time to go for fair weather is from mid-January to late February and from late August through to September. A decent pair of boots are an advantage but not strictly necessary. A pair of joggers are quite adequate most of the time though it's useful to have a pair of thongs or canvas tennis shoes available for the evenings if your shoes get wet.

A tent is a very good idea if you don't want to or can't pay the lodge and hut fees. It's more or less essential if you are planning to use the Chogoria route. A stove and a billy are very useful not only for cooking dried soups but for that hot drink when the night descends. You should also have a water container with a capacity of at least one litre per person and water purifying tablets for the lower levels of the mountain. All this sort of gear can be hired in Nairobi – see the National Parks & Game Reserves section for details.

Getting to the Trail Heads

There are seven different routes to the summit but the majority of travellers take the Naro Moru route. This isn't obligatory so if you're not simply interested in getting to the top and back down again it's worth considering the Sirimon and Chogoria routes too. With your own transport you can get much closer to the trail heads on the Naro Moru and Sirimon tracks than you can using public transport so this gives you a head start.

To Naro Moru Your starting point is the town of Naro Moru on the Nairobi to Nanyuki road. There is at least one daily OTC bus per day from Nairobi to Naro Moru which costs KSh 39. The depot in Nairobi is at the junction of Cross Rd and Racecourse Rd.

You can also take a public bus from the country bus station in Nairobi to Nyeri for KSh 30 and a *matatu* from there to Naro Moru for KSh 10 (they often ask for KSh 15 to KSh 20 because they see a lot of tourists).

This two-stage journey is not recommended. The buses are very crowded and you end up hurtling down hills at high speed and crawling up them at a snail's pace.

To Sirimon Take the same OTC bus as to Naro Moru but continue on to Nanyuki or do the same two-stage journey except that on the final leg you need a *matatu* to Nanyuki (KSh 15). If you want to ascend the mountain the same day you leave Nairobi, take the earliest possible bus from Nairobi. Otherwise you'll probably have to stay in Nanyuki for the night and leave the following day.

To get from Nanyuki to the start of the Sirimon track take one of the frequent *matatus* going to Timau and tell the driver you want to be dropped off at the start of the track (signposted). If you go over a fairly large river (the Sirimon River) then you've gone too far. It's about 15 km out of Nanyuki and the fare should be KSh 5.

To Chogoria Take an OTC bus from Nairobi direct to Chogoria village or one first to Embu (KSh 30) then another to Chogoria (KSh 20). You will probably have to spend the night in Chogoria before setting off up the mountain as the first day's hike is a long slog up the forest track with nowhere to stay en route.

The Trails

The normal weather pattern is for clear mornings with the mist closing in around 11 am to 1 pm. The mist sometimes clears again in the early evening for a while. This means that if you want to make the most of the trek you should set off early every morning and for the final assault on Point Lenana (the highest point for walkers) you need to make a 5 am start if you want to see the sunrise from the top.

In describing the following trails it's assumed that you are reliant on public transport.

Naro Moru Trail This is the most popular and the quickest. It's also the steepest and the one on which you are most likely to come down with altitude sickness if you rush the hike. It can be done in three or even two days starting from the Meteorological Station but what's the point in climbing up to the top and back down again just so you can say you've done it? If you take four or five days you can adopt a far more leisurely pace and see something along the way.

Day 1 The first day is spent walking from Naro Moru to the Meteorological Station at 3050 metres, a distance of about 26 km. On the way there you will pass the *Youth Hostel* (tel 2471) (about 10 km out of Naro Moru). To stay there costs KSh 25 for members and KSh 30 for others. It's a beautiful old converted farmhouse with kerosene lanterns and log fires. Cooking facilities are provided and, although it's a good idea to bring food along, you can buy things like eggs, milk, carrots, cabbages as well as prepared food nearby. You can also rent essential camping gear. Tents cost KSh 125 per day and boots and stoves cost KSh 25 each per day. *Minto's Safaris* also have a rest house nearby where it's possible to find a bed. Half way between the Youth Hostel and the Meteorological Station is the park entrance gate where there is a camp site. It's sometimes possible to get a lift all the way from Naro Moru to the Meteorological Station.

At the *Meteorological Station* which is where most people stay you can camp for KSh 15 per person or rent a bunk in the lodge there for KSh 100 per person.

Day 2 The second day you start out for Teleki Valley (4000 metres) which will take five to six hours. About one hour out of the Meteorological Station you come to the so-called 'vertical bog' which, if you have ever been up the Ruwenzori, is normally, by comparison, little more than a gentle slope with occasional wet patches. Once you reach the crest of the

ridge overlooking Teleki Valley, the trail veers off to the right above Teleki Hut and down to the valley floor and on to Mackinder's Camp. This camp is just a series of tents set up on platforms and if you haven't got your own equipment it's going to cost KSh 80 per person for a bunk. If you have your own tent the fee is KSh 15. The warden is very friendly and may let you cook on his stove.

Day 3 The third day takes you from Mackinder's Camp to the rocky bluff on which the Austrian Hut sits below Point Lenana. It's a steep four-hour climb. Next to the Austrian Hut is Top Hut but the latter is for the exclusive use of Kenya Mountain Club members. In theory, you're supposed to pay the normal fee for use of the Austrian Hut at the Naro Moru River Lodge but the hut is unattended.

Day 4 On the fourth day you need to get up very early – at the latest by 5 am – in order to make the hour-long trek to Point Lenana (4985 metres) which is the highest one can go without specialist climbing equipment. Follow the rocks (or snow) close to the ridge all the way (not on the glacier). When you have taken in the sunrise and the views, return the same way or descend along either the Chogoria or Sirimon trails.

Sirimon Trail This is the least used of the three trails which we cover.

Day 1 On the first day you walk from the start of the track on the Nanyukic to Timau road to the park entrance gate (about 10 km) and on from there to the camp site (3350 metres) which is a further 11 km. It's a fairly easy stroll and you don't gain much in altitude. If you prefer, you can stay at the park entrance gate and continue the next day.

Day 2 On the second day you walk from the camp site to Liki North Hut (3993 metres). It's an easy morning's walk. This hut belongs to the Mountain Club but is unattended. If it's still early in the day and you prefer to continue, don't take the trail off to the left at the Liki North stream (which takes you to Liki North Hut) but cross the stream and the ridge beyond and descend into Mackinder Valley. There is a clearly defined track from here which follows the eastern side of the valley, eventually crosses the main Liki stream and leads you to Shipton's Cave – a formation of obvious rock overhangs where you can camp for the night. From the camp site to Shipton's Cave takes about seven hours.

Day 3 On the third day (assuming you start from Liki North Hut) you descend into the main Liki valley and pick up the track which takes you past Shipton's Cave and on to Kami Hut. The last part of this walk is heavy going as it's steep but there are cairns to guide you. Kami Hut is another Mountain Club hut but, again, it's unattended.

Day 4 On the fourth day you go from Kami Hut to the Austrian Hut. There are two possibilities here and unless you have experience of rock climbing it's not recommended that you take the direct route since it involves a fairly precipitous rock scramble. Instead, cut left into the head of the Gorges Valley then round the east side of Point Lenana to the Austrian Hut along a well-defined track.

Day 5 On the fifth day your options are the same as on the Naro Moru route.

Chogoria Trail This trail, from the eastern side of the mountain, is perhaps the most beautiful of the access routes to the summit and certainly the easiest as far as gradients go. From Minto Hut there are breathtaking views of the head of the Gorges Valley and the glaciers beyond.

Day 1 On the first day you walk from the start of the track on the Nanyuki to long 24 km slog to the park entrance gate where there is a lodge with *bandas* for KSh 80 per person. If you have a tent and prefer to camp, there is a camp site two km beyond the park entrance gate. This is free unless the park warden comes round to collect fees in which case it will cost KSh 10 per person. En route you pass the Chogoria Forest Station a few km past Chogoria village.

If you can't make it as far as the park entrance gate on the first day it's possible to camp at the Bairunyi Clearing (2700 metres, indicated simply as 'Clearing' on the tourist map of Mt Kenya).

It's possible to get a lift all the way from Chogoria village to the park entrance. There is at least one vehicle per day which goes between the Forest Station and the park entrance lodge. It generally leaves the forest station between 6.30 and 7 am and returns between 9 and 10 am. There may also be people staying at the lodge who can help out with lifts.

Day 2 The second day is spent walking from either the lodge or the camp site to Minto Hut with spectacular views all the way. The hut belongs to the Mountain Club but is unattended.

Day 3 On the third day you walk from Minto Hut to the Austrian Hut (about 3½ hours) up to the head of the Gorges Valley then round the head of the Hobley Valley.

Day 4 From the Austrian Hut your options are the same as on the Naro Moru trail.

EMBU

There are many cheap hotels spread out along the main road especially near where the buses stop. One recommended place is the *Kwiremia Guest House* which is clean and costs KSh 35/40 for a single/double.

NANYUKI

This is a small town on the western side of Mt Kenya which services the predominantly agricultural activities of the surrounding area. For travellers it's an overnight stop either on the way to Lake Turkana or for those who are planning to climb Mt Kenya along the Sirimon trail.

Places to Stay

The best place to stay is the *Sirimon Guest House* near the *matatu* park which costs KSh 45 for a room (one or two people). It's spotlessly clean including the showers and toilets, plus soap and towels are provided. They also have rooms with shower and toilet for KSh 70/90 for a single/double. There is hot water 24 hours a day. The meals are very good and excellent value.

There's a *Youth Hostel* (tel 2112) at the Emmanuel Parish Centre, Market Rd near the post office, which costs KSh 35 for a bed. People who have stayed there report that a membership card is not needed and the staff are very friendly.

NARO MORU

The *Naro Moru River Lodge* (tel 23), about two km from the town on the west side of the main Nairobi to Nanyuki road, maintains a bunk house for budget travellers where a bed costs KSh 60 per night. The private rooms cost considerably more. Meals are available.

In the town itself there is the *Naro Moru 82 Bar & Restaurant* which costs KSh 35/55 for a single/double but we don't recommend that you stay here. It's a scruffy, poorly maintained place and the mattresses often stink of urine.

Northern Kenya

This vast area covering thousands of square km to the borders with Sudan, Ethiopia and Somalia is an explorer's paradise and hardly touched by the 20th century. The tribes which live here – the Samburu, Turkana, Rendille, Boran, Gabra, Merille and el-Molo – are some of

the most colourful and fascinating people in the world. The whole area is a living ethnology museum. Like the Masai, most of them have little contact with the modern world preferring their own centuries-old traditional lifestyles and customs. Many have strong warrior traditions and, in the past, it was the balance of power between the tribes which defined their respective areas. Change is coming slowly to these people as a result of missionary activity, employment as rangers and in anti-poaching patrols in national parks and game reserves, and the tourist trade.

Not only are the people another world away from Nairobi and the more developed areas of the country but the landscapes are tremendous. Perhaps no other country in Africa offers such diversity. Much of it is scrub desert dissected by *luggas* (dry river beds which burst into brief but violent life whenever there is a cloudburst), and peppered with acacia thorn trees often festooned with weaver bird nests. There are also extinct and dormant volcanoes, barren, shattered lava beds, canyons through which cool, clear streams flow, oases of lush vegetation hemmed in by craggy mountains and huge islands of forested mountains surrounded by sand deserts. And, right at the top, the legendary Lake Turkana (the 'Jade Sea') – Kenya's largest lake and, as a result of the Leakeys' archaeological digs, regarded by many as the birthplace of humankind.

A remote region like this with such diverse geographical and climatic features naturally supports a varied fauna. Two species you will see a lot of (but not elsewhere) are Grevy's zebra, with their much denser pattern of stripes and saucer-like ears, and the reticulated giraffe. Lake Turkana also supports the largest population of Nile crocodile in Kenya which feed mainly on the fish living in the lake but which will quite happily dine on those not so cautious humans swimming there. The giant eland finds a sanctuary in the forested hills around Marsabit.

There are several national parks and game sanctuaries in the area, three of them along the Ewaso Ngiro River just north of Isiolo. Further north are the national reserves of Maralal, Losai and Marsabit. Others may shortly be gazetted for the Mathew's range and the eastern side of Lake Turkana near the Ethiopian border.

GETTING THERE & AROUND
Hitching
Apart from three routes – Kitale to Lodwar, Nyahururu to Maralal, and Isiolo to Marsabit to Moyale – there is no public transport in this area of Kenya. You can certainly hitch as far as Lodwar (from Kitale) on the western side of Lake Turkana and Maralal or Marsabit (from Nyahururu or Isiolo) on the western side of the lake but that's about the limit of reliable hitching possibilities. Other routes have *very* little traffic.

The mission stations/schools invariably have their own Land Rovers (and some have their own light planes) but they usually only go to regional centres once a week or once a fortnight. So, although most will try to help out if you're stuck, you cannot be guaranteed a lift.

Own Vehicle
For most travellers it comes down to hiring a vehicle or going on a tour. Vehicle hire rates are covered in the Getting There & Around section of this chapter. Remember if you are taking your own vehicle to have with you a high-rise jack, sand ladders, a shovel, a long, strong rope (that you can hitch up to camels) plus enough fuel and water. The only regular petrol pumps you will find are at Isiolo, Maralal, Marsabit and Lodwar. Elsewhere there's nothing except religious mission stations that will reluctantly sell you limited amounts of fuel at up to three times the price in Nairobi.

A 4WD is obligatory if you want to get off the beaten track though you wouldn't have too many problems in a 2WD in the dry season if you stuck to the main routes as far as Lodwar or Loyangalani.

Tours
Most of the tours last eight to nine days and all seem to follow much the same route. Starting from Nairobi, they head up the Rift Valley to Lake Baringo, over to Maralal then up the main route to Loyangalani on Lake Turkana via Baragoi and South Horr. On the return journey, again via Maralal, they take in Samburu National Reserve and Buffalo Springs National Reserve. No more than one or two tours take in Marsabit National Reserve since the only way of getting there from Loyangalani is directly across the Koroli Desert (hazardous after rain) or via the long loop north through North Horr and Maikona. Even this involves crossing the Chalbi Desert which, like the Koroli, is hazardous after rain. There are also the restrictions on the Marsabit to Isiolo road to contend with – all transport must go in convoy at a certain time of day, usually between 10 and 11 am.

The cost of these tours varies between KSh 2750 and KSh 3300 which includes transport, all meals, park fees and necessary camping equipment. There are all-camping safaris which use open-sided 4WD trucks and are not for those in search of luxury. Everyone has their favourite company but a lot depends on the people you find yourself with, what you see en route, and the drivers and guides. The following companies all offer a Turkana tour usually once a week but sometimes once a fortnight:

Safari Camp Services Ltd
  PO Box 44801, on the corner of Koinange St and Moktar Daddah St, Nairobi (tel 28936, 330130)
Best Camping
  PO Box 40223, Nanak House, 2nd floor, on

the corner of Kimathi St and Banda St,
Nairobi (tel 28091, 27203)
Zirkuli Expeditions Ltd
PO Box 34548, Banda St, Nairobi (tel
23949, 20848)
Birds Paradise Tours & Travel Ltd
PO Box 22121, Nairobi (tel 25898)
Special Camping Safaris
PO Box 51512, Gilfillan House, 3rd floor,
Kenyatta Ave, Nairobi (tel 338325)

WEST OF TURKANA

The main route is from Kitale to
Kapenguria then along the A1 to the
junction with the B4 highway then north
along the B4 to Lodwar and Ferguson's
Gulf on Lake Turkana. It's also possible to
go much further north on the C47 from
Lodwar to Lokitaung.

Getting There & Away

There are daily buses in either direction
between Kitale and Lodwar for KSh 80 to
KSh 90 (depending on the company)
which take about eight hours. You can
also hitch trucks for about KSh 60 but
they generally take longer than the buses.
The road is now sealed all the way so it's a
comfortable journey.

Saiwa Swamp National Park

If you are in your own vehicle there are a
number of interesting stops you can make
en route. The first is Saiwa Swamp
National Park about 15 km north of Kitale
to the east of the main road. The entrance
fee is KSh 30 as usual. It's a very small
park and one of the few that you are
allowed to walk around. The main
attraction is the shy and elusive Sitatunga
swamp antelope.

Cherangani Hills

Further north the road passes over the
beautiful Cherangani Hills and simple
accommodation is available at Ortum in
the Marich Pass for around KSh 25 per
person. This is one of the great unknown
trekking areas in the world. It's possible to
climb up to over 3030 metres in the
vicinity of Ortum and the views are really
stunning. The area is inhabited by the
Pokot tribe which, like many others in
northern Kenya, have been virtually
untouched by the 20th century.

Lodwar

In Lodwar there's a good choice of
accommodation. The *Mombasa Hotel*
costs KSh 29/40 for a single/double but
doesn't have fans. The *Ngonda Hotel*
costs KSh 28 a single without a fan and
KSh 40/70 a single/double with fan. For
those who would prefer something slightly
better, the *Turkwel Lodge* is worth the
extra at KSh 75/105 for a single/double
with fan. You might also be able to get a
very cheap bed (KSh 10 per person) at the
TRP Guesthouse but it's supposedly only
for those working on the Turkana
Rehabilitation Project.

One of the cheapest places to eat in
Lodwar is the *New Loima Hotel* which
offers very filling meals. The *Turkwel
Lodge* is also popular if you prefer
western-style food (steak and chips,
mixed grills, beef stew and rice, etc).
Prices are reasonable.

Kalekol

From Lodwar many travellers head to
Kalekol (the village about one km from
the lake shore at Ferguson's Gulf). There
is an infrequent *matatu* service (KSh 25)
between the two which is usually an open-
backed Land Rover or Land Cruiser with
bench seats. By Turkana standards,
though, this road is quite busy and most
people will manage to get a lift if they are
prepared to wait around for a day or two.
There are also VSOs in this area so you
may be able to arrange a lift with them.

Places to Stay & Eat There are two fairly
primitive lodges in Kalekol. One of them
is the unnamed *Guesthouse* across the
main street from the Safari Hotel. It costs
KSh 30 a single and good cheap meals are
available. The other is the *Ojavo Mieni*

Hotel also known as George's Hotel because it's owned by George Ojavo. It's a grass hut with kerosene lamps and the people are extremely friendly. Many travellers have found a welcome here. It costs KSh 25/50 a single/double. The people will prepare food for you very cheaply if you make advance arrangements – subject to what's available. The Safari Hotel is a good place to enquire about lifts back to Lodwar.

The *Lake Turkana Fishing Lodge* is for well-heeled tourists only and not a possibility for budget travellers though it might be worth a visit. To get there you have to take a boat from the lake shore across Ferguson's Gulf which costs KSh 40 return. Lunch there costs KSh 50. Meals are based around lake fish and are excellent. It's also the only place where you can find a cold beer.

Central Island National Park

If you want to visit Central Island National Park the lodge lays on a launch which costs KSh 150 to KSh 200 per person for a four-hour trip. The island is a dormant volcano and the three crater lakes provide a breeding ground for large numbers of Nile crocodile and water birds.

Eliye Springs

Getting to Eliye Springs is far more difficult and demands a 4WD because there is soft sand in places. The little traffic that comes here is reluctant to pick up extra passengers. It's a beautiful place with palm trees, white sand and, of course, the lake.

Places to Stay & Eat The lodge is very run-down these days and quotes ridiculous figures for the price of a room. Depending on the season, though, you can haggle this down to KSh 50 for a very basic double. You can camp on the beach close to the lodge but they'll still charge you KSh 40 for this dubious privilege. Food is very limited and consists mainly of ugali, chips and fish. Bring your own with you if you

want to be sure. They have a refrigerator where food can be stored and if you make arrangements they will cook for you.

Other Places

West of Lodwar the **Loima Hills** are an interesting area to explore. They rise up to 2121 metres out of the desert and are topped with cedar forests inhabited by elephant, lion, buffalo and other game. If you are thinking of going there, bring all your own supplies, camping equipment and hire a Turkana guide at the Forestry Camp at the base of the hills.

If you are interested in **Turkana handicrafts**, the best places to buy them are either in **Lokichar**, 75 km south of Lodwar, or in **Lodwar** itself at the Diocesan Handicrafts shop. Prices are five to six times cheaper than in Nairobi.

EAST OF TURKANA

There are two main routes. The first is the A2 highway from Nanyuki to Marsabit via Isiolo and Laisamis and north from there to Moyale on the Ethiopian border. The other is from Nakuru to Maralal via Nyahururu and north from there to Loyangalani on Lake Turkana via Baragoi and South Horr. From Loyangalani you can make a loop all the way round the top of the Chalbi Desert to Marsabit via North Horr and Maikona.

Getting There & Away

None of these roads are surfaced and the main A2 route is corrugated *piste* which will shake the guts out of both you and your vehicle. The road from Maralal to Loyangalani, however, is surprisingly smooth though there are bad patches here and there.

The main cross route between the two is via Wamba and Parsaloi. This road leaves the main A2 about 20 km north of Archer's Post and rejoins the Maralal to Loyangalani road about 15 km south of Baragoi. Although a very minor route, the Maralal to Loyangalani road is smooth most of the way with occasional rough patches. You'll probably only use it if you want to visit the Mathew's Range.

Hitching This is definitely possible between Isiolo, Marsabit and Moyale and between Nyahururu and Maralal. On the Maralal to Loyangalani road, however, you are unlikely to get beyond Baragoi or South Horr.

Bus There are public buses three times per week in either direction between Isiolo and Marsabit (at 11 am on Wednesday, Friday and Sunday from Marsabit) and between Marsabit and Moyale (at the same time on the same days from Marsabit). The fare is KSh 100 on either route and the journey takes about six hours. A convoy system is in operation in order to deter *shifta* (bandits) from stopping and robbing trucks, buses and cars.

National Reserves

Just north of Isiolo are three national reserves, **Samburu National Reserve, Buffalo Springs National Reserve** and **Shaba National Reserve**, all of them along the banks of the Ewaso Ngiro River and covering an area of some 300 square km. They are all mainly scrub desert and open savannah plain broken here and there by small rugged hills. The river, however, which is permanent, supports a wide variety of game and you can see rhino, elephant, buffalo, cheetah, leopard, lion, dik dik, Grevy's zebra and the reticulated giraffe. Crocodiles can also be seen on certain sandy stretches of the river bank.

If you are driving round these parks in your own vehicle it's useful to have a copy of the Survey of Kenya map, SK 85 *Samburu & Buffalo Springs Game Reserves* which costs KSh 30.

There are four public camp sites close to the Gare Mara entrance gate of the Buffalo Springs Reserve and three other special camp sites spread between this reserve and the Samburu Reserve. There

are also three lodges but they are outside the range of budget travellers.

Parsaloi

Further north, Parsaloi (sometimes spelt Barsaloi) is a small scattered settlement with a few basic shops but no petrol station. It has a large Catholic Mission which may offer accommodation or allow you to camp. There are no lodges.

Baragoi

Next on is Baragoi, a more substantial settlement full of tribespeople, a couple of lodges, and a few shops. Petrol is sometimes available here. Quite a few people speak English. The town seems to get rain when everywhere else is dry so the surroundings are quite green.

Places to Stay & Eat If you have to stay in Baragoi the *Mt Ngiro Lodging* is probably the best. It costs KSh 25 a single. Facilities are primitive. It's the first building on the left as you enter the town from the south. For food, eat at *Hussein Mohammed's Hotel* across the street. They have tea and mandazi for breakfast, and for lunch or dinner meat and potato karanga with rice or chapatti.

South Horr

The next village is South Horr set in a beautiful lush canyon between the craggy peaks of Mt Nyiro (2752 metres), Mt Porale (1990 metres) and Mt Supuko (2066 metres). There's no petrol available.

Places to Stay There is one small, basic hotel in the centre of the village and a large Catholic Mission opposite where you may – but most likely will not – be offered accommodation. They have been hostile to travellers in the past.

The best place to stay is the *Kurungu Camp Site*, a few km out of the village on the road to Loyangalani on the right hand side (signposted). This is the place where a lot of Turkana tour trucks put their people up for the night. There's also a lodge but it's semidefunct because the person who owns it is having problems with the government. There are, however, three double *bandas* with beds which you can rent (rates are negotiable). The camp site still functions (pitch your tent on the sand under trees) and there are staff. It costs KSh 20 per person per night. Whenever a large group stays (a tour truck) the local tribespeople will put on a traditional dance (at a price). Local people are used to tourists taking photographs but it's going to cost you money.

Lake Turkana

Going further north, the lushness of the Horr Valley gradually peters out until, finally, you reach the totally barren, shattered lava beds at the southern end of Lake Turkana. The lake is a breathtaking sight, vast yet totally barren. You'll see nothing living except a few stunted thorn trees. The reason for this is that Turkana is a soda lake. Watch out for crocodiles if you go swimming in the lake.

Loyangalani

A little further up the lake shore and you are in the Turkana village of Loyangalani. There is an airstrip, post office, fishing station, luxury lodge (with the only cold cleansing ales for hundreds of km), two camp sites, and a Catholic Mission (which will reluctantly sell petrol).

If you want to explore the surrounding area get in touch with Francis Langachar, a very friendly young Turkana man who speaks fluent English. His father went on John Hillaby's epic trek to Lake Turkana, which is recounted in the saga *Journey to the Jade Sea*.

Places to Stay Of the two camp sites, it's hard to favour one over the other. Both are staffed by very friendly people but the *Sunset Camp* is the cheaper of the two. Camping costs KSh 20 per person with good showers and toilets. They also have nine simple *bandas* at KSh 100 per person with sheets and blankets. Safari Camp

Services utilise this camp site for their Turkana buses.

The second camp site, *El Molo Camping*, costs KSh 30 per person to camp plus they have several *bandas* for KSh 200 per person (singles, doubles and triples). There are good shower and toilet facilities. Best Camping put their people on the Turkana bus. Both camp sites are fenced but neither have electricity or firewood though they do have kerosene lanterns.

Both camp sites have a bar and dining area. Whichever place you camp at, beware of the sudden storms which can descend from Mt Kulal. If there is a storm, stay with your tent otherwise it won't be there when you get back and neither will anything else.

Other than the camp sites there is the luxury *Oasis Lodge* which is well outside the range of budget travellers – even for meals – and if you want to use any of their facilities (bar, swimming pool, etc) it will cost KSh 100 per day.

North Horr

North of Loyangalani the road loops over the lava beds to North Horr. There is a short cut across the desert through the village of Gus. There are no lodges or petrol but the Catholic Mission is very friendly and will probably offer you somewhere to stay if you are stuck. It's staffed by German and Dutch people.

Maikona

Next down the line is Maikona where there is a large village with basic shops (but no lodges) and a very friendly Catholic Mission and school, staffed by Italian people. You will undoubtedly be offered a place to stay for the night. Please leave a donation before you go if you do stay. The mission usually has electricity and the father goes into Marsabit once a fortnight in his Land Rover.

Marsabit National Park & Reserve

South of Maikona is Marsabit and you are

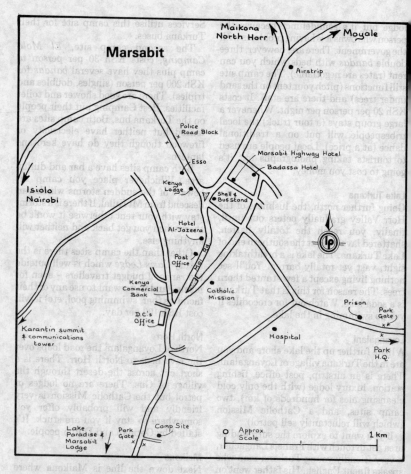

Marsabit

Maikona
North Horr

Moyale

Airstrip

Police
Road Block

Esso

Marsabit Highway Hotel

Badassa Hotel

Kenya
Lodge

Shell &
Bus Stand

Isiolo
Nairobi

Hotel
Al-Jazeera

Post
Office

Kenya
Commercial
Bank

Catholic
Mission

Prison

D.C.'s
Office

Park
Gate

Karantin summit
& communications
tower

Hospital

Park
H.Q.

Lake
Paradise &
Marsabit
Lodge

Park
Gate

Camp Site

Approx.
Scale

1 km

back in relative civilisation. The main attraction is the Marsabit National Park & Reserve centred around Mt Marsabit which rises to a height of 1702 metres.

The hills are thickly forested and in stark contrast to the desert on all sides. Mist often envelops them in the early morning. The view in all directions from the communications tower on the summit above town is magnificent. In fact, it's probably as spectacular as any of the views from Mt Kenya or Kilimanjaro. The whole area is peppered with extinct volcanoes and volcanic craters (or *gofs*), some of which have a lake on the crater floor.

The National Park & Reserve is home to a wide variety of the larger mammals including lion, leopard, cheetah, elephant, rhino, buffalo, wart hog, Grevy's zebra, the reticulated giraffe, hyena, Grant's gazelle, oryx, dik dik and greater kudu among others. Unfortunately, it's difficult to see them because the area is thickly forested.

The Survey of Kenya's map, SK 84 *Marsabit National Park & Reserve*, KSh 35, is a good buy if you are touring this park.

Places to Stay There is a good camp site next to the entrance gate (water and plenty of firewood) but the so-called showers are a joke. Camping costs KSh 5 per person. Entry to the park, open from 6 am to 7.15 pm, costs the usual KSh 30 per person. There's also a luxury safari lodge overlooking a lake but it's beyond the range of budget travellers.

If you don't have camping equipment there's a good choice of lodges available in town. One of the best is the *Kenya Lodge*. It's very clean and pleasant and costs KSh 40/60 for a single/double with soap and toilet roll provided. The showers are communal and the hotel has a bar and restaurant at the front. Almost as good is the *Marsabit Highway Hotel* which costs KSh 50/85/120 for a single/double/triple with shower and toilet. It's a large place and very clean. The hotel has a bar/restaurant open from 11 am to 2 pm and 5 pm to 12 midnight. There is a disco on Friday and Saturday nights. The cheapest place, though not such good value, is the *Hotel Al Jazeera* which costs KSh 25 per person with communal showers. There's a bar and restaurant out front. For something vaguely mid-range, try the *Badassa Hotel*.

National Parks & Game Reserves

Kenya is East Africa's safari country without compare. Its national parks may not be as large as those in Tanzania, Zambia, Namibia or South Africa but you'll be hard pressed to better the variety and numbers of wild game.

Most of the parks have a standard entry fee of KSh 80 per person plus KSh 30 per vehicle but Masai Mara costs KSh 30 per person plus KSh 50 per vehicle. If you are taking your own transport it's a good idea to equip yourself with maps of the parks before you set out. The maps published by the Survey of Kenya can be bought either from the Map Office or bookshops in Nairobi. The ones you will need are SK 87 *Amboseli National Park* (KSh 35), SK 86 *Masai Mara Game Reserve* (KSh 35), SK 82 *Tsavo East National Park* (KSh 30), and SK 78 *Tsavo West National Park* (KSh 30). The new Macmillan maps of *Amboseli, Masai Mara* and *Tsavo East & West* are expensive but even better.

If you are travelling independently you will also need camping equipment unless you can afford to stay at the (very expensive) lodges of which there are several in each park. Camping equipment can be rented from several places in Nairobi though the main places are Atul's (tel 25935), Biashara St, Nairobi, which is mainly a fabric shop, and Habib's Cars Ltd (tel 20463, 23816), Agip House, Haile Selassie Ave, Nairobi.

Rental charges are less, proportionally, the longer you rent equipment but typical short-term charges per day are: tent (two person) – KSh 75 (deposit KSh 900); tent (three person) – KSh 120 (deposit KSh 1200); sleeping bag – KSh 30 (deposit KSh 500); mattress – KSh 12 to KSh 16 (deposit KSh 200 to KSh 300); mosquito net – KSh 10 to KSh 15 (deposit KSh 300 to KSh 450); gas stove – KSh 15 to KSh 50 (deposit KSh 400); gas tank (three kg) – KSh 45, indefinite period (deposit KSh 500); and kerosene lamp – KSh 8 (deposit KSh 120).

You are not allowed to walk in the national parks in Kenya (except in certain designated areas) so you will have to hitch a ride with other tourists, hire a vehicle or join an organised tour.

Hitching is really only feasible if the people you get a ride with are camping. Since this requires some considerable preparation in terms of food, drink and equipment, tourists with their own cars are naturally reluctant to pick up hitch

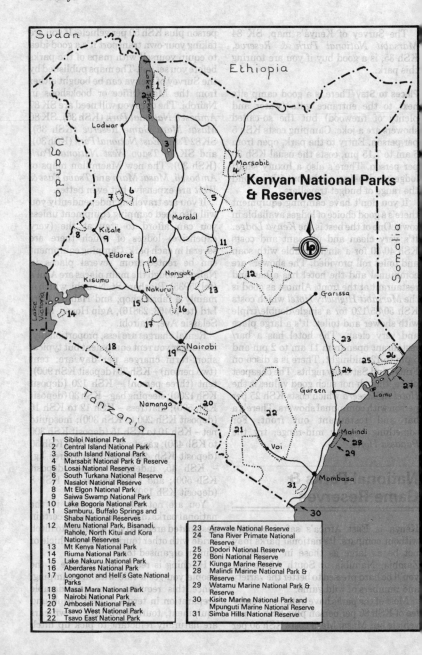

Kenyan National Parks & Reserves

1 Sibiloi National Park
2 Central Island National Park
3 South Island National Park
4 Marsabit National Park & Reserve
5 Losai National Reserve
6 South Turkana National Reserve
7 Nasalot National Reserve
8 Mt Elgon National Park
9 Saiwa Swamp National Park
10 Lake Bogoria National Park
11 Samburu, Buffalo Springs and Shaba National Reserves
12 Meru National Park, Bisanadi, Rahole, North Kitui and Kora National Reserves
13 Mt Kenya National Park
14 Riuma National Park
15 Lake Nakuru National Park
16 Aberdares National Park
17 Longonot and Hell's Gate National Parks
18 Masai Mara National Park
19 Nairobi National Park
20 Amboseli National Park
21 Tsavo West National Park
22 Tsavo East National Park

23 Arawale National Reserve
24 Tana River Primate National Reserve
25 Dodori National Reserve
26 Boni National Reserve
27 Kiunga Marine Reserve
28 Malindi Marine National Park & Reserve
29 Watamu Marine National Park & Reserve
30 Kisite Marine National Park and Mpunguti Marine National Reserve
31 Simba Hills National Reserve

hikers. If the people who give you a lift are staying at the lodges then you have the problem of how to get from the lodge to the camp site at the end of the day. Lodges and camp sites are often a long way apart and driving in the parks is not allowed between 7 pm and dawn.

If you're looking for other people to join you on a safari using a rented vehicle check out the notice boards at the Youth Hostel and Mrs Roche's in Nairobi.

Safari Tours

Most travellers opt to go on one or more organised safari. There are scores of different companies offering safaris and they cater for all pockets and tastes. The cheaper ones involve camping and a degree of self-help (erect your own tent, help with the catering, etc) and they are for people who don't mind roughing it. Camping out in the bush is, of course, the authentic way of going about a safari. There's nothing quite like having just a sheet of canvas between you and what you would normally see in your own country only on the other side of a cage or other impenetrable barrier.

Which Park?

There are all manner of different safari combinations to choose from depending on how long you want to be away and how many parks you want to explore. Masai Mara definitely has the edge on sheer numbers and variety of game but you can find the same variety in Amboseli and, of course, you have the magnificent backdrop of snow-capped Mt Kilimanjaro. Game in the Tsavo parks is much more sparse (a lot of poaching goes on) but, because it's hilly country, you will see species which you won't find in the plains parks of Amboseli and Masai Mara.

Which Safari Company?

There is no doubt that some safari companies are better than others. The main factors which make for the difference are the quality and type of vehicles used, the standard of the food

and the skills and knowledge of the drivers/guides. It's equally true to say that any particular company can take a bunch of people on safari one week and bring them back fully satisfied, yet the following week take a different set of people on the same safari and end up with a virtual mutiny. That's an extreme example but you will hear these sort of contrary comments among travellers in Kenya. Whether a company gets praised or condemned for its safaris can hinge on something as simple as a puncture which takes half a day to fix and for which there are no tools on board, or a broken spring which involves having to wait around for most of the day whilst a replacement vehicle is sent out from Nairobi. There's obviously a lot which companies can do to head off unnecessary delays but what you get is what you pay for.

Companies offering camping safaris which can be recommended are:

Best Camping Tours
  Nanak House, 2nd floor, on the corner of Kimathi St and Banda St, Nairobi (tel 28091, 27203)
Special Camping Safaris
  Gilfillan House, 3rd floor, Kenyatta Ave, Nairobi (tel 338325)
Safari-Camp Services Ltd
  on the corner of Koinange St and Moktar Daddah St, Nairobi (tel 289336, 330130)
Zirkuli Expeditions Ltd
  Banda St, Nairobi (tel 23949, 20848)
Gametrackers
  Banda St, near Koinonge St, Nairobi (tel 338927)
Ahmedi Expeditions
  NCM House, 1st floor, Tom Mboya St, Nairobi (tel 334480)
Let's Go Travel
  Caxton House, Standard St, Nairobi (tel 29539/40)

How Much?

There's a lot of competition for the tourist dollar among the safari companies and prices for the same tour are very similar. Most offer a range of possibilities and combinations taking in one or more of Amboseli, Tsavo, Masai Mara, Nakuru, Naivasha, Baringo, Mt Kenya, Samburu and Buffalo Springs. The longer you go for, the less, proportionally it costs per day. For camping safaris you are looking at around KSh 700 per day for three days down to KSh 600 per day for eight days. This will include camping equipment, transport, camping site and park entry fees, plus three cooked meals a day. You will be expected to provide a sleeping bag. Safari companies which are based on renting rooms for the night rather than camping, generally charge about double these rates for the same trip and normally expect two people to share a room. If you are a single traveller and want a room to yourself there is a supplement of between 15% and 20% to pay.

AMBOSELI NATIONAL PARK

This park must have one of the world's most stunning settings. Right there on the plain in front of Mt Kilimanjaro with nothing in the way to interrupt the views! Game is very easy to see in Amboseli because of the terrain and the lack of forest. It's a small park, too, so you don't have to do too much driving. The lake which covers much of the western section of the park is generally dry except during a prolonged wet season.

Places to Stay

There used to be a camp site near the Ol Tukai Lodge but it's now been moved outside the boundaries of the park southwest of the Amboseli Serena Lodge. It's run by friendly Masai who live in a small house on the site but there are no facilities other than a plentiful supply of firewood for collection nearby. It's used principally by safari tour groups. Camping costs KSh 50 per person per night (a bit of a ripoff considering there are no facilities). Warm beers and sodas can be bought from the Masai in the house at normal prices.

Elephant, leopard and lion wander through this camp site at night when everything has gone quiet but no-one has ever been eaten or crushed. Yet it's food for thought in the mornings sometimes when you see how close the piles of dung and footprints are to your tent!

There are three lodges in the park, the *Amboseli Serena Lodge*, the *Kilimanjaro Safari Lodge* and the *Amboseli Lodge*. They have restaurants and bars open to nonresidents and the Serena Lodge, which overlooks a watering hole, has a swimming pool and bookshop. Nonresidents can have a hot shower at the Kilimanjaro Safari Lodge for KSh 50 per person.

MASAI MARA NATIONAL PARK

Masai Mara is much larger than Amboseli and is contiguous with Serengeti National Park in neighbouring Tanzania. Though it offers one of the widest range of big and small game in East Africa it is also famous for the annual migration of the wildebeest (gnu) of which there are up to two million. The herds are mixed with hundreds of thousands of zebra, gazelle and antelope, and it's a truly magnificent sight to see all these animals move across the plain. Since the North American bison were wiped out, it has to be the last of the world's greatest animal spectacles. Naturally, you won't see all of them at one time – they're spread out across the plains wherever the grass is greenest – but that isn't going to diminish the sight.

During the rainy season (March, April and early May), the herds spread out across the plains of the Serengeti and Mara but as it starts to dry out (during May and June) they begin to concentrate on the better watered areas. Huge herds are gradually formed which finally move off westwards in search of better pasture. Hundreds can be drowned fording a large river on some of these migrations. The animals mate at about the same time that the herds begin to gather so there is a lot of rutting, with bull wildebeest defending temporary territories against rival males while trying to assemble a harem of females. Much of the dry season is spent in the west of the Serengeti but towards the end they begin to move back east in anticipation of the rainy season. Calves are born at the start of the wet, but if the rains are late and the herds are still on the move, then up to 80% of the calves may die.

These vast herds of wildebeest, zebra, gazelle and antelope support healthy populations of predators like lion, cheetah, leopard and wild dogs, and scavengers like hyena and vulture. You'll see all these and much more on a visit to Masai Mara. For numbers and variety, it's Kenya's best game park.

Places to Stay

There are numerous camp sites scattered through Masai Mara though many of them are luxury tented ones which cost about half the price of a room in a lodge. These include *Fig Tree Camp* (tel Nairobi 332170), *Governors' Camp* (tel Nairobi 331871/2), *Mara River Camp* (tel Nairobi 331228), *Mara Cottar's Camp* (tel Nairobi 27932), and *Mara Sara Camp* (tel Nairobi 21716). The other camps where you can pitch your own tent offer few facilities except for river water and firewood so bring everything else with you.

As in the other national parks, there are luxury lodges which include *Keekorok Game Lodge* and the *Mara Serena Lodge*. They're both very expensive but, like lodges in other parks, nonresidents can eat and drink in the restaurants and bars.

TSAVO NATIONAL PARK – EAST & WEST

Tsavo East & West National Parks constitute the largest wildlife reserves in Kenya and although you can see a wide variety of game here poaching has been – and continues to be – a problem. The poachers are mainly interested in ivory and rhino horn so the populations of these animals have been considerably reduced. The main area people visit is the north end of Tsavo West where most of the game

lodges and camp sites are located. It's also worth a visit to the **Taita Hills** which are sandwiched between the two parks but themselves are not a national park. There's a famous salt lick here (and the inevitable lodge).

In Tsavo West, probably the most famous spot is **Mzima Springs** where there is a glass-panelled underwater observation chamber which some inspired soul once set up so that visitors could observe the private lives of the hippos which live here. It would appear, however, that the hippos were not too impressed by this invasion of their privacy since they've moved to the far end of the pool. You'll be very lucky to catch sight of them from the under-water chamber. There are plenty of fish to distract your attention in the meantime.

Not far from Mzima Springs is the interesting and recent **Shetani Lava Flow** which sweeps right across the road close to the Chyulu gate on the road from Amboseli. It's also worth visiting the high point of **Roaring Rocks** in this same area for the magnificent views over the surrounding countryside.

Places to Stay

There are a number of public camp sites where you can stay, most of them close to a park entrance gate and most of them pretty dilapidated. Water connected to a makeshift shower, one or two open-sided shelters and firewood for the gathering is usually all there is but, in most cases, no-one comes round to collect a camping fee. This is certainly true at the Chyulu gate but not at the Mtito Andei gate which is a noisy site due to the proximity of the main Mombasa to Nairobi highway. Chyulu is peaceful and quiet but there is a mob of baboons living here who will steal anything. When out viewing game make sure tents are closed securely and food is put into sealed containers.

As in the other parks, there are a number of lodges in Tsavo. In the western side they are concentrated in the north and include the superb *Kilaguni Lodge, Ngulia Safari*

Lodge and *Tsavo Safari Camp*. In the Taita Hills there are the *Taita Hills Lodge* and the *Salt Lick Lodge*. In the eastern side of the park the lodges are concentrated just outside the town of Voi and include the *Voi Safari Lodge*.

Lesotho

Lesotho came together as a nation in the 1820s, at a time when large numbers of refugees were fleeing from Zulu expansionism. It was united by a remarkable military and diplomatic strategist, Moshoeshoe I, who by the 1850s had built a powerful kingdom, which covered the fertile plains of the Caledon River as well as present-day Lesotho. By that time the country had a single language, a unified army and a system of government based on a national assembly of chiefs, each of whom retained a considerable degree of autonomy.

Moshoeshoe I was able to keep both the Zulu and the Boers at bay until shortly before his death in 1870, but when his forces were defeated by those of the Orange Free State in 1868 he was forced to seek help from the British. A protectorate was declared shortly afterwards, but it was too late to prevent the loss of the rich grazing lands west of the Caledon.

Despite these setbacks the chiefs were able to retain their power by loaning cattle to the often destitute newcomers. They also retained their rights to both allocate and evict people from land as well as to demand tribute labour. Yet, at the same time, the country gradually changed from the granary of the high veld to a mere labour reserve for South African mines and farms. In 1904 alone some 86,000 passes were issued to Basotho labourers out of a total population of 350,000. This pattern of labour movement has continued right up to the present. Some 150,000 Basotho labourers currently work in South Africa.

Nationalist policies got off to a very early start but it wasn't until the Basutoland Congress Party was founded in 1952 under the leadership of Ntsu Mokhehle that a militant campaign for self-rule was launched. The BCP's radicalism, though not its goal of national independence, was opposed by the Basutoland National Party, founded under the leadership of Chief Jonathan in 1958. As a result of the BCP's campaign the British were forced to grant self-government in 1965 and full independence in 1966, but in the elections leading up to independence it was the BNP which scooped the lion's share of the votes.

Part of the reason for this was the massive help given to it by various outside interests. These included the 215,000-member Catholic Church which used its considerable ideological, financial and organisational resources to condemn the radicalism of the BCP and promote the BNP. The South African government of Dr Verwoerd provided helicopters, trucks and other assistance such as giving the BNP sole access to the 100,000 Basotho expatriate workers inside South Africa. The British colonial administration also threw in its lot with the BNP, though it would have preferred to support the royalist party.

The country thus became independent in 1966 under the leadership of Chief Jonathan on a platform of friendship and cooperation with South Africa, rabid anticommunism and the muzzling of South African political refugees. Barely two months after independence Chief Jonathan consolidated the hold of the BNP by forcing King Moshoeshoe II to renounce everything but a purely ceremonial role as head of state. The BCP nevertheless remained active, but when it was clearly heading for victory in the elections of

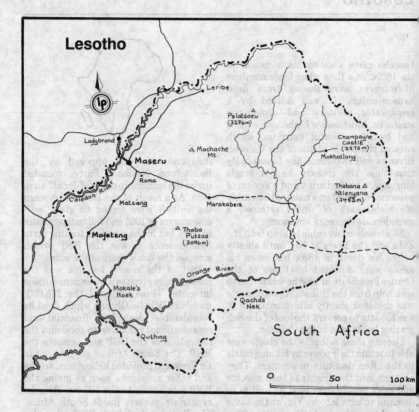

1970, Jonathan staged a coup d'état, suspended the constitution, arrested opposition leaders, banned all political parties except his own and put the king under house-arrest.

Moshoeshoe II subsequently went into exile in Holland but was allowed to return in the early 1970s but on the understanding that he would keep out of the political arena. At the same time the pro-royalist Maremthlou Freedom Party adopted a neutral position in the bitter quarrel between Jonathan's ruling BNP and the opposition BCP.

Jonathan's dictatorship, however, was opposed by many sections of the population and so, in 1972, in an attempt to defuse an increasingly tense political situation, he announced an amnesty for political prisoners. This was followed by the creation of an all-party national assembly the following year.

Though there were a few defections from the BCP, the hard-core leaders refused to cooperate in what was a transparent exercise to legitimise Jonathan's regime. In 1974 serious disturbances broke out, including armed attacks on a number of police stations. In the ensuing witch-hunt of BCP supporters, at least 250 people were killed by the BNP militia and many more were arrested. Mokhehle, along with several other important members of the BCP, fled into exile.

With many of the leaders of the opposition effectively removed from the scene, Jonathan attempted to create a one-party state, though with very limited success. Serious disturbances continued to plague his regime. To stifle it, Jonathan resorted to assassination by unleashing his paramilitary forces on prominent critics, one of whom, Edgar Matuba, was the editor of the independent newspaper *Leselinyana la Lesotho*. Matuba and two companions were taken from his home one night, murdered and their bodies dumped by the side of the road. The same fate befell Odilon Sehri, the king's private secretary.

Jonathan might still have been in power today had he continued to placate the South African authorities. However, his flirtation with Mozambique and, particularly, Cuba, and his alleged support of ANC guerrillas who were granted sanctuary in Lesotho, led to his downfall. As relations continued to deteriorate between Lesotho and South Africa, the latter imposed a blockade on Lesotho preventing the movement of goods into or out of the country. They also shelved the Highlands Water Project. This huge scheme costing Ml 2.3 billion was to have provided hydroelectricity to Lesotho and enable the country to export water to South Africa.

The pressure precipitated a crisis and, in an attempt to solve it, a Lesotho delegation led by General Justin Lekhanya, the commander of the paramilitary forces, went to Pretoria to negotiate with the South African authorities. Three days later in late January 1986, Jonathan was overthrown in a coup d'état led by Lekhanya. Though naturally denied, it is more than likely that the South African authorities gave the go-ahead for the coup.

Within hours of the announcement that Jonathan had been ousted, the blockade was lifted and South Africa's deputy director-general of foreign affairs arrived in Maseru for consultations with the new government. The Highlands Water Project was also restarted.

Despite obvious covert support for the coup by South Africa, there was little resistance, and residents of Maseru took to the streets to celebrate. Even when a curfew was announced a little while later it was generally ignored as people continued to throng the streets.

The new government enjoys considerable popular support. Many Basotho regard Moshoeshoe II as the one man who can reunite the divided country and it's widely expected that he will adopt a more prominent role in the affairs of the nation.

Meanwhile, Lesotho remains largely a political and economic hostage of South Africa even though it has been quite successful in attracting development loans from several western countries, principally from the EC. Any government in Maseru wanting to break out of this stranglehold is faced with enormous difficulties. Not only is the country surrounded by South Africa and its 'homeland' puppet states but Lesotho's main export is about half its able-bodied men. They work in South Africa under a pernicious migrant labour system which has wreaked havoc with the social stability of the country. Their remittances home are a vital part of the country's economy.

There has also been an enormous investment of capital by several South African companies in the search for coal and minerals, including the De Beers company which has sunk R 23 million into a diamond mine near Letseng. Much of the wholesale and retail trade within the country is also South African owned.

Jonathan was forced to adopt a style similar to that of the leaders of the Black 'homelands', while occasionally risking rhetorical outbursts of condemnation of the apartheid regime. He did, on the other hand, refuse to recognise the so-called independence of the Transkei. When this led to the closure of their common border in 1978, he used it as a gambit to secure substantial loans and emergency aid from various western governments who were not averse to polishing up their anti-apartheid images.

Nevertheless, the platform on which Jonathan came to power at independence remained basically the same. When Pieter Botha, the South African prime minister, first met him in 1980 Jonathan is widely thought to have sought South African help in dealing with insurgents crossing the border from South Africa.

One of the country's chief aims is to become self-sufficient in food, but it suffers from erosion stemming from overgrazing. The lowlands remain infertile because of the lack of tree cover, which means that animal manure is used for fuel instead of being returned to the soil.

Facts

GEOGRAPHY & CLIMATE

Lesotho is one of the world's poorest nations, with few mineral resources, limited agricultural land and a harsh and changeable climate. It makes up for this, however, with its stunning natural beauty and its friendly, generous people.

While the majority of the 1½ million population live in the lowlands at around 1500 metres, much of the land is wild mountain country with occasional peaks rising to over 3000 metres. Because of this it is excellent for trekking, though you need to take precautions against the very changeable weather. Never go out into the mountains, even for an afternoon, without a sleeping bag, tent and sufficient food for a couple of days in case you get fogged in. Even in summer it can freeze and thunderstorms are an ever-present danger (quite a few people are killed by lightning here every year). It's generally clear between May and September but cold and windy higher up. The highest parts often experience frost at night. Down in the valleys, summer days can be hot with temperatures in the 30°Cs.

There is no trouble finding clean drinking water for most of the year but towards the end of the dry season it can become very scarce. If you take water from below a village, boil it before drinking. You can pick up hepatitis, dysentery and even cholera if you don't.

VISAS

Visas are required by all except nationals of Commonwealth countries, Belgium, Denmark, Finland, Greece, Iceland, Irish Republic, Israel, Italy, Japan, Luxembury, Netherlands, Norway, South Africa, South Korea, Sweden and the USA. Where there are no Lesotho diplomatic missions visas can be obtained from British embassies. Visas are generally obtainable on entry at Maseru Bridge (overland) or Maseru Airport if arriving by air.

There are very few Lesotho embassies or high commissions in Africa, those in Maputo (Mozambique), Nairobi (Kenya) and Pretoria (South Africa) being the only ones.

MONEY

US$1 = Ml 2.46

The unit of currency is the loti (plural maloti) = 100 lisente. The loti is on a par with the South African rand. There are no restrictions on the import or export of local currency but make sure you change excess maloti back into rand before leaving.

The cost of living is high, especially for such things as food and public transport. Inflation is running at around 13.5%.

The airport departure tax for international flights is Ml 2.

ACCOMMODATION

There's very little purpose-built accommodation for travellers outside of Maseru though there are small hotels in Butha-

Buthe, Teyateyateng, Mokale's Hoek and Quthing.

Outside these places you won't have any difficulty finding somewhere to stay. People are very friendly, especially in the mountains. If you ask the village chief for permission to camp he'll not only make sure you get a good spot but he'll often fix you up with a *rondavel* for the night.

In other places try the missions and training centres. There are Agricultural Training Centres in many places and they can all provide beds for travellers. The usual price is Ml 2.50. Facilities include cold showers and toilets but there are rarely any cooking facilities.

There is a Youth Hostels Association (tel 313766) PO Box 970, Maseru, but it only has two hostels, one at Phomolong (Lancer's Gap), four km from Maseru, and another outside Butha-Buthe. The latter is highly recommended.

The Fraser Group have three lodges (known as Fraser's Lodges) at Quaba, Semonkong and Marakabeis which cost Ml 10 per person plus 10% tax. They all have cooking facilities but bring your own food. Beer and soft drinks are usually available. You can make bookings at Fraser's Furniture Store (tel (050) 322601) on Kingsway opposite the post office in Maseru, or by writing to PO Box MS5, Maseru.

LANGUAGE

The official languages are Sesotho and English. Greetings are an important social ritual in Lesotho, so if you want to create a favourable impression on people it's useful to know some of them.

Greetings

Greetings father	*lumela ntate* (du-may-lah n-tah-tee)
Peace father	*khotso ntate* (ko-tso n-tah-tee)
Greetings mother	*lumela 'me*
Peace mother	*khotso 'me*
Greetings brother	*lumela abuti*
Peace brother	*khotso abuti*
Greetings sister	*lumela ausi*
Peace sister	*khotso ausi*

There are three possible ways to say 'How are you?' They are:

	singular	plural
How do you live?	*o phela joang?*	*le phela joang?*
How did you get up?	*o tsohele joang?*	*le tsohele joang?*
How are you?	*o kae?*	*le kae?*

The answers to these questions are:

	singular	plural
I live well	*ke phela hantle*	*re phela hantle*
I got up well	*ke tsohile hantle*	*re tsohile hantle*
I am here	*ke teng*	*re teng*

These questions and answers are quite interchangeable. Someone could ask you *o phela joang?* and you could answer *ke teng*.

When trekking, people always ask *lea kae?* (Where are you going?) and *o tsoa kae?* or the plural *le tsoa kae?* (Where have you come from?).

When parting, use the following expressions:

	singular	plural
Go well	*tsamaea hantle*	*tsamaeang hantle*
Stay well	*sala hantle*	*salang hantle*

You must always add *ntate* or *'me* (or *bo* for the plural).

'Thank you' is *kea leboha* (pronounced 'keya lebowah'). The herd boys often ask for money (*chelete*) or sweets (*lipompong*) (pronounced dee-pom-pong). If you want to say 'I don't have any', the answer is *ha dio* (pronounced 'ha dee-oh').

Getting There & Around

AIR

Air Lesotho, the national airline, has a fairly extensive network of internal flights and is worth considering if your time is limited or if you get stuck. Fares are very reasonable but schedules are another matter. The office in Maseru is reluctant to take bookings, so most people have to go out to the airport and sit it out until a flight is announced. This can take all day.

The main reason for this state of affairs is that the planes are quite small and most of the airstrips are only grass tracks, so cancellations are frequent in bad weather. The free baggage allowance on these flights is 15 kg. Anything over that and you will have to pay excess baggage rates. Examples of fares are: Maseru/Semonkong Ml 32; Maseru/Qacha's Nek Ml 40.

ROAD

In the mountains roads can be incredibly rough and lifts difficult to find, so to get to the heart of this country you need plenty of time and very few expectations. In the more remote areas the only way you'll be able to get around is by walking or by hiring or buying a horse. The few Basotho who own horses regard them as their most valuable possessions and are extremely reluctant to part with them. That being so, expect to pay handsomely for one. On the other hand, it is superb walking country and there's no danger of robberies or anything of that nature.

Bus

In the lowlands minibuses are the usual form of transport. They are cheap and most of the roads are surfaced but they're also dangerous and many people are killed in accidents. These so-called accidents are often the result of drunken driving – alcohol consumption is a real problem in this country and bus drivers are not immune from this. The Maseru to Roma road is particularly bad. Hitching is easy and much faster than taking buses but you should expect to pay for lifts. Some examples of bus fares are:

Maseru to Roma – Ml 1.50
Maseru to Morija – Ml 1
Maseru to Semonkong – Ml 5
Maseru to Marakabeis – Ml 4.55
Marakabeis to Qacha turn-off – Ml 1.30
Qacha turn-off to Qacha – Ml 2
Qacha's Nek to Quthing – Ml 15

TO/FROM SOUTH AFRICA

Many people enter Lesotho via the capital, Maseru, which is connected by road and rail to South Africa. The two-km rail link from Maseru to the South African border is the only railway line in the country but there are no through services. Trains have to be caught from Marseilles. There are minibuses from Maseru to the border for 40 lisente and buses from there to Marseilles station for R 1.20.

The border between Lesotho and the Transkei is open to non-Lesotho nationals.

Around the Country

BUTHA-BUTHE

About half way between Butha-Buthe and Leribe are the **Subeng River Dinosaur Footprints**. The river is signposted but the footprints are not. Walk down to the river from the road until you reach a concrete causeway (about 250 metres). The footprints, of at least three species of dinosaur, are about 15 metres downstream of the causeway on the right bank. They're a little bit worn these days, but still clearly visible. When the river is in flood they may disappear under the water.

There are no direct buses between Maseru and Butha-Buthe. You must change at Maputsoe. Maseru to Maputsoe costs Ml 4 and Maputsoe to Butha-Buthe costs Ml 1.50.

Places to Stay

There are signs on the road pointing to the *Youth Hostel* though you may have to ask directions from the local people (ask them for *ha-sechele*). It's about four km from the village. The hostel is run by Mr and Mrs Ramakatane who are very friendly and helpful. It consists of four beds in two rooms with a kitchen and bathroom. The kitchen has kerosene stoves and a limited assortment of utensils. Water comes from a pump and is clean and fresh. A bath is a bucket shower. Buy food in the village before coming. The hostel costs Ml 5 per night and is excellent value.

LERIBE

The most convenient place to stay is the *Agricultural Training Centre* just outside town. If they don't have room, try the *Catholic Mission* about 10 km past Leribe. You can camp in the grounds, but you'll probably be invited to stay in one of the rooms if there's one available. It's a centre where people come to stay and attend classes (such as foreign volunteers on 10-day language classes). Please leave a generous donation if you're given hospitality and/or meals.

MARAKABEIS

Fraser's Lodge is beautifully situated in the mountains outside town. They have clean, comfortable *rondavels* for Ml 10 per person with gas water heaters in the bathroom, and flush toilets. The kitchens are provided with a gas stove, pots, pans, cutlery and crockery, but the only light is by candle. There's a good dining room and bar (with the only electric lights in the place) and a store which sells a limited range of foodstuffs. Very good meals can be had, though the price depends on what you eat and/or what the manager feels like charging. A whole roast chicken costs Ml 7. There are other shops up the hill in town but it's quite a walk. Camping is also possible.

There is at least one daily bus (and sometimes two) in either direction between Maseru and Marakabeis. They continue on to Thaba Tseka. The buses leave Thaba Tseka around dawn and Maseru late morning. The fare to Marakabeis is Ml 5 and the journey takes four hours. Buses are sometimes cancelled in June and July when there can be up to half a metre of snow on the ground.

MASERU

In 1959 Maseru had a population of just 2000 and even 10 years ago it was little more than a one-street village of single-storey buildings. Today it has over 80,000 inhabitants with enough supermarkets, restaurants and the like to make frequent trips over the border to South African towns unnecessary.

Information

The tourist office is on Kingsway next to the Victoria Hotel, about two km from the centre of town on the road to the border. American Express is on Kingsway on the same side as the GPO. If you are looking for lifts into the interior, check out the CIDA office.

Things to See

A good short excursion in the immediate vicinity of Maseru is to **Thaba Bosiu**, a flat-topped hill where the Basotho made a heroic stand against the Boers and where the graves of the chiefs killed in that battle are found. Buses go right past the mountain (ask the conductor for the right spot). There is a guide up there who may treat you to a (free) two-hour history and culture lecture which is worth listening to.

North of Roma are the **Ha Khotso Rock Paintings**, sometimes known as *ha baroana* (Home of the little Bushpeople). These are some of the best Bushpeople paintings in the country though they're quite worn and faded and considered by some to be inferior to those at Giant's Castle.

The most usual way to get there is to take a minibus from Maseru to Nazareth and get off about 1½ km before Nazareth.

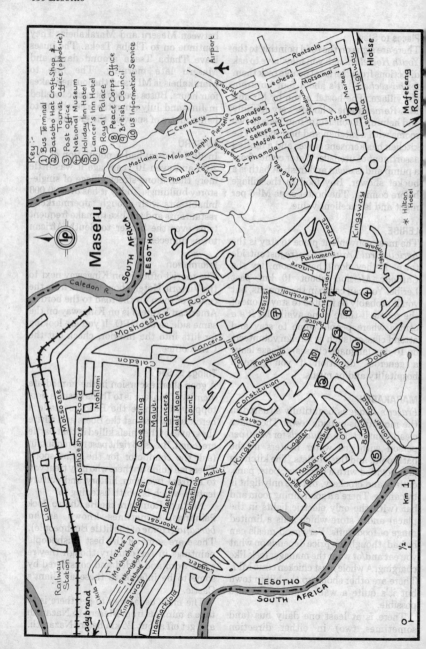

Key:-
1. Bus Terminal
2. Basotho Hat Craft Shop &
   Tourist office (opposite)
3. Post Office
4. National Museum
5. Holiday Inn Hotel
6. Lancer's Inn Hotel
7. Royal Palace
8. Peace Corps Office
9. British Council
10. US Information Service

Maseru

LP

SOUTH AFRICA
LESOTHO
Caledon R.

Hlotse
Mafeteng Roma
Leabua Highway
Market
Rantsala
Lechesa
Motsamai
Pitso
Stadium
Ramafole
Fako
Ntsane
Sekese
Mafole
Phamola
Airport
Airport Road
Maseru
Cemetery
Molomaomphi
Short Street
Phamola Street
Matlama
Paepaeng
Paepaeng
Patsela

Parliament
Kingsway
Nightingale
Hilton Hotel
Moshoeshoe Road
Caledon Road
Mohlomi
Matseene Road
Moshoeshoe Road
Constitution Road
Assissi
Caldwell
Linare
Ierofeoli
Constitution Place
Lancers
Tonakholo
Flint
Dove
Bowker
Pioneer Road
Kingsway
Constitution Road
Maluti
Half Moon Mount
Lancers
Qoqolosing
Maluti
Moorosi
Mathebe
Tonakholo
Maluti
Lagden
Margaret
Mabile
Orpen
Qubodina
Lagden

Matete
Machachako
Sekongola
Leabake
Likila
Kingsway
Hammarkold
Moshoeshoe Road
Lioli

Railway Station
Ladybrand

LESOTHO
SOUTH AFRICA

km 1
½
0

Here there is a signpost indicating the way to the paintings off to the left. Follow this gravel track three km to the village of Ha Khotso then turn right at a football field. Follow this track a further 2½ km to a hilltop overlooking a sandstone gorge. A footpath zigzags down the hillside to the rock shelter where the paintings are found. Entry costs 30 lisente and the site is open daily from 9 am to 5 pm.

A shorter route involves staying on the minibus as far as the village of Nazareth. Get off at the crest of the hill and take the dirt road which forks off to the left about 100 metres before the large Caltex sign (ignore the smaller Caltex sign painted on the side of a tank). Follow this dirt road for about four km until it joins the track from the village of Ha Khotso. From here the paintings are about half a km off to the right down the zigzag footpath. Whichever route you take, you'll probably have to ask local people for directions.

If you can't find a minibus to Nazareth take a Maseru to Roma bus and get off at St Michael's where the untarred Mountain Rd to Nazareth forks off left from the main road. From here it's 14 km to the turn-off for Ha Khotso village. Vehicles are few and far between so you might as well start walking.

Places to Stay

Many travellers stay at the *Youth Hostel* at Lancer's Gap. There's a large sign outside so you can't miss it. A recent price increase has raised the cost of this place to Ml 7.50 with a Youth Hostel card and Ml 10.50 without, but there are electric cooking stoves, electric lights and plenty of cooking and eating utensils. The water supply has been a problem for many years and there's no hot water except in the kitchen. The dormitories have six beds each but most of the time you'll be on your own. It's a very pleasant and friendly place. There are plenty of buses between Maseru and Lancer's Gap (25 lisente). If coming into Maseru by bus from Roma ask the conductor to let you off at the hostel as the bus goes right past the gate.

There's a small store opposite the Youth Hostel offering takeaway food until about 9 pm.

As well as the Youth Hostel, it's worth checking out the *Peace Corps* office on Constitution Rd or the *IVS* and *UN* volunteers behind Lancer's Inn but be prepared to pay for your keep. They can usually provide a bunk, floor space or somewhere to put up your tent. The *Danish Volunteer Service* run a guesthouse which costs around Ml 10 (usually full at weekends but not during the week) as does the *German Volunteer Service* with beds for Ml 4.50. Also try the *Anglican Centre* which is quite friendly and offers beds for Ml 6.

Hotel accommodation is quite expensive. The *Maseru Hotel* next to the bus station costs Ml 19.50 a double with a bathroom and the *Lancer's Inn* costs Ml 21.50 a double with a bathroom.

QACHA'S NEK

There's only one hotel and it offers indifferent accommodation for Ml 23 and up, but there's no competition.

A bus service to Sehlabethebe leaves daily at around 1 pm and costs Ml 6.55. It's a beautiful journey.

SEHLABETHEBE

The *Sehlabethebe Park Lodge* is good value and comfortable, though a little run-down. There are 18 double rooms which cost Ml 10 or Ml 20 per bed. They also have dormitory accommodation for Ml 5 and you can camp for Ml 1. The lodge has cooking facilities.

SEMONKONG

Fraser's Lodge is a 10-minute walk from the airstrip and costs Ml 10 for a bed or Ml 3 to camp. It's a pleasant place with a 'Wild West' atmosphere, a well-equipped kitchen, bar and small store. You can also find a bed at the *Roman Catholic Mission* for a small contribution. It's run by two French-

Canadian priests, Father Latremouille and Father Leo.

A bus service from Maseru to Semonkong leaves around 10 am daily from outside the Beehive Restaurant by the market. It costs M1 9 and takes about seven hours.

Trekking in Lesotho

Lesotho offers some of the most spectacular trekking country in southern Africa. Straddling the Drakensberg, which includes the highest peaks in this part of the continent, it is one of the most beautiful areas in the world. Much the same is true of the South African side of this massif. The most fascinating area of Lesotho is along the south-east border region between Transkei and South Africa, and if you had two weeks to spare you could walk all the way around this region from Ramanbanta to Butha-Buthe via Qacha's Nek, the Sani Pass, Mokhotlong and the Mont aux Sources.

Beautiful it certainly is, but the climate is very changeable so prepare for this before trekking into the mountains. Temperatures can plummet to near zero even in summer, and thunderstorms are very common.

A good book to take is David Ambrose's *Guide to Lesotho* (Winchester Press). Good maps are available from the Department of Survey behind the Department of Mines, which in turn is behind Barclays Bank in Maseru. They have a large-scale map of the whole country (1:250,000) for M1 5 and section maps (1:50,000) for M1 2.90. The large-scale map is somewhat out of date.

First take a bus from Maseru to Ramanbanta. These depart daily around noon and arrive at 4.30 pm. The fare is M1 3. There's also a flight, which costs M1 21. From Ramanbanta you can either walk to Semonkong (about two days) or hitch a ride in a 4WD truck, which costs around M1 10 between three people and takes

about 5½ hours. There are also supply trucks between Ramanbanta and Semonkong departing daily around 5 pm.

While in Semonkong pay a visit to the **Maletsunyane Falls** (also known as Lebihan Falls). It's a four-km walk. The falls are some 200 metres high and are particularly spectacular in the summer months.

From Semonkong either head off to Ha Qaba then back to Maseru or continue on to Qacha's Nek and the Sani Pass. If you take the former it's a three-day walk and you need to take food as there are no shops en route except for a very basic store at Thakabanna. It's also difficult to find water along this trail until you're past the halfway mark, so take some with you. From Ha Qaba there is a road to Maseru and it's easy to hitch.

Taking the second route you head off walking to Qacha's Nek, or you can get there direct by road from Maseru or Matatiele on the Natal-Transkei border. There's also a flight from Maseru to Qacha's Nek for M1 40. From there take the bridle path to Ramatseliso's Gate (Ramatselisohek, about 1½ days) where there is a store, then continue on to the **Sehlabethebe National Park**, which takes a further day. From here it takes another two days to climb and walk along the escarpment to the Sani Pass. There are no villages along the way, so take supplies.

At Sani Pass there's a shop and chalet with sleeping accommodation. From Sani you can walk to the top of Thabana Ntlenyana (at 3482 metres the highest point in southern Africa) in about four hours.

The next leg of the route takes you along a ridge and down to Mokhotlong. Here there is a hotel for M1 6 to M1 10. Or you can stay at the *Agricultural Training Centre* for M1 2, ask for Mr Kele-Kele. There are stores at Mokhotlong and buses to other parts of the country. A good place to eat is the *Salang Restaurant* which offers cheap filling meals and coffee.

From Mokhotlong to Oxbow there is a daily bus which costs M1 6 and takes about

4½ hours. Oxbow is a skiing centre in the winter months and it has a lodge. From Oxbow to Butha-Buthe there's a daily bus for Ml 3.

From Mokhotlong to Thaba Tseka you can walk (it takes about five to six days staying at missions en route) or hitch. There's also a direct flight from Mokhotlong to Maseru (Ml 44). Mokhotlong is a good take-off point for the **Mont aux Sources National Park** and down to Butha-Buthe.

PONY TREKKING

Pony trekking is now really well organised by the Basotho Pony Trekking Centre from their stables and lodge at Molimo Nthuse between the Bushman's Pass and the Blue Mountain Pass on the Maseru to Marakabeis road. The road is paved all the way from Maseru to the centre and you should be able to get there within 45 minutes.

There's quite a choice of treks ranging from two-day round trips (Ml 40 per person) to five-day ones (Ml 100 per person). Non-return treks range from four days (Ml 80 per person) to seven days (Ml 140 per person).

These charges include horses and gear and a guide but exclude the cost of overnight accommodation, food and transport to the Centre. Bring your own waterproof clothing, sweaters, sleeping bags and cooking utensils. The Centre prefers groups of between five and 10 people. Trekkers have the choice of using their own tents at overnight stops or renting *rondavels* from the villagers (usually Ml 5 per person per night). There are also lodges at some places (eg, Qaba and Semonkong), where gas cookers and hot showers are available.

Treks must be booked in advance through Basotho Pony Trekking (tel Maseru 314165), PO Box 1027, Maseru 100, Lesotho. If you write or telephone they'll send you a leaflet containing full details and prices of all the treks.

You can sleep on the floor of the Centre before starting out, otherwise there is the *Molimo Nthuse Lodge* nearby which costs Ml 39/56 a single/double. Dinner costs Ml 10.

If you don't have the time or the inclination to plan your own trek, you can have all this prepared by the Lesotho Tourist Board (tel 050 322896, 323760), PO Box 1378, Maseru. Naturally the treks cost more this way. For example, a four-day trek is Ml 253 and a five-day trek is Ml 315. These charges are inclusive of all food and lodging, a guide, horses, tackle, transport between Maseru and the starting point, and flights (where applicable). Bring your own sleeping bag, rain gear, warm clothes and eating utensils.

Liberia

Liberia began as a venture by American philanthropists in 1822, the idea being to resettle in Africa freed slaves no longer wanted by the plantations. Not all those who were offered 'repatriation' in this way accepted it. Many regarded it as humiliating and refused to go. The few thousand who did accept had a hard time establishing themselves, having to contend with the hostility of the indigenous people, who resented being alienated from their land, and the settlers' attempts to dominate them. Not until 1847 did the new country declare itself to be an independent republic, and even its foster parent, the United States, took until 1862 to formally recognise it.

Ironically, the settlers didn't see any need to extend to the indigenous population the same love of liberty which supposedly had brought them to Liberia in the first place. They saw themselves as part of a mission to bring civilisation and Christianity to Africa, and imposed a form of forced labour on the local people, which anywhere else would have gone under the name 'slavery'. This continued for almost 100 years and in 1930 both Britain and the USA broke off diplomatic relations for five years as a result of a scandal over the sale of such labour to Spanish colonialists in what was then Fernando Póo (now Bioko).

As late as 1960 Liberia was still being condemned for its labour recruitment methods by the International Labour Organisation. Yet, despite the exploitation of the indigenous people, the settlers were never able to develop an independent economic base and were heavily dependent on foreign capital. The country also lost large chunks of its territory to the British and French during the scramble for colonies in the late 19th century.

Early in Liberia's history power was monopolised by the True Whig Party and it continued to maintain its grip on the political machinery right up until the 1980 coup. Despite the country's labour recruitment policies, the party was able to project an image of Liberia as Africa's most stable country. During William Tubman's presidency, from 1944 to 1971, this led to massive foreign investment. So eager was Tubman to hand out concessions to foreign companies that Liberia acquired the disparaging tag of the 'Firestone Republic' for a number of years.

The huge influx of foreign money, however, soon began to distort the economy and to exacerbate social inequalities. This led to increasing hostility between the descendants of the settlers and the indigenous people. Viewing this development with alarm Tubman was forced to concede that the indigenous people would have to be granted a measure of political and economic involvement in the country, and one of his concessions was to enfranchise them. Incredible as it may seem, some 97% of the population had been denied the franchise until 1963. William Tolbert, who succeeded Tubman in 1971, was one of South Africa's strongest supporters in its efforts to maintain diplomatic and economic relations with the rest of Black Africa.

Tolbert continued with Tubman's policies but, while upholding the values of 'free enterprise', he sought to broaden the country's contacts. For the first time diplomatic relations were established with Communist countries such as the People's Republic of China. At the same

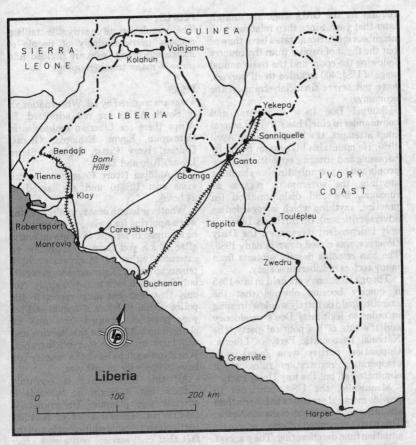

time, however, Tolbert clamped down on opposition and brought in harsh laws to deal with anyone considered to be a threat to the regime. Even his staunchest ally, the USA, began to complain about violations of human rights.

In the end the resentment boiled over. There were demonstrations against a proposed increase in the price of rice in early 1979 and several demonstrators were shot. Then, in April 1980, Tolbert was overthrown in a coup led by Master Sergeant Samuel Doe. In the fighting which accompanied the coup Tolbert and

many high-ranking ministers were killed and their bodies dumped into a common grave. Of those who survived, the majority were briefly 'tried', beaten up, then publicly shot while tied to stakes on the beach at Monrovia.

Although the coup gave the indigenous population real political power for the first time since the settlers had arrived, it was condemned by most other African countries as well as by Liberia's other allies and trading partners. Nigeria, for instance, refused to allow the new foreign minister, Baccus Matthews, into the country for the OAU economic summit later that year. Since then relations with neighbouring African states have thawed but the flight of capital from the country following the coup, and the basic annual wage of US$2400 awarded to all workers, have put severe financial strain on the economy.

Samuel Doe (now a general and commander in chief) has survived several coup attempts, the latest being in April 1985. He maintains his grip on power by harassing and arresting opposition spokespeople and by promulgating laws banning anything the government regards as rumours, lies and disinformation (in practice, anything which is regarded as adverse criticism). On this basis, Liberia's only independent newspaper, the *Daily Observer*, was closed down in early 1985. The ban remains despite protests from many sectors of Liberian society.

Though elections were held in late 1985 it quickly became obvious that the exercise would be merely window dressing in order to legitimise Doe's presidency and the rule of his political party, the National Democratic Party of Liberia. Opposition parties were faced with exasperating registration rules which eliminated all but the tiny Unity Party.

Meanwhile, the USA continues to provide more aid per capita to Liberia than any other country in sub-Saharan Africa. This hasn't prevented Liberia's economic situation from deteriorating. The wages of civil servants and soldiers are often months in arrears and the external debt has risen to over US$1.4 billion.

Facts

CLIMATE
Liberia has a warm, humid climate. Temperatures range from 21°C to 32°C. The best time to visit is between November and April, which roughly corresponds with the dry season.

PEOPLE
The population of nearly 2½ million consists overwhelmingly of people of indigenous origin, who are divided into some 16 major tribal groupings.

VISAS
Visas are required by all. White nationals of South Africa are not admitted. In Africa there are Liberian embassies in Cameroun, Egypt, Ethiopia, Ghana, Guinea, Ivory Coast, Nigeria, Sierra Leone, Togo and Zaïre.

In Abidjan (Ivory Coast) one-month visas cost US$10 and are issued in 24 hours.

Whatever length of stay you're granted when applying for a visa, you'll probably be stamped in for just 48 hours on entry, after which you have to apply for an extension either in Monrovia or at a provincial capital. Extensions are generally only for a week each time you apply. Not only that, but you must report to the police within 48 hours of arrival and get your passport stamped. You may be charged up to US$20 for this 'service' and will have to supply four photographs. When you want to leave the country you have to apply for an exit visa.

All this bureaucracy is certainly tedious, but it might be bearable if officials were pleasant. Unfortunately, they're not. There's a lot of hostility particularly towards white people and the fact that civil service, police and army wages are sometimes not paid for months at a time means they're going to squeeze travellers for every cent they can get.

Many travellers have had very bad experiences in Liberia recently. Typical was the experience of a Dutch visitor who came in from Ivory Coast. The first thing they objected to was his camera ('not allowed'); then he didn't have an identity card (what's a passport for!?); then they accused him of spying because he looked at their radio; then they invented a US$3.50 'inspection fee' – a total of three hours of unpleasant nonsense. By the time he got to Ganta he was charged US$5 for a 15-day visa extension even though his original visa was for 30 days. At the same time, another officer was going to charge him US$60 for a 'camera fee' (he got them down to US$5).

All these Mickey Mouse 'fees' can amount to a lot of money and if you refuse to pay they may deport you, confiscate your camera or passport, or accuse you of being a spy. You're up for this nonsense every time you cross paths with officialdom unless you're lucky enough to meet an officer with an ounce of sense. There are frequent passport checks on all the main roads. Expect to hand out 'presents' at every one of them.

Exit visas are required before you can leave Liberia. Get them in Monrovia before setting off for Ivory Coast or Sierra Leone.

If you only want to stay 48 hours in the country and are flying in and out of Robertsfield Airport (Monrovia), you can get a transit visa on arrival. However, you must have an onward ticket if you are going to do this. You will also be a sitting duck for 'fees', 'presents' and all manner of other hassles.

Other Visas
In Monrovia there are embassies for Algeria, Cameroun, Egypt, Ethiopia, France, Germany (West), Ghana, Guinea, Israel, Italy, Ivory Coast, Japan, Morocco, Nigeria, Sierra Leone, Spain, Sweden, Switzerland, UK, USA and Zaïre.

Ivory Coast In Monrovia these cost US$20 (!) and are issued while you wait. Get them elsewhere if possible.

Sierra Leone The embassy is on Tubman Blvd out towards Robertsfield Airport. Visas cost US$30 (!), require two photos and take 24 hours to issue. You must have a valid vaccination certificate when applying.

MONEY
US$1 = L$1.00

The unit of currency is the Liberian dollar, which is on a par with the US dollar. American notes and coins are legal tender in Liberia. There is no restriction on the import or export of 'local' currency.

Many banks (even large international ones) won't change travellers' cheques so have cash (US dollars) handy. Despite the fact that the Liberian dollar is on a par with the US dollar, it appears there is a black market on which you can get as much as US$1 = L$1.30 from Lebanese shopkeepers.

Liberia is a very expensive country.

LANGUAGE
The official language is English but a number of African languages (such as Golla, Kpelle and Kru) are also spoken, especially in the interior.

Getting There & Around

ROAD
There is a schedule of MTA (Monrovia Transit Authority) buses, but it's mostly wishful thinking as the buses generally leave late and arrive even later. The terminal in Monrovia is at Center and Front Sts. The routes are as follows:

Monrovia to Ganta – minibuses cost US$10 including baggage and take four hours, or take a minibus first to Kakata (US$5) then another to Ganta (US$6)
Ganta to Sanniquellie – a taxi costs US$1
Sanniquellie to Kahnplay – buses are US$1
Kahnplay to Ivory Coast border – a taxi costs US$1
Buchanan to Monrovia – buses are scheduled to depart at 9 am, 2.15 and 4 pm, and take 2¼ hours

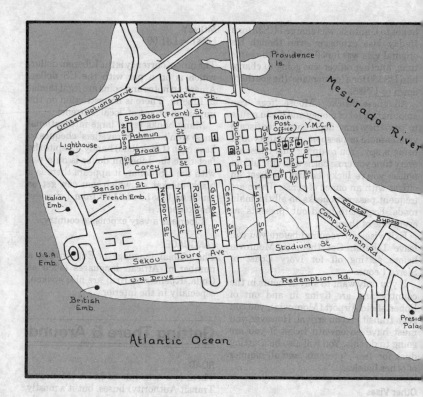

Monrovia to Buchanan – buses depart at 9 am, 12 noon and 4 pm

Monrovia to Harper – to do this journey you have to go via Ganta, a gruelling 30-hour trip over rough roads; the taxi fare is US$22.50

TRAIN

Passenger services on the Liberian railway system have been suspended.

BOAT

A Firestone Rubber boat plies between Harbel (near Monrovia) and Harper (close to the Ivory Coast border) in either direction roughly once a week. It's usually possible to get a free ride if you talk to the captain and buy him a few beers.

Otherwise it costs US$20. The journey takes about 36 hours on the open sea.

TO/FROM IVORY COAST

The main route into Ivory Coast from Monrovia goes to Man via Sanniquellie and Danané. The taxi fares and journey times as far as the border are listed in the Bus & Taxi section.

At the border you cross the bridge to the Ivory Coast side where customs officers will date and sign your passport, but you must then get a stamp from immigration in Danané. If you don't you'll be sent back there the next time your passport is examined. Try to get hold of CFA before leaving Liberia or you'll be charged US$8 for a taxi from the border to Danané.

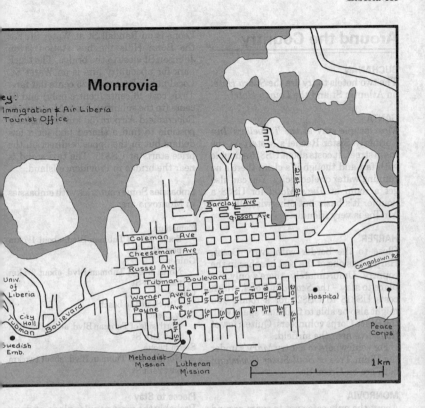

Monrovia

Key:
Immigration & Air Liberia
Tourist Office

Barclay Ave
Gibson Ave
Coleman Ave
Cheeseman Ave
Russel Ave
Tubman Boulevard
Warner Ave
Payne Ave

Congotown Rd

Univ.
of
Liberia

City Hall
Tubman Boulevard

Swedish Emb.

Methodist Mission
Lutheran Mission

21st St

20th St

Hospital

Peace Corps

0   1 km

You can also cross into Ivory Coast from Harper (close to the border on the coast) to Tabou. It's a six-hour journey over rough roads by a combination of bus and taxi, and canoe across the Cavally River which forms the border. The whole trip should cost about US$3. Travellers who have gone this way say there are no exit formalities when leaving Liberia.

There used to be a route from Monrovia to Abidjan via Ganta, Tappita and Toulépleu, but travellers who have attempted it recently say there is so little traffic that it's not worth trying.

TO/FROM SIERRA LEONE

The main crossing point between Liberia and Sierra Leone is the Mano River Union Bridge. Taxis are available from Monrovia to the border for US$5 but it's probably best to get a taxi all the way from Monrovia to Kenema in Sierra Leone. These cost US$25 and leave from Randall St at the junction with Water St in Monrovia. The roads are rough and get rougher the further you go from Monrovia. Before setting off get your exit permit for Liberia in Monrovia. The border closes at 8 pm.

The north-eastern route via Kolahun and Kailahun has been closed by the Sierra Leone government because too much smuggling was going on.

Around the Country

BUCHANAN

The two hotels to try are the *Sabra Hotel* on Atlantic St and the *Louiza Hotel*.

GANTA

Most people stay at the *Travellers' Inn* (formerly Sister Rachel's Motel) on the main street. It costs about US$15 a double with fan and though it's clean there's no running water or electricity. You can also get a room at *Toe's Motel* for US$8 a double. It's basic but otherwise OK and Mr Toe is very friendly.

HARPER

Close to the border with Ivory Coast, Harper has one of the best beaches in the country. Unfortunately, there's only one place to stay – the *Seafoam Hotel*, which costs US$18 to US$25 for a room. You might also be able to find floor space with the Peace Corps volunteers. Quite a few of them live near the airfield.

For somewhere to eat try *Mary's* under the Plum Tree or *Soul Sister Cookshop*; both are on Green St.

MONROVIA

About the only safe spot to swim around Monrovia is **Kenema Beach**. It costs 50 cents to get there by taxi plus US$1 to get onto the beach. Be careful as there are riptides and strong undercurrents on all the beaches in Liberia.

Information

You can get a visa for Mali from the street vendor on the corner of Carey and Gurley Sts. He sells Malian handicrafts and will come up with a Malian visa if you give him US$15, two photos and your passport. According to a local expatriate resident the operation is legitimate (sounds very dubious all the same!). You can get passport photos (four for US$2) from street vendors on Randall St.

The bus station for buses to Sierra Leone is on Randall St at Water St. For the Bomi Hills the bus station is on Johnson St close to the bridge. The truck park for upcountry lifts is on Water St. Local public buses cost 25 cents flat fare. Taxis cost 40 cents (centre only) and 65 cents (to the suburbs). From Monrovia to Robertsfield Airport (50 km) it's usually possible to find a shared taxi for a few dollars but in the opposite direction the price starts at US$35. The taxi stand is near the bridge to Providence Island.

Embassies Some countries with embassies in Monrovia are:

Cameroun
    South side of Tubman Blvd, about 1½ km past 24th St
Guinea
    North side of Tubman Blvd, about 2½ km past 24th St
Ghana
    11th St at the beach
Ivory Coast
    North side of Tubman Blvd, about three km past 24th St
Sierra Leone
    North side of Tubman Blvd, about two km past 24th St

Places to Stay

Probably the most popular place, and one of the cheapest, is the *Lutheran Mission*, 13th St, on the beach. The staff are very friendly and it costs US$15 a double with shower, fan and toilet. Cooking facilities are available. To get there take a taxi to the Sinkor Shopping Centre.

Virtually right next door to the Lutheran Mission is another popular place, the *United Methodist Mission*, 12th St on the corner of Tubman Blvd, and close to the beach. A room costs US$15 a double, but without shower and toilet. There are better cooking facilities than at the Lutheran Mission.

If these places are full try the mid-range *Ambassador Hotel* which costs US$20 a double with shower, toilet and fan.

There are quite a few other hotels in

Monrovia, but they're mainly for whores and their clients so don't expect too much in the way of comfort and facilities. Try the *Star Hotel & Disco*, on the road to the free port about two km from the centre of town over the bridge. It's in a rough area and is very basic but you can get their best rooms for US$8 or even US$6.50 after negotiation.

Right in the city centre are the *Central Hotel*, on the corner of Broad and Center Sts, and the *Hotel Center*, on Center St around the corner from the Central Hotel. They both have rooms for US$14/20 a single/double though it is possible to bargain them down to as little as US$10 a single. Other travellers have stayed at the *Florida Hotel* which costs US$14 a double with shower and air-con. It's mainly a brothel, but is not too noisy.

Other hotels travellers have used in the past are: the *Park Hotel*, on the corner of Broad and Buchanan Sts, with singles for US$13 plus 10% tax; the *Palm Hotel*, on the corner of Broad and Randall Sts, which costs US$22 a single plus 10% tax; the *Carlton Hotel*, Broad St, where a single costs US$25 plus 10% tax; the *Nevada Hotel*, on the corner of Benson and Gurley Sts, which costs US$25 a double with air-con plus 10% tax, though

you can sometimes get rooms for US$20 a double including tax; and the *Hotel Plaza*, Water St at Michlin.

There is also a *YMCA*, on the corner of Broad and McDonald Sts, where you can get a bed for US$5, but it's hard to get in and it's often full.

Don't sleep on the beaches in Monrovia; you'll either be mugged or arrested for spying.

Places to Eat

Try the restaurants and rice-chop houses on Gurly St off Broad St. The *City Restaurant* on this street has been recommended. Be careful down Gurly St – it's the bar area and muggings are common. The Lebanese restaurant next to the Shelia Cinema, Carey St, offers excellent falafel sandwiches for US$1.50. The *Gondole Restaurant* has been recommended for hamburgers and Lebanese sandwiches.

ROBERTSPORT

Robertsport has some of the best beaches in Liberia. To get there take a truck ride (one hour, US$4) up the coast from Monrovia. There is a cheap hotel (US$5) and a number of cheap rice and soup cafés in town.

Libya

Libya has been conquered and settled at one time or another by Greeks, Romans, Berbers, Arabs and Turks. Remains from these various periods can still be seen in the ruined cities along the coast. The Greek remains at Leptis Magna are particularly interesting and are some of the best preserved in the world.

From the middle of the 16th century until 1911 Libya was part of the empire of the Ottoman Turks and was the empire's last possession along the North African coast. It was taken from them by the Italians in that country's last-minute bid for colonies. Following WW II Libya was placed under United Nations trusteeship until 1951 when it became an independent nation.

In 1969 the old King Idris was deposed in a military coup led by Colonel Muammar Gaddafi, a man then in his late 20s, deeply religious and inspired by a vision of pan-Arabism. Gaddafi has succeeded in placing the country in the forefront of Middle Eastern and even world politics and has drastically changed Libya's former status as a UK-USA client state. His regime is pledged to the equitable distribution of Libya's enormous income from the sale of oil and is currently spending thousands of millions of dollars on roads, schools, houses, hospitals and agriculture. Soon after Gaddafi came to power the British and Americans were ordered to leave the bases they had occupied since WW II, and the 25,000 descendants of the Italian colonists were also forced to pack their bags and leave promptly.

Some promising moves are being made in the devolution and sharing of political power based on Gaddafi's *Green Book*. In it he states that the parliamentary system practised in the west is undemocratic since it is used by politicians to take power away from the people. It also states that a

multi-party system is detrimental to political progress, encouraging sterile opposition for opposition's sake, while in reality the parties in power pursue much the same policies. Though the book contains some refreshing insights and promising new directions which have revolutionised Libyan society, a fair amount of it is pure eccentric eyewash.

Almost wholly foreign-owned and controlled at the time of King Idris' overthrow, Libya's vast oil deposits have gradually been taken over by a government determined to return control of the country's natural resources to its people. Despite an attempt to form a cartel to resist such a development, by 1973 all the foreign oil companies had been forced to accept a minimum 51% Libyan participation.

The National Oil Corporation began independent operations in 1971 and by 1973, with its own operations and the participation agreements it had wrung from the oil companies, it controlled 70% of oil production. Soon after that it embarked on its own refining, distribution of refined products and direct export of crude to overseas state concerns. Before these events took place, despite being one of the world's largest producers of crude oil, Libya was forced to import all of its refined requirements since none of the foreign oil companies had built refineries in Libya. Refined oil is now being exported, often in Libyan tankers, and the natural gas which had been flared in the

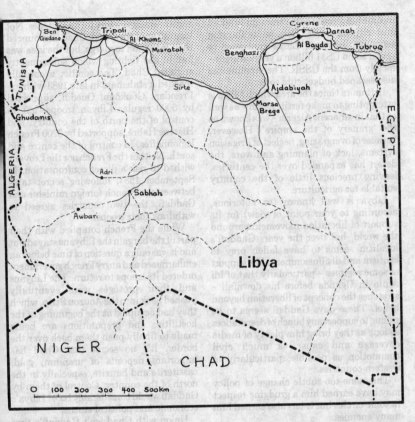

past is now harnessed to fuel power stations.

Ambitious plans to make Libya self-sufficient in food have brought agriculture into a dominant position in the country, with forestry and fishing following closely behind. Vast areas of land are in the process of reclamation and the government is encouraging farmers to adopt cooperative methods. Dams have been constructed to catch what little water falls, and many novel methods of turning desert back into arable land have been utilised.

The largest agricultural project, however, involves the construction of a huge desert-to-coast water pipeline which will be fed by water contained in massive aquifers deep in the south-eastern desert. The project has a total budget of US$25 billion and dominates the economy at the expense of other projects. The first phase, budgeted at US$3.3 billion, was awarded to a South Korean consortium in 1983. The water will be used to supply the area between Sirte and Benghazi. The second phase of the project involves constructing pipelines in the west of the country to supply the area around Tripoli.

It's a very ambitious project and may never be fully completed since Libya's oil exports have dwindled to half what they were in the late 1970s. The resulting loss of income has forced the government to adopt austerity measures. Despite its flagging economy, however, Libya continues to spend some US$1 billion a year on arms – mostly from the USSR. The pipeline has also escaped budget cuts so far.

In Roman times the area which Libya is attempting to make fertile again – as well as that in adjacent Algeria – was known as the 'granary of the empire'. However, because of overgrazing, neglect of irrigation systems, lack of planning and wars, the desert has expanded over the centuries, leaving precious little of the country suitable for agriculture.

Libya is well known (or notorious, according to your point of view) for its support of liberation movements around the world, but over the years Gaddafi's idealism seems to have fallen prey to egotism and disillusionment. His support of some regimes – particularly that of Idi Amin in Uganda before his downfall – stretches the concept of liberation beyond belief. These days Gaddafi seems to be willing to support any bunch of desperadoes as long as they bring him plenty of media coverage and cause as much civil commotion as possible, particularly in western countries.

This none-too-subtle change of policy may have earned him a grudging respect in some circles but it has also earned him many enemies.

His attempts to eliminate exiled Libyan opponents living in various western countries by unleashing death squads in the early 1980s was surely the end of the line as far as his credibility was concerned. Even radical Arab regimes generally prefer to keep him at arm's length and are very lukewarm about his proposals for Arab unity. Many African countries have also expressed serious concern about Libya's involvement in Chad.

When the civil war broke out in Chad several years ago, Libya occupied a section of the northern part of that country and shortly afterwards poured in troops and arms to ensure victory for its protégés. Not long after, Libya and Chad announced their intention to merge, but the idea was lost in the fighting which subsequently engulfed Chad. The conflict eventually reached a stalemate in late 1983 with ex-President Goukouni Oueddi, supported by 5000 regular Libyan troops, left in control of the north of the country, and Hissene Habré, supported by 3200 French legionnaires, in control of the centre and south. Neither the French nor the Libyans wished to risk a direct confrontation. In September 1984, following secret talks between the French foreign minister and Gaddafi, the two countries agreed to withdraw their troops.

While the French complied with their part of the bargain the Libyans stayed put and it was only a question of time before an embarrassed and angry French government ordered its troops to return. The Libyans and their protégés were eventually pushed back into the Aouzou Strip, which they had occupied at the beginning of the hostilities and preparations are being made to finally push them back over the border. It's no secret that Chad has important deposits of uranium, gold, cassiterite and bauxite, especially in the north of the country. Control of them by Gaddafi would considerably boost Libya's economic and political status.

Union with Chad isn't Gaddafi's first attempt at pan-Arabism. He has tried it before with Tunisia, Sudan, Syria and Egypt, but the attempts have all come to grief. Indeed, since negotiations with Egypt were broken off, the two countries have twice been on the brink of war, the first time as a result of the treatment of Egyptian workers in Libya (all of whom were subsequently expelled), then again as a result of the Camp David peace treaty with Israel. A similar hiatus was reached with Tunisia following the expulsion of Tunisian workers from Libya. Gaddafi's latest fantasy was a loose federation with Morocco, but the political differences between the two countries were such that the whole idea verged on the absurd, and soon foundered.

While most Libyans will willingly admit that Gaddafi has done a lot for the Libyan people since he took over, there is opposition to his rule. Most of it is centred in the military establishment and there have been a number of attempted coups, though news of them is generally suppressed.

Though the armed forces were once Gaddafi's main power base, he is aware of the opposition within its ranks and has attempted to erode their influence by the creation of revolutionary committees staffed by young zealots answerable only to him. They have gained a lot of power at the expense of the armed forces recently, and there is a movement afoot to disband the regular forces and replace them with a 'people's army'.

As long as Gaddafi can maintain the initiative, his control of the political scene will probably remain undisputed. The problem is that ordinary Libyans are beginning to feel the pinch of the austerity measures after the halcyon days of the 1970s, when there was more money than things to spend it on.

Economics, however, are not the only issue concerning Libya's near 4½ million people. The extremely rapid transition from a largely nomadic to a modern consumer society has resulted in many problems. City streets are full of garbage, inflation is high and food is not only expensive but scarce. Fruit and vegetables are almost impossible to find, as are meat, eggs and butter.

Not only does Libya have to import about 90% of its food but there are also an estimated one million expatriate workers in the country, many of whom – especially those in the oil industry – are indispensable. So indispensable that, despite American military provocation and the shooting down of Libyan jets in the Gulf of Sirte, many Americans continued to remain there even after diplomatic relations were severed. Most were finally induced to

leave, however, when Reagan ordered the American Mediterranean fleet to attack a number of Libyan mainland targets – including Gaddafi's headquarters – in April 1986. The attack was in retaliation for alleged Libyan complicity in a number of airport massacres in Europe carried out by an extremist Palestinian group. Gaddafi narrowly escaped, though members of his family were killed in the bombings.

Though Gaddafi certainly payrolls some of these fringe groups and has recently been casting his net as far as the South Pacific, the attack was a contentious issue which had more to do with Reagan's and the CIA's personal animosity towards Gaddafi than it had to do with facts. Far more culpable was Syria, yet the US administration preferred to turn a blind eye. This was because Assad's cooperation in any US-sponsored Middle East peace initiative is vital, as is his willingness to negotiate the release of hostages held in Lebanon.

Meanwhile, it is unlikely that Gaddafi will tone down his vitriolic tirades against countries he regards as imperialist or counter-revolutionary, though, quietly, there is a lot of concern about the country's increasing isolation. Several requests have been made for closer economic ties with the EC but they have all been vetoed, leaving Libya, along with Albania, as the only Mediterranean countries which have no economic cooperation agreements with the EC.

Facts

VISAS

Visas are required by all except nationals of Algeria, Malta and Mauritania. Nationals of West Germany must get visas from the Libyan Embassy in Bonn; visas obtained elsewhere will not be accepted.

If you are going to Libya you must have in your passport a translation in Arabic of your particulars. Without this the Libyan embassies won't accept any visa application. Most western embassies in North Africa will provide such a translation free of charge.

Nationals of Israel and South Africa are not admitted nor are those with either Israeli or Egyptian stamps in their passport.

Unmarried women under 35 years old are generally refused visas or are made to wait so long (weeks and even months) that it simply isn't worth trying. So much for Gaddafi's much-lauded policies for women's liberation.

MONEY

US$ 1 = LD 0.30
UK£ 1 = LD 0.48

The unit of currency is the Libyan dinar = 1000 dirham. The import and export of local currency is allowed up to LD 20.

The airport departure tax for international flights is LD 5.

TOURIST INFORMATION

Entry into Libya is conditional on your having at least US$500 to show immigration authorities.

Searches at Libyan borders and airports are very thorough. Alcohol, pork products, pornography and anything considered to be anti-Libyan propaganda will be confiscated – paperbacks and cassettes fall into this category regardless of content. 'Marks & Sparks' underwear is definitely suspect. Also, anything vaguely connected with Israel will be confiscated. It's rumoured that radios with short-wave bands will soon be on the list as the government doesn't like what it hears about itself on the BBC World Service.

You must report to a police station within 48 hours of arriving. Usually your hotel can take care of this but if not you'll have to ask someone to help you find a place called Balladia, where you fill in forms and get your passport stamped. You haven't a hope of finding this place or of

filling in the forms unless you read and speak good Arabic.

The borders with Egypt and Tunisia are closed.

PHOTOGRAPHY

Remember to be careful taking photographs. Libyans are generally very suspicious of foreigners with cameras, if only because the government-controlled media are forever rabbitting on about imperialist/racist enemies of the Libyan people.

LANGUAGE

Arabic is the official language, and Gaddafi is so keen on promoting its use and discouraging the use of any other language that a phrase book is essential. You'll be very lucky to find a sign in any other language anywhere in the country.

Getting There & Around

Because the borders with Egypt and Tunisia are closed, and visas are such a hassle to get, very few travellers are going to Libya these days.

ROAD

Hitching is easy in the north and lifts are often for long distances, especially between Tripoli and Benghazi – there's very little habitation between these two cities. Lifts are often with expatriate workers and are usually free, though if you're heading down into the desert you should expect to pay.

There are fast and efficient daily buses between the main Libyan coastal towns but you need to buy tickets at least a day in advance as there's heavy competition for seats.

Around the Country

TRIPOLI

There's no such thing as a cheap hotel in Tripoli so be prepared for a shock. Perhaps the best place to try is the *Youth Hostel*, about 500 metres outside the old city on Sharia Ibn El As (otherwise known as Omar ben Alas). It's just past the cinema on the opposite side of the road. It is comfortable and spacious with clean linen, TV lounge, and hot and cold showers – and sometimes they even have movies.

If the Youth Hostel is full, or you can't find it, try the *Libyan Palace Hotel* which costs LD 10 a single. It's usually full but the staff on the desk speak English and might be able to recommend another place.

If you arrive by air, the yellow government taxis will take you into Tripoli for LD 4. Buy your ticket inside the terminal building. Private taxis charge LD 8.

GREEK & ROMAN RUINS

Even if you're not a ruins buff you will thoroughly enjoy a visit to the Greek and Roman ruins along the northern coast. Undoubtedly the best is **Leptis Magna** close to Al Khums (Homs) east of Tripoli.

Others worth visiting are **Sabrantha**, between the Tunisian border and Tripoli, and **Cyrene**, close to Shahhat and half way along the Benghazi to Tobruk road.

Madagascar

Madagascar (or the Democratic Republic of Madagascar as it's officially called) is a fascinating enigma in Africa. Travelling through this beautiful country you will begin to wonder where you are. Is it Africa, Asia, Polynesia or Europe? Cobblestoned streets wind through villages, which could be straight out of rural France, but somehow in the 1950s, if the cars are anything to go by. Yet the people have African and Asian features.

Some towns, such as Toamasina and Antsirabe, are crowded with rickshaws and resemble Asia, and the countryside is cultivated with terraced rice fields. On the other hand, in the winter in the central highlands, seeing all the people wearing hats and swaddled in large blankets you might think you were in Ethiopia or even the Peruvian Andes. Actually, it's not simply any one of these, but a mixture (except there's no South American input) of them all.

The majority of its 11 million inhabitants are descended from Malay and Polynesian migrants. They began arriving from the 6th century onwards, particularly during the 9th century when the powerful Hindu-Sumatran empire of Srivijaya controlled much of the maritime trade in the Indian Ocean. These people brought with them the food crops of South-East Asia, so that even today the agriculture of the island resembles that of the peoples' origins rather than of the mainland.

It has been suggested that the gradual spread of these crops to the mainland assisted the Bantu tribes of the interior in migrating to the coasts of Kenya and Tanzania by providing them with potentially greater food surpluses.

Malagasy agriculture, however, isn't the only factor distinguishing the island from the mainland. None of the mainland apes, antelopes, poisonous snakes or the lion or elephant are found on the island.

A number of different kingdoms came into being side by side on the island, and it wasn't until the end of the 18th century that the kingdom of Merina, using weapons and advisers from European nations, was able to unite the island. During the 19th century a sort of modern state with a trained army and administration, an established church and formal education system was created by uniting both traditional and European models of government. The country was invaded by the French in 1895 and was declared a colony the following year after the Merina queen had been deposed.

Colonisation followed the typical pattern: expropriation of land by foreign settlers and companies, the exploitation of the peasantry through forced labour and taxes, the imposition of an import-export economy (in this case based on coffee) with the construction of roads and railroads to serve it, and the training of an intellectual elite to French standards. Resentment grew in all levels of society and eventually culminated in the insurrection of 1947-48. This was crushed by the French with the loss of several thousand Malagasy lives. In 1960, however, the French (taking advantage of the tensions existing between the coastal and inland peoples) granted independence on terms very favourable to themselves.

Under the Malagasy Republic's first president, Philibert Tsiranana, the French were allowed to retain their hold over trade and financial institutions and keep their military bases on the island.

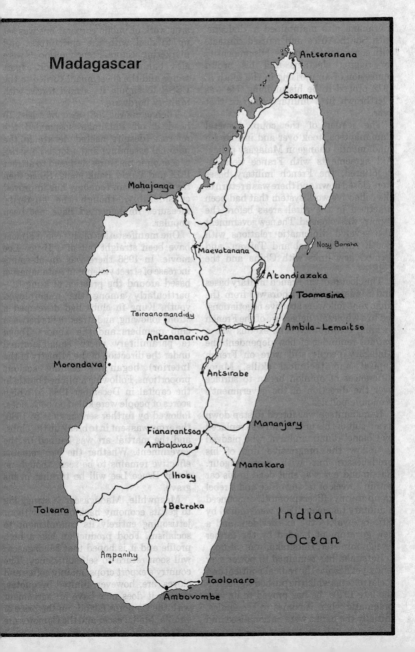

Madagascar

Antseranana

Sasumav

Mahajanga

Maevatanana

Nosy Boraha

A'tondiazaka

Toamasina

Tsiroanomandidy

Ambila-Lemaitso

Antananarivo

Morondava

Antsirabe

Mananjary

Fianarantsoa

Ambalavao

Manakara

Ihosy

Betroka

Toleara

Indian Ocean

Ampanihy

Taolonaro

Ambovombe

Tsiranana also maintained a 'dialogue' with South Africa and refused contacts with communist countries. His propensity for rigging elections and his brutal repression of an uprising in the south in 1972 proved to be his undoing. He was overthrown in a military coup in that year.

The leader of the coup, General Ramanantsoa, took over and initiated a fundamental change in Malagasy policy. Aid agreements with France were re-negotiated, the French military bases were closed down and there was a return to the collective work system that had been practised in the rural areas before the country was colonised. The new government also severed diplomatic relations with South Africa, Israel and Taiwan, and formed new links with China and the USSR.

The closure of the French military bases and Madagascar's withdrawal from the franc zone following abortive negotiations, led to a wholesale departure of the French farming community. The exodus was a painful reminder of how dependent the Malagasy people still were on French capital and technical skills. Major differences of opinion began to surface over the direction of the government's economic policies.

Ramanantsoa was forced to step down as a result of this unrest and was replaced by Colonel Ratsimandrava, who pledged to follow the progressive line of his predecessor but with more vigour. Ratsimandrava was shot dead in his car within a week of taking office and a rebel group of army officers promptly announced a military takeover. They were routed by officers loyal to the ex-president and a new government headed by the former foreign minister, Ratsiraka, was set up.

Ratsiraka has remained in power ever since, yet despite the radical political and social reforms which he pushed through in the late 1970s, he has proved to be very pragmatic when it comes to economics. Initially the banks were nationalised and a network of public corporations was set up to deal with the agricultural and marketing sectors. French nationals were also banned from the import-export sector and the government turned to the USSR to supply its armed forces with military hardware.

Then came the 1981-82 debt crisis. To head it off Ratsiraka suspended the reforms (despite heated debate in the national assembly) and adopted a series of economic measures designed to attract IMF and World Bank loans. Since then the Madagascan economy has improved considerably, though the austerity measures implemented have not been popular.

One manifestation of this could almost have been straight out of a Bruce Lee movie. In 1986 there was an alarming increase of street violence in Antananarivo based around the practice of kung fu – particularly among the unemployed youth. Kung fu clubs had developed a strong following, and street fights between club members and the Tanora Tonga (a paramilitary youth squad formed under the direction of the Ministry of the Interior) began to assume serious proportions. Following a pitched battle in the capital in December 1985 in which scores of people were killed on both sides, followed by further serious riots in 1986, the army was sent in to break up the clubs, and the martial art was banned by the government. Whether the ban remains effective remains to be seen, though no doubt Bruce Lee will be turning in his grave.

Meanwhile, Madagascar is struggling to get its economy back on line without jettisoning entirely its commitment to socialism. Food production has a high profile and it is hoped that Madagascar will soon return to self-sufficiency. The country's export crops, mainly coffee and cloves, are, however, limited by quotas, though it does now have an agreement with the Comoros Islands on the price of vanilla. Madagascar and the Comoros are the world's foremost exporters of this flavouring material, though there is now strong competition from artificial substitutes. Agreements have been signed with a number of oil companies to begin drilling (three of them US concerns), and another with British Petroleum to develop coal deposits, but in all of them the Madagascan government has retained a 51% stake.

The days of near-xenophobic suspicion of foreigners appears to be over and the government has accepted that if it sells some 45% of its exports to France and the USA, then it might be reasonable to address these countries' legitimate concerns. This is a far cry from the days of Bob Denard's coup in the Comoros in 1978. At that time, relations with the tiny island republic were severed and Madagascar sought to acquire a more sophisticated airforce and stronger relations with the socialist states of the mainland.

The regime in Antananarivo is obviously feeling more confident these days, though there does remain the dispute over sovereignty of several small islands off the northern tip of Madagascar – such as Iles Glorieuses, Juan de Nova and Europa – which the French continue to occupy. This is not likely to be resolved in the near future, especially as the French have built extensive air facilities on Juan de Nova.

This description may give you the impression that Madagascar is a dangerous place to visit. It isn't. It's certainly different from the mainland and travelling around requires a degree of persistence, but people are friendly, the landscape is stunning and the sounds, smells and sights unique.

Facts

GEOGRAPHY & CLIMATE

Madagascar is set almost entirely in the tropics. Because of the rugged mountain chain which runs down the centre of the island there are dramatic differences in the vegetation and climate between the west and east sides of the island. The eastern coastal strip is fairly narrow and partly covered with tropical rainforests. The west side of the island has a wider plain of savannah and forest. The south is considerably more arid and features cactus-like vegetation. The mountain chain is dissected by deep valleys.

The rainy season stretches from November to March. Cyclones are common along the east coast, with the monsoon between December and March.

VISAS

Visas are required by all. They are valid for a stay of one month, cost the equivalent of about US$12, require four photos and take up to seven days to issue. You need an onward ticket for entry into the country, but this isn't usually asked for when you apply for the visa. In Africa they have the following embassies:

Algeria
    22 Rue Aouis Bologhine, Algiers
Mauritius
    6 Sir William Newton St, Port Louis
Tanzania
    Magoret St, Dar es Salaam

There is no longer a Malagasy embassy in Nairobi but you can apply for the visa through Air Madagascar (tel 25286, 26494) at the Hilton Hotel block, City Hall Way (PO Box 42676), Nairobi. They only take applications on Mondays as the forms have to be sent to Antananarivo for approval. You get the visa on Thursday the same week. The visas cost KSh 170, require four photos and you need to show an onward ticket.

If arriving in Madagascar from continental Africa you must have valid cholera and yellow fever vaccinations.

Outside Africa there are Malagasy embassies in Bonn, Brussels, Geneva, London, Paris, Rome, Tokyo and Washington.

One of the easiest places to obtain a visa

is in London (UK). It costs UK£20, requires five photos and you need an onward ticket. The visa is issued while you wait (usually about 20 minutes). The honorary consulate is at Hobbs & Partners, 69-70 Mark Lane, London EC3R 7JA, near Fenchurch St railway station.

Visas are easy to extend for up to two months in Antananarivo at the Ministry of the Interior. The cost is MFr 15,000 and you must supply three photos, a photocopy of your visa and a short letter in French explaining why you want an extension. They take three days to come through.

MONEY

US$1 = MFr 1295

The unit of currency is the Malagasy franc (Franc Malgache) = 100 centimes. The import or export of local currency is prohibited and any found on you when you leave will be confiscated.

There is a very strict currency control on arrival and your cash will be checked down to the last cent. The same happens when you leave. Currency declaration forms are issued. Malagasy francs are almost impossible to get rid of outside the country (they're officially nonconvertible).

The black market is difficult to find, but useful if you're on a budget. It is best to change money with a Malagasy abroad as you will get up to twice the bank rate. Inside the country try approaching Indian and Chinese traders. Be discreet when doing this as penalties are severe. The cost of living is relatively high and many goods are only available in limited quantities and at high prices on the black market, though things are definitely improving. Fashionable western clothes, electrical goods and calculators sell well.

In the markets prices are quoted in piastres, ariary, drala or parata. The MFr 50 coin is known as 10 ariary; the MFr 100 coin as 20 ariary.

The airport departure tax for international flights is MFr 1500.

ACCOMMODATION

The Direction du Tourisme recently classified all of Madagascar's hotels from one to four star and laid down rules for the tariffs in each grading. In some cases this has led to an increase in prices, but in others to a decrease.

Accommodation prices at lodges are per room – you pay the same whether you're on your own or travelling with others. You can always find cheap hotels by making enquiries locally. Small lodging places can be very cheap indeed, but beware of body lice (a real pest in Madagascar) and bedbugs.

LANGUAGE

French and Malagasy are the official languages. Very little English is spoken.

Getting There & Around

AIR

Air Madagascar flies to Nairobi, Comoros, Mauritius, Réunion, Seychelles and Paris. This airline is fond of appearing to be fully booked, so if you can't get a confirmed seat (on domestic or international flights), try standby – it often works. Be sure to reconfirm flights. It's best to have a confirmed flight out of the country otherwise you could find yourself staying there longer than intended. Allow plenty of time for formalities when leaving by plane.

Air Madagascar also has a domestic network. If you're thinking of using their services extensively, enquire about the Air Tourist Pass which allows unlimited travel for a fixed period of time – usually one month. Since the domestic network is dense (58 destinations) this represents quite good value especially if you want to cover a lot of ground. You have to buy the pass from an Air Madagascar office outside the country or from an Air France office in countries where they act as general sales agents for Air Madagascar.

You don't have to buy your international flight from Air Madagascar to qualify.

ROAD

Road transport is slow, expensive and infrequent, and the roads are all in bad shape, except for the Antananarivo to Toamasina road recently rebuilt by the Chinese. All the same, travelling between those two cities is much faster by taxi than by train and costs about the same. The views are also more spectacular.

Avoid coming in the rainy season if possible as many roads are impassable. Regardless of the type of transport you take, be prepared for very uncomfortable journeys and breakdowns – Fianarantsoa to Taolanaro (Fort Dauphin) can take up to five days even in the dry season! Take warm clothes if travelling in the mountains during winter. The locals wear up to four blankets in some areas.

Hitching is a joke as there are so few vehicles and you pay for rides anyway.

Bus & Taxi

There are four categories of public transport. The *taxi-be* is the quickest and most comfortable but expensive. Next best is the *taxi-brousse* which is fast but uncomfortable and seats about 15 people. After that there is the van-type bus which seats 25 to 30 people. This is more uncomfortable than the *taxi-brousse* and makes more stops, but is quite tolerable. Last are the proper buses, which seat over 30 people. You're advised to give these a miss as they're slow and don't handle the Malagasy roads very well (most of the island's roads are unsurfaced). The only reliable bus service in Madagascar is operated by the railways. The buses cover the Antsirabe to Fianarantsoa route in 7½ hours. Always book transport in advance.

All vehicles stop for meals. Bus stations have *hotelys* – restaurants where you can buy a hot meal at a reasonable price. Unless you want a large meal, it's best to order a *demi-plat*. These are smaller and cheaper than the larger *plat*.

It helps to know when market days are in neighbouring towns otherwise you can get stuck in a place for days because there's no transport available.

Examples of road transport are:

Antananarivo to Tulear – a *taxi-brousse* costs MFr 15,000 and takes about 24 hours
Toleara (Tulear) to Taolanaro (Fort Dauphin) – a *taxi-brousse* costs MFr 10,000, but they only go on Fridays at 4 am

TRAIN

There are railway lines from Antananarivo to Toamasina (Tamatave) on the coast via Ambila-Lemaitso, and from Antananarivo north to A'tondrazaka and south to Antsirabe. There is also a short line from Fianarantsoa to Manakara along the scenically spectacular coast.

Rail fares are based on MFr 5 per km but there are reductions on return tickets depending on the number of days you want to spend at your destination. Journey times are slow because of the difficult terrain and the narrow gauge track. On Nosy Be there are 60-cm-gauge plantation trains which you can ride free.

Antananarivo to Toamasina (Tamatave)

There are daily trains in either direction, except on Sundays, at about 5 am. Trains are comfortable and relatively fast but you must make reservations in advance. The fares are MFr 9350 (1st class) and MFr 4000 (2nd class). Going 1st class saves a lot of time queuing up. The journey takes 12½ hours. This is a spectacular journey with many twists and turns as the train follows the river gorges up onto the plateau.

Antananarivo to Antsirabe

There are two trains daily in either direction at about 4.50 am and 1 pm, which take 5¼ hours and cost MFr 3995 (1st class). It's a very pleasant journey with good views of the countryside.

Fianarantsoa to Manakara
There is at least one train daily (some days there are two) and the journey time is six hours.

BOAT
There is a boat from Hell-Ville (on Nosy Be) to Mahajunga every three to four days. It's a good trip and costs only MFr 7000 (as opposed to MFr 20,000 by land). There is no firm departure time – just make sure you're around when it's likely to be leaving.

There are boats from Toamasina to many Madagascan ports and coastal villages. Most of these are cargo boats but they usually take passengers. Fares are more or less fixed; Toamasina to Antseranana, for example, costs MFr 25,000.

There are no schedules except for the one going to Nosy Boraha (Ile Ste Marie), which leaves Toamasina every Tuesday. This boat is called the *Rapiko*; it takes about 10 hours to get to Ste Marie and costs MFr 7000. There's a cabin with two bunks on the boat and foreigners are generally given it without charge as long as it's not occupied. Buy your tickets from the SCAC office in Toamasina.

After arriving at Nosy Boraha the *Rapiko* continues on to Maroantsetra, which it reaches the next morning (fare from Nosy Boraha is MFr 5000). The *Rapiko* returns to Nosy Boraha on Friday evening and leaves there for Toamasina on Saturday mornings.

If you go as far as Maroantsetra you're virtually obliged to take the boat out again. There's no road north from there and the road south to Toamasina involves crossing about 15 rivers. Small barges operate as ferries at these points, but there's always at least one broken down which means there's no traffic at all to rely on as a stopgap.

For information on other boats ask around at the Auximad and Trans 7 offices in Toamasina.

Other ferries operate between Hell-Ville and Antsahampano and between Mahajunga and Katsepy.

Around the Country

AMBALAVAO
One hour by taxi from Fianarantsoa is Ambalavao, known throughout Madagascar as the 'home of the departed'. In a country where ancestors are periodically exhumed as a mark of respect, this place is of great spiritual importance.

Nearby are **Ambondrome Crag**, said to be the paradise of all Malagasy ancestors, and **Ifandana Crag**, the site of the mass suicides of 1811. If you visit Ifandana Crag it's important to observe the *fady* (taboo) of the local people. In the past tourists have apparently attempted to take away the bones that are still very much in evidence – unbelievable, isn't it!

Ambalavao is also a crafts centre where you can find *antaimoro* paper, made by arranging patterns of flower petals in the wet pulp; and *lamba arindrano*, a hand-woven silk rectangle with geometric patterns.

Places to Stay
There's only the *Hotel Verger*, which has eight rooms and costs MFr 5100 per night. You can reserve a room from Fianarantsoa by ringing Ambalavao 5.

AMBOSITRA
The main attraction of Ambositra is the **woodcarving cooperative**, whose work is famous throughout the island. The originators of this craft are the Zafimaniry families. The best way to visit them is to contact the Jesuits, many of whom work around here. If you're lucky enough to be taken along to these peoples' villages you'll probably be offered a glass of *toaka gasy*, the local firewater, often distilled to 125° proof. Whether you're a hard drinker or not, refusal offends – but expect violent headaches within 24 hours.

The *Grand Hotel* with 15 (often empty) rooms and an indifferent reputation has been forced to cut its prices dramatically to MFr 7500 per night.

AMPEFY

This is an interesting town on the shores of Lake Itasy. Stay at the *Kavitaha Hotel* which costs MFr 4000 per night.

ANTANANARIVO (Tananarive)
Information

The tourist office is closed. To get a map of Antananarivo go to the reception desk of the Hilton Hotel. Many of the streets now have Malagasy names.

It's suggested you stay off the streets after dark in this city as it's not particularly safe.

Embassies Some countries with embassies in Antananarivo are:

France
  3 Rue Jean Jaurès, BP 204
UK
  Immeuble Ny Havana, Cité des 67 Ha (tel 27749, 27370)
USA
  14 Lalana Rainitovo (tel 21257)

Things to See

The **Zuma** is the big Friday market. It is supposedly the second largest in the world and people flock to it from all over the island. Bargains can be found but some travellers regard it as overrated. Beware of pickpockets and muggers. Don't go there alone and don't carry bags.

Also worth visiting is the **Rova** (Queen's Palace) on the highest hill, and the small streets around it. There are superb views over the city from here. The palace is closed on Mondays and is only open in the afternoons on weekdays and Saturdays. Entry is free. Similar is the **Ambonimanga** (King's Palace), about 30 km north of the city.

The **zoo** and the **botanical gardens** are also worth a visit, though the zoo is nothing special except for the lemurs. The **archaeological museum** is, according to many travellers, not worth visiting, though it is free.

Places to Stay

Good accommodation in the capital is expensive, though there are a number of cheap places to the right as you come out of the railway station. To find a room there you need to be early. Cheapies include the *Hotel Lapan'ny Vaniny* and the *Hotel Ivarivo*. Both are dirty.

Also cheap is the *Boulidor Hotel & Restaurant*, which you get to by turning left coming out of the station, then taking the first right past the Perle de l'Orient Restaurant. It costs MFr 3500. For the same price you can also get a basic room at the *Hotel Ravinala*, 10 Lálana Ratianarivo, which has a restaurant and bar.

Other travellers have recommended the *Centre d'Accueil Haley* off Ave de l'Indépendence. It's very clean, secure and is staffed by friendly people who will help you with your proposed itinerary.

If looking for something better, there's a good choice of places under US$10. One of the cheapest is the *Hotel Select*, Ave 18 de Juin next door to Alitalia, where a small room costs MFr 16,000. It's very clean and conveniently located. The *Hotel Terminus* (tel 25440), Ave de la Libération 2, just by the railway station, is similar, with rooms for MFr 7000/9500 a single/double, and breakfast for MFr 800. The *Lido* (tel 23848), Escalier Ranavalona 1, costs MFr 4500; the *Hotel Glacier*, has rooms for MFr 7000 (dirty and no locks on the doors); and the *Bridge Hotel*, Ave Marguerite Barbier, costs MFr 7000 and has a bar, restaurant and nightclub. If you opt for the Lido you need to know that it's run by an evangelical Christian who won't allow two men to share the same room.

Also in this range is the *Hotel Mellis* (tel 23425), 3 Rue de Nice, Tsaralakana, which costs MFr 5600. Another traveller recommended the *Hotel-Restaurant Pavillion de Jade* (tel 22690), 20 Rue

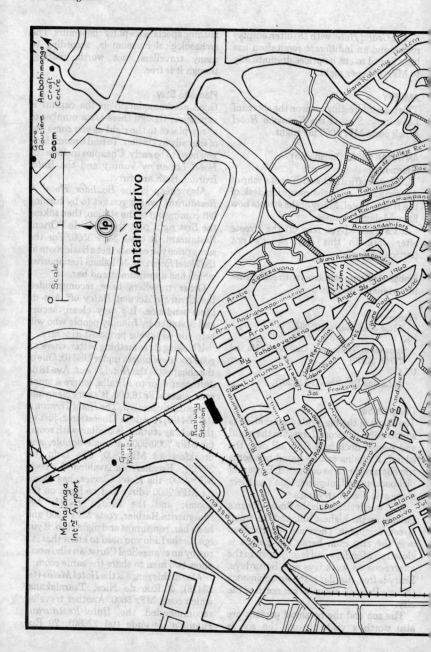

Antananarivo

Mahajanga Inter' Airport

Railway Station

Gare Routière

Gare Routière

Ambohimanga Craft Centre

500m

0   Scale

Lálana Rabearivelo Pastora

Lalana de Villeje Rev

Lálana Rakotomalala

Joe

Lálana Ramandriamampan...

Andriandahifo...

Lálana Andriahatoandra

Zuma

Arabe 26 Juin 1960

Lálana Paul Dussac

Arabe Rabezavana

Arabe Andriahamponimena...

Araben

Ny Fahaleovantena

Lálana Ratsimilaho

Arabe Lumumba

Lálana Razafindramanitra

Lálana Reisana

Lálana Jean Jaurès

Sol Frantsay

Arabe Grandidier

Arabe Ravoninahitriniarivo

Lálana Rasoamanarivo

Lálana Ranaivo Jul

Lálana Pasteur

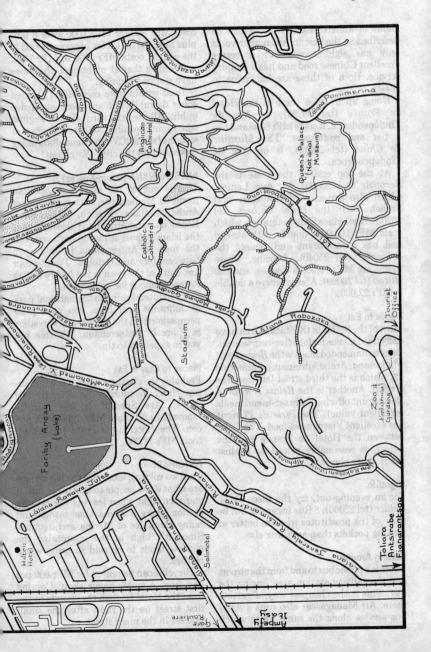

Emile et Juliette Ranarivelo, which he described as the best in Antananarivo. It only has eight rooms but it serves excellent Chinese food and has a laundry service. Both of these are half-price to guests.

Going up in price there is the *Hotel de France* (tel 20293), 34 Ave de l'Indépendence. It costs MFr 8000 and has a bar and restaurant. The *Muraille de Chine* (tel 23013), is on Ave de l'Indépendence.

At the top end of the scale is the *Acropole* (tel 23380), 71 Ave Lenine, which also serves good Malagasy and French food; the *Hotel Colbert* (tel 20202), Rue Prince Ratsimamanga, which costs MFr 16,000 a double with air-con and has a restaurant and casino; the *Solimotel* (tel 25040), Anosibe, where rooms are MFr 12,500 a double; and the *Hilton* (tel 26060), Anosy, where a double is MFr 22,000.

Places to Eat
Most of the hotels in the station area have daily fixed menus for for a five-course meal. One recommended place is the *Restaurant Fiadanana*, Arabe Adrianampoinimerina 12, which is the third street left from the station. Another is the *Relais Normand Restaurant* offering daily set-menu meals (excellent value). The *Perle de l'Orient* has excellent Vietnamese food. The *Lola*, between the Hotel de France and the Select, is reasonably priced as against many other places.

Nightlife
For an evening out, try the disco at *Le Cellier* (tel 22060), 8 Rue Ingereza, but be wary of the prostitutes who are better at picking pockets than anything else.

Getting Around
There is a public bus to and from the airport and the railway station area during the day. This is the cheapest way of getting there. Air Madagascar also runs a daily bus service along the same route which costs MFr 800 (or MFr 1000 after 8 pm) plus MFr 100 for excess luggage. A taxi to the airport costs MFr 5000 to MFr 7000, and double that at night once the buses have stopped running.

Taxis within town cost MFr 150 when going downhill but are more expensive uphill! All the taxis turn off their engines when going downhill so there's a constant stream of silent 2CVs and Renaults cruising downhill into the city! Watch out!

ANTSERANANA (Diego-Suarez)
This is one of the most cosmopolitan towns in Madagascar, with a mixture of Arabs, Indians, French, Malagasies, Réunionais and Africans. It also has one of the island's most stunning harbours, but the road to Antseranana is only open between July and October. Twenty four km south of the town is the **Ambre Nature Reserve** famous for its lemurs.

If you intend going to the national park at **Joffreville** near here, you need prior permission from the Ministre de Forestière et Eaux in Antseranana. It's free but you're expected to tip.

Places to Stay & Eat
Probably the cheapest place is the Indian-run *Hotel Restaurant La Racasse* (tel 22024), Ave Surcouf. It was recently renovated and costs MFr 7800 with air-con. The *Hotel de la Poste* (tel 22044) costs MFr 12,000.

ANTSIRABE
The two **volcanic lakes** and the **hot springs** are what draw people to this place but, if you turn right when leaving the railway station, there is also a huge **market** and many examples of Merina architecture. Since it's high in the mountains the climate tends to be cold so bring warm clothes.

Bicycles can be rented for MFr 800 per day from a small repair shop. Coming from the Hotel Baobab the shop is in the first street on the right after the small market in the main street.

Places to Stay

One of the cheapest places is the *Hotel Baobab*, Ave de l'Indépendence, which costs MFr 2500 to MFr 4000 and serves reasonable Malagasy food (soup, fish and rice for MFr 1200). Similar is the *Trianon Hotel*, run, as one traveller commented, 'by an ever-shouting old French colonial'. It costs MFr 4000.

For a touch of luxury try the *Hotel des Termes*, a huge, classical-style building with swimming pool and a bar-terrace set in pleasant gardens, which costs MFr 12,000. The bar is open to nonresidents.

FIANARANTSOA

Fianarantsoa is regarded as the intellectual capital of Madagascar. Not only that, but it is also a Christian centre (unusual on this island) and the main wine-producing area. Getting around the town can be perplexing as there are three distinct levels.

There are three reasonably priced hotels: the *Hotel Le Papillon*, the *Sud-Hotel* and the *Relais du Betsileo*. All cost between MFr 4500 and MFr 5600.

IHOSY

This is an unremarkable town in itself but is a frequent overnight stop between Fianarantsoa and Toleara as well as between Fianarantsoa and Taolonaro.

The *Zahamotel* has rooms for MFr 7000.

MAHAJANGA (Majunga)

This town is a large port on the estuary of the Betsiboka River (Madagascar's largest) but its main attraction is the shark-free **beach**. There are road connections here between July and October by bush taxi from Antseranana. The journey can be interesting as it goes through the Mahajamba Valley, famous for its fossils and forests full of lemurs.

Places to Stay

There are three reasonably priced hotels. The *Nouvel Hotel* (tel 2110), 13 Rue Paul Henri Paul, costs MFr 5800; the *Les Roches Rouges* (tel 2161), Blvd Marcoz Corniche, costs MFr 6100; and the *Village Touristique de la Plage* (tel 2079), Port Schneider has rooms for MFr 7500.

More expensive are the *Hotel de France* (tel 2607), Rue Marechal Joffre, with rooms for MFr 9500, and the *Zahamotel* (tel 2334), Amborory, which costs MFr 12,000.

MANAKARA

This is a pleasant coastal town, though you'll probably only find yourself here if you have taken the railway from Fianarantsoa.

Stay at the *Hotel de Manakara* (tel 21141) for around MFr 4000.

NOSY BE

Nosy Be is the Zanzibar of Madagascar. The plantations here provide the perfume industry with its raw materials – macassar oil (or ylang-ylang as any self-respecting hippie will tell you), lemon grass and patchouli – as well as vanilla, which even Reagan eats from time to time.

There are also **sugar cane plantations** with miniature railways so, if you're from northern New South Wales or Queensland and are feeling nostalgic, here's balm for your eyes. Visits to the sugar plantations can be arranged in advance at the Sucrerie Nosy Be Côte Est, 14 Rue Radama 1, Bôite Postale 482, Antananarivo.

For history buffs there's a ruined **Indian village** 11 km east of Hell-Ville dating from the 17th century, when there was a wave of immigration from that subcontinent.

Road connections with Nosy Be are impossible outside the dry season (July to October), though the ferry to and from the mainland operates all year round. To go there during the rest of the year you'll have to consider flights – there are connections from Antananarivo, Mahajanga and Antseranana.

Between Nosy Be and the mainland is the smaller island of **Nosy Komba**. It is a lemur reserve and has no resident human population. To visit you'll need authorisation from the Direction des Eaux et Forêts in Hell-Ville.

Places to Stay

The cheapest place in Hell-Ville is the *Hotel de la Mer* (tel 61353) which costs MFr 5600 and has a restaurant. More expensive is *Les Cocotiers* (tel 61284) at Dzamandzar with rooms for MFr 9800. The hotel has a yacht club and diving centre. Another mid-range hotel is the *Residence d'Ambatoloaka* (tel 61368) which costs MFr 12,000 and has a restaurant and yacht club. At the top end of the market are the *Palm Beach* (tel 61284) at MFr 16,000 and the *Holiday Inn* (tel 61176) at MFr 17,000.

NOSY BORAHA (Île Ste Marie)

This is a beautiful unspoilt island off Madagascar's eastern coast about 120 km north of Toamasina. It's much less touristy than Nosy Be and the people are extremely friendly. The largest village (which itself is tiny) is **Ambodifototra** where both ferries and flights land.

If you don't take the ferry from Toamasina, there's a three-times weekly flight from the same place for MFr 25,450.

Once on the island you can easily explore it on a hired bicycle (MFr 2000 per day with a MFr 5000 deposit), which you can rent in Ambodifototra or Ravoruna. Otherwise it's ideal for walking. There are ample opportunities for deep-sea fishing if you have the money. There are no banks on Nosy Boraha so bring enough cash with you.

Places to Stay & Eat

In Ambodifototra there are two small adjacent hotels with rooms built from fronds of the 'travellers' palm' (the local construction material). Each one has a small restaurant. The *Hotel Falafa* costs MFr 3500 and the one next door MFr 3000.

Much of the village was destroyed some time ago by a cyclone, but it now has a few small shops with very limited stock, a post office and Madagascar's oldest church. There is only one bus, which runs from the

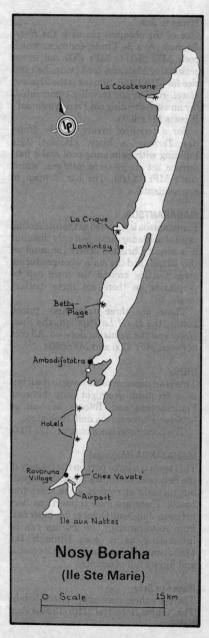

Nosy Boraha

(Île Ste Marie)

village to the airport when planes arrive or leave. Some of the hotels elsewhere on the island have their own cars but they only make the trip to the airport when a plane arrives. Otherwise there is no traffic at all.

Outside Ambodifototra the best place is *Chez Vavate*, about two km from the airport on a hilltop. Mr Vavate, the proprietor, offers travellers'-palm bungalows for MFr 4500 a double including breakfast. Chez Vavate has a very mellow Malagasy atmosphere and people are much friendlier than at the touristy La Crique Hotel. There is a shop in nearby Ravoruna village but it has an even more limited range than the shops in Ambodifototra. There's a nice beach at the back of the hill from Chez Vavate.

La Crique Hotel certainly has a better beach but has no Malagasy atmosphere as it's just a row of touristy bungalows. It costs MFr 9000 with a bathroom and the food is apparently poor value.

Further up the coast, *La Cocoterie* is in a very beautiful spot and only slightly more expensive. It is impossible to get to, unless you're willing to walk the 40 km, or have arranged beforehand to be met at the airport. Another possible place to stay is the *Hotel Bar Restaurant Betty Plage* with rooms for MFr 7000 to MFr 8000.

Off the southern tip of Nosy Boraha is the **Île aux Nattes**. Ask around for a man named Napoleon with whom you can stay for MFr 3000 and who can provide meals. He used to be quite famous for his stories, but the cyclone which ravaged the island left him depressed. You can get to the island by dugout canoe from the tip of Nosy Boraha – ask around among the fisherpeople. The price is negotiable but reasonable.

Most of the restaurants are able to supply fresh and tasty seafood meals including ridiculously cheap lobster.

TAOLANARO (Fort Dauphin)
This town has a really fine location and was the scene of much colonial rivalry between the French, Portuguese and Dutch. Parts of the actual fort are still in existence, though it's now occupied by the Malagasy army.

About 15 km away by road and canoe is the remains of the **fort** built by the Portuguese. The area is noted for its wide variety of carnivorous pitcher plants (*nepenthes* species) and spectacular orchids. If you have an interest in them, it's worth visiting the **Réserve de Berenty** at Sainte-Luce Bay. This bay is one of the few places where you can swim safely and there's delicious seafood available.

It's difficult to get into or out of Taolanaro during the rainy season. At this time it can rain for four or five days nonstop and be very cold and miserable, so bear this in mind.

Places to Stay
The cheapest place is the *Centre Touristique de Libanona*, Place de Libanona, which offers self-catering bungalows for MFr 6500. Otherwise there is the *Hotel Le Dauphin* (tel 21238). It has air-con and costs MFr 11,000.

TOAMASINA (Tamatave)
This is a beautiful town with streets lined with flame trees and old colonial houses. There was, unfortunately, a lot of damage caused by the cyclone which hit the coast in 1986.

Places to Stay & Eat
The cheapest place is the *Hotel Soahiahary* a few blocks from the railway station. It is small, pleasant and clean and has rooms for MFr 2000 a single. The hotel also has a restaurant. Relatively cheap and with a restaurant is *Les Flamboyants* (tel 32380), Blvd de la Libération, which costs MFr 7500. If it's full, try the *Hotel Plage* (tel 32090), Blvd de la Libération opposite the football stadium. It has singles for MFr 7000 and much better rooms with balcony, bathroom and sea views for MFr 15,000. This hotel also has a restaurant.

More expensive is the *Hotel Joffre*

(tel 32390), Blvd Joffre, which costs MFr 12,000 with air-con. The *Hotel Neptune* (tel 32226), 35 Blvd Ratsimilaho, has rooms for MFr 15,000 with air-con, and has a restaurant, nightclub, casino and swimming pool.

For food, try *Restaurant Vietnamien*, Rue Aviateur Goulette 16 off Blvd Joffre, or one of the many 'soupe Chinoise' restaurants which lay on cheap soup. The best of these is the *Double Heaven*, offering excellent Malagasy, Chinese and French food.

TOLEARA (Tulear)

This town has some good colonial architecture and excellent beaches, but otherwise isn't that interesting. One traveller also commented that the town was badly hit by anti-Asian riots recently and, as a result, the shopping centre is very much like a ghost town.

If you have an interest in palaeontology you might like to visit **Morombe**, about 150 km north of Toleara, where dinosaur fossils have been found at the Lamboharano Reserve, and **Betioky-Sud**, about 80 km from Toleara, where there is the Tsimanampetsotra petrified forest. To visit either place you need authorisation from the Direction des Eaux et Fôrets in Toleara.

Places to Stay

Two cheap places are the *Hotel Plaza* (tel 42766), costing MFr 5100, and the *Hotel La Pirogue* (tel 41537), which costs MFr 7900 and has air-con.

Malawi

Malawi consists of a thin sliver of densely populated territory running the whole length of beautiful Lake Malawi (Lake Nyasa), and a southern extension which dips down deep into Mozambique, almost cutting that country in half. Before the arrival of Europeans it was settled by various Bantu tribes who traded their small agricultural surplus and ivory with Portuguese merchants from the coast. European interest in the area was kindled by David Livingstone's travels, and it wasn't long after his return to Britain that Scottish missionaries began to arrive in the country in considerable numbers.

Employing the well tested policy of 'divide and rule' the missionaries were able to overwhelm the warlike Ngoni and Yao tribes, suppress slavery, open up missions and begin to make inroads into traditional agricultural practices by establishing estates. Following the declaration of a Protectorate in 1891 (over what was then known as Nyasaland) and the introduction of coffee, the number and size of these plantations began to grow rapidly.

More and more land was expropriated, a 'hut tax' was introduced and traditional slash-and-burn methods of agriculture discouraged. As a result, increasing numbers of Africans were forced to seek work on the White settler plantations or become migrant workers in Zimbabwe and South Africa. By the turn of the century some 6000 Africans were leaving the country every year, and by the 1950s this number had grown to 150,000.

Opposition to colonial rule surfaced early in the southern highlands, but didn't become a serious threat until the 1950s. At this time, the Nyasaland African Congress was formed to oppose both federation with Northern and Southern Rhodesia and intolerable colonial interference in traditional agricultural methods.

Its support, however, remained limited until Dr Hastings Banda was invited to return home and take over the leadership. By that time Banda had spent 40 years abroad in the USA and Britain studying and practising medicine. He was so successful in whipping up support that just one year after he took over, the colonial authorities declared a state of emergency, threw Banda and other leaders into jail and went on a rampage of suppression in which 52 Africans were killed.

Nevertheless, opposition continued and in 1961 the colonial authorities were forced to release Banda and invite him to London for a constitutional conference. In the elections which followed, Banda's Malawi Congress Party swept to victory. Shortly afterwards the Federation of Rhodesia and Nyasaland was dissolved and Malawi became independent in July 1964.

Despite his fierce oratory, however, Banda was no radical, and when major political differences began to surface between him and his ministers, Banda demanded they declare their allegiance to him. Rather than do this, many ministers resigned and took to violent opposition. Drawing his support from the peasant majority, Banda was quickly able to smash opposition and drive the leaders into hiding or into exile, where they have remained ever since.

With the opposition muzzled, Banda has continued to strengthen his dictatorial powers by having himself declared

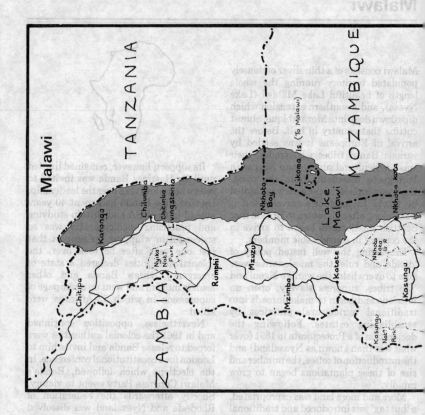

'president for life', banning the foreign press whenever it suits him, outraging the OAU by refusing to ostracise the South African regime (for which he has been handsomely rewarded financially), and waging pogroms against any group he regards as a threat. Although a slight liberalisation was attempted in 1977, when some 2000 detainees were released (many of whom immediately fled the country), thousands more continue to languish in jail and it's virtually impossible to discuss politics with a Malawian. Spies and informers abound.

Typical of Banda's dictatorial powers is his control over the largely rubber-stamp parliament, whose function is not to discuss the merits of his policies but to decide how best to implement them. Criticism is regarded in the same light as treason and is likely to result in dismissal and imprisonment. In 1978, in the only general election to be held since independence, Banda personally vetted everyone who intended to stand as a candidate, demanded that each pass an English examination (thereby precluding 90% of the population), and even reinstated supporters who were defeated.

Banda's control over the country isn't just political. Foreign capital investment, particularly from Britain, Israel, Taiwan and the USA, is actively encouraged. Government ministers, likewise, are

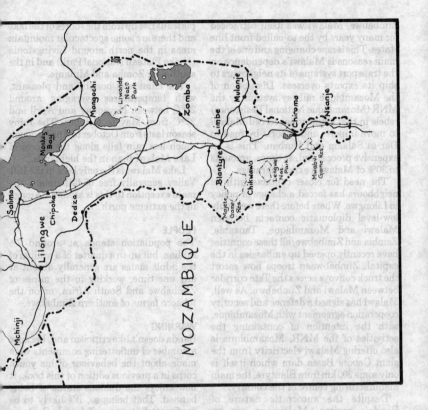

encouraged to acquire land, start businesses and grow cash crops. Thus land is becoming more and more concentrated in the hands of the Malawian elite, with the peasants being forced to move onto land that is largely unsuitable for agricultural use, or to seek employment on the estates. Management of these estates is often placed in the hands of white expatriates from what was Rhodesia. Banda himself owns all but one of the 5000 shares of Press Holdings, a conglomerate of companies with wide interests including an agricultural subsidiary, which accounts for an estimated 30% of the country's economic activity.

All this is in complete contrast to the situation in Zambia and Tanzania where ministers are banned from business activities. At the same time, education and medical facilities are a low priority in the allocation of development funds, while roads and railways serving plantations and prestige projects like the new capital at Lilongwe are given precedence.

On the other hand, the emphasis on estate agriculture (and favourable weather during the 1983-84 season) enabled Malawi to post its first ever balance of payments surplus on its current account. Few African countries have come close to achieving this.

Because of Banda's unwillingness to ostracise South Africa or to support the liberation movements in Mozambique and

Zimbabwe, Malawi was itself ostracised for many years by the so-called front line states. This is now changing and one of the main reasons is Malawi's dependence on the transport systems of its neighbours to ship its exports overseas. Disruption of the Mozambique railway system by the MNR (Mozambique National Resistance) rebels in that country has forced Malawi to move imports and exports by road to Dar es Salaam and Durban. This is an expensive process and, at times, amounts to 30% of Malawi's export earnings.

The need for closer contacts with its neighbours has forced a change of policy in Lilongwe. Where before there were only low-level diplomatic contacts between Malawi and Mozambique, Tanzania, Zambia and Zimbabwe, all these countries have recently opened up embassies in the capital. Zimbabwean troops now escort the truck convoys across the Tete corridor between Malawi and Zimbabwe. As well, Malawi has signed a defence and security cooperation agreement with Mozambique, with the intention of containing the activities of the MNR. Mozambique is also offering Malawi electricity from the giant Cabora Bassa dam which itself is only some 200 km from Blantyre, the main manufacturing centre of the country.

Despite the autocratic nature of Banda's regime, Malawians are an extremely friendly and hospitable people. The countryside is lush and beautiful, and it is safe to walk around anywhere. There are no hassles for single women whatsoever. Malawi should be on everyone's African itinerary.

Facts

GEOGRAPHY & CLIMATE
Of Malawi's total area of just over 118,000 square km, 20% is taken up by the waters of Lake Malawi. The only other countries having sovereignty over part of the lake are Mozambique and Tanzania. High plateaus rise up from the shores of the lake and there are some spectacular mountain areas in the north around Livingstonia (Nyika Plateau National Park) and in the south near Zomba and Mulanje.

The climate is healthy and pleasant, with temperatures averaging around 20°C between November and April and 27°C from May to October. The rainy season lasts from October to April, though much less rain falls along the shores of Lake Malawi than in the highlands.

Lake Malawi is the only lake in the Rift Valley generally free of bilharzia – the main exception to this is around Karonga in the extreme north.

PEOPLE
The population stands at around 7½ million, but up to a quarter of a million of the adult males are generally absent at any one time, working in the mines of Zimbabwe and South Africa, or on the tobacco farms of southern Zimbabwe.

WARNING
Banda doesn't like criticism and, because a number of unflattering comments were made about the behaviour of his youth corps in a previous edition of this book, it now enjoys the dubious status of being banned. That being so, it's likely to be confiscated on entry if found. Customs officers on the borders with Zambia and Tanzania will certainly ask if you are carrying a copy and will probably search your bags looking for it. This rarely happens at the Mozambique border.

There's no foolproof way around this except perhaps to leave it somewhere in Zambia and collect it on your return or paste the cover of another book on the front and take a chance. From all accounts, only a small proportion of travellers actually get their copy confiscated.

VISAS
Visas are required by all except nationals of Commonwealth countries, Belgium, Denmark, Finland, Germany (West),

Iceland, Irish Republic, Luxemburg, Netherlands, Norway, Portugal, South Africa, Sweden and the USA. Those who don't require visas are generally given 30-days stay on arrival.

Visa extensions are free and available at Lilongwe, Blantyre, Zomba, Monkey Bay, Mzuzu, Karonga and any other regional police station. If you think you might be staying for more than 30 days you can apply for an entry visa (as opposed to a tourist visa). They're free but two photos are needed.

Other Visas
Mozambique Visas for Mozambique used to be quite difficult to get, but since the accord was signed with that country they are now generally easy. A transit visa costs Kw 6, requires two photos and takes 24 hours to issue. Tourist visas can take seven to 14 days. The embassy in Lilongwe is in the Commercial Bank of Malawi building in the city centre. It's open in the mornings only.

South Africa South African visas are free and issued while you wait at the embassy in Lilongwe near the Capitol Hotel.

MONEY
US$ 1 = Kw 2.20
UK£ 1 = Kw 3.75

The unit of currency is the kwacha = 100 tambala. The import or export of local currency is allowed up to Kw 30. Currency declaration forms are issued on arrival, and officials may ask to see how much foreign cash and travellers' cheques you are carrying. The same might happen when you leave.

There is a black market on which you can get US$1 = Kw 3.75 but you will only find it in the major towns. Enquire at Asian-owned shops.

The only permanent bank north of Mzuzu is at Karonga. Many population centres between these two towns have a system of 'roving banks', which operate on one or two days of the week only. In Nkhata Bay it's on Friday; in Chilumba on Monday and Thursday; at Rumphi it is Thursday. Livingstonia gets the mobile bank on the first and third Monday of each month.

If entering Malawi at a border post where there is no bank, or you find yourself needing to change money in a town without a bank, go along to the local district commissioner's office. Most of these people can fix you up. With a Eurocheque card you can cash personal cheques at the National Bank of Malawi in Lilongwe, Blantyre, Mangochi and Mzuzu. The bank tellers are familiar with this and you get a better rate than for travellers' cheques.

Changing travellers' cheques at banks can take time so prepare for this. The commission on travellers' cheques varies from 1.5% to 3%. You can reconvert up to Kw 30 per day of your stay into hard currency at the banks. This transaction is often not recorded on your currency form so it's possible to visit several banks.

The airport departure tax for international flights is Kw 10.

TOURIST INFORMATION
Despite the use of scantily-clad female models in Malawi's tourist literature, it's officially illegal for women to wear either trousers or skirts which don't completely cover the knees (except at certain holiday resorts). Likewise, men with long hair (loosely defined as hair falling in bulk to the collar), shorts or flared trousers are barred from entry. And they mean it!

If entering Malawi via Lilongwe International Airport you may be asked to show an onward ticket.

Clearing customs on arrival can be a lengthy process. It is likely that you'll be subjected to two separate and detailed searches of your baggage and possibly your person. Communist literature, girlie magazines and this book are banned and will be seized if found. We have also had one report that oral contraceptives were confiscated.

ACCOMMODATION

In almost every town there is either a government rest house or a district or council rest house, or both. The council rest houses are cheaper and generally more crowded but usually clean. They cost Kw 2/7 for a single/double and sometimes have dormitory style accommodation for as little as 75 tambala.

The government rest houses are generally of a higher standard. Expect to pay around Kw 15 to Kw 17 for a double including breakfast, but in some places you can pay up to Kw 27.50 for a double (Likoma Island, Mzuzu and Nkhata Bay for instance). You can generally camp at either type of rest house but the charge varies considerably.

MARKETS

Virtually every town has a market selling vegetables, rice, peanuts, fruit, dried fish and utensils. A few have local crafts for sale, such as ebony carvings and bracelets, ivory necklaces, reed and raffia baskets. The further north you go, the cheaper things get. Market traders, as a rule, don't hike their prices for travellers. Bargaining is certainly possible in some places but it often doesn't secure a reduction in the original price asked. The Zomba market is outstanding.

LANGUAGE

English and Chichewa are the official languages. There are a number of other African languages spoken. The following words in Chichewa could be useful:

hello	*moni*
How are you?	*muli bwanji?*
I'm fine	*ndili bwino*
good/fine/OK	*chabwino*
thank you/ excuse me	*zikomo*
thanks very much	*zikomo kwambiri*

goodbye (to person leaving)	*pitani bwino*
goodbye (to person staying)	*tsalani bwino*
please	*chonde*
yes	*inde*
no	*iyayi*
to eat	*kudya*
water	*madzi*
milk	*mkaka*
chicken	*nkuku*
meat	*nyama*
fish	*nsomba*
lake perch	*chambo*
eggs	*mazira*
potatoes	*mbatata*
where?	*kuti?*
here	*pano*
over there	*uko*
in there	*umo*
house	*nyumba*
to sleep	*kugona*
how much?	*mtengo bwanji?*
I want	*ndifuna*
I don't want	*sindifuna*
father/man (polite greeting)	*bambo*
mother/woman (polite greeting)	*mayi*
women (polite greeting)	*amai*

On toilet doors, *akazi* means women and *akuma* means men.

Getting There & Around

AIR

Air Malawi flies to Harare, Johannesburg, Lusaka, Mauritius and Nairobi. UTA (in conjunction with Air Malawi) flies from Paris via Libreville and Lusaka. Other airlines servicing Malawi are SAA, Zambian Airways, Air Tanzania, KLM and Kenya Airways. All international flights go through Kamuzu International Airport, 27 km north of Lilongwe.

ROAD

Roads have been considerably improved and the main north-south highway is surfaced all the way to Karonga. Hitching is OK in the south, especially along the Blantyre to Lilongwe road, but elsewhere you should be prepared for long waits as there's little traffic. Pick-up trucks and council trucks are not supposed to take passengers, but they often do in order to supplement their income.

At weekends white expatriates living in Blantyre and Lilongwe make a beeline for Monkey Bay and Cape McLear, so it's easy to get a lift there on Fridays. It's equally easy to get a lift in the opposite direction on Sundays.

If you are going to Livingstonia you will probably have to walk up the escarpment to the town from the main north-south highway as there is no public transport and the road is too steep for buses. There is a short cut through the hairpin bends but it's very steep, and slippery in the wet season. It takes about four hours to walk up.

If heading to the Nyika National Park, you may be lucky and connect with the mail Land Rover, which comes from Rumphi three times a week on Monday, Wednesday and Friday. It leaves Rumphi at 9 am and arrives at Livingstonia at 11 am. It then leaves Livingstonia at 11.45 am and arrives at Rumphi at 1.45 pm.

Most travellers prefer to use the Lake Malawi steamers to get around but there is also a useful network of public buses. If using the buses make sure you ask for the 'express' bus. They are much faster since they don't stop every 100 metres or so. Some examples of routes, fares and journey times are as follows, but enquire locally about schedules as they change from week to week:

Blantyre to Zomba

There are many buses daily in either direction for Kw 1.70.

Blantyre to Lilongwe

There are several ordinary and express buses daily in either direction. The express buses cost Kw 17 to Kw 25 (depending on the company) and take five hours. The ordinary buses cost Kw 8 to Kw 12.20 but take much longer. One of the early express buses from Blantyre goes all the way to Kamuzu International Airport for the afternoon flights.

Blantyre to Karonga

There are two express buses daily in either direction (at 6.30 am and 2.30 pm from Karonga). They cost Kw 40 and take about 19 hours. The buses stop for the night at Mzuzu and continue on the following morning at 6.30 am. Book in advance as there's heavy demand for tickets.

Lilongwe to Monkey Bay

There are several buses daily in either direction via Salima (the fastest route). The express bus leaves at 2 pm, costs Kw 10 and takes about four hours. Other buses go via Dedza, Ncheu and Balaka but cost Kw 15 and take nine hours.

Lilongwe to Mzuzu

There are several buses daily in either direction which cost Kw 16.40 and take about 10 hours. About 150 km of this route is not yet surfaced.

Mzuzu to Chitimba

There are several buses daily, the first at 6.30 am. Express buses cost Kw 6.50 and take about three hours. The buses go via Rumphi.

Chitimba to Karonga

There is one ordinary bus (at 7 am from Chitimba) and one express bus (at 10 am from Chitimba) daily in either direction. The ordinary bus costs Kw 3.70 and takes about five hours. The express takes three hours.

Karonga to Chitipa

There are buses on Monday, Tuesday, Thursday and Saturday. They depart around 1 pm and arrive at 5 pm. In the opposite direction they leave at 8 am and arrive at 11 am. The fare is Kw 2.40.

TRAIN

There is a railway line connecting Limbe with Salima via Blantyre, Nsanje and Chipoka with a small branch line to Zomba, but it's unlikely that anyone other than a railway buff would use the line. Not only are the trains very slow but 2nd class is more expensive than the buses.

There is a daily train in either direction. It leaves Blantyre at 5 am and costs Kw 8.32 (2nd class) and Kw 3.93 (3rd class) as far as Chipoka. There is very little difference between 2nd and 3rd classes – both are overcrowded.

BOAT
Lake Malawi Steamers

There are two boats, the MV *Ilala* and the MV *Mtendere*. Many travellers consider the *Mtendere* to be the better as it only has 2nd and 3rd classes and 2nd class takes up the entire floor at deck level. Above this are the crew's quarters, a bar and another open area for the use of 2nd class passengers. There's plenty of room to sleep up here and the crew are very friendly (they'll often lock up your bags during the day). Third class is below deck and usually crowded. Third class passengers regularly get chased off the promenade deck.

The *Ilala*, on the other hand, is a much older boat and has room for only 10 1st class cabin passengers, who have the exclusive use of two-thirds of the boat. This means that about 800 2nd and 3rd class passengers are crammed into the remaining one-third. There's very little difference between 2nd and 3rd class on the *Ilala*. Indeed, it's probably true to say that 2nd class on the *Ilala* is worse than 3rd class on the *Mtendere*, and as tickets are hardly ever checked it's not worth paying the extra for 2nd class. First class tickets are checked regularly and if you're on the wrong deck you'll be removed.

First class tickets without a cabin are available on the *Ilala* enabling you to sleep on the deck of 1st class, but it's only a few kwacha less than the cost of a 1st class cabin ticket. If you want a cabin (1st class), book as far ahead as possible (especially during South African school holidays) by writing to the Marine Traffic Manager (tel 640 844), Box 5500, Limbe.

There's no restaurant on the *Mtendere* but you can buy reasonable food (rice/maize with fish or meat) from people who come out to the boats. On the *Ilala* you eat in the 1st class dining room regardless of the class you're travelling in. Notify the staff in advance if you want a meal. Otherwise, as on the *Mtendere*, you can buy fish, eggs and fruit from local people who come out to the boats.

Tickets for the *Mtendere* are only sold when the boat is sighted, so queuing tends to start about a day before it's due to arrive. On the other hand, there's no question of anyone being refused – it just gets filled up, and up, and up!

On the *Mtendere* you are not allowed on the deck except when the boat docks. This appears to apply specifically to the upper decks – there is a promenade deck around the 2nd class level.

Schedules for the boats should be taken as approximate, but they generally leave earlier rather than later.

There are occasionally nasty storms out on the lake, so watch out.

Fares (in kwacha) from Monkey Bay are as follows:

port	1st class	2nd class	3rd class
Monkey Bay	–	–	–
Chilinda	6.40	1.92	0.86
Makanjila	10.00	3.00	1.35
Chipoka	11.60	3.48	1.51
Nkhotakota	49.80	13.14	5.69
Likoma Island	65.20	17.76	7.70
Chizumulu Bay	65.20	17.76	7.70
Nkhata Bay	77.20	21.36	9.26

port	1st class	2nd class	3rd class
Mangwina Bay	77.20	21.36	9.26
Usisya	94.00	24.60	10.66
Ruarwe	97.20	25.56	11.08
Tcharo	97.20	26.22	11.36
Mlowe	104.60	27.78	12.04
Chitimba	108.00	28.80	12.48
Chilumba	110.80	29.64	12.84
Kambwe	110.80	33.90	14.69
Kaporo	110.80	33.90	15.18

MV Mtendere

port	arrive	depart
Monkey Bay	–	10.00 Tue
Chipoka	12.30	22.30
Nkhotakota	05.30	06.30 Wed
Likoma Island	12.00	13.00
Chizumulu Island	14.00	14.30
Nkhata Bay	17.30	–
–	–	06.00 Thu
Mangwina Bay	07.00	07.30
Usisya	09.00	09.30
Ruarwe	10.30	11.00
Charo	11.30	12.00
Mlowe	13.30	14.30
Chilumba	16.30	–
–	–	06.00 Fri
Kambwe	09.30	10.30
Kaporo	11.30	12.30
Chilumba	17.00	–
–	–	06.00 Sat
Mlowe	08.00	08.30
Charo	10.00	11.00
Ruarwe	12.00	13.00
Usisya	13.30	14.30
Mangwina Bay	15.30	16.30
Nkhata Bay	17.30	–
–	–	02.30 Sun
Chizumulu Island	05.30	06.00
Likoma Island	07.00	08.00
Nkhotakota	13.30	14.30
Chipoka	21.30	–
–	–	06.30 Mon
Monkey Bay	09.30	–

On the northbound sector there is a connecting train which arrives at Chipoka on Tuesday at 12.48 pm. Second class is available. On the southbound sector the connecting train arrives at Chipoka at 5.42 am, but no 2nd class is available on this train.

MV Ilala

port	arrive	depart
Monkey Bay	–	08.00 Fri
Chilinda	10.00	10.30
Makanjila	12.30	14.00
Chipoka	17.00	22.00
Nkhotakota	05.30	06.30 Sat
Likoma Island	12.30	13.30
Chizumulu Island	15.00	16.00
Nkhata Bay	19.30	–
–	–	04.00 Sun
Usisya	06.30	07.30
Ruarwe	08.30	09.30
Mlowe	11.30	12.30
Chitimba	13.30	14.30
Chilumba	16.00	–
–	–	04.00 Mon
Chitimba	05.30	06.30
Mlowe	07.30	08.30
Ruarwe	10.30	11.30
Usisya	12.30	13.30
Nkhata Bay	16.00	–
–	–	03.00 Tue
Likoma Island	08.30	10.00
Nkhotakota	16.00	21.30
Chipoka	05.30	09.00 Wed
Makanjila	12.00	13.00
Chilinda	15.00	15.30
Monkey Bay	17.30	–

On the northbound sector there is a connecting train which arrives at Chipoka on Friday at 3.02 am. Second class is available. On the southbound sector the train arrives at Chipoka at 6.08 am on Wednesday.

TO/FROM MOZAMBIQUE

Overland travel by rail or road from Malawi to the Mozambique coast is very dangerous at present because of the activities of the MNR rebels, who are fighting the central government. Even if you are given permission by the authorities to attempt it (very unlikely), there's a very good chance you'll either be shot or taken hostage. Forget it!

It is, however, *relatively* safe to take the Tete corridor through Mozambique to Zimbabwe because the Zimbabwean army escorts truck convoys. For details see the To/From Zimbabwe section.

TO/FROM TANZANIA

A direct route between Malawi and Tanzania was opened up a few years ago and is becoming the preferred passage between the two countries (rather than via Nakonde and Chitipa).

The easiest way to do this trip is to take the daily bus from Karonga to the Malawi-Tanzania border on the Songwe River Bridge (known as Iponga). It departs between 2.30 and 3 pm and takes about four hours. The bus goes via Kaporo and this is where you get your Malawi exit stamp.

By the time you get to the Songwe River Bridge (where there's another Malawi immigration post) it will be dark and that's where you stay for the night. There are absolutely no facilities here – no accommodation, food or running water – so you'll need a sleeping bag. You won't be allowed to sleep on the bus overnight either. Next morning you cross to the Tanzanian side and go through customs and immigration.

The Tanzanian authorities on this border have acquired a reputation for being very officious. Your passport will be minutely scrutinised for any indication that you have visited South Africa – overland entry stamps into Zimbabwe, Botswana, Lesotho and Swaziland; missing dates which can't be matched up, etc. If they even suspect you have been there you're in for a long haul. Many travellers have been refused entry and those that have argued about it have had 'Prohibited immigrant' stamped in their passports. Others have been refused entry because they had dual nationality and (quite legitimately) two passports. If it looks like you are going to be refused entry, get your passport back before they

stamp it 'Prohibited immigrant' and try a different border crossing (Nakonde-Tunduma or Kigoma via the Lake Tanganyika ferry from Mpulungu in Zambia).

The bus to the border very conveniently returns to Karonga at 6 am so, if you are refused entry, you'll be stuck at the border for another night unless you can find a lift back into Karonga.

Assuming you get through, you'll probably have to walk the four km from the Tanzanian border post to the main Mbeya to Kyela road. Once on the main road there are buses and trucks to Mbeya.

If all this sounds like a lot of messing around, try to arrange a lift through to Mbeya before setting off. Otherwise, there is a weekly bus from Mzuzu to Dar es Salaam, which leaves at 6.30 am on Wednesday, costs Kw 70 and takes three days with stops at night.

TO/FROM ZAMBIA

There are two entry points: via Chipata on the Lilongwe to Lusaka road in the centre of the country, and via Chitipa on the Karonga to Nakonde road in the extreme north of the country.

Direct UBZ buses depart from Lilongwe to Lusaka at 7 am on Monday, Wednesday, Friday and Saturday, cost Kw 24 and take between 17 and 21 hours. In the opposite direction they leave Lusaka on the same days at the same time. The border can be very slow and there are several police checks. It's advisable to book the buses in advance.

You can also do this journey in stages if the through buses are booked up. There are daily buses from Lilongwe to Chipata. From there it's about 12 km to the Zambian border post and it's fairly easy to hitch a ride. From the Zambian side of the border there is a daily bus to Lusaka for Kw 13 and takes about nine hours.

There is a shortage of tyres in Zambia and bus companies often do not provide their buses with spare tyres (the drivers are apparently inclined to sell them to supplement their incomes). This means that if you get a puncture which cannot be repaired, you'll be stuck until another bus comes through with a spare from Lusaka.

The other route between Chitipa and Nakonde should not be attempted in weekends or during bad spells in the wet season as there is no traffic at those times. During the week there are usually buses at 7 am on Monday, Wednesday and Friday from Nakonde to Chitipa, though some only go as far as the Zambian border (Nyala) and you must walk from there. In the opposite direction there are buses, usually on the same days, which leave Chitipa at 2 pm. The journey takes about three to four hours.

The two border posts are about three km apart and if there is no transport available you'll have to walk. Some travellers have suggested it's a bad idea to walk this stretch on your own as you might be robbed, but if you're in the company of a lot of local people who have got off a bus at the border, just follow them through the clearly marked paths across the fields. There should be transport from the Malawi border post to Chitipa, but if there is none it's about 1½ km to Chitipa downhill all the way.

TO/FROM ZIMBABWE
An overland route between Malawi and Zimbabwe via the Tete corridor in Mozambique has been operating for a few years so it's possible to travel directly between the two countries without going via Zambia. Convoys of trucks leave in either direction everyday except Saturday and take about 16 hours. It's known as the 'Gun Run' and, although you'll see burnt-out trucks by the side of the road or might hear gunfire, it's relatively safe. All convoys are accompanied by Zimbabwean soldiers in case of attack. However, they are very reluctant to let passengers travel in trucks now.

The trucks set out from Mwanza, west of Blantyre, and to get a lift you must be

there the day before. The cost is negotiable. You'll also need a Mozambique transit visa and (if required) a Zimbabwean visa, which can be obtained in Lilongwe. Normal Zimbabwean entry requirements apply at the opposite end. There are more details about this route in the Zimbabwe chapter.

Around the Country

BLANTYRE
Blantyre is the main commercial and industrial centre of Malawi and has a population of around 300,000. It stretches for about 20 km but most of the places of interest and importance to travellers are well within walking distance of the rest house.

The bus to the airport leaves from outside the Mt Soche Hotel and costs Kw 5.50.

Things to See
The **National Museum** is midway between Blantyre and Limbe, just off the main highway. Entry costs 10 tambala. The British Council has an excellent reading room and library.

Places to Stay
The *District Rest House* (tel 634460; also known as the Travellers' Rest House) is on Chileka Rd facing the bus station. There are three classes of accommodation from Kw 3 to Kw 4.50 a single and Kw 4.50 to Kw 6.75 a double. VIP suites with mosquito nets cost Kw 8. The management are friendly and the rooms are good value. The restaurant has a varied menu, but stocks only a fraction of the foods listed, though what it has is usually good. It's a popular place for travellers, but try to make a reservation in advance by telephone, or you may find that it's full.

Also popular is the guesthouse in the grounds of *St John's Mission* about one km up Chileka Rd from the bus station. It's clean and quiet, and meals can be

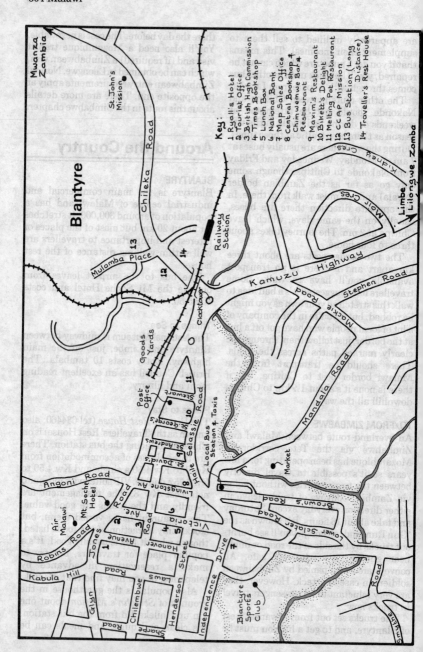

Blantyre

Key:
1 Ryall's Hotel
2 Tourist Office
3 British High Commission
4 Times Bookshop
5 Lunch Box
6 National Bank
7 Map Sales Office
8 Central Bookshop &
   Chimwemwe Bar &
   Restaurant
9 Maxim's Restaurant
10 Bikett's Delight
11 Melting Pot Restaurant
12 CCAP Mission
13 Bus Station (Long
   Distance)
14 Traveller's Rest House

provided if ordered in advance. Rooms cost Kw 15 a double including breakfast.

If you wish to camp, however, it's worth paying the Kw 2 per day per person temporary membership fee for the *Blantyre Sports Club*, since this not only allows you to camp free on the gravel car park but lets you in on the swimming pool, film nights, darts nights and the bar. It has become a popular place to camp over the last few years. The club also has rooms for rent at Kw 7.50 per person. Meals are excellent and cost Kw 5.

The other hotels marked on the street map are outside the range of budget travellers.

Places to Eat
A very good cheap takeaway is the *Lunch Box*, Victoria Ave, which offers beef, beans and rice. *Bikett's Delight*, Haile Selassie Rd, offers chicken and meat dishes as well as vegetable samosas. Another cheap place is the *Chimwemwe Bar & Restaurant* where you can get fish, chicken, chips and salad. The bar is usually very lively.

Also very good is *Maxim's Restaurant & Bar*, Haile Selassie Rd, offering very good Indian vegetarian food, soup, curry, rice, chapati, salad and fish curry. It's open from 11.15 am to 1.30 pm and 6.15 to 10 pm. The Greek-owned *Melting Pot Restaurant*, Haile Selassie Rd, is the place to go for a splurge. It's not cheap, but the food is very good. Curry seems to be the best deal as the portions are huge, though they also offer European-style food.

For somewhere to sit around with a cold beer and relax, try the terrace bar of the *Mt Soche Hotel*. They also do good meals and, if you order wisely, they're not too expensive.

CHITIPA
You will pass through this town if going to Zambia from the extreme north of Malawi. Chitipa is about five km from the Zambian border (Nyala), and although

there are usually three buses per week between here and Nakonde, you may have to walk.

There is a roving bank which operates on two days of the week but if it's not there you can change up to US$20 at the district commissioner's office.

Places to Stay
There is an excellent *Rest House* with doubles for Kw 4, or you can sleep on the verandah for just 25 tambala. Mosquito nets are provided in the rooms. It's best to stay here rather than in Nyala, as Nyala has nowhere to stay and no shops. Other travellers have recommended the *Javet Rest House* run by Mr Suali. It costs Kw 4 a double.

KARONGA
The best place to stay is the *Kankununu Guest House* behind the market to the right. It costs Kw 5/8 a single/double for a very basic room. There is an attached restaurant serving good, cheap food, and lots of it. Otherwise, try the *District Council Rest House*, also near the market. Double rooms are Kw 6. Somewhat upmarket is the *Government Rest House* the only hotel facing the lake. It costs Kw 11 per person and has hot showers.

If you're not eating at your rest house try the *Sumuka Restaurant*. A good place to enjoy a cold beer and play darts is the *Club Marina* opposite the Government Rest House.

LIKOMA ISLAND
It's worth staying here between steamers if you have the time. Unlike most of Malawi, this island is dry and sandy and baobab trees are a common feature of the landscape. There are also a lot of mango trees. The beaches on the island are excellent and you can swim safely in the crystal-clear water, which teems with fish. Also, visit the amazing **Anglican Cathedral** 15 minutes uphill from the beach.

Places to Stay

You can pitch a tent anywhere on the island. The villagers are very friendly.

The enormous two-bedroom *Government Rest House* on the beach is a great place but costs Kw 22/27.50 a single/double (they let four people use a double room for that price). You can also camp for Kw 5.50 per tent including the use of cooking facilities, toilets and sinks with running water. The cook can prepare meals on request and there's a refrigerator which you can use. Cheaper is the *Akuzike Rest House*. It's pretty cramped but costs only Kw 5 per person. They have a restaurant and bar (subject to beer being available).

Food supplies are limited in the island's markets and shops, though you can always find fruit, fish and rice. Bring other supplies with you. There's only one restaurant in the town, and it offers poor quality fish and rice.

LILONGWE

The capital of Malawi is still being constructed but most of the embassies and government departments have moved here. It's a pleasantly landscaped city, but otherwise, is of limited interest.

Information

All the travel agents, embassies, banks, the National Parks & Wildlife office and a PTC supermarket are clustered around the city centre.

The South African Embassy (tel 730 888) is in the Impco Building and the Zambian High Commission (tel 731 911) is up the hill on Convention Drive. Air Malawi is in Gemini House and Air Tanzania is on City Square. Manica Freight Service is the American Express agent but they don't cash travellers' cheques. The National Parks & Wildlife office is upstairs in the arcade along with all the travel agents. It's open from 8 am to noon and 1 to 4 pm, and has plenty of good information.

Things to See

The **Lilongwe Nature Reserve** is three km out on Kenyatta Rd near the Capital area. Entry is free.

Places to Stay

Campers should head for the *Lilongwe Golf Course* almost opposite St Peter's Church, which has been recommended by many travellers as well as resident expatriates. For Kw 8 per person per day you can pitch a tent on the golf course and have access to the bathrooms (which are clean and have toilet paper and soap), the restaurant, bar and swimming pool. The pool costs 20 tambala extra. The camp site is guarded. The members are almost entirely expatriates and many travellers have been treated with great generosity. You may not even have to use that tent you erected because someone has offered you a room.

The *Council Rest House*, Malangalanga Rd opposite the bus station, has two classes of accommodation, one in the old wing and another in the new wing. The old wing costs Kw 5 per person or Kw 10 a double plus there's an overcrowded dormitory for 50 tambala per person. The new wing costs Kw 12/20 a single/double. The old wing is not particularly good value as it's badly maintained, the showers don't work and it has a lot of mosquitoes, but the new wing is very good. Cheap meals are available. The rest house is often fully booked. There's also a baggage storeroom where you can leave gear for 10 to 20 tambala per bag per day depending on the size.

Another cheapie is the *Kholowa Rest House* on the other side of the market from the bus station. This costs Kw 6 for a dormitory bed, Kw 8 to Kw 12 a single and Kw 15 a double. There are cold showers and the staff are friendly, but some of the rooms are very dark and there are no locks on the doors. Better is the *Likonde Rest House & Restaurant* recommended by many travellers. It's a very clean and friendly place and it costs Kw 10/15 a

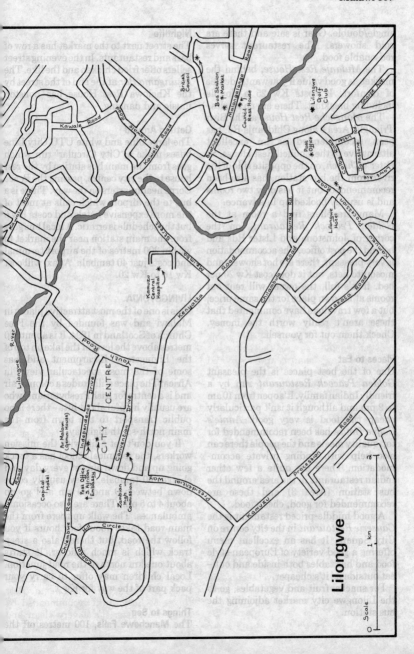

Lilongwe

Scale

0   1 km

single/double. Gear is safe and there are cold showers. The restaurant serves reasonable food.

The *Mulanje Rest House*, behind the market, is good value if you want a degree of comfort. It costs Kw 25 a double including breakfast. There are no singles.

The *Mangoche Rest House* at the Biwi Triangle, Area 8 along Chidzanja Rd, has been recommended as an excellent alternative to the Council Rest House. *St Peter's Church*, on the opposite side of the river from the bus station, has also been recommended, but it has only two rooms and is usually booked up in advance.

Many travellers find a room at the *Golden Peacock Restaurant*, on the corner of Johnstone and Lister Rds and behind the post office. The accommodation is very pleasant, there are hot showers and mosquito nets, but it does cost Kw 20 per bed. If it's full, the owner will rent out rooms at his own place for the same price, but a few travellers have commented that these aren't really worth the money. Check them out for yourself.

Places to Eat

One of the best places is the pleasant *Golden Peacock Restaurant* run by a friendly Indian family. It's open from 10 am to 2 pm and although it isn't particularly cheap the food is very good. *Annie's Coffee House* has been recommended for top quality meals and the people there can also help with finding private accommodation. There are quite a few other Indian restaurants in the area around the bus station (Area 3) and these are recommended for good, cheap food.

A good middle-priced restaurant is the *Causerie Restaurant* in the city centre on City Square. It has an excellent menu offering a good variety of European-style food and has tables both inside and out – eat outside as it's cheaper.

For snacks, fruit and vegetables, go to the Lilongwe city market adjoining the bus station.

Nightlife

The street next to the market has a row of bars and restaurants. In the evening street sellers offer fried chicken and the like. The *Msungama Bar* at the end of the street by the Kholowa Rest House has nonstop music and dancing.

Getting Around

The large blue and white UTC City Line buses make a 'City Circular' run which goes from the main bus station by the rest house to the city centre, passing the Peace Corps headquarters on the way. There is a bus to the airport which calls at most of the more expensive hotels and costs Kw 6 but the schedule is erratic. A local bus goes from the main station near the market to within 200 metres of the airport terminal and costs just 40 tambala. A taxi will cost Kw 16 to Kw 20.

LIVINGSTONIA

This is one of the most attractive places in Malawi and was founded by the Free Church of Scotland in 1894. It is about 800 metres above the level of the lake on top of the Livingstone Escarpment and has some of the most spectacular views in Africa. The place still exudes a colonial air and is a centre for Irish Presbyterians, who are usually helpful about lifts – there is no public transport to the town from the main north-south highway.

If you don't get a lift with the mission workers, the technical school has a truck going up and down almost every day and charges 50 tambala. They usually come down between 9 and 10 am and go up about 4 to 5 pm. There are also occasional ambulances. The walk up there from the main road takes about four hours if you follow the road, but there's also a steep track which is much quicker. It starts about one km north of the road junction. Local children may offer to carry your pack part of the way for Kw 1.

Things to See

The **Manchewe Falls**, 100 metres off the

road down the escarpment and about four km from the rest house, are worth a visit. They are over 60 metres high and the caves behind the falls were once used by Phoka tribespeople hiding from the Ngoni slavers some 100 years ago. If unsure how to get there, ask one of the local children to guide you.

The stone house about 200 metres up from the clocktower is now a **museum**; entry costs 50 tambala.

Places to Stay & Eat

The *Rest House* about 500 metres down from the clocktower is one of the best in Malawi and has hot water, flush toilets and a friendly warden. It's clean and costs Kw 6 per person. If it's full, they'll reluctantly let you sleep on the verandah for less. You can also camp on the lawn for Kw 2.50 per person plus 50 tambala for use of the stove. The staff can rustle up meals which are little short of banquets, but fix the price first. Otherwise, simple meals of beans and rice are available. Bread and eggs are also for sale if you want to cook for yourself.

Camping is also possible behind the petrol station free of charge.

One wing of the museum offers rooms to travellers but they're somewhat expensive at Kw 15 per person though very pleasant. You generally have to book them in advance by writing to PO Box 7, Livingstonia.

MCHINJI

This is the village on the Malawi-Zambia border.

A cheap place to stay is the *Asungeni*

Lodge about three km from the customs post. The rooms cost Kw 3 or you can camp for Kw 1. The manager is friendly and good cheap meals are available. The *District Rest House* has rooms for Kw 5 as does the *Kasalika Rest House* though rooms here are very small.

MONKEY BAY

'Roving bank' days at Monkey Bay are Tuesday and Friday from 9 to 11 am (Commercial Bank) and Monday and Thursday from 10.45 am to 2.30 pm (National Bank). They generally won't change US$50 or US$100 bills or travellers' cheques, but they will take smaller denominations.

Monkey Bay is a weekend watering hole for expatriates living in Malawi and, if you're lucky, you may be invited to stay with someone. The beach, however, isn't up to much, and most travellers head for **Cape McLear**, about 18 km north of Monkey Bay.

Offshore from Monkey Bay is the quiet nature reserve of **Thumbi Island**, which has birds and reptiles, and free camping. You should bring food with you from Monkey Bay, though fisherpeople often come across in the afternoons to sell fish.

Places to Stay & Eat

Before you even get to Cape McLear you'll hear about *Mr Stevens'* place on the travellers' grapevine as it's a very popular place to stay. 'Mr Stevens' is actually two remarkably similar brothers (George and Ernest). They have a range of very pleasant beach huts with prices starting at Kw 2.50 per bed with others for Kw 5 a single (shared bathroom), Kw 10 a double (own bathroom) and Kw 15 a double (a larger hut with bathroom). Almost all travellers give Mr Stevens' a rave recommendation and it's the sort of place people go back to time and time again. However, we do get the occasional letter from people who, for one reason or another, are not at all impressed.

Cape McLear is certainly a beautiful

spot with a pebble beach and warm lake water, and the Stevens' place is very easy-going. You help yourself to beers, Cokes, etc and write what you take into an old exercise book. It all works on the honesty of the people staying there. The restaurant offers fish, salad, rice and chips, but you need to order a meal hours in advance and be prepared for the restaurant to close early. Have candles and mosquito coils handy as there is no electricity in the huts. George has a boat which you can use to row across to the island opposite the beach. It takes eight to 10 people at a time. Otherwise local children will ask if you want to rent motor boats (Kw 8 per hour) or rowing boats (Kw 2 per hour).

Mr Stevens (one of them) generally meets buses and boats arriving at Monkey Bay and takes people out to Cape McLear in the back of his truck for Kw 1. Other than this, there's no public transport between Monkey Bay and Cape McLear after 5 pm. If you have to ring up Mr Stevens and ask him to collect you it costs Kw 30 shared between however many are in your group.

Meals can also be found in a sort of local 'restaurant' a few hundred metres south of Mr Stevens'. They are just as good.

If you don't want to stay at the Stevens', try the *Golden Sands Holiday Resort* at scenic Otter Point, about 1½ km past Mr Stevens'. It has *rondavels* for Kw 12 a single or double and camping for Kw 2.50 per person. They have meals and a nice bar, and there's good diving and snorkelling available. If you prefer to put your own meals together there are no problems – young men constantly come round offering fish, chicken, eggs and vegetables for sale.

In Monkey Bay itself there is the *District Rest House* next to the bus station and 15 minutes' walk from where the boats dock. It costs Kw 5/6 a single/double, but it's not particularly clean and the showers have only cold water. Mosquito nets are provided and good meals are available. There's also the *Monkey Bay Guest House* for Kw 5 per person. The *Champion Hotel* and the *Zikoma Hotel* are out on the road to Cape McLear. The Zikoma has no running water.

For a better standard of accommodation, go to the more expensive *Government Rest House*.

MULANJE

The town of Mulanje is at the foot of Mt Mulanje and is the centre of the tea-growing region. It's also a popular mountain-climbing and bushwalking area. If you're interested in doing some of the treks, get hold of *Guide to Mulanje Massif* by Geoffrey Eastwood. You won't find maps for sale in Mulanje itself so buy them beforehand in Blantyre. It's also worth contacting the Mountain Club (tel 636899 during the day) in Blantyre since they frequently do a trip to the top.

Otherwise, it's easy and cheap to arrange a trek yourself. You first have to get to the Likhubula Forestry office from Mulanje (10 km). There are local buses daily at 10 am and 3 pm from Mulanje (12.30 and 3 pm in the opposite direction), which cost 35 tambala and take 15 minutes.

At the office you can book to stay in the excellent huts higher up. There are six of these huts altogether and they're spaced about three to six hours walking distance apart. They all have huge fireplaces with wood and water supplied. There's a care-taker at each hut and he makes the fire. As you have to sleep on the floor, it's a good idea to have an inflatable mattress or sleeping mat. The charge for the huts is Kw 2.50 per night. It's probably a good idea to book ahead for the huts in case there are groups trekking on the mountain. You can do this by ringing Mulanje 218 or by writing to PO Box 50, Mulanje.

Porters are available at the forestry office for Kw 2 per day plus something like Kw 3 for their food, which they will buy locally. There's only a limited range of foods for sale in Mulanje itself so bring anything else you want from Blantyre.

Although a map of the area is certainly useful, the most popular trekking routes are well signposted, so there's little chance of getting lost. There are also maps in the huts. Take warm clothes as it gets very cold up there at night.

Many different climbs and walks are available, ranging from easy to difficult. If your time is limited and you only want to go to the top of Mt Mulanje you can do it in about 5½ hours at a relatively brisk pace, or 7½ hours at a more leisurely pace. Avoid walking after dark as there are poisonous snakes around. It's said you can see the Indian Ocean in clear weather from the 3000-metre summit.

Woodcarvings made from local fallen cedar are available in the villages around the base of the massif.

Places to Stay

In Mulanje itself the best place is the *Mulanje Motel* next to the bus station. It is fairly new, very clean and excellent value at Kw 5/8 a single/double. The staff are friendly and excellent meals are available (beef stew with rice for Kw 2.25 and fish & chips for Kw 3).

There's also the *Wayside Rest House* about 1½ km from the bus station back down the road to Blantyre and near the market. It's clean and friendly and costs Kw 4.50/6.50 a single/double.

MZIMBA

The cheapest accommodation is the *Council Rest House*, next to the market, for Kw 2 per bed. Also cheap is a private guesthouse at the left, on the main road from the bus stop, which costs Kw 4 a single. It's clean and there's food available. There's also a more expensive *Government Rest House* next to the police station.

MZUZU

The *Jambo Rest House* opposite the bus station is one of the cheapest places to stay

at 40 tambala for a dormitory bed. Close by is the *Mulinda Rest House* at Kw 3.50 a double, but it has been described as 'disgusting'. Better, but still not very clean, is the *Council Rest House* with doubles for Kw 8.

Much better is the *Mtwalo Rest House* out along the Nkhata Bay road which offers decent doubles at Kw 12. The *Government Rest House* is very pleasant and clean but costs Kw 18 per person.

The luxury *Mzuzu Hotel* offers half-price accommodation at weekends, but that's still Kw 35 a double.

NKHATA BAY

Although some of the beaches further south are very pleasant (eg, Cape McLear), they are somewhat commercialised because of their popularity with expatriates. Nkhata Bay is much quieter (as is the beach at Chikale, south of Nkhata Bay, where you can camp free). These beaches are practically deserted except for a few travellers and when the fishing boats come in at dusk to sell their catch. If you like fresh fish buy it directly from the boats and take it to the rest house where they will cook it for you. In the town itself all the stores and bars are situated around a central 'meeting place'. Dancing goes on just about all the time in the bars.

There's a 'roving bank' on Tuesday and Friday (9.30 am to 1 pm) which will change cash and travellers' cheques. The Commercial Bank also comes on Monday, but it won't do foreign exchange.

Places to Stay

The best place by far is the *Heart Hotel* and anyone who has ever stayed here has praised it highly. It costs Kw 3 per person for bed and breakfast or you can camp for Kw 1.50 per person. The owner, Phillip, is an excellent cook and turns out the most amazing meals from an open fire, including his world famous pancakes. The toilets are OK, but there's no electricity or running water, though they will heat up a tub of water so you can get a wash behind a bamboo screen. It's a very friendly and cosy place. To get there from the boat jetty turn left by the forestry commission and carry on for about 200 metres, then turn right after the police station. Continue on a further 150 metres, cross the bridge then turn right by the Fumbani Rest House. It's a little further on from there.

If the Heart Hotel is full, try the *Fumbani Rest House* at Kw 3 a single (no electricity), or a private rest house behind the PTO superette and Southern Bottlers wholesalers. It is good value at Kw 4.50/6 a single/double, though the toilets are usually dirty. Try to avoid the *Council Rest House* if possible as it's noisy, dirty and the sanitation is appalling. It costs Kw 3/6 a single/double.

The *Government Rest House* is very expensive at Kw 22/30 a single/double. You can also camp for Kw 4.50.

If intending to camp, head for Chikale Beach about two km south of town around the headland. This has become very popular with travellers over the last two years. Camping is free and it's a beautiful place. Children come around everyday selling firewood, fish and other things. Since it became so popular the thieves have also arrived so watch your gear, but there has been no violence.

NKHOTAKOTA

This is reputedly one of the oldest market towns in Africa and was once the centre of the slave trade in this region. There's a **Chinese agricultural mission**, which has been very friendly in the past towards people interested in their work.

The town itself is about one km from the lake, whereas the post office, banks and other government buildings are clustered together about two km from the lake. Buses for Lilongwe and Salima leave from the bus station opposite the Pick & Pay Rest House.

Places to Stay

The best place is the *Pick & Pay Rest House*, run by Philip Banda, opposite the bus station. It's clean and friendly and has electricity, showers (cold water only) and mosquito nets in all the rooms. It costs Kw 6/8 a single/double and Kw 10 a double with bathroom. Campers can put up their tents on the lawn for Kw 1 – the lawn is surrounded by a wall so gear is safe. Meals are available for Kw 1 to Kw 2.50.

If it's full, try the *Kulinga Rest House* next door. It is clean and pleasant, and costs Kw 4/6 a single/double. Mosquito nets are provided.

The *District Rest House* by the boat jetty is very run-down and is a dump. There's no electricity and the rooms are small and dark with no food available. It's poor value at Kw 4 for a single or double. It is a great pity that this rest house has sunk to such a level as it was once an amazing place made out of parts of old boats, trucks and cars. There are still windows made from car doors. It also has a beautiful 2nd-storey terrace overlooking the lake.

The *AFA Restaurant* opposite the market is OK but it has only double rooms for Kw 5, and has a very loud bar.

RUMPHI

Rumphi, between Nkhata Bay and Livingstonia, is a good starting point to get to Chelinda in the **Nyika National Park**. Getting to the national park can be problematical without your own transport. See the National Parks section for details.

Places to Stay

The *Government Rest House* in Rumphi is about one km from the market. There's no electricity and you need to take your own food, but they do have hot showers. It costs Kw 22/27.50 a single/double. The *District Rest House* next to the market near the bus station is more convenient and costs Kw 2.50 per person. It has pit toilets and good showers. There's also the *Universal Rest House*, which has friendly staff and costs Kw 2 a single.

If you have your own transport there's the *Simphawaka Inn* several km before

Rumphi. It's quiet, clean and costs Kw 4/10 a single/double. Meals cost Kw 1.50 and there's a bar.

There's good nightlife in the bars of Rumphi, and women come round selling fried chicken, liver and beef.

SALIMA

The town is about 15 km from the lake and is where many people stop for the night before heading down to the beach.

It's worth visiting **Lizard Island**, a beautiful national park home to a wide variety of eagles and huge lizards. The whole island is spattered white with cormorant droppings, and stinks, but don't let that put you off. Rowing boats (Kw 6 per hour shared between three or four people) and motor boats are available to get you there.

Places to Stay

One of the cheapest places is the *Consul Rest House*, opposite the bus station, which costs Kw 5 a single or double but it is scruffy. Close by is the clean *Council Rest House* with doubles for Kw 6. Also opposite the bus station is the *Everest Rest House*, which has small dark rooms for Kw 6/12 a single/double. The rest house has a restaurant where you can get beef and salad for Kw 1.50.

For better accommodation try the *Salima Rest House*, near the post office. It is clean, but only has double rooms at Kw 6. Even more expensive is the *Maltsalani Motel* opposite the National Bank. Rooms cost Kw 10/15 a single/double and Kw 20 a double with a bath. It's clean and there are hot showers, a restaurant (good food) and bar.

Campers should head for the *Livingstonia Beach Hotel* (previously the Grand Hotel) where you can camp for Kw 4 per person including hot showers, toilets and firewood. This is a long way from town at Senga Bay so take a local bus (Kw 1, 30 minutes) or hitch. The hotel itself is very expensive at Kw 50/88 a single/double. The hotel rents windsurfers for Kw 6 per hour.

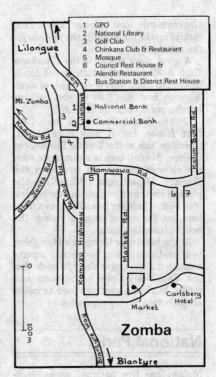

1	GPO
2	National Library
3	Golf Club
4	Chinkana Club & Restaurant
5	Mosque
6	Council Rest House & Alendo Restaurant
7	Bus Station & District Rest House

Zomba

ZOMBA

Zomba is the old capital of Malawi. It is a good place from which to explore the 2000-metre-high **Zomba Plateau**, or visit **Chingwe's Hole**, reputedly so deep that no one has ever been able to measure its depth.

Places to Stay & Eat

The *Council Rest House* opposite the bus station is pretty good, clean and costs Kw 5/7.50 a single/double. It has only cold showers and is often full. It also has a good restaurant. The *Welcome Inn* around the corner is a dump and is very noisy so avoid it if possible.

The *Carlsberg Hotel* is reasonable value at Kw 6/9 a single/double. There are cold showers only and the hotel has a restaurant and lively bar. There's also the

Government Rest House about 100 metres up the hill towards the plateau for the usual price.

A good place to eat is the *Chinkana Club & Restaurant* which serves lunch from 12 to 2 pm. Very good meals of steak & chips cost Kw 3.30 or you can get hamburger & chips for Kw 1.60.

On the Zomba Plateau is the *CCAP Rest House*, but it may have closed. Check on this at the Zomba Theological College. Also up here is a camp site with hot showers, etc, which is run by the Forestry Department. While on the plateau visit the *Kuchawe Inn* for tea or a cold beer. There are beautiful views from here, but the cost of rooms is outside the budget travellers' range.

At the hotel near Chingwe's Hole there is a good camp site, but recent reports suggest it's no longer there. Check this out. Facilities include hot showers and toilets, but bring your own food as meals at the hotel are very expensive.

National Parks

Malawi has five national parks, each protecting certain species of animals and their habitats. All but Lake Malawi National Park have government-run accommodation available. Booking for accommodation in the national parks (except for the Kasungu National Park) should be made through the Chief Game Warden (tel 730 944), Department of National Parks & Wildlife, PO Box 30131, Capital City, Lilongwe 3.

All parks and game reserves have an entry fee of Kw 1.50 per person per day plus Kw 4.50 per day per vehicle under 2000 kg, and Kw 6.50 per day over 2000 kg.

KASUNGU NATIONAL PARK

This park has rolling *miombo* woodlands and there is excellent game viewing available late in the dry season, when fires have burned off the tall grass. The wildlife roads are open from mid-June to early January, and at those times you can see elephant, buffalo, zebra, antelope and many others. A game-viewing vehicle is sometimes provided. Guides cost Kw 2 per trip and are compulsory for walks. There are Bushpeople paintings to be seen. The park is closed during March. The entrance is 38 km from Kasungu town.

Places to Stay

Fourteen km inside the park is the *Lifupa Lodge* overlooking a small lake. It has twin-bedded *rondavels* with showers, toilet and electricity for Kw 30/35 a single/double. Meals are available and there's a bar. There are also seven tents with three beds each for Kw 12 per person. They are provided with linen and you can use a kitchen and a cool room. Camping in your own tent costs Kw 10 per person. Make your booking through Hertz/Hall's Car Hire.

LENGWE NATIONAL PARK

Some 75 km from Blantyre (the last nine km on dirt), Lengwe's woods and thickets are home for nyala antelope and other ungulates as well as a large and varied bird population. You can view game from the 'hides' at artificial water holes. The best season to visit is during the dry season (May to December).

For permission to visit the **Majete Game Reserve** north of Lengwe or the **Mwabvi Game Reserve** to the south, check with the Wildlife Management Officer (tel 0-1203), Lengwe NP, PO Box 25, Chikwawa. Majete has elephant, kudu, sable antelope and waterbuck. There's only one chalet which costs Kw 8 regardless of how many people stay there. Mwabvi has hills, sandstone ridges and rocky gorges with black rhino, leopard, hyena and antelope. There are two *rondavels* for Kw 4 regardless of how many people stay.

Places to Stay

There are four chalets at Lengwe National Park, each with double rooms and hand basins, fully equipped kitchens and refrigerators, but you must bring your own food.

LIWONDE NATIONAL PARK

Fifty-six km north of Zomba on the Shire River, this park includes part of Lake Malombe and the eastern Upper Shire plain. Hippos and crocodiles live in the river and there are about 300 elephants. The bird life is very varied.

The second half of the dry season is the best for game viewing because the animals congregate along the river at that time. The park roads are closed in the wet season.

Places to Stay

At the *Mvuu Camp* on the Shire River are adequate twin-bedded *rondavels*. There are pit toilets and you get water from the river, but you must bring your own bedding, cooking utensils and food; firewood is provided. In the wet season you can get there by boat.

NYIKA NATIONAL PARK

This was the first of the Malawian national parks. It encloses a beautiful montane plateau over 2000 metres high and covered in moor-like open rolling grassland that is completely treeless. For this reason it is very easy to see the animals. Trees only grow in occasional patches in the valleys. During the rainy season when the grass grows on the plateau you can see herds of zebra, eland, roan antelope, reedbuck, bushbuck and wart hog without even moving from the Chelinda Camp. You may also be lucky and sight leopard from the camp.

Due to the absence of lions and elephants, you're allowed to walk anywhere in this park, and there are trails where you may camp on walks taking up to five days, escorted by a game scout. The best game-viewing times are between November and May. You can fish for trout in the streams the whole year, or in the dams from September to April.

Thazima Gate, where the park head-quarters is located, is 67 km from Rumphi

and about 10 km north of the Rumphi to Katumbi road. Without your own vehicle it can be problematic getting to the park. There are several possibilities. First try contacting the district commissioner in Rumphi (on the edge of town) and ask if there is any possibility of getting a lift with the park truck, which comes down regularly for supplies and wages.

Alternatively, take a morning bus from Rumphi or Katumbi to the park turn-off. From here you'll have to hitch or walk to Thazima, where there may be a park vehicle going the 60 km to Chelinda Camp. You may have to wait a day for this – possibly more. If nothing comes through, the park staff have government-issue sleeping bags and will let you sleep in the gate house.

If you'd like to know with more certainty what your chances are, you can call either Chelinda Camp (tel Chelinda 1) or the Thazima headquarters (tel Rumphi 50) and find out what day a park vehicle will go. Every Thursday is bank day in Rumphi so the park staff often come down by vehicle to do the banking and they'll give you a lift back.

Places to Stay

Chelinda Camp is on the edge of a beautiful pine forest overlooking a small artificial lake and rolling grass hills. It has six double rooms with one bathroom for every two rooms; these bathrooms are equipped with a bathtub (no showers) and hot water. The bedrooms each have a fireplace. There's a fully equipped kitchen/dining room with wood stoves. These double rooms cost Kw 9 per person (even if you occupy them singly).

In addition, there are four chalets, each with two bedrooms, a huge living room, bathroom, fireplace and kitchen. There's electricity in the evenings. A chalet costs Kw 36, but in the off season you can book one for Kw 9 per person. There is also a camp site nearby with pit toilets, running water and picnic shelters. It costs Kw 3 per person.

The *Drivers' Rest House* consists of two small buildings with beds and kerosene lamps, and an outside toilet and shower shack. You can use the kitchen at the bedroom block. The park office will say that you can't stay here but that's not true – just tell them you're very short of money. It costs Kw 1.50 per person. The rest house is right next to the shop which sells beer and a few basic canned goods. Bring most of your food with you.

If you have your own transport you can stay at the *Juniper Forest Cabin*, 45 km south-east of Chelinda Camp on a dirt track in the most southerly part of the park. It consists of one rustic cabin with four bunk-beds, blankets and some kitchen equipment, but there's no electricity or running water. It costs Kw 6 per person.

Lastly there is the *Zambian Rest House* just off the road to Chelinda and about 40 km from the Thazima Gate in the Zambian part of the park. There's no customs or immigration and you don't need a Zambian visa to go there. It costs Kw 6 per person. Nearby is **Chowo Forest** – the last remnant of natural forest – which has walking trails through it.

Mali

The area occupied by the modern states of Mali and parts of Niger and Senegal was one of the most important trading centres of the entire Islamic world in mediaeval times. The reputation of some of its trading cities – like Djenné, Timbuktu and Gao – as centres of wealth and cultural brilliance became world famous and surrounded by a mystique which has endured through the centuries right up to the present day. Others, famous in their day, like Kumbi and Audagost, are now ruins on the edge of the Sahara. The development of these places owed much to the spread of Islam, which became the religion of trade in those days. However, the religion itself made little impact on the peoples of the Sahel until the 15th and 16th centuries, except it was commercially convenient. Throughout this time the traditional beliefs continued to be of paramount importance and still survive today among peoples like the Dogon, Songhai and Mossi.

The wealth of these trading cities was based primarily on the taxes levied on the transport of West African gold to North Africa and the Middle East, and of salt from the Saharan oases to West Africa. So important was West African gold that without it there would have been no general use of the metal as a medium of exchange in mediaeval times. Monarchs as far away as England struck their coins in gold which had originated in West Africa. A long series of powerful empires grew up and collapsed in this part of the world, from the 9th to the 16th century. They only came to an end following invasion from Morocco and the breaking of the Muslim monopoly on trade in Africa and the Indian Ocean by the European maritime nations.

Berber traders who plied the trans-Saharan routes west from Morocco through Mauritania and south through

the Fezzan to the Middle Niger and Lake Chad had been important during Phoenician and Roman times. This trade was disrupted by the invasions of the Vandals, Goths and Visigoths and was not to be revived until the advent of Islam.

Islam brought with it an accepted system of law and order which enabled trade to thrive once again. Ghana, the first empire to spring up among the Soninke people in the area of the Upper Niger and Senegal rivers, came into being in the 9th century. By that time the Soninke had come to dominate all the important relay stations along the western trade routes and had established their capital, Kumbi, 200 km north of modern Bamako.

Like the wealth of all the empires which were to grow in this part of the world, their prosperity was principally based on the movement of gold and ivory from West Africa to the Mediterranean and Middle East, and on the movement of salt from the Saharan oases to West Africa. It also encompassed copper, cotton, fine tools and swords initially from Arabia and later from Italy and Germany, horses from Morocco and Egypt, kola nuts and slaves from southern West Africa. The empire of Ghana was, like most early mediaeval empires, based almost exclusively on the personal rule of the king and his immediate companions. There was no system of bureaucracy or civil service as developed later by the empires of Mali and Songhai. None of Ghana's kings converted to Islam. Instead they retained

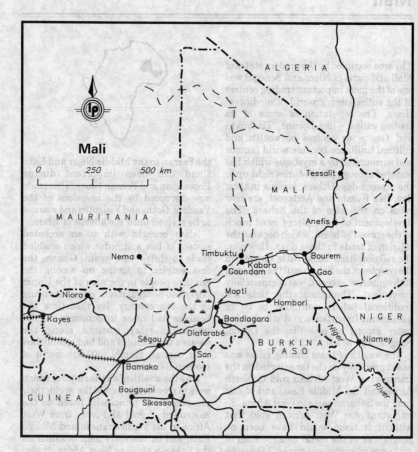

Mali

their traditional beliefs based on a community of the ancestors, the living and the still-to-be-born.

After nearly 500 years of existence, Ghana was finally destroyed by the invading Muslim Berber armies of the Almoravides from Mauritania in 1076 – the same people who took possession of Moorish Spain. The Almoravides were unable to hold onto power, being restless raiders, and what was left of Ghana struggled on until 1230 when the capital, Kumbi, was taken by people from the Tekrur area in northmost Senegal.

Shortly afterwards a new empire arose among the Mandinka under the leadership of Sundiata Keita. He converted to Islam as a gesture of friendship to the trading partners in the north, and also to take advantage of the efficiency and organisation which allegiance to Islam brought with it. Nevertheless, Sundiata owed his political success as much to the exploitation of traditional religion as to Islam, and also to the fact that the Mandinka were the most successful cultivators of the Gambia and Casamance rivers.

This new empire of Mali, with its

capital at Niani, was at its height under Mansa Musa (1312-1332) when it stretched from the Atlantic to the borders of present-day Nigeria. It was about this time that trans-Saharan trade reached its peak. So wealthy was the empire under Mansa Musa that when he passed through Egypt on his pilgrimage to Mecca he ruined the value of the Egyptian gold-based dinar for several years by his lavish gifts of the precious metal.

Musa's reign was a period of stability and prosperity during which Timbuktu and Djenné's long career of scholarship and cultural brilliance began. Musa brought back architects from Arabia to construct new mosques in these cities. He improved his administration by making it more methodical and literate, but the advent of an actual civil service had to wait until the rise of Songhai.

The Songhai still survive as a group of some 750,000 people farming, fishing and trading along the banks of the Niger River, from the borders of Nigeria to the lake region west of Timbuktu. Their villages, especially around Bandiagara near Mopti, are the major attraction for travellers in Mali after the old trading cities of Gao, Timbuktu and Djenné.

Although originally vassals of Mansa Musa, by 1375 the Songhai had founded a strong city-state based on Gao and were able to throw off Malian overlordship and make a bid for empire themselves. By 1400 they were strong enough to raid the Malian capital of Niani, and in 1464, under the leadership of Sunni Ali, finally embarked on a systematic conquest of the Sahel which was to eclipse the Malian Empire.

The final collapse of Mali came under Ali's successor, Askia Mohammed Ture, who came back from Mecca with the authority to act as Caliph of Islam in west Sudan. Ture pushed his armies west towards the Atlantic coast and east as far as Kano, overrunning the Hausa states in the process. Following these successes the armies turned north to take the Tuareg

stronghold of the oasis of Aïr, establishing a community of Songhai settlers there whose descendants still survive today.

Like the rulers of Mali, those of Songhai converted to Islam but took care to preserve and respect the traditional beliefs of the peasants of the countryside. Where Songhai excelled over Mali was in the creation of a civil service controlled by provincial governors on long-term appointments, a professional army and the beginnings of a professional navy on the Niger River. The sympathies and power base of the early rulers of Songhai lay in the peasants of the countryside, but gradually this was transferred to the Muslim-dominated trading cities. In this lay the basic weakness of the empires in this region. Such an arrangement was fine as long as the rulers could rely on the Islamic system of beliefs and government for promoting centralised rule and long-distance trade and credit. In times of crisis, however, these town-based empires were an easy prey to collapse.

This was the main reason Songhai was rapidly eclipsed in 1591, following an invasion from Morocco and the ensuing internal revolt of subject people. Even if Songhai had been able to withstand the invasion from Morocco, it's doubtful that the prosperity of the Niger trading cities would have lasted long. The European maritime nations were soon able to circumvent the cities' middle role by trading directly with the primary producers along the West African coast and further south.

With the rise of European naval hegemony, the trans-Saharan trading routes lapsed into relative obscurity, though even as late as the 1950s caravans were still transporting salt from the Saharan oasis of Bilma (in Niger) south to Nigeria.

Towards the end of the 19th century, Mali became a French colony. As in other French colonies, its people were gradually forced into cultivating cash crops – mainly groundnuts, cotton and gum arabic – initially through a system of forced labour then later by taxation. As in neighbouring Burkina Faso (formerly Upper Volta), the legacy of the emphasis on cash cropping and the neglect of food crops continues to plague the nation's agriculture.

Mali became independent in 1960, though for a few months it was federated with Senegal. Modibo Keita, the first president, quickly put his country on a socialist road to development and opposed French imperialism. The French were required to vacate their military bases in the country and, in 1962, Mali left the Franc Zone and set up its own currency (though the country did return to the Franc Zone in 1967). State corporations were set up and industrialisation was encouraged. However, some four years later, mismanagement and excessive bureaucracy forced the government to announce austerity measures which the general public were very reluctant to accept since there was a lot of obvious profiteering going on.

Keita was overthrown in a bloodless military coup in 1968 and the country has been ruled by the leaders of that coup ever since. The military are not particularly popular and the regime has been challenged on a number of occasions by student and labour organisations. The death in detention in 1977 of Modibo Keita, in particular, provoked spontaneous demonstrations throughout the country.

Being a part of the Sahel, Mali suffered disastrously from the droughts of the 1970s. The drought turned enormous areas of once marginal grazing and crop raising land into desert and resulted in massive losses of crops and livestock. When a further drought struck in 1984-5, not only were emergency supplies of grain held up in the ports of Dakar, Abidjan and Lomé but when they finally arrived in Mali, the nomads of the country's vast northern regions were beyond reach. The roads and other transport infrastructure simply did not exist. Some 80% of the cattle on which they depend perished and the nomads themselves were decimated. The survivors now crowd the cities of Mali as refugees.

The effects of these droughts will dominate Malian politics and economics for years to come but they have resulted in Moussa Traore, the president, demanding that foreign aid in future be linked to the country's social priorities.

Facts

GEOGRAPHY & CLIMATE

Only in the extreme south is rainfall sufficient to permit cultivation without irrigation. Cultivation depends largely on the flooding of the Niger and its tributaries, but rearing livestock remains the predominant occupation of most of the peasants in the countryside. Resources are so limited that many Malians are forced to migrate into neighbouring countries in search of work. The rainy season in the south lasts from June to September and sometimes October. The dry season stretches from October to February.

PEOPLE

The population of about eight million consists mainly of Bambara. Minority groups include the Songhai, Malinke, Senoufo, Dogon and Fula. The north is populated mainly by Tuareg.

VISAS

Visas are required by all except nationals of France. There are very few Malian embassies or consulates around the world so you need to plan ahead. In Africa, there are embassies only in Abidjan (Ivory Coast), Accra (Ghana), Algiers (Algeria), Cairo (Egypt), Conakry (Guinea), Dakar (Senegal) and Tripoli (Libya) plus consulates in Niamey (Niger) and Tamanrasset (Algeria). Outside Africa they are available at Mali embassies in

Berlin, Bonn, Brussels, New York, Ottawa, Paris and Washington. You cannot get a visa at the border.

Malian visas are expensive – FFr 100 or CFA 5000 – require two or three photos and are issued the same day or within 24 hours. No onward ticket or 'sufficient funds' are required. Visas are usually for a one-month stay and are extendable.

Some years ago, Malian bureaucracy used to be horrendous but things have eased up considerably these days. You only have to report to police and get your passport stamped in Bamako, Mopti, Gao and Timbuktu. The stamp is free except in Gao where they may charge you CFA 100 for it.

Tourist cards (cartes d'identités) and photography permits are no longer required, though this hasn't percolated down to all SMERT (the Malian tourist organisation) offices yet, so you may find yourself being forced to buy a tourist card for CFA 600.

Visa extensions for a further month are easy to obtain and are no fuss but the procedure for getting them varies depending on where you apply. In most cases you first have to go to SMERT for the application forms and then go onto the police. In other places (Mopti and Djenné, for example), you simply go to the police. Extensions cost CFA 5000 and are issued while you wait.

Exit visas are no longer required.

Other Visas

In Bamako there are embassies for Algeria, Burkina Faso, Egypt, Ghana, Guinea, Libya, Mauritania, Morocco and Nigeria. The French Embassy deals with other African Francophone countries' affairs which are not represented in Bamako.

Burkina Faso The embassy is in the Hippodrôme suburb about three km from the centre. Visas cost CFA 6000 with two photos and are issued in 24 hours. The staff are friendly and there's no fuss.

Senegal There is no Senegalese embassy in Bamako, so you may be in for a few problems if you're going there by rail or road without a visa (where required). This applies particularly on the train. Some people have been turned back. Most travellers seem to get through, however.

MONEY

US$1 = CFA 284

The unit of currency is the CFA franc (until May 1984 Mali retained its own currency – the Mali franc – but this was phased out shortly afterwards). There are no restrictions on the import or export of local currency. There is a commission of CFA 1500 plus CFA 100 duty stamp for changing travellers' cheques. This applies to all transactions. Allow up to two hours for changing money at a bank. Banking hours are generally 8 to 11 am (and sometimes 12 noon). The bank at Bamako Airport hardly ever seems to be open. Bring sufficient French francs with you if you arrive in Mali on a Friday. Some of the large hotels in Bamako can change travellers' cheques though their commission rates are higher than those at the banks.

The airport departure tax is CFA 2500.

LANGUAGE

French is the official language but the most widely spoken is Bambara. Other languages spoken in various areas are Senoufo, Sarakolle, Dogon, Tuareg and Arabic.

Getting There & Around

AIR

Air Mali merged with Air Afrique some years ago so the latter handles their international flights. For the internal sectors they presently have only one reconditioned Antonov 24 so flights are few and far between and you should treat schedules with a pinch of salt. Flights are often cancelled. Examples of fares are: Mopti to Timbuktu (CFA 17,500, usually once per week); Mopti to Gao (CFA 18,900); Bamako to Gao (CFA 32,700).

ROAD

Most roads in Mali are pretty rough at the best of times, and when it rains they often get washed out completely. However, there are a few roads which are fairly well maintained. Bamako to Mopti is reasonable these days and there is a new road between Mopti and Gao. How long they will stay that way remains to be seen. Where roads are subject to wash out, barriers are erected during and after heavy rain to prevent the roads being churned up and destroyed.

Hitching is generally a waste of time. You should arrange lifts the day before with truck drivers, or take a taxi. If you intend going north from Gao on the Route du Tanezrouft to Adrar in Algeria, you may have to wait around for up to a week before you find a truck going that way (there are generally no more than five or six vehicles crossing the border between the two countries per day). There are a lot of police checks on the roads in Mali so expect delays and have your passport handy.

There are shared taxis and trucks from Mopti to Bandiagara, Sangha and Bankass. To Bandiagara costs CFA 1750 plus CFA 100 to CFA 300 for a backpack (cheaper in a *taxi-bachée* – a passenger truck). Beware of the children who meet incoming taxis and offer all manner of nonsense 'services' at very inflated prices. From Mopti to Bankass there are shared taxis for CFA 1550 plus CFA 250 for a backpack which take about four hours. Shared taxis are also available from Bankass to Ende village on market days.

Examples of local road transport, costs and journey times are as follows:

Bamako to Mopti

There is a choice of trucks and taxis along this route. A shared taxi costs CFA 5000 to CFA 6000 plus CFA 500 for a backpack and takes about 10 hours. There's a lot of demand for seats so you must be at the Sogo Niko taxi stand before 8 am if you want to give yourself a reasonable chance. (Sogo Niko is six km from the centre of Bamako so take a taxi there.) If you miss out then take a taxi first to Ségou (CFA 2000 plus CFA 250 for a backpack) and another from there to Mopti (CFA 4000). The last taxis leave Ségou for Mopti around noon.

There are also Courier Postale buses once a week on Tuesday which cost CFA 4600 and are very comfortable. They leave from the rear of the main post office. Book the previous night.

Bamako to Sikasso

A taxi costs CFA 3000 plus CFA 300 for a backpack and takes about six hours. There are five police checkpoints en route.

Mopti to Djenné

This journey is best done in a taxi rather than a Land Rover. It costs CFA 1550 plus CFA 250 for a backpack.

Mopti to Timbuktu

Land Rovers are available for CFA 7500 plus CFA 500 for a backpack and the journey can take up to two days. Be prepared to push when you get stuck. Women stay in the vehicle when this happens so it's quite a task!

Mopti to Gao

There are daily taxis for CFA 6700 and a once weekly Courier Postale bus which leaves Mopti on Wednesday.

Bamako to Djenné

There are converted trucks on Monday and Tuesday which leave around 12 noon, cost CFA 5000 including baggage and take about 14 to 15 hours. It's an uncomfortable journey, crowded and there are many police checkpoints.

Selling Cars

The most sought-after cars are Peugeot 504 sedan or station wagons. A sedan in good condition sells for CFA 600,000 to CFA 750,000 and a station wagon for CFA 1,000,000 to CFA 750,000. You needn't go looking for customers – they'll find you. The best prices are in Gao and Mopti. When you find a buyer expect to spend two to three days haggling over the price. Watch out for the *affaire economique* tax which can be as high as 105% of the selling price! Most customers will bribe the customs so that you don't have to pay the tax (why would you sell otherwise?!) but be careful and don't hang around once you've sold it. Get moving.

TRAIN

There is only one railway line in Mali which connects Bamako with the Atlantic coast at Dakar, Senegal, but it's one of the country's most important transport links. Virtually all the passengers and freight between the two countries pass along this line. The road link is hardly used at all.

There are two trains in either direction per week. They are scheduled to depart Wednesday and Friday at 11 am but often run late. Make enquiries about this. Although the fares on the two trains are the same, the Senegalese train (from Bamako on Friday and from Dakar on Wednesday) is far superior to the Malian train (from Bamako on Wednesday and from Dakar on Friday). The Senegalese train is comparable with any West European train. It's clean, pleasant, has air-con and a buffet car serving soft drinks, beer and good food. First class on the Malian train, by comparison, would be called 4th class in any other country. Even the insects prefer going 1st class! So do yourself a favour and take the Senegalese train.

If you have to take the Malian train, get to the station several hours before it's due to leave. It can be unbearably overcrowded even though seats in 1st and 2nd classes are now reserved. The fares from Bamako to Dakar are CFA 27,600 (sleeper), CFA 18,500 (1st class) and CFA 11,700 (2nd class). Book your berth or seat in advance.

Student reductions of 30% are available during school holidays but not at other times. To get them you have to go and see the *chef de la gare* (station chief).

You must get off the train at the border and report to the police. Their office is quite some distance from the train.

Although you can buy food in the buffet car on the train it tends to be a little expensive. If you're trying to save money buy food from vendors on the platforms at various stops along the way.

These passenger trains are not the only trains which use this line. Many freight trains run along it too. It's possible – but difficult – to get a ride on them by speaking to the engine driver and agreeing on a price. It won't work out much cheaper than going on the passenger trains and they are noisy and dusty, but you'll definitely get a lot more room to yourself. Local people jump onto and off them all the time for short free rides. Make sure you have a visa for Senegal (if necessary) before you leave.

Beware of robberies on the passenger trains, especially at night.

BOAT

In theory there are three river boats which ply up and down the Niger River between Mopti, Timbuktu and Gao, but, until recently, because of the Sahel drought and the lack of water in the Niger River, none of them were operational. They're now back in operation although only between August and November. Depending on the level of the river, they may cover the whole route between Bamako and Gao. However, most of the time they only ply between Koulikoro (57 km east of Bamako), Mopti, Kabara (Timbuktu) and Gao and sometimes only between Mopti and Gao.

The only trouble with these boats is that schedules are a complete figment of the imagination, so there's no way of knowing when they're going to turn up and how long they are going to take, so you can't plan ahead. If you have the chance, though, they're an experience not to be missed.

The *Kanga Moussa* is the best of the boats whereas the *Timbouctou* and the *General Soumare* are about as near to Noah's Ark as you're likely to get. There's an even older boat known as the *Liberté* which is like an 18th century prison hulk. Despite obvious differences, all the boats have the same fares but, even on the *Kanga Moussa*, if you want anything approaching basic amenities then you'll have to travel 2nd class.

The fares on the *Kanga Moussa* are:

class	Mopti to Gao	Mopti to Koulikoro
super deluxe	CFA 104,769	CFA 65,782
1st	CFA 37,240	CFA 23,398
2nd	CFA 25,492	CFA 16,076
3rd	CFA 16,857	CFA 9,410
4th	CFA 5,218	CFA 3,345

First class consists of two-berth cabins and includes food; 2nd class is a four-berth cabin with food; and 3rd class is either an eight-berth or 12-berth cabin with food. Fourth class is just deck space without food. Fourth class was recently described as 'utter swill – it is too crowded to pick your nose, it smells like a burning pig farm and there are more screaming babies than at the Bellevue Hospital maternity ward'. Third class allows you to sleep on the upper deck, which is much less crowded, much nicer and a pleasant place to hang out during the day. The food, however, is bland and boring. You will also need your own bowl and fork. Soda, beer and mineral water can be bought on the boat, though they sometimes run out. The landscape is interesting but

there's a lot of it, so bring something to pass the time with.

Additional food can be bought on the boats or at the stops en route, but take as much water as possible with you. Water on the boats is drawn from the river and 'purified' by the addition of bleach.

The journey from Mopti to Gao takes five days on average but can take 10 days (engine trouble and getting stuck on sandbars are the most common reasons for delays).

Timbuktu is no longer on the river – which has changed course over the centuries – so if you're heading there you must get off at Kabara (11 km from Timbuktu). Taxis are available from Kabara to Timbuktu. If there is a lot of cargo to unload at Kabara then you may have time to take a taxi there, have a look around and return in time for the boat. If not, you may have to stay in Timbuktu for up to a week waiting for the next boat to come along.

If you don't want to take a large boat (or can't because of the level of the river), motorised and nonmotorised pirogues are available between Timbuktu and Mopti. The trip in a motorised pirogue should cost about CFA 4500 including your pack, but you'll only get this price after hard bargaining. The starting price might well be CFA 10,000 excluding pack (the locals pay CFA 3500). You need to take lots of food and water with you and, if you want to eat on board, donate a couple of handfuls of rice to the meal; you'll be rewarded with a share of the communal bowl of fish and rice (plus take the odd CFA 100 for fish and salt, etc). There's very little food you can buy on the way.

The journey time between Mopti and Timbuktu varies from six to 15 days depending on the amount of cargo carried, the size of the pirogue, the water level in the river and whether the pirogue is motorised or not. You should expect delays when the boat owner goes off to see friends and family on the riverbank – often for up to half a day at a time.

There are somewhat more predictable pirogues between Mopti and Djenné, primarily for local people taking produce to various markets. They generally leave Mopti on Friday and Djenné on Monday and Tuesday mornings. The journey takes two days and two nights and costs CFA 1300 to CFA 1500. Bring food with you unless you don't mind eating rice and fish all the time. If you're starting from Djenné you must get to the Bani ferry point, from which the pirogues depart. A taxi there from Djenné costs CFA 300 (shared), or you can get there by truck for CFA 125.

TO/FROM ALGERIA

It's not easy to find rides going from Mali to Algeria and you're going to need a lot of patience. Some travellers have waited up to 10 days in Gao before they found a ride. Whatever else you do, never hand over money until you are on the truck. The best place to find lifts in Gao is at the police station in the morning when truck drivers come in to get their papers stamped before leaving. Don't be too surprised if you get turned down even if you have the money in your hand.

The usual route is Gao to Adrar via Tessalit and Bordj Moktar – the Route du Tanezrouft. A truck along this route will cost CFA 17,000 to CFA 22,000 including food and water. Make sure that the truck you take is going through the border post otherwise you won't have an Algerian entry stamp and that will cause a lot of problems later on. The trip takes about four days (ie, a total of 38 to 40 hours driving over four days). The road is easy to follow on the Algerian side as there are solar-powered beacons every 10 km or so.

There's a bank at Bordj Moktar so you'll be up for your obligatory AD 1000 change. Water is available too from a borehole opposite the customs at 6 pm.

There's another route to Algeria between Gao and Tamanrasset via Timeiaouine. Transport along this route will either be Tuareg who drive Land Rovers across the desert, or Malian trucks. Most of these vehicles will be smuggling and the Algerians know it, so you could be stuck at the border for days. Again, make sure the driver intends going through a border post otherwise you won't have an entry stamp. The cost between Gao and Tamanrasset should be CFA 20,000 to CFA 30,000 including food and water. The journey takes about three days assuming there are no delays at the border.

TO/FROM BURKINA FASO

The main routes to Burkina Faso are Bamako to Bobo Dioulasso via Koutiala, and Sikasso and Mopti to Ouagadougou via Bankass and Koro. The roads are bad along either route so you're in for an uncomfortable journey but transport is more predictable along the Bamako to Bobo Dioulasso route.

Taxis leave from the Sogo Niko taxi stand in Bamako for Bobo Dioulasso daily in the early morning and cost up to CFA 8000. The journey takes about 11 hours but can take longer. There are quite a lot of checkpoints along the way on both sides of the border and although they're generally no hassle, they do get tedious. You can also do this journey in stages, first to Sikasso (around CFA 3500 plus CFA 600 for a backpack, six hours) and then from Sikasso to Bobo Dioulasso (about CFA 3500 plus CFA 300 for a backpack, five hours).

From Mopti to Bobo Dioulasso there is usually one taxi daily but they're often in a bad state of repair. The fare is CFA 7500.

There's very little traffic along the Mopti to Ouagadougou road so it's best to wait until you find something going the whole way. If you don't, then allow two days for the journey. There are taxis from Bankass to Koro and Koro to Ouahigouya but they only go when full and some travellers have waited two to three days for them to fill up.

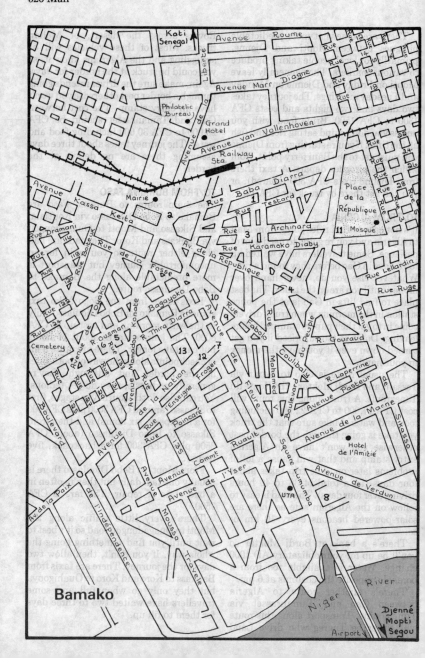

Bamako

1	American Embassy & US Information Centre
2	Place de la Liberté
3	GPO
4	Market & Place du Marché
5	Bar Mali
6	Conseil Diocesien des Religieuses
7	Hotel Majestique
8	French Embassy
9	Bar Berry
10	Cathedral
11	Artisans' Market
12	Air Mali
13	Sûreté

TO/FROM IVORY COAST

There are two main routes, the first between Bamako and Ferkéssédougou via Sikasso and Pogo, and the more westerly between Bamako and Odienné via Bougouni and Manankoro. Traffic isn't as frequent on the latter route so expect delays while taxis wait for sufficient custom.

On the Sikasso to Ferkéssédougou route, there are regular buses and taxis which cost CFA 5000. The buses take around 11 hours and the taxis around eight hours.

TO/FROM NIGER

The only practicable route between the two countries is Gao to Niamey. There are three SNTN buses weekly in either direction which depart Gao on Monday, Wednesday and Friday, cost CFA 5550 plus CFA 35 per kg of your baggage and take about 30 hours. You can buy tickets up to 48 hours in advance and you're advised to do this. There are also occasional trucks for CFA 5000 but these generally take longer.

You need patience to do this trip. One traveller described it recently as, 'A horrific journey of hassles, bureaucracy, time wasting and general lunacy'. Take plenty of water with you and be prepared to line up at the Niger border and take your anti-cholera pills (Fanasil) for which

you pay CFA 200. If you refuse to take the pills, they send you back to Mali.

There are thorough baggage searches on both sides of the border.

TO/FROM SENEGAL

The only practicable route is to take the train from Bamako to Dakar via Tambacounda. See the Train section for details.

Around the Country

BAMAKO
Information

The tourist office is opposite the mosque but they have no maps of the city. The Institut Géographie National is worth checking out if you're thinking of doing some walking trips around Mali, especially in the Dogon country. To get there, take the road that has the Banque du Commerce on its right and follow it for about one km. It's open Monday to Friday from 7 am to 1.30 pm and on Tuesday and Thursday from 3.30 to 5.30 pm.

If possible, avoid using Bamako as a poste restante address as the post office isn't very efficient.

The truck/taxi park is known as Sogo Niko and is about six km from the city centre. A taxi there costs CFA 1500. A taxi to the airport costs CFA 2500 to CFA 3000.

The Peace Corps office (tel 24 479) is on El Hadja Samba Kone, Quartier Niarella, near the Hotel Dakan. It's open Monday to Thursday from 7.30 am to 3 pm and on Friday and Saturday from 7.30 am to 12.30 pm. The office isn't really open to outsiders, so if you're interested in seeing what they get up to in the villages, you'll have to make personal contact with a volunteer.

Things to See

The National Museum on the road to the zoo is very well laid out and interesting, especially as far as weaving and Dogon artefacts are concerned. Entry is free. The **zoo** itself costs CFA 100 (CFA 50 for students). There are artisans' workshops worth visiting near the Grand Mosque.

It's worth making a day trip out of Bamako to **Lafibougou**, a western suburb, where there are beautiful cliffs, market activity and weavers.

Places to Stay

Hotel accommodation in Bamako is generally quite expensive, but paying a lot of money doesn't always guarantee a good room, so it's worth checking out the missions before you try the hotels.

One place which has been popular for years is the *Conseil Diocesien des Religieuses* (also known as the Centre d'Accueil Catholique and the Centre d'Accueil des Soeurs Blanches), on the corner of 130th and 133rd Sts (this is also Rue El Hadj Ousmane Bagayoko). Look out for a pink coloured building. Here they have a dormitory with 12 beds at CFA 1500 per person plus singles/doubles/triples at CFA 4000/5000/6000. Mosquito nets are provided (even in the dormitory) and the toilets and showers are clean. Baggage left here is usually secure. You can cook your food in the courtyard if you have your own stove. The Conseil Diocesien is closed from 1 to 4 pm and 10 pm to 8 am. They won't let you in during these hours so don't stay out late.

Also cheap, but very often full, is the *Maison des Jeunes*, opposite the French Embassy and adjacent to the river. It's a blue-coloured, five-storey concrete building. You can get a dormitory bed for CFA 1000 (10 to 12 beds) but there are no locks on the doors so it's not wise to leave gear here. The bathrooms could do with a good scrub out.

If it's full, try the *Pension Djoliba* close to the US Embassy where you can get a bed for CFA 1500 with mosquito net. The people who run it are very pleasant but it's a noisy place at night. The *Bar Mali* is also in the same category at CFA 1500 per person but it's a filthy dump and the water supply is erratic.

One of the cheapest hotels is the *Hotel Majestique*, Ave de Fleure, which offers rooms for CFA 4000/7500 for singles/doubles. It's a little seedy these days but tolerable.

If you arrive late at night at the Sogo Niko truck/taxi park it might be best to stay for the night at one of the *chambres de passage* around here. They all offer very basic accommodation (a mat on the floor) for around CFA 250 but they're usually very dirty indeed.

Campers should head for the *Hotel les Colibris* which is about two km over the bridge across the river and out of town and then off to the left about 500 metres. You can camp here for CFA 3000 for two people, a tent and a car (if you have one). You may be able to bargain for less. It has good facilities.

Places to Eat

Bamako is a good city to find cheap street food stalls selling all manner of things such as brochettes, ragout, fish, rice, fried plantain, potatoes, sweet potatoes, couscous and much more.

If staying at the Conseil Diocesien, there's a small café within 100 metres which offers good cheap food. To get to it, turn right when you leave the Conseil, then take the first street to the right and you'll see it on the left hand side. Also cheap are the *Restaurant Au Bon Coin*, Ave de la Nation; *Le Capitaine* (very tasty fish); the *Café Phoenicia*; the *Istanbul* near the large market; and *Le Bambou*.

The *Ho Chi Minh Restaurant* offers excellent Vietnamese food but it's a little on the expensive side. Similar are the *Restaurant Mikado* and the *Snack Bar Hanoi*. For a reasonable splurge, try the *Restaurant Central*, close to the Mali Mag supermarket or *Le Gondole*, Ave de la Nation, which offers good French and Lebanese dishes.

The *Café Sabbaque*, opposite the Mille

et Un Merveilleux store, is the main expatriate hang-out these days. They offer good food at reasonable prices and the bar is popular. The *Berry Bar* is also popular but it's very expensive and there are a lot of touts around. If you want to hear some music while you eat an excellent meal go to *Les Trois Caimans*. This is another expatriate watering hole and is popular with the Peace Corps. Another is the *Bar Central*. Peace Corps volunteers who sometimes go here may offer you a place to sleep for the night.

DJENNÉ

Djenné is a city full of legends. It's possibly the oldest and most impressive of the trading towns which once straddled the lucrative trans-Saharan caravan routes. Precious little has changed for centuries. In fact, the town remains much as it was when the opening of direct sea links between West Africa and Europe put paid to the trans-Saharan caravanserai. It's a mud-brick town right down to the famous mosque. There's not a single modern building to detract from the atmosphere and very few places have electricity either. This is a kerosene lantern and candle town and it's easy to imagine you're living in mediaeval times.

The Djenné of today dates from about 1400 AD and had its heyday during the 15th and 16th centuries. Old Djenné (Jenné-jeno), a few km upstream, has its origins around 250 BC and was a thriving city by the 9th century AD. It was abandoned around 1400 AD for reasons which are not clear, though it's thought that the Muslim elite considered the city too contaminated by pagan practices. A lot of travellers miss this place because it isn't easy to get to, but it's worth the effort.

Things to See

The **Monday Market** is very interesting and shouldn't be missed – 'The men with their straw and leather hats and the women

adorned with amber and associated finery are an unforgettable sight'. It's the highlight of many people's trip though there tend to be a lot of overland expedition tourists here. The rest of the week it's very quiet. Make sure you visit the **mud-brick mosque** but prepare yourself for a hassle before you get in. The first price asked is CFA 1500 which includes a visit to the roof but it is possible to haggle down to CFA 250. Whatever you pay, however, the tour will be short, sharp and sweet. Why complain though? Name another functional mosque where infidels are allowed in outside of Turkey. From the roof there's an excellent view of the town and the market below (on Monday). The narrow alleyways of the town are also worth exploring.

A four-km walk from Djenné is **Jenné-jeno**. Walk to the last village you passed on the way into Djenné, turn right and head for the rise with trees on it. All this area is part of the abandoned city. There are broken fragments of pottery everywhere and major archaeological excavations going on.

Because Djenné has attracted a lot of tourist interest recently, there are many youths touting their 'services' as 'guides'. You don't need a guide to Djenné but if you don't take one of these insistent people, expect aggression and hassles. Even SMERT attempts to press you into accepting a 'guide' for CFA 1250 and will tell you it's compulsory. This is rubbish and, although a refusal won't get you into trouble, it will bring you a lot of hassles. If you can't handle the nonsense, take a guide and put it down to experience (CFA 1250 for one person or CFA 1500 shared by up to four people). Remember Marrakesh?

Places to Stay & Eat

Just about the only immediate place to stay is *Le Campement*. It's very basic and the manager is OK but the water supply is erratic and the food is expensive. Rooms cost CFA 2500 a double. If it's full – and only if it's full – they'll let you sleep on the roof for CFA 1500 per person. The only way you'll get a shower is to plead on your bended knee for the management to fetch more water from the well (it's a long way and they're not keen). Only some of the beds have mosquito nets. There is erratic electricity from 6 to 10 pm. It's suggested you avoid the children who hang around as they're basically con-merchants.

The other place to stay is the *SMERT Building*! They offer very pleasant rooms in a beautiful old mud-brick house at CFA 750/1500 for singles/doubles. The manager, Mr Ba, is very friendly. The building overlooks the mosque and main square (where the market is held). There are bucket showers and kerosene lanterns and you can sleep on the roof if you choose. The roof is a good place to take photographs of those below without them noticing.

Good food is very difficult to find except on market days. There are a few food stalls in the main square which offer rice, sauce and meat (meat = bones) but, according to many travellers, it's virtually inedible. If you ask around, on the other hand, you will quickly find yourself eating in the back of a mud-brick house somewhere down a back alley.

GAO

Like Djenné, Gao was another prosperous Sahelian trading city which flourished during the 15th and 16th centuries. It's been more affected by the 20th century than Djenné, but it's still very interesting. Make sure you visit the curious **Tomb of Askia** and the associated **mosque**, the two good **markets**; and the **river area** (where you'll see pirogues, sand dunes, cultivation patterns and people washing clothes).

There are still many refugees in Gao from the drought which affected Mali during 1984-85.

Changing money in Gao at the bank can be a bureaucratic nightmare so allow two to three hours.

Places to Stay & Eat

The cheapest place to stay if you have your own tent is *Camping Askia* next door to the now long defunct Camping Dominique. It costs CFA 600 per person to camp or sleep on the roof. They also have rooms but these are more expensive. There are good showers but the toilets are home to giant cockroaches (ever been to New York!?) and there's no shade for the tents though baggage left in the tents is safe. Similar is *Chez Yarga* but this is 40 minutes' walk from town. It offers mats on the floor for CFA 750. It's clean and there are good showers.

If you don't have a tent try the *Union Democratique du Peuple Malien* which is a large pink building offering rooms for CFA 2000/3000 a single/double. The guard here is very friendly and helpful.

The *Hotel Atlantide*, about 200 metres from the above, is the only hotel in town. It costs CFA 2535/3825 per single/double without bathroom and CFA 3095/4315 per single/double with shower and a small fan. These prices include breakfast (coffee, bread and jam). The beds have rigging for a mosquito net but you need your own. It's basic but friendly. The water supply, like the electricity supply, is erratic. It's also possible to camp in the enclosed and guarded courtyard next to the hotel with the use of the hotel's facilities for CFA 500 per person. There are also huts for CFA 750 per person but they're dirty hovels and can't be recommended. It's no longer possible to camp at Le Village.

The cheapest places to eat in Gao are the street stalls where you can buy grilled fillet of lamb or beef. The usual goat meat is available, as are spicy sausages.

Good Senegalese food is available from the *Restaurant Soundiata*. Otherwise, try *Le Camerouni* near the market. Everyone knows the owner, so just ask. He has learned the art of hamburgers, omelettes and salads and is, according to many travellers, excellent. The *Sahel Vert*, about five km from the centre, is also

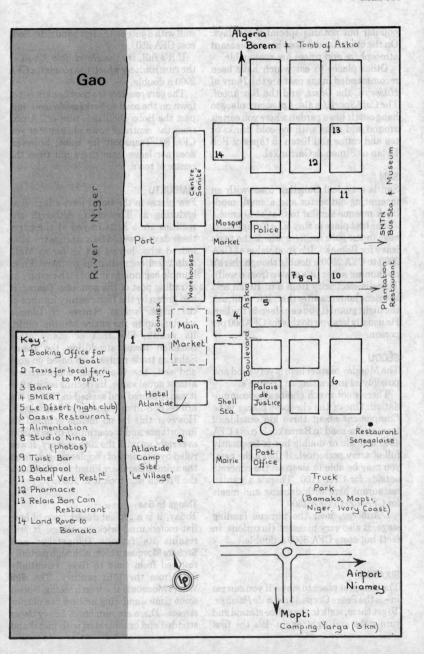

Gao

River Niger

Port

Centre Santé

Mosque

Market

Police

Warehouses

SOMIEX

Main Market

Hotel Atlantide

Shell Sta.

Atlantide Camp Site 'Le Village'

Mairie

Palais de Justice

Post Office

Boulevard

Askia

Plantation Restaurant

SNTN Bus Sta.

Museum

Restaurant Senegalaise

Truck Park
(Bamako, Mopti, Niger, Ivory Coast)

Algeria
Borem ✝ Tomb of Askia

Airport
Niamey

Mopti
Camping Yarga (3 km)

Key:
1 Booking Office for boat
2 Taxis for local ferry to Mopti
3 Bank
4 SMERT
5 Le Désert (night club)
6 Oasis Restaurant
7 Alimentation
8 Studio Nina (photos)
9 Twist Bar
10 Blackpool
11 Sahel Vert Rest^{nt}
12 Pharmacie
13 Relais Bon Coin Restaurant
14 Land Rover to Bamako

popular but nothing special these days. On the other hand it does have a pleasant atmosphere and prices are reasonable.

Other places to eat which have been recommended in the past are the *Touré al Husseini*, the *Oasis*, and the *Blackpool*. The *Café Sportif* is also a pleasant place to hang out. It has a garden where you can sit around and relax with ice-cold drinks or tea and coffee and listen to tapes of Bob Dylan or Simon & Garfunkel.

SAN

San is a typical Sahelian town with an interesting old sector and a small mud-brick mosque similar to that at Djenné.

The best place to stay is *Le Campement* next to the *gare routière* where the taxis leave for Bamako. It's good value at CFA 2000 to CFA 2500 a double though there's no running water (it's drawn from a well). There is electricity from 6 to 10 pm and kerosene lanterns after that. If it's full, ask the night guard if you can sleep in the bar. He usually lets you do this for CFA 500 per person.

SÉGOU

The Monday market here is very good and possibly as interesting as Djenné's.

There's not much choice of accommodation. One of the cheapest places is *Le Campement* about three km outside of town on the road to Bamako. It costs CFA 4500 a single or double but is frequently full of army personnel. If that's the case, you may be able to sleep on the concrete outside for CFA 1100. There's a garden restaurant here with dancing and meals for CFA 750 to CFA 1500.

L'Auberge, near the pirogue landing stage, is also very pleasant (luxurious, in fact) but costs CFA 8500 a double.

SIKASSO

The cheapest place to stay – if you can get in – is the Peace Corps *Maison de Passage*. To get there, walk to the police station and turn right and right again. It's the first

wall with a gate on the left hand side. Beds cost CFA 250.

If it's full, try the *Hotel Solo Khan* at the *gare routière* which has rooms for CFA 2000 a double.

The *gare routière* is about one km out of town on the road to Ferkéssédougou, just past the Bobo Dioulasso turn-off. A taxi from the centre of town should cost you CFA 80. Transport for Bobo, however, does not leave from there but from the centre of town.

TIMBUKTU

Few places in the world have a legend as enduring as Timbuktu. Although the realities are a little frayed at the edges these days, it would be a strange traveller indeed who, having got as far as Mali, didn't feel compelled to go there. From humble beginnings in the 11th century as a trading post of the nomadic Tuareg, it had grown by the 15th century into one of the most famous centres of Islamic scholarship in the entire Muslim world. Its wealth, like that of many other Sahelian towns straddling the trans-Saharan trade routes, was based on gold and salt, the two being considered of almost equal value. Its decline set in after it was captured and sacked in 1591 by the armies of Sultan Mansour of Marrakesh. However this by no means eclipsed its importance and it continued to be fought over right up until the 20th century. It was ruled by a variety of peoples ranging from the animist Bambara kingdom of Ségou to the French who took it in 1894.

Things to See

Today, it is a typical desert town of low, flat-roofed mud-brick buildings. It still retains its famous **Djingerebur** and **Sankore Mosques** which, although partially restored from time to time, essentially date from the 15th century. The **Sidi Yahaya Mosque** is also worth seeing. Spend some time wandering around the narrow streets. There are numerous heavy doors studded and ornamented with metal and

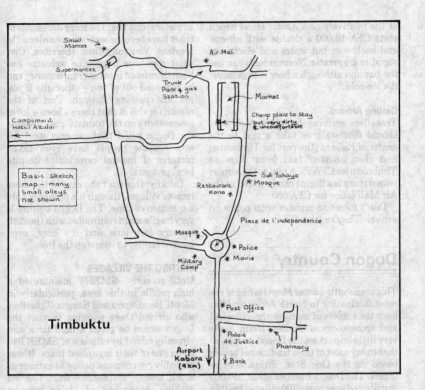

Basic sketch map – many small alleys not shown.

Timbuktu

surrounded with ornate frames – and even plaques to various western explorers who came through here such as René Caillie (1828) and Alexander Gordon Laing (1826). Such 20th-century intrusions as trucks and planes haven't entirely put a stop to traditional means of transport and sources of income. A salt caravan, often consisting of over 3000 camels, sets out for Taoudenni twice a year in March and November.

Places to Stay & Eat

Probably to get the best deal for accommodation ask around in the market place for the *Restaurant Sundiata* (otherwise known as Le Senegalais). This place is owned by a man called Abdulaye Arafa who will offer you a room or roof

space in the restaurant itself, or a room at his own house which is near the Sidi Yahaya mosque. At either place the accommodation is very basic and the water supply limited (it's drawn from a well). You must haggle over the price but expect to pay around CFA 1500 for a room. Some travellers had breakfast thrown in for this price but don't count on it. Other meals are relatively expensive and the quality is poor. Baggage left in the rooms is secure.

Le Campement costs up to CFA 8000 a double for the better rooms, but cheaper rooms may be available. The more expensive rooms come with breakfast, otherwise it costs CFA 1000. Other meals are expensive at around CFA 3000.

Luxury accommodation can be found

at the relatively new *Azalai Hotel* which costs CFA 18,000 a double with air-con and bathroom but water and electricity supplies are erratic. Nonresidents can use the bar and although a beer is expensive, it's ice-cold.

Getting Around

Travellers arriving by pirogue or boat should first walk or take a taxi to the centre of Kabara (the port for Timbuktu) and then another taxi from there to Timbuktu for CFA 75. A taxi to the airport (when there is a flight) can be found at the Air Mali office for CFA 500.

Don't forget to register with police on arrival. They're friendly.

Dogon Country

This area south-east of Mopti is one of the most fascinating in North Africa and has been the subject of many anthropological and archaeological studies. Islam made very little impact on the Dogon people, so that today most of their traditional beliefs based on the Dog Star, Sirius, survive intact. The Dogon number about 250,000 distributed over some 700 villages built in pairs either up against the 200-km-long Bandiagara Cliff (*Falaise de Bandiagara*) or nearby on the adjoining plateau.

The design of their houses is unique and very characteristic. There are two basic types. The first is the plateau type built on flat rock outcrops between arable fields, while the second and most spectacular are erected on the steep slopes of the cliff itself. Each house, collectively built and made of rock and mud-brick, consists of a number of separate rooms surrounding a small yard and interlinked with stone walls. Roofs are flat and families will sleep there during the hot, dry season. The granaries, on the other hand, have conical straw roofs which are assembled on the ground then lifted into place.

Unfortunately, the Dogon villages are so picturesque that the more accessible of them have become somewhat hardened to tourism. You may find, therefore, that what was once a genuine welcome has been translated into how much money can be squeezed out of you – especially if you are just passing through. Part of the reason for this is that there's been a lot of insensitivity on the tourists' part towards the Dogon belief that cameras steal the soul – some people have even taken pictures of funeral ceremonies despite local protests.

Luckily, this isn't the case in the more remote villages, though it's probably only a question of time. The Dogon culture is very fragile when confronted with the 20th century fast lane and it's easy, even inadvertently, to overstep the line.

VISITING THE VILLAGES

Until recently, SMERT maintained a high profile in this area, particularly in Mopti, Bandiagara and Sangha. Travellers who arrived there wanting to visit the Dogon would be given a hard time and virtually forced by officials of SMERT to go on one of their organised tours. It was probably government policy to extract as much money as possible from tourists wishing to see one of Mali's premier attractions.

For whatever reason, those days have apparently gone and only in Sangha do SMERT still have a high profile (except on market days). This may only be a temporary change of policy. Nevertheless, the damage (if that's what it is) has been done. There's now a price for everything and, although there's still room for negotiation on an individual basis, there are definitely minimum rates. Other than that it remains an experience you shouldn't miss.

Whatever you are told to the contrary, it's still possible to visit this area on your own without a guide though you won't be allowed into certain villages without one (such as Kanikombole). And without a guide, you'll be at the mercy of all the

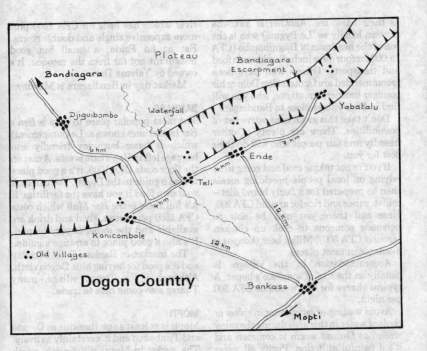

Bandiagara

Plateau

Bandiagara
Escarpment

Djiguibombo

Waterfall

Yabatalu

6 km

Ende

7 km

Teli

4 km

4 km

Kanicombole

6.5 km

Old Villages

12 km

Dogon Country

Bankass

Mopti

cadeau-seeking children and whatever 'fees' various Dogon chiefs think you are capable of paying. Many will conveniently pretend they don't speak any French for the purposes of maximising income. While it may be true that some don't, there are quite a few who do and their sons – many of whom make an income by acting as guides – certainly do. All the same, this doesn't prevent some determined travellers from making it on their own. The choice is yours and will depend largely on how much time you have to spare.

Most travellers take a guide if only to avoid pitfalls and hassles but, if you're going to do this, do it locally either in Bandiagara or Bankass. However good you are at haggling, if you arrange a trip in Mopti, it's going to cost about double what it would in Bandiagara or Bankass (though not always).

A typical price would be CFA 3000 to CFA 4000 per person per day including the guide's fee, a donkey/horse and cart, and all your food and lodging for a five-day, four-night trip. The guide's fee is usually CFA 2000 to CFA 3000 per day per group. It makes sense to be part of a small group so you can share that part of the cost. Some of the villages also demand a fee before allowing you to enter and this can be up to CFA 1000 (Kanikombole charges CFA 500 per person).

Some guides are greedy so try to get the measure of someone before you agree to a trip. Others are very friendly and fair. Mamadou Kansaye, who owns the Bar Kansaye in Bandiagara, was one of the original 'patriarchs' of guided tours in this area but now he leaves these things up to various younger members of his family. Two of them are Pascale and Abdoulaye. They charge CFA 3000 per day per group as their basic fee. Another is Yakouba (known locally as 'Le Pygmé) who is the son of the headman of Djiguibombo (CFA 15,000 for four days including his own food and transport). Others who have been recommended are Ogotemelon Dolo or his younger brother, Amatigue, who you will find in Dini village close to Bandiagara.

Don't take this as an exhaustive list of possibilities. There are plenty of other friendly and fair people who will do their best for you.

If you're not taking food and going to be relying on local people providing meals then be prepared for a fairly bland diet – millet, sauce and rice for around CFA 200. Here and there you may be able to persuade someone to cook up chicken (around CFA 500). Millet beer (konyo) is available in most places.

Accommodation in the villages is usually on the roof of someone's house. A typical charge for this would be CFA 500 per night.

Avoid wading or swimming in rivers or pools of water in this area during the rainy season as Guinea worm is common and it's a painful affliction. Purify all water which you draw from village wells.

While Dogon goatskin bags are very attractive, they'll cost more in the villages than in Mopti itself because too many well-heeled tourists have been through already and local people are not prepared to haggle. About CFA 1500 would be average.

BANDIAGARA

The most popular place to stay is the Bar Kansaye (also known as Le Conseil) which is on the riverbank on the right hand side before you cross the bridge. This place is owned by Mamadou Kansaye and offers beds with clean sheets for CFA 1000 per person. It's a good place to arrange a guide to the Dogon and a popular place for travellers to meet in the evenings. Mamadou is very personable and the place is relaxing. If it's full try Le Campement across the other side of the

river which has beds for CFA 1500 plus more expensive single and double rooms. Eat at La Faida, a small but good restaurant not far from the mosque. It's owned by Yalema Dara.

Market day in Bandiagara is Monday.

BANKASS

The most popular place to stay is Ben's Bar (sometimes known as Le Campement) which is basic but very friendly and baggage left in Ben's care is safe. A mat on the floor costs CFA 1000. It's a good place to find a guide to the Dogon. You can cook your own food if you have the facilities. If it's full there is the Bar Mali which costs CFA 1500 per person. Food and drink are available and the owner is very helpful. It's also a good place to arrange a guide.

The market in Bankass is on Monday and it's good for buying blue Dogon cloth. Although it's a Dogon village, many Tuareg also come here to trade.

MOPTI

Mopti is at least as picturesque as Djenné and Timbuktu and it's certainly as lively. The market in Mopti is definitely worth visiting if you're looking for crafts (beautiful carpets, beads, silver jewellery, etc). Also don't pass up what local Tuaregs offer you individually. Similar things for sale in the Dogon area are often more expensive because too many well-heeled tourists have been through and the people are unwilling to haggle. You can hire dugout canoes in Mopti with a poler/guide for around CFA 1500 to visit nearby fishing villages and Tuareg camps.

Banking hours are 8 to 11 am. Commission on travellers' cheques is CFA 500.

Places to Stay

The Hotel Bar Mali in the old part of town has been popular for many years, but opinions about it vary widely. It certainly goes through good times and bad times and is definitely a whorehouse. Perhaps some people expect too much of a cheap

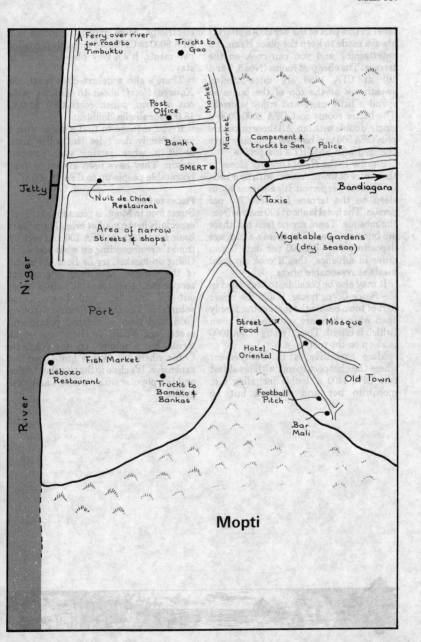

Ferry over river for road to Timbuktu

Trucks to Gao

Post Office

Market

Bank

Market

SMERT

Campement & trucks to San

Police

Jetty

Nuit de Chine Restaurant

Area of narrow streets & shops

Taxis

Bandiagara

Vegetable Gardens (dry season)

Niger

Port

Street Food

Mosque

Hotel Oriental

Fish Market

Lebozo Restaurant

Trucks to Bamako & Bankas

Old Town

Football Pitch

River

Bar Mali

Mopti

hotel in this part of the world. An effort is always made to keep the place clean, it's entertaining and you can cook on the terrace. The cheapest rooms (Nos 8, 9 and 10) at CFA 1750 are mice-infested sweatboxes at the top of the house so spend a little more and enjoy yourself. The better rooms cost CFA 2000/3000 a single/double with fan. All these prices are plus CFA 500 tax, however, this may have changed with SMERT's low profile.

Similar is the *Hotel Oriental* closer to the centre of town. A room with four beds is CFA 1750 per person. It's also possible to sleep on the terrace for CFA 750 per person. The hotel is about 100 metres from the mosque. There are no fans but there are bucket showers and there's a baggage depository for CFA 500 per day. If you order in advance, they'll cook up good meals at reasonable prices.

It may also be possible, to find a bed in the *Peace Corps* house. It's in the newer part of town beside the market but is only open when there are volunteers in town (which is often). They'll charge CFA 1000 to sleep on the roof.

More expensive is *Le Campement* where the cheapest rooms with breakfast cost CFA 4400 a double including fan, mosquito net and showers but no electricity. More expensive rooms cost CFA 8000 to CFA 9300 a double including two meals. It's a very pleasant place to stay.

There's also a deluxe-class hotel, the *Kanaga Hotel*, about 15 minutes' walk out of town, which costs CFA 12,000/18,000 for singles/doubles.

If you manage to find a room with a local family don't let the police know about it when getting your passport stamp. They have been known to 'fine' hospitable people up to CFA 18,000.

Places to Eat

Street food in Mopti is generally excellent, especially in the market area. The price of basic food starts at CFA 100 and goes up from there depending on what you want. Going up-market, try *Le Bozo* at the end of the harbour. The food is good but service can be very slow. It's also a hangout for travellers and Peace Corps volunteers. The *Douma Restaurant* offers good food such as mashed potato and sauce, egg salad, omelette and steak meals. For a splurge, try the *Nuits de Chine* where the food is quite good but expensive. It's close to the river boat office and is a popular with travellers and local guides.

Mauritania

Much of Mauritania forms part of the Sahara desert – a region of shifting sand dunes, rugged mountain plateaus and rocky outcrops. Only in the oases and along a narrow strip bordering the Senegal River can food crops be grown. The country exists almost entirely on the export of iron ore from the deposits around Zouerate, which until recently, provided some 80% of the country's income. Unfortunately, the high-grade ores are nearly worked out and although new mines have been opened at El Rhein Guelb, the ore there is of low-grade quality. Recently, an enrichment plant was built that cost US$90 million.

An attempt has been made to diversify mining and industry but the options are very limited. A copper mine was opened north of Nouakchott and the fishing industry had a shot in the arm after an agreement was reached with Lisbon for trawling the coastal waters. All the same, Mauritania will remain dependent on outside aid – particularly from the Arab world – for the foreseeable future. Mauritania produces only some 7% to 8% of its own food needs.

Mauritania may be dry and inhospitable these days, but once one of the most lucrative of the trans-Saharan trade routes from West Africa to the Mahgreb ran through it. So rich were the pickings in gold, slaves and salt along this route that the Almoravide dynasty in Morocco sought to control the trade. In 1076 they defeated the empire of Ghana, which held sway over what is today Senegal and parts of Guinea and Mali. The Almoravide commanders who had taken part in the campaign quickly asserted their independence from Morocco. Their descendents ruled over this area until defeated by the Arabs in 1674. The conquest resulted in a rigid caste system which has survived largely intact to the present.

Incredibly, it was only in July 1980 that slavery was officially abolished in this country, and even then it depended on compensation for the former owners! Nevertheless, it's thought that slavery still continues in remote areas of the country. The freeing of the slaves also complicated the problem of land tenure reform. The government was constrained to announce that ex-slaves were not automatically entitled to the land on which they lived. Part of the reason for this was that the nomadic Berbers who formally owned the slaves have been forced by drought to settle down. By doing so, they have placed themselves in competition for land with the established peasants.

Very little interest in Mauritania was shown by the European nations until the 19th century, when France took over the area. Even then Mauritania was little more than an administrative appendage of Senegal, and it wasn't until 1934 that sporadic resistance to French rule came to an end. Self-government of a sort was granted in 1957 under the Loi cadre, and independence in 1960 under the presidency of Mokhtar Ould Daddah. Nevertheless, the French continued their stranglehold over the economy. In fact, one reason why they granted independence was to prevent the country's absorption by Morocco, which maintained a historical claim to the area and refused to recognise Mauritania until 1969.

In the early years of Mokhtar Ould Daddah's regime, opposition first came

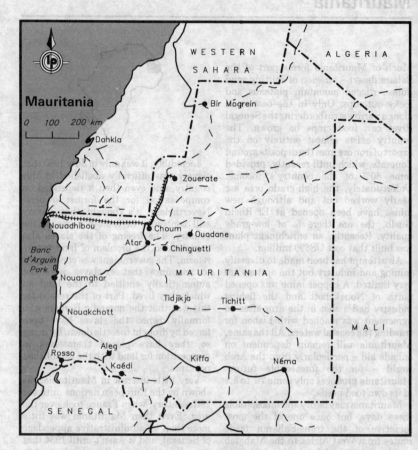

Mauritania

0   100   200 km

WESTERN SAHARA

ALGERIA

• Bir Mogrein

• Dahkla

• Zouerate

Nouadhibou
• Choum
• Ouadane
Banc d'Arguin Park
• Atar
• Chinguetti

MAURITANIA

• Nouamghar

• Tidjikja
• Tichitt

• Nouakchott

MALI

• Aleg
Rosso •
• Kaédi
• Kiffa
• Néma

SENEGAL

from the black people of the south who resented his decision to make Arabic, along with French, an official language. The next challenge came from the trade unions who objected to the racial inequality in the mining community at Zouerate (the 3000 expatriates there earned a staggering two-thirds of the country's entire wage bill). Ould Daddah survived that challenge by nationalising the mines in 1974 and withdrawing from the Franc Zone. The event which led to his overthrow was the signing of the tripartite agreement between Spain, Morocco and Mauritania. This resulted in the partition of what was the Spanish Sahara between Morocco and Mauritania, against the wishes of the people of that colony. The Mauritanians took the largely worthless southern third of the colony while the Moroccans took the centre and phosphate-rich north.

Both countries immediately found themselves fighting a vicious war with the guerrillas of the Saouarhi Polisario Front who were supported by Algeria, Libya and Cuba. Mauritania was totally incapable both militarily and economically of fighting such a war. Its weak spot was the railway line between the iron mines of Zouerate and the port of Nouadhibou, and the guerrillas knew it. They repeatedly sabotaged the track and also conducted daring bombing raids on the capital of Nouakchott. Though Ould Daddah attempted to reinforce the Mauritanian army of 1800 men with a further 17,000 (at enormous cost), they proved to be no match for the guerrillas. Even with Moroccan troop reinforcements and French air-power, he was still unable to contain the guerrillas and in 1978 he was overthrown in an army coup.

The new regime dithered for over a year about how to extricate Mauritania from the war. Eventually, however, renewed guerrilla attacks and demonstrations by the black population of the south against the increasing Arab influence, forced the regime to renounce all territorial claims to the Western Sahara. The guerrillas have now ceased attacking Mauritanian targets, but Morocco has annexed the whole of the Western Sahara, and the war continues.

In order to curry Arab favour, the new regime, headed by Haidallah, threw in its vocal support for Polisario and this quickly led to a break in diplomatic relations with Morocco (restored in early 1985). Support for the guerrilla movement certainly had its benefits, such as increased aid on very generous terms from Algeria, but it didn't prevent the economy from continuing to deteriorate.

With the country slipping further and further into unsustainable debt, Haidallah, who had refused to devalue the currency on World Bank advice, was overthrown in December 1984 by Colonel Maaouya Sid'Ahmed Ould Taya. Within two months of the coup, the currency was devalued by 16% and food prices rose by 25%. The measures were greeted with satisfaction by Mauritania's creditors and the national debt rescheduled.

As a result of the war between Morocco and Polisario, the trans-Saharan route (Route du Mauritanie) from Algeria to Senegal via Mauritania has been a no-go area for travellers for many years and remains so. The only way to get to Mauritania is either from the Canary Islands, Mali or Senegal. Most possible routes into Mauritania, except from Senegal, are both rough and inconvenient. As a result very few travellers go there these days.

Facts

GEOGRAPHY & CLIMATE

Mauritania is a harsh land of largely untouched desert, sandstorms, overwhelming poverty, lack of resources and ethnic conflict between 'white' Moors, 'black' Moors and black Africans. It's a very traditional and strictly Muslim society with an atmosphere of timelessness about it. Travelling around is difficult at the best of times and Muslim rules of dress should be observed always. Some indication of how difficult life is in Mauritania can be gleaned from the fact that it has the highest Peace Corps drop-out rate of any country in the world.

PEOPLE

The population stands at about two million of whom some 26% are urban dwellers. Islam is the main religion.

VISAS

Visas are required by all except nationals of France.

There are very few Mauritanian embassies around the world, the nearest are in Algiers, Dakar, Paris, Rabat and Madrid. There is also a vice-consulate in Las Palmas (Canary Islands) at 'Pecheurs Mauritaines'. It's in a poorly marked office in Calle Raffael Cabrera. Visas take a long time to come through here as your passport has to be sent to Madrid. In Paris (the embassy is at Rue de Cherche Midi 89, 75006 Paris) they cost FFr 56, require two photos and are issued while you wait. You must put your application in between 9 am and 12 noon and collect your visa in the afternoon of the following day between 2.30 and 5 pm. Yellow fever vaccination certificates are demanded. The embassy is closed on Fridays.

In Dakar visas cost CFA 3500, require two photos, a letter of recommendation from your embassy and take 24 to 36 hours to issue.

There are heavy searches at the border. There is no UK embassy in Nouakchott. If you are British and have problems, the US Embassy may help.

MONEY

US$1 = UM 74

The unit of currency is the ouguiya = 5 khoums. The import or export of local currency is prohibited. The ouguiya is pegged to the CFA system on the basis of UM 1 = CFA 5 and UM 10 = FFr 1. Currency declaration forms are issued on arrival and the authorities are very strict about them. It's rare you will be searched and officials are usually very friendly, but that doesn't mean they're lax.

The only place where a black market exists is at Rosso.

If you're arriving from Senegal, there is a bank at Rosso on the Mauritanian side of the border where you can buy ouguiya. It's closed between 12.30 and 3 pm. Banks are closed on Thursdays and Fridays.

Airport departure tax for domestic flights is UM 70. For international flights to African countries it is UM 220. Elsewhere the tax is UM 560.

LANGUAGE

French and Arabic are the official languages. The Moors speak an Arabic dialect known as Hassaniya, whereas the Black peoples of the south speak Pulaar, Soninke and Wolof.

Getting There & Around

AIR

There are two flights daily between Nouakchott and Nouadhibou.

ROAD

Ever since Spain handed over the Western Sahara to Mauritania and Morocco and the guerrilla war began with the Polisario Front, the most westerly trans-Saharan route – the Route du Mauritanie from Algeria to Senegal – has been out of service. The only way of getting into Mauritania now is from Senegal or by ship from the Canary Islands. The prospects for change are not good either as the guerrilla war against Moroccan occupation continues and there are frequent hot-pursuit raids by Moroccan armed forces into Mauritanian territory.

There are only two roads as such in Mauritania: Nouadhibou to Rosso (Senegal border) via Nouakchott, and the Route du Mauritanie from Nouakchott to Tindouf (Algeria) via Atar, Choum, F'Dérik and Bir Moghrein. The former is surfaced all the way. The latter is surfaced only between Nouakchott and Akjoujt. The road between Nouakchott and Nouadhibou is diabolical and most people go via Choum. There are small, very overcrowded buses on some routes but it's better to pay the extra and go by taxi.

Rosso to Nouakchott

By taxi this will cost UM 450 to UM 500 plus UM 150 for a backpack, and takes about 2½ hours. A bus or pick-up truck costs UM 260 to UM 350 plus UM 50 for a backpack and takes about three times as long.

Nouakchott to Choum via Atar

This costs UM 1200 in an open truck or UM 2000 by shared taxi and takes about 12 hours. The taxis leave when full, but they usually coordinate departures with the arrival of trains in the opposite direction.

TRAIN

There is one railway line which runs between Nouadhibou and Zouerate, where the iron ore mines are located. The trains which travel along this route are among the longest in the world – often three km long! As you might expect, they consist of open-topped ore bogies which make no concessions to comfort and are slow and very dusty. Until very recently it was possible to travel free on this train by simply hopping on top of an ore wagon. It was a bone-shattering experience while you and everything you owned would end up caked in ore. It may still be possible to travel free but the Société Nationale Industrielle et Minière, which owns the railway, decided to clamp down on free travel in 1986. They now attach a passenger coach to one of the daily trains and you're officially obliged to travel in that.

Despite this change of policy, some travellers still travel free by speaking to the engine driver and getting a ride in the cab with him. If you don't get a free ride or jump on one of the ore bogies then the fare from Nouadhibou to Zouératé costs UM 650. The trains depart Nouadhibou daily from the Pointe Central outside of town at 2 and 5 pm. The journey takes about 10 hours. Trains depart in the opposite direction at about the same times.

TO/FROM CANARY ISLANDS

Two boats ply regularly between Las Palmas and Nouadhibou but you need to make enquiries locally to find out the schedule.

All the flights from Las Palmas to Nouadhibou and Nouakchott are fully booked weeks in advance but there's a good chance of getting a seat if you get listed as standby and hang around at the airport. There are four flights weekly.

TO/FROM MALI

There are two possible routes between Mauritania and Mali. The first is between Ayoûn al Atroûs and Nioro and the second is between Néma and Nara further east. The road between Nouakchott and Nema is sealed as far as Ayoûn al Atroûs.

Fares on road transport are determined by frequency of use rather than distance (the less competition, the dearer they are), and expect to pay for your baggage. A shared taxi from Nouakchott to Néma should cost UM 1500. Find out what the local people are paying before you hand over the fare. Don't forget to clear immigration in Néma before leaving for Mali otherwise you'll be sent back.

The route between Ayoûn al Atroûs and Nioro is much more difficult and transport is very hard to find.

TO/FROM SENEGAL

The usual route is between Nouakchott and Dakar via Rosso.

Make sure you have a Senegalese visa (where required) before attempting to cross the border. You cannot enter Senegal otherwise. There is no Senegalese embassy in Nouakchott. One traveller who needed a visa but didn't have one was refused entry even after the French Embassy in Nouakchott had telexed Dakar for a visa. Get rid of all excess ouguiya before you leave Mauritania as no other country will exchange it, but keep UM 15 for the ferry across the Senegal River at Rosso.

Around the Country

If you do go to all the time and expense of coming to Mauritania, don't hang around in Nouakchott but head out into the more remote parts of the country which are far more interesting.

Near Atar is **Azougi**, a pleasant oasis and once a stronghold of the Almoravides. Also close by is **Chinguetti**, Islam's 7th holiest city. It's a classic oasis surrounded on three sides by sand dunes and there are a number of interesting old buildings, a fort, and a mosque said to be 1000 years old. A place to sleep can probably be found in exchange for medicine or old clothes. The route from Atar across the mountains is dramatic with a number of hair-raising switchbacks, which are too tight for vehicles to negotiate in one turn.

Further south, to the north of Néma, is **Oualata** which was once as famous throughout the Sahara as Timbuktu. There are quite a few archaeological sites and many houses decorated with designs in relief and lacy white patterns. Try to get into the Prefect's house with its much photographed courtyard. Transport is difficult from Néma, but not impossible if you are persistent.

NOUADHIBOU

There are some beautiful deserted **beaches** to explore in this region on both sides of the peninsula. It's sometimes worth a visit to **Port Mineralier**, 15 km from Nouadhibou, where the ore is loaded onto ships. You may meet bored crew members from European cargo ships who will take you back to their ship for a weekend of inebriation and high living. They may even offer you a lift further south or back to Europe.

There are two hotels in Nouadhibou, but they're very expensive at around US$40 per night. The *Hotel Sabah* (tel 2377), for instance, offers rooms for UM 2160. Meals cost UM 580. The *Mission Catholique* is small and not geared to catering for travellers but they may offer you accommodation. Anyway, travellers are such a rare breed here that if you hang around in a café or shop and keep a smile on your face, it's more than likely a local person will take an interest in you and offer you somewhere to stay.

For a quiet drink and something to eat, try the *Cabanou* about 12 km from Nouadhibou beyond the airport.

NOUAKCHOTT

Nouakchott is the capital of Mauritania. There's very little of note to see but the **mosques** are worth visiting. The one constructed by the Saudi Arabians is stunning. In the Zone Industrielle du Ksar is the **National Carpet office** where you can see some of Mauritania's famous carpets being made – and buy them if you are feeling flush.

The airport is about two km from town.

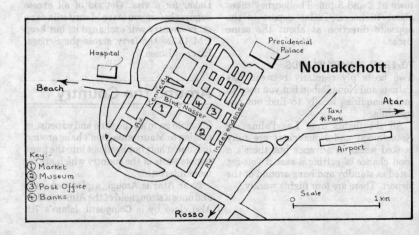

Nouakchott

Key:-
① Market
② Museum
③ Post Office
④ Banks

Places to Stay & Eat

The Mission Catholique will not accommodate travellers so forget it. The cheapest place to stay is the *Hotel Adrar* which costs UM 800 a double including breakfast. The manager is unfriendly but it's clean and relatively quiet. A little more expensive is the *Hotel Fouta*, a long way from the centre of town, which costs UM 1200 a double with air-con.

More expensive still are the *Hotel Park* and the *Hotel El Amane* which both charge UM 2500/3000 a single/double with bathroom.

There are many restaurants along the Ave Nasser where you can buy a simple meal at a reasonable price. For a splurge, try the *Restaurant Sindibad* opposite the market.

There's an *American Club* that serves the only cold beer in town, but it's members only. Hang around and wait for a member to invite you in.

Mauritius

Though visited by Malay and Arab mariners before the arrival of the Europeans, Mauritius remained uninhabited until the end of the 16th century. The first Europeans to call there were the Portuguese under the command of Pedro Mascarenhas, after whom the island group is named. The Portuguese laid no claim to the island and it wasn't settled until the Dutch landed a party there in 1598. The island subsequently became an important port of call for Dutch, French and English trading ships. It was from here that the Dutch captain, Tasman, set off on the voyage which was to lead to the discovery of Australia.

The Dutch colonial period saw the introduction of sugar cane and slaves to harvest it, the decimation of the ebony forests and the extermination of the dodo and other indigenous birds. The Dutch settlement lasted until 1710, when it was abandoned.

Eleven years later the island was claimed by France and its name was changed to Île de France. The French imported large numbers of slaves from the African mainland and Madagascar, and set up extensive plantations for the cultivation of sugar, cotton, indigo, cloves, nutmeg and other spices. They also used Mauritius as a base from which to harass British merchant ships on their way to and from India as well as to mount invasions of Britain's Indian colonies.

It remained a thorn in Britain's side until 1810, when the French forces were defeated by a British naval squadron that launched its attack from the island of Rodrigues. At the end of the Napoleonic Wars the island was ceded to Britain, though under the terms of the treaty the French way of life – its religion, customs, language and laws were safeguarded.

Under British rule, life continued in much the same way until 1835 when, despite strident opposition from French *colons*, slavery was abolished. Most of the freed slaves left the plantations and settled in the coastal towns, resulting in a labour crisis. It was solved by importing indentured labourers from India, mostly from Bihar and the southern provinces. At the end of their contracts most of the Indian labourers chose to remain on the islands so that by 1860, out of a population of some 300,000, two-thirds were Indian.

The sugar plantations continued to thrive until competition from European grown sugar beet began to make large inroads on the market. The importance of Mauritius as a port of call further declined with the opening of the Suez Canal.

Political activity in the 19th century centred mainly around the struggle of the Franco-Mauritian plantation owners for more representation in the colonial government, and it wasn't until 1936 that the Labour Party was formed. Strikes and demonstrations by this party between 1937 and the end of WW II were repressed with much bloodshed.

Meanwhile, a group of Indo-Mauritian intellectuals, traders and planters had come together under the leadership of Dr Ramgoolam. They succeeded in getting a number of their members nominated to the Legislative Council, and in 1948, under the banner of 'defenders of Hindu interests', picked up most of the rural vote. By the next elections in 1953 they had succeeded in taking over leadership of the Labour Party and won a comfortable majority. The working class, however,

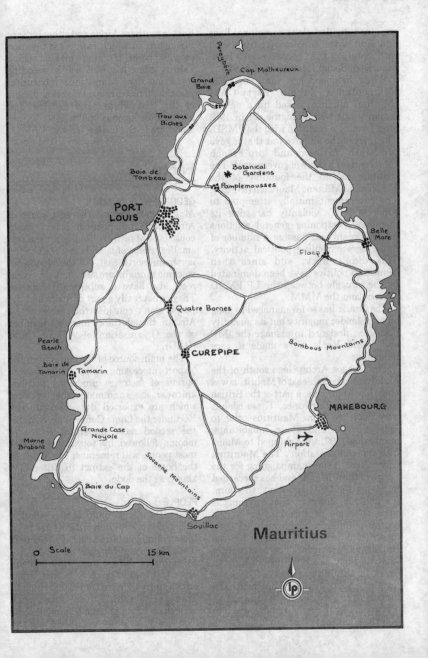

Mauritius

Peregrèbe

Cap Malheureux

Grand Baie

Trou aux Biches

Baie de Tombeau

Botanical Gardens

Pamplemousses

PORT LOUIS

Belle Mare

Flacq

Quatre Bornes

CUREPIPE

Pearle Beach

Baie de Tamarin

Tamarin

Bambous Mountains

MAHEBOURG

Grande Case Noyale

Airport

Marne Brabant

Savanne Mountains

Baie du Cap

Souillac

0 Scale 15 km

remained divided along communal lines and most of the Creoles were frightened into joining the conservative Parti Mauricien Social Démocrate (PMSD).

When independence came in 1968, Ramgoolam's Labour Party-CAM (Muslim) alliance picked up a narrow majority but was strengthened in 1969 after forming a coalition with the PMSD. The price of the alliance was that it gave pro-South African and pro-French conservatives a share of government. The coalition led to the founding of the Mouvement Militant Mauricien (MMM). The government initially attempted to suppress it by violently harassing its members, postponing general elections for four years and passing a number of harsh laws curtailing political activity. This didn't work, and since then Mauritian politics have been dominated by the struggle between the LP-PMSD alliance and the MMM.

The former has so far managed to hang on to a slender majority but its austerity measures, designed to assuage the IMF and World Bank, have made it very unpopular.

The Chagos Archipelago south of the Maldives and north-east of Mauritius was once, like Mauritius, a part of the British Indian Ocean Territories. These islands were detached from Mauritius prior to independence and their inhabitants, numbering 1200, were shipped to Mauritius for 'compensation'. The Mauritian government is now campaigning for the return of those islands and has succeeded in having the OAU endorse their claim. It's unlikely, however, that anything is going to come of this in view of the enormous military base which has been constructed on Diego Garcia by the British and Americans. This is to counter what they say is a build up by Russian forces in the Indian Ocean. The issue remains a hot political one into which the Indian government has been drawn.

It's unlikely that you'll find yourself in Mauritius unless you are flying between East or southern Africa and either India or Singapore, in which case it's a common stopover point. If you are making such a journey then it's well worth spending some time here. Mauritius is a beautiful island with picturesque villages and some of the best white sand beaches and aquamarine lagoons you're likely to find anywhere in the Indian Ocean.

Facts

GEOGRAPHY & CLIMATE

Almost 2000 km off the east coast of Africa, this independent island group consists of Mauritius, Rodrigues and two smaller groups of islands and reefs to the north and north-east. All the islands are volcanic in origin, are surrounded by coral reefs and have a subtropical climate. They're not really a part of Africa and the people don't consider themselves to be African, though the country is a member of the Organisation of African Unity (OAU).

The main source of income is from the 'export processing zone' which covers dozens of factories producing textiles, knitwear, shoes and many other products which are exported duty-free into the EC under the Lomé Convention. Sugar is the second most important source of income followed by tourism. Probably most people will remember Mauritius as the home of the extinct flightless bird known as the dodo.

PEOPLE

Most of the islands' multiracial population of just over one million is descended from Indian immigrants and contract labourers (both Hindu and Muslim).

Mauritius differs from almost every other third world country in that it has no peasantry living in traditional villages. There is absolutely no subsistence agriculture. People have to buy all their food except for a few vegetables and the occasional chicken or goat. Villagers work either as labourers on estates or for small producers, or as blue and white-collar workers in the towns. This is one reason why costs are high on the island.

VISAS

Visas are required by all except nationals of Commonwealth countries, EC countries, Finland, Israel, Japan, Norway, South Africa, Spain, Sweden, Turkey and the USA. If you don't need a visa, you get 30 days on arrival which can be extended up to six months. You must have an onward ticket to enter.

Other Visas

Madagascar The Madagascan Embassy (tel 6-5015/6) is on Ave Queen Mary, Floreal. This is the plush suburb of Curepipe. The Mauritian receptionist speaks English and is very helpful. Visas cost MRs 220, require four photos and are issued in 48 hours.

MONEY

US$1 = MRs 15.40

The unit of currency is the Mauritian rupee = 100 cents. The import of local currency is allowed up to MRs 700 and export up to MRs 350. Avoid changing cash at banks, as the exchange rates are poor. The rates for travellers' cheques are much better. There is no black market.

There is a 10% government tax on all hotel and restaurant bills. There is an 11% government tax on all airline tickets bought within the country. Airport departure tax is MRs 100 for international flights.

ACCOMMODATION

There are good camp grounds around the beaches if you have a tent, but the best deals are the self-catering apartments and bungalows near the beaches. These apartments are often cheaper than the *pensions de famille*, and radically so if you can get a group together to share a two-bedroom apartment. *Pensions de famille* cost MRs 45 to MRs 100 or over, depending on facilities and quality, the season and whether you're a tourist. There are a few cheap hotels, but they're mostly in the cities and not at the beaches. Hotels fill up quickly once a plane arrives, so don't waste time getting there. You can also camp anywhere on the island free of charge. If you do this in inland areas, you may be visited by curious local people, who more often than not will invite you to have a meal with them.

FESTIVALS

Check out *Le Mauricien*, the French daily, for announcements of fire-walking or *kavadee* ceremonies. These take place many times during the year though February and May are when the largest *kavadee* processions occur. Penitents skewer themselves through cheeks, tongue, arms and back, walk on nail shoes, drag carts on hooks fastened in their flesh as well as carrying heavy wooden frames festooned with images of deities. Visitors with cameras are always welcomed – no hassles.

In January or February there is the Hindu pilgrimage of Mahashivaratri at Grand Bassin in the south-centre of the island. The crater here (known as Ganga Talab) is believed to be connected to the River Ganges by an underground river! There are temples all around the lake, troops of monkeys and great views. Up to 300,000 people – a little under 30% of the entire population – make the pilgrimage.

LANGUAGE

English and French are the official languages, but many people don't speak English. About 80% to 90% of the people speak Creole (a French-Bantu-Malagasy mixture) which is, in effect, the lingua franca. Many of the Indo-Mauritians speak Bhojpuri (derived from Bihar), but they also speak Creole.

Getting There & Around

AIR

British Airways, Air France, Air India, Lufthansa, Air Malawi, South African Airways and Zambia Airways are among the airlines which call at Mauritius. Most allow a stopover without further charge.

If you're in Nairobi or Dar es Salaam, it's worth looking into the cost of airline tickets. There are quite a few airlines which fly to Mauritius via the Comoros, Madagascar and Réunion and you can stop off at all these places.

From Australia, the cheapest way to get to Mauritius is via Singapore.

La Plaisance International Airport is near Mahebourg in the south-east corner of the island. It is 43 km from the capital, Port Louis. There is a tourist office here, but travellers say it's useless. There is, however, a Chamber of Commerce & Industry 'accommodation desk', which is helpful and will book a hotel room, guesthouse or apartment anywhere on the island. You must pay a deposit of 20% of the first night's rent, but this is then deducted from your hotel bill. There is a bank at the airport which opens when flights arrive. Make sure you reconfirm your flight out of Mauritius.

A taxi to Mahebourg (about seven km) will cost MRs 60 (up to MRs 100 at night) but there are also public buses from the airport to Mahebourg (MRs 1.50) and Curepipe (MRs 4). Ask a police officer or a security guard where the buses stop (there's no sign). The conductors speak French and English and they won't charge you for luggage. Other people on the bus can be very helpful about telling you where to get off.

ROAD

Roads around the island are sealed and good. There's an excellent bus service to most places, though the last buses often leave at 7 pm or even earlier. The only drawback to the buses is that there are so many private bus lines. You may have to change buses several times to get from one place to another, but they're often more convenient than hitching. You may be charged extra for luggage.

From Mahebourg to Curepipe (via the airport) costs MRs 4 and takes one hour. From Curepipe to Port Louis costs MRs 3.50 and takes one hour. There are also express buses available which take 30 minutes and cost MRs 5. These buses run every 10 minutes or so. From Mahebourg to Port Louis you must change at Curepipe.

Taxis are very expensive unless you can find a group taxi (not always easy). Mahebourg to Port Louis, for instance, will cost MRs 250.

On the other hand, hiring a taxi to tour the island is cheaper than hiring a car. Ask for the Muslim banker at Péreybère who's a really pleasant and honest man. A full day tour costs around MRs 500 which is good value split between four or five of you.

BOAT

People from nearby Réunion often visit Mauritius and vice versa. They may help out with transport between the two places (with boats and light planes).

Around the Island

CUREPIPE

There's not a great deal to do in this sedate little town in the centre of Mauritius though the **central market building** is one of the weirdest structures on the island – like a 'tacky pipe organ' according to one traveller. The central bus stand is right in front of the market.

The **Trou au Cerfs**, an ancient crater close to Curepipe, is worth a visit for the fantastic views over the whole island. There are buses close by. Another place is the **Carela Bird Park** close to Tamarin Bay. Apart from the Mauritius pink pigeon, it has two Bengal tigers. A barbeque is available there for MRs 80. This entitles you to free entry to the park. Otherwise you pay MRs 30 on weekdays and MRs 20 at weekends.

The *Hotel Shanghai* in Curepipe offers rooms for MRs 185 a single including breakfast.

A good place to eat is the *Amigos Hotel* which offers excellent beef or chicken biryani. Avoid the *Taiwan Snack* which is horrendously overpriced compared to what you would get much cheaper at a snack bar anywhere else on the island. There's also a *Kentucky Fried Chicken*.

MAHEBOURG

Mahebourg was the capital of Mauritius in French colonial days and is a very attractive small town. It's also close to the airport.

It's worth visiting the **Historical Naval Museum** out on the highway towards the airport. The museum is housed in an old French-colonial 18th-century house and has displays of old ships' bells, cannons, charts and furniture. It's open daily from 9 am to 4 pm except on Tuesday, Friday and public holidays.

Places to Stay & Eat

If you're a woman travelling alone, the best place to stay is the *Pension Notre Dame* (tel 71 587), Souffleur St, which is run by nuns. It's very good, quiet, and provides breakfast, lunch or dinner. A refrigerator is available. One correspondent said, 'Soeur Anette is dynamite!' but didn't elaborate.

Also recommended is *Chez Jacqueline* (also known as Auberge Sea Fever) which is 200 metres south of the Monte Carlo and on the seashore. A room costs MRs 100 including breakfast.

The *Pension de Famille 'St Tropez'*, by the sea on the way to Blue Bay, is also worth considering. It's very friendly and costs MRs 100 a double plus they have incredible Creole food for MRs 50. Bicycles are for hire for MRs 50 per day. Outside Mahebourg there is the *Blue*

Lagoon Hotel (tel 71 529) at Blue Bay, which charges MRs 90/180 for singles/doubles with bathroom and breakfast. They also have one self-catering bungalow with two beds for MRs 150 (no breakfast). Meals at the hotel are quite expensive (MRs 50). There are buses to and from Blue Bay, only in the morning and afternoon.

Avoid the *Monte Carlo Bar & Restaurant*. They have rooms for MRs 150 but they're no larger than a cupboard.

If you're looking for some action or a drink and a meal, try *Chez Joe* (also known as Le Corailler). It's popular with local people and offers excellent curries (turtle, fish and chicken), with rice. They have egg dishes as well.

PORT LOUIS

Port Louis is the island nation's capital.

Information

The tourist office is in the new Registrar's building, William Newton St, but reports suggest it's not worth visiting. The Indian High Commission is on the 5th floor, Bank of Baroda Building, William Newton St near Royal Rd. Hours for visa applications are 9.30 am to 12.45 pm Monday to Friday. Visas take two to three days, cost MRs 57 and require three photos.

There are two bus stations in Port Louis, one for buses going north to the beaches (Immigration Square Bus Station) and another for the southern routes (Victoria Square Bus Station). They are about 10 blocks apart. There are buses to Tombeau Bay from Port Louis for MRs 1.25.

Things to See

The **Natural History Museum** is recommended, if only to see the exhibits of the extinct dodo. Entry is free. It's open Monday, Tuesday, Wednesday and Friday from 9 am to 4 pm and on Saturday from 9 am to noon.

Other interesting places to visit are the **French Government House**, built in 1738;

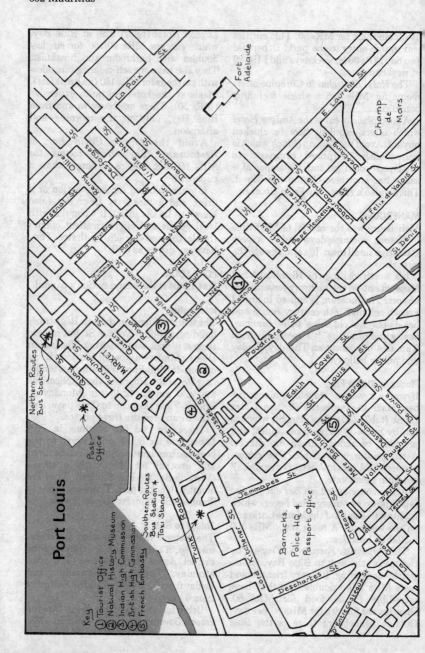

Port Louis

Key:
① Tourist Office
② Natural History Museum
③ Indian High Commission
④ British High Commission
⑤ French Embassy

Northern Routes Bus Station

Post Office

Southern Routes Bus Station
Taxi Stand

Barracks, Police HQ
Passport Office

Fort Adelaide

Champ de Mars

the **Jummah Mosque** on Royal St; **Fort Adelaide**, built in the reign of William IV; and the **Chinese Pagoda** on Volay Pougnet St in Chinatown.

A bus ride from town is **Pamplemousses Botanical Gardens**, a large, very old garden with ponds and cages full of 100-year-old tortoises. It's a beautiful spot to spend a morning or afternoon. Entry is free. The garden's headquarters is an old colonial house which used to be the governor's residence.

Places to Stay

There are plenty of cheap hotels and pensions around the bus stations. One of the cheapest places in Port Louis is the *Hotel Président Tourist*, which is very friendly but there are no singles or reductions for single occupancy. *Le Grand Carnot* (tel 083054) also offers relatively cheap rooms with shower, toilet and breakfast. Others worth trying are the *Suntours City Hotel* for MRs 40/50 for singles/doubles including breakfast, and the *France Tourist Hotel* which has rooms for MRs 75/100 for singles/doubles including shower, fan and breakfast.

Avoid the *Tandoori Hotel* (tel 20 031), Victoria Square across from the southern routes bus station. It's a 'real dump' according to one traveller and charges MRs 165/235 for singles/doubles – 'fumes and noise free of charge'. It's also a good idea to avoid the *Ambassador Hotel* well overpriced at MRs 200 a double.

If you intend to stay for a week or so, it's better to look for a *pension de famille*. Highly recommended is the one run by Mme Jean Louis at 13 Ave des Capucines, Quatre Bornes. With a room you get a tin of Nescafé, excellent breakfasts and a hot meal on Sundays. The owner is an elderly woman who really enjoys the company of travellers. It's centrally located.

Places to Eat

Mauritian food is usually curry with rice or noodles, or curry with roti. Curries with many different spices are known as daube; those with fewer hot spices and more tomatoes are known as rougaille.

For local food at its cheapest, try the food stalls lined up on Poudriére St between the Natural History Museum and Company's Garden Park where you can sit and eat. They feature roti, fried rice or fried noodles with curries of octopus, fish, chicken and beef. There are also egg dishes, desserts and drinks.

Another very cheap place is *Les Copains*, a Chinese schlock gift house across from the Mauritius Institute Museum, which serves takeaway chicken, cheese, beef rolls and the like. Other cheap restaurants include: *Namaste*, on the corner of Farquhar and Louis Pasteur Sts (cheap curries and biryanis; *Barracks Snack Bar*, Route des Casernes near the Police HQ (friendly, good meals); *Lotus Snack Bar*, Mère Barthelemy St between Poudrière and Edith Cavell Sts (good noodles with meat and vegetables, fried rice, etc); *Teenage Snack*, Place Victoria (noisy but cheap noodles and soup); *Café Hong Kong*, Joseph Rivière St (no English or French spoken); and the *Ciel Bleu*, close to the Hong Kong (mainly a bar with a bored barlady but quite good food).

The *Resto Ravinale*, Bourbon St, is a pleasant place for a meal and the inner walls are lined with *ravinala* – the Madagascan traveller's palm. Also very pleasant is *La Paloma*, upstairs on Leoville l'Homme St between Bourbon and Corderie Sts. There are fans and a balcony overlooking the street. It's a first rate café and the octopus daube is a must! The *Snow White*, upstairs on Queen St, on the corner of William Newton St, is a popular lunch-time haunt with a pleasant atmosphere and balconies. The menu is basically Chinese. Similar is the *Shamrock Restaurant*.

Le Café de la Cité, Place du Cathédrale, offers more elaborate cuisine in a pleasant setting. Lunches include pork chops, steak, chips, curries and blood sausage (boudin).

The *Underground Restaurant & Snack*, Bourbon St between Leoville l'Homme and Remy Ollier Sts, was recommended in the past but the quality of the food has gone downhill. They still have a good sound system though.

For a splurge, try either *La Palmerie*, 7 Rue Sir Colicourt Antelme, run by Franco-Mauritians, or *La Flor Mauricienne*, Intendance St near the Parliament buildings. *La Palmeraie* offers dishes like green pepper sauce with rice and mushroom omelettes with French rock music and pink tablecloths. *La Flor Mauricienne* is definitely top end with wine, tablecloths and super-polite, bilingual waiters. The meals are delicious.

Just about everything in Port Louis closes between 5 and 6 pm except for some street vendors in the Chinese quarter. You can get a filling meal from these people at a reasonable price.

THE NORTHERN BEACHES

If beaches are what you're looking for, the best of them are on the north-western tip of the island.

Beware of the people who offer trips in glass-bottomed boats – they're rip-off merchants. If you want to go snorkelling buy gear in Port Louis – there's none for rent at Péreybère. The best snorkelling areas are off the private beaches. You can use these but be discreet.

Tombeau Bay

There are two relatively cheap places to stay. *Le Clapotis* (tel 37 724) has rooms with common bath for MRs 95/115 for singles/doubles including breakfast. At the *Hotel Capri* rooms cost MRs 90/130 for singles/doubles also with breakfast.

Péreybère

This is one of the best beaches. There is a bus service to Grand Baie and Port Louis every 15 minutes until 7 pm. The fare to Port Louis is MRs 4. After 7 pm you will have to hire a taxi and they're extortionate – MRs 100 from Port Louis.

Places to Stay & Eat For somewhere to stay try the *Etoile du Nord* (tel 038 303) just opposite the Péreybère public beach and close to the bus stop. It's managed by two very friendly Creole guys and offers small, self-catering apartments equipped with kitchen, fan, etc for MRs 150 a single or double. This is a fairly standard price for units at Péreybère but in the low season you can bargain down to MRs 125.

There are many other places in this same price range including *Sylvilla, Le Beryl, Rajoo, Sabina, Fred's* (Fred is a German married to a local), *La Côte d'Azur, Le Bénitier, Jolicoeur Guest House, Merry Cottage Pension, Ville de Joie* and *Samila Villa*.

More expensive are the *Péreybère Beach Apartments, Hibiscus Hotel* and *Hotel Charleroi*. The first offers self-catering flats for MRs 175 a double and the last has rooms with shower, toilet, air-con and breakfast for MRs 110/154 for singles/doubles.

Restaurants at Péreybère are, as you might expect, on the expensive side. The *Cafeteria Péreybère* has takeaway Chinese food but it's mainly a bar and sit-down restaurant. *Le Bénitier* on the main road has little atmosphere but the food isn't bad. *La Sainière* next door to Le Bénitier is similar. The *Café Péreybère*, also on the main road, is a Chinese restaurant but has a better atmosphere though it's not cheap. If you are self-catering then food is cheaper at Grand Baie (a bus there is MRs 1) or at the two shops about one km up the road towards the east. In Péreybère itself you can buy bread, jam, peanut butter, eggs and canned fish from *Stephen Boutique*.

Grand Baie

This is another popular beach with a wide choice of accommodation, but it's more touristy. Many yachts are anchored here. Camping is permitted.

For somewhere to eat, try *La Jonque* which has delicious venison steak. *Phil's Pub* is also good. It offers meals and beers and there's often live music. Avoid the

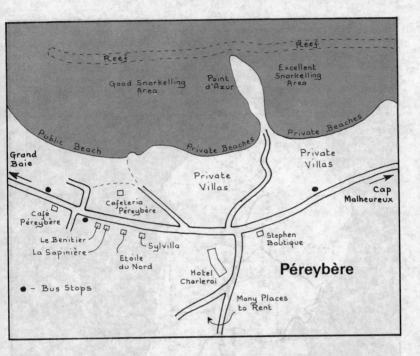

On the map:
Reef
Reef
Good Snorkelling Area
Point d'Azur
Excellent Snorkelling Area
Public Beach
Private Beaches
Private Beaches
Grand Baie
Private Villas
Private Villas
Cap Malheureux
Cafeteria Péreybère
Café Péreybère
Le Benitier
La Sapinière
Sylvilla
Etoile du Nord
Stephen Boutique
Péreybère
Hotel Charleroi
Many Places to Rent
● – Bus Stops

Sakura Japanese restaurant, which is very expensive indeed. Better for a splurge would be *Pearle Noire* which offers excellent food.

Trou aux Biches
The **Aquarium**, one km from Trou aux Biches on the road towards Pointe aux Piments, has eels, sharks, turtles, rays, octopi and tropical reef fish. It's open every day from 9 am to 4.30 pm. Entry costs MRs 27.50.

Rodrigues Island

This small (108 square km) volcanic island with a population of around 30,000, lies about 650 km east of Mauritius and is only 10 km long by five km wide. It's very rugged apart from some flattish ground in the south-west. The population is almost entirely of African or Malagasy descent and predominantly Roman Catholic.

Until recently the staple diet was maize. The most striking aspect of the agriculture is that the hillsides are extensively terraced – something unheard of in Mauritius. This, originally Asian, technique of farming was introduced by the Malagasy slaves who were brought here during the colonial era. Without it, erosion would probably render farming impossible.

The island has been a backwater for centuries and was almost completely ignored by Mauritius until independence. The first attempts to settle failed miserably, partly due to its isolation and partly to the unsuitable nature of the land for agricultural purposes. The first settlers were only able to survive by supplying passing ships with turtle meat and various other provisions.

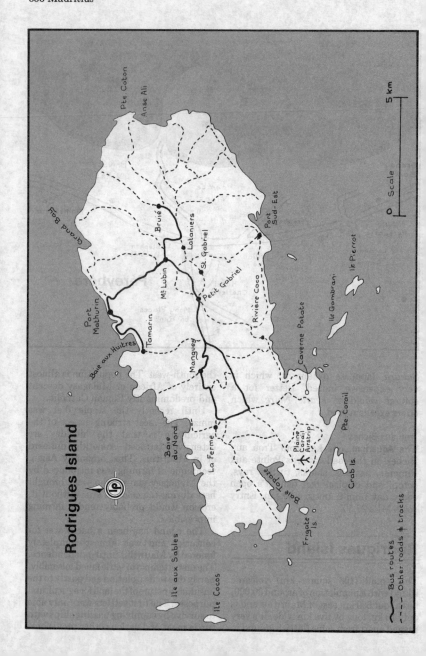

Rodrigues Island

Pte Coton
Anse Ali
Grand Baie
Brûle
Lotaniers
St. Gabriel
Petit Gabriel
Port Mathurin
Mt Lubin
Rivière Coco
Port Sud-Est
Tamarin
Baie aux Huîtres
Manguey
Caverne Patate
Île Pierrot
Île Gombrani
Baie du Nord
La Ferme
Pte Corail
Plaine Corail Airstrip
Baie Topaze
Crab Is.
Île aux Sables
Frégate Is.
Île Cocos

0   Scale   5 km

Bus routes
Other roads & tracks

When the turtles became scarce, the ships no longer called at the island, but by then the settlement was firmly established and a regular service to Mauritius introduced. The island is still very undeveloped. There's no radio or TV, and electricity and telephones are confined to Port Mathurin. Due to the lack of educational facilities, most skilled workers are Mauritians on contract. There is a lot of development going on – mostly financed by the EC and UN – some of it constructive but quite a bit of it short-sighted.

There are wind power and water management schemes under way which can only benefit the island. Electricity is a real problem, and Rodrigues is much drier than Mauritius and suffers regularly from devastating droughts – often followed by equally devastating cyclones. The road development scheme, however, seems hard to justify. There are very few vehicles on the island and this has resulted in agricultural workers being drawn into urban centres in search of paid employment. In turn this has led to a drop in agricultural production, land lying uncultivated and the need to import rice from Mauritius (that is, in turn, imported from elsewhere).

Rodrigues has two representatives in the Mauritian parliament. Although the Rodriguans cultivate a fiercely independent nature and there is a vague independence movement afoot, the island is highly dependent on Mauritius for almost everything.

GETTING THERE & AROUND
Air
If your time is short, Air Mauritius can whisk you to Rodrigues in two hours on one of their Twin Otters. There are five flights a week and the one-way fare is MRs 1538.

Road
There are three bus routes from Port Mathurin: to Baie aux Huitres, La Ferme and Grande Montagne (otherwise called Bruié). Since the island is so small,

nowhere is more than two or three hours' walk from a bus route. Walking is really the only way to see the island and meet the people who are unbelievably friendly and always ready to pass the time of day. Most tourists are rich, come from Réunion and travel in jeeps, so they're often quite startled to see a tourist on foot. Hitching is easy bearing in mind there are very few cars, though getting to the airstrip can be a problem. If arriving by air, someone will give you a lift to town but if you are leaving by air it can be more difficult. Enquire at the hospital, fire department, police department, Air Mauritius or the Relais Mont Venus Hotel. They all send vehicles to meet incoming flights. The island's administration also sends a vehicle if there's an official visitor arriving. Try these organisations in the order they are mentioned.

Boat
Until the construction of the airstrip in 1973, Rodrigues' only link with the outside world was the MV *Zambezia* which made the 36-hour trip from Port Louis every three weeks or so. The *Zambezia* has now been replaced by the slightly less antiquated MV *Mauritius* and this is the most interesting way of getting there. It usually leaves Port Louis on Saturdays and arrives at Rodrigues on Monday where it stays for five days. It leaves again on the following Saturday and arrives in Port Louis on Monday. You need to book well in advance (though you may get a place at the last minute). Write or call Rogers & Co (tel 086 801, ex 239), Rodrigues Service, President John Kennedy St, PO Box 60, Port Louis.

The fares are MRs 1260 (1st class), MRs 600 (2nd class) and MRs 350 (3rd class) return (one-way fares cost half). First class is worth the extra for colonial-style service, double cabins and reasonable food. Second class is in the hold, where it's hot and stuffy and packed full of people, mattresses, chickens, vegetables, bicycles, clothes, electrical goods, suitcases, you name it. Third class is on deck and is probably slightly better – so long as it doesn't rain. It's as crowded as 2nd class but not hot and stuffy and, if you are discreet, you can sleep on the 1st class deck. All fares include food but it's pretty basic in 2nd and 3rd classes. You can buy beer, soft drinks and duty-free cigarettes on board. The trip across – particularly the loading at Port Louis – is an experience to be remembered. And when the boat arrives at Port Mathurin, most of the population will be there to welcome it.

THINGS TO SEE

The **caves** in the south-west of the island (near the airstrip) are worth a visit but you have to get permission first (free) from the island's administration, or the police and you must have a guide (MRs 30).

The best beaches are at **Pointe Coton** and **Anse Ali** at the eastern tip of the island – golden sands, crystal-clear water and completely deserted. Take the bus to Grande Montagne (Buié) then walk.

There are two low-lying sandy islands off the west of Rodrigues **Île Cocos** and **Île de Sable** which are nature reserves. If you want to go, ask in Port Mathurin or one of the fishing villages.

PLACES TO STAY

There are four hotels on the island all in or near Port Mathurin. They're almost always full, so book in advance if you want to be sure of a room. The cheapest is the *Ciel d'Été* (tel 587), Jenner St, which is run by a Chinese family and costs MRs 90

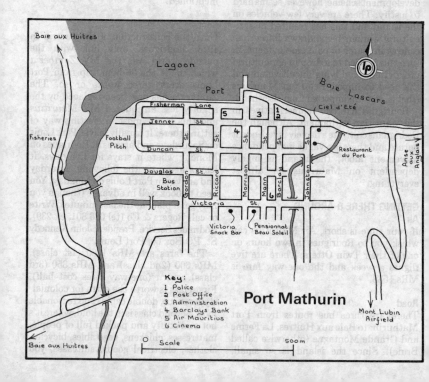

per room including breakfast. Similar are the *Pensionnat Beau Soleil* in Victoria St, and the *Pensionnat Les Filaos*, 10 minutes from town on the ocean front at Anse aux Anglais. They cost MRs 100/185 for singles/doubles including breakfast; half board costs MRs 125/250 for singles/doubles.

Going up in price, the *Relais Mont Venus Hotel* at Pointe Venus east of Port Mathurin costs MRs 260 per room with breakfast.

If you haven't booked a hotel or find them all full, ask around in Port Mathurin as there are people who occasionally take lodgers. Be quick about this if you arrive by boat. There will be 100 other people doing exactly the same thing. Campers can more or less please themselves.

Many thanks to Bob Newman (Australia) for providing information on Rodrigues.

Morocco

Morocco, unlike other North African countries, is still largely populated by the descendants of its original Berber settlers. The Berbers came to this area thousands of years ago and at one time controlled all of the land between Morocco and Egypt. Little is known about the origin of the early Berbers, other than that they occupied the Mahgreb in the New Stone Age period. (Rock carvings in the Saharan regions and a stone circle at Larache date from around this time.) However, there is some indication that Morocco was settled even earlier. Several fragments of fossilised human remains with the characteristics of Neanderthal man of Palaeolithic times have been found near Rabat, Casablanca and Tangier. There are no written records of these early people though, nor is there any evidence linking them with the original Berbers.

What we do know about the latter is that they were never united, except for brief periods when expediency dictated such an arrangement in the face of a threat from a common enemy. Even today, the various tribes in Morocco jealously guard their independence. Berber society is based on the clan and village. Each village is autonomous, ruled by a council of adult males. Sometimes villages will come together in a loose confederation to better administer something of mutual concern, but the autonomy of each village is always respected. This entrenched unwillingness to forfeit independence has muted the effects of various conquerors who have come and gone over the centuries, and has resulted in the preservation of one of Africa's most fascinating and colourful cultures through to the 20th century. It has understandably been a travellers' mecca for many years, though excessive tourism is beginning to spoil many of its unique features.

The Berbers' language is different from that of the Arabs, who began arriving here in the wake of the Muslim expansion after the death of the Prophet Mohammed. Arab horsemen failed to penetrate the Rif and Atlas mountains, and, as a result, these areas remain firmly Berber. A considerable amount of intermixing has gone on elsewhere, however. Examples of the art and buildings left by the many brilliant cultures and empires that have grown up in Morocco can still be seen today, ranging from the Roman city of Volubilis to the Muslim kingdoms, which had their capitals variously at Marrakesh, Fès, Meknès and Rabat.

The Berbers were first recorded in history as the merchants who traded with the Phoenician coastal cities by virtue of their control of the trans-Saharan gold and ivory trade. They were never much influenced by the urban culture of the Phoenicians, though they sometimes helped them fight the Romans if this paid in terms of trade. Likewise, when the Romans finally established themselves here, the Berbers were willing to trade with them (even fight for them if it paid), but they were unwilling to give up their independence. So, at best, Roman rule remained tenuous in this part of North Africa.

All the same, Roman rule ushered in a long period of peace and prosperity during which many cities were founded, and Berbers of the coastal plains became city dwellers. Christianity arrived in the 3rd century AD, and again the Berbers asserted their traditional dislike of centralised authority by taking advantage of doctrinal differences and adopting the heretical Donatist line like the Copts of Egypt.

The Roman Empire began to disintegrate in the 5th century with the arrival of the Vandals from Spain, but the end came slowly. The invaders were unable to graft themselves onto the urban culture and relaunch it under new management. Their principal effect was to disrupt the agriculture of the coastal plains and the trans-Saharan trade routes, which were not to recover until the arrival of Islam.

Islam burst onto the world in the 7th century when the Arab armies swept out of Arabia, taking Byzantine Egypt, then moving west to conquer the whole of the north African coast and eventually much of Spain. The Arabs' lightning success probably had as much to do with the chaos and provincialisation that followed the collapse of the Roman Empire, as it had to do with the attraction of the idea of a universal bond of humanity, in which all people, regardless of the circumstances of their birth, could, in theory, be members of a new and broad community based on equal dignity and worth. In this respect, the Arab conquest was markedly different from that of the Romans. While their success was dependent on delivering some of the goods, the reality was far from the utopia they promised. Once the initial flush of enthusiasm had subsided, the basic tribal divisions and animosities began to reappear. As with the Christians, there emerged doctrinal differences based on the interpretation of Mohammed's teaching, and disputes over where power should reside in the Islamic community. The basic schism between Sunnis and Shi'ites dates from this time.

The Berber tribes were not slow to see these schisms as a convenient way of expressing their independence, while at the same time remaining Muslim. They developed their own brand of Shi'ism, known as Kharijism. The Kharijite brotherhood was essentially a puritanical movement of the oases and distant plains, which denounced the decadent and easy-going tendencies of the cities. While it was rejected by Islam as a whole, it attracted many followers, especially around Sigilmasa - the great caravan centre in southern Morocco - and Tahert, in what is now Algeria. These Kharijite communities were able to carve out successful kingdoms during the 8th and 9th centuries in the western Mahgreb. One of them, the Idrissids, with their capital at Fès, was to sow the seed that would later germinate into the idea of a united Moroccan kingdom.

The Idrissids were led by Idriss ibu Abdullah (Idriss I), a descendant of Ali and Fatima, the daughter of the Prophet. The kingdom was later divided between the two sons of Idriss II, but in 921 AD the new states were destroyed. Fighting broke out among the numerous Berber tribes in a bid to take control of the area, a situation that was to continue until the 11th century. At this stage, a second Arab invasion took place. Much of North Africa was plundered and many tribes became nomadic.

Out of the chaos, another fundamentalist movement got under way among the Berbers of the plains of Mauritania and Morocco, and was enthusiastically supported by the peasants of the area. The Almoravides, as they became known, quickly overran Morocco and Muslim Andalusia. They then turned south to destroy the kingdom of Ghana in western Sudan, which had expanded to a point where it had succeeded in imposing tribute on Audaghost, the principal southern trading centre of the Berbers. The Almoravides went on to found Marrakesh and build a rich and prosperous empire over the western half of the Mahgreb. In doing so, however, they gradually lost the simple faith, military energy and cohesion of their desert days. A revolt among the tribes of the Moroccan Atlas Mountains led to their overthrow and replacement by another dynasty, the Almohades.

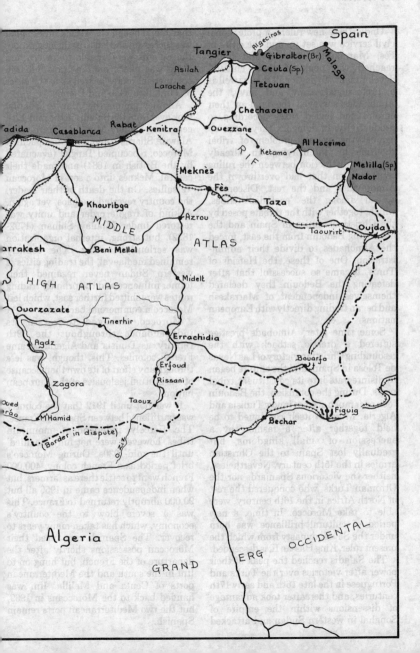

Under these new rulers, a professional civil service was set up and the cities of Fès, Marrakesh, Tlemcen and Rabat reached the peak of their cultural development. To pay for all this, as well as a professional army and navy, the Almohades surveyed the land of their empire and levied taxes according to productivity. In doing so, they came up against the age-old problem of tribal rivalries by intensifying an already apparent distinction between the ruling confederation that had overthrown the Almoravides and the rest. Discontent spread among the 'excluded' tribes, which, together with the threats posed by the Christian armies in Spain and the advancing Bedouin from the east, forced the Almohades to divide their administration. One of these, the Hafsids of Tunis, became so successful that after defeating the Bedouin they declared themselves independent of Marrakesh and began trading directly with European nations.

Some time later, Almohade prestige suffered a drastic setback with the resounding Christian victory of Las Nevas de Tolosa in Spain, and the empire began to disintegrate into its constituent tribal parts. During the confusion, the Bedouin took over much of what is now Tunisia and Algeria. Morocco itself continued to be held together after a fashion by a succession of small kingdoms, but gradually lost Spain to the Christian armies in the 15th century. Nevertheless, neither the victorious Spaniards nor the Ottoman Turks, who conquered the rest of North Africa in the 16th century, were able to take Morocco. In time, a new period of cultural brilliance was born under the Sa'adi dynasty from which the present ruler, King Hassan II, is descended.

The Sa'adis reached the peak of their power after victories over the Turks and Portuguese in the late 16th and early 17th centuries, and thereafter took advantage of dissensions within the empire of Songhai in western Sudan and attacked that too. Though the attack on Songhai was successful and led to its disintegration, the Sa'adis were unable to govern and there was chaos on the trans-Saharan commercial routes as well as in the cities of Timbuktu, Gao and Djenné.

Another group, the Alawite Sharifs, took over from the Sa'adis in the mid-17th century. Under Moulay Sharif, the Alawite Sharifs subjugated and pacified Morocco, reoccupied Tangier (evacuated by the British in 1684) and made their capital, Meknès, into a sort of Moroccan Versailles. On the death of their leader, the country reverted to chaos, yet again. A kind of fragile order and unity was restored under Moulay Shinan (1792-1822), but strong, internal organisation was seriously lacking. The country remained mediaeval, the trading cities of western Sudan never regained their former influence and the primary trading routes were shifted further east, which left Morocco a commercial backwater.

Morocco managed to retain its independence throughout the 19th century, as Tunisia and Algeria became French colonies. This, though, was less through any effort of its own than because of the mutual jealousies of the European nations.

It was not until 1912 that the country was partitioned between Spain and France. The fiercely independent mountain tribes, however, were not fully 'pacified' until the mid-1930s. During Morocco's brief period as a French colony, 400,000 French went to settle there as farmers, but when independence came in 1956 all but 90,000 abruptly returned to France. This was a severe blow to the country's economy, which has taken many years to recover. The Spanish renounced their Moroccan possessions shortly after the departure of the French, but hung on to Ifni in the south and the Mediterranean ports of Ceuta and Melilla. Ifni was handed back to the Moroccans in 1969, but the two Mediterranean ports remain Spanish.

King Hassan II, the present ruler, has been threatened with attempted coups several times, but seemingly remains a despotic ruler with the prerogatives of absolute monarchy. In the early years of his reign, political repression was the order of the day, with troops and police much in evidence along main roads and in towns. The former leader of the opposition party, Ben Barka, was abducted and murdered while living in exile in Paris in 1965, following his alleged complicity in the conspiracy against Hassan in 1963. Subsequent French investigations into his murder led to the issue of arrest warrants for several high-ranking members of Hassan's government, including the Minister of the Interior. This led to a temporary break in diplomatic relations with the French.

There has been much apparent liberalisation of the political structure in recent years, including elections, in which even the Moroccan Communist Party (banned until 1983) was allowed to put up candidates. But it remains a façade. The king retains the power to appoint and dismiss his prime minister and cabinet, to dissolve parliament, change the constitution and reject legislation. Frustration with the system has led to an upsurge in Islamic fundamentalism, which, to date, has been contained. It may, however, prove to be the monarchy's undoing, and it wouldn't be the first time this has happened in the history of Morocco.

Perhaps the greatest threat to Moroccan stability, however, is the seemingly endless war over Western Sahara, which is costing an estimated US$1 to US$2 million a day, not to mention the (undisclosed) amounts contributed by Saudi Arabia and the Gulf states. The conflict began in 1975 when Hassan, recalling Morocco's historical claims to the area, organised several hundred thousand men, women and children to walk over the border into what was the Spanish Sahara, in an attempt to force Spain to hand over the territory. There

was a great flurry of diplomatic activity and military posturing at the time, but in the end, Spain, unwilling to get embroiled in a colonial war, agreed to hand over the territory to Morocco and Mauritania for partition between the two.

The partition was much against the wishes of the indigenous Saouarhis, who wanted independence. The result was the start of a guerrilla war fought by the Saouarhi Polisario Front supported by Algeria, Libya and Cuba, against Mauritania and Morocco.

The Mauritanians were incapable of containing such a revolt and even less capable of withstanding the economic consequences of sabotage to their ore-extraction industry. It wasn't long before they withdrew, recognising the Saouarhis' right to independence. Their withdrawal was quickly followed by total Moroccan occupation of Western Sahara and a break in diplomatic relations with Mauritania (restored in 1983).

Morocco's occupation of Western Sahara is not recognised internationally, though the self-proclaimed Sharawi Arab Democratic Republic (Polisario's government in exile) is – by 62 countries. The decision by the Organisation for African Unity (OAU) to give them a seat at the 1984 summit led to Morocco's resignation from the organisation and brought Morocco and Algeria to the brink of war.

Meanwhile, Morocco has been strengthening its defences in Western Sahara by building an enormous sand wall from Dakhla to the Moroccan border – a distance of some 900 km. The wall certainly has curtailed many of Polisario's activities, but it has not stopped them. They were even able to weather the temporary drying-up of funds after Morocco and Libya announced they were to federate. The intended federation was undoubtedly one of Gaddafi's wildly optimistic ideas. It came to nothing – much to the relief of the United States.

While both Morocco and Polisario have indicated their willingness to hold a referendum, neither has agreed to the other's preconditions, and the conflict is far from resolved. The most significant development to date was the 1988 agreement between Morocco and Algeria to re-establish full diplomatic relations. This is going to put a lot of pressure on both Morocco and Polisario to resolve the conflict.

The war's main effects on travellers has been to put a large part of southern Morocco and the trans-Saharan Route du Mauritanie out of bounds. It has also complicated the border crossing procedure between Morocco and Algeria.

Facts

GEOGRAPHY & CLIMATE

Morocco is one of Africa's most geographically, socially and culturally diverse areas. Only in parts of East Africa and southern Africa is it possible to find a similar degree of diversity. The country is traversed by three distinct ranges of mountains, some of them the highest in Africa. From the north, they are the Rif, the High Atlas and the Anti-Atlas. Certain peaks of the High Atlas remain snow-capped year round. Between the ranges and the Atlantic Ocean are plateaus and plains, which are often fertile and well-watered by the melting snow. This is not always the case though. Agriculture on many of the plains further south is tenuous to say the least, except along river courses. In the extreme south, at the edge of the Anti-Atlas, the country is characterised by vast, eroded gorges, which, like the rivers that flow at their base, gradually peter out into the endless sand wastes of the Sahara Desert.

The climatic variations in a country like this are vast. Generally, in winter, the lowlands vary between pleasantly warm to hot during the day and cool to cold at night. In summer, it's very hot during the day and only less so at night. In the higher regions, winter demands clothing suitable for Arctic conditions. In summer, it's hot during the day and cool at night (depending on the altitude).

The principal crops are cereals, dates, olives, citrus fruits and grapes. There is also a good deal of market-garden vegetables – principally tomatoes. In the mountains, large flocks of goats and sheep are reared.

Morocco is the world's third largest producer and exporter of phosphate ore (used as fertiliser), bringing around 30% of its export earnings. There are other significant amounts of minerals, such as uranium, coal, zinc, manganese, cobalt and copper, which remain unexploited. The only oil/gas field being exploited is off the coast of Essaouira and its reserves are limited.

PEOPLE

The population stands at about 22 million, but at present growth levels it is expected to double by the end of the century. The majority of the people are Sunni Muslims.

WARNING

A lot of travellers leave Morocco with very negative feelings about the country – and we hear about it all the time in the feedback mail. These comments are typical of those who felt they were skinned alive:

Morocco was an amazing experience. I have never been hassled so much, treated so rudely and felt so threatened as I was there.
The place is a true nerve-wracking, high-pressure sales war zone.
Three rules: 1. Never accept an invitation into someone's house, or only enter with as much as you're willing to lose. 2. Never trust anything a young man tells you on the street and, if he's persistent, flag down a cab. 3. Never divulge where you are staying.

It would be fatuous and inaccurate to pretend that you will not come up against similar situations in Morocco. Without wishing to be frivolous: 'Been there, done that'. At times, I've come very close to punching someone out in Morocco because of their totally obnoxious, aggressive, insulting and insinuating behaviour. Nothing racist about this – it's just a fact, it happens. But I've found myself in far more life-threatening situations than what amounts to verbal abuse, in cities in England, the Philippines, India and the USA.

I've also come across the exact opposite in Morocco, where the hospitality was second to none, where no 'gift' or anything of that nature would have been accepted, and where insistence would have been regarded as an insult. I've also been pleasantly surprised by the degree of honesty that can be expected from most people.

If you haven't done much travelling, there are a few things you should understand. Morocco has been dragged screaming into the 20th century. Poverty is widespread. Educational opportunities are minimal: over half the population is illiterate. Unemployment is high and social security hand-outs nonexistent. Austerity is the name of the economic climate. Moroccan 'guest workers' in France and Germany have been the subject of racist attacks, both on a personal level and in the media of those countries. At the same time, millions of well-heeled tourists from Europe have flocked to Morocco for years throwing (for ordinary Moroccans) incredible amounts of money around, flouting traditional Islamic values of propriety and condescendingly treating people like they were a bunch of stupid peasants. The hippies, likewise, have assumed that here is a nation of stoned-out freaks just waiting for the impecunious hordes of Europe's and America's dropouts to bring them gems of wisdom about the 'revolution'. Not so.

Life is hard for most people. So when you get hassled and before you get angry or frustrated, just remember where you came from and ask yourself how many Moroccans you have come across sightseeing in your country, and why.

That doesn't mean you have to be wet-eyed about your dealings with hustlers. You certainly don't, or you'll be taken for an expensive ride. Be clear, up-front and definitive. They thrive on vagueness and hesitancy and, if that's what you display, they'll wrap you round their little finger. These people have a long history of barter and you have a very desirable commodity – money. They'll readily trade you dubious 'services' or trash for hard cash, or even desirable goods at outrageous prices. Wake up! You're not at home and normal rules do not apply.

VISAS

Citizens of West European countries, except Belgium, the Netherlands and Portugal, do not require visas. Citizens of Australia, Brazil, Canada, Chile, Japan, Mexico, New Zealand, Peru, Philippines, USA, Venezuela and most Arab countries do. Israelis and South Africans are not admitted.

Visas cost US\$3, or the equivalent, and are valid for a stay of up to 90 days with a maximum of two entries.

Moroccan immigration officials do not believe 'hippies' are an endangered species, but rather that this offal of western society is a moral pollutant that must be turned back before it sullies the soil of Morocco. A 'hippy' is any male with long hair, a preferably untidy beard, and/ or untidy or outlandish clothes. Females face no such discrimination. For males who fit the description, the rules are applied with a frustrating capriciousness. Some people get through, others don't. The ferry from Algeciras to Tangier is notorious for arbitrary refusals. The one from Algeciras to Ceuta doesn't have this problem as Ceuta is Spanish territory and the border with Morocco is usually easy-going. On the other hand, the Melilla border (Spain's other Moroccan enclave) is often staffed by officials whose main qualifications for the job appears to be obnoxiousness. If entering Morocco at this border, males should make sure they're wearing their Sunday best and that their razor was sharp that morning.

Visa extensions are free of charge, but you need a letter of recommendation from your embassy. In theory, they're obtainable from any regional capital. In practice, you'll be told to go to Rabat to get them. In Rabat you have to go to Sûreté National, Rue Soekarno. You can collect them the same day (at 6 pm) if you get there early.

If you intend to stay more than three months, you must make an application for this within 15 days of arrival. French and Spanish nationals are allowed an unlimited stay, so long as they report to the police within three months of arrival.

Travel south of Tan Tan into Western Sahara is prohibited without a special permit, obtainable from the military authorities. Depending on the state of the war in that disputed part of Morocco, you may be able to get a permit. If you do, it will usually allow you to travel south as far as Layoune and even Dakhla. The war usually affects only the border area with Algeria, so it's safe to travel if you get the permit.

Other Visas

There are embassies for CAR, Egypt, Equatorial Guinea, Gabon, Guinea, Ivory Coast, Libya, Mauritania, Nigeria, Senegal, Sudan, Tunisia and Zaïre in Rabat.

Algeria There are Algerian consulates in Rabat (tel 24215, 24287), 8 Rue d'Azrou, just off Ave du Fas; Oujda (tel 3740/1), Blvd Bir Anzarane; and Casablanca, 159 Blvd Moulay Idriss. The consulate in Rabat shares a building with the United Arab Emirates Embassy and is open Monday to Friday from 8.30 am to 12 noon. Visas cost Dr 50, require four photos and can be issued the same day if your application does not have to be referred to Algiers.

If you have a West German passport *do not* apply for your visa in Morocco. You will be refused. I even met a West German man married to an Algerian who was refused a visa in Rabat. Get your visa in Bonn before leaving. Much the same applies to Dutch nationals, who will be made to wait up to six weeks for a visa (though they do come through in the end as a rule).

Egypt Visas cost Dr 170 with two photos, and are issued in 24 hours. There's no fuss or request to show money. The embassy is at 31 Charia Al Jazair (formerly called Ave d'Alger) on Place Abraham Lincoln, Rabat.

Mauritania These cost Dr 50 and are issued while you wait. The embassy is at 6 Rue Thami Lam Souissi, Rabat.

Niger There is no Niger embassy in Rabat and the French Consulate cannot issue visas – you'll have to get it in Algiers or Tamanrasset.

Spain Visas cost Dr 60 with three photos and are issued on the spot.

Tunisia Visas are issued free on the spot.

MONEY

US$ 1 = Dr 7.97 (official rate)
UK£ 1 = Dr 14.05
DM 1 = Dr 3.78
FFr 1 = Dr 1.24

The unit of currency is the dirham = 100 centimes. The import and export of local currency is prohibited. There's no black market as such, though you will occasionally be made an offer. If you are, it will only be a few cents above the bank rate. If it's any more than that, you are being set up for a rip-off.

Banks do not usually charge commission on travellers' cheques, though the Banque Populaire may take Dr 5 in some places (eg Azrou, Errachidia).

If you are going to Algeria it is worth

buying Algerian dinars in Ceuta, Melilla or Oujda before you go. In Oujda the going rate is US$1 equals AD 23. Even dirhams hold their value well – you should be able to get AD 1 for Dr 2. It is illegal to import Algerian dinars into Algeria and the searches at the borders can be thorough – hide them well. There are plenty of moneychangers doing the rounds in Oujda and Melilla.

Stock up on petrol in Ceuta or Melilla if you have your own vehicle as they are both duty-free ports. Petrol will cost you more in Morocco.

ACCOMMODATION

You can camp anywhere in Morocco so long as you have the permission of the owner. There are a large number of official camp sites that vary in price, depending on the facilities provided. Tourist offices have details of their location. Also, there are a number of youth hostels (*auberges de jeunesse*) and, if you're travelling alone, they are among the cheapest places to stay. The charge is usually Dr 10 a night with a Youth Hostel card or Dr 12.50 without. If you buy a Youth Hostel card in Morocco it will cost Dr 35. Meals generally are not available at hostels and you have to pay extra for hot showers (cold showers are free). There are hostels at Asni, Asrou, Casablanca, Chechaouen, Fès, Ifrane, Marrakesh, Meknès, Mohammedia and Rabat. Where there is no youth hostel, there is usually a *centre de sportif/ jeunesse*, where basic accommodation can be found for a small charge. Sometimes it's just floor space, other times a bed.

Youth hostels are all very well if you don't mind dormitory accommodation and you're carrying no valuables, which could attract the attention of thieves. A cheap hotel will often not cost much more especially if two people are sharing. Only very rarely will you find a dirty room and dirty sheets, even in the cheapest hotels. The vast majority are remarkably clean and excellent value. The toilets and bathrooms also tend to be clean. Hot showers are the exception rather than the rule, and, if you want one, there's usually a small additional charge for it (most hot showers in cheap hotels are run off bottles of liquid propane gas). Baggage usually is safe left in rooms. I never had a single thing stolen and found the level of honesty to be very high (Tetouan hustlers notwithstanding). For those wanting more comfort than a budget hotel, there's usually plenty of choice, except in the very small places.

LANGUAGE

Moorish Arabic, French and Spanish are the main languages. English is also spoken in many places. Spanish is more common in the north and French in the south.

The Berbers must be among the world's most accomplished linguists. There is probably no other country in the world where you will come across so many people, even children, who can speak so many different languages passably. The motivation – unemployment amid hordes of well-heeled tourists – might be obvious but their skill can only be admired. Even food stall dish-washers can manage one or two sentences of passable Japanese, not to mention any European language. Most of the people in this category are, naturally, involved in the tourist trade and hang around the souks. It is extremely hard to shake them off. Every ruse in the book will be used to get you talking in your own language, from 'I'm just a student who wants to practise my English/German/ French', etc to 'Are you a racist?' if you refuse. Some can be abusive if refused, even when the ruse is paper-thin. But as you'll probably get lost on your first visit to the souk in any major town, you may as well employ one of these people as a guide. Agree on a price for their services before you set off.

Getting There & Around

For many travellers, Morocco will be their first taste of Africa. The cheapest way to get to Morocco from Europe is to take one of the ferries from Spain to Tangier, Ceuta or Melilla. On the other hand, it can cost more to travel through France and Spain, even if you are hitchhiking, than to fly direct from northern Europe.

AIR

Depending on the time of year, there may be some incredibly cheap charter flight tickets available to Morocco from London and northern European cities such as Amsterdam and Paris. They're always return tickets and generally must be paid for in advance, though some agents will sell you a one-way ticket a few days before the flight or even on the day itself if there are spare seats.

The same goes for flights to Madrid and Malaga. These charter tickets are often tied to a minimum number of nights at a specific hotel and, in theory, can't be bought without also paying for the accommodation. In practice, most agents will sell you the air ticket and give you a bogus voucher for the accommodation so it all looks normal in case you're questioned by officials. Naturally you can't use the bogus voucher. Even if you have to buy a return charter ticket, they're often so cheap you can afford to throw away the return half. A London/Agadir return charter ticket can cost as little as UK£40. Finding these tickets can involve a lot of leg and phone work and they get snapped up quickly. Trying to arrange them through provincial agents usually is a waste of time.

If your time is very limited and you want to see as much of Morocco as possible, it's worth considering the occasional internal flight offered by Royal Air Maroc. If you're 26 years of age or under, it works out particularly cheap as they offer 40% 'youth fare' discounts.

ROAD

Hitching

Hitching is OK, but demands a thick skin and considerable diplomatic expertise in the north, due to aggressive hustlers who simply won't take 'no' for an answer or who feign outrage if you express lack of interest in whatever they're trying to sell you – usually drugs. It's particularly bad on the road between Tetuan and Tangier.

In the south you can only go by road without special permission as far as Tan Tan because of the war with Polisario in Western Sahara. In this area, there are numerous army and police roadblocks where vehicles are searched for arms, though foreign-registered vehicles are often waved through.

Bus

Buses can take you all over the country. Departures are frequent so a timetable is superfluous. Most Moroccan cities and towns have a central bus terminal though this isn't the case in Meknès and Tangier. Where there is no central terminal, the various bus companies usually are all in the one area.

The main company CTM is Compagnie de Transports au Maroc. Between the main towns it generally offers 1st-class buses, plus 2nd-class buses along some routes. On minor routes the buses are usually 2nd-class. CTM buses are slightly more expensive and no faster than those of the other companies, such as SATAS, Maroc Express and FAK. CTM sometimes has its own separate bus terminal, but when it does it also operates from the central terminal. Sufficient leg-room is no problem on CTM buses, but the width of the seats is another matter. On non-CTM buses you're usually squeezed both ways. On well-subscribed routes and those that only have one bus a day, book in advance.

Bus transport is cheap and isn't going to be one of your major expenses. Marrakesh to Ouarzazate, for example, is Dr 31.20 (about US$3.30) for the five to six-hour journey. Ouarzazate to Errachidia is Dr 36 for the nine-hour journey. Marrakesh to Essaouira is Dr 18 for the three-hour journey.

There are no official charges for baggage placed on the roof or in the side compartments, but, if it goes on the roof, the baggage handlers will demand a tip no matter how much help you offer. They're usually happy with Dr 1, though locals pay less. On dusty journeys your baggage is better off on the roof as a tarpaulin is pulled over it and it won't end up the colour of the road. Theft of baggage is not a problem, though it might be wise to keep an eye on it if the bus is standing for any length of time at an intermediate terminal.

Don't expect any bus to have heating, even on the journeys over the Atlas Mountains in winter. Therefore, warm clothing is essential, particularly if there's any chance of being stranded on the passes due to snow drifts. The Marrakesh to Ouarzazate road is prone to this. It's extremely unlikely you'll be stranded for longer than overnight, as snowploughs usually clear a path by early morning.

CTM also operates international buses from Casablanca and Rabat to Bordeaux and Paris. But at US$107 one-way and US$165 return, it's poor value. You'd be able to do the same independently for less.

Cycling
The other way of getting around by yourself is to cycle, and quite a few travellers do.

Driving
If you are driving your own vehicle, make sure you have a valid 'Green Card'. Police can fine you Dr 35 on the spot if you can't produce one.

Self-hire cars are great to get to those out-of-the-way places in Morocco if you don't want to hire a taxi, but they're not cheap. With four people, however, they're affordable. The cheapest cars are Renault 4 and Fiat 127. Charges vary slightly from company to company and you may be able to do a bit of bargaining in the off-season. Typical charges are Dr 1230 for three days and Dr 2170 for a week with unlimited mileage. You will have to pay a government tax of 19%. It's advisable to buy extra personal insurance (Dr 20 per day) and the collision damage waiver (Dr 30), or you'll be liable for the first Dr 3000 of any damage. The estimated cost of the rental is payable at the time you take delivery (minimum deposit Dr 2000). The minimum age for drivers is 21 years, with at least one year's driving experience. An International Driving permit usually is required though some agencies will accept your national driving licence.

Renting the car is the major cost, but fuel is not especially cheap. Super petrol costs Dr 6.05 a litre.

Taxi
Shared taxis are worth considering on some routes – particularly scenic ones, which buses might cover at night. They cost about 50% more than the equivalent bus fare – but make sure you know what local people are paying beforehand, as they often try to conceal this so you end up paying more. They're a particularly good idea if there are enough of you to fill one and you'd like to stop occasionally for photographs or to stretch your legs. It will cost more if you want the driver to stop, so negotiate a price before setting off. They won't stop if you are sharing with local people. The Ziz and Dr'aa valleys and the Tiz-n-Test pass are among those that lend themselves to shared taxis. Shared taxis are often old Mercedes Benz, bought by their owners when they were 'guest workers' in France and Germany in the days when those countries were short of manual labourers.

TRAIN
As with the bus system, there is a good network of railways connecting all the main centres. Through services to Algeria, however, were suspended years

ago because of political tension between Morocco and Algeria over the war in Western Sahara.

If you have a choice, trains are the best way to travel in Morocco. A lot of money has been spent on upgrading the railways and rolling stock in recent years, so it's not only comfortable, fast and reliable, but the fares are little more than the equivalent 2nd-class bus fare. Third class, known as *economique*, is cheaper than going by bus, but can be overcrowded. First class is luxurious and an unnecessary expense. Second class consists of separate six-seat compartments and usually has air-con. It would be the equivalent of 1st class on trains elsewhere in Africa and is the one most travellers opt for.

On the fringes of the railway system – Meknès to Fès to Oujda, for instance – you may come across some older-type 2nd-class carriages that won't have air-con (or heating in winter). Third class is more like a community experience and perfectly adequate for short journeys.

The Rabat to Casablanca line is an experience on its own. The track is electrified and superfast. It takes just 55 minutes (nonstop) and costs Dr 22 (2nd class). It's a bargain.

Most trains offer a choice of all three classes, but there are some that offer only 1st class and 2nd class. Sleepers are available on night trains. A refreshment trolley usually does the rounds, offering hot coffee, soft drinks and snacks, and, on the longer journeys, there is a buffet car with lunch and dinner available.

Timetables are prominently displayed in the railway stations, and are available from the ticket offices so you can plan ahead. It's also possible to buy a small booklet from major stations for Dr 1, which lists the schedules of all the major trains throughout the country.

Advance booking is advisable for 1st class, though it would be rare for all the trains to be booked out on any particular day. For 2nd class and 3rd class, buy the ticket on departure. You can buy the ticket in advance, but as there are no seat reservations, there seems little point.

TO/FROM ALGERIA

There are only two possible crossing points between Morocco and Algeria – Oujda-Tlemcen in the north and Figuig-Beni Ounif in the south. If you're driving your own vehicle, you can cross at either point. If you're on foot, you can cross only at Figuig-Beni Ounif.

However, while the Algerians won't allow you to cross the Oujda-Tlemcen border on foot, the Moroccans won't stop you from walking to the Algerian side. It's their idea of a joke. On the other hand, you can cross on foot from Tlemcen to Oujda.

If you have a lift in a car crossing at Oujda-Tlemcen, the date of your Moroccan entry stamp must be the same as that of the driver's. Algerian immigration check this, and if it's not the same you'll be sent back. If you get a lift, have the driver put your backpack in the boot of the car.

For those with their own vehicles, both crossings are straightforward in either direction. The only thing you should be aware of when taking a vehicle to Morocco from Algeria, is that your embassy in Rabat must send a telex to the border post saying you will be exporting the vehicle. These letters usually take a couple of weeks to organise, so don't leave it till the last minute. Although this telex is supposedly compulsory, it is often possible to get through with just a 'Green Card' or carnet.

TO/FROM SPANISH NORTH AFRICA

The Spanish border is 33 km to the north of Tetouan at Fnideq. *Grands taxis* leave frequently from the corner of Rue de Mouquauama and Rue Sidi Mandri, just up from the bus station. There are dozens of blue Mercedes taxis in the two ranks for the frequent departures to Fnideq (for Ceuta, Dr 14) and Tangier (Dr 20). Although the border is open 24 hours, transport dries up from about 7 pm to 5 am. A seat costs Dr 14 for the 20-minute trip.

On the Spanish side of the border, the No 7 public bus runs every 30 minutes or so into the centre for Ptas 40.

This is a much easier way to enter Morocco than via Tangier. The border is fairly easy-going, if crowded at times. It is possible to visit Ceuta in a day trip from Tetouan, but why anyone would want to is another matter, unless to buy a bottle of cheap duty-free liquor.

Around the Country

AGADIR

Agadir was destroyed by an earthquake in 1960 and although it has been rebuilt, it's no longer a typical Moroccan city. Most of the activity is centred around catering for the short-stay package tourists from Europe, who flock in by the plane-load daily in search of sun, sand and an acceptably sanitised version of the mysteries of the Barbary coast. The reek of *Ambre Soleil* and the rustle of *Paris Match, Der Spiegel* and the airmail *Sunday Times* fills the air. Not that it's unpleasant, it's just that it could be any resort town on the northern Mediterranean coast. It's one of the more expensive cities in Morocco and the jumping-off point for visits east and further south, so you'll probably have to stay overnight at least.

Information

The national tourist office is on Ave Prince Sidi Mohammed and there's a syndicat d'initiative on Blvd Mohammed V at the corner of Ave du General Kettani. Both these places offer a free map of Agadir, but otherwise are not of much help to budget travellers.

There are consulates for Belgium, Finland, France, Italy, Norway and Spain.

The bus terminals are all at the corner of Rue Allal ben Abdallah and Blvd Mohammed Cheikh Saadi. CTM has buses to Tiznit (3.30 pm) and Essaouira

(7.30 am, 7.30 and 9 pm) daily, but none to Marrakesh. SATAS has buses to Marrakesh (8 am and 6.30 pm), Tiznit (3, 5, 6, 9 am and 2 pm) and Goulimime (6 am and 2 pm) daily. Express Sud-Est has a bus to Marrakesh daily at 9.30 am.

Things to See

For **beaches** head north of Agadir. There are plenty of beautiful sandy coves every few km. Most of the ones nearer Agadir have been heavily colonised by obviously affluent Europeans. Further north, the European villas give way to a sea of campervans. By the time you are 20 to 25 km north of Agadir you might find something resembling space, and even peace and quiet.

Places to Stay

Most of the budget hotels and a few of the mid-range hotels are around the bus terminal and along Rue Allal ben Abdallah. In the high seasons, you must get into Agadir early in the day if you want to be sure of a room. If you arrive late, you may have to sleep out or pay through the nose at an expensive hotel. Disappointed backpackers wandering around with nowhere to go are a common sight by 8 pm.

Best value is *Hotel Amenou*. It is clean with pleasant decor and furnishings. Rooms cost Dr 31/42 for singles/doubles without bathrooms. The communal bathrooms have hot showers and, although you're supposed to pay an extra Dr 3 for one, they rarely ask for it. If it's full, try *Hotel Tifaut*, at Dr 35/50 a single/double, or *Hotel Excelcior* for Dr 30/42 a single/double without bathroom, and Dr 60 a double with bathroom. Both these hotels will tell you they have hot water, but it can be a long time coming at the Excelcior.

Going down Rue Allal ben Abdallah, try either *Hotel Select, Hotel Diaf* or *Hotel de la Braie*. The latter costs Dr 29/38 a single/double without bathroom and Dr 44/50 a single/double with bathroom. It's a clean place and there's hot water. The *Hotel de Paris*, Ave President Kennedy, is clean

and comfortable, but has no hot water. It costs Dr 32/44 a single/double. Breakfast is available for Dr 6.

If you still have no bed, try *Hotel Moderne*. It is a little more expensive, but likely to have room as it's not in an obvious position. Avoid *Hotel Massa* if possible. It's dingy and there's no hot water, so at Dr 40 a double it's definitely overpriced.

If you have to go for *Hotel Sindibad*, you're looking at around Dr 95/130 a single/double with bathroom.

Places to Eat

There are a number of cheap restaurants and sandwich bars on the same street as the bus terminals and they're good value. You can get almost anything, from seafood to kebabs to sandwiches and yogurt.

Behind the bus terminal street is a small plaza, where there are two restaurants next to one another that are popular with travellers and night strollers from the tourist district in search of a change. They are *Restaurant Chabib* and *Restaurant Mille et Une Nuit* (*sic*). They might look expensive (judging from some of the clientele) but they're not, and the food is very good. Both offer a choice of dining inside or outside. A three-course meal of bread, soup, tajine and a sweet costs Dr 13 to Dr 15. It's excellent value.

If you're looking for a cleansing ale or a bottle of Moroccan wine, the tourist palaces on Blvd Mohammed V will empty your pockets. The clientele will regard you with disdain, unless you have just emerged from the launderette. There are much livelier Moroccan-style bars to be found if you wander around. For takeaways, go to one of the two supermarkets opposite Hotel Erfoud, Blvd Hassan II. There's an excellent choice of local and imported beers, wines and spirits.

AZROU

Azrou is primarily a Berber town in the mountains surrounded by pine forests. It is a pleasant place to relax when you've

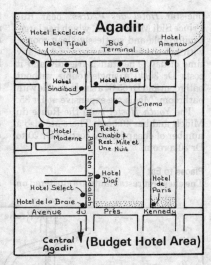

had enough of souks and handicraft hustlers on the plains. There's not a great deal to do other than trek into the mountains, but the people are friendly and there is absolutely no hassle. It's another dimension of Morocco.

A visit to the **Coopérative Artisanale** on the right hand side of the road to Khenifra (signposted) is worthwhile. Here you can find craftwork in cedar and iron, as well as the Berber carpets typical of the Middle Atlas.

Places to Stay

Behind the main street is a small square around which you'll find four budget hotels – *Hotel Ziz, Hotel Atlas, Hotel Beau Séjour* and *Hotel Salam*. The first three are of equal standard and cost Dr 17 a single and Dr 20 to Dr 25 a double. None has hot water (and it's cold in the mornings at 1250 metres). The Ziz is parsimonious with blankets, too, and it's a hassle to get more out of the management. Slightly better is Hotel Salam. It is more modern and costs Dr 30 a double.

For only a little more you can stay at the

one-star *Hotel des Cedres*, near Rue Prince Sidi Mohammed, which has large, comfortable and spotlessly clean rooms, with hot showers at no extra cost at any time of day. The staff is friendly and it costs Dr 30/40 a single/double without bathroom and Dr 55/64 a single/double with bathroom. Meals are expensive at Dr 35.

The *Youth Hostel* is on the Route du Midelt and has 40 beds. There are also a number of cheap hotels, costing Dr 20 to Dr 30 a room.

Places to Eat
The cheapest restaurants are clustered on the street opposite the park, below the main roundabout. You can get a good meal for around Dr 10 to Dr 15. Two pieces of fish, sauce, salad, bread and tea cost me Dr 15 and was very tasty.

BOUARFA
This town is between Oujda and Figuig and a good place to stay if you plan to explore the towns and villages on the edge of the Sahara to the south-west, such as Erfoud and Rissani.

There's only one hotel, *Hotel Hauts Plakas*, on the main street. It's very basic and costs Dr 30 a double.

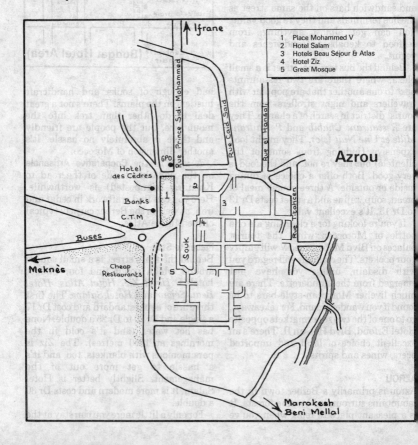

1 Place Mohammed V
2 Hotel Salam
3 Hotels Beau Séjour & Atlas
4 Hotel Ziz
5 Great Mosque

Azrou

↑ Ifrane

Hotel des Cèdres

GPO

Rue Prince Sidi Mohammed

Rue Caid Said

Rue el Hansali

Banks

C.T.M

Buses

Souk

Rue Tanger

← Meknès

Cheap Restaurants

↓ Marrakesh Beni Mellal

CASABLANCA

With a population of 3½ million, Casablanca is Morocco's largest city by far, and is still growing at the rate of 50,000 people a year. This growth is a fairly recent phenomenon, dating from the early days of the French Protectorate when it was chosen as the centre of the colonial administration. The first settlement on this part of the coast was by the Portuguese in the 15th century. It was abandoned by them in 1755 after an earthquake not only levelled Casa Branca, as the Portuguese called it, but also much of Lisbon. By the late 19th century, the site had been resettled by local tribes and developed into a modest commercial centre with a population of some 20,000.

Casablanca is like many modern cities around the world and not at all typically Moroccan. There are few sights as such, except perhaps some good examples of Mauresque architecture (a French idealisation of Moorish design), and the old medina is nowhere near as interesting as those at Fès, Meknès and Marrakesh. Those travellers interested in contrasts might find it worth visiting for a day or two, but if it's the more exotic flavours of Morocco that you want, you can safely give it a miss.

Information

The national tourist office (ONT) is at Rue Omar Slaoui 55 and the syndicat d'initiative is at 98 Blvd Mohammed V. The central post office is at Place des Nations Unies. The poste restante is in the same section as the international telephones, and the entrance is the third door on the right hand side of the building.

American Express (tel 222946) is represented by Voyages Schwartz, 112 Ave du Prince Moulay Abdallah. Thomas Cook and Wagon-Lits (tel 261211) have an office at 60 Ave de Foucauld. The Touring Club du Maroc is at 3 Ave de l'Armée Royale. It's open Monday to Friday from 9 am to 12 noon and 3 to 6.30 pm and on Saturday from 9 am to 12 noon.

Most airline offices are between Place de l'Unité Africaine and Place Zellaqa. The staff usually speak English, French and Arabic. Air Afrique (tel 249653) is in the Tour Atlas office, Place Zellaqa; Air France is at 15 Ave des Armées Royales. The airport is 35 km to the south of Casablanca and buses leave the CTM station every 30 minutes from 5.30 am to 7 pm. The 45-minute trip to the city centre costs Dr 20. From Casablanca's Mohammed V Airport there are regular flights to most West European countries and to West Africa, Algeria, Tunisia, Egypt and the Middle East.

The CTM bus terminal is between Ave des Armées Royales and Rue Vidal, close to where the two streets intersect Blvd Hassan Seghir at the back of Hotel Safir. There are other bus stations scattered around, but most also use the terminal on Rue Strasbourg, two blocks from Place de la Victoire. The latter terminal is quite a distance from the city centre, so take a taxi from Place Mohammed V. There are regular CTM departures to Marrakesh, Fès, Rabat Tangier, but the trains are faster and more comfortable.

There are hundreds of red *petits taxis*, whose drivers are unwilling to use the meters because they are out of date. Expect to pay Dr 10 for a ride in or around the city centre.

Most train departures are from Casa-Voyageurs station, which is a Dr 10 taxi ride from the centre or a 30-minute walk. Departures to the following places are:

Tangier – 12.45 and 11.10 pm; seven hours
Fès – five daily from 6 am to 10 pm; 5½ hours
Marrakesh – six daily from 1.20 to 7.13 pm; four hours

Departures from the much more convenient Gare du Port ('Casa-Port' on the platform

1	Chleuh Mosque
2	Great Mosque
3	Youth Hostel
4	Hotel Toubkal
5	Touring Club of Morocco
6	Place Mohammed V
7	Hotel Casablanca
8	GPO
9	Fountain
10	Place des Nations Unies
11	Law Courts
12	French Consulate
13	Hotel Excelsior
14	Hotels de Foucauld & du Périgord
15	Thomas Cook/Wagons Lits
16	Syndicat d'Initiative & Post Office
17	Hotel Kon Tiki
18	Hotel Mon Rêve
19	Main Bus Station
20	Hotel Safir
21	Hotel Mahaba
22	Hotel el Mansour

Casablanca

Docks

Gare du Port
(Casa-Port Railway
Station)

0   500m

Rabat

Boulevard Moulay Abderrahmane

Boulevard du Forbin

Moh El Hansali

id ou Hmed

21

enue   de
l'Armée   Royale

19   20

Vidal

18

Abdallah

armmed

Hassan   Seghir

Rue   Mohammed   V

Fetouaki

el Maani

R. Strasbourg

Lalla

Blvd

Yagoute

Smiha

Meskini

al el   Blvd Lahcen Ider

New
Medina

Marrakesh

Avenue   Pasteur

Blvd.   Mohammed   V

Blvd. Emile   Zola

Blvd. de la Résistance

Main
Railway
Station

Boulevard Abdallah ben Yacine

Blvd Ibn Tachfine

Route des Ouad Ziane

Rue d'Ouida

Blvd de Khouribaa

R. E. Barathon

Place
de
la Victoire

Strasbourg Blvd de la Résistance

Rue de
Libourne

Rue de

signs) at the southern end of Blvd Mohammed el Hansali are:

Tangier – 7.15 am and 5.57 pm
Fès – 8.04 am, 12.27 and 8.50 pm
Oujda – 8.50 pm; 10½ hours
Marrakesh – 1 pm
Rabat – 14 local trains daily from 6.50 am to 7.30 pm (50 minutes); plus mainline departures

Things to See

The old **medina** is worth wandering through, though it has seen more dynamic days. Most of the surviving craft industries are along Blvd Mohammed el Hansali, where they catch sailors on shore leave and tourists coming out of the railway station. Prices, as you might imagine, are relatively high. On the other hand, one of the plusses about exploring this medina is that there are no hassles with 'guides'.

Some of the best examples of **Mauresque architecture** are to be found around or close to Place des Nations Unies. They include the law courts, post office, French Consulate and the Sacré Coeur Cathedral.

Places to Stay

The hotels in the medina have all seen better days, but you wouldn't know it from the prices they charge. It is possible to find good rooms at some of them, but don't count on it. There's not a lot to choose between them – few have hot showers and many have no showers at all. During the winter prices would be negotiable, but in the summer months prices reflect demand and you'd get much better value at the hotels outside the medina.

The cheapest place to stay, if you're happy with dormitory accommodation, is the *Youth Hostel* (tel 74301), 6 Place Admiral Philbert, on the boundary of the old medina. It costs Dr 10 a person (without breakfast) and is large, comfortable and clean. It's closed daily between 10 am and noon and from 2 to 5 pm. From Casa-Port railway station, walk to the first major intersection and turn right along Blvd des Almohades. Turn left when you get to the first opening in the medina wall. Go through it and the hostel is on the right-hand side.

The other cheapies in the medina are all best approached from the entrance on Place Mohammed V. One of the cleanest places is *Hotel Geneve*, 44 Rue du Marché aux Grains, which costs Dr 30/35 a single/double and Dr 40 a twin. The staff is friendly and there are cold showers. *Hotel Candide*, 33 Rue du Marché aux Grains, has some sunny rooms at Dr 30 a double, but most are dark and there are no showers. *Hotel Soussi*, Rue de Fès, is also reasonable value, clean and well-maintained, but with cold showers only. It costs Dr 26/40 a single/double.

The rest of the budget hotels are much of a muchness. Expect to pay Dr 25 a single and Dr 35 to Dr 40 a double. They include *Hotel Widad, Hotel Brezil, Hotel Helvetia*, 50 Rue Dar el Makhzen; *Hotel Gibraltar, Hotel Medine, Hotel des Amis, Hotel de Pacha, Hotel Restaurant London, Hotel de la Reine*, 37 Rue Chakab Arsala; and *Hotel Kaouarib Maghrib*.

In the middle bracket and out of the medina area, most of the tourist hotels are in the side streets between Ave de l'Armée Royale and Ave Houmane el Fetouaki, close to Place Mohammed V. Try *Hotel Touring* (tel 310216), 87 Rue Allal ben Abdallah; *Hotel Lincoln* (tel 222408), 1 Rue ibn Batouta; *Hotel Kon Tiki*, 88 Rue Allal ben Abdallah, which costs Dr 27/37 a single/double with cold showers; or *Hotel du Périgord*, 56 Rue de Foucauld, for Dr 27/37 a single/double without bathroom and Dr 53 a double with bathroom. Hot showers cost Dr 3 extra.

Going up-market, try *Hotel de Foucauld* (tel 222666), 52 Rue de Foucauld, costing Dr 45/57 a single/double without bathroom, and Dr 57/66 a single/double with bathroom. It's clean and pleasant and there are hot showers for Dr 3.

Campers should head for *Camping Oasis* on Ave Mermoz, which is the main road to El Jadida. It's a long way from the centre, so unless you have your own transport it's hardly worth it. Bus No 31 from the CTM terminal gets you there.

Places to Eat

Most of the cheap eats are in the medina. None stands out, but one that is clean, bright and good is *Restaurant Widad*. Attached to the hotel of the same name, it is just inside the medina from Place Mohammed V. It serves good Moroccan food in generous helpings – Dr 19 for main dishes, and Dr 2 for good soups and salads. Beware of their habit of bringing you things you haven't ordered and then adding them to the bill. A similar place, but in the new city, is *Café Restaurant Point Central* at 89 Rue Allal ben Abdallah, next door to the Touring Hotel. The food is good and the colour TV a big drawcard with the locals.

Another good place in the new city is the kitsch *Restaurant de l'Etoile Marocaine* at 107 Rue Allal ben Abdallah, not far from Touring Hotel. It's a friendly place, the food is good and they have individual serves of pastilla (pigeon pie), great value at Dr 30.

For something a little better, *Las Delicias* at 168 Blvd Mohammed V has a good range of tajines – such as chicken with prunes and onions or beef with raisins. The big surprise comes at the end of the meal when you find you have been charged not only the standard 10% service charge but also a 10% 'tax'. The tax is a ruse to get extra money from tourists. It is not legitimate and you should not feel obliged to pay it, here or anywhere else.

If you have money to spare, try *Le Marignan Restaurant* (tel 309817) at 63 Rue Mohammed Smiha, on the corner of Blvd Mohammed V. It serves Korean and Japanese food, cooked at your table. Set menus range from Dr 80 to Dr 100. Main courses cost around Dr 40. It is open for lunch and in the evenings from 7 pm

till midnight. Another Asian place is *Restaurant Saigon* (tel 286007) at 40 Rue Colbert, which has a very pleasant outdoor terrace for summer evenings. Main courses range from Dr 20 to Dr 40.

CHECHAOUEN

Also called Chaouen, Chefchaouen and Xauen, this delightful town in the Rif Mountains is a favourite with travellers and for good reason. The air is cool and clear, the people are noticeably more relaxed (stoned?) than those on the coast (there's more *kif* than you can poke a stick at) and it's small, making it a great place to hang out for a few days.

Founded by Moulay Ali ben Rachid in 1471 as a base from which to attack the Portuguese in Ceuta, the town prospered and grew considerably with the arrival of Muslim refugees from Spain. It remained isolated, however, up until its occupation by Spanish troops in 1920.

Today the town sleeps beneath the Djebel ech-Chaouan (The Horns) and, although it sees its fair share of package-tour buses, it is still a remarkably easy-going place. The touts are relatively few and keep a fairly low profile – a blessed relief if you have just come from Tetouan or Tangier.

Information

Both the post office and the branch of the BMCE (Banque Marocaine du Commerce Extérieur) are on Ave Hassan II, the main street running from Place Mohammed V to Bab el Ain and curving around the south of the medina.

The bus station is an open yard next to the market. All buses leave from here. There are daily departures to Tetouan (four hours), Meknès (five hours) and Fès (seven hours). It's worth booking at least 24 hours ahead as demand is high, especially to Meknès. Buses coming from Tetouan are much quicker in getting to Meknès, but there's no guarantee of a seat – in fact, in summer you can be fairly well assured there *won't* be seats.

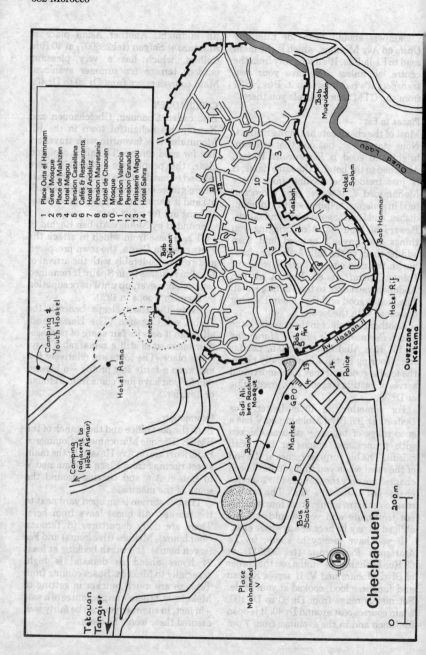

Key

1 Place Outa el Hammam
2 Great Mosque
3 Place de Makhzen
4 Hotel Magou
5 Pension Castellana
6 Cafés & Restaurants
7 Hotel Andaluz
8 Pension Mauretania
9 Hotel de Chaouen
10 Mosque
11 Pension Valencia
12 Pension Granada
13 Patisserie Magou
14 Hotel Sahra

Chechaouen

200 m

0

Bab Muqqddam

Oued Laou

Hotel Salam

Kasbah

Bab Hammar

Bab Salam

Bab Djenan

Cemetery

Bab el Ain

Av. Hassan II

Hotel Rif

Ouezzane Ketama

Hotel Asma

Camping & Youth Hostel

Camping (adjacent to Hotel Asma)

Tetouan Tangier

Sidi Ali ben Rachid Mosque

GPO

Market

Bank

Police

14 13

Bus Station

Place Mohammed V

Grands taxis leave from the bus station to Tetouan, Meknès, Fès, Ketama, Al Hoceima and Ouezzane.

Things to See

The **market** is on Ave Al Khattabi, one block south of Ave Hassan II. It is very much the centre of things on market day, Mondays and Thursdays, when merchants come from all over the Rif to trade. The emphasis is on second-hand clothes and food, although sometimes there are a few things of interest in the way of souvenirs.

The old **medina** is small, uncrowded and very easy to find your way around. For the most part, the houses and buildings are a blinding blue-white and, on the northern side especially, you'll find many with tiny ground-floor rooms crowded with weaving looms. The guys working these looms often as not, are bored out of their brains and may invite you in for a smoke and chat to break the monotony. There is also a fair smattering of tourist shops, particularly around Place de Makhzen and Place Outa el Hammam – the focal points of the old city.

The shady, cobbled **Place Outa el Hammam**, with the **kasbah** along one side, is busiest in the early evening when everyone starts to get out and about after the inactivity of the afternoon. It's great to sit in one of the many cafés opposite the kasbah and relax. The atmosphere is sedate and almost mediaeval, it's just a pity that cars are still allowed in. The ruins of the 15th-century kasbah dominate the square and its walls enclose a beautiful garden. An entrance fee of Dr 1 also gives you access to the museum, where you'll be shown the cells, complete with neck chains at floor level, in which Abd el-Krim was imprisoned in 1926. In the corner of the garden opposite the prison is a small pavilion that has been restored to house a display of traditional crafts, utensils, musical instruments and clothes.

The **Place de Makhzen** is the lesser of the two town squares, with an enormous old gum tree at its centre. Instead of cafés, it has mostly tourist shops, although on market days you still get people squatting under the tree selling their bundles of mint and vegetables. The lane heading east from the square comes out at Bab Onsar, and behind it, the river, with a couple of very agreeable shady cafés on its banks. This is where the women come to do the washing while the men drink tea.

Places to Stay

The cheapest places are the pensions in the medina. For the most part they are OK, if a little gloomy and claustrophobic at times.

Pension Castellana, just off the western end of Place Outa el Hammam, is the cheapest at Dr 7 a bed in rooms with two, three or four beds. A bit roomier is *Hotel Andaluz* for Dr 14 a person in twin rooms. There are no double rooms. The rooms all face an internal courtyard, so are poorly ventilated. Cold showers are Dr 2; hot showers Dr 4. The pension is signposted off to the left, about 50 metres inside Bab el Ain.

Another popular place with travellers is *Pension Mauretania*, which is unusual in that it has single rooms, although they would be better used as cupboards. It costs Dr 10 a person in singles, doubles or triples.

The best of the medina places is *Pension Valencia* because it is on the northern slope and gets some breeze and good views. It's a little more expensive than the others at Dr 15 a person, but the rooms are larger and more airy. To find it, take the lane off to the north from Place Outa el Hammam; it twists back and forth up the hill, but after a few minutes you come to Restaurant Granada and the pension is at the back and to the right.

Right up on the side of the hill, behind the ghastly Hotel Asma, is the camping ground and *Youth Hostel*. They are only worth considering if you have your own vehicle, as it's a 30-minute walk by road (follow the signs to Asma Hotel), or a 15-

minute scramble up the hill through the cemetery, which shouldn't be attempted on a Friday as the locals don't take kindly to it. The camping area is pleasantly shaded and cheap at Dr 2 per vehicle and the same per person. The Youth Hostel is extremely basic and although it is cheap at Dr 5, you can do much better in the medina.

Going up in price, *Hotel Sahra*, close to the market, lacks atmosphere but is good value at Dr 17 a person. Better is *Hotel Salam* (tel 6239) at 39 Rue Tariq Ibn Ziad, the street that loops around the southern edge of the medina wall. The rooms are bright and clean and some look out over the valley. Both the comfortable lounge and the shaded rooftop terrace have views. Rooms are reasonable at Dr 42/64 for singles/doubles with hot shower. The meals, Dr 36 for a set menu, are not great value.

Further up the scale is the two-star *Hotel Magou* (tel 6275) at 23 Rue Moulay Idriss. It is close to the market and bus station and is often used by small tour groups. If you are looking for comfort, it's not bad at Dr 80 a double with bathroom.

Places to Eat

Among the cafés on Place Outa el Hammam are a number of small restaurants that serve good local food. One is *Restaurant Granada*, near Pension Valencia, which is run by a cheery character who cooks a variety of food at reasonable cost. Apart from these places, the only other restaurants are in the hotels, and prices start at around Dr 35 for a set meal.

Patisserie Magou in Ave Hassan II has OK pastries and fresh bread.

Most of the cafés on Place Outa el Hammam have seedy rooms upstairs where the hard smoking goes on – you can cut the air with a knife in some of them – and there certainly are worse ways to pass a few hours than by sitting around playing dominoes with the locals.

EL JADIDA

El Jadida was founded by the Portuguese in 1513 in the days when these sea-faring people were undertaking voyages of discovery around the world and pouring their meagre resources into establishing a maritime trading empire stretching as far as China and Japan. They were to hold on to El Jadida, in those days known as Mazagan, until the 1769 siege by Sultan Mohammed ben Abdallah. Though the Portuguese were forced to evacuate the fortress with little more than the clothes they stood in, at the last moment they blew the ramparts to smithereens, taking with them a good part of the besieging army.

The walls of the fortress lay in ruins until 1820, when they were rebuilt by Sultan Moulay Abderrahman. The Moors, who took over the town after the Portuguese withdrew, preferred to settle outside the walls. The medina inside was largely neglected until the mid-19th century, when it was recolonised by European merchants after the establishment of a series of 'open ports' along the Moroccan coast. Also established at this time was a large and influential Jewish community, which controlled the trade with the interior and particularly with Marrakesh. Not only that, but almost alone among Moroccan cities, the Jews were not confined to living in a separate quarter (the *mellah*). As a result, the massive fortress with its enclosed medina, churches and enormous cistern, is remarkably well preserved. Indeed, despite having been reconstructed by the Moroccans, it's one of the most spectacular European-style mediaeval fortresses to be found anywhere in the world.

These days, El Jadida is a popular beach resort.

Information

The bus terminal is at the northern end of town on Rue Abdelmoumen el Mouahidi, close to the corner of Ave Mohammed V. It's a 10-minute walk to the main hotel

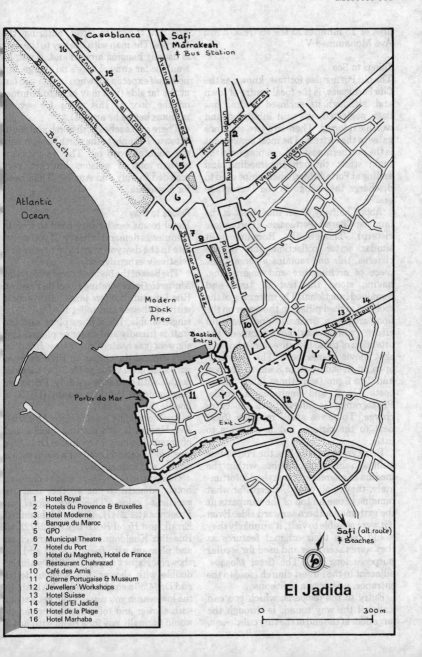

Map legend:

1 Hotel Royal
2 Hotels du Provence & Bruxelles
3 Hotel Moderne
4 Banque du Maroc
5 GPO
6 Municipal Theatre
7 Hotel du Port
8 Hotel du Maghreb, Hotel de France
9 Restaurant Chahrazad
10 Café des Amis
11 Citerne Portugaise & Museum
12 Jewellers' Workshops
13 Hotel Suisse
14 Hotel d'El Jadida
15 Hotel de la Plage
16 Hotel Marhaba

El Jadida

0   300 m

Labels on map: Casablanca, Safi Marrakesh & Bus Station, Avenue & Jamia al Arabia, Boulevard Almount, Avenue Mohammed, Beach, Atlantic Ocean, Rue Ibn Khaldoun, Ave Moh Errachi, Avenue Hassan II, Place Hansali, Boulevard de Suez, Modern Dock Area, Bastion Entry, Porte de Mar, Exit, Rue Zerktouni, Safi (alt route) & Beaches

area or 15 minutes to the fortress, down Ave Mohammed V.

Things to See

The old Portuguese fortress, known as the **Cité Portugaise**, is the focal centre of town and, although its enclosed medina has been neglected, it's still inhabited and worth exploring. There are two entrance gates to the fortress. The most convenient is the northernmost one, opening onto the main street through the medina and ending at **Porta do Mar**, where ships used to discharge their cargo in the Portuguese era.

About halfway down this street is the famous **Citerne Portugaise** (Portuguese cistern). Though the Romans built similar water collection and storage cisterns, this one remains a remarkable piece of architecture and engineering, having stood the test of time and remained functional. The mirroring of the roof and arched pillars in the water on the floor creates a dramatic and beautiful effect, which has not escaped the attention of those film directors who have shot movie scenes here. The cistern is open on weekdays from 8 am to 12 noon and 2 to 6 pm (sometimes later). Entry costs Dr 2 and includes a guide. Photography is allowed at no extra charge. There's a small **museum** (free) next to the cistern, but it amounts to little.

Being zealous Catholics, the Portuguese built a number of churches within the medina in characteristic style. Unfortunately, they're all closed, except for what remains of one on top of the ramparts at the extreme southern seaward side. Even if it were possible to visit, it's unlikely they would retain their original features as they were taken over and used for secular purposes long ago. The **Great Mosque**, adjacent to the largest church close to the entrance, was once a lighthouse.

Entry to the **ramparts**, which you can walk all the way round, is through the large door at the end of the tiny cul-de-sac,

first on the right after entering the fortress. The man with the key to the door is usually hanging around and, if not, he won't be far away. There's no charge, but he'll half expect a tip when he lets you out at the far side (you may have to hammer on the door at this point for several minutes before he arrives).

There are **beaches** both north and south of town. The ones to the north occasionally are polluted with oil. They're pleasant enough out of season, but get very crowded in July and August. Then head for Essaouira.

Places to Stay

Hotel rooms can be very hard to find in summer as demand is heavy. If you arrive late in the day you may have to stay at a relatively expensive one.

The best of the budget hotels is *Hotel du Mahgreb* (incorporating Hotel de France), Rue Lescoul. It offers large, clean rooms without shower and toilet for Dr 17/26 a single/double. It's a huge place and the staff is friendly and eager to please. Hot showers (gas heated) cost extra. *Hotel du Port* around the corner on Blvd de Suez isn't such good value at Dr 27/36 a single/double with cold showers only. Prices are negotiable in the low season (Dr 30 a double, for instance).

Another budget hotel is *Hotel Moderne*, Ave Hassan II. It's nothing special and offers small, dimly-lit rooms for Dr 17/26 a single/double and Dr 40 for a room with a double and a single bed.

Going up in price, there are two one-star hotels adjacent to one another that are excellent value. They are *Hotel de Provence* (tel 2347), 42 Ave Mohammed Errafi, and *Hotel Bruxelles* (tel 2072), 40 Rue Ibn Khaldoun. They're very clean and pleasant with friendly staff and hot showers. Expect to pay Dr 38/46 a single/double with shower, but without toilet and Dr 44/56 a single/double with both. In the low season you usually can get a room with shower and toilet for the price you would normally pay for a room with just a shower. Similar are *Hotel Royal* (tel 2839), 108 Ave Mohammed V; *Hotel d'El Jadida*, Ave Zerktouni, and *Hotel Suisse* (tel 2816), 145 Ave Zerktouni.

Places to Eat

There are very few cheap restaurants in El Jadida. One of the best, however, is *Restaurant Chahrazad*, 38 Place Hansali. It offers a meal (soup, salads, tajine, etc) for around Dr 30. It might look full, but it has a mezzanine floor as well. Otherwise, try *Café des Amis* at the southern end of Place Hansali. There are quite a few

restaurants opposite the post office and Théâtre Municipal, but you'd be well advised to check prices before ordering. They can be expensive.

For bars, check out *Hotel de la Plage* and *Hotel Marhaba*, both on Ave Jamia el Arabia. There are others opposite the post office.

ERFOUD

Erfoud is the principal town in the Ziz Valley south of Errachidia, but like many small, modern Moroccan towns it offers little of interest to the traveller. There is

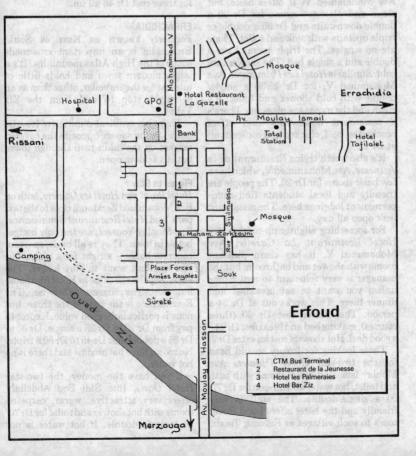

Erfoud

1 CTM Bus Terminal
2 Restaurant de la Jeunesse
3 Hotel les Palmeraies
4 Hotel Bar Ziz

no labyrinthine souk, just a small square with fruit and vegetable stalls and three or four handicraft shops with super-aggressive sellers. The town is the jumping-off point for visits to Rissani and Merzouga, further into the desert.

There are two or three buses daily in either direction between Erfoud and Errachidia which cost Dr 8.50. A shared taxi from Erfoud to Rissani costs Dr 5 and takes about 30 minutes.

Places to Stay

The best of the cheapies is *Hotel Bar Ziz*, 3 Ave Mohammed V. It offers basic, but clean and pleasant rooms for Dr 20 a double downstairs and Dr 35 a double or triple upstairs with sink and toilet. There are no singles. The triple rooms have a double and a single bed. The showers are cold. Similar is *Hotel Les Palmeraies*, Ave Mohammed V, for Dr 25/30 a single/double with cold shower and toilet. It's clean and the rooms are pleasant. There's a restaurant downstairs that offers brochettes, beef, chicken and couscous all at Dr 13.

It's also worth trying *Restaurant de la Jeunesse*, Ave Mohammed V, which has a few basic rooms for Dr 20. The people are friendly and local students find semi-permanent lodgings here. The restaurant isn't open all day.

For something slightly up-market, try *Hotel Restaurant La Gazelle*, Ave Mohammed V. It has clean pleasant rooms with shower and bathroom, but the manager is very reluctant to rent rooms unless you want to eat breakfast and dinner there. This works out at Dr 54 a person. The dinner cost Dr 30 (three courses), making bed and breakfast Dr 24 – a good deal. Hot showers cost an extra Dr 2.

Those looking for luxury should head for the two-star *Hotel Tifilalet*, Ave Moulay Ismail. It offers rooms with bath and toilet, hot water and air-con for Dr 77/90 a single/double. The staff is very friendly and the hotel offers Land Rover tours to such villages as Rissani, Taouz,

Merzouga etc. They also run the hotel at Merzouga.

There is a camp site near the river that charges Dr 5 for a basic room with bunks, and Dr 5 per vehicle. There are supposed to be hot showers, but it's a holocaust of a place with no character or life whatsoever.

Places to Eat

The extremely friendly *Restaurant de la Jeunesse*, Ave Mohammed V, is the place to go in the evenings. The food is excellent and very reasonably priced. Soup, salad, tajine, brochettes, dessert and soft drinks for three cost Dr 46 all up.

ERRACHIDIA

Formerly known as Ksar es Souk, Errachidia is an important crossroads south of the High Atlas mountains. It's a large, modern town and holds little of interest for the traveller, other than as an overnight stop to and from the Ziz Valley.

There is a syndicat d'initiative (tourist office) in the square opposite the covered market on the main road through town, but it's seldom open.

Places to Stay

Hotel Royal and *Hotel les Oliviers*, both on Rue Mohammed Zerktouni close to the taxi park, and *Hotel Restaurant Renaissance*, Rue Moulay Youssef, are the only budget hotels in town. They're all basic, spartan, concrete boxes - alright for a night, but you wouldn't want to stay longer. The Hotel Royal is the same as Hotel Marhaba, but the signs suggest otherwise. The Renaissance is the best of the three, but none is particularly good value. Expect to pay from Dr 20 to Dr 25 a single, Dr 30 to Dr 35 a double and Dr 45 to Dr 50 a triple. No rooms have bathrooms and there is no hot water.

If you have the money, the two-star *Hotel Oasis*, Rue Sidi Bou Abdellah, offers very attractive, warm, carpeted rooms with hot shower and toilet for Dr 70/90 a single/double. If hot water is not

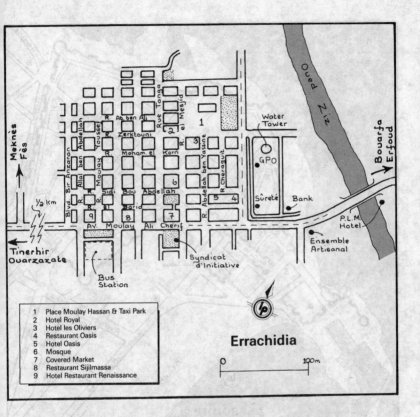

1 Place Moulay Hassan & Taxi Park
2 Hotel Royal
3 Hotel les Oliviers
4 Restaurant Oasis
5 Hotel Oasis
6 Mosque
7 Covered Market
8 Restaurant Sijilmassa
9 Hotel Restaurant Renaissance

Errachidia

0   100m

available, a complaint usually secures a Dr 20 reduction in tariff. The restaurant is expensive at Dr 40 a meal, but beer and wine are on sale (to drink in or takeaway).

Places to Eat

One of the most popular places is *Restaurant Sijilmassa* on the main street – look out for the sign 'All food is here'. You can get an excellent meal for Dr 15 to Dr 20 (soup, bread, salad, tajine, chicken & chips, brochettes). Eat inside or at the tables on the footpath.

There is a wide variety of food at the covered market for those wishing to put their own together.

ESSAOUIRA

Essaouira is the most popular of the coastal towns with independent travellers. Rarely will you see package tourists here. Not only does it have a magnificent beach curving for miles to the south, but the atmosphere of the town is in complete contrast to the souk cities of Marrakesh, Fès, Meknès and Tangier. It can be summed up in one word – relaxation.

The old town was founded in the 16th century by the Portuguese, who continued to occupy it until the mid-18th century when the trans-Saharan trade routes fell apart. The present town dates from 1765, when Sultan Sidi Mohammed ben Abdallah re-established it as a fortress

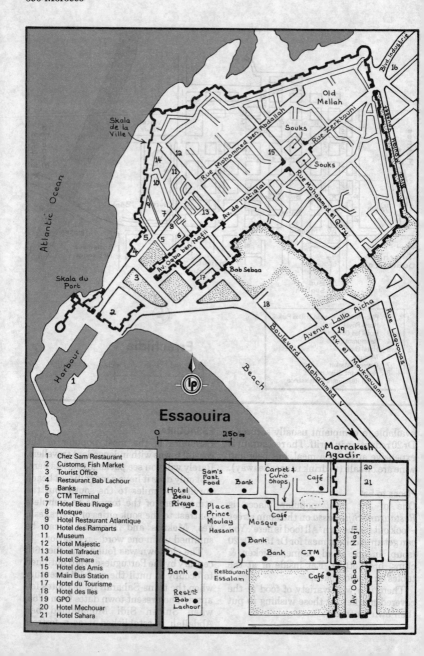

Essaouira

0 ————— 250m

Marrakesh
Agadir

1 Chez Sam Restaurant
2 Customs, Fish Market
3 Tourist Office
4 Restaurant Bab Lachour
5 Banks
6 CTM Terminal
7 Hotel Beau Rivage
8 Mosque
9 Hotel Restaurant Atlantique
10 Hotel des Ramparts
11 Museum
12 Hotel Majestic
13 Hotel Tafraout
14 Hotel Smara
15 Hotel des Amis
16 Main Bus Station
17 Hotel du Tourisme
18 Hotel des Iles
19 GPO
20 Hotel Mechouar
21 Hotel Sahara

town and base from which to suppress a revolt at Agadir. Thus fortifications are an interesting mixture of Portuguese and Berber military architecture, though the walls around the town are mainly from ben Abdallah's time. They're certainly impressive, and their massiveness lends a powerful mystique to the town. Inside the walls though, all is light and charm – narrow, freshly whitewashed streets, painted blinds, tranquil squares, thuya carvers in tiny workshops beavering away with mallet and chisel, friendly cafés and not a hustler in sight. It's one of the few places in Morocco where you can feel that the locals aren't categorising you as a 'tourist'.

Information

There is a tourist office in the square between Place Prince Moulay Hassan and the fishing harbour, but it's often closed during winter. The CTM bus terminal is in the square opposite the tourist office, round the corner from Place Prince Moulay Hassan. All other bus companies have their terminals at Bab Doukkala, just outside the ramparts at the northern end of town.

All buses leave from Bab Doukhala. Ticket office No 6 for CTM buses to Casablanca (9.30 am, Dr 48) and Agadir (12 noon, Dr 28), and office No 2 for Marrakesh.

Things to See

You can walk along most of the **ramparts** on the seaward part of town and visit the two main **forts** (*skalas*) during daylight hours. The Skala du Port is locked at lunchtimes. There is no charge and no-one will hassle you to employ them as a guide. The Skala de la Ville is particularly impressive with a collection of 18th and 19th-century brass cannon from various European countries.

Just off the coast to the south-west is the Île de Mogador, on which there's another massive fortification. It's actually two islets and in Phoenician and Roman times

served as a warehouse for Mediterranean merchants. These days it's a sanctuary for a particular species of falcon, as well as other birds, and visits normally are prohibited.

On Rue Laalouj there is a **museum** with displays of jewellery, costumes and weapons. Given the history of this town, it could be better. It's open daily, except Tuesday, from 8.30 am to 12 noon and 2 to 6 pm. Entry is Dr 3.

Essaouira is a centre for **thuya carving** and the quality of the work is superb. Most of the carvers have workshops under the Skala de la Ville. They're very laid-back, so you can walk around and examine what they are doing without any pressure to buy. It's unlikely you won't want to buy something, but because there's no pressure, the prices are not negotiable, except perhaps for the smallest fraction. Nevertheless, this sort of craftwork will not be found cheaper anywhere else in Morocco. There are also quite a few craftshops in the immediate vicinity with an equally impressive range.

Carpet and rug shops, as well as bric-a-brac, jewellery and brassware shops, are clustered in the narrow street and small square between Place Prince Moulay Hassan and the ramparts that flank Ave Oqba ben Nafii.

The **beach** stretches some 10 km down the coast to the sand dunes of Cap Sim. On the way you'll pass the ruins of an old fortress and pavilion, partially covered in sand. Close to Cap Sim and inland through sand dunes and scrub for about a km is the Berber village of Diabat, which became a legend among hippies in the 1960s after a visit by Jimi Hendrix. It subsequently became a freak colony similar to those on the beaches of Goa, India, but was cleared by the police in the mid-1970s after the murders of several freaks by local junkies. There's still a camp site some three km past the village and parallel to the sea, but you need your own transport to get there. Adjacent to the camp site is *Auberge Tangaro*, a small but attractive place to stay which is usually empty during the week. Take your own food as meals normally are available only at weekends.

Places to Stay

Hotel Beau Rivage, Place Prince Moulay Hassan, is excellent value and very popular with travellers. It's clean, friendly, overlooks the square and has hot showers at any time of day (for Dr 3). Rooms cost Dr 28 a double. Singles are also available. At a similar price, though not quite in such an interesting position, is *Hotel Majestic*, Rue Laalouj. It is friendly, clean, has cold showers (Dr 1.50) and costs Dr 25/40 a single/double. It's popular and is often full by midday, even in winter. Also in this category is *Hotel du Tourisme*, Rue Mohammed ben Messaoud. The staff is friendly and there are good rooftop views, but no hot showers. Rooms cost Dr 17/25/37 a single/double/triple without sea views and Dr 27/40 a double/triple with sea views. It also has rooms with four beds (Dr 50) and five beds (Dr 60).

A hotel right next to the ramparts with a view of the sea (at least from the top rooms) is *Hotel Smara*, Rue de la Scala. It is excellent value – clean, pleasant and friendly. A double room costs Dr 42/52 without/with sea views. There are hot showers and great views from the top of the building. Similar is *Hotel Restaurant Atlantique*, in a cul-de-sac off the same street but closer to Place Prince Moulay Hassan.

For a simple room in the souks, check out *Hotel Chakir* or *Hotel des Amis*.

More expensive, classified hotels include the one-star *Hotel des Remparts*, Rue Ibn Rochd, and the two-star *Hotel Tafraout*, off Rue Allal ben Abdallah. The Remparts has seen better days, but retains a lot of charm. It is a better choice than the Tafraout. It costs Dr 45/60 single/double with bath. If it's full, try either *Hotel Mechouar* or *Hotel Sahara*, more or less adjacent to one another on Ave Oqba ben Nafii.

The best camp site is about three km past the village of Diabat and adjacent to Auberge Tangaro. You get there by driving about six km south of Essaouira on the Agadir road before turning off to the right. It should be signposted (if the sign hasn't disappeared). You will need your own transport. Otherwise there's *Camping Municipal* on Blvd Mohammed V, some 600 metres before you get to the ramparts of the old town. If arriving by bus, ask the driver to drop you there as it's a long walk from the bus terminal.

Places to Eat

There are quite a few small Moroccan-style restaurants that offer good, tasty food. For around Dr 10 to Dr 15 you get bread, vegetables, a salad, tajine or kefta and chips. All these little places display their wares in the front window. There's a cluster of them about three-quarters of the way up Rue Allal ben Abdellah, walking away from Place Prince Moulay Hassan, where the road begins to narrow. There are also some in the narrow street and small square between the mosque on Place Prince Moulay Hassan and the ramparts, which flank Ave Oqba ben Nafii. The restaurant in the small square is a popular hang-out with travellers.

Restaurant Bab Lachour, at the bottom of Place Prince Moulay Hassan next to the bank, is worth checking out. It looks expensive, but offers four-course set-menus for Dr 50. There's also an à la carte menu. Similar, and diagonally opposite, is *Restaurant Essalam*.

For a splurge on seafood, head to *Chez Sam* in the harbour area. This restaurant is in a somewhat eccentric building that looks something like a cross between an old wooden boat and an antique shop. The atmosphere, however, is delightful. You can eat a fish meal for as little as Dr 20 to Dr 30. A four-course, set-menu costs Dr 35 and a three-course meal, with lobster as the main dish, costs Dr 80. The restaurant also has local (Dr 7) and imported (Dr 10) beers and Moroccan wines (Dr 35).

Hotel Beau Rivage, with its outdoor tables, is a popular place with both locals and tourists to sit and have coffee or mint tea and watch the world go by at any time of day, but especially in the evening.

For cheap fresh barbequed fish, try the umbrella stalls just past Restaurant Bab Lachour. Don't be put off by stall owners rushing up to you trying to coax you into their stalls, just pick one and sit down to five sardines, a chunk of bread, hot sauce and lemon for Dr 4 – great value.

Entertainment

If you're looking for a bar, there's not much choice. *Chez Sam* serves beer and wine, but otherwise it's down to the bar *Chalet de la Plage* at Hotel des Remparts, on the promenade. Opposite is *Hotel des Iles*, which has a bar and you don't have to be a resident to drink there.

FÈS

Fès is the oldest of Morocco's imperial cities, founded shortly after the Arabs swept across North Africa following the death of the Prophet. It has been the capital of Morocco a number of times and for long periods. Like Marrakesh and Meknès, it's full of magnificent buildings that reflect the incomparable brilliance of Arab-Berber imagination and artistry.

The souk is one of the largest in the world and the most interesting in Morocco. Its narrow winding alleys and covered bazaars are crammed with every conceivable sort of craft workshop, teashop, restaurant, meat, fruit and vegetable stall, mosque and dye pit. But it's not just the sights that are going to draw you here, it's the exotic smells, the hammering of metalworkers, the call of the *muezzin*, the need to jostle past a team of uncooperative donkeys. You will have an experience you're never going to forget. You can easily spend a week wandering through this endless labyrinth and still not be ready to leave.

Idriss I founded Fès on the right bank of the Oued Fès around 789 AD, in what is now the Andalous Quarter. His son, Idriss II, extended the city to the left bank in 809 AD, and the two parts are now known as Fès el Bali. The 11th and 12th-century Berber rulers, the Almoravides and Almohades, used Marrakesh as their capital and it wasn't until the Merenids (the last of the Berber dynasties) came to power in 1248 that Fès once again became the pre-eminent city in North Africa. It was the Merenids who established the city of Fès el Jdid (Fès the New) alongside Fès el Bali in 1276.

With the rise to power of the Sa'adis in the 16th century, Marrakesh once again became the capital, though Fès enjoyed a revival under the Alawite ruler Moulay Abdullah in the 19th century.

Construction of the Ville Nouvelle was begun by the French in 1916 on the plateau to the south-west of the two ancient cities.

Information

Tourist Office The ONT office is on Place de la Résistance in the new city. It has little of interest other than the printed brochures available all over the country, but you can get an official guide to take you through the medina. They cost Dr 35 for half a day and are not necessary unless you are really bothered about getting lost. The office is open from 8 am to 12 noon and 2 to 6 pm Monday to Friday, and 8 am to 12 noon on Saturday.

The local syndicat d'initiative is inside the bank on Place Mohammed V, also in the new town. It is open the same hours as the bank and has the same maps and brochures as the ONT office.

Official guides are available at the tourist office, but there are plenty of unofficial ones hanging around Bab Bou Jeloud. These guys can be good, and are usually cheap (about Dr 10). Before agreeing to go with one though, make sure you know exactly which sites you will be seeing, and if you don't want to be shown

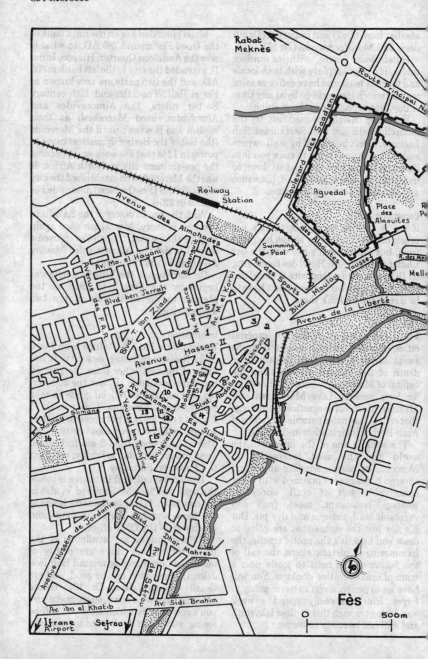

Fès

0   500m

Rabat
Meknès

Route Principal Ne

Boulevard des Saadiens

Aguedal

Place
des
Alaouites

Blvd des Alaouites

Railway
Station

Avenue des Almohades

Swimming
Pool

Av des Sports

Blvd. Moulay Youssef

Avenue de la Liberté

Av. Mo. el Hayani

B. Chenguit

Avenue des FAR

Blvd. ben Jerrah

Blvd. T. Ibn Ziad

Av. de France

Av. M. el Korbi

5

3   2

Avenue   Hassan II

6

7

Av. Mohammed

Mohammed

Abdallah Chefchaouni

10

25

Blvd.

Es Slaoui

4

13

18

Av. Moulay Slimane

16

15

Boulevard Youssef ben Tachfine

Avenue Hussein de Jordanie

Blvd. Dhar Mahres

Av. de Sefrou

Av. Sidi Brahim

Av. ibn el Khatib

Ifrane
Airport

Sefrou

R. des Me

Mell

Hô des
ma

R.
Pe

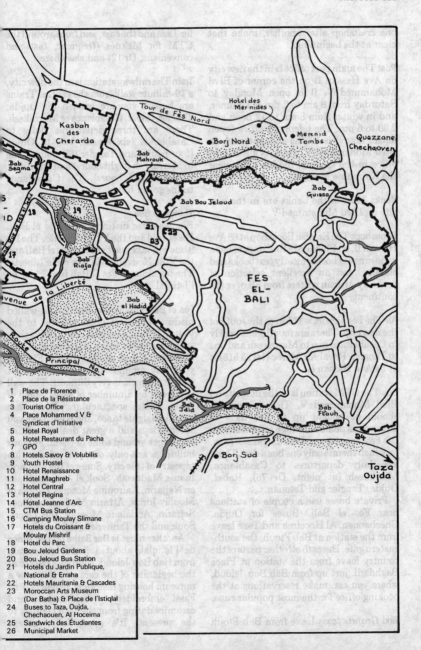

1	Place de Florence
2	Place de la Résistance
3	Tourist Office
4	Place Mohammed V & Syndicat d'Initiative
5	Hotel Royal
6	Hotel Restaurant du Pacha
7	GPO
8	Hotels Savoy & Volubilis
9	Youth Hostel
10	Hotel Renaissance
11	Hotel Maghreb
12	Hotel Central
13	Hotel Regina
14	Hotel Jeanne d'Arc
15	CTM Bus Station
16	Camping Moulay Slimane
17	Hotels du Croissant & Moulay Mishrif
18	Hotel du Parc
19	Bou Jeloud Gardens
20	Bou Jeloud Bus Station
21	Hotels du Jardin Publique, National & Erraha
22	Hotels Mauritania & Cascades
23	Moroccan Arts Museum (Dar Batha) & Place de l'Istiqlal
24	Buses to Taza, Oujda, Chechaouen, Al Hoceima
25	Sandwich des Étudiantes
26	Municipal Market

one craftshop after another, make that clear at the beginning.

Post The main post office is in the new city on Ave Hassan II on the corner of Blvd Mohammed V. It is open Monday to Saturday from 8 am to 2 pm in summer, and in winter from 8 am to 12 noon and 2.30 to 6 pm. The telephone office (open longer hours) is off the side entrance on Blvd Mohammed V. There is also a post office in the medina, hidden away near the Kairouine Mosque.

Banks Most of the banks are in the new city on Blvd Mohammed V.

Bookshops The English Bookshop at 68 Ave Hassan II, on Place de la Résistance, has a wide range of books, mostly textbooks and classics, and an excellent selection of books by African writers from all over the continent.

Air The Fès airport is 15 km to the south of the new city. There are four flights weekly to Casablanca, two to Marrakesh and one to Tangier. Royal Air Maroc (tel 25 516) is at 54 Ave Hassan II.

Bus The CTM station is in the new city on Blvd Mohammed V. Tickets can and should be bought up to five days in advance as demand is high, especially on the Fès-Tangier and Fès-Marrakesh runs, on which there is only one bus a day. There are daily departures to Casablanca, Marrakesh (at night, Dr 76), Rabat, Oujda, Tangier and Tetouan.

Private buses use a couple of stations near Fès el Bali. Buses for Oujda, Chechaouen, Al Hoceima and Taza leave from the station at Bab Ftouh, the southeastern gate. Buses to all other parts of the country leave from the station at Place Baghdadi, just up from Bab Bou Jeloud, where you can make reservations at the booking office for the most popular runs.

Taxi *Grands taxis* leave from Bab Ftouh

for Taza and the east, and from around the CTM for Meknès (frequent, fast and convenient, Dr 12) and elsewhere.

Train The railway station is in the new city, a 10-minute walk from the centre. Trains are best if you are headed for Oujda, Tangier, Rabat, Casablanca or Marrakesh. There are three departures daily to Casablanca (six hours), two to Oujda (four hours) and Tangier (6½ hours), one to Marrakesh (eight hours) and one direct to Rabat (4½ hours). The Casablanca trains go via Rabat.

Things to See

Fès has three distinct parts: Fès el Bali, Fès el Jdid and the Ville Nouvelle. The No 9 bus will take you between Fès el Bali and the Ville Nouvelle, via Ave de la Liberté. The terminus in Fès el Bali is at Place de l'Istiqlal.

Fès el Bali This is the original old-walled medina and is of great interest to the visitor. Its walls encircle one massive souk – an incredible maze of twisting alleys, blind turns and smaller souks. Finding your way around, at least for the first couple of times, is very difficult. The wall is pierced by a number of gates, some of them quite spectacular. There are countless sights to see, and it will take you several days and a great deal of walking just to get around some of them. Famous buildings are only one part of the rich tapestry of this city. Some of the best are: Inania Madrasah, Souk el Attarin, Place en Nejjarin, Kairouine Mosque, Zaouia of Moulay Idriss, Attarin Madrasah, Place Seffarin, Andalous Mosque, the Dyers' Souk and the Tanneries (Dabbaghin).

Another must is **Dar Batha** on the Place de l'Istiqlal, about a five-minute walk from Bab Bou Jeloud. Built as a palace at the beginning of the century, it is now a museum housing historical artefacts, fine Fassi embroidery, tribal carpets and ceramics dating from the 14th century to the present. It's open daily, except

Tuesday, from 9 am to 12 noon and 3 to 6 pm.

While the buildings are interesting, they aren't really the essence of Fès. This is more likely to be found by letting your senses lead you slowly through the crowded bazaars, pausing, wherever the mood takes you, to watch something of interest, to rummage through the infinite variety of articles for sale, or simply to experience the heartbeat of this Aladdin's Cave. Like most Moroccan souks, this one is divided into areas representing different craft guilds and commodity shops, and it will take days before you discover where some of them are.

Although not strictly necessary, it's a good idea to take a guide for your first two or three visits to Fès el Bali, if only to get an idea of the layout of the streets and the location of the activities that most interest you. Even if you don't take a guide and get hopelessly lost, which you will, it's no problem. For a couple of dirham, there are any number of street urchins who will lead you out of the maze to a familiar landmark.

If you take a guide, beware of the usual pitfalls. The way guides make their money (apart from what you pay) is from commissions from shopowners for taking you to their shop. Naturally, the guide's cut is built into the price of anything you buy, so if you see something you like, remember the shop and go back later without the guide. And if you have acquired a hanger-on (very easy!), make this quite clear from the outset. It's one of their favourite tricks to tag along and get a commission even though you haven't engaged them as a guide.

Another important point is to make sure you have a common language with your guide. If you don't speak French, make sure the guide speaks your own language well enough for you to understand. Many of them speak enough to point out the obvious features of what you're seeing, but not enough to answer any questions.

The main entrance to Fès el Bali is **Bab**

Bou Jeloud and, like the main entrances to most large Moroccan cities, you will encounter people offering to be guides. But here, there is very little hassle if you tell them you don't want a guide. Should they persist, tell them you're staying at one of the cheap hotels just inside the gate. If they simply won't let go, sit down and have a mint tea at one of the numerous cafés just inside the gate and wait until they go away.

Fès el Jdid This is the other walled city, built next to Fès el Bali by the Merenids in the 13th century. Although it has the old Jewish quarter and a couple of mosques, it is far less interesting than Fès el Bali. It is, however, much easier to get around and no-one will hassle you for guide services. There are some spectacular buildings, including the entrance to the **Royal Palace** on Place des Alaouites, which is a stunning example of modern restoration work. Also, at the northern end of the main street – Grande Rue de Fès el Jdid – is the enormous Merenid gate of **Bab Dekakene**, the formal entrance to the royal palace. Between this gate and Bab Bou Jeloud are the **Bou Jeloud Gardens**, which are very well maintained and a quiet place to relax.

The Grande Rue de Fès el Jdid, though lined with shops, a few hotels and cafés, lacks the atmosphere of the main street of Fès el Bali.

For a spectacular overview of Fès, walk to the end of Grande Rue de Fès el Jdid and through Bab Dekakene. Then, instead of turning right towards Bab Bou Jeloud, go straight on through the Old Mechouar and out through Bab Segma, taking the road that follows the left hand wall of the Kasbah des Cherarda to the corner of Tour de Fès Nord. Turn right and walk towards Borj Nord. Fès lies before you. Borj Nord was once a fortress, but is now the **Arms Museum**.

Further along, past Hotel des Merinides, are a number of **Merenid Tombs**.

The **Ville Nouvelle** lies to the south-east

of Fès el Jdid. It is laid out in the usual French manner with wide, straight streets. Here you'll find the majority of restaurants and hotels, as well as the post office, banks and transport connections. It lacks the atmosphere of the medina, but if you don't want to stay in either a medina cheapie or a five-star palace, this is where you'll end up. It is about a 10-minute bus ride to Bab Bou Jeloud, and the buses run frequently.

Places to Stay

In summer, demand for accommodation is high and the smaller hotels fill up early. If you arrive late in the day, you may have to take what's closest and look for something better in the morning. Many of the cheapies in Fès el Jdid and Fès el Bali put up their prices in summer to around what you would pay for the far better accommodation in the Ville Nouvelle. Also, they let single rooms out to two and three people and charge accordingly.

The most colourful and interesting places to stay are the cheapies clustered around Bab Bou Jeloud at the entrance to Fès el Bali. They're all pretty basic and most don't have showers (or a functioning shower). That's no problem as there's a good *hammam* very close by with separate times for men and women. The best is *Hotel du Jardin Publique*, down a side lane (signposted) just outside the Bab. It's clean, quiet, friendly and good value at Dr 30/35/42 a single/double/triple. There are a couple of rooms on the 3rd floor with windows facing outwards, rather than the more claustrophobic lower rooms which face the internal courtyard. These upper ones are hotter in summer though. The hotel has cold showers.

If the Jardin Publique is full, try the nearby *Hotel Erraha* or *Hotel National*. The National is down an alley on the left-hand side going uphill from the Erraha. Just inside Bab Bou Jeloud are another couple of hotels on the right-hand side, including *Hotel Mauritania* and *Hotel Cascades*. The Cascades probably is the better of the two, as the rooms at the Mauritania are very basic and small. Both charge Dr 25/30 a single/double.

If all these are full (which they often are late in the day during summer) or if you would like to be closer to the medina, try the three cheapies in Fès el Jdid along Grande Rue de Fès el Jdid (the main street). Prices are similar to those at Bab Bou Jeloud. The one closest to Bab Bou Jeloud is *Hotel du Parc*, near the end of the street. It is clean and good value for money. At the bottom of the street, just inside Bab Smarine (Semmarin), are *Hotel du Croissant* and *Hotel Moulay Mishirf*.

In the new town there's a good choice of cheap to middle-range hotels. Most have showers, though not all have hot water. The cheapest is the *Youth Hostel*, 18 Rue Mohammed El Hansali, which costs Dr 10 a person with cold showers. It's a fairly new building and they will let you sleep on the roof if there are no beds left.

The cheapest hotels are *Hotel Moghreb*, 25 Ave Mohammed es Slaoui, *Hotel Regina*, 25 Rue Moulay Slimane, and *Hotel Renaissance*. The Moghreb and Regina are basic and clean, but have no showers. They cost Dr 20/30/38 a single/double/triple. The Renaissance is an old, cavernous place, with an entrance lobby resembling an art gallery. It's friendly and clean, but has no showers and costs the same as the Moghreb and Regina.

Better value, and only slightly more expensive, are *Hotel Volubilis*, Blvd Abdallah Chefchaouni and, just around the corner from it, *Hotel Savoy*. Both have good, clean, airy rooms with handbasins and communal cold showers, costing Dr 30/35 a single/double. Very similar is *Hotel Jeanne d'Arc*, 36 Ave Mohammed es Slaoui, which costs Dr 30/40 a single/double. Another is *Hotel Restaurant du Pacha*, 32 Ave Hassan II. It has large, clean, airy rooms overlooking the avenue and very friendly staff. A double room costs Dr 60 (less in winter).

Those looking for better amenities and hot showers should first check out the one-star *Hotel Central*, 50 Rue Samuel Biarnay, at the corner of Blvd Mohammed V. It is excellent value – friendly, clean, secure and easy-going. Rooms with hot shower (mornings and evenings), bidet and handbasin cost Dr 40/48 a single/double. Baggage can be left at the reception desk safely if you're catching a late bus or train. Also very comfortable, pleasant and friendly is *Hotel Royal* (tel 24656), 36 Rue d'Espagne, which costs Dr 51/62 a single/double. All the rooms have their own shower and toilet and there's hot water all day except occasionally in winter when there are not enough guests to warrant it. Another that has been recommended is *Hotel CTM*, costing Dr 57 a double.

The one-star *Hotel Excelsior* (tel 255 602) on Blvd Mohammed V has good doubles with bathroom and hot water for Dr 62. It is not a good choice if you are catching a late bus or train and want to leave your baggage during the day as they charge Dr 10 for the privilege!

For campers, there's a good site at *Camping Moulay Slimane*, Rue Moulay Slimane. It costs Dr 4 a person plus Dr 2 a vehicle. The camp site is very popular with travellers in their own vehicles, and an excellent place to ask around for share-expenses lifts, especially if you're heading to Algeria to go down through the desert to Niger, Mali and the West African coast. Quite a lot of the people who stay here have vehicles, which they intend to sell in Togo, Burkina Faso or Ivory Coast. There are no tents for hire and cold showers only. There's a swimming pool (often empty) and a shop (expensive).

Places to Eat

The best place to find a cheap meal in Fès el Bali is around Bab Bou Jeloud and Bab Guissa, though the ones around the Bab Bou Jeloud are pretty indifferent to quality as they now see too many tourists. The best of the bunch probably is *Restaurant Bouayad*, next to Hotel Cascades, which offers reasonable tajine

and is open until late at night. *Restaurant des Jeunes*, closer to the gate, has good set meals, but beware. They have two menus and give you the one they think you can afford – Dr 25 or Dr 35 for the same meal. Good tajines for Dr 15, soup Dr 2 (with bargaining). There are similar restaurants along Grande Rue de Fès el Jdid, close to Bab Smarine.

For something better, try the restaurant in the Bou Jeloud Gardens. It is popular with young Moroccans, but expect to pay considerably more for a meal.

For a splurge in Fès el Bali head for *Palais Jamais*, close to Bab Guissa, which has a terrace overlooking the medina. The food is excellent, but you'll be up for a minimum of Dr 140 a head for the sumptuous buffet (it's a five-star hotel as well.)

In the new town there's a good choice of relatively cheap restaurants along or just off Blvd Mohammed V, with most of them around the municipal market. One of the best is *Sandwich des Etudiantes*, one block back from Place Mohammed V, on the right hand side walking towards the post office. (Next door is one of the few liquor stores in Fès.) It's popular and cheap. A soup, salad, kefta and sauce would cost about Dr 14. Another very good and nameless place is the blue and white tiled restaurant on Rue 5, which is the second street on the left walking away from Place Mohammed V towards the post office. It's popular, reasonably priced and has an extensive choice of food.

Café Restaurant Mounia at 11 Blvd Med Zerktouni, just around the corner from Hotel Jeanne d'Arc, is a stylish place (waiters with bow ties!). But the prices are reasonable and it has a decent wine list.

You should try the Fassi specialty, pastilla – pigeon pie. It is available in some restaurants, where it is expensive, or from the small shops around Bab Bou Jeloud. Sometimes it can be difficult to find, but one place that seems to have it regularly is the tiny shop on the corner of Talaa Kebira and the small 10-metre-long lane that connects it with Bab Bou Jeloud.

The pie is sweet, spicy and rich. Half a kg (Dr 15) is plenty for two people.

Getting Around
The red *petits taxis* are cheap and plentiful. The drivers use the meters without any fuss. Expect to pay about Dr 5 from the CTM station to Bab Bou Jeloud. Fès has a fairly good local bus service, although the buses are like sardine cans at certain times of the day. The bus number is displayed on the side of the bus near the back door. Useful routes include:

No 3 – Place de la Résistance to Bab Ftouh (for Andalous Quarter)
No 9 – Ave Hassan II to Place de l'Istiqlal (Dar Batha and Bab Bou Jeloud)
No 19 – railway station to Place Baghdadi

FIGUIG
This is a beautiful old Berber village and the last Moroccan town before you get to the Algerian border. Also it is the only crossing point possible for those without vehicles going into Algeria. Palm trees blanket the ruins of the old city.

There's no black market for Algerian dinar and you cannot exchange excess dirham for hard currency.

It's a three-km walk to the border, and from there another km to Beni Ounif. Don't forget to visit the police before walking to the border. The officials on the Algerian side can be a pain in the neck at times, so be prepared for this.

Places to Stay & Eat
There are only two places to stay. The cheapest is *Hotel Sahara*, which is poor value and dirty. It costs Dr 20/30 a single/ double. Much better is *Tourist Hotel*, about one km up the road towards the border. It costs Dr 30 a single and has good clean showers and a terrace café with good views. It's worth making the effort to stay here, even though the buses drop you in front of Hotel Sahara.

Good food is cooked by 'Mohammed the Berber' for Dr 10 (couscous) or Dr 15 (tajine and tea).

GOULIMIME
The enduring myth of the Goulimime Saturday camel market persists despite the fact that for years there have been more tourists than camels to be seen, and precious few of the latter. The ones that are brought here are purely for the benefit of the package tourists, who arrive by the bus-load from Agadir. It's really just a tourist trap and one you can afford to miss.

The town itself is featureless and boring. It's remarkable only for its lack of interest and because it's the furthest south you can go without a military permit, and, therefore, continues to attract a few die-hards. But, depending on the military situation in Western Sahara, you may be able to get as far south as Tan Tan without a permit.

Information
The bus terminal is about one km from the centre of town, which you get to by turning right coming out of the terminal. There are a few buses daily to and from Tiznit. There is one bus daily to Sidi Ifni, departing around 2 pm, costing Dr 8 and taking about two hours. The landscape makes it an interesting journey.

Things to See
If you feel you must contribute to the myth of the camel market, it takes place outside town (take a taxi) on Saturday mornings. Get there just after sunrise, otherwise you won't be able to see the camels for the tourists.

Places to Stay & Eat
Hotel Place bir Inzarane is one of the cheapest places to stay. For Dr 35 a double it is poor value as it has cold showers only. It is, however, better than *Hotel Oued Eddahab*, which is primitive – many of the rooms are dark and dingy, the locks on

the doors are a joke and there are cold showers only, but the sheets are clean. It costs Dr 30 a double. Both these hotels are on the main roundabout in the centre of town.

The only decent hotel is *Hotel Salam*, but they know it and charge Dr 70 to Dr 80 a single.

A cheap but basic meal of fried fish, chilli sauce and bread, for Dr 6 can be had at the café a few doors up from Hotel Place bir Inzarane as you walk away from the roundabout. The only two decent restaurants are *Café de la Poste* and *Café Jour et Nuit*, opposite the post office, where the main road from Tiznit and the road from the bus terminal meet. It's around Dr 35 for a three-course meal.

MARRAKESH

There can be few travellers who have not heard of Marrakesh. During the 1960s and 1970s it was the travellers' mecca, along with Istanbul and Kathmandu – and rightly so! This turn in the fame and fortunes of Marrakesh is only the most recent of the city's ups and downs.

With the snow-capped backdrop of Morocco's highest mountain, Marrakesh's setting is hard to beat. Once one of the most important artistic and cultural centres of the Islamic world, Marrakesh was founded in 1062 AD by Yussef Ibn Tashfin, who built the underground irrigation canals that still supply the city's gardens with water. The city was razed by the Almohades in 1147, but was rebuilt shortly afterwards in the Omayyad style and became the capital of that empire until its collapse in 1262. For the next 300 years, the focus of Moroccan brilliance in the arts moved to Fès. But after the defeat of the Merenids by the Sa'adis in 1520, Marrakesh again became the capital of the empire. In time, decadence set in and Morocco was taken over by the Alaouites, who made Meknès their capital, but Marrakesh regained some of its former prestige when Moulay Hassan was crowned there in 1873.

Information

The tourist office is on the corner of Ave Mohammed V and Ave du President Kennedy. It has the usual range of leaflets, but is a long walk from the budget hotel area. The main post office is on Place 16 du Novembre in the Ville Nouvelle. There is a branch office on Djemaa el Fna. There is a branch of the Banque du Maroc on the bottom side of Djemaa el Fna.

Even though CTM and SATAS have garages on Djemaa el Fna, there is now a centralised bus station from which all buses (regardless of the company) leave. It is just outside the walls of the medina, close to Bab Doukkala, and is a 20-minute walk from the Djemaa el Fna or a Dr 5 taxi ride. The railway station is on Ave Hassan II – a long way from Djemaa el Fna. Take a taxi or bus into the centre.

Things to See & Do

The focal point of Marrakesh is **Djemaa el Fna**, a huge square in the old part of town where many of the budget hotels are located. Other than the souks, this is where everything happens in Marrakesh. Although it's a lively place at any time of day, it comes into its own in the late afternoon and evening. There's no place quite like it anywhere else in Morocco.

Almost without warning, the curtain goes up on one of the world's most fascinating and bizarre spectacles. Rows and rows of open-air food stalls are set up and mouthwatering aromas quickly fill the square. Jugglers, storytellers, snake charmers, magicians, acrobats and benign lunatics quickly take over, each of them surrounded by an audience of jostling spectators, which alternately listens or watches intently and falls about laughing. Meanwhile, assistants hassle spectators for contributions. In between the groups weave hustlers, thieves, knick-knack sellers and bewildered tourists, while, on the outer edges, kerosene lanterns ablaze, are the fruit and juice stalls. Overlooking one end of the square are the huge, eerily-

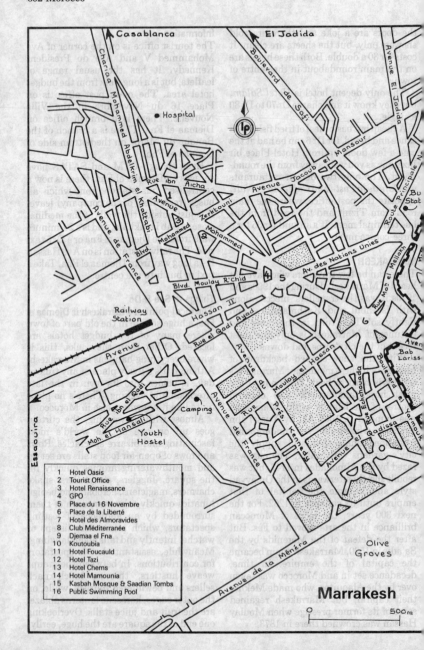

1   Hotel Oasis
2   Tourist Office
3   Hotel Renaissance
4   GPO
5   Place du 16 Novembre
6   Place de la Liberté
7   Hotel des Almoravides
8   Club Méditerranée
9   Djemaa el Fna
10 Koutoubia
11 Hotel Foucauld
12 Hotel Tazi
13 Hotel Chems
14 Hotel Mamounia
15 Kasbah Mosque & Saadian Tombs
16 Public Swimming Pool

Marrakesh

0   500m

Ouarzazate
Meknès
Fès

Bab
el Khemis

Bab Kechich

Zaouia
of Sidi
Bel Abbes

Route

des

Remparts

Rue de Bab Taghzout

Rue Assouel

Rue de Bab Kheuis

Bab
Debbarh

Ben Youssef
Mosque &
Medressa

R. de Bab Debbarh

Tanneries

Bab Doukkala
Mosque

Rue de Bab Doukkla

Rue el Gza

Rue de Dar el

Fatima Zohra

Sidi Abd el

Souk Attarine

Rue Mouassine

R. Azbezt

Bab
Ailen

K. de Bab Ailen

Rue Jesabaine

Rue Dabach

Rue Ba Ahmad

Rue el Koutoubia

Mohammed

Abbes Sebki

7

8

9

10

11

12

13

Museum of
Moroccan Arts
(Dar Si Said)

Graoui

Bab
Rhemat

Ouarzazate

Houmane el Fetouaki

Rue Sidi Mimoun

Rue ben Aggau

Rue Houmane el Kedim

Houmane el Fetouaki

Bab
Jdid

14

Palais de
la Bahia

Rue Yarmouk

Bab
Agnaou

15

Palais
el-Badi

Mellah

Royal
Palace

Bab Ahmar

rport

Bab
Kaiba

Taroudannt

lit Berber tents on the terrace of the Club Méditerranée hotel. From within them you will occasionally hear snatches of folk music being played for the well-heeled up there. Down below, however, the mediaeval pageant unfurls its nightly cornucopia of delights, totally unaffected by the needs of those who prefer their experiences sanitised. Breughel would have had a field day here!

While Djemaa el Fna is justifiably famous for its energy and life, its **souks** are known as some of the best in Morocco for their variety and quality of crafts.

Marrakesh's streets are as labyrinthine as those in Fès and just as busy. But here is a difference. It's a long time since *Marrakesh Express* was written but it sure put the place in the limelight. You will not be able to get within sniffing distance of any entrance to the medina without being beseiged by 'guides', and for every one you *can* shake off, another will be there within seconds. They'll pursue you every inch of the way. Trying to go there without a 'guide' is a waste of time and extremely frustrating, so take one. Just remember that the only thing they are basically interested in is the commission they make by getting you to buy things in the shops. Some are better than others, of course, but that's the bottom line.

The tourist blurb benignly raves on about 'merchants sit cross-legged on heaps of merchandise, a fan waving indolently in the hand'. Nothing could be further from the truth. You are about to confront high-pressure selling, high prices and contempt bordering on abuse if you refuse to buy or baulk at the quoted price. Never spend a lot of time in any one shop unless you seriously want to buy something, otherwise you may well be in for a traumatic experience. Almost all the shops in the souks have stickers saying they take American Express, Diners Club, Visa and many other cards.

This is *not* Fès! It's more like Barter Town in *Mad Max Beyond Thunderdome*! Never believe a word you are told about anything silver, gold or amber. It's never solid, but always plated. The amber is plastic (put a lighted match to it and smell it). Anything said to be 'authentic', 'tribal' or 'antique' is nothing of the sort. Techniques for ageing things are well known here. Thousands of tourists are conned every year, wasting their money on trash.

Having said that, there are some things that can't be faked, such as brass plates, leatherwork, woodwork and, up to a point, carpets.

Away from the souks it's definitely worth a visit to the **Palais de la Bahia**, an old, walled palace with numerous secluded shady courtyards, fountains, living quarters and pleasure gardens. Entry is free, but you must take a guide and he will expect a tip at the end.

There is an incredible **donkey market** every Monday in the nearby valley of **Ourika**. Take a bus from Marrakesh.

If you'd like to do some trekking in the **High Atlas**, ask for either Houssein or Lacem Izahan at *Café Azagya*, about two km before the village of Setti Fatma in the Ourika Valley. These two are young guides that know the Atlas backwards. They can take you for a 30-minute walk or a trek lasting 10 or more days – and they're reliable.

Climbing Mt Toubkal Mt Toubkal (4165 metres) is Morocco's highest mountain. From Marrakesh you will go through some spectacularly beautiful countryside to get to it. Take a bus from Marrakesh to Asni – they leave every hour. There is a *Youth Hostel* at Asni that costs Dr 10 per person a night.

From Asni take a taxi to Imlil, where there is a hostel known as the *CAF Refuge*. Take your own food, unless you are happy to eat omelettes, cheese, bread and oranges, which is all you'll get in Imlil. The refuge costs Dr 17 per night. It has beds, but no sheets or blankets, so take a sleeping bag. There are cooking facilities, pots, pans, crockery and cutlery and the warden takes good care of the place. This is the best place to hire guides. If it's full, there's a pension opposite, where you can stay for Dr 10.

Although it's possible to buy maps of the hiking trails up Mt Toubkal in Imlil, it may be wise to come to Morocco equipped with the guide *Atlas Mountains* by Robin G Collomb (West Col Productions, UK, 1980). This guide covers the region comprehensively. If you are just going up the normal route to the summit via the Mizane Valley, you don't need a guide until you get to the first refuge. From there to the summit you may need one. The guide's fees are usually fixed, though they'll probably expect a tip at the end as well.

On the first day of the trek you walk from Imlil to the Neltner Hut (3207 metres) via the villages of Aroumd and Sidi Chamharouch. This takes about five hours. Bottled drinks are usually available at both villages. The Neltner Hut is a stone cottage built in 1938. It has beds for 29 people in two dormitories, though you have to provide your own sheets and blankets. There's a kitchen with Calor gas stove and a range of cooking utensils. Hot water is available. The charge is Dr 17 a person per night, plus extra if you use the cooking facilities or need hot water. There's a resident warden. Take all your food as there's none for sale. Given plenty of notice, the warden may prepare meals for you.

The ascent from Neltner Hut to the summit should take about four hours, and the descent about two hours. It's best to take water in summer, though generally it isn't necessary in winter. It can be bitterly cold at the top even in summer, so take plenty of warm clothing. On clear days, there are incredible views in all directions, but especially south to the Sahara.

Places to Stay

There are scores of reasonably priced hotels between Rue Oqba ben Nafaa and Rue Riad Zitoun el Kedim. There's not a lot to choose between most of them, except whether they have hot showers or not. Most of the cheapies will charge extra for hot showers (usually Dr 5). Average prices for cheapies would be from Dr 15 to Dr 25 a single and Dr 25 to Dr 45 a double, depending on the season, their standard and your haggling capacity.

Most of the ones available are marked on the detailed map of this area. Which one you choose may very well depend on where there is room. Take your pick.

Hotel El Atlal is a very friendly, family-run place with clean showers and toilets. It has rooms with handbasins for Dr 40 a double (Dr 10 extra during holidays). Hot showers are Dr 5 extra. Baggage is safe left in the rooms. *Hotel Afriquia* is also very pleasant, friendly and has a quiet courtyard. Rooms cost Dr 25 a double with handbasin, but there are cold showers only. *Hotel Central* has good rooms on the upper floors, but the lower ones are dark and dingy. It costs Dr 20/30 a single/double and has cold showers only. Similar, is *Hotel de la Paix*.

Excellent value for a few dirham more is *Hotel Gallia*. It is a beautiful and spotlessly clean place with a quiet courtyard, luxurious TV lounge and hot showers. It costs Dr 38/47 a single/double without bathroom, and Dr 47/58 a single/double with bathroom. It's a gem!

Very popular with travellers who want to stay on Djemaa el Fna is *CTM Hotel*, costing Dr 27/42 a single/double without shower, and Dr 37/49 a single/double with shower (hot water), plus tax (10%). The rooms are pleasant and there's a courtyard on the 1st floor, plus a rooftop terrace where you can watch the activity in the square below. Don't complain about anything here or they may throw you out – they have, after all, a guaranteed clientele.

Hotel de France (tel 22319), also overlooks the square from Djemaa el Fna. There are no singles, and doubles cost Dr 25 to Dr 30, triples Dr 45 and rooms with four beds Dr 60, all without bathrooms.

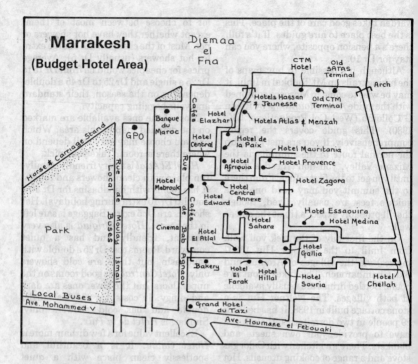

Marrakesh
(Budget Hotel Area)

The hotel has cold showers only. There is a terrace restaurant on both the ground floor and roof.

There are a lot of other hotels in the Ville Nouvelle, but they're more expensive than those around Djemaa el Fna, so there's not much point in staying there unless you need a touch of luxury.

For the die-hards, there's a *Youth Hostel* close to the railway station that costs Dr 10 a night. It's clean and pleasant, and although the warden is something of a strange character, he's harmless. The hostel maintains strict youth hostel hours.

Places to Eat

There are cheap restaurants all around Djemaa el Fna and along Rue Oqba ben Nafaa, which offer a mixture of Moroccan and European-style food. Many of them

do the cooking on the footpath outside the café, so you can see what they have on offer. Some of the cooks and waiters can be very entertaining in at least five or six languages. Again, take your pick. There's not a lot to choose between them. An average meal costs around Dr 10 to Dr 15.

In the evenings, you can't beat eating at the food stalls in Djemaa el Fna between 5 and 9 pm. There's an incredible range of food to choose from – tajine, kebabs, soup, even fish & chips – for around Dr 10 a meal. Just about everyone eats here in the evening.

MEKNÈS

Although a town of considerable size even in the days of the Merinids (13th century), it wasn't until the 17th century that Meknès experienced its heyday. In 1672, having fought for and won the succession to the throne, Sultan Moulay Ismail, the second Alaouite sultan, made Meknès his capital. Over the next 55 years an enormous palace complex, surrounded by some 25 km of wall, with 20 gates, was built by armies of slaves and workers, often whipped on by Moulay Ismail himself. By the time he died in 1727, Meknès had been transformed beyond recognition.

It wasn't to last. After Moulay Ismail's death, the traditional balance of power between Fès and Marrakesh reasserted itself and two reigns later, under Sultan Sidi Mohammed, the capital was moved back to Marrakesh. The earthquake that destroyed Lisbon in 1755 and severely damaged many other Moroccan cities took its toll on Moulay Ismail's construction. No restoration was undertaken and the city has been allowed to crumble and decay ever since, but enough remains to make a visit to this city worthwhile.

The old medina and the French-built Ville Nouvelle are neatly divided by the small valley of the Oued Boufekrane ('oued' is Arabic for river). Train and CTM bus connections are in the new city, while the private buses, cheap hotels, camping and sights are in the old city. It's a 30-minute walk between the two, although there are regular (and very crowded) local buses as well as service taxis.

Information

The syndicat d'initiative is just inside the gates of Esplanade de la Foire, at the top of the valley on Ave Hassan II. Finding someone on duty, however, is a hit and miss affair.

The main post office is in the new town on Place de France. There is another large post office in the medina on Rue Dar Smen, near the corner of Rue Rouamzine. Opening hours are Monday to Saturday from 8 am to 2 pm in summer. The banks are concentrated in the new city, mainly on Ave Hassan II and Ave Mohammed V. Royal Air Maroc (tel 20 963) has an office at 7 Ave Mohammed V.

The CTM terminal is on Ave Mohammed V, near the corner of Ave Forces Armées Royales. There are seven departures daily to Casablanca and Rabat, six to Fès, two to Oujda and one to Tangier. Other buses use the terminal below Place el Hedim in the old city. There are regular departures to Chechaouen, Fès and elsewhere. All the *grands taxis* leave from opposite the bus station in the old town, down from Bab el Mansour. There are regular departures to Fès (Dr 12) and Moulay Idriss (for Volubilis) Dr 5.

The main train station is some way from the centre of the new city on Ave du Senegal. It's much more convenient to use the Abdelkader station, one block down and parallel to Ave Mohammed V, as all trains stop here. All trains to or from Fès, stop in Meknès.

Things to See

The focus of the old city is the massive gate of **Bab el Mansour**, the main access to Moulay Ismail's 17th-century Imperial City. The gate is exceptionally well preserved, and highly decorated with (faded) *zellij* tiles and inscriptions running right across the top.

The gate faces onto Place el Hedim. On the far north side of this square is **Dar Jamai**, a palace built in the late 19th century and recently turned into a good museum. As is often the case in museums housed in historic buildings, the building itself is as interesting as the exhibits. The domed reception room upstairs is furnished in the style of the time, complete with plush rugs and cushions. It is open daily, except Tuesday, from 9 am to 12 noon and 3 to 6 pm. Entry costs Dr 3.

The **medina** proper stretches to the north behind Dar Jamai. The most convenient access is through the arch to the left of Dar Jamai. Though nowhere near as extensive or as interesting as the medina at Fès, it is nevertheless worth a visit and you won't be hassled by 'guides'. Perhaps the most interesting parts are the carpet souks, just off to the left of the main

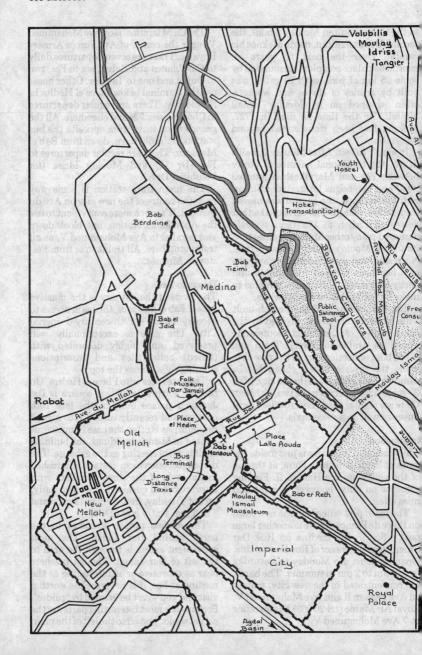

1 GPO
2 Hotel Palace
3 Hotel Touring
4 Hotel Moderne
5 Hotel Majestic
6 Abdelkadar Railway Station
7 Hotel Central
8 CTM Bus Terminal & Hotel Volubilis
9 Hotel Excelsior
10 Hotel Continental

Meknès

0   500m

medina street, about five minutes' walk from Dar Jamai. If you are looking for rugs to buy, Meknès is not a bad place as the shopkeepers are a little more relaxed than elsewhere, particularly Fès. Bargains are still as rare as hen's teeth, but at least the bargaining starts at a reasonable level.

Further along the covered main street is **Bou Inania Medressa**, a contemporary of one with the same name in Fès, having been built in the mid 14th-century. It is not all that conspicuous, apart from the dome over the street, which is easy to spot. With the same layout and features as the Fès madrasahs, this is about the only one where you can get on the roof as it has all been restored. It is open from 9 am to 12 noon and 3 to 6 pm. Entry costs Dr 3.

A visit to the **Imperial City** starts from Bab el Mansour. Once through this gate, the road runs straight ahead before turning right. On the right is an open grass area and a small white building, the **koubba**. Once a reception hall, it is now plain in the extreme and not worth the Dr 3 entry fee. The grassed area actually covers an enormous vaulted granary – the concrete rings are vents. If you bought a ticket for the koubba, it will get you in here too.

On the opposite side of the road is another arch. Through this and on the left is the city's main monument, the **Mausoleum of Moulay Ismail** – one of the few Islamic monuments in Morocco open to foreigners. Despite his extreme brutality, Ismail was and is held in very high esteem, hence, his tomb is a shrine. Once inside, everything is fairly modestly decorated. Although entry is free, the attendant who shows you around will expect a tip. The mausoleum is open from 9 am to 12 noon and 3 to 6 pm. It's closed on Friday morning.

The road continues through another long narrow arch, and from here it's a 20-minute walk around the walls to the southern corner, where there are the excellent **Heri as-Souani** granaries and storerooms. The narrow street here has four-metre-high walls on either side, and,

as it carries a lot of traffic, the diesel fumes hang low on still days and are stifling. The storerooms are impressive in size, and wells for drawing water can be seen. The first few vaults have been restored. The ruins of others, with no roofs, stretch away at the back. Such is the atmosphere here that it is occasionally used as a film set. Entrance is Dr 3 and the opening times are 9 am to 12 noon and 3 to 6 pm.

Steps on the outside of the as-Souani (towards the basin) lead up to a beautiful roof café and garden – an excellent place to rest. Just before you reach the as-Souani, the shady and well-equipped camping ground is through an arch to the left.

The **Agdal Basin**, originally built to serve the dual purposes of reservoir and recreational lake, now supplies the locals with a ready supply of fish.

At **Volubilis**, about 33 km from Meknès, are the largest and best preserved Roman ruins in Morocco. Volubilis dates largely from the 2nd and 3rd centuries AD, though excavations show that the site was originally settled by Carthaginian traders in the 3rd century BC.

Volubilis was one of the Roman Empire's most remote centres and capital of the province of Mauretania, as North Africa was then known. While direct Roman rule lasted for only 240 years after the area's annexation by Claudius in 45 AD, Volubilis's population of Berbers, Greeks, Jews and Syrians continued to speak Latin and practise Christianity until the coming of Islam. The city was finally abandoned in the 18th century when its marble was plundered for the building of Moulay Ismail's palaces in Meknès.

If you like ancient ruins, it's worth a visit to Volubilis. It is an easy day trip from Meknès and you can take in the nearby town of Moulay Idriss.

The whole site has been well excavated and is open daily from sunrise to sunset; entry is Dr 15. The major points of interest are the **House of Orpheus**, the **Basilica, Capitol** and **Forum**, the **Triumphal Arch** and the stunning **mosaics**, the most attractive feature. These are all found in the ruins of the houses lining the Decumanus Maximus, which stretches away up the slope to the north-east. The best mosaics are those in the **House of the Cortege of Venus**, where there's a viewing platform.

Back at the entrance, there is a good café where you can rehydrate yourself.

To get there from Meknès it's best to get a small group together and hire a taxi from just below Place el Hedim in the old city (about Dr 6 a person each way – not including waiting time). Alternatively there are buses to nearby Moulay Idriss from the same place. They leave when they're full and cost Dr 3.50 each way. *Grands taxis*, however, are more frequent. If you take a bus or *grand taxi*, ask the driver to drop you off at the turn-off (signposted) about two km from Moulay Idriss and walk the 2½ km in. As long as it's not stinking hot, it is a pleasant one-hour walk and there is a good chance of hitching back to Meknès with tourists from the car park at the site.

The other main place of interest outside Meknès is **Moulay Idriss**, about 4½ km from Volubilis. The town is named after its founder, Morocco's most revered saint, a great-grandson of the Prophet and the creator of the country's first Arab dynasty. Moulay Idriss fled Damascus in the late 8th century AD after the great civil war, which split the Muslim world into the Shi'ite and Sunni sects.

Moulay Idriss is a very attractive town from a distance, nestled in its cradle of lush mountains. It is heavily promoted in the tourist literature and a profound disappointment.

For Moroccans it's a place of pilgrimage. Non-Muslims, however, get the feeling they are only grudgingly tolerated (it has only been open to infidels for the past 70 years or so). You cannot visit any of the mosques or shrines, and you are not allowed to stay overnight. This being so, it's hardly worth the effort, but if you do want to check it out take a taxi (Dr 6) or bus (Dr 3.50) from just below Place el Hedim in the old city. These are the same taxis and buses that go to Volubilis.

The best day to go to Moulay Idriss is Saturday, market day, when the place is a lot more lively. Also, there are many more buses and *grands taxis* running on Saturday morning.

Places to Stay

Most of the cheapest places are clustered in the old city along Rue Dar Smen and Rue Rouamzine. The best of the lot and excellent value is *Hotel Maroc* on Rue Rouamzine. It's quiet, clean, pleasantly decorated and furnished, all the rooms have a handbasin and most face onto a well-kept courtyard. The cold showers and toilets are also clean and well-maintained. It's a bargain at Dr 20/30 a single/double. Not quite as good is *Hotel de Paris*, also on Rue Rouamzine. This is an older hotel with large airy rooms, table and chair and handbasin, but there are no showers. Rooms cost Dr 25 a double (two beds).

The rest of the cheapies are nothing special and many don't have showers. Cheapest, but basic, are *Hotel Victoria* and *Hotel Agadir*, Rue Dar Smen, which cost Dr 18/20 a single/double (no showers and tiny, scruffy rooms). Slightly better is *Hotel Regina*, Rue Dar Smen, which is a cavernous edifice with the air of a Dickensian workhouse. Rooms cost Dr 20/30 a single/double. Try to get a room on the top floors as the ground-floor rooms are very dingy. Again, there are no showers. Similar is *Hotel de Meknès* a few doors up from the Regina.

In the new town there are only two cheap places to stay. The first is the *Youth Hostel*, very close to the large Hotel Transatlantique. You'll see signs for the Transatlantique in several places, so just follow them to get to the hostel (about one km). It is open from 8 to 10 am, 12 noon to 3, and 6 to 10.30 pm. More convenient is *Hotel Central*, 35 Ave Mohammed V, close to the CTM bus station and Abdelkader railway station. It's relatively

1 Berdaine Mosque
2 Musical Instrument Souk
3 Textiles Souk
4 Carpet Souk
5 Slipper Souk
6 Dar Jamai (Folk Museum)
7 Mansour Palace
8 Hotels de Meknès & Nouveau
9 Hotel Regina
10 Hotel Agadir
11 Hotel Victoria
12 GPO
13 Hotel de Paris
14 Hotel Maroc

Meknès
(The Medina)

good value at Dr 20/30 a single/double. There are cold showers only.

For a hotel with hot showers, check out the one-star *Hotel Touring*, 34 Blvd Allal ben Abdallah. It's good value at Dr 45/57 a single/double without shower and Dr 57/66 a single/double with shower. Similar are *Hotel Volubilis* and *Hotel Excelsior*, both close to one another and the CTM bus station, on Ave des Forces Armées Royales.

The unclassified *Hotel du Marché* on the corner of Zankat Abou Hassan M'Rini and the main street, Ave Hassan II, is reasonable value at Dr 50 double. It fills up early.

Further up-market and more expensive are *Hotel Palace*, Rue de Ghana, *Hotel Majestic*, 19 Ave Mohammed V, *Hotel Panorama*, and *Hotel Continental*, both on Ave des Forces Armées Royales.

For campers, there is an excellent site on the south side of the Imperial City right up against its walls. But it's quite a walk. A taxi from the railway station or the CTM bus station will cost Dr 10. The camp site is a little expensive at Dr 7 a person, Dr 3.50 a vehicle, and Dr 4 a tent space, but it has very clean toilets and showers, washing facilities, a shop and restaurant (three-course meals for Dr 30). Hot showers are Dr 5 extra. The site is open 24 hours.

Places to Eat
Meknès isn't an outstanding city for gastronomic delights. There are very few cheap places to eat that stand out above the rest. If you are staying in the old town, there's a fair choice of simple restaurants doing standard fare along Rue Dar Smen, between Hotel Regina and Place el Hedim. One of the best is *Restaurant Economique* at No 123, one of the few with a sign. It is opposite the gate, just up from Bab el Mansour. There are a few others along Rue Rouamazin.

In the new town, check out *Rotisserie Karam* at 2 Ave Ghana, near the corner of Ave Hassan II. It does some of the best

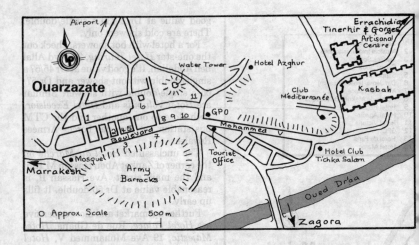

1	Hotel Atlas
2	Restaurant Chez Dimitri
3	Hotel es Salam
4	Hotel Royal
5	Bank
6	Truck & Taxi Park
7	Texaco Station
8	Bank
9	Transportes FAK
10	CTM Bus Station
11	Hotel es Saada

chips in the country, and the set-meal of salad, meat and dessert is good value at Dr 24. *Restaurant Walima* at 2 Ave Hassan II near Ave Mohammed V, does mostly takeaway food, but you can sit upstairs and eat quite cheaply.

For something a bit up-market, try *Restaurant Gambrinus* on Rue Loubnane, opposite the market.

Getting Around

Local buses run between the medina and the new city, but are invariably full. Bus No 2 goes from Bab Mansour to Blvd Allal ben Abdallah, returning to the medina along Ave Mohammed V; No 7 goes from Bab Mansour to the CTM station.

A useful service-taxi route connecting the new and old cities starts in the new city from Ave Ghana, near the corner of Ave Hassan II, opposite Rotisserie Karam. The service taxis are always silver Mercedes with black roofs. The fare is Dr 1.50 a person.

OUARZAZATE

Ouarzazate was built by the French as a garrison and regional administrative centre. It did not exist as a Moroccan town before their arrival, though the Glaoui kasbah of Taourirt, at the far end of town on the road to Tinerhir, has been there a long time. Other than the kasbah, it's a rather nondescript town with little of interest, though Club Méditerranée has built a huge hotel resort on the hill overlooking the town. The best part about Ouarzazate is getting there from Marrakesh over the Tizi-n-Tichka pass. There are superb views over the mountains and down the valleys from many points on this journey. Most travellers spend the night in Ouarzazate on their way to or from Zagora in the Dr'aa Valley or the Todra and Dades gorges. In winter you need plenty of warm clothes to protect against the bitterly cold winds that whip off the snow-covered High Atlas mountains.

Information

The tourist office is in the centre of town, opposite the post office. They're helpful and have a useful bus timetable chart, but precious little else. The taxi and truck park is in a small square behind the main street below the water tower.

Bus The main bus companies (CTM and Transportes FAK) have their terminals on Blvd Mohammed V, close to the post office. CTM has buses to:

Agadir – 3, 8 and 10 pm; Dr 42.50; nine hours

Errachidia – 1 pm; Dr 36; nine hours

Marrakesh – 6 and 10 am, 12 noon, 2 and 4 pm; Dr 31.20; five hours

Taroudannt – 3, 8, 10 and 10.30 am; Dr 35; eight hours

Tinerhir – 6 am and 12 noon; Dr 27.75; 4¼ hours

Zagora – 12 noon; Dr 27.65; four to five hours

Some of the Zagora buses continue on to M'Hamid, but you must get permission to go to M'Hamid from Zagora, so you'll have to stop at Zagora anyway.

Things to See

The only place worth visiting in Ouarzazate is the **kasbah** at the eastern end of town. In its heyday in the 1930s, at the time of the Glaoui chiefs, it was one of the largest kasbahs in the area. In those days it housed numerous members of the Glaoui dynasty, along with hundreds of their servants and workers. But it appears to have been largely abandoned after the government took it over at independence. Wandering through its narrow streets you'll be struck by how deserted and derelict it feels. Indeed, part of the outer walls facing the Oued Dr'aa appear ready to collapse. The actual 'palace' which the Glaouis occupied, consisting of courtyards, living quarters, reception rooms and the like, is open daily, except Sundays, from 9 am to 12 noon and 3 to 6 pm. A guide is provided. It's worth a visit, but you'll only be shown part of it. The rest of the kasbah can be visited at any time.

Opposite the entrance to the kasbah is another building in the same style, which houses an **artisanal complex**, where you can find stone carvings, pottery and woollen carpets woven by the region's Ouzguita Berbers. It's open Monday to Friday from 8.30 am to 6 pm, closing for lunch between 12 noon and 1 pm, and on Saturdays from 8.30 am to 12 noon.

From any vantage point in Ouarzazate if you look south across the Dr'aa Valley you'll be able to see a magnificent mud-brick fortress. This is the kasbah of **Tifoultoutte**, which, like the one in Ouarzazate, formerly belonged to the Glaouis. It certainly looks romantic from a distance, and indeed, was converted into a hotel in the 1960s for use by the cast of *Lawrence of Arabia*. It is now somewhat kitsch, and used by package tour groups for supposedly authentic tribal music and dance evenings. If that doesn't deter you, take the road to Zagora for about nine km and then turn off (the road bypasses the kasbah). You'll probably have to take a taxi.

In the opposite direction, off the road to Marrakesh and some 31 km from Ouarzazate, is the village of **Ait Benhaddou**, which offers some of the most exotic and best-preserved kasbahs in the Atlas region. This is hardly surprising as it had money poured into it as a film set, notably for *Lawrence of Arabia* and *Jesus of Nazareth*. Much of the village was rebuilt for filming *Jesus of Nazareth*. Its fame lives on, but the population has dwindled. To get there, take the main road to Marrakesh and turn off after 22 km when you see the signpost for the village. Ait Benhaddou is another nine km down a good bitumen track. There are occasional local buses from Ouarzazate, though it's a lot easier to get there by share taxi. Otherwise, ask around among tourists in the restaurants or at La Gazelle. Hitching is difficult.

There are also some very impressive kasbahs in the oasis town of **Skoura**, some 38 km east of Ouarzazate on the road to Tinerhir.

Places to Stay

It can sometimes be difficult to find budget accommodation in Ouarzazate if you arrive late in the day. There are not many budget hotels but two of the cheapest are *Hotel Atlas* and *Hotel Royal*. The Royal fills up earlier because it's more obviously placed on Blvd Mohammed V. They're both clean, have hot water and their staff are friendly. The Atlas costs Dr 15/30/35 a single/double/triple without bathroom and Dr 40 a double with bathroom and toilet. It also has a room for five (two double beds and a single) for Dr 63, the walls of which are covered completely with an amateur oil painter's rendition of scenes from *Ali Baba & the Forty Thieves*. The communal bathrooms are reasonably clean and hot showers cost Dr 4 extra. The hotel has its own restaurant, which is very popular with travellers. Prices and facilities at the Royal are similar. It, too, has a restaurant.

In the same category are *Hotel es Salam*, Blvd Mohammed V, and *Hotel es Saada*, Rue de la Poste. Both were closed for renovations, but by now should be open again. There's also *Hotel La Vallee*, on the road to Zagora about two km from the centre of Ouarzazate, which has similar prices to the Atlas and Royal.

There is a camp site past the kasbah on the road to Tinerhir, but it's very run-down, inconvenient and almost the same price as a hotel.

Going up-market, there is *La Gazelle* about 1½ km out of town on the road to **Marrakesh**. If you're busing from Marrakesh, ask the driver to drop you there. It's well-lit, so you can't miss it. It's a two-star hotel with its own swimming pool and restaurant. The rooms are clean and comfortable and there are hot showers. Quite a few tourists with their own cars stay here, so there's a good chance of arranging lifts to nearby places of interest.

Places to Eat

Most travellers eat either at *Hotel Atlas* or *Hotel Royal*. Both offer reasonably priced couscous, tajine, soups and omelettes, though the Royal often has nothing left in the evenings except omelettes.

For a minor splurge, or if you're simply looking for good Moroccan food, you can't beat *Restaurant Chez Dimitri*, Blvd Mohammed V, in the next block to the Royal. It's very popular and the food is excellent. A three-course meal will cost Dr 43 and it's the only restaurant (apart from the large hotels) where you can buy beer, wine (Dr 18 to Dr 35 per bottle) and spirits. It's definitely the only place to go on a winter's evening as it has a pot-belly stove from which you can soak up enough heat to keep you warm throughout the night. Get there early if you don't want to wait for a table.

OUJDA

This is the last town before the Algerian border, and if you have just come from Algeria, make the most of the very relaxed, un-Moroccan atmosphere – there are no hassling touts, apart from the occasional offers to change money.

There are no buses to the border, 13 km away. A taxi will cost up to Dr 50, depending on your bargaining power. Hitching may be slow as there are few cars.

The town itself is of little interest – the medina is quite small and the French new city lacks character. If you are heading for Fès, there are evening trains which will get you there early the next morning.

Information

The main post office is in the centre on Ave Mohammed V, the main street. The banks are concentrated on Ave Mohammed II. *Grands taxis* to Nador leave from Place du Maroc and from outside the bus station.

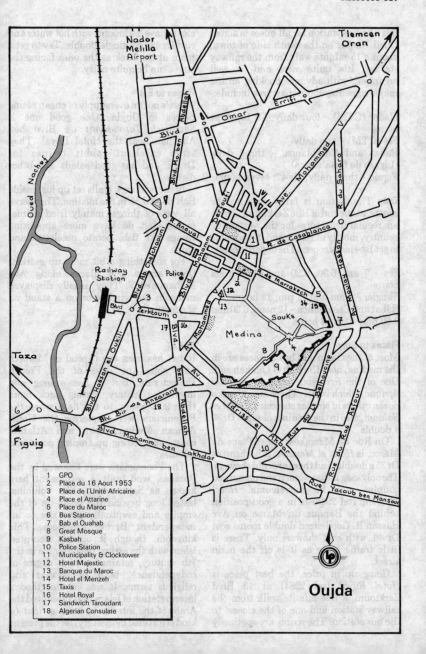

1 GPO
2 Place du 16 Aout 1953
3 Place de l'Unité Africaine
4 Place el Attarine
5 Place du Maroc
6 Bus Station
7 Bab el Ouahab
8 Great Mosque
9 Kasbah
10 Police Station
11 Municipality & Clocktower
12 Hotel Majestic
13 Banque du Maroc
14 Hotel el Menzeh
15 Taxis
16 Hotel Royal
17 Sandwich Taroudant
18 Algerian Consulate

Oujda

Bus The bus station for all buses is across Oued Nachef on the south side of town, about a 15-minute walk from the railway station. It's quite new and is well organised, with advance booking on the major runs. Regular departures include:

Nador (CTM) – four daily; Dr 15; three hours
Fès (CTM) – two daily
Rabat and Casablanca – three daily (Lignes de Casablanca)
Figuiq – three daily; Dr 42; seven hours

Train The station is fairly close to the centre, at the end of Rue Zerktouni. There are regular departures for the west of the country, mostly at night, and it's possible to get 1st-class sleepers. The departures are:

Fès – 7 am, 6.30, 9.20 and 11 pm; six hours
Tangier – 7 am and 11 pm; 13 hours
Rabat and Casablanca – 12 noon, 6.30 and 9.20 pm; 10 to 12 hours

Places to Stay
Most of the cheap and basic places are in the medina, near the Bab el Ouahab end. One of the first you come to is *Hotel Afrique*, which is OK. There are at least a dozen others of similar standard. *Hotel es Salaam*, also in the medina, charges Dr 30 a double.

On Rue de Marrakesh, near Place du Maroc, is *Hotel el Menzeh*. It is cheap at Dr 35 a double, and there are cold showers. The only snag is that women and unmarried couples may be unwelcome. *Hotel Majestic* (tel 2948) is in a good position behind the Banque du Maroc on Ave Hassan II. Good-sized double rooms cost Dr 40, with cold showers only. There is little traffic noise as it is off the main street.

Going up in price, the best place is *Hotel Royal* (tel 2284) at 13 Blvd Zerktouni, a five-minute walk from the railway station and one of the closest to the bus station. The rooms are spotlessly clean, have bathrooms with hot water and cost Dr 49/65 a single/double. Try to get a room at the back as the ones facing the street can be quite noisy.

Places to Eat
There's not an oversupply of cheap eating places in Oujda. One good one is *Sandwich Taroudannt* on Blvd ben Abdellah near the Hotel Royal. They serve excellent rabbit tajines for Dr 12, and has good salads and other dishes.

In the evenings, stalls set up just inside Bab el Ouahab in the medina. They serve all sorts of things, mainly fried animal organs, but do have more appetising things like fish, potato omelettes and chips.

For something a bit more up-market, there are a few places along Ave Mohammed V. They usually display a menu in the window or on a stand on the footpath.

RABAT

Rabat has been the capital of Morocco only since the days of the French Protectorate. But it has a long and interesting history, dating back more than 2000 years, to the days when the Phoenicians were exploring the North African Mediterranean and Atlantic coasts and setting up trading posts and colonies.

The Phoenicians were followed by the Romans, who built a settlement here known as Sala, which, like Volubilis, lasted long beyond the break-up of the empire and eventually gave rise to an independent Berber kingdom. This kingdom, though it quickly accepted Islam with the arrival of the Arabs in the 7th century, retained a high degree of independence, both in secular and religious terms. It was its unorthodox interpretation of Islam that prompted the Arabs of the interior to build a *ribat* (a kind of fortified monastery) on the present site of the kasbah to try to bring the Berbers into line.

The orthodox authorities were relatively successful in this venture, and by the time a new settlement was established at Salé, on the opposite side of the estuary in the 11th century, the original town had all but been abandoned.

Next on the scene were the Almohades in the 12th century. They built a new kasbah on the site of the *ribat* and used it as their base for the conquest of Spain. The city was further expanded by Yacoub el Mansour, who built the magnificent Oudaia Gate of the kasbah and the never-finished Hassan Mosque. This period of glory, however, was brief, and on the death of Mansour, the city rapidly declined in importance.

It was to remain that way until the early 17th century when it was resettled by Muslims expelled from Spain. Their numbers augmented by renegade Christians, Moorish pirates and adventurers of many nationalities, the settlement asserted its independence once more and the stage was set for the most colourful era of Rabat's history – that of the Sallee Rovers. The pirate corsairs who set sail from here attacked and plundered thousands of merchant vessels returning to Europe from Asia, West Africa and the Americas throughout much of the 17th century. They were feared far and wide. Only towards the end of the century were they finally subdued by the Alaouites under Moulay Ismail.

All the different influences and architectural styles that have swept through Rabat have left an interesting legacy, and it's worth spending a few days here. Though it definitely retains a distinctive Moroccan flavour, Rabat is unlike other Moroccan cities as so few of its people are involved in the tourist trade. Most are government and office workers. That being so, you are in for a treat – no hassles. You can even walk through the souk without fear of high-pressure selling.

Tourist Office & Banks There are two places you can find information and maps: ONT, 22 Ave al Jazair, and the syndicat d'initiative, Rue Patrice Lumumba. Neither has much for budget travellers. The banks are concentrated along Ave Mohammed V. The Banque Marocain du Commerce Extérieur is open from 8 am to 8 pm Monday to Friday, and weekends from 10 am to 2 pm and 4 to 8 pm.

Useful Addresses The main embassy area is around Place Abraham Lincoln and Ave de Fas (Fas appears on street signs and means Fès). The Algerian, Egyptian and Mauritanian embassy addresses are given in the Visa section. The main airline offices are on Ave Mohammed V: Royal Air Maroc, Air France and Iberia. Some useful addresses are:

French Consulate
    Ave Allal ben Abdallah
Senegal Embassy
    11 Ave de Marrakesh, (tel 26090)
Spanish Embassy
    3 Rue Mohammed el Fateh
Tunisian Embassy
    6 Ave de Fas, (tel 25644)
UK Embassy
    17 Blvd Tour Hassan, (tel 20905)
USA Embassy
    Ave de Fas

British Council The British Council (tel 69361) is at 3 Zankat Descartes, one block from the railway station. It has a library, and shows feature films twice a week. It is open from 9.30 am to 12.15 pm and 2.30 to 5.45 pm Tuesday to Friday, and from 2.30 to 5.45 pm on Mondays.

Bookshops There's a good English-language bookshop at 7 Zenkat Alyamama, behind the British Council, run by Mohammed Belhaj. He's a friendly person and stocks a good selection of mainly second-hand English and American novels, guides, language books, dictionaries, etc. They're cheap and if you take a book back in less

Boulevard Mostafa as Saih

Blvd. Mokhtar Gazoulit

Ave. Sidi Mohamed ben Abdallah

Avenue

Av. Abdelkrim

al Moukaouam

Ave al Maghrib al Arabi

Avenue du Mali

Ave de Madagascar

Pl. Moham. Zerktouni

Avenue Hassan II

Casablanca
Bus Station

Rabat-Agdal
Station

Ibn al Ouzzane

Avenue an Nasr

Av. Abdelhamid el Marrakchi

Avenue Pasteur

Avenue Ibn Toumerte

Rue Oqbah

Rue Oqbah

Ibn Khaldoun

Av. M. Youssef

Blvd. al Amir

Al Abtal

Ibn Khattab

Avenue

Ave. ibn Hamz

Ave. ibn Batota

Ave. Moulay

Great
Mosque

Avenue al Omar

Oumam al Mouttahida

Royal
Palace

R. Lumumb Mohammed V

Ave. Yacoub el Mansour

Boulevard ad Doustour

Blvd.

0   Scale   ½   1 km

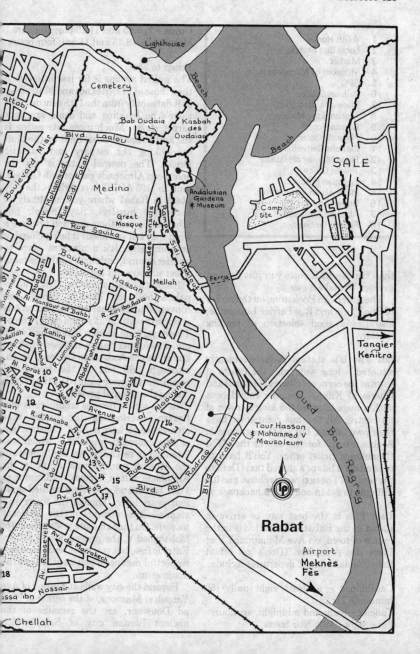

1	Youth Hostel
2	Local Bus Station
3	Market
4	Museum of Moroccan Arts
5	GPO
6	Railway Station
7	Place des Alaouites
8	Archaeology Museum
9	Balima Hotel
10	Place du Golan
11	Catholic Cathedral
12	Place Moulay al Hassan
13	Tourist Office
14	Egyptian Embassy
15	Place Abraham Lincoln
16	British Embassy
17	Algerian Embassy
18	French Embassy

than two weeks it costs you just Dr 2 on average to make a swap.

The American Bookstore, on the corner of Rue Tanja and Rue Patrice Lumumba, also has a good selection of reading matter.

Bus The bus station is inconveniently situated a long way from the centre of town at the corner of Charia Hassan II and Charia al Kifah – a major roundabout with a huge illuminated king's crown at its centre. All the bus companies have their own offices, but all the signs are in Arabic, except for the one at the CTM Casablanca ticket office. You'll have to take either a bus or a shared taxi (Dr 6) to the centre. (The taxi rank is chaos, and it's difficult to get in one with a backpack.)

Train This is the best way to arrive in Rabat as the Rabat Ville station is in the centre of town, on Ave Mohammed V at Place des Alaouites. (Don't get off at Rabat Agdal.) Direct departures include:

Casablanca – at least eight daily (50 minutes); Dr 22
Tangier – 8 am and midnight, six hours
Fès – eight daily; four hours

Oujda – 2, 9.45 and 11.15 pm; 10 hours
Marrakesh – 8.45 and 11 am; four hours

Things to See
The walled **medina** is far less interesting than those at Fès, Meknès and Marrakesh as it dates only from the 17th century. But there's no hassling and some excellent carpet shops. Much more interesting is the **Kasbah des Oudaias**, built on the bluff overlooking the estuary and Atlantic Ocean. The normal entry is via the enormous Almohade gate of Bab Oudaia, built in 1195 AD. This is perhaps the only place in Rabat where you are likely to encounter hustlers. Say 'hello', but otherwise ignore them and don't believe a word they tell you about it being closed or anything else. It's a pleasant place to wander around, and there's only one main street so you can't get lost.

Inside the kasbah is the 17th century palace built by Moulay Ismail, but converted to the **Museum of Moroccan Arts** and worth visiting. It's open daily, except Tuesdays, from 8 am to 12 noon and 4 to 6 pm. The former palace encloses what are known as the **Andalusian Gardens**, which, although laid out in the traditional Spanish style, were planted by the French during the colonial period.

Rabat's most famous landmark is **Tour Hassan**, overlooking the bridge that crosses the estuary to Salé. Construction of this enormous minaret – which was intended to be the largest and highest in the Muslim world – was begun by the Almohade sultan Yacoub el Mansour in 1195, but abandoned when he died some four years later. Though the tower still stands, little remains of the adjacent mosque. On the same site is **Mausoleum of Mohammed V**, the present king's father. Entry is free, but you must be dressed in a respectful manner if you want to visit the mausoleum.

Beyond the city walls at the end of Ave Yacoub el Mansour, at the corner of Blvd ad Doustour, are the remains of the ancient Roman city of Sala, which subsequently became the independent Berber city of **Chellah**. When abandoned in 1154, it was used by the Almohades as a royal burial ground. Most of what stands today, however, dates from Merenid times when Sultan Abou el Hassan built the enclosing walls and gates. Entry is free and you don't need a guide to take you through, although you'll run into a few touts offering their services.

Lastly, a visit to the **Archaeological Museum**, close to the Grand Mosque on Place Djemaa Assouna, is recommended. It contains some excellent collections of Phoenician, Carthaginian and Roman relics. Some of the Roman exhibits were collected from Volubilis, but others were found at Chellah. The museum is open daily, except Tuesday, from 8.30 am to 12 noon and 2.30 to 6 pm.

Places to Stay

The *Youth Hostel* is on Blvd Misr, between Ave al Moukaouama and Ave al Maghrib al Arabi, opposite the walls of the medina. It costs Dr 10 a night. There are cold showers, but no cooking facilities.

There are several rock-bottom budget hotels on, or just off, Ave Mohammed V as it enters the medina. Few of them make any concession to creature comforts and some don't have showers, cold or otherwise, so they're not good value. An extra dollar or two will buy you far better accommodation outside the medina.

The best of the cheapies is *Hotel Marrakesh*, Rue Sebbahi just off Ave Mohammed V, which costs Dr 25/40/45 a single/double/triple. The management is friendly, but the communal showers are cold. *Hotel des Voyageurs*, on Rue Souika, just off Ave Mohammed V, is similar. Cheaper are *Hotel du Centre*, on the right as you enter the medina, which costs Dr 30 a double (no singles), and the hotel that bears only an Arabic name on Rue Sidi M'Amed el Ghazi, just off Ave Mohammed V, which costs Dr 20/30 a single/double. Neither has showers of any description.

Just outside the medina, *Hotel Berlin*, Ave Mohammed V, is excellent value. It's on the 2nd floor above the Vietnamese restaurant Hong Kong. It's clean, secure and friendly, and the rooms cost Dr 25/35 a single/double. Hot showers are Dr 3 extra. Get there early as there are only a few rooms.

Also excellent value is *Hotel Central*, 2 Zenkat al Basra near the huge *Balima Hotel* on Ave Mohammed V. This hotel offers clean, large, airy rooms with handbasin (warm water) and bidet for just Dr 30 to Dr 35 a single and Dr 40 to Dr 43 a double without shower. Hot showers (mornings only) are Dr 7 extra – somewhat expensive, but there are gallons of hot water available. There are also more expensive rooms with showers. The staff is friendly and breakfast is available. It's a large place and unlikely to be full. *Hotel de France*, behind the market, but visible from Blvd Hassan II, has also been popular with travellers in the past.

The more expensive *Hotel Splendid*, 24 Zenkat Ghazzah just off Ave Mohammed V, costs Dr 49/60 a single/double with hot shower, but without toilet, and Dr 60/74 a single/double with both. The staff here seem bored and indifferent. Going further up-market, there are *Hotel de la Paix*, Zenkat Ghazzah, *Hotel Gaulois*, 1 Zenkat Hims, just off Ave Mohammed V, and *Hotel Majestic*, Blvd Hassan II.

The camp site is at Salé Beach. It's open all year and has showers, toilets and a shop.

Places to Eat

Rabat abounds with coffee shops where office workers, businesspeople, students and travellers pass the time of day. Some of these places serve snacks but most are not restaurants as such. Finding good, cheap food is surprisingly difficult but there are a few places that can be recommended.

Restaurant El Bahia, Blvd Hassan II, close to the corner of Ave Mohammed V and actually built into the medina walls, offers a shady open-air section set around a fountain. It has a comfortable, traditional Moroccan-style section upstairs. The staff is friendly, it's very popular and the food is remarkably cheap and tasty. A delicious tajine (some of the best you will taste in Morocco) costs just Dr 14, plus it has kebabs (prices depend on what you want), salads for Dr 2.50, omelettes for Dr 4 to Dr 10 and more.

A traditional travellers' hang-out is *Restaurant de la Jeunesse*, Ave Mohammed V, just inside the medina. It's great value and you can get a meal of kebabs, chips, salad, bread and a soft drink for Dr 20. On the ground floor there are even cheaper takeaways.

Another good one is *Café Restaurant Mona Lisa*, in a small square called Passage Derby at 258 Ave Mohammed V. There's a sign on the footpath pointing to it. Although the place is used more by locals as a coffee shop, the food is good and the prices reasonable – excellent tajines and salads.

Restaurants and cafés tend to close by 9.30 pm, except during Ramadan when they stay open much later.

Bars are few and far between, but for a beer try *Hotel Balima*, which is a popular place in the evenings. A more earthy establishment is the bar at the corner of Zenkat al Basra and Ave Allal ben Abdallah, which runs parallel to Ave Mohammed V.

SAFI

Safi is largely a modern fishing port and industrial centre that sits in a steep crevasse, formed by the River Chaabah, on the Atlantic coast. It does, however, have a lively, walled medina, souk and fortresses dating from the Portuguese era and is well known for its traditional pottery.

Though Safi's natural harbour was known to the Phoenicians, and probably used later on by the Romans, it's main European connection came with the arrival of the Portuguese in 1508, when they began building a fortress using Essaouira as their base. Though what they built at Safi was of monumental proportions (as all Portuguese military installations tended to be), their stay was short and they voluntarily left in 1541.

Their leaving didn't signal the end of European contact. In the 17th century, the French established a consulate at the port, enabling the signing of many trading treaties with the indigenous rulers. But by the 19th century, the port had faded into insignificance. It was revived in the 20th century with the establishment of a fishing fleet (taking mainly sardines) and a huge industrial complex to the south for the manufacture of fertilisers and sulphuric and phosphoric acids, using local pyrites and phosphate ores.

While Safi may not be the most attractive of Moroccan towns, it's worth a day of your time if you are in the area.

Information

There's no tourist information centre and maps of the city are hard to find.

Both the bus station (Ave President Kennedy) and railway station (Rue de R'Bat) are some distance from the centre of town (Place de l'Indépendence), and are best reached by bus or shared taxi. Buses, however, don't actually go through the centre of town, as a bypass (Blvd Hassan II) circles it.

Things to See

In the walled city, which the Portuguese built and to which the Moors added, the **Qasr el Bahr** is usually the first port of call. It was built by the Portuguese to protect the old port and house the governor. It was restored in 1963. There are good views from the south-west bastion, as well as a number of old Spanish and Dutch cannons dating from the early 17th century, notably two manufactured in Rotterdam in 1619 and another two from the Hague in 1621. Visiting hours are 9 am to 12 noon and 3 to 7 pm. A guide is provided.

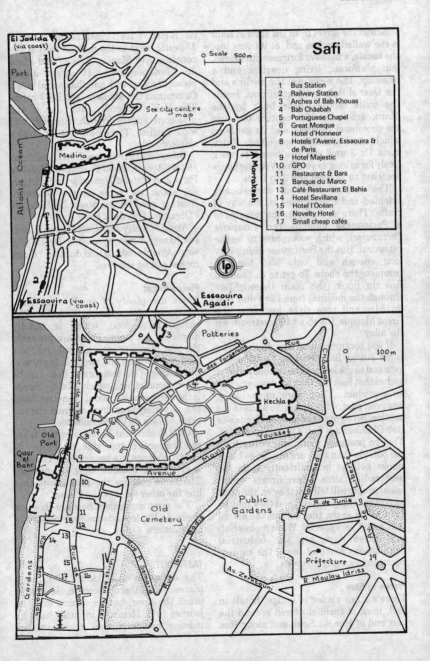

Safi

1 Bus Station
2 Railway Station
3 Arches of Bab Khouas
4 Bab Châabah
5 Portuguese Chapel
6 Great Mosque
7 Hotel d'Honneur
8 Hotels l'Avenir, Essaouira & de Paris
9 Hotel Majestic
10 GPO
11 Restaurant & Bars
12 Banque du Maroc
13 Café Restaurant El Bahia
14 Hotel Sevillana
15 Hotel l'Océan
16 Novelty Hotel
17 Small cheap cafés

Across the street from the Qasr el Bahr is the walled **medina** and, at its very top, the **kechla**, a massive fortress with ramps, gun platforms, living quarters and a museum. The views over the medina and the Qasr el Bahr are magnificent. Inside the walls is the **palace** built by the Moroccans in the 18th century to house the provincial governor and its gardens, which are beautifully conceived. Entry costs Dr 3 and you're allowed to walk freely for as long as you like. Visiting hours are 9 am to 12 noon and 3 to 7 pm.

The **medina** itself is domestically oriented and there's little in the way of crafts. There is, however, the remains of a **Portuguese church** (the *Chapelle Portugaise*), which was meant to be the cathedral. But the Portuguese didn't stay long enough and only had time to complete the choir. To get to it, head up Rue du Souk (the main thoroughfare through the medina) from Blvd du Front du Mer and turn right just after the Great Mosque. It's about 100 metres down the alley.

If you continue along Rue du Souk you come out at **Bab Chaabah**. Outside this gate and to the left is an enormous series of arches that look like they were once part of an aqueduct. They were more likely, however, part of the defensive walls of the medina. Straight ahead on the hill opposite Bab Chaabah are Safi's famous **potteries**. They're probably more interesting from the outside than they are inside, as black smoke bellows intermittently from the beehive-like kilns when firings occur. Local people will tell you they're 'the most important thing in Safi', and they may be right as far as the tiles go, but the actual pots aren't very special. What makes Safi tick these days are the industrial installations south of town, the sardine boats and canning factories.

Places to Stay

There's a fair choice of budget hotels in Safi, most of them clustered around the port end of Rue du Souk and along Rue de R'Bat. Exceptional value is *Hotel Majestic*, next to the medina wall at the corner of Ave Moulay Youssef and Place de l'Indépendence. It offers clean, pleasant rooms with handbasin and bidet. Communal hot showers cost Dr 3 extra. The staff is friendly, and one of the managers speaks French, Spanish and some English. The rooms cost Dr 17/25 a single/double.

Others worth trying are *Hotel Sevillana*, *Hotel l'Avenir*, *Hotel Essaouira*, *Hotel de Paris* and *Hotel d'Honneiur* (*sic*). Prices are about the same as the Majestic. Another good choice would be *Hotel de l'Océan* on Rue de R'Bat.

Avoid *Novelty Hotel*, off Rue de R'Bat. It's hardly a novelty paying Dr 15/30 a single/double only to find dark and dingy rooms and no showers.

Places to Eat

There are plenty of small, traditional Moroccan cafés on Rue du Souk that offer cheap, tasty food, which is usually displayed out front. These are probably the best places to eat – not only for their food but because the street is lively and interesting. One restaurant that can be recommended, and which is fairly cheap, is the one on the left about 10 metres down the only alley branching off from the top side of Place de l'Indépendence.

Café Restaurant El Bahia, which takes up the entire top side of Place de l'Indépendence, is a tourist trap. The food is expensive, without being exceptional. The same goes for the restaurants that line the other sides of the Place.

The most convenient bars are those on Place de l'Indépendence, but beware of the hustlers.

TAFRAOUTE

The attraction of Tafraoute, like many places in southern Morocco, is not so much the town, but its setting and the journey to it. Hemmed in on all sides by massive boulder-strewn mountains, its

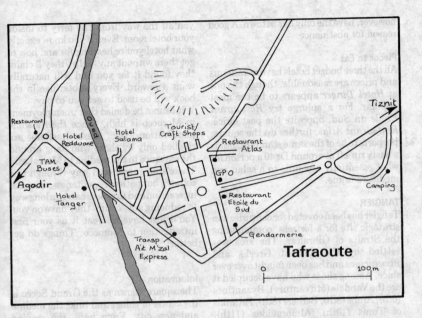

surroundings are spectacular. Its nearest equivalent is Hampi in India, except here the prevailing colour is pink instead of grey. The boulders are smooth and well-weathered – quite a contrast to the craggy *djebels* (hills) elsewhere in Morocco. *Palmeraies* and small cultivated areas line the river, though almond trees are the economic base, and there are plenty of mud-brick villages nearby. It's good walking country and the town itself is very laid-back. Stay here a few days and you'll find it hard to leave. Market day is Wednesday.

The road between Tafraoute and Agadir is spectacular and there are some excellent photographic opportunities – abandoned Berber mud-brick villages and kasbahs perched on hair-raising precipices; others, inhabited, on the tops of conical rock outcrops; and, of course, the vistas from the summits of passes. Some of the road is rough in parts, but nothing an ordinary car can't handle.

The road south to Tiznit also is breath-taking, though much more forbidding and barren, particularly towards the end when you begin to feel you've taken the wrong turning and won't see another village until Timbuktu.

Places to Stay

Camping is the cheapest accommodation in Tafraoute provided you have a tent (there are none for hire). It's Dr 3 a person, plus Dr 2.50 a one-person tent or Dr 3 a two-person tent and Dr 3 a car. The camp site has hot showers, electricity and is friendly and pleasant.

There are three budget hotels in the centre, offering much the same in facilities and all with their own restaurants. They are *Hotel Tanger*, *Hotel Redduane* and *Hotel Salama*. They all charge Dr 25 a double with communal bathrooms and toilets. None has hot water. Those seeking comfort should check out *Hotel les Amandiers*, an amateur architect's travesty of a kasbah that sits on the crest of the hill overlooking the town. It does, however, have the only bar in town. A good reason for abstinence.

Places to Eat

All the three budget hotels have restaurants and prices are reasonable, though the one at *Hotel Tanger* appears to be the most popular. For a splurge try *Restaurant Etoile du Sud*, opposite the post office. *Restaurant Atlas*, further up the square, purports to be of the same standard, but is a nasty rip-off at around Dr 40 a person for what essentially amounts to a salad and mediocre tajine.

TANGIER

Tangier has been coveted for centuries as a strategic site for a fortress, commanding the Straits of Gibraltar. The area was settled by the ancient Greeks and Phoenicians and has been fought over ever since. Among those who have occupied it are the Vandals (5th century), Byzantines (6th), Arabs (8th), Berbers (8th), Fatimids of Tunis (10th), Almoravides (11th), Almohades (12th), Merinids (13th), Portuguese (15th and 16th), Spanish (16th), British (17th) and French (19th).

In the 19th and early 20th century it was the object of intense rivalry between France, Spain, Britain and Germany, and this led to it being declared an international zone in 1923. It retained that status until after WW II, when it was reunited with Morocco. All the various peoples who have ever settled here have left their mark on the city. It has an atmosphere markedly different from that of other Moroccan cities, though there's little left of the sophisticated decadence for which it was notorious during the 1930s and 1940s.

What has replaced the sleaze and opulence, as a result of it being the major port of entry for tourists, are hordes of the world's best hustlers. Pick any language, any situation, any time of day or night and they'll find you. Nothing you say will make any difference to their persistent superglue patter, which will accompany

you all the way from the ferry to inside your hotel room. Even if you know exactly what hotel you're heading for and how to get there without any 'help', they'll claim they found it for you and will naturally want a reward. Every subterfuge in the book will be used to get you to pay.

It cannot be denied that unemployment in Morocco is high, hence there's some justification, but these hustlers are rivalled only by those who hang around the entrance to the medina in Marrakesh. There's no guaranteed way through this cobweb, but patience, politeness, minimal interaction and firmness can go a long way to reducing any 'claim' they have on you. You'll just have to treat it as your first introduction to Morocco. Things do get better!

Information

The square known as the Grand Socco is the centre of things and links the medina and new city. From here, the medina covers the hillside below, and the crowded main street, Rue es Siaghin, leads down to the Petit Socco, a smaller square that forms the heart of the medina. Below the medina, the port and bus and train stations are all within easy walking distance. The kasbah occupies the north-west corner of the medina – dominating a cliff-top position. The medina is fairly small, and although it is the usual tangle of twisting narrow lanes, it is easy to find your way around. The new city lies to the west and south of the medina and, as usual, contains the bulk of the banks and middle and top-class accommodation.

The tourist office is at 29 Blvd Pasteur. It is fairly well stocked with maps and brochures, bus and railway timetables and several languages are spoken (you can usually rely on English, French, German and Spanish). *The Rogue's Guide to Tangier* is a humorous and well-written alternative guide to the city. It's worth buying, but is only sporadically available from the larger hotels. The main post office is on Blvd Pasteur, a 15-minutes walk from the Grand Socco.

Useful Addresses Some useful addresses are:

French Consulate
    Place de France (tel 320 39)
Portuguese Consulate
    9 Place Sahat Umame (tel 317 08)
Spanish Consulate
    85 Rue Sidi Boabid (tel 356 25)
UK Consulate
    Rue d'Angleterre (tel 358 95)
Royal Air Moroc
    Place de France (tel 347 22)
Air France
    Rue du Mexique (tel 364 77)
Iberia Airlines
    35 Blvd Pasteur (tel 361 77)
American Express
    Voyages Schwarz, 76 Ave Mohammed V
    (tel 334 59)
Thomas Cook/Wagon-Lits
    86 Rue de la Liberté
Comanov Shipping Company
    43 Ave Abou Alaa el Maari, to Sete (tel
    326 552)
Comarit Shipping Company
    7 Rue du Mexique, to Algeciras (tel 367 82)

Bus All buses leave from the square at the port entrance. The CTM office is to the left of the port entrance. Other bus companies have their offices on Ave d'Espagne, between Rue Portugal and Rue de la Plage.

Taxi *Grands taxis* leave from around the square; there are regular departures to Tetouan (Dr 20), Asilah and Rabat.

Train There are two railway stations – Tangier Gare and Tangier Port. Most trains start from Tangier Port, at the port, and stop at the Gare. The main departures are:

Rabat and Casablanca – 7.20 am (Gare only), 4.10 and 11.15 pm; four to 5½ hours
Marrakesh – 11.15 pm; 10 hours

Meknès and Fès – 8.10 am (Gare only), 4.10 pm; five to six hours
Oujda: 8.10 am and midnight (both Gare only); 12 hours

Ferry It's only a few minutes' walk from the ferry terminal to the medina, though it will seem longer because of the accompanying touts. The ferry ticket offices are closed on weekends, but you can buy tickets from a number of travel agents around town. The Wasteel agency by the port entrance is a popular one. There are ferries to both Algeciras (Spain) and Sete (France). In summer there are hydrofoils to Algeciras and Gibraltar.

Things to Buy Tangier is not the ideal place to buy souvenirs – too many people come here on day trips from Spain and the prices are generally way over the top. While it is possible to get things for a reasonable price, it involves a lot of hard work. If you have to buy something here, keep clear of Blvd Pasteur and shop in the medina.

Things to See
The **Petit Socco**, with its cafés and restaurants, is very much the centre of things. It's easy to sit here for an hour or two, sipping mint tea and watching the world go by. In the days of the international zone, this was the sin and sleaze centre of the city. Today it retains something of its seedy air – the whispers of 'something special, my friend?' (or the equivalent phrase in French, German or Spanish) in your ear are amazingly constant.

The narrow **Rue des Chrétiens** takes you to the **kasbah**. When you walk along here, you have to run the gauntlet past the shopkeepers who practically leap out and grab you to come and have a look.

The kasbah is built on the highest point of the city and is accessed from Bab el Assa, at the end of Rue Ben Raisouli in the medina. The gate opens on to a large open courtyard that leads to **Dar el Makhzen**, the former sultan's palace and now quite a

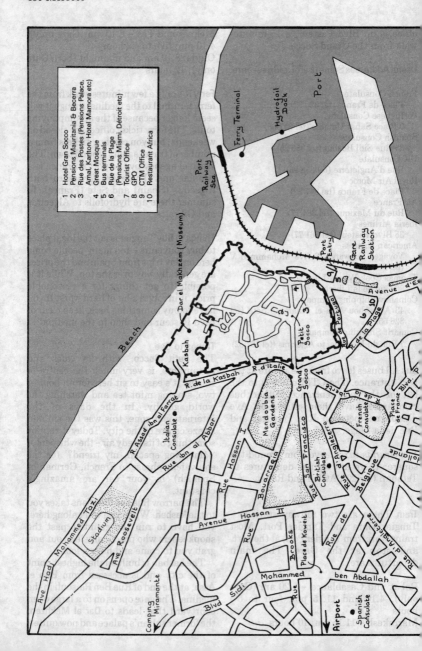

1 Hotel Gran Socco
2 Pensions Mauritania & Becerra
3 Rue des Postes (Pensions Palace, Amal, Kariton, Hotel Mamora etc)
4 Great Mosque
5 Bus terminals
6 Rue de la Plage (Pensions Miami, Détroit etc)
7 Tourist Office
8 GPO
9 CTM Office
10 Restaurant Africa

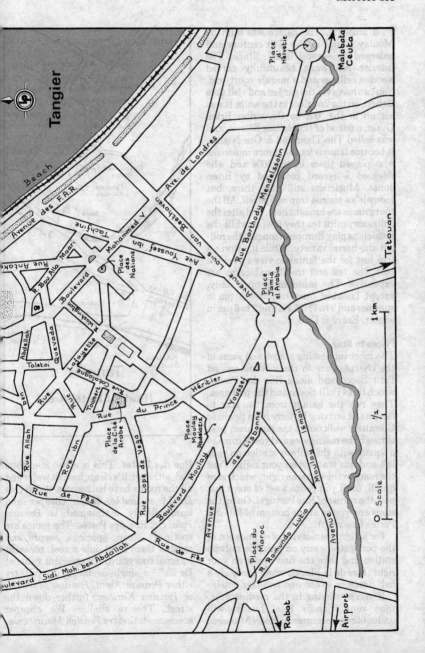

Tangier

good museum. The palace was built by Moulay Ismail in the 17th century and enlarged by several later sultans. The interior has some beautifully carved wooden ceilings and a marble courtyard. You can leave via the garden and visit **Café Detroit**, on the 2nd floor in the walls. It was set up in the '60s by the writer Brian Gysin, a friend of the Rolling Stones, and was called The Thousand & One Nights. It became famous for the trance musicians who played there in the '60s and who released a record produced by Brian Jones. Musicians still play there, but today it's a tourist trap *nonpareil*. All the tour groups are brought here, and after the obligatory mint tea they file out while the musicians play European songs of the roll-out-the-barrel variety. While it's worth a trip just for the fantastic views over the port, the tea and traditional cakes are expensive. The museum is open daily, except Tuesday, from 9 am to 3.30 pm in summer and 9 to 11.45 am and 3 to 6 pm in winter. Entry is Dr 5.

Places to Stay

The most interesting places and some of the cheapest are in the medina around Petit Socco and along Rue des Postes, which links Petit Socco and the port area. They run the gamut from two-star to fleapits. If arriving by ferry from Spain or Gibraltar, walk out of the port area, pass through the main gates and you'll come to a square with the railway station on your left and bus stations on your right. Take the road on the extreme right, which goes uphill, until you get to a set of steps just past the corner of Rue Portugal. Go up the steps and you're at the bottom of Rue des Postes (see map).

For a European-style hotel, once out of the port gates, carry on past the railway station and take the first street on your right (Rue de la Plage), where there are a half dozen or so one and two-star hotels.

If you're staying in the medina area, then your friendly local hustler will undoubtedly recommend *Hotel Mamora*,

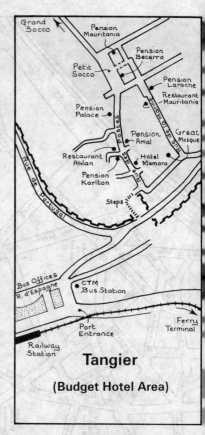

Tangier
(Budget Hotel Area)

Rue des Postes. This is a two-star hotel and, although it's clean, has hot water and all the rooms have bathrooms, it will cost Dr 74 a double. Much cheaper and immaculately maintained is *Pension Palace*, 2 Rue des Postes. The rooms are spotlessly clean, spacious, secure and most of them front onto a cool, pleasant internal courtyard. It's excellent value at Dr 20/35 a single/double. If it's full, try either *Pension Amal*, *Pension Marhaba* or *Pension Karlton*, further down the street. They're similar. For cheaper accommodation try *Pension Mauritania*,

Pension Fuentes and Hotel Becerra, all on the Petit Socco, and Pension Larache, just off the Petit Socco. They're all traditional, basic Moroccan hostelries.

If all these are full, head to the Grand Socco (a very short walk) and Hotel Gran Socco. While it has a variety of rooms, the best deals for groups of three or four are the large rooms overlooking the Socco. If you're staying in a place with no showers, there's a hamman at 80 Rue des Chrétiens, which runs off the Petit Socco by Café Central. It's open from 8 am to 8 pm and a shower costs Dr 5.

Campers have a choice of two sites. The cheaper and more convenient is Camping Miramonte, about three km west of the centre of town. It's a good site, close to the beach and has a reasonable restaurant. To get there, take bus No 1, 2 or 21 from the Grand Socco. Don't leave valuables unattended at this site – things disappear. The other site is Caravaning Tingis, about six km to the east of the centre of town. It is much more expensive, but has a tennis court and swimming pool. To get there, take bus No 15 from the Grand Socco.

Going up in price, the hotels along Rue de la Plage will set you back Dr 40 a double or more, excluding the cost of hot showers. Two of the most popular are Pension Miami and Pension le Détroit. These hotels are both at the bottom of the hill, near Ave d'Espagne. Hotel Continental, at the end of Rue Dar el Baroud in the medina, is great value. It dates from the turn of the century and is not without charm. The view from the terrace over the harbour is one of the best around. Rooms cost Dr 80 a double with bath and hot water.

Hotel el Muniria, on Rue Magellan, is an English-owned one-star hotel and good value at Dr 65 a double. Its Tangerine bar is a great place for a drink in the evening: open 9 pm to 2 am. Finding the place, however, can be difficult. From Hotel Rembrandt on Blvd Pasteur, turn down Rue Rembrandt and walk down the steps

to the right next to the church. You are now on Rue Magellan. From the port, go along Ave d'Espagne until you get to a service station on the right, take the steps next to it, then the second left and first right. The hotel is on the right. Hotel Ibn Batouta, opposite the El Muniria, also is not a bad place.

Places to Eat

There are plenty of small rustic cafés and restaurants around the Petit Socco and Grand Socco, offering traditional fare at reasonable prices. One of the cheapest is Restaurant Mauritania, which may look like Lucifer's waiting room (if you've just come from Europe), but has very tasty food at an unbeatable price and the staff is friendly. Get there early – the food runs out quickly as the night wears on. For more substantial meals, try Restaurant Ahlan, Rue des Postes. It's a popular place and offers excellent tajines with soup for around Dr 14 a meal. Also good value is the cosy Restaurant Moderne at No 21.

There are a couple of stalls at the bottom of the stairs at the end of Rue des Postes. The one closest to the port looks a bit rough, but does excellent fried fish with a tomato sauce and bread for Dr 1.50 each, and three or four of these make a fair meal.

For a splurge, or for food with a more European flavour, head to Place de France. Here you'll find several restaurants and cafés where you can get a good meal; though for substantially more than you would pay around the Petit Socco.

At 83 Rue de la Plage, almost on the corner of Ave d'Espagne, is Restaurant Africa, which has good three-course set-menus for Dr 23 as well as good individual dishes. The restaurants either side of the Africa are also worth investigating.

TAROUDANNT

Taroudannt, with its magnificent and extremely well-preserved red mud walls, has played an important part in the history of Morocco since 1056 when it was overrun by the Almoravides at the start of their conquest of Morocco. It played only a peripheral role in the dynasties that followed until, in the 16th century, it was made the capital of the Sa'adis. This dynasty was responsible for building the old part of town and the kasbah, though most of the rest dates from the 18th century. The Sa'adis eventually moved to Marrakesh, but not before the fertile Sous Valley, in which the city stands, was developed into the country's most important producer of sugar cane, cotton, rice and indigo – valuable items of trade along the trans-Saharan caravan routes.

The city narrowly escaped destruction at the hands of Moulay Ismail in 1687 after it became the centre of a rebellion opposing his rule. Instead, Moulay Ismail contented himself with slaying its inhabitants. It regained some of its former prominence when Moulay Abdallah was proclaimed sultan here at the end of the next century. However, it was to remain a centre of intrigue and sedition against the central government throughout much of the 19th century, though, by then, its importance in the overall scheme of things had begun to decline rapidly.

Unlike many Moroccan towns of its size and importance, the French never chose Taroudannt as an administrative or military centre, so there is no 'European' quarter of wide boulevards and modern buildings tacked onto the original city. Perhaps this is why, despite its proximity to Agadir, very few well-heeled tourists visit.

Information
The CTM buses arrive in Place Talmoklate, while SATAS and Ait M'Zal Express buses have their depot in Place Assarag. The taxi park is at Place Assarag, as are most of the city's hotels and banks.

Things to See
While you can explore the **ramparts** of Taroudannt on foot, it would be better to

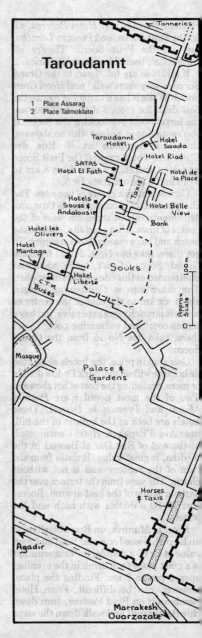

Taroudannt

1 Place Assarag
2 Place Talmoklate

- Tanneries
- Taroudannt Hotel
- Hotel Saada
- Hotel Riad
- SATAS
- Hotel El Fath
- Hotel de la Place
- Hotel Belle View
- Hotels Souss & Andalousie
- Bank
- Hotel les Oliviers
- Hotel Mantaga
- Souks
- C.T.M. Buses
- Hotel Liberté
- Taxis
- Mosque
- Palace & Gardens
- Horses & Taxis
- Agadir
- Marrakesh Ouarzazate

Approx Scale
100m
0

hire a bicycle or engage one of the horse and cart drivers, which can be found just inside the main entrance (see map). It's a long way round the walls!

The **souk** at Taroudannt is relatively small, but its craftwork is of high quality. It features limestone carvings and traditional Berber jewellery, which has been influenced by the tribes of the Sahara and the Jews, who were a significant part of the community until the late 1960s. You might come across a few half-hearted attempts by youths to press you into engaging them as 'guides', but this isn't Marrakesh and a guide isn't necessary.

There are **tanneries** similar to the ones at Fès, though smaller. Follow the main street out of Place Assarag, on the opposite side from the bank, and continue down to the ramparts. Turn left out of the gate, continue for about 100 metres and take the first right. Let your nose guide you from there. Most of the skins (which you can buy) are from sheep and cattle, but they also cater for those that don't care about the extermination of wildlife.

The road between Taroudannt and Marrakesh goes over the spectacular **Tizi-n-Test** pass – one of the highest in Morocco. It's a good road all the way, though it twists and turns endlessly and, in some places, is hair-raising. The views from many points are magnificent. If you can't arrange a lift with tourists, SATAS has buses daily at about 5 am, which arrive in Marrakesh around 2 pm. The road passes **Asni** towards the end of the journey, which is the starting point for treks up **Mt Toubkal**, the highest mountain in North Africa.

Places to Stay

Most travellers like to stay as close to the centre of activity as possible and in Taroudannt you can do this without paying a lot of money. There are many hotels around Place Assarag, but one of the cheapest is *Hotel de la Place*. Though basic, it is pleasant and clean, and the friendly owner is eager to please. A rooftop double overlooking the square costs Dr 30. There are cold water showers only. Similar are *Hotel Souss* and *Hotel Andalousie*, on the main street coming into the square.

Further up the main street close to Place Talmoklate is *Hotel les Oliviers* – good value at Dr 25 a double. It's pleasant, clean, friendly and has a rooftop terrace, but, like the other hotels in this range, has cold water showers only. *Hotel Liberté* in Place Talmoklate is similar.

If you're looking for something better, I can recommend the one-star *Hotel Taroudannt* on Place Assarag. It has a bar and is owned by a garrulous and somewhat eccentric, but thoroughly entertaining French woman. It's a great place to stay, is clean, has hot water and costs Dr 43/55 a single/double. If it's full, try *Hotel Belle View* in the same square, but expect to pay a little more.

Places to Eat

There are quite a few small cafés along the main street, just before you get to Place Assarag, where you can get traditional food, such as tajine, salads and soups. The terrace of *Hotel Belle View* is also popular, but relatively expensive. For a splurge, have a meal at *Hotel Taroudannt*, which offers very good French cuisine at reasonable prices.

TETOUAN

With its interesting medina, beautiful setting and nearby beaches, Tetouan isn't a bad place, although if you have just come from Ceuta, the thing that will probably strike you most is the touts. While not threatening, they are persistent enough to send most people packing after a day. As an introduction to Morocco, it is not very encouraging, but things improve rapidly from here.

Information

The tourist office is on Rue Mohammed V, just near the corner of Rue ben Tachfine. The guy is helpful and speaks quite a bit of

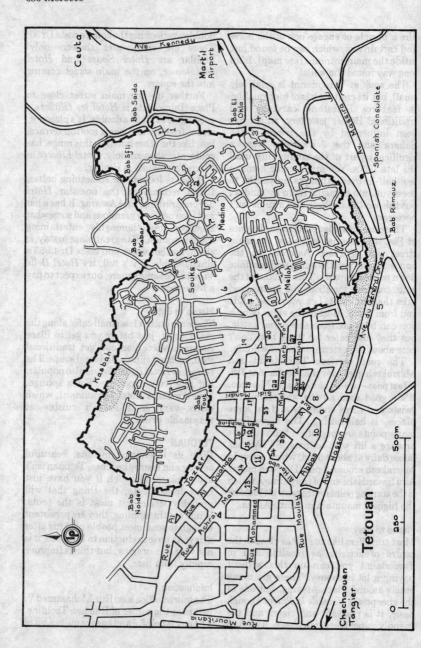

Tetouan

1	Saidi Mosque
2	Great Mosque
3	Museum of Moroccan Art
4	Artisan School
5	Artefact Emporium
6	Royal Palace
7	Place Hassan II
8	Bus Station
9	Taxis to Ceuta
10	Taxis to Tangier
11	Place Moulay el Mehdi
12	Tourist Office
13	Pensions Fès, Bienvenida & Florida
14	Pension Riojana
15	GPO
16	Hamman
17	Hotel Regina
18	Pension Cosmopolita
19	Museum
20	Restaurant Granada
21	Pension Bilbao
22	Hotel Nacional
23	Restaurant Restinga
24	Pension Iberia
25	Hotel Príncipe
26	Sandwich Ali Baba
27	Restaurant Saigon

English. Don't be talked into hiring a guide (unless you want one) as the medina is small and manageable on your own. The post office is on the roundabout known as Place Moulay el Mehdi, in the Spanish-built new town. There are plenty of banks along the main street, Rue Mohammed V, and around Place Moulay el Mehdi.

The Spanish Consulate is on Ave Massira. Visas can be issued on the spot, although none of the staff speaks English.

The bus station for all buses is behind the municipality building on the corner of Rue Sidi Mandri and Rue Moulay Abbas. It is a dark and gloomy old place with the ticket windows upstairs and the buses downstairs. There are daily departures to al Hoceima, Casablanca, Rabat, Nador, Chechaouen, Ouezzane, Meknès, Fès and Tangier. Book in advance where possible, and check at all the windows to find out

what's available. Tickets for buses to the beaches at Martil and Cabo Negro are available from window 12.

Grands taxis to the Spanish border at Ceuta, 33 km away, leave frequently from the corner of Rue de Mouquauama and Rue Sidi Mandri, just up from the bus station. The trip to Fnideq, for Ceuta, will cost Dr 14, and to Tangier will cost Dr 20. For more details see the To/From Spanish North Africa section.

Things to See

As is often the case in Morocco, the place that links the old and new cities is the real centre of activity. Here it is **Place Hassan II**, the town's showpiece. It underwent 'beautification' and is now resplendent with its four massive concrete pillars.

The interesting and surprisingly busy **medina**, is great for just wandering around at random. The busiest entrance is **Bab el Rouah**, to the right of the old Spanish consulate. The area towards the eastern gate, **Bab el Okla**, was the up-market end of town and still has some of the finest houses built in the last century. At least one has been turned into a carpet showroom (there are plenty of touts hanging around who will take you to one).

Just inside Bab el Okla is the excellent **Museum of Moroccan Art**, housed in an old bastion in the town wall – there are still cannon in place in the garden. The exhibits of everyday Moroccan and Andalusian life are well presented, but it's a pity the staff rush you through as fast as they can so they can go back to their seat at the door. It is open daily, except Tuesday, from 9 am to 12 noon and 2 to 6 pm. Entry is Dr 3.

Just opposite Bab el Okla is the **Artisan School**, where you can see young kids being taught the traditional crafts, such as enamel (*zellij*) tiling, leatherwork and woodwork. The building in itself is worth a visit. The school is open from 9 am to 12 noon and 2.30 to 5.30 pm, closed Tuesday and Saturday. Entry is Dr 3.

To the south of the medina on Ave du Général Orgaz is a government-run **Artefact Emporium**, where you can get an idea of the real prices of things. What you would pay here is at the top end of the price scale. Upstairs, out the back, and then downstairs, you can see young men and women making all sorts of handicrafts. It is open daily from 9.30 am to 1 pm and 3.30 to 6.30 pm.

There is a small **Archaeological Museum** opposite the end of Rue Prince Sidi Mohammed, but it is only for the dedicated. They have a few prehistoric stones, some Roman coins and a few small mosaics and bits and pieces from Lixus. It is open daily, except Sunday, from 9.30 am to 12 noon and 2.30 to 5.30 pm. Entry costs Dr 3.

In the evenings, Rue Mohammed V becomes a pedestrian precinct and fills with hundreds of people promenading, mostly young men from the university campus.

Places to Stay

There are plenty of typical cheap hotels around Place Hassan II and the entrance to the medina, but they tend to be on the noisy side. *Hotel Marrakesh* and *Hotel Seville* are typical. There are a couple of dozen pensions dotted about, some representing good value for money. Many are run by women who speak only Spanish.

Pension Bilbao (tel 7939), at 7 Rue Mohammed V, is close to Place Hassan II and is cheap at Dr 20 a person. It has no showers, but it's only a five-minute walk to the nearest *hamman*. At the other end of Rue Mohammed V, past Place Moulay el Mehdi, is *Pension Fès*. It is on the 3rd floor, so look for the sign over the street entrance. Beds cost Dr 20 and there are cold showers. A bit more expensive but with a homely atmosphere is *Pension Iberia*, on the 3rd floor above the BMCE bank on Place Moulay el Mehdi. There are only a few rooms and the cost is Dr 28/

40 a single/double. Cold showers are free and hot showers cost Dr 3.

A couple of other cheap pensions include *Pension Bienvenida* and *Pension Florida*, in the same building on Rue Achra Mai near Place Moulay el Mehdi. Neither is especially friendly, but would do for a night.

Going up in price and probably the best place to stay in town is *Hotel Regina* (tel 2113), 8 Rue Sidi Mandri. All rooms have a bathroom with hot water, the management is friendly and at Dr 48/60 for singles/doubles it is excellent value. *Hotel Nacional* (tel 3290), 8 Rue Mohammed ben Larbi Torres, is another reasonable one-star place costing around Dr 70/85 for singles/doubles with bath, and Dr 55/75 without. Another similar place is *Hotel Príncipe* (tel 2795), 20 Rue Youssef Tachfine. Its front rooms, however, can be noisy as they are right by the place where the *grands taxis* queue.

There is a *hamman* on Rue ben Tachfine.

For campers, the nearest camp site is by the beach at Martil, eight km away. There's another near Club Méditerranée, about halfway between Tetouan and the border.

Places to Eat

The best cheap place is *Sandwich Ali Baba* on Rue Mourakah Anual. Despite the name, they also do chicken, chips, soups and tajines. It's very popular and you practically have to fight through the crowd at the front to get to the seats out back.

For something a bit more formal try *Restaurant Restinga*, in a small alley off Rue Mohammed V. The menu is a bit limited and it closes early in the evening, but it has a small open courtyard. There's nothing Asian about *Restaurant Saigon* on Rue Mourakah Anual, despite the name. The food is OK, that is if you're not put off by the display case full of rather old meat by the door. *Restaurant Granada* on Rue Mohammed V at Place Al Jala, is clean, cheap and serves the usual tajines, couscous and soups.

TINERHIR & THE TODRA GORGE

Some 14 km from Tinerhir (Tineghir on some maps), at the end of a lush valley full of *palmeraies* and mud-brick villages hemmed in by barren, craggy mountains is the Todra Gorge. About 300 metres high, just 10 metres wide at its narrowest point and with a crystal clear river running through it, it's one of Morocco's most magnificent natural sights, especially in the mornings when the sun penetrates to the bottom. On winter afternoons it gets very dark and cold, cool in summer.

The main part of the gorge can be explored in half a day, and for those with more time it is an interesting walk further up and through the *palmeraies* on the way to Tinerhir (people are friendly). There are numerous ruined kasbahs flanking the *palmeraies*.

There's little of interest in Tinerhir itself.

Places to Stay

There are three places to stay at the gorge. The cheapest, at the entrance, is *Hotel Restaurant El Mansour*. It's a friendly place, has sun for most of the day, a good selection of western music and costs Dr 30 a double for a clean, basic concrete box. The toilets are clean, but primitive, and there's neither hot water nor electricity – kerosene lamps light the night's activities. The hotel has a restaurant, and although it is a little expensive, the food is good. Tajine and salad costs Dr 25 to Dr 30, a salad on its own Dr 8, omelette Dr 7 and tea or coffee Dr 2.50. The staff and management try hard to make you welcome.

A little further inside the gorge itself are *Hotel Yasmina* and *Hotel les Roches*, where most of the package tourists and well-heeled stay. Both have hot water and wood fires at night in winter. Despite this, they charge only Dr 35 a double. In summer they charge more. Both offer good set menus for Dr 35 (soup or salad, tajine and dessert). There are Berber tents in the grounds, with tables, chairs and divans, making them an excellent place to eat in the summer (in winter you'd freeze your butt off). Both places are good for finding lifts with other tourists.

Neither of these hotels would ever be allowed in a country where environmental impact studies are required before construction. While they keep their doorsteps clean, they use the upper gorge as a private garbage tip. Incredible!.

Some four km back along the main road to Tinerhir are three camp sites all next to one another in the *palmeraies*. They all have facilities (showers and toilets) and charge Dr 3. There's a small shop in the village nearby that sells the basics (but no cigarettes – get these from Le Lac). The sites are *Camping Les Poissons Sacres*, *Camping Le Lac* and *Camping Le Source Sacre*. Take your pick.

If you want to stay in Tinerhir, there are three hotels around the main square. The two cheapest are *Hotel Oasis* and *Hotel Salam*. The former is Dr 25/30 a single/double without bathroom, but you can sleep on the roof for less. It's basic and there's no hot water. Similar is the Salam, which also houses the CTM office. The restaurant is good value. The most expensive is *Hotel du Todra*, which sports bizarre concrete fantasies of monkeys and the like around the balcony and costs Dr 57/68 a single/double with both hot shower and toilet. Breakfast costs Dr 9 and a three-course dinner Dr 35.

Getting There

There are no buses from Tinerhir to the gorge, but there are frequent shared taxis from the main square for Dr 5.50 a person. They will take you to the entrance of the gorge. If you can't afford a taxi and must hitch, walk out of Tinerhir towards Errachidia until you get to the bridge. Turn left and wait for a lift (the only sign here is in Arabic). Unless tourists come along, you may have to pay for your lift anyway.

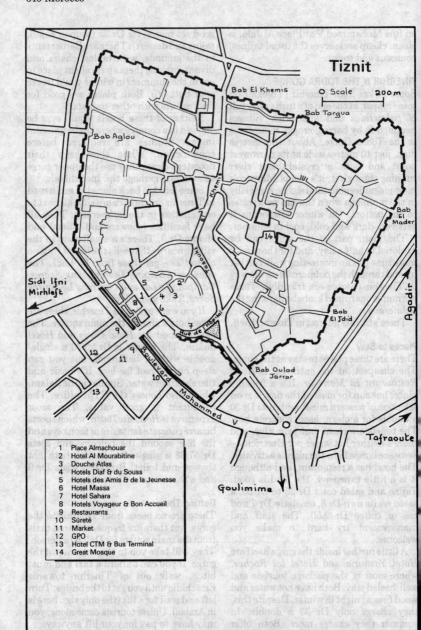

Tiznit

0 Scale 200m

- Bab El Khemis
- Bab Targua
- Bab Aglou
- Bab El Mader
- Bab El Jdid
- Bab Oulad Jarrar

Sidi Ifni
Mirhleft →

← Agadir

→ Tafraoute

Goulimime ↓

Boulevard Mohammed V

Rue de l'Hôpital

1 Place Almachouar
2 Hotel Al Mourabitine
3 Douche Atlas
4 Hotels Diaf & du Souss
5 Hotels des Amis & de la Jeunesse
6 Hotel Massa
7 Hotel Sahara
8 Hotels Voyageur & Bon Accueil
9 Restaurants
10 Sûreté
11 Market
12 GPO
13 Hotel CTM & Bus Terminal
14 Great Mosque

TIZNIT

In an arid corner of the Sous Valley, at the very end of the Anti-Atlas range, Tiznit looks like an old town with its six km of encircling red mud walls. It is actually fairly new. Though there was a settlement of sorts here previously, the town dates substantially from 1881, when it was chosen by Sultan Moulay Hassan as a base from which to assert his authority over the semiautonomous and rebellious tribes of the Sous and Anti-Atlas, as well as the nomadic Tuaregs further to the south. He was only partially successful in this quest and it wasn't until the 1930s – 20 years after Spain and France had partitioned Morocco between them – that the tribes were finally 'pacified'.

In the first decade of the 20th century, Tiznit became a focal point of resistance against foreign incursions under the leadership of El Hiba, an Idrissid chief from Mauritania who was regarded as a saint and credited with performing miracles. In 1912 he had himself proclaimed sultan àt the mosque in Tiznit and succeeded in uniting the tribes of the Anti-Atlas and the Tuaregs in a fanatical effort to repel the French invaders.

The best time to be in Tiznit is after the package tour buses from Agadir leave (between mid-to-late afternoon and mid-morning). Then, it reverts to normality and is a pleasant place to hang around and explore. This is also the best time to have a look at the silver jewellery, reputedly some of the best in the south.

Places to Stay

The best hotels are in Place Almachouar. Many have rooftop terraces, where you can escape the tourist hordes during the middle of the day. They're all much the same price and offer similar facilities. Most travellers stay at *Hotel Atlas*, which has one of the best and liveliest restaurants. It's clean and costs Dr 30 a double. Almost identical are *Hotel des Amis* and *Hotel de la Jeunesse*. Next best would be *Hotel Voyageur* and *Hotel du*

Bon Accueil, on the opposite side of the square. For something up-market, try *Hotel Massa*. Another nearby and worth checking out if the others are full is *Hotel Sahara*, at the start of Rue de l'Hôpital.

Off Place Almachouar is Rue Bain Maure, along which are several other cheapies. Perhaps the best of them is *Hotel Al Mourabitine*, which is clean and costs Dr 30 a double. It's adequate and secure, but poor value considering it has only one handbasin and toilet for the whole hotel. There's a tearoom on the 1st floor. Out of this immediate area is *CTM Hotel*, next to the CTM bus terminal. It is clean and costs Dr 25/30 a double downstairs/upstairs. The staff is friendly and there's a bar and restaurant on the 1st floor.

None of the hotels has hot showers, but there is a public *douche*, the *Douche Atlas*, halfway down Rue Bain Maure at the end of a cul-de-sac. It costs Dr 3.50 for unlimited hot water. There are separate showers for men and women and it is open till late evening.

Places to Eat

There are several good cafés opposite the main entrance (Les Trois Portes) to Place Almachouar, and just outside the Place, on Blvd Mohammed V. In the evening, the best place to go is the restaurant at Hotel Atlas. For those wanting to prepare their own food, the market is on the left-hand side up the road opposite Les Trois Portes. It has an excellent selection of meat, vegetables, fruit (fresh and dried) and many other foodstuffs.

ZAGORA

The journey down through the Dr'aa Valley, with its innumerable crumbling red-mud kasbahs and lush green *palmeraies*, hemmed in on both sides by forbidding, barren and craggy cliffs, has to be one of the world's most colourful and exotic experiences. It's pure magic from what feels like another world, and all the more reason to expect something special of Zagora. Unfortunately, Zagora, like

Ouarzazate, is largely a fairly new town, dating from the French colonial times when it was an administrative centre. Nevertheless, the town does have its moments, particularly when a dust storm blows up out of the desert in the late afternoon and the lighting becomes totally surreal. There are plenty of interesting places to explore in its vicinity.

Information

Market days are Wednesdays and Sundays, when fruit, vegetables, herbs, hardware, handicrafts, sheep, goats and donkeys are brought in to be bought and sold.

Bicycles can be rented from a repair shop on Ave Hassan II for Dr 5 an hour (negotiable). They're ideal for visiting Amezrou and Tamegroute to the south, and Tinezouline to the north. Otherwise you can go to the expense of hiring a taxi.

There's one CTM bus daily in either direction between Zagora and Ouarzazate, but if you want to stop along the way it is best to get a group together and hire a taxi. Make sure you fill the taxi as they won't stop if you are sharing with locals. Negotiate the price before you set off, and make sure the driver understands what you intend to do.

Things to See

The spectacular djebel, which rises up across the other side of the Oued Dr'aa, is worth climbing for the views – if you have the stamina and you set off early enough.

Also on the other side of the river, about three km south of Zagora, is the village of Amezrou, with its interesting old Jewish kasbah, which is still a centre for the casting of silver jewellery. Jews lived here for centuries and formerly controlled the silver trade. But they all took off for Israel in 1947, leaving the Berbers to carry on the tradition. If you look like you might buy something, they'll be willing to show you the whole process. Being so close to Zagora, local children will leap on you

offering to be guides, but it's fairly low-key. Elsewhere in the *palmeraie* life goes on much like it always has. It's worth at least a half day, wandering through the shady groves and along the many tracks that dissect it. The dates grown are reputed to be the best in Morocco, but in the last few years a disease has been attacking and killing the palms.

About 18 km south of Zagora, is Tamegroute which, for many centuries and until recently, was an influential religious and educational centre. The town consists of a series of inter-connected kasbahs, at the centre of which is the zaouia, or confraternity sanctuary, and its famous library. The library houses a magnificent collection of illustrated religious texts, dictionaries and astrological works, some of which are printed on gazelle hides, with the oldest dating back to around the 13th century. Visitors are allowed into the outer sanctuary and library in the morning and late afternoon (it's generally closed from 12 noon to 3 pm). You'll be expected to leave a donation for its upkeep. There is no shortage of local people willing to act as guides. Also in Tamegroute is a small potters' souk.

About three km south of Tamegroute you can get your first glimpse of the Sahara Desert. Off the road to the left are a number of isolated sand dunes, which, if you've never seen the desert proper or are not intending to go there, might be worth a visit. Otherwise, it's hardly worth the effort. There are the inevitable craft tents selling everything from silverware to carpets, but the guys who own them are pleasant and will invite you in for mint tea. Sales pressure is at a minimum.

Most people who come to Zagora go on to the end of the road and M'Hamid, about 95 km further south. M'Hamid in itself is nothing special, though its people are friendly and half the villagers will follow you around. The attraction of M'Hamid is the journey to it. The Dr'aa Valley widens dramatically after Zagora and there are magnificent vistas, vast tracks of stony

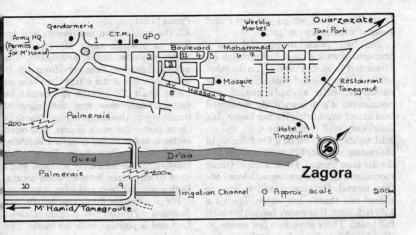

1. Hotel de la Palmeraie
2. Restaurant Timbouctou
3. Market
4. Hotel du Vallée
5. Hotel des Amis
6. Bank
7. AGIP Station
8. Bicycle Hire
9. La Fibule Hotel & Restaurant
10. Camping d'Amezrou
11. Hamman

desert, oases and two passes, as well as the beginning of the Sahara Desert as you get close to M'Hamid (though nothing like a *grand erg*). There's also the interesting village of **Oulad Driss**, with its traditional mud-brick mosque and kasbah. Great for photographers.

To visit M'Hamid you must first get a permit from the army barracks opposite Hotel de la Palmeraie. Go through the gates where there is a sign – 'Timbuctou: 52 jours'. The permit is free, but they'll want to see your passport. For those without transport, you will first have to arrange a lift or a taxi. Taxis charge around Dr 300 return (negotiable) and take up to six people. The driver will arrange the permits. There are also irregular transit vans and pick-up trucks plying between Zagora and M'Hamid, and they're much cheaper than taxis. Ask around.

Tamegroute is the furthest south you can go without a permit.

Places to Stay

In Zagora itself there are just four hotels. The cheapest is *Hotel des Amis*, for Dr 18/30/35 a single/double/triple without bathroom and Dr 20/30/37 a single/double/triple with bathroom. It's popular with travellers and the staff is friendly. Many of the rooms, however, are small and dark and there's no hot water. Slightly better, especially if you can get a front room, is *Hotel du Vallée* for Dr 32/42 a single/double without bathroom, and Dr 57/65 a single/double with bathroom. Better still is *Hotel de la Palmeraie*, where the staff is friendly and the rooms – most with their own balcony – cost Dr 59/83 a double/triple with shower or Dr 68/92 a double/triple with both shower and toilet. There are no singles. The showers have hot water. They also have one room on the bottom floor for Dr 43 a double, but it's stuffy and not worth the money. All these hotels are on Blvd Mohammed V. The only other hotel in Zagora itself is the large and expensive

Hotel Tinzouline, which you can forget about if you're on a budget.

The best place to stay, if you're prepared to walk a km or hire a taxi, is *La Fibule* (tel 4), Boite Postal 11, on the other side of the Oued Dr'aa. Set in the *palmeraie*, with a shady garden and restaurant, it's a beautifully converted traditional mud-brick Berber house. It's deliciously cool during the day, and on cold nights there will be a fire burning in the restaurant/bar. The rooms cost Dr 45 a double (two rooms), Dr 60 a triple (three rooms) and Dr 75 for a room with four beds (two rooms). Bathrooms and toilets are shared and there's hot water. There's a 15% reduction if you stay two nights with full board. There are only a few rooms, so it's advisable to book. It's excellent value and a much more pleasant place to stay than in the town itself.

Campers have a choice of two sites. The most convenient is *Camping d'Amezrou* about 400 metres past La Fibule along the dirt track that runs beside the irrigation channel. The other is *Camping Montagne*, at the foot of the *djebel*, which you get to by crossing the bridge over the irrigation channel immediately past La Fibule, then turning right. Follow the dirt track for about two km. It's run by friendly people and cold drinks are available, but take your own food.

Places to Eat

All the hotels have restaurants and try hard to produce tasty Moroccan-style dishes – soups, tajine, salad, etc. The quality, however, does vary from day to day. *Hotel des Amis* offers the cheapest meals at Dr 25, but the service can be excruciatingly slow and the tajine of minimal size, though great play is made of clean plates for each course. It's often better to eat at either *Hotel du Vallée* or *Hotel de la Palmeraie*. Both have excellent meals for Dr 35, and you won't have to wait ages between each course. Both also stock beer and wine.

For a change from the hotels, try *Restaurant Timbouctou*. It offers excellent food and is popular with the locals. The complete menu costs Dr 25, or, separately, soup (Dr 1.50), salad (Dr 5), tajine (Dr 14). Even if you are not staying at *La Fibule* you should eat there at least once. The food is excellent and the surroundings relaxing, but the service can be painfully slow. La Fibule has a bar, with beer and wine (you don't have to eat to drink). *Cafe Restaurant Essahara*, in the market square, has a good complete menu of soup, tajine and salad for Dr 20.

Mozambique

Although the Portuguese first arrived here in the late 15th century, their early activities were restricted to setting up a number of trading enclaves and forts along the coast which acted as collection points for the gold, ivory and slaves brought from the interior. The inland African principalities remained independent and conducted vigorous trading systems of their own. Not until the late 17th century did colonisation begin in earnest with the setting up of privately owned agricultural estates on land granted by the Portuguese crown or obtained by conquest from African chiefs.

Later, in the 19th century, when the country's borders were defined during the European scramble for colonies, huge concessions were granted to foreign charter companies which remained virtually autonomous until Salazar came to power in Portugal in the 1920s. A protectionist policy was introduced then in an attempt to seal off the colonies from non-Portuguese investment and to tie the colonies' economies more closely to that of Portugal. The outbreak of the liberation wars in the 1960s, however, forced Portugal to abandon this policy and to turn to its western allies for assistance.

Portuguese colonialism was a particularly backward and unbalanced affair. In the early days it relied heavily on slave labour, and, when that was abolished in the 19th century, forced labour took over. Every man was compelled to do six months unpaid work a year, and in the south most of the workforce was sent to the mines of South Africa in exchange for the routing of a part of South Africa's transit traffic through Mozambiquan ports.

There wasn't even a pretence of social investment in the African population. At independence 90% were illiterate and, after the large-scale exodus of Portuguese specialists, there were only 40 doctors left in the entire country. In the towns a sprawling service economy generated parasitic classes, and only towards the end of the colonial era did the large bureaucracy begin to take in Africans at its lower levels.

Resistance to colonial rule coalesced in 1962 with the formation of Frelimo, the Mozambique liberation front. It was made up of exiled political groups, radical intellectuals and underground organisations which had begun to operate inside the country. Frelimo launched its first military campaigns two years later and by 1966 had driven the Portuguese army out of much of the two northern provinces of Cabo Delgado and Niassa. But the Front wasn't just a guerrilla army. In the areas which it liberated, a socialist economy was put into operation and essential services were provided. By the time the Portuguese were overthrown in 1975 Frelimo had accumulated a lot of experience in organising production and devising participatory structures. This guaranteed that the post-independence government would be committed to a policy of radical social change and not merely the Africanisation of the existing colonial structure.

Nevertheless, when independence was won in 1975, Frelimo was faced with an enormous task made worse by the wholesale exodus of Portuguese skilled labour and capital, plus the looting and deliberate destruction of machinery, heavy vehicles and other technical resources by the departing whites. The economy took a

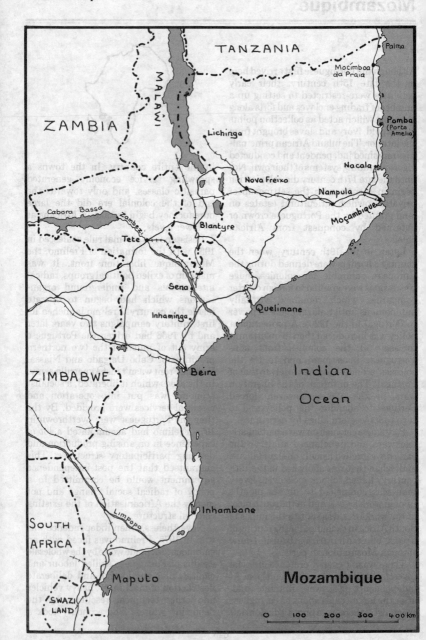

TANZANIA

Palma

Macimboa
da Praia

ZAMBIA

MALAWI

Pomba
(Porto
Amelia)

Lichinga

Nacala

Nova Freixo

Nampula

Moçambique

Cabara Bassa

Zambezi

Blantyre

Tete

Sena

Quelimane

Inhaminga

Indian
Ocean

ZIMBABWE

Beira

SOUTH
AFRICA

Inhambane

Limpopo

Maputo

Mozambique

SWAZI
LAND

0   100   200   300   400 km

nosedive which led to serious food shortages. Yet, at the same time, Mozambique bravely reaffirmed its commitment to African liberation by faithfully complying with the UN-sponsored sanctions against Ian Smith's Rhodesia even though this hit the economy hard with the loss of transit trade from that country.

There was a further balance-of-payments crisis in 1978 when South Africa suspended gold payments for Mozambiquan mine labour. The system of gold payments was set up in colonial days. Under it, a proportion of the mine workers' wages was retained until the completion of the work contract when it was paid in gold to the Portuguese government. Portugal was thus able to sell the gold on the free market, pay the workers in local currency, and retain the speculative profit from the deal.

Despite all this, Frelimo forged ahead with its programme. Private ownership of land was abolished, paving the way for the creation of state farms and companies, peasant cooperatives and collectives. Rented property was nationalised, as were schools. On the one hand, this eliminated landlords and desegregated the colonial towns, while on the other, it dealt a blow to elitist education and the raising of youth with the values of a propertied individualist society.

Banks and insurance companies were likewise nationalised while private practices in medicine and law were abolished. These moves were intended to disperse skilled labour where it was most needed and, as far as law was concerned, to enable lay participation in the administration of justice. Because of the scarcity of skilled labour, however, the going was rough and education assumed a high priority. Crash literacy programmes were launched with the aim of teaching 100,000 people to read and write each year. Much assistance was received from foreign volunteers, notably from Sweden.

At the same time, emphasis was placed on breaking the barriers between manual and intellectual work and orienting education to the demands of production. Rural schools were expected to be self-sufficient in food, and university students were compelled to undertake manual work or teaching as well as study. To increase awareness of the realities of rural life, brigades of university students were despatched to work in the countryside for a month every year. Similarly, basic health services were provided by the creation of the Mozambiquan equivalent of the Maoist 'barefoot doctors'. The principal aim of this programme was mass vaccination against the most common diseases and the teaching of the basic rules of hygiene and sanitation.

Mozambique also provided the bases and support for Robert Mugabe's forces during their war of liberation against the Smith regime in Rhodesia. The cost of this support was high and reprisals were frequent. There was wholesale destruction of agriculture, roads, bridges and social amenities. On one occasion, there was a full-scale invasion of Tete province by Rhodesian ground and air forces.

By the time Frelimo held its fourth congress in 1983, the country was almost bankrupt. Foreign reserves were non-existent, while production in both the agricultural and industrial sectors was at an all time low. There seemed little prospect of any improvement for a long while to come. There were several reasons for this – not all of them connected with South Africa's and Rhodesia's deliberate policy of doing their utmost to destabilise the Mozambiquan economy.

While collectivisation of agriculture had worked well in some cases, in many others it was a complete disaster which Frelimo failed to recognise for many years. The peasants may have been prepared to make great sacrifices during the war of liberation from the Portuguese, but after independence they had somewhat higher expectations. When these were not forthcoming and when workers on the state farms found they could not even buy food with their wages, they began to leave in droves to grow their own. The food producers on the collectives were likewise reluctant to sell their crops to the government in return for worthless money. The system was quickly heading back to mere subsistence agriculture.

On top of this there was the expulsion of Mozambiquan mine workers from South Africa with the accompanying loss of their vital hard currency earnings. It also created the problem of how to accommodate tens of thousands of unemployed miners in areas which had been traditionally dependent on work in South Africa. To make matters worse, a severe drought was, at that time, covering a large part of southern Mozambique.

Into this picture of gloom, and feeding on the discontent, came the MNR (Mozambique National Resistance). Though the rebels of this group had been active for a number of years, they now stepped up their activities with the encouragement and support of Pretoria. If things weren't already bad enough, the MNR were determined to make them impossible. Anything used to transport goods or people was destroyed or sabotaged. Villagers were rounded up and anyone with skills considered to be beneficial to the people – teachers, medical workers, etc – were shot. Schools and clinics were destroyed and even Maputo itself was not safe from their activities. Because of Machel's support for the exiled ANC, there was even direct military intervention by regular South African forces.

Machel claimed at the time that the MNR had cost the country US$333 million and caused the destruction of 900 rural shops, 495 primary schools, 86 health posts and 140 communal villages.

The country could not sustain losses of this magnitude and the aid expected from its socialist allies proved to be insufficient to help the country back onto its feet. Something had to give and it came in the form of a radical change of policy.

Though Frelimo's hatred of apartheid was in no way diminished, it was clear that an accommodation had to be reached with the South African regime and Mozambique opened up to western capital investment. The alternative was to tie the country even more closely into the Soviet-dominated economic and political system – a course of action which Frelimo had always shied away from, preferring to retain a degree of independence. The upshot was the signing of the Nkomati Accord with South Africa. Pretoria undertook to withdraw its support from the MNR in return for the expulsion of the ANC from Mozambique and the opening up of the country to South African business investment. At the same time, Machel made a tour of a number of western countries in an attempt to drum up further aid and investment.

For Mozambique, the Accord was a strange mixture of desperate courage and naiveté. Yet, from the moment it was signed, the country abided by the terms of the agreement. Pretoria, however, as subsequently became clear, was determined to exploit the situation to the full.

Despite the Accord, MNR activity did not diminish in the slightest yet Pretoria vehemently denied any involvement. The truth finally surfaced in late 1985 following a successful joint Zimbabwean-Mozambiquan military offensive against the most important MNR base in the Gorongosa Game Reserve north-west of Beira. Some 1500 guerrillas were killed or captured, huge amounts of arms and ammunition recovered. Most damning of all, incontrovertible proof was found that not only had Pretoria continued to supply the rebels, but that senior officers and advisers had regularly flown into Mozambique to train MNR recruits and check on the progress being made.

Although South Africa was forced to come clean on their involvement, the MNR are still active within Mozambique. Their activities, however, have been curtailed to some degree and, with the help of the

Zimbabwean army, Mozambique has been able to reopen the Beira to Harare railway and the road link between Zimbabwe and Malawi via Tete. It will be a long time, though, before Mozambique returns to any semblance of peace and economic health. Civil war, austerity, hunger and poverty seem destined to stalk the country for many years to come.

The country's first president, Samora Machel (along with several other members of the government) met his end in an air crash whilst returning to Maputo from Zambia following a meeting with other front line presidents in Lusaka. His plane, flown by Soviet pilots, crashed just inside South African territory on the final approach to Maputo Airport. The South African government was inevitably blamed for the disaster and there was widespread outrage at what was regarded as the assassination of a well-respected African leader. Yet it appeared from reports that, at least on this occasion, there had been no South African involvement. It seems that it was simply a case of pilot error though the South African government did insist on conducting its own enquiry and refused to accept international participation.

Since it had other, more important, concerns following independence, Mozambique did not encourage tourism and visas were very difficult to get. This has changed considerably over the last few years since the country has been attempting to strengthen its economic ties with the west and quite a few travellers are going there these days. If you do go, be prepared for very limited services – suspended road and rail connections, sporadic electricity and water supplies. Food is scarce and many shops are closed. Services in hotels, too, are minimal.

Facts

GEOGRAPHY & CLIMATE
The land consists of a wide coastal plain rising to mountains and plateaus on the Zimbabwean, Zambian and Malawian borders. Two of Africa's major rivers – the Zambezi and Limpopo – flow through the country. The huge Cabora Bassa dam is sited on the Zambezi. The dry season runs from April to September, during which time the climate is pleasant. In the wet season it's hot and humid with temperatures ranging from 27°C to 29°C on the coast but cooler inland.

PEOPLE
There are many different tribal groups in Mozambique, including the Shona, the main tribal grouping in Zimbabwe, but the largest group is the Makua-Lomwe, which accounts for some 40% of the people.

The population stands at around 14½ million.

VISAS
Visas are required by all. They can be obtained in Dar es Salaam (Tanzania), Lilongwe (Malawi), Lusaka (Zambia), Harare (Zimbabwe) and Mbabane (Swaziland). There are also embassies in the USA and Portugal.

In Harare visas cost Z$6, with three photos and take three days to issue. The embassy is at 152 Rhodes Ave. If you are told at reception that visas are only issued to Zimbabwean residents and nationals ask to see a more senior official. Tell that official you are interested in the country and sympathetic towards its problems. This usually does the trick. The application form asks for intended dates of entry and exit so have this worked out beforehand.

Visas are also reputedly relatively easy to get in Lusaka and Dar es Salaam. If you experience problems getting a tourist visa read up on Mozambique, work out an acceptable reason for wanting to spend some time there then write, citing your reasons, to Sr José Augusto Ferrao, Empresa Nacional de Turismo, Avenida 25 de Setembro 1203, CP 2446, Maputo.

While obtaining tourist visas may be

problematical, transit visas to take you across the Tete corridor between Zimbabwe and Malawi are no problem whatsoever. They are easily obtained in both Harare and Lilongwe.

Depending on the security position at any particular time, you may need a special permit (known as a *Guía de Marcha*) to travel anywhere outside Maputo province. You can get this from ministries and official institutes. Make enquiries in Maputo.

MONEY

US$1 = Me 450 (official rate)

The unit of currency is the metical (plural meticais) = 100 cents. The import and export of local currency is prohibited. Customs officials are usually very strict about this and you may be thoroughly searched. Others have said that customs and immigration are among the most easy-going on the continent. Currency declaration forms are issued on arrival but may not be collected when leaving. You may be required to change money on arrival but this is usually only a small amount – around US$20 to US$30.

There is a lively black market for hard currency, but be very discreet when changing as there are heavy penalties. Asian traders are the best people to approach. The current rates are about US$1 = Me 1000 to Me 1500 or Zimbabwean $1 = Me 700 to Me 900. Rands are also acceptable. Don't get too excited about the black market rate, however, as there's very little you can buy with metical. You need ration cards for food, fuel and clothes so the only place you can get rid of excess is in the markets.

The airport tax for international flights is US$10. The tax for internal flights has been abolished.

TOURIST INFORMATION

You can actually take things out of the country which you've bought, but you do need a permit from the Ministerio de Cultura e Educacão. Before they'll issue one you have to show receipts, the item itself and tell them where you bought it. Patience is required for such a permit and a bribe is helpful.

PHOTOGRAPHY

Don't take photographs of public buildings or soldiers. They're naturally very sensitive about things like that.

LANGUAGE

Portuguese is the official language but there are many African languages. In the more remote provinces, you may not find many people who speak Portuguese.

Getting There & Around

AIR

There are several relatively cheap international flights available. One possibility is the once-weekly Harare to Maputo service which costs Z$166 return, but there's usually a waiting list for it. Lesotho Airways flies Manzini to Maputo on Thursdays and LAM (Lineas Aereas Moçambique) flies Maputo/Manzini/Maseru and vice versa on Saturdays. There's also a charter company which offers Nelspruit (SA) to Maputo flights.

Due to the current street exchange rate, flying internally is cheap and the obvious answer to long-distance travel. Most of the main towns have an airport. Flights are frequently delayed or cancelled, so it's advisable to get to the airport well in advance. Overbooking is endemic so book as far ahead as possible and pay a hard currency bribe to be sure of getting onto any particular flight. Maputo to Beira costs Me 24,000.

Bank receipts only have to be shown for international flight tickets.

ROAD

Because of the war it is no longer safe to hitch in Mozambique. Between the

Zimbabwean and Malawian frontiers and Beira there is little traffic, and the buses which do exist are in bad shape and very unreliable. Treat all schedules as a figment of the imagination.

TO/FROM MALAWI & ZIMBABWE

The railway lines between Beira and the Malawian and Zimbabwean frontiers are probably the best bet if entering from the north, but services can be disrupted for weeks on end due to sabotage by the MNR. The Chicualacuala crossing between Zimbabwe and Mozambique is closed even though there is usually a daily train between there and Maputo.

All that can be said about road transport is that nothing is definite and you'll have to play it by ear. The MNR do their utmost to destroy and disrupt road and rail transport but there's also a desperate shortage of spare parts, tyres and batteries so nothing can be guaranteed. The only route in the country which is reliable is the one between the Zimbabwean and Malawian frontiers via Tete since all traffic has to go in convoy and is accompanied by a unit of the Zimbabwean army. For details of this route, see either the Malawi or Zimbabwe chapters.

If there are no problems with sabotage, there is generally a bus from Milanje (Malawi-Mozambique border) to Quelimane on Tuesday and Saturday. From Quelimane to Caia there is a daily bus, and from Caia to Beira there is a daily train (if it's not a passenger train you're likely to get a free ride on a freight train).

TO/FROM SOUTH AFRICA

If coming in from the east, the best bet is to take the train between Johannesburg and Maputo via Ressano Garcia. There is a daily train in either direction which leaves Johannesburg at 6.15 pm and Maputo at 4.35 pm. The journey takes about 17 hours and costs R 34.20 (1st class), R 23.10 (2nd class) and R 10.25 (3rd class).

TO/FROM SWAZILAND

There are twice-weekly buses between Mbabane (Swaziland) and Maputo operated by Oliveiras Transportes e Turismo. They leave on Friday and Sunday from Maputo, Sunday and Monday from Mbabane. The journey takes all day. Customs and immigration at Namaacha are very easy-going.

TO/FROM ZAMBIA

From Zambia the best point of entry is Chanida-Cassacatiza just south of Chipata. A new road has been built between the two border towns. If coming this way be prepared for long waits, as there is very little traffic. The customs people are friendly and may let you stay with them while you wait for transport.

Around the Country

BEIRA

This is one of Mozambique's most important ports and the terminal of the oil pipeline and railway line to Zimbabwe and Malawi. There are a few public buses and an even smaller number of taxis around the town. However, they are not worth waiting for because schedules are erratic, and the buses are extremely overcrowded.

There are some beautiful beaches and you'll rarely meet another traveller here. There's been no electricity since 1986 (though it may be fixed by the time you read this). The beaches are open for a fair stretch to the north and a little to the south of town. They get cleaner as you head north (the one close to the Hotel Dom Carlos is good), but you can't go too far north as they are closed off by the army.

Places to Stay & Eat

One of the best places to stay is the popular *Estoril Hotel* which costs Me 500 a double. There's no running water but the hotel usually has sufficient food for its guests. Most of the people at reception speak English. The hotel is near the lighthouse to the north of town. Next door to it is the *Hotel Dom Carlos* which costs Me 1500 a double and includes a very basic breakfast (usually an egg and something to drink). The *Hotel Moçambique*, though closer to the centre, is thoroughly run-down, filthy, and overrun with rats and other rodents. It costs Me 470/1200 a single/double. Breakfast, at Me 150, consists of 'two dry rolls and rubbery, powdered egg'. The lift doesn't work either. Lunch or dinner costs Me 350 and consists of noodle soup followed by fish and noodles (it's the same every day).

The *Hotel Embaixador* costs Me 1400 a double but there is hot water all day. Like other hotels, the lifts don't work. The quality of meals is said to be poor and the place is overrun with cockroaches. Only one of the people at reception speaks any English and he's often not there.

There are a number of smaller hotels and *pensão* but they're often full. In any case, you need to be in a hotel which provides food otherwise you are limited to food bought from the foreign currency shop, where goods have to be paid for in hard currency (expensive). If you do decide to plump for a cheap place, try either the *Messe dos Trabalhadores* one block from the Hotel Embaixador, or the *Pensão Imperio*. They both cost around Me 100 to Me 200 a single.

The *Voleiro* by the roundabout at the coast has been recommended as a good restaurant if you like pork and mealie meal. They also have good bread.

There are two nightclubs which are worth visiting if you're looking for some action or want a beer without having to buy a meal. The *Oceana* near the Grand Hotel is open every night except Monday from 9 pm to 4 am and every day for lunch. Entry costs Me 500. If intending to go at night you must reserve a place the day before. Good prawns are available at night, and beef (sometimes) at lunch.

The market has a good selection of vegetables but there are no other food shops in Beira except for bakeries and the Interfranca shop where you must pay in hard currency. They take travellers' cheques (including Zimbabwe dollar cheques but not cash) and give change in US dollars and rand.

MAPUTO

Maputo is the capital of Mozambique. If you have an old map, it may still be marked as Lorenço Marques (the old Portuguese name). There are a few buses around the centre but there is no regular transport to the airport. Bus Nos 22, 13 and 14 are scheduled to go there. Taxis are few and far between because of fuel shortages. Most of the cafés and restaurants are closed and, at the ones which still remain open, you must make a reservation the day before to be sure of getting a meal.

Useful Addresses

Tourist Office
1179 Avenida 25 de Setembro (tel 5011). Helpful with information and hotel bookings outside Maputo.
Banco de Moçambique
Avenida 25 de Setembro 1695
LAM terminal (Mozambique national airline)
Avenida 25 de Setembro 1747 (tel 26001)

Things to See

The **Museum of the Revolution**, Avenida 24 de Julho is worth a visit and costs Me 10 but you really need to go with a guide unless you can read Portuguese.

A lively and colourful place to visit is the **market** on Avenida 25 de Setembro – there are fruit, vegetables, spices and basketwork.

The beaches in Maputo are very dirty and it's difficult to get buses south where the better beaches are located.

If you're looking for some music or want to buy seafood, take the early morning boat across the harbour to **Costa del Sol** (about five km north). There are good beaches there and a good cosmopolitan restaurant where you can get a meal for about Me 150. There is live music at

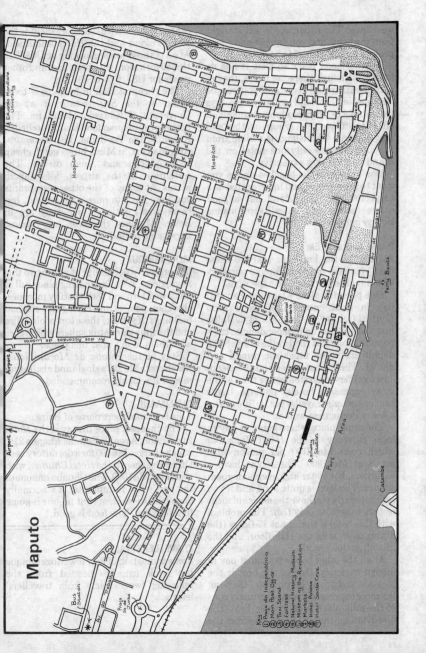

Maputo

Key

1. Praça de Independência
2. Main Post Office
3. Taxi Stand
4. Fortress
5. Natural History Museum
6. Museum of the Revolution
7. Markets
8. Hotel Polana
9. Hotel Santa Cruz

weekends. The fisherpeople sell straight from the boats and you can get two dozen prawns for about US$4.

Another good place to visit is **Ilha do Inhaca**. Although there are boats, they're very irregular and risky and you can be stranded on the island for four or five days before another comes along to take you off. It's better to get a group together and rent a plane. The island is visible from Maputo. There's only one hotel on the island and it's very expensive.

Don't sleep on the beaches unless you want to get arrested and interrogated as a suspected spy. The island has a good **nature reserve** and a well-kept **marine biology museum**.

Places to Stay & Eat

At most of the hotels in Maputo these days you have to pay in foreign currency which makes things quite expensive.

One pleasant place where you can still pay in local currency is the *Pensão Central* (tel 24476), Avenida 24 de Julho just above Praça da Independéncia. It's a popular place and good value at Me 800 a double including breakfast, lunch and dinner. There's hot water and it's clean. The food served is often better than at the more expensive hotels. perhaps that's because (as one traveller put it) 'it's run by a bossy Portuguese woman'.

The other place where you can pay in local currency is the *Hotel Tourismo* which costs Me 2100 per person with meals at Me 1300. The rooms have a bathroom, hot water and telephone room service. The food is quite good and if you get there early you have the choice of meat or fish, otherwise only fish. The problem with this hotel is that it has 12 floors (the dining room is on the 11th floor) and the lifts often don't work.

At all the other hotels you must pay in foreign currency. One of the best is the pleasant and privately run *Hotel Cordoso*. It's more expensive than the ordinary run-of-the-mill place and it does have the disadvantage that it's a long way from the centre. Others in this category include the *Hotel Polana* and the *Hotel Andalusia*. At all of these you are looking at US$35 to US$50 for a room with breakfast and other meals for US$10 to US$13.

The cheapest food in Maputo is to be found at the *Self* restaurant at the University of Eduardo Mondlane. The best Mozambiquan food is at *Matchedje*, Avenida Mao Tse Tung. The *Coxemira*, Avenida Ho Chi Minh, offers good, cheap East African and Asian dishes. The restaurant at the airport does superb pizzas. At many of the other restaurants you may have to queue for a meal, but beers aren't rationed like they are in Beira. Matches, however, are almost impossible to find.

MOÇAMBIQUE

If there's any possibility of getting to this town, do so. It's a fascinating place full of mildewed 17th and 18th-century mosques, churches, palaces and Portuguese colonial buildings. If you like these sort of old relics and the time warp atmosphere which goes with them, don't miss this place.

Stay at the *Posada de Moçambique*, which costs Me 250 a single and also serves meals. It's highly recommended.

QUELIMANE

This is a small port north of Beira.

The cheapest place to stay is the *Hotel 24 de Julho*, Avenida Samuel Magaia 216, which charges Me 100 for a dormitory bed. Otherwise there is the *Hotel Chuabo*, with rooms for Me 1000. The Chuabo has one of the port's few restaurants. It's normally open only to residents but no-one is going to refuse you. The food is good.

TRAVELLERS' TALES

Some indication of how low Mozambique has sunk can be gleaned from the following two extracts from travellers' letters:

Mozambique makes Tanzania seem like a prime holiday resort. It's one thing having meticais to spend, quite a different thing finding something to spend them on! Great if you like *perri perri* sauce, furniture polish or wooden buttons. There are some very nice carvings available but it's impossible to post them home from Mozambique, as you need a permit to send anything other than a letter out of the country.

You can't get food at any restaurant and you can only eat at the hotel you are staying in. The only other place we found that sold meals was at the airport both in Beira and Maputo – just say you are waiting for a flight if anyone asks. You can sometimes find a café which sells tea and plain bread rolls, but you have to stand in line for hours to get this treat! There are two foreign currency stores – one small one in Beira and a large one in Maputo called the IF (Interfranca) on 24 de Julho up the hill from the Pensão Central. The one in Beira is near the post office. They both sell all manner of imported goods at prices which are very competitive with, say, South Africa. The checkouts only accept foreign currency. The Maputo store sells some fresh produce.

Namibia

Namibia has one of the world's most barren and inhospitable coastlines which is the main reason why this part of Africa was largely ignored by the European maritime nations until fairly recently. The first European visitors were Portuguese mariners seeking a way to the Indies in the late 15th century but they confined their activities to erecting stone crosses at certain points as navigational aids. Next came American whalers in the late 18th century. However, it wasn't until the last minute scramble for colonies towards the end of the 19th century that Namibia was annexed by Germany except for the enclave of Walvis Bay taken in 1878 by the British for the Cape Colony.

The indigenous tribes, the Herero, Nama and Ovambo, vigorously attempted to preserve their independence. When it became clear by 1904 that this couldn't be done using peaceful means, the Herero rose in rebellion. They were joined later that year by the Nama. The colonial authorities responded with over a year of genocide in which some 60% of the native population of the south and centre were wiped out, including 75% to 80% of the Herero. The Ovambo in the north were luckier and managed to avoid conquest until after the start of WW I when they were overrun and 'pacified' by Portuguese forces in 1915 fighting on the side of the Allies. In that same year the German colony came to an end after its forces surrendered to a South African expeditionary army also fighting on behalf of the Allies.

At the end of WW I, South Africa was given a mandate to rule the territory (then known as South West Africa) by the League of Nations. The mandate was renewed by the United Nations following WW II but the organisation refused to sanction the annexation of the country by South Africa.

Undeterred, the South African government continued to increase its control over the territory with each passing year, beginning with the granting of representation in the South African parliament for the white population in 1949. The bulk of the country's viable farming land was steadily parcelled out into some 6000 farms owned by white settlers, while male black workers with their families were restricted to their workplace by labour and pass laws. The rest – women, children, the elderly, the sick and the unemployed – were dumped in 'reserves' which they could only leave with a work-seeker's pass.

The more populous Ovamboland in the north was virtually sealed off and left to stagnate while a pernicious labour contract system was imposed on black migrant labour. Under this system a worker had no choice of employer, no negotiating rights over wages or the length of the contract period and no right to quit. Tribal leaders in the 'reserves' were appointed by the South Africans regardless of whether they enjoyed popular support or not. Finally, following UN cancellation of the South African mandate in 1966, apartheid and security laws were introduced. Shortly afterwards, the status of the 'reserves' was altered to bring them in line with the bantustans (homelands) in South Africa itself.

South Africa continued illegally to occupy and rule the country despite almost total worldwide condemnation. It seemed unlikely that they would ever voluntarily relinquish control or agree, in

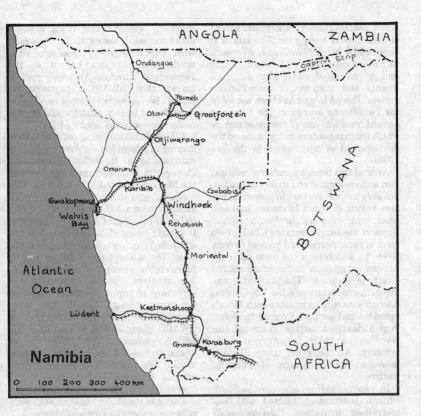

good faith, to negotiations on independence for the country. Everytime a breakthrough appeared to be achieved on this issue during the last decade or so, it turned out to be yet another exercise in political skulduggery by the South African government. They were encouraged in this by the Reagan administration in the USA, which linked the removal of Cuban troops from Angola with the removal of South African troops from Namibia.

Meanwhile, the guerrilla war mounted by SWAPO (South West Africa People's Organisation) continued to escalate. This led to the stationing of over 10,000 South African troops there (alongside some 21,000 Namibians of the South West

Africa Territorial Force). It also led to a number of full-scale invasions of southern Angola by those troops, on the pretext of wiping out guerrilla bases there and in support of UNITA, the rebel Angolan faction.

South African intransigence over Namibia was based on its fears of having yet another antagonistic government on its doorstep and on losing the income which it derives from the mining operations there. Namibia is rich in minerals such as uranium, copper, lead and zinc and is the world's foremost source of gem diamonds. These are all mined by South African and other western multinational companies under a very generous taxation scheme which enables them to export up to a third of their profits every year. The labour is supplied by black Namibians, who work in bad conditions at rock bottom wages and are recruited under what is, to all intents and purposes, a forced-labour system. Forced labour has been the lot of the Namibians ever since the Germans arrived, and was one of the main factors which led to mass demonstrations and the development of nationalism in the late 1950s.

Around this time, a number of political parties were formed and strikes organised, not only among workers in Namibia, but also among contract labourers who had been sent to work in South Africa. Support was sought from the UN. By 1960 most of these parties had merged to form SWAPO, which took the issue of South African occupation to the International Court of Justice. The outcome was inconclusive but in 1966 the UN General Assembly voted to terminate South Africa's mandate and set up a Council for South West Africa (renamed the Commission for Namibia in 1973) to administer the territory. At the same time, SWAPO launched its campaign of guerrilla warfare.

In response to this campaign the South African government reacted with unrestrained brutality. Casting aside international opinion, its security forces fired on demonstrators and arrested thousands of activists. Torture was commonplace and thousands were banished to the reserves. At the same time funds were pumped into white and compliant black organisations in an effort to pave the way for a unilateral exercise in self-determination. In this way South Africa hoped to upstage the UN and discredit SWAPO by presenting to the world what appeared to be a representative government enjoying support from all sections of Namibian society. In terms of stalling for time and currying the favour of the five western members of the UN Security Council who continued to veto

sanctions against South Africa, it was a major success. It lost credibility, however, when Dirk Mudge – the leader of what would later become known as the Democratic Turnhalle Alliance – made it known that SWAPO's participation would be severely limited and that defence and foreign affairs would remain under the control of South Africa.

While all this was going on, events were coming to a head in neighbouring Angola culminating in its independence from Portugal in 1975, and the ascendancy of the Marxist-oriented MPLA forces. This was anathema to South Africa who, in an attempt to smash the MPLA, launched a full-scale invasion of Angola in support of the right wing UNITA forces which controlled much of southern Angola at the time. The attempt was a failure and by March 1976 the troops had been withdrawn. Nevertheless, South African forces continued to regard southern Angola as fair game though latterly the main 'justification' was the destruction of SWAPO guerrilla bases. Certainly the MPLA supported SWAPO's war of liberation (as did many other countries around the world) and South African attacks severely limited its scale of operations, but, from all accounts, the majority of deaths in these attacks were refugees rather than active fighters.

Back in Namibia itself, the Democratic Turnhalle Alliance (DTA, named after the site of its meetings) was officially established in 1975. Formed from a combination of White political interests and artificial ethnic parties, it turned out to be little more than a toothless debating chamber which spent most of its time in litigation with the South African government over its scope of responsibilities. The DTA was dissolved by its sponsors in 1983 after it had indicated it would favour some kind of accommodation with SWAPO. It was replaced by yet another puppet administration, the Multi-Party Conference, which had even less success than the DTA and quickly faded into insignificance. Thereafter, total control of Namibia was resumed by the South African-appointed administrator-general who retained absolute authority and had the right of veto over all decisions coming from below.

The failure of these two attempts to foist an internal government beholden to South Africa on an unwilling population did not deter South Africa from continuing to play a double game. While it was careful not to reject UN initiatives entirely, it clearly had no intention of allowing a SWAPO-dominated government to take over in Namibia. The existence of an estimated 19,000 Cuban troops in Angola had now become the prima facie reason for its refusal to negotiate on a UN-supervised programme for the independence of Namibia. SWAPO was well aware of this and, accordingly, intensified the guerrilla campaign. As a result, movement in the north of the country became severely restricted.

In the end, it may not have been the activities of SWAPO alone or international sanctions which forced South Africa to negotiate. The dissatisfaction among the white Namibian population over the effects of the war on the economy and their personal lives, the attitude of the multinational companies towards the extraction of the country's mineral resources and South Africa's own internal troubles had a significant effect.

The war was already costing some R 480 million per year by 1985 and conscription was becoming widespread. The export of minerals which once provided around 88% of the country's gross domestic product had plummeted to just 27% by 1984. Part of the reason for this was falling world demand and depressed prices on the stock markets, but it was also discovered that mining concerns had been defrauding the Namibian economy for years.

Prominent among them was the diamond extraction company, Consolidated Diamond Mines. (Diamonds are the country's second most valuable export after uranium.) Not only had this company been understating the value of diamonds it extracted for tax purposes, but its accounts had not been audited by the Auditor General, as required by law. It turned out that the Auditor General himself was none other than the chairman of the board of CDM!

There is evidence, too, that mining companies had adopted a policy of grabbing what they could while the opportunity lasted, with dire consequences for the future of the Namibian economy. It is estimated that by 1993, at the current rate of extraction, diamond mining would no longer be viable. International sanctions against the purchase of Namibian minerals have also had their effect.

Minerals apart, the once rich inshore fishing grounds were rapidly being depleted by foreign trawlers taking unfair advantage of the refusal of the international community to recognise South Africa's administration of Namibia. As a result, fish-processing factories in Lüderitz and Walvis Bay were forced to close, causing serious unemployment amongst the black workers and the demise of a previously important industry. Drought in the early 1980s also seriously depressed the agricultural sector, and stocks of beef cattle and sheep remain low. Agriculture now accounts for only some 40% of the contribution it made to the economy before the drought.

SWAPO (which now had full observer status in the UN General Assembly) was profoundly resentful about South Africa's obduracy and its (and the multinationals') rapacious attitude towards mining in the country. The fear is that the country's inhabitants will eventually be handed a worthless independence with a crippled economy and totally dominated by South Africa for the foreseeable future. Not only that, but South Africa has so far refused to negotiate on the issue of Walvis Bay – Namibia's only viable sea port and a vital communications base. Pretoria regards the enclave as an integral part of the republic. Their claims are based on the British annexation of 1878 even though it had been administered from Windhoek between 1922 and 1977 after which it was transferred back to Cape Province. Should it remain in South African hands it would amount to a virtual stranglehold over Namibia's exports and imports.

With all things taken into account, it would appear that the South African government has bowed to both internal and external pressures in agreeing to grant Namibia its independence. How genuine that independence will be, and how much subject to the wishes of Namibia's powerful neighbour to the south, remains to be seen.

Facts

While uncertainty may be the state of the political situation for the foreseeable future, this should not cloud your appreciation of what the country has to offer. It's a stunningly beautiful land and quite different from anywhere else in Africa. Parts of the countries bordering the Sahara and Somalia bear superficial similarities but the people and the fauna and flora are totally dissimilar. It is also much easier to travel around than it is in the areas bordering the Sahara. Anyone who visits Namibia is in for a uniquely memorable experience.

VISAS

As for South Africa. Special permits for visiting the Black 'homelands' (bantustans) are no longer necessary. Permits are necessary for travelling through the Caprivi Strip in which case they can be obtained from a police station in any large town. Most travellers either get them from Rundu in the west or Katima Mulilo in the east.

MONEY

As for South Africa.

TOURIST INFORMATION

Well-illustrated and informative tourist literature is readily available from the SWA-Namibia Publicity Association, PO Box 1868, Windhoek 9000, or from the SWA-Namibia Information Service, PO Box 2160, Windhoek. Make sure you get hold of the publications, *Africa's Gem*, the annual, *SWA Accommodation Guide for Tourists* and one of the road maps. All these are free of charge. There's also an excellent publication by Shell entitled, *Tourist Guide, SWA-Namibia* (free), in English, German and Afrikaans with excellent regional maps as well as a full-scale map of Windhoek and the Etosha National Park.

ACCOMMODATION

There's a whole range of accommodation available in most of the places of interest. Prices are R 5 to R 18 for a bungalow (two to six beds) and R 2.50 to R 6 for a camp site (for up to eight people and two vehicles). Facilities are excellent. Before going to Namibia, obtain the small but comprehensive booklet *SWA Accommodation Guide for Tourists*, which lists virtually all the camp sites, bungalows and hotels in the country with their prices, facilities and seasons (where applicable). You can get these booklets from either the Directorate of Nature Conservation (tel 061-36975/6/7/8), Private Bag 13267, Windhoek 9000, Namibia; or from the South West Africa Tourist Commission, New St North, Johannesburg, South Africa (postal address: PO Box 11405, Johannesburg 2000). The Directorate of Nature Conservation (DNC), in particular, is very helpful and it's worth calling in at their Windhoek office.

Included in this guide is a list of the resorts and game parks which the DNC operates. They're often in the most scenic parts of the country and the accommodation is good value. The resorts have restaurants, small shops, hot showers and bedding but you must bring your own cutlery, crockery and cooking utensils. They're often full during school holidays. Try to make reservations in advance. These will be confirmed and are paid for on arrival. If you arrive after 5 pm, especially without a reservation, you may not be able to stay as the night guard will not have the keys to the vacant bungalows. Plan ahead and arrive early.

There are also various municipal bungalows, caravan sites (some with on-site caravans) and camping sites but most hotels and guesthouses will be outside the range of budget travellers (R 40 a double per day and up).

Student card holders are entitled to a 50% reduction on the full rate at all Namib-Sun Hotels throughout Namibia. They have hotels in Keetmanshoop, Swakopmund and Walvis Bay. The regular price is around R 22 so it will cost R 11 for bed and breakfast.

If you'd like to test the waters of local hospitality stop at a hotel bar and talk to the locals. They'll often offer you a place to stay free of charge. Be prepared to drink a fair swag of the amber nectar, however!

LANGUAGE
English and Afrikaans are the official languages but German is also widely spoken. African languages fall into two groups – Khoisan and Western Bantu.

Getting There & Around

AIR
Keetmanshoop is included in the South African Airways 'See South Africa' fare so bear this in mind if you buy one of those tickets.

Namib Air, which services internal routes, flies to many destinations including Lüderitz, Swakopmund, Walvis Bay, Cape Town and various Caprivi Strip towns from Windhoek. A few sample fares are: Windhoek to Lüderitz – R 212 one-way; Windhoek to Swakopmund – R 95 one-way; Windhoek to Katima Mulilo – R 235 one-way.

ROAD
Hitching
Roads in Namibia are generally excellent and hitching is easy along the main routes although you may have to wait a while until a vehicle comes along. When it does, however, it invariably stops and you'll often be offered accommodation. Off the main routes, hitching is problematical since there's so little traffic but the gravel tracks are well maintained. Take food and water when hitching off the main roads.

Between Windhoek and Ghanzi-Maun (Botswana) there are about 30 vehicles per day and it's fairly easy to arrange a lift. You may have to pay for lifts with black drivers but with white drivers it's often free. The journey takes about two days. If you meet with a blank try going via Katima Mulilo in the Caprivi Strip. En route, check at the military base in Rundu to see if they can fix you up with a lift to Katima Mulilo. There are plenty of vehicles going that way.

Driving
The main difficulty for those dependent on hitching or without their own vehicle is that the railways are the only form of public transport. There are no public buses. This being the case, if you want to explore the country and have limited time, it's worth renting a car even if you are just two people. Organised tours are very expensive. A conventional vehicle will get you to most places and there are signs indicating where a 4WD is necessary.

It's also possible to pick up hire-cars in Windhoek and drive them down to Cape Town for just the cost of fuel, especially during November and December.

TRAIN
A single rail line connects South Africa with Namibia. The route is De Aar, Prieska,

station	frequency Suidwester Tues	Tues	daily ex Tues
De Aar	10.30 pm	5.00 pm	6.00 pm
Prieska	2.21 am	9.26 pm	10.18 pm
Upington	7.10 am	3.45 am	5.05 am
Karasburg	1.20 pm	10.35 am	12.05 am
Keetmanshoop	7.05 pm	4.35 am	6.15 pm
Windhoek	7.00 am	5.40 am	7.35 am

station	frequency Suidwester Mon	daily
Windhoek	11.30 am	8.20 pm
Keetmanshoop	11.15 am	10.10 am
Karasburg	4.40 am	4.45 am
Upington	11.30 am	12.15 am
Prieska	3.40 pm	6.26 am
De Aar	6.45 pm	10.50 am

Upington, Karasburg, Keetmanshoop and Windhoek. The schedule is shown above. The Suidwester takes only 1st and 2nd class passengers. On all trains there is an hour's stop (approximately) at both Upington and Keetmanshoop.

From Windhoek there are branch lines west to Swakopmund and Walvis Bay and north to Tsumeb and Grootfontein via Otavi. There's also a branch line from Keetmanshoop to Lüderitz. Trains are very slow on these branch lines and, with hitching being so good, you'll probably only be interested in taking them if stuck for a ride.

The schedules for these lines are displayed below and on the opposite page.

The fare is R 37 from Keetmanshoop to Lüderitz.

The other branch line from Windhoek to Gobabis is for freight only.

Windhoek to Tsumeb station	frequency Sun, Thurs, Fri	Mon, Thurs, Fri, Sat	Tues, Wed
Windhoek	20.10 pm	–	–
Kranzberg	2.15 am	–	7.35 am
Otjiwarongo	7.42 am (arr)	–	3.10 pm
–	11.50 am (dep)	10.10 am	–
Otavi	4.25 pm	2.15 pm	–
Tsumeb	6.18 pm	–	–

The 10.10 am train from Otavi to Otjiwarongo continues on to Grootfontein.
The 7.35 am train from Kranzberg to Otjiwarongo originates in Grootfontein.

Tsumeb to Windhoek

station	frequency Wed, Fri, Sat, Sun	Wed, Fri, Sat, Sun	Mon, Tues
Tsumeb	7.00 am	–	–
Otavi	9.25 am	11.37 am	–
Otjiwarongo	1.34 pm (arr)	3.18 pm	–
–	6.30 pm (dep)	–	6.55 am
Kranzberg	12.14 pm	–	2.23 pm
Windhoek	5.30 am	–	–

The 11.37 am train from Otavi to Otjiwarongo originates in Grootfontein.

Windhoek to Walvis Bay

station	frequency daily	station	frequency daily
Walvis Bay	6.25 pm	Windhoek	7.10 pm
Swakopmund	7.22 pm	Karibib	11.39 pm
Usakos	12.17 pm	Kranzberg	12.55 pm
Kranzberg	1.30 am	Usakos	1.45 am
Karibib	2.05 am	Swakopmund	5.20 am
Windhoek	6.10 am	Walvis Bay	7.20 am

Otavi to Grootfontein

station	frequency Mon, Thurs, Fri, Sat	station	frequency Wed, Fri, Sat, Sun
Otavi	2.15 pm	Grootfontein	7.30 am
Grootfontein	6.10 pm	Otavi	10.55 am

Keetmanshoop to Lüderitz

station	frequency Thurs, Sat	station	frequency Fri, Sun
Keetmanshoop	6.30 pm	Lüderitz	6.30 pm
Aus	2.09 am	Aus	11.25 pm
Lüderitz	6.20 am	Keetmanshoop	6.20 am

Around the Country

CAPRIVI STRIP

This strange and lengthy extension of Namibia which separates Botswana from Zambia is the result of a deal in 1890 between Britain and Germany. In that year, the two agreed on an exchange of territory which left Britain with Zanzibar and Germany with Heligoland (an island in the North Sea) and what would become known as the Caprivi Strip, after the name of the German Chancellor, General Count von Caprivi.

It's a very different part of Namibia and through it flow two of Africa's greatest rivers – the Zambezi and the Okavango.

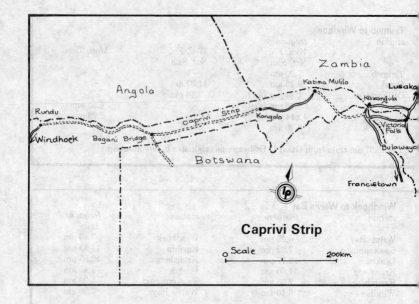

Caprivi Strip

0 Scale 200km

Few travellers have visited this region of Namibia in the past because it's been generally assumed that the area was out of bounds due to guerrilla activity. This is not the case, though you do need to get a permit from the military authorities either at Rundu (if travelling east) or Katima Mulilo (if travelling west) and travel is prohibited after sunset. Also, facilities have improved considerably since the construction of a sealed road from Grootfontein to Rundu, the upgrading of the gravel road from Rundu to Katima Mulilo and the establishment of a rest camp at the Popa Falls. The Caprivi Strip is also the easiest route between Zimbabwe and Namibia, the only alternative being what can be a nightmare journey through Botswana between Maun and Buitpos.

Places to Stay

The rest camp at Popa Falls on the Okavango River near Bagani Bridge has a camp site and three five-bed huts provided with toilets, hot and cold water

and fridges. Booking ahead shouldn't be necessary but can be arranged through the Directorate of Nature Conservation in Windhoek. It's a convenient base from which to visit the Mahango and Khaudum Game Reserves nearby. Permits to visit these reserves are obtainable either at the entry gates or at the Nature Conservation office in Rundu.

Katima Mulilo

The regional capital of the Caprivi Strip is Katima Mulilo on the banks of the Zambezi. It's a pleasant town with lush vegetation, enormous trees and plenty of wildlife in the surrounding area. The Namibian border post at Katima Mulilo is very easy-going and there's no fuss about onward tickets or 'sufficient funds'. There is no Botswanan frontier post at Ngoma south-east of Katima Mulilo so if entering Botswana through here get your passport stamped in Kasane.

Boat trips can be taken on the Zambezi to see hippos and other river dwellers

There are chalets and a caravan/camping site behind the golf course where you can stay at the usual prices. There's also the *Gasthaus Zum Fluss* which offers bed and breakfast for R 25.

A good place to go for food, a beer and to hear about lifts is the club run by an Austrian – ask around, everyone knows where it is.

Rundu

There's a Barclays Bank in Rundu. For accommodation try the *Kavango Hotel* next to the police station which, though excellent, is expensive at R 30/45 a single/double. There's nowhere else to stay.

GROOTFONTEIN

Apart from the official camp site, you can erect a tent at the rugby stadium, Rundu Rd, free of charge.

The *Hotel Nord* offers rooms for R 20 a single. Dinner costs R 7.50.

KEETMANSHOOP

Keetmanshoop is an important rail and road junction and one of Namibia's largest towns with a population of some 15,000. It was founded by the Rhenish Mission Society in 1860 and the stone church which they built there in 1895 is now a museum.

While in Keetmanshoop it's worth visiting the **Kokerboom (Quivertree) Forest** some 14 km north-east of the town on the road to Koës. Here is one of the last remaining stands of the bizarre tree-plants, *Aloe dichotoma*, which grow to a height of about eight metres. Their hollowed-out branches were formally used by the Bushpeople as quivers for their arrows – hence the name of the tree. Quivertrees are now a protected plant in Namibia. Though on private property (the Gariganus farm), the forest is open to the public.

Places to Stay & Eat

The camp ground is just beyond the museum and costs R 3 for one or two people.

Extra people cost 60 cents each. This is the only camp site between the South African-Namibian border and Windhoek. The two hotels in town are expensive so, if you're dependent upon hotels, head further south to Grünau where cheaper accommodation is available.

A good place to eat is the *German pub* 100 metres down the road from the camp site. It has an excellent bar.

LÜDERITZ

Lüderitz is an almost surreal living colonial relic – a German-style town huddling on the barren, windswept coast of the Namib Desert and almost untouched by the 20th century. It was founded by the Bremen merchant, Adolf Lüderitz, who persuaded Bismarck to place South West Africa under German 'protection' in 1884. It has everything you would expect of a small German town, from delicatessens to coffee shops and Lutheran churches. The desert is slowly encroaching on the town.

Things to See

Make sure you visit the **Lüderitz Museum** which has some excellent historical displays. It's open Tuesday, Thursday and Saturday from 4 to 6 pm.

Also definitely worth visiting is the diamond mining ghost town of **Kolmanskop** nearby. To see it you must book a place on a guided tour with Consolidated Diamond Mining at their office next to the powerhouse. There are tours from Monday to Saturday which cost R 2 (50 cents with a student card). There is no public transport from Lüderitz to Kolmanskop so you must arrange your own (it's about nine km) and show your permit when you get there. There are plenty of old buildings, a museum and mining installations slowly being engulfed by sand. It's an eerie place.

Places to Stay & Eat

The *Government Tourist Camp*, right on the bay, offers two-bed *rondavels* for R 8.50 (including hot plate) and four-bed self-contained bungalows with fridges

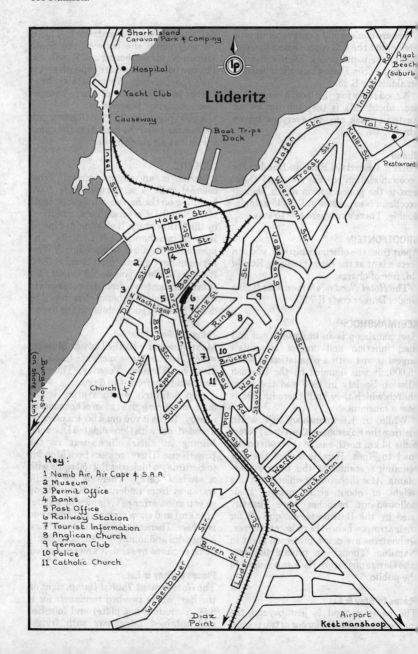

Lüderitz

Shark Island
Caravan Park & Camping

Hospital

Yacht Club

Causeway

Boat Trips
Dock

Agat
Beach
(suburb)

Industry Rd

Tal Str.

Kreler Str.

Restaurant

Hafen Str.

Troost Str.

Woermann Str.

Hafen Str.

Usel Str.

Moltke Str.

Bismarck Str.

Bahn Str.

Vogelsang Str.

Schinz Str.

Ring Str.

Nachtigall Str.

Berg Str.

Kinch Str.

Zeppelin Str.

Bülow Str.

Brücken Str.

Woermann Str.

Stauch Str.

Diaz Str.

Church

Bungalows
(on shore ~1 km)

Old Bay Rd

Bay Rd

Werft Str.

Bay Rd

Schuckmann Str.

Lüderitz Str.

Buren Str.

Wagenbauer Str.

Diaz
Point

Airport
Keetmanshoop

Key:
1 Namib Air, Air Cape & S.A.A.
2 Museum
3 Permit Office
4 Banks
5 Post Office
6 Railway Station
7 Tourist Information
8 Anglican Church
9 German Club
10 Police
11 Catholic Church

nd hot plates for R 11 to R 16.50. There is no charge for vehicles. The keys are kept at the tourist information office. At these prices, you'd be crazy to camp. If that's what you want to do though, there is a site close to the lighthouse where you can pitch a tent for R 6.50 regardless of numbers. The site is exposed.

One traveller described Lüderitz as the crayfish capital of the world' and suggested splurging on a meal of them at the café opposite the museum. Another recommended restaurant is the *Strand Café* close to the Government Tourist Camp which offers excellent seafood and relatively cheap wine. If you're stuck for somewhere to stay, it's worth asking here.

MARIENTAL

The main attraction of this place is the **Hardap Recreation Resort** about 15 km from town. It's a good place to relax and there's a camp site for R 8 and *rondavels* for R 10 a double. There's a shop and swimming pool at the site. In Mariental itself the *Mariental Hotel* offers rooms for R 15 with air-con.

SWAKOPMUND

This is another attractive old German colonial town though not quite as ethereal as Lüderitz as it has suffered from modernisation. It does, however, have plenty of flower gardens, old buildings, a restored pier, lighthouse, a *circa* 1901 railway station, the old German barracks, the Hansa brewery and the beautiful Woermannhaus, which once housed the crews of a shipping line, but was later converted into a library and declared a national monument. Its tower, the Damara Tower, once served as a lookout for shipping out at sea. In German colonial times, Swakopmund was South West Africa's only natural harbour along this part of the coast giving access to Windhoek. These days it is a resort town.

Things to See

The **Swakopmund Museum** is excellent with displays of Namibian ethnology and colonial history. It's open daily from 10.30 am to 12.30 pm and 4 to 6 pm and costs R 0.50. Free tours of the **Hansa Brewery** are available during December and January each year.

The world's largest **uranium mine** operated by Rössing (a subsidiary of Rio Tinto Zinc) is 70 km east of town. Visits are possible on Thursdays. You need to buy a ticket (R 1.50) on Wednesdays from the museum then take the bus leaving from close to the Café Anton at 9.30 am on Thursday.

The **seal reserve** at Cape Cross is 120 km to the north of Swakopmund. The reserve is open to the public daily from the middle of December until the end of February and after that during the Easter holidays and every weekend until 30 June. From July until mid-December it is only open on Wednesday afternoons from 12 noon to 4 pm. Entry permits can be obtained at the colony.

Places to Stay

Accommodation can be difficult to find during December and January as that is when settlers from the inland areas come here for their holidays.

The best deal in town is the *Swakopmund Restcamp* which offers two-bed bungalows for R 12.90; four-bed bungalows for R 16.35 and six-bed bungalows for R 24. All the bungalows have a fridge, hot plates, bedding, private bathrooms and hot water but you must bring your own cooking cutlery and crockery. There's a laundromat next door.

If the bungalows are full, there are others owned by the Rheinische Missionswerk where you can stay for R 12 a double. Crockery and cutlery are provided.

For campers there is the *Mile 4 Campsite*, north of town, but it's expensive at R 9.80 per site. It's often full at weekends and school holidays. You can book ahead through Swakopmund Tourism (tel 0641 2488), Municipality of Swakopmund, Private Bag 5017, Swakopmund, between

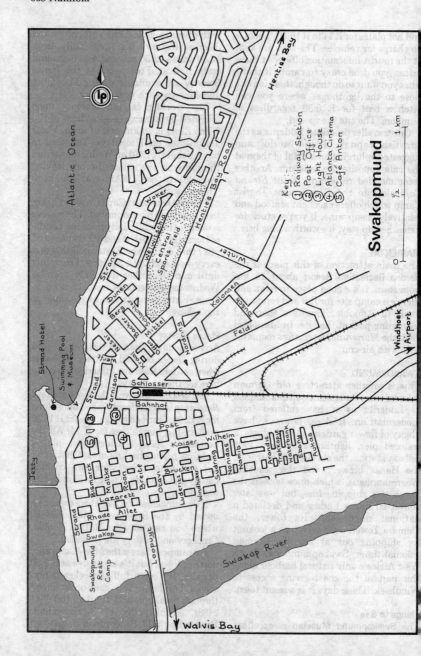

Key:-
① Railway Station
② Post Office
③ Light House
④ Atlanta Cinema
⑤ Café Anton

Swakopmund

Atlantic Ocean

Strand Hotel

Swimming Pool
& Museum

Jetty

Strand

Garrison

Schlosser

Bahnhof

Post

Kaiser Wilhelm

Bismarck
Moltke
Roon
Breite

Rhode
Lazarett
Allee

Swakop

Swakopmund
Rest Camp

Loopye

Strand
Dünen
Berg
Nesser
Packer
Mittel
Schlosser
Kolping
Brücken
Lüderitz
Windhuker
Süding
Nordring
Namidas
Namib
Arandis
Treekseke
Waterbank
Ebony
Aukos

Woker
Welwitschia

Central
Sports Field

Henties Bay Road

Nordring
Garnison

Winter
Kolonnen
Busch
Feld

Henties Bay

Windhoek Airport

Swakop River

Walvis Bay

1 km
½

8 am and 1 pm and 2 to 5 pm from Monday to Friday.

If these are full try *Dig by Sea Private Hotel*, 4 Brücken St, just up from the beach. It's friendly and costs R 12.50 per person for bed and breakfast with common bath, and R 16 per person with private bathroom. The price includes a large breakfast. The *Atlanta Hotel* is also a possibility at R 18 per person. More expensive is the *Pension Prinzessin-Rupprecht-Heim*, which offers beds for R 14 and up. The *Grüner Kranz Hotel* costs R 35 a double with breakfast. If all else fails, ask around at *JJ's Restaurant* which is also a good place to pick up a cheap meal.

Places to Eat

A good place to eat in Swakopmund is the *Strand Hotel* on the mole. They offer German-style meals and draught Hansa lager. The *Café Anton* overlooking the lighthouse and park is another popular place. It offers home-baked pastries and cakes and good coffee. It's open daily except between 12.45 and 3 pm. The main watering hole for young people and travelling businesspeople is *Köke's Bar*. There's good draught beer for sale.

Self-caterers will find what they need at the *Model Supermarket*, on the corner of Roon and Kaiser Wilhelm Sts – cheeses, bread, cold cuts, wurst, etc.

TSUMEB

Tsumeb is the railhead in northern Namibia just north-west of Grootfontein.

There's a camp site for R 2 per head. For hotel accommodation, try the *Hotel Minen* (tel 3071) which costs R 25 for bed and breakfast.

WALVIS BAY

Though nominally a part of South Africa on the basis of the British annexation of 1878, Walvis Bay is Namibia's only viable seaport. Sited 30 km south of Swakopmund along a coastal road bordered by sand dunes, it's a busy harbour town with important fish processing factories and a salt works. There's also a bird sanctuary on the outskirts of town. If you come in from Swakopmund, watch out for the huge wooden platform (known as Bird Island) about 10 km north of Walvis Bay built in the sea to provide a roosting place for coastal birds and from which guano is collected from time to time. The annual yield is in the region of 1000 tonnes. This platform is one of several such structures along this coast.

Things to See

Walvis Bay isn't exactly a tourist attraction by any stretch of the imagination and, if the wind is blowing the wrong way, it stinks. However, the **bird sanctuary** – a lagoon which hosts, at times, up to 20,000 flamingoes and many other species of freshwater and coastal birds – is worth a visit. You can also visit the **port** (with permission from the police station just before the port gate) if you have a mind though it's nothing special.

Some 50 km south of Walvis Bay is **Sandwich Harbour** which was used many years ago by whalers and trading vessels in preference to Walvis Bay. These days the inlet has silted up considerably and is no longer used as an anchorage but it is an ornithologist's paradise. Fresh water seeps through underneath the sand dunes to form freshwater pools which, with the seawater lagoon, provide an important refuge for migrating birds. Over 100 species of birds have been recorded here and, at times, the bird population can exceed half a million.

Places to Stay & Eat

There is a camp site near the lagoon end of the docks (signposted) which has good facilities and costs R 5 per site. There's often no-one there to collect the fee. *Willi Probst Bakery & Café*, 12th Way and 9th St, is possibly the best German restaurant in Namibia. They have huge servings of kasseler rippchen and spätzle plus incredible pastries and good coffee.

WINDHOEK

Windhoek, meaning 'windy corner', is the capital of Namibia. At a height of 1650 metres above sea level, it was once the headquarters of one of the principal Hottentot chiefs opposing the German advance but is now a typical prosperous, modern, southern African town. It has, however, managed to preserve many old colonial buildings which include the Alte Feste, once a fort but now converted into a museum, three other forts each on their own hillock overlooking the city (all now private houses), a Lutheran church, the old railway station and a number of shops, houses and hotels.

Information

It's worth visiting the Directorate of Nature Conservation (tel 061 29251), Kaiser St (at the opposite end to the post office). They're extremely helpful and they have excellent detailed information as well as maps of Windhoek and Namibia. If you'd like this information in advance, telephone or write to them at PO Box 13267, Windhoek 9000. Camping equipment can be hired from SWA Safaris or from Budget car hire (tel 061 28720), 72 Tal St, PO Box 1754, Windhoek.

American Express is on Peter Muller St off Kaiser St.

For share-expenses lifts ring 291911 and ask for the person who arranges these. For lifts to Etosha National Park, ring up the SWA radio station and broadcast a request. The new J G Strijdom International Airport is 42 km from the centre of the city. If hitching, the only cars you'll see along this road are those going to meet outgoing or incoming flights. There is a public bus for R 7.

Things to See

The two museums in Windhoek are worth a visit. The **Alte Feste**, which features historical displays, is open Monday to Friday from 9 am to 6 pm, on Saturdays from 9.45 am to 12.45 pm and 3 to 6 pm, and on Sundays from 10.45 am to 12.30 pm

and 3 to 6 pm. Entry is free. The **Staatsmuseum**, Lüderitz St near the GPO, features ethnology and natural history, and is open Monday to Friday from 9 am to 6 pm, Saturdays from 10 am to 12.45 pm and 2 to 6 pm, and on Sundays from 11 am to 12.30 pm and 3 to 6 pm. Entry is free.

Places to Stay

Campers can erect tents free of charge at the small site near the Windhoek stadium about two km past the Safari Motel on the Rehoboth road but there are no facilities and no security.

The most convenient camp site close to town with facilities is that at the *Safari Caravan Park* which is attached to the Safari Motel and is four km from the centre. It costs R 7 plus R 2 per person to camp. They also have 34 on-site caravans for hire at R 14 per van plus R 2 per person. The caravans have four beds. There's a bottle store and a steakhouse offering takeaways. The only trouble with this site is that if you are staying in a caravan or camping the management won't allow you access to their minibus shuttle service into and out of town, and you can't use the swimming pool. The motel itself is expensive.

A better place to head for is the *OASE Caravan Park* (tel 061 62098), 15 km from town, which offers a good grassed site, immaculate showers and toilets (hot water). It's run by very friendly and helpful owners. To get there go to Okahandja Rd and head north. Follow the signs to Brakwater. When you arrive you will see a sign for the caravan park. It's very easy to hitch into and out of this caravan park since there are many permanent residents there who drive into Windhoek daily. You'll never have to wait more than a few minutes for a lift.

If you have a car there's the government-run *Daan Viljoen Game Park*, 24 km from Windhoek along a paved road, where you can camp or rent a bungalow surrounded by zebras, oryx, kudus and springbok. It's a pleasant weekend resort and during

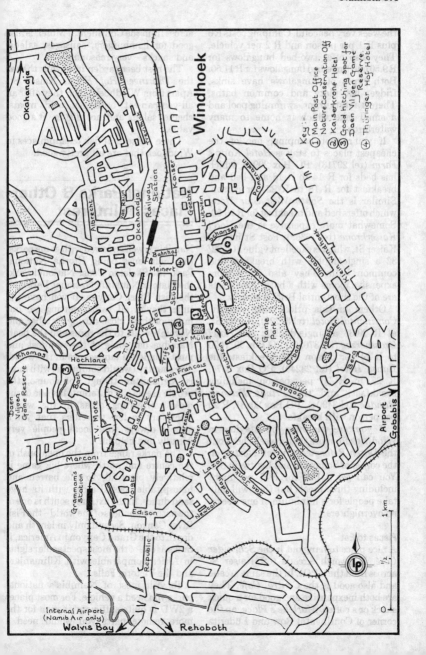

Windhoek

Okahandja

Railway Station

Game Park

Khomas

Daen Viljoen Game Reserve

Marconi

Edison

Republic

Internal Airport
(Namib Air only)

Walvis Bay   Rehoboth

Airport
Gobabis

Key:-
① Main Post Office
② Nature Conservation Off
③ Good hitching spot for
   Daen Viljoen Game
④ Thüringer Hof Hotel

① Kaiserkrone Hotel

1 km

1/2

0

the week very peaceful. Camping costs R 6 plus R 1 per person and R 2 per vehicle. They also offer two-bed bungalows for R 9.50 and three-bed bungalows for R 11.50. Both types of bungalows have sinks, fridge, hot plate and common baths. There's a restaurant, swimming pool and a small lake which is home to many waterbirds.

If you're not camping, one of the cheapest places to stay is *Hotel Kapp's Farm* (tel 29713), PO Box 20946, which has beds for R 14 to R 18 and bed and breakfast for R 18 to R 22 per person. Similar is the *South West Star Hotel* which offers bed and breakfast for R 16.50. Somewhat more expensive is the *Hotel Kaiserkrone* (tel 26369), Post St just off Kaiser St, which is excellent value at R 22/32 a single/double with breakfast and common bath. They also have more expensive rooms with a bath. Breakfasts are of the substantial British variety.

Others in this price range are the *Continental Hotel* (tel 37293), Kaiser St, at R 20/38 a single/double; the *Hotel Grossherzog* (tel 37026), PO Box 90, R 20 to R 24 per person with breakfast; the *Hansa Hotel* (tel 23249), PO Box 5374, R 22 to R 26 per person including breakfast; and the *Privat Pension Handke* (tel 34904), PO Box 20881, R 20 per person with breakfast.

If you are planning on staying in Windhoek for more than a week check out the *Dutch Reformed Church Hostel*, on the corner of Schanzen and Leutwein Sts. You can get a bed for R 7 per night including three meals but they will only take people for a minimum of one week – no overnighters.

Places to Eat

A nice place to hang out is the *Schneider Café*, Hepworth Arcade (off Kaiser St across from the GPO). In the same arcade and also good is the *Central Café*. They are both inexpensive and good for a quick snack or a coffee. *Marlene's Place*, on the corner of Continental Row and Lüderitz

across from the Continental Motel, is also good for hamburgers, sausages, salads, and snacks – very reasonable.

The best beer garden in town is that at the *Thüringer Hof Hotel*, Kaiser St. Apart from Windhoek lager, they offer an all-you-can-eat buffet of cold meats, cheese, salads and hot dishes. It's good value.

There are several fish & chip places in Windhoek that are all pretty good.

National Parks & Other Places of Interest

Namibia is well endowed with game parks, the main ones being Etosha National Park, the Skeleton Coast National Park, the Namib-Naukluft National Park and the Fish River Canyon. If you have the time they're all worth getting to, but many of them close during October and November due to the rains and the heat. Namibia has some of the weirdest and most wonderful landscapes in the world. The country I would compare it with most is Afghanistan though, of course, the people are totally different. It's one of the most captivating areas in the world. There are so few travellers that you'll almost always find local people very friendly and helpful.

The parks range from the open bush of the centre and north where big game is relatively plentiful, to the barren and inhospitable coastal strip with its huge sand dunes. In the extreme south is one of the natural wonders of the world – the Fish River Canyon. Second only in length and depth to the Grand Canyon in America, it ranks as one of the most spectacular sights in Africa comparable with Kilimanjaro and the Victoria Falls.

To visit most of Namibia's national parks you need a vehicle. For most places a 2WD is quite sufficient though for the more remote parts you would need a

4WD. Hitchhikers are not allowed in parks containing big game unless they happen to have secured a lift beforehand. Apart from this, even in the parks where there is no big game, it's often not a viable proposition to attempt to hitch. Lifts are rare off the main routes.

If you are a group, it would be best to hire a 4WD which certainly works out cheaper than going on an organised tour. There are car rental firms in Windhoek, Swakopmund, Keetmanshoop and Walvis Bay. The cheapest place at present to rent a truck is Budget. They charge R 32 per day with unlimited mileage.

If there's no chance of getting a group together and you haven't got the time to hitch, check out the following safari companies:

SWA Safaris Ltd
    PO Box 20373, Windhoek 9000 (tel 37567/8/9)
Springbok-Atlas Safaris Ltd
    PO Box 2058, Windhoek 9000 (tel 24252)
SAR Travel Bureau
    PO Box 415, Windhoek 9000 (tel 298-2532, 34821)
Toko Safaris
    PO Box 5017, Windhoek 9000 (tel 25539)
Charley's Desert Tours
    PO Box 1400, Swakopmund

All these companies have regular departures during the season (March to October). Charley's Desert Tours specialises in tours of the Namib Desert and offers one-day trips for R 50 and longer tours up to 14 days. We've had several recommendations for this outfit.

ETOSHA NATIONAL PARK

Etosha National Park in the north of the country is one of Africa's most beautiful and interesting game parks. The season runs from the second Friday in March to 31 October except for the Namutoni camp which is open throughout the year. You'll have no problem getting there and you're unlikely to see anything quite like it anywhere else in the world. As one correspondent put it: 'Where else could you drive all day through the bleakest landscape in the world and suddenly see three oryx under the only tree for 100 miles?'

Covering some 22,270 square km, the heart of the park is the giant Etosha Pan – a shallow depression which, for most of the year, is dry, flat and blinding white. It's an eerie, quiet and lifeless landscape of dust devils and mirages. On the edge of the pan, however, there are perennial springs which draw huge concentrations of birds and game animals during the dry winter months. Exceptionally rainy periods result in the pan filling with water up to a metre in depth and, when that happens, enormous numbers of waterfowl come to feed and breed. Further to the east, the scrub gives way to mixed woodland.

As in most parks containing big game, you need to be in a vehicle – either your own or a tour company's – to explore Etosha. Hitchhikers are not allowed.

Places to Stay

There are three camps in the Etosha National Park at Okaukuejo, Halali and Namutoni, all with restaurants, swimming pools, petrol pumps, bungalows and camp sites. Namutoni is an old German fort, which has been converted into a safari lodge. A pleasant room costs R 5 a double. At Halali a room costs R 6 a double. At Okaukuejo you can watch game all night if you like, as they have a floodlit water hole which is very popular with black rhino, elephant and lion late at night. Tents can be rented for R 7.50 for up to four people and huts with three beds for R 8.50. If you have a tent the cost is R 6 for up to eight people. Another camp will open soon at Otjovasandu.

The three main camps are on the southern edges of the pan and are connected by good, well-signposted gravel roads.

NAMIB-NAUKLUFT PARK

The Namib-Naukluft is Namibia's largest

national park covering an area of over 23,000 square km. It offers a wide variety of eco-systems, and geological and topographical features ranging from granite mountains, canyons and estuarine lagoons to what are claimed to be the highest sand dunes in the world – up to 300 metres high at Sossusvlei.

The Namib desert is one of the oldest and driest in the world. Like the Atacama along the coast of Chile, it's there by virtue of the fact that a cold current sweeps up the coast from Antarctica which resists evaporation and captures moisture blown towards the land from mid-ocean. In this case, it is the Benguela current. The central area is a sea of sand consisting of apricot-coloured dunes but with the occasional dry pan here and there. The most surreal of these – particularly when the Tsauchab River contains enough water to flow into the pan – is that at Sossusvlei. You will never ever see anything quite like this; 300 metres high, dry as dust dunes as far as the eye can see surrounding a shallow lake with a sprinkling of stunted trees with gemsbok, springbok, ostriches and a variety of aquatic birds. It's totally unreal!

The dunes end suddenly and dramatically at the Kuiseb River after which the Namib assumes a completely different character and appearance. Here is a land of endless, grey-white gravel plains with isolated rocky outcrops. It supports gemsbok, springbok and mountain zebra as well as the incredible Welwitschia plants whose only source of moisture is dew and fog.

The most eastern part of the park contains the Naukluft Mountains where there are gorges, caves and springs which cut deeply into the dolomite formations. There are good trekking possibilities here starting from the Koedoesrus camp site.

Places to Stay

There are eight camp sites in this park (R 1.50 per person) but you must book in advance in Windhoek as only one party

per night is allowed at each one. There is no camp site at Sossusvlei and only day trips are permitted there. The most convenient camp site to Sossusvlei is at Sesriem and a 4WD vehicle is recommended to get between the two, though it is possible to drive most of the way in a normal car and walk across the dunes from where you would have to leave it.

FISH RIVER CANYON & AI-AIS

Nowhere else in Africa is there anything quite like this canyon. It's immense – 160 km in length, up to 27 km wide and up to 550 metres deep in places. But these figures convey little of the breathtaking vistas which are possible from various vantage points, particularly at dawn and dusk. The Fish River, which joins the Orange about 70 km to the south, has been gouging out this canyon for thousands of years and no words could ever describe the magnificence of what is waiting for you here.

Though the most spectacular views are easily accessible by car for those in a hurry, there is a three to four-day hiking trail available which is very popular among travellers with imagination and the necessary stamina. The trail, which runs along the bed of the canyon and is about 85 km long, starts from the main lookout point and ends at Ai-Ais. It's only open from May to August because outside this period flash floods and extreme summer heat make it hazardous. Only one group per day is permitted to start on the trail (a minimum of three people, a maximum of 40) and a hiking tour permit must be obtained beforehand from the Directorate of Nature Conservation, Reservations Office, Private Bag 13267, Windhoek. When applying for this you'll need a medical certificate of fitness – it's a strenuous hike! Book as far ahead as possible.

There are simple overnight camping facilities at the main lookout point but none along the rest of the trail so you'll need to bring along all your own bedding, wood, water and food.

At the southern end of the canyon is the hot springs resort of Ai-Ais which is open from mid-March to the end of October. The water which bubbles up from springs in the riverbed averages 60°C and is piped into a variety of indoor baths as well as an outdoor swimming pool. The resort includes a restaurant and accommodation is available in bungalows, caravans and tents all equipped with beds and bedding. You can rent a tent with four beds for R 7.50, a caravan with four beds for R 10 or, if you have your own tent, you can camp for R 6 for up to eight people.

WATERBERG PLATEAU PARK

The Waterberg, which rises east of Otjiwarongo, is a flat-topped, well-watered and well-wooded mountain notable for its rock paintings and engravings (at Okarakuwisa on the northern side of the park). Many of the plants growing in this park are not found elsewhere in the country and the vegetation is particularly lush around the springs on the south-eastern side. The plateau is also a sanctuary for rare and endangered animal species. The latter include sable and roan antelope, white rhino and buffalo.

A camp site has been established at the foot of the plateau on the southern side with toilets and hot water and there are three hiking trails to the top. There are plans to establish a rest camp on the slopes of the mountain.

SKELETON COAST PARK

Taking up the last third of the Namibian coastline all the way to the Angolan border, this park covers an area of 15,000 square km and consists of sand dunes, gravel plains and a desolate, fogbound coastline. Countless ships have run aground here over the centuries but, despite this, it's an area of rare beauty.

Only the southern section of the park is open to the public and access is not easy.

A 4WD vehicle will be necessary. Permits must be obtained from the Directorate of Nature Conservation (address in Fish River Canyon section) before setting out. At the same time you must reserve accommodation at one of the two small fishing villages, Torra Bay and Terrace Bay. The former has tents and a tent site and is only open during the December/January holiday period. Terrace Bay is open all year and has bungalows with full board only. Both resorts are essentially for angling and visitors are restricted to certain areas so it's probably not of too much interest unless you are keen on fishing and have the equipment.

THE PETRIFIED FOREST, TWYFELFONTEIN, BURNT MOUNTAIN & BRANDBERG

Though not part of any national park, this area between Khorixas and Karibib has a number of fascinating and unique geological, archaeological and biological features. It is worth exploring and a convenient base from which to do it is the rest camp three km from Khorixas on the Torra Bay road. The camp offers fully-furnished bungalows for R 20, a camp site for R 4 per tent, some barbeque areas, swimming pool and a general store.

The Petrified Forest

Going west from Khorixas, this is the first place of interest. Many petrified tree trunks are found scattered over the open veld, the largest of which is 30 metres in length with a circumference of six metres. Details of the bark and wood can be plainly seen. It's been estimated that the age of the fossilised trunks is around 200 million years, and evidence suggests they were not native to the region, but were uprooted from another area and deposited here during a gigantic flood. Growing in among the fossils are a number of species of drought resistant plants including Welwitschias.

Twyfelfontein

A further 36 km west of the Petrified

Forest is the turn-off for Twyfelfontein. Close by is a spectacular collection of rock paintings and engravings – perhaps the largest of its kind in Africa. Many of them are thousands of years old, dating back to the Early Stone Age, whilst others are as recent as the 19th century and probably the work of Bushpeople. Many of them depict animals no longer found in the area such as elephants, rhinos, giraffes and lions.

The sandstone rocks in this area have a hard patina covering them and it was by cutting through this skin that the engravings were executed. In time, the skin reformed over the engravings thus protecting them from erosion. Flintstone chisels which were used for the engravings can be seen at the base of some of the rocks.

Burnt Mountain

South-east of Twyfelfontein is the 12-km-long ridge of hills known as Burnt Mountain which has the appearance of having literally been exposed to fire. It's an eerie panorama of desolation where virtually nothing grows, but the rocks are vividly coloured and quite spectacular at sunset. Nearby there is an unusual rock formation consisting of a mass of perpendicular slabs of basalt which resemble the organ pipes of a cathedral – hence their popular name.

Allow at least one day to visit these two sites.

Brandberg

Further to the south is the misty massif of the Brandberg whose peak, the Königstein, is the highest in the country at 2573 metres. Though popular with climbers, its main focus of interest is the rock paintings found there. One of these, known as the 'White Lady', has been the subject of controversy for many years. The Abbé Breuil, who studied the paintings in the mid-1940s speculated, on the basis of the dress, hairstyle and colouring, that the White Lady was of Egyptian or Cretan origin though this is highly unlikely since the latest research has dated the famous frieze at between 15,000 and 16,000 years old. The paintings, in the valley of the Tsisab River, were first discovered in 1918 by the German surveyor, Dr Reinhard Maack, on his descent from the Königstein when he sought shelter from the blazing sun under a huge rock overhang.

The hike up the ravine to the paintings is about three km from the entry gate and will take about 1½ hours. Take water as it's usually very hot. Allow about four hours in total for the round trip. There is no accommodation at the Brandberg but it's possible to camp at the beginning of the trail to the rock paintings if you have the necessary equipment.

Niger

Like the other countries of the Sahel belt, Niger suffered horrendously from the droughts of 1969 and 1972-74. At least 60% of the livestock was lost, there were no food harvests for two years, and many rural dwellers were forced to leave the land for good and migrate to the cities. The effects of the drought might not have been so catastrophic had there not been an ill-considered and rapid expansion of stockbreeding in the north during the 1960s which had already overburdened the delicate ecological balance of the pastures. What saved Niger from economic disaster (though perhaps not the rest of the world from ecological disaster) were the uranium mines at Arlit. So valuable were deposits that Niger's trade balance actually went into surplus by 1976. By 1980 uranium accounted for 75% of the country's exports and this was due to rise to 90% by the mid-1980s.

However, these hopes were not realised since the world market for uranium collapsed in the mid-1980s, though the French still buy the bulk of Niger's yellow cake at prices said to be 50% above prevailing world prices. Also the income derived from sales of uranium has not proven to be a universal blessing. It has led to high inflation and social discontent among students and trade unionists as a result of the disparity in income levels.

Long before the country was colonised by the French, a number of prosperous and well-organised states occupied all, or part of, the Niger republic as it stands today. They include the Songhai Empire in the west, the Hausa kingdoms in the centre and the empire of Kanem-Bornu in the east around Lake Chad. The wealth of these states was based on control of the trans-Saharan trade routes which were of vital importance to West Africa and the countries bordering the Mediterranean. The principal commodities were slaves,

gold and salt. The wealth of Sahel empires diminished rapidly during the 18th and 19th centuries as a result of the European maritime nations' increasing trade with the West African coastal kingdoms. Even so, trans-Saharan trade has never actually ceased even today. Until quite recently, annual caravans consisting of thousands of camels were loading up with salt at the oasis of Bilma and heading south for Nigeria and Cameroun.

Islam was introduced into the area during the 10th and 11th centuries, but for a long time it remained the religion only of the aristocracy and the wealthy urban elite. The rural population continued to follow traditional beliefs, and when Islam began to make headway with these people in the 19th and particularly the 20th century, it did not undermine traditional creeds. Pagan rituals are not only practised alongside Islam but are accepted without question. Indeed, Niger has managed to preserve a remarkable number of its precolonial traditions and institutions, and these often carry far more weight in social relations than the country's constitutional laws. Even urban dwellers rarely question traditional values.

Despite the fact that the British were the first to explore the upper reaches of the Niger beginning with the Scotsman, Mungo Park, who disappeared in the area in 1806, it was the French who colonised it between 1891 and 1911. The country was not fully 'pacified' until much later, however, and there were a number of resistance movements which severely tested the mettle of the colonial authorities. The most serious of these was the siege of Agadez by Tuaregs in 1916-17.

Niger suffers from poor soils. This, together with the fact that most crops are watered only by rain, makes the production of food entirely dependent on the hazards of the climate. Such factors hampered the development of the colony for a long time until groundnuts were introduced in 1930. These quickly became the country's most important export and, along with cattle, remained so until uranium took over in the 1970s.

Independence was granted in 1960 under the presidency of Hamni Diori. The earlier years were troubled with insurgency from Sawaba commandos until an agreement reached in 1965 with Algeria, Ghana and China put an end to their activities. Sawaba, a communist/radical left political grouping, had gone into exile when it failed to win control of the government in elections prior to independence. The drought of 1973, however, provoked severe economic and social upheavals which Diori was unable to control. He was overthrown in a coup the following year by Lieutenant General Seyni Kountché, who has remained in power ever since.

Unfortunately for Niger, the end of the uranium boom years coincided with yet another serious drought and for the first time in recorded history the River Niger actually dried up at Niamey. Though there is some truth in the claims by Nigeria that the various hydroelectric and irrigation projects built on the river by both Mali and Niger are responsible for the low levels of the river, there is no doubt that the area is again gripped by drought. Not only did the river dry up but Lake Chad almost disappeared too.

To counter the effects of the drought and to push back the desert, a scheme was launched in 1984 to plant hedges and wind-breaks to prevent further desertification. The scheme was expanded a year later into a major reafforestation programme.

Peasants have been encouraged to set up nurseries wherever they have room, and this has been backed up by a reform of the taxation system in order to reduce regional disadvantages. Firewood is presently being cut at an unsustainable rate and this is most obvious around the capital, Niamey, whose environs have been virtually stripped of forest.

Facts

GEOGRAPHY & CLIMATE
A good part of Niger's 1,267,000 square km lies in the Sahara Desert, with most of the remainder lying in the Sahel. The climate is hot and dry except for a brief rainy period in July and August. November and January are the coolest months, when the Harmattan blows off the desert. Vegetation in the north is sparse or nonexistent gradually merging into scrub in the Sahel and into lightly wooded grassland in the extreme south. Most of the country's land mass receives less than 500 mm (20 inches) of rain per year. Even so, millet and sorghum fields are found in some of these drier areas. The only permanent river is the Niger, which flows parallel to the south-west border. The sole permanent lake is Lake Chad on the south-east border.

Though most of the country is a vast plain, the Aïr Mountains (pronounced 'eye-ear') in the north rise to 2000 metres.

PEOPLE
The population of Niger is estimated at nearly seven million. Population densities range from .007 people per square km in the north to 40 people per square km in the heavily populated agricultural areas in the south. The annual rate of increase is close to 3.2% – one of the world's highest. The average life expectancy is 43 years for males and 46 for females. Eighty percent of the population is sedentary, living

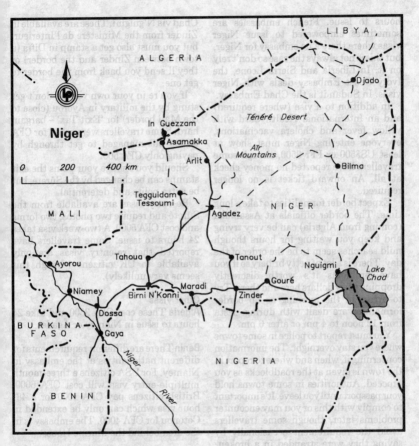

Niger

0   200   400 km

either in cities, urban areas or farms, while 20% remains nomadic.

There are five principal ethnic groups: Hausa, Djerma-Songhai, Peuhl-Fulani, Tuareg and Kanuri Beri Beri. The Hausa represent half of the total population and the Djerma-Songhai a further quarter. Each ethnic group has its own language and customs but the Hausa language is the most widely spoken. Eighty-five percent of the population is Muslim.

VISAS

Visas are required by all except nationals of Belgium, Denmark, Finland, France, Germany (West), Italy, Luxemburg, Netherlands, Norway, Sweden and the UK.

There are very few Niger embassies around the world, so plan ahead. In Africa you can obtain visas in Abidjan (Ivory Coast), Accra (Ghana), Addis Ababa (Ethiopia), Algiers and Tamanrasset (Algeria), Cairo (Egypt), Cotonou (Benin), Dakar (Senegal), Freetown (Sierra Leone), Khartoum (Sudan), Lagos and Kano (Nigeria), and Monrovia (Liberia).

In Tamanrasset a visa from the Niger Consulate will cost AD 65 and takes 48 hours to issue. French embassies are sometimes empowered to issue Niger visas where there's no embassy for Niger, but this is not always the case so don't rely on it. In Liberia and Sierra Leone, the Ivory Coast Embassy deals with Niger visas. In Sudan it is the Chad Embassy.

In addition to a visa (where required) and an International Health Card with yellow fever and cholera vaccinations, everyone entering Niger must show at least US$500 or FFr 3500, though some travellers have reported no money check at all. An onward ticket is no longer required.

Expect border formalities to take a long time. The border officials at Assamaka (coming from Algeria) can be very trying and keep you waiting for hours though mild searches seem to be the order of the day. There is a lot of petty bribery so if you have problems it's worth discreetly dropping a few dollars here and there. Try to arrive in the morning as no border formalities are dealt with during siesta from 12 noon to 4 pm or after 6 pm.

You must report to police in some towns where you stay overnight. The information concerning if, when and where to report in the town is given at the roadblocks as you proceed. Authorities in some towns hold your passport until you leave. It's important to comply with this or you may encounter problems later, though some travellers avoid the requirement occasionally by saying they were stranded in a broken-down truck overnight, etc. Make sure your story is convincing, however, as some travellers have been sent back all the way from Niamey to Arlit for failing to register.

Exit visas are no longer required if you're going to either Nigeria or Benin, but it would be a good idea for the time being to confirm this with other travellers or with immigration. The stamp you get in your passport from the Sûreté National in Niamey doubles as both an entry and exit stamp.

You do need an exit visa if you're travelling to Chad around the top of Lake Chad via N'guigmi. These are available in Zinder from the Ministère de l'Intérieur, but you must also get a stamp in Diffa (a town between Zinder and the border) or they'll send you back from the border to get one.

If you're in your own vehicle don't get stung by the military in Ayorou (close to the Mali border) for 'Exit Tax' – bargain hard. Some travellers were asked for CFA 25,000 but managed to get through by paying only CFA 500.

Should you change your plans the exit stamps can be changed by the Sûreté, but be extra polite and deferential.

Re-entry visas are available from the Sûreté and require two photos, two forms and cost CFA 5000. A two-week visa takes 24 hours to issue. Some travellers have reported that re-entry visas are only available to UK citizens (though this seems very unlikely).

Other Visas

Algeria These cost CFA 3500 and take 24 hours to issue in Niamey or Agadez.

Benin There are different requirements for different nationalities at the embassy in Niamey. For USA citizens a three-month multiple-entry visa will cost CFA 6000. British citizens pay CFA 1000 for a 48-hour visa which can only be extended in Cotonou for CFA 4000. The embassy is in the area behind the Marine House.

Burkina Faso These are obtainable from the French Consulate. A 90-day visa costs CFA 3000, requires two photos and is issued in 24 hours. The visas are for multiple entry.

CAR Obtainable from the French Consulate, a 48-hour visa costs CFA 3000 and is valid for two months.

Chad Obtainable from the French Consulate, a one-month visa will cost CFA 3000 and is issued the same day if you go early.

Ivory Coast Obtainable from the French Consulate in Niamey, visas cost CFA 1500 and are issued in 24 hours.

Mali There is now a Mali Consulate in Niamey in an obscure little office on the left of the former Grand Marché. It costs CFA 5500 for a seven-day visa, requires two photos and is normally issued in 48 hours. However, if you're really pressed for time it may be possible to get it the same day.

Nigeria These are very difficult to obtain at the embassy in Niamey. Most travellers are refused with no reasons given and no amount of pleading or bribery seems to help. To be sure of getting one apply elsewhere. They're easily available in Benin, Cameroun, CAR and Ghana, and not too hard to get in Burkina Faso, Chad and Togo. For UK citizens they are available at the embassy in London for UK£10.54 and take two days to issue.

Togo These are obtainable from the French Consulate, cost CFA 3000, with two photos and take 24 hours to issue. The political situation there has eased up considerably, so they will even consider applications for a three-month visa these days.

Visas for Egypt, Liberia and Morocco can also be obtained in Niamey.

MONEY
US$1 = CFA 284

The unit of currency is the CFA franc. There are no restrictions on the import of local currency but export is limited to CFA 175,000.

When entering Niger it's good to have CFAs or French francs on hand especially if you arrive on the weekend when the banks are closed. French francs are interchangeable at a lot of places like restaurants and hotels. If coming from Algeria, Arlit is the only town before

Niamey where you can change travellers' cheques. You can't change them in Agadez or Tahoua and if you're travelling to Chad make sure you change what you need in Zinder as it is not possible after there. Most banks will change hard cash of any description but French francs are preferred.

If you're driving your own vehicle, in Birni N'Konni and Maradi you can buy cheap petrol smuggled from Nigeria. It costs CFA 130 per litre (official price is CFA 240 a litre). The petrol should be dyed red and you need to check for added water. Black market diesel costs CFA 75 per litre.

POST
If you are collecting mail in Niamey, be sure to check not only the Hotel des Postes near the Sûreté National, but also the larger and older main post office. There is a charge of CFA 180 for each letter collected.

PHOTOGRAPHY
If intending to use a camera, you must get a photography permit. These cost CFA 5000! In Agadez you can get one at the tourist office, but it's only valid for that particular department. The ones issued in Niamey are valid for the whole country. To get it you must buy a CFA 5000 *timbre fiscal* from the Prefecture, on the corner of Rue du Souvenir and Rue du Président Luebke near the tourist office. Take this stamp to the Ministère de l'Intérieur, Ave Charles de Gaulle, where they will attach the stamp to the photo permit. It generally takes about 1½ hours. No photos are necessary.

LANGUAGE
French is the official language but the main spoken languages are Hausa, Zarma, Fulani, Tamachek and Kanuri.

Getting There & Around

ROAD

A few years ago, roads in Niger – where they existed – used to be dreadful and you'd get off at the end of a journey bruised and battered from head to toe. A lot of money has been poured into surfacing roads since then, primarily to improve access to the uranium and other mineral mines in the Aïr Mountains. There are now good, sealed roads all the way from Niamey to Arlit via Tahoua and Agadez and between Niamey and Zinder (the road is the same for these two routes as far as Birni N'Konni). Work should also be complete on the new Agadez to Zinder road.

There are a lot of police checkpoints on the roads in Niger so have your passport handy.

Because of the improvement in the roads there is now a fairly good network of buses between the main centres of population in Niger. They generally cost much the same as trucks over the same distance, but they're often crowded so you may prefer to go by truck anyway. Try to arrange a lift by truck in advance (say, the night before) and don't hand over any money (even a deposit) until you are on the truck. This includes giving money to people who are touting for passengers.

Travelling by *taxi-brousse* will cost approximately CFA 1000 per 100 km but waiting for the taxi to fill and negotiating the numerous road blocks (with at least 20 between Agadez and Niamey) will take a lot of your day.

Some examples of transport costs and journey times along the main routes are:

Arlit to Agadez There are daily trucks for CFA 2500 and a once-weekly bus by SNTN which costs CFA 3100 and takes three hours.

Agadez to Zinder There are daily trucks as well as buses which run twice a week. The trucks cost CFA 3700 and take up to 20 hours. They generally stop between 2 and 6 am so that the driver can catch some sleep. The buses leave Agadez on Wednesday morning (arriving late evening the same day) and on Saturday afternoon (arriving before noon the following day; staying overnight in Tanout). They cost CFA 5200 plus CFA 35 per kg of baggage. These buses are the same as those which start from Arlit. Book tickets on these buses two days in advance.

Agadez to Niamey There are daily trucks along this route and a SNTN bus three times per week in either direction (departing at 8 pm from Agadez and on Monday, Wednesday and Friday at 4 pm from Niamey). The bus costs CFA 12,000 and takes 15 hours on average. The trucks are slightly cheaper at CFA 10,000. The bus leaves Niamey on Thursdays and the terminus is upriver from the Hotel Gaweye. There are 20 police checkpoints to go through on this journey.

Agadez to Tahoua There are trucks most days of the week in either direction throughout the dry season which cost CFA 3500. You can also take the SNTN bus described previously since this goes via Tahoua. There are also minibuses which go when full, cost CFA 3000 and take about 7½ hours.

Birni N'Konni to Dosso There is a daily bus for CFA 2000 including baggage.

Birni N'Konni to Niamey The SNTN bus costs CFA 3000 and takes nine hours. There are also minibuses available for the same price which go when full.

Niamey to Gaya A daily SNTN bus leaves at 9 am, costs CFA 2500 and takes five hours. Minibuses are also available for CFA 1800 plus CFA 300 for a backpack. They leave when full and take between four and six hours. There are plenty of police checkpoints en route.

Niamey to Maradi The SNTN buses run in either direction three times per week on Tuesday, Thursday and Saturday from 7 to 9 am and cost CFA 6500. *Taxis-brousses* leave from the *autogare* by the Grand Marché early every evening and cost CFA 4000 including baggage charge. They take about 14 hours.

Niamey to Zinder The SNTN bus runs three times per week in either direction. It departs Niamey at 6 am on Tuesday, Thursday and Saturday and arrives in Zinder at 9 to 10 pm. You can buy the ticket from 4 pm the day before and the fare is CFA 9600. It's also possible to get a truck from the *gare routière*. These leave when full but not always daily.

Driving

For people with their own vehicles, driving is prohibited after 7.30 pm which means you won't be allowed past the next checkpoint unless it's just before a town where you intend to stay for the night. Police, customs and military stop and search all cars. Expect to be hassled for *cadeaux* – Walkmans, pocket knives, photos and cigarettes.

TO/FROM ALGERIA (Route du Hoggar)

There are no buses between Agadez and Tamanrasset (Algeria) except for the occasional bus between the Algerian border post and Tamanrasset (usually once per week), so you'll have to arrange a lift on a truck. Expect to pay around CFA 10,000. Food and water are usually included, but you should confirm this before you pay the 'fare'. The journey usually takes 2½ days but can take five depending on breakdowns and/or punctures.

There are two routes from Agadez to the border: one goes via Arlit (a sealed road from Agadez to Arlit) and the other goes via Assaours and Tegguidam Tessoumi. The trucks often take the latter route. On the truck route you can only get water at Tegguidam and at In Guezzam (Algerian border post). There is water at Assamaka

(Niger border post), but it comes from a sulphur spring and tastes really foul. Expect long delays at the Algerian border.

If you can get a group of 10 people together, you have the option of chartering a Land Cruiser which will cost CFA 20,000 per person but will only take a day and a half if the border times and the guards who staff them are congenial. The price may or may not include food, so you need to confirm this before you set off.

There is another possibility, too, but you shouldn't be in a hurry if you're thinking of trying it. Between August and December Algerian date trucks come down to In Gall west of Agadez, dump their loads then return to Algeria. You might be able to get on one of them. A *taxi-brousse* from Agadez to In Gall should cost about CFA 1500 and the truck from there to Tamanrasset ought to be about CFA 10,000. The journey should take four to five days once your ride is found.

At In Guezzam the customs may try to charge money if you arrive on a Friday, but refuse to pay.

TO/FROM BENIN

There are daily SNTN buses from Niamey to Gaya which leave at 9 am and take about five hours. The fare is CFA 2500. You can either stay overnight in Gaya (eg at *Amir Asmir's hanger*) or continue into Benin. The scenery around Gaya is a lot greener and you are finally out of the dry, dusty, desiccating Sahel. There are *taxis-brousses* from Gaya to the border (Malanville – eight km) for CFA 500 which wait for you at the border points. There are no problems with the immigration or customs here and no searches. From the border you can take the STB bus to Parakou. It costs CFA 1800 plus CFA 200 for a backpack, takes five hours and leaves between 9 and 10 am (when full). Otherwise there are Peugeot taxis which will cost CFA 2500.

TO/FROM BURKINA FASO

SNTN buses no longer do the run between Niamey and Ouagadougou so the best thing to do is to take a *taxi-brousse* which will cost CFA 6300 plus CFA 200 for a backpack. Even so, the journey will take up to two days because of long delays at the Burkina Faso border. Whatever you do, don't take a truck as there are always endless hassles at customs on the Burkina Faso side. It's a very smooth new road all the way with fruit, bread and coffee available en route.

TO/FROM CHAD

There is a once weekly SNTN bus on Friday from Zinder to Diffa and N'guigmi. The bus does the return journey on Saturday morning. There are also daily Hiace minibuses from Zinder to Diffa which depart from the *gare routière*. These cost CFA 3100 plus CFA 250 for a backpack and take about 12 hours. Be sure to get an exit stamp in Diffa from the Sûreté to prevent any problems at N'guigmi. The only transport available from N'guigmi are the very occasional truck or traveller driving their own vehicle. We've had reports of only one vehicle passing through the border in 23 days and of travellers waiting up to two weeks for a lift. Some travellers who got a lift from N'guigmi to Nokou paid CFA 5000 per person.

The road is sealed all the way from Zinder to Nguigmi.

If driving your own vehicle, border formalities in N'guigmi will take two to three hours and will cost CFA 2300 in 'administrative charges'. You will also be obliged to take a guide across part of the dry lake bed of Lake Chad to the official borderline and pay CFA 8000 for the service. It is not advisable to cross this area with only one vehicle and the terrain is reportably much more difficult to get a 4WD vehicle through than the Sahara. Note also that fuel consumption will double, driving across this route. The Chadian customs are at Bol and if they try to charge you any money, demand to speak to the District Prefect who will see that you get through without paying anything. The villages from Bol across the dry lake are: Bol to Ngarangou (25 km); to Isserom (20 km); to Ameroum (30 km); to Dourn-Dourn (40 km); to Baladja, then another 30 km to a good road.

TO/FROM MALI

There are usually two SNTN buses a week from Niamey to Gao which leave on Tuesday and Friday, and cost CFA 5550 plus CFA 35 per kg of your baggage. Try to book this bus in advance as departures depend on demand. This route has been described as an 'horrific journey of hassles, bureaucracy, time wasting and general lunacy'. So be prepared and take plenty of drinking water. It is also possible to take a Toyota bus from the taxi park next to the Mali Consulate in Niamey to Tillaberi then a Land Cruiser to Ayorou. From there, take the SNTN bus to Gao for CFA 3975.

If you have to stay overnight in Ayorou there is accommodation available in mud huts for CFA 500 at *Le Campement* which has water but no real facilities.

If you have the time and money to spare you could take a pirogue from Niamey to Ayorou along the Niger River. For CFA 40,000 these come with a poler (but no motor) and take five to six days. For more information about this trip ask at the Port du Pêche.

Expect long delays at the borderland, if coming from Mali. Niger immigration will also line you up to administer your anticholera pills (which are Fanasil manufactured by Roche) and charge you CFA 200 for the privilege. If you don't take them you don't get through. If you're in a hurry there is an Air Mali flight from Niamey to Gao – sometimes!

TO/FROM NIGERIA

The three main routes into Nigeria from Niger are Birni N'Konni to Sokoto, Maradi to Katsina to Kano, and Zinder to

Kano. There are usually daily trucks between Zinder and Kano, but the best days to find a lift are Thursday and Friday, as there are a lot of trucks which do the run on those days after loading up with supplies from the Zinder market. On the Birni N'Konni route there are taxis for CFA 1000 to Sokoto. If you're going via Maradi there are SNTN buses from Niamey to Maradi on Tuesday, Thursday and Saturday between 7 and 9 am. The fare is CFA 6500.

Around the Country

AGADEZ
Agadez is certainly a welcome sight after the desert and an interesting town to explore, though its character is changing as more and more tourists go there and the wealth from the uranium mines at Arlit filters through. The old town is a maze of narrow alleyways, rarely more than three metres across, which weave between the single-storey, mud-brick buildings. It's a market town where the nomadic Tuareg and their former slaves, the Bouza, come in from outlying areas to barter their goods for those of the Hausa traders from the south.

You must register with police in Agadez. This is no hassle but some travellers have been charged CFA 500 for the stamp.

Information
If changing money, the bank in the market square is relatively quick.

Things to See
The **Camel Market** on the edge of town has goats and donkeys as well as camels and is worth a visit. Entry into the tower of the **Mosque** costs CFA 200. The **market** has the usual assortment of clothing, hardware, souvenirs and constant offers to swap your wristwatch for a sword. The **Old Quarter** of Agadez has some notable traditional façades with carved or painted designs; look for houses with horn-like spikes on the roofs (spot them from a distance) or ask people in the street where you can find houses with 'belles façades'.

Check out the **Tuareg market** outside town. They're keen to trade anything.

Places to Stay
An excellent place to stay is the *Hotel Agreboun* (formerly the Family House Hotel) which is very clean and friendly and offers rooms at CFA 3000/5000 a single/double with shower, but communal toilet. They also have more expensive air-con rooms (CFA 4000 a single). You can get good meals too. Other travellers sleep on the roof of the *Hotel Sahara* opposite the market, for CFA 500 though you have to pay extra for a mat on the floor or use of the showers. If you'd prefer a room, these cost CFA 2500 with fan and shower or CFA 3000 if you want a toilet as well, and CFA 4000 for air-con.

The *Hotel Telwa* offers similar rooms for CFA 4000 a double. Also worth checking out is the *Auberge Le Caravane* which costs CFA 6500 a double with shower and toilet. If you have your own vehicle they offer guarded parking for CFA 500 per night.

More expensive is the *Hotel de L'Aïr*. It's a popular place and offers rooms for CFA 5500 to CFA 7500 a double depending on the features, and has good toilets and western-style showers. You can also sleep on the roof for CFA 1500 - great views! Even if you don't stay at the Hotel de L'Aïr, it's worth visiting for its architectural qualities and the view of the mosque from there.

A popular camp site is *L'Oasis* (formerly Joyce's Garden), which is eight km from town on the Arlit road and costs CFA 1000 per person per night plus CFA 500 if you have your own vehicle. It has a swimming pool which isn't always in working condition, ice-cold beer and orange juice for CFA 350. The food is expensive so bring your own. There are

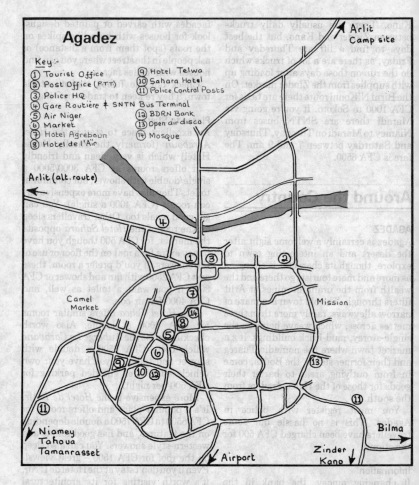

Agadez

Key:-
1. Tourist Office
2. Post Office (P.T.T)
3. Police HQ
4. Gare Routière & SNTN Bus Terminal
5. Air Niger
6. Market
7. Hotel Agreboun
8. Hotel de l'Air
9. Hotel Telwa
10. Sahara Hotel
11. Police Control Posts
12. BDRN Bank
13. Open air disco
14. Mosque

Arlit Camp site

Arlit (alt. route)

Camel Market

Mission

Niamey Tahoua Tamanrasset

Bilma

Airport

Zinder Kano

bucket showers and the toilets aren't too bad. If you are using water from the well, purify it before drinking as there are bats around and they're none too fussy about where they shit.

There is another camp site, *L'Escale*, about three km out of town on the new Arlit road past the police roadblock. It costs CFA 1000 per person, has cold showers, not very special toilets and a restaurant/bar that's like a barn. You can

get a plate of rice and sauce for CFA 400 and a warm beer for CFA 400. It's important to wear shoes at night around the camp sites because of the scorpions and camel spiders.

You can also camp for CFA 1000 at the *Tourist Centre* which is much more central. Many travellers have said it's as good as L'Oasis.

It's illegal to camp out in the bush anywhere within five km of Agadez.

In addition to these places, you may be offered rooms in private houses by local children. If you find one you like, bargain madly.

Places to Eat

There are many small restaurants in the market area serving rice and sauce and there is excellent hot food on the road outside the *autogare* in the morning and evening. These are about the cheapest places to eat. The *Restaurant Tamgale* has good food and is a friendly place to eat. You can get an excellent couscous served by nice Tuareg guys. The *Hotel Saraha* and *Restaurant Agreboun* have some of the best meals around. The *Restaurant Chez Nous*, behind the mosque, has excellent chips and is very good value. For a treat there's an ice cream parlour run by an Italian expatriate near the Hotel de L'Aïr.

ARLIT

Arlit is the uranium mining town in the Aïr Mountains north of Agadez and is often the first overnight stop in Niger if you're coming south from Algeria. It isn't marked on Bartholomew's maps but it is on the Michelin ones.

Report to the police immediately on arrival and leave your passport with them. There are two banks in Arlit but they charge heavy commissions for changing travellers' cheques, so have some French francs handy. Banks are closed from 12 noon to 4 pm. The police station is a good place to wait for a lift out as all vehicles have to call there before leaving. If you're in need of medical attention the hospital is French-run and very good.

Arlit has become a tourist trap in recent years. There are plenty of artefacts and jewellery for sale but it's always overpriced and poor quality.

Places to Stay

There are two camp sites in this town. The one to the south on the road to Agadez is the worst of the two. It costs CFA 600 per person plus CFA 500 for a car and it's best to give the food a miss as several million flies seem to commute freely between the toilet and the kitchen. It's always crowded with jewellery sellers.

The other site is between Arlit and the Somair mine (about one km from town) just off the improved road and is the better of the two. It costs CFA 1000 plus CFA 500 for a car. There are clean showers and toilets while meals and beer are available but at a hefty mark-up. If coming south from Algeria, stock up on fruit and vegetables at the government-sponsored gardening project about five km before Arlit (signposted).

Places to Eat

There is good food available from the street stalls in the evening – for example you can have a meal of omelette or steak and salad. The *Restaurant Sahel* is cheap and friendly. The *Restaurant N'Wala* (just past the large hotel) and the *Ramada* near the PTT in the centre of town opposite the main bakery have also been recommended as having good, reasonably priced food. Good steaks can be found at the *Tamesna* but they're fairly expensive.

Entertainment

A popular watering hole is the *Cheval Blanc*, where you can get ice-cold beers. If there is music on that evening there will be an entry charge.

BIRNI N'KONNI

There is a camp site to the west of town on the road to Niamey which costs CFA 1000 plus CFA 500 for a car. The staff are friendly but the water supply is poor. The restaurant is fairly expensive but beer prices are reasonable. The site is guarded 24 hours a day and the staff are keen about this. Reliable supplies of petrol can be found. It's a little more expensive than on the street but the latter is often adulterated with water.

For hotel accommodation, try the *Hotel Kado* which offers very clean rooms for CFA

4000 with fan and CFA 6000 with air-con. Next door is an annexe known as 'Camping' which has single rooms for CFA 3000.

DIFFA

Diffa is a pleasant unspoilt rural Hausa town. It has seen many refugees from the drought and their wicker dwellings have sprung up outside the mud-brick town. There are no hotels but you can camp in the grounds of the police station for free. Any luggage left during the day is safe with the friendly caretaker/gardener. Food is available in the square off the main road opposite the SNTN office. Tea, coffee, brochettes, rice, macaroni, wheat cakes, beans and sauce are on sale at various times of the day. The market is in front of the *gare routière*.

DOSSO

There are only a few places to stay. One of the cheapest is the *Relais Carrefour* which has rooms for CFA 3000. It's on the road to Niamey. Far more expensive is the *Hotel Djerma* which offers air-con rooms with shower and toilet.

MARADI

Maradi is one of the main commercial and industrial centres of Niger. The present town is only some 40 years old but the original settlement at Sohongari in the lush Maradi valley dates back to about 1790 and was founded by the animist Barki. At that time it was part of the territory controlled by the rulers of Katsina whose regional governor, known as the *maradi* (chief of the fetishers), gave his name to the town. Maradi was a way station on the traditional caravan routes between the Aïr Mountains and northern Nigeria and, consequently, there was a lot of fighting for its control. These conflicts eventually led to the city's decline in favour of Kano.

When colonisation by the Europeans began in earnest in the late 19th century, the city was originally taken by the British in 1902 but was ceded to the French a year later at the London Convention.

The main industrial products are peanut oil, tanned hides, blankets and bricks made of traditional indigenous materials. The Maradi market is held twice a week on Monday and Friday, when it is filled with local people as well as those from the outlying villages of Sofo, Soura, Madarounfa, Guidan Roumdji and Dan Issa. Bicycles are available for hire and to explore this city it's a good idea to use one – Maradi is very spread out.

Places to Stay & Eat

The *Hotel de la Liberté* has rooms with fans and showers for CFA 2100/3100 a single/double. It also has good cheap food. There is another hotel just below the road in from Niamey on the edge of town as well as *Le Campement* between the new city and the old town down in the valley. The *Jangozzo Hotel* is outside the reach of budget travellers.

Entertainment

There are numerous bars in town. One of the best places to go is *Le Club Privé* where all the expats hang out. In theory it's for members only but passing tourists generally have no problem getting in. There is a pool, bar, tennis court, and other facilities. Another good place is the *Pacific Bar* where there is always music, dancing and plenty of people. Other bars and hang-outs are *Chez Raymond*, *Hirondelle* and the airport which is nonfunctional for flights but has beer, good music and comfortable chairs.

There are two cinemas: the *Vox* which shows films from Niamey and the *Jangozzo* which shows English language films from Nigeria.

N'GUIGMI

There are no hotels in this border town but you can camp at the police station. There is a lively market area to the south of town where you can buy brochettes and nearby is a periodically stocked bar.

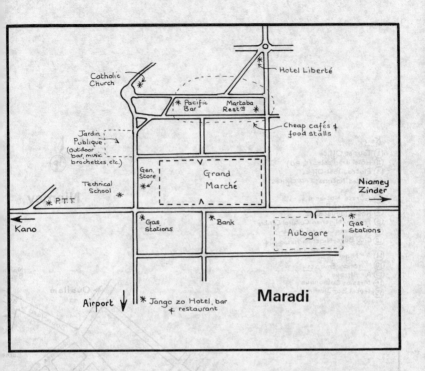

Map labels:
Catholic Church
Hotel Liberté
Pacific Bar
Martaba Rest^{nt}
Cheap cafés & food stalls
Jardin Publique (outdoor bar music brochettes etc.)
Gen. Store
Grand Marché
Niamey Zinder →
Technical School
← Kano
P.T.T.
Gas Stations
Bank
Autogare
Gas Stations
Airport ↓
Jango zo Hotel, bar & restaurant
Maradi

NIAMEY

Niamey has been the capital of Niger since the administration moved here from Zinder in 1926. It has grown rapidly in recent years and now has a population of nearly half a million, yet in 1940 there were still only 2000 people living there. It has most of the amenities you would expect to find in a modern capital city.

Information

On arrival you must report to the Sûreté National with one photo. The tourist office (tel 73 24 47) is on Rue du President Laubke. They have maps for CFA 1000. The agents for Thomas Cook are Transcap Voyages, in the Sonora II building (next to El Nasr). The Algerian Embassy is on the road to Gao. The Mali Consulate is in an obscure little office to the left of the Grand Marché. The poste restante is at the Hotel des Postes near the Sûreté National.

If your personal belongings are stolen in Niamey and you need an official declaration (for insurance purposes), you may find the police uncooperative, so be persistent. Don't go there at lunch hour, you'll be wasting your time.

For changing travellers' cheques, the BIAO Bank (near the Petit Marché towards the Sûreté) gives the best rates and doesn't charge any commission. If you need to change money outside bank hours, go to the *bureau de change* at the Hotel Gaweye near the Pont Kennedy. To change Central African CFA for West African CFA, go to the Banque Centrale des États de l'Afrique Ouest. You can get a straight swap without commission.

For books and magazines Camico-

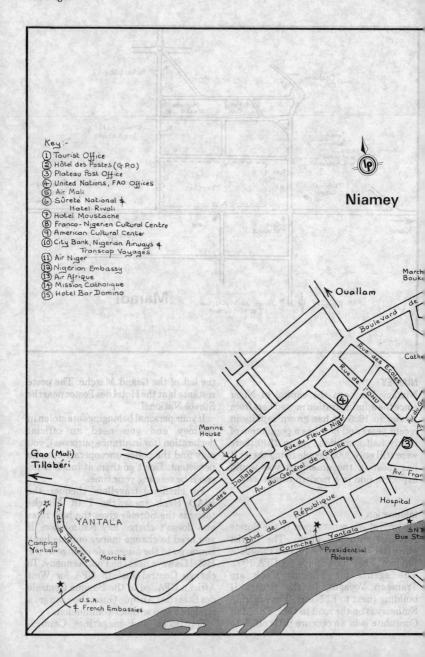

Key:-
1. Tourist Office
2. Hôtel des Postes (G.P.O.)
3. Plateau Post Office
4. United Nations, FAO Offices
5. Air Mali
6. Sûreté National &
   Hotel Rivoli
7. Hotel Moustache
8. Franco-Nigerien Cultural Centre
9. American Cultural Center
10. City Bank, Nigerian Airways &
    Transcap Voyages
11. Air Niger
12. Nigerian Embassy
13. Air Afrique
14. Mission Catholique
15. Hotel Bar Domino

Niamey

Ouallam

Boulevard de

Rue des Ecoles

Cath

Rue de

PONU

Marine
House

Rue du Fleuve Niger

Rue des Dallais

Av. du Général de Gaulle

Av. Fran

Gao (Mali)
Tillabéri

Blvd. de la République

Hospital

YANTALA

Corniche Yantala

SN
Bus Sta

Camping
Yantala

Av. de la Jeunesse

Marché

Presidential
Palace

U.S.A.
& French Embassies

Marché
Bouke

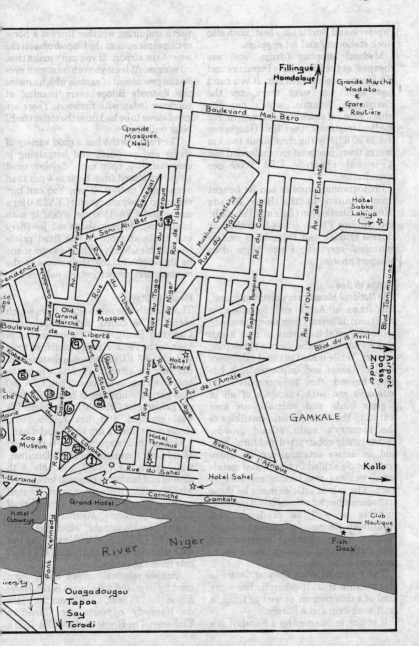

Papeterie and Burama are best. Both also stock stationery and art supplies.

Medical supplies (drugs, etc) are cheapest at the Pharmacie Populaire and the Pharmacie Soni Ali Ber. If you can't find what you want there, try the Pharmacie Centrale, which has the widest range of stock but is expensive. For medical treatment, the Clinic Gamkalley (tel 73 20 33), by the river about two km east of town, has been recommended but it is not cheap – CFA 6500 per consultation.

Photographic supplies can be bought from Mouren in the Bata Arcade (Kodak); Studio Kap (Agfa and Polaroid); and Optique Photo, across from the Vox cinema (Kodak and Polaroid as well as opticians' services). Photo Niger does passport photos.

Things to See

The National Museum is worth a visit and, like those in Accra and Kampala, is structured differently from most European-conceived establishments so that it can play a vital role in the life of a developing country. While it has the usual exhibits of local costumes and implements, it has gone beyond this to incorporate an extensive zoo with examples of all of Niger's birds and animals; an area featuring the characteristic dwellings of the country's main ethnic groups, authentically constructed and furnished; and an active artisanal section where craftspeople skilled in traditional metal-work, weaving and leather are busy at work. The sale of articles made by these craftspeople helps fund ambitious outreach projects as well as academic and vocational courses for underprivileged children. Entry is free and the museum is open daily except Monday from 8 am to noon and 4 to 6 pm.

The Franco-Nigerien Cultural Centre is also worth a visit. It generally has some kind of exhibition on as well as films, a craft workshop and a library.

If you're in Niamey on a Sunday, it's worth enquiring whether there is a horse or camel race out at the Hippodrome on the way to the airport. If you can't make this, no worries. At least you can feast your eyes on the procession of camels which crosses the Kennedy Bridge every evening at sundown laden with firewood. There are great views to be had from the top of the El Nasr building.

The Petit Marché has a good variety of shops and products and bargaining is essential. It is open every day but most shops are closed from noon to 4 pm then open again until 6.30 pm. You can buy very good mosquito nets for CFA 1200 for a single and CFA 1500 for a double with bargaining. Artisan shops sell jewellery and crafts at more or less fixed prices (reasonable). Many of the items are made by those who exhibit their wares at the museum and are particularly well crafted.

Places to Stay

There is only one camp site in town which seems to be called both *Yantala* and *Camping Touristique*. It's five km out of town on the Tillabéri road. A taxi from town will cost CFA 100 per person and a taxi from the *gare routière* in Wadata where the buses and trucks arrive will cost CFA 200 plus extra for luggage. It costs CFA 1000 per person plus CFA 500 for a vehicle. It's well guarded and has toilets, cold showers, drinkable tap water and a bar.

One of the cheapest hotels is the *Bar/Hotel Lede* (formerly the Hotel Domino), which costs CFA 4400 a double with shower and fan but communal toilets. It is within walking distance of town, the staff are friendly and the owner is a great help if you have problems. Another is the very clean *Chez Moustache*, which has small rooms for CFA 3225 a double with fan but with shared showers and toilets. It's a taxi ride from the centre.

Another relatively cheap hotel, often used by overland tour buses is the *Hotel Rivoli* (tel 733 849), uphill from the Place de Kennedy opposite the Canadian Embassy. The Rivoli charges CFA 7250 a double with air-con, shower and toilet. Lunch and dinner are available with dinner being served outside at the pavement restaurant. There is a bar inside which serves draught beer (*pression* in French).

The *Mission Catholique*, behind the cathedral, will no longer take travellers.

If you're looking for semi-luxury try the *Terminus Hotel* (tel 732 692) which costs CFA 6000/7000 a single/double. They also have bungalows for CFA 8000/9000 for singles/doubles. All the rooms have air-con, bathroom and the place is very clean. An extra bed in any of these is another CFA 1000. Breakfast costs CFA 700. Lunch and dinner are also available. The Terminus is popular with expatriate volunteer workers and there's a swimming pool.

Up-market are the following hotels: *Hotel Sahel* (tel 732 231), which costs CFA 7700/8300 a single/double; *Les Roniers Hotel* (tel 723 138), at CFA 8000/8700 a single/double; *Grand Hotel* (tel 732 641), at CFA 9150/10,050 a single/double; *Tenere Hotel* (tel 732 020), where rooms are CFA 9150/10,050 a single/double; *Sabka Lahiya* (tel 732 933), which costs CFA 9150/10,050 for a single/double; and *Hotel Gaweye* (tel 733 400), the most expensive at CFA 18,000 to CFA 19,000 for a single and CFA 20,000 to CFA 21,000 for a double.

All these hotels have restaurants and swimming pools. The pools are generally open to nonresidents though the fee for use varies. The cheapest is probably the Olympic-sized pool behind the Sahel which costs CFA 250. Both the Sabka Lahiya and the Tenere charge CFA 500. The Gaweye charges CFA 800. The pool at the Terminus is really only open for people who are prepared to pay a monthly fee of CFA 4000. The pool at the Grand Hotel (CFA 500 per day) is popular with many travellers and is a good place to make contacts for lifts. There are also beautiful views of the Niger River from here especially at sunset.

It's no longer possible to stay at the Peace Corps Hostel. It's strictly PC volunteers only.

Places to Eat

You'll find good cheap food in the Petit Marché and good eating stalls at a place called the *Texaco Table* at the junction of Blvd de l'Indépendence, Ave Soni Ali Ber and Ave de l'Arewa. A very good and cheap place to eat is the *Restaurant Doro* opposite the Hotel Chez Moustache, which serves meals of rice with meat, vegetables and hot (or very hot) sauce. The *Bar Restaurant Le Refuge* near the Bar Domino has also been recommended as having very good, reasonably priced food.

A bit more up-market is the *Restaurant M'Backe* behind the Hotel Terminus which has very good Senegalese cuisine. You can try the *Nam Dinh* across from the Hotel Tenere for some Vietnamese food. It is only open for dinner. In the same bracket is *L'Ermitage*, which offers steak & chip dinners in the outdoor beer garden. There is an air-con bar inside and occasional live music on Saturday. The *Epi d'Or* snack bar is reasonably priced and popular with local people and expatriates after the cinema. It has a French café/bar atmosphere. The *American Recreation Centre* snack bar (open from noon to 8 pm daily) allows entry to nonmembers and is moderately expensive for hamburgers and meals. The pool is free and there is a tennis court and table tennis.

The other restaurants in Niamey are expensive and only worth considering if you feel like a splurge. Two that have been recommended are the *Chez Nous* which has excellent French cuisine and the *Au Feu du Bois* which has very good African cuisine. Others in this bracket include the *Lotus Blue*, Vietnamese food, dinners only, pleasant garden setting, closed Tuesday; the *Oriental*, Middle East cuisine with daily specials, dinners only, closed Wednesday, return taxis difficult to get; the *Vietnam*, Vietnamese and

European dishes, dinners only, closed Monday; *La Cascade*, French and Italian cuisine, dinners only, refreshing atmosphere, closed Tuesday; *Chez Nous*, excellent French cuisine, dinners only, air-con, closed Sunday; and *La Flottille*, Russian cuisine, lunch and dinner, closed Sunday.

Most of the main hotels also have restaurants. These include the *Tenere Hotel*, French cuisine, dinner à la carte, open daily; *Terminus Hotel*, French cuisine, lunch and dinner, open daily; *Sahel Hotel*, fair French cuisine and good salads plus pizza in the evenings, open daily (the outdoor portion has a superb view over the Niger River but you need to have mosquito repellent handy); *Sabka Lahiya*, has Tunisian cuisine, lunch and dinner, is open daily, off the airport road near the Wadata Market; *Les Roniers Hotel* on the old Tillabéri Rd past the US Embassy, offers French cuisine, lunch and dinner, open daily; *Rivoli Hotel*, steaks and brochettes with a menu for lunch and dinner, open daily; *Grand Hotel*, mediocre French cuisine but very good omelettes, lunch and dinner, air-con dining room, open daily, attractive terrace overlooking the Niger River, good for breakfast; and the *Gaweye Hotel*, two restaurants serving excellent pizzas on Friday nights at 9 pm by the pool with good live music.

Entertainment

If you're looking for some action in the evenings, one of the most popular places is the *Marine House* next to the Tunisian Embassy which is open to the public on Monday, Wednesday and Friday nights (and sometimes on Saturday too). They have a bar and swimming pool (which can be used every day of the week). They show movies on Monday and Wednesday nights which cost CFA 300 to CFA 500. The movies start at 8 pm though most people get there earlier – it opens at 6 pm. The place is run by the boys of the US

Marine Corps who guard the embassy. They're a good bunch of guys.

There are a number of nightclubs/discotheques which open early but really only start moving about 11 pm and go on till the wee hours. They're all relatively expensive, but the best is probably the *Fo-Fo Club* in the Sahel Hotel which plays African music. Few Europeans go there and drinks cost CFA 1000. Others include the *Hi-Fi*, drinks are CFA 1000; the *Satellite*, drinks cost CFA 1000; and the *Kakaki* in the Gaweye Hotel where drinks are CFA 2500.

Getting Around

Taxis are plentiful and cost CFA 100 per journey in the main part of town. If you go outside town the fares increase. A taxi to the US Embassy, for instance, will cost CFA 200. To the airport a taxi will cost CFA 1000. Expect to pay CFA 50 for a pack, though this is negotiable. Bicycles cost CFA 200 per hour to hire or CFA 1000 for the day.

Bus The Grand Marché burned down about two years ago and was moved along with the *gare routière* to Wadata. This is where the trucks and buses depart from these days.

TAHOUA

For many years, Tahoua was closed to tourists and a detour was necessary but it has been open again since November 1987.

You must have your passport stamped by police here and you'll need one photo. The bank will not change travellers cheques – cash only. Market day is on Sunday.

Places to Stay & Eat

The cheapest accommodation in town is at *Le Campement* which is a 20-minute walk from the *gare routière*. Single or double rooms with a shower and fan cost CFA 3100 and CFA 4600 with air-con. Camping costs CFA 600 per person

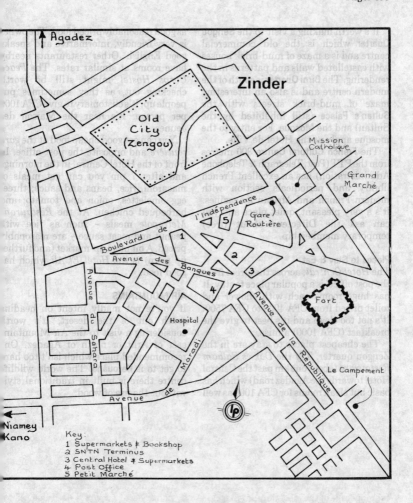

There's also another place where you can camp for CFA 1100 per person plus CFA 1100 for a vehicle. The staff are not very friendly. Meals can be bought for CFA 650 and up.

The *Hotel Galabi Ader* is nice and clean with single or double rooms with a fan at CFA 3600, and CFA 4600 with air-con. Very central is the *Jardin Publique* with rooms at CFA 7000 with air-con.

ZINDER

Zinder is a very pleasant town and, like Agadez, is one of the traditional market towns of Niger. It was the capital until 1926. Don't miss the beautiful large **market** which takes place on Thursday. There is a lot of good quality leatherwork. The market is also a good place for securing lifts to Kano with Nigerians who come up for the market.

It's worth making a visit to the **Sengou Quarter** which is the old commercial centre and is a maze of mud-brick houses with castellated walls and patterns in the rendering. The **Birni Quarter** is south of the modern centre and is also an interesting maze of mud-brick streets with the **Sultan's Palace** (still inhabited by the Sultan) and the **Mosque**. For entry to the mosque apply at the Hotel de Ville.

The **French Cultural Centre** 300 metres from the PTT (Post, Telegraph & Telephone Administration) has an excellent French library and periodicals section with modern French and African magazines. It's a very pleasant, quiet place and you can ask the Directeur about (free) temporary membership.

Places to Stay & Eat

The *Hotel Central*, across the street from the post office, is a popular place to stay. It has huge rooms each with shower and toilet priced from CFA 4000 to CFA 7500. It's not too clean and it's best to give the breakfast (CFA 1000) a miss.

The cheapest places to stay are in the Zengou quarter. Try the *Dar es Salaam Restaurant* (about one km past the Central Hotel towards the Agadez road) which has basic but clean rooms for CFA 1000 as well as good reasonably priced food. The owner is very friendly, informative and speaks good English. Other restaurants nearby have rooms at similar rates. The *Peace Corps Hostel* might still be worth checking out, as they sometimes put people up. It's customary to give CFA 1000 per person. It's near the Maison des Jeunes.

You can get good cheap food at the *gare routière* and opposite the post office. In front of the Hotel Central in the morning and after 7 pm you can get meals of macaroni, rice, beans and sauce; three egg omelettes, onion and tomato; and barbequed chicken. At the *Restaurant Metropole* meals – such as rice with peanut and meat sauce – are reasonably priced. A bit more up-market (and further up town) is the *Hotel El Ali* which has good food.

AÏR MOUNTAINS

If you're not madly intent on heading south out of the desert, it's worth considering a visit to the Aïr Mountains east of Arlit or north of Agadez. One recommended place which isn't too hard to get to is **Iferouâne**. The world wildlife centre there is built in traditional style without the use of wood.

Nigeria

Nigeria is Africa's most populous state and, for a while during the 1970s, one of its wealthiest. It consists of a fascinating collection of different peoples, cultures, histories and religions. Never united at any period in the past, today it is trying to find a sense of nationhood out of the rivalries and bloodshed which bedevilled the country for years after independence. Its diversity is a powerful attraction to travellers, but there is another, rather negative side to the country. This is the unbridled and often ill-considered 'development' that has taken place, particularly in the cities, which was fuelled by what appeared to be an endless source of easy money through the sale of oil.

As a result, most Nigerian cities have been transformed beyond recognition. Overcrowding, pollution, noise and traffic chaos, a soaring crime rate, and inadequacy of public utilities combine to make most urban centres hell-holes. Rapid development has also led to massive migration from the country to the cities, and a consequent decline in agricultural production. This in turn, has meant more and more importation of food. Inflation has also taken its toll. There can be no other country in Africa where corruption has reached such staggering and widespread proportions. If you come to the conclusion that things have got out of hand, you won't be alone. Many Nigerians feel the same.

It has become an expensive country to live in, but, with the two-tier exchange system (see Money section) it's not as bad for foreign visitors.

The first recorded state which grew up in this part of Africa was Kanem, located north-east of Lake Chad. Its wealth was based on control of one of the most important trans-Saharan trade routes from West Africa to the Mediterranean. On the strength of this, it was able to raise a powerful army and extend its control over neighbouring areas. Islam became the state religion quite early on in the empire's history. Like other empires in the Sahel, it occasionally fell on hard times and in the 14th century was invaded and forced to move south to Borno. In time, however, the empire regained its vigour and reconquered the area it had originally occupied. Meanwhile a number of Islamic Hausa states flourished between the 11th and 14th centuries, based around the cities of Kano, Katsina, Zaria and Nupe.

In the south-west a number of Yoruba empires grew up between the 14th and 15th centuries, centred in Ife, Oyo and Benin. These three cities became important trading and craft centres. Goods produced there and from the area under their control were much in demand in Morocco and the other Islamic Mediterranean states. The political systems of these states rested largely on a sacred monarchy with a strong court bureaucracy and, unlike the states to the north, they retained their traditional pagan religions. Islam made very little headway until the late 18th century. The Obas (kings) of these states still survive, though of course, their influence has declined considerably. In the south-east the Ibo and other peoples never developed any centralised empires but instead formed loose confederations.

The first contact between the Yoruba states and the Europeans came in the 15th century with the Portuguese who began

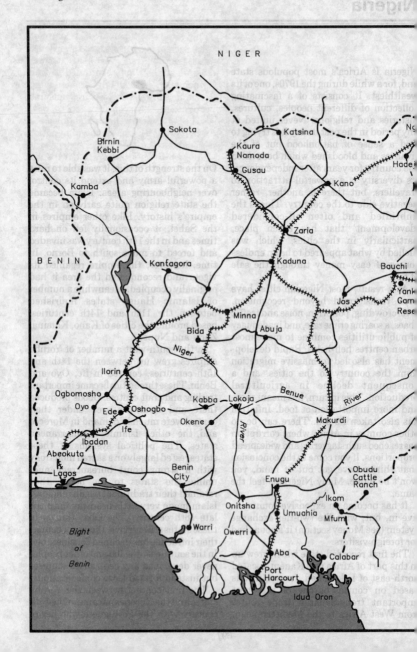

NIGER

Lake Chad

Baga

Maiduguri

Dikwa

otiskum

Biu

Gombe

Yola

CAMEROUN

Nigeria

0   100   200 km

trading in pepper. This was later supplanted by trade in slaves. Commerce was increasingly directed towards the coast, in contrast with the northern Islamic states which continued to trade principally across the Sahara and which remained untouched by Europeans until well into the 19th century.

The Portuguese were gradually displaced by the northern European maritime nations throughout the 16th and 17th centuries during which time the slave trade expanded dramatically. It's estimated that up to 40 million West Africans were dragged off in chains to the Americas while this sordid traffic continued, but human misery wasn't the only result. The internal effects of the trade were catastrophic, resulting in continuous wars, political instability and the neglect of agriculture and other possible avenues of commerce. By the time slavery was abolished in the early 19th century, the coastal kingdoms had become so dependent on the trade and so inured to the decadence it engendered that they were unable to make the transition. By that time, however, the British had begun to lay the foundations for direct political control of the hinterland in order to protect their commercial monopoly from being challenged by the French.

Another change of importance which took place towards the end of the slave trade era was a revolutionary upheaval in the Hausa kingdoms of the north. This led to the replacement of Hausa kings with Fulani, and the setting up of the Sokoto caliphate.

Once military conquest was completed, the British were content to rule indirectly through local kings and chiefs, as they were in most other places in their empire. This was not only less costly but guaranteed a stable environment from which economic surplus could be extracted without undue disruption. The policy worked quite well in the north but much less smoothly in the south-west, where none of the traditional rulers had ever extracted taxes. The imposition of these taxes led to widespread resentment among the Yoruba. In the south-east the policy was even less successful, largely because the British did not understand that there had never been any centralised authority in this part of the colony.

As the demand for independence gathered force after WW II, the British attempted to put together a constitution which would take into account the interests of the three main areas of the colony – the north, mainly Muslim with an ethnic majority of Hausa and Fulani; the east, Catholic and mainly Ibo; and the west, mixed Muslim and Anglican and mainly Yoruba.

It proved to be an extremely difficult task. The northerners feared that the southerners had an educational advantage which would allow them to dominate politics and commerce, and so demanded 50% representation in any central government. There was likewise considerable mistrust among the southerners, the result of fierce competition for jobs in the civil service and for business contracts. The British favoured appeasing the north since the more conservative leaders of this region were seen as the best way of safeguarding British interests after independence. So, in the end, each region was given its own civil service, judiciary and marketing boards (the main earners of foreign exchange). Thus, when independence was granted in October 1960, Nigeria was essentially three nations.

The first six years of independence were disastrous. National politics degenerated into a vicious power game, corruption became rampant and the elite took to accumulating wealth by any means at their disposal. With their interests ignored and faced with extortionate rents and rising food prices, the workers organised a general strike in 1963. This was followed by another strike in 1964 after the government had totally rejected a commission of enquiry's recommendation

for an increase in the minimum wage. Their grievances finally exploded in an orgy of looting and violence which swept the country following blatantly rigged elections in the western region in 1965. It was obvious that something had to give, and in early 1966 a group of army majors, most of whom were Ibos, attempted a coup. The prime minister, the premiers of the west and north, and most of the senior army officers were assassinated, but the coup failed when General Ironsi, himself an Ibo, managed to rally the military. What was left of the cabinet hurriedly agreed to hand over power to the army.

Ironsi's accession to power was welcomed by many sections of the Nigerian public, but his regime had no sense of direction or any idea of how to sort out the disastrous political situation. A few months later he was toppled in a coup staged by a group of northern army officers after anti-Ibo riots had broken out in the north. Ironsi and a number of Ibo officers were killed in the coup and a new regime was set up under the leadership of Lieutenant Colonel Yakubu Gowon, a Christian officer from a minority group in the north.

The coup was viewed with horror in the east and the military commander of the area, Lieutenant Colonel Ojukwu, refused to recognise Gowon as the new head of government. His antipathy to the new regime was sealed when large-scale massacres of Ibo took place in the north, triggering a return to the east by thousands of Ibo from all over the country. In May 1967, Ojukwu announced the secession of the east and the creation of the independent state of Biafra.

Biafra was recognised by only a handful of African countries, and the civil war dragged on for three years as the Ibo forces fought tooth and claw for every inch of territory which the federal forces took back. By late 1969, however, Biafra faced famine and its forces were compelled to capitulate. Despite the hatreds which had been fanned by civil war, reconciliation was swift and peaceful. Gowon was careful not to treat the Ibo as a vanquished people. Unfortunately, he was unable to use the same degree of imagination to get the economy moving again, and corruption once more grew to intolerable proportions. He was overthrown in a peaceful coup by General Murtala Mohammed while attending an OAU summit meeting in Kampala in 1975.

The new government set a brisk pace and launched a clean-up of the civil service, the judiciary and the universities. Some 10,000 officials were sacked or forced to retire and a start was made on trying to break up the antagonisms between the various regions by creating seven more states – four in the north and three in the south. A decision was also made to move the capital from Lagos to Abuja in the geographical centre of the country. Mohammed was assassinated in an attempted coup in early 1976, but the other members of the regime survived and continued to implement his policies until power was handed back to a civilian government following elections in 1979. The new civilian regime of President Shagari proved itself to be no better and possibly even worse than previous administrations.

With Nigeria at the height of its political influence on the continent and encouraged by what appeared to be an endless supply of oil money, Shagari squandered the country's wealth on grandiose and ill-considered projects in much the same way as Nkrumah had done two decades before in Ghana. Billions of dollars were poured into schemes which were never completed, so badly constructed that they fell apart or simply never left the drawing board despite vastly expensive feasibility studies. The lion's share of all this profligate waste went to overseas concerns. Only small contracts were awarded to local businesses. Some contractors, having been paid substantial advances to begin work, just disappeared. Meanwhile corruption took on huge proportions. Nothing could be done

without the right permits and that meant substantial bribes.

It wasn't long before the cracks started to appear and when the price of oil plummeted in the early 1980s the situation became serious.

As the money supply dried up, payments to contractors fell into such arrears that they simply packed up and abandoned whatever they were working on. In an attempt to shore up the crumbling edifice, Shagari turned to bartering oil for essential commodities such as foodstuffs, transport and spare parts. It rarely worked, however, because of wholesale theft of the oil and imported products which it had supposedly been bartered for. Whole tankers full of oil simply 'disappeared'.

Shagari next turned on the millions of other West Africans who had flocked to Nigeria in search of work during the oil boom of the 1970s. Some three million of them, including an estimated two million Ghanaians, were suddenly expelled causing massive dislocation, unemployment and food problems in neighbouring countries. Nigeria's action almost destroyed ECOWAS (the Economic Community of West African States) and certainly dented its standing among African nations.

The army was not prepared to sit back and watch the country sink into chaos and on New Year's Eve 1983, Shagari was overthrown in a military coup headed by General Mohammed Buhari.

Buhari clamped down heavily and made bold moves to get the country back together. There was a currency changeover to halt the export of naira (for black market speculation), the country's land borders were closed to prevent smuggling, and many of the grandiose projects begun by the Shagari regime were postponed or cancelled altogether. Members of the former government deemed to be involved in embezzlement or corruption were brought before secret military courts and given long jail sentences.

Yet Buhari overdid it and his second-in-command, General Tunde Idiagbon, was even worse. Widespread abuses of civil liberties, torture, arbitrary arrests and incarceration without trial became common. When the Nigerian Bar Association refused to cooperate with the new regime, Buhari resorted to rule by decree. His arrogance and particularly that of his lieutenant, Idiagbon, quickly came to be regarded with extreme distaste by the senior officers of the army. Under the direction of Idiagbon, the Nigerian Security Organisation (the secret police) became a law unto itself, loathed and feared by almost everyone. It quickly became apparent that under Buhari, the country was slipping into a police state and by 1985 rumours of an impending coup became common.

The coup took place in August of that year. It was headed by General Ibrahim Bagangida, the army chief of staff and the man who had played a key role in putting not only Murtala Mohammed in power but also Mohammed Buhari.

Since then, Bagangida has made much headway in restoring some semblance of order to Nigeria without the iron-fisted approach of his predecessor. The country's debts have been rescheduled, political prisoners released, a number of respected civilians brought into the government and some progress made in rooting out corruption. It will not be an easy task. The mess left by previous administrations is nothing short of disastrous. Nevertheless, a reasonable start has been made.

Facts

GEOGRAPHY

Oil is the country's main export income earner, accounting for some 95% of the total and around 20% of the GDP. At current rates of production, this makes Nigeria OPEC's fifth largest producer and the largest on the African continent (Libya is the second largest). The major drilling area is in the Niger delta where there are over 70 drilling rigs out of a total of around 150.

Agriculture is the second most important economic activity and still employs a large proportion of all male workers though its importance has declined. Although normal agricultural practices were first disrupted during the colonial era in favour of cash crops, the decline has accelerated since then. Thus for over a decade now, Nigeria has been forced to import massive amounts of foodstuffs, much of it to suit the modern tastes of urban dwellers. As a result, food is an expensive commodity. Successive governments have tried hard to reverse the drift of the rural population to the cities in order to stimulate agricultural production but their efforts have only been partially successful.

The crops of the north are mainly groundnuts, cotton, sugar cane, rice, wheat and tobacco, which reflect the comparatively short rainy season in that area and the use made of riverine lands flooded during the rains. In the south the most important crops are cocoa, rubber, palm oil and kola nuts. From the central area comes beniseed, ginger and yams. The Fulani of the north keep large herds of cattle, sheep and goats.

CLIMATE

The climate is hot and dry in the north and hot and wet in the south. The rainy season in the north is between April and September while in the south it is from March to November. A long dry season stretches from December to March when the cooling Harmattan blows off the desert. The coast is an almost unbroken line of sandy beaches and lagoons running back to creeks and mangrove swamps. It's very humid most of the year.

PEOPLE

The population stands at about 100 million and is rising rapidly. There are many different ethnic groups the main ones being the Yoruba in the west, the Ibo in the east and the Hausa-Fulani in the north. About half the people are Muslim, with 34% Christian and the rest following tribal religions.

WARNING

Watch out for members of the NSO (National Security Organisation) – secret police – as they can be particularly irksome. The main trouble is that they cannot understand why someone would want to travel around for fun. Therefore you must be a spy. When talking to these people or the ordinary police the greatest courtesy and firmness is needed. Fatuous questions should be answered with the same courtesy as serious ones. Photography is not appreciated. The situation has eased up a lot recently but it might be best to keep a low profile. The ordinary people are very friendly and hospitable.

VISAS

Visas are required by all. Nationals of South Africa are not admitted nor is anyone with a South African stamp in their passport. Obtaining a visa for Nigeria depends on applying in the right country. The policy of some embassies is to issue visas only to residents and nationals of the country in which that embassy is located. In other countries it doesn't seem to matter. UK nationals can expect to pay considerably more for a visa than others because, although it's business as usual in all other respects, relations are not so sweet on a diplomatic level.

In Cotonou, Benin, a seven-day visa costs CFA 9730. In Yaoundé, Cameroun, a seven-day visa costs CFA 7935 and is issued in 24 hours. In Bangui, Central African Republic, the price of visas varies for different nationalites but a one-month visa requires three photos and takes 24 hours. In Accra, Ghana, a seven-day visa costs C 210 for most and C 2500 for UK nationals and is issued in 24 hours, but they will only take visa applications on

Mondays. Visas used to be hard to get in Niamey, Niger, but it seems things are easing up there and they now take just a few days to issue. In London visas for UK citizens cost UK£10.54. You hand in your passport between 9 am and 12 noon and collect it two days later between 2 and 4 pm (3.30 pm is best as there's always a long queue at 2 pm).

You can't get visas at the border or on arrival at an airport and if arriving by air an onward ticket is required.

Regardless of what it says on your visa, immigration officials may reduce your permitted length of stay on arrival.

If you want to stay longer than your visa says ask immigration on arrival and you may get an extension there and then. If you have no luck, extensions are fairly easy to get from the Ministry of Internal Affairs, 23 Marina, Lagos. Extensions are free for most but for UK nationals they cost N 15, require one photo and a letter from a citizen or resident who will vouch for you. Look smart or they won't even let you into the building. Extensions can also be obtained in the state capitals from the immigration department of the Federal Secretariat.

Other Visas

Algeria The embassy is on Maitama Sule St, off Awolowo Rd, Ikoyi, Lagos. Visas cost N 32, with four photos and a letter of introduction from your embassy.

Benin The embassy is at 4 Abudu Smith St, off Ahmadu Bello Rd, Victoria Island, Lagos. A seven-day visa costs N 10, with one photo and is issued the same day. The staff are very helpful.

CAR Thirty-day visas cost N 15, but recent reports suggest that the embassy is longer on Awolowo Rd, Ikoyi Island, Lagos. You'll need to check this out.

Cameroun The embassy is on Adeola Odeku St, off Ahmadu Bello Rd, Victoria Island, Lagos. There's also a consulate at

21 Marian St, Calabar. Many travellers have been turned away at the embassy in Lagos and told that visas are only issued there to residents of Nigeria, Benin, Togo and Niger. It's even possible to run up against this sort of nonsense at the consulate in Calabar but usually it's a much safer bet. Some people have had no trouble at all. The visas cost N 45 with two photos. At the consulate in Calabar put your passport in as soon as the office opens and collect it in the early afternoon.

Niger The embassy is on Adeola Odeku St, off Ahmadu Bello Rd, Victoria Island, Lagos. A 15-day visa costs N 30 and a one-month visa costs N 40. They both require three photos and take 24 hours to issue. You have to tell them your proposed date of entry and the visa is valid from then.

Zaïre The embassy is on Kofa Abayomi Rd (next street south and parallel to Ozumba Mbadiwe Ave), Victoria Island, Lagos. A three-month, multiple-entry visa costs N 60, with three photos and a letter of introduction from your embassy. It's issued in 24 hours. The British High Commission charges N 54 for the letter!

MONEY
US$1 = N 3.80

The unit of currency is the naira = 100 kobo. The import and export of local currency is limited to N 20.

Following the introduction of the Second Tier Foreign Exchange Market (SFEM) in October 1986, Nigeria has gone from being one of the most expensive countries in Africa to being relatively cheap. The value of the naira is now adjusted on a weekly basis but it seems the banks don't always have the latest rates so it's definitely worth shopping around. Most banks charge a heavy commission for changing travellers' cheques. The banks are very slow and you must deal with endless bureaucracy and a likely rugby scrummage at the cashier. One traveller worked out that it took one minute for every naira he got! The big hotels are much faster for changing money but take a punitive commission.

On arrival in the country you are required to fill in a yellow currency declaration form and declare all foreign currency. Keep this form carefully and make sure it's stamped everytime you change money. If you arrive by air you'll be required to change the equivalent of US$100 at the airport (and have a hefty commission deducted).

In 1984 Nigeria changed its currency so you do need to be able to recognize the old and new notes – the old notes are now worthless. The design on the new notes has not changed but the colour has. Here's what to look for:

value	new notes	
	front	back
N 1	red & green	olive green
N 5	blue & crimson	crimson
N 10	red & orange	red
N 20	blue & green	green

The 50-kobo notes remain unchanged. The new N 5 notes (crimson and blue) are the most trusted of all denominations because they have the least resemblance to any of the old colour schemes. When you cash a travellers' cheque at a bank you are likely to receive N 5 notes as the largest denomination. A trick which some money dealers (in Lomé, etc) might try to use is to insert a few old naira notes into a wad of new N 10 notes – so watch out. Also the green N 20 note is not desirable as there are forged ones in circulation.

There is a black market for hard currency on which you can expect US$1 = N 4.20 (small bills) and US$1 = N 4.40 (large bills). Also CFA 1000 = N 15. The black market is centred around the Bristol Hotel in Lagos but be very careful! There's a five year jail sentence for those caught dealing.

In theory, it's possible to convert excess naira back into hard currency if you have receipts to prove you changed at a bank. In practice, it takes forever and is not worth the effort.

The airport departure tax for internal and international flights is N 50.

LANGUAGE

English is the official language. The main African languages are Hausa (in the north), Yoruba (in the south-west) and Ibo (in the south-east). There are also large numbers of Edo and Efik speakers.

Getting There & Around

Since the period of political turmoil and the closing of its borders in 1984, Nigeria has now become more stable and at present all the land borders are open.

AIR

You must pay for international flight tickets with either hard currency or with naira accompanied by a bank receipt.

On arrival by air you will be faced with a lot of bureaucratic nonsense, so be extra polite and patient. You'll need to show an onward ticket, an International Health Certificate and you'll be required to change the equivalent of US$100. Customs can be very thorough or very cursory depending on which official you're dealing with. Make sure you're not the last off the plane and make sure all your papers are in order otherwise you can expect to start handing out the bribes.

Departing from the international airport at Lagos can also be a nerve-wracking experience. A taxi to the airport is much cheaper than one from it. The best place to catch them is Eko Bridge (north side) from the Oshodi bus stop. At the airport avoid the departure lounge touts by entering at the arrivals level.

An OK rating on your airline ticket doesn't mean much as overbooking is endemic. You need to arrive hours in advance and find out where the queue is

going to form. It won't matter how early you arrive if you don't make it near the head of the queue. You can't be checked in until a customs officer has looked at your luggage. There is a mandatory death sentence for carrying drugs. Collect a yellow Immigration Departure Card and a blue Currency Departure Card from where you check in. The latter has to be handed in together with the yellow currency form you received on arrival but only when the flight has been called and you are going out to the departure gate. If someone says that they have to take your travellers' cheques and show them to a customs official before you'll be allowed to leave the country, don't believe them. Anyone who says this is a rip-off merchant.

For internal flights follow the Nigerians in running onto the tarmac as soon as the plane arrives. Nigeria Airways are absolute chaos so try to use Jambo, Kabo, Okada or Gas airlines which are privately owned and much better. Some sample fares for domestic Gas Air flights are:

route	fare
Lagos to Maiduguri	N 135
Lagos to Kano	N 105
Lagos to Kaduna	N 90
Lagos to Ilorin	N 42
Lagos to Yola	N 135
Lagos to Enugu	N 68
Kano to Yola	N 70
Kano to Maiduguri	N 70
Ilorin to Kaduna	N 55

Flights are usually in a BAC 111 leased from Tarom, the Rumanian airline.

ROAD

The roads in this country are very good and most are sealed, so journey times tend to be relatively short and predictable compared with those in some of the neighbouring countries. The devaluation of the naira has also made internal transport quite cheap.

Hitching

Hitching is usually easy, especially in the north, where it is mainly trucks and private cars, but less so in the south where it's mainly private cars. You will be offered quite a few free lifts. All the same, you should ask about this when getting into a car because if the driver didn't intend to give you a free lift and you haven't agreed on a price, you're likely to end up paying twice what the locals pay. You may have to pay for lifts in the south. When hitching a ride make a few waves to attract attention then hold you're palm out like you're begging which means 'no money'. Avoid over-full trucks if possible. Road safety isn't a high priority in Nigeria.

There have been alarming stories of highway robbery on the Ibadan to Lagos expressway and on the expressway to Benin which branches off it. Avoid these roads at night or around dusk. Vans are safer than taxis which in turn are safer than private cars.

Bus & Taxi

One of the best forms of road transport is the 'passenger transport cars' which are Ford Transit vans or shared taxis. They're fast and leave when full. Check out what the other passengers are paying before you get in, otherwise the drivers will ask for as much as they think they can get away with. Taxi drivers are pirates and the fares posted on cab windows are merely a joke. A few large companies run buses between the main centres of population.

Some examples of fares and journey times follow:

Lagos to Calabar – The two bus companies which cover this sector are Inyang Ete Line, 13 Ikorodu Rd, and Utuk Motors Ltd, 3 Western Ave, Serelera. Both operate luxury buses on which it's possible to sleep. Buses depart daily around 7.30 am though you need to be at the depot by 5 am. The fare is N 25 and the

journey takes 12 to 13 hours. The buses are fast and the drivers are crazy
Calabar to Ikom – N 15 by taxi
Ikom to Mfum (Cameroun border) – N 3 by taxi
Maiduguri to Kano – N 10 by bus; takes 11 hours. Costs N 25 for a taxi
Maiduguri to Jos – N 25 by taxi
Enugu to Jos – N 13 by taxi; takes six hours. Costs N 15 by bus; takes eight hours
Jos to Kano – N 15 by taxi; takes three hours
Jos to Kaduna – N 14 by shared taxi; takes three hours
Kaduna to Lagos – N 40 by shared taxi; N 30 by bus
Lagos to Onitsha – N 20 by bus

TRAIN

There are two main railway lines which run north from the coast. The first starts in Lagos and goes to Kano via Kaduna and Zaria. The other goes from Port Harcourt to Jos and Maiduguri via Aba, Enugu and Makurdi. These two lines are connected between Kaduna and Kafanchan. As Jos is a terminus and not a station on the way to Maiduguri the trains to these two towns run as a unit from Lagos or Port Harcourt to Kafanchan then split. There is a daily train to Jos but only three times a week to Maiduguri. When travelling south from Jos, go on the days when it doesn't have to wait for the Maiduguri section at Kafanchan.

Kano to Port Harcourt There is a daily train in either direction (at 11 am from Kano). If you're only going as far as Aba (en route to Calabar and Oron then by boat to Cameroun), the train arrives in Aba at 4 pm the next day. Along this same route there is also the daily express bus which leaves from Sabon Gari in Kano around 5.30 to 6 am and takes about 12 hours. It isn't as safe as the train.

Jos to Lagos The train departs at 5 pm

daily and takes 36 hours. First class costs N 66 and 2nd class costs N 17.50.

BOAT

A popular way of getting to Cameroun from Nigeria (or vice versa) is to take a boat from Idua Oron near Calabar to a small place near Limbe (formerly Victoria) which isn't marked on the map. There are daily ferries from Calabar to Idua Oron at 7.30 and 10.30 am and 1 and 3.30 pm. The fare is 50 kobo and it's a pleasant 1½-hour journey.

There are two types of boat available from Idua Oron to Limbe. The first type are very fast, fairly safe and expensive. The other type are long wooden boats fitted with two to three outboard motors and usually loaded with smuggled goods – petrol, alcohol, hi-fi, food and anything else worth smuggling. The fare depends on the boat and where they drop you but it should be around N 40 to N 60. Not all these boats go to Limbe itself but it shouldn't take you too long to get to Limbe if you are dropped elsewhere. To find these boats you need to ask around at the port in Oron. Even if the captain of the boat has paid off all the officials, the trip can turn into a thriller. Not only is the Nigerian navy on the lookout for these boats but the Cameroun navy is too. Getting caught can be a chilling experience and violence is not unknown – though usually not to 'clean' passengers – but you will be hassled for everything you have got. Be prepared to talk about embassies and follow them off the boat. Remember, however, that if you are listed on the boat's manifest then you are there *legally*. The crews of the boats, on the other hand, get a hard time and the captain usually has to pay large bribes (up to N 500). Sensible people not looking for drama on the high seas should seriously consider going overland instead or taking the speedboats to Nyenge (3½ hours) though to get from here to Limbe is a lot of hassle involving two pirogue trips and a 45 to 60-minute walk along the beach.

On arrival in Limbe, immigration may hassle you for CFA 3000 to stamp your passport.

Have some Central African CFA handy on arrival as many people in Cameroun won't accept West African CFA.

TO/FROM BENIN & TOGO

Driving across the border is very easy and a *taxi-brousse* from Cotonou to Lagos will cost CFA 1500. The Nigerian border officials are casual and pleasant and the road is excellent. In Lagos to get a bus or taxi to Benin you need to go to the Mile Two bus stop and you'll need to take a bus or taxi to get there.

If you like, you can get a Peugeot taxi all the way from Lagos to Lomé (Togo). The time taken for this depends very much on border formalities rather than on the distance (it's quite a short run). Taxis doing this run leave from Lagos Island at the end of Carter Bridge.

TO/FROM CAMEROUN

One of the popular routes has already been covered in the Boat section. The usual road route is between Ikom and Mamfé. You can get to Ikom from Enugu or from Calabar. From Ikom take another taxi to Mfum (the Nigerian border village) for N 3. Unless you have through transport, it is a km walk from Mfum to Ekok (the Cameroun border village). From Ekok there are taxis to most of the towns in western Cameroun via Mamfé.

There is also another crossing in the far north between Maroua and Maiduguri. From Maroua to Benki (Nigerian border) a taxi costs CFA 2000. From here a taxi to Maiduguri costs N 10.

If you wish to fly, there's an Air Nigeria flight from Douala to Calabar on Fridays which costs CFA 20,000.

For travellers in their own vehicles driving the northern route, the Garoua to Dourbeye and Mubi road is a better route than the Garoua to Demsa and Belel road which can be impassable due to mud and truck ruts.

TO/FROM CHAD

On leaving Chad at N'Djamena your baggage is searched very thoroughly before the boat crosses the river to Kousseri (Cameroun). The boat costs CFA 100 plus extra for luggage. Here, check in with port immigration/emigration who will tell you to take a taxi (for CFA 500) to the commissariat where, *if* you have a Nigerian visa they will give you a free permit for nonstop transit to Maiduguri. A bus from Kousseri to Gambaru (Nigerian border) will cost CFA 850 plus CFA 200 for luggage and takes five hours. It's a very rough road. There is a bar cum hotel/brothel to stay in if need be in Gambaru for N 10 a night.

To Lake Chad

If you want to visit Lake Chad, make sure you go about it the right way. The only place to get a permit (and you must have one) is from the Maiduguri military base. Don't zip through Maiduguri and expect to get permission from the Mile 4 military base in Baga near the lake. Two travellers who attempted to do this a while ago were arrested by a psychotic commander who accused them of being mercenaries and spies. He took them under military escort to Maiduguri where they were interrogated all day. When the travellers asked why they would be so stupid as to go to a military base to ask for a permit if they were spies, they were accused of making fun of the military and of plotting to kill the commander's driver and steal the truck! When those in charge of the interrogation got bored with asking questions the two were transferred to a military barracks and guarded by 30 fully armed soldiers. The next day they were taken to the police, asked what tribe they were from (!!), had their bags searched and were finally allowed to go. What a farce! All the same, get that permit in Maiduguri.

You can take a Peugeot taxi or minibus from Maiduguri to Baga via Dikwa. The last stretch of road from Baga to the lakeside is very rough.

TO/FROM NIGER

The main route between these two countries is from Kano to Zinder. You can get transport from Kofar Ruwa Motor Park where the Katsina road meets the road to Kofar Ruwa (on the northern edge of the old city). You have to pay 10 kobo to enter the motor park. Direct taxis cost N 30 per person but the driver may demand more from tourists. Direct buses cost N 25 and take seven hours. The Nigerian customs are very cursory but the Niger customs are extra thorough and you may get an 'everything out' search from the police on arrival at Zinder. You can also go from Birni N'Konni to Sokoto and from Maradi to Kano via Katsina. If you're hoping to find a free lift, Tuesday and early Wednesday are the best from Kano to Zinder, and Thursday is the best in the opposite direction. At least 30 trucks do the run to pick up produce from the Zinder market which takes place every Thursday.

Between Maradi and Kano there are taxis (taking five hours) and trucks. You may have to change vehicles in Katsina, but this doesn't cost extra.

Around the Country

BAUCHI

A friendly comfortable place to stay is *De Kerker Lodge* for N 10 a night. The rooms have fans and there is hot water if requested. Ask the management where there's a decent restaurant. There is also the new luxury *Zaranda Hotel*, just before the dual carriageway starts on the Jos road. The cheapest rooms are N 40 a double.

Bauchi is the nearest town to the **Yankari Game Reserve**. It is a 1½-hour journey and the local bus costs N 4. A minibus which leaves from the car park of the Zaranda

Hotel at about 10 am costs N 10. (There are some sharks around who will offer a personal taxi service for N 70!) There is a tourist complex at the reserve where huts cost N 15/22 a single/double. (A double holds up to five people.) The water and electricity supply at the complex is erratic and scarce. Bookings can be made at the State Hotel in Bauchi. Camping costs N 5 per night. The restaurant at the complex has three course meals for N 8 although the menu is rather limited.

You can go game viewing in a truck for two to five hours for N 2 (March being the best time to see lions). The trucks leave at 7.15 am and 3 pm. A highlight of the reserve is the **Wikki Warm Springs** with its wonderful thermal waters, while downstream you can see crocodiles and hippos.

BENIN CITY

Benin is one of the old Yoruba capitals. A highlight of a visit is the **museum**, with its very interesting collection of artefacts from the kingdom which flourished here for centuries before the advent of colonialism. It's also possible to visit the **Oba's Palace**, but you need to make arrangements in advance. Try to do this in Lagos.

Places to Stay & Eat

A cheap place to stay is *Tommy's Guest House* near the Seven Sisters' Hotel. It costs N 10 and is fairly standard with clean rooms, bucket showers and a good bar. The *Eroja Hotel* in Uribi St costs N 15 a night and there are other cheap hotels in this street. There is a *YWCA* (but no YMCA) which costs N 5 per person. Other places used in the past are the *Seven Sisters' Hotel*, a whorehouse with character but no running water, and the *Hotel Crispo*.

CALABAR

Calabar is a pleasant town to relax in, there are hardly any tourists and the local people are friendly and eager to strike up a conversation. It's quite safe to walk around even at night and there are a number of lively bars.

The excellent **museum** is housed in the Old Residency overlooking the Calabar River. It has a large exhibit on the history and effects of the slave trade and another on trade patterns after the abolition of slavery in 1830 and their effects on the Nigerian people, especially the Epik and Eput tribes of southern Nigeria.

Places to Stay & Eat

The *Catholic Mission* and the *Methodist Mission* are worth trying before resigning yourself to a hotel. One of the cheapest hotels is the *Rolsol Guest House* (tel 220328), 91 Palm St near the Cameroun Consulate. It's clean, quiet, has a pleasant garden, the staff are friendly and it's probably the best deal in town at N 10 a double with fan or N 15 a double with air-con. There's also another *Rolsol Guest House* (tel 224391) at 15 Yellow Duke St which costs the same as the other but lacks a garden. Both are owned by Chief Roland P Salomon.

More expensive is the *Guesthouse Vic-Los* just off Marian St and about 100 metres from the Cameroun Consulate. It costs N 45 a double with bathroom, toilet and air-con.

IBADAN

Ibadan is as large as Lagos but is much easier to get around. It's an educational centre and also has one of the largest markets in Nigeria – the Dugbe Market – next to the post office (No 3 on the street map).

Places to Stay & Eat

The best place to stay is the *CUSO* hostel. (CUSO is the Canadian volunteer service.) You can pick up the key to this place at the office (tel 414032) at 836 Adelabu Rd, which is a short walk from the hostel. To get to the office take a minivan from Dugbe Market to 'Ring Challenge' and get dropped off at 'Joyce B' pharmacy. From there it's a 200 metre-walk down the street which runs beside Joyce B (look for the small CUSO signs).

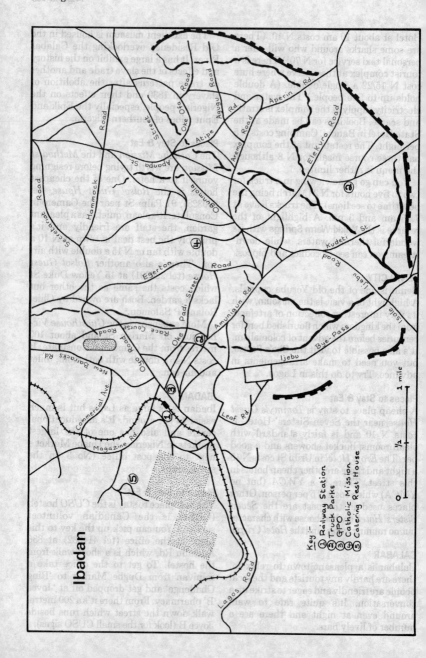

Ibadan

Key:-
1 Railway Station
2 Truck Parks
3 GPO
4 Catholic Mission
5 Catering Rest House

There are some Lebanese restaurants in Ibadan where you can get excellent food, though they're a little pricey. If you want some real luxury bluff your way into the IOTA (Institute of Tropical Agriculture), where you can go for a swim and eat at the subsidised restaurant. They will hardly question you at the front gate, but have an expatriate name handy (any will do) and prefix it with 'Dr' if asked who you want to see. IOTA is a luxurious research station staffed mainly by highly paid expatriate scientists.

IKOM

This is the last Nigerian town on the southern route into Cameroun. Depending on when you arrive, you may have to spend the night. If so, try the *Ikom Guest House* whose excellent management will even cook meals especially for you. Rooms cost N 15 a double with bathroom and fan. The hotel is opposite the taxi park.

JIMETA

This is a town near **Yola** which is the first sizeable town you reach after crossing the Cameroun border from Garoua. Situated on the Benue River, it's a more scenic place than Yola. There are lots of hotels near the waterfront, all of them around N 10 a night. The *Bani Hotel* has fans and large beds but a communal and dirty toilet. The management are friendly.

Trips up the river by boat can be arranged with Alhej (who owns the bank). Expect to pay around N 20 for a half-day trip but you'll have to haggle.

JOS

After the steamy mayhem of Lagos, a trip to Jos might be the highlight of a visit to Nigeria. The Jos plateau has a cool climate all year and is green, shrubby and surrounded by small undulating hills.

Things to See

Within walking distance of the missions are the **Jos Museum**, **Railway Museum** and the **zoo**. The most important attraction is the **Museum of Traditional Nigerian Architecture**. Here you can see a series of life-size reproductions of historic buildings in Nigeria which, in their original setting, are either run-down or demolished, or to which entry is prohibited. They include the Kano wall and the Zaria mosque as well as traditional huts and villages of the various tribes in Nigeria. It's worth a visit and free of charge.

Places to Stay & Eat

The *Universal Hotel* on Pankshin Rd is a friendly place to stay with singles for N 10.35. It is fairly central and good value with a fan and hot water on request. Otherwise try the *Micky Guest Inn* on Boundary Rd which has good rooms for N 15 a single. The manager will ask for N 25 so you need to haggle.

There are two church missions across from each other where you might be able to stay. They're behind the Challenge bookshop. The *CBM* mission has rooms for N 10 per night and has hot water if the boiler hasn't broken down. The other is the *SIM/ECWA* mission with rooms for N 15 a night. Discounts may be given for stays of more than four or five nights, but check this out. Breakfast, lunch and dinner are available.

KADUNA

A cheap place to stay is the *CUSO Hostel* on Kwato Rd behind the racecourse. A bed will cost N 3 per night. The *Central Guest Inn* on Benue Rd has singles/doubles for N 15/20. It's very comfortable with air-con, showers and friendly staff. The *International Restaurant* on Lagos St also has doubles for N 20.

You can get a meal of yam, egg and rice for N 3 at the *Fina White Restaurant* on Lagos Rd. For drivers in their own vehicle the *Jacaranda Restaurant* at the 20 km peg on the Kachia road is up-market but enchanting.

KANO

Kano is the largest city in northern

Nigeria and one of the country's most interesting. It has a history going back 1000 years and was once a very important trading centre and crossroads of the trans-Saharan trade routes. The old city consists of thousands of narrow, winding streets which were once enclosed by an impressive city wall though much of this has been allowed to fall apart in recent years. The old city markets are excellent with stall after stall of beautiful leatherwork and exquisite fabrics. On the surface, little has changed for centuries, though outside the city walls oil money has made a major impact.

Information

The tourist office (tel 2341) is in the Ministry of Home Affairs & Information building, New Secretariat, Zaria Rd. There's also an information kiosk at the airport. The Niger Consulate (tel 2882) is on Kasinda Rd near Airport Rd roundabout.

Things to See

Inside the old city are the famous **Kofar Mata** (dye pits) which are still used and said to be the oldest in Africa. You can, if you wish, have some of your clothes dyed with real indigo. Prices are negotiable of course but a T-shirt should cost around N 2 to N 3. Other attractions include the **Emir's Palace** (an outstanding example of Hausa architecture), the **Central Mosque** (or Grand Mosque) and the **Gidon Makama market**. Opposite the Emir's palace is a very good **museum** that is open every day and entry is free. It is housed in a lovely old building which was itself a former palace complete with its own dye pits.

Although much of the city wall has disappeared some of the original gates remain and are still maintained as national monuments and worth a look. They include the **Kofar Na Isa**, **Kofar Dan Agundi** and **Kofar Sabuwar** on the southern edge of the old city.

For a view over the old city climb **Dala Hill**. It's north of Kurmi Market and on a reasonably clear day easily visible from the Central Mosque.

Places to Stay

A popular place to stay is the state government *Kano Tourist Camp* on Club Rd near the Central Hotel. It costs N 10 for a bed in the dormitory, N 15 for a double room, or you can camp with your tent for N 4 per night plus N 3 for a vehicle. Facilities are fairly basic with fans, sporadic electricity and water. Meals are available and cost N 2.50 for breakfast, N 3.50 for lunch and N 5 for dinner. Also in the same price bracket is the *SIM Guest House*, on Tafawa Balewa Rd off Airport Rd, where a double costs N 15.

Other moderately priced places are the *Challenge Guest Inn* (tel 7719), 87 Yoruba Rd, Sabon Gari; the *Universal Hotel*, 86 Church Rd, Sabon Gari; *Hotel de France*, 54 Tafawa Balewa Rd a small place with 12 rooms, each with private toilet, and meals available; and the *Criss Cross Hotel* (tel 3305), 2A Church Rd, Sabon Gari, which has a choice of air-con or fan-cooled rooms.

More expensive are the *Daula Hotel* which has air-con rooms for N 50 a double with refrigerator and hot water; the *Duniya Hotel* (tel 8754, 8398), 12 Festing Rd, Sabon Gari; the *Akija Hotel* (tel 3514, 5327), 13 Murtala Mohammed Way; the *Usman Memorial Hotel*, 288 Kurmawa Quarters; and the *J Heman Hotel*, Sarkin Yaki Rd, Norman's Land, Sabon Gari. All these hotels have restaurants.

Places to Eat

Highly recommended for good cheap food is the *Bet Restaurant* at 3 Bello Rd near the Nigeria Arab Bank. It's only a small place that looks closed even when it's not so don't be put off. It's clean with good food and pleasant staff. You can also try *Baba's Restaurant*, State Rd near the High Courts building, which has cheap, filling meals of rice, beans, salad and stew. Don't order chicken or you'll get three bones floating in a bowl of sauce. If that

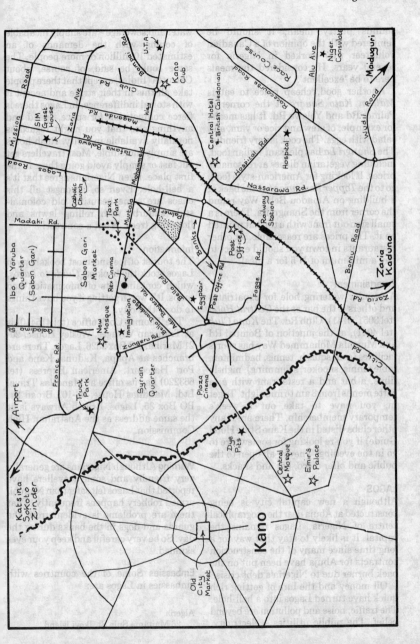

Kano

sounds pretty mean, it should be tempered with the opinion of a Canadian volunteer who worked in Nigeria for several years. He considered the meals here to be 'excellent'.

Another good, cheap place to eat is *Mallam Kato Square* at the corner of Palmer Rd and Yolawa Rd. It has meals, for example, of stew and rice or yam, and salad with eggs. The cook is very friendly. The *Shangri La* has pleasant Indian food, including vegetarian dishes at reasonable prices. If looking for American-style food, go to the *Topper Restaurant* at the back of a building on Amadou Bello Way round the corner from the Shangri La. There is a small sign out front with a top hat painted on it. The prices are reasonable. At other restaurants in town you should expect to pay a minimum of N 5 for a meal.

Entertainment

A popular watering hole for expatriates and others is the bar at the *Central Hotel* (tel 3051, 5141), Club Rd. The *Kano Club* (tel 4041), at the junction of Bompai Rd and Murtala Mohammed Way has sports facilities (golf, squash, tennis, badminton, table tennis, snooker, swimming), nightly films, a bar and a restaurant with à la carte menus from 8 am to midnight. To get in, you have to take out a week's temporary membership. There are many other clubs (listed in the Kano State Hotel Guide) if you're looking for somewhere to go in the evening. They're all open to the public and offer disco, bar and snacks.

LAGOS

Although a new capital city is being constructed at Abuja near the geographical centre of Nigeria, Lagos remains the capital. It is likely to stay that way for a long time since many of the construction contracts for Abuja have been put on the back burner due to Nigeria's debt crisis.

Oil money and the lure of getting rich quick have turned Lagos into a hell-hole. The traffic, noise and pollution are beyond belief. The public utilities – electricity, water and sewerage – are simply incapable of coping with the demands of an estimated 10 million or more people. The same could be said, of course, about Calcutta (India), except that there people take all this in their stride and accept it with stoical indifference. In Lagos there is fierce competition for space, speed and anything else that you might regard as normally available in a city. Rush hours are simply incredible. Most travellers get out fast or simply avoid going there in the first place. Even Nigerians agree that it's a hell-hole. Even so, amongst all this chaos are some beautiful old colonial-style suburbs with rolling lawns and flowering trees. What a contrast!

Information

The tourist office and most bookshops in Lagos stock the booklet, *Guide to Lagos*, which contains lots of information and maps. It's worth getting if you have things to do in this city.

The Thomas Cook office (tel 415410) is at Transcap Voyages, Wesley House, 20-21 Mariba, PO Box 2326, Lagos. There are branches at Apapa, Kaduna, Kano and Port Harcourt. American Express (tel 663220) has its office at Mandilas Travel Ltd, Mandilas House, 96-102 Broad St, PO Box 35, Lagos. British Airways is at the same address as the Australian High Commission.

Warning Although Nigerians are generally very friendly and some travellers have reported that Lagos felt safer than Nairobi, armed robbery happens frequently. That there are problems is evident from the guards and dogs in the banks during the day. So be very careful and keep your eyes skinned.

Embassies Some of the countries with embassies in Lagos are:

Algeria
    26 Maitama Sule St, Ikoyi Island

Belgium
    1A Bank Rd, Ikoyi Island
Benin
    4 Abudu Smith St, Victoria Island (tel
    614411)
Burkina Faso
    15 Norman Williams St, Ikoyi Island
Central African Republic
    Plot 1630 Oko Awo Close, Victoria Island
Egypt
    81 Awolowo Rd, Ikoyi Island
France
    1 Queen's Drive, Ikoyi Island
Gabon
    8 Norman Williams St, SW Ikoyi Island
The Gambia
    162 Awolowo Rd, Ikoyi Island
Germany (West)
    15 Eleke Crescent, Victoria Island
    (tel 58430)
Morocco
    Plot 1318, 27 Karimu Kotun St, Victoria
    Island
Netherlands
    Western House (12th floor), 8-10 Broad St,
    Lagos Island
Senegal
    14 Kofo Abayomi Rd, Victoria Island
Togo
    96 Awolowo Rd, Ikoyi Island
UK
    11 Eleke Crescent, Victoria Island
USA
    2 Eleke Crescent, Victoria Island
    There are consulates in Ibadan and
    Enugu.

High Commissions Some countries with
high commissions in Lagos are:

Australia
    Nurses House (3rd floor), Plot Pc 12, off
    Idowu Taylor St, Victoria Island (tel
    618875)
Canada
    4 Idowu Taylor St, Victoria Island
Ghana
    21-23 King George V Rd, Lagos Island
India
    107 Awolowo Rd, Ikoyi Island
Kenya
    52 Queen's Drive, Ikoyi Island (tel
    682768)
Sierra Leone
    29 Ademola St, SW Ikoyi Island

Tanzania
    45 Ademola St, Ikoyi Island

Things to See
The Nigeria 2000 exhibition is worth
seeing at the **Nigerian Museum** on
Awolowo Rd near Tapwa Balewa Square.
The admission is N 1 and the air-con is
great.

Places to Stay
Finding hotel accommodation in Lagos
can be difficult as there's heavy demand.
If at all possible, try to make a booking
before you arrive.

Many travellers make for the far end of
Bar Beach on Victoria Island, about three
km past the Federal Palace Hotel. Despite
the holocaust which has hit most
parts of Lagos, this place still has many
redeeming features and you may be
offered accommodation. To get there take
a yellow *molue* bus which it's best to get at
the CMS bus stop rather than at the
racecourse. If you're at the racecourse end
of Lagos Island you can pick it up on the
Marina outside NET (the cable office).
The conductor will shout 'Maroko – Bar
Beach'. Don't get on a 'Maroko – Law
School' bus by mistake as this goes on the
north side of Victoria Island.

If you need somewhere more definite
immediately, try the *YMCA*, 77 Awolowo
Rd, Ikoyi Island, which takes men only.
You can get a bed in a four-bed dormitory
for N 6.50 or N 10 for a two-bed room. It's
also possible to camp. It's a good place to
stay and centrally located. The rooms
have fans and showers that actually work
and don't just dribble. Meals are available
and cold beers are on sale.

For women the *YWCA* at Maloney St,
Victoria Island, has clean rooms with
handbasins for N 15 which includes a
breakfast of eggs, bread and tea. The
communal showers have cold water only.

In the more expensive bracket are the
Excelsior Hotel, 3-15 Ede St, Apapa
which costs N 55 a single, and the *Drubar
Hotel* (tel 880600), Badagry Rd, which

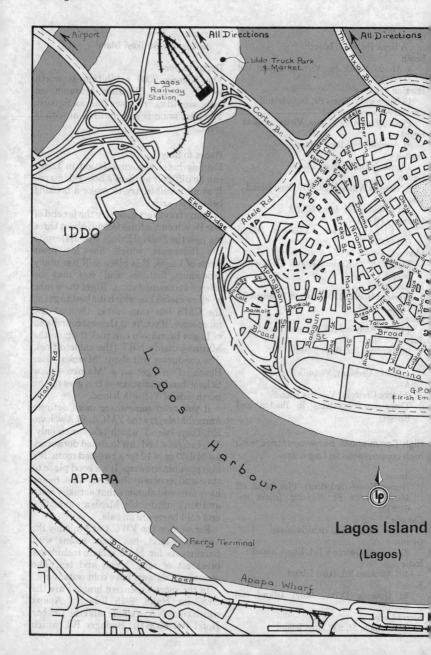

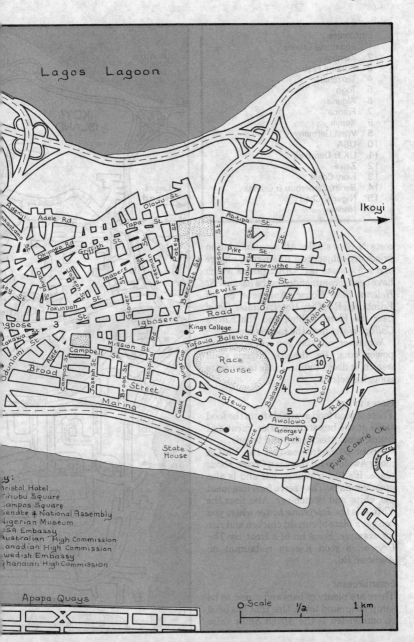

Lagos Lagoon

Ikoyi

Adeniji
Onikantamo
Adele Rd
Okpopo Rd
Odunsi
Griffith St
Tapa St
Olowu St
Abitipa St
Simpson St
Howley St
Forsythe St
Pike St
Freeman St
Inabere St
Glover St
Patey St
Beecroft St
Lewis Road
Igbosere Road
Tokunboh St
Okesuna St
Stracian St
Moloney St
Mission St
Tafawa Balewa Sq
Kings College
Race Course
Balawa Sq
George Rd
Campbell St
Hospital Rd
Brook St
Joseph St
Campos St
Ale St
Kings Coll
Cable
Tafewa
Awolowo
George V Park
Force Rd
King Rd
Broad Street
Marina
State House
Five Cowrie Ck
Eteko Cres
Ikoyi Island
Odunlami St
Kakawa St
Kakawa St
Ngbose St
Sey St
Odunja St
Bristol Hotel
Tinubu Square
Campos Square
Senate & National Assembly
Nigerian Museum
USA Embassy
Australian High Commission
Canadian High Commission
Swedish Embassy
Ghanaian High Commission

Apapa Quays

0 Scale   1/2   1 km

Embassies
1 Equatorial Guinea
2 Zambia
3 Burkina Faso
4 Tanzania
5 Togo
6 Algeria
7 France
8 Kenya
9 West Germany
10 USA
11 UK & Denmark
12 Zaïre
13 Ivory Coast
14 Benin, Cameroun & Guinea
15 Niger & Chad
16 Norway

costs N 65 a single. All accommodation prices are subject to a 10% service charge and a 5% state tax. Other places which have been recommended in the past are *St Helen's Rest House*, Aninwede St off Edinburgh Rd; *City Hotel*; *Jubilee Hotel* near the Hotel Bobby; and the *King's College Hotel* near the racecourse.

Wherever you stay you will encounter power cuts, for despite Nigeria's oil wealth, it doesn't appear able to generate enough electricity.

Places to Eat

There is good food available from the food stalls at the bus stations (rice, meat and beans, omelettes, coffee and bread).

About 50 metres east of the YMCA along Awolowo Rd there is a *Crown Foods* place. It's like a Wimpy bar and is also open Sundays. They serve food like meat pie, chips and Scotch egg. Also near the YMCA is the *Josephine Lodge* where you can get a plate of curried chicken and rice for example. For a bit of a treat try *The Crystal*, a good Korean restaurant on Awolowo Rd.

Entertainment

There are plenty of bars and music to be sampled around town. One that has been recommended is the *Afrika Shine* (also

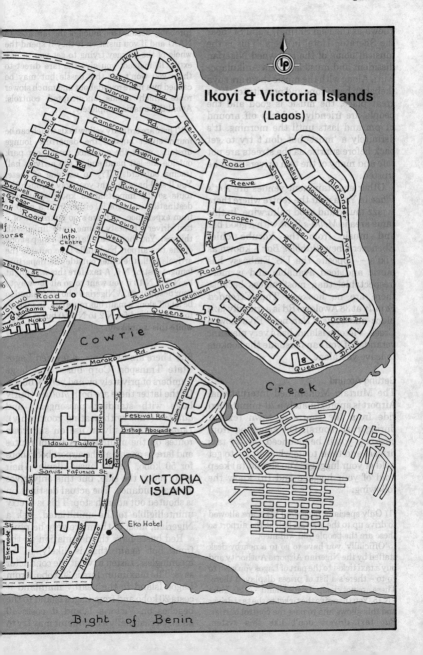

known as the Fela Shrine), Pepu St, near the Sheraton Hotel in Ikeja. This is the musical home of the renowned Nigerian dissident and musician, Fela Anikulapo-Kuti. Along with the music there are suya (kebabs), beer, dope and prostitutes. It's a great place, the music is good and the people are friendly. It kicks off around 11 pm and lasts until the morning. It's definitely a 'must' but don't try to get back before sunrise as the streets are not safe and many of the taxi drivers can't be trusted.

Other entertainment venues are *Art's Place* in Yaba near the centre where there is jazz music and good palm wine. In this same area is *Melki's Spot* with a good bar and music from the Yoruba chief Ebenezer Obey. *Bubbles Bar* – known as Fiki's – opposite the US Embassy has music and food available and is more 'respectable' than most places because there are no hookers. The *Extended Family* at 38 Awolowo Rd is a friendly jazz place and *Julie's Bar* near Five Lowne Creek, Victoria Island, has a very pleasant verandah if you can persuade the hookers to leave you alone.

Getting Around

The Murtala Mohammed International Airport is approximately a 20-minute taxi ride from the centre of town (except during rush hours). On emerging from customs you'll be pounced on by taxi drivers and their touts who will try to get hold of your luggage. You should (a) keep hold of your luggage and (b) know the following:

(1) Only specially registered taxis are allowed to drive up to the arrivals hall at the airport so these are the people you will meet.
'Officially' you have to go to a nearby desk staffed by the Nigerian Airports Authority and buy a taxi ticket to the part of Lagos you wish to go to – there's a list of prices displayed there. These are not cheap: Lagos Island – N 20, Yaba – N 15. You then give the ticket to the taxi driver and this allows him to pass the control barrier. *But* taxi drivers don't like this system

(probably because too much of the fare goes to NAA) and if you insist on it they'll spend the whole of the journey trying to get you to pay extra. If, instead, you give the fare direct to them you won't get this hassle but may be carried by a more roundabout and much slower route which avoids uncorrupted controls. Avoid these taxis completely.

(2) There are ordinary yellow taxis which can be found either outside the departure lounge upstairs, or at the entrance to the car park outside the left hand end of the arrivals hall (facing outwards). Try to use one of these. You'll still have to fight your way through the touts so it's important to know what your destination in Lagos is, either from a map or from experience, as there's no guarantee of a taxi driver's honesty (some have links with thieves). You should be able to get a map at one of the two airport bookstalls (one outside the arrivals hall, the other outside the departure lounge) costing N 6. A taxi fare this way might be N 5 to N 10 if you want to go all the way to your destination. A Nigerian who is prepared to be let off along a main bus route can, in fact, go to Lagos Island for N 2 to N 2.50 but if you're white this is unlikely.

Bus There are two types: a few red Lagos State Transport Corp buses and large numbers of privately owned yellow buses. Of the latter there are both *molues* (fairly large with standing passengers) and *damfos* (vans with seating room only). *Damfos* are mostly in use on suburban routes on the mainland. A list of routes and fares is on sale at the airport bookshops for 50 kobo. Yellow buses display their route along the side, but this only gives general guidance. The actual destination is shouted out at each stop. This is pretty unintelligible to the uninitiated. Ask a Nigerian, most of them are very helpful.

Red buses have the destination on the front but again this is likely to be meaningless. Listen to what the conductor says. The maximum fare is 30 kobo. From Lagos Island to the nearby mainland it costs 20 kobo and from Lagos Island to the beaches on Victoria Island it costs 10 kobo. Occasionally a conductor may try to overcharge – it's a joke usually. Treat it as one, offer the correct fare and the whole bus will roar with laughter. Only red buses normally have tickets. Sometimes you may have to pay twice (eg for Stage 1 and Stage 2). Queueing for buses is rare – fight to get on and do it vigorously. Learn the technique of jumping onto a moving bus.

Taxi Use them like buses. They're cheap – 50 kobo as opposed to 10 kobo on the bus. Give a bus stop as your destination – not an address and especially not a smart hotel. Don't discuss the fare with the driver when you get in – this will indicate you don't know it. Expect to share. Offer the correct fare as change is hard to come by. Don't pay any attention to the fare table in the window – it is ignored. Watch what other passengers are paying. You'll pay more at rush hours and if you have unweildy loads. Ignore taxi drivers who attract your attention spontaneously. Ignore taxis parked outside large hotels. To get a taxi, wave as it comes and shout out your destination. If he's not going that way he'll ignore you.

Never cross an expressway in Lagos – always use a footbridge. The penalty for not doing this is N 100.

Train The suburban railway system is unknown to 99% of westerners and even to many Nigerians. It connects five stops which visitors may be interested in:

Lagos terminus (Iddo) – from here you can walk across the western side of Carter Bridge to Lagos Island. You can also walk across the eastern side, but the walkway is an unofficial lavatory.

Apapa – the port area across the lagoon from Lagos Island. From here you can get a ferry (10 kobo) to the CMS bus stop on the island. If the ferry is out of action there will be private launches (50 kobo).

Yaba – an important bus stop on the nearer mainland. From here you can get shared taxis to Ibadan or Benin.

Oshodi – an important bus stop further out. From here there are taxis and vans to Ibadan and possibly elsewhere. It's also the nearest major bus stop to the international airport.

Ikeja – from here it's about 10 minutes walk to the domestic airport.

There's no service from Iddo to Apapa – you have to do this by bus. A train fare costs 30 kobo for all or most journeys. Timetables may be on sale at Iddo or Apapa, otherwise get details from one of the smaller stations. Don't trust boards displaying times at stations as they are often out of date. Most trains are in the rush hours (early morning and after 3 pm). They're not all full but avoid Ikeja Yaba early morning and Iddo Oshodi in the evening. There are only three trains a day to/from Apapa but they're not overcrowded. Tickets are not usually sold until the approach of the train is signalled. Never board a train without a ticket however great the temptation.

Ferry

There are two ferries from Lagos Island. One runs to Apapa, departing Lagos on the hour and Apapa on the half hour and costs 10 kobo. The one to Festac Town (western mainland) is probably of interest only for the ride.

MAIDUGURI

An interesting excursion to make is to the village of **Gwoza**, south-east of Maiduguri.

Places to Stay

In Gwoza the *Government Rest House* with rooms for N 10 is one of two places to stay. It is a comfortable, run-down version of a once smart establishment. The management is very helpful and there is hot water if you ask. From here go for a walk into the hills – approximately a 2½ hour trip. On the way there are very primitive villages steeped in local custom. A guide would probably be useful. The other place to stay offers beds for N 5.

In Maiduguri accommodation at the

Royal City Hotel is clean and comfortable for N 10/15 a single/double. It has air-con and fans and hot water for bathing. There is also the *Mauri Palace Hotel* which costs N 20 a single, and the *Lake Chad Hotel* where you pay N 42 a double and are plagued by millions of mosquitoes.

ONITSHA

The *Hotel Plaza* in the centre of town has been recommended. It costs N 30 a double.

ORON

This is the town south of Calabar where you get the ferries to Cameroun. It's something of a weird place and you should avoid hanging around too long. Everyone and everything is connected with smuggling. There is, however, a good **museum** with some very interesting carvings and masks. Entry is free.

Never give your passport to anyone except immigration who are pleasant. They might even arrange a boat to Cameroun for you. Make sure your name goes on the boat's manifest and is stamped officially.

There are very few hotels in this town and you can expect to pay up to N 40 a double. One of the cheaper places is the *King Kong Hotel* where they'll let you put up to three people in a room.

SOKOTO

The cheapest place to stay is the *SIM Mission Guest House*, which is not easy to find (even the taxi drivers generally don't know where it is). The *Good Food Restaurant* at 3 Maituta St costs N 10 a double and is clean and secure with electric light and fan. The management is friendly and helpful. There is also a government rest house in town.

A leading tourist attraction is the **Argungu Fishing & Cultural Festival** in early March in Sokoto. There is now a *Grand Fishing Hotel* at Argungu where a round hut costs N 20 or N 35 with aircon.

ZARIA

The **Emir's Palace** is worth a visit but don't photograph the colourful guards as they just might hit you. The Union Bank is incredibly slow for changing travellers' cheques. One recommended place to stay is the *Zaria Motel* which has chalet rooms for N 30 a double. They are clean and comfortable and have air-con and ceiling fans. There is good beer and the staff are friendly though the food is expensive. There are also one or two good restaurants in the newer part of town.

OTHER TOWNS

Following is a list of accommodation available in other towns around the country:

Gusau The *Catholic Mission* sometimes has rooms.

Ilorin The *White House Guest House* on Lagos Rd costs N 30 a double and is comfortable with a bar, restaurant, TV and a friendly manager.

Katsina *Abuja's House* costs N 20.

Lafia The *Catholic Mission* is very hospitable and friendly.

Lokoja The cheapest room at the (luxurious) *Niger Guest House* is N 15 but you may be able to get it for N 10.

Makurdi *The Lamp & the Ward* is a mission hostel on the south bank.

New Bussa The *Student Hostel* near the post office costs N 3.

Port Harcourt Try the *Cedar Palace Hotel* on Harbour Rd or the *Land of Canaan Hotel* at 226 Niger St.

Yelwa The *Hillside Hotel* costs N 10/20 a single/double.

Réunion

About 650 km off the east coast of Madagascar and close to Mauritius lies the volcanic island of Réunion. It is one of France's last colonies or, more correctly, an overseas *département* of France administered by a prefect with an elected local council which sends three deputies to the French national assembly.

The island has a history very similar to that of Mauritius and was visited, though not settled, by Malay, Arab and European mariners. It was first claimed by the French East India Company in 1664, who put in French settlers and Malagasy slaves. Until 1715 they were content to provide only for their own needs and those of passing ships, but when coffee was introduced the island's economy changed dramatically and demanded the large-scale use of slaves – this occurred despite the company's rules specifically forbidding the use of slave labour. As a result of bad management and the rivalry between France and Britain in the 18th century, government of the island passed directly to France in 1764.

In the late 18th century there were a number of slave revolts, and those who managed to escape made their way to the interior. They organised themselves into villages run by democratically elected chiefs and fought to preserve their independence from the colonial authorities.

While the Mascarenes (Réunion, Mauritius, Rodrigues, etc) remained French colonies, Réunion had the function of providing the island group with good food while Mauritius made the profits in the form of sugar exports. When Mauritius was ceded to the British after the Napoleonic wars, sugar was introduced to Réunion. The change took place to the detriment of food crops and quickly became the only agricultural activity. It resulted in the dispossession of many small farmers (forced to sell out to those with capital to invest in the new monoculture), and in their migration to the interior. Like Mauritius, Réunion experienced a labour crisis when slavery was abolished in the first half of the 19th century and, in exactly the same way, the crisis was 'solved' by the importation of contract labourers from India. Many of those imported in the 19th century were Hindus. They remain largely distinct from the Muslim Indians who arrived in the early years of the 20th century.

With competition from Cuba and sugar beet from Europe, Réunion's economy stagnated and resulted in a further concentration of land and capital in the hands of a small French elite. Since then the situation hasn't essentially changed. A left-wing group, the Comité d'Action Démocratique et Sociale, was founded in 1936 on a platform of integration with France. When the island eventually became a *département* after WW II, however, they turned against it because of the obvious futility of it all. The conservatives who initially opposed this integration with France for fear of losing their privileges as colonists eventually did an about-face too. They realised that independence would release the resentment of those who had been dispossessed for so long and they would have to face it without French police or military protection.

The last two decades have seen a push, led mainly by the left, for greater autonomy and for improvements in working conditions and wages.

Facts

GEOGRAPHY

This tropical, volcanic island has lush forested mountains, picturesque villages and hiking trails rivalling those in Hawaii. The beaches have coral reefs offshore.

PEOPLE

Like Mauritius, Réunion is populated by descendants of French plantation owners, African slaves and contract labourers from India. There are also about 20,000 Chinese people in Réunion. The total population is around 600,000.

VISAS

These are required by all nationalities except the EC countries and Swiss nationals. Since the island is a French possession, visas must be obtained from a French embassy or consulate. Make sure the visa is stamped valid for Réunion otherwise it won't be accepted.

You must have an onward ticket to get into Réunion. An MCO is not acceptable. Also, you might have difficulties at the airport on arrival if unable to name a place where you intend to stay, so have one on hand.

Other Visas

Madagascar The consulate (tel 21 66 52) is at 77 Rue Juliette Dodu, St Denis. Visas cost FFr 70, require four photos and normally take a week to issue, but they will speed up the process if you have an earlier flight.

South Africa The consulate (tel 21 50 05) is in the Résidence Compagnie des Indes (1st floor), 18 Rue de la Compagnie near Rue Jean Chatel, St Denis. A 12-month, multiple-entry visa is free and issued while you wait. One photo is required but you don't need to show an onward ticket. Remember to ask for your visa on a separate piece of paper so you don't get stamps in your passport.

MONEY

US$1 = FFr 3.05

The unit of currency is the French franc. Banks, including the one at the airport, are closed on Sunday. If you arrive on a Sunday, the Hotel Meridien will change money.

Réunion is a very expensive island and as one traveller put it, 'expect to blow half your budget in this place'. The cost of living is higher than in France and there are *no* bargains. This also applies to food because the bulk of it is imported, mainly from France! It is nevertheless worth visiting if you can afford it, as the scenery is spectacular.

There is no airport departure tax.

ACCOMMODATION

Hotels and *pensions de famille* are very expensive. Not only that, but the relatively cheaper *pensions* are often permanently full (especially in St Denis) or are in towns of little touristic interest (Le Tampon). There are, however, some cheap accommodation possibilities such as the *Youth Hostel* in Hell-Bourg, the seven camping sites around the island, the 12 mountain huts (*gîtes de montagne*) on the hiking trails, the three government-run vacation villages and a few cheap hotels detailed later.

Another interesting and inexpensive form of accommodation is the *chambre d'hôte*. This is generally two to three guest rooms in houses which offer *tables d'hôte* – traditional meals of local produce served family-style. Bed and breakfast at these places generally costs FFr 70 to FFr 100 a double. Meals cost about FFr 45 to FFr 60 per person including wine and coffee. For a list of these places, contact the office (tel 20 31 90) at 2 Ave de la Victoire, St Denis, one block from the tourist office. This office also has information about *gîtes ruraux* – country houses – for two to 12 people which cost FFr 550 to FFr 1550 per week.

There are municipal camp sites at St

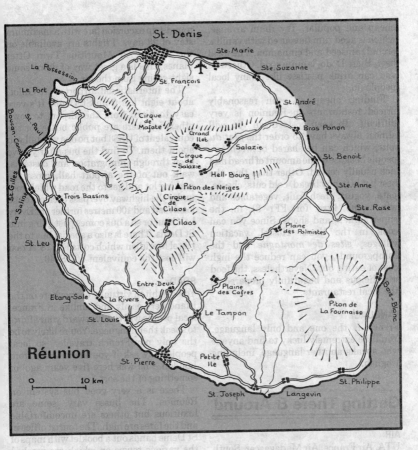

St. Denis

La Possession

Le Port

Boucan-Canot

St. Paul

St. François

Ste. Marie

Ste. Suzanne

St. André

Bras Panon

Cirque de Mafate

Grand Ilet

Cirque de Salazie

Salazie

St. Benoît

Hell-Bourg

Ste. Anne

▲ Piton des Neiges

St. Gilles

La Saline

Trois Bassins

Cirque de Cilaos

Ste. Rose

St. Leu

Cilaos

Plaine des Palmistes

Etang-Sale

La Rivers

Entre-Deux

Plaine des Cafres

Bois-Blanc

St. Louis

Le Tampon

▲ Piton de La Fournaise

Réunion

St. Pierre

Petite Ile

0   10 km

St. Joseph

Langevin

St. Philippe

Gilles les Bain, St Leu, Etang-Sale, Grand Anse, Bois Court and Cilaos. These sites cost FFr 25 per day plus FFr 3 extra for electricity. Water is available on site. You need your own tent to make use of these sites. The one at Etang-Sale is quite small (75 metres wide) and is sandwiched between the main St Denis to St Pierre highway and the black sand beach. There are showers, (dirty) toilets, a restaurant and a shop about 200 metres away.

FOOD

Creole cuisine in Réunion is a combination of influences from India, Madagascar and France. Spicy curry is the most common dish, usually chicken, beef or goat. Two speciality curries are turtle and octopus. Brede, a delicious green vegetable somewhat like spinach, is often served. Rougail, usually of tomatoes, is a hot sauce similar to Mexican salsa that accompanies most meals.

Regional specialities include the famous lentils and home-made sweet wines of Cilaos, the trout of Hell-Bourg and turtle supplied by the turtle farm in St Leu.

Locally distilled white rum is very

cheap and popular. Try rhum arrangé, which is aged rum flavoured with vanilla, orchid, aniseed and cinnamon. The local beer, Bière Dodo, is quite good. Otherwise you can drink pastisse like many local people do.

Finding cheap or even reasonably priced restaurants in Réunion is very difficult. To keep costs down you will almost always have to order the *plat du jour*, which can be shared between two people because of the amount of bread and rice usually served. Other than this, the best bet is to buy bread, cold cuts, cheese, paté, yogurt, fresh fruit, vegetables and wine (one litre for FFr 8) in the supermarkets and shops. Since you can cook in the Youth Hostel, vacation villages, *gîtes de montagne* and the campgrounds, you can reduce the high cost of eating out. Nevertheless, the food is delicious and beautifully prepared in the local restaurants.

LANGUAGE
French is the one and only language. You'll be extremely lucky to find anyone who speaks another language, including English.

Getting There & Around

AIR
UTA, Air France, Air Madagascar, South African Airways and Air Mauritius operate international flights to Réunion. The French charter company, Le Point, has Boeing 707 flights from Lyon, France to Réunion for FFr 4800 return. This works out far cheaper than taking the regular airlines.

Réunion/Antananarivo (Madagascar) can be done for FFr 1790 return on an excursion ticket – minimum stay of six days, maximum of 30 days. The regular one-way fare on Air France or Air Madagascar costs FFr 1195. Réunion/Mayotte (Comoros Islands) costs FFr 2960

round-trip excursion fare with a maximum stay of 23 days. Flights are available on the 16-seat Air Mauritius Twin Otter planes; this is a great way of doing some sight-seeing from the air.

The international airport is at Gillot, about eight km from St Denis. It's very easy to hitch from the airport to town otherwise there are public buses for the equivalent of US$3 but no one will tell you about them. To find the bus after you've been through immigration and customs, walk out of the airport hall, cross the parking lot and get to the road which goes under the highway overpass then onto the local road and 100 metres further on. Every half hour or so a bus comes past going into St Denis. There is also a special bus to the Hotel Meridien which costs FFr 18. A taxi will cost the equivalent of US$40.

ROAD
You can hitch virtually everywhere on the island very easily and, unlike in France, local people will richly reward your efforts to speak their language. You're likely to be the only non-French traveller, so local people may ask if you know 'John from London – he was here five years ago' or something of the sort.

There is a very good bus system on Réunion. The buses vary, some are luxurious but others are uncomfortable and the fares are high. The tourist office in St Denis hands out a booklet with maps of the various towns on which are marked the bus stations.

Some examples of bus fares and journey times are:

St Denis to St Louis – FFr 30.60 and takes two hours
St Louis to Cilaos – FFr 19 and takes two hours
St Denis to St Pierre – FFr 29.90
St Denis to Ste Rose – FFr 20.70
St André to Hell-Bourg – FFr 9.70
St André to Grand Ilet (Cirque de Zalazie) – FFr 16.10

Shared taxis are also available and to go from St Pierre to St Joseph costs around FFr 10.

Around the Country

CILAOS

Cilaos is an absolute must. It is the most impressive of the craters and is worth it for the breathtaking road alone. The mountain scenery is comparable to any in the world. It was once famous as a refuge for runaway slaves.

Things to See & Do

It's 113 km from St Denis and at a height of 1220 metres. Hitching the 113 km from St Denis to St Louis is easy but there's also a bus which costs FFr 30.60 and takes two hours. However, it's harder to hitch out of St Louis and you may have to take the minibus to Cilaos for FFr 19 (36 km). Almost immediately on leaving St Louis you enter a gorge. After crossing the river the road flings itself up the mountainside in a gleeful frenzy of twists and turns, switchbacks and zigzags with cuttings, embankments, tunnels, a flying buttress and even a bridge over itself. The road is very narrow and often the minibus only has a clearance of inches. You should sit on the right hand side for maximum vertigo.

Cilaos is famous for Les Thermes (hot springs) where you can get a private tub for FFr 15. To get to them take a short hike down into a river valley from town. They're open from 6.30 to 11.30 am and from 1 to 4.30 pm. They are closed on Sunday afternoons in winter. Swimming in the river is also good. It's possible to go wine tasting in homes and shops which sell the locally made sweet wines – look for signs saying 'Vin à vendre'.

The Cirque de Cilaos is noted for its fine hiking possibilities and splendid views. Two popular day hikes are to Le Bras Sec (14-km round trip) and to Îlet a Cordes

plateau (22-km round trip). Another hike is the ascent of Piton des Neiges, manageable in a day if you don't have a heavy pack. It is a steep 2000 metre ascent and return (a 16-km round trip). The track is clearly marked though rough in stretches and over two-thirds of the distance is staircased. There is a hut at the crater rim which is more expensive than other hiking huts. You can plan longer treks using the gîtes de montagne to Cirque de Salazie and Cirque de Montagne.

Places to Stay & Eat

There is a camp site if you have the gear. Otherwise, one of the cheapest places is the Marla Hotel (tel 27 72 33), which has doubles with common bath for FFr 100. Double rooms with shower and bidet but common toilet cost FFr 125. The Marla is a very pretty, friendly place and has the cheapest Creole restaurant in town. Rabbit, goat, lentils and sausages are specialities. One plat du jour is quite adequate for two people.

If the Marla is full, try the VVF Fleurs Jaunes (tel 27 71 39), which costs FFr 150 per person with full board.

CIRQUE DE MAFATE

To really see rural Réunion this is the place to go. There are no roads into Mafate and you have to walk in. Count on taking a day to get in and a day to get out again. You can walk in from various points (Salazie, Cilaos or via Rivière des Galets from Le Port, amongst others). The paths are fairly obvious and signposted, but it's best to take a map, as well as food and water. You can fill up with water at the springs here and there (some of them hot, so don't forget the tea bags). There are gîtes (huts) to stay in along the way.

HELL-BOURG

Hell-Bourg is in the Salazie Cirque, the most beautiful and verdant of the three cirques on Réunion. (A cirque is a large, volcanic cul-de-sac valley surrounded by high mountains.)

Things to See & Do

There are some amazing waterfalls in the vicinity, especially **Le Voile de la Mariée** between Salazie and Hell-Bourg which you can walk to. There are many streams where you can bathe.

Hiking in the Cirque de Salazie is the other main attraction of the area and an excellent way of taking in all the best of what Réunion has to offer. Ask for the Youth Hostel brochure which has a map and a description of several local day-long hikes. You can also use Hell-Bourg as a base for longer hikes, resting in the *gîtes de montagne*. One such hike would be to the **Piton des Neiges**, the highest point on the island (3069 metres), then back to Hell-Bourg via Grand Îlet. Another would be up to the same point then down to Cilaos.

While you're here it's worth a visit to the **Trout Farm** (tel 23 50 16) run by Paul Irigoyen and his wife. It's just a short walk from the Youth Hostel. You can buy freshly caught trout for FFr 50 a kg and cook it at the Youth Hostel.

The nearby village of **Grand Îlet** is worth a day trip from Hell-Bourg. It's famous for its *tables d'hôte* – country-style, several-course set meals.

Places to Stay & Eat

The best accommodation deal is the 20-bed *Auberge de la Jeunesse* (Youth Hostel) (tel 23 52 65), Rue de la Cayenne, Maison Morange, 97433 Hell-Bourg. It costs FFr 30 per person and is in a beautiful old colonial building built in 1938 in the centre of town. You must have a Youth Hostel card to use the place (you can buy membership for FFr 100). There is a huge, well-equipped kitchen, dormitories and private rooms, hot water, patios, pretty grounds and good views as well as plenty of food shops nearby. If you plan to come here direct from the airport, hitch or take a bus to St André (30 km). From there get another bus to Hell-Bourg – a beautiful 25-km run.

If the Youth Hostel is full, there is the *Relais des Cimes* two blocks away which costs FFr 165 a double including breakfast.

In Grand Îlet people worth checking out are Madame Grondin (tel 23 59 29), Madame Nourry (tel 23 51 27) and Madame Boyer (tel 23 52 81), all of whom serve *tables d'hôte* including wine and coffee.

PITON DE LA FOURNAISE

A visit to this still active volcano is one of the 'must sees' on the island. The easiest way to visit it is to take one of the tours which go every Wednesday and take two days. Ask at the tourist office in St Denis for information. The tour takes you up to the edge of the crater where you can watch the 'bubbling and gurgling and the flaming inferno and, if you're lucky enough, witness a minor eruption'. The landscape is strange and moonlike. If you want to go on your own, there is a *gîte* at Pas de Bellecombe, two to five hours' walk from the crater depending on the individual. You really need your own transport to get to the *gîte* as it's 20 km to the main road at Le Vingt-Septième. You can hitch, but obviously there's very little traffic, so don't count on it. It's worth the visit, but be sensible – don't go too close to the edge and don't go if it's erupting.

ST DENIS
Information

The tourist office (tel 21 24 53) is at 4 Rue Rontaunay. The people are very friendly and speak English 'with the Peter Sellers accent'. The post office has a good poste restante, but you must pay FFr 2.10 for each letter collected.

Things to See

It's worth visiting the **Leon Dierx Art Gallery** on Rue de Paris, open from 10 am to noon and 3 to 6 pm every day except Tuesday. The gallery has a good collection of French Impressionists. The **Natural History Museum** in the Jardin de l'État is also worth a visit. It's open Wednesday, Saturday and Sunday from 8 am to noon and 2 to 5 pm.

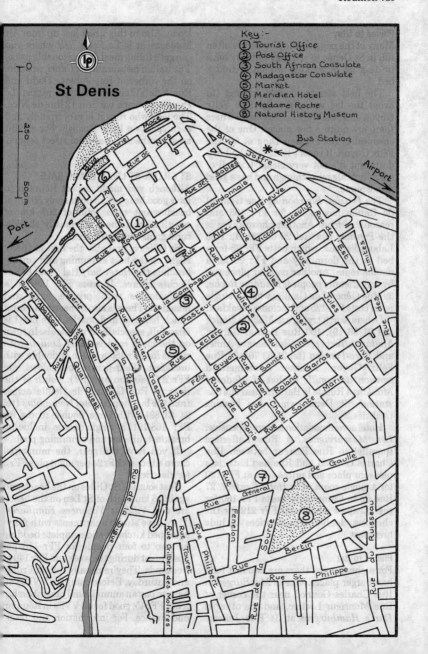

Places to Stay

Many of the *pensions de famille* are often full in St Denis, so you may initially have to do a lot of walking around to find a bed.

The best streets to start looking (to avoid the leg work) are the Rue Félix Guyon and Rue Général de Gaulle where there are quite a few places. One of the cheapest is the *Pension Dina* at 56 Rue Félix Guyon. It costs FFr 25 for a bed in a dorm but it's not very clean. It's full of friendly Malgaches though and has a good atmosphere.

The *Pension Bourbon* 54 Rue Général de Gaulle has rooms for FFr 105 and reasonable food. Another cheap place is the *Pension Hik* (tel 20 05 08), 12 Rue Labourdonnais, which costs FFr 35 for a bed in the dormitory and FFr 90 for a double room. Another popular place run by very friendly people is *Madame Roche*, 39 Rue Général de Gaulle, where a single room costs FFr 125 and includes breakfast.

Others worth trying are *Madam Smith* (tel 21 36 19), 100 Rue Roland Garros; *Madame Techer*, 18 Rue Sainte-Anne; and *Euro-Pension* (tel 21 53 70), 21 Rue Félix Guyon. Another recommended *pension de famille* is that of *Madame Moulan*, 4 Rue de la Batterie near the bus station, St Denis, which has cooking facilities.

Hotel accommodation is more expensive. *Les Mascareignes*, 3 Rue Lafférière (parallel to Rue Pasteur between Rue Charles Gounod and Rue de l'Est), is a pleasant place and prices start at FFr 120 for a single room. The *Hotel Central*, 27 Rue de la Campagnie, costs FFr 160 for the cheapest single and FFr 212 for the cheapest double. These prices include breakfast.

Places to Eat

For a cheap meal there are two fast food hamburger places. One is *MacBurger* in Rue Charles Gounod near the corner of Rue Monsieur Leclerc, and the other is *Dan's Hamburgers* at 34 Rue Juliette Dodu. Also in this street just up from Air Madagascar is *Le Resto-Self* where you can get a filling meal at a reasonable price. The Italian restaurant, *Le Capri*, upstairs on the corner of Rue Juliette Dodu and Rue A de Villeneuve has good pizzas. *Le Provençal* snack bar is at 12 Rue de Nice. The lady who runs it is very friendly and even speaks a little English. For a light meal try the samosas from street sellers.

ST GILLES, ST LEU & ETANG-SALE

Although you might expect Réunion to have good beaches, there are only 30 km of beaches out of a total of 207 km of coastline, and these are mostly shallow coral going out to the reef.

St Gilles is probably the best of them. Right on the best swimming and surfing beach is the *Hotel Surf* (tel 24 42 84) at Roches Noires. It costs FFr 128/145 a single/double with private bath and breakfast. There is also a cheap restaurant which has beer and snacks. The hotel is often full, especially at weekends. In town on the main road is *Hotel Loulou* with rooms for FFr 150 a single or double with breakfast. Four-person bungalows are FFr 200 (air-con and TV). South of the river on Rue Général de Gaulle across from the bus stop is *Hotel Nenuphars* (tel 24 43 89), with large double rooms for FFr 168/191 a single/double including breakfast, air-con and swimming pool.

If you have the gear, the municipal camp site costs FFr 24 per night plus FFr 3 for electricity.

Just south of St Gilles on the beach and again 16 km south of St Leu on the beach are two *Villages Vacances Familiares*. They have studio apartments with fully-equipped kitchens and complete bedding for two to four people for FFr 118 per apartment during the week and FFr 140 at weekends. They're usually full on Friday and Saturday. Before using the VVFs you have to pay an annual family membership fee of FFr 45, good for all VVFs in Réunion and France. For information and reser-

vations phone 24 47 47. The VVFs also
serve good family-style lunches for FFr 27.

Two km north of St Leu is the **Corail
Turtle Farm**, which is free and worth a visit.
The farm supplies the island's turtle meat
and shell, but due to export restrictions is
facing bankruptcy. For a meal of turtle
meat prepared in the local style, try the
beachfront restaurant across from the
VVF in St Leu.

ST PIERRE
This is a good place to while away a few
days. There is a *pension de famille* in Rue
des Bons Enfants, 2nd floor, opposite the
one-hour photo express place. It has a very
small sign and the entrance is around the
back so it's easy to miss. It costs FFr 85 for
a single. Otherwise try *Pension de
Madame Decanonville*, 17 Rue Auguste
Babet, but this may be for women only.
However, the woman in charge is friendly
and helpful so try it whatever your sex and
she may be able to arrange somewhere for
you to stay.

For a place to eat try the excellent and
very popular *L'Osteria*, an Italian
restaurant at 16 Rue M et A Leblond,
which offers good pizzas and pasta, with
wine available. There are several bars and
restaurants on Blvd H Delisle, down by
the beach. *Le Cabanon* has good pizzas
and is run by a friendly Armenian who will
probably speak your language and talk
about his relatives in Australia.

HIKING
To really see this island go up into the
mountains. There are nine *gîtes de
montagne* you can use for overnight stays
which are maintained by the tourist office
in St Denis. They're all situated on one or
other of the 600-km network of maintained
hiking trails. The cabins have from 10 to
38 beds, two blankets per bed (bring
sheets), cold water and fireplaces or wood
stoves for cooking, but no electricity. They
cost FFr 36 per night and there's a two-
night limit at any one cabin. Meals are
available at some huts but not all.

Make reservations in advance at the
tourist offices (tel 21 24 53, 21 65 23) in St
Denis, St Paul, St Penoit or Plaine des
Palmistes. You also have to put down a
deposit of an additional FFr 36. Remember
when hiking that the clouds and rain come
in very fast and obscure views making it
somewhat dangerous in some areas.

If you're thinking of hiking along the
popular GRR1 trail which goes to all three
cirques (Salazie, Cilaos and Mafate), get
hold of a copy of the book *GR1 Le Tour du
Neiges* for FFr 34 from the tourist office.
They also sell the excellent Institut
Géographique National 1:25,000 topographical maps. Map No 4405 R covers
the cirques (FFr 50).

*Thanks to Jan King & Tom Harriman
(USA) for supplying the bulk of the
information and the maps for Réunion.*

Rwanda

As in neighbouring Burundi, the original inhabitants of Rwanda, the Twa pygmies, were gradually displaced from 1000 AD onwards by migrating Hutu tribespeople who, in turn, came to be dominated by the Tutsi from the 15th century onwards. The Tutsi used the same methods for securing domination over the Hutu as in Burundi, namely, the introduction of a feudal land system and a lord-peasant relationship with regard to services and the ownership of cattle which represented wealth. The similarities with Burundi end there, however. The Rwandan *mwami's* (king's) authority was far greater than his opposite number in Burundi and the system of feudalism which developed here was unsurpassed outside Ethiopia.

Not only was the Rwandan *mwami* an absolute ruler in every sense of the word with the power to exact forced Hutu labour and to allocate land to peasants or evict them from it but here Tutsi overlordship was reinforced by ceremonial and religious observances. Military organisation, likewise, was the sole preserve of the Tutsi. Rwanda, however, was more intensively farmed than Burundi and, in the process of growing food on all available land, the Hutu eventually denuded the hills of tree cover. The resulting erosion, lack of fuel and competition for land with the Tutsi pastoralists frequently threatened the Hutu with famine. Indeed, in the 20th century alone there have been no less than six famines.

Faced with such a narrow margin of security, something was bound to give sooner or later among the Hutu who, in this country, account for some 89% of the population. The process was interrupted, however, by the colonial period.

In 1890 the Germans took the country and held it until 1916 when their garrisons surrendered to the Belgian forces during WW I. At the end of the war, Rwanda was mandated to the Belgians along with Burundi by the League of Nations. From then until independence the power and privileges of the Tutsi were increased as the Belgians found it convenient to rule indirectly through the *mwami* and his princes. They were not only trained to run the bureaucracy but had a monopoly on the educational system operated by the Catholic missionaries. The condition of the Hutu peasantry meanwhile deteriorated and led to a series of urgent radical demands for reform in 1957. Power and its props are rarely given up voluntarily in Africa, however, and in 1959, following the death of Mwami Matara III, a ruthless Tutsi clan seized power and set about murdering Hutu leaders.

It was a serious miscalculation and led to a massive Hutu uprising. Some 100,000 Tutsi were butchered in the ensuing bloodletting and many thousands more fled into neighbouring countries. The new *mwami* likewise fled into exile. Faced with carnage on this scale, the Belgian colonial authorities were forced to introduce political reforms and when independence was granted in 1962 it brought the Hutu majority to power under the prime ministership of Gregoire Kayibanda.

Certain sections of the Tutsi, however, were unwilling to accept the loss of their privileged position. They formed a number of guerrilla groups which mounted raids on Hutu communities but this only provoked further Hutu reprisals. In the

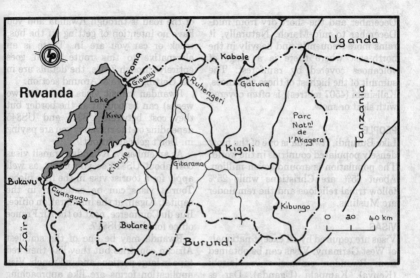

Rwanda

Lake Kivu

Bukavu

Goma
Gisenyi
Ruhengeri
Kabale
Gatuna
Uganda

Kibuye
Kigali
Gitarama

Parc
Nat¹
de
l'Akagera

Tanzania

Cyangugu
Kibungo

Zaïre
Butare
Burundi

0   20   40 km

bloodshed which followed thousands more Tutsi were killed and tens of thousands of their fellow tribespeople fled to Uganda and Burundi. Since those dark days, things have cooled down though there was a resurgence of anti-Tutsi feeling in 1972 when Hutu tribespeople were massacred by the tens of thousands in neighbouring Burundi. Disturbances in Rwanda during this time prompted the army commander, Juvenal Habyarimana, to oust Kayibanda. He has ruled the country ever since.

Facts

Unlike Burundi, many travellers come to Rwanda though mainly to visit the Parc National des Volcans in the north where the borders of Rwanda, Uganda and Zaïre meet. The thickly forested slopes are one of the last remaining sanctuaries of the mountain gorilla. This is the place where Dian Fossey did her research until she was murdered there having made herself very unpopular with the poachers.

GEOGRAPHY

In order to feed everyone, almost every available piece of land except for the Akagera along the border with Tanzania and the higher slopes of the volcanoes is under cultivation. Since most of the country is mountainous, this involves a good deal of terracing and the banded hillsides may remind you of Nepal or the Philippines. Tea plantations (tea is one of Rwanda's major exports) take up considerable areas of land in certain parts. The country is a major recipient of international aid, particularly from the Chinese People's Republic and you may come across Chinese aid workers engaged on various projects, usually agricultural or hydroelectric.

CLIMATE

The average daytime temperature is 24°C with a possible maximum of 34°C except in the highland areas where the daytime range is between 12°C and 15°C. There are four discernible seasons: the long rains from mid-March to mid-May, the long dry from mid-May to mid-September, the short rains from mid-September to mid-

December and the short dry from mid-December to mid-March. Naturally, it rains more frequently and heavily in the north-east where there is a range of volcanoes covered by rainforest. The summit of the highest of these volcanoes, Kalisimbi (4507 metres), is often covered with sleet or snow.

PEOPLE

Like Burundi, Rwanda is one of the most densely populated countries in the world. The population is around seven million. About 65% are Christians while 25% follow tribal religions and the remainder are Muslims.

VISAS

Visas are required by all except nationals of West Germany. Visas can be obtained from Rwandan embassies in Nairobi (Kenya), Kampala (Uganda), Dar es Salaam (Tanzania), Bujumbura (Burundi) and Kinshasa (Zaïre). There is a consulate in Mombasa (Kenya). Some other embassies in Africa include:

Egypt
    13 Midan Aswan, Agouza, B P 485, Cairo
Ethiopia
    Africa Ave, Higher 17 Kebele 20, House 001, Addis Ababa
Ivory Coast
    B P 3905, Abidjan 01

Avoid applying for a visa outside East Africa if possible as this often involves a lot of red tape. They cost about US$12.50 in most countries (less in Tanzania if paying in local shillings bought on the street market) with two photos for a one month stay and generally take 24 hours to issue.

It's a good idea to request a multiple-entry visa on the application form (no extra cost for this) especially if you are intending to go to Zaïre and Burundi. The most convenient route between Bukavu (Zaïre) and Bujumbura (Burundi) is via Rwanda and for this you *may* need a Rwandan visa even though only one-third

of the road is through Rwanda and you have no intention of getting off the bus, truck or car you are in. There is an alternative to this route which goes entirely through Zaïre, the details are in the Getting There & Around section.

Rwandan transit visas (valid for two weeks) can be bought at the border but they cost between US$35 and US$45 depending on the currency you are paying in. Don't get caught out!

At an embassy, Rwandan transit visas cost about US$10 so you might as well apply for a tourist visa in the first place. Tourist visas can be extended in the capital, Kigali, at the immigration office, Rue du Commerce, next to the Air France office for about US$17.

Rwanda may be one of the smallest African countries but they like their red tape in large portions and in French. Visa application forms are like approaching *Lord of the Rings* or *Poor Fellow My Country* on a one-hour lunch break. Don't be put off. A separate form which comes with the visa application will have you signing a bond where you promise to spend at least US$20 per day. Sign it. Nobody wants to know when you get there or when you leave. The same goes with mistakes or 'don't knows' on the visa application form. You'll get the visa. Letters of introduction from your embassy and onward tickets are no longer required. No-one will ask to see (or count) how much money you are carrying.

The only thing to think carefully about when filling in the application form is the date on which you intend to enter Rwanda as this is written on the visa stamped in your passport. You cannot enter before that date (though you can leave before it expires). This *may* not be strictly enforced and I would imagine from my own and others' experiences at Gatuna (on the Rwanda-Uganda border) that it isn't.

There are no Rwandan consulates in Bukavu or Goma in eastern Zaïre so it's advisable to get your visa in Kinshasa (or elsewhere) if coming from the west.

However, several travellers have reported that it's possible to get a *permis provisoire*, valid for one week (a sort of transit visa), for about US$46 on demand at the Goma-Gisenyi border. Or, assuming you have the time, a tourist visa from the Belgian Consulate in Goma for about US$17. The tourist visa takes two weeks to issue and you have to leave your passport with them. The same may be true for the Belgian Consulate in Bukavu. The regulations about these things change constantly so don't rely on this possibility.

If travelling between Bukavu (Zaïre) and Bujumbura (Burundi), the most convenient (and comfortable) route is via Rwanda. You don't have to go this way. There is a road all the way through Zaïrois territory to Uvira, at the head of Lake Tanganyika (where both routes end). Many trucks use this route but the road isn't in good shape. Rwandan roads are surfaced most of the way whereas Zaïrois roads are not. Nevertheless, many travellers use the all-Zaïre route.

We've had a lot of letters from travellers in the past who have taken the Rwandan route and have been fleeced for a US$10 Rwandan transit visa at the border (in the absence of a Rwandan multiple-entry visa). In updating this edition I travelled on a minibus from Bukavu to Uvira without a multiple-entry Rwandan visa. Not only did the Zaïrois authorities not want to stamp my passport on exit or re-entry – or the Rwandans on entry or exit – but I was never asked for a Rwandan visa (or a Zaïre visa for that matter). And I stood out. I was the only white person on the bus.

I would suggest, though I cannot confirm, that the no-visa deal is connected with the minibus alone. It may be different if you are in a private car or hitching a ride on a truck. The driver of the minibus had a list of names and passport/ID numbers on a clipboard which had to be completed before we left Bukavu but that was the extent of the red tape. We also had to state how much cash and how many travellers' cheques we were each carrying but there was never any check. This may change.

Other Visas

Kigali, the capital, is a small city and most of the embassies are within easy walking distance of the centre.

Burundi The embassy is on Rue de Ntaruka off Ave de Rusumo. The staff are abrupt and unhelpful. Visas must be applied for one week in advance and are only issued on Fridays. They cost about US$17 (RFr 1500), require two photographs and are valid for a stay of one month.

Kenya The embassy is on the Blvd de Nyabugogo just off the Place de l'Unité Nationale next to the Panafrique Hotel and is open Monday to Friday from 8.30 am to 12 noon and 2 to 4.30 pm. Visas cost about US$5, require two photographs and are issued in 15 minutes to one hour. No onward tickets or minimum funds are asked for.

Tanzania The embassy is on Ave Paul VI close to the junction of Ave de Rusumo. Visas generally take a week to issue though you can often get one in 24 hours if you enlist the assistance of your embassy (some embassies will do this, others won't). Other travellers who have spent a lot of time hassling on their own generally make it in less than a week but, if you do this, you may need to show an onward ticket.

There is a scale of charges for visas depending on your nationality. They seem to be the lowest for French nationals at about US$8, a little higher for the Germans and Swiss while for others they're between US$15 and US$17. Two photographs are needed and the visas are usually for a single-entry three-month stay.

Uganda The embassy is on Rue de Kalisimbi opposite the post office. It's open Monday to Friday from 8 am to 12 noon and 2 to 5 pm but visa applications are only accepted on Monday, Wednesday and Friday. They are issued in 24 hours, cost about US$22, require two photographs and are valid for three months (multiple-entry). Transit visas (valid for six days) are free. Visas may be available at the Gatuna border (very easy-going) for about US$15 on demand but don't count on it.

Zaïre The embassy is on Rue Depute Kamuzinzi off Ave de Rusumo. One-month, single-entry visas cost US$10; two-month, multiple-entry visas cost US$17.50 and three-month, multiple-entry visas cost US$22.50. Four photographs are needed for any visa and they are generally issued in 24 hours. Generally travellers do not require a letter of recommendation from their embassy or an onward ticket but these regulations change from time to time.

In addition there are embassies for Belgium, Egypt, France, Germany (West), Switzerland and the USA. There's also a British Consulate at 55 Ave Paul VI.

MONEY

US$ 1 = RFr 78
UK£ 1 = RFr 130

The unit of currency is the Rwandan franc = 100 centimes (you're very unlikely to come across centimes). These official bank rates fluctuate according to the international currency markets (the Rwandan franc is tied to the Eurodollar).

Travellers with only travellers' cheques are at a considerable disadvantage in this country since the commission rates at banks for these are little short of outright banditry. Even at the Banque Commerciale de Rwanda in Kigali it is RFr 250 per transaction. In other banks expect RFr 370 per transaction. This commission is charged regardless of the amount changed.

The moral of the story is to bring cash to Rwanda and change it on the street market or in the shops. The best rates are to be found in Kigali and Cyangugu (around US$1 = RFr 115 to RFr 120) and Gatuna (US$1 = RFr 110). The rates in Gisenyi are relatively poor (around US$1 = RFr 105) probably because there are a lot of rich expatriate Belgians who come here for their holidays and have more money than sense.

The street market in Kigali is more or less controlled by a few individuals and, if you find it, you'll get up to 40% above the official rates. Try walking around the Rue du Travail or the Blvd de la Révolution. You can often change money in *matatus* on the way to Kigali. Expect around US$1 = RFr 120 in Gisenyi and Rusumo, US$1 = RFr 110 in Gatuna and Kigali and US$1 = RFr 100 in Ruhengeri.

Travellers' cheques can also be changed on the black market but the rate is poor (less than 10% above the official rate) though at least you avoid bank commission charges. The Banque Nationale de Kigali will change US dollar bank cheques into US dollar travellers' cheques for a 1% commission (they will be Bank America travellers' cheques). Rwandan banking hours are Monday to Friday from 8 to 11 am. Outside these hours, armed only with travellers' cheques you are in dire straits. Currency declaration forms are not issued at the border.

Rwanda is an expensive country. The national parks, in particular, will burn a hole in your pocket.

POST

The poste restante in Kigali is quite well organised. They'll give you piles of letters corresponding to the first letters of both your given name and surname to sort through. You're unlikely to miss anything sent to you for collection, including parcels. Each letter collected will cost RFr 20. The overseas postal rates are quite high.

HEALTH

As with most African countries take

precautions against malaria whilst in Rwanda.

Expatriate residents suggest that if you get sick in Rwanda you should be extremely careful especially if the treatment involves a blood transfusion. A recent study of prostitutes in this country indicated that around 80% of them carry the AIDS antibody. If you think you'll need any injections buy your own disposable syringe.

There are certain parts of Lake Kivu where it is very dangerous to swim as volcanic gases are released continuously from the bottom and, in the absence of a wind, tend to collect on the surface of the lake. Quite a few people have been asphyxiated as a result.

Bilharzia is also a risk in Lake Kivu so stay away from shore areas where there is a lot of reedy vegetation. The same goes for slow-moving rivers.

It's advisable not to drink tap water. Purify all water used for drinking except that obtained from mountain streams and springs above any human habitation. Soft drinks, fruit and beer are available in the smallest places.

Other than this, Rwanda is a fairly healthy place to live as much of the country is considerably higher than neighbouring Tanzania, Uganda and Zaïre. Mosquitoes are not a problem.

Cholera vaccination certificates are compulsory for entry or exit by air. Entering overland the check is cursory but they do ask about it.

FILM & PHOTOGRAPHY

Bring all your own equipment and film as they are very expensive to buy. If you have to buy film the choice will be extremely limited. Don't take photographs of anything connected with the government or the military (post offices, banks, bridges, border posts, barracks, prisons, dams, etc). Your film and maybe your equipment will be confiscated.

LANGUAGE

The national language is Kinyarwanda. The official languages are Kinyarwanda and French. You'll be able to get along in most areas with French. Little English is spoken though Swahili can be useful in some regions.

Getting There & Around

There are no railways in Rwanda. Possible entry points are by air and road. There are lake ferries on both the Rwandan and Zaïrois sides of Lake Kivu but they connect only their respective sides of the lake.

AIR

International airlines flying into Rwanda are Air Burundi, Air France, Air Tanzania, Air Zaïre, Ethiopian Airlines and Sabena. Plane tickets bought in Rwanda for international flights are very expensive and compare poorly with what is on offer in Nairobi.

Internally, Air Rwanda flies from Kigali to Butare, Gisenyi, Kamembe and Ruhengeri. The flights to Butare and Gisenyi are subject to demand (you go onto stand-by and, if there are enough passengers, the plane will leave). There is at least one daily flight to Kamembe and flights to Ruhengeri on Tuesday, Friday and Saturday. The planes are Twin Otters.

ROAD

Rwanda used to be a rough country to travel through by road. This is no longer the case. There are now excellent sealed roads from the Gatuna and Cyanika (Uganda) borders to Kigali; Kigali to Ruhengeri and Gisenyi; Kigali to Bujumbura (Burundi) via Butare; and Kayanza and Kigali to the Tanzanian border. The Butare to Cyangugu road should be completely sealed by the time you read this. The government has also placed a high priority on sealing the Ruhengeri to Gitarama and Gitarama to Kibuye roads.

There are plenty of modern, well-maintained minibuses serving all these these routes (many of them bearing the Japan/Rwanda assistance programme logo). You can almost always find one of these going your way between dawn and about 3 pm (depending on the distance) from the *gare routière* in any town. Destinations are displayed in the front window and the fares are fixed (ask other passengers if you're not sure). Minibuses leave when full and this means when all the seats are occupied unlike in Kenya, Uganda, and Tanzania where most of the time they won't leave until you can't breathe for the people sitting on your lap and jamming the aisle. There should be no charge for baggage.

Shared taxis are also available though there's often little advantage in taking one rather than a minibus. Private taxis are expensive.

Some sample fares and journey times on minibuses are:

Gatuna (Ugandan border) to Kigali – RFr 250, about 2½ hours, beautiful journey through many tea plantations
Cyanika to Ruhengeri – RFr 100
Kigali to Ruhengeri – RFr 300, about two hours, magnificent ascents and descents over the intensively cultivated mountains between these two places
Kigali to Butare – RFr 400, about three hours
Kigali to Kibuye – RFr 400, the road is part-sealed
Kigali to Gitarama – RFr 200
Ruhengeri to Gisenyi – RFr 150, about 1½ hours, beautiful journey through upland forest, villages and finally panoramic views of Lake Kivu as you descend into Gisenyi
Kigali to Kibungo – RFr 300, about 2½ hours, a rucksack may cost half as much again on this route
Kibungo to Rusumo – pick-up for RFr 150
Gitarama to Kibuye – RFr 250
Gitarama to Butare – RFr 200

Butare to Cyangugu – RFr 700 (though this should get cheaper when the road is sealed)

For those hitching, it may be useful to know the province abbreviations on the vehicle licence plates. They are:

AB	– Kigali	FB	– Kibuye
BB	– Gitarama	GB	– Gisenyi
CB	– Butare	HB	– Ruhengeri
DB	– Gikongoro	IB	– Byumba
EB	– Cyangugu	JB	– Kibungo

If you are looking for a lift on a truck to either Uganda, Kenya, Burundi or Zaïre from Kigali go to the STIR truck park in the Gikondo suburb about two to three km from the centre. You can have your pick from scores of trucks at the customs clearance depot. To get there head down Blvd de l'OUA and turn right when you see the sign. It's sometimes possible to find a free lift all the way to Mombasa.

BOAT

The ferries on Lake Kivu used to connect Rwandan ports with Zaïrois ports but these days Rwandan ferries only call at Rwandan ports and Zaïrois ferries only at Zaïrois ports. The small modern motor ferry, *Nyungwe*, covers the route Cyangugu, Kirambo, Kibuye, Gisenyi leaving Cyangugu at 7 am on Wednesday and Saturday. (In the opposite direction make enquiries at the Hotel Izuba-Meridien.) Watch out for thieves on the boats.

Fares and times are:

Gisenyi to Cyangugu – RFr 780, takes 9½ hours
Gisenyi to Kibuye – RFr 215, takes about three hours
Kibuye to Cyangugu – RFr 520, takes about 6½ hours

TO/FROM BURUNDI

The main crossing point between Rwanda and Burundi is via Kayanza on the Butare to Bujumbura road. The road is sealed all the way. There are Peugeot shared taxis between Butare and the border for about US$4, and minibuses from there to Kayanza on Tuesday, Friday and Sunday for about US$1.25 (otherwise hire a taxi). There are daily minibuses from Kayanza to Bujumbura for about US$2.90.

TO/FROM TANZANIA

Getting into Tanzania from Rwanda is now much easier than it used to be. First take a minibus to Kibungo (RFr 350). From there a shared taxi to the border at Rusumo (Chutes de Rusumo) (RFr 200) or take the direct bus from Kigali to Rusumo at 7 am. From Rusumo you will have to hitch a ride to Ngara or Lusahanga. The Lusahanga, Rusumo, Kigali road is the main one used by petrol trucks supplying Kigali and Bujumbura so there's plenty of traffic.

From Ngara, there's a bus (usually daily) to Mwanza via Lusahanga which sets off very early in the morning around 4 am and costs TSh 400. It arrives after dark. The buses are operated by the New El-Jabry Bus Co in Mwanza. There's the possibility, that if you get a ride with a truck driver in Rusumo you could go all the way to Dar es Salaam or Mwanza.

Lusahanga is an overnight truck-stop for all these petrol tanker drivers and it is where the tarmac road starts.

If coming into Rwanda from Tanzania get the bus from Mwanza to Ngara but make sure you get off at Lusahanga. The buses leave Mwanza (usually daily) at 4 am and arrive after dark. To make sure you catch the bus, stay at the *Penda Guest House* in Mwanza right next to the bus terminal. It's a dump and costs TSh 340 for a room but it's convenient.

Other travellers have suggested it is much easier to arrange all this in Kigali at the truck park. If you're interested, take a minibus (marked 'Gikondo') from the Place de l'Unité Nationale in Kigali about three km down the Blvd de l'OUA (RFr 20) to the STIR truck park and ask around there. There are a lot of trucks leaving daily around 9 am for Tanzania from this place. Most of the drivers are Somalis and, if you strike up a rapport with them, you may get a free lift all the way to a major city in Tanzania. If not, it'll be about US$20 from Kigali to Mwanza.

TO/FROM UGANDA

Between Rwanda and Uganda there are two main crossing points: Katuna-Gatuna (from Kabale) to Kigali and Cyanika (from Kisoro) to Ruhengeri. If going from Rwanda to Uganda, make sure you get there before 11 am as there is an hour's time difference between Rwanda and Uganda (so 11 am in Rwanda is 12 noon in Uganda) and the Ugandans take a *long* lunch break. The Gatuna border is very easy-going and is only 100 metres from the Ugandan post. There are frequent minibuses from the border to Kabale which take about 30 minutes and cost about US$0.30 (at the street exchange rate).

TO/FROM ZAÏRE

The two main crossing points between Rwanda and Zaïre are between Gisenyi and Goma (at the northern end of Lake Kivu) and Cyangugu and Bukavu (at the southern end of Lake Kivu). These borders are open (for non-Africans) between 6 am and 6 pm. For Africans they are open from 6 am until 12 midnight. There are two border crossing points between Gisenyi and Goma – the 'Poids Lourds' crossing (a rough road) along the main road north of the ritzy part of town, and a sealed road along the lake shore. It's only two to three km either way. Minibuses run to the border along the Poids Lourds route but not along the lake shore. Along this route you will have to hitch or walk.

If you have a camera the Zaïrois officials may try to extract a 'fee' for this. We suggest you ask a lot of questions and sweat this one out. It goes straight into their back pockets. The 'fee' is nonsense. If you pay, you'll be handed a 'receipt' written on official paper headed 'Republic of the Congo' with 'Congo' crossed out and 'Zaïre' substituted in handwriting. Buy them a bottle of beer instead.

Around the Country

BUTARE

Butare is the intellectual centre of Rwanda. The **National Museum** is worth a visit for its ethnology and archaeology displays. They will also be able to tell you if any folklore dances have been planned. These dances often take place at the **Institut National de Recherche Scientifique** (INRS) – National Institute for Scientific Research. The **National University** is also here. Those interested in trees should visit the **Arboretum de Ruhande**.

In the surrounding area there are a number of craft centres such as **Gihinda-muyaga** (10 km) and **Gishamvu** (12 km). If you're thinking of buying anything at these places first have a look at quality and prices of what's for sale at the two top-end hotels in town, the Hotel Ibis and Hotel Faucon.

Places to Stay & Eat

One of the cheapest hotels is the *Hotel Chez Nous* which costs RFr 500/600 a single/double. Similar, but somewhat more expensive is the *Hotel Weekend* next to the market and petrol station (where the minibuses depart). This costs RFr 600/1000 a single/double. Many travellers, however, stay at the *Procure de Butare* which is a very attractive building surrounded by flower gardens. It costs RFr 400 per person and, although they do have double and triple rooms, usually only singles are available. They serve breakfast and excellent dinners (three courses, all-you-can-eat). There are no signs for this place so ask directions.

CYANGUGU

At the southern end of Lake Kivu and close to Bukavu (Zaïre), Cyangugu is an attractively located town and an important centre for the processing of tea and cotton. Nearby is the **Rugege Forest**, home to elephant, buffalo, leopard, chimpanzee and many other mammals as well as numerous birds, the waterfalls of the Rusizi River and the hot springs of Nyakabuye. It's also the ferry departure point for other Rwandan towns on Lake Kivu – Kibuye and Gisenyi.

Places to Stay

A convenient place if you're taking the ferry to Kibuye or Gisenyi (which departs at 7 am) is the *Hotel des Chutes* though it's quite expensive at RFr 1300 a single.

Some travellers have suggested that rather than stay in Cyangugu, it's better to head for Kamembe Market where cheap lodging is available.

GISENYI

Gisenyi is a resort town for rich Rwandans and expatriate workers and residents. Their beautifully landscaped villas, plush hotels and clubs take up virtually the whole of the Lake Kivu frontage and are quite a contrast to the African township on the hillside above. For those with the money, there's a wide variety of water sports available, nightclubs and restaurants. For those without, there are magnificent views over Lake Kivu and, looking north-west, the 3470-metre-high volcano of Nyiragongo. Swimming and sunbathing on the sandy beach are also free.

Information

There is no Zaïrois consulate so you must obtain your visa elsewhere if intending to go to Zaïre. The nearest embassy is in Kigali. Moneychangers (cash transactions only) approach all incoming minibuses. The rest of the time they can be found around the petrol station on the main street close to the market and the craft shops at the back of the Hotel Izuba-Meridien.

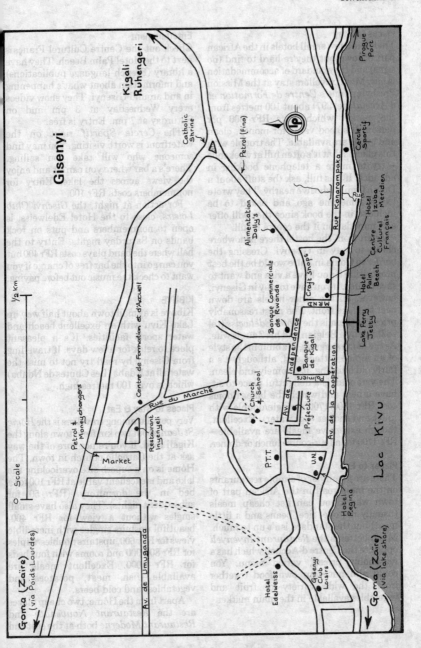

Gisenyi

Kigali
Ruhengeri

Goma (Zaïre)
(via Poids Lourdes)

Goma (Zaïre)
(via lake shore)

Lac Kivu

½ km

0   Scale

Catholic Shrine

Petrol (Fina)

Rue Konarampaka

Cercle
Sportif

Pirogue
Port

Rue

Hotel
Izuba
Meridien

Centre
Culturel
Français

Alimentation
Dolly's

Hotel Palm
Beach

Craft Shops

M.R.N.D

Lake Ferry
Jetty

Banque Commerciale
de Rwanda

Banque
de Kigali

Rue de
l'Indépendence

Church +
School

Premiers

Av. de la
Coopération

Préfecture

Av. de la Coopération

P.T.T.

U.N.

Hotel
Regina

Centre de Formation et d'Accueil

Rue du Marché

Restaurant
Ingenyeli

Petrol +
Moneychangers

Market

Av. de Umugaada

Hotel
Edelweiss

Gisenyi
Club Loisirs

Places to Stay

There are a few small hotels in the African part of town but they're hard to find (no signs) and the standard of accommodation is low. Most travellers stay at the Mission Presbytérienne's *Centre de Formation et d'Acceuil* (tel 397) about 100 metres from the market which costs RFr 300 per person. It's good value for money, clean and meals are available. The trouble with this place is that it's often full at weekends – try to make a telephone booking in advance. If it is full, ask the staff about a Dutch family who live nearby. They wrote to us sometime ago and asked to be included in the book since they will offer accommodation if the centre is full.

Apart from the hostel there is nowhere cheap to stay in Gisenyi. Crossing the border to Goma in Zaïre would be the best proposition if you have a visa and want to save money. If you have to stay in Gisenyi, however, all the other hotels are down near the lake front. The most reasonably priced of them is the *Hotel Edelweiss* (tel 282) run by a Belgian and his Zaïrois wife. As the name suggests, it's built in the style of an alpine cottage and, although it's a fairly old building, it's homely and clean. The verandah is a delightful place to sit, have a beer and watch the lake. Rooms cost RFr 1300/1700 a single/double with toilet and shower (hot water). Excellent, though expensive meals are available – RFr 1100 for a four-course lunch or dinner.

Places to Eat

There are a number of simple restaurants on the main road in the African part of town where you can get cheap meals (usually matoke, rice, beans and a little meat) but the standard isn't up to much. Much better is the *Restaurant Inyenyeli* opposite the Centre d'Accueil which has a reasonably priced, varied menu. You could also put your own food together from the wide variety of fruit and vegetables available in the main market.

Entertainment

Check out the Centre Culturel Français next to the Hotel Palm Beach. They have a library (French-language publications) and information about what's happening in and around Gisenyi. They show videos every Wednesday at 3 pm and on Saturday at 7 pm. Entry is free.

The *Cercle Sportif* right on the waterfront is worth visiting. You may find someone who will take you sailing. There's a bar where you can sit and enjoy the views across the lake. Entry for nonmembers costs RFr 100.

For action at night, the *Gisenyi Club Loisirs*, close to the Hotel Edelweiss, is open to nonmembers and puts on rock bands on Saturday nights. Entry to the hall where the band plays costs RFr 400 but you can go into the bar free of charge if you want to check the music out before paying.

KIBUYE

Kibuye is a small town about half way up Lake Kivu with an excellent beach and water sports facilities. It's a pleasant place to relax for a few days. If travelling from Gisenyi by road try not to miss the **waterfall** at Ndaba (Les Chutes de Ndaba) which is over 100 metres high.

Places to Stay & Eat

Very popular among travellers is the *Hôme St Jean* about two km from town along the Kigali road. If you're not sure of the way ask at the Catholic church in town. The Hôme is on a superb site overlooking the lake and is excellent value at RFr 100 for a bed in the dormitory (RFr 50 for subsequent nights). They also have small singles without a view for RFr 400, beautiful upstairs singles with incredible views for RFr 600, upstairs doubles/triples for RFr 800/900 and rooms with four beds for RFr 1000. Excellent meals are available (fish, meat, potatoes and vegetables) and cold beers.

Apart from the Hôme, two cheap places are the *Restaurant Nouveauté* and *Restaurant Moderne* both at the east end of town. They have the same menu (goat stew, beans, rice, potatoes, omelettes) and you can eat well from around RFr 30. Cold beers and sodas are available.

KIGALI

The tourist organisation describes Rwanda as the 'Land of Eternal Spring'. It's a very appropriate description and Kigali, the capital, displays it to the full. Built on a ridge and extending right down into the valleys on either side, it's a small but beautiful city full of an incredible variety of flowering trees and shrubs. From various points on the ridge there are superb views over the surrounding intensively cultivated and terraced countryside. The mountains and hills seem to stretch forever and the abundant rainfall keeps them a lush green.

Information

The national tourist office, Office Rwandais du Tourisme et des Parcs Nationaux (tel 6514), BP 905, Kigali, is on the Place de l'Indépendence on the far side from the post office (PTT). It's open every day including public holidays from 7 am to 9 pm. They have a lot of free leaflets (all in French) about the mountain gorillas, the volcanoes and other areas of interest. There are other booklets/leaflets for sale such as the *Passeport Touristique* (about US$3 – not worth it) and the *Parc National de l'Akagera* (worth it if you are going there). Detailed maps of Rwanda (but not of Kigali) can be bought, though they're pretty expensive. You must make your reservations here to see the mountain gorillas in the Parc National des Volcans (except for those groups which don't require prior reservation). To be dealt with in a civil manner you must speak French. Budget travellers are often virtually ignored.

Street maps of Kigali can be bought from bookshops for about US$1. Immigration is on the Ave du Commerce next door to the Air France office in a building set back from the road. There are a few bookshops in Kigali with predominantly French-language publications. The best is probably that on the Ave de la Paix close to the junction with the Ave des Milles Collines. The US Embassy has a library (English-language books only) and will exchange books on weekdays from 8 am to 12 noon and 2 to 4 pm.

The international airport is at Kanombe, 12 km from the city centre. A taxi will cost RFr 1000 but you can get there cheaper by taking a minibus to Kabuga (RFr 30) and getting off at the airport turn-off. It's a 500-metre walk from there.

Places to Stay

Most travellers stay at the *Auberge d'Accueil* (tel 5625) at the Eglise Presbytérienne au Rwanda, 2 Rue Deputé Kayuku. The staff are very friendly and the accommodation excellent though there is only cold water in the showers. It costs RFr 300 for a bed in the dormitory and RFr 550/1100 for a single/double. The private rooms have a wash basin and clean sheets are provided. There's no objection to you doing your own laundry. Breakfast is available (good value). Soft drinks and beer can be obtained from the bar which is usually open in the early evening (otherwise ask one of the staff). The Auberge closes at 10 pm except by prior arrangement.

Equally popular, though a considerable way from the centre of town, is the guesthouse (tel 6340) at the *Eglise Episcopale au Rwanda*, 32 Ave Paul VI. The rooms are clean and bright and there are plenty of them so you should always be able to find accommodation. There's hot water in the showers every day and a large laundry area. A bed in one of the six triple rooms costs RFr 500 including breakfast (eggs, bread, coffee or tea). The three double rooms cost RFr 800 without breakfast. Lunch and dinner are available and there's a small shop in the compound.

The Mission Catholique, Blvd de l'OUA, no longer accepts travellers.

The cheapest available hotel is the *Lodgement Metropole* (part of the

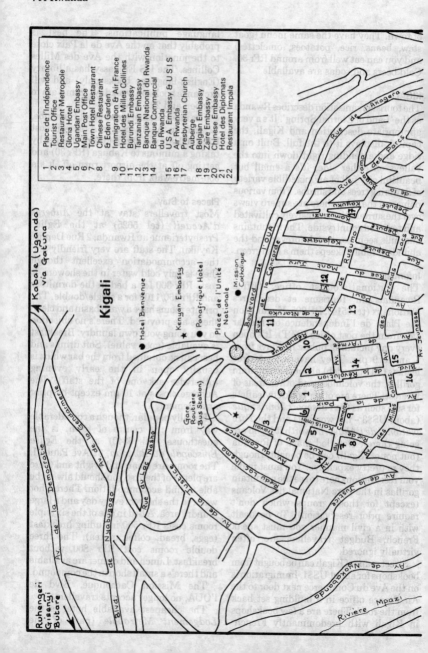

Kigali

1 Place de l'Indépendence
2 Tourist Office
3 Restaurant Metropole
4 Gloria Hotel
5 Ugandan Embassy
6 Main Post Office
7 Town Hotel Restaurant
8 Chinese Restaurant & Eden Garden
9 Immigration & Air France
10 Hotel des Milles Collines
11 Burundi Embassy
12 Tanzanian Embassy
13 Banque National du Rwanda
14 Banque Commercial du Rwanda
15 U S A Embassy & U S I S
16 Air Rwanda
17 Presbyterian Church
18 Belgian Embassy
19 Zaire Embassy
20 Chinese Embassy
21 Hotel des Diplomats
22 Restaurant Impala

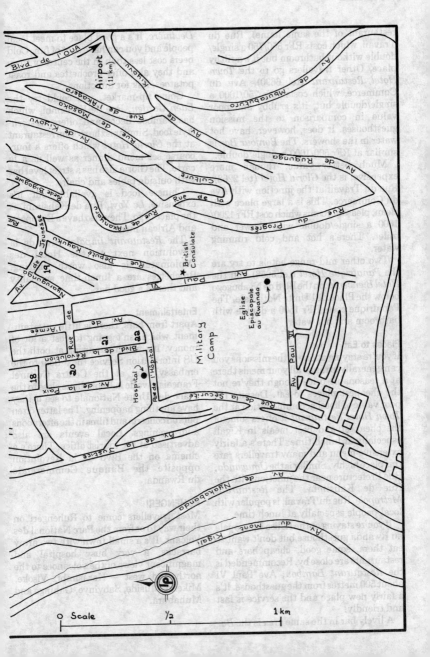

restaurant of the same name), Rue du Travail, which costs RFr 550/750 a single/double without bathroom but it's a filthy place. Other travellers go to the *Town Hotel Restaurant* (tel 6690), Ave du Commerce, which costs RFr 750/1000 a single/double but, it's grubby and poor value in comparison to the mission guesthouses. It does, however, have hot water in the showers. The *Bonjour Bar* is similar at RFr 500/1000 a single/double.

Much better value, though more expensive, is the *Gloria Hotel* (tel 2268), Rue du Travail at the junction with Ave du Commerce. This is a large place with clean, pleasant rooms which cost RFr 1200/1600 a single/double with shower and toilet. There's hot and cold running water.

Two other mid-range hotels to try are the *Panafrique Hotel* (tel 5056) and the *Hotel Bienvenue* on the Blvd de Nyabugogo below the Place de l'Unité Nationale. The Panafrique costs RFr 1500 a double with bathroom and hot water.

Places to Eat
If you're staying at one of the missions you can generally arrange all your meals there at a reasonable price though they're not the cheapest places to eat. Despite the poor value of hotel accommodation at the *Town Hotel Restaurant* it offers some of the cheapest and best meals in Kigali especially at lunch time. There's a fairly extensive menu and many travellers rate this place highly. Similar is the *Umuganda*, Rue Prefecture near the junction with the Rue de Kalisimbi. The *Restaurant Metropole*, Rue du Travail, is popular with local people especially at lunch time.

If you're staying at the Eglise Episcopale au Rwanda guesthouse but don't want to eat there, some good, cheap bars and restaurants are close by. Recommended is the *Restaurant Bambou*, Ave Paul VI about 500 metres from the guesthouse. It's a fairly new place and the service is fast and friendly.

A lively bar in the same area is the *Bar Devinière*. It's a good place to meet local people and you can have a lot of fun. Cold beers cost less than in the centre of town and they also offer brochettes and roast potatoes. Ask for directions.

Going up-market, you could try the *Eden Garden*, Rue de Kalisimbi, which has bamboo decor and offers western-style food. Similar is the rooftop restaurant at the *Gloria Hotel* which offers a four-course set menu dinner as well as à la carte. The Gloria also has a street level bar with outside tables and chairs.

Chinese food is available but it's expensive. *Le Yoyi*, Rue de Kalisimbi, is the place to go. They also have a European and African menu.

The *Restaurant Impala*, Blvd de la Révolution next to the Hotel des Diplomates, is also worth visiting. Brochettes are a lunch-time speciality and there's a good bar.

Entertainment
Apart from bars, there is little entertainment which isn't going to cost a lot of money. It's worth enquiring at both the US Information Service (next door to the embassy) and at the Centre Culturel Français, Ave de la République close to the Place de l'Unité Nationale to see if they have anything happening. The latter often puts on concerts and films in the afternoons and evenings. Local events are also advertised at the tourist office. There's a cinema on the Blvd de la Révolution opposite the Banque Commerciale du Rwanda.

RUHENGERI
Most travellers come to Ruhengeri on their way to or from the Parc National des Volcans. It's a small town with two army barracks, a very busy hospital and magnificent views of the volcanoes to the north and west – Karasimbi, Visoke, Mikeno, Muside, Sabyinyo, Gahinga and Muhabura.

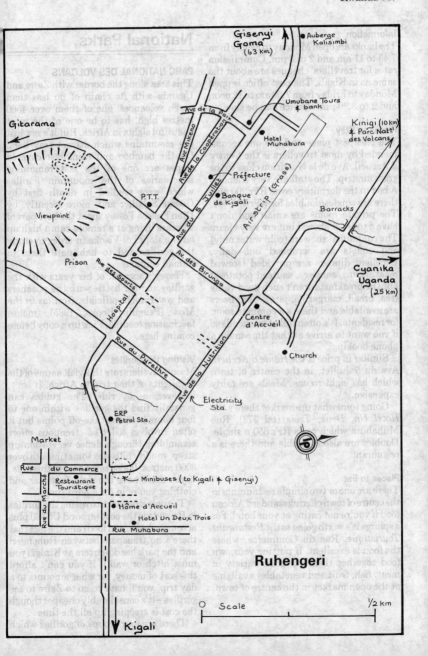

Ruhengeri

Information

The banks are open Monday to Friday from 7.45 to 11 am and 2 to 3 pm. Commission rates for travellers' cheques are about the same as in Kigali. The post office is open Monday to Friday from 7.30 am to 12 noon and 2 to 3.30 pm. Service can be slow.

Places to Stay

The cheapest place and the one recommended by most travellers is the *Centre d'Accueil*, Ave de la Nutrition close to the grass airstrip. The staff are very friendly. A bed in the dormitory costs RFr 200 plus there are singles/doubles for RFr 400/600. The private rooms are small and don't have a toilet or shower but are very clean. The communal showers (cold water only) and toilets are scrubbed out daily. Excellent dinners are provided (stewed meat, beans, cabbage, sautéed potatoes) but the breakfasts aren't such good value (tea, bread, margarine, jam). Cold beers are available and there's a common room for residents. It's often full at weekends so if you want to arrive at that time make a phone booking.

Similar in price is the *Hôme d'Accueil*, Ave du 5 Juillet, in the centre of town which has eight rooms. Meals are fairly expensive.

Going somewhat up-market there's the *Hotel Un, Deux, Trois* (tel 373), Rue Muhabura which costs RFr 650 a single. Doubles are also available and there is a restaurant.

Places to Eat

There are one or two simple restaurants in the centre of town offering standard African food if you're not eating at your hotel. For a splurge it's worth going to the *Restaurant Touristique*, Rue du Commerce, where the food is excellent. If putting your own food together there's a good variety of meat, fish, fruit and vegetables available at the open market in the centre of town.

National Parks

PARC NATIONAL DES VOLCANS

This area along the border with Zaïre and Uganda with its chain of no less than seven volcanoes, one of them over 4500 metres high, has to be one of the most beautiful sights in Africa. But it's not just the mountains which attract travellers. On the bamboo and rainforest covered slopes are one of the last remaining sanctuaries of the mountain gorillas which were studied in depth first by George Schaller and, more recently, by Dian Fossey. Fossey spent the best part of 13 years living at a remote camp high up on the slopes of Visoke in order to study the gorillas and to habituate them to human contact.

Fossey's account of her years with the gorillas and her battle with the poachers and government officials, *Gorillas in the Mist* (Penguin Books, 1985), makes fascinating reading. Pick up a copy before coming here.

Visiting the Gorillas

Many travellers rate this visit as one of the highlights of their trip to Africa. It isn't, however, a joy ride. The guides can generally find the gorillas within one to four hours from the take-off points but it often involves a lot of strenuous effort scrambling through dense vegetation up steep, muddy hillsides sometimes to over 3000 metres. It also rains a lot in this area. If you don't have the right footwear and clothing you're in for a hard time.

The only drawback to seeing the gorillas in Rwanda is the cost (around US$60 plus accommodation and food) and the fact that there's no transport between Ruhengeri and the park headquarters at Kinigi (you must hitch or walk). If you can't afford this sort of money, for what amounts to a day trip, you'll have to go to Zaïre to see gorillas – it's considerably cheaper though the cost is creeping up all the time.

There are four groups of gorillas which

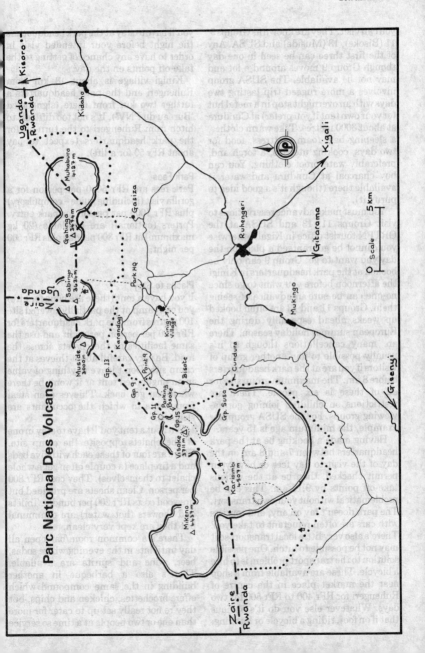

Parc National Des Volcans

you can visit. They are known as Groups 9, 11 (Bisoke), 13 (Muside) and SUSA. Any of the first three can be seen in one day though Group 9 moves around a lot and may not be available. The SUSA group involves a more rugged trip lasting two days with an overnight stop in a metal hut (or your own tent if you prefer) at Cundura at about 3000 metres. Take warm clothes, a sleeping bag, foam mattress, food for two days, cooking utensils, a torch and, preferably waterproof clothing. You can buy charcoal at Cundura and water is available there (though it's a good idea to purify it).

You must make advance reservations to visit Groups 11, 13 and SUSA at the ORTPN tourist office in Kigali otherwise you cannot be guaranteed a place on the day you want to go. Group 9 can only be booked at the park headquarters in Kinigi the afternoon before you want to go since no-one can be sure in advance of seeing them. Groups 11 and 13 are often booked up weeks ahead especially during the European summer holiday season. There are many cancellations though so it's usually possible to join another group of visitors if you are at the park headquarters before 8 am. The maximum group size for all of these is six people. There are restrictions on children joining gorilla-viewing groups. For the SUSA group, for example, the minimum age is 15 years.

Having made a booking be at the park headquarters between 7 and 8 am on the day of the visit to pay fees or have your permit checked, then be at the various take-off points by 9.15 am. This can be problematical without your own transport. The park doesn't lay on any, and tourists with cars are often reluctant to take you. There's also very little local transport so it may not be possible to hitch. One possible solution to the transport problem is to hire a bicycle. These are available from a shop near the market place in the centre of Ruhengeri for RFr 400 to RFr 500 for two days. Whatever else you do it's obvious that if on foot, riding a bicycle or hitching,

you'll have to stay at the park headquarters the night before your intended visit in order to have any chance of getting to the take-off points on the day.

Kinigi village is about 18 km from Ruhengeri and the park headquarters a further two km from there (signposted 'Bureau du PNV'). It's not too difficult to hitch from Ruhengeri to the turn-off for the park headquarters (expect to pay about RFr 50 for a lift).

Park Fees
Park fees are RFr 5000 per person for a gorilla visit (including guide – compulsory) plus RFr 1000 per person for park entry. Porters (optional) are available (20 kg maximum) at RFr 300 per day plus RFr 500 per night.

Places to Stay
If you have a tent (there are none for hire) you can camp at the partially covered site 100 metres from the park headquarters for RFr 250 per person per night and use the same facilities as the chalets across the road. Be very careful about thieves at the camp site. Don't leave anything of value in an unguarded tent or it won't be there when you get back. Thieves even steal from tents in which the occupants are sleeping.

Without a tent you'll have to stay in one of the chalets opposite the camp site. There are four of these each with five beds and a fireplace (a couple often get a whole chalet to themselves). They cost RFr 800 per person. Clean sheets are provided but firewood costs RFr 200 per bundle. Toilets and showers (hot water) are communal but they are kept very clean.

There's a common room/bar open all day until late in the evening where sodas, beer, wine and spirits are available. There's also a barbeque in another building in the same compound which offers brochettes, chicken and chips, but they're not really set up to cater for more than one or two people at a time so service can be slow. Valuables left in the chalets appear to be safe.

Climbing the Volcanoes

There are a number of possibilities for trekking to the summit of one or more of the volcanoes in the park – from several hours to two days or more. For all of these a guide is compulsory (at the usual fee) but porters are optional. The ascents take you through some remarkable changes of vegetation ranging from thick forests of bamboo, giant lobelia or hagenia onto alpine meadows. If the weather is favourable you'll be rewarded with some spectacular views over the mountain chain.

Among the more popular treks are:

Visoke (3711 metres) Return trip six to seven hours (from Bisoke Parking).

Lake Ngezi (3000 metres) Return trip three to four hours (from Parking Bisoke).

Karisimbi (4507 metres) Return trip two days. There is a metal hut where you stay for the night at about 3660 metres (the key for this hut is available at Parking Bisoke).

Sabinyo (3634 metres) Return trip five to six hours (from the park headquarters at Kinigi). There's a metal hut just before the start of the lava beds.

Gahinga & Muhabura (3474 & 4127 metres respectively) Return trip two days (from Gasiza). There is a metal hut offering a modicum of shelter but it's in a bad state of repair.

PARC NATIONAL DE L'AKAGERA

Created in 1934 and covering an area of 2500 square km, Akagera is one of the least visited but most interesting wildlife parks in Africa. One of the reasons for this is its three distinct types of environment. Large areas of the park are covered with treeless savannah but there is an immense swampy area some 95 km long and between two and 20 km wide along the border with Tanzania. This contains six lakes and numerous islands, some of them covered with savannah, others with forest. Lastly, there is a chain of low mountains (ranging from 1618 metres to 1825 metres high) which stretches through much of the length of the park. The vegetation is variable ranging from short grasses on the summits to wooded savannah and dense thickets of xerophytic (ie adapted to a dry habitat) forest on the flanks.

As you might imagine, there's an extraordinary variety of animals to be seen and they're often much easier to find than in other wildlife parks. In just a two to three day trip you can usually come across topi, impala, roan antelope, giant eland, bushbuck, oribi, various types of duiker, buffalo, wart hog, red river hog, baboon, vervet monkeys, lion, leopard, hyena, zebra, hippo, crocodile and, at night, hare, palm civet, genet, galago (bushbaby) and giant crested porcupine. There are also herds of elephant. The best time to visit the park in terms of access is between mid-May and mid-September (the dry season). November and April are the wettest months.

The only trouble with getting to Akagera is that you need your own transport or need to join an organised safari. Safaris do not, as in Kenya and Tanzania, cater to budget travellers. Check out current car hire and safari prices in Kigali. Some companies are:

Rwanda Travel Service
    Hotel des Diplomates, 45 Blvd de la Révolution (tel 2210)
Umubano Tours Agency
    BP 1160, Kigali (tel 2176)
Agence Solliard
    2 Ave de la République, Kigali (tel 5660)

The best entry into the park is either at the Gabiro Hotel in the mid-north or the Akagera Hotel in the south but the quickest is the Nyamiyaga entrance about 16 km from the sealed road going through Kayonza.

Hiring a guide is a waste of money. You won't find any more animals with a guide than you will without. Take all your own food, drinking and washing water and fuel. It's best to assume you won't be able to get these in the park (fuel *may* be available at the hotels sometimes but they're very reluctant to sell it).

Park Fees

The park entry fees are RFr 1500 per person plus RFr 800 for a vehicle. Camping costs RFr 1000 per person. A guide costs RFr 500 per day.

Places to Stay

The hotels in the park are very expensive

(RFr 3100/4300 a single/double) so to keep costs down you'll have to camp. You can do this on good sites at both of the hotels. There are also designated camping sites at various other points inside the park but that's all they are – 'designated'. There are no facilities and no protection. Some people do camp out but it's not really recommended and can be dangerous (sleep in the car instead).

One exception to this is Plage Hippos, half way up the park close to the Tanzanian border. There are covered picnic tables, good waste bins and toilets but the site is no more protected than anywhere else.

São Tomé & Principe

Remote islands have always been a magnet for travellers and these two, in the Gulf of Guinea some 320 km off the coast of Gabon, are no exception. They constitute one of Africa's smallest countries and you could easily be forgiven for thinking that this chapter has somehow escaped from a guidebook to South America. The two volcanic islands, with a population of only 108,000, are a legacy of the Portuguese empire, achieving independence in 1975. The capital, the town of São Tomé has a population of 25,000. It's not easy to get there, but the few travellers who have made it describe the rugged, forested islands as among the most beautiful in the world.

Despite their relative obscurity, these islands have been of more than passing interest to the outside world. They were first sighted by Portuguese navigators between 1469 and 1472, and the town of São Tomé was founded in 1485. Principe was not settled until 1500.

The islands quickly became the largest sugar-producing country in the world, but in 1530 a Black revolt scared the plantation owners off to Brazil. However, slavery, on which the brief sugar boom had been built, remained the cornerstone of the colony's economy. São Tomé and Principe became staging posts for the slave trade between West Africa and the Americas. The coffee and cocoa plantations set up in the 18th and 19th centuries likewise depended on slave labour. Even when slavery was abolished in 1875, it was replaced by a system of forced labour with minimal wages.

The people of the islands, including those brought in to work the plantations from Angola, Mozambique and Cape Verde, fought the Portuguese on numerous occasions in a bid to win their freedom. Each time, the revolts were put down bloodily by the colonial forces. The worst example was the notorious massacre of 1953 when, in an attempt to suppress a strike, over 1000 plantation workers were gunned down by Portuguese troops on the orders of Governor-General Carlos Gorgulho. Despite the repression, the spirit of nationalism continued to grow. A liberation headquarters was set up in Libreville, Gabon, under the leadership of Pinto da Costa, and from there further strikes were organised.

With the fall of Salazar in Portugal in 1974, followed shortly afterwards by a mutiny of black troops, the colonial authorities were finally forced to come to terms with the liberation forces. A transitional government was set up in December 1974 to steer the country to independence. Even at that late date the Portuguese governor-general, in an attempt to ensure that a moderate post-independence government came to power, undertook a purge of radical elements, particularly those who had advocated nationalisation of the cocoa estates and the disbanding of the colonial army. It was a pointless exercise. When independence was declared in July 1975 there was a mass exodus of the 4000 or so Portuguese settlers who feared reprisals – just as they did in their other African colonies.

The European exodus left the country with virtually no skilled labour, a 90% illiteracy rate, only one African doctor and many abandoned cocoa plantations. An economic crisis was inevitable. Da Costa, until then a moderate, was forced to concede to many of the demands of the

sighted frequently in São Tomé's territorial waters and air space during 1978.

The invasion never took place, but resulted in the dispatch of 1000 Angolan troops to the islands to augment the 140 or so Cuban soldiers and advisors already there. Since then the country has strengthened its ties with the Marxist regime of Angola. The president of São Tomé, Manuel Pinto da Costa, along with other leaders of the party, has also made official visits to Cuba, East Germany and the USSR.

Nevertheless, the islands remain economically aligned with Western Europe. Their principal trading partners are still Portugal and the Netherlands (a traditional market for São Tomé's cocoa). Politically the country looks increasingly towards the communist world, and 75% of the islands' skilled labour is provided by Cuba. Much of the remaining labour force, in the form of teachers, technicians and agricultural experts, is provided by Portugal. Relations with Gabon remain tense as a result of President Bongo's support of da Graça, but this is treated with a degree of lassitude rarely to be found in other Marxist-leaning regimes.

more radical members of his government. The majority of the plantations were nationalised four months after independence, laws were passed prohibiting anyone from owning more than 100 hectares of land, and a people's militia was set up to operate in the workplaces and villages. Since independence the government's priorities have been to revive the cocoa industry (which accounts for the majority of the islands' export earnings) and to diversify into other areas.

Another major cause of the sharp turn to the left after independence was the fear of a Comoros-type invasion, or the one which nearly happened in the Seychelles. The fears were not entirely unjustified. Many São Tomé opposition figures, including the former health minister, Carlos da Graça, were living in exile in Gabon (a staunch pro-western country), and unidentified ships and planes were

Facts

VISAS
Visas are required by all. 'Tourists' are no longer officially forbidden and it is now much easier to get a tourist visa. The best place to obtain the visa is in Libreville (Gabon) where it is issued within 24 hours and costs CFA 7500.

To get a visa for business reasons you must provide proof of an invitation, usually a letter from the government. Expect considerable delays before a visa is issued.

There are embassies in Lisbon (Portugal), Conakry (Guinea), Libreville (Gabon) and Luanda (Angola). It's advisable to apply at one of the first three, since getting into Angola itself is quite a feat. One traveller suggested applying direct by registered letter to the Ministerio de Negocias Estrangeros, São Tomé. If you do it this way, you need to supply the following formidable list of details:

full name (and parents' family name if a married woman)
country, date and place of birth
nationality
sex
marital status
father's and mother's full name and nationality
passport number, type, date and place of issue and validity
permanent home address
profession
which employer/organisation you work for and your position
the nature of the business your employer/ organisation is involved in
if you have ever been to São Tomé before and, if so, the dates when you entered and left, and your residential address there
the names, nationalities, relationship, address and telephone number of any friends or relatives you have in São Tomé
your proposed date of entry, departure and length of stay
proposed place where you will stay and the address
the name of any religious or associated organisation you belong to
the reason for your proposed visit
the address to which a reply should be sent

If that seems excessive, you might be right, but the main reason for the poor success rate of visa applications by post is that not enough information is provided.

If granted a visa, you can pick it up on arrival. You must have a yellow fever vaccination before being allowed in. Exit visas are no longer required.

Travel around the island of São Tomé is no problem, but travel to Principe is subject to all manner of special provisions.

There are a lot of Russian, Cuban, East German and North Korean advisors on the islands, and the regime is very paranoid about 'imperialist' infiltration.

The fears of invasion have still not subsided, so use some discretion when wandering around. It's forbidden, for instance, to walk along the boulevard next to the sea in São Tomé town at night smoking a cigarette. You could be suspected of sending messages to submarines. Also, when the flag is raised you're supposed to stand still even if you can't see the flag but can hear a remote trumpet.

MONEY

US$ 1   = D 42.4   (official rate)
CFA 1000 = D 130

The unit of currency is the dobra = 100 centavos. There is a black market, but it's dangerous to trade in it here. While there are no restrictions on the import of local currency, export is limited to D 30,000.

Getting There & Around

The only regular air services to São Tomé are the weekly flights from Luanda by the national airline, Transportes Aéreos de São Tomé and by TAAP, the Angolan airline. TAP – Air Portugal – and Aeroflot also fly there. A return excursion fare from Luanda costs about US$225.

There are three flights per week from Libreville with Equatorial International Airlines. Representatives of organisations like the UN and the World Bank usually rent small planes in Libreville to take them to and from São Tomé. Ask around in Libreville at the offices of the UNPD or the European Development Fund. If you don't have any luck there, try the offices of Air Service and Air Affaires. If there's a spare seat going, it's more than likely you'll get on, and it's unlikely you'll have to pay. When you want to leave the island, ask around at the same offices in São Tomé or try the Russian, East German and Chinese embassies.

There is a ferry from Libreville which costs CFA 25,000 one-way, and from Douala

(Cameroun), which costs CFA 35,000 one-way.

Around the Islands

Unlike many other parts of Africa, all the roads are sealed and there's a good network of buses to almost everywhere. Buses are cheap at around D 1 per two km. Hitching is simplicity itself.

SÃO TOMÉ

The island is extremely beautiful. It's full of strange remnants of extinct volcanoes which look like huge pillars, some rising 600 metres straight up out of the jungle. The north of the island is drier with rolling hills and baobabs. The coasts are ringed with beautiful, deserted beaches of white sand fringed with palms, and the water is turquoise. The town of São Tomé itself is a picturesque, little place full of Portuguese colonial buildings and shady, colourful parks, and it's very, very clean.

Places to Stay & Eat

The *Boa Vista*, about 20 km from town, is often full (there are only 10 rooms) and costs D 750 per night. More than likely, one of the few western volunteers (Portuguese, Dutch and French) will invite you to stay with them, as they never see any tourists there.

There is now a tourist-class hotel, the *Hotel Miramar*. Singles/doubles cost US$70/80 and you must pay in US$. The hotel has a good restaurant.

Food can be a minor problem. The many once-filled shops are empty except for sardines and toilet paper, though things are improving. There's little bread, meat, soft drinks or cigarettes. At the market you can buy breadfruit, manioc and sometimes tiny tomatoes and pineapples.

There are three restaurants in São Tomé The *Omstep* is the cheapest, but you can only get one meal (usually rice or breadfruit with fish). Be sure to get there by 7 pm or there will be nothing left. Beer and coffee, when available, are cheap. The *Club Nautico* and *Celestino's* both have fixed menus and are similar in price. The Club Nautico also has a free swimming pool.

You can get good value meals in the pensions.

PRINCIPE

If you can persuade the authorities to allow you to go to Principe, there is a flight on a locally owned AN 245, which costs D 200. There is also a ferry run by Transcolmar.

At the *Residencia Official* you can stay for D 500 per night. It's quite smelly as it's near a tuna processing factory. Meals are available and will inevitably consist of fish.

Other than the crews of Russian trawlers which frequently visit the tuna processing plant, you'll probably be the only foreigner on the island. One traveller spent the afternoon lying on the beach drinking vodka with a Russian trawler crew to celebrate the fact that they'd found a foreigner there – the first time, apparently, in 18 visits!

Senegal

Senegal has been inhabited for many thousands of years, as the neolithic stone circles to be found in the country (and in The Gambia) bear witness. Its recorded history, however, began when part of it was ruled by the empire of Ghana between the 8th and 11th centuries. The rest of the country came under the control of the Tekrour empire which came together here in the 9th century and was converted to Islam shortly after as a result of Almoravide raids from Morocco. As these empires waned a new kingdom arose – the Djolof – during the 13th and 14th centuries, in the area between Cape Verde and the Senegal River. It was with this kingdom that Europeans had first contact.

Initial contact was through the Venetian, Cada Mosto, who, in 1455, was employed by the Portuguese prince, Henry the Navigator, to explore the coast of West Africa. Fifty years later a Portuguese explorer spent four years travelling through the country. On the basis of his reports, the Portuguese established a monopoly of trade with the Senegalese coastal kingdoms which was to last until the 16th century when they were displaced by the British, French and Dutch. These last three nations hoped to gain control of St Louis and Ile de Gorée, which were strategic points where slaves bound for the Americas could be collected. After changing hands several times, St Louis was finally secured by the French and a fort was built there in 1659. Although slaves formed the bulk of the trade, gold, ivory, leather and gum arabic were also purchased.

When slavery was finally abolished in the 19th century and the trade in gum arabic was on the decline, France turned to cultivating cash crops such as indigo and cotton, but the venture was unsuccessful because of the hostility of the inhabitants.

The expansion of the colony was largely the work of Louis Faidherbe who was appointed governor in 1854. He undertook the systematic conquest of the Senegal basin and developed the cultivation of groundnuts as the dominant cash crop of the area. His successor destroyed the rising power of al-Hajj Umar, a Tucolor, who, on his way back from Mecca, had married a daughter of the Sultan of Sokoto and raised a *jihad* (holy war) against the French and what he regarded as the decadence of his Islamic neighbours. By 1863 Umar had raised an army of 2000 and created an empire stretching from the land occupied by the French to Timbuktu. His downfall, however, was not so much due to French military superiority as to the penchant of his troops to plunder, which alienated the people who had been conquered and led to a number of uprisings against him.

The conquest of Senegal by the French was completed in the last decade of the 19th century and Dakar was built up as the administrative centre and showpiece of France's empire in West Africa. Roads, railways and port facilities were constructed and a university was opened. As early as 1848 Senegal had sent a deputy to the French parliament, but it wasn't until 1914 that the first black deputy, Blaise Diagne, was elected to the position.

The franchise was limited to the citizens of the four communes of St Louis, Gorée, Rufisque and Dakar. Diagne was soon to lose the support he had previously enjoyed as a result of his collaboration

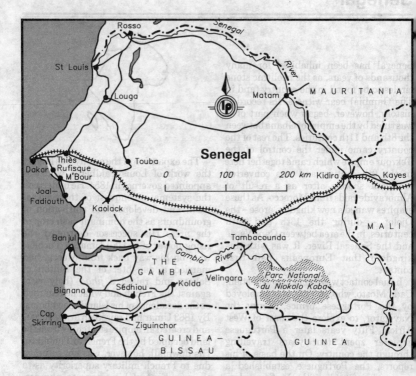

with French interests in the colony. A new generation of black politicians came to the fore, led by Lamine Gueye and Leopold Senghor. They campaigned for the granting of French citizenship to the colony's subjects, the abolition of forced labour, a general improvement in the standard of living, and repudiation of the right of the colonial authorities to hold in detention without trial anyone deemed subversive.

In the run-up to independence, Senegal joined French Sudan to form the Federation of Mali in early 1959. The Federation became independent in 1960 but, only two months later, Senegal seceded and declared itself independent as the Republic of Senegal under the presidency of Leopold Senghor. For many years after, Senegal followed a very

moderate course and was one of the few Black African states in favour of 'dialogue' with South Africa. It was apparent that not everyone was happy with the political set-up and, from time to time, student unrest exploded leading to violent demonstrations in the streets of Dakar. The government managed to contain most of their grievances but there were further crises when farmers refused to plant groundnuts in the late 1970s because of drought and falling prices on the world market. The World Bank also uncovered a racket whereby the state organisation responsible for the groundnut crop had been underpaying farmers for their crops.

At the end of 1980, Senghor stepped down as president and his place was taken by Abdou Diouf. Senghor nevertheless, remains head of the ruling party in Senegal.

There was further trouble for the government in 1984, once again centred around the farmers and the groundnut crop. The amount officially exported that year was the lowest on record since independence though, in actual fact, it could have been one of the largest ever. The reason for this was that an estimated 650,000 to 700,000 tonnes had been smuggled out of the country to Mali, Mauritania and The Gambia by disgruntled peasants – about three times the official exported amount! The loss of revenue forced the government to cut back its diversification projects though it did report overall growth in the fishing and phosphate industries.

Facts

GEOGRAPHY & CLIMATE

Senegal has suffered a great deal from the droughts which have affected the Sahel recently. North of the Gambia River much of the country is barren and unproductive. Wind erosion and increasing salinity have made the problem worse. Few crops can be grown in this area except on the flood plain of the Senegal River, where millet and groundnuts are cultivated. Irrigation projects now under way may help alleviate this problem and allow rice to be grown there, but it could also lead to increased salinity.

The best time to travel in Senegal is between December and May, when it is cool and dry. However, at this time of year be prepared for the Harmattan – a strong, dry wind which blows off the desert for lengthy periods of time.

PEOPLE

The population is around seven million, an eighth of whom live in Dakar. The main groups are the Wolofs (36%), the Fulani (18%) and the Serer (17%).

Nomadic groups include the Moors and the Bassaris.

VISAS

Visas are required by all except nationals of Belgium, France, Germany (West), Italy, Luxemburg and the Netherlands. Nationals of the UK and other EC countries spending less than one week in Senegal don't need a visa. Nationals of South Africa and Zimbabwe are not admitted.

There are Senegalese embassies in Addis Ababa (Ethiopia), Algiers (Algeria), Bissau (Guinea-Bissau), Cairo (Egypt), Conakry (Guinea), Lagos (Nigeria), Libreville (Gabon), Nouakchott (Mauritania), Rabat (Morocco), Tunis (Tunisia) and Yaoundé (Cameroun). Visas can be obtained from French embassies where there is no Senegalese embassy (eg Mali). They may, however, refuse to give Americans visas unless they're prepared to wait six to eight weeks. You are officially required to have an onward ticket but this is rarely enforced.

You can sometimes get into Senegal without a visa (where one is required). This is often true of the Senegal-Mali border if entering by train but expect a lot of hassle. There is no Senegalese consulate in Bamako (Mali), so you'll have to get a visa (where required) elsewhere. On the other hand, you won't be allowed entry at Rosso on the Senegal-Mauritania border without a visa.

Senegalese visas in Banjul (The Gambia) cost Da 22.25 (CFA 1000), require three photos, and take a few days to issue depending on demand. Senegalese visas are not being issued in Guinea-Bissau (though this may change).

Other Visas

Burkina Faso These are available from the French Embassy, 1 Rue El Haji Amadou Assane Ndoye on the corner with Rue Mage, Dakar. A one-month visa costs CFA 3000, with three photos and is issued in 24 hours.

Gabon Dakar is a good place to get a Gabon visa since there is no waiting and no hassles. They cost CFA 5000.

The Gambia The embassy is on Rue de Thiong. Visas cost CFA 4000, require two photos and are issued in 24 hours. You'll have seven to 14 days stamped on entry into The Gambia and this can be extended at Banjul or Basse.

Guinea The embassy is on Route de Quakam opposite the main hospital. Visas cost CFA 5000, require two photos and a letter of recommendation. They take 72 hours to issue. If you have a vehicle this costs CFA 2000 with photocopies of your driver's licence, ownership documents and insurance.

Ivory Coast Visas cost CFA 3000 for a 90-day single-entry visa and take 24 hours to issue.

Mali The embassy is at 46 Blvd de la République, opposite the cathedral in Dakar. A one-month visa costs CFA 5000, requires three photos and is issued the same day or within 24 hours.

Togo Visas are outrageously expensive in Dakar at CFA 10,000. Try to get them elsewhere.

MONEY
US$ 1 = CFA 284
UK£ 1 = CFA 535

The unit of currency is the CFA franc. There are no restrictions on the import of local currency. Export is limited to CFA 20,000. There is no black market.

Opening hours vary from bank to bank but are usually from 8.30 am to noon and from 2.30 to 4.30 pm. You can change money on Sunday in Dakar at the Chamber of Commerce office. In Dakar it's best to check around as rates vary and some banks don't charge commission. One such bank is the Banque Internationale pour le Commerce et l'Industrie du Sénégal on the Place de l'Indépendance. The BIAO Bank on the Place de l'Indépendance in Dakar allows withdrawals of up to CFA 45,000 on Mastercard (Access). In the smaller towns don't rely on being able to change travellers' cheques at the banks. The bank in Tambacounda gives a lousy rate and charges commission.

If you're heading for Guinea-Bissau you can buy pesos on the street in Ziguinchor at the rate of CFA 5000 = P 11,500.

Petrol costs CFA 325 a litre in Dakar.

LANGUAGE
French is the official language. Wolof is the most widely spoken African language.

Getting There & Around

AIR
There are no ferries to the Cape Verde Islands. The only way to get there is to fly. Air Senegal flies on Saturday and TACV (the Cape Verde airline) on Tuesday. The planes land on São Tiago Island. There are flights from Dakar to Casablanca for CFA 145,000 but some travellers have reported that it's cheaper to go to Nouakchott (Mauritania) and take a flight from there to Casablanca or from Nouadhibou to Las Palmas and from there to Agadir.

Student reductions of 40% are possible with Air Mali. Their office is close to the Mali Embassy on Ave Lamine Gueye.

For cheap charter flights to France, enquire at Nouvelles Frontières, Rue Sardinière. They can generally fix you up for CFA 100,000. Otherwise Aeroflot has similar flights for CFA 140,000.

ROAD
The main routes through Senegal run north-south from the Mauritanian border at Rosso to the Guinea-Bissau border at São Domingo via St Louis, Dakar, Kaolack, the Gambia River and Ziguinchor.

There are two possible routes between Kaolack and Ziguinchor. The direct road takes the Trans-Gambia highway, which cuts across the centre of The Gambia. (There is still no bridge across the Gambia River so you have to take a ferry.) The other route goes via the capital of The Gambia, Banjul, and requires taking the ferry across the Gambia River from Barra Point to Banjul.

West-east routes run from Dakar to Kayes (Mali) via Tambacounda and from Ziguinchor to Tambacounda via Kolda and Velingara. There are good networks of buses, taxis and trucks on these routes, though it's unlikely you'll take road transport if heading for Mali as the train is much more convenient.

Some examples of transport on these routes are:

Rosso (Mauritanian border) to St Louis – shared taxi costs CFA 1200 plus CFA 100 for luggage

St Louis to Dakar – minibus costs CFA 3000 and takes five hours

Dakar to Diourbel – truck costs CFA 1025

Diourbel to Touba – truck costs CFA 350

Dakar to Rufisque – city bus costs CFA 75

Rufisque to Kaolack – takes three hours in a minibus and costs CFA 1300

Dakar to Joal – bus costs CFA 900

Joal to M'Bour – taxi costs CFA 500

M'Bour to Kaolack – bus cost CFA 1000

Kaolack to Barra Point (The Gambia border) – bus costs CFA 1000 and taxi costs CFA 1300

Tambacounda to Kidira – costs CFA 5000 in a taxi. There is no hotel in Kidira if you're waiting for the train

TRAIN

Dakar to St Louis

There are trains three times per week in either direction on Tuesday, Thursday and Saturday from Dakar but make enquiries because they are sometimes cancelled. The fare is CFA 1485 (2nd class) and the journey takes about seven

hours. Make sure you're at the station at least an hour before the train is due to leave in order to have any chance of getting a seat.

Dakar to Bamako (Mali)

This is the most important railway line in the country and the one used by most travellers going between Senegal and Mali. The road link is hardly used at all.

There are two trains in both directions every week. They are scheduled to depart in either direction on Wednesday and Friday at 11 am. Although the fares on the two trains are the same, the Senegalese train (from Dakar on Wednesday and Bamako on Friday or Saturday) is far superior to the Malian train (from Dakar on Friday and Bamako on Wednesday). The Senegalese train is comparable to any West European train. It's clean, pleasant, has air-con and a buffet car serving soft drinks, beer and food. First class on the Malian train, by comparison, would be called 4th class in any other country. It's the pits. Wait for the Senegalese train.

If taking the Malian train be at the station several hours before it's scheduled to leave. It can be extremely overcrowded even though seats in 1st and 2nd class are now reserved. The fares from Dakar to Bamako are CFA 27,600 (sleeper), CFA 18,500 (1st class) and CFA 11,700 (2nd class). Book your berth or seat in advance. The journey takes 36 to 48 hours.

Student reductions of 30% are available during school holidays but not at other times. To obtain them you have to see the *chef de la gare* (station chief).

You must disembark from the train at the border and report to the police. Their office is some distance from the station.

Food in the buffet car tends to be expensive so, if trying to conserve funds, buy food from the vendors on the platforms at various stops en route.

If you get on these trains at Tambacounda, the chances are they'll only have 1st class tickets available. Second class is invariably booked out so it would be cheaper to take a taxi to Kidira (border) and another from there to Kayes. From Kayes, there is at least one local train per day to Bamako which costs CFA 5000 (2nd class).

Beware of thieves on the trains especially at night.

BOAT

Dakar is a major West African port and many passenger and cargo ships call here. You can get passenger ships from France, Spain (including the Balearic Islands), Morocco and the Canary Islands to Dakar, but none of them cater to budget travel. Even the cheapest fares will cost more than the price of a flight.

There is the weekly 'Casamance Express' boat that travels from Dakar to Karabane to Ziguinchor. This departs Ziguinchor on Thursdays at 10 am and costs CFA 3000 (3rd class) one-way. It's better to sit outside in 3rd class than in 2nd class (Pullman seats) since it's very crowded and, if the sea is slightly rough many people are sick. The journey time is 18 to 20 hours. Take food and water as the food on the boat is expensive and the water frequently runs out. There is no need to book the ticket in advance.

TO/FROM THE GAMBIA

The best and cheapest transport from Dakar to Barra Point is the Gambian government bus (GPTC) which is much more orderly than the Senegalese buses. These depart daily at 9 and 11.30 am from the Place Leclerc near the junction of Blvd de la Liberation and Rue Dagorne. Don't rely on the 11.30 am bus – if there are enough passengers at the terminal at 9 am to fill both buses, the second one will leave straight away rather than wait until the 11.30 am departure time. The fare is CFA 2500 plus CFA 350 to CFA 900 for a backpack depending on size. The journey takes about five hours. A taxi costs CFA 3000 plus luggage and is no faster.

The ferry from Barra Point to Banjul costs Da 1.75 or CFA 200 and takes 20 minutes. The first departs at 8.30 am. After that they leave from either side every two hours throughout the day.

A minibus from Banjul to Ziguinchor takes four hours and costs CFA 1100.

TO/FROM GUINEA BISSAU

From Ziguinchor you can take a service taxi directly south to São Domingos on a reasonable dirt road for CFA 600 plus a baggage charge. At São Domingos there is a daily ferry through the mangroves to Cacheu around 11 am which takes about 1½ hours and costs P 1200. From Cacheu you may be lucky and find a truck all the way to Bissau. The usual fare is P 1200. If you don't find one you'll have to do the journey in stages, first to Canchungo, then to Safim and finally to Bissau. There is a ferry across the river at Safim. If it's out of fuel (which happens often) you cross the river by canoe. The fare is the same. The ferry doesn't operate between 12.30 and 2.30 pm. There are no hotels in either São Domingos or Cacheu.

Another route is via the Senegal border at Tanaf to Farim (33 km). A taxi from Ziguinchor to Tanaf costs CFA 1400; a minibus costs CFA 1100. From Tanaf a taxi to Farim will cost CFA 750 or else there are trucks that depart when full (about 30 passengers). It is a rough pot-holed road and will take about six hours by the time you clear customs on both sides. At a garage in Tanaf you can buy Bissau pesos at a favourable rate but keep them hidden from customs.

There is a ferry across the river at Farim which runs every hour except at siesta time from 12.30 to 2 or 3 pm. From Farim to Bissau it is a two-hour trip on a good road for P 350.

There are flights to Bissau from Dakar twice a week which cost US$66 and from Ziguinchor which cost US$30.

TO/FROM MALI

See the Train section.

Around the Country

DAKAR

The capital of Senegal and a major West African port, Dakar is a large modern city where an eighth of the country's population lives. It's an expensive place to stay and it gets a variable press. Some travellers don't like it and consider it to be dangerous because of incidents of robbery with violence. While this has been on the increase, it's no worse than in any other large city around the world. You certainly need to exercise discretion about going back to a house alone or wandering down small alleyways, and you should definitely stay away from the beach at night.

Apart from that, Dakar seems a welcome sight to most travellers, especially after they've been roughing it in the desert. Watch out, however, for young men who will try to give you so-called 'presents' (usually trash) in exchange for a few drinks in a café then demand money for their 'present' several hours later. Also beware of touts who will attach themselves to you and finally demand money for all the time they've taken to hassle you. Every newcomer is a potential victim and it is very hard to get rid of these people. There are, however, many other people who go out of their way to be helpful without any strings attached.

Information

The tourist office, Bureau de Renseignements de Tourisme (tel 211300) is in Ave André Peytavin. The American Express office (tel 222416) is at 51 Ave Albert Sarrant. The poste restante at the main post office charges CFA 125 per letter collected. If you need to insure your car see Mr Fall at 'La Foncière' (tel 210176), 79 Ave Peytavin. He has been highly recommended.

Public buses, No 7 and 8, run between the airport and the city centre and cost CFA 120. Taxis between the two are exorbitant and you're looking at CFA 2500 during the day or CFA 3000 at night. Buses No 6 and 18 will take you to the bus terminal. Taxi rides in the city should be CFA 100 (cabs are metered) but be sure the meter is switched on. 'Tourist taxis' run the meter five times faster than they are supposed to, so if it reads CFA 500 before you turn the corner, get out and find another taxi.

Note these street name changes: Rue Thiers is now Rue El Haji Amadou Assane Ndoye; Ave Ponty is now Ave Pompidou; Rue de Bayeux north of Ave Ponty is now Rue Raffenel.

Things to See

The **Ifan Museum** in Place Soweto near the Palais de l'Assemblée Nationale is worth a visit. It has a superb collection of West African masks, furniture and royal paraphernalia. Entry costs CFA 200 (CFA 100 with student card). It's open 8.30 am to 12.30 pm and from 2 to 6 pm; closed on Monday.

One of the 'musts' in Dakar is a visit to **Ile de Gorée**. An old fortified slaving station, the island was one of the very first French settlements on the African continent. There is an excellent historical museum on the island, slaves' houses and old colonial mansions. Entry to the museum is CFA 200 (CFA 100 with student card). The 'House of Slaves' is free; don't miss the 3 pm visit when you are shown around by the interesting and very amusing *conservateur* (curator). There are regular ferries from Dakar and the fare is CFA 1000 return.

The museum is closed all day on Monday and on Wednesday morning. The food at the cafés on the beach near the wharf is good and reasonably priced. Cheap beers are available at *Chez Michou*, a small shop behind the museum. It's a much less pressured environment than Dakar and accommodation is available with the locals if you ask at the cafés. Also on the island is a Muslim sect, certain members of whom live in the old naval gun installations on the hill. They are a lot like

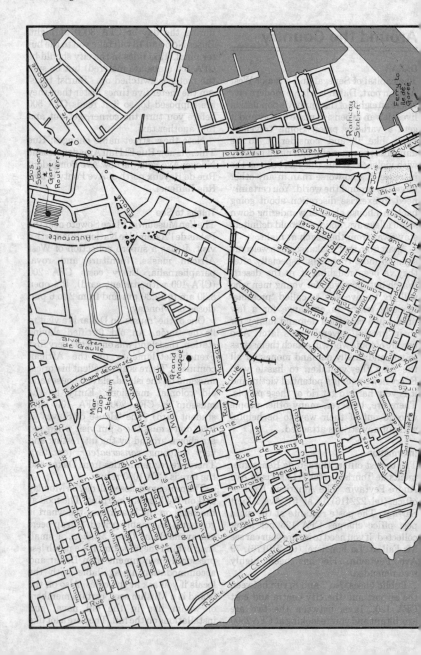

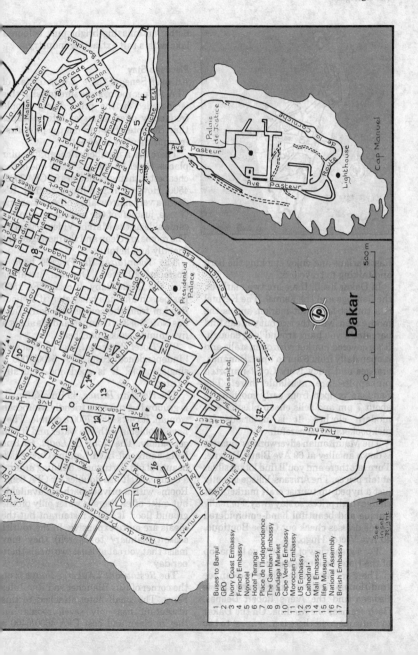

1 Buses to Banjul
2 GPO
3 Ivory Coast Embassy
4 French Embassy
5 Novotel
6 Hotel Teranga
7 Place de l'Independence
8 The Gambian Embassy
9 Sandaga Market
10 Cape Verde Embassy
11 Moroccan Embassy
12 US Embassy
13 Cathedral·
14 Mali Embassy
15 Ifan Museum
16 National Assembly
17 British Embassy

Dakar

500 m

See
Inset
Right

Ile de Gorée

Rastafarians and enjoy smoking the herb and talking to travellers.

In Dakar itself, there are two markets, the **Sandaga** and the **Kermel**. The Kermel is a tourist and fruit market and is the more expensive of the two but you can find bargains if you hang around long enough. It's a covered market with open stalls and is open daily from 6 am to 1 pm. Bananas, oranges and juicy Ivory Coast-imported pineapples are available here. The Sandaga is open from early morning to about 7 pm and sells cheap plastics and modern clothes. It is notorious for pickpockets, so be careful.

The Mauritanian silverworkers' quarter is down an alley at 69 Ave Blaise Diagne. Turn left there and you'll find lots of silver at fair prices. The **Artisans' Village** is really just a hyped-up tourist craft market that charges high prices, so stay away. For really unique and beautiful hand-embroidered Gorée dresses check out Gorée Boutique, 40 Ave Victor Hugo.

For a great view of the city, go to the top of the **Hotel de l'Indépendence**.

There are two arenas where you can see traditional fighting; the **Arène Émile Badiane** and the **Arène Robert Delmas**. Both are near the Medina. On the Dakar to Rufisque road there is a signpost to **Lac Retba**, an amazing bright pink coloured lake with a salt extracting industry.

Places to Stay

All over Senegal there is a hotel tax of CFA 400 per room, so be sure to ask if this is included in the price. Local people frequently offer rooms at rates cheaper than the hotels but sort out the price first (even if they say it's free).

There are a number of cheap, popular places. *Hotel Mon Logis* is still one of the cheapest with singles/doubles for CFA 3000/ 4500. However it is difficult to find. It's down a very narrow alley off Ave Lamine Gueye, just left of the mosque and on the same side as the Marché Video-Cassette. The rooms are clean and the management friendly and helpful.

The *Volontaires du Progrès* have a hostel at 5661 Rue 13, Dieuperl, just along from the Clinic Raby. It costs CFA 1500 per person and has hot water. It's about five km from the centre of Dakar. Take bus No 9, 2 or 3 to Dieuperl and it's about a five-minute walk from there.

The *Hotel Provençal*, just off Place de l'Indépendence, costs CFA 5400/7000 a single/double. It is good and centrally located.

The *Hotel du Prince*, 49 Rue Raffenal is grubby but run by a friendly Moroccan woman. It costs CFA 7000 a double. They have problems with the water and it can get smelly. The *Hotel St Louis*, 68 Rue Félix Faure, off Blvd Lamine Gueye is a beautiful old Portuguese building around a courtyard. It has doubles for CFA 6800. Rooms with a private bath are available but quite often there is water only on the ground floor. It has a restaurant but the meals are quite expensive. In the tourist season (January to March) they may insist that you eat at least two meals there per day.

The *Restaurant l'Auberge Rouge* is on the corner of Rue Blanchet and Rue Jules Ferry. The small hotel attached to this restaurant has only seven rooms but they're clean and cost CFA 4600/6400 a single/double. The *Hotel Continental*, Rue Galandou Diouf, costs CFA 5700 for a single with shower and CFA 8000 a double but there are no fans or air-con. *Hotel Continental Annex* in Rue Blanchot, is 500 metres from the Hotel Continental and around the corner. The front of the building looks like a garage and it's easy to miss. It is run by the same person but is cleaner, quieter and has fans. It costs CFA 6200 a single.

The *Hotel Central*, Ave Pompidou, has rooms for CFA 8600 a double. The *Hotel Atlantic*, 52 Rue El Amadou Ndoye, is clean, friendly and centrally located. The ordinary rooms cost CFA 5600/6800 a single/double plus they have rooms with bathroom and air-con for CFA 8800 a double.

For something more up-market try the *Hotel de la Paix*, 38 Rue El Amadou Ndoye, which has rooms for CFA 6500/12,000 a single/double. The *Hotel Al Barakka*, 35 Rue Abdou Karim Bourgi (250 metres from Place de l'Indépendence) is very clean, has a nice little garden at the back and is run by friendly people. It costs CFA 14,000/16,000 for a double/triple.

Places to Eat

You can get cheap, tasty food at any *dibitterie*. These are generally run by Mauritanians and are small places, usually without a sign, where meat is grilled in front of you. You take the grill away in a twist of newspaper. Eaten with a hunk of bread (available everywhere), it's a filling meal and the cost is minimal. At other street stalls ask for chawarma, a Lebanese-derived dish which consists of a piece of pitta bread filled with grilled meat, chips and onions. It's hot, juicy and filling. The street stalls next to the railway station serve good breakfasts and brochettes.

The *Keir Ndeye Restaurant*, Rue Vincens, serves superb traditional Senegalese food – but check your bill carefully, as their imagination sometimes runs away with them. One traveller described their peanut stews as 'one of the great culinary experiences of my life'.

The *Chez Lutchea*, 14 Rue Wagane Diouf, is also clean and has good food. Try the maffé – rice and groundnut sauce containing meat and potatoes. Breakfast (bread, butter and coffee with milk) is available. Also on the same street at No 20 is *Chez Ousmane* where they have excellent Senegalese food. There's an excellent, cheap restaurant next to the Hotel de la Paix with a menu in French and English. There's a good choice of meals and snacks.

There are also many small restaurants along Ave Jean Jaurès and Rue Sandinière. Try the *Modern Restaurant* on the corner of Sandinière and Blanchot.

Le Rustic on the corner of Rue de Bayeux and Ave Pompidou, is a pleasant shady sidewalk café that has wonderful hors d'oeuvres and beer on tap. *Le Hanoi Restaurant* is on 90 Rue de Bayeux. *Chez Nava*, 40 Rue Blanchot, has good meals, and has beers as well as cheap wine.

Other recommended restaurants include *Gargotte Diarma* 56 Rue Félix Faure; *Chez Nanette*, Rue Wagane Diouf just south of the Ave Pompidou (European food); *Gargotte du Plateau*, Rue Félix Faure; and the *Gargoutier* (delicious cheap dinners). *La Latticia Patisserie* across from the cathedral has also been recommended. It's closed between 1 and 3 pm. Right next to Chez Nanette is the *Restaurant Sénégalaise*; it's an unassuming little place but has a far better menu than Chez Nanette.

Soft drinks are expensive everywhere. Cheap bars in which to have a cold beer include *Bar Nana*, on the corner of Blanchot and Escarfait, and the beer garden behind the Hotel de Ville (where they speak English). The *Bar M'Bollache*, on the corner of Rue Carnot and Blanchot is popular. You'll find exotic and strange people here such as male prostitutes and huge fat female ones – but it's not a rough place. It's open till 3 am. Somewhat more up-market than this is *Yang-Yang* at Jaura Guiberry. It's a bit more civilised and slightly more expensive too. The bars along Ave Pompidou are very expensive.

Although there are good views from the top of the *Hotel de l'Indépendence* you must buy a drink and they're not cheap. The swimming pool is open to everyone but costs CFA 2000 which includes a soft drink.

The *New Experience Jazz Club* has a band playing every Friday and Saturday night. There's another really good jazz club on the corner of Rue Jules Ferry and Mohammed V.

N'Gor

A pleasant weekend excursion from Dakar is to the beach at N'Gor near the airport. Take bus No 7 (CFA 80) from the Place de l'Indépendence or from the Ave Lamine Gueye but make sure the bus is signposted 'Yoff'. The other No 7 only goes as far as Ouakam. Tell the fare collector to let you know when you reach N'Gor Village. Walk about 200 metres through the village to the bay behind the village. From there you can take an outboard-powered dugout canoe 200 to 300 metres across the bay to the island opposite and the most pleasant beach in the Dakar area. It's patronised mainly by middle-class Senegalese. The canoe fare is CFA 300, and is paid on the return trip.

Snorkelling equipment is available for hire on the island for CFA 2500 per day. The best area for this activity is between the rocks in front of the Hotel Meridien and the open sea. It's not dangerous if you are careful.

There are small stands on the beach selling sandwiches and soft drinks.

JOAL

Joal itself isn't particularly interesting and has been described as the fly capital of the world. Nearby, however, is the village of **Fadiouth** where the houses are built out of shells. There are no roads or cars though the village is connected to Joal by a bridge.

It's very touristy these days so expect to be hassled by the kids demanding *cadeaux*. Get there either on foot or by pirogue. A tour of the lagoon in a pirogue costs CFA 700.

The place to stay is the *Mission Catholique* about 100 metres before the bridge to Fadiouth. You can sleep in the hut in the garden of the mission for a donation but there are no facilities. Bring your own candles, mosquito coils, matches and bedding. Showers are available.

For food, it's best to eat on the waterfront where vendors sell rice and fish. Forget about the ridiculously expensive Relais 114.

KAOLACK

One option for accommodation is the *Hotel Napoleon*, Ave Cheikh Ibra Fall one block from the cathedral and three blocks east of the market. It costs CFA 4000 for a single and CFA 5000 if you want air-con. It's old and dirty and some rooms have no windows. The hotel *Chez Aida Ba* has doubles for CFA 3500 (negotiable). Otherwise try the *Mission Catholique* where you can get a nice room with bathroom. The Peace Corps Hostel no longer accepts travellers.

The taxi park for Tambacounda and Banjul is on Ave John Kennedy at the junction with Ave Ababacar Sy.

M'BOUR

M'Bour is a typical package holiday village in the high season (November to April), but during the rest of the year it's all yours. There's a good beach.

The *Centre Touristique de la Petite Côte*, Ave Diogoye Senghor near the Prefecture, costs CFA 8500 a double and is a really nice place with a good swimming pool and bar. The food is good but expensive. For somewhere cheaper try the *Restaurant La Torre* which has doubles for CFA 3000.

RUFISQUE

If you don't like Dakar, head off for Rufisque and stay there – take bus No 10 from opposite the Hotel de l'Indépendence and in front of the Sabena office in Dakar. It costs CFA 75.

The *Hotel Koussin* (the sign is broken and faded) is just across from the cinema and has big, clean, airy rooms for CFA 2500 a double with clean communal showers and toilets. Near the market there are several cheap, small restaurants where you can get meals and a drink. They're unnamed. If you're obviously short of money, you may be invited to stay with a local family. Money would be welcome to some (indeed some are very greedy), but to others it might cause offence. If you stay with a family for a fortnight or so, make sure you buy them enough food to cover your stay at least.

Rufisque is a nice place with open-air bars and two cinemas, though the quality of the films is generally poor. There are friendly people everywhere.

ST LOUIS

Like Ile de Gorée, St Louis was once a fortified collection point for slaves bound for the Americas. It's the oldest French settlement on the continent. Its old Portuguese architecture (predating the French settlement) set against the river makes it a very attractive place to visit.

Things to See

While in St Louis it's worth visiting the nearby **National Park of Jolan Djoudj** (50 km to the north). The newly built dam of Maka Diama ensures that there is water all year round in the park. The best season is winter when you can see thousands of pelicans and cormorants and dozens of other types of birds. Entry to the park is CFA 2000 and the hire of a pirogue costs CFA 3000 per person. There is a *campement* in the park where you can stay and camping is allowed.

Transport to the park can be difficult without your own vehicle so it's probably best to see Mrs Anne-Marie Philip, at the Hotel de la Poste, who organises trips out to the park. They charge CFA 10,000 per

person which includes the park entry fee and a meal. You need a minimum of four people. The jeep leaves at 8 am and returns at 3 pm.

There is also the **National Park of La Langue du Berberie** 18 km to the south of St Louis. Entry to the park costs CFA 2000 and you'll have to pay CFA 2000 to CFA 3000 for a pirogue to take you to the sandbar. Winter is the best time as there's very little bird life during the summer months.

About three km south of the city is an excellent **beach** for swimming.

Places to Stay & Eat

The cheapest place to stay is the *Maison des Combattants* in front of the hospital where you can get a bed for CFA 1000 per person. It's nothing special and not particularly clean.

The best of the cheap hotels is the *Hotel Battling Siki* where a double room costs CFA 4000 or you can camp on the roof for CFA 1500. The hotel is named after the first African heavyweight champion of the world. His real name was Mbarick Fall and he was born in St Louis in 1897. He was murdered in the USA in 1925, a victim of racism. The people of St Louis are still very proud of him. The hotel is clean but it can be very noisy.

If looking for something better, try the *Hotel de la Poste*, an old colonial-style hotel which has been run by the same French family for four generations. It has shaded terraces, a bar and good food. Rooms cost CFA 7000/12,000 a single/double. Finally there is the *Hotel de la Résistance*, which is more expensive at CFA 16,000 a double.

A pleasant place to eat is *La Signaree*, Rue Brière de l'Ile at the ninth intersection north of the post office, which serves basic French cooking.

TAMBACOUNDA

Neither the Mission Catholique nor the Volontaires du Progrès will take travellers any longer. Some travellers have managed to persuade the people at the *Peace Corps*

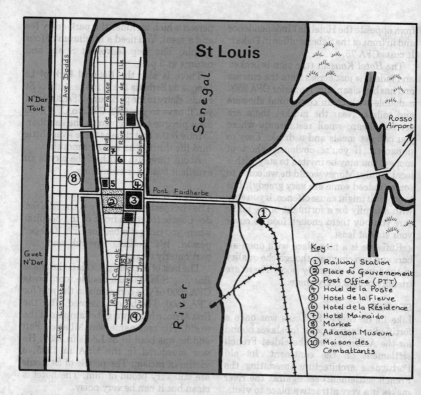

St Louis

Key:—
1. Railway Station
2. Place du Gouvernement
3. Post Office (PTT)
4. Hôtel de la Poste
5. Hôtel de la Fleuve
6. Hôtel de la Résidence
7. Hotel Maïmaïdo
8. Market
9. Adanson Museum
10. Maison des Combattants

house to rent them a bed for the night but don't take this for granted. To get there, turn left out of the railway station and carry on until the petrol station on the left hand side of the street. Turn left here, cross the tracks and take the first right. It's the first house on the left on the second block.

If you can't find anything else your choice is extremely limited. The *Maison des Jeunes* is just about the only cheap place to stay but it's a filthy brothel and very run-down. Other than these, there's only the very expensive *Hotel Aska Kebe*. Nonresidents can use the swimming pool for CFA 500.

The friendly *Restaurant Khadim* on the main road has a shady terrace and offers good food.

TOUBA

This is the most important pilgrimage town in Senegal for the Mouride Muslims, for the tomb of their founder, Amadou Bamba, is here. The town is dominated by **La Grande Mosquée** with its 86-metre-high central minaret. Non-Muslims are allowed to go up to the top and, as you might imagine, there are fantastic 360° views from the top. It is worth a day trip from Diorbel, or it's a three-hour drive from Dakar.

ZIGUINCHOR

The best place to stay is *Hotel Bel Kady* behind the Grand Marché (which makes it noisy at night). It costs CFA 3000 a double and is clean and friendly. Good, cheap meals are available. The *Restaurant* de la Gare Routière, opposite the bus and taxi stand, has rooms for CFA 2300 a double. The *Hotel Bambadinka* on the road into town from the main market (Marché St Maur) on the left hand side has small but clean doubles for CFA 2300 and meals from around CFA 1000.

There's also the *Hotel l'Escale* which has rooms for CFA 2400 or CFA 5000 with air-con. The *Hotel Aston Gaudiaby* near the big market, costs CFA 2400 a double, and the *Hotel Mama Djanke Waly Sames* has rooms for CFA 4000 a double.

More up-market, the *Hotel du Tourisme* is popular with travellers and costs CFA 6000 a double with bathroom and fan; it isn't bad value if you can get a room upstairs. The hotel has a good restaurant. Also at this hotel there is a guy called Mario who organises trips in a yacht through the Bijago Islands of Guinea-Bissau departing from Ziguinchor.

If you have time to spare and are prepared to help patch up sails and rigging, you can find accommodation down at the harbour. If you can speak a modicum of Wolof you might also ask around in the bakery for either John or Joe, who may be able to put you up.

The *Restaurant SeneGambiene* at the parking station has good cheap rice.

There is a **craft market** near the Bel Kady.

Around Ziguinchor

West of Ziguinchor is the Casamance region with its beautiful beaches, palm trees, mangrove swamps and estuarine vegetation. All along the coast are numerous small villages with *campements* where you can stay.

Cap Skirring This is a popular tourist resort. There is a *Club Med* here. The *Hotel Paillote* has pleasant bungalows near the beach and a double room costs CFA 14,000. Some cheaper *campements* are the *Moussouwan* and the *Paradise* at the end of the second small alley about 500 metres past the Hotel Paillote in the direction of Kabrousse village. Moussouwan is very pleasant with doubles for CFA 3000 (singles the same price) and three-bed rooms for CFA 4200. You have to take at least one meal there every day for CFA 1750 (these are low season prices before November). There is a car leaving here for Ziguinchor everyday at 7 am. Paradise has singles for CFA 1300 but the doors look totally unreliable and the only water available is taken out of a pit with a bucket.

There are cheap eating places in the village of Cap Skirring.

Diembering A really pleasant place to stay is the much quieter village of Diembering about 12 km north of Cap Skirring. There are a few *campements* to stay at. The *Campement sur la Colline* has clean doubles for CFA 2000 and friendly management. Meals are available. There are also the *campements Chez Albert* near the beach and *Khelil* as you come into the village. If you have not been on a tour of the mangroves in a pirogue this is the place to ask around. Don't miss Sunday mass at this village with its choir and tam-tam (gong).

The beach walk from Diembering to Cap Skirring is very beautiful and there are a number of fairly isolated beaches along the way.

Boucotte This is a lovely quiet village, three km from Cap Skirring. It has a good *campement* that costs CFA 1000 per person and serves breakfast and dinner. It is two km from the beach.

Oussouye Here the *campement* is very good value for CFA 1000 per person. It is clean and friendly, has mosquito netting, a good shower and toilets. It is hard to find at night but the man that runs the bar near the market will take you there if you need help.

An interesting trip is to take a pirogue from Oussouye to the **islands** in the Casamance River. Here it's possible to visit the Diola people's villages.

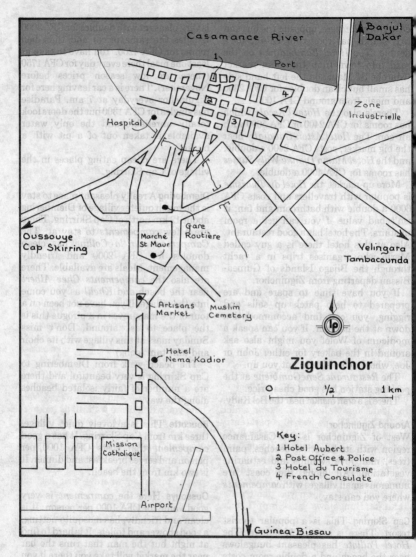

Casamance River

Port

Banjul
Dakar

Zone
Industrielle

Hospital

Oussouye
Cap Skirring

Marché
St Maur

Gare
Routière

Velingara
Tambacounda

Artisans
Market

Muslim
Cemetery

Hotel
Nema Kadior

Ziguinchor

0   ½   1 km

Mission
Catholique

Airport

Guinea-Bissau

Key:
1 Hotel Aubert
2 Post Office & Police
3 Hotel du Tourisme
4 French Consulate

Elinkine The *campement* at Elinkine is excellent – three-bed dormitory accommodation with toilets and showers costs CFA 1000 per person. Meals are good too – fish, rice, fruit, etc.

Karaban This island is worth visiting with its old Breton church and the remains of a colonial settlement as well as a local village.

Pointe St Georges This is another village in the area that is worth a visit.

National Parks

BASSE CASAMANCE NATIONAL PARK

This park is 12 km from Oussouye. You can try to hitch (but there is very little traffic) or walk, or wait for the park vehicle to come to town and get a lift with it – but it doesn't come every day. Entry to the park costs CFA 1000. Camping at the park headquarters is free; at the *campement* it's CFA 1500. Meals are available. This is a small park with many monkeys and duikirs, big birds and hyenas (hard to see as usual) and a few buffalo.

NIOKOLO KOBA NATIONAL PARK

It can be very difficult to get a lift right into this park south of Tambacounda. Buses from Tambacounda charge the fare all the way to Kessegou even though you're only going one-third of the distance. A better way is to take a shared taxi from Tambacounda to Dialokota (which leaves when full) for CFA 700 and walk the several km (a one-hour walk) to Badi at the park entrance. From here they radio Siminti for transport to *Le Campement* which costs CFA 3000 one-way plus park entry fee of CFA 2000 per day. If you're lucky you may be able to hitch a ride with tourists.

The park provides a truck and guide for 4½-hour safaris for CFA 5000 per person. If the truck breaks down you don't get a refund. Bungalows at Siminti cost CFA 4000 a night and you can fit as many people as you want in them. Camping is available at *Le Campement des Lions*, nine km from Siminti, free of charge (there's nobody there). It is a really good place to see the wildlife by the river. The guard's camp at Buttlabe is about one km away across the river so you can get a ride back to Siminti with them. Food is expensive so bring your own if possible.

If you spend a few days here you can expect to see bushbuck, Bouffon cobs, waterbucks, buffaloes, dikdiks, baboons, vervets, wart hogs, hippos, sables, porcupines, civets and lions. Unfortunately poaching has reduced the elephant population to a mere 50 animals and there probably won't be any left in a few years.

SINE SALOUM DELTA NATIONAL PARK

This national park takes in the delta area of the Saloum River and is made up of thousands of islands surrounded by mangroves (the most northern in Africa) with amazing bird and marine life. One part of this park – the **Fathala Forest** – is where the Red Colobus monkey has made its home. To get to the forest, take a bush taxi from Kaolack to Tabacouta for CFA 900 including luggage. (Tabacouta is 44 km before the Gambian border on the Dakar to Kaolack and Banjul road.) From here you will have to walk 10 to 16 km to Missira and from there another three to five km to the park headquarters. It's a nice walk (although hot) and the villagers along the way are very friendly. The entry fee is CFA 2000 a day and you can camp pretty much anywhere – just ask the guards.

Seychelles

If you're looking for that unspoilt tropical paradise thousands of miles from anywhere, where you can lie on palm-fringed beaches, go swimming in warm, crystal-clear seas and relax among friendly, easy-going people, the Seychelle islands fit the bill.

Scattered over a vast expanse of ocean but with a total land area of only about 445 square km, the Seychelles lies some 1500 km east of the African mainland and about 3000 km west of India. There are 92 islands in all, 38 of them granitic (the only mid-oceanic group of granite islands in the world) and the remainder coralline. Since they remained uninhabited until fairly recent times, a unique assembly of plants and animals were able to develop on these tiny fragments of land. As a result, they're of immense botanical and zoological interest and the government is intent on keeping them that way. Conservation is a major consideration and all development is carefully regulated and controlled to protect the natural beauty of the islands.

Some 80 species of indigenous trees and plants have been discovered in the Seychelles, ranging from the giant coco de mer to a tiny insectivorous pitcher plant. The double nuts of the coco de mer are the heaviest seeds in the plant kingdom and can weigh over 27 kg! The seed nut takes seven years to mature and a year to germinate, and many of the 30-metre-high palms on which it grows are estimated to be 800 years old. Long before the Portuguese rounded the Cape of Good Hope, the empty nuts were found on the shores of lands surrounding the Indian Ocean and gave rise to cults which attributed mystic powers to the fruit. Since no one had ever discovered their origin, the tree was thought to grow under the sea – hence the name.

It isn't just strange plant life which the Seychelles supports. The lagoons teem with marine life: giant tortoises are a common sight on some islands, and there are many unique frogs, geckos, chameleons and flying foxes to be seen, all of them harmless. As you might expect, snorkelling and scuba diving are popular.

The islands were sighted by Vasco da Gama, the Portuguese navigator, at the beginning of the 16th century, but no settlement was attempted until French planters and their slaves arrived in the 1770s. They introduced cinnamon, cloves, nutmeg and pepper, but the British took control of the islands in 1810 and administered them from Mauritius until they were made a separate Crown Colony at the beginning of the 20th century. Political organisations didn't surface until 1964, when two rival parties were formed: the Seychelles People's United Party (SPUP) led by France-Albert René and the Democratic Party (SDP) led by James Mancham.

The SPUP stood for complete independence while the SDP wanted association with Britain. The first full elections in the colony resulted in a stalemate between the two parties, but in 1970 the SDP won a majority. However, Mancham was unable to persuade the British authorities that association would be better than independence, which was granted in 1976. The first postindependence government was a coalition between the SPUP and the SDP, with Mancham as president and René as prime minister. Mancham remained in power only a short time. His flamboyant style and his plans to make

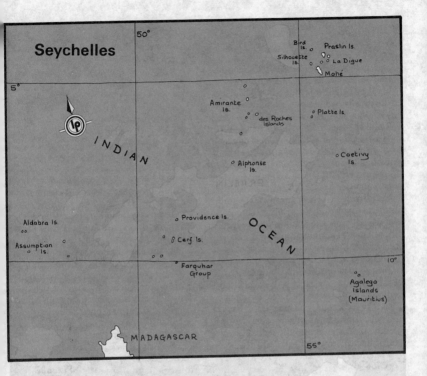

the Seychelles into a tax haven for the rich and powerful were completely at odds with René's commitment to social change. So when Mancham was away attending a Commonwealth Conference in London in 1977 a coup was staged and the presidency was assumed by René.

René is well aware of the ease with which a well-armed group of mercenaries could take over a scattered island group with such a small population (about 70,000). The perfect example was provided by the coup in the nearby Comoros Islands in May 1978. Since then, an effort has been made to provide the islands with a degree of security. The measures have included setting up a regular army backed by a 3000-strong militia and joint manoeuvres with Tanzanian and Malagasy forces.

Nevertheless, this didn't prevent a group of mercenaries (including some of the most notorious in Africa) from attempting to do the very thing René most feared. The attempt took place in late 1981 and very nearly succeeded, but its cover was blown when an airport customs officer discovered a sub-machine gun in the baggage of what appeared to be a party of business people on holiday. A gun battle ensued at the airport, and while some of the most notorious mercenaries managed to escape by hijacking a plane and flying it to South Africa, many others were arrested.

There was also a rapidly suppressed army revolt in mid-1982.

Mancham and his supporters, meanwhile, have continued to lobby for western support in toppling René, painting him as

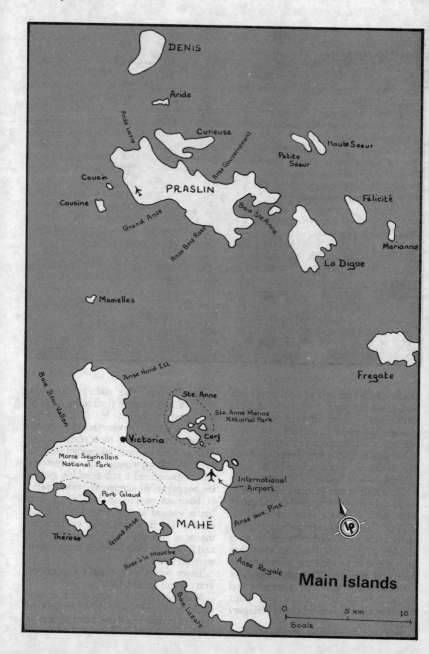

DENIS

Aride

Curieuse

Anse Lazio

Anse Gouvernement

Haute Soeur

Petite Soeur

Cousin

PRASLIN

Cousine

Grand Anse

Anse Bois Rose

Baie Ste Anne

Félicité

La Digue

Marianne

Mamelles

Fregate

Anse Nord Est

Baie Beau Vallon

Ste. Anne

Ste. Anne Marine National Park

Victoria

Cerf

Morne Seychellois National Park

International Airport

Port Glaud

Anse aux Pins

MAHÉ

Thérèse

Grand Anse

Anse Royale

Anse à la Mouche

Main Islands

Baie Lazare

0   5 km   10

Scale

a communist who is about to offer a site for a military base to the Russians. While it is true that the Seychelles has become a militant member of the nonaligned group and pressed ahead with the centralisation of economic and political power, no western country has so far accepted Mancham's claims. René himself has declared that not only have the Russians not asked for a base, but that it would be refused anyway. In any case, the Seychelles has been actively diversifying its diplomatic contacts in many directions of late.

Facts

GEOGRAPHY & CLIMATE
The main islands of Mahé, Praslin and La Digue lie only a few degrees south of the equator, but because they're so far out in the ocean, weather patterns can be variable. Unlike Mauritius, they are outside the cyclone belt. There are two monsoons. The south-east monsoon from May to October is strong, cool and dry, bringing with it overcast skies and choppy seas. The north-west from December to March is calmer though hotter and rainy. In view of this, the best time to visit the islands is from May to October.

Mahé, on which stands the capital, Victoria, is by far the largest island, with mountains rising to a height of almost 1000 metres in parts. The coral islands are unpopulated and rise only a few metres above sea level.

PEOPLE
The population stands at about 70,000 most of whom are Roman Catholics.

VISAS
Visas are not required by anyone. A one-month visitor's pass is issued on arrival subject to possession of an onward ticket or sufficient money to pay a returnable 'security bond'. You must have a valid cholera vaccination certificate if arriving from Africa. Customs are very thorough. Visitor's passes can be renewed up to one year.

MONEY
US$1 = SRs 7.24

The unit of currency is the Seychelles rupee = 100 cents. There are no restrictions on the import of local currency, but export is limited to SRs 100. There is no black market. Everything is expensive even for the locals so be prepared. There is no airport departure tax.

ACCOMMODATION
Avoid the high seasons if possible – July and August and again in December and January – as the price of accommodation rises and it's often difficult to find somewhere to stay.

There are hotels, guesthouses, self-catering apartments and beach bungalows on Mahé, Praslin and La Digue. You can get a full list of them from the Tourist Office, Independence House, Independence Ave, Victoria, Mahé (closed Sunday). They're very helpful and will telephone free of charge to check room availability and prices. This can save a lot of hassle. Off-season prices can be as little as half the high-season prices, so do bargain if you're there in the off-season. Most places offer full board, but you're advised to take half board because it's hot during the day and you generally don't feel like eating much. Dinners are enormous in most restaurants – average costs are SRs 80 (dinner) and SRs 50 (lunch).

The high-season prices of hotels and guesthouses are in the following range:

One Star – SRs 90 to SRs 175 a single and SRs 165 to SRs 240 a double, with breakfast. SRs 140 to SRs 220 a single and SRs 245 to SRs 330 a double, for half board.
Two Star – SRs 150 to SRs 270 a single and SRs 210 to SRs 365 a double, with

breakfast. SRs 200 to SRs 320 single and SRs 300 to SRs 465 double, for half board.

In addition to hotels, guesthouses and beach bungalows, accommodation is offered by some local families. This is mostly in the same price range as the one-star hotels and guesthouses.

Camping is frowned on so don't do it unless you can find a truly remote spot like Anse Matelot on Praslin.

FOOD
Seychellois food is a blend of French, Indian and Chinese influences. Most meals consist of fish or a curry served with white rice and salad or fruit. Octopus (usually curried and very tender) is a common local delicacy, as is grilled bourgeois (red snapper) and becune (mackerel). Other favourites are rougaille of local sausage cooked with green pumpkin; daube of pork with potatoes and tomatoes; and chicken, beef or fruit bat curry. Desserts include mashed bananas mixed with sugar and nutmeg, and yams in coconut milk. Drink *calou*, the local toddy sold in bamboo containers.

LANGUAGE
English and French are the official languages, but as the vast majority of the people are Creole, this is the first language of most Seychellois. Creole is a phonetic language similar to that found in other territories with French influence like Mauritius, Martinique and New Orleans. It has grown from a local patois in which French words have been hardened in pronunciation and syllables not pronounced have been dropped entirely. There are also substantial grammatical differences between Creole and French. A working vocabulary of Creole is outside the scope of this book, but to give those who know French an idea of what's happened to the language, here are a few examples:

What's your name? *koman ou apele?*

My name is George	*mon apel George*
I'm English	*mon Angle*
What time is it please?	*keler i ete silvouple?*
Would you like a drink?	*oule en bwar?*
Where are you?	*oli ou?*

Not easy, eh? No worries. The tourist office will give you a booklet with an extended list of phrases on arrival. Make sure you ask for it.

Getting There & Around

AIR
Air France, Air India, British Airways, Kenya Airways, Air Mauritius, Aeroflot and Air Seychelles all fly to the Seychelles. You can get there from any one of the following places: Europe (London, Paris, Frankfurt, Zurich); Asia (Jeddah, Bahrain, Colombo, Bombay, Hong Kong, Tokyo); and Africa (Djibouti, Nairobi, Johannesburg, Réunion, Mauritius). On arrival immigration may want to know the name of the place where you will be staying, so have one ready.

Air Seychelles has several daily flights between Mahé and Praslin (SRs 135 one way and SRs 270 return) twice a day, seven days a week, and the same to Fregate. Bird and Denis Islands are served by charters. Enquire about flights to Bird Island in the office across from the tourist office in Victoria.

ROAD
Mahé and Praslin are the only two islands with sealed roads and a regular bus network. On Mahé the buses operate between 5.30 am and 7 pm (more infrequently around midday) and cost SRs 3 to SRs 5, making taxis expensive and unnecessary. A bus from the airport to Victoria costs SRs 3. The bus stop is directly across from the airport parking

lot on the road in front of the petrol station. A bus from Victoria to Beau Vallon Beach is SRs 2. Taxis are available on both these islands at rates fixed by the government. It's worth taking a day to drive around the island for the beautiful scenery, lovely beaches, small Seychelle villages and friendly people. To hire a mini-moke for the day costs SRs 150 or a taxi will cost SRs 200.

On the other islands the roads are gravel, and about the only form of transport is the ox-cart. Bicycles can be rented on most of the larger islands. Hitching is excellent.

BOAT

Cruise ships and cargo vessels call at Mahé, but there is no regular passenger ship calling there these days. For several years there have been no passenger boats between India and Africa (these used to call at the Seychelles).

Ferries connect the islands of Mahé, Praslin and La Digue on a regular schedule. Details are as follows:

Mahé-Praslin-La Digue

ferry	days	depart	arrive	price
La Belle Praslinoise	Tue	Praslin 6 am	Mahé 9 am	SRs 25
		Mahé 1 pm	Praslin 4 pm	
	Wed	As above	As above	
	Fri	As above	As above	
Louis Alfred	Mon	Praslin 6 am	Mahé 9 am	SRs 25
		Mahé 1 pm	Praslin 4 pm	
	Wed	As above	As above	
	Fri	As above	As above	
La Bellone	Mon	Praslin 6 am	Mahé 9 am	SRs 25
		Mahé 1 pm	Praslin 4 pm	
	Thu	As above	As above	
Aroha	Mon	La Digue 6 am	Mahé 9.30 am	SRs 25
		Mahé 1 pm	La Digue 4.30 pm	
	Wed	As above	As above	
	Fri	As above	As above	

Praslin-La Digue

ferry	days	depart	arrive	price
Silhouette	Daily	Praslin 10.30 am	La Digue 11 am	SRs 25
		La Digue 11.30 am	Praslin 12 pm	
		Praslin 2.30 pm	La Digue 3 pm	
		La Digue 3.30 pm	Praslin 4 pm	
Ideal	Daily	La Digue 7.30 am	Praslin 8 am	SRs 25
		Praslin 10.30 am	La Digue 11 am	
		La Digue 3.30 pm	Praslin 4 pm	
		Praslin 5.00 pm	La Digue 5.30 pm	

The port of call/departure point in Praslin is Baie Ste Anne.

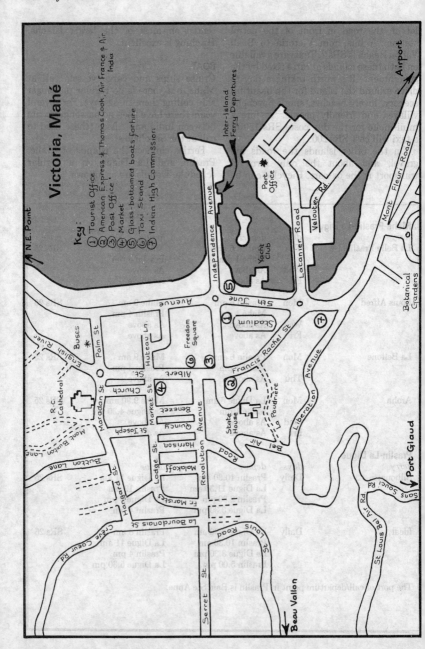

Victoria, Mahé

Key:
1. Tourist Office
2. American Express & Thomas Cook, Air France & Air India
3. Post Office
4. Market
5. Glass-bottomed boats for hire
6. Taxi Stand
7. Indian High Commission

Around the Country

COUSIN, BIRD & ARIDE ISLANDS
Those who have an interest in bird life should make a point of visiting one or more of these islands, where they are most numerous.

Cousin Island is administered by the International Council for Bird Preservation and can be visited on Tuesday, Thursday and Friday in groups of no more than 20. The trip there takes 1½ hours by boat from Mahé or half an hour by boat from Praslin. Getting to Bird Island requires more time. Boats take six to eight hours from Mahé (they depart Mahé at 9.15 and 11 am and Bird Island at 10.30 am and 3.30 pm). There's also a plane which takes 30 minutes.

There is a lodge on the island which costs SRs 495/705 a single/double for half board.

Aride Island is owned by the Society for the Promotion of Nature Conservation and is the home of the greatest concentration of seabirds in the entire region. Tours can be arranged through local travel agencies in Victoria but they only run from 1 October to 30 April.

LA DIGUE
The island has some fine examples of plantation owners' houses from the last century. There are many fine beaches, mostly deserted. With a rented bike you can explore most of the island in five to six hours.

Places to Stay
Chateau St-Cloud is a beautiful old plantation house about five minutes' walk from the boat jetty. Maston, who runs it, charges SRs 65 per person with breakfast and SRs 100 for half board which includes an excellent creole meal. Bicycles can be rented for SRs 30 per day.

Choppy's Bungalow (tel 342240), Anse Réunion, costs SRs 105/185 a single/double for bed and breakfast. The *Bernique Guest House* (tel 34229), La Passe, has singles/doubles with breakfast for SRs 100/150. Half board costs SRs 175/250 a single/double. An evening meal is also available. *Cabanes Des Anges* costs SRs 270/365 a single/double including breakfast in the high season, and SRs 320/465 a single/double for half board. In the low season it can cost as little as SRs 250 a double for half board. It's a great place right on the seafront, offering delicious food and run by friendly people.

La Digue Island Lodge has dormitory style rooms with shared amenities for SRs 85 including breakfast.

MAHÉ
Things to See
The **Botanical Gardens** in Victoria are worth strolling through to see the coco de mer palms, orchids and giant tortoises. There's no charge for entry, but the orchid house costs SRs 10. The **National Museum** opposite the Pirates Arms Hotel is open Monday to Friday from 10 am to 6 pm. It's free and is worth a visit.

Some excellent walks are possible into the interior of the island where there are forests, coconut, cinnamon and vanilla plantations as well as magnificent views of the smaller islands and the coastline.

There's a small colony of giant tortoises on **Therese Island** off the west coast. Off the east coast opposite Victoria are the five small islands of **Ste Anne, Cerf, Long, Round** and **Moyenne**, which together make up one of the marine national parks. Glass-bottomed boats and snorkelling equipment are available for hire.

For scuba diving go to the Seychelles Underwater Centre at the Coral Strand Hotel, Beau Vallon. You can go diving for SRs 150, which includes all the equipment. Two dives on the same day would cost SRs 230. This makes it cheaper than Le Diable de Mer at the Northome Hotel.

Places to Stay
The *Eureka Guest House* (tel 44349), La Louise, has a high season tariff at SRs 160/

300 a single/double with breakfast
(though depending on the season you may
be quoted SRs 175 a double with
breakfast). Half board is SRs 250/400 a
single/double. The cuisine is excellent
and the owners, France and Rosemary
Adrienne, are very friendly and hospitable.
The *Bel Ombre Holiday House* (tel
23616), Bel Ombre, offers a whole house
which can be rented for SRs 280 (four
people) or SRs 380 (six people) in the high
season, or for SRs 150 (two people) in the
low season. It's clean, pleasant, close to
the sea and has good bus connections.

The *Beau Vallon Bungalows* (tel
47382), Beau Vallon, is very pleasant and
beautifully situated. Single rooms in the
owner's house cost SRs 100 including
breakfast. The regular rooms cost SRs 125/
225 a single/double for bed and breakfast.
Madame Michel's Les Mangiers (tel
41455), Machabee near North Point, has
three houses which overlook a beautiful
cove. They come complete with equipped
kitchens, towels, all bedding, fans and a
daily maid service. One house is SRs 150
for four to five people (two bedrooms) or
SRs 100 for a couple. Another two-
bedroom house is SRs 175 for four people.
The Madame will do a Creole dinner for
four delivered to your house for SRs 60.
There are free mangoes in the yard during
the season (December) and several beautiful
beaches nearby. An excellent deal.

North Point Guest House (tel 41339)
Fond des Lianes, Machabee, has rooms for
SRs 150/220 a single/double with breakfast.
There are also self-catering bungalows for
SRs 700 a week. The *Villa Napoleon* (tel
47133), Beau Vallon, has self-catering
bungalows for SRs 125/225 a single/
double. *Le Niol Guest House* (tel 23262),
between Beau Vallon and Victoria costs
SRs 150/195 a single/double including
breakfast. The *Panorama Guest House*
(tel 44349), Beau Vallon, has rooms for
SRs 175/240 a single/double.

Places to Eat

There are many excellent restaurants on
Mahé and you'll be spoilt for choice.

At Pointe Au Sel *Hoi Tins* has excellent
Creole and Chinese food, and plenty of it
at reasonable prices. *Sundowner*, Port
Launay, is beautifully set below the
mountains on the other side of the island
from Victoria. It has excellent food and a
varied menu. The *Pirates' Arms*, Victoria,
has good meals and excellent fruit juices.
Sony's, Victoria is good for take-away
food. The *Yacht Club*, again in Victoria, is
a very popular and inexpensive spot for
local dishes. Ask around about crewing on
yachts through the Red Sea and to South
Africa.

The *Beau Vallon Beach Restaurant &
Macquerel Pub*, Beau Vallon, directly on
the beach, offers good octopus curry,
grilled fish and other local dishes served
with salad. They also have grilled
sandwiches, hot dogs and hamburgers.
Draught *Seybrew* beer is on tap.

The Garden of Eden at the Coral Strand
Hotel has cheap sandwich-type dinners.
Pizzas and other dishes are a bit more
expensive. Beers are available. For cheap
take-away curries (octopus, fruit bat,
beef, chicken or pork) served with rice and
salad, go to *Confex The Second*, Francis
Rachel St, Victoria, near Cable & Wireless.
It's very popular with local people.

PRASLIN

The major focus of interest is the **Vallée de
Mai**, the home of some 4000 coco de mer
palms, many of them estimated at over
800 years old. There are also plenty of
good, secluded beaches.

Places to Stay

The *Cocobello* (tel 33311) (formerly the
Merry Crab Guest House), Grand Anse, is
a bar and restaurant. It has singles for
SRs 100 (including breakfast) or SRs 150
(half board), and doubles for SRs 175
(with breakfast) or SRs 275 (half board).
The *Orange Tree House* (tel 33248), Baie
Ste Anne, has singles/doubles at SRs 90/

175 with breakfast. The *The Beach Villa* (tel 33445), Plage d'Or, offers singles/doubles with breakfast for SRs 150/204.

The *Britannia Guest House*, Grande Anse, has a high season tariff of SRs 90/170 a single/double including breakfast, and SRs 140/270 a single/double for half board. In the low season it can cost as little as SRs 60 a single with breakfast and SRs 200 a double for half board. It's clean and pleasant and the food is excellent.

The *Maxim*, Baie Ste Anne, offers self-catering rooms for SRs 75 per night. The *First and Last Guesthouse* near the boat jetty, about 10 minutes' walk from Baie Ste Anne, has singles for SRs 40 without meals and half board for SRs 100 per day.

Places to Eat
The *Indian Ocean Fishing Club* has a

good atmosphere and serves excellent seafood. They also arrange trips to **Cousin Island** for SRs 50 and you pay another SRs 50 on the island. Well worth a visit.

SILHOUETTE
To get some idea of what the Seychelles were like last century, take a boat to Silhouette from either Victoria (two hours) or Beau Vallon (one hour) on Mahé. Only group tours depart from Victoria, but you can charter boats individually for US$1 at Beau Vallon. Before visiting the island, however, you must first get a permit from the government. There are no vehicles on this beautiful island with a population of only 450. The planter's house is one of the finest examples of wooden Seychellois houses.

Sierra Leone

Sierra Leone owes its origins to a convergence of interests between British philanthropists seeking to establish a homeland for freed slaves and commercial concerns in the country wanting to expand trade links with West Africa. The first 411 settlers (who included 100 whites) landed at Freetown in 1787, but three years later their numbers had dwindled to 48. The next batch of 1200 freed slaves landed in 1792 and were soon augmented by another 550 brought from Jamaica.

The colony was initially governed by the Sierra Leone Company, but financial problems forced the British government to takeover in 1808. Over the next 60 years the settlers were joined by about 70,000 West Africans liberated from slave ships intercepted by the British navy and by tribespeople migrating from the interior. Freetown, the capital, thus ended up with a very mixed population divided by religion, language and economic status. The result was the development of largely separate ethnic communities with their own leaders and internal organisation.

The colonial authorities naturally favoured those settlers who identified with British culture and values, but there was very little friction between the different communities until the late 19th century. The event which changed all this was the imposition of a hut tax in 1898. The result was a war in which many of the settlers were killed by the indigenous population. The xenophobia this produced has not entirely subsided even today. In the run-up to independence in 1961 one group of Creoles actually petitioned against the granting of independence because it was obvious that political power would be monopolised by the indigenous groups since the Creole community numbered less than 2% of the entire population.

In the last years of the colonial regime two parties emerged: the Sierra Leone People's Party (SLPP) led by Milton Margai, which identified with the Mende of the south; and the All People's Congress (APC) led by Siaka Stevens, representing the interests of the Temne in the north. With Creole support, the SLPP won the elections prior to independence and Milton Margai took over as the country's first prime minister. He died in 1964 and his place was taken by Albert Margai.

Ever since the 19th century the Creoles had monopolised positions within the civil service and Albert Margai set about replacing them with people from the southern provinces. Alarmed at seeing their hold on power eroded in this way, the Creoles threw weight behind the APC in the 1967 elections, and, although the party gained a majority, it was prevented from taking its place by a military coup. This was followed two days later by a second coup led by Brigadier Juxon-Smith, who ruled the country for a year. Siaka Stevens, meanwhile, went into exile in Guinea and there raised a guerrilla army in preparation for invading Sierra Leone. As it turned out, this wasn't necessary because another coup in 1968 re-established civilian rule and Stevens was able to take his place as the country's new prime minister.

The return to civilian rule, however, did not bring peace. The country remained under a state of emergency. Large numbers of SLPP supporters were tried for treason, political parties were banned

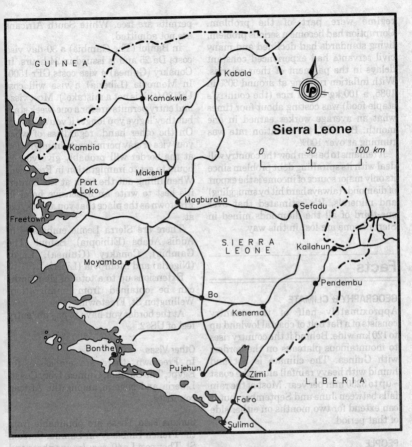

and intertribal rivalries led to violence. At one point Guinean troops were flown into Freetown to support the government. Things have cooled down considerably since those dark days, and the APC has gone on to win two further elections. In the process the country has become a republic and, since 1978, a one-party state. Siaka Stevens became the country's first president.

His rule was to last some 18 years but with his popularity and that of the APC rapidly declining towards the end, the net was cast for a suitable successor who would cover his exit. Over the heads of two obvious candidates for the job, Major General Joseph Momah, commander of the armed forces, was chosen.

Though an outsider, Momah was considered to be not too closely associated with any single tribal grouping so it was hoped that there would be a relatively smooth transition. This proved not to be the case and the elections which he called a short time later were overshadowed by high political and economic tension.

The country's economic problems inherited from the days of Siaka Steven's regime were part of the problem. Corruption had become a serious problem, living standards had declined and many civil servants had experienced constant delays in the payment of their salaries. With inflation running at around 60% in 1985, a 100 kg bag of rice (the country's staple food) was costing about four times what an average worker earned in one month. By 1987, the inflation rate was running at over 100%.

It remains to be seen how the country will deal with its spiralling debt problem since its only major source of income is the export of diamonds (always hard hit by smuggling) and minerals. It's estimated that over one-third of all the diamonds mined in Sierra Leone are lost in this way.

Facts

GEOGRAPHY & CLIMATE
Approximately half of the country consists of a flat belt of coastal lowland up to 120 km wide. Behind it the country rises to mountainous plateaus on the borders with Guinea. The climate is hot and humid with heavy rainfall along the coast – up to 3250 mm per year. Most of the rain falls between June and September, but it can extend for two months on either side of that period.

PEOPLE
The population stands at around four million, of which some 60% is composed of Temne and Mende peoples in about equal numbers. There are significant minorities of Europeans, Lebanese and Indians.

VISAS
Visas are required by all except those who are entitled to an entry permit. Entry permits are available to nationals of Commonwealth countries, Belgium, Denmark, Greece, Irish Republic, Iceland, Italy, Luxemburg, Netherlands, Norway, Spain, Sweden and Turkey. Entry permits are free. White South Africans are not admitted.

In Banjul (The Gambia) a 30-day visa costs Da 25 and is issued in 24 hours. In Conakry (Guinea) a visa costs GFr 1500. In Monrovia (Liberia) a visa will cost US$30 (this is not a mistake!). Most visas and entry permits are for a one-week stay, but they'll give you longer if you ask for it. On the other hand, regardless of what your visa or stay permit says, immigration at the border will probably give you 48 hours to get to immigration in Freetown. When filling out the form at the border, it's best to write an expensive hotel in Freetown as the place that you are staying at.

There are Sierra Leone embassies in Addis Ababa (Ethiopia), Banjul (The Gambia), Conakry (Guinea), Lagos (Nigeria) and Monrovia (Liberia).

Extensions up to a total of six months can be obtained from immigration, Wellington St, Freetown.

At the border you have to pay an 'entry fee' of US$2.

Other Visas
In Freetown, there are embassies for Egypt, The Gambia, Guinea, Ivory Coast, Liberia and Nigeria among the African countries.

Burkina Faso These are obtainable from the French Embassy on Lamina Sankoh St. They cost Le 40, require one photo and take 24 hours.

Guinea These are available from the Guinea Embassy, 4 Liverpool St, Freetown. A 15-day visa costs Le 200 and you need a letter of recommendation from your embassy. The British Embassy charges UK£6 (payable in leone) for a letter. The visa is issued with a fixed date of entry.

Liberia Visas are available from the embassy at 30 Brookfields Rd. They cost Le 20, require two photos and take two days to issue. Keep all copies of forms even if told otherwise as you will need them at the border.

MONEY

US$ 1 = Le 38
UK£ 1 = Le 56

The unit of currency is the leone = 100 cents. The import or export of local currency is allowed up to Le 20. The street rate is much the same as the official rate. As a result of a number of recent devaluations though, there is a slight difference. Expect up to Le 40 for US$1 and up to Le 60 for the UK£ sterling. You can also buy leones in the large bank on Ashmun St in Monrovia, Liberia, for close to the prevailing black market rate. (They won't, however, buy leones from you.) Be discreet if changing money on the street in Sierra Leone.

Currency declaration forms are issued on arrival at the airport and the land borders. Border officials will want to check these when you leave, but probably will not do so too carefully. There are large signs in all the hotels in Sierra Leone saying that foreign guests must pay either in hard currency or with leones bought at a bank (a bank stamp on your currency form is necessary to prove you obtained the leones at a bank). In practice, only the expensive hotels enforce this.

You cannot re-exchange leone at the airport or anywhere else on exit so use up all your leones beforehand. The airport departure tax for international flights is Le 20.

ACCOMMODATION

Until recently there were no hotels outside Freetown and Bo, but there are now a number of small boarding houses/hotels in the provincial towns such as Kabala and Kenema. The Peace Corps operates a number of hostels in outlying towns such as Kenema, Kabala, Makeni, Bo and Kambia. You might be able to stay in one of them for a small charge, if they have room. In other places you'll have to ask

around – someone will generally help out if you're willing to pay for your keep.

Getting There & Around

Very few travellers go to Sierra Leone, largely because it usually involves a lot of backtracking to get out. Apart from the road between Conakry (Guinea) and Freetown, communications with neighbouring countries are poorly developed.

AIR

If you can't handle the overcrowded bush taxis and trucks, it's worth considering flying. Quite a few travellers have recommended the flights in this country because the planes fly low enough for you to see all the detail below. Sierra Leone Airlines flies from Hastings Airport near Freetown to Bonthe and Kenema.

The cost of a flight from Freetown to Monrovia (Liberia) is US$100 and to Lomé (Togo) is US$173 with a student discount.

ROAD

Public transport or lack of it can be a real problem. Hitching is slow even along the main routes, and there are many police and army checkpoints where your baggage will be searched and papers scrutinised.

A reasonably good bus service operates between Freetown and all the larger centres such as Bo, Kenema, Makeni and Sefadu. The buses are fast and fairly cheap, but arrive well before they're due to leave if you want to be sure of getting on. (They are as cheap as private vehicles but much more comfortable, so there is a lot of competition for tickets.) Some examples of fares are:

Makeni to Freetown – Le 20
Freetown to Kambia – Le 25, once a day
Freetown to Bo – Le 32, twice a day

Bo to Kenema – Le 20
Freetown to Kenema – Le 40, twice a day

Other than buses, passenger cars called *poda poda* are the main means of transport. They're crowded, uncomfortable and at times hazardous – up to 24 people are crammed inside a VW-sized minibus or Toyota pick-up. A cheap taxi service is available between Bo and Kenema along the excellent German-built highway (the best road in the country). A minibus between Bo and Freetown costs Le 32. Very few start from Bo but one departs at 7 am outside the old cinema. Try and reserve a seat the night before (but you can't buy one until the day).

TRAIN

The railway between Freetown and Kenema shown on most maps of Sierra Leone has been out of operation since 1971.

TO/FROM GUINEA

There are direct buses in either direction between Conakry (Guinea) and Freetown, usually on a daily basis, which leave when full. However it's best not to take through transport especially with foreign number-plates – you'll be stopped at all the numerous checkpoints and it will take 24 hours to get from Freetown to Conakry. Instead go to Free St. From here buses leave for the border daily at about 8 am and take five to six hours. They cost Le 50. Peugeot taxis also leave from here and cost Le 60 plus Le 20 for luggage. There will be taxis waiting at the border to take you to Conakry. The Guinea border officials are friendly and baggage searches are cursory.

TO/FROM LIBERIA

There used to be two routes you could take to Liberia, but the route via Kailahun in the north-east has been closed because a lot of smuggling was going on. This means that the only route open at present is the one via Kenema, Zimi, the Mano River and Monrovia via the Bomi Hills. There

are taxis through from Kenema to Monrovia for Le 400 and trucks for Le 300 or, if coming from Monrovia it will cost US$25. This is a scenic drive with some beautiful, largely unspoilt forest. Expect to have to deal with hassles and bribery at the checkpoints en route.

If you want to do the journey in stages, there are taxis or minibuses (Le 32) from Freetown to Bo which take about four hours and taxis from Bo to the border which will cost Le 80 to Le 100. You can do the journey in smaller stages but you are likely to get stuck in one of the towns along the way due to lack of transport. The border is actually a bridge called the Mano River Union Bridge and it closes at 8 pm daily. You can just about get from Freetown to Monrovia in one day during the dry season, but not during the wet. If you are caught overnight at the border there are two cheap hotels (both unnamed) in Malema on the Sierra Leone side that cost Le 40 for a double.

Around the Country

BO

A good place to stay is the *Southern Motel* which costs Le 80 a double and has a fan, shower and toilet. It is out of town and a bit difficult to find. More central, though very run down, is the *Denby Hotel*.

FREETOWN

Freetown has a very British atmosphere and retains some fine old colonial wooden buildings and, as one traveller put it, 'a steamy, run-down decadence which is thoroughly enjoyable'. The electricity supply is still very erratic so that in the evenings there are often no fans, air-con or cold drinks. The city did, however, benefit from Siaka's role as chairperson of the OAU conference held here in 1980, when new ferries were purchased, roads widened, street lighting installed and improvements made to the public transport system.

Information

Taxis within town have yellow licence plates – this is their only difference from other vehicles. To get to the airport there is a Sierra Leone Airlines bus from the Paramount Hotel for Le 100 but you can do it much cheaper by taking a taxi to the ferry terminal, crossing by ferry for Le 1 then taking another taxi to the airport. International flights depart from Lungi Airport. Domestic flights depart from Hastings Airport, which is much closer to the city and does not involve a ferry crossing.

The government bus station in Freetown is in Rawdon St at Wallace Johnson St in the old railway station. You may be offered places in the queue by small boys, but it's generally not worth it. Private buses leave from Dan St or Fyabon or from the Shell station in Kissy St. These buses are usually very crowded and uncomfortable.

The truck park for trucks going to Conakry (Guinea) is on Free St at Regent Rd.

For travel information try Yazbeck's Travel Agency on Siaka Stevens St. It's a good place to change money and inquire about cheap flights. Bucket Shop Travel is also worth checking out.

Useful Addresses Some useful addresses are:

Immigration
   Siaka Stevens St on the corner with Rawdon St
Barclays Bank
   Siaka Stevens St at the junction with Charlotte St
American Express
   22 Siaka Stevens St
Ghana Embassy
   18 Pultney St
Ivory Coast Embassy
   1 Wesley St
Peace Corps Office
   8 Lamina Sankoh St
VSO Office
   Rawdon St, upstairs across from Yum Yums

Things to See

The **Basket Market** at the bottom of Lamina Sankoh St is worth visiting with its wonderful collection of new and old baskets, spoons, rattles, gourds and miscellaneous 'juju' medicines.

There are some lovely beaches close to Freetown. The closest and most touristy is **Lumley Beach**. A minibus there costs Le 1 or a shared taxi costs Le 3 to Le 4. It's then a 10-minute walk to the beach. It's best not to sleep on the beaches because of the dangers of being mugged or robbed.

The most spectacular beach is **River No 2**, which is 30 km from Freetown. It's very difficult to get there without private transport. A daily bus to York passes by and will drop you off but getting back is a problem. Sundays are best for hitching back as there are more tourists. A taxi one-way costs Le 140 for four people. The beach has pure white sand with a river winding down to the sea and rainforested hills behind. You can buy cooked fish on the beach.

Places to Stay

Cheap hotels can be a bit of a problem as they are often full of local residents. This is true of the *Lido Hotel*, Garrison St at the junction with Charlotte St, which costs Le 50 a double. The same applies to the *City Hotel*, Lightfoot Boston St on the corner with Gloucester St, which is dirty and run-down, and costs Le 40 a double.

Opposite the City Hotel is the *Tropic of Cancer Restaurant*, 4 Gloucester St, which has rooms upstairs for Le 40 a single. It's an old wooden colonial place with a lot of character and nice, clean rooms run by a pleasant lady called Mrs Williams. The restaurant downstairs is the cheapest in town.

The *YMCA* (for both men and women) on Fort St has been renovated and has a cafeteria and clean rooms that cost Le 30/45 a single/double. Women can stay at the *St Joseph Sisters' Convent* on Charlotte St which is clean with mosquito nets and cooking facilities. It's possible to sleep on

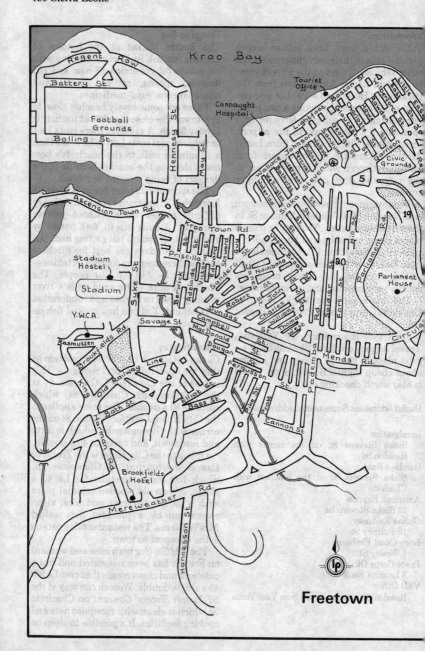

Freetown

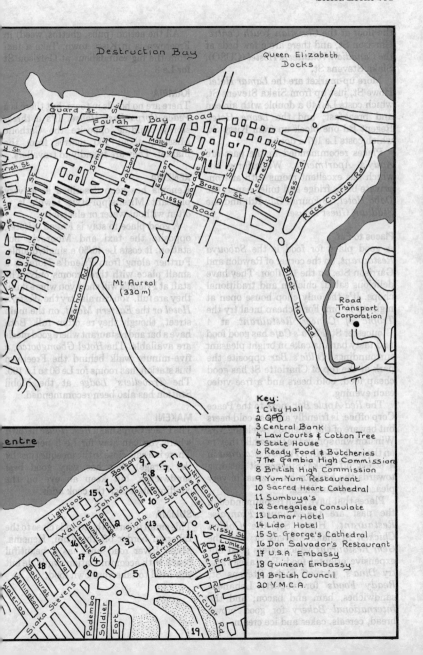

Key:
1 City Hall
2 GPO
3 Central Bank
4 Law Courts & Cotton Tree
5 State House
6 Ready Food & Butcheries
7 The Gambia High Commission
8 British High Commission
9 Yum Yum Restaurant
10 Sacred Heart Cathedral
11 Sumbuya's
12 Senegalese Consulate
13 Lamar Hotel
14 Lido Hotel
15 St. George's Cathedral
16 Don Salvador's Restaurant
17 U.S.A. Embassy
18 Guinean Embassy
19 British Council
20 Y.M.C.A.

the floor at the *Christian Youth Centre*, Garrison St, and there are a few beds at the *Canadian Volunteers Hostel* (CUSO), Siaka Stevens St.

More up-market are the *Lamar Hotel*, Howe St, just up from Siaka Stevens St, which costs Le 140 a double with air-con and breakfast; and the *Leone Hotel*, Regent Rd one block up from Kissy St, which costs Le 107 a double.

Places recommended in the past are *Andy's Apartments*, Wilberforce St, which has excellent rooms with air-con, private bath, fridge and toilet paper; the *Dabo Hotel*, 18 Fourah Bay Rd; and the *Stadium Guest House*.

Places to Eat

A good place for food is the *Sabouya Restaurant*, on the corner of Rawdon and Garrison Sts, on the 1st floor. They have delicious salad, chicken and traditional chops. It's the only chop house open at night to 10 pm. For a cheap meal try the *Tropic of Cancer Restaurant* at 4 Gloucester St. *Flora's Café* has good food and tasty banana cake in bright pleasant surroundings. *Dillie's Bar* opposite the park at the top of Charlotte St has good cheap food, cold beers and a free video each evening.

The *Red Apple Bar*, next to the Peace Corp office, is friendly and has cold beers but beware of the 'Shelltox'-wielding Mrs Winston who sprays the flies while they're on the food. The *Don Pedro Restaurant* in a street off Siaka Stevens St heading towards the harbour has pizzas, in very pleasant surroundings.

Places that have been recommended in the past are the *Alliance Française Restaurant*, Howe St; the *Golden Chicken* in Siaka Stevens St; and the *Gem Restaurant* which offers good but expensive oriental food. For takeaways, try *Dina's*, just off Siaka Stevens St; *Ready Foods* for yogurt, Lebanese sandwiches, ham and bacon; and the *International Bakery* for good brown bread, cereals, cakes and ice cream.

All the action (pubs, ghettos, weed) in Freetown is in Kissy town. Take a taxi from the big roundabout at Garrison St for Le 3.

KAMBIA

There are no hotels in town, but there is a *Peace Corps Rest House*. It's a three-storey building opposite the Catholic Mission, about 200 metres from the market. They are friendly to travellers.

KENEMA

Kenema has been described as a 'very pleasant Mississippi-style town'. It is often without water or electricity.

A good place to stay is *Friend's Hotel*, opposite the taxi and Monrovia bus station. It costs Le 40/50 a single/double. Further along from Friend's Hotel is a small place with three rooms only. The staff at Friend's will show you where it is if they are full. You can also try the *Western Hotel* or the *Eastern Motel*, on the main street, though they're often full. Both have a bar and restaurant where good meals are available. The *Hotel Gbomgbotch*, a five-minute walk behind the Freetown bus station, has rooms for Le 60 to Le 100. The *Travellers' Lodge* at the Mobil Station has also been recommended.

MAKENI

The Peace Corps has a *Rest House* in town where you can stay for Le 5 per night. There is a café close to the mosque (just by the garage) that has very good beef sandwiches, but keep an eye on the condiments which the cook adds.

SULIMA

This small town on the coast is close to the Liberian border off the Zimi, Kenema, Mano River road and has a beautiful beach with accommodation available but you need to take your own food.

National Parks

KAMAKWIE NATIONAL PARK

This park is north of the village of the same name in the north-eastern part of Sierra Leone. To get there, start out early by car (7 am at the latest) from Kamakwie No 2 – the twin village – to the river. The ferry is broken so cross by canoe. Hopefully there will be another car on the other side which goes to Fintonia but you get off before there at the turn-off to the park. It's a walk of seven km from here. On the return journey you usually have to walk all the way to the river (14 km) because cars from Fintonia leave very early.

There are tents and showers at the park with electricity in one tent. Canoes can be hired to see the hippos. If you ask the staff nicely they might prepare food for you otherwise bring your own and cook by the river.

OUTAMBA-KILIMI NATIONAL PARK

This is a small peaceful game reserve north of Kamakwie but it's impossible to get to without private transport. There are tent-like huts available to stay in but bring your own food. There is a lovely river and canoes for hire. Hippos can be seen two km downriver.

Somalia

The Somali coast once formed part of the extensive Arab-controlled trans-Indian Ocean trading network. Its ports of Mogadishu and Brava were part of the East African chain which stretched through Malindi, Mombasa, Zanzibar and Kilwa as far as Sofala in Mozambique. The prosperity of these ports, and indeed the trading network itself, were largely destroyed by the Portuguese in the early 16th century following the latter's discovery of a sea route to India and beyond, via the Cape of Good Hope. As a result, Somalia lapsed into obscurity, ignored by European traders because of its lack of exploitable resources.

In the 19th century much of the Ogaden desert – ethnically a part of Somalia – was annexed by the empire of Ethiopia during Menelik I's reign. This loss has never been accepted by the Somalis, and has not only poisoned Somali-Ethiopian relations for over half a century, but has also led to war on more than one occasion.

Throughout the 1970s Somali guerrilla organisations dedicated to recovering the Ogaden were supported by the Somali government. At one point they had succeeded in not only throwing back regular Ethiopian army troops from the desert area, but also in taking Jijiga and almost capturing Harrar and Dire Dawa – the major towns in southern Ethiopia. They were eventually pushed back over the Somali border only with massive Russian and Cuban assistance. This followed Moscow's switch of allegiance from Mogadishu to Addis Ababa in the wake of Haile Selassie's overthrow and the Marxist takeover in Ethiopia. Somalia also claims parts of northern Kenya, which were detached during the late 19th century by the British, though these claims are on a much lower key than those relating to the Ogaden.

At the turn of the century Somalia was divided between the British, who took the northern part opposite South Yemen, and the Italians, who took the southern part alongside the Indian Ocean. The two parts were reunited when independence was gained in 1960. Nine years later a military coup brought current President Mohammed Siyad Barre to power on a ticket of radical socialism, which has resulted in enormous changes in Somali society. The government places great emphasis on self reliance and on the use of team work. Many roads, houses, hospitals and agricultural projects have been created by such methods, paralleling similar redevelopments around the world.

As a result of the coup which brought Barre to power, the USA withdrew the Peace Corps and in 1970 imposed a trade embargo on the country following news that Somalia was trading with North Vietnam. The USSR immediately stepped into the vacuum with economic and military aid, and several years later Somalia's armed forces became one of the best equipped and best trained on the whole continent. The honeymoon came to an end, however, when Russia threw in its lot with Mengistu's Marxist regime in Ethiopia, Somalia's traditional archenemy. The Russians were summarily ordered to leave Somalia in the late 1970s. Since then there has been a *rapprochement* with the west, which has included the use of port and airbase facilities by the USA at Berbera.

Unusual among African countries, the people of Somalia are all from the same

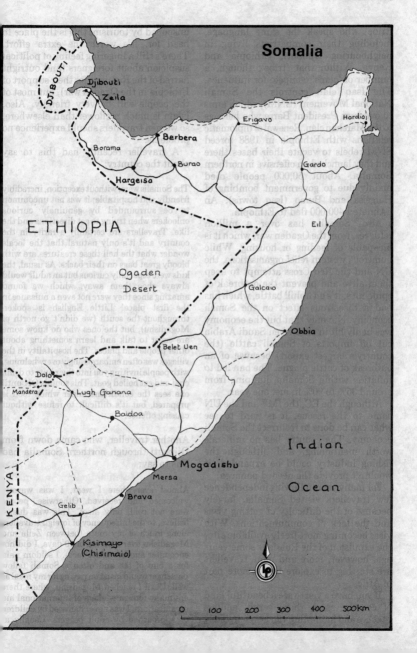

'tribe' who speak the same language, including their compatriots living in neighbouring Djibouti, Ethiopia and Kenya. Within that 'tribe', though, a number of 'clans' compete for influence. The Isaq clan controls the Somali National Movement (SNM), which aims to overturn President Barre who belongs to the Marehan clan. Renewal of diplomatic relations with Ethiopia in 1988 forced SNM rebels to vacate their bases there and they launched an offensive in northern Somalia. About 50,000 people died mainly due to government bombing of Hargeisa and Burao (Isaq towns). An estimated 400,000 fled to Ethiopia.

Also, Somalia has over a million refugees, from the Ogaden war, which it is incapable of feeding or housing. While numerous western relief organisations, the UN and the Red Cross attempt to keep them alive and prevent the outbreak of epidemics, it's an uphill battle, which has had a disastrous effect on the Somali economy. Not only that but the economy was badly hit in 1984 when Saudi Arabia cut off imports of Somali cattle (the country's largest export) because of an outbreak of cattle plague. The ban led to inflation within Somalia, jumping from around 35% to 90% in just one year.

Although the EC, the IMF and the UN came to the rescue, it is hard to see what can be done to resurrect the Somali economy. The country has no minerals worth mentioning, and although the fishing industry could be expanded, it wouldn't provide the needed panacea.

For many years following independence few travellers visited Somalia, largely because of the difficulty of getting visas and the lack of communications. With visas becoming more freely available after the expulsion of the Russians some years ago, however, more and more travellers are starting to explore this remote part of Africa.

If you have a yen to see a beautiful land of camels, sand, thorn scrub, endless beaches and interesting villages completely unspoiled by tourism, this is the place to head for. It's worth the extra effort. There's still a lingering feeling of political suspicion about foreigners (and outright hatred of the Russians for their support of Ethiopia in the Ogaden war), but most of the people will be very friendly. Also, Islam is much mellower than elsewhere, so women travellers should experience no problems.

A traveller recently had this to say about the country:

The Somalis were, without exception, incredibly friendly and hospitable; it was not uncommon to be surrounded by genuinely curious onlookers when trying to get directions and the like. Travellers are certainly a rarity in the country and it's only natural that the locals wonder what the hell these creatures are with bloody great bags on their backs. As usual, the kids were especially curious but an adult would always shoo them away, which we found amazing since they were not even a nuisance in the first place! Little English is spoken throughout the south (we didn't go north of Mogadishu), but the ones who do know some are eager to talk and learn something about other people and places. The hospitality in the villages was often embarrassingly overwhelming, with people inviting you into their huts to drink chai and eat boiled goat. This sounds OK until one sees the conditions under which food is prepared, but it's difficult to refuse without causing offence.

Another traveller, who came down from Djibouti through northern Somalia had this to say:

Almost everywhere I went, I was warmly welcomed and received. Otherwise, people were not cold, only aloof. This was due, I believe, to the infrequency of foreign travellers along much of my route (between Zeila and Mogadishu over a period of 10 days, I did not encounter another white face). I seldom paid for a cup of tea and often a Somali fellow passenger would insist on paying for my meal as well. Until I reached Mogadishu, where there are many foreign workers of international aid organisations, I was never harassed by children or approached by adult beggars. Usually at least one person of the 10 or 20 people on the back of the truck could speak reasonable English and was happy to talk with me. On a couple of occasions it was made abundantly clear that hatred of the Russians runs very deeply because of their support of the Ethiopians in the war in the Ogaden. I maintained as low a profile as possible with regard to officials and met with no hostility from them.

Facts

GEOGRAPHY & CLIMATE

Severe droughts are a continuing problem in this part of the world. The one which struck in the mid-1970s had a devastating effect on the people living in the Ogaden area and necessitated their relocation to more favourable areas. Another drought at the end of the 1970s, combined with renewed fighting over the Ogaden, has left Somalia with the almost impossible task of incorporating an estimated one million refugees.

The Somali coastline has some of the longest beaches in the world but it is unsafe to swim on most of them because of the danger of sharks. Also, because there is no shady fringe of coconut palms on these beaches, visits to them can become a searing affair.

The climate is hot and humid during the rainy seasons (March to June and again between September and December) but otherwise very pleasant. In the mountains and plateaus of the north it is hot and dry with little vegetation and few people. You won't see any evidence of agriculture, only the scattered herds of domestic sheep, goats and camels of the nomads. You can make some beautiful journeys in this part of the country, especially from Hargeisa to Berbera, and along the switchback ascent up the 1000-metre-high escarpment from the coastal plain to the central plateau along the Berbera to Burao road. South of Mogadishu the land becomes greener, though flat and monotonous. Corn and bananas can be seen growing in the fields.

PEOPLE

The people who make up the population of around five million are perhaps the most beautiful in the world, being tall with aquiline features, ebony skin and long flowing robes. They are quiet and dignified and tend to ignore strangers, although Somalis who have learned to speak English are quite ready to talk, unless they are politically suspicious of you.

WARNING

Northern Somalia is in the throes of a civil war. There have been reports of atrocities committed by Somali forces on members of the Isaq clan, and other human rights abuses. The safety of foreign relief workers in this area is no longer guaranteed and the Australian agency, Community Aid Abroad, has withdrawn its health-care programme in protest at the government's repressive actions.

VISAS

Visas are required by all.

In Nairobi, Kenya (the embassy is in International House, Mama Ngina St), a three-month visa costs KSh 200 and requires two photos and a letter of introduction from your embassy. This letter is free from the Irish and Australian embassies for their citizens but the British Embassy charges KSh 260. The visa takes 24 hours to issue. Check the dates on your visa before leaving the embassy as they sometimes make mistakes.

In Cairo, Egypt (the embassy is just west of Dokki St, 10 minutes on foot north of 6 October St), they only issue visas if you will be arriving by air and have onward air tickets. No overland-entry visas are issued. Visas take 24 hours to issue, cost E£21.70, and require three photos and a letter of recommendation. This letter costs E£7.50 from the British Embassy for their citizens. The visa is valid for one month and must be used within one month of issue. Visa applications are accepted on Wednesday, Saturday and Sunday between 10 am and 12 noon.

You can also get visas easily in Dar es Salaam (Tanzania) where they are issued by the Italian Embassy. A three-month multiple-entry visa costs TSh 250. They are also easily obtainable in Djibouti.

In London the Somali Embassy won't issue tourist or transit visas without a letter or invitation from a company or similar organisation in Somalia.

You cannot get a visa at the border or on arrival by air.

You must have valid vaccination certificates for entry, including one for yellow fever. If you arrive in Mogadishu by air without a yellow fever vaccination certificate, they may insist on vaccinating you there and then. Get it done before arriving.

MONEY
US$1 = SSh 89

The unit of currency is the Somali shilling = 100 cents. The import and export of local currency is allowed up to SSh 200. There is a black market for hard currency (US dollars and Saudi ryals are preferred, with the pound sterling a poor third) but be discreet. Expect around SSh 140 for US$1 in Kisimayo and SSh 135 for US$1 in Mogadishu. Credit cards are a waste of time.

If arriving by air you must buy a currency declaration form for SSh 20. Make sure you declare everything they're likely to find during a thorough search or you could find yourself spending a week in jail and being deported afterwards. At Liboi (the land border with Kenya) and Loyada (the land border with Djibouti), currency forms are not normally issued, but it's worth asking for one anyway to avoid hassles later. If you try to change money at a bank inside the country without a currency form, for instance, you

may be referred first to customs. This can soak up time.

The January 1985 devaluation made Somalia a very reasonable place to visit in terms of costs. Likewise, international phone calls are quite cheap and the service is efficient (you'll never have to wait more than one hour).

The airport departure tax is SSh 80 in Mogadishu and SSh 30 in Hargeisa.

ACCOMMODATION
Outside Mogadishu and Kisimayo there are few hotels to choose from. All are very basic with considerable variation in cleanliness. If you're an unmarried couple you should say you're married when asking for accommodation. If you sleep out in the desert (as is often necessary on long truck trips) you need a sleeping bag or warm clothes. It gets quite cold at night.

FOOD
The staple diet everywhere is rice, macaroni or spaghetti with a splash of sauce. A joint of sheep or goat costs SSh 50 and the endless cups of tea cost a standard SSh 5.

In the Mogadishu market there is a fair choice of food such as tomatoes, bananas, grapefruit, bread rolls, onions and peppers. The standard breakfast throughout Somalia is fried liver (of sheep, goat or camel) with onions and bread for SSh 50 – very tasty if you like liver.

Cafés hardly ever serve vegetables. Normally it's just meat, spaghetti and mofu, a local bread that resembles a chapatti but would be better used as a cushion – it's thick and rubbery like the traditional fermented bread of Ethiopia.

QAT
Another feature of life, in common with Ethiopia and the two Yemens, is the consumption of qat. The leaves of this bush give a kind of mild amphetamine high when chewed and is one of the few stimulants sanctioned by Islam. Its sale and distribution is big business. Even at

the height of the Ogaden war the daily DC 3 Air Somali qat flight from Dire Dawa to Mogadishu was always on time and shooting at it by either side was strictly out of the question.

More recently, the supply of qat has been driven in at high speed across the scrub from Kenya and Ethiopia in specially modified Toyota Land Cruisers. These delivery runs present a very good source of lifts, provided you can endure the punishment which your head and kidneys receive along the rough desert roads. Qat is now officially illegal in Somalia, though the supply continues to pour in. Does this sound like something else you might have come across?

HEALTH

Malaria is a serious problem in Somalia and even if you are taking chloroquine you might still get a light bout that will knock you off your feet for a few days. If this happens, go to the nearest refugee aid centre rather than a Somali hospital.

Although the World Health Organisation claims smallpox has been wiped out, you shouldn't take this for granted if going near any refugee camps. It's a good idea to have a smallpox vaccination beforehand, just in case.

The tap water in Mogadishu is said to be alright for drinking, but elsewhere it should be avoided because of the risk of hepatitis.

PHOTOGRAPHY

People with cameras must have a photography permit. These cost SSh 100, require three photos and take two days to issue. They are available from the National Censorship Office near the Dalsan Hotel and the US Embassy in Mogadishu. You'll also need two copies of your Somali visa (there are photocopying stores on the same road) and you have to state reasons for wanting a permit. Even with a photography permit you should be very discreet about taking photographs because many people object.

LANGUAGE

Somali is the official language. English is widely used in the north but Italian dominates in the south. However, it is almost essential that every traveller knows some Somali. Here's a basic English-Somali vocabulary:

Useful Phrases & Words

good morning	*subah wanaqsan*
good afternoon	*galab wanaqsan*
good evening	*habeen wanaqsan*
How are you?	*iska waran?*
I'm fine	*ficaan*
thank you	*mahadsamid*
Where do you come from?	*hage ka timio?*
I come from . . .	*wahan ka imid . . .*
What is your name?	*maga?*
My name is . . .	*maga aniga . . .*
How much . . . ?	*waa imissa . . . ?*
I want to eat	*inaan ahno baan raba*

yes	*ha*
no	*maya*
I	*aniga*
you	*adiga*
he	*isaga*
she	*iyada*
we	*anaga*
they	*iyaga*
today	*maanta*
tomorrow	*berri*
yesterday	*sheley*

Food

food	*ahnto*
water	*beeyu*
milk	*anno*
meat	*hillip*
camel	*gil* (hard 'g')
goat	*ari*
liver	*ber*
rice	*baris*
bread	*roti*
vegetable	*kudar*
salt	*milih*
tea	*shah*

spaghetti	*basta*
lobster	*argosto*
fish	*khallun*

On the Road

Is this truck going to (Erigavo)?	*baaburr ke tagaya (Erigavo)?*
How much?	*imisa?*
How many km?	*imisa km?*
How many hours?	*imis sa'adood?*
Where do you go?	*hage u so'ofa?*
where?	*hage?*
when?	*mahrki?*
who?	*kuma?*
before	*qor*
now	*had*
maybe	*lege yaba*
far	*fuq*
fast	*degdeg*
slow	*tartip*
big	*wean*
small	*yahr*
road	*djit*
town	*magalo*
truck	*gari*
bus	*bus*
toilet	*musghul*

Remember that Somali script is Romanised. Arabic script is only used for religious purposes.

Numerals

1	*kow*
2	*laba*
3	*sader*
4	*afar*
5	*shan*
6	*ligh*
7	*todoba*
8	*seeded*
9	*sagal*
10	*toban*
20	*laba tau*
30	*sodon*
40	*afar tan*
50	*koh tan*
100	*bogol*
200	*laba bogol*
1000	*kuhn*

Getting There & Around

AIR

There are two flights per week in either direction between Nairobi and Mogadishu on Sunday by Kenya Airways and on Thursday by Somali Airlines. The fare is normally about US$150 but if you buy a round-trip ticket (US$164) in Mogadishu you can get US$62 refund in Nairobi in Kenyan shillings (at least that's what Kenya Airways tell you).

At Mogadishu the airport is very disorganised and delays can be expected. Theft from luggage is a common problem. Make sure all your papers are in order or you'll have real hassles, and be prepared for a major search when leaving Mogadishu.

Somali Airlines has two flights a week in either direction between Mogadishu and Berbera for SSh 6400. This is an excellent flight if you don't mind ex-airforce pilots who still think they're flying MiG fighters. There is one flight a week, on Tuesdays, in both directions from Mogadishu to Kisimayo for SSh 2400. Mogadishu to Hargeisa costs SSh 5600.

If you're travelling south through Africa and want to see northern Somalia without having to backtrack, it might be worth considering the flights from Cairo to Djibouti – details are in the Djibouti chapter.

ROAD

There are surfaced roads between Mogadishu and Kisimayo and, except for a few stretches of desert track, between Mogadishu and Hargeisa. Elsewhere the roads are gravel or just tracks through the bush. In the dry season the unsealed roads and tracks are no problem and you'll get from one point to another quickly. In the wet season, however, the stretch between Kisimayo and Garissa (Kenya) alone can take up to two weeks!

The road between Hargeisa and Djibouti gets into a similar state, but it isn't quite so radical. One traveller, who went along this road in the wet, described it as the only one he'd come across in Africa where you could be covered in dust and bogged in the mud at the same time.

You cannot go overland into Ethiopia at present. Toyota Land Cruisers on the qat run do it every day, but unless you're in the game, you're *persona non grata*.

Hitching

A good alternative to buses is lifts with one of the relief agencies. These lifts are relatively easy to get and are a cheap way of moving around the country. The vehicles run by these agencies are officially for relief workers only, but if you are interested in the work they do, the chances are they'll give you a lift.

One of the best places to try is the United Nations High Commission for Refugees (UNHCR) in Mogadishu on the 'Volag' (voluntary agencies) notice board. There are often 'lifts offered' notices here. The Anglo-American Beach Club, Lido Rd, Mogadishu, is a good place to ask around for lifts, as are the Finnish TB Centre (Finnish medical aid) and the GTZ Bureau near the West German Embassy (enquire there). Good lifts can also be obtained via the traffic police once you're out of the city.

Bus

There is a regular network of buses between the main centres of population in the south, but very few in the north. Most of them travel at night to avoid the heat of the day.

Examples of current bus fares and schedules are as follows:

Liboi (Kenya-Somalia Border) to Kisimayo There are several daily buses, some of them direct, others via Afmadu. The cost is SSh 700 (plus there might be a baggage charge) and the trip takes about 10 hours. The 'road' is just a sandy track through the scrub. There are numerous security checks which involve 'everybody off/

baggage search/document check/everybody back on'. They're mainly concerned with Somalis smuggling goods in from Kenya. Officials are generally courteous to western travellers.

Kisimayo to Mogadishu Daily buses leave about 6 am (though they're often late leaving) from the square next to the police station. There are usually plenty of seats if you get there by 5 am. It costs SSh 550 and takes all day with army checkpoints every hour (they're looking for qat, and there's no luggage search). In Mogadishu tickets must be bought in advance from a street vendor at the bus station. Trucks cost SSh 300.

Mogadishu to Hargeisa or Berbera This is a three-day journey and you need to have a sleeping bag. It costs SSh 1500 and there are about 30 checkpoints along the way.

Berbera to Hargeisa There are a number of minibuses available along this paved road for SSh 400 plus SSh 100 to SSh 300 for a bag. It takes about four hours with a lunch stop and the minibus will take you to any hotel in the city centre.

Mogadishu to Mersa Buses cost SSh 80. They leave when full.

Hargeisa to Loyada (Djibouti border) Trucks along this unpaved route usually cost SSh 1200. It's two days of rough travelling but it's probably the most scenic route in Somalia.

BOAT

The Russians virtually killed the dhow trade while they were in Somalia, but there is still a few boats plying up and down the coast. If you have time it is worth making enquiries at the old port in Mogadishu or in the small port at the end of the beach in Kisimayo. In the latter you should be able to find dhows travelling to Mombasa. The price is around SSh 3000 including food (though bring your own fruit and extra food) and it takes about three to four days to travel the 530 km. The captain will probably arrange your exit stamp at immigration. It is a great experience. The dhows going south to Kenya only do so at certain times of the year (November to March); at other times the wind is blowing in the wrong direction and it can take two weeks to get from Mogadishu to Lamu!

From Mombasa to Kisimayo it costs around KSh 400 on an ordinary boat and takes two to three days. On arrival at Kisimayo you must clear customs at the old port, the new port and immigration. This will involve a taxi ride. Negotiate the price first: it will be anything up to SSh 500.

TO/FROM DJIBOUTI

Regular trucks travel this route. The trip is short, but it can take two days. The landscape is stunning and worth the discomfort. First check with the UNHCR in Hargeisa for any refugee vehicles that might be going that way. If travelling in the opposite direction, the best place to find a lift is at the Somali border post around mid-afternoon – ask the drivers as they stop at the border. Get a visa for Djibouti (where required) at the embassy in Mogadishu near the UNDP compound. They are cheaper than at the border and there's a lot less hassle if you have one when you arrive at the border. You must have an onward ticket to get into Djibouti.

TO/FROM KENYA

There are two possible routes, one from Kisimayo to Garissa via Liboi, and the other in the extreme north of Kenya from Lugh to Garissa via Mandera. The route via Liboi is the most predictable as far as transport and road conditions go, and there's a full description of it in the Getting There & Around section in the Kenya chapter.

The route via Lugh requires more initiative. There are some trucks along this route but usually you will have to find a lift in a Toyota Land Cruiser on the qat run. Ask around in any of the border towns about these, but remember they drive very fast and you'll feel like a piece of jelly at the end. On the other hand, it isn't that difficult to find a lift.

As you come from the Kenyan side after leaving Mandera, walk the two km to Beled Hawo in Somalia then try to find the immigration office (it's in a whitewashed concrete compound). After this go to the customs house and try to find the customs officer. Both the customs checks at Mandera and Beled Hawo are pretty thorough. There is no bank or any place to change money in Beled Hawo and you are only allowed to bring in SSh 200 and KSh 100 which won't go very far. This probably means you will need to bring in more Kenyan shillings, but hide them well.

There's a bus once in a while to Lugh (Lugh Ganana), which goes through the bush in no apparent specific direction. Lugh is like a huge refugee camp and you may be able to get a lift to Mogadishu with the relief agency CARE (Emergency Logistics Unit).

Travelling from Somalia to Kenya you must first have permission from the district commissioner before crossing the border from Lugh. If you start from Kisimayo and are heading to Kenya via Liboi, you must get an exit stamp from the National Security Service before setting out.

Around the Country

BAIDOA

There are plenty of cheap hotels. The *Bar Bekin* at the start of town coming from Mogadishu has been recommended as a good place to meet people and have cold drinks.

BERBERA

There is nothing much of interest in Berbera although the people are really friendly and helpful. One traveller reported that it was 'hot, humid and hell – and that's in the cool season'. If arriving by plane, Somali Airlines have a free bus service to their office in town. People are sometimes hassled by immigration officials looking for illegal immigrants. Play it cool and be polite. Also check before taking photos, even if you have a permit.

Places to Stay & Eat

The *Hotel Wabera* is clean and has singles for SSh 100; or the *Hotel Saaxil* costs SSh 160 for a double with fan, air-con is extra. More expensive is the *Hotel Sahel* for SSh 450 a double with air-con.

There are many small eating places, where you can get good meals of fish, rice and salad for around SSh 100. Otherwise, there are more expensive restaurants on the seashore where an excellent spaghetti costs about SSh 150, though it often comes accompanied by anything up to 50 ravenous cats. It's best to avoid the water and drink Coke or Fanta.

BRAVA

This is a beautiful old Arab town five km off the main Kisimayo road. Take a visit to the **leather tannery** where you can get cheap leather sandals for SSh 80 to SSh 150 a pair. A cheap place to stay is the *Kolombo Hotel* on the right at the entrance to town. It has large airy rooms for SSh 150 a double. There are no good eating places in town.

HARGEISA

Hargeisa is the former capital of British Somaliland but is now very run-down and, like Berbera, there is nothing much of interest, although the people are really terrific.

The taxis are painted red and white and are even more expensive than in Mogadishu. The Air Djibouti office is next to the Hotel Oriental and there is a daily flight to Djibouti. For trucks or buses to Mogadishu go to the Hamar station in the centre of town.

Places to Stay & Eat

A good place to stay is the clean and secure *Hotel Daali*, which has singles/doubles for SSh 135/230. The *Hotel Maaweel* is also clean and costs SSh 140 for a single. There are rooms available at the *Hargeisa Club* for SSh 200 per night. The *Hotel Oriental* is cheaper at SSh 150 a double but, despite its expensive exterior, the rooms are bad, the beds are uncomfortable and the toilets unusable. However, the food is surprisingly good and cheap. Also recommended in the past is the *State House* two km outside town. The staff are friendly and you can camp in the park.

The *Lake Victoria Restaurant* is a good place to get a meal of shish kebabs, chips and a cold drink for SSh 75. On the edge of town is *Gouled's*, a fancy outdoor restaurant with slick USA-educated proprietors. The food is good but expensive.

KISIMAYO

Remember to report to the National Security Service on arrival. If you're heading for Kenya, you must also get an exit stamp before setting off.

To give you a taste of what to expect on your first night in Somalia, here is one traveller's recent impression of Kisimayo:

Here's a place that seems to be timeless – almost. Donkey cart drivers loll about in their carts as the donkeys plod away at their own speed along streets lined by robust palm trees, whose overhanging fronds half obscure, here and there, the old town. Perhaps it's the sandy streets themselves which exude an air of timelessness, but then maybe it's the narrow, low adobe buildings with darkness boding on their perimeters.

On one such row of structures can be seen a series of dark men in equally dark holes, each with his own fire pounding away on hot metal. In another area, sheltered from the sun, are others cutting and sewing leather to make shoes. At night, kerosene lanterns line the streets illuminating Breugelesque figures moving about their business, selling wares or sitting in front of conical piles of peanuts, roasted maize, little trinkets or bars of soap.

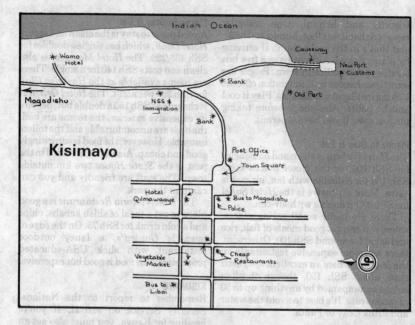

Every so often a dark shadow blankets your view as a flock of women, clothed in enormous gowns and veils, flit furtively from one stall to another like conspirators from the tales of Sheherazade, mysterious and unknowable. Add to this the warm gentle breeze wafting in from the Indian Ocean bringing with it the flavours and aromas from the Hejaz, Oman, Pakistan and India.

Such have been the nights here for centuries and you can still find goods from those places in the shops – fabrics, spices and incense from countries as far flung as China. Here is a place where you can relax and indulge in fantasy.

Places to Stay & Eat

One of the best places to stay is the clean and friendly *Hotel Quilmawaaye*, which costs SSh 150 for a bed or SSh 200 a double. It is set in a nice garden and the local big wigs go here. Not as central is the *Hotel Africa* with good rooms for SSh 200 a double, but no electricity. More expensive is the *Hotel Wamo* with singles/doubles for SSh 250/500. This is a good

place to meet expatriates and locals, especially if looking for a lift to Mogadishu and elsewhere. There is a disco on Friday nights.

One traveller suggested it might be worth asking around for accommodation at the ARABCO compound, which is an expatriate hangout. Someone there might offer to put you up for the night. Take some western cigarettes and whisky and leave them as a contribution to your keep.

At the restaurant attached to the Hotel Quilmawaaye you can get spaghetti, fish, and chicken for SSh 50 per item. The *Shoreline Restaurant* also has very good food that is reasonably priced.

LIBOI

This border town is a fascinating little place. Local people bring in their camels, goats and cows for water at the borehole. Accommodation is available in mud-brick houses for SSh 60 a room (double or triple) on the Somali side and KSh 15 on the Kenyan side. Food is limited to chai, chapatti, boiled goat and a few tomatoes in the market under the tree.

MERSA

This is a wonderful old Arab town on the coast 100 km south of Mogadishu. Five km from Mersa (an easy hitch) you can stay right on the beach in huts at **Sinbusi Beach** where it's clean, quiet and there are few people. A hut for two costs SSh 400 with a basic bathroom. The sea is calm, clear and warm with no sharks due to a sand bank further out. There is a restaurant that has good grilled fish.

MOGADISHU

Founded in the 10th century AD by Arab immigrants from the Persian Gulf, Mogadishu was at its height in the 13th century. It was then that the mosque of Fakr al Din and the minaret of the Great Mosque were built. The city's wealth was based on trade across the Indian Ocean with Persia, India and China and this is what attracted the Portuguese during the 16th century. Unlike the other Arab city-states further south along the coast of East Africa, Mogadishu was never conquered by the Portuguese and continued to be ruled by its sultans until it accepted the overlordship of the Sultan of Oman in the 19th century.

Information

The Al Aruba Hotel has a duty-free shop where you can get booze, cigarettes, film and cosmetics.

Things to See

The **Hammawein** is the original city of Mogadishu and was once one of the most beautiful sights on the east coast of Africa, rivalling such places as Lamu, Mombasa and Zanzibar. These days its gleaming whitewashed walls have been allowed to deteriorate, but it's still worth a visit. Make sure you see the two **mosques** mentioned earlier.

Other travellers have recommended a visit to the Italian-constructed Roman Catholic **cathedral** and the **museum** next to the Al Aruba Hotel. The museum is open daily from 9 am to 12 noon except on Thursday and Friday.

The **market** (by the main bus station) is very interesting and worth looking around. The best buys are Somali cloth and carved meerschaum objects. The jewellers will make up gold and silver to order. In the craft shops next to the Anglo-American Club you can get nice camel-bone items, carvings and fabrics.

The beach most popular with expatriates and Somalis, especially on Friday, is **Gezira Beach**, but to get there you need to have your own transport or know someone who has. There is a hotel there with a beach supposedly protected from sharks. The restaurant is reasonably priced and serves fish, lobster, rice and spaghetti.

Further along the coast are a number of isolated **coves**, though not all are protected from sharks. (One of them is appropriately called Shark's Bay, though the name is derived from a shark-shaped coral reef that juts up out of the water.) Keep an eye out for them if you go swimming. It's not an uncommon event for someone to be gobbled up. You can buy fresh fish. It's suggested you do not take a local woman to these areas as there are military checkpoints along the way staffed by armed soldiers. Most of them are 'young lads' (as one traveller put it) and are not likely to behave in the way you might want.

Places to Stay

There are lots of cheap hotels on Makha Rd on the way to Km 4. One of the best is the *Hotel Kaffa* (formerly the Zeno) near the Kenyan Embassy. A double with fan costs SSh 250. The electricity works, it's clean and quiet and the rooms are arranged around a pleasant courtyard.

The *Hotel Dalsan* near the American Embassy is very popular amongst travellers, but is small and often full. It has bright

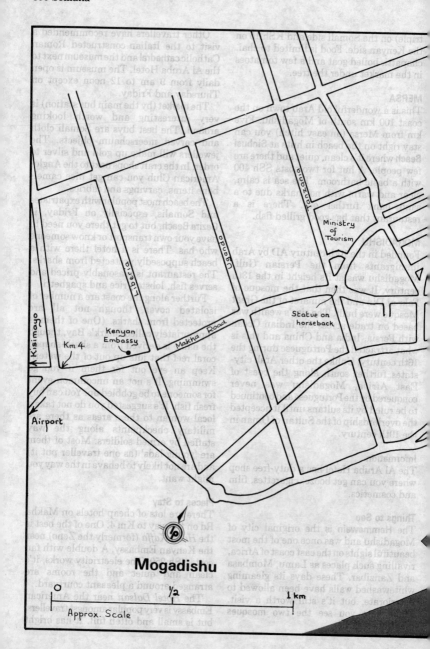

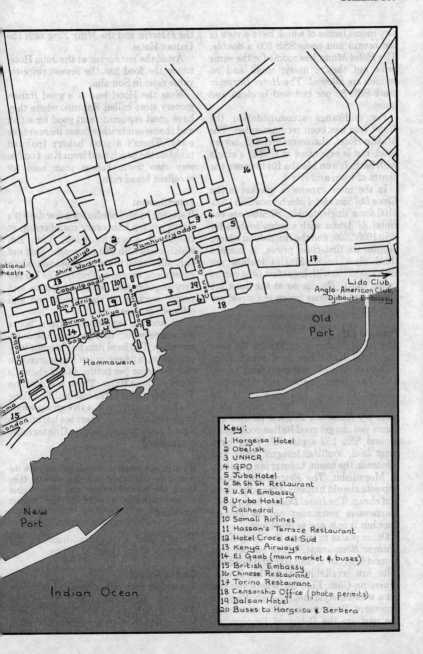

Key:
1 Hargeisa Hotel
2 Obelisk
3 UNHCR
4 GPO
5 Juba Hotel
6 Sh Sh Sh Restaurant
7 U.S.A. Embassy
8 Uruba Hotel
9 Cathedral
10 Somali Airlines
11 Hassan's Terrace Restaurant
12 Hotel Croce del Sud
13 Kenya Airways
14 El Gaab (main market & buses)
15 British Embassy
16 Chinese Restaurant
17 Torino Restaurant
18 Censorship Office (photo permits)
19 Dalsan Hotel
20 Buses to Hargeisa & Berbera

airy rooms (some of which have a view of the ocean) and costs SSh 300 a double. The *Hotel Muna* has rooms for the same price but they're noisy, small and no women are allowed. The *Hotel Hargeisa* costs SSh 80 per bed and is clean and quiet.

For mid-range accommodation the *Hotel Issa* has been recommended. The *Makha Hotel*, also recommended, is very good, but is expensive at US$29 a single with bath. It's on Makha Rd between the centre of town and Km 4.

In the more expensive bracket is the *Croce Del Sud Hotel* which costs SSh 1400/2100 for a single/double. Similar are the *Hotel Al Aruba* with singles/doubles for SSh 1600/2300, and the *Hotel Juba* which, despite its first-class prices, is more a third class hotel. Singles/doubles are SSh 1300/2100 with breakfast (if it can be called that). The rooms at the Juba are alright but the ones facing the street are very noisy.

Places to Eat

The *Hotel Mubarak* on Makha Rd near the Hotel Kaffa has good meals from SSh 50 to SSh 150 and great fruit juices, and has been highly recommended. Similar in price and quality is the *Restaurant Seafood*. For a really good meal try *Hassam's Rooftop Restaurant* where you can get good Italian cooking for around SSh 180 a plateful. They have roast beef, soufflés, lasagna, tuna and lobster on the menu. Lobster is a good buy in Mogadishu. The *Restaurant Torino* opposite the old harbour is friendly, clean and cheap. The *Hotel Dalsan* has a good, inexpensive restaurant on the ground floor but it only serves breakfast.

Other places to try are the *Hong Kong Chinese Restaurant*, where entrées cost around SSh 100 to SSh 300, and good egg rolls are available; and the *Anglo-American Club*, Lido Rd, where you can get a western-style meal though it's quite expensive. Restaurants recommended in the past are the *Pakistani Restaurant*, the *Pizzeria* and the *Ming Sing* near the Dalsan Hotel.

Avoid the restaurant at the Juba Hotel where the food has the lowest price-to-value ratio in Somalia.

Near the Hotel Issa is a good Italian grocery store called Kaputo, where they have great espumuto and good tuna fish and cheese sandwiches to eat there or take away. There's a good bakery (painted pink) on the beach road from Km 4 on the way into town. Follow your nose for excellent bread rolls.

Entertainment

If staying in Mogadishu for a few days it's worth getting temporary membership at the *Anglo-American Club*, Lido Rd, which costs SSh 500 per week. This not only allows you to get in, it lets you take a guest along except on Friday. The bar is a very popular spot with expatriates and people working at the various aid and refugee agencies.

All working expatriates have a 'booze allowance' which they get from the duty-free shop. The local rum has become very expensive, but beer, when it is scarce, can cost the same per bottle, so the choice is yours at those times. There is a disco on Thursday nights in the last building along the Lido, usually with a live group which sings western music. There is a bar and it's a good place to meet people. One traveller commented:

If you go as a couple, a Somali guy may ask the man if he can dance with the woman, then thank the man afterwards and have a chat without uttering a word to the woman concerned!

There's also a popular disco in the basement of the Hotel Al Aruba.

Getting Around

Taxis (red and yellow) around town are relatively expensive at SSh 200 to SSh 300, and the buses are unreliable. The best form of transport are the minibuses which run continuously along set routes. There are no actual stops, so just stand at the roadside and flag them down. When you want to get off, shout out, 'Jojii!'. They cost SSh 5 for any trip. Buses to other parts of the country leave from El Gab, the big expanse of sand, dust and chaos at the southern end of Lido St, which is also the market place.

The cheapest way to get to the airport is to take a pick-up to Km 4, then walk the remaining 1½ km. If you can't hack that, a taxi will cost around SSh 500 (but they will start at anything up to SSh 3000).

South Africa

The earliest recorded inhabitants of this area of Africa were the !Ke (Bushpeople), who lived in the mountains of the southern Cape region, and the Khoi-Khoi (Hottentots), who lived further east along the Cape coast. Both were essentially hunters and gatherers organised into small family units without any centralised tribal authority. The next arrivals were a number of Bantu-speaking tribes (including the Tsonga, Nguni, Swazi, Zulu and Xhosa) who, by the 13th century, had settled most of the land between the Drakensberg mountains and the south-east coast. These tribes were primarily pastoral, held land in common and undertook some form of agriculture.

Because they were better organised and their food supply was more predictable, their numbers rapidly increased and this forced them to find new unpopulated areas further to the south and west. In the process, the !Ke and Khoi-Khoi were forced further and further west and north into more remote areas.

Into this shifting migration pattern came the early Portuguese mariners towards the end of the 15th century in search of a sea route to the Indian Ocean. They made no attempt to settle the area and were content to erect a number of stone crosses, which acted as navigational aids. The Portuguese were mainly interested in plunder and the takeover of the Arab monopoly on the transport of spices from India and the East Indies. It wasn't until the mid-17th century that any attempt was made to colonise this part of Africa.

The first European settlement was established in 1652 by the Dutch East India Company at the Cape of Good Hope. Its purpose was not only to establish a supply point for Dutch merchant ships on their way to or from India and the East Indies, but also to find slaves, raw materials and precious metals to fuel the expanding merchant capitalist economy of Holland. They were joined 36 years later by a group of Huguenot refugees from France.

What remained of the lands occupied by the Khoi-Khoi were quickly brought under Dutch control and the settlers themselves, being so isolated, developed a close-knit community with their own dialect (Afrikaans) and Calvinist sect (the Dutch Reformed Church). To develop the land, slaves were imported from both the west and east coasts of Africa as well as from South-East Asia.

Over the next 150 years the Dutch colonists gradually spread east, taking land from the indigenous people and coming into increasingly violent contact with various Bantu tribes expanding westwards. The Dutch had already crossed the Orange River by 1760 and the stage was set for the inevitable confrontation. It came in 1779 when the eastward expansion of the Boers (the Dutch-Afrikaans farmers) was temporarily halted by the Xhosa. This first so-called Bantu War was one of many fought with great bitterness by the two opposing groups, and in them lie the roots of apartheid.

Further Boer expansion was given a powerful shot in the arm during the Napoleonic Wars as a result of permanent British annexation of the Cape in 1806 and the abolition of slavery in 1834. The latter was regarded by the Boers as an intolerable interference in their affairs and it led to the wholesale migration of the Boers across the Orange River two years later. This event became known as the Great Trek and has become enshrined in as much myth and legend as the arrival of the First Fleet in the settlement of Australia.

Meanwhile the British busied themselves with the creation of another colony in the eastern Cape by driving some 20,000 Xhosa from their lands and bringing in 5000 settlers.

The stage was set for a blood bath between the Boers and Bantu tribes on the one hand, and between the British and the Bantu on the other. Pressure on the Bantu meanwhile had led to profound political and social changes among the tribes of the Natal area.

The changes were spearheaded by Dingiswayo, a chief of the Zulu, who reorganised and unified his tribe into a military nation along European lines. Shaka, the commander of Dingiswayo's regiments, discontinued the traditional Bantu methods of conducting warfare based on ritualised single combat and the ransom of fallen champions. Instead he used rigorously trained soldiers who fought in formation - to the death if necessary - and who were intent on annihilating their enemies.

So began the many grim years of intertribal warfare that left a scene of carnage and devastation previously unknown in this part of Africa, and created an impression in the minds of Europeans who came across it that this was the normal state of affairs. It also led to the wholesale migration and dispersal of defeated tribes. One such migration, led by Mzilikazi (who had quarrelled with Shaka), even got as far as Lake Tanganyika, destroying, in the process, the effete Rozwi Empire based on Great Zimbabwe and Khami. Other groups fled south and west over the Drakensberg, clashing with settled tribes there and leaving similar scenes of devastation. The genesis of both Swaziland and Lesotho

and, to some extent, Botswana, dates from these struggles.

It was into this scene of fanatical Zulu militancy that the Boers came in search of new lands. Not far behind them were the British, who were settling in ever increasing numbers in Cape Province and Natal. The spears and shields of the Zulu, however, were no match for the guns of the Europeans, and the Zulu were eventually forced into submission. Relations between the Boers and the British, meanwhile remained tense, and frequently led to armed conflict, particularly after the formation of the autonomous Boer republics of the Orange Free State and the Transvaal.

Nevertheless, when diamonds were discovered in 1867 at Kimberley, then gold in 1886 on the Witwatersrand, the Boer republics needed to attract British capital in order to develop the deposits. Capital poured into the republics and the demand for labour soared. The wars of conquest had created the ideal labour pool and many Africans, unable to feed themselves or pay colonial taxes, were forced to seek work in the mines. The supply of labour, however, was never equal to the demand, and in the early years the African workers were able to turn this to their advantage by demanding higher wages or deserting when better conditions were not forthcoming.

Against this background the British, along with other industrialised European nations, were in the process of grabbing what was left of Africa. Bechuanaland was made into a British protectorate in response to the German annexation of Namibia, and Cecil Rhodes was encouraged to send expeditions north into what is now Zimbabwe and Zambia. When these areas failed to promise the bonanza that the Transvaal had realised, Rhodes turned his attention back to the Transvaal, where he encouraged a rebellion amongst the heavily taxed white non-Afrikaner mine workers with a view to destabilising the Boer republics and inviting British

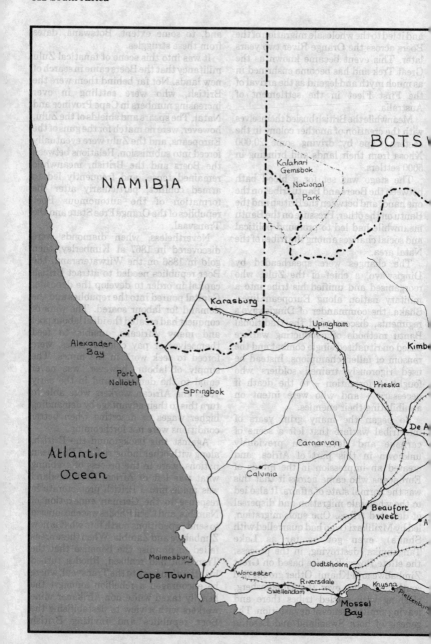

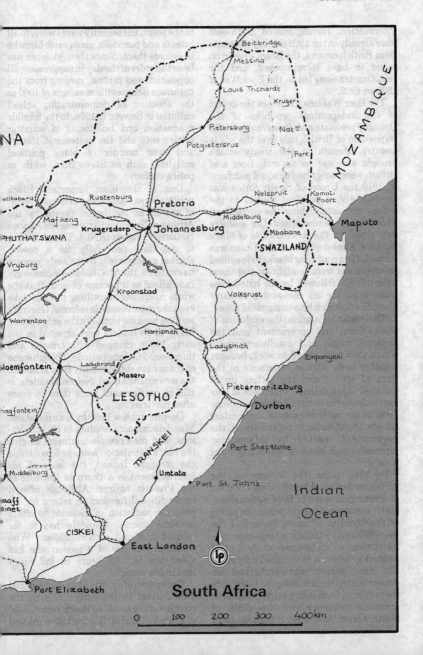

South Africa

0   100   200   300   400km

intervention. Having moved north-east once already in the 19th century to escape from British control, the Boers were in no mood to have it reimposed, and the resulting tensions led to the Boer War of 1899 to 1902.

The Boer War brought about the defeat of the independent republics of the Orange Free State and Transvaal, and the imposition of British rule over the whole country, though in the treaty which brought the war to an end, Boer and British were recognised as equal partners. In 1910 the Union of South Africa was created, giving political control to the whites and establishing the conditions, which have characterised the country ever since, for the strict control of black workers. Almost as soon as the Union was formed, laws confining blacks to specified reserve areas were brought in and these were quickly followed by the hated Pass Laws requiring all non-whites to carry identification in white-designated areas.

This racist legislation, the exclusion of blacks from the government and the abysmal wages and conditions under which they were forced to work, brought together early African resistance in the form of strikes and the setting up of political organisations, which would give expression to the demands of black workers. Despite the moderate tone of the charters adopted by these early organisations, the government reacted by intensifying repression and banning one party after another.

In 1948 came the victory of the Afrikaner National Party riding the crest of a resurgent wave of Boer nationalism, and it was determined to pursue its policy of apartheid at all costs. Instead of the more informal – though no less onerous – restrictions which had previously applied to blacks, Asians and so-called coloureds, the new government embarked on draconian legislation designed to exclude these groups from ever having political or economic influence over the affairs of South Africa. And what is perhaps more

to the point, the security forces were, to all intents and purposes, given carte blanche to enforce them. Since then, violence has been the order of the day in suppressing all opposition and protest, ranging from the notorious Sharpeville massacre of 1960 to the shooting of demonstrating school children in Soweto in 1976, to the forcible evacuation and bulldozing of squatter settlements and the systematic torture and even murder of black political activists, such as Steve Biko, while in police custody.

One of the most important Black political organisations to arise as a result of the racist legislation passed by the Afrikaner National Party was the African National Congress (ANC). Though willing to negotiate peacefully for a power-sharing arrangement in the early years of its existence, the ANC became increasingly radicalised as it became obvious that the white rulers were unwilling to undertake even the most cosmetic reforms. Guerrilla warfare became virtually the only option. Many of its leaders were arrested in the early 1960s, charged with treason and imprisoned for long periods. Though some of them have subsequently been released, the movement's head, Nelson Mandela, is still in confinement more than 25 years after his 'trial'.

Despite such a lengthy incarceration, Mandela remains resolute in his convictions, and his example continues to give the black population courage to continue the struggle. Indeed, the issue of his imprisonment is a thorn in the side of the Pretoria regime. Although offered unconditional freedom in return for his public repudiation of violence to effect political change, Mandela has so far refused to accept such conditions. Who would expect less of a person who has spent the last 25 years in jail for a legitimate cause?

The system of apartheid was entrenched even further in the early 1970s by the creation of the so-called Black 'homelands' of Transkei, Ciskei, Bophuthatswana and

Venda which were, in theory, 'independent' countries with their own governments. All this was window-dressing and was recognised as such internationally. However, by creating the 'homelands' Pretoria could claim that all blacks within white-designated South Africa belonged to one or other of these 'homelands' and that they were, therefore, foreign guest-workers not entitled to political rights. Not only that, but any black person found without an official residence pass (such as the family of a legal pass-holding worker) or any unemployed black person could be unceremoniously 'deported' back to a homeland.

Despite the fact that some of the 'homelands' came into existence without those pillars of apartheid such as the Mixed Marriages Act and the Immorality Act (which outlawed marriage or sexual relations between whites and blacks), the whole exercise has been exposed for the fraud it is. All the 'homelands' are ruled by compliant black opportunists beholden to the White South African regime not only for their political survival (as witness the failed coup in Bophuthatswana), but also for their economic survival. They are largely uneconomic because they encompass some of the least fertile land in South Africa, and their industrial base is negligible.

The main purpose of the 'homelands' as far as Pretoria is concerned is to provide a convenient pool of cheap labour for the mines, factories and farms of White South Africa. Not only that, but the convoluted borders of some of the 'homelands' makes a mockery of their claim to be independent – Bophuthatswana, for instance, consists of no less than seven separate enclaves, all of them completely landlocked and all but one of them completely surrounded by South African territory.

While all this was taking place, however, South Africa was becoming increasingly isolated as a result of the success of various African liberation struggles in Angola, Mozambique and Zimbabwe, which all brought Marxist-leaning governments into power. As a result, a war psychosis came to dominate government thinking and resulted in ever higher defence budgets; invasions of southern Angola by South African armed forces; the encouragement of counter-revolutionary guerrilla groups in both Mozambique and Angola; the refusal to enter into genuine negotiations for the independence of Namibia; and the development of a nuclear capacity with the clandestine assistance of West Germany. US satellites monitored what appeared to be a nuclear bomb test in the South Atlantic in the early 1980s, but it has never been established exactly what happened.

At about the same time, South Africa found itself on centre stage internationally. There were widespread calls both from the UN and the Commonwealth for economic and political sanctions against the regime unless it embarked on a course leading to genuine democracy – meaning one person one vote, regardless of skin colour. While this is certainly anathema to President Pieter Botha's ruling party, he was forced to make concessions to keep the international community at bay and prevent wholesale disinvestment by western business concerns in South Africa. The concessions included the abolition of such things as the Pass Laws, the Mixed Marriages Act and the Immorality Act as well as the establishment of a new tricameral parliament of whites, 'coloureds' and Indians on the basis of a 4:2:1 ratio. This parliament, while it accurately represents the current population balance between those three communities, still excludes blacks from any say in the central government.

Even these mild reforms resulted in the breakaway of a radical right-wing faction from his party led by die-hards intent on maintaining the structure of apartheid to the end. They have since become a powerful factor restricting the regime's freedom of movement.

Since then the politics of South Africa have become very complicated both internally and externally. There is no doubt that the repugnant, degrading and racist edifice of apartheid has to be dismantled and a reasonable power-sharing arrangement set up between the various ethnic groups in South Africa. How to reach such an agreement, and what form it might take given the confrontationist and entrenched positions now being adopted by the various factions, is another thing entirely.

South Africa is a pot on the boil. Disregarding international pressure, anyone who commands support within South Africa is on the stoop, ranging from Bishop Tutu (Anglican Christian) to Chief Buthelezi (of the Zulu-dominated Inkatha movement) to the supporters of Nelson Mandela (ANC) and the multiracial anti-apartheid United Democratic Front (UDF), not to mention the die-hards of the extreme White right-wing. What remains a fact, however, is that anyone classified as black in South Africa has no political rights whatsoever as far as the central government is concerned.

Unfortunately, another factor which has complicated the issue is that South Africa has become a fetish of the international media. Nothing excites the appetite of these networks more than violence. It's almost as though they are waiting for the final conflagration and are doing their best to encourage it. While most people would support the freedom of the press to report events, how often do these media undertake a detailed analysis of the issues involved? In most cases, never. Were such a conflagration to occur in Uganda, Burundi, Zaïre, Equatorial Guinea or Sudan, would events be reported in such consistent fashion or would they be a two-day flash in the pan? Part of the reason for the intense press coverage (as much as the government clampdown on foreign journalists will allow anyway) is that the rulers of South Africa claim that the country is – and would like it to be

regarded as – a civilised nation. Some of its actions betray it as otherwise. And, while it's true that far fewer people have been killed in the struggle here than in conflicts and civil wars elsewhere in independent Africa, that's hardly something of which to be proud.

Whether disinvestment, international political and economic sanctions, recession, labour unrest or guerrilla warfare eventually force a change of policy, it is clear that Pretoria must come to the negotiating table before it is too late. Economically, the country is the most important in Africa south of the Sahara and, despite all the rhetoric which pours forth from the so-called Front Line states in particular, it is obvious that if South Africa were to be engulfed in a civil war the effects would be felt far and wide. Its armed forces are also acknowledged to be more than a match for those of its neighbours combined.

Were Pretoria to refuse to negotiate a sharing of power, and the extreme right-wing were to decide on a scorched-earth approach in anticipation of a Black majority government, the effects would reverberate for decades and demand an international rescue operation the like of which has never been seen.

Anger (and unemployment as a result of the recession) has been rising steadily in the Black townships not only because blacks are excluded from political power, but also because of the murder and/or abduction of a number of prominent activists – thought to be the work of the secret police. Several black mayors, councillors and police officers were 'necklaced' (burnt to death by having a tyre doused in petrol rammed down over their shoulders and set alight) and hundreds more were forced to resign out of fear for their lives. This has proved to be a major setback in Botha's attempts to contain dissent.

Meanwhile, if recent statements are anything to go by, it seems that Pretoria, internally at least, is actually hardening its stance rather than moving to an accommodation. Such attitudes can only continue to fan the flames of war and make a final conflagration inevitable.

Facts

GEOGRAPHY & CLIMATE

Much of the interior of South Africa consists of a high, semiarid plateau, known as the veld, broken occasionally by mountain massifs as in Lesotho and the far south-west of Cape Province. This plateau is traversed by some of the major rivers in southern Africa – the Vaal, Orange and Limpopo. On the eastern side of the country the Great Escarpment of the Drakensberg sweeps across the provinces of Transvaal and Natal and gradually peters out in Cape Province. This whole area is one of outstanding natural beauty.

The narrow coastal plain is rugged and equally beautiful, though more fertile and subtropical than the high veld. These coastal regions have a Mediterranean climate with hot summers and mild winters – ideal for cultivation of grape vines (South Africa is well known for the quality of its wines).

WILDLIFE

The country is rich in wildlife though most of the large game is now concentrated in the national parks and, particularly, the huge Kruger National Park on the border with Mozambique.

Conservation of this game is an active national concern and you will not find anywhere near the same amount of poaching (and corruption of park officials which that entails) as in the national parks further north, especially in East Africa. The so-called Garden Route between Cape Town and Durban is noted for its rich variety of forest timber and wildflowers, though the most famous wildflower area is Namaqualand in the north-eastern Cape.

PEOPLE

Of the population of 32½ million, some 22 million are black, just under five million white, some 2½ million 'coloured' (ie, mixed race) and around 1½ million of Indian descent. Some 60% of the whites are of Afrikaner descent and the rest of British descent. The 'coloureds' are concentrated mainly in Cape Province and the Indians (descended from indentured labourers imported by the British in the 19th century) mainly in Natal. The majority of the population is Christian, though the Indians remain largely Hindu.

ARTS

Despite government censorship of the media and the repression of Black political aspirations as well as support for them by the minority English-speaking whites, there are many theatres, cinemas and lecture halls. They regularly feature plays, films and other cultural activities, which are remarkably radical in the opinions and ideas they promote.

While it may be true that, in some ways, South Africa is a police state – and a brutal one at that – it certainly isn't in other respects. Much of what goes down in some of these theatres would be anathema to even such relatively liberal governments as Kenya.

VISAS

Visas are required by all except nationals of Botswana, the Irish Republic, Lesotho, Seychelles, Swaziland, Switzerland and the UK.

Visas are free to nationals of Australia, Austria, Belgium, Canada, Denmark, Finland, France, Germany (West), Greece, Israel, Japan, Luxemburg, Mauritius, Netherlands, New Zealand, Norway, Spain, Sweden, and USA. For anyone not in these categories visas cost R 2.50.

Most people are issued with a three-month triple-entry visa allowing visits to Lesotho and Swaziland without having to apply for another visa. If you don't get a multiple-entry visa, you must get one before visiting these two countries. Re-entry visas can be obtained from the Department of the Interior, Civitas Building, on the corner of Struben and Andries Sts, Pretoria 0002 (Private Bag X1114); or from similar offices in Johannesburg, Cape Town, Durban, Bloemfontein, Port Elizabeth, East London and Kimberley.

In Africa there are South African embassies only in Lilongwe (Malawi), Port Louis (Mauritius) and St Denis (Réunion) but visas are obtainable from South African trade missions in many southern African nations including Botswana, Lesotho, Mozambique, Swaziland and Zimbabwe.

The South African authorities are very strict about onward ticket requirements, especially if visitors arrive by air or via Beitbridge. At Jan Smuts Airport, Johannesburg, for instance, they won't accept any excuses. The same is true for entry via Cape Town International Airport. If you have no onward ticket they will insist that you buy one and it will be stamped 'Nonrefundable'. The only alternative is to deposit a R 1200 bond (refundable on exit).

You can actually get a refund on a ticket stamped 'Nonrefundable' if you buy an alternative onward ticket (a rail ticket from Mafikeng to Gaborone (Botswana) is acceptable) but it can involve a lot of hassle. You must go along to customs and immigration, show them your alternative onward ticket and get a letter from them instructing the airline to refund your money. If you want the refund in cash and it's a South African Airways ticket, this has to go through headquarters in Johannesburg and the process takes weeks. Even if you fly in with a return ticket, it may be stamped 'Nonrefundable', making it impossible to cash in.

If you had to pay a deposit (through not having an onward ticket) and are leaving via Ramatlhabama (South Africa-Botswana border), go to the South African 'Embassy' in Mafikeng (officially in Bophuthatswana) first. They'll take the deposit to the border with you and give it back to you at that point.

You're advised to look clean and tidy on entry.

Many South African businesspeople go through the Tlokweng Gate as this is the shortest route from Gaborone (Botswana) to South Africa. It is undoubtedly the most easy-going border crossing.

The biggest problem with South African visas, however, is that once you have one stamped in your passport, you'll have great difficulties getting into many other countries in Africa, and will be refused entry to quite a few. Zambia and Tanzania are the main two where this is most likely to happen. South African immigration officials are aware of this and will, if you ask, insert a loose card with the stamps on it, in your passport. When you leave, throw the card away.

However, that's not the end of your problems as far as entry into Tanzania is concerned. Officials at the southern borders are very clued up about which entry and exit stamps for Botswana and Zimbabwe are picked up on the South African border. If you can't prove that you haven't been to South Africa or don't have a cast-iron explanation for the various stamps in your passport, they'll refuse entry and stamp 'Undesirable Immigrant' in your passport. This is happening to a lot of travellers these days.

The Homelands

There's a further complication because of the creation of the so-called 'homelands' – Transkei, Bophuthatswana, Ciskei and Venda. Unless you want specifically to visit one you can get around them most of the time. The exceptions are if you're travelling direct from Cape Town to Durban (through Transkei) or coming from Botswana between Gaborone and Mafikeng (through Bophuthatswana).

Entry requirements for the 'homelands' are:

Bophuthatswana No visas required for a visit up to 14 days so long as you have a valid passport and a South African visa (where required). If planning on staying longer, visas can be obtained from the Bophuthatswana Embassy (tel 436001), 39 Glyn St, Colbyn, Pretoria 0001; or from the consulate-general (tel 001 215931), Nedbank Mall, 145 Commissioner St, Johannesburg 2001.

Ciskei No visas required.

Transkei Visas are required by all except South African nationals and can be obtained at the border on entry. They can also be obtained beforehand from the Transkei Embassy (tel 215626) on the 2nd floor, Tomkor Sentrum, Du Toit St just north of Vermeulen St, Pretoria. The embassy is open from Monday to Friday from 8 am to 1 pm and 2 to 4.30 pm.

Visas are also available from the consulate-general (tel 011 215935), 164 Commissioner St, Kariba House, Johannesburg 2001. There are consulates in Durban, Port Elizabeth, Bloemfontein, Cape Town and East London. There's a small charge for tourist visas, which are issued while you wait. No photos are required.

Venda No visas required.

If you need a visa for any of the 'homelands', you will also need a South African re-entry visa. You can avoid this by getting a multiple-entry visa for South Africa in the first place. This applies equally if you're going to visit Lesotho and Swaziland.

These are the official requirements. In practice, however, you may find that at many crossing points between South Africa and the various 'homelands' there are no customs/immigration posts, so you simply drive through (or ride undisturbed on the train). The same may apply when re-entering South Africa. On the other hand, there are all sorts of permutations on this theme. You may be stamped as leaving South Africa, but not stamped for entering, say, Transkei, or you may be stamped leaving, say, Transkei, but not stamped re-entering South Africa.

It's generally true to say that if you don't have a visa for a 'homeland' (where required), it can be obtained on the border. This is invariably true if you're travelling by train. We've only had one report of a traveller being fined for not having a Transkei visa (he entered by road and was fined R 40). As with South Africa, officials on these borders will put stamps on a separate card in your passport, though we did have one report of the officials at Kei Bridge (Transkei) north of East London insisting that stamps went directly into the passport.

Visa extensions for South Africa can be obtained at the same office that re-entry visas are issued.

Other Visas
Lesotho & Swaziland Neither of these countries maintains diplomatic relations with South Africa. Visas must be obtained from the British Consulate-General, Nedbank Mall, 145 Commissioner St, Johannesburg 2001 (open Monday to Friday from 9 am to 2 pm), or from British consulates in Cape Town and Durban. The British Embassy in Pretoria does not issue visas.

Mozambique Mozambique does not maintain diplomatic relations with South Africa, but visas can be obtained from the Mozambique Trade Mission (tel 234907), 73 Market St, Johannesburg.

Zimbabwe Like Mozambique, Zimbabwe does not have official diplomatic relations with South Africa, but visas can be obtained from the Zimbabwe Trade Mission, 10th Floor, Sanlam House, on the corner of Sauer and Commissioner Sts, Johannesburg. Visas cost R 12 and are issued as soon as a telex to Harare is answered.

Working in South Africa

South Africa is experiencing a serious recession coupled with disinvestment by many multinational companies. Jobs are getting hard to find and the demand for skilled labour has dropped considerably. As a result, the authorities are making it more difficult for foreigners to obtain work permits or residence permits. Don't come here expecting to find immediate work – you might, but then might not.

Having said that, there is work for people with qualifications in electronics, engineering, medicine and teaching. Of course you will need to be able to produce certificates, degrees, references, etc.

If looking for teaching work it's advisable first to write to the Committee of Heads of Education, Department of National Education, Var der Stel Building, Pretoria 0001, and ask for a questionnaire. This then has to be signed by the registrar or senior tutor at your college or university. Without such a document they cannot determine what your salary should be so you'll be on the bottom rung. Perhaps you don't care?

For other work you can usually rely on your employers to sort out this stuff and your residence permits – if they really need you.

Casual work in restaurants is still fairly easy to get, but is becoming more difficult and the pay isn't too great.

In the 'homelands', on the other hand, there's an enormous shortage of skilled workers especially teachers. In Bophuthatswana, mechanical and civil engineers are in high demand. Even people who are prepared to take on a contract as a game warden get better wages than in South Africa itself. Those without qualifications might like to try for a job at the Sun City Casino Hotel. Most of the slot machine mechanics, croupiers and maintenance staff are expatriates and the pay and allowances are good.

In the Ciskei, there's an enormous shortage of qualified teachers and work is easy to find, though there are 60 to 70 students per class in the lower grades. Not only that, but only one in three children will have a textbook. The pay is about R 130 a month without qualifications and R 750 a month with an honours degree or an ordinary degree with a Diploma of Education.

Payment is often late, but does eventually arrive. It's suggested you don't get a job if you only want to stay a couple of months as this disrupts the children's education and means the authorities might have passed up someone who would have stayed longer. You must be able to show the authorities in Zwelitsha your certificates, or at least copies of them.

MONEY

US$ 1 = R 2.14
UK£ 1 = R 3.25

The unit of currency is the rand = 100 cents. The import and export of local currency is limited to R 100. There is no black market though this may change as South Africa's economy continues to deteriorate.

TOURIST INFORMATION

The South African Tourist Corporation (Satour) maintains offices in many large cities in America, Western Europe, Australasia and Japan as well as a number of other places. If you're planning on spending any length of time in South Africa, it's worth writing to them for information before setting off. They turn out some excellent literature – maps, accommodation and transport digests, booklets containing detailed descriptions of the national parks, game reserves, hiking trails and just about everything else you're likely to want to see.

Inside the country itself there are tourist offices at Bloemfontein, Cape Town, Durban, East London, George, Jan Smuts Airport, Johannesburg, Kimberley, Nelspruit, Port Elizabeth and Pretoria.

There is a network of youth hostels. You can get full details of these by writing for the brochure published by the South African Youth Hostels Association (tel 43 5693), PO Box 4402, Cape Town 8000, or ask at any Satour office.

An interesting magazine put out by the Educational Wildlife Expeditions, in association with the Wilderness Trust, has articles by travellers not only on South Africa but other places on the continent. The subscription address is: *Great Outdoors Magazine*, PO Box 84436, Greenside, 2034, Johannesburg.

ACCOMMODATION
Youth Hostels
South Africa has a network of Youth Hostels in all four states. At R 5 per night for members and R 6 for nonmembers (sometimes less) it's the cheapest accommodation you're likely to find, so it's worth having a membership card. If you haven't got one from your own country you can join here. The national office (tel 419 1853) is at 606 Boston House, Strand St, Cape Town 8001.

House-Sitting
If staying for a month or more in any of South Africa's larger cities, the cheapest form of accommodation is house-sitting. This is very efficiently organised by House Sitters Service, who have offices in many cities and put out a quarterly newsletter called *House Sitter*.

The sort of people they look for generally need short-term accommodation for a few weeks to a few months. They prefer couples without children, but this doesn't necessarily exclude single people. Twenty-five is considered a reasonable lower age limit, though this isn't rigidly applied (they are looking for people with sufficient experience in looking after a home and its contents).

Sitters are expected to undertake basic maintenance of the house, garden and swimming pool if there are no servants. Three hours of watering and one hour of mowing per week is regarded as a reasonable stint, if required. Current fees

for sitters are: daily fee of R 3 plus R 1.50 per person in excess of two, or R 150 per month for sits over three months long, and a refundable deposit of R 100. Electricity, water and servant costs are normally paid by the owners, subject to negotiation if the sit is over two months.

If you're interested, get in touch with the following offices:

Head Office
Mackay Chambers, 11 Mackay Ave, Blairgowrie, Randburg 2194 (tel 789 1250/1)
Cape Town
Mount Olive, Lindeshof Rd, Constantia Hills, 7800 (tel 021 72 5634)
Durban
12 Canal Drive, Westville, 3630 (tel 031 86 1541)
East Rand
P O Box 13434, Northmead, 1511 (tel 849 4432)
Johannesburg, Pretoria, West Rand
As for Head Office (tel after hours 787 9203)
Pietermaritzburg
7 Carbis Rd, Scottsville, 3201 (tel 0331 62943)
Windhoek (Namibia)
PO Box 20607, Windhoek 9000 (tel 061 33266)
Zimbabwe
18 Percy Fynn Rd, Belvedere, Harare (tel 01910 82721)
UK (June to Sept)
5 Ridgeway House, The Crescent, Horley, Surrey RH6 7NP (tel Horley 772514)

LANGUAGE
Afrikaans and English are the official languages. Several African languages are spoken, of which the most common are Xhosa and Zulu.

Getting There & Around

AIR
You can fly into South Africa direct from many places around the world, but no longer from Australia because the Australian government has banned South

African Airways. So the only way of getting there is to fly Qantas from Perth to Harare, where there is an immediate connection on South African Airways to Johannesburg.

Perhaps the cheapest flights out of South Africa to Europe are with Luxavia to Luxemburg. The carrier is not an IATA member, but the flights generally work out cheaper than you are likely to find on Hillbrow notice boards in Johannesburg. Check out these flights at 87 Rissik St, Johannesburg.

If you fly into South Africa and your time is limited, it's worth enquiring about deals SAA is offering. This can include 28-day unlimited-excursion tickets, which are a bargain by any standard: return trips offering 40% discount if booked four days in advance, certain night flights, which offer almost 50% discount on certain sectors, and stand-by flights generally offering 20% discount. Some of the deals available make flying cheaper than going by rail or bus.

ROAD

South Africa's roads are excellent.

Overland travellers have a choice of two main border crossing points – Beitbridge (Zimbabwe-South Africa) or Ramatlhabama (Botswana-South Africa). Both have road and rail connections with the Republic. Ramatlhabama is by far the easier of the two crossings. Officials at Beitbridge are well known for their strictness regarding onward tickets, sufficient funds and the like. There are, however, a number of smaller crossing points between Botswana and South Africa, which are even easier than these two.

Hitching

South Africa is one of the easiest countries in the world to hitch through – if you're white. So easy, in fact, that most white travellers rarely use the bus and train networks. Get out of the suburbs before starting (most cities sprawl for miles).

Johannesburg to Durban should take about a day, and Johannesburg to Cape Town about three days, with long waits here and there en route. One route which can be very slow is from Mafikeng to Vryburg, and travellers may have to take public transport along this stretch. Your country's flag on the front of your pack and a destination sign is a great help in securing lifts.

The majority of people who pick up hitchers will be extremely friendly and hospitable – so friendly that many travellers don't see the inside of a hotel room from one end of the country to the other. With some lifts, however, you may have to put up with long lectures on the virtues of apartheid. Afrikaans speakers are generally keen on this, English speakers much less so.

The worst areas for hitching are around Kimberley, along the Atlantic coast and in the Transkei. If you're hitching from Cape Town to Durban, and your lift is only going to some place in Transkei, get out at the border and wait for a through lift. If you don't, you could find yourself stuck.

The licence plate system works on the basis that the first letter indicates the state (C, O, N, T) and the subsequent letters indicate the city or town, eg, CA – Cape Town, CB – Port Elizabeth. Transvaal plates end with T but don't indicate the town.

Bus

There are a number of long-distance buses operating between the main centres, usually on a daily basis, but most of them are not particularly cheap. One which isn't too bad is the International Express which offers Johannesburg to Kimberley for R 30 and Durban to Johannesburg for R 35. On the other lines, such as Translux, prices tend to be higher and you are looking at around R 57 between East London and Durban (9¼ hours) and R 10 for Durban to Pietermaritzburg (one hour). Nevertheless, travelling by bus is still both cheaper and quicker than going 2nd class on the trains.

Elsewhere there are many more local buses which operate between smaller towns, and are mainly used by the non-white population. Even if you're white, these buses are safe to use though you'll undoubtedly attract a good deal of curiosity. They don't offer the same degree of comfort or speed as the long-distance buses, but they are quite cheap. International Express bus services are available between Johannesburg and Harare (Zimbabwe).

Renting Vehicles

Although all the normal international hire companies are represented – Hertz, Avis, Budget – they are no cheaper than anywhere else in the world and in fact are usually more expensive. However, since South Africa has its own car manufacturing industry, alternatives are available including local outfits, which rent relatively old vehicles at budget rates. Holiday Car Hire (Sir Lowry St, Johannesburg), for instance, offers old Volkswagens at R 8 per day plus 3 cents per mile, which is cheaper than public transport and certainly cheaper than the Hertz and Avis rates of around R 45 per day plus mileage. Also cheap is Rent-A-Wreck (tel 402 7043), again in Johannesburg.

TRAIN

South Africa has an extensive network of railways, and since desegregation was introduced a little while ago it's now possible for anyone – regardless of skin colour – to travel in any class. Whites were previously banned from travelling in 3rd class, so this made railway transport quite an expensive proposition for those budget travellers.

If you're thinking of using the railways extensively get hold of a copy of the *Intercity Train Time-Table* from any office of the South African Railway Travel Bureau. The addresses of these bureaus in the main cities are:

Bloemfontein
   FVB Centre, Shop 29, 40 Maitland St (tel 7 6352)
Cape Town
   Travel Centre, Station Building, Adderley St (tel 218 2391, 218 2282)
Durban
   Trust Ban Centre, 475 Smith St (tel 310 3376/63/71)
East London
   Southern Trident House, 56-58 Terminus St (tel 2 3952)
Johannesburg
   Intown Centre, on the corner of Rissik and Kerk Sts (tel 713 5541, 713 4941, 713 4163)
Pietermaritzburg
   Capital Towers, on the corner of Commercial Rd and Prince Edward St (tel 55 2461/2)
Port Elizabeth
   Fleming Building, Market Square (tel 2 2922, 2233)
Pretoria
   African Eagle Life Centre, 236 Vermeulen St (tel 294 2222/3/4)

Trains in South Africa are comfortable and not too slow, but are definitely slower (though cheaper in 3rd class) than the express buses. Durban to Pietermaritzburg costs R 6.30 (3rd class) and takes about three hours. Durban to Johannesburg costs R 41 (3rd class) and takes 17 hours.

Through services are available to Mozambique, Namibia and Zimbabwe, but the service from South Africa to Zimbabwe is only available via Botswana; there are no longer any through services direct via Beitbridge.

TO/FROM BOTSWANA

The most popular border crossings are between Mafikeng and Ramatlhabama; Zeerust, Pioneer Gate and Lobatse; and Zeerust, Tlokweng Gate and Gaborone. Travelling sales representatives and businesspeople recommend the last of these places as customs and immigration formalities are minimal. Going by one or other of the latter two routes, you will either have to hitch or take public transport. Hitching isn't all that easy until you get to Zeerust, and even then you may have to take public transport to Johannesburg. Make an early start if you don't want to be stuck.

For crossing at Mafikeng-Ramatlhabama, the easiest thing to do is to take the train, although there are infrequent buses between Mafikeng and Johannesburg for R 15.50. The trains going through this border are the ones which connect Johannesburg to Bulawayo (Zimbabwe) via Gaborone and Francistown (Botswana). Depending on the present state of relations between South Africa and Botswana, you may not have to get out at the border and walk across, but don't count on this. For details of the schedule and fares, see the To/From Zimbabwe section.

TO/FROM MOZAMBIQUE

The easiest way is to take the train from Johannesburg to Maputo via Ressano Garcia. The trains depart daily (except Tuesday) from Johannesburg and daily (except Wednesday) from Maputo. The journey takes about 17½ hours. Some time ago, the rebels of the MNR blew up the bridge at the border, so if it still hasn't been repaired you'll have to walk across and take a train from the other side.

TO/FROM ZIMBABWE

You have a choice of taking the train from Johannesburg to Bulawayo via Botswana and the Plumtree border, or a bus from Johannesburg to Harare via the Beitbridge border.

There are buses three times per week in either direction between Johannesburg and Harare. They depart Johannesburg on Monday, Wednesday and Friday at 10 pm and arrive the next day at 7 pm. In the opposite direction they depart Harare on the same days at 6 pm and arrive the following day at 4 pm. The fare is R 132.50 one way and R 228.50 return. You must change buses at the border. The terminal in Johannesburg is at the main railway station.

There is a weekly train in either direction between Johannesburg and Bulawayo, which departs Johannesburg on Thursday at 1.30 pm, arriving the next day at 2.20 pm; the fare is R 123.75 (2nd class). There are no through trains from Johannesburg to Harare any longer, though it is possible to take the train as far as Messina, then road transport across the border and another train from the other side.

Around the Country

BEAUFORT WEST

The tourist office is on Donkin St next to the museum. If on a tight budget try the *Catholic Mission* across the bridge. Father Muller may find floor space or a couch for you to sleep on. Otherwise, try one of the following hotels, all of which are in the lower price category.

Donkin House (tel 4287) is at 14 Donkin St. A room costs R 9 and up per person. More expensive rooms have bathrooms. The *Royal* (tel 3241/2) is at 20 Donkin St, or there's the *Park Rooms* in Danie Theron St. At *Young's Halfway House*, 143 Donkin St, a room costs R 9 per person and up. At the *Safari Tourist Rooms* (tel 2439), Pritchard St, a room costs R 6. Meals are available at all these places.

BLOEMFONTEIN

The tourist office is on the ground floor, FVB Centre, Maitland St. A visit to the **Voortrekker Museum and Park** is a must. It's much larger than the one in Pietermaritzburg. The **Sand du Plessis Opera House** is also worth a visit and is the most modern of its kind in Africa. Guided tours are available.

Other travellers have suggested a visit to **Kings Park**, one of the Republic's finest. It's full of colour all through the year. Take a walk through it and the adjacent **President Swart Park**, which also contains the zoo.

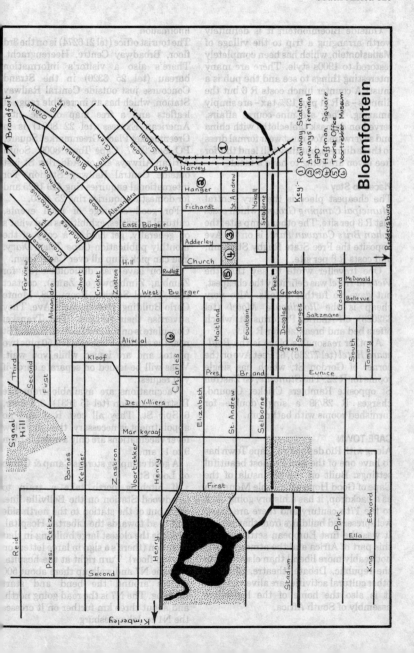

Bloemfontein

Key:—
1. Railway Station Airways Terminal
2. GPO
3. Hoffman Square
4. Tourist Office
5. Voortrekker Museum

Outside Bloemfontein it is definitely worth arranging a trip to the village of **Matiesfontein**, which has been completely restored to 1900s style. There are many interesting things to see and the pub is a must! A counter lunch costs R 6 but the dinners – at R 11 plus 12% tax – are simply amazing. They are nine-course affairs, served on damask tablecloths with china and silverware. You must wear formal dress to these dinners, but they will lend this for free if you are going to have a meal.

Places to Stay

The cheapest place is the very central *Municipal Camping Ground* which costs just R 3 per site. The other camp site, the *Johan Brits Caravan Park*, is on 1st Ave opposite the Free State Rugby Stadium, and costs R 8 per site.

One traveller wrote to say that the *Victoria Hotel* was definitely the cheapest, but gave no further details. Also very cheap is the *Roadhouse Motel* (tel 332023), off Andries Pretorius St, which offers bed and breakfast for R 10.

Another reasonable place is the *Boulevard Hotel* (tel 77236), 61 Peet Ave on the corner of Gordon St, which has single rooms for R 22. The *Stanville*, 85 Zastron St opposite Ramblers Cricket Ground, charges R 28/39 a single/double for furnished rooms with bathroom.

CAPE TOWN

Along with Rio de Janeiro, Cape Town has to have one of the world's most beautiful settings. Built on the peninsula of the Cape of Good Hope with Table Mountain as a backdrop, it has a history going back to the 17th century and there are many well-preserved buildings from that period. It was the first European settlement in this part of Africa and the atmosphere is noticeably more liberal than elsewhere in the republic. Debate, theatre, film and other cultural activities are alive and well. It is also the home of the legislative assembly of South Africa.

Information

The tourist office (tel 21 6274) is on the 3rd floor, Broadway Centre, Heerengracht. There's also a visitor's information bureau (tel 25 3320) in the Strand Concourse just outside Central Railway Station, which has an incredible range of leaflets and a free map of the city. American Express (tel 22 8591) is in Greenmarket Place, Greenmarket Square, PO Box 2337, Cape Town 8000. South African Airways are on Adderley St just outside Central Railway Station. For international enquiries ring 419 1525 and for domestic enquiries ring 25 4610.

For good coverage of local events, cultural activities, exhibitions and what's on generally, get hold of a copy of the monthly publication *Cape Town Diary*. You can pick it up all over Cape Town.

If you have visa difficulties (eg, for Zambia, Zimbabwe or Zaïre), contact Ross Travel Service, Room 308, Monte Carlo Building, Heerengracht Ave. They advertise their services. The Transkei Consulate is on the 2nd floor, 42 Strand St near the station. Visas cost R 2.50 plus two photos and are issued while you wait. Visas will be issued on separate cards if you request.

Vaccinations are available from the District Surgeon (tel 45 1631), 3rd floor, 6 Spir St. They all cost R 3 and no appointment is necessary, though yellow fever vaccinations are only available from 9 to 11 am.

A good camping store is Camp & Climb on Loop St.

If hitching north take a train to Goodwood Station on the Bellville line. Walk out of the station to the north side and head towards the Libertas Hospital, which is the closest large building in that direction (there's a sign in large letters on the top floor). Turn right at the hospital onto the N7 and walk up there about 500 metres around the bend and start hitching. The N7 is the road going north, and about three km further on it crosses the N1 to Johannesburg.

Things to See

In a city the size of Cape Town, and with such a spectacular setting, there are endless things to see and do.

Signal Hill View Point This hill (350 metres high) more or less divides the centre of the city in half. There are excellent views over most of central Cape Town and Table Bay Harbour. To get there, take Kloof Nek Rd and turn off to the right into Signal Hill Rd.

On the slopes of Signal Hill is the Malay quarter, an area of cobblestoned streets peppered with mosques, the oldest of them (the Anwal Mosque on Dorp St) dating from 1798.

Table Mountain Cableway Like to see the view from the top of Table Mountain (1067 metres)? In Africa this is the nearest you'll get to something comparable to the Sugar Loaf or Corcovado in Rio de Janeiro. Cable cars make the ascent every 30 minutes, weather permitting, every day between 9 am and 6 pm. From December to May they keep going until 10.30 pm. The ride costs R 5 return. To get to the cable car station from Kloof Nek bus terminal walk up Tafelberg Rd or take the minibus.

It's not advisable to go walking up there without a map or a good guide book. Several are available but the *Table Mountain Guide* by the Mountain Club of South Africa is probably the best. It's available at bookshops and camping stores for R 6.25. If that's too expensive buy the *Cape Peninsula* map (R 1) from tourist offices or the National Hiking Way Board. It shows walks and trails between Signal Hill and Cape Point, and describes some of the easier ascents of Table Mountain, but it's not as detailed as the guide book.

Castle of Good Hope Right in the centre of town and built in 1666, the castle used to house the first governors of the Cape colony. There are three different museums within the walls. Tours are conducted daily at 10 and 11 am, at 12 noon, and at 2, 3 and 4 pm; entry is 30 cents.

Greenmarket Square A very picturesque cobbled square, this is now a national monument and was once the site of Cape Town's market.

Museums There are several of these, but if you're a museum buff don't miss the Cultural History Museum open Monday to Saturday from 10 am to 4.45 pm and on Sunday from 2 to 4.45 pm. Initially it was the Dutch East India Company's slave lodge in 1679 and later became the Old Supreme Court. Entry is free for students and for everyone else on Mondays and Fridays, otherwise the entry fee is 50 cents. The museum also runs the Cape Dutch Koopmans de Wit House, Strand St, and the Malay Bo-Kaap House, Orange St. Both of these are essentially period furniture museums.

The South African Museum, open Monday to Saturday from 10 am to 5 pm and on Sunday from 2 to 6 pm, offers excellent ethnological displays including a good exhibition of Bushpeople artefacts, reconstructed villages and authentic music. Entry is free on Mondays and 50 cents on any other day.

Botanical Gardens The gardens are between Government Rd and Queen Victoria St, and are a beautiful spot to rest and relax in the middle of the city. They're superbly maintained and there are tame squirrels everywhere.

Beaches There's a string of great beaches all the way down the coast to Simonstown. Just take the train and get off when you see something you like. Kalk Bay is especially recommended. The *Brass Bell Restaurant* overlooks the sea and fishing harbour and offers all-you-can-eat fish and meat dishes for R 5.50. It also hosts open-air rock concerts on Saturday nights

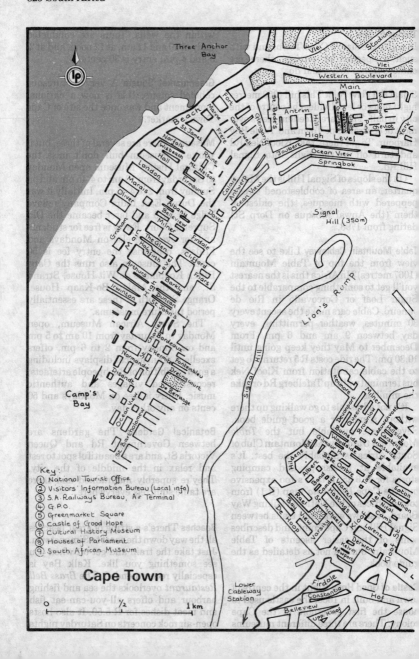

Cape Town

Key
1. National Tourist Office
2. Visitors' Information Bureau (Local info)
3. S.A. Railways Bureau, Air Terminal
4. G.P.O.
5. Greenmarket Square
6. Castle of Good Hope
7. Cultural History Museum
8. Houses of Parliament
9. South African Museum

0   ½   1 km

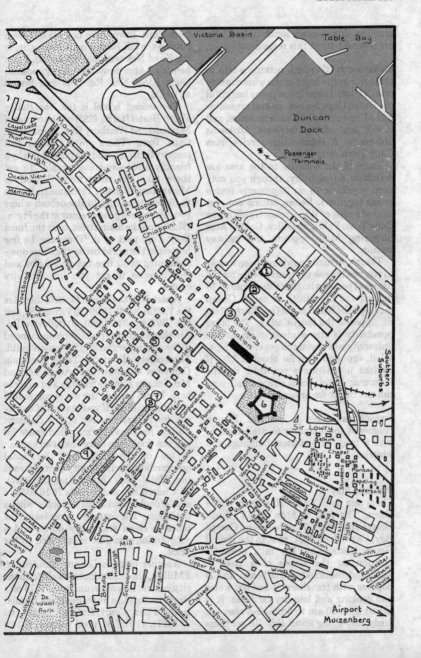

plus live singers every lunch time. There are several bars at this restaurant.

Stellenbosch It's worth making a trip to this town in the heart of the wine country east of Cape Town. It has many beautiful old Dutch Cape houses, several museums including an excellent wine museum, and is the seat of the foremost Afrikaans university. A regular bus service from Cape Town costs R 4.

Tours of the wineries in the area are definitely a possibility, though you may need a vehicle to do it properly (get a group together). Before setting out, get hold of a copy of *Wine Route Guide* at the Cape Town Publicity Office, Golden Acre Shopping Mall opposite the railway station.

There's virtually nowhere cheap to stay so you need to ask the tourist office for the names of people who offer this service (R 10 for bed and breakfast), or camp. Cheap meals can be found at the *Ons Pleck*, Plein St, opposite the tourist office. The other possibility is the student union at the university where you can get steak, chips, salad, eggs and ham for about R 2.50. If student unions leave you cold, try the *Lanzarac Hotel* which offers an all-you-can-eat buffet for around R 4.50.

Franschhoek This is an old French Huguenot town similar to Stellenbosch, with a range of historical buildings and wineries.

Places to Stay

There are two Youth Hostels in Cape Town. The first is *Stan's Halt Youth Hostel* (tel 48 9037), The Glen, Camps Bay, Cape Town 8001, next to the Round House Restaurant. It's in a beautiful position on the slopes of a pass in woodland overlooking the beach and is popular with travellers. It has hot water and cooking and laundry facilities. It is closed from 10 am to 5 pm, but they are fairly easy-going about this. To get there

from Cape Town, take bus No 062 from outside the OK Bazaar on Adderley St, to the Kloof Nek terminal (65 cents). From here it's 1.4 km down the hill (signposted) along Kloof Nek Rd. The last bus is at 10 pm.

The second hostel is the *Abe Bailey Youth Hostel* (tel 88 4283) on the corner of Maynard and Westbury Rds, Muizenberg, Cape Town. There are hot water and laundry facilities, and the place is run by a friendly and easy-going couple. To get there take the train from Central to Muizenberg (R 2.40). The same train goes to Simonstown and to Rondebosh where you can spend a good evening at the *Pig 'n' Whistle* on the main street, or at the *Hard Rock Café* next to it. There can be few hostels in the world better than this one – swimming pool, free tea and coffee and free bicycles to get you into the city centre.

Apart from the Youth Hostels there are the *YMCA* (tel 41 1848), 60 Victoria St, and the *YWCA* (tel 22 1886), 20 Belleview Rd. Another good cheap place recommended in the past is *Bergheim*, 12 Constantia Rd, Tamboerskloof, on the Table Mountain Cableway bus route. It is run by Mr and Mrs Schafer who are friendly and eager to help. Prices include the use of communal cooking facilities. If you're short of money ask for Father Doolley at the *Salesian College for Boys*. He may find space for you but don't stay more than two nights.

One of the best deals for hotel accommodation in the city centre area is the *Hotel Café Royal* (tel 22 9047), 23 Church St, which costs R 16.50/33 a single/double and R 40 a double with a bathroom. The manager is pleasant, the place is clean and fairly quiet, and a substantial breakfast is included in the price.

Another place is *Lennox Residential*, 2 Mill St, about 15 minutes' walk from the city centre. It is clean and costs R 13.50 a single including a huge breakfast. Similar is the *Palm Court Holiday Lodge* (tel 23 8721), 11 Hof St, good value at R 14 a single with breakfast. Make a reservation in advance if possible.

Other reasonably priced hotels recommended in the past include the *Castle Hotel* (tel 46 6306), 42 Canterbury St; the *Good Hope Hotel* (tel 22 3369), 87 Loop St; the *Stag's Head* (tel 45 4918), 71 Hope St; and *Mrs B Mayer*, 6 Upper Orange St, Oranjezicht. The last has been described as 'a veritable museum of a guesthouse' by one traveller, but others have been much less complimentary and strongly suggest you give it a miss. Try the *Lennox Lodge* in the same street instead.

More expensive is the *City Hall Hotel* (tel 46 5947), 50 Darling St, which costs R 45 a double plus tax and is very noisy. The *Tudor* (tel 24 1335), Greenmarket Square, costs R 22/42 a single/double without a bathroom, and R 28/50 a single/double with bathroom. Prices for both hotels include breakfast.

Places to Eat

There are hundreds of good cafés and restaurants in Cape Town. Since many of them have taken a leaf out of continental Europe's book they often spill out onto the pavements, so you have a choice of eating inside or outside.

Mike's Kitchen, in the Golden Acre Centre next door to Satour, offers endless coffee and serve-yourself salads (some 20 different types!) – it's excellent value. Another good coffee house is *House of Coffee*, Adderley St. *Simmer 'n' Spice*, 25 Church St, two doors south-east of Berg St, has excellent, reasonably priced and nutritious breakfasts, lunches and snacks.

The *Rozenhof Restaurant* (tel 24 1968), 18 Kloof St Gardens, is deservedly popular and well known all over Cape Town for its excellent yet very reasonably priced food. It's open for lunch Tuesday to Friday from 12.30 pm onwards and for dinner Tuesday to Sunday from 7.30 pm onwards. A reservation is essential as it's so popular.

A little more expensive is the *Kaapsie Tafel*, Grey Pass, opposite the South African Museum. This restaurant specialises in Cape dishes such as bobotie (rice casserole covered with meat and egg sauce), venison and Malay curries. It's open for lunch and dinner.

Authentic German food can be found at the *Bacchus Room* in the Tudor Hotel on Greenmarket Square from 10 am to 3 pm and from 6 pm till late. There are many low budget dishes on the menu.

For excellent eastern cuisine (Persian, Chinese, Burmese and Thai) try the *Marco Polo Restaurant*, 41 Regent Rd, Sea Point, which offers all-you-can-eat meals.

Entertainment

The Baxter Theatre at the University of Cape Town in Rosebank (15 minutes train ride from Cape Town Central) is well known for its programme of plays, concerts, shows and movies on socially relevant topics. Check the newspapers for what's on. Entry usually costs R 2 for students. The Labia Theatre across the street hosts similar programmes and prices are much the same.

For something more 'ocker', the *Castle Brewery* in Newlande (10 minutes from downtown) offers tours of the brewery once a week after which you can drink your fill (free of charge). Ring them up and ask when the next tour is happening.

DURBAN
Information

The tourist office (tel 6 7144) is on the 3rd floor at 320 West St. The American Express office is on the 1st floor, Westguard House, Gardiner St. The Transkei Consulate is in Commercial City (3rd floor), Commercial St, not far from the GPO. The Ciskei Consulate is on the 4th floor at 320 West St. The best book exchange is the Arcade Book Exchange at 14 Ajmeri Arcade off Grey St.

Things to See

The **Snake Park** on the beachfront is worth a visit. It has a good snake collection (mainly poisonous) from South Africa and many other parts of the world, and is a major producer of antivenin for the southern half of the continent.

It is also worth visiting the **Old Fort**, an important bastion of the British forces during the war with the Boers in 1842. The fort is open daily, except Saturday and public holidays, from 10 am to 12 noon and 1 to 4 pm.

For a taste of the orient, try the **Indian market** at the top end of West St. It's usually packed full of people, food stalls and curios and the all-pervading aroma of spices. For an uncrowded beach go to **Umhlanga Rocks** (pronounced 'Um-shlun-ga') north of the city. The scenery is fantastic, and in the off season the long beaches are almost deserted. Buses run there all day long during the week from downtown Durban outside the Metro Theatre – the tourist office has the schedule.

Other travellers have suggested a trip to **Port St Johns** (Transkei). The bus from Durban departs at 7.30 am, arriving at 3 pm. The route is wild and beautiful, with plenty to see on the way.

Places to Stay

The cheapest place is the *Youth Hostel* (tel 84 2050), 15 Cadogan Place, Durban North, run by Mrs D A Griffiths. It costs R 4 per night but only has four beds! Even so it's rarely full as only foreigners seem to stay here. There are no cooking facilities, but hot water is provided for making hot drinks. To get there take bus No 2 from the centre, or No 22 from the railway station and get off at Broadway-Kensington where there is a shopping centre. From here walk two blocks uphill to Chelsea St and turn right. Then turn left into Gloucester St, and Cadogan Place is on the right hand side.

Another very cheap place worth considering is *Trallee Court*, 38 Mona Rd, which offers double rooms from R 5 to R 15. It's excellent value.

The *YMCA* (tel 42 8106), on the corner of Beach Rd and Victoria Embankment, offers bed and breakfast for R 17.25 per person, but is said to be relatively poor value.

Other than these, the best place to go looking for cheap hotels is Gillespie St. This street is full of holiday flats of one sort or another, and the average price is R 15 per room in the low season. Among them are the *Baltimore Holiday Flats*, one of the cheapest and cleanest; the *Impala Holiday Flats* (tel 32 3232), R 19 per room; the *Grand Hotel*, 84 Gillespie St; the *Hilton Heights Holiday Flats* (tel 37 1535), 5 Gillespie St, R 15 a double; the *Palm Beach Hotel*, R 22.50 per person including breakfast; the *Ocean Beach Hotel*, R 15 per person; the *Sea Breeze Hotel* (tel 37 8696), 55 Gillespie St; the *White Hotel*; the *Killarney*; the *Casa Mia*; the *Miramar Hotel* next to the Sea Breeze; and the *Beachsider Holiday Rooms*, 14 Rochester St.

Other good value places are the *Hawaii Holiday Flats*, Rutherford St, which costs R 16 for a four-bed flat with TV, cutlery and two rooms; and the *Balmoral Hotel*, Marine Parade, which costs R 18/19 a single/double (but including three meals in the low season only). The *White House* and the *New City Hotel*, Russell St, have also been recommended in the past.

The prices of virtually all accommodation in Durban doubles during the high season and it's very difficult to find any accommodation at Christmas, Easter or during the summer school holidays.

Places to Eat

A good place is the small dining room beside the Balmoral Hotel in Marine Parade. It serves the same food as in the main dining room, but at much lower prices, and you can order course by course.

The *XL Café*, Marine Parade, is also worth considering. It's a bit seedy, but it is open all night and has a good atmosphere and videos. The Chinese takeaway around the corner from the Hawaii Holiday Flats on Point St is very good value. The *One Rander Steak House* has

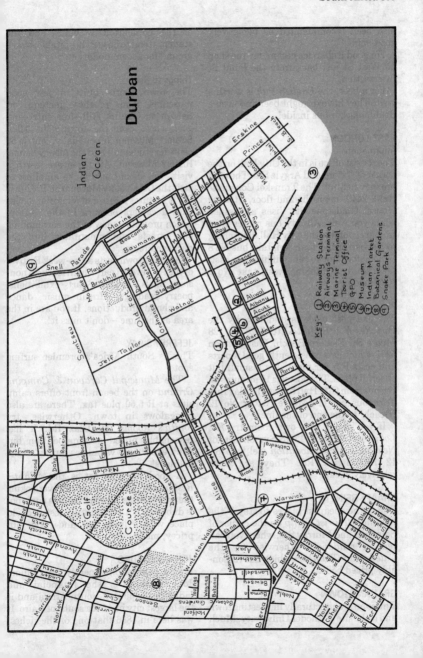

Durban

Indian Ocean

Key:
1 Railway Station
2 Airways Terminal
3 Marine Terminal
4 Tourist Office
5 GPO
6 Museum
T Indian Market
8 Botanical Gardens
T Snake Park

also been recommended as being very good value.

For good Italian ice cream, try the shop on West St just back from the Point St intersection.

For a beer, the *English Pub* is worth a visit. They have draught beer and even a double-decker bus inside!

EAST LONDON
Information
The tourist office is in the City Hall on the corner of Oxford and Argyle Sts. The staff are very helpful. The Transkei Consulate (tel 2 2446) is on the 2nd floor, Sterling House, Gladstone St. Visas are issued while you wait. All city bus routes start from just outside the City Hall. If hitching to Durban or the Transkei, take bus No 8 (Abbotsford) for 40 cents; if hitching east, take No 3; if hitching west, take No 2 (Collingdale).

Places to Stay
The cheapest place is undoubtedly the *Port Rex Youth Hostel* (tel 5 2855), 128 Moore St, Eastern Beach, East London 5201, which gets consistently good reports and costs R 5 per night. It's a small but cheerful place. The hostel is 10 minutes on the bus from City Hall by the Holiday Inn. Take bus No 11 (Moore St) or No 12 (Beach) to the end of the line.

If you prefer your own room try *Kei Lodge* (tel 2 8105), 13-15 Symons St, or *Newlands Accommodation* (tel 2 0548), 12 Fitzpatrick Rd. They are both relatively cheap.

GRAAFF REINET
One of the cheapest places to stay is the *Urquhart Tourist Camp* on the corner of Somerset and Murray Sts, where you can rent a *rondavel*. Otherwise try the *Caledonian Chambers* which has reasonably priced beds.

GRAHAMSTOWN
This is an architecturally interesting town and is the site of Rhodes University. Much of the population is black and the students tend to be very hospitable, so ask around for accommodation.

Things to See
The town sports quite a few good museums. Some of these include **Fort Selwyn** on Gunfire Hill (free entry and good views over the town); the **1820 Settlers Museum** (open daily, entry 50 cents for students); and the **Albany Natural History Museum**. All three are worth a visit. You should also make an effort to visit the **Observatory Museum** on Bathurst St. It features a restored Victorian house with a camera obscura in the rooftop, which projects a view of the surrounding city streets and mountains into the darkened room.

Grahamstown hosts a two-week Festival of the Arts every year, which features non-stop plays, concerts, art exhibitions, poetry readings, African music, dance and choral productions. If you are in the area at the time – don't miss it!

JEFFREY'S BAY
This is South Africa's premier surfing spot.

The *Municipal Caravan & Camping Ground* on the beach front offers camp sites at R 5.50 plus tax. There are also bungalows in town. Otherwise, try *Smith's Rooms*, 50 Diaz Rd. It has reasonably priced accommodation but don't expect any vacancies during school holidays!

A good place to eat is the *Atlantis Restaurant* (tel 348) on the hill overlooking the 'super tubes' (as the famous surf spot is dubbed). It's a beautifully restored, old place with a lively bar and good, but pricey, meals.

JOHANNESBURG
With a population of nearly two million, Johannesburg is the financial and industrial capital of South Africa and is the largest city in Africa south of Cairo. It was here in 1886 that one of the richest

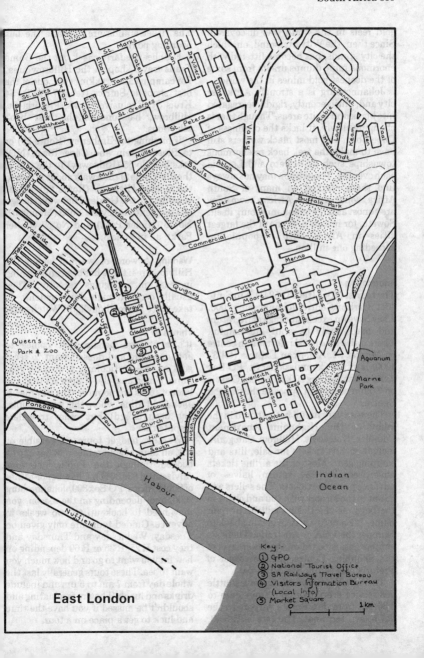

East London

Key:—
1. GPO
2. National Tourist Office
3. SA Railways Travel Bureau
4. Visitors Information Bureau (Local Info)
5. Market Square

0   1 km

gold reefs in the world was discovered. Since then, the Witwatersrand, on which the city stands, has become littered with enormous mine dumps drawn from some of the deepest gold mines in the world.

Johannesburg is a strongly Afrikaner city and, until recently, rigidly segregated into black and white areas. Though that is changing slowly, it lacks the openness of Cape Town and most black workers still have to make the trek back to enormous townships such as Soweto and Lenasia each evening. Though you may not always find them marked on maps of South Africa, some of these African townships are almost as large as Johannesburg itself. Soweto, for instance, is one of the largest cities in Africa with a population exceeding one million.

Information

The tourist office (tel 331 5241) is in Suite 4611, Carlton Centre, Johannesburg 2000. They have an excellent range of literature and maps and the staff are helpful. There's also a visitors' information centre on Market St. American Express (tel 37 4000) is at 123 Commissioner St, PO Box 9395, Johannesburg 2000. Thomas Cook is on Commissioner St opposite the Carlton Centre.

There's a very useful notice board in the lobby of the Highpoint Apartment Complex, Kotzee St, Hillbrow. Categories include airline tickets for sale, lifts and camping gear. Most of the airline tickets advertised are the return halves of advance purchase tickets. The sellers will go out to the airport with you and check in the bags, as the tickets will be in their name. It's a cheap way of getting back to Europe, the USA or Australia. There's a similar notice board on the lower level of the Shopping Centre, on the corner of Pretoria and Claim Sts, Hillbrow.

There is a South African Airways shuttle bus service every half hour from 7 am to 9.30 pm from Jan Smuts Airport to the downtown terminal. The fare is R 3.50.

The ticket stands are opposite the bus boarding points.

For cheap safaris check out the Game Trails travel shop in the Hillbrow area. For camping and trekking gear, one of the best shops is Safrics (tel 337 7917), 54 Kruis St. Exclusive Books, Pretoria St, Hillbrow, has one of the best book selections.

If hitching to Kimberley (Route 29) or to Bloemfontein and Cape Town (N1), take bus No 55 (Ridgeway) to the end of the line (Zone 2) then walk about 1½ km to the Golden Highway (Route 29). Buses run direct to the Golden Highway, though less frequently: they are No 52 (Mondeor), No 56 (Kibler Park) and No 57 (Power Park), all in Zone 3.

Warning A word of warning about the Hillbrow area: there has been an alarming increase in muggings recently. They usually occur at night but incidents do take place in broad daylight. Watch out!

Things to See

It's a strange person that comes to Johannesburg and doesn't want to see a gold mine – particularly a working gold mine. Unfortunately, it appears that the budget tours are no more (the Simmer & Jack Gold Mine, where this was possible, has been closed) but other travellers dispute this.

Whether budget tours are possible or not, all tours of gold mines now have to be booked through the Public Relations Adviser (tel 838 8011), Chamber of Mines of South Africa, PO Box 809, Johannesburg 2000, and, depending on the season, you may need to book up to two weeks in advance. Guided tours are only given on Tuesday, Wednesday and Thursday and they cost R 25, R 35 or R 60 depending on how far you want to go and how much you want to see. These tours generally last the whole day from 7 am to 5 pm and include drinks and lunch. They're fascinating and shouldn't be missed if you have the time and luck to get a place on a tour.

The **Gold Mine Museum**, Alamein St by Kimberley Freeway, is also worth a visit. The entry fee includes an underground tour.

The **Gold Reef City** has also become popular of late. It's a kind of amusement park, though is worthwhile for its old gold mine and Zulu dancers. Make enquiries at the tourist office.

Tours of **Soweto** are available for those who are interested and a permit is no longer necessary (though this may change so make enquiries beforehand). You don't have to go on a tour, of course, you can simply catch the train. If you do go on your own, however, it would be very wise to make it obvious that you are not South African – put a flag on your bag.

For those people interested in hiking there's the well-signposted **Mervyn King Ridge Trail** which stretches from Hillbrow along the crest of the Witwatersrand.

Places to Stay

The *Youth Hostel* (tel 26 8051), 32 Main St, Townsview, is the cheapest place and is excellent value at R 5. It's clean, well run and has a good notice board with details of cheap accommodation all over South Africa. Some days it's open all day but on others it's closed from 10 am to 5 pm. To get there take bus No 47 from the terminal on the corner of Eloff and Main Sts and get off at stop No 24 (Zone 2). The hostel is also a good place to ask around about jobs.

The *YMCA/YWCA* (tel 724 4541), 104 Rissik St near the train station, is usually full of long-term residents as far as the private rooms are concerned, so they generally have only dormitory beds available for R 10, including breakfast. There's also an annexe on the corner of Rissik and Smit Sts.

Most travellers, however, stay in the Hillbrow-Berea area north-east of the railway station. Some of the cheapest places in this area include: *Kolping House* (tel 643 1213), 4 Fife St, Berea, where rooms are R 12 but invariably full;

the *Hawthorne* (tel 642 5915), 45 Olivia St, Berea, for R 35 a double with breakfast including tax, but it has been described as 'a depressing place full of ageing, low-income whites'; the *Ambassador* (tel 642 5051), 52A Pretoria St, Hillbrow, which costs R 24 for bed only and R 40 a double; the *Europa* (tel 724 5321), 63 Claim St, Hillbrow, a good place at R 20 a single without bath and R 22.40 a single with bath (no breakfast included); the *Mark*, also in Hillbrow, which is R 34 a double (with rooftop swimming pool); the *New Stephanie Hotel*, 46 High St, Berea, for R 10 per night; the *Huguenot*, Claim St, Hillbrow, a single with bathroom for R 16.50; and the *Golden Crest Hotel*, Able St, Hillbrow, which costs R 15 per person plus 12% tax.

For weekly rentals in this area, check out *Hilton Plaza*, on the corner of Court and Esselen Sts, Hillbrow, which offers cheap weekly rates of R 110 per room or R 35 a double per day.

Others in this area which have been recommended in the past include the *Chelsea* (tel 642 4541), in Catherine St, Berea; *Constantia* (tel 725 1046), 35 Quartz St, Hillbrow; the *Rondebosch* (tel 724 9421), 24 Edith Cavell St; the *Whitehall* (tel 643 4911), 8 Abel St, Berea; and the *Odyssey*, 8 Lily St near Soper St.

Outside this area are the *Cosmopolitan* (tel 614 3315), 285 Commissioner St; the *Federal* (tel 29 4584), 180 Commissioner St; the *East London* (tel 836 5862), 54 Loveday St; and the *Gresham* (tel 834 5641), 13 Loveday St.

The *Boulevard Rest House* next to the Chelsea Hotel has also been recommended.

Places to Eat

If you're not paying for breakfast at your hotel, *Jo'burg* department stores do very good, cheap breakfasts for early shoppers, including a full British-style breakfast with coffee.

For a meal at other times of the day try the *Kasbah Steak & Snack*, Katze St, Hillbrow, a Greek restaurant. The *Three*

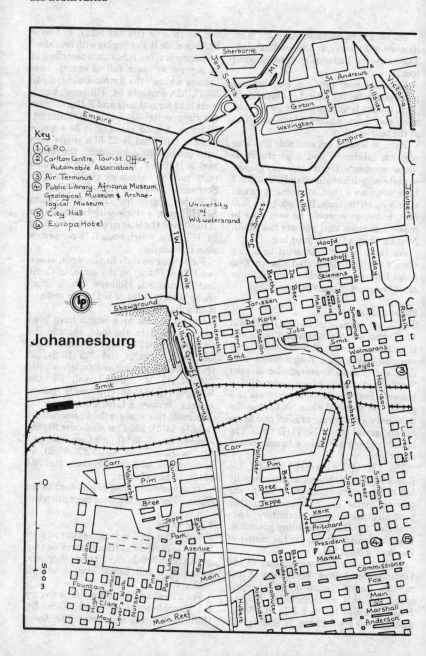

Key:
1. G.P.O.
2. Carlton Centre, Tourist Office, Automobile Association
3. Air Terminus
4. Public Library, Africana Museum, Geological Museum & Archaeological Museum
5. City Hall
6. Europa Hotel

Johannesburg

0
500 m

Sisters Greek Restaurant, Elkam Building, Pretoria St, is also very good value for hot or cold all-you-can-eat lunches and dinners.

Entertainment

For action in the evenings, two good hangouts are the *Chelsea Theatre* under the Chelsea Hotel on Catherine St, with very good bands and pleasant atmosphere; and *Lucky Luke's*, which has a friendly manager called Steve. Both are in the Hillbrow area. *Plum Crazy*, also in Hillbrow, has good jazz on Sunday afternoon. The *Hard Rock Café* is the only pub in Johannesburg open on Sundays.

The *Market Theatre Complex*, Bree St on the corner of Wolhuter in the western part of the city, is a radical intellectuals' watering hole (for both blacks and whites). There are several levels to this complex including a pub, café, restaurant and exhibition areas. There's a good crowd normally and it's worth a visit.

KIMBERLEY

The tourist office is in City Hall, Market Square.

Kimberley is the site of the world's largest human-made hole, known as **The Big Hole**. In 1871 diamonds were found on what used to be a hill here. From then until 1914, the hill was not only completely dug away but a huge crater 756 metres deep and covering 15 hectares was gouged out of the earth. Thousands of people came to seek their fortune and quite a few of them made it. Of the 28 million tonnes of earth removed by hand, some three tonnes of diamonds were found, worth R 94 million.

Next to the Big Hole is a **museum** where the streets of Kimberley as they were in Victorian times have been reconstructed. There's a diamond exhibition as well. The museum is open daily from 8 am to 6 pm and costs R 2.

Diamond mining has now moved to the other side of town in the shape of the **De Beers Mine** and, in time, it promises to rival the Big Hole in terms of size. There's an observation platform where you can see how far things have got, but most of the workings are now underground.

Those who would like to see a working diamond mine are in luck. Take yourself along to the **Bultfontein Mine** which offers two-hour tours starting at 9 am from Tuesday to Friday for just R 1. This includes a slide show on diamond mining, a tour of the recovery plant, a good look at what constitutes a day's production from the four mines currently operating, plus a film on the history and development of Kimberley followed by free tea and coffee. It's excellent value.

The **Duggan-Cronin Bantu Gallery**, Egerton St, has an interesting collection of black & white photographs of the Bantu tribes taken in the 1920s and 1930s.

Places to Stay

The *Kimberley Youth Hostel* (tel 0531 28577), Bloemfontein Rd, Kimberley 8301, is about five km from the centre of town just before Hull Rd meets the intersection with Route 64. It's an excellent hostel with swimming pool, hot showers, free tea and coffee, and bicycles which can be used to get into town. The people who run it are friendly and it costs just R 3.50 for members.

For something closer to the centre of town, try the *Grand Hotel* (tel 2 65251/2/3) on the corner of Southey St and Transvaal Rd. This hotel offers beds-only for R 16.50 or doubles for R 40 plus 12% tax. The *Cresent Hotel* (tel 2 2413), Darcy St, offers beds-only for R 17.40. The *Queens Hotel* (tel 2 3299), off Stockdale Rd, has beds-only for R 14.75 and doubles for R 45 plus 12% tax. At the *Halfway House Hotel* on the corner of Main and Egerton Sts a bed costs R 16.25.

There is a camp site on the Transvaal road about two km from the centre next to the mosque; sites cost R 7.20.

KNYSNA

Quite a few people come to Knysna to visit

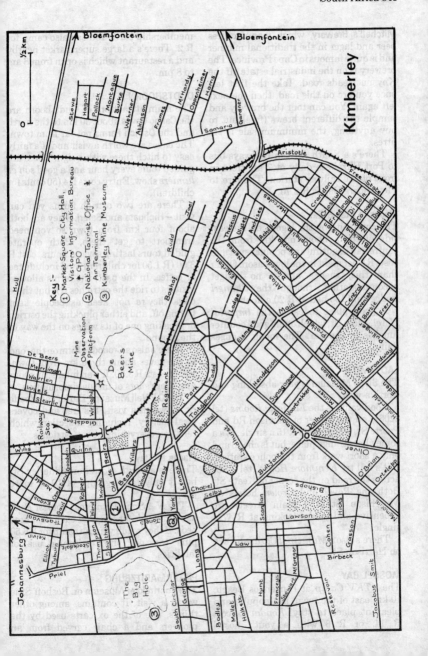

Kimberley

↑ Bloemfontein

↑ Bloemfontein

← Johannesburg

½ km

0

Key :-
① Market Square, City Hall, Visitors Information Bureau
② GPO
National Tourist Office
Air Terminal
③ Kimberley Mine Museum

Mine Observation Platform

De Beers Mine

The "Big Hole"

Railway Sta.

Mitchell's Brewery, which manufactures beer and lager in the traditional manner and is quite famous in Cape Province. The brewery is on the industrial estate off the Knysna Heads road. Take the first left once you are on this road, then the next left again. You can tour the brewery and sample the different brews (free) but to buy anything, the minimum sale is six litres.

There's a South African Railways bus to Port Elizabeth daily at 7 am from in front of the railway station. The fare to Plettenberg Bay is R 2.70.

Places to Stay & Eat

The camp site by the lagoon on the east side of town, about one km from the centre, is a beautiful and popular spot and costs R 5 per night in the low season. Other than this, there's almost no budget accommodation, though the *Shangri Lodge* isn't too bad at R 20 a double.

A good place to eat is the *Imperial Hotel*, Main St, which offers good counter lunches in the bar. The menu changes daily.

LADYSMITH

The **Siege Museum** is very absorbing and worth a visit.

Good value is the *El Marie Rooms* (tel 22061) on the corner of Harrison Rd and Poorte St, which costs R 15 a single. It's a somewhat strange place, but is cheap and only a short walk from the police station. If it's full try *Kenimore House* (tel 2018) across the road on the corner of Keate St. Both the *Royal* and *Crown* hotels on Murchison St (the main street) are expensive and you're looking at R 47 a single.

There's also a *Municipal Caravan Park* on Harrison St.

MOSSEL BAY

The *ATKV Camp* at Hartenbos Beach, 10 km east of the town, is a popular and pleasant place to stay. *Rondavels* cost R 14, or R 8 with a youth hostel

membership card. You can also camp for R 2. There's a large supermarket nearby and a restaurant which is open from 8 am to 8 pm.

OUDTSHOORN

The main attractions of Oudtshoorn are the **Cango Caves** about 30 km to the north and the **Ostrich Farms** not far from town. The caves are worth a visit and it's fairly easy to hitch there with a sign. There are guided tours every hour and a good *son et lumière* show. Entry costs R 4 (50 cents for children).

There are two ostrich farms you can visit – **Highgate** and **Safari**. They are both about four km from town so you need transport to get there. Both operate guided tours lasting several hours, cost R 3.50 (R 1.50 for children), and include tea or coffee. In the past, the farms allowed visitors to ride the ostriches (!), but these days they're not keen as people kept falling off, and either plucking the ostrich or breaking one of its wings on the way to the ground.

There's also a **Crocodile Farm** on the road to the caves about three km from town. Entry costs R 3.50. It's an interesting tour and there's lots of factual information.

The **C P Nell Museum**, Baron van Reede St, is worth a visit. It's free and covers local history, including a section which tells you everything about ostriches.

Places to Stay

There is a *Youth Hostel* on Adderley St, but it only takes groups of 10 or more people.

The *N A Smit Municipal Tourist Park* has *rondavels* for R 9, and each has three beds. If they're full you can camp for R 6.50 plus tax per site including use of facilities.

PIETERMARITZBURG

The **Voortrekker Museum** on Boshoff St is worth a visit. It contains, among other things, one of the ox carts used by the pioneers and a chair carved from an

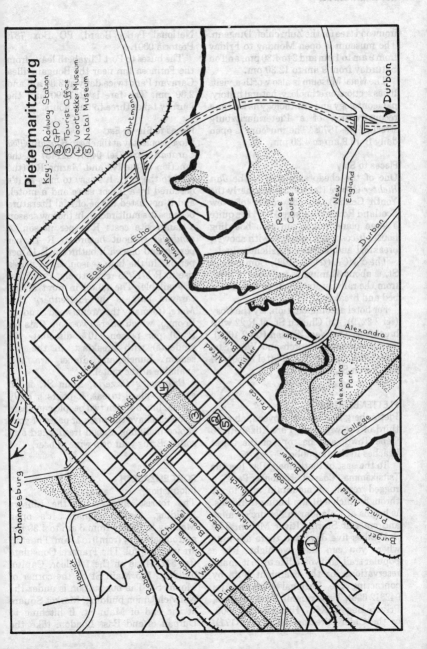

Pietermaritzburg

Key:-
① Railway Station
② GPO
③ Tourist Office
④ Voortrekker Museum
⑤ Natal Museum

ironwood tree for the Zulu chief, Dingaan. The museum is open Monday to Friday from 9 am to 1 pm and 2 to 4.30 pm, and on Saturday from 9 am to 12.30 pm.

The **Natal Museum** is also worth a visit. It has sections on ethnology, natural history, palaeontology and ornithology as well as a reconstruction of a Pietermaritzburg street of the 1870s. The museum is open daily from 9 am to 4.30 pm.

Places to Stay

One of the cheapest places is the *Jan Richter Centre* (tel 6 9252) (formerly the Youth Centre), on the corner of New Scotland Rd and Stalkers Alley. It's quite a large place and is run as a boarding house. It costs R 15 a single with shower, breakfast and dinner – excellent value!

The *YMCA* (tel 42 8106), Commercial St, is about 30 minutes walk out of town from the railway station. It costs R 18 for bed and breakfast.

For hotel accommodation, try the *Cosy* (tel 2 3279), 456 Church St, at R 22 with breakfast. The *New Watson* (tel 2 1604), on the corner of Church and West Sts, costs R 32; and the *Norfolk* (tel 2 6501/2), 23 Church St, costs R 22.

PLETTENBERG BAY

Plettenberg Bay is near Knysna, about a third of the way from Port Elizabeth to Cape Town, and has one of the finest beaches in the Republic.

To the east of Plettenberg Bay lies the **Tsitsikamma Coastal National Park**, a rugged region of mountain and forest through which a 61-km hiking trail runs. It begins at Calandar in Nature's Valley and ends at Storms River Mouth. The trek takes five days and there are huts where you can stay overnight. It's a popular trail, so if you'd like to do it, make reservations for the overnight huts by contacting the Regional Director (tel 042312 656), Tsitsikamma Forest Region, Private Bag No X557, Humansdorp 6300; or the Chief Director (tel 012 441171),

National Parks Board, PO Box 787, Pretoria 0001.

The buses to Port Elizabeth leave from the Formosa Inn near the Bougainvillea Caravan Park twice daily at 3.30 am and 2.30 pm. The fare is R 16.90 and the journey takes three to four hours.

Places to Stay & Eat

Most people stay at the cheap *Bougainvillea Caravan Park* (tel 04457 32146) at the junction of the N2 and Marine Rd (the road to the bay). It's easy to miss as it's obscured by a liquor store and a motel, and is not listed in the official literature because it's multiracial. In the low season a camp site costs R 4 per person, a *rondavel* without bathroom R 12 per person and one with bathroom R 18 per person. In the high season, these prices rise to R 5/17/25 respectively. Breakfast is available. The motel in front of the caravan park is the *Plettenberg Bay Motel* (formerly the Archerwood Student Rooms), which offers two-room flats for R 20 per person (10% discounts for students) with breakfast, in the low season. Lunch and dinner are also available at the motel.

Cranzgot's Pizzeria, Main St, is an excellent place to eat. It offers a daily special lunch which two people can share – you can have the pizza or pasta of your choice including a good fresh salad and coffee. Bring your own wine or beer.

PORT ELIZABETH
Information

The tourist office is in the Library Building, Market Square. It's open Monday to Friday from 8 am to 4.30 pm and on Saturday from 9 to 11 am. The staff are very helpful. The Transkei Consulate (tel 542224) is on the 1st floor, Capitol building, 545 Main St on the corner of Mount St. The bus station is under the Norwich Union building, Market Square at the end of Main St. If hitching to Durban or/and East London, take the

Uitenhage train or bus No 86 or No 89 from stand No 7 to Swartkops.

Things to See

Port Elizabeth is quite proud of its links with the past. Many of the old colonial houses have been restored and some are open to the public, such as that at No 7 Castle Hill (built in 1827), and the Cora Terrace Houses (built in the 1830s).

The oldest stone building in the Eastern Cape is **Fort Frederick**, erected by British troops in 1799. It's now a national monument and from it there are good views over Algoa Bay. The key to the fort can be obtained from the visitors information bureau.

Port Elizabeth's **museum** is worth visiting. In the grounds is a **snake park** where there are daily demonstrations of snake handling and the milking of venom from adders in the summer months. There is also a **tropical house** a unique feature of which is a section which simulates full-moon conditions so you can see nocturnal animals and birds! There's also an **oceanarium** with performing dolphins. All these sections of the museum are open daily from 9 am to 12.45 pm and 2 to 5 pm.

Places to Stay

There is a sort of *Youth Hostel* at 4 Roseberry Ave which costs R 7 per night. To get there take bus No 45, 54, 55 or 56 from the terminal in town to the crossroads known as 'Fiveways'. Another very cheap place is *Naulty Tower*, 12 Fort St, which costs R 5 per person. It's very clean, friendly and has hot water.

The *Municipal Camping Ground*, Hawthorne Rd, Humewood, is now privately owned and offers beach huts for R 10, and (very primitive) *rondavels* with three beds for R 20 per night. No bedding is provided. To get there take bus No 2 to Humewood from stand No 5.

More expensive is the *YMCA* (tel 2 3913), 31 Havelock St, which offers dormitory beds (four per room)/singles/ doubles for R 10.96/18.80/34.24, all including breakfast.

Two of the cheapest hotels are the *Laurel Lodge* (tel 2 8870), 6 Fort St, and the one run by Mrs Wendy Jackelman at 12 Fort St. Both are clean and well appointed.

Some other cheaper hotels include: the *Belle Aurora* (tel 58 1415), 58 Kirkwood St, North End; *Canadia Accommodation* (tel 2 4832), 50 Belmont Terrace; *Central Lodge* (tel 2 8831), 12 Western Rd; *Cuylerholme* (tel 2 9032), 42 Western Rd; *Hornby Holiday Accommodation* (tel 2 5120), 39 Beach Rd; *Inchkeith* (tel 2 6216), 7 Havelock St; *Richly House* (tel 39 1570), 80 Cape Rd; *St Croix* (tel 2 2614), 10 Havelock St; *Town House* (tel 33 1072), 81 Cape Rd; or *Valhill Accommodation* (tel 2 4700), 17 Prospect Hill.

Places to Eat

One of the best deals in town is the *Maverick Spur Steak Ranch* on Rink St below the Kine cinema. They offer all-you-can-eat salads with fruit for R 3.25.

PRETORIA

Just 50 km north of Johannesburg, Pretoria is the administrative capital of South Africa and before that it was the capital of the Transvaal Republic. It's quite a small, but pleasant city with a leisurely, old-world atmosphere not unlike Canberra (Australia).

There's not a great deal to do, but it is a pretty city in the springtime when the jacaranda trees bloom.

Information

The tourist office is on the 3rd floor, Frans du Toit Building, Schoeman St, Pretoria 0001. There's also a visitors' information bureau on the corner of Vermeulen and Van der Walt Sts, which has plenty of information and maps, and the staff are very helpful. American Express (tel 2 9182) is in the SAAU Building, 308 Andries St, Pretoria 0001. The South African Airways terminal is on Andries St at Vermeulen.

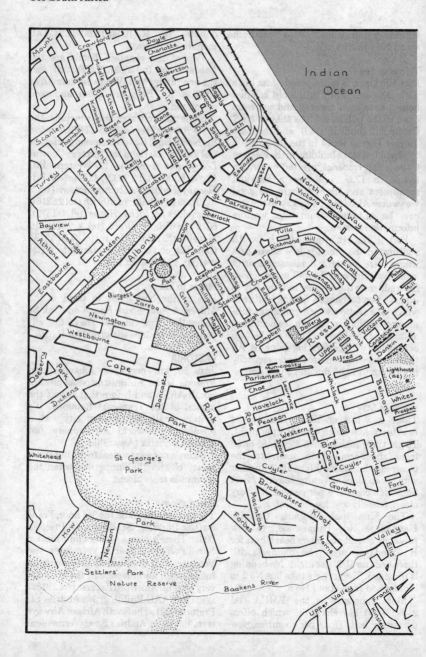

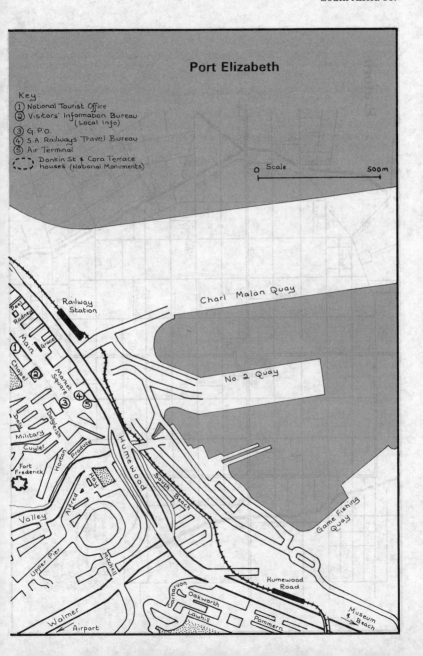

Port Elizabeth

Key:
1. National Tourist Office
2. Visitors' Information Bureau (Local Info)
3. G.P.O.
4. S.A. Railways Travel Bureau
5. Air Terminal
- - - Donkin St & Cora Terrace houses (National Monuments)

0 Scale 500m

Charl Malan Quay

No. 2 Quay

Game Fishing Quay

Railway Station

Peel
Rodney
Main
Grace
Chapel
Market Square
Military
Cuyler
Fort Frederick
Valley
Upper Pier
Alfred
Horton
Produce
Humewood
South Beach
Mitchell
Walmer
Airport
Carnarvon
Oakworth
Lawhill
Pommern
Humewood Road
Museum & Beach

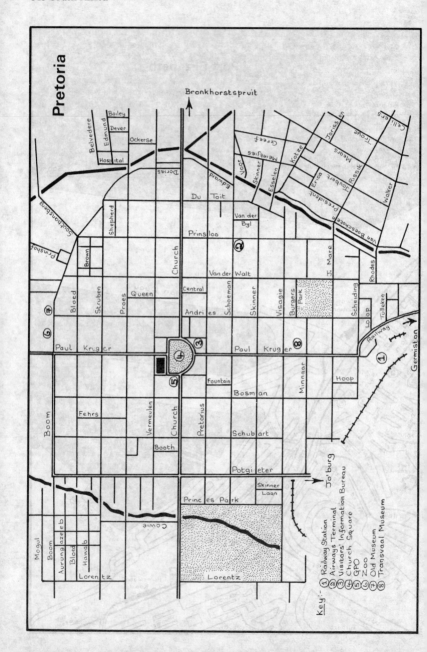

Pretoria

Key:- ① Railway Station
② Airways Terminal
③ Visitors Information Bureau
④ Church Square
⑤ GPO
⑥ Zoo
⑦ Old Museum
⑧ Transvaal Museum

A shuttle bus runs to Jan Smuts International Airport for R 3.80. If hitching to Johannesburg (Route 28 changing to National 1), go down Potgieter St to the start of the freeway about 750 metres from the railway bridge.

Things to See

There are tours of the **Premier Diamond Mine**, 40 km north-east of Pretoria, Tuesday to Friday at 9.30 and 11 am, except on public holidays. You need to make reservations in advance with the Public Relations Officer (tel 368), Premier Diamond Mine, PO Box 44, Cullinan 1000. The tourist office will advise you about transport to Cullinan.

Two places worth visiting in Pretoria itself are the **National Cultural History Museum** and the **Fort Klapperkop Museum**. The former is devoted mainly to the black tribes of the Transvaal and has a collection of prehistoric rock paintings, but there are also sections on the cultural history of the European population and Voortrekker furniture. It's open Monday to Saturday from 8 am to 5 pm and on Sunday from 10.30 am to 5 pm; entry is 50 cents. Fort Klapperkop was built in 1898 and has been converted to a museum of the military history of the Republic from 1852. It's open Monday to Friday from 10 am to 4 pm and on Saturday and Sunday from 10 am to 6 pm.

The **Transvaal Museum**, Paul Kruger St opposite City Hall, is one of the best natural history museums you are likely to come across. The displays are comprehensive, informative and well laid out. Entry is 50 cents (20 cents for students) and it's open from 9 am to 5 pm Monday to Saturday and 11 am to 5 pm on Sunday.

The **Krugerhuis**, on the corner of Church and Potgieter Sts, was completed in 1883 and is also worth a visit. It's essentially a monument to Paul Kruger and contains his carriage, private railroad car and a reconstruction of the room in which he died in Switzerland. The museum is open Monday to Friday from 7 am to 4.30 pm

and on Saturday and Sunday from 11 am to 4.30 pm. Entry is 50 cents.

Places to Stay

The *YMCA*, 122 Skinner St, has a number of youth hostel-type beds which cost R 3. There is hot water and kitchen facilities. This place is due to be demolished in 1989 to make way for a new hospital. Some of the cheapest hotels are the *Belgrave* (tel 3 5578), 22 Railway St; the *Louis* (tel 44 4238), 599 Schoeman St; the *Pretoria* (tel 42 5062), 611 Schoeman St; and the *Republique* (tel 3 2025), 47 Schoeman St.

VRYBURG

If you're on a tight budget ask for Father Bastian next to the Catholic Church. He'll probably find you somewhere to sleep on a floor, couch, or even a bed, but take your own food. If you can't get in try the relatively cheap *Afrikaner Boarding House*.

The 'Homelands'

BOPHUTHATSWANA

The main 'attraction' (if it can be called that) of this homeland is **Sun City**, the capital. However, it's really only an attraction for white South African revellers who come here at weekends to gamble at the casino and take advantage of cheap sex. There's also nowhere to stay except at the *Sun City Hotel*, which is, as you might imagine, very expensive.

On the other hand we did have one letter from a volunteer health worker some time ago, which said the people in Bophuthatswana were incredibly friendly once you had broken through the old Black-White barrier. He said people were dying for a chance to be friendly and to invite you into their homes despite their poverty. It's just that they're suspicious at first that. you're going to push them around like most of the Afrikaners do.

If you are not camping, there's almost nowhere to stay except in a few of the larger villages with Afrikaner hotels, but these are dreary places and the atmosphere is heavily apartheid. There's not much to see either, apart from the huge maize plantations run by Afrikaner farmers, and lots of squalid little settlements where the Tswana people from Johannesburg and Cape Town were dumped after the homeland was created in 1976. Infectious diseases are apparently rife in these places since no one in any position of authority really cares.

Mafikeng
Previously Mafeking of Baden Powell and Boer War fame, Mafikeng is now in Bophuthatswana. There is little reason to stay.

Places to Stay Should you need to stay, there is the *Protea Hotel* on the main street, which costs R 40 per night without breakfast. Cheaper rooms may be available at the *Café Welkom*.

TRANSKEI
It's probably not worth the trouble of getting a visa before arrival as these are issued at the border at Umzimkulu and Kei Bridge for 50 cents (Transit) and R 2.50 (Tourist). At the Kei Bridge crossing, in particular, there are no formalities, no rubber stamps and the officials are swift and efficient. Entry via a road without a border gate is officially illegal for a foreign passport holder. Transkei officials usually aren't too concerned about this (though we heard from one traveller who was fined R 40 for not having a visa), but South African officials can be difficult.

A simple rule to observe: if you enter on a road with a border gate, leave on a road with a border gate (eg, the main Pietermaritzburg to East London road). If you enter via a road without a border gate (34 to choose from), keep your mouth shut and leave the same way.

As well as Umtata and Port St Johns several other places have been recommended as good to visit. These are the

Hluleka Nature Reserve, Mazeppa Bay and the Dwesa Game Reserve. The Hluleka Nature Reserve is a very secluded and beautiful place to spend a few days. *Rondavels* and cabins are available.

Umtata
There is a somewhat basic camp site with showers on the edge of town. To get there take Alexandra Ave towards the hospital and turn left. For hotel accommodation, the *Grosvenor Hotel* has been a popular place for years. Although it's now under new management, it may still be possible to get a 'hiker's discount' if they're not full, in which case it will cost R 15 a single with bathroom and TV. Otherwise, the price is R 39 a single including an all-you-can-eat breakfast. It's a pleasant place and since a lot of commercial travellers stay, lifts to East London, Durban and Port St Johns are easy to find.

There are daily buses from Umtata to Port St Johns which cost R 4.60 and take about three hours.

Port St Johns
This coastal town is in a beautiful location and the journey there, along a wild and rugged coastline, is even more spectacular.

Things to Do If you have the time, it's worth considering doing the Port St Johns to **Coffee Bay** trail, which takes about five days. It involves a lot of uphill, downhill walks, but there are plenty of attractions to make it worth your while - superb views, wildflowers, small villages, forests, grasslands, rocky reefs, beaches, sand dunes, estuaries and occasional fisherfolk and other people searching for shellfish. Excellent seafood can be bought at many points. The trail is well provided with simple, but adequate accommodation for overnight stays.

If you go swimming beware of the strong currents and sharks.

The Department of Agriculture & Forestry, on the 3rd floor of the Botha Sigcay Building, on the corner of Leeds and Owen Sts, Umtata, handles bookings for this trail. Entry costs R 9 and a map is available for R 1.50.

Places to Stay & Eat The cheapest place to stay is the *Municipal Camp Ground* at **First Beach** about one km from the centre of town. A camp site costs R 5 and there are also bungalows for R 10 a double, plus larger ones which will sleep up to five people for R 20.

Everyone seems to gather in the *Cape Hermes Hotel*, next to the camp ground, in the evenings to talk and drink a few beers. The hotel also has accommodation, but it's somewhat expensive at R 40 per night plus 12% tax, though this does include breakfast and dinner. *Neats Eats* on the way to the Cape Hermes Hotel just before the turn-off for Second Bay offers reasonable takeaways.

Over the next headland there is **Second Beach**, a really beautiful spot. There's another *Municipal Camp Ground* which costs R 6.50 per person with a restaurant, although this is somewhat overpriced. If it's full, there are other sites at the *Second Beach Holiday Resort* another km further down the road for R 5 plus R 1.50 per person (low season), or R 9 plus R 1.50 per person (high season). *Rondavels* cost R 25.50 and up in the low season.

The *Mabuhay Restaurant* on Second Beach has been recommended as a good place to eat. It offers Filipino seafood cuisine at reasonable prices. Bring your own wine or beer. They'll also do takeaways if you prefer. If you are catering for yourself bring food from Port St Johns, as the choice is limited at Second Beach.

You can go further along this coast (via a trail) to **Third Beach**, which is even more laid back.

National Parks & Game Reserves

The national parks are one of South Africa's premier attractions, and because of the abundance of wildlife and, in some, the spectacular mountain scenery, you should make an effort to spend time in at least one of them – preferably more than one.

They all have rest camps that offer a wide variety of accommodation, from cottages and *rondavels* to dormitory huts and camp sites. Most of the camps have restaurants and shops, and there is usually camping equipment for hire. There are also petrol stations at most of the main camps.

Very popular are the horseback and wilderness trails, which you take through areas where cars and other vehicles are banned.

Accommodation and trails should be booked in advance with the National Parks Board (tel 44 1194), PO Box 787, Pretoria 0001. The parks are very popular during the school holidays, so if you propose to go there at these times you should book as far in advance as possible. If you don't, you'll probably find them fully booked and will be turned away. This is especially true of the Kruger National Park.

Probably the best way to go to the parks is to get a small group together and rent a vehicle. Otherwise you'll have to hitch, relying on someone else to take you to a rest camp and to drive you around those sections of the parks where vehicles are allowed (most South Africans are very helpful when it comes to things like this).

Those people who would prefer to have a company organise transport, accommodation and food should check out Game Safaris Wildlife Tours (tel 838 4321/2), Suite 203, Kattis Mansions, 66 Harrison St, Johannesburg 2001. This company is very well organised with excellent guides, and the food is top value. A four-day tour of the Kruger National Park costs US\$250 (or US\$175 if you are willing to accept double occupancy in the accommodation which they use).

In addition to the national parks and game reserves listed, there are a number of others, which are smaller or less well known. The National Parks Board office in Pretoria has details.

ADDO ELEPHANT PARK

This park is about 72 km north of Port Elizabeth and has elephants, black rhinos and antelopes. Most people visit on the coach tour, which leaves Port Elizabeth every Friday at 2 pm (weather permitting) and returns the same evening, but there is a small camp of self-contained *rondavels* with a restaurant if you want to stay. Entry to the park costs R 1.10 per vehicle with up to five passengers plus 10 cents for each additional passenger. Accommodation costs R 9.35 per hut (one or two people) plus R 2.25 for each additional person.

GIANT'S CASTLE GAME RESERVE

On the eastern face of the Drakensberg up against the Lesotho border and about half a day's drive from Howich, this park is a must if you're in the area. It's wild, remote and is the home of 12 species of antelope and two rare species of eagle. Horseback trails of two to six days duration can be arranged with the Parks Board Office in Pietermaritzburg.

A visit to the so-called **Main Caves** is worthwhile to see the museum (R 1 entry) and the Bushpeople paintings. Both of them are within two km of the main camp.

Places to Stay

Two and four-bed bungalows with beds, table and chairs, kitchen facilities and fresh water are available both at the main camp and at another some three to four hours away. There are also larger, self-contained cottages available for rent at the main camp. Camping is not allowed at the main camp. There is no food of any

sort available, so bring all your own supplies. Prices and reservations are the same as for the reserves in Zululand.

GOLDEN GATE HIGHLANDS NATIONAL PARK

This national park is close to the northern border of Lesotho in the Orange Free State. The main attraction is the spectacular scenery, but there are plenty of eland, red hartebeest, black wildebeest, blesbok and springbok.

The best way to see the game is to walk. There is a two-day trail with an overnight hut about half way. The hike covers about 13 km per day, but it's all up and down and so is quite hard going. It's also easy to lose the trail in places, though the map which is available helps sort that out. The scenery is superb and the hut comfortable, but it would be very cramped if the full complement of people (18) turned up. There is a gas stove, lamps, pots and pans and plenty of wood for the *braai*. It costs R 6 per person.

Horse riding can be arranged at the Brandwag Hotel for R 6 per hour.

Places to Stay

There are two rest camps within two km of one another. *Brandwag Camp* has a restaurant and shop. Camping costs R 5.50 per site plus R 1.50 per person. The showers are piping hot, but there are no cooking facilities except for *braai* places. In addition there are family cottages for R 15.60 (two people) plus R 2.30 for each additional person as well as single/double rooms for R 8.85/13. The *Brandwag Hotel* is about 500 metres down the road and is a good place to go in the evenings as there's a bar and restaurant and it's warm. The breakfasts are enormous – juice, yogurt, cereal, porridge, eggs, bacon, sausage, toast, tea and coffee! Dinners and Sunday lunch are available. The cafeteria serves lunches and snacks all day.

Glen Reenan Camp has a shop but no restaurant. Accommodation is in self-contained *rondavels* (two people) for

R 9.35, and in ordinary huts (two people) for R 7.80. You can also camp.

KALAHARI GEMSBOK NATIONAL PARK

Located in the northern reaches of Cape Province up against the Namibia and Botswana borders, this is South Africa's second largest park. Animals here include lion, cheetah, gemsbok and springbok. The park is open all year, but the best time to visit is between March and October.

Entry to the park costs R 7 per vehicle plus R 1.50 per person.

Places to Stay

There are three rest camps: *Twee Rivieren*, the park headquarters; *Mata Mata*, on the Namibian frontier; and *Nossob*, 139 km north of Twee Rivieren. There are no restaurants but limited supplies of canned goods as well as petrol and diesel are available.

The costs are as follows: family cottage with kitchenette (up to four people), R 16.15; hut with shower and toilet (one or two people), R 10.70; ordinary hut (one or two people), R 5.75. Additional people in any of these are charged R 2.30 (bed provided) or R 1.15 (provide your own bed). Camping costs R 2 per person. You are not permitted to leave Mata Mata for any of the other camps after 12 noon.

KRUGER NATIONAL PARK

This huge park, stretching virtually all the way along the Transvaal border with Mozambique, is one of the largest in Africa and the largest in the Republic. It's claimed to have the greatest variety of animals in any game park in Africa, and includes lions, leopards, cheetahs, elephants, giraffes and many varieties of antelope.

Three-day wilderness trails are available from Skukuza Rest Camp. The trails are led by experienced rangers and all necessary equipment (tents, rucksacks, sleeping bags, water bottles, etc) is provided. Food is included in the cost of the trail. Trails commence every week on

Tuesday and Friday and must be booked in advance at the National Parks Board, Pretoria. There is a set maximum of eight people in a group.

If you don't have your own vehicle, it's easy (and permitted) to hitch from camp to camp.

Entry to the park is R 4.50 per visit plus R 4.50 for a vehicle.

Places to Stay

There is a total of 11 rest camps, the largest of them situated in the heart of the park. Others are located at four of the seven entrance gates. Reservations can be made up to a year in advance, but during school holidays, not for more than five nights at any one camp. When accommodation is fully booked, only a limited number of day visitors are admitted.

All types of accommodation provide mattresses, bedding, towels and soap. Lamps are provided in those camps with no electricity. The accommodation available includes cottages with kitchenette, two double bedrooms and bathroom (R 28 for four or fewer persons); cottages without kitchenette (R 19.75); self-contained huts (R 9.45 to R 10.75 for one or two persons); ordinary huts (R 6.25 to R 8.10 for one or two persons); and camping (R 3.35 to R 5.50 per site plus R 1.50 per person depending on facilities).

MOUNTAIN ZEBRA NATIONAL PARK

This park is on the northern slopes of the Bankberg, 27 km from Cradock in Cape Province. The main attraction is, as the name suggests, the mountain zebra, but there are also baboons and herds of eland, gemsbok, springbok, hartebeest, etc. Entry to the park costs R 1.10 per vehicle with up to five passengers plus 30 cents for each additional person. There is a communal kitchen and barbeque.

ROYAL NATAL NATIONAL PARK

The Royal Natal is one of the smallest of South Africa's national parks but in terms of landscape it's the most spectacular.

Right up against the Lesotho border, the Drakensberg forms an eight-km-long wall of rock known as the Amphitheatre, behind which is the Mont aux Sources summit where both the Orange and the Tugela Rivers originate. The area is well watered by countless streams and has forests of cypress, cycad and sagewood as well as a profusion of birds and wildflowers.

Entrance to the park costs 60 cents. Camping costs R 4.50 per person per night (minimum of R 6.75 per site) and horses are available for R 6 per hour. Hot showers are available at the camp site. Maps of the park can be bought for around R 1.

ZULULAND GAME PARKS

There are five main game reserves in Zululand (northern Natal) – Hluhluwe, Umfolozi, Mkuzi, Ndumu and St Lucia.

Accommodation in the reserves is in two-bed and four-bed self-contained huts, which cost R 5 per person, with a minimum charge of R 8 for the four-bed huts. A number of larger, self-contained cottages at Hluhluwe cost R 6 per person with a minimum charge of R 12 for a four-bed cottage and R 18 for a six-bed cottage. Camping costs R 6 per person with a minimum of R 9 per site. Reservations, which can be made up to six months in advance, must be made at the Game & Fisheries Preservation Board (tel 5 1514), PO Box 662, Pietermaritzburg 3200, Natal.

There are no restaurants or stores at these reserves so take your own provisions. Petrol and diesel are available and cooking and eating utensils are provided. The kitchen staff prepare all meals. Admission to the parks costs R 4 per vehicle plus 50 cents per passenger.

Hluhluwe

This reserve is famous for its rhino, but there's also a large variety of other game, including buffalo.

Mkuzi

This is mainly a waterfowl reserve, but

you can also see the timid suni antelope as well as impala, giraffe, kudu, zebra and wart hog. If you want to camp, there is a site about one km in from the gate on the main road through the park, which costs R 4.50 per person (minimum charge of R 6.75 per site). The tap water is brackish but fresh tank water is available. Entry to the park costs R 1. Reservations must be made in advance with the Officer-in-Charge (tel Mzuki 3), Mzuki Game Reserve, PO Mzuki, 3965, Zululand.

There are a number of 'hides' which you can use to observe game and birds from during the day. It's usually fairly easy to hitch to them if you don't have a car.

Ndumu

Right on the Mozambique border, Ndumu is another reserve mainly for waterfowl. Tours are available around the pans with one of the rangers.

St Lucia

The reserve consists of an island-studded bay almost 72 km in length and from two to eight km wide. It was established primarily as a fishing reserve but also contains buck, hippo and crocodile.

Five-day wilderness trail trips are available from **Charter's Creek** under the supervision of a ranger every week between April and September. They cost R 50 per person. Those who go on the trail are taken 24 km up the lake to the wilderness area by boat. The same conditions apply as for the wilderness trail in the Umfolozi Reserve. Reservations for the huts in this reserve and for the wilderness trail must be made with the Parks Board Office in Pietermaritzburg.

There are launch tours of the **St Lucia Estuary** and Charter's Creek which leave St Lucia daily at 8.30 am and 2.30 pm when tidal conditions permit; they cost R 8. It's unlikely you'll see much more than hippos.

Places to Stay There are two camping areas and two hut camps. *St Lucia Estuary* and

Eden Park offer camping. Reservations should be made to the Ranger-in-Charge (tel St Lucia 20), PO St Lucia Estuary 3936, Zululand. Eden Park is closest to the town of St Lucia (about 20 minutes walk).

Charter's Creek has huts available. *Fanies Island* offers camping and huts (reservations to the Camp Superintendent, Fanies Island, Private Bag X7205, Mtubatuba 1431). Camping costs R 6 per person and there is a minimum charge of R 9 per site.

Umfolozi

Umfolozi is primarily a sanctuary for the 'white' rhino, although there are many other species of game to be seen.

One of the features of Umfolozi is the three-day wilderness trail. Trips take place throughout the year but reservations must be made in advance with the Game & Fisheries Preservation Board, Pietermaritzburg. If you plan to take part in one during May to August you are advised to book ahead as far as possible. The trail costs R 50 per person or R 200 for a group of six people (six is the maximum for a group). You must provide your own food, clothing, soap and towels, but sleeping bags, tents and cooking and eating utensils are provided. Transport of food, bedding, camping gear, etc is by pack animal.

Spanish North Africa

All that remains of the Spanish colonies in Africa are the two tiny enclaves of Ceuta and Melilla on the northern Moroccan coast, and the tiny islands of Alhucemas, Chafarinas and Peñon de la Gomera just off the coast. Ceuta and Melilla are two intensely Andalusian cities, which came under Spanish control in the 15th century at a time when the Muslim armies were gradually being pushed out of Spain and Portugal. They remained under Spanish control when Morocco gained its independence in 1956, and both are administered as city provinces of Spain.

About 90% of the inhabitants are Spanish. The main function of the cities is to supply the Spanish troops stationed there and to service the NATO base and other ships. Fishing and the export of iron ore from the Rif Mountains are the other main activities. The Moroccan government occasionally campaigns for the return of the provinces to Morocco.

These places are of interest to the traveller mainly because the cheapest ferries between Spain and Morocco operate through them, and because customs formalities tend to be easier than going through Tangier. However, because Morocco resents the continuing Spanish occupation of these enclaves, Moroccan customs and immigration can be obstructive and extremely rude, though this usually applies only to the Melilla border. If you have problems, wait until the shift changes and try again.

Facts

VISAS

As for Spain, visas are not required by nationals of any West European country (including Yugoslavia), any country in the Americas (including the Caribbean), Japan, South Korea, Philippines, Singapore, and many countries in Africa (eg, The Gambia, Kenya, Mauritius, Morocco, Seychelles, Sierra Leone and Tunisia).

Nationals of Israel and South Africa require visas.

MONEY
US$ 1 = Ptas 112

The unit of currency is the Spanish peseta.

Getting There & Around

TO/FROM MOROCCO

In Ceuta there are buses to the border every 15 minutes or so from Plaza de la Constitución. The No 7 bus costs 40 Ptas (exact change only) and the trip takes about 20 minutes. If you arrive by ferry and want to head straight for the border, turn right out of the port area. There is a bus stop 50 metres along, on the right hand side, opposite the ramparts and moat. The border crossing is straightforward enough and once through, there are plenty of taxis doing the trip to Tetouan. A seat in one of these costs Dr 14. Unless the border is really crowded, the whole trip from Ceuta to Tetouan should take no more than two hours; often a good deal less.

In Melilla there are local buses from the Plaza de España to the border, which run

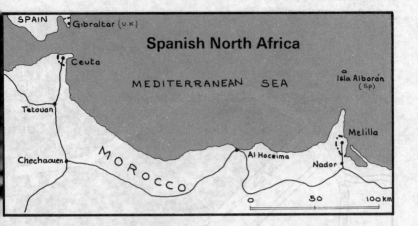

from about 7.30 am to late in the evening. From where the buses stop, it's about 150 metres to the Spanish customs, then another 200 metres to the Moroccan customs. On the other side of the Moroccan customs there are frequent buses to Nador.

TO/FROM SPAIN

The ferry terminal in Ceuta is at the western end of the town centre. Monday to Saturday there are six departures daily, the first at 8 am, the last at 9 pm; on Sunday there are only three sailings, between 9.30 am and 9 pm; the fare is 1100 Ptas. The journey to Algeciras on the Spanish mainland takes one hour.

Melilla is connected to Spain by ferries from Malaga. There is usually at least one per day, though they are occasionally cancelled in the winter due to rough weather.

Ceuta

Known as Sebta in Arabic, Ceuta's *raison d'être* is as a supply and service centre for the military base, but it does also prosper with its duty-free status. You're not going to find any great bargains, but if heading for Algeria it's worth picking up a bottle of whisky for sale later on. Fuel is also worth buying as it's cheaper than in Morocco, so stock up if you're driving.

As a place to visit, Ceuta doesn't offer a great deal and there's nothing to keep you here, especially as it's not particularly cheap. If you're heading for Morocco, your best bet is to catch an early ferry from Algeciras and move straight through to Tetouan or Chechaouen.

A lot of people enter Morocco via Ceuta as a way of avoiding the hundreds of touts who hang around in Tangier. They're just waiting for the ferries to arrive so they can attach themselves to the new arrivals.

Information

The small tourist office (tel 51 1379) is right by the ferry terminal, so you can pick up the useful brochure, map and accommodation list. The guy staffing the office speaks reasonable English and is helpful with any enquiries. It is open from 8 am to 2 pm and 4 to 6 pm daily except Sunday. Outside these hours, the ferry times, maps and other handy information are displayed in the window. The main post office (*Correos y Telégrafos*) is the big yellow building at Plaza de España, a

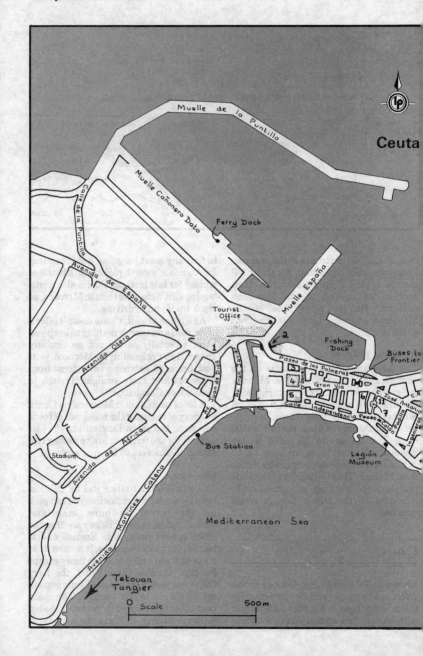

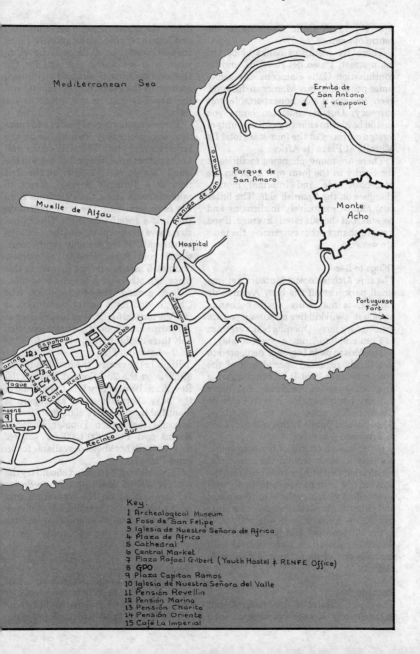

Key:
1 Archeological Museum
2 Foso de San Felipe
3 Iglesia de Nuestra Señora de Africa
4 Plaza de Africa
5 Cathedral
6 Central Market
7 Plaza Rafael Gilbert (Youth Hostel & RENFE Office)
8 GPO
9 Plaza Capitan Ramos
10 Iglesia de Nuestra Señora del Valle
11 Pensión Revellin
12 Pensión Marina
13 Pensión Charito
14 Pensión Oriente
15 Café La Imperial

square just off Calle Camoens in the centre of town.

There are plenty of banks along the main street, Paseo del Revellin, and its continuation Calle Camoens. It's sometimes possible to buy Moroccan dirhams, even though it's a nonexportable soft currency. Outside business hours you should be able to change small amounts of foreign currency at the four-star Hotel La Muralla at Plaza de Africa.

There are moneychanging facilities at the border in the form of a bank on the Moroccan side and informal money-changers on the Spanish side. The latter deal almost exclusively in dirhams and pesetas, but the rate is only average. If you want to change other currencies, the rates are worse.

Things to See

The tiny **Archaeological Museum**, set in a small park just off the busy Avenida de España, is not really worth bothering with, but it will kill five minutes if you are waiting for a ferry. Opening hours are 9 am to 1 pm and 5 to 7 pm; closed Monday.

The **Museo de la Legión** is dedicated to this highly regarded special unit of the army created in 1920. It holds a staggering array of weapons, uniforms and other military paraphernalia. It is on Paseo de Colón and is open only on Saturdays, Sundays and public holidays from 11 am to 2 pm and 4 to 6 pm.

If you have a couple of hours to spare, it's easy to walk around the peninsula, which is capped by Monte Acho. From the convent of **Ermita de San Antonio**, there is an excellent view over the Mediterranean, and Gibraltar is plainly visible on a clear day. At the convent itself, originally built in the 17th century and reconstructed in the 1960s, there is a large festival held annually on 13 June to mark St Anthony's Day.

Places to Stay

The *Youth Hostel* is the cheapest, but unfortunately it only operates as such during the school vacation periods of July and August. It's hidden away on the Plaza Rafael Gilbert, just off Paseo del Revellin, where you see a big red sign for the Restaurant China. Stairs lead up through an arch to the Plaza Rafael Gilbert, and the hostel is just in the corner to the right.

There is no shortage of *fondas* and *casas de huéspedes*, easily identifiable by the large blue and white 'F' or 'CH' on the wall at the entrances. Cheapest of these is the small *Charito* (tel 51 3982) on the first floor at 5 Teniente Arrabal, about 15 minutes' walk along the waterfront from the ferry terminal. The only indication that it is a guesthouse is the 'Chambres' sign above the footpath, and the 'CH' sign on the wall. There are only eight rooms, which cost Ptas 500/900 for singles/doubles. There are no hot showers in this place, but otherwise it is quite adequate.

Just around the corner from the Charito, and right on the waterfront, is the *Marina* (tel 51 3206) on the 3rd floor at 26 Marina Española. It is a tiny place with only three double rooms, which go for Ptas 1200 – basic but OK.

Right in the centre, the *Revellin* (tel 51 6762) is on the 2nd floor at 2 Paseo del Revellin. The doorway is in the middle of the busy shopping street and again is identifiable by the 'CH' sign. It is directly opposite the Banco Popular Español. Rooms cost Ptas 800/1500 for singles/doubles, with hot showers available for an extra Ptas 150.

Those looking for comfort should try the *Atlante* (tel 51 3548) at 1 Paseo de las Palmeras, right on the waterfront and handy for the boat terminal. It is a two-star *hostale residencia* and charges Ptas 2000/2600 for singles/doubles with washbasin.

Places to Eat

Finding a good cheap meal is a real problem in Ceuta. There are plenty of cafés, which just have snacks, but these are still quite expensive and not really filling. Things get cheaper as you go further from the centre along Calle Real. The *Café La Imperial* at No 27 has set menus.

Melilla

Melilla is smaller than Ceuta, and even today its population stands at less than 80,000. Its very well preserved mediaeval fortress, however, is what gives the city a lingering fascination. Right until the end of the 19th century virtually the whole of Melilla was contained within these massive defensive walls, and the garrison was well able to withstand the occasional siege from Morocco. This old part of town has a distinctly Castilian flavour with its narrow, twisting streets, squares, gates and drawbridges. The area has been declared a national monument.

The new part of town to the west of the fortress was begun at the end of the 19th century and was laid out by Don Enrique Nieto, one of Gaudí's contemporaries. When it was originally built it reflected the dictates of Spanish modernist architecture and there were many façades of stucco and gypsum with a covering of Sevillan tiles. Unfortunately, many of these have now disappeared behind the plate glass and aluminium frames of duty-free shops and the like, while others have been allowed to deteriorate.

Information

The tourist office is at the junction of Calle de Querol and Avenida del General Aizpuru close to the Plaza de Toros (bullring). It's a well-stocked office and the staff are friendly and helpful. Most of the banks are along the main street, Avenida de Juan Carlos I. There are always a lot of moneychangers hanging around the cafés on the Plaza de España who will do deals for Moroccan and Algerian money. Make sure you know what the rates are before agreeing to a deal.

Both RENFE and Transmediterranea ferry companies have offices in town (see map) where you can buy tickets for the ferries to the Spanish mainland. Otherwise, buy tickets at the ferry terminal itself (Estación Maritima).

Things to See

It's definitely worth half a day of your time exploring the incredible fortress of **Medina Sidonia**, and there are good views over the town and out to sea from the ramparts. Inside the walls, make sure you visit the **Iglesia de la Concepción** with its gilded reredos and shrine to Nuestra Señora la Virgen de la Victoria (the patroness of the city); and the **Museo Municipal**, which has a good collection of Phoenician and Roman ceramics as well as a coin collection and displays of historical documents.

The main entrance to the fortress is through the massive Puerta de Santiago with its drawbridges, tunnels and chapels, though there is another gate on the eastern flank opposite the ferry terminal. Known as the Foso de Hornabeque, this entrance provides vehicular access via a stone tunnel under the walls.

Places to Stay

There's not a lot of cheap accommodation in Melilla so you may find yourself staying in a one or two-star hotel especially if you arrive late in the day. There are a couple of cheap *pensiones* on the Calle de Jardines, which runs parallel to the Paseo General Macías, but these are pretty rough and ready and are mainly brothels.

A better bet is the *Hostal Residencia Montero*, Avenida del General Aizpuru, one block back from the western end of the Parque Hernández. It's a clean, well-maintained place but is quite a walk from the ferry terminal. More convenient is the *Hostal Residencia Miramar*, Paseo General Macías, a two-star establishment

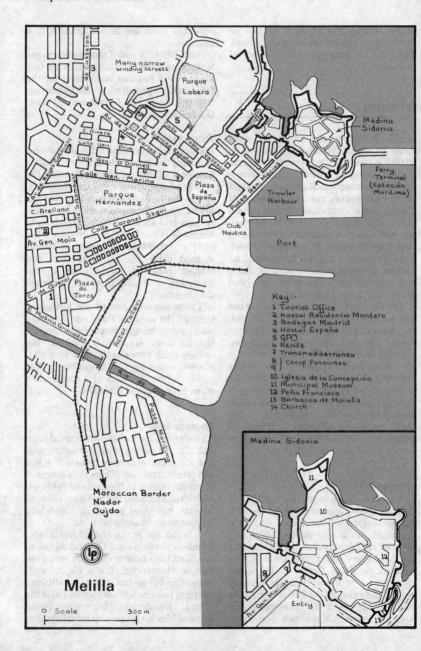

Key:-
1 Tourist Office
2 Hostal Residencia Montero
3 Bodegas Madrid
4 Hostal España
5 GPO
6 RENFE
7 Transmediterranea
8 } Cheap Pensiones
9 }
10 Iglesia de la Concepción
11 Municipal Museum
12 Peña Francisca
13 Barbacoa de Muralla
14 Church

Parque Lobera

Medina Sidonia

Ferry Terminal (Estación Maritima)

Trawler Harbour

Club Nautico

Port

Many narrow winding streets

Parque Hernández

Plaza de España

Plaza de Toros

C. de Castelar

Av. de Juan Carlos I

C. Rivera

Calle Gen. Prim

Calle Gen. O'Donnell

Calle Gen. Marina

Av. de Rejes Catolicos

C. Arellano

Calle Sotomayor

Calle Coronel Segui

Av. Gen. Mola

C. de Gueroi

C. Musico Granados

Calle Ejercito Español

Calle Pablo Vallesca

Paseo Gen. Macias

Actor Tallavi

Rio de Oro

Paseo Maritimo

Moroccan Border
Nador
Oujda

Melilla

0   Scale   300m

Medina Sidonia

Av. Gen. Macias

Entry

with plenty of room. It is almost next to the Puerta de Santiago.

My recommendation, however, is the *Hostal España* (tel 684645), on the corner of Avenida de Juan Carlos I and Calle del General Pareja, which is in a delightful old building and is run by a very friendly family. Many of the rooms have balconies overlooking the street. The place is kept well scrubbed and hot showers are available at no extra cost.

Places to Eat

There are a number of good restaurants to choose from in the streets bounded by the Avenida de Juan Carlos I, the Avenida de Reyes Catolicos and the Parque Hernández, but check prices before you eat, as most are quite expensive.

A better hunting ground for budget travellers is the Calle de Castelon where there are number of rustic bar/restaurants, most of which only open in the evenings. In all these places there is a range of fresh seafoods, meat and salads on display and you can eat very well indeed at a reasonable price. All of them offer cheap Spanish wines and beer and, by dinner time in the

evening, they are packed out by revellers. Highly recommended is the *Bodegas Madrid* with its old wine casks for tables.

For a splurge you can't beat the *Barbacoa de Muralla* inside the fortress on top of the Foso de Hornabeque. The restaurant is housed inside a refurbished building, which retains all the original features including the barred windows overlooking the port. If you're not sure you can afford a meal, pop in first, order a beer and have a look at the menu.

Also inside the fortress are a number of small bar/restaurants where you can get simple meals and snacks, and drink away to your heart's content. They're open lunch times and evenings.

Nightlife

Other than spending your evenings in the many bars around town, or promenading up and down the main street, there's a folk music club, the *Peña Francisco* inside the fortress (see map), which is open in the evenings. As well, there are a number of discos: their addresses are in the tourist leaflet.

Sudan

Sudan, Africa's largest country, stretches from the deserts of Nubia to the equatorial rainforests and swamps of the Sudd, just north of the great lakes and source of the Nile. Like neighbouring Chad, it straddles the dividing line of two cultures, that of the Arab north and Black south. Also, like Chad, it was torn by civil war between the two groups for many years after independence in 1956.

The conflict ended in 1972 when a large degree of autonomy was granted to the south. This was one of the great achievements of the former leader Jaafar el-Nimeiry. It allowed the country to concentrate on social and economic developments, especially in the less developed south. It was, therefore, hard to believe when Nimeiry unilaterally scrapped autonomy for the south and decreed Islamic Law over the whole country in 1983. As a result, Sudan was again torn by civil war and there is still no settlement in sight.

The international fame of Egypt's exceptionally long and rich cultural heritage has tended to overshadow the equally interesting heritage of the Sudan. As early as 2300 BC, the Pharaonic kingdoms had begun to extend south. By 1000 BC, Nubia had become an Egyptian colony and the empire's prime source of gold, producing an estimated peak of 40,000 kg a year. Further south lay numerous Egyptian towns, the most important being near Merowe, just below the fourth cataract of the Nile. Out of this town around 1000 BC grew the independent kingdom of Kush, whose rulers conquered Egypt in the 9th century BC, making Napata their capital and one of the most important centres of the ancient world.

After the sacking of Thebes by the Assyrians in 666 BC, the kingdom retreated further south into what was then well-wooded country and established a new capital at Meroe, near today's Shendi. Here it survived virtually untroubled for centuries, while Egypt was overrun by the Persians, Macedonians and Romans.

The legacy of this Egyptianised kingdom can be seen in the temples, tombs and other ruins along the banks of the Nile from Wadi Halfa to Khartoum.

The kingdom's wealth was based on the export of ivory, slaves, rare skins and ebony. But after the 1st century AD, it came under pressure from its rival trading state of Axum in Ethiopia, falling to it in the 4th century. Meroe was sacked by the Christian rulers of Ethiopia and its rulers were forced to flee west to Kordofan and Darfur, where they eventually set up a successor state. From there, Egyptian influences spread far and wide over the centuries and have been traced as far away as Mali and Zimbabwe by archaeologists and anthropologists.

After the destruction of Meroe, a Christian kingdom grew up in Nubia with its centre at Dongola. It was sufficiently powerful to stop the advance of the Arab armies that seized Egypt from the Byzantine Empire in 641 AD. But 10 years later, Dongola was besieged and the Nubians were forced to sign a treaty with the Arabs guaranteeing Muslim traders freedom of access and worship in return for Arab respect of Nubia's independence. This treaty lasted for five centuries, until Egypt came under the control of the Mamelukes in 1250. Shortly afterwards, Nubia was conquered and Arab migration to the Sudan grew from a trickle to a flood.

As Mameluke power in Egypt waned, control of the Sudan passed to two Sultanates whose prosperity was based on taxing the trans-Saharan caravan trade. They were the Fung and the Fur. The Fung centred around Sennar and controlled the Nile Valley between the Egyptian border and Ethiopia, and the Fur centred in the Jebel Marra mountains of Darfur. Continuing Arab migration into these areas and the resultant intermarriages with the indigenous population, led to the adoption of Arabic as the common language and a legal system based on the Muslim Shari'ah.

While all these developments were taking place in the north and west, the swamps of the Sudd remained an effective barrier against Arab penetration. The south was not opened to trade until 1821, when the Turkish Viceroy of Egypt, Muhammad Ali, conquered northern Sudan. The effect was catastrophic. Within a few decades, the population plummetted as a result of pillage, slavery and disease. Meanwhile, the towns of the north grew rich on the proceeds.

After the construction of the Suez Canal in 1869 (and Egypt's subsequent indebtedness to foreign creditors) the process was further complicated by British mercenaries who, with the active encouragement of Westminster, were employed by the Khedive Ismail as explorers and governors of the Sudan. The most famous of these was General Gordon, governor of Sudan from 1877.

At this time, British colonial policy centred around controlling the Nile, containing French expansion from the west and drawing the south into a British-East African federation. The western intrusion, and in particular the Christian missionary zeal that accompanied it, was resented by many Muslim Sudanese, as were the taxes imposed by the Egyptians to finance their growing foreign debt. In 1881, when the British occupied Egypt,

the Sudanese rebelled under the leadership of the Mahdi. Five years later, Gordon and his forces were massacred at Khartoum, and for the next 13 years Sudan was ruled by the Mahdi.

Though nationalist in many respects, the Mahdist uprising was also religious. Based on the *tariqa*, a form of brotherhood brought from Arabia in the 1770s that advocated a government founded on the Koran, the Mahdiya preached Sufi asceticism and declared a *jihad* (holy war) in defence of Islam and against corruption. They didn't enjoy universal support, however. They were opposed by the Khatmia, who were closely associated with the Turko-Egyptian regime and had been brought to the Sudan in the early 1800s. In its short life, the Mahdiya also had to confront the Turko-Egyptian armies, the Ethiopians, the forces of the Darfur sultanate, the Italians and the Belgians. It was finally defeated by Kitchener and the Anglo-Egyptian army in 1898.

After the Mahdist defeat, the British finalised a 'condominium' agreement with Egypt that effectively made the Sudan a British colony. Over the next 25 years, an export-oriented economy based on cotton and gum arabic developed, railways and harbours were built and a modern civil service was established. The British accorded privileged status to the Khatmia, as opposed to the defeated Mahdist brotherhood, the Ansar. But as the Khatmia increasingly identified with emerging Egyptian nationalism, the colonial authorities switched allegiance and rehabilitated the Mahdists. The brotherhood quickly re-established itself as a semifeudal aristocracy, advocating independence from Egypt as a way of safeguarding the Sudan's economic interests.

At the end of WW II, two political parties had emerged in Sudan – the Ashiqqa Party, formed by the educated supporters of the Khatmia and eventually to become the National Union Party

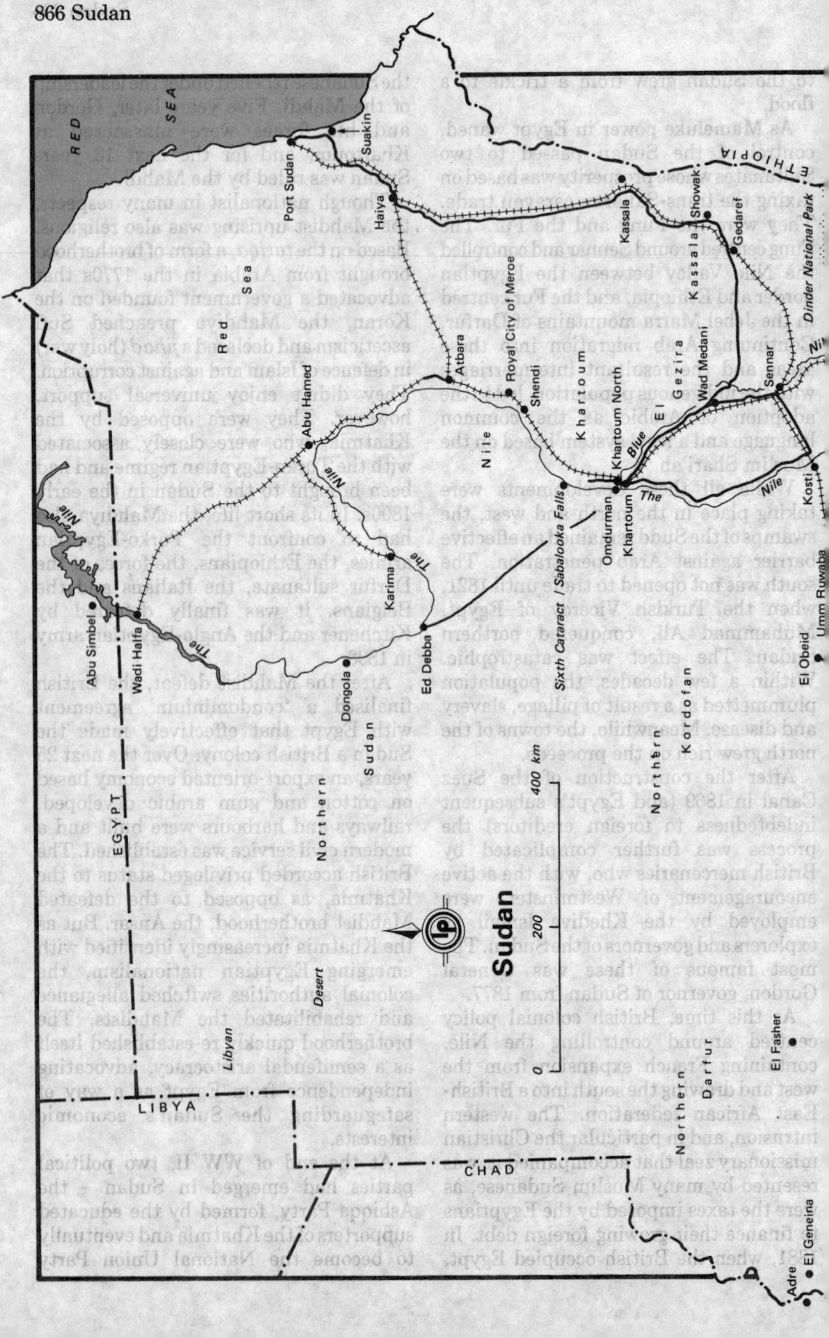
Sudan
0
200
400 km
RED SEA
Red Sea
EGYPT
LIBYA
CHAD
ETHIOPIA
Libyan Desert
Northern Sudan
Northern Kordofan
Northern Darfur
Nile
Khartoum
El Gezira
Kassala
The Nile
The Blue Nile
Port Sudan
Suakin
Haiya
Atbara
Abu Hamed
Royal City of Meroe
Shendi
Khartoum North
Omdurman
Khartoum
Sixth Cataract / Sabalooka Falls
Karima
Ed Debba
Dongola
Wadi Halfa
Abu Simbel
Kassala
Showak
Gedaref
Wad Medani
Sennar
Kosti
Umm Ruwaba
El Obeid
El Fasher
El Geneina
Adre
Dinder National Park

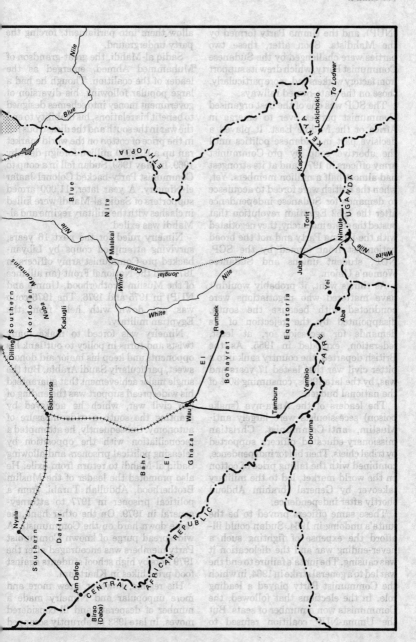

(NUP), and the Umma Party formed by the Mahdists. Soon after, these two parties were challenged by the Sudanese Communist Party, which drew its support from factory workers and, more particularly, those on the state-owned railways.

The SCP was one of the best organised Communist parties ever to emerge in Africa or the Middle East. It played a decisive part in Sudanese politics until the abortive coup by pro-Communist army officers in 1971, and at its strongest had almost half a million members. Yet, when the British were forced to acquiesce to demands for Sudanese independence after the 1952 Egyptian revolution that ousted the effete monarchy, they negotiated with the Umma Party and not the broad nationalist front formed by the SCP, NUP, student unions and Sudanese Women's Union.

As things went, it probably wouldn't have mattered who negotiations were conducted with because the south, disappointed by the rejection of its demands for secession or, at least, federation, exploded in 1955. As the British departed, the country sank into a bitter civil war that lasted 17 years and was, by the late 1960s, consuming 30% of the national budget.

The leaders of the Anya-nya (snake poison) secessionists were largely anti-Muslim, anti-Communist, Christian missionary-educated officers supported by tribal chiefs. Their bid for independence, combined with the falling price of cotton on the world market, led to the military takeover by General Ibrahim Abdoud shortly after independence.

These same officers proved to be the junta's undoing in 1964. Sudan could ill-afford the expense of fighting such a never-ending war and the dislocation it was causing. The junta's failure to end the war led to a general strike in 1964, in which the Communist Party played a leading role. In the elections that followed, the Communists won a number of seats. But the Umma-NUP coalition refused to allow them into parliament, forcing the party underground.

Sadiq al-Mahdi, the great-grandson of Muhammed Ahmed, emerged as the leader of the coalition. Though he had a large popular following, his diversion of government money into schemes designed to benefit his relations, his inability to end the war in the south and the disastrous fall in the price of cotton on the world market ran up a US$260 million foreign debt by 1969. In May 1969, Sudan fell in a coup to Communist Party-backed Colonel Jaafar el-Nimeiry. A year later, 11,000 armed supporters of Sadiq al-Mahdi were killed in clashes with the military regime and al-Mahdi was exiled.

Nimeiry ruled for the next 16 years, surviving attempted coups by Libyan-backed pro-Communist army officers in 1971 and the National Front (an alliance of the Muslim Brotherhood, Umma and NUP) in 1975 and 1976. The 1976 coup was put down with help from the Egyptian military.

Nimeiry was forced to make many twists and turns in policy to outflank his opponents and keep his major aid donors sweet, particularly Saudi Arabia. But the single major achievement that guaranteed his widespread support was the ending of the civil war, which he achieved by granting the south a wide measure of autonomy. Subsequently, he attempted a reconciliation with the opposition by releasing political prisoners and allowing Sadiq al-Mahdi to return from exile. He also promoted the leader of the Muslim Brotherhood, Abdullah Turabi, from a political prisoner in 1977 to attorney-general in 1979. On the other hand, he came down hard on the Communists. A widespread purge of known Communist Party members was encouraged after the 1979 riots by high school students against food price hikes in Khartoum.

His regime, however, grew more and more unpopular and Nimeiry made a number of desperate and ill-considered moves. In late 1983 he abruptly scrapped the autonomy accord with the south in favour of 'regionalisation' and imposed Islamic Law over the whole country. Reports soon began to trickle out of Sudanese courts ordering multiple amputations for such crimes as robbery, and public floggings for the possession of alcohol and for real or imagined adultery. Foreigners were not exempt from these laws, as several found out. Nimeiry went on to dismiss many of his experienced lieutenants and advisers, replacing them with what amounted to a gaggle of mystics and Islamic fundamentalists. Not only did this provoke widespread disaffection in the north, it was an anathema in the south and led to the resurgence of civil war.

Within a couple of months the central government virtually lost control of the south as the railway was sabotaged, the Kosti-Juba Nile ferry was blown up and roads were mined. At the same time, Gaddafi announced his support for the rebels, now known as the Sudanese People's Liberation Movement (SPLM). Nimeiry reacted by declaring a state of emergency that suspended the constitution and banned all strikes, public gatherings and demonstrations. As subsequent events proved, this was the straw that broke the camel's back.

Faced with a ridiculously high external debt he couldn't service, the worst drought in living memory, austerity measures and food price hikes that most people couldn't tolerate, Sudan hovered on the brink of collapse. After massive street demonstrations in Khartoum, which most of the junior and many of the senior army officers supported, Nimeiry was deposed in a coup in April 1985 while returning from a visit to Washington. He initially stayed in Cairo, but was forced to flee to the Bahamas when Sudan applied for his extradition from Egypt.

The new military regime, headed by the former defence minister General Abdul Rahman Swar el-Dahab, pledged a return to civilian rule after a one-year transitional period. Meanwhile, it began purging all those associated with the former regime. While it sacked the chief justice, a Muslim fundamentalist and strict interpreter of the Shari'ah, it did not repeal Shari'ah law. As a result, attempts to negotiate peace with the SPLM were stillborn and the civil war continues. Almost the only success the new government has had regarding this conflict is to achieve a rapprochement with Libya, which had been arming the rebels.

A general election was held in April 1986, with the Umma Party, led by the former prime minister Sadiq al-Mahdi, taking the majority of seats in the new National Assembly. Al-Mahdi again became Prime Minister and Defence Minister. A six-member Supreme Council was appointed to serve as Head of State.

With the ongoing civil war and resultant dislocation of services, continuing drought and famine and an economy constantly on the brink of bankruptcy, it will be a long time before peace and a measure of prosperity return to Sudan.

Facts

GEOGRAPHY & CLIMATE

Sudan, with a population of about 21 million, is one of Africa's poorest and least developed nations. In its north and west are vast areas of desert that support little life, and in its east is the semi-desert of Nubia. Rain hardly ever falls in these areas, and when it does it creates raging torrents in the *wadis* (dry river beds) that can cut communications for days. In summer there are frequent dust storms.

The only areas that support crops of any size are the Gezira, between the Blue and White Niles, south of Khartoum, and a small area south of Suakin on the Red Sea coast. Elsewhere in the north, life centres around date palms, camels and raising stock.

The desert gradually gives way in the south to savannah and then to the rainforests on the borders with Uganda and Zaïre.

Very few sealed roads exist. Travel is largely over desert tracks or rail. It can be slow and unpredictable, but is more than compensated for by the incredible hospitality found everywhere – not just from ordinary people but from government officials and the police. This is something experienced by every traveller. We've received countless letters raving about the friendliness and hospitality of Sudan.

Before the resurgence of the civil war, Sudan was well on the way to completing one of the largest irrigation projects ever attempted in Africa. The Jonglai Canal was being cut through the swamps of the Sudd from Bor to Malakal. It was designed to drain off much of the water that normally flowed to the swamps and was lost through evaporation, thereby increasing the amount of water joining the Nile further north. The extra water was to irrigate the Gezira, where Sudan's main export crop – cotton – was grown.

A number of people have suggested the scheme may backfire by destroying the ecological balance of the area. The swamps are a natural habitat for large herds of buffaloes, elephants and hippopotami and are essential for the cattle-herding activities of the indigenous tribes. The scheme is being monitored by a UN ecology unit.

If it's going to rain in the north, it normally happens between July and September and is rarely more than 100 mm per annum – often less. In the south, annual rainfall can exceed 1000 mm and usually occurs between April and November. Temperatures are generally high, climbing to more than 38° C in Khartoum in summer.

WARNING

Though some travellers do make it to places in the south, because of the civil war it's best to assume that anywhere south of Kosti is off limits.

As a result of Islamic law, you can get S£200 for a bottle of whisky on the street. But you're taking a great risk as you can be publicly flogged if caught with it. When Islamic Law was declared, the authorities went through all the hotels, confiscated all alcohol and threw it into the Nile, or simply smashed the bottles on the street. You're in for a dry time. The revolution hasn't changed this.

VISAS

Visas are required by all. Nationals of Israel and South Africa are not admitted. If your passport contains Israeli stamps or Egyptian stamps from the Egyptian-Israeli border at Rafah, you will be refused a visa.

There are Sudanese embassies in Abidjan (Ivory Coast), Addis Ababa (Ethiopia), Algiers (Algeria), Bangui (CAR), Cairo (Egypt), Dar es Salaam (Tanzania), Kampala (Uganda), Kinshasa (Zaïre), Lagos (Nigeria), Nairobi (Kenya), N'Djamena (Chad), Rabat (Morocco), Tripoli (Libya) and Tunis (Tunisia).

At the Sudanese Embassy in Cairo (3 Al Ibrahim St, Garden City), one-month visas cost E£10.10, require three photos and a letter of introduction from your embassy and are issued in 24 hours or less.

In Nairobi (7th Floor, Minet ICDC House, Mamlaka Road), a one-month visa costs KSh 100, requires an onward ticket, one photo and takes 24 hours to issue (up to three weeks if it has to be referred to Khartoum).

Visa extensions are issued by the Ministry of the Interior, near the post office in Khartoum. They cost S£10, require one photo and take 24 hours to issue. There are no hassles.

Other Visas

In Khartoum there are embassies for Algeria, CAR, Egypt, Ethiopia, Kenya,

Libya, Morocco, Niger, Nigeria, Somalia, Tanzania, Uganda and Zaïre.

CAR CAR visas are easy to get in Khartoum, taking between one and 10 days to issue depending on whether they have to telex Bangui. A one-month visa costs S£60.

Chad Chad visas cost S£40, require a letter of recommendation from your embassy and are issued in 24 hours.

Kenya These cost S£15 and take 48 hours to issue.

Zaïre A multiple-entry visa for one/two/three months costs US$27/$52.60/$65.75. They require three photos and can take up to four days to issue. The embassy, on 13th St in El Ammerat, will not accept Sudanese pounds.

MONEY

US$1 = S£2.45 (official bank rate)
US$1 = S£4.05 (official tourist rate)
UK£1 = S£6.72 (official tourist rate)

The unit of currency is the Sudanese pound (S£) = 100 piastres. The import and export of local currency is prohibited. If you're coming south from Aswan on the Lake Nasser ferry, however, no one will mind you bringing in sufficient local currency to see you through to Khartoum. But plenty of moneychangers meet the boat in Wadi Halfa and will give a better rate for Egyptian pounds than you'll get in Aswan.

There are two official rates of exchange – the tourist rate and the bank rate. The higher tourist rate is for changing travellers' cheques or cash at a bank. The lower bank rate is for buying an international airline ticket in Sudan, where you must produce your bank receipt to show you have changed money at the bank rate, or else pay in hard currency.

Avoid changing money at the bank in Wadi Halfa. It only gives you the official bank rate. Likewise, some of the banks in western Sudan are unaware that an official tourist rate exists. The Bank of Khartoum charges S£2 commission plus S£2 stamp duty for changing travellers' cheques.

There is a lively black market but the rates are volatile. Avoid changing with people on the street: instead, go to shopkeepers and be discreet. Expect US$1 = S£6.20 to S£7.00 and UK£1 = S£10. The best rates are in Port Sudan. Travellers' cheques can be sold on the black market for 20 pt to 40 pt less than what you would get for cash. It's also possible to exchange Egyptian pounds for Sudanese pounds, especially at Wadi Halfa. Expect E£1 = S£3. This is better than the rate inside Egypt.

For selling alcohol, see the 'Warning' section.

The airport tax is S£30 for international flights.

ACCOMMODATION
Hospitality in the Sudan can be incredible. Half the time you may have no need of a hotel. Rarely will you board a train or truck and get off at the other end without an invitation to stay with someone. Offers of money for your keep will probably be politely refused, but it's important to offer. A thoughtful gift or helping to do something is a different matter. It is the correct way to show your appreciation. If you neglect your obligations as a guest, these people will start to assume that travellers are a bunch of uncultured yobbos and the invitations will cease. Please keep it sweet. There are very few places like Sudan left in the world.

Hotels in both Khartoum and Kassala tend always to be booked out. To get a room you have to be there in the early morning, otherwise you may have to put up with very primitive accommodation.

FOOD
Local food is mainly fasulia, a bean stew

served with bread and dura (cooked maize or millet). There are several meat dishes – kibda (liver), shoya (charcoal barbequed meat) and kebab (fried meat). Along the Nile you can find dishes of Nile perch. Mangoes, dates, figs and bananas are plentiful and cheap, as are tomatoes and grapefruit in the south.

PHOTOGRAPHY

Photography permits are issued by the tourist office in Khartoum and are free.

LANGUAGE

Arabic is the official language and is spoken by about half the population, mainly in the north and centre. Nilotic and Nilo-Hamitic languages are spoken in the south. Darfur is spoken in the western province of the same name. English is widely spoken among government officials.

Getting There & Around

Wherever you arrive in Sudan, you must register with the police. This will cost S£2.50, except at Wadi Halfa where it costs S£5.

Before you can travel anywhere within Sudan you must have the appropriate travel permits, available from the Foreigners Registration Office in all regional capitals. The permits cost S£5 each, plus 75 pt in fiscal stamps, require two photos and are issued while you wait. The office in Khartoum is on Sayed Abdul Rahman Ave, between Abu Sina and 18th St, next to a travel agency. The entrance is easily missed.

Quite a few travellers deliberately neglect to get permits to travel around Sudan because of the hassle or cost. While a number of them may make it through undetected – either because the police in remote areas are unaware of the regulations or simply don't care – they are taking the risk of being sent back to Khartoum

immediately if they can't produce their permit to police on demand. I have never, however, heard of anyone who has landed in hot water by not having a permit.

No permits are issued for travel south of Kosti, and you would be ill-advised to go there as much of the area is controlled by the SPLM.

Whatever route you take through Sudan, you'll travel on an interesting array of trucks, riverboats, trains, international agency jeeps, mail vans and even get the occasional free flight in a light plane. Apart from the flights, all travel is slow. Many routes are impassable during the rainy season from June to September. In the more remote areas of the south it can take a week to find transport going your way, especially between Wau and Juba and anywhere south of Juba. Moreover, it isn't just road transport that is slow. The trains, too, are notoriously slow and subject to long delays. This extract from a letter by two people who visited Jebel Marra, Nyala, Khartoum, Kassala and Port Sudan gives you some idea of what to expect:

You need lots of time to see Sudan. The transport is diabolical and expensive. We took three months to see these few places. Most of the time was taken up being transported or waiting for transport. An example is when we left Jebel Marra with Ramadan starting. It took three days to do 65 km on a truck in the rain, and then when we arrived in Nyala we missed the train by half a day so we had to wait a week for the next one. This was then five days late for no apparent reason. When it arrived, it sat for ages in the station and then finally got moving. After 16 hours it stopped for 24 hours while the engine went back to get a train-load of cars. We couldn't believe it! Other delays entailed waiting for sand to be dug off the track; travelling at less than walking pace because the rain had washed away the foundations of the track; four hours going backwards to pick up the last carriage that had fallen off; derailments; mechanical failures and stopping to pick up people who had fallen off the roof. This was additional to waiting hours at little stations in the middle of nowhere. We eventually reached

Khartoum 6½ days after we left Nyala. The 1000-km journey between Jebel Marra and Khartoum had taken about three weeks. It was fun though!

AIR

It is advisable to buy your ticket and make reservations for the flight out of Sudan before entering Sudan. Tickets are very expensive in Khartoum. If you intend to fly to Kenya from Khartoum, buy your ticket in Cairo where student discounts of up to 30% are possible. Student discounts of 25% are sometimes available in Khartoum but are extremely hard to find. One travel agent who will do his utmost to secure you a discount if you have an international student card is Omer el-Hadd, the manager of Towawa Travel Agency (tel 80145), Parliament St. If he's out, ask for Mohammed Ali, who is equally helpful. To buy an airline ticket in Sudan you must produce bank receipts to show you changed the money at the official bank rate. Sample fares are: Khartoum to Nairobi US$425; Khartoum to Entebbe US$360.

Because of the civil war, the direct overland route down the Nile Valley from Khartoum to Juba, via Kosti, is no longer open. Many travellers now fly from Khartoum to Nairobi, with some stopping over in Juba to get a glimpse of southern Sudan, as Juba is just about the only southern town still in central government hands. Most companies have not flown to Juba since a plane was shot down by the SPLM, therefore, those that do fly are usually booked out solid at least two weeks in advance. This is often the case for flights from Juba to Kenya. You won't save any money flying to Nairobi via Juba as the fare from Khartoum is S£366 (US$140) one-way.

If you desperately need to get to Juba but all flights are booked out, try Ganjari Air, a subsidiary of Trans-Arabian. Its 'office' is on the runway, a long hot walk over the tarmac. It flies to Juba daily, but at unscheduled times. You may be able to get a flight as cargo, for free. If they direct you to their town office (walking distance from the airport and near the Kenyan Embassy), be prepared to be redirected to the Department of Civil Aviation, on the Nile near the post office, to get a special permit to fly as cargo. This permit simply requires that you agree to accept all responsibility for your personal safety, in case the plane is shot down or you are otherwise injured. It takes a few hours to issue, and there is no fuss if you say Sudan Air flights are booked weeks in advance and you need to fly as soon as possible. Flights from Khartoum to Nyala are similarly booked out weeks in advance. The fare is S$207.

ROAD

There are very few sealed roads. The main one is the Khartoum to Port Sudan road, via Wad Medani, Gedaref and Kassala. Most other roads are just a set of tyre tracks in the sand, dust or mud, or a dirt-track through the forest.

Buses now ply the Khartoum to Port Sudan highway, if you don't like truck trips.

Trucks frequently get bogged in bulldust (or mud in the rainy season) and everyone has to get off and start digging. This can be immense fun in retrospect, and a good way of getting to know your fellow travellers. But it doesn't always happen at convenient times of the day and night. Many roads in the south are closed for months during and after the rains, as they get washed out. Do your travelling between February and April.

Protect yourself from sunstroke when travelling on top of trucks. Take plenty of water when travelling through the desert, otherwise you will have to rely on wells and waterholes and may end up with hepatitis or dysentery. Free lifts are rare, but fares are more or less standardised. Mostly, you will be charged the same as the locals. Travelling inside the cab generally costs double the load-top journey.

Petrol shortages are fairly common and can delay or cancel your lift. Punctures and mechanical problems are another bugbear. Everyone has their own story to tell.

Arrange lifts the day before you want to go, but don't pay until you get on the truck. As in most African countries, trucks generally leave early in the morning from either the marketplace or a truck park nearby. There are two truck parks in Khartoum – Khartoum North and Omdurman. Trucks heading west generally leave from Omdurman.

TRAIN

There's a good rail network in Sudan connecting Wadi Halfa and Khartoum, Atbara and Port Sudan, and Khartoum and Sennar. At Sennar the line branches, one going east to Kassala and Port Sudan, the other going west to Kosti, Nyala and Wau. The track between Wau and Babanusa, where it joins the Nyala-Kosti line, is often sabotaged by the SPLM.

Student discounts of 50% are easy to get, but you must know exactly what routes you'll be taking. They are available from the Ministry of Youth in Khartoum, one block west of the post office on the Nile. They are not available in Wadi Halfa.

There are three classes on the trains – 1st, 2nd and 3rd. In 2nd and 3rd class, there are effectively two categories – ordinary and *mumtaz*. The latter is the better, with padded seats as opposed to slatted wooden benches, and costs a little more. Unless you're particularly robust, avoid ordinary 3rd class. It can turn into a nightmare on long journeys. You can reserve seats only on 1st class.

Trains never run on time. Also, be warned that when a train is parked beyond its originating platform, the local boys board all the 3rd-class carriages and 'reserve' seats for every man and his dog. By the time it gets to the platform, it's 'full'. So, either join the local lads or pay one of them to 'reserve' you a seat.

BOAT

Lake Nasser For details of services between Wadi Halfa and Aswan, see the Egypt chapter.

River Nile There are no longer any steamers along the Nile between Kosti and Juba because the SPLM rebels shot and sank one in February 1984. In any case, foreigners are prohibited from travelling overland south of Kosti.

Red Sea The Egyptian Steamship & Navigation Company has steamers from Port Suez to Port Sudan and Jeddah. For more details see the Egypt chapter.

OVERLAND ROUTES

To avoid hassles apply for permits before travelling around Sudan. There are no problems travelling north or east of Khartoum, and there shouldn't be any travelling west from Kosti to Nyala. In theory, you should also be able to get a permit for travel south from Nyala to Wau, but of late there has been intense rebel activity around Wau.

You will *not* be able to get permits to travel from Wau to Juba, Kosti to Juba or south of Juba to either Kenya or Uganda, and you would be foolish to try. Though some intrepid adventurers were still making it through to the Ugandan border without permits in early 1986, it's very doubtful you would make it now without exposing yourself to great danger.

Wadi Halfa to Khartoum

When you get off the boat at Wadi Halfa, it's still five km to town. To get there will cost you S£4 in a taxi or small van. From Wadi Halfa the cheapest, but most uninteresting, way to Khartoum is by train. In theory, the trains should connect with the steamers. In reality, you may have to wait a day or two in Wadi Halfa. Again, in theory, the trains depart from Wadi Halfa in the late afternoon on Thursday and Sunday and from Khartoum in the early morning on Sunday and

Wednesday. They are crowded and it's a dusty 50-hour journey if no breakdowns or derailments occur. On the first night, the trains stop in the desert so everyone can get out and get some sleep.

The fares are: S£80 sleeper, S£56 1st class, S£42/34 2nd class *mumtaz*/ordinary and S£23/17.50 3rd class *mumtaz*/ordinary.

To travel 1st class, you must hurry from the boat and make a reservation. Travelling on the roof is free, but you have to jump on without being seen by the conductors while the train is moving and there are few hand holds. It's impossible to take your pack up with you. That must be left inside for fellow travellers to watch. If you do ride on top use plenty of sunscreen and cover up well.

Take plenty of water on the train, and try to get it boiled beforehand at one of the hotels.

If you'd prefer to follow the course of the Nile and visit the antiquities, of which there are hundreds, take a truck from Wadi Halfa to Kerma. This should cost about S£25 to S£35 and take between 15 hours and 1½ days. It's as rough as hell and the nights are very cold. Try and get a place at the front of the lorry or pay more to ride in the cab. Next, take a lorry or shared taxi from Kerma to Dongola for S£10. It will take about 2½ hours. The ferry across the Nile will cost 25 pt, and a taxi into the town centre about 50 pt. From Dongola there are trucks and buses to Karima for S£20 to S£25 and taking between seven and 10 hours.

Alternatively, take a river steamer between Dongola and Karima. These boats, however, only operate after the level of the Nile rises, usually in August, and until it drops again towards the end of the year. Their schedules are erratic, but it is a pleasant trip. There usually are two sailings in either direction per week. The journey takes three days and cost S£14 (1st class) and S£9 (2nd class). You can get off the boat at villages and towns along the way, where you'll find plenty of interesting souks. Bean soup and tea are available on the boat, but it's advisable to take extra food.

From Karima, take the 36-hour train journey to Khartoum. There are trains in either direction every Wednesday and Sunday. The fares are: S£45.25 1st class, S£36.25/29.70 2nd class *mumtaz*/ordinary and S£20.10/15.30 3rd class *mumtaz*/ordinary.

Also, there are buses twice a week between Karima and Khartoum, leaving Khartoum on Tuesday and Saturday mornings. They take about 24 hours and cost S£11 to S£15, depending on whether you sit in the front or the back, and go via Shendi, Atbara and Abu Hamed.

Khartoum to Nyala, via Kosti

A truck all the way from Khartoum to Nyala will cost between S£50 and S£80 and take five to six days in the dry season (considerably longer in the wet). They leave from the souk in Omdurman, as do the occasional buses doing this trip.

Most people, however, prefer to do the journey in stages. There are buses from Khartoum to Kosti for S£10, taking 4½ hours, and a truck from Kosti to Nyala for S£40, taking four to five days.

If you don't want to do the trip by road, take the train. Schedules are erratic, but, in theory, there is a train from Khartoum to Nyala on Mondays, and Khartoum to El Obeid on Tuesdays. The journey to El Obeid takes around 32 hours in the dry, and up to 64 in the wet. The fares to El Obeid are: S£37.30 1st class, S£25.15/30.05 2nd class and S£12.95/17.00 3rd class. To Nyala: S£72.60 1st class, S£43.05/59.40 2nd class and S£25.10/33.00 3rd class. The higher fares in 2nd and 3rd class are for 'special' carriages.

There are also trucks direct from Khartoum to El Fasher – a great way to go – straight across the desert in five days. You can buy the ever available bowl of foul and chai from the villages along the way. It is a good road from El Fasher to Nyala, and easy hitching as there are plenty of aid workers driving up and down.

Along the Kosti to Nyala route an interesting place to visit is Kadugli, a lovely little town in the Nubian mountains. To get there, take a bus from Kosti to El Obeid, then a bus or truck (S£10) for the five-hour trip to Kadugli. From Kadugli there are buses and lorries to Babanusa, via El Fula. The first part of this road is very picturesque.

Khartoum to Port Sudan, via Kassala

Though there is a rail link between Khartoum and Port Sudan, via Sennar and Kassala, the journey is agonisingly slow and most people go by road.

Trucks and buses to Wad Medani, Gedaref, Kassala and Port Sudan leave from the Shabi souk in south Khartoum. There are several buses daily, leaving between 6 and 7.30 am. The best companies are Sugipto, Arrow and Taysir. Their buses have comfortable seats and some are air-con. Fares are S£15 to S£22 and you must book a day in advance. Sugipto and Arrow have their offices at Shabi souk. Taysir has its office on El Qsar Ave, in the same building as the French Cultural Centre in central Khartoum. Even if the bus is scheduled to go all the way to Port Sudan, it will stop overnight in Kassala. The journey from Khartoum to Kassala takes seven to nine hours.

TO/FROM CAR

In the wet season there are no trucks between Nyala and Bangui and the police will refuse to grant travel permits to head west at this time. But this doesn't mean you can't make it. If you choose to ignore the permit regulations, there are trucks from Nyala to as far as Rahad el Berdi for around S£20 and taking about 12 hours. You can stay at the police station in Rahad. From Rahad to the border town of Am Dafog, its either camel or donkey. Camel trains are the usual transport. They cost about S£5 for your bags, plus S£30 for you if you don't want to walk.

The 160 km is very hard going, through shallow swamps and coarse grasses, but you should be there within five days. Donkeys and guides are available for about S£50. Again, at Am Dafog you can stay at the police station. Food is available at a café.

The journey from Am Dafog to Birao, or Daba as the Sudanese often call it, takes another two days. It involves fording five deep wadis and staying with cattle-herding nomads. Two camels and a guide should cost S£25 a person. The nomads are usually very hospitable and helpful, serving you prime steak, fresh milk and yogurt, and, if you're lucky, treating you to some tribal music. In Birao you can stay at the Catholic Mission, though the people there are not particularly friendly and the mosquitoes are ferocious. There are no cafés in Birao and only limited supplies at the market. Shopkeepers might serve you a meal, such as meat and spaghetti. There's only one moneychanger and his rates are very poor.

In the wet, the only way from Birao to Bangui is to fly. Apart from the commercial flights, the French military regularly fly between Bangui and Birao with supplies and return empty. A lot of travellers have managed to talk their way onto a free flight. If you do have to go commercial, don't change money for it in Birao. Pay when you get to Bangui.

During the dry season, trucks leave from the Texas souk in Nyala for CAR. You could possibly get a truck all the way to Bangui for between S£120 and S£250. But you may have to settle for one to Birao or Ndélé. To Ndélé will cost around S£100 and take about seven days. The road as far as Ndélé is really bad.

TO/FROM KENYA

The same applies as for Uganda. There are direct flights from Khartoum to Nairobi.

TO/FROM UGANDA

It is impossible to go overland south to

Uganda because of the civil war. You must fly direct from Khartoum to Entebbe. Stopovers may be possible in Juba, depending on the fighting. Most companies, however, have not flown to Juba since the SPLM shot down a plane.

TO/FROM ZAÏRE

The same applies as for Uganda and Kenya.

Around The Country

ABU HAMED

There is a *Government Rest House*, with a huge verandah and showers, next to the railway station. To stay you need authorisation from the police station, which is about 500 metres from the mosque.

ATBARA

There's a small hotel about 500 metres from the railway station. It's clean, but there are a lot of mosquitoes. *Hotel Atbara* has been recommended. If you're short of money, ask at the police headquarters. They may give you a bed for the night. Cheap, basic meals are available.

DONGOLA

One of the best places to stay is *Hotel el Mana*. It is very pleasant, has clean rooms with fans for S£5. There are cold showers. If it's full, try *Hotel Mecca wa Jeddah* for S£2. There's one more hotel in town if these are full. Good cheap food is available in the cafés opposite the market. There are well-stocked shops and excellent pharmacies.

EL OBEID

Try the *Government Rest House* or *John's Hotel*, which has reasonable prices. If camping at John's Hotel, they'll let you use the showers.

JEBEL MARRA

Nyala is the jumping-off point for a visit to Jebel Marra, at 3088 metres the highest mountain in Sudan. There are lots of rivers and orchards, an extinct volcano and good, hilly walking country. The trails are a maze of goat and sheep tracks, winding all over the gullies and gorges that dissect the countryside. It's difficult to find the right track and asking directions won't necessarily help. Also, the locals work on African time – 30 minutes could mean anything from one to five hours. Ask at the Dafur Hotel in Nyala about an English teacher who lives in the area and has drawn some excellent maps of the Jebel Marra region. He's willing to let you copy them.

To get there, take a bus from Nyala to Nyetiti. It takes 3½ hours and costs S£10. Then start walking towards the mountains. Trucks also run between Nyala and Nyertiti for S£7 and take about 5½ hours.

Halfway to Quaila, just past the first village, is an excellent waterfall and pool where you can camp and swim. From Quaila walk to the hot springs. Then, up to the crater of Jebel Marra, halfway round the rim and down again to the crater floor. From there, walk out through the canyon to Taratonga, where there is a weekly truck to Nyala. From Taratonga visit nearby villages; Sunni in the north, or Gandator and Kalu Kitting in the south-west are interesting. From Kalu Kitting you can get back to the tarmac at Nyama, where there is a camp for the German construction gang building the road. They often have transport going to Nyala. Some travellers have been allowed to use their swimming pool. In Quaila, the schoolteacher may find accommodation for you and point you in the right direction for the crater.

It's possible to go in the opposite direction, as the sketch map in the 'tourist office' in Nyala suggests. There is a truck that leaves Nyala once a week to Taratonga. It costs S£15 and takes 24 hours. Any combination of routes is possible. To give you an idea:

Take a truck from Nyala to Menawashi (S£4), which is little more than a truck stop – no resthouse but plenty of food vendors. You can sleep in the food vendors' huts.

From Menawashi it's a two-hour walk to Marshing over flat scrubland, where you should ask the local schoolteacher about accommodation (there's usually an empty hut). There's a café serving soup and bread (S£1) and tea (25 pt). There is a market on Wednesday and Sunday.

A five-hour walk from Marshing will bring you to Melemm, which is a beautiful, fairly large village with a resthouse next to the police station. The police are friendly and will probably supply you with firewood, water and other things. There is a market on Monday and Friday. From Melemm to Deribat it's an all-night truck ride (S£4 to S£5) through beautiful hills, some of which are so steep it may be necessary to winch the truck up! There's no resthouse in Deribat but there are several teahouses, a café and a Monday market.

A two-hour walk from Deribat will take you to Jawa, where you should stay in the huge new hospital. It's empty, but there is one bed. Market day is Thursday. About 1½ hours away is Sunni, one of Jebel Marra's most scenic settlements. A large old resthouse with four beds costs S£1.50 each. There's no souk, but a small shop sells rice, nuts, dates, cigarettes and the occasional chicken. Don't forget to visit the 35-metre-high waterfall behind the power station.

From Sunni it's a five-hour walk/scramble to Lugi, with beautiful views. But it gets cold and there are only a few huts in the fields along the way. There's a small store at Lugi that sells basic supplies.

Next you walk to Taratonga (2¼ hours) through a landscape of conifers and heather, somewhat similar to the Scottish lowlands. Taratonga is very picturesque and set on wooded, grassy slopes. There's a market on Saturday and a shop that sells basic supplies. The resthouse is in bad repair, and it's better to look for an empty hut in the wet season. The schoolhouse is another possibility (the teacher speaks English and can put you in touch with guides to the crater).

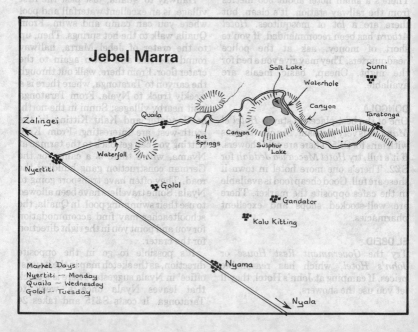

Jebel Marra

Zalingei ← Nyertiti Waterfall Quaila Hot Springs Golol Gandator Kalu Kitting Nyama Nyala → Salt Lake Waterhole Canyon Sulphur Lake Canyon Sunni Taratonga

Market Days:
Nyertiti — Monday
Quaila — Wednesday
Golol — Tuesday

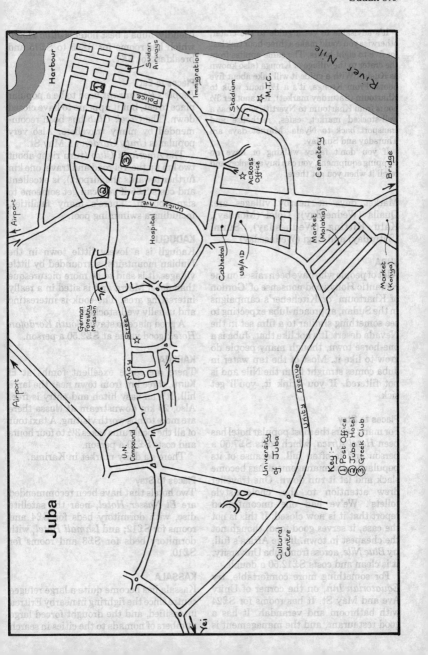

Juba

Key:-
1 Post Office
2 Juba Hotel
3 Greek Club

It's advisable to get a guide to the crater, otherwise you could make a three-hour trek last for five to eight hours. The same applies from the crater to the village of Kronga (also known as Kuela). With a guide it will take about five hours. From Kronga, it's a 1½ hour walk to Khartoum (Saturday market). It's another 3½ hours from Khartoum to Nyertiti, which has a well-stocked market, cafés, resthouse and transport back to Nyala. Market days are Thursday and Sunday.

If you don't fancy walking or have no camping equipment, you can buy a donkey and resell it when you get there.

Market days at nearby villages are: Quaila (Wednesday); Golol (Monday), Kalu Kitting (Wednesday), Sunni (Saturday) and Lugi (Wednesday).

JUBA

A lot of people who have been raised on the romantic Hollywood nonsense of 'Gordon of Khartoum' or Kitchener's campaigns in the Sudan, approach Juba expecting to see something similar to a film set in the Nevada desert. It's not like that. Juba is a one-horse town, though many people do grow to like it. Most of the tap water in Juba comes straight from the Nile and is not filtered. If you drink it, you'll get sick.

Places to Stay

For many years the most popular hotel has been *Hotel Africa*, which costs S£7.50 a person and is often full. Because of its popularity, the management has become slack and let it run down. One traveller drew attention to the 'cholera-style toilets'. We've had one uncomfirmed report that it is now closed. If this is not the case, it serves good food, though not the cheapest in town. If the Africa's full, try *Blue Nile*, across from Juba University. It is clean and costs S£12.50 a double.

For something more comfortable, try *Equatorian Inn*, on the corner of Unity Ave and May St. It has rooms for S£24 with bathroom and verandah. It has a good restaurant, and the management is friendly. Juba's best hotel is *Juba Hotel*, which has rooms for S£45 to S£75 and breakfast for S£7.

Places to Eat

People's Restaurant used to be a popular place to eat, but it appears to have closed down. The *Greek Club* has been recommended by many travellers. Also very popular is *Unity Garden* on May St.

The *American Club* (turn right about two km up the Yei road and travel one km further towards the airport), is excellent and costs S£5 if you can get someone to sign you in. There's many facilities, including a swimming pool.

KADUGLI

Kadugli is a lovely little town in the Nubian mountains, surrounded by little villages. It is said to be more picturesque than Jebel Marra and is sited in a really interesting area. The souk is interesting and usually well-stocked.

A good place to stay is *South Kordofan Hotel*: good value at S£2.50 a person.

KARIMA

There are some excellent tombs at **El Kurru**, three km from town near the large hill. It's an easy hitch and entry is free. Also, 20 km downstream at **Nussa** there are more tombs worth visiting. A taxi tour of all the local ruins takes 3½ to four hours and costs S£10 a person.

There's a daily market in Karima.

Places to Stay

Two hotels that have been recommended are *El Nasser Hotel*, near the satellite disc, with dormitory beds for S£4 and rooms for S£12; and *Ishmali Hotel*, with dormitory beds for S£3 and rooms for S£10.

KASSALA

Kassala has become quite a large refugee centre since the fighting in nearby Eritrea intensified, and the drought forced large numbers of nomads to the cities in search

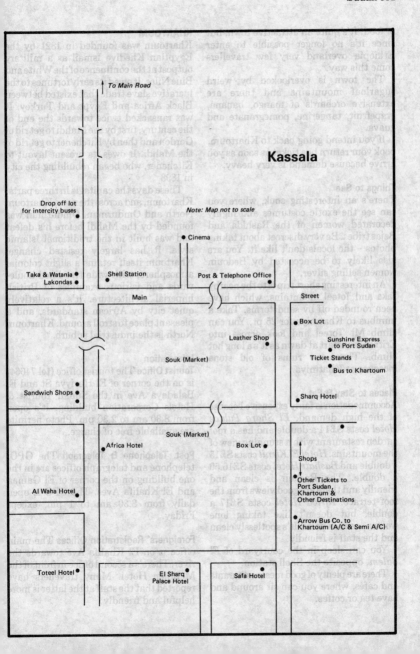

To Main Road

Kassala

Note: Map not to scale

Drop off lot for intercity buses

Cinema

Taka & Watania
Lakondas

Shell Station

Post & Telephone Office

Main   Street

Box Lot

Leather Shop

Sunshine Express to Port Sudan

Souk (Market)

Ticket Stands

Bus to Khartoum

Sandwich Shops

Sharq Hotel

Souk (Market)

Africa Hotel   Box Lot

Al Waha Hotel

Shops

Other Tickets to Port Sudan, Khartoum & Other Destinations

Arrow Bus Co. to Khartoum (A/C & Semi A/C)

Toteel Hotel

El Sharq Palace Hotel

Safa Hotel

of food. It's quite an attractive town, but since it's no longer possible to enter Ethiopia overland very few travellers come this way.

The town is overlooked by weird sugarloaf mountains and there are extensive orchards of mango, banana, grapefruit, tangerine, pomegranate and guava.

If you intend going back to Khartoum, book your return bus ticket as soon as you arrive because demand is very heavy.

Things to See
There's an interesting **souk**, where you can see the exotic costumes and highly decorated women of the Rashida and Bejas tribes. Be very discreet about taking photos – the locals don't like it. You are also likely to be accosted by Bedouin women selling silver.

An interesting short trip is to the nearby **Taka** and **Toteel** mountains, which have been rounded off by sandstorms. Take a minibus to Khatmiya for 25 pt. You can climb Mt Toteel and look across into Eritrea, but start at dawn as it's a long hot climb. There are ruins of **old stone mosques** at Khatmiya.

Places to Stay & Eat
Accommodation is fairly expensive because of the high demand. *El Sharq Palace Hotel* costs S£14 a double and has a roof garden restaurant with a stunning view of the mountains. *Hotel El Kirnil* costs S£15 a double and *Bashair Hotel* costs S£16.50 a double. The Bashair is clean and friendly and there are good views from the roof terrace. *Africa Hotel* costs S£17 a double, but doesn't like taking lone women, or even pairs. It's spotlessly clean and the staff is friendly.

You can sleep in the courtyard of *El Salem*, opposite the Shell station.

There are plenty of good meat restaurants and cafés, where you can sit around and have tea or coffee.

KHARTOUM
Khartoum was founded in 1821 by the Egyptian Khedive Ismail as a military outpost at the confluence of the White and Blue Niles. It owed its early fortunes to the lucrative slave trade that existed between Black Africa and Egypt and Turkey. It was ransacked twice towards the end of the century, first by the Mahdi to get rid of Gordon and then by Kitchener to get rid of the Mahdi. It owes its present layout to Kitchener, who began rebuilding the city in 1898.

These days the capital is in three parts: Khartoum, and across the river, Khartoum North and Omdurman. Omdurman was founded by the Mahdi before his defeat and was built in the traditional Islamic style. It has largely resisted change. Khartoum itself retains a slight colonial atmosphere, with wide tree-lined boulevards and various examples of British imperial architecture. It's a relatively quiet city by African standards, and a pleasant place to stroll around. Khartoum North is the industrial suburb.

Information
Tourist Office The tourist office (tel 74664) is on the corner of El Huriyya St and El Baladaya Ave in the Sudan Tourist & Hotels Corporation building. It's open from 8.30 am to 2.30 pm. Photo permits are available free of charge.

Post, Telephone & Telegraph The GPO, telephone and telegraph offices are in the one building on the corner of El Gamaa and El Khalifa Aves. The GPO is open daily from 8.30 am to 1 pm, except Friday.

Foreigners' Registration Offices The main office is on El Khalifa Ave towards the river. There's a second office in front of the Meridien Hotel. Many travellers have reported that the staff at the latter is more helpful and friendly.

American Express This is opposite British Airways on a small side street just off El Gamhuriyya Ave, between El Taiyar Morad Ave and El Khalifa Ave. It's upstairs, above KLM, and is open daily from 8.30 am to 1.30 pm and 5.30 to 7.30 pm, except Friday and Sunday evening. Financial services are not available here.

Air The airport is 10 to 15 minutes from central Khartoum. A taxi will cost S£15. There are buses for 25 pt from the main road, but they're often full as they come in from outlying suburbs. The addresses of some airlines are:

EgyptAir
  Abouela New Building, El Qasr Ave (tel 70259)
Ethiopian Airlines
  El Gamhuriyya Ave (tel 77180)
Kenya Airways
  El Qasr Ave (tel 73429)
Sudan Airways
  El Gamhuriyya Ave (only internal flights and Egypt) and El Barlaman Ave (international flights, except Egypt)

Bus & Truck Parks There are three departure points for all transport. Behind the central post office in Omdurman (northern bound to such places as Atbara, Karima and Dongola), Souk Shabi in south Khartoum (east, north-east and south bound) and Omdurman Souk (west bound).

Things to See
The **souk** in **Omdurman** is the largest in Sudan. It has an amazing variety of wares, though it doesn't compare with Cairo's Khan el Khanili. A quick look (which is all you'll get because foreigners are not allowed inside) at the **Madhi's Tomb** in Omdurman is worth the effort, though the original was destroyed by Kitchener and only rebuilt in 1947. More rewarding is **Khalifa's House**, opposite. It was built in 1887 for the Madhi's successor and is now a museum, featuring exhibits from the

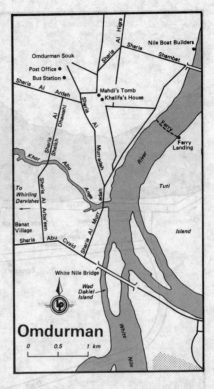

Omdurman

0   0.5   1 km

late 19th century. It's open Tuesday to Sunday from 8.30 am to 8.30 pm and on Friday from 8.30 am to 12 noon and 3.30 to 8.30 pm. Entry costs 22 pt.

The most spectacular sight in Omdurman, however, is the **whirling dervishes** who stir up the dust in no uncertain fashion every Friday afternoon in front of the Hamed al Niel Mosque. The dervishes are members of the Sufis, a mystical Islamic sect. Don't miss them. Take a green bus from in front of the Arak Hotel and get off at the Al Murradah Stadium on El Arbein Ave. Walk straight past the stadium and through the village to a field. It's then a 10-minute walk to the mosque on the other side. Get there by 4 pm at the latest. If you are lucky, there may be

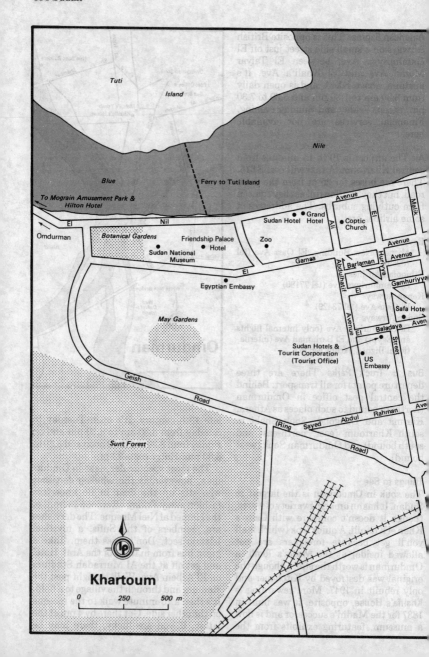

Khartoum

0   250   500 m

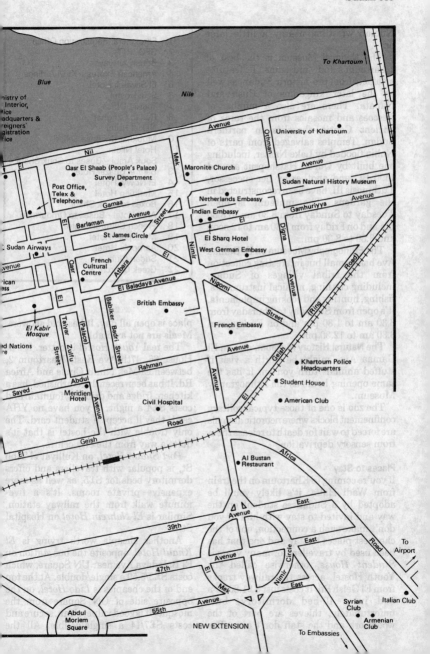

Blue

Nile

To Khartoum

Ministry of
Interior,
ice
headquarters &
reigners'
gistration
ice

Nil

El

Qasr El Shaab (People's Palace)

Survey Department

Post Office,
Telex &
Telephone

Mek

Othman

Avenue

University of Khartoum

Avenue

Maronite Church

Avenue

Sudan Natural History Museum

Gamaa

Avenue

Netherlands Embassy

Indian Embassy

Gamhuriyya

Avenue

m

Barlaman

Street

El

Digna

Avenue

El Sharq Hotel

Sudan Airways

St James Circle

Atbara

El

Nimir

West German Embassy

Nigomi

Street

Road (Ring

venue

Qasr

French
Cultural
Centre

El Baladaya Avenue

rican
ss

El

Babiker Badri Street

Talyar (Palace)

British Embassy

French Embassy

Avenue

El Kabir
Mosque

d Nations

Zulfu

Street

Rahman

Geish

Khartoum Police
Headquarters

Student House

American Club

Sayed

Abdul

Meridien
Hotel

Avenue

Civil Hospital

El

Road

Geish

Africa

Al Bustan
Restaurant

East

Avenue

East

39th

Avenue

Nimir Circle

To
Airport

47th

Avenue

m

Road

East

Abdul
Moriem
Square

Mek

Avenue

NEW EXTENSION

Syrian
Club

Italian Club

Armenian
Club

To Embassies

Nubian wrestling nearby a little later on.

The **National Museum** is the best of Khartoum's four museums. It features artefacts from pre-historic Sudan, as well as the later kingdoms of Cush and Napata. There are also a number of frescoes and mosaics from the ruins of ancient Coptic churches in northern Sudan. Temples salvaged from parts of Nubia flooded by Lake Nasser, including one built by Queen Hatshepsut around 1490 BC and another by her successor, Tuthmosis III, have been reconstructed in the gardens. The museum is open Tuesday to Sunday from 8.30 am to 8.30 pm and on Friday from 8.30 am to 12 noon and 3.30 to 8.30 pm.

The **Ethnography Museum** on El Gamaa Ave has a small but interesting collection from the tribal villages of Sudan, including clothing, musical instruments, fishing, hunting and cooking implements. It's open from Saturday to Thursday from 8.30 am to 1.30 pm and on Friday from 8.30 am to 12.30 pm.

The **Natural History Museum**, also on El Gamaa Ave, might be worth a visit if stuffed animals turn you on. It has the same opening hours as the Ethnography Museum.

The **zoo** is one of those typical solitary confinement blocks where neurotic animals are forced to wait for death to release them from sensory deprivation.

Places to Stay

If you're coming to Khartoum on the train from Wadi Halfa, it's likely you'll be adopted by a Sudanese student on the way and invited to stay with him. If you don't make such a connection, one of the cheapest places to stay and one that has been used by travellers for many years is *Student House*, otherwise called the Youth Hostel, across the railway tracks from El Geish Rd. It costs just S£1.80 for a bed in a 10-bed dormitory, but, unfortunately, thieves are part of the woodwork and the staff don't care. The

1	Foreigners' Registration Office
2	GPO (PTT)
3	British Airways
4	American Express/KLM Airlines
5	El Sawahli Hotel
6	Safa Hostel
7	Tourist Office
8	Bus to Sanghat
9	Nakiel Hotel
10	Mubkhar (Incense Seller)
11	Hotel Nilein
12	Souk Arabi – Buses to Souk Shabi
13	Bahr el Ghazal Hotel
14	El Nowyi Hotel
15	Meridien Hotel
16	Boxes to Souk Shabi
17	Arak Hotel - Buses to Omdurman
18	French Cultural Centre
19	Metropole Hotel
20	Acropole Hotel
21	Sudan Club
22	Greek Church

place is open all day. It has cold showers. Meals are not available.

The real *Youth Hostel* is better. It's at House 66, 47th Ave East, Khartoum 2, between El Mek Nimir Circle and Africa Rd. It has been recently refurbished, has a kitchen, fridge and drinking fountain and costs S£4 a night. If you have no YHA card, they'll accept a student card. The only trouble with the hostel is that it's quite a way from the city centre.

Port Sudan Hotel, on Kulliyat el Tibb St, is popular with travellers and offers dormitory beds for S£5, as well as more expensive private rooms. It's a five-minute walk from the railway station. Similar is *El Nahrein Hotel* on Hospital St.

Another cheapie worth trying is *El Khalil Hotel*, opposite the bus station on El Baladaya Ave near UN Square, which costs S£3/5.50 a single/double. At the top end of the cheapies is *Lido Hotel*, on the opposite side of UN Square from the mosque. It is good value, clean, secure and costs S£7/14 a single/double. All the

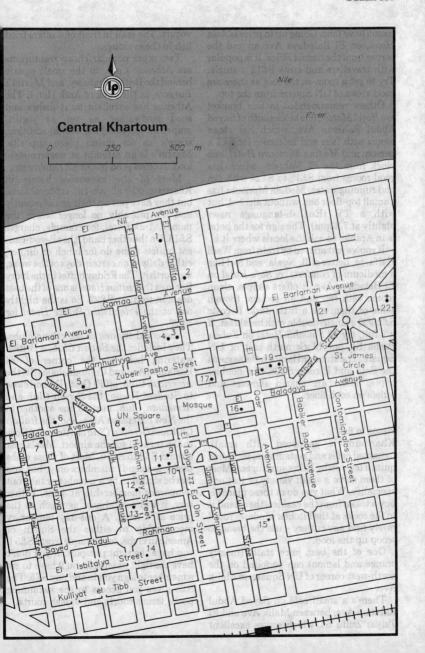

Central Khartoum

rooms have fans. Going up in price is *Asia Hotel*, on El Baladaya Ave around the corner from the tourist office. It is popular with travellers and costs S£12 a single. Try to get a room on the roof as there are good views of UN Square from the top.

Others recommended in this bracket are *Hotel Marwi*, one block south of Sayed Abdul Rahman Ave, which has clean rooms with fans and balconies for S£7 a person; and *Medina Monoura Hotel*, one block from the El Nahrein, which has good rooms from S£12 to S£24 with fan and running water. Medina Monoura has a small top-floor bar, without alcohol, but with a TV (English-language news nightly at 7.30pm). The sign for the hotel is in Arabic, so ask the locals where it is.

If you've just arrived by train from Wadi Halfa, or, better still, Nyala, and feel like a modicum of comfort, try *Safa Hotel* on El Baladaya Ave. It offers simple, clean rooms with fan and air-coolers, though some of them are a little dark. It costs S£20/30 a single/double with breakfast. If it's full, try *El Sawahli Hotel* on Zubeir Pasha St, one block north-east of UN Square. The standard is much the same as the Safa and it costs S£28/42 a double/triple. There are shared showers and toilets on each floor.

Places to Eat

Khartoum is peppered with small, unnamed cafés and restaurants, including quite a few run by Eritrean refugees. Most of them serve a small variety or just one speciality. What you do at these places is buy a token from the cashier, then hand it to the cooks at the kitchen window. You'll rarely find any cutlery – use the bread to scoop up the food.

One of the best juice stalls (mostly orange and lemon) can be found on the north-west corner of UN Square on Malik Ave.

There's a small café on Sayed Abdul Rahman Ave, between Malik Ave and El Taiyar Zulfu St, which serves excellent yogurt. The stall in front of it offers fried fish in the evenings.

Two other popular cheap restaurants are *Athenae Café*, in the small square behind the British Embassy, and *Maxim's Burgers*, at the back of Arak Hotel. The Athenae has excellent meat dishes and good sandwiches, as well as yogurt, grapefruit juice and the like. In addition, there's an ice cream place opposite. Maxim's is an attempt at western-style food. It offers good but small hamburgers.

Most of the expensive hotels in Khartoum offer all-you-can-eat breakfasts, but they have put up their prices recently and it's probably no longer worth the money. *Arak Hotel*, for example, charges S£18. On the other hand, the all-you-can-eat buffets some do for lunch or dinner, either daily or on certain days of the week, are worth it. The Friday buffet in the Ivory Room at the *Hilton Hotel* is one of the best deals in town at S£27. So is the nightly one at the *Friendship Palace Hotel* for S£28.

You could try one of the ethnic clubs. They include: the *Sudan Club*, a British watering hole on the corner of El Barlaman Ave and Contomichalos St; the *American Club*, off El Geish Rd and close to Student House; the *Syrian Club* and *Armenian Club*, next to one another in the New Extension Area; and, the *Italian Club* and *German Club* on Africa Rd close to the turn-off for the airport. Meals cost around S£8 to S£10. Most of these clubs prefer to keep it members only, but you can be signed in by a member or take out temporary membership at some. Either way, it will cost almost as much as the price of a meal. A one-day temporary membership to either the Sudan or American clubs, for example, costs S£5 if you have the right passport. If you don't have the right passport, you'll have to get a member to sign you in and pay S£5. The S£5 gives you access to the swimming pools, tennis courts and squash courts.

Entertainment

Most of the clubs have film nights, lectures and other cultural events. The *British Council* screens free films on Tuesday or Saturday evenings; at *Acropole Hotel* on Friday and Sunday; and *Arak Hotel* on Tuesday. There's also the *Blue Nile Cinema*, beyond the Ministry of Education, which shows English-language movies.

The English teachers in Khartoum frequent Gasser El Niel Hotel and are a friendly well-informed group.

Getting Around

To Omdurman you can get buses from El Taiyar Zulfu St in front of the Arak Hotel, plus *boxes* (small pick-up trucks running on fixed routes) from the corner of El Gamhuriyya Ave and El Huriyya St. Buses to Souk Shabi leave from the dirt lot near Hotel Nilein, and minibuses depart from the dirt lot opposite the mosque on El Taiyar Zulfu St. *Boxes* to the New Extension and airport go from El Jami Ave.

KOSTI

Take a boat to **Abba Island** for 25 pt. The villagers are friendly and unspoiled. You'll probably be invited in for a tea.

Places to Stay

You can camp free at the police station near the Telecom tower, but be aware that there are five or six police stations in Kosti. Otherwise, try *Kosti Hotel*, which costs S£6 a double, or *Lokanda El Medina*, which is clean and popular with the locals.

NYALA

Nyala is a fascinating, lively town with a good souk and restaurants. It is full of refugees displaced by the drought and war with Chad.

Transport to Jebel Marra leaves from the Suq Al Gemena, about 1½ km from the main souk past the police station. For hikers there are many trucks leaving to various towns in the mountains from where you can start walking. Guides are available in the villages. They're cheaper if shared.

Places to Stay

One place is *Dafur Hotel* – good value at S£2 a person. You can sleep on the roof. They are a bit cool towards foreigners, so it helps if you speak a little Arabic. They will store excess baggage if you want to go trekking. Another good place to stay is the *Government Rest House*. It is very clean and costs S£10 a person. *Laconda Hotel* is reputed to be good, but the staff tend to tell foreigners it is full.

Places to Eat

Nyala has two good eating places: *Camp David*, near the Dafur Hotel; and the 'hole in the wall' near the mosque in the centre of town. Food is expensive but plentiful.

PORT SUDAN

Port Sudan isn't particularly interesting. Avoid coming to Port Sudan in the pilgrimage season (the last boats leave in November) as accommodation can be very tight. The tourist office is friendly and helpful. Buses for Suakin depart from Diem Suakin and cost S£2.20. Hitching, however, is fairly easy along the tarmac road.

Places to Stay & Eat

Most hotels are fairly expensive. At *Pension Khartoum* you can sleep outdoors for S£2.50. For a private room, try *Olympia Park Hotel* near the post office. It's popular with travellers at S£13 a person. If it's full, try *Hotel Sinkat* or *Hotel Africa*. The *Youth Hostel* is a 10-minute bus ride outside town at Salabona. It has dormitory beds for S£1.50. You must hold a YHA card. Catch a red and yellow bus to Ab Hashish-Salabona. It will cost you 10 pt. The hostel is clearly signposted. Salabona has an area of excellent food stalls, selling fried fish,

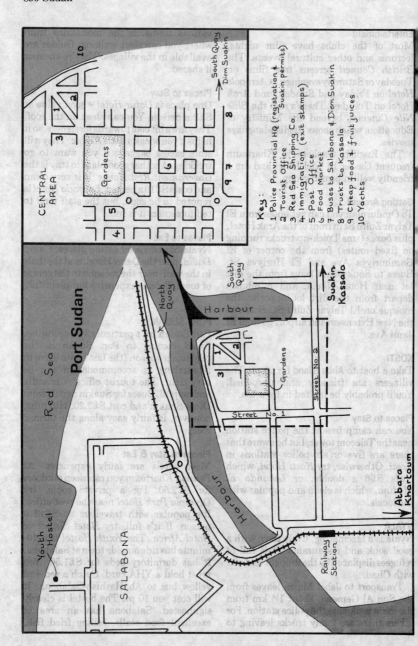

Key:
1 Police Provincial HQ (registration +
  Suakin permits)
2 Tourist Office
3 Red Sea Shipping Co.
4 Immigration (exit stamps)
5 Post Office
6 Food Market
7 Buses to Salabona ≠ Diem Suakin
8 Trucks to Kassala
9 Cheap food + fruit juices
10 Yachts

salads, foul and banana fritters. Yogurt is widely available.

In Port Sudan itself there's a good restaurant at *Port Sudan Palace Hotel*, and the café next door is a meeting place for travellers. The hotel has free English-language video movies. Details are posted in the foyer.

Another place to eat and visit that has always been highly recommended is the *Red Sea Club*, but it seems club members are no longer keen on the idea of temporary memberships or signing in unknown guests. Check it out for yourself. The members are largely British. Temporary membership will cost you S£5.

SENNAR

Hotel Tourism, behind the market and opposite the cinema, is very clean but by no means the cheapest place to stay.

SUAKIN

Before the construction of Port Sudan, Suakin was Sudan's only port. It was abandoned by the British in the 1930s and is now full of decaying coral houses. It's a fascinating place to wander through and, because very few people visit, you'll probably have the place to yourself. Before you set out you must get a special permit from the Red Sea Province headquarters in Port Sudan, regardless of whether you have already done this in Khartoum. You'll be sent back to Port Sudan if you don't have it.

The **mainland village** opposite Suakin is worth visiting. Swimming and diving at Suakin is excellent. Ask around in the village for a mask. Beware of conger eels in the sea wall. They may attack if cornered. Also be careful when walking around the ruins. There was one report of two women being pursued through the ruins by men out to rob (or sell) them, and of the police chief taking rather *too close* an interest in their welfare. Go with company, especially if you're female.

There is no accommodation in Suakin, but ask at the police station if you can camp there. They are friendly and may insist that you sleep (for free) on the floor of their office.

WADI HALFA

It is very difficult to get a bed in Wadi Halfa as there are only two small hotels and often hundreds of people waiting for the boats and train. *Bohaera Hotel* is 700 metres from the station and costs S£7.50 a night. *Hotel Nile* is 500 metres from the station and costs S£5 a night. Both are clean and have their own restaurants, which sell basic meals. They may let you sleep in the yard and use the showers. Many Sudanese sleep out under the stars and it seems to be OK for travellers to do so too, but don't leave valuables unattended. Taxis to the port cost S£5. Before leaving, however, you must get an exit stamp in Wadi Halfa.

Trucks going south leave from one of the hotels at least twice a week.

National Parks

The following is an account of one traveller's experience in **Dinder National Park**.

Surely one of the least accessible places in Sudan, despite tourist office posters of it's giraffes, lions, etc. This was the pattern of an attempt to reach it that I made with a Finnish girl who had already been defeated on a first effort to get there.

Day One Invited to travel with people from Khartoum Zoo who were going there to take the warden's wages – two weeks overdue already. All day spent waiting for action in the zoo. Amongst other problems, the driver got a piece of metal wedged in his eye! Finally set off, only to break down on the outskirts of town and have to come back again.

Day Two All day spent waiting for action at the zoo. Mainly because a mechanic couldn't be found to fix the truck.

Day Three Abandoned truck. Set off with the wages by bus to Singa where we ferried across the Blue Nile. Collected on the other side by a park pick-up which took us to Park HQ in Dinder – 100 miles from the park! Too late to go any further.

Day Four Friday, so no-one going anywhere in an Islamic state. Spent our time sweltering round Dinder souk.

Day Five All day sweltering round Dinder while our companions attended a meeting in Sennar. Evening departure along horrendously bumpy, dusty road, but glad to be on our way at last. Arrived at the park to a warm reception. Accommodated in a straw hut equipped with mosquito net and electric light. Sudan Airways plane crashed in the field outside the gate.

Day Six to Day Eight In park, a marvellous wilderness of borassus palms with every imaginable type of bird and plentiful waterbuck, reedbuck, baboons, etc. Interesting to see the life of the wardens in such a remote spot. Often their time is taken up with driving out marauding sheep. Ethiopians camping by a river. One lone female occupant of camp never seen to leave her hut.

Day Nine My vegetarian friend running low on food. Lift available, no certainty when another would appear. Decided to leave camp and set off in the relative cool of evening. Some wardens being relocated, so back of truck loaded with bed frames, etc. Also a dozen sheep, some standing on top of each other. We perched on top and ducked to avoid low branches. All went well, until a puncture. Unloaded the truck to find the spare tyre, only to find two dead sheep whose bodies were removed. Tool broke, so unable to remove old wheel. Escort vehicle so far ahead they didn't realise we were in trouble. Got down bedrolls, lay down and prepared to wait.

Day 10 Finally we were missed and help arrived to replace the wheel. Rolled into Dinder freezing (temperatures drop sharply at night here) and determined to be back in Khartoum eating pizza the next evening. So up early to take a bus to Singa and a bus back to Khartoum.

For me the Dinder episode encapsulated Sudan. the incredible heat, the food shortages, the appalling transport, the friendliness of the people, the interminable waiting. Hard to get to certainly, but worth it in the end!

SLOW TRAIN TO WAU

And here's that amusing story about rail transport, which many travellers enjoyed in the last edition:

The Wau (pronounced wow) Express covers the 480 km of track between Babanusa and Wau in a little over three days. 'When', the reader may ask, 'will I ever have occasion to take the Wau Express?' The answer is probably never, unless you are prone to seasickness, detest mosquitoes and are in a 'hurry' to get from Khartoum to Juba overland on the way to Nairobi. In that case the two-to-three-week riverboat journey up the Nile to Juba is out and the Wau Express is for you.

Actually, the train trip is only a small part of the journey to Juba. Before it you have to get from Khartoum to Babanusa. This is accomplished by taking a fairly comfortable and punctual train from Khartoum via Kosti. At Babanusa you change trains and board the Wau Express – if it is there and running, of course.

Heather and I were lucky; the train was standing in the station ready to go. It looked as if it were built about the same time as the railway, the early 1900s, and consisted of a steam locomotive and about 25 decrepit carriages. We were told it would leave in an hour's time at 9 pm. Feeling extravagant, we decided to splurge on a couple of 2nd-class tickets (there was no 1st class that day). This entitled us to a comfortable, reserved seat in a six-seat compartment. The compartment was empty when we boarded and, expecting the train to leave soon, we bedded down for the night hoping that no one else would enter. No one else did, but since the train was still sitting in the station the next morning, this was understandable. Around 7 am, eight Sudanese, who also had the wisdom to travel 2nd class, crowded into our compartment and the train chugged out of the station.

Although initially annoyed about the over-booking of the compartment, we were pleased with our choice when we saw the conditions in the 3rd and 4th classes. Third class consisted of a carriage filled with wooden benches. The benches were jammed and every square cm of floor space was covered with squatting people and their baggage. The luggage racks were filled with children. Fourth class, a cattle car, was beyond description.

The corridors of the 2nd-class carriages were crammed with people, making passage impossible. We were therefore forced to use the window to enter and exit our compartment. This would have made it difficult to get to the dining car when the train was moving but, as someone had forgotten to attach the dining car, this was of no great consequence. On the roof of the train there must have been about a thousand people. They were the lucky ones as far as space was concerned, but that must have been outweighed by the intense heat of the day and the cold of the night. 'Why are there so many people?' I asked my fellow passengers. I was told that the twice-weekly Wau Express was making its first trip in three weeks.

So the journey began. The train travelled very slowly to start with. Later we came to the bracing realisation that it was travelling at top speed: 12 km per hour. Every 25 km or so the train would stop at a station for an hour or two. This was so the engine could be watered and rested. Each time, many of the passengers would disembark. Fires were built, pots produced and food cooked. Children and clothes were washed and five times a day Mecca was faced in prayer. A quick blast of the whistle and the train was off again with hundreds of people scrambling to get back on.

We actually welcomed these delays because they gave us the opportunity to stretch, cool down and go out for food and water. Water was usually available, but food was limited to boiled eggs, bananas and raw beans. These were sold by scores of vendors who would appear from nowhere at even the most remote stations.

Halfway to Wau, in the middle of an uninhabited, roadless desert, the train suddenly stopped yet again, this time for no noticeable reason. Mechanical failure, we were told soothingly. After a few hours we began to get a little uneasy. Was the engine beyond repair? If so, would we have to complete our journey on foot? Happily the answer to both questions was no. Eight hours later the problem was apparently solved and we were again on our way. During the last hundred or so km a number of extra stops were made. These were due to the antics of the playful Dinka tribe, who enjoy placing large boulders on the track.

Finally, over three long days, thoroughly sick of our monotonous diet and crowded sitting and sleeping arrangements, we wheezed into Wau station. Heather and I looked at each other, flushed with the special relief that accompanies great endeavours. 'Wau!' we said.

Swaziland

Swaziland is one of only three remaining African monarchies, and until King Sobhuza II died at the end of 1982 he was the world's longest reigning monarch. The country, like Lesotho, had its origins in the early 19th century when the Zulu nation was expanding. Swaziland's first king, Sobhuza I, was able to merge refugees fleeing from the Zulu with his own people, and build a powerful military nation that would withstand Zulu pressure. When he died in 1839, Swaziland was twice its present size. It was whittled down to today's boundaries by the Boers between 1840 and 1880. Finally, after a protracted period of rivalry between the Boers and the British for control over what remained of the country, it became a British protectorate and the king's powers were restricted to internal civil matters.

Sovereignty, however, wasn't all it lost. In the land rush of the 1880s, virtually all the natural resources were placed in the hands of concession hunters. In 1907, all but 38% of the land was expropriated from the Swazi peasantry and distributed among concessionaries and the monarchy in about equal amounts. But by 1930, the majority of Swazi Crown land had been sold off to white settlers.

British interest in the colony was minimal right up to independence. The development of cash cropping on small holdings by the peasants was actively discouraged by white farmers and mining concerns, who preferred to have a pool of manual labour. The arrangement suited the monarchy in many ways because the growth of a system of small holdings would have threatened the king's traditional rights over the land and his subjects. The king was entitled to demand an annual tribute in the form of labour or crops, and give or reclaim land as he pleased. After independence, however, Sobhuza pursued a policy of buying back concessionary land and converting it to Swazi Nation Land for the use of the nation as a whole.

There was a brief flirtation with a constitutional monarchy after independence. But in 1972, when the parties of urban workers and intellectuals collected sufficient votes to begin to erode the overwhelming dominance of the Imbokodvo (traditionalist party), the king suspended the constitution, dissolved all political parties and declared a state of emergency. This remained in force for many years. Sobhuza II subsequently banned trade union meetings.

Swaziland is now governed by a traditional tribal assembly, the Liqoqo. The Liqoqo meets in the Royal Cattle Kraal at Lombamba, outside Mbabane. The monarch and his ministers sit on the ground in traditional dress, facing the sacred hills across the valley. The audience, regardless of rank, sits in front of the king. Policy is debated and the king issues decrees.

Critics of this ancient form of government are answered with the claim that direct rule by the monarchy has resulted in Swaziland being one of Africa's most stable countries. While there is some truth in this, it is not the whole story. There have been a number of popular revolts. In 1975, striking railway workers marched on Lobamba only to be dispersed with tear gas. Some 400 teachers did the same thing in 1977, which resulted in the banning of the National Teachers' Association. Further demonstrations by school and

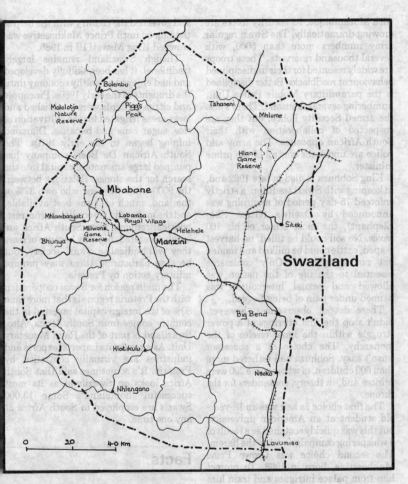

university students, with parental support, took place later that year. These were broken up by baton charges and tear gas, but in the rioting that followed, a lot of government property was badly damaged. There has also been discontent among professional and white-collar workers.

Certainly the post-independence government of Mozambique didn't think much of the Swazi political system. It condemned it as western-orientated and capitalist.

Relations between the two neighbours were tense in the late 1970s. They have since improved. Swaziland needs the cooperation of Mozambique in order to maintain some degree of economic independence from South Africa. There's also the consideration of the railway line from Mbabane to Maputo, which carries the bulk of Swazi exports to the outside world.

While Swaziland is cultivating friendship

with Mozambique, its security forces are growing dramatically. The Swazi regular army numbers more than 5000, with several thousand reservists. These troops are widely resented for their undisciplined behaviour at roadblocks. Better disciplined is the paramilitary Mobile Police Unit, numbering several thousand. There's also the armed Security Police, but they are suspected of collaboration with their South African opposites. The army and police are under the control of the prime minister.

King Sobhuza II died in late 1982 and, in keeping with Swazi tradition, a strictly enforced 75-day period of mourning was announced by Dzeliwe (Great She-Elephant), the most senior of his 100 wives. No soil could be tilled, no harvest reaped, cattle could be milked and tended but not slaughtered. Only commerce essential to the life of the nation was allowed and sexual intercourse was banned under pain of being flogged.

These devout observances, however, didn't stop the first stirrings of a power struggle within the inner circles of the monarchy. The choice of a successor wasn't easy. Sobhuza had fathered more than 600 children, of whom some 200 were princes and, in theory, contenders for the throne.

The first choice as heir was an 18-year-old student at an American university, but this was quickly scotched as a result of a whispering campaign within the harem. The second choice was Crown Prine Makhosetive, born in 1968. To protect him from palace intrigues and train him for the kingship, he was removed to a secret hideaway to be taught Swazi customs and traditions by royal counsellors, tribal elders, soothsayers and others appointed by the Great She-Elephant. He was also taught by selected western tutors.

In August 1983, Queen Mother Dzeliwe was ousted in favour of Ntombi, another of Sobhuza's wives and the mother of Prince Makhosetive. She acted as regent and governed the country with the help of the Liqoqo until Prince Makhosetive was crowned King Mswati III in 1986.

Though Swaziland remains largely traditional, it has been skilfully developed and had enjoyed a healthy economy until the droughts of the early 1980s. Pineapple and citrus orchards were established and large areas irrigated for the cultivation of rice, sugar cane and bananas. Diamond mining began in the early 1970s. The South African De Beers company has pumped large amounts of capital into the search for the stones. Relations between the 9000 white farmers, who own 37% of the land, much of it the best available, and the monarchy are cordial. In contrast, political refugees from South Africa are barely tolerated, not only because of fears they will radicalise Swazi society, but because harbouring them may prompt military action by Pretoria.

The main reason for Swazi cooperation with the Pretoria regime is that more than 80% of the foreign capital invested in the country comes from South Africa. Also, Swaziland is part of the Rand Monetary Unit. As a result, its imports, exports and industries are virtually controlled by Pretoria. It's sometimes said that South Africa looks on Swaziland as its most successful 'homeland'. Some 13,000 Swazis are employed in South Africa at any one time.

Facts

Surrounded on three sides by South Africa and on the other by Mozambique, Swaziland sits on the edge of the southern African escarpment. Beautiful rugged mountains in the west descend to low-lying plains in the east. Abundant rainfall in the mountains falls mainly in summer (October to March). Ninety per cent of the 700,000 people are Swazi, the other 10% are Zulu, Tonga, Shangaan and European.

VISAS

Visas are not required by nationals of Commonwealth countries, Belgium, Denmark, Finland, Iceland, Irish Republic, Israel, Italy, Luxemburg, Netherlands, Norway, Portugal, South Africa, Sweden and the USA. If you intend to stay longer than two months, you must apply for a temporary residence permit from the Chief Immigration Officer, Box 372, Mbabane. Where there are no Swazi embassies or consulates, visas can be obtained from British embassies (eg in Johannesburg).

There are Swazi embassies in Maputo (Mozambique) and Nairobi (Kenya).

Vaccination against cholera is no longer required for entry. Malaria, however, is still common, especially in low-lying areas.

MONEY

US$1 = E 2.15

The unit of currency is the lilangeni (plural emalangeni) = 100 cents. The lilangeni is on a par with the South African rand, which is also legal tender in Swaziland. Swazi currency, however, is hard to get rid of in South Africa. Banks there will discount it by 10% to convert it to rand. There are no restrictions on the import or export of emalangeni.

ACCOMMODATION

In rural areas, travellers on a tight budget could ask the principal of a school if they might sleep in a classroom. Swazis are very friendly and hospitable, and few would refuse. You would probably get a brick-built room and some sort of toilet and water supply, almost certainly clean.

Also, you may be able to find accommodation with Peace Corps volunteers, many of whom are teachers. While most PCVs are willing to help out, they exist on very little money. Please supply your own food and contribute to meals and other expenses, and don't overstay your welcome.

You can camp anywhere, but it's important to introduce yourself to people living nearby to reassure them that you're not a danger or there to steal their cattle. Be careful with water as there is a lot of cholera and bilharzia about.

Hotels are expensive. However, a number of smaller ones exist that don't cost too much, and are clean and comfortable.

There are some relatively inexpensive places to stay in the smaller towns. In Hlatikulu the *Assegai Inn* (tel 16) has full board (dinner and breakfast), a good bar and plenty of local colour. In Mankayane the *Inyatsi Inn* (tel 12) provides rooms with full board. The *Robin Inn* (tel 160) in Nhlangano has rooms with breakfast. The *Lavumisa Hotel* (tel 7) in Lavumisa has singles/doubles with bath and breakfast. In Siteki the *Stegi Hotel* (tel 26) has singles/doubles with full board, and a good bar. *Bamboo Inn*, next door, is very inexpensive. Finally, at Pigg's Peak the *Highlands Inn* (tel 12) has rooms with bath and breakfast.

FOOD

Traditional Swazi food is cornmeal porridge and stew. Swazis are great lovers of meat, meaning beef. The closest you get to real Swazi food is in one of the innumerable cafés where you should order either stew and porridge or curry and porridge. You might want to try 'bunny chow', a dish from the Indians of South Africa. It consists of half a loaf of bread with the inside torn out so that the crust forms a bowl, which is filled with stew.

There are many inexpensive Portuguese restaurants. For a splurge, try the chicken peri-peri, or even better, the famous Mozambique prawns. For an inexpensive lunch, ask for a prego. Fast-food addicts will be pleased to know there are Kentucky Fried Chicken outlets in both Mbabane and Manzini!

THINGS TO BUY

There is a wide variety of local crafts for sale in Swaziland. Tishweshwe Cottage Crafts, between Mbabane and Manzini (turn off at Mhlanya and go about one km till you get to a cottage on the right) and run by Jenny Thorne, has curios from all over Africa, mohair sweaters and pottery, as well as a good collection of books on southern Africa. The prices are high, but that is the case throughout Swaziland.

In Manzini check out Manzini Handicrafts on Ngwane (President) St, just past the Town Hall on the corner of Mhlakurane St. If you're here in September, the best crafts from all around the country are on show at the Trade Fair at the showgrounds. At Pigg's Peak, there are 10 or 12 small stands selling Swazi carved wooden bowls. On the road from Mbabane to the Oshoek border post 14 km away, there is a mohair rug factory and glass-blowing factory.

Finally, at Mantenga Falls, on the road from Mbabane to Manzini, in the Ezulwini Valley near the Mlilwane Game Reserve, there is a large handicraft outlet for pottery, mohair, cloth and some imported curios and jewellery.

LANGUAGE

The official languages are SiSwati and English. SiSwati is very similar to Zulu, and the two speakers can understand one another. Until the early 1970s, school children learned Zulu instead of SiSwati because there were no textbooks in SiSwati. All other subjects, however, are supposed to be taught in English.

Useful Words & Phrases

hello	*sawubona*
yes	*yebo*
How are you?	*unjani?*
I'm fine	*ngikhona*
I thank you	*siyabonga*
We thank you	*ngiyabonga*

Sawubona literally means 'I see you'. *Yebo* is often said as a casual greeting, and sometimes in response to a greeting.

It is the custom to greet everyone you meet. Often you will be asked *u ya phi?* (Where are you going?).

Getting There & Around

AIR

Royal Swazi Airways flies to Dar es Salaam, Durban, Gaborone, Harare, Johannesburg, Lusaka and Nairobi.

ROAD
Hitching

Hitching is very easy. The more remote the area, the more likely you are to get a lift. You have to be very determined about it though: Swazis jump out in front of a vehicle to get a lift. Most rides are free, though you may occasionally be asked to pay.

If you're hitching to Swaziland from South Africa, bear in mind that many weekenders from Johannesburg go there on the Friday and return on the Sunday. Hitching anywhere along the road to Benoni (just outside Johannesburg) on Fridays is a snack. It's a large, well-travelled motorway. On other days, the traffic can be pathetic and it will take you ages to get there.

If you're heading to Durban and other parts of Natal, try hitching from Helehele, about eight km from Manzini. Here, the road to south-east Swaziland and Natal forks from the one going to Maputo.

Bus

There are regular and punctual buses all over the country. On sealed roads, they're quite comfortable. On dirt roads, expect a bumpy and dusty journey, especially towards the end of the dry season. Most buses are modern, with fares averaging around 3½ cents a km. Mbabane to Manzini costs E 1.45. The daily bus from

Lavumisa to Manzini (on the route from Natal) costs E 4.60, departs at 7.30 am and takes 4½ hours. There are buses twice weekly in either direction between Mbabane and Maputo (Mozambique), via Namaacha. They depart Mbabane between 8 and 9 am on Monday and Sunday (check departure time the day before) and take all day. From the border town of Lomohasha, a two-km walk from the Mozambique border, there is a bus to Manzini at 1.30 pm for E 3.50. It arrives in Manzini at 5 pm.

South African railways (SAR) run buses between the republic and Swaziland. There is a bus every weekday from Mbabane to Johannesburg, departing at 9.30 am and arriving at 4.15 pm. The SAR office is on Coventry Crescent, Mbabane.

TRAIN

The railway line from Mbabane to Maputo is for freight only, but some travellers have got lifts by speaking to the driver or guard. The line is often sabotaged by the Mozambique National Resistance guerrillas.

TO/FROM SOUTH AFRICA

The border posts with South Africa are staffed on both sides. The smaller ones close at 4 pm; the larger ones, including Mahamba, Oshoek and Lavumisa, stay open till either 8 or 10 pm. The main crossing point is Oshoek (open from 6 am to 10 pm), which gets a bit crowded and slow on Friday evening (entering Swaziland) and Sunday afternoon (entering South Africa) because of the weekend traffic. Other border posts are quiet all the time. No customs duties are payable on anything you bring into the country. Fresh meat, fruit and vegetables are not allowed in. (One traveller turned up at the border with about R 400 worth of booze in his car, but customs' only concern was whether he had any oranges!)

Around the Country

MANZINI

This is Swaziland's second largest town. An absolute must to see is the **market** on Thursday and Friday mornings. Get there at dawn if possible as the rural people bring in their handicrafts to sell to retailers.

Places to Stay

The cheapest places to stay are: *Highway Motel* (tel 50614), about seven km east of Manzini and costing E 30/42 a single/double (restaurant, bar and nightclub); and *Uncle Charlie's Hotel* (tel 52297), opposite the showgrounds on the edge of town and costing E 25/35 a single/double with breakfast. It gets quite rowdy on a payday weekend.

A place worth trying if you intend to stay for a week or more is *Mrs Smith's* boarding house on Meintuust St, past the Mozambique restaurant, over the bridge and on the corner on the left. *Paradise Camp Site* is seven km from Manzini on the Mbabane road, near Matsapha and the university. For something up-market, try the colonial-style *George* for E 31 a night.

Places to Eat

For cheap, Portuguese-style food try *Mozambique*, on Meintuust St, or *Gil Vincente*.

MBABANE

Mbabane, the capital of Swaziland, is a small, pleasant city heavily influenced by South Africa. South Africans flock here in droves at the weekends to see films banned by their own censors, visit the brothels and gamble at the Holiday Inn's casino. The same kind of thing happens in Swaziland's second city, Manzini, but to a lesser extent. Because of this, hotel accommodation is geared to affluent weekenders and it's difficult to find a cheap place to stay.

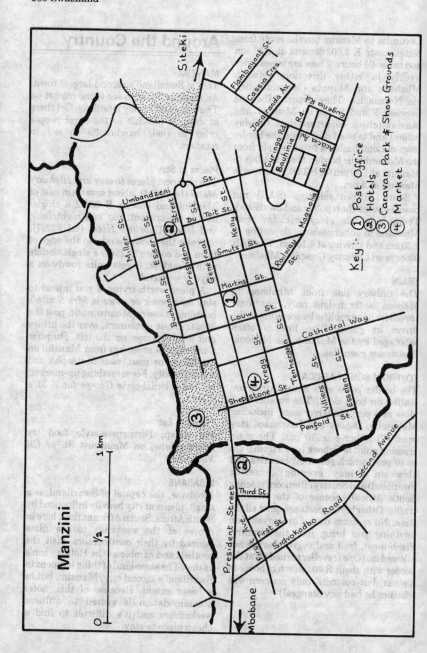

Manzini

Siteki

0   ½   1 km

Mbabane

Flamboyant St.

Cassia Cres.

Jacaranda Av.

Engebula Rd.

Suriaga Rd.

Acacia Av.

Bauhinia St.

Railway

Magnolia St.

Umbandzeni

Street

Miller St.

Esser St.

Du Toit St.

President St.

General

Buchanan

Smuts St.

Kelly St.

Martins St.

Louw St.

St.

Kregg St.

Tenhegen St.

Villiers St.

Esselen St.

Shepstone St.

Penfold St.

Cathedral Way

Second Avenue

Third St.

President Street

First Ave.

First St.

Sidvokadbo Road

Caravan Park

Show Grounds

Market

Key:-
1 Post Office
2 Hotels
3 Caravan Park & Show Grounds
4 Market

It's advisable not to wander alone or even in small groups at night because of the *sidlani* - gangs named after the question they ask: *utsi sidlani?* (What do you think we eat?).

Information

The tourist office, Swazi Place, is worth visiting. It offers a free booklet with plenty of good suggestions for walks, things to see and places to visit (hot springs, waterfalls).

There is a British Embassy on Allister Miller St, and a USA Embassy in the Central Bank Building.

Things to See

The Swazi **market**, although worth visiting, has high prices and is geared to the weekend trade. If you're looking for crafts, try the cheaper market at Manzini.

The **National Museum** at Lobamba has a good display of handicrafts, historical displays and explanations of Swazi culture. Close by, along the Lozitha road (turn left at Lobamba coming from Mbabane), you can see the light blue dome of the **Royal Palace** and the mountains behind it. Sobhuza is said to have been buried here along with a live goat and his faithful retainer, who was groomed from birth for his ritual death. The university is along this road.

Places to Stay

One of the best places to stay is the *Thokoza Church Centre* (tel 46681), Mhlanhla Rd, behind the police station and near Mater de la Rosa High School. (From Allister Miller St turn onto Walker St, go past Johnston St and Market St and over the bridge, turn left at the police station and then keep left along a dirt road up the hill for about 10 minutes. It's signposted.) It is nondenominational and run by Mennonites. A nice clean double room with hot showers costs E 14. There are no singles. Reasonably priced meals are available. The place is often used for conferences, in which case you may have

to stay in a dormitory (E 2). It's a good place to meet Peace Corps and VSO volunteers. The staff is very friendly.

Another cheap place to stay is the *Mbabane Youth Centre* (tel 42406), Msunduza. It costs E 5 a person. From the police station, turn right (south) and go about one km.

More up-market is *Jabula Inn*, Allister Miller St, next door to Wimpy's. It's the cheapest hotel in Mbabane and good value at E 18/28 a single/double with bath. There is a restaurant, and the bar is a popular place for white-collar workers. *Studio 21* disco rages until 2 am on weekdays and 5 am on weekends.

More expensive is *Mountain View Hotel* (tel 42773), about one km from the town centre on the Manzini road overlooking Ezulwini Valley. It costs E 51/64 a single/double with bath. There's a restaurant, swimming pool, bar and disco. *Tavern Hotel* (tel 42361) costs E 40/53 a single/double with breakfast. There is a charcoal grill, bar and nightclub. *Swazi Inn* (tel 42235), three km from Mbabane, costs E 64/86 a single/double with breakfast.

If you want to camp, *Highland View Caravan Park & Campsite*, near Mountain View Hotel, costs E 3.50 a site plus E 1.50 a person. The management is friendly and there is a small shop and bottle store opposite. *Timbali Caravan Camp* (tel 61156), 11 km from Mbabane (turn off at the Midway Spar before Holiday Inn), has *rondavels* for E 10 for the first person and E 3 for each additional person. There's a swimming pool and a shop.

Many South Africans stay in the Ezulwini Valley where the casinos are, about nine km from town. None of the hotels comes anywhere near being 'budget', and if you don't want to look out of place you had better have some well-pressed, snappy gear. The cheapest of the hotels are: *Mantenga Falls Hotel* (tel 61049), E 32/40 a single/double with breakfast; *Happy Valley Motel* (tel 61261); and *Diamond Valley Motel*

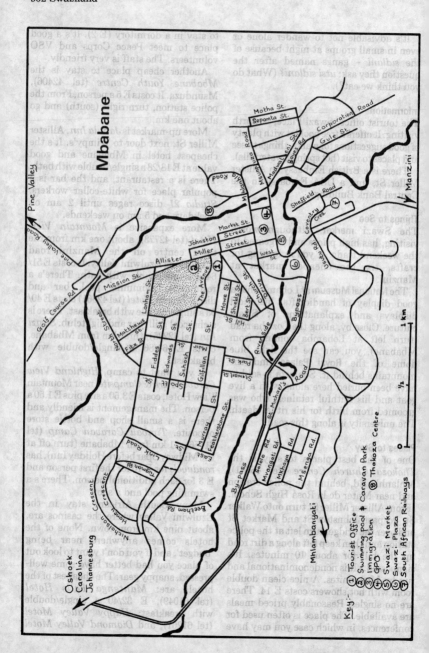

Mbabane

Key:
1. Tourist Office
2. Swimming pool
3. Immigration
4. GPO
5. Swazi Plaza
6. South African Railways

⊕ Caravan Park
⑦ Thokaza Centre
⑧ Swazi Plaza

(tel 61041/2), E 55 a double with bathroom and breakfast. The *Why Not Disco* at Happy Valley Motel is said to be the place to go if you want a taste of very decadent Swaziland.

At *Smokey Mountain Village* in the Ezulwini Valley, there are A-frame family cabins, a swimming pool and restaurant.

Camping and accommodation is available at the Mlilwane Game Sanctuary (tel 61037), in the Ezulwini Valley close to Mbabane. For details see the Camping & Trekking section.

Places to Eat

For cheap, Portuguese-style food try *Lourenco Marques* at Gilfilliam St and Allister Miller St. *Indingiliza Art Gallery & Restaurant* at 112 Johnston St has a pleasant tea room and restaurant, where you can get light meals. It also has good crafts on display. It is open Monday to Saturday from 8 am to 5 pm. For some Italian ice cream try *Flaminia Kiosk* in Swazi Place.

Camping & Trekking

Transport for most people in rural Swaziland is on foot, which has left trails all over the country. As long as you observe local customs and don't camp near houses or graveyards, and as long as you ask the chief's permission to camp, you are limited only by your imagination.

HLANE GAME RESERVE

Hlane Game Reserve on the road to Simunye has camping facilities and 'a friendly giraffe who likes to have his photo taken'. Other game includes rhino and buck.

KOMATI RIVER

There are Bushpeople paintings near Pigg's Peak (you'll need a guide), and spectacular gorges nearby with incredible

camp sites. Ask permission before camping.

MALOLOTJA NATURE RESERVE

Malolotja Nature Reserve is halfway between Mbabane and Pigg's Peak in beautiful high veld country. There is only a limited variety of game, and no big animals. It is used mostly by walkers. There are extensive trails for one to six-day hikes in the mountainous country, featuring forests (including a cycad forest), waterfalls, clean streams and rivers.

You can camp only at designated sites, of which there are ample.

A map of the park costs E 2.50. Entry into the reserve costs E 3 and camping E 2 a night. Hire tents cost E 3 a night. There are hot showers and clean toilets. The very pleasant wooden bungalows cost E 30 to E 40 a night. You will need to bring all your own food and a camp stove as fires are not permitted outside the base camp.

MBULUZI NATURE RESERVE

Mbuluzi Nature Reserve is in the north-east of the country, 10 km from Simunye. Take a bus from Manzini to Simunye for E 3.40 and another from Simunye to Mbuliyi for 50 cents. The reserve is in a beautiful setting and has rhino, zebra, waterbuck, impala, wildebeest, wart hog and hyena. The wardens are friendly and helpful. It costs E 2 to enter and E 1 to camp. The camp site has water and showers. There are marked trails for hiking along the mountain ridges and river bed.

Mbuluzi, however, is being incorporated into **Mlawula Nature Reserve**, 18,000 square km run by the Swaziland National Trust Commission. In future, therefore, there will only be the 'Mbuluzi Gate' into that section of Mlawula Nature Reserve and Mbuluzi will cease to exist in name. The camping facilities will be retained.

MLILWANE NATURE RESERVE

The Mlilwane Nature Reserve, near

Mbabane in the Ezulwini Valley, is a beautiful and peaceful place with plenty of game, mostly impala and hippopotamus. The hippos and wart hogs are fed at the base camp each afternoon at 3 pm. There are some Bushpeople paintings within walking distance of the accommodation area. Entry to the park is E 3 a person and E 6 a car. You are not allowed in the reserve on foot without a guide (E 5 an hour), but you can hitch or hire a horse for E 11 an hour.

Camping costs E 4 a night. A bed in a dormitory (a large building with thatched roof and walls about one metre high) costs E 5, and a *rondavel* E 40 a double plus E 4 tax. The *rondavels* are arranged around a barbeque area next to a hippo pool. There

is a kitchen with pots and pans, and a shop with tins, packets and meat (impala, wart hog and wildebeest chops and sausages). There is also a restaurant that serves good meals for E 6 to E 8 (plus 10% tax).

SAND RIVER DAM
This has no facilities, but good camping and hiking. Don't swim in the water as it's full of bilharzia.

USUTU RIVER
Along this river are some excellent camp sites, but if there are houses nearby ask permission before setting up camp. Some of the best camps are in the forest past the pulp mill at Bhunya.

Tanzania

Probably no other African country has been moulded so closely in the image of its president as Tanzania. Known as Mwalimu (teacher) in his own country and often referred to as the 'conscience of Black Africa' elsewhere, Julius Nyerere is one of Africa's elder statesmen who ruled his country as president for over 20 years. He stepped down in November 1985 but has continued as chairman of his party, Chama Cha Mapinduzi (CCM – Party of the Revolution). Ali Hassan Mwinyi has been the president since, though out of respect their photographs appear side by side in all offices, hotel foyers etc.

Like many other first presidents of post-colonial Africa such as Nkrumah, Sekou Touré and Kaunda, Nyerere was firmly committed to radical socialism and non alignment. He has always been in the forefront of African liberation struggles and Dar es Salaam, the capital, has been home to many a political exile or guerrilla fighter seeking asylum or a base to operate from. Likewise, Nyerere has never missed an opportunity to condemn the South African regime for its racism and denial of political rights to the Black majority. Certainly his sincerity cannot be faulted but a greater pragmatic attitude to solving his country's problems in the face of repeated failure might well have been more realistic than rigid adherence to ideology. On the other hand, his popularity among the people cannot be doubted. In both the election of 1975 and that of 1980 he picked up over 90% of the vote. None of his party colleagues have come even close to matching this performance. Tanzania came into existence as a result of the political union between mainland Tanganyika and the offshore islands of Zanzibar and Pemba. The two halves of the union attained independence from Britain separately, the mainland in 1961 and Zanzibar in 1963.

Though the coastal area had long been the scene of maritime rivalry first between the Portuguese and Arab traders and later between the various European powers, it was Arab traders and slavers who first penetrated the interior as far as Lake Tanganyika in the middle of the 17th century. Their main depots were at Ujiji on the shores of Lake Tanganyika and Tabora on the central plain. Their captives were generally acquired by commerce rather than force and were taken first to Bagamoyo and then to Zanzibar where they were either put to work on the plantations there or on Pemba, or shipped to the Arabian peninsula for sale as domestic servants. Zanzibar, which had been ruled for decades from Oman at the mouth of the Persian Gulf, had become so important as a slaving and spice entrepôt by the first half of the 1800s that the Omani Sultan, Seyyid Said, moved his capital there from Muscat in 1840. Though cloves had only been introduced to Zanzibar from the Moluccas in 1818, by the end of Seyyid Said's reign it was producing 75% of the world's supply.

Britain's interest in this area stemmed from the beginning of the 19th century when a treaty had been signed with Seyyid Said's predecessor to forestall possible threats from Napoleonic France to British possessions in India. They were only too pleased that a friendly oriental power should extend its dominion down the East African coast rather than leave it open to the French. So when Seyyid Said

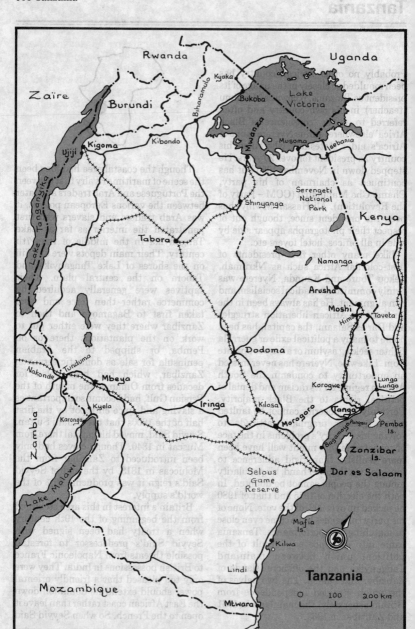

moved to Zanzibar, the British set up their first consulate there. These were the days when Britain was actively trying to suppress the slave trade. Various treaties limiting the slave trade were signed with the Omani sultans but it wasn't until 1873, under the threat of a naval bombardment, that Sultan Barghash (Seyyid Said's successor) signed a decree outlawing the slave trade. The decree certainly abolished the seaborne trade but the practice still continued on the mainland for many years since it was an integral part of the search for ivory. Indeed the decree probably intensified the slaughter of elephants for ivory since ivory was now one of the few exportable commodities that would hold its value despite the cost of transport to the coast. Slaves were used as the means of transport.

In 1890, Zanzibar was made a British Protectorate and was to remain that way until independence in 1963. The Sultan was toppled about a year after independence in a communist-inspired revolution in which most of the Arab population of the island was either massacred or expelled. He was replaced by a revolutionary council formed by the Afro-Shirazi Party. A short time later, Zanzibar and Pemba merged with mainland Tanganyika to form Tanzania.

European explorers began arriving around the middle of the 19th century, the most famous of which were Livingstone and Stanley. Stanley's famous phrase, 'Dr Livingstone, I presume', stems from their meeting at Ujiji on Lake Tanganyika. Other notable explorers in this region included Burton and Speke who were sent to Lake Tanganyika in 1858 by the Royal Geographical Society. It was the Germans, however, in the form of the German East Africa Company who first colonised the mainland though in 1891 the colony was administered directly by the German government. Like the British in Kenya, the Germans set about building railways to open up the colony to commerce.

Unlike Kenya, however, where there were fertile and climatically pleasant highlands suitable for European farmers to colonise, much of Tanganyika was unsuitable and the tsetse fly made cattle grazing or dairying over large areas of central and southern Tanganyika impossible. The German occupation continued until the end of WW I after which the League of Nations mandated the territory to the British.

Nationalist organisations came into being after WW II but it wasn't until Julius Nyerere founded the Tanganyika African National Union (TANU) in 1954 that they became very effective. The British would have preferred to see a 'multiracial' constitution adopted by the nationalists so as to protect the European and Asian minorities but this was opposed by Nyerere. Sensibly, the last British governor, Sir Richard Turnbull, ditched the idea and Tanganyika attained independence in 1961 with Nyerere as the country's first president.

Nyerere inherited a country which had been largely ignored by the British colonial authorities since it had few exploitable resources and only one major export crop, sisal. Education had been neglected, too, so that at independence there were only 120 university graduates in the whole country. It was an inauspicious beginning and the problems which it created eventually led to the Arusha Declaration of 1967. Heavily influenced by the Chinese communist model, it was a masterplan for socialism. The cornerstone of this policy was the *Ujamaa* village – a collective agricultural venture run along traditional African lines. The villages were intended to be socialist organisations created by the people and governed by those who lived and worked in them. Self-reliance was the keyword. Basic goods and tools were to be held in common and shared among members while each individual had the obligation to work on the land. Hundreds of these villages were set up. Nyerere's proposals for education were seen as an essential part of this scheme and were designed to foster constructive attitudes to cooperative endeavour, stress the concept of social equality and responsibility, and counter the tendency towards intellectual arrogance among the educated.

At the same time, the economy was nationalised as was a great deal of rental property over a certain value. Taxes were also increased in an attempt to redistribute individual wealth. Nyerere also sought to ensure that those in political power did not develop into an exploitative class by banning government ministers and party officials from holding shares or directorships in companies or from receiving more than one salary. They were also prohibited from owning houses which were rented out.

Since they were first established, the *Ujamaa* villages have undergone considerable transformation. In the early days, progressive farmers were encouraged to expand in the hope that other peasants would follow their example but this resulted in little improvement in rural poverty and the enrichment of those who were the recipients of state funds. This approach was abandoned in favour of direct state control of planning, organisation and the resettlement of peasants into planned villages with the object of modernising and monetising the agricultural sector of the economy. The settlement schemes were to be provided with potable water, clinics, schools, fertilisers, high-yielding seeds and, where possible, irrigation. Again they failed. They were well beyond the country's ability to pay for them and there was a lot of hostility and resentment among the peasants to what they regarded as compulsory resettlement without any consultation or influence over the decision-making process. Corruption also remained widespread.

Following the second failure a third scheme was adopted. This was based on persuading the peasants to amalgamate their small holdings into large, communally

owned farms using economic incentives and shifting the emphasis onto self-reliance. In this way, the benefits reaped by the members of such *Ujamaa* settlements would be a direct reflection of the dedication of those who lived there. This scheme had its critics but was relatively successful and prompted the government to adopt a policy of compulsory 'villagisation' of the entire rural population.

Since western nations were very tardy about providing development aid for his country despite their lip service to his policies, Nyerere turned to the People's Republic of China as his foreign partner. The Chinese built Tanzania a brand-new, modern railway from Dar es Salaam to Kapiri Mposhi in the copper belt of Zambia (the TAZARA railway) costing some US$400 million. For a time it was the showpiece of eastern and southern Africa and considerably reduced Zambia's dependence on the Zimbabwean (at that time Rhodesian) and South African railway systems. OPEC's oil price hike at the beginning of the 1970s, however, led to a financial crisis and Tanzania was no longer able to afford any more than essential maintenance of the railway. There were also serious fuel shortages. As a result, the railway no longer functions anywhere near as well as it did when first built, though recently things have been improving slightly.

Tanzania's experiment in radical socialism and self-reliance might have been a courageous path to follow in the heady days following independence and even during the 1970s when not only Tanzania but many other African countries were feeling the pinch following the oil price hikes. Only romantics these days, however, would disagree with the assessment that the experiment has failed. The transport system is in tatters, agricultural production is stagnant, the industrial sector limps along at well under 50% capacity, the capital Dar es Salaam is dusty and down-at-heel and all economic incentives seem to have been eliminated.

Obviously, many factors, particularly the extreme poverty, have contributed to Tanzania's woes and are beyond her control. At least, that is true of the mainland. Zanzibar, however, was one of the most prosperous countries in Africa at the time of independence.

The trouble is, Nyerere had no intention of changing and he tolerated no dissent. It is a little-known fact that in 1979, Tanzanian jails held more political prisoners than South Africa, though over 6000 were freed late that year and a further 4400 the following year. Dissent is, of course, much more difficult in a one-party state such as Tanzania than in a western-type democracy but this system isn't peculiar to Tanzania. Most African countries with civilian governments are one-party states. Even now that Nyerere has stepped down as president, it is unlikely there will be any significant changes until after his death.

Tanzania has been one of the most consistently outspoken supporters of African liberation movements particularly in the south. Nyerere joined with Kaunda in supporting the guerrillas fighting for the independence of Angola and Mozambique against the Portuguese and also those fighting to overthrow the White minority government of Rhodesia (now Zimbabwe) during Ian Smith's regime. This support cost both countries dearly and they are still counting the cost. Tanzania also provided asylum to Ugandan exiles during Idi Amin's regime including Milton Obote and the current president, Yoweri Museveni. This support was to cost Tanzania so dearly that it almost bankrupted the country. In October 1978, Idi Amin sent his army into northern Tanzania and occupied the Kagera district as well as bombing the Lake Victoria ports of Bukoba and Musoma. It was done, so he said, to teach Tanzania a lesson for supporting exiled groups hostile to his regime but it's more likely it was a diversionary move to head off a mutiny among his restless troops.

Since Tanzania had hardly any army at the time worth mentioning, it took several months to scrape together a people's militia of 50,000 men and get them to the front. They were ill-equipped and poorly trained but when they struck, the Ugandans – supposedly one of Africa's best trained and best equipped armies at the time – threw down their weapons and fled. The Tanzanians pushed on into Uganda and routed Amin's forces after which a 12,000-strong contingent stayed in the country for some time to maintain law and order and to ensure that Nyerere could exert a strong influence over the choice of Amin's successor. The war cost Tanzania around US$500 million and it received not a single contribution from any source. Furthermore it was half-heartedly condemned by other African countries within the OAU (Organisation of African Unity). One of the OAU's cardinal principles is that African borders are inviolable and member states must not interfere in the internal affairs of others. It wasn't the first time that Tanzania had interfered in the affairs of its neighbours. Nyerere had helped to topple two other regimes, once in the Comoros Islands in 1975 and again in the Seychelles in 1977.

Perhaps Tanzania's economy wouldn't have got into such a parlous state if the East African Economic Community had been allowed to work. At independence, Kenya, Tanzania and Uganda were linked together in an economic union which shared a common airline, telecommunications and postal facilities, transportation and customs. Their currencies were convertible and there was freedom of movement. Any person from one country could work in another. It fell apart in 1977 due to political differences between socialistic Tanzania, capitalistic Kenya and the military chaos that passed as government in Uganda.

As a result of Kenya's action in grabbing the bulk of the community's assets, Nyerere closed his country's border with Kenya. It remained closed for years but is now open again.

The long border closure with Kenya did a great deal of damage to Tanzania's tourist industry. Facilities are much fewer and not as easily accessible as Kenya's except in the northern parks and game reserves.

Facts

GEOGRAPHY & CLIMATE

A land of plains, lakes, mountains and a thin coastal belt, Tanzania is East Africa's largest country with a wide variety of different climates. The bulk of the country consists of highland plateaus, some of which are desert or semidesert and the rest savannah and scattered bush.

The altitude considerably tempers what would otherwise be a tropical climate and it can be quite cool at nights in many places. Many of these plateaus are relatively uninhabited because of the tsetse fly which prevents stock raising. The thin coastal strip along the Indian Ocean, together with the offshore islands of Pemba, Zanzibar and Mafia, enjoys a hot, humid climate tempered by sea breezes. The vegetation is tropical. The highest mountains – Meru (4556 metres) and Kilimanjaro (Africa's highest at 5895 metres) – are to be found in the north-east along the border with Kenya and the area around these enjoys an almost temperate climate for much of the year. Over 53,000 square km of the country is covered by inland lakes, most of them in the Rift Valley. The long rainy season is from April to May when it rains almost every day. The short rains fall during November and December.

PEOPLE

The population stands at around 22.6 million. There are more than 100 different tribal groups in the country but most of them are Bantu in origin. The Arab influence on Zanzibar and Pemba Islands is shown in the people who are a mixture of Shirazis (from Persia), Arabs and Comorans (from the Comoros Islands).

VISAS

Visas are required by all except nationals of Commonwealth countries, Scandinavian countries, the Republic of Ireland, Rwanda, Romania and Sudan. For all these people a free Visitor's Pass is obtainable at the border on entry and valid for a stay of one to three months (you will be asked how long you want to stay). Nationals of South Africa are not admitted.

The cost of visas varies depending on your nationality and are generally issued in 24 hours. Two photographs are required. Be very careful when filling in the application form for a visa because there is now a rule (enforced at some embassies; ignored at others) that you must have US$80 for each day of your proposed stay! This means that if you want to stay two weeks you must write on the form that you have a minimum of US$1120 or, if you want to stay a month, that you have US$2400. Only very rarely would you be asked to prove that you have the amount you declare. Even if you get caught out on the application form you can always renew your visa in Dar es Salaam or at another immigration office.

In Africa, there are Tanzanian embassies in Addis Ababa (Ethiopia), Bujumbura (Burundi), Cairo (Egypt), Conakry (Guinea), Harare (Zimbabwe), Kampala (Uganda), Kigali (Rwanda), Khartoum (Sudan), Kinshasa (Zaïre), Lagos (Nigeria), Luanda (Angola), Lusaka (Zambia), Maputo (Mozambique) and Nairobi (Kenya).

In Bujumbura the embassy is on Ave Patrice Lumumba opposite the PTT. There is a varying scale of charges for visas depending on your nationality and they're issued in 24 hours. Two photographs are required. The embassy is open Monday to Friday from 8 to 11.30 am and from 2 to 4.30 pm but visa applications are only accepted in the morning.

In Kampala the embassy (tel 56755) is at 6 Kagera Rd. Visas cost USh 1500 with two photographs and can be issued the same day if you're lucky. There's no fuss about sufficient funds. The embassy is open Monday to Friday from 9 am to 3 pm.

In Kigali the embassy is on Ave Paul VI at the junction with Ave de Rusumo. Visas cost RFr 715 (French), RFr 890 (Icelandic and Swiss), RFr 1000 (West German) and RFr 1315 (Belgian) and can take up to one week to issue though five days would be average. Two photographs are required. If you make a polite fuss or enlist the support of your own embassy you may get it in 24 hours but they may insist on you producing onward tickets. Visas are for three months and single entry.

In Nairobi the embassy (tel 331056/7) is on the 4th floor, Continental House, on the corner of Harambee Ave and Uhuru Highway. Visas cost KSh 35 (Icelandic and Swiss), KSh 50 (Dutch), KSh 56 (French), KSh 118 (West German) and KSh 139 (Belgian) and you'll need two photographs. They take 48 hours to issue. The US$80 per day rule is enforced here (but they don't ask to see the money). The embassy is open Monday to Thursday from 9 am to 12.30 pm and 2 to 5 pm but visa applications are only accepted in the morning.

If you take a car across the border into Tanzania you will have to buy a temporary import licence valid for 90 days which costs US$60.

Some Tanzanian borders have acquired bad reputations for hassling travellers. The main ones are the Tunduma-Nakonde (Tanzania-Zambia) and Kyela-Karonga (Tanzania-Malawi) borders. At the former you can expect hassles whether you cross by road or on the TAZARA railway. Make sure your papers are in

order and everything else is hunky-dory. The border crossing points into Kenya are generally a breeze (Namanga and Lunga Lunga but not Taveta which is strict). They don't even collect currency forms at Namanga.

Warning

You will probably be refused a visa or entry if you have South African stamps in your passport or the border post stamps of countries adjacent to South Africa. They're very keen on this. New passports also evoke suspicion. Even stamps showing that you entered *and* left Lesotho or Swaziland by air are treated suspiciously. If they're sure you've been to South Africa your passport may well be endorsed 'Undesirable Alien'.

Other Visas

Dar es Salaam is a good place to stock up on Francophone country visas (West Africa, Central African Republic, Chad, etc). Since there are very few of these embassies in the capital you have to get them all from the French Embassy. They generally cost TSh 110 each, are issued without fuss and valid for a stay of one month. The French Embassy (tel 68601/3) is on Bagamoyo Rd.

Burundi It's probably best to get your visa for Burundi at the embassy (tel 29282), 1007 Upanga Rd, in Dar es Salaam. You can also get one at the Burundi Consulate in Kigoma on Lake Tanganyika. This consulate is open for applications on Monday and Wednesday only from 8 am to 3 pm. Visas cost TSh 200, are valid for a stay of one month and take three days to issue (pick them up on Thursday and Saturday respectively).

Kenya The embassy is on the 14th floor, NIC Investment House, Samora Ave at the junction with Mirambo St, Dar es Salaam. Visas cost TSh 120, take 24 hours to issue and you'll require three photographs.

Rwanda The embassy (tel 20115) is at 32 Upanga Rd, Dar es Salaam. Visas cost TSh 250, take 24 hours and two photographs are required. They're valid for a stay of one month.

Zaïre The embassy (tel 24181/2) is at 438 Malik Rd, Dar es Salaam. You'll need four photographs and a letter of recommendation from your own embassy. Visas cost TSh 300 and are issued in 24 hours but they will only issue one-month, single entry visas.

There's also a consulate in Kigoma on Lake Tanganyika which is open for visa applications on Monday, Wednesday and Friday from 9 am to 12.30 pm and 3 to 6.30 pm. Visas cost TSh 200 but take *two weeks* to issue. You'll need four photographs and you do not need a letter of recommendation from your own embassy.

MONEY

US$ 1 = TSh 90
UK£ 1 = TSh 175

The unit of currency is the Tanzanian shilling = 100 senti. It's value on the international market has been declining and its import or export is prohibited.

There's a lively black market. The rate you get not only depends on where you change your money but also on the size of the bills you change (US$50 and US$100 bills are preferred). Dar es Salaam and Zanzibar are the best places (US$1 = TSh 180 to TSh 200) followed by Arusha and Namanga (US$1 = TSh 150). The rates in Kigoma, Moshi, Tanga and Bujumbura (Burundi) are usually well below par (around US$1 = TSh 120 to TSh 130) so only change as much as you need to get to Dar.

Be careful who you change money with on the black market especially in Dar. There are some very dubious characters hanging around Maktaba St who you'd be well advised to stay clear of. It's not necessary to do business with them anyway. Just take your time. You'll get offers from much more reliable quarters.

As in Uganda, Kenyan shillings are almost as good as hard currency when you want to change money (though it's officially illegal to take them out of the country). You can expect KSh 1 to be worth about TSh 6 to TSh 7.

Currency declaration forms are issued on arrival and officials may demand to see the cash and cheques which you declare on the form so you must hide any excess. It's very unlikely, however, that you'd be subjected to a body search and baggage searches are cursory except at the southern border posts. It is probably a good idea to change *something* at a bank just to get a stamp on the currency form and a bank receipt in case anyone official wants to know where you have been changing money. This is important if you are crossing the Tanzania-Zambia border between Tunduma and Nakonde on the TAZARA train or the Tanzania-Malawi border between Kyela and Karonga. It's probably best to assume that you will be thoroughly searched at these borders though it doesn't happen to everyone. Crossing the Tanzania-Kenya border is a different matter. You probably won't even be asked for the currency form and, if you are, it won't be scrutinised.

In the past there was a lively trade on the black market in forged bank stamps and bank receipts which you paid for by a lower exchange rate. This was especially so in Arusha. You're not only wasting your time and money getting involved in this but the authorities are wise to it.

Don't mix 'official' and 'black market' shillings when travelling in Tanzania especially by air. Make sure that any excess shillings not covered by bank receipts and stamps on your currency form as well as any undeclared hard currency is well hidden. Discovery would involve confiscation and other problems.

These schemes to make travelling in Tanzania cheap and to get realistic exchange rates for your hard-earned dollars are all very well but they only go so far. The Tanzanian authorities are not devoid of imagination either. In order to clamp down on the black market and bring in much needed foreign currency, you must now pay for all entry fees to national parks and park lodges in hard currency (cash or travellers' cheques). Shillings are not acceptable even with bank receipts. And if you don't happen to have the exact amount in foreign currency then you'll get the change in shillings (at the official rate of exchange). The same goes for the big hotels on the mainland and for all hotels on Zanzibar.

Likewise, you must pay for all international flight tickets in hard currency. You can still pay for all your food (even at national park lodges), transport, accommodation at budget hotels, souvenirs and internal flights on Air Tanzania in shillings and you don't need to produce bank receipts for this.

Banking hours are Monday to Friday from 8.30 am to 12.30 pm and on Saturday from 8.30 to 11.30 am.

The departure tax for international flights is US$10 – payable in cash dollars. Travellers' cheques are not acceptable. You have to change them at the airport bank and they'll only give you US$19 for a US$20 travellers' cheque! The departure tax for internal flights is TSh 300 – payable in shillings.

POST & TELECOMMUNICATIONS

The poste restante is well organised and you should have no problems with expected letters not turning up. The same is true for telegrams. There's no charge for collecting letters. Due to the very favourable street exchange rate for hard currency posting parcels from Tanzania is much cheaper than doing it from Kenya. If you need to make an international telephone call try to do it, where possible, from either a private house or from one of the large hotels (there will be a surcharge if you do it from the latter – usually 25% of the cost of the call). The reason for this is

that the Extelcoms office on Samora Ave in Dar es Salaam has the grand total of *two* (!) international lines for use by the public. If they're busy – and they often are – you'll be waiting for hours before you get the use of one of the telephones. It's totally inadequate.

TOURIST INFORMATION

The Tanzania Tourist Corporation (tel 2761/4) PO Box 2485, is on Maktaba St close to the junction with Samora Ave and opposite the New Africa Hotel. It's open Monday to Friday from 9 am to 5 pm and on Saturday from 9 am to 12 noon. It has a limited range of glossy leaflets about the national parks and other places of interest, a city map of Dar es Salaam and a road map of Tanzania (1:2,000,000) but it's often out of stock of all of these.

The TTC can make bookings for you at any of the large hotels in Tanzania and at most of the national park lodges but you must pay for these in hard currency. However, it's better to book the national park lodges through a travel agency, because officially you have to pay in hard currency, but in practice some of them may be able to arrange a deal where you pay in shillings.

There are branch offices of the TTC in Zanzibar at the Tanzania Friendship Tourist Bureau (tel 32344) PO Box 216, Zanzibar and in Arusha (tel 3842) on Boma Rd. At the former they have excellent maps of Zanzibar town and the island (1:200,000 – DOS 608 Edition 1-DOS 1983) for sale. It's well worth buying one if you're going to spend some time on the island.

The national parks are managed by a different government body. This is the Tanzania National Parks Authority (tel 3471) PO Box 3134, Arusha. Their main administrative office is on the 6th floor, Kilimanjaro Wing, Arusha International Conference Centre. If you call in they may have a range of descriptive leaflets about the national parks and a reasonably good road map of the Serengeti National Park (there's a nominal charge for these). They're also in the process of rewriting their series of guides to the national parks. The Director is a hard-working but friendly man and he may have copies of the *Quarterly Report* which the authority puts out. If you're interested in what they do these make fascinating reading.

FILM & PHOTOGRAPHY

Bring all your photography requirements with you to Tanzania as very little is available outside Dar es Salaam, Arusha and Zanzibar. Even in these places the choice is very limited and prices are high. Slide film is a rarity – most of what is available is colour negative and black & white. If you're desperate for film then the large hotels are probably your best bet. You'll be extremely lucky to find film at any of the national park lodges.

Don't take photographs of anything connected with the government or the military (government offices, post offices, banks, railway stations, bridges, airports, barracks, etc). You may be arrested and your film confiscated if you do. People are worried about South African-instigated sabotage and spying. If you're on the TAZARA train from Dar to Kapiri Mposhi (Zambia) and want to take photographs of game as you go through the Selous Game Reserve, get permission first from military personnel if possible or, failing that, from railway officials. You might think that what you are doing is completely innocuous; they may think otherwise.

LANGUAGE

Swahili and English are the official languages but there are also many local African languages. Outside the cities and towns far fewer local people speak English than you would find in comparable areas in Kenya. It's said that the Swahili spoken in Zanzibar is of a much purer form than in Kenya. Quite a few travellers come here to learn it since the Institute of Swahili & Foreign Languages is on the island.

Getting There & Around

All fares translated into US dollar prices in this section are on the basis that US$1 = TSh 150 (the average street rate). If you're changing money exclusively at the official rate of exchange then the fare, in dollar terms, will obviously be much higher.

AIR

Quite a few travellers use Tanzania as a gateway to Africa though the most popular one is Nairobi. There's not a lot of difference between Nairobi and Dar/Kilimanjaro in the one-way fare from the most price competitive agents in Europe (about UK£20). For some strange reason, however, there's a considerable difference between the return fares (up to UK£65). You're looking at around UK£260 one-way and UK£440 to UK£450 return from London.

International flight tickets bought in Tanzania have to be paid for in hard currency. You cannot buy them in shillings (even with bank receipts to prove that you have changed money officially). Air Tanzania, the national carrier, services internal routes. Small jets are used between the main airports – Dar, Kilimanjaro, Mwanza and Zanzibar. Propeller planes are used on other routes which service smaller airports such as Bukoba, Dodoma, Iringa, Kigoma, Kilwa, Lindi, Mafia, Mbeya, Musoma, Mtwara, Pemba, Shinyanga, Songea, Tabora and Tanga. There are usually several flights a day between the main airports and at least three flights a week through the smaller ones. Internal flights can be paid for in shillings without having to produce bank receipts or a currency form. This makes them an incomparable bargain if all you want to do is to get from A to B and you're changing money at the unofficial rate.

If arriving by air you must change US$50.

ROAD

Tanzania's economy is in dire straits and part of the reason for this is the crippling bill it has to pay every year for oil imports, vehicles and spare parts. As a result, petrol and diesel are in short supply and buses are often very ramshackle. Many services have been suspended indefinitely – there are no longer any buses, for example, between Arusha and Musoma through the Serengeti National Park – and other services are liable to cancellation at short notice. Breakdowns are frequent. This means that, where there is no train service to fall back on, there's a lot of competition for a place on a bus. Off the main routes (Dar, Moshi, Arusha and Dar, Iringa, Mbeya) it is possible to get stuck for days. Even safari company buses or Land Rovers have been known to run out of fuel on occasion.

Given these circumstances, it's not surprising that there is a black market in diesel and petrol and if driving your own vehicle you'll have to get to grips with this. In most places, you will only be allowed to buy a certain amount at official prices. More will have to be paid for at black market rates which can be up to three times the pump prices.

The Sunday driving rule – where only foreign registered vehicles and those with special plates were allowed to operate – has been abolished.

A few Tanzanian towns have central bus and *matatu* stations (Moshi and Arusha, for example) so it's easy to find the bus you want. Other places – and Dar is the prime example – don't have a central stand and buses depart from several locations, some of them not at all obvious. In circumstances like this you will have to ask around before you find the bus you want. Buses and *matatus* leave when full but pick up more people en route. Fares are usually fixed though you may be charged extra for baggage.

Don't, under any circumstances, allow your bag to be put on the roof if there's any possibility of other people travelling up there with it. There won't be much left in it by the time you arrive. The safest thing to do is insist that it goes under your seat or in the aisle where you can keep your eye on it. Most of the time you won't have to dispute this with the driver. You also need to be very wary of pick-pockets at bus stations – there are usually hundreds of them and they're all waiting just for you! Arusha is notorious for this.

Some examples of bus fares and journey times follow.

Dar to Moshi There are several buses daily in either direction which cost TSh 500 to TSh 600 depending on the bus line and they take about 12 to 13 hours to Moshi. In Dar they leave from the bus station on the corner of Morogoro Rd and Libya St. It's a rough journey.

Moshi to Arusha There are plenty of buses and *matatus* every day in either direction from early morning until late afternoon which cost TSh 50 and take about two hours. They leave when full. It's relatively easy to hitch along this road but you'll generally be charged more than the bus fare.

Moshi to Mwanza There are usually two buses per week in either direction which cost TSh 300. It's a rough road and it does not go through the Serengeti.

Arusha to Musoma There are no longer any buses between Arusha and Musoma which means there is no public transport going through the Serengeti.

Dar to Tanga There are usually one or two buses daily which cost TSh 160 and take about seven to eight hours. They leave from the bus station bounded by Lumumba St, Uhuru St and Libya St in Dar.

Dar to Mbeya There are usually two buses daily in either direction which cost TSh 465 and take about 20 hours. They leave from the same terminus as the Dar to Tanga buses. There's a lot of competition for these buses so, if they're full, you can do the journey in stages by taking a bus first to Iranga (TSh 240) and another from there to Mbeya. It's possible to get stuck in Iranga for a day or two if you do the journey this way. The Dar to Mbeya road goes through the Mikumi National Park and there's a lot of game, including elephants, giraffes, zebras and gazelles, visible during the day.

If heading for Malawi, there are other buses between Dar and Kyela via Mbeya. There are usually two buses daily which cost TSh 722 and take about 27 hours.

TRAIN

Most of Tanzania's major centres of population are connected by railway except for Arusha, Bagamoyo and Kilwa. The Central Line linking Dar es Salaam with Kigoma via Morogoro, Kilosa, Dodoma and Tabora was built by the German colonial authorities between 1905 and 1914 and subsequently extended by the British from Tabora to Mwanza. Dar es Salaam is also linked by rail to Moshi and Tanga via Korogwe.

The other major line is the TAZARA Railway linking Dar es Salaam with Kapiri Mposhi in the heartland of the Zambian copper belt via Morogoro, Mbeya and Tunduma/Nakonde. This line was built by the People's Republic of China in the 1960s and passes through some of the most remote country in Africa including part of the Selous Game Reserve. It is Zambia's most important link with the sea but, unfortunately, maintenance hasn't matched the energy with which the Chinese first constructed the railway. The schedules can be erratic though there are usually two trains in either direction each week.

There are three classes on Tanzanian trains – 1st class (two-bunk compartments), 2nd class (six-bunk compartments) and 3rd class (wooden benches only). You'd have to be desperate to go any distance in

3rd class. It's very uncomfortable, very crowded and there are thieves to contend with. Second class is several quantum levels above 3rd in terms of space and comfort (though the fans may not work) and it's an acceptable way to travel long distances. The only real difference between 2nd class and 1st is that there are two people to a compartment in the latter instead of six. On some trains meals can be served in your compartment (the food is usually good). Otherwise there are always food and drink sellers on the platform at stations en route.

Even when you try to book a ticket several days in advance you may be told that 1st and 2nd class is sold out. The Central Line station in Dar es Salaam is notorious for this. The claim is usually pure, unadulterated rubbish but it helps to secure 'presents' for ticket clerks. If you are told this then go to see the station master and beg, scrape and plead for his assistance. It may take some time but you'll get those supposedly 'booked' tickets in the end. The claim is generally true, on the other hand, on the day of departure.

Dar to Kigoma to Mwanza In theory, there should be a train in either direction daily but fuel shortages generally reduce the service to four trains per week usually on Tuesday, Wednesday, Friday and Sunday at 8 pm from Dar and on Tuesday, Thursday, Friday and Sunday from Kigoma. Dar to Mwanza takes about 36 hours and Dar to Kigoma about 38 hours. Trains can be up to four hours late at the final destination. If going from Mwanza to Kigoma you can only get 1st and 2nd class reservations as far as Tabora. Beyond that you cannot be guaranteed a reservation in the same class on the connecting train. If you are doing this journey go to see the station manager at Tabora as soon as you arrive and ask for his assistance. He's a very helpful man and will do his best to get onward reservations for you.

The fares in Tanzanian shillings are:

class	1st	2nd	3rd
Dar to Kigoma	2025	925	315
Dar to Mwanza	2045	940	370
Dar to Tabora	1465	655	225

Dar to Moshi to Tanga There are three trains per week to both Moshi and Tanga on Tuesday, Thursday and Saturday at 3 pm. In the opposite direction they depart both Moshi and Tanga on Wednesday, Friday and Sunday at 4 pm. The journey to Tanga takes about 13 hours and to Moshi about 15 hours.

Sample fares from Dar to Moshi are TSh 730 (1st class), TSh 450 (2nd class sleeper) and TSh 335 (2nd class seat).

Tanga to Moshi There are trains on Tuesday, Friday and Saturday at 7 pm. The train arrives at Korogwe at about 11.30 pm and waits until about 3 am for the Dar to Moshi train to arrive. There's a lively platform café at Korogwe if you need food or drink while you are waiting. The journey takes about 16½ hours in total.

The TAZARA Railway – Dar to Kapiri Mposhi There are two and sometimes three trains in either direction per week but the actual days on which they go varies so much that the only way to find out is to go to the station and buy a ticket. It is usually on Wednesday and Saturday at 11 am or on Tuesday at 4 pm and Friday at 9.15 am. The journey takes 48 to 54 hours (about 24 hours to Mbeya). In Dar you need to go to the TAZARA station on Pugu Rd to buy tickets. This is not the same station as the one in central Dar (from which Central Line trains depart and arrive). The TAZARA station is about half way to the airport and you can catch the same buses as for the latter to get there. They leave from the junction of Sokoine Drive and Kivukoni Front opposite the Cenotaph and Lutheran Church. You need to book tickets in advance (at least five days is advisable) – don't expect any 1st or 2nd

class tickets to be left up to two days before departure.

The fares from Dar to Kapiri Mposhi are TSh 1297 (1st class), TSh 872 (2nd class) and TSh 359 (3rd class).

Student discounts of 50% are available on these fares for international student card holders. Getting authorisation for this can be time consuming. The normal procedure is first to pick up a form from the TAZARA station on Pugu Rd and then take it to the Ministry of Education (beside State House) where you fill in more forms and get the appropriate rubber stamp. You then take the form back to the TAZARA station and buy your ticket. It's a lot of fuss for two or three dollars!

Meals are usually available on the TAZARA train and can be served in your compartment. Otherwise, there are always plenty of food and drink vendors at the stations en route.

Don't take photographs on this train unless you have discussed the matter beforehand with police.

If you're going all the way to Kapiri Mposhi then you have the Tunduma-Nakonde border to contend with and it's notorious. It's best to expect the worst which is a very thorough search right down to your knickers (women included). The officials who do the searching would have no problem finding employment with the Mafia. And if they find anything which you shouldn't have or haven't got something which you should have then you're in for a hard time. Fines and bribes are the order of the day. If they don't find anything that they can give you a hard time about you may well be hassled for 'presents' – we've had letters from a few travellers who have actually been thrown off the train for refusing to cross someone's palm. Beware!

BOAT

Lake Tanganyika

The main ferry on Lake Tanganyika is the historic MV *Liemba* which connects

Tanzania with Burundi and Zambia. It's a legend amongst travellers and must be one of the oldest steamers in the world still operating on a regular basis. Built by the Germans in 1914 and assembled on the lake shore after being transported in pieces on the railway from Dar es Salaam, it first saw service as the *Graf von Goetzn*. Not long afterwards however, following Germany's defeat in WW I, it was greased and scuttled to prevent the British getting their hands on it. It stayed there for many years until brought back to the surface by the British colonial authorities, then reconditioned and put back into service in 1927 as the MV *Liemba*.

The MV *Liemba* runs on a regular weekly schedule though it can be delayed for up to 24 hours at any point if there is a lot of cargo to be loaded or off-loaded or if there is engine trouble. It departs Bujumbura (Burundi) on Monday at about 4 pm and arrives Kigoma at 8 am the next day. It sets sail from Kigoma later on Tuesday and arrives at Mpulungu (Zambia) on Thursday at 8 am calling at many small Tanzanian ports en route (usually for not much more than half an hour). On the return journey, it departs Mpulungu at 5 pm on Friday and arrives at Kigoma at 10 am on Sunday. It leaves Kigoma again later on Sunday and arrives at Bujumbura at 7.30 am on Monday.

The fares in Tanzanian shillings are:

class	1st	2nd	3rd
Kigoma to Bujumbura	257	203	92
Kigoma to Mpulungu	856	679	308

There's also a port fee of TSh 40 at Kigoma. Fares from Bujumbura can be found in the Burundi chapter. First class is a cabin with two bunks; 2nd class is a cabin with four bunks, and 3rd class is deck space on the lower deck. It's worth going 1st or 2nd class if only because you're on the upper deck but don't expect anything in the way of luxury. It's more quaint than luxurious. Third class is tolerable and rarely crowded between

Kigoma and Bujumbura but between Kigoma and Mpulungu it's very crowded.

Meals (beef curry, rice, soup and desserts) can be bought on board and are reasonably priced. Breakfast (omelette, bread, tea or coffee) is particularly good value. Beer is also available. All meals and drinks have to be paid for in shillings.

There used to be another ferry, the MV *Mwongozo*, which doubled up on the Liemba's schedule but this boat no longer sails to Burundi and Zambia and now only connects Kigoma with the small Tanzanian ports to the south.

There are no longer any ferries between Tanzania and Zaïre but there are cargo boats. To get a lift on one of them to Kalemie, you'll have to speak to the captains. The fare is negotiable. The boats generally leave in the evening and arrive the next morning. If you draw a blank then go via Burundi on the MV *Liemba*.

The MV *Liemba* is not the only way of getting to Burundi. Indeed, there's now a very popular alternative which takes you via the **Gombe Stream National Park** (mainly a chimpanzee sanctuary) and onto Kagunga (the Tanzanian border village). Small, motorised, wooden boats ply between Kalangaabu (two to three hours' walk from Kigoma) or Ujiji and Kagunga via Gombe Stream everyday except Sunday and are used by local people to get to villages up the shore and to bring their produce in to market. They normally depart between 11 am and 12 noon and arrive at Gombe Stream around 4 pm and Kagunga around 6 pm. In the opposite direction they depart Kagunga about 7 am and arrive in Ujiji between 12 noon and 1 pm. The fare is TSh 150.

These boats used to leave from Kigoma just up the railway line from the station and go all the way to Banda (the Burundi border village). Although this was more convenient, it appears the Tanzanian authorities stopped them doing this because too much smuggling was going on. Keep your ear to the grapevine because the situation may change. The boats are partially covered, often overcrowded and offer hardly any creature comforts but they're fun in fine weather. In rough weather they might give you cause for concern.

If you intend leaving Tanzania on one of these small boats (whether you drop off at Gombe Stream or not) you will first have to get an exit stamp from immigration in Kigoma. They're sometimes reluctant to give you these (and may go as far as telling you that it's illegal to leave Tanzania this way). Be firm, polite and make it clear you have all day to wait. You'll get the stamp.

Lake Victoria

There are two ferries which serve ports on Lake Victoria, the MV *Victoria* (which connects Bukoba and Mwanza) and the MV *Bukoba* (which serves Bukoba, Mwanza, Musoma and Kisumu). Since the latter sails to Kisumu you can use it to get to Kenya. The table below details the ferry schedules.

First class on these boats is a four-bunk cabin on the upper deck. Second class is a four-bunk cabin on the lower deck. Third class is simply wooden seats.

Meals on board are the same as on the MV *Liemba*. Since the fighting in Uganda came to an end in early 1986, a new ferry service has started up between Mwanza

MV Victoria			
day	port	arrive	depart
Sunday	Mwanza	–	9 pm
Monday	Bukoba	6 pm	9 pm
Tuesday	Mwanza	6 pm	9 pm
Wednesday	Bukoba	6 pm	9 pm
Thursday	Mwanza	6 pm	
Friday	Mwanza		9 pm
Saturday	Bukoba	6 pm	9 pm
Sunday	Mwanza	6 pm	9 pm

MV Bukoba			
day	port	arrive	depart
Monday	Mwanza	–	9 pm
Tuesday	Musoma	6 am	9 pm
Wednesday	Mwanza	6 am	
Thursday	Mwanza		9 am
	Musoma	7 am	9 pm
Friday	Kisumu	6 am	9 pm
Saturday	Musoma	6 am	9 am
	Mwanza	6 pm	9 pm
Sunday	Bukoba	7 am	9 pm
Monday	Mwanza	7 am	–

The fares on either of these boats are:

class	1st	2nd	3rd
Bukoba to Mwanza	TSh 257	TSh 203	TSh 97
Mwanza to Musoma	TSh 283	TSh 226	TSh 103
Mwanza to Kisumu	TSh 571	TSh 453	TSh 206

and Jinja which runs once a week in either direction. The schedule varies so you need to confirm. The ferry is mainly for freight and railway freight cars but it has room for 30 passengers. The fare is around US$5 and the boats are in good shape.

Indian Ocean

There are two shipping companies which operate boats from Dar es Salaam to the offshore islands (Zanzibar, Pemba and Mafia) and to ports on the mainland. The Zanzibar Shipping Corporation (tel 30749) at Jengo la Vijana, Morogoro Rd, Dar es Salaam (PO Box 1395), owns the MV *Mapinduzi* and the MV *Mandeleo*. The latter, according to a recent newspaper article, is permanently laid-up for lack of funds to repair it. That leaves the MV *Mapinduzi* which, if fuel is available, sails from Dar to Zanzibar twice a week usually on Tuesday and Saturday at 12 noon arriving about four to five hours later. In the opposite direction it sails from Zanzibar to Dar on Monday and Friday at 7 am.

The fares are TSh 510 (1st class); TSh 250 (2nd class), and TSh 190 (3rd class). In addition, there is a harbour tax of TSh 40. The schedule of this boat varies so you need to confirm in Dar (the office is marked as 'CCM Youth' on tourist maps of the city).

The other shipping company is the Tanzanian Coastal Shipping Line (NASACO) (tel 26192) in Sokoine Drive, Dar es Salaam, (PO Box 9461). One manager of this shipping line is a very friendly German man who speaks English and who will help you if he can. The company operates boats which connect Dar with Tanga, Mafia Island, Kilwa, Lindi and Mtwara. They normally sail to Tanga twice a week taking about 12 hours and, although passengers are rare, you are welcome on board (seats only) for TSh 150. They also sail to Mafia Island and Kilwa on average about once every two weeks. To Mafia takes about eight hours and costs TSh 40 (seats only). To Kilwa

takes about 16 hours and costs TSh 80 (seats only). This same company also occasionally sails to Mombasa and the Comoros Islands. There is no regular schedule for any of these boats so you need to make enquiries at the office (it's at the junction of Sokoine Drive and Mission St).

There are small, motorised, passenger boats – often overcrowded – between Zanzibar and Mkoani on Pemba island which take about 12 hours and cost TSh 250. Ask around down at the wharf in Zanzibar.

Dhows

Dhows have sailed the coastal waters of East Africa and across to Arabia and India for centuries. They're greatly reduced in number these days and the only regular services are from Dar to Zanzibar, Zanzibar to Pemba and Pemba to Tanga.

Before you can go on a dhow you need to get the District Commissioner's permission to sail. This is just a formality and shouldn't take more than a few minutes.

Since they rely entirely on the wind, dhows only sail when the winds are favourable otherwise too much tacking becomes necessary. This may mean that they sail at night but, on a full moon especially, this is pure magic. There's nothing to disturb the silence except for the lapping of the sea against the sides of the boat and the occasional conversation. Remember they are open boats without bunks so you have to bed down wherever there is space and where you won't get in the way of the crew when the sail has to be moved. Fares are negotiable but often are more than you would pay on a modern ship for the same journey.

Most of the towns and cities on the coast and on the islands have a dhow dock where you go to make enquiries. This dock is often in a different place to the modern shipping wharves. In Dar es Salaam, for example, it is the Malindi Dock alongside Sokoine Drive.

The fare between Dar and Zanzibar is TSh 270 and the journey takes about seven hours. The dhows leave from Dar around midnight but you need to be there by 9 pm. In the opposite direction, they depart Zanzibar around 8 am.

The fare between Zanzibar and Pemba is TSh 150 and between Pemba and Tanga it is TSh 300.

You may also be able to pick up a dhow from either Zanzibar or Dar to Mombasa at times, but the red tape is a little more involved.

TO/FROM BURUNDI

There are essentially no road links between Tanzania and Burundi except between Kagunga and Banda on the shore of Lake Tanganyika. The normal way of getting between the two countries is to take the Lake Tanganyika steamer, MV *Liemba*. See the Lake Tanganyika segment in the Boat section.

TO/FROM KENYA

There are several points of entry into Kenya but the main overland routes are from Arusha to Nairobi via Namanga, and from Dar or Tanga to Mombasa via Lunga Lunga. Other lesser used routes are Musoma to Kisii via Isebania, and Moshi to Voi and Mombasa via Taveta. There's also the possibility of the Lake Victoria ferry from Musoma or Mwanza to Kisumu. There are no through rail services.

International buses are available between Dar and Nairobi, between Dar and Mombasa and between Moshi and Mombasa. The bus companies covering these routes include Goldline, Rombo Investments and Hood between Dar and Nairobi and Rombo and Hood between Dar and Mombasa. Hood is sometimes known as the Cat Bus. These buses leave from Msimbazi St in Dar. Rombo and Hood share the two routes on alternate days so there is usually at least four buses per week. Depending on the company, the fare to either Nairobi or Mombasa is TSh 1000 to TSh 1300. The buses generally leave early in the morning and arrive early the following morning.

Although these buses are convenient if you just want to get from A to B, they're probably no more convenient than doing the journey in stages and going through the border on foot. There are plenty of daily buses (TSh 60) and *matatus* (TSh 150) from Arusha to Namanga which take less than two hours. The two border posts are adjacent to each other and easy going so you shouldn't experience any delays. From the Kenyan side there are buses (KSh 30) to Nairobi which take four hours. More convenient are the shared taxis of East African Road Services which cost KSh 50 but take only two hours.

From Tanga there are shared taxis and *matatus* to Lunga Lunga which cost TSh 100 and take about one hour. There is a six km gap between the two border posts but pick-ups are usually available. Otherwise hitch. From the Kenyan side of the border there are frequent buses (KSh 30), *matatus* and shared taxis to Mombasa which take about 1½ hours.

TO/FROM MALAWI

The usual route between the two countries is from Mbeya to Karonga via the Songwe Bridge along the shore of Lake Malawi. There are no buses from Mbeya or Kyela to the border post though there are buses from Mbeya to Kyela (at least two daily in the early morning and late afternoon, TSh 100, about three to four hours). From Kyela (or Mbeya if no bus) you will have to take a shared taxi to the border. All border formalities are taken care of at Songwe Bridge so you don't need to go to immigration in Kyela.

The Tanzanian officials at this border have acquired a bad reputation among travellers for their officious manner, so watch out. However, it's travellers who are coming *from* Malawi who get hassled most (the Tanzanians are looking for any trace of evidence that they have visited South Africa and if there is they refuse entry). Going *to* Malawi, your main concern is that the Malawian officials will be looking for this book and, if they find it, it will usually be confiscated. Hide it!

On the Malawian side of the border there is a once-daily bus to Karonga but it 'conveniently' leaves at 6 am which means you will have to hitch or find a shared taxi.

There is also supposed to be an international bus service between Dar es Salaam and Mzuzu (Malawi) once a week but it takes three days.

TO/FROM RWANDA

There is now a well-used road link between the two countries from Mwanza to Kigali via Lusahanga and Rusumo. Full details of this route can be found in the Rwandan chapter.

TO/FROM UGANDA

The road route from Bukoba to Masaka and Kampala via Kyaka is hardly used at all and, if you attempt it, you're liable to get stuck for days as there's very little traffic. It's also an extremely bad road.

The most direct way to Uganda is by boat from Mwanza to Jinja across Lake Victoria. See the Boat section for details.

TO/FROM ZAMBIA

Most travellers take the TAZARA railway between Tanzania and Zambia via Tunduma and Nakonde though you can also cross by road. Details are in the Train section.

The Tanzanian border officials here have, like their counterparts on the Malawi-Tanzanian border, acquired a very bad reputation among travellers so expect the worst and be prepared.

The other entry point into Zambia is via Mpulungu on Lake Tanganyika on the MV *Liemba*. Details are in the Boat section.

Around the Country

As with transport, all prices translated into US dollar figures in this section are on the basis that US$1 = TSh 150. If you are changing money at the official rate of exchange then accommodation will obviously cost you considerably more.

ARUSHA

Arusha is one of Tanzania's most attractive towns and was the headquarters of the East African Community in the days when Kenya, Tanzania and Uganda were members of an economic, communications and customs union. It sits in lush, green countryside at the foot of Mt Meru (4556 metres) and enjoys a temperate climate throughout the year. Surrounding it are many coffee, wheat and maize estates tended by the Waarusha and Wameru tribes whom you may see occasionally in the market area of town. For travellers, Arusha is the gateway to Serengeti, Lake Manyara and Tarangire National Parks and the Ngorongoro Conservation Area and it's here that you come to arrange a safari. Mt Meru can also be climbed from here.

Information

There is a tourist office on Boma Rd just down from the New Safari Hotel. It generally has a few glossy leaflets about the national parks but its main function is to make bookings for the national park lodges. Safari companies will generally do this for you and it's often preferable since they may be able to fix you up with deals where you pay in local currency, especially in the low season. The tourist office will only accept hard currency for bookings.

The Tanzania National Parks headquarters (tel 3472) is on the 6th floor, Kilimanjaro Wing, International Conference Centre (PO Box 3134). They usually stock a few leaflets about the national parks for which there's a nominal charge. Many of the safari companies have their offices in the International Conference Centre and the remainder are along Boma Rd, Sokoine Rd and India St.

The State Transport Corporation, on the corner of Temi Rd and Sokoine Rd, runs minibuses which connect with all incoming and outgoing flights at Kilimanjaro International Airport. The fare is TSh 150. Air Tanzania, Ethiopian Airlines and KLM all have offices on Boma road close to the New Safari Hotel.

Things to See

Arusha is a pleasant town to walk around and take in the sights. The **market area** is particularly lively but, of course, the main concern of most travellers will be to arrange a safari and take off for the national parks.

There are a number of very good **craft shops** along the short street between the clock tower and Ngoliondoi Rd which offer superb examples of *makonde* carving at prices cheaper than you will find in Dar es Salaam.

Places to Stay

The cheapest place to stay and one which has been popular with budget travellers for years is *St Theresa's Catholic Guest House* next to the Catholic church in the valley between the two parts of town. It's a pink coloured building which you can see from the bridge over the river. It costs TSh 100 for a bed in triple rooms or TSh 50 to sleep on the floor. There's no hot water in the showers and nowhere to lock up your gear during the day but it's unlikely anything will be stolen. Very similar is the *Anglican Guest House* next to Christchurch off Moshi Rd but few people seem to stay here. We once received a very tartly worded letter from the very reverend gentleman who runs the place saying that it was 'not for those who wish to scrounge cheap accommodation as they travel around the world, but for missionaries from the bush'.

If you want a private room the best value by far in Arusha is the *Lutheran Centre*, Boma Rd opposite the New Safari Hotel, but they're often full and sometimes reluctant to take travellers. It costs TSh 100/200 for a single/double. For this you get a spotlessly clean, modern room with mosquito nets and bathroom (hot water).

There are a lot of budget hotels in the market area of town, all more or less of a similar standard and price as well as a few mid-range hotels. Budget hotels include the *Friends' Corner Hotel*, on the corner of Sokoine Rd and Factory Rd; *Greenlands Hotel*, Sokoine Rd, which is decaying somewhat; *Central Guest House*, Market St, which is clean and fairly good value; *Naaz Hotel*, Sokoine Rd, a strange place with a restaurant and hot water sometimes available; and the *Karibu Guest House*, Sokoine Rd, which is fairly rough and ready. Others in this range are the *Meru Guest House*, *Town Guest House*, *New Central Hotel*, *Silver Guest House*, *Robannyson Hotel*, *Aspro Hotel* and the *Twiga Guest House*.

For mid-range accommodation two places stand out above the rest. One very popular with travellers is the *YMCA/ Arusha Inn*, India St. It's an older building but clean and well-furnished and the staff are very friendly. Standing on the balcony Mt Meru is in front of you. It costs TSh 250/350 for a single/double including breakfast (omelette, toast, butter, jam and tea or coffee). The communal showers and toilets are kept clean and there's hot water. Clothes left to dry on the line will be there when you get back. Downstairs is the *Silver City Bar* which has a pleasant, shady courtyard and offers tasty, cheap, barbequed meat. It closes early in the evening so there's no problem about noise.

The other hotel is the *Miami Beach Hotel* off Stadium Rd at the back of the bus station. This is a fairly new place and very clean. It costs TSh 150/300 for a single/double without bathroom. There is hot water in the showers and the hotel has its own reasonably priced restaurant.

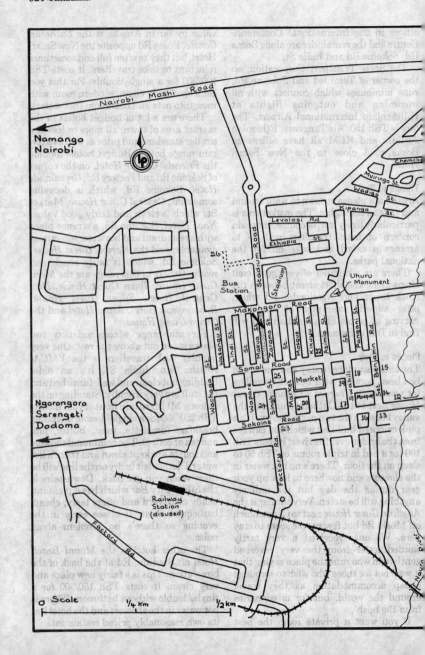

Nairobi Moshi Road

Namanga
Nairobi

Ngorongoro
Serengeti
Dodoma

Stadium Road

Chemchem

Mviringo St.
Wadigo St.
Kipanga St.

Levolosi Rd
Ethiopia St.

Uhuru
Monument

26

Bus
Station

Stadium

Makongoro Road

Wasangu St.
Lindi St.
Makua St.
Zaramo St.
Mosque St.
Kikuyu St.
Azimio St.
Pangani St.
Benjamin Rd

22

Somali Road
Wochaga St.
Wapare St.
Singh St.
Market St.

25

Market

18 15

19

Sahill St.

24 30 Mosque St. 14 12

17 16 13

Sokoine Road

23

Factory Rd

Railway
Station
(disused)

Factory Rd

Naura River

Scale
0   ¼ Km   ½ Km

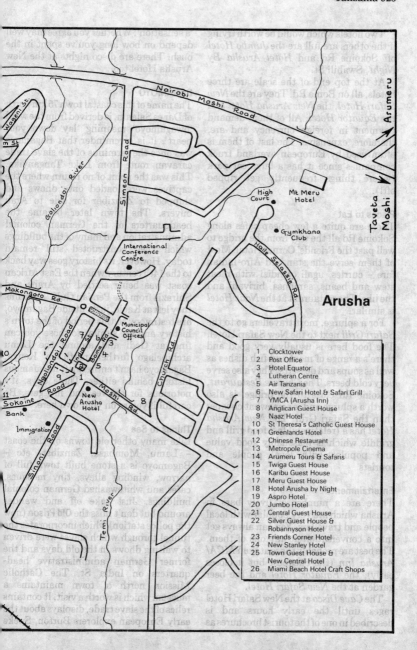

Arusha

1 Clocktower
2 Post Office
3 Hotel Equator
4 Lutheran Centre
5 Air Tanzania
6 New Safari Hotel & Safari Grill
7 YMCA (Arusha Inn)
8 Anglican Guest House
9 Naaz Hotel
10 St Theresa's Catholic Guest House
11 Greenlands Hotel
12 Chinese Restaurant
13 Metropole Cinema
14 Arumeru Tours & Safaris
15 Twiga Guest House
16 Karibu Guest House
17 Meru Guest House
18 Hotel Arusha by Night
19 Aspro Hotel
20 Jumbo Hotel
21 Central Guest House
22 Silver Guest House & Robannyson Hotel
23 Friends Corner Hotel
24 New Stanley Hotel
25 Town Guest House & New Central Hotel
26 Miami Beach Hotel Craft Shops

Two hotels which would be worth trying if the others are full are the *Jumbo Hotel* off Sokoine Rd and *Hotel Arusha By Night*, Swahili St.

At the top end of the scale are three hotels, all on Boma Rd. They are the *New Safari Hotel*, the *New Arusha Hotel* and the *Equator Hotel*. All of them demand payment in foreign currency and are, therefore, expensive. The last of them is often used by European overland truck companies since it has a large car park (where things frequently get ripped off!).

Places to Eat

There are quite a few cheap cafés along Sokoine Rd all the way from the bridge to well past the Friends' Corner Hotel. Most of them serve the standard Afro-Indian fare – curries, ugali or ndizi with meat stew and beans, sambusa, biriyani and the like. The restaurant at the *Naaz Hotel* is similar.

For a splurge, most travellers go to the *Safari Grill* next to the New Safari Hotel. The food here is usually very good and there's a range of meat and fish dishes as well as soups and desserts. They also serve *very* cold beers. The *Chinese Restaurant*, Sokoine Rd close to the bridge, is also worth a splurge and is somewhat cheaper than the Safari Grill. The *New Arusha Hotel* has a (relatively) fast food grill and griddle which is reasonably good value and popular with local people and tourists.

Entertainment

There are a number of lively bars in Arusha which are very popular with local people and travellers. You can always get into a conversation at any one of them. The best are probably those at the *YMCA/ Arusha Inn* (the cheapest but it closes early), the *Equator Hotel* and the beer garden at the *New Safari Hotel*.

The *Cave Disco* at the New Safari Hotel rages until the early hours and is described in one of the tourist brochures as 'a sensation'. Whether you agree may well depend on how long you've spent in the bush. There are disco nights at the New Arusha Hotel too.

BAGAMOYO

The name of this coastal town 75 km north of Dar es Salaam, is derived from the word 'bwagamoyo' meaning 'lay down your heart'. It is a reminder that Bagamoyo was once the terminus of the slave trade caravan route from Lake Tanganyika. This was the point of no return where the captives were loaded onto dhows and shipped to Zanzibar for sale to Arab buyers. The town later became the headquarters of the German colonial administration and many of the buildings which they constructed still remain today. However, its history goes way back to the 14th century when the East African coast was being settled by Arabs and Shirazis from the Persian Gulf. The ruins they left at Kaole, just outside Bagamoyo, are testimony to this period of the town's history and are similar to those you can find at Gedi and around the Lamu archipelago further north in Kenya. Bagamoyo hasn't entirely left its infamous history behind either. These days, it's notorious for thieves and muggers. Be careful if you're on your own here.

Things to See

Like many other old towns on the coast – Lamu, Mombasa, Zanzibar, etc – Bagamoyo is a stone built town full of narrow, winding alleys, tiny mosques, cafés and whitewashed German colonial buildings. Just take off and wander around but don't miss the **Old Prison** (now the police station) which incorporates the tunnel through which slaves were driven to waiting dhows in the old days and the former German administrative head-quarters on India St. The Catholic Mission north of town maintains a **museum** which is worth a visit. It contains relics of the slave trade, displays about the early European explorers Burton, Speke and Stanley and the chapel where Livingstone's body was laid before being taken to Zanzibar en route to Westminster Abbey. Don't walk to this museum alone. There's a good chance you'll get mugged. To visit the 14th century ruins at Kaole you'll need to hire a taxi.

Places to Stay

Almost all the travellers who come to Bagamoyo stay at the *Badeco Beach Hotel* which costs TSh 50/90 for a single/double without bathroom. It's somewhat run-down and the water supply tends to be erratic but the excellent beach compensates for any hardship.

A good place to eat is the evening market by the bus station, where you'll find many street food stalls.

BUKOBA

Bukoba is one of Tanzania's principle ports on Lake Victoria but few travellers come here these days because it's something of a backwater. If you arrive by one of the lake ferries, the jetty where they tie up is about 2½ km from the centre of town.

Places to Stay

One of the cheapest places to stay if you want dormitory accommodation is the *Nyumba na Vijana* (Youth Centre) at the Evangelical Lutheran Church on the road to the hospital. It costs TSh 50 for bed. Your bags are safe here. The *Catholic Mission* also maintains a similar place. For a cheap private room there are many budget hotels around the bus station. If you don't mind spending the money, however, it's worth staying at the *Lake Hotel* (tel 237), which is a beautiful old colonial building with a verandah which overlooks the lake. The hotel is about two km from the centre of town past the police station and the council offices. It costs TSh 225 a double with bathroom including breakfast. Lunch or dinner costs TSh 150. Similar is the *Coffee Tree Inn* (tel 412).

DAR ES SALAAM

Dar es Salaam (meaning 'Haven of Peace') started out as a humble fishing village in the mid-19th century when the Sultan of Zanzibar decided to turn the inland creek (which is now the harbour) into a safe port and trading centre. It became the capital in 1891 when the German colonial authorities transferred their seat of government from Bagamoyo, a move prompted by the unsuitability of the port at Bagamoyo to receive steamships.

Since that time it has continued to grow and is now a city of almost 1½ million people. Nevertheless, although quite a few high-rise buildings have appeared, it remains substantially a low-rise city of red-tiled roofs with its colonial character intact. The harbour is still fringed with palms and mangroves and it's one of the few places where you can see Arab dhows and dugout canoes mingling with huge ocean-going freighters and liners. Dar has a long way to go before it matches the same frenzied pace of life encountered in Nairobi.

Information

The tourist office (TTC), is at Maktaba Rd near the junction with Samora Ave and opposite the New Africa Hotel. It offers a limited range of glossy leaflets about the national parks and other places of interest, and a city map but is often out of stock. They can also make reservations at any of the TTC-managed hotels in the country (payment in foreign currency only) but they can't help you with budget accommodation.

Embassies Foreign embassies represented in Dar es Salaam include the following.

India
    NIC Investment House, Samora Ave (tel 28197)
Madagascar
    Magore St (tel 68229)
Mozambique
    25 Garden Ave (tel 33062)

Somalia
    31 Upanga Rd (tel 32104)
Sudan
    64 Upanga Rd (tel 32022)
Zambia
    5/9 Sokoine Drive/Ohio St (tel 27261)
Zimbabwe
    Umoja wa Vijana Building, Morogoro Rd
    (tel 30455)

Airline Offices The majority of these are in Samora Ave.

Banks Banking hours are Monday to Friday from 8.30 am to 12.30 pm and on Saturdays from 8.30 to 11.30 am. If you need to change money at a bank outside these hours there is a branch of the National Bank of Commerce in the Kilimanjaro Hotel which opens daily except Sunday from 8 am to 8 pm.

Things to See
The **National Museum** in the **Botanical Gardens** between Samora Ave and Sokoine Drive is worth a visit. It houses important archaeological collections especially the fossil discoveries of Zinjanthropus ('Nutcracker people') as well as displays of handicrafts, witchcraft paraphernalia and traditional dancing instruments. Entry is free and the museum is open daily from 9.30 am to 7 pm.

Another museum definitely worth visiting is the **Village Museum** about 10 km from the city centre along the road to Bagamoyo. This is an actual village. It consists of a collection of authentically constructed dwellings from various parts of Tanzania that display several distinct architectural styles. It's open daily from 9 am to 7 pm and there's a small charge for entry plus a further charge if you want to take photographs. Traditional dances are performed here on Thursday and Sunday. Another three km further down the same road at Mpakani Rd is a *makonde* carving community. It would be a good place to pick up examples of this traditional art form.

Those with an interest in local oil, water and chalk paintings should visit the **Nyumba ya Sanaa** building on Upanga Rd at the roundabout overlooking the Gymkhana Club. You can see the artists at work here and there are also *makonde* carvers and batik designers.

The **Kariakoo Market** between Mkunguni St and Tandamuti St is still worth visiting for its colourful and exotic atmosphere – fruit, fish, spices, flowers, vegetables, etc – but there are very few handicrafts for sale here any more.

The nearest beach is at **Oyster Bay**, six km north of the city centre but most people head up to the beaches around the Kunduchi Beach, Bahari Beach, Silver Sands and Rungwe Oceanic hotels, 24 km north of the city. From the New Africa Hotel there's a shuttle bus to the Rungwe Oceanic Hotel. Be careful walking around on its beach if you are on your own. Mugging is not unknown.

Boat trips are available from some of these hotels to offshore islands such as **Mbudya Island** where you can go swimming, snorkelling or sunbathing. The Rungwe Oceanic Hotel charges TSh 1000 for a boat (shared with up to eight people) while the Kunduchi Beach Hotel charges TSh 150 per person.

The Kunduchi also offers longer boat trips to **Zanzibar** for TSh 1000 per person. They take off between 3.30 and 7 am depending on the tides and return in the evening. The journey in either direction takes four to five hours and leaves you with a few hours to wander around Zanzibar town. The man who operates this boat will only take groups – a maximum of 18 people.

Places to Stay
Finding a place to stay in Dar is often like trying to find rocking horse dung or chicken lips. And the later you arrive, the harder it gets. It's not that there aren't a lot of hotels – there are – but they seem to be semi-permanently full. This applies to expensive places as much as to budget hotels. So,

whatever else you do on arrival in Dar, *don't* pass up a room at a hotel if one is vacant. Take the room then go looking for another if you're not happy with it. If you draw a blank everywhere else you still have that room to fall back on.

With a few exceptions, most of the cheaper hotels are to the south of Maktaba St between there and Lumumba St and most of the expensive places are either on or to the north of Maktaba St. At the very bottom end of the market you shouldn't expect too much for your money – a scruffy room with equally scruffy communal showers and toilets. Again, there are one or two exceptions.

Best value for money by far is *Luther House* (tel 32154), Sokoine Drive (PO Box 389), next to the characteristically German church at the junction of Sokoine Drive and Kivukoni Front. It costs TSh 250/500 for a single/double. The rooms are very clean, comfortable and have a fan and mosquito net. Hot showers and breakfast are available. The only trouble with this place is that you'll be lucky to find a room unless you have booked in advance and it's a long walk back to the other budget hotels.

Also very popular is the *YWCA*, Maktaba St, next to the main post office, which takes couples as well as women but they won't take two men. It's very clean and secure. There are a lot of rules which are enforced, but things work as a result. Mosquito nets and laundry facilities are provided. It costs about TSh 450/640 for a single/double including breakfast, and lunch is available for TSh 100. You can only stay for a maximum of seven days. Like Luther House, it's often full so try to book in advance.

There's also a *YMCA*, Upanga Rd, which costs the same but it isn't such good value and, like the YWCA, is often full. They may be willing, however, to let you sleep on the floor if you're desperate.

The cleanest and best value budget hotels are the *Mbowe Hotel* (tel 20501), Makunganya St (PO Box 15261), which is

a pleasant, old, rambling house with a verandah and airy rooms costing TSh 300 a double (no singles) and a sign which says, 'Women of moral terpitude strictly prohibited'; the *City Guest House* (tel 22987), Chagga St (PO Box 1326), which is pretty clean and costs TSh 150/200/250 for a single/double/triple without bathroom (10 am checkout); and the *Florida Guest House* (tel 22675), Jamhuri St (PO Box 132), which costs TSh 200 a double and TSh 300 a triple (no singles).

Some basic places you could try are the *Clock Tower Guest House* (tel 21151), Nkrumah St; the *Windsor Hotel* (tel 20353), Nkrumah St; and the friendly *Traffic Light Motel* (tel 23438), on the corner of Jamhuri St and Morogoro Rd. Other budget hotels, marked on the city map are *Princess Hotel*, *Wananchi Guest House* (tel 20736), *Royal Guest House*, *Zanzibar Guest House* (tel 21197) and the *Pandya Guest House*.

Going up in price there are several reasonable places you can try. The *De Lux Inn* (tel 20873), Uhuru St, is very good value, clean and costs TSh 300/400 a single/ double some with attached bathroom. Breakfast is included in the price. Similar is the *Tamarine Hotel*, Lindi St, which costs TSh 250/325 for a single/double (very few singles). Next to the Tamarine is the *Hotel Internationale* (tel 22785), Lindi St, which consists of two buildings facing each other on opposite sides of the street. It costs TSh 280 per person for bed and breakfast or TSh 580 per person for full board.

Going further up-market, the *Rex Hotel* (tel 21414), Nkrumah St, is clean and not bad value at TSh 350/460 a single/ double. There's a bar and restaurant downstairs.

In mid-range hotels probably the best value would be the *Jambo Inn* (tel 35359, 21552), Libya St. This place is very clean and pleasant and has its own reasonably priced restaurant. It costs TSh 400/500 a single/double and TSh 450/550 a single/ double with air-con. All prices include

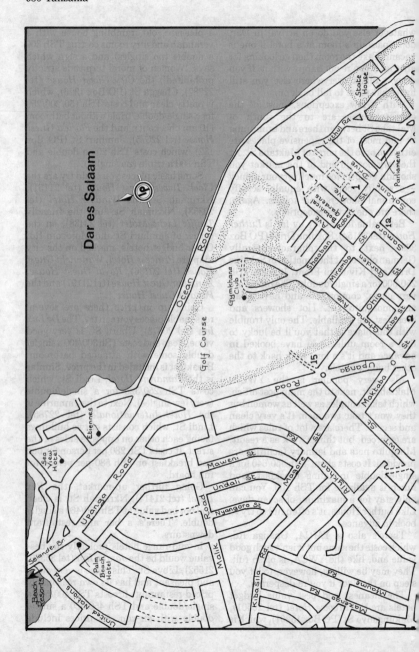

Dar es Salaam

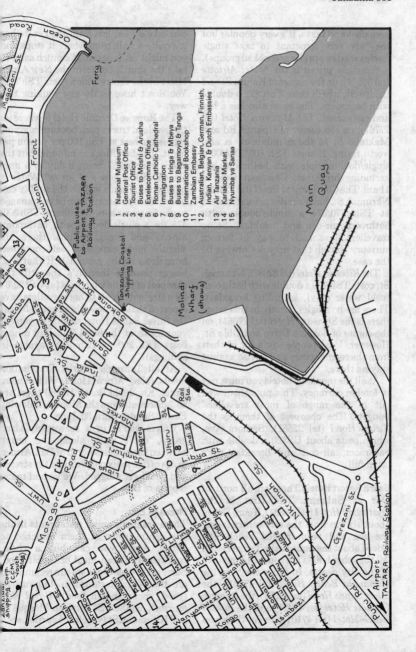

1 National Museum
2 General Post Office
3 Tourist Office
4 Buses to Moshi & Arusha
5 Extelecomms Office
6 Roman Catholic Cathedral
7 Immigration
8 Buses to Iringa & Mbeya
9 Buses to Bagamoyo & Tanga
10 International Bookshop
11 Zambian Embassy
12 Australian, Belgian, German, Finnish,
Indian, Kenyan & Dutch Embassies
13 Air Tanzania
14 Kariakoo Market
15 Nyumba ya Sanaa

breakfast and taxes. It's very popular but they are very reluctant to take single foreigners (they prefer prebooked groups).

Similarly priced is the *Motel Afrique* (tel 31034), on the corner of Kaluta St and Bridge St, which costs TSh 472 a double with bathroom. The hotel also has a bar and restaurant. The *Mawenzi Hotel* (tel 27761), on the corner of Upanga Rd and Maktaba St at the roundabout, is also worth trying. It costs TSh 400/500/600 a single/double/triple with bathroom but excluding breakfast. Checkout time is 11 am. The *Continental Hotel* (tel 22481), Nkrumah St, has a similar price structure at TSh 570/674 a single/double with bathroom, air-con and breakfast. Some travellers have had to pay in foreign currency though that may not always be the case.

The *Kibodya Hotel* (tel 22987), Nkrumah St, costs TSh 700 a double with bathroom (cold water only), including breakfast. There are no singles. Lastly in this range there is the *Skyways Hotel* (tel 27061), on the corner of Sokoine Drive and Ohio St. However, local people say a lot of theft from the rooms occurs and advise against staying there.

At all the top range hotels you must pay in foreign currency. This puts them well out of the range of most travellers' budgets. The cheapest of them is the *Twiga Hotel* (tel 22561), Samora Ave, which costs about US$20 a double with bathroom, air-con and breakfast. It's often full.

Beach Resort Hotels These are all north of Dar es Salaam. The first is the *Oysterbay Hotel* (tel 68631), Touré Drive, about six km from the city centre facing the sea and palm-fringed beach. It's priced about the same as the Twiga Hotel. All the other hotels are some 24 km north of the city centre. In order they are the *Kunduchi Beach Hotel* (tel 47261), the *Silver Sands Hotel* (tel 47231), the *Rungwe Oceanic Hotel* (tel 47021) and the *Bahari Beach Hotel* (tel 47101). To get there you can take a local bus from the centre but it's quite a walk from where it stops and you might get mugged. It's much safer to take the shuttle bus from the New Africa Hotel in the centre which costs TSh 300. You don't have to do any walking this way.

The Rungwe Oceanic Hotel is where all the overland trucks park because camping is possible here at TSh 100 per person per night. The facilities are minimal but the site is guarded 24 hours a day by a man armed with a bow and arrow! Water is pumped up from a well so the supply can be erratic. Some travellers have managed to pay for rooms here in shillings (TSh 300/575 for a single/double with bathroom, air-con and breakfast plus there are slightly more expensive self-contained bungalows in the grounds). If that's no longer possible then it's the still the cheapest of the beach hotels (at US$20/34 for a single/double). Other travellers have reported that it's possible to camp free at the Silver Sands Hotel so long as you eat your meals at the hotel (lunch or dinner costs TSh 200 to TSh 250 payable in shillings).

At all Tanzania Tourist Corporation hotels (New Africa Hotel, Kilimanjaro Hotel, Kunduchi Beach Hotel) there are 50% discounts from the Monday following Easter Sunday until 30 June.

Unless you're in a reasonably sized group, don't walk along the beach between these hotels north of Dar. Armed gangs of five to six people roam the stretch and you'll get mugged. We've had many reports of this.

Places to Eat
There are many small restaurants in the city centre, some of them attached to hotels, where you can buy a cheap traditional African meal or Indian food. Some of the ones which we can recommend are the *Naaz Restaurant*, Jamhuri St (good, cheap Indian food); *Royal Restaurant*, Jamhuri St between Mosque St and Kitumbini St (vegetable curries, etc);

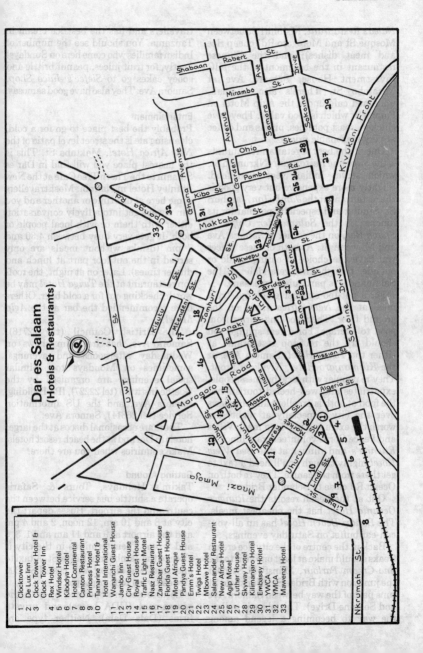

Dar es Salaam
(Hotels & Restaurants)

1 Clocktower
2 De Lux Inn
3 Clock Tower Hotel &
   Clock Tower Inn
4 Rex Hotel
5 Windsor Hotel
6 Kibodya Hotel
7 Hotel Continental
8 Canton Restaurant
9 Princess Hotel
10 Tamarine Hotel &
   Hotel International
11 Wananchi Guest House
12 Jambo Inn
13 City Guest House
14 Royal Guest House
15 Traffic Light Motel
16 Naaz Restaurant
17 Zanzibar Guest House
18 Florida Guest House
19 Motel Afrique
20 Pandya Guest House
21 Emm's Hotel
22 Twiga Hotel
23 Mbowe Hotel
24 Salamander Restaurant
25 New Africa Hotel
26 Agip Motel
27 Luther House
28 Skyway Hotel
29 Kilimanjaro Hotel
30 Embassy Hotel
31 YWCA
32 YMCA
33 Mawenzi Hotel

Nawaz Restaurant, Msinhiri St between Mosque St and Morogoro Rd (cheap rice and meat dishes); and the Chinese restaurant in the basement of the NIC Investment House, Samora Ave at Mirambo St. There's also a small, unnamed café under the Agip Motel on Pamba St which is good value. They have chicken, roast potatoes, pizzas and coffee at very reasonable prices.

One of the best vegetarian restaurants is the *Supreme Restaurant*, Nkrumah St, which serves Indian vegetarian food. Slightly more expensive but very good is the restaurant at the *Jambo Inn*, Jamhuri St. Similar and especially popular for its lunches is the *Salamander Coffee & Snack Bar*, on the corner of Samora Ave and Mkwepu St. At both of these places you have the choice of eating inside or outside though the verandah of the Salamander is particularly pleasant.

For a not-too-expensive splurge, try a meal at the *New Africa Hotel* on the ground floor. Their cooking varies from good to average. For a real splurge you should try the roof-top restaurants at either the *Twiga Hotel*, Samora Ave, or the *Kilimanjaro Hotel*, Kivukoni Front. They're popular with local businesspeople, expatriates and well-heeled tourists but the food at both is excellent and the views over the city (especially at night) are worth the extra you pay for a meal. VSOs and Peace Corps volunteers rate lunch at *Etienne's* and dinner at the *Sea View Hotel* highly though you'll need a taxi to get there from the centre. They're both on Ocean Rd close to Selander Bridge.

Out at the beach resorts the *Rungwe Oceanic Hotel* has the cheapest meals. The *Bahari Beach Hotel* has an all-you-can-eat buffet on Saturday evenings.

Back in the centre of the city, ice cream freaks should make at least one visit to the *Sno-Cream Parlour*, Mansfield St near the junction with Bridge St (Mansfield St runs part of the way between Samora Ave and Sokoine Drive). This place is well on the way to becoming a legend among travellers and has the best ice cream in Tanzania. You should see the number of Indian families who come here on Sundays! Lastly, for fruit juices, peanut brittle and gooey cakes go to *Siefee's Juice Shop*, Samora Ave. They also have good samosas.

Entertainment

Probably the best place to go for a cold, cleansing ale is the street level patio of the *New Africa Hotel*, Maktaba St. This is the nearest place you will find in Dar es Salaam to the Thorn Tree Café at the New Stanley Hotel in Nairobi. Most travellers come here at one time or another and you can always get into a lively conversation either with them or with local people or both. It gets very busy between 4.30 and 7 pm (drinks without meals are only served in the outdoor part at lunch and dinner times). Later on at night, the roof-top restaurant at the *Twiga Hotel* may be worth checking out for a cold beer. Others have recommended the bar at the *Agip Motel*.

The British Council (tel 22716), Samora Ave, has free film shows on Wednesday afternoons and evenings, sometimes on Mondays too. Similar social evenings are organised by the Goethe Institute (tel 22227), IPS Building, Samora Ave, and the US Information Service (tel 26611), Samora Ave.

There are occasional discos at the larger hotels in Dar and at the beach resort hotels. Make enquiries when you are there.

Getting Around

Takim's Holidays, Tours & Safaris operate a shuttle bus service between the centre and the airport. Buses depart the city at 8 and 10 am, 12 noon, 2 and 4 pm and the airport at 9 and 11 am and 1, 3, 6 and 7 pm. Their terminus in the city is close to the Jambo Inn, Libya St. A taxi to and from the airport will cost TSh 300 shared by up to four people.

Local buses are operated by both the government (UDA buses) and private firms (Dala Dala). Neither type are numbered. Instead they have their first and last stop indicated in the front window (the one to the TAZARA railway station is marked 'Posta-Vingunguti'). Fares are fixed and cost a few shillings.

The State Travel Service operates shuttle buses between the city centre and the beach hotels to the north. These depart the city Monday to Friday at 9 am, 12 noon, 2 and 5 pm and on Saturdays and Sundays at 9 and 11 am and 1, 3 and 5 pm. The fare is TSh 100. The terminus in the city is the New Africa Hotel.

DODOMA

Dodoma is the CCM party political headquarters and slated to become the capital of Tanzania sometime towards the end of the century though economic constraints may delay implementation of this. In the meantime there's little of interest here for the traveller. It is, on the other hand, the only wine-producing area of Africa south of Morocco and north of South Africa. Bacchanalians shouldn't get too excited though. Viticulture has a *long* way to go before they'll interest anyone but a Bowery bum in their product. It's foul.

Places to Stay

A reasonable place to stay is the *Central Province Hotel* (tel 21177) which costs TSh 100 a double. To get there, leave the front entrance of the railway station and turn right along the road running parallel with the tracks. Continue to the first roundabout and turn right. Walk to the next roundabout and turn right again then it's the first street on the left and the hotel is 50 metres down that road. Other travellers have recommended the *Christian Centre of Tanzania* which is clean and costs TSh 280 a double. Another place worth trying is the *Ujiji Guest House* near to the bus station. It costs TSh 75 a double, is clean and provides mosquito nets.

KIGOMA

Kigoma is the most important Tanzanian port on Lake Tanganyika and the terminus of the railway from Dar es Salaam. Many travellers come through here en route to or coming from Bujumbura (Burundi) or Mpulungu (Zambia) on the Lake Tanganyika steamer, the MV *Liembe*. The town has little of interest in itself but it is a jumping off point for visits to Ujiji and the Gombe Stream National Park.

Information

There are consulates for both Burundi and Zaïre in Kigoma but don't apply for a Zaïrois visa here as it takes at least two weeks to issue. See the Visas section.

If you are flying out of Kigoma, Air Tanzania runs a minibus from their office in town for the airport. There's a small charge for the service.

The railway booking office is open daily from 8 am to 12.30 pm and 2 to 4.30 pm.

Things to See

Just down the coast from Kigoma is **Ujiji**, one of Africa's oldest market villages, which is a good deal more interesting than Kigoma itself and the place where the famous words, 'Dr Livingstone, I presume', were spoken by the explorer and journalist, Stanley. There's the inevitable plaque. There are frequent buses there from the railway station in Kigoma for TSh 6 which take 15 minutes or you can hire a car for TSh 200 if there is a group of you. Boat building and repairs go on down by the lake shore. If you need a meal whilst you are here the *Kudra Hotel* has good food and fruit salads.

North of Kigoma, half way to the Burundi border, is **Gombe Stream National Park** which is primarily a chimpanzee sanctuary. For more details see the National Parks section.

Places to Stay

The cheapest place to stay is the *Kigoma Community Centre* which costs TSh 90/120 for a single/double with hand basin and running water but they're not very

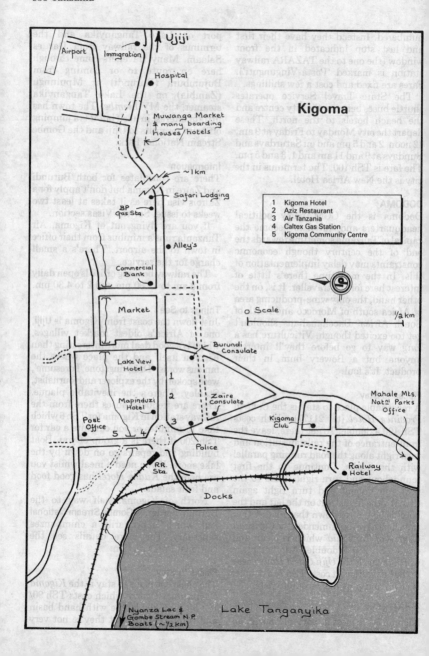

Kigoma

1 Kigoma Hotel
2 Aziz Restaurant
3 Air Tanzania
4 Caltex Gas Station
5 Kigoma Community Centre

Airport

Immigration

↑ Ujiji

Hospital

Muwanga Market & many boarding houses/hotels

~1km

Safari Lodging

BP Gas Sta.

Alley's

Commercial Bank

Market

Lake View Hotel

Mapinduzi Hotel

Post Office

5   4

Police

R.R. Sta.

Burundi Consulate

Zaire Consulate

Kigoma Club

Mahale Mts. Nat'l Parks Office

Railway Hotel

Docks

0 Scale   ½ km

Lake Tanganyika

↓ Nyanza Lac & Gombe Stream N.P. Boats (~½ km)

friendly towards travellers. To find it, turn left out of the railway station, go over the bridge and then look for the sign 'Tanzania Electrical Supply Co' on the left hand side. The Community Centre is the last door of this building. If you'd prefer a normal hotel then the best value for money is the *Lake View Hotel* on the left hand side about 350 metres uphill from the railway station just before the market. There's no view of the lake as the name suggests but it's a very clean, comfortable place and the staff are friendly. It costs TSh 80/100 a single/double without bathroom. The attached restaurant is one of the best places to eat in Kigoma.

Not such good value because it's tatty and there are a lot of mosquitoes (and no nets) is the *Kigoma Hotel* a few metres down the road on the opposite side. It costs TSh 120/175 for a single/double. The showers could do with a good scrub to get rid of the slimy algae on the floor and walls, too. There's an attached restaurant which is good value. Further down the hill is the *Mapinduzi* which is owned by the same people as the Kigoma Hotel. It's primitive and grubby and poor value at TSh 140 a double.

The most expensive hotel in Kigoma is the *Railway Hotel* on the west side of the port. If you can't get in at the Lake View Hotel it's worth spending the extra and staying here. It has a superb location overlooking the lake and the grounds are landscaped with flowering trees and palms. Rooms cost TSh 270/490 for a single/double with bathroom, including breakfast. The hotel has its own restaurant and bar.

There are a lot more budget hotels but they are several km up the hill from the market – very inconvenient if you are catching the train or lake steamer.

Places to Eat

There are several good places to eat in Kigoma. One of the cheapest is the *Kigoma Hotel* where you can get a reasonably priced meal of fish, sauce and fried rice. Breakfasts are good value, too. Every second day they will have beer for sale but only between 6 and 7.30 to 8 pm. The limit is three bottles. The rest of the time it's konyagi, the local firewater. Lunch at the *Lake View Hotel* is excellent value and it's also a good place to pick up breakfast. The kitchen here is much cleaner than at the Kigoma Hotel. Their ice-cold pineapple juice is superb. Many travellers have recommended the *Aziz Restaurant* just down from the Kigoma Hotel. You can pick up a good meal here at lunch times and they run a clean kitchen. No beer is served as it's a Muslim establishment. *Alley's*, up the hill from the market, is a good place for snacks and African music. Some travellers have said they've raged all night here but there wasn't much evidence of that when I was last there.

For what amounts to a splurge in Kigoma try eating at the *Railway Hotel*. The meals aren't bad but nothing to write home about. This is the only other place in Kigoma where you can find beer but they generally won't serve any unless you're staying or eating there. Unlike at the Kigoma Hotel, however, there's no limit.

MBEYA

Until recently, few travellers stayed overnight in Mbeya but since the opening of the direct route to Karonga in Malawi via Kyela it has become a busy one-night stopover town. The surrounding area where bananas, tea, coffee and cocoa are grown is very fertile, but there's little of interest for the traveller.

Buses for Kyela depart from the bus station up the hill from the railway station. The fare is TSh 80 and the journey takes about three hours.

Places to Stay

If at all possible try to get here early in the day as accommodation fills up rapidly by late afternoon. One of the best places to stay is the *Moravian Youth Hostel* near

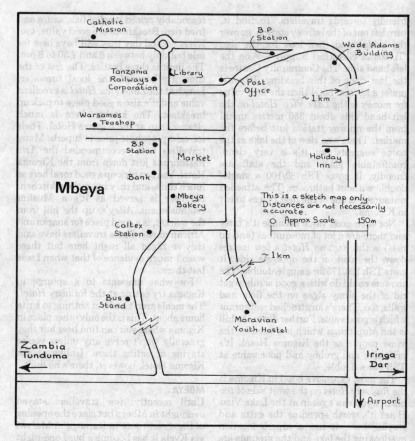

Catholic Mission

B.P. Station

Wade Adams Building

Library

Tanzania Railways Corporation

Post Office

~1 km

Warsames Teashop

Holiday Inn

B.P. Station

Market

Mbeya

Bank

Mbeya Bakery

This is a sketch map only. Distances are not necessarily accurate.

○ Approx Scale   150m

Caltex Station

~1 km

Bus Stand

Moravian Youth Hostel

Zambia Tunduma

Iringa Dar

Airport

the radio tower which costs TSh 175 a double. It's very clean and the staff are friendly. A reasonably priced breakfast and dinner are provided. Cheaper rooms are available at guesthouses but they're nothing special.

For a mid-range hotel, the *Mbeya Hotel* opposite the football stadium and managed by the Tanzania Railways Corporation is recommended. It's a very pleasant, colonial-style hotel with comfortable rooms, clean sheets, mosquito nets and hot showers. It costs TSh 800 a double.

MOSHI

Moshi is the gateway to Kilimanjaro and the end of the northern railway line from Dar es Salaam but otherwise not a very interesting place. Rather than stay here, many travellers head straight out to **Marangu** and arrange a trek up the mountain from there but this might not always be the best thing to do. The pros and cons are discussed in the National Parks section.

Information

There is an immigration office in Moshi

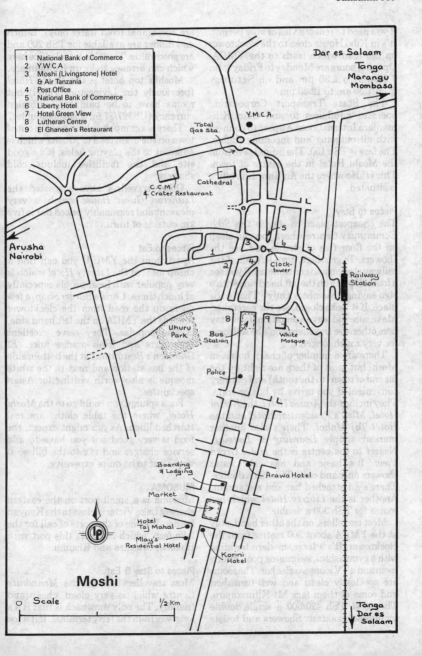

Moshi

1. National Bank of Commerce
2. YWCA
3. Moshi (Livingstone) Hotel & Air Tanzania
4. Post Office
5. National Bank of Commerce
6. Liberty Hotel
7. Hotel Green View
8. Lutheran Centre
9. El Ghaneen's Restaurant

Dar es Salaam

Tanga
Marangu
Mombasa

Y.M.C.A.

Total Gas Sta.

C.C.M. & Crater Restaurant

Cathedral

Arusha
Nairobi

Clocktower

Railway Station

Uhuru Park

Bus Station

White Mosque

Police

Boarding & Lodging

Arawa Hotel

Market

Hotel Taj Mahal

Mlay's Residential Hotel

Korini Hotel

Scale

0   1/2 Km

Tanga
Dar es Salaam

if you need to renew a visa or stay permit. It's in Kibo House close to the clocktower on the road which leads to the YMCA. Opening hours are Monday to Friday from 7.30 am to 2.30 pm and on Saturday from 7.30 am to 12.30 pm.

The State Transport Corporation operates minibuses to and from Kilimanjaro International Airport to connect with all outgoing and incoming flights. The fare is TSh 150. The buses leave from the Moshi Hotel in the centre of town. This is also where the Air Tanzania office is situated.

Places to Stay

The cheapest place to stay is the *Sikh Community Centre* where you can sleep on the floor free of charge and use the showers. To get there, turn left out of the railway station and continue until you see a football pitch on the left hand side with a sign saying, 'Members Only'. That's the place. If it looks closed, see the caretaker. Make sure you leave a donation if you stay here otherwise travellers won't be welcome for very much longer.

There are a number of cheap hotels in Moshi but most of them are right up the far end of town (to the south) and not very convenient if you arrive by bus or train. They include the *Arawa Hotel*, the *Korini Hotel*, *Mlay's Residential Hotel* and the *Hotel Taj Mahal*. There's also another marked simply *Boarding & Lodging*. Nearer to the centre is the *Hotel Green View*. It's basic and has cold water showers only and costs TSh 200 a double. There's an attached bar and restaurant. Another is the *Liberty Hotel* which has rooms for TSh 300 a double.

Most travellers, on the other hand, stay at the *YMCA* about 300 metres from the clocktower. It's a large, modern building with a gymnasium, swimming pool, dining room and a TV lounge/coffee bar. The rooms are spotlessly clean and well-furnished and some of them face Mt Kilimanjaro. They cost TSh 420/600 a single/double including breakfast. Showers and toilets are communal (cold water only). Lunch and dinner are available for TSh 200 and are good value. There's a travel office here which can arrange treks up Kilimanjaro.

Moshi's top hotel is the *Moshi Hotel* (previously the Livingstone Hotel) but rooms have to be paid for in foreign currency (US\$27/37 for a single/double).

There is a camp site about two km out of town on the main road to Arusha which is adjacent to the playing fields. It's a good site and the facilities include cold showers.

Other travellers have suggested the *Lutheran Guest House* which is very pleasant and reasonably priced but is five km outside of town.

Places to Eat

Apart from the *YMCA*, you can find a cheap meal at the *Liberty Hotel* which is very popular with local people especially at lunch times. *Chris's Burger Shop*, a few doors up the road from the clocktower towards the YMCA on the left hand side, is also popular. They serve excellent eggburgers and fresh orange juice. *El Ghaneen's Restaurant* at the bottom side of the bus station and next to the white mosque is also worth visiting for Asian specialities.

For a splurge you could go to the *Moshi Hotel*, where the table cloths are real starched linen. As you might expect, the food is very good but you have to add service charges and tax to the bill so it works out to be quite expensive.

MUSOMA

Musoma is a small port on the eastern shore of Lake Victoria close to the Kenyan border. It's one of the ports of call for the lake ferry which connects this port with Bukoba, Mwanza and Kisumu.

Places to Stay & Eat

Most travellers stay at the *Mennonite Centre* which is very clean, cheap and friendly. The only drawback is that it's a long way from the ferry terminal. If it's too far away for you try the *Embassy Lodge* in the centre of town which costs TSh 90 a double or the *Musambura Guest House* round the corner which is slightly more expensive. Similar is the *Rafiki Guest House*, Kivukoni St, which costs TSh 82 a single and TSh 104 a double. The *Sengerema Guest House* close to the market and bus station has also been recommended by travellers in the past. For a mid-range hotel the *Railway Hotel*, about half an hour's walk from the centre of town, is probably the best value. It's also worth coming for a meal even if you don't stay here.

MWANZA

Mwanza is Tanzania's most important port on the shore of Lake Victoria and the terminus of a branch of the central railway line from Dar es Salaam. It's a fairly attractive town flanked by rocky hills and its port handles the cotton, tea and coffee grown in the fertile western part of the country. In the area live the Wasukuma people who make up the largest tribe in the country. There are lake ferries from Mwanza to the other Tanzanian ports of Bukoba and Musoma as well as to Kisumu (Kenya) and Jinja (Uganda).

If you're heading for Kenya there are buses to the border around 5 am for TSh 300, and they are usually daily.

Things to See

About 15 km east of Mwanza on the Musoma road is the **Sukuma Museum** (sometimes called the Bujora Museum) which was originally put together by a Quebecois missionary. It contains displays about the culture and traditions of the Wasukuma tribe as well as an excellent drum collection. Once a week, on average, it puts on traditional dances of this tribe including the spectacular Bugobogobo and the Sukuma Snake Dance. It's well worth making enquiries in town as to when the next performance is due. Entrance to the museum costs TSh 50 and that includes a guide. To get there take a local bus from the bus station in Mwanza to Kisessa (TSh 20) and from there it's about a km walk. It's also possible to camp at the museum or rent a *banda*.

There are regular ferries from Mwanza to **Ukerewe Island** further north if you'd like to explore the surrounding area.

Places to Stay

Mwanza is plagued with hordes of mosquitoes and malaria is prevalent so get a hotel room with a net.

Perhaps the best place to stay and one which is popular with travellers is the *Sukuma Museum*. It's a lovely spot and camping is generally free. If you don't have a tent there are two-bed *bandas* for rent for just TSh 80.

In Mwanza itself there's quite a choice of reasonably priced hotels. The *Zimbabwe Guest House* near the bus station is adequate for most budget travellers' needs and the staff are friendly. It costs TSh 135 per room (one or two people) and mosquito nets and towels are provided. Similar are the *Furaha Guest House* at the railway station and *Wageni Salim's Guest House* both of which cost TSh 100/120 for a single/double; *Jafferies Hotel* at TSh 120/166 for a single/double; the *Capital Guest House* at TSh 120 a double and TSh 200 a triple; and the *New Safari Lodge* which costs TSh 150/200 for a single/double.

Going up in price, try the *Kishinapanda Guest House*, a new place which is very good but fills up early in the day. It costs TSh 200 a single without bathroom, TSh 250/350 for a single/double with bathroom. Fans and mosquito nets are provided. To get there from the bus station, take the first street on the right hand side (off Nyerere Rd) after the Mutimba Guest House and then the second on the left hand side. About 50 metres down this road you come to the Delux Hotel; the Kishinapanda is just round the corner from there. If coming from the harbour, take the first street on the left hand side before the Mutimba

Guest House and after that the second street on the left.

The *Mutimba Guest House* has rooms for TSh 360 a double without shower and TSh 460 a double with bathroom. The *De Lux Hotel* is also worth checking out if you want a mid-range hotel. It costs TSh 350 a double with breakfast. The restaurant is excellent. The *Victoria Hotel* at TSh 200/255 a single/double is pretty tatty for the

price. The *Shinyanga Guest House* has doubles at TSh 350.

If you want to camp you can do this free of charge at the *Saba Saba Showground* near the airport. There is a waterpump but no toilet or shower.

Places to Eat

For local food there are a number of good cheap restaurants along Lumumba St. Try

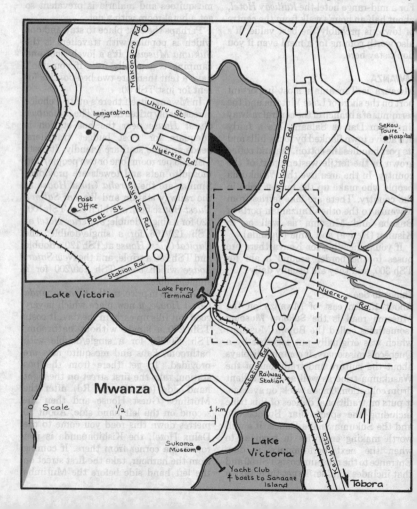

Mwanza

the *Cairo* next to the Shinyanga Guest House. In the evenings between 5.30 and 6.30 pm there are a lot of food stalls set up opposite the Victoria Hotel where you can eat well for a song. A favourite with travellers is *Al Shah's African Restaurant* where you can get a meal of fish or meat, vegetables and potatoes or rice. At the rear of this place there is a lively disco on Saturdays and Sundays (African music). You have to pay an entry fee unless you eat there, in which case it's free. The *Delux Hotel* is definitely worth a visit if you like Indian Moghlai food. One dish would be enough for two people. They have cheaper dishes like kebabs and fried chicken as well as samosas and other snacks. Cold beers are also available.

Other reasonably priced restaurants which have been recommended are the *Kunaris Restaurant*, the *Furaha Restaurant* and the *Rex Hotel*.

If you are catering for yourself then you can buy cheap fish at the market near the ferry terminal.

TABORA

Tabora is a railway junction town in western Tanzania where the central railway line branches for Mwanza and Kigoma. You may have to stay the night if you're changing trains but can't get immediate onward reservations.

Places to Stay

The *Moravian Guest House* is probably the best place to stay and is certainly cheap at TSh 25 per person. It's pleasant and the staff are friendly. If the accommodation isn't to your liking you could try the somewhat expensive *Railway Hotel* which also has reasonable meals.

TANGA

Tanga is Tanzania's second largest sea port though you would hardly be aware of this strolling around the town since it has retained a sleepy colonial atmosphere. It was founded by the Germans in the late 19th century and is a centre for the export of sisal. Not many travellers come here, except those who are either looking for a dhow to Pemba Island or heading north to Mombasa, but there are a few things worth visiting in the area.

Things to See

Not too far from town off the road to Lunga Lunga are the **Amboni Caves**. The area is predominantly a limestone district. Some 20 km south of Tanga on the Pangani road are the **Tongoni Ruins** which consist of a large ruined mosque and over 40 tombs. This is the largest concentration of such tombs on the whole of the East African coast. They supposedly date from the 10th century.

Places to Stay

A very twee place to stay which many travellers rate highly is the *Bandorini Hotel*, Independence Ave overlooking the harbour. It offers matchless English colonial style living (reflecting the owner's nationality) but is often full because they only have seven rooms. Bed and breakfast costs TSh 150 per person. If it's full try the *Planters Hotel* (tel 2041) on Market St which is a huge, rambling, old wooden hotel surrounded by an enormous verandah with its own bar and restaurant downstairs. It costs about TSh 300/600 a single/double including breakfast. The rooms are clean and equipped with a hand basin. The communal showers have cold water only.

If these hotels are too expensive try the *Mkwakwani Lodgings* behind the maternity hospital and dispensary where you can get a room for TSh 100 a double. The rooms are clean and have fans. Other reasonable hotels in Tanga include the *Sunset Guest House*, the *Equator Guest House* and the *Splendid Hotel* (tel 2031).

The most convenient mid-range hotel in town is the *Marina Inn* which is a modern, well-maintained hotel offering air-con double rooms for TSh 595 including breakfast. There are no singles. The hotel has its own bar and restaurant.

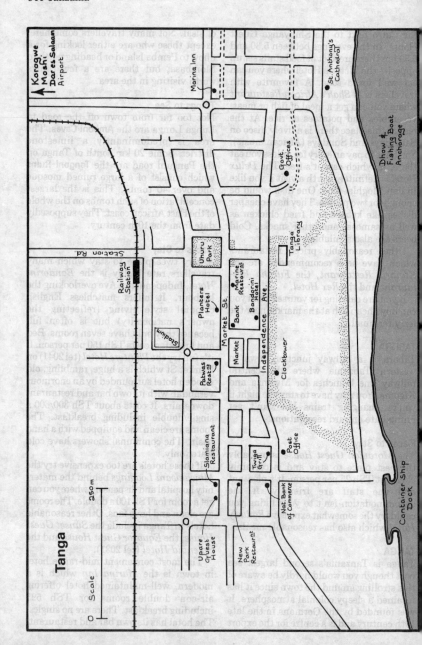

Tanga

0 Scale 250m

Korogwe
Moshi
Dar es Salaam
Airport

Station Rd

Railway Station

Stadium

Market St.

Uhuru Park

Planters Hotel

Patwas Rest.

Siamiana Restaurant

Bank
Marine Rest.
Bandarini Hotel

Market

Independence Ave.

Clocktower

Twiga Grill

Post Office

Upare Guest House

New Park Restaurant

Nat. Bank of Commerce

Govt. Offices

Tanga Library

St. Anthony's Cathedral

Marina Inn

Dhow & Fishing Boat Anchorage

Container Ship Dock

If you're going to spend this amount of money, however, it's probably better to stay at the *Baobab Hotel* (tel 40638) about five km from the centre. Prices are similar to the Marina Inn.

Places to Eat

The best place to go in Tanga for a cheap, tasty meal is the *Patwas Restaurant* opposite the market in the centre of town. It's a very clean, Asian-run restaurant which offers very reasonably priced meals at lunch and dinner times, and snacks and tea in between. The owner is very friendly. The *Marine Restaurant* on Market St is popular with local people at lunch time and meals are cheap but the food is average – boiled meat, sauce and potatoes etc. For a minor splurge, eat at the *Planters Hotel*. They're a bit on the slow side getting food together but it's worth waiting for.

The Offshore Islands

ZANZIBAR

The annals of Zanzibar read like a chapter from the *Arabian Nights* and doubtless evoke many exotic and erotic images in the minds of travellers. Also known as the Spice Island, it has lured travellers to its shores for centuries, some in search of trade, others in search of plunder. The Sumerians, Assyrians, Egyptians, Phoenicians, Indians, Chinese, Persians, Portuguese, Omani Arabs, Dutch and English have all been here at one time or another. Some stayed to settle and rule, notably the Shirazi Persians and the Omani Arabs. It was under the Omani Arabs that the island enjoyed its most recent heyday in the 19th century. The clove tree was introduced in 1818 and the Omani sultan's court was transferred from Muscat (near the entrance to the Persian Gulf) to Zanzibar not long after.

By the middle of the century Zanzibar had become the world's largest producer of cloves. At the same time it also became the largest slaving entrepôt on the east coast with some 40,000 to 45,000 slaves drawn from as far away as Lake Tanganyika passing through its market every year. Under these sultans, Zanzibar became the most important town on the East African coast. All other centres were subject to it and all trade passed through it until the establishment of the European Protectorates towards the end of the 19th century and the construction of the Mombasa to Kampala railway. The Omani sultans continued to rule under a British Protectorate right up to 1963 when independence was granted, but were overthrown the following year prior to the union of Zanzibar with mainland Tanganyika.

The many centuries of occupation and influence by various peoples has left its mark, particularly on the old stone town of Zanzibar which is probably one of the most fascinating places to visit on the whole east coast. Much larger than Lamu or Bagamoyo it is honeycombed with narrow, winding streets lined with whitewashed houses and magnificently carved, brass-studded doors. Regrettably, many of these have disappeared in recent years.

There are quaint little shops, bazaars, mosques, courtyards and squares, even a fortress and sultan's palace. Outside of town there are more palaces, Shirazi ruins, the famous Persian baths and that other perennial attraction – magnificent, palm-fringed beaches with warm, clear seas ideal for swimming.

Information

The tourist office (Tanzania Friendship Tourist Bureau) (tel 32344) on Creek Rd has an excellent map of Zanzibar town and the island for TSh 40. It is a worthwhile investment for exploring the alleys of the old town, though you'll probably still get lost from time to time.

Municipal buses run between the airport and town for a few shillings. They're marked 'Uwanja wa Ndege'. A taxi will cost about TSh 20.

There is an American-sponsored Malaria Centre in the old American Embassy building near the Starehe Club right across from the Ministry of Education. If you think you have the disease or would like to get checked out, they'll do this free of charge and give you an answer often the same day.

If you arrive by air it is no longer compulsory to change US$30 into shillings for every day of your intended stay at the official rate of exchange. *All* hotels on the island though must be paid for in foreign currency. They do not accept shillings bought on the mainland at the official rate of exchange and backed up by bank receipts. There is no compulsory change if you arrive by boat or dhow.

The Bank of Zanzibar changes travellers' cheques into US dollars cash, usually US$50 per day with a commission of US$1 but may change more with a little persuasion.

Things to See

Among the places you should make a point of seeing whilst strolling around the old stone town are the **Beit el Ajaib** (House of Wonders), one of the largest structures in Zanzibar; the **People's Palace**, formerly the sultan's palace; the **Arab Fort**, built by the Portuguese in 1700; the **Shirazi Mosque**, which dates back to 1107; the **Old Slave Market** where the first Anglican cathedral in East Africa was built; **Livingstone House**, the base for the missionary-explorer's last expedition before he died; and the **Dhow Harbour**. The **National Museum** is also worth a visit for its displays cataloguing the history of the island though it's becoming run-down these days. Entry costs TSh 10.

On the outskirts of the town, it's worth visiting the **Maruhubi Palace** built by Sultan Sayyid Bargash to house his harem. Further afield are the well-preserved **Kidichi Persian Baths** built by Sultan Sayyid Said for his Persian wife on

Zanzibar

the highest point on the island (153 metres), and the **Old Slave Caves** near the famous Mangapwani beach about 15 km north of Zanzibar. The caves were used for illegal slave trading after it was finally abolished by the British in the late 1800s. There are buses to within one km of the caves from the bus station in town. Otherwise it's possible to rent a bicycle for the day either from a shop close to the Malindi Guest House or from an old man named Isaac opposite the Air Tanzania office. The charge is usually TSh 10 per hour or TSh 60 per day. Bicycles can be put on the roofs of local buses if you get tired of pedalling.

Just off the coast of Zanzibar town are a number of islands. The most famous of these is **Prison Island** (Kibandiko Island), about five km from Zanzibar, on which there is, as the name suggests, an old prison (which was never used), a disused hospital, a beautiful beach and bunch of giant land tortoises which are large enough to ride (but don't even consider it!) There is a bar and restaurant on the island.

To get there you have to take a boat from the dhow harbour. The fare is whatever you can bargain it down to according to the amount of time you want to spend there. Get a small group together so you can share the costs. Foreigners have to pay an entrance fee of US$1 to visit the island.

There are other ruins around the island. Some of them are Portuguese – at **Mvuleni** north of Mkokotoni; and others are Shirazi – near Kizimkazi in the south, and on the island of **Tumbatu** (13th century), which is off the north-west coast. The ruins of **Dimbani Mosque** in Kizimkazi carries an inscription round the *mihrab*, dated 1107, which is the oldest inscription yet found in East Africa.

Those with an interest in wildlife might like to arrange a visit to **Jozani Forest** which is the last remaining red monkey sanctuary in the world.

The **Festival of Idd el Fitr** (the end of Ramadan) lasts about four days here and is worth trying to get to if you're in the area when it's on. At the same time there is the Zanzibarian equivalent of the tug o' war at Makunduchi in the south of the island where men from the south challenge those from the north by beating each other silly with banana branches. After that the women of the town launch into a series of traditional folk songs then the whole town eats and dances the night away. Don't miss it.

The Zanzibar beaches are dealt with later.

Places to Stay

All hotel accommodation on the island has to be paid for in foreign currency. Although this was the case at most of the hotels for years, until the new ruling came into force in July 1985 some of the budget hotels would always allow you to pay in local currency subject to certain conditions. There are now no exceptions. Even staying with friends who live there requires a special permit (though it's easily obtained).

Although the hotels all demand payment in hard currency there is one place where you can pay in shillings. The person to ask for is Musa Maisara who offers accommodation in his house on Nyerere Rd just after the junction with Abdallah Mzee Rd on the sea front. He has six rooms which vary in price between TSh 450 and TSh 700 a double (negotiable). He's a very pleasant man and can help if you need information. Everyone knows him so just ask if you can't find the house.

The cheapest hotel is the *Wazazi Guest House* which costs US$3 per person. To find it, face Africa House and go right taking the first alley on the left. About five metres from the corner above a darkened doorway you'll see the sign. It's often full and even if it isn't the manager is likely to tell you that it is. There's water only from midnight until early morning.

Similar is the *Warere Guest House* behind the Ciné Afrique near the port.

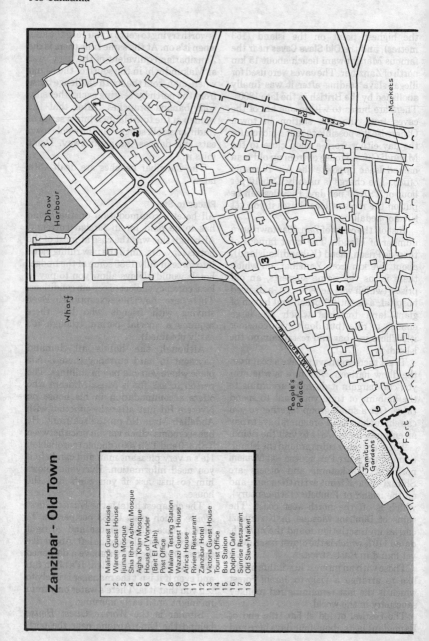

Zanzibar - Old Town

1   Malindi Guest House
2   Warere Guest House
3   Ijunaa Mosque
4   Shia Ithna Asheri Mosque
5   Agha Khan Mosque
6   House of Wonder
    (Beit El Ajaib)
7   Post Office
8   Malaria Testing Station
9   Wazazi Guest House
10 Africa House
11 Riviera Restaurant
12 Zanzibar Hotel
13 Victoria Guest House
14 Tourist Office
15 Bus Station
16 Dolphin Café
17 Sunrise Restaurant
18 Old Slave Market

Dhow Harbour

Wharf

People's Palace

Jamituri Gardens

Fort

Markets

CREEK RD

MIZINGANI RD

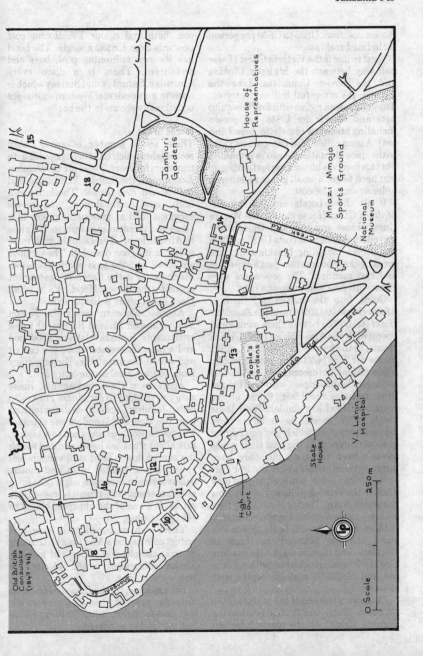

Rooms cost from US$5 to US$6 per person including breakfast.

Next in line is the *Victoria Guest House* half way between the Majestic Cinema and the Soviet Consulate. Like the Wazazi, it's often full but worth trying. They offer clean rooms with fan, mosquito nets and shower for US$6 per person including breakfast (omelette, bread and tea). A man called Miti can arrange visits to the spice plantations if you're interested but this involves hiring a car for the day, so you need to get a small group together in order to share the cost.

If all these hotels are full try the *Malindi Guest House* close to the Warere Guest House and the port. Quite a few travellers stay here. It costs US$5 to US$6 per person including breakfast but the breakfasts are poor value – just a cup of tea and two mandazi. The rooms are very clean with fans and mosquito nets.

Going into the mid-range, there is *Africa House* (tel 30708) and the *Zanzibar Hotel* (tel 30309) both of them owned and operated by the Afro-Shirazi Party. Africa House, in the former 'British Club', offers rooms for US$14/24/32 a single/double/triple without bathroom and US$15/28/34 a single/double/triple with bathroom. Price includes breakfast. Prices at the Zanzibar Hotel are similar. Both these hotels offer meals to residents and nonresidents alike which you can pay for in local currency. In the past their meals haven't been too good but they have improved considerably over the last year or so. Africa House, however, is good for a drink in the evening while you're watching the sun go down. The bar is on the 1st floor with a terrace overlooking the ocean.

More expensive still is the *Spice Inn* about half way between the House of Wonders and the market. Rooms are US$22/27 a single/double without air-con and US$28/33 a single/double with air-con.

At the very top end of the market is the *Bwawani Hotel* (tel 30200) overlooking Funguni Creek. All the rooms have air-con, bath and colour TV. Rooms cost upwards from US$30 a single. The hotel has its own swimming pool, bars and restaurant. There is a disco every Thursday, Saturday and Sunday which is open to nonresidents. Western videos are occasionally shown in the bar.

Places to Eat

There are a number of good, cheap restaurants which have been popular with travellers for years. These are the *Dolphin Restaurant*, the *Sunrise Restaurant* and the *Riviera Restaurant*. The latter is a fairly new establishment and serves excellent food at reasonable prices in a clean and pleasant atmosphere. It's close to Africa House. The Dolphin used to be good but it's gone downhill. The servings are small and the food poorly prepared. Much better is the *Camlurs Restaurant* opposite the Africa Hotel. It's a small place but it offers delicious food.

Another place to try is the *Falcon Restaurant* off Malawi Rd near the new apartments. It offers relatively good food and a pleasant terrace where you can sit and watch the street life. For hot, spicy food, go for a meal at the *Spice Inn*.

Apart from these restaurants, make sure you go along to *Forodhani Park* (also called Jamituri Gardens) on the waterfront near the House of Wonders one evening. The townspeople gather then to socialise, talk about what has happened and watch the sun go down. Food stall vendors sell spicy curries, roasted meat and maize, cassava, smoked octopus, sugar cane juice and ice cream at extremely reasonable prices. It's one of the cheapest places to eat in Zanzibar.

There's an unnamed fruit juice and yogurt café run by a Mrs Luis on Gizenga St near the old post office and near Dr Metha's dispensary in the old city. It's well worth a visit.

For a splurge, try the *Bwawani Hotel* on Saturday evening when they have an all-you-can-eat buffet. It's a little expensive but the food is wonderful.

The Beach Resorts

There are some superb beaches in Zanzibar, the majority being on the east coast. Ask any traveller who has stayed there what they think of them and you're going to wonder whether they're describing some born-again paradise. 'Perfect honeymoon destination' and 'I loved every minute of it. Fresh fish and lobster every day and a beautiful deserted beach less than six metres from the front step' are typical of what we get through the mail. Tranquil and beautiful they certainly are but they are not for those who cannot enjoy paradise without artificial sweeteners like electricity, hot and cold running water, luxury apartments, swimming pools and discos. Paradise here is simple and uncomplicated. That's why the beaches are largely deserted and you don't have to give a second thought to getting mugged just by walking up the beach.

Places to Stay The tourist office in Zanzibar maintains a number of bungalows at the best beaches – Bwejuu, Chwaka, Jambiani, Makunduchi and Uroa. Most of them are priced on the basis that they will sleep five people comfortably but will easily take six at a pinch. As with other accommodation on Zanzibar, you must pay for these bungalows in foreign currency though we have heard of travellers who have simply gone to one or another village and asked around for accommodation in local houses. Naturally you'd pay for this type of accommodation in local currency. Most people rate Jambiani and Bwejuu as the best beaches.

Rates for the tourist bungalows vary but are between US$20 per night (for the whole bungalow) for up to five people plus US$2 per person per night over five people. Kerosene lanterns are provided and water is usually drawn from a well. At Jambiani, the caretaker, Hassan Haji, is very helpful and friendly. If you ask him, he'll catch crabs and fish during the day for you and his wife will cook them up with coconut rice and spicey sauces in the evening. Their charges are very reasonable indeed. During the day people will come round with coconuts and other fruits for sale. All you have to do is relax. There is one public bus daily in either direction between Jambiani and Zanzibar town (it departs Jambiani about 5.30 am and can take up to four hours).

PEMBA

While many travellers make it to Zanzibar, very few ever make the journey to Pemba Island north of Zanzibar. Nevertheless, it's a very laid back, friendly island and completely untouched by tourism, although the beaches tend to be difficult to get to. Cloves are the mainstay of its economy. The island was never as important as Zanzibar or other settlements on the coast but it has had some remarkable associations during its history.

There is a fortified settlement and the remains of a palace destroyed by the Portuguese in 1520 at Pujini on the east coast which were apparently built by conquerors from the Maldive Islands! It seems, however, that they were not particularly welcome – one of the rulers of this town was known as Mkame Ndume (Milker of Men) because of the amount of work he extracted from his subjects. Later on, after the expulsion of the Portuguese from this part of East Africa, Pemba was taken over first by the rulers of Paté (in the Lamu archipelago), then by the rulers of Mombasa and finally by the sultans of Zanzibar.

There are dhows from Tanga and from Zanzibar. The former usually dock at Wete, the most northerly of the islands' three towns and the latter at Mkoani, the most southerly. From Tanga the fare is generally around TSh 200 and the boats take all night plus you need permission from the District Commissioner before you can sail. The boats from Zanzibar are fairly frequent, cost about TSh 250 and take about 12 hours.

Air Tanzania flies to Chake Chake from Tanga three times per week.

Places to Stay

There is a government-owned hotel in each of the three main towns and they're all reasonably priced. All the rooms in these three hotels have a bath though you shouldn't expect the services (water and electricity) to work too often.

MAFIA

You'll be extremely lucky to come across any traveller who has ever been to Mafia Island. The reason for this is fairly simple: accommodation and transport. There's very little of either. Transport alone can involve waiting around in Dar es Salaam until the Tanzania Coastal Shipping Company has a boat going there (which is not frequent). On the other hand Air Tanzania usually has a flight at least once a week.

Places to Stay

If you have your own tent then you could find a suitable spot to pitch it and buy fruit, vegetables and fish from local people. If not, you'll have to ask around among local people for a room or stay at the *Mafia Island Lodge* (tel 23491), Fisherman's Cove. It has 30 air-con rooms with private showers, etc, overlooking the sea. Single rooms with breakfast cost US$24 (payment in foreign currency only).

Mt Kilimanjaro

Kilimanjaro is Africa's highest mountain at 5894 metres. Snow capped and not yet extinct, it is an almost perfectly shaped volcano which rises sheer from the plains. It is one of the continent's most magnificent sights.

From cultivated farmlands on the lower levels, it rises through lush rainforest onto alpine meadow and finally across a barren lunar landscape to the snow and ice capped summit. The rainforest is home to many animals including elephant, buffalo, rhino, leopard and monkeys. You may even encounter herds of eland on the saddle between the summits of Mawenzi and Kibo. There are few travellers to East Africa who do not dream of reaching the summit and watching the dawn rise over hundreds of km of bushland below.

COSTS

These dreams are all very well but the government has decided to cash in on the idea and there is now a fee of US$380 per person (payable in US dollars) to do a trek. That sum pays for park entry fees, guides and porters but does not include food, equipment or transport to the trail heads. Add the cost of those and you are looking at US$500 unless you pay for the latter in local currency bought on the street market. All this for a five day trek!

The sheer expense has put many budget travellers completely off the idea, which is very sad. Unlike on Mt Kenya, most people who climb Kilimanjaro opt to go on an organised tour. There are good reasons for this. Most of the charges are standard and a guide is compulsory in any case. Also, since the minimum trip takes five days, organising your own involves a lot of running around and this is difficult without your own transport. Food supplies are very limited at Marangu so you'll be forced to do most of your shopping in Moshi. By the time you have the whole thing together you will have saved very little.

Not only that, but most people find they have very little energy left for cooking at the end of a day's climb. Having someone to do it for you can very well make the difference between loving and hating the trek.

The YMCA in Moshi and both the Kibo and Marangu Hotels in Marangu are the best places to arrange an organised tour. The Marangu Hotel has the best reputation (though it's not the cheapest).

Their guides are very good, the food is excellent and there are no extra charges for equipment which you may need – boots, blankets, etc. Whatever else you do, don't go through the Tanzania Tourist Corporation in Dar es Salaam. They will organise you a trek up Kilimanjaro – everything included – but it will cost you US$930 (payable in hard currency).

There may still be scope for negotiation on the US$500 minimum price for climbing Kilimanjaro. It's worth pursuing this at both the Marangu and Kibo Hotels but you might not get anywhere. The YMCA in Moshi, on the other hand, is still offering the trek at considerably less than this. Their price (for a minimum of three climbers) is US$240 per person (payable in hard currency) which covers park entry fees, rescue fees and hut fees; plus TSh 1620 for guides and porters and a further TSh 500 for food. The last two items are payable in local currency. These prices don't include transport to the park gate. The trek is for five days. If this is still within your budget then the summit of Kilimanjaro is within reach. If not, you'll have to give it a miss. It *is* possible to find deals as good as the YMCA if you ask around and negotiate, but don't count on it. It seems the government is determined to control the market on this trek. Don't forget that the guides and porters will expect a tip at the end of the climb. A T-shirt and/or TSh 100 is about average.

THE TRAILS

As on Mt Kenya, there are a number of routes to the summit but the most usual is the Marangu Trail (starting at Marangu village). The Mweka Trail (direct from Moshi), Umbwe Trail (west of Moshi), Machame Trail (west again from the Umbwe Trail), Shira Trail (from west of the mountain), and the northern routes from Loitokitok in Kenya are other possibilities. However, you are strongly advised to avoid the northern routes from Kenya until further notice. There are

stories in Nairobi of murders along these routes.

There are huts where you stay for the night on all these routes except the northern ones. The Mandara (about 2700 metres) and Horombo (3720 metres) huts might be better described as lodges in some ways. They consist of a large central chalet surrounded by many smaller huts and both can accommodate up to 200 people at a time. The Kibo hut (4703 metres) further up is more like a mountain hut of the type you are likely to find on Mt Kenya.

Too many people try to scale Mt Kilimanjaro without sufficient acclimatisation and end up with altitude sickness or, at least, nausea and headaches. This is obviously going to detract from your enjoyment of going up there and prevents quite a few people from reaching the summit.

To give yourself the best chance of reaching the top it is a very good idea to stay at the Horombo hut for two nights instead of one, though this will not guarantee you plain sailing. You won't get the same benefits staying two nights at the Kibo hut because it's too high and you're not going to be able to sleep very much. Remember the old adage about mountaineering – 'Go high, sleep low'. And, whatever else you do, walk *pole pole*, drink a lot of liquid, suck glucose tablets and don't eat too much (you won't feel like eating a lot anyway!). You also won't be the first person not to make it to the summit. Bear in mind that staying two nights at the Horombo hut is going to make the trek into a six day affair and increase your costs. Make sure that the guides and porters understand what your intentions are before you set off.

No specialist equipment is required to climb Kilimanjaro but you do need a good, strong pair of boots and plenty of warm clothing including gloves, a woollen hat and waterproof overclothes. If you lack any of these they can be hired from the YMCA in Moshi, the two hotels in

Marangu village or at the park entrance. Gear hired at the park entrance is reputedly of poor quality. You can climb Kilimanjaro at any time of year but you will probably encounter a lot of rain during April, May and November.

Before you go up Kilimanjaro we strongly recommend that you buy or at least read the Mountain Club of Kenya's, *Guide to Mount Kenya & Kilimanjaro* (1981), edited by Iain Allan. You can get it either direct from the Mountain Club (PO Box 45741, Nairobi) or from bookshops in Nairobi. You will not be able to buy it in Tanzania.

The Marangu Trail

This is the trail which most visitors take.

Day 1 Starting from the Marangu National Park gate at 1800 metres. It's a fairly easy three to four hours walk through thick rainforest to the Mandara hut. There's often quite a lot of mud along this route so wear good boots.

Day 2 Next day the route climbs steeply through giant heath forest and out across moorlands onto the slopes of Mawenzi and finally onto the Horombo hut. It's a difficult 14 km walk and you need to take it slowly. If your clothes are soaked through by the time you arrive at the Horombo hut, don't assume you will be able to dry them there. Firewood is relatively scarce and reserved for cooking.

Day 3 & 4 If possible, spend two nights at this hut and on the fourth day go to Kibo hut – about six to seven hours. Porters don't go beyond the Kibo hut so you'll have to carry your own essential gear from here to the summit and back. Don't skimp on the warm clothing. It's extremely cold on the summit and you'll freeze to death if you're not adequately clothed.

Day 5 Most people find it difficult to sleep very much at Kibo. Since you have to start out for the summit very early (around 1 or

2 am) to get to the summit just before sunrise, it's a good idea to stay awake the evening before. You'll feel better if you do this rather than trying to grab a couple of hours of fitful sleep. The mist and cloud closes in and obscures the views by 9 am and sometimes earlier. On the fifth day you descend from the summit to the Horombo hut, spend the night there then return to Marangu the following day.

Places to Stay – Trail Head If you are doing the trek through the YMCA and don't mind paying for their expensive transport to the park entrance on the first day of the climb, you can stay at their hostel in Moshi the night before. If you want to save money, and have camping equipment, you can camp either at the park entrance gate or at the *Marangu Hotel* for TSh 20 per person plus TSh 20 extra if you want a hot shower. The Marangu Hotel isn't too friendly to campers these days, however. If you have no tent, the national parks have a hostel near the entrance gate. It costs TSh 60 per person per night (with cold water showers only) or TSh 80 per person per night (with hot water showers). The cook at this hostel turns out delicious meals. Those who need a good rest and comfort before or after a climb can stay at the *Marangu Hotel* (tel Marangu 11), 32 km from Moshi. It costs TSh 350/700 for a single/double with own bathroom (hot water) and half board. You can also stay at the *Kibo Hotel* (tel Marangu 4), 40 km from Moshi, which costs about a third as much again as the Marangu Hotel. You may well have to pay for both these hotels in foreign currency. However, there will probably be scope for negotiation if you are organising the Kilimanjaro trek through them.

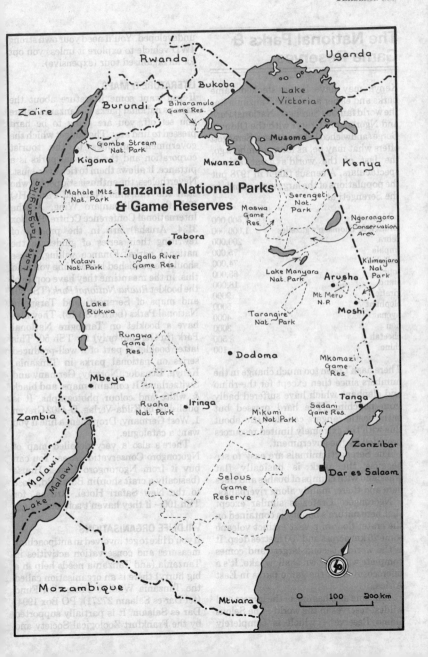

Tanzania National Parks & Game Reserves

The National Parks & Game Reserves

Kenya may have better stocked game parks and easier access but Tanzania has the world famous Serengeti National Park and Ngorongoro Crater with the Olduvai Gorge sandwiched between them. Serengeti offers what may be, as far as numbers go, the last of the world's great animal spectaculars. A census taken in 1978 put the populations of the largest mammals in the Serengeti at:

wildebeest	1,500,000
Grant's & Thomson's gazelles	1,000,000
zebra	200,000
impala	75,000
buffalo	74,000
topi	65,000
eland	18,000
giraffe	9000
elephant	5000
hyena	4000
lion	3000
cheetah	500
rhino	100

There hasn't been too much change in the numbers since then except for the rhino and elephant which have suffered badly from poaching. The hard pressed but enthusiastic rangers can do little about this with the extremely limited resources provided by the government.

The Serengeti animals are easy to see because the park is basically flat grassland with clumps of bushes and trees here and there, mainly along riverbanks.

Ngorongoro Crater is similar except that here nature's bounty is contained on the crater floor of a vast extinct volcano some 20 km across and 700 metres deep. It is the world's second largest and comes complete with its own shallow lake. It's a microcosm of all the game parks in East Africa.

Tanzania also has one of the largest and wildest reserves in the world – the Selous Game Reserve – which is completely undeveloped. You'll need your own strong 4WD vehicle to explore it unless you opt for an organised tour (expensive).

LITERATURE & MAPS

If you want some literature about the various national parks in Tanzania before you set off, you are going to be hard pressed to find any. The budget which the government provides to the tourist corporation and the national parks is a pittance. It allows them to tick over – just. Nevertheless, the enthusiastic people who staff the Tanzania National Parks HQ (6th floor, Kilimanjaro Wing, Arusha International Conference Centre, PO Box 3134, Arusha) are in the process of rewriting their series of guides to the national parks. Finance willing, these should be published by the time you read this. In the meantime they have copies of the booklet *Ruaha National Park* (TSh 50) and maps of Serengeti and Tarangire National Parks (both TSh 15). They also have a booklet on Tarangire National Park (in German only) for TSh 50. This latter booklet is part of a well-produced series on national parks in Tanzania, Kenya, Ecuador, Norway, Germany and Switzerland. It contains maps, and black & white and colour photographs. It is published by Kilda-Verlag, D-4402 Greven 1, West Germany. Drop them a line if you want a catalogue.

There's also a very detailed map of Ngorongoro Conservation Area. You can buy it from Ngorongoro Crater House (basically a craft shop) in Boma Rd, close to the New Safari Hotel, Arusha, for TSh 100 – if they haven't sold out.

WILDLIFE ORGANISATIONS

If you'd like to get involved in antipoaching measures and conservation activities in Tanzania (and Tanzania needs help in a big hurry) there is an organisation called the Tanzania Wildlife Protection Fund (tel Dar es Salaam 27271), PO Box 1994, Dar es Salaam. It is partially supported by the Frankfurt Zoological Society and does what it can, given the funds available, to protect wildlife and their habitats. It helps in the recovery of endangered animal and plant species. It also funds research into the management of wildlife and the impact on their habitats by human beings. Enquiries are welcome.

PARK FEES

As with Mt Kilimanjaro, the government has excelled itself in squeezing the maximum number of tourist dollars out of visitors to the national parks. It now costs US$10 per person per day plus US$75 per day for a non-Tanzanian registered vehicle (but only about US$12.50 per day for a Tanzanian registered one). Then there's the cost of camping. It is US$15 per person per day for established sites and US$20 per person per day for nonestablished sites. All these fees are payable in foreign currency only. Furthermore if you pass through two park entry gates in one day (Lake Manyara to Ngorongoro and Ngorongoro to Serengeti, for instance) then you pay twice. This means it's going to cost you US$50 in park fees alone to go on a five day safari of Lake Manyara, Ngorongoro and Serengeti. None of these fees are 'negotiable'. The national parks are open daily from 6 am to 7 pm.

PLACES TO STAY

Accommodation at all the park lodges must also be paid for in foreign currency. They're all priced around US$40/50 for a single/double for bed and breakfast. However, there is a 50% discount on prices from the Monday following Easter Sunday until 30 June. Unlike the park entry fees though, there may be scope for negotiation in paying for the lodges in local currency depending on which safari company you go through. We obviously can't be specific about this otherwise it would lead to problems for the companies concerned. A little leg work should unearth them. Certainly all meals and drinks at the lodges can be paid for in local currency. So make sure that in reserving and paying for lodges in advance you only book for bed and breakfast. If you book for full board in advance you will pay for the lot in foreign currency.

GETTING THERE & AROUND
Hiring Vehicles

Except for those with their own transport, most travellers go through safari companies when visiting the national parks. There are sound reasons for this as opposed to hiring your own vehicle. Not only does hiring a vehicle cost an arm and a leg but most vehicles are poorly maintained and fuel is scarce if not impossible to find outside of the cities. Even in places where there are petrol and/or diesel pumps, they will usually only sell you a limited amount. If you want more, you pay for it at black market rates – up to three times the pump price. Taking your own vehicle will also preclude any possibility you might have of negotiating a deal for paying in shillings at the lodges.

If you decide to hire a vehicle you are looking at a minimum of TSh 500 per day including insurance plus TSh 20 per km for a 4WD Land Rover (petrol or diesel). Don't take anything less than a 4WD except in the dry season and even then you might have problems in places.

Hitching

Hitching a lift to the national parks in Tanzania is usually a complete waste of time. You may be able to get to Lake Manyara and even to Karatu (between Lake Manyara and Ngorongoro) but you won't get any further.

Organised Safaris

Safaris to Arusha National Park, Tarangire National Park, Lake Manyara National Park, Ngorongoro Conservation Area and Serengeti National Park are all best arranged in Arusha where there are plenty of companies to choose from. Visits to Sadani Game Reserve, Mikumi National Park, Ruaha National Park and Selous Game Reserve should be arranged in Dar es Salaam. Most of the safari companies offer a range of possibilities to suit all tastes and pockets, though cost and reliability vary widely. To a large extent you get what you pay for but this isn't always the case.

Naturally, if a bunch of people go on a safari with a certain company, have an excellent time and there are no hitches like vehicle breakdowns then they are going to recommend that company to others. If the company also fixes them up with prebooked accommodation at the park lodges payable in local currency then that's a double plus for them. The trouble is, all that's required to convert an enthusiastic recommendation into a scathing condemnation for many travellers is if the vehicle breaks down for half a day, especially on a four to five day tour of Ngorongoro and Serengeti.

We get letters all the time with these two opposing points of view about particular companies. Some of the complaints are justified. Others are simply bad luck. There's obviously a lot which companies can do to head off foreseeable problems. The main one is to have well-maintained vehicles. But, in Tanzania, this is easier said than done. Spare parts demand the expenditure of scarce foreign currency and there are harsh government restrictions on this. Also, if the company you go through tries hard to cater for budget travellers and allows you to pay in local currency without seeing your currency declaration form, then it's hardly fair to make the most of this and then turn around and be totally condemnatory if you lose half a day because of a breakdown. All the same, you'd be surprised how many people want their bread buttered on both sides.

We have received a lot of scathing letters in the recent past about a certain company in Arusha whose vehicles were supposedly unreliable and their drivers or guides unable to do much more than change a wheel or put on a new fan belt. There were, it's true, a few more serious allegations

such as drivers substituting water for brake fluid in leaking hydraulic systems but it's impossible to substantiate this.

I tried this company out a little while ago. The trip was to Manyara, Ngorongoro and Serengeti in a full Land Rover in the middle of the wet season. The road between Manyara and Serengeti was just a sea of mud and there were whole lines of bogged trucks and buses broadside across the road. Other than one puncture, we didn't have a single breakdown or delay. The driver was superb and we all paid for the entire trip including lodges (though not, of course, park entry fees) in local currency. And it was all done with one bald back tyre. Alright, you can be lucky, but that's the name of the game in Tanzania.

So, if you break down, don't whinge; count your blessings, get out and lend a hand, get your hands dirty and get back on the road. This is a safari after all! The only thing I was disappointed about was the parsimony of two or three of the passengers when it came to giving the driver a tip at the end of the safari. You wouldn't believe how tight fisted some people can be!

Bear in mind all these details when you're choosing which safari company to go through and get several quotes first. At least in Arusha, you'll come across many companies which can offer budget prices at comparable rates. You pay your own park entrance fees (in foreign currency), the transport, driver, guide and maybe accommodation in local currency. Most of the cheaper companies (though not all) have offices in the Arusha International Conference Centre. They include Star Tours (Room 138); Sengo Safaris (Room 155); Wapa Safaris (Room 225); Ranger Safaris (Room 332); Lions Safaris (Room 435); Wilderness Safaris/Takims Holidays, and Sable Safaris (Room 517). There are others scattered around town.

It wouldn't be fair to suggest that the following list of companies in Arusha is exhaustive but we do recommend that you check them out before deciding who to go with. They are the ones most used by budget travellers.

Star Tours
    PO Box 1099, AICC, Ngorongoro Wing, Room 138/140, Arusha (tel 3181 ext 2281 or 2285 after hours)
Arumeru Tours & Safaris
    PO Box 730, Seth Benjamin St, Arusha (tel 2780)
Taurus Tours & Safaris
    PO Box 1254, Boma St (next door to the New Safari Hotel), Arusha (tel 2388 - 24 hours per day)
Wildersun Safaris & Tours
    PO Box 930, Sokoine Rd, Arusha (tel 3880)

These companies will give you a fair spectrum of the prices which you'll have to pay to visit Manyara, Ngorongoro and Serengeti ranging from budget to relatively expensive. Whatever else you do, don't go through African Wildlife Tours, India St, close to the YMCA. The prices of their tours are pure banditry.

Costs For the cheapest safaris you are looking at a minimum of TSh 28,000 for a five day, four night safari of Lake Manyara, Ngorongoro and Serengeti. This includes transport, a driver and guide plus a (compulsory) accompanying guide down onto the crater floor at Ngorongoro. So, shared between six people that's about TSh 4700 per person. This does not include the park entry fees or accommodation. Park entry fees will be US$60 per person and accommodation at the lodges, if you can pay for them in local currency, will be about TSh 2050 (including breakfast and dinner). A self catered lunch (buy food in Arusha before leaving) will be extra as will drinks at the lodges and a tip for the driver and guide. All up, it comes to about US$125 per person.

All the US dollar prices in this section (except the park entry fees) assume that you are buying your local currency at the street rate of exchange. If that's what you

are doing then the safari prices are comparable to those in Kenya. If you have to pay in dollars then you're going to need a rich uncle.

TARANGIRE NATIONAL PARK

This national park covers quite a large area south-east of Lake Manyara mainly along the course of the Tarangire River and the swamp lands and flood plains which feed it to the east. During the dry season, the only water flows along the Tarangire River. The park fills with herds of zebra, wildebeest and kongoni which stay until October when the short rains allow them to move to new pastures. Throughout the year, however, you can see eland, lesser kudu, various species of gazelle, buffalo, giraffe, waterbuck, impala and elephant and you may see the occasional rhino. For ornithologists, the best season is from October to May.

The only trouble with this park is that there is no cheap accommodation regardless of what you might be told in Arusha or Dar es Salaam. There's only a luxurious tented camp at TSh 500 a double with own shower and toilet with meals at TSh 125 a pop.

The animals in this park are very timid because there are so few visitors.

LAKE MANYARA NATIONAL PARK

Manyara National Park is usually visited as the first stop on a safari which takes in this park, Ngorongoro and Serengeti. It's generally a bit of a let down apart from the hippos since the large herds of elephant which used to inhabit the park have been decimated in recent years. Because the park is too small they invade adjoining farmland for fodder during the dry season. Naturally, local farmers have been none too pleased and once outside the park boundaries the elephants are fair game (and their ivory worth a lot of money).

Even the waterbirds which come to nest here (greater and lesser flamingoes in particular) can usually only be seen from a distance because there are no roads to the lake shore. You will certainly see wildebeest, giraffe and baboon. It's probably true, however, that what you see here depends on how long you are prepared to stay. For most people (and most tours) that's just a day.

Places to Stay

There are two camp sites just outside the park entrance which itself is just down the road from the village of Mto wa Mbu (River of Gnats or Mosquito Village according to various translations but, whichever one you choose, it's true). Camp site No 2 is probably the best. It costs TSh 40 per person. It also has *bandas* for TSh 200 which contain two beds, blankets and sheets and have running water, toilets and firewood. However, you need to beware of thieving baboons. Insect repellent and/or a mosquito net would be very useful. There's also a *Youth Hostel* of sorts here but it can't be recommended unless you're in love with mosquitoes. *Fig Tree Farm*, about two km from the park entrance has also been recommended by some travellers. It offers accommodation for TSh 75 per person and excellent meals.

You can stay in budget accommodation in the village of Mto wa Mbu. There are three very basic hotels. The *Mzalendo Guest House* and the *Rombo Guest House* are both on the main road. The *Rift Valley Bar & Guest House* is on the dirt 'square' next to the petrol station.

The best place to stay, however, especially if you don't have a tent, is the *Starehe Bar & Hotel* on the escarpment up above Lake Manyara. It's about 100 metres off to the left on the turn-off for Lake Manyara Hotel (signposted) on the main road from Mto wa Mbu to Ngorongoro. It's not an obvious place but there is a sign. It's rustic, very clean, very comfortable and there are no bugs, mosquitoes or electricity (though candles are provided). It costs TSh 200 a single (without bathroom) and TSh 300 a double (with bathroom). There are only cold water showers but the staff are eager to please

and very friendly. They'll cook you superb and generous meals which you will not be able to finish for TSh 120 per person. They also have great breakfasts which are excellent value.

There is a reasonably interesting market in Mto wa Mbu – mainly fabrics and crafts. However, they see a lot of tourists so you'll discover few bargains that you can't already find in Arusha.

Lake Manyara Hotel (tel 3300,3113) is where the rich people stay. It sits right on the edge of the escarpment overlooking Lake Manyara about three km along the same turn-off as the Starehe Bar & Hotel. It costs about US$40/50 for a single/double with breakfast (only foreign currency accepted). There are flower gardens, a swimming pool, curio shop and what one guide to Tanzania calls a 'specious restaurant and bar' (!?).

NGORONGORO CONSERVATION AREA

There can be few people who have not heard, read or seen film or TV footage of this incredible 20-km-wide volcanic crater packed with just about every conceivable species of wildlife to be found in East Africa. The views from the 700-metre-high crater rim are incredible. Though the wildlife might not look too impressive from up there, when you get to the bottom you'll very quickly change your mind. It has been compared to Noah's Ark and the Garden of Eden. Though a little fanciful, it might have been almost true at the turn of the century. That is, before so much of the wildlife in East Africa was destroyed by the 'great white hunters' armed with the latest guns and an egoistic mentality. It doesn't quite come up to those expectations these days but you certainly won't be disappointed.

You'll definitely see lion, elephant, rhino, buffalo and many of the plains herbivores like wildebeest, Thomson's gazelle, zebra and reedbuck. As well, you'll see thousands of flamingoes wading in the shallows of Lake Magadi – the soda lake on the floor of the crater.

The animals don't have the crater entirely to themselves. Local Masai tribespeople have grazing rights down there and you may come across some of them tending their cattle. In the days when Tanzania was a German colony, there was also a settler's farm but that has long since gone.

Places to Stay

On the crater rim there is a choice of four places to stay and a camp site. The cheapest place is the *Usiwara Guest House* (often known as the Drivers' Lodge) where you can get a bed for TSh 90. Only one sheet is provided and there are no blankets so you are going to need a sleeping bag. You'll also need a padlock. The guesthouse is near the post office in Crater Village. You can buy cheap, simple food here. Otherwise you can eat at the *Ushirika Co-op Restaurant* which also offers good, cheap food.

Of the three lodges, the *Ngorongoro Rhino Lodge* is the first one you will come to, off to the left. It is the cheapest if there isn't much demand for rooms. In this case they'll offer you a 'special price' of US$9 for a room which will sleep up to three people. In the tourist season, however, it will cost US$16. The lodge is clean, tidy and hot water is available when the generators are running. Dinner costs TSh 350. It's on a beautiful site but somewhat out of the way and doesn't overlook the crater. You can also camp here, if you have your own tent, for US$6.

Next is the *Ngorongoro Crater Lodge* (tel Arusha 3530, 3303), an old rustic lodge built in 1937 which overlooks the crater. It has many detached cabins all with bath and toilet and is a very pleasant place to stay. The rooms are very clean, with towels, soap, toilet paper, a gas fire and hot water all the time (from gas heaters which work when you turn on the water). It's privately owned, so it may be possible to negotiate a price in local currency. You should do this in Arusha before you set out. They probably only accept foreign currency at the lodge itself.

If you can pay in shillings it costs TSh 450 a double for bed and breakfast during April, May and June and TSh 900 a double for bed and breakfast during the rest of the year. If you want eggs with your breakfast, however, this costs an extra TSh 40! If you have to pay in hard currency it will cost US$32/48 for a single/double (except during April, May and June when it's half price). Morning tea is delivered to your door at 6.30 am. A three course lunch or dinner here costs TSh 200 and may include something exotic like roast wildebeest leg. Lunch boxes to take with you down into the crater cost TSh 150. The bar, stuffed with hunting trophies from the old days, is a good place to meet people in the evening. Whenever it's cold, there will be a roaring log fire.

The *Ngorongoro Wildlife Lodge* (tel Arusha 3300, 3114) is between the Rhino Lodge and the Crater Lodge. It is a very modern building built right on the edge of the rim with superb views out over the crater. The rooms all face the crater and are centrally heated with bath and toilet. You must pay in foreign currency whatever time of year it is. Rooms cost around US$40/50 for a single/double with breakfast. There is a 50% discount during April, May and June. Meals are excellent and you can pay for them in local currency. The bar is a good place to meet people and, like the one at the Crater Lodge, has a log fire.

Most campers stay at the *Simba* site on the crater rim about two km from Crater Village. It costs US$15 per person. The site is guarded and has hot showers, toilets and firewood. It's also possible to camp on the floor of the crater but you must have a ranger with you and it costs US$30 per person per night! There's a general store at Crater Village but it only has a limited range of foodstuffs. So bring food with you from Arusha or eat at the lodges.

At Karatu about half way between Lake Manyara and Ngorongoro is *Gibb's Farm* run by a white Tanzanian family. According to most of the people who have stayed there, they offer the best accommodation and meals to be found in the whole country. It costs TSh 750 a double for bed and breakfast. If you don't want to stay there, you can buy either lunch or dinner. The food is excellent and the farm is beautifully situated. Gibb's Farm is signposted on the main road as you drive into Karatu from Manyara.

Getting There & Away

Only 4WD vehicles are allowed down in the crater except at times during the dry season when the authorities *may* allow 2WD combies to go down. The roads down into the crater are very steep, however, so if you are driving your own vehicle make sure it will handle the roads. It takes about 30 to 45 minutes to get down to the crater floor. Whether you are driving a vehicle or are on an organised tour, you must take a park ranger with you at a cost of TSh 75 per day (though they expect more). You can pay this in local currency.

It's also possible to hire a 4WD Land Rover at Crater Village from the same place where you collect a ranger. They cost TSh 1750 for half a day and TSh 2400 for the whole day (payable in shillings) However, there are often fuel shortages so don't count on being able to hire one. If they are not going down for this reason then enquire at the lodges about tours.

If you are trying to get to the crater under your own steam, there are private buses from Arusha at least as far as Karatu but it may be difficult to find anything going beyond there. There are also plenty of trucks as far as Karatu.

The State Transport Corporation in Arusha used to have buses to Lake Manyara, Ngorongoro and Seronera village in Serengeti. Shortages of fuel and buses have led to the service being suspended.

THE OLDUVAI GORGE

The Olduvai Gorge made world headlines in 1959 following the discovery by the Leakeys of fossil fragments of the skull of one of the ancestors of Homo sapiens. The fragments were dated at 1.8 million years old. The Leakeys were convinced by this and other finds that the fragments represented a third species of early humans which they dubbed *habilis*. They proposed that the other two (known as *Australopithecus africanus* and *A robustus*) had died out and that Homo habilis had given rise to modern humankind. The debate raged for two decades and is still unsettled. Meanwhile, in 1979, Mary Leakey made another important discovery in the shape of footprints at Laetoli which she claimed were of a man, woman and child. They were dated at 3.5 million years old. Since they were made by creatures which walked upright, this pushed back the dawn of the human race much further than had previously been supposed.

The gorge itself isn't of great interest unless you are archaeologically inclined. It has, however, acquired a kind of cult attraction among those who just want to visit the site where the evolution of early humans presumably took place. There is a small museum on the site too, which is only a 10 to 15 minute drive from the main road between Ngorongoro Crater and Serengeti. The museum closes at 3 pm but in the rainy season it's often not open at all. It's possible to go down into the gorge at certain times of year if you would like to see the sites of the digs.

Places to Stay

There is nowhere to stay in Olduvai. At the western end of the gorge though, where the creek which flows through it empties into Lake Ndutu there is the *Ndutu Safari Lodge* on the borders of the Serengeti National Park. There is both tent accommodation and chalets as well as a bar and restaurant. It costs approximately US$20 per person for bed and breakfast (payable in foreign currency).

You can also camp here if you have your own tent. It costs TSh 75 per person but there are no facilities at the camp site.

SERENGETI NATIONAL PARK

Serengeti, which covers a total of 14,763 square km, is Tanzania's most famous game park and is contiguous with Masai Mara in neighbouring Kenya. Here you can get a glimpse of what much of East Africa must have looked like before the 'great white hunters' began their mindless slaughter of the plains animals from the late 19th century onwards. To this, trophy hunters and poachers in search of ivory and rhino horn, have added a sickening toll. On the seemingly endless and almost treeless plains of the Serengeti are literally millions of hooved animals. They are constantly on the move in search of pasture, watched and pursued by those predators which feed off them. It's one of the most incredible sights you will ever see in your life. The numbers are simply mind boggling. Nowhere else will you see wildebeest, gazelle, zebra and antelope in such concentrations. It's pure magic!

The wildebeest, of which there are up to two million, is the chief herbivore of the Serengeti and also the main prey of the large carnivores such as lions and hyenas. They are well known for the annual migration which they undertake. It's a trek with many hazards. Not the least of these is the crossing of large rivers which can leave hundreds drowned, maimed or taken by crocodiles.

During the rainy season the herds are widely scattered over the eastern section of the Serengeti and Masai Mara in the north. These areas have few large rivers and streams and quickly dry out when the rains cease. When that happens the wildebeest concentrate on the few remaining green areas and gradually form huge herds which move off west in search of better pasture. At about the same time that the migration starts, the annual rut also begins. For a few days at a time while the herds pause, bulls establish territories which they defend against rivals. Meanwhile they try to assemble as many females as they can with which to mate. As soon as the migration resumes, the female herds merge again.

The dry season is spent in the western parts of the Serengeti at the end of which the herds move back east in anticipation of the rains. Calving begins at the start of the rainy season but, if it arrives late, anything up to 80% of the new calves may die due to lack of food.

Serengeti is also famous for its cheetahs and lions. (Many of the latter have collars fitted with transmitters so that their movements can be studied and their location known.) If you want to give yourself the chance of being in on a 'kill', however, then you are going to need a pair of binoculars. Distances are so great in this park that you'd probably miss one unless it happened close to the road.

The main road from Ngorongoro to Seronera village is a gravel road which is well maintained with the occasional *kopje* to one side or another. Kopjes are slight rises strewn with huge, smooth boulders which generally support a few trees and are often the lookouts of cheetahs.

You'll see plenty of Masai herding cattle all the way from Ngorongoro as far as Olduvai Gorge.

Places to Stay

Most budget travellers stay at either the camp site or the hostel close to the lodge near Seronera village. The camp site normally costs US$6 per person but there is usually scope for negotiation here. The hostel has dormitory style rooms with cold showers and toilets. They also cost US$6 per person per night. You need to bring your own bedding. Candles and a torch are also useful since there's no electricity. Basic meals are available in the village but the quality of the food is poor.

The other place to stay is the *Seronera Lodge* (tel Arusha 3842). This is a stunningly beautiful and very imaginative building constructed on top of and around a kopje with hyrax running around everywhere. They're so tame you can almost touch them. The bar and observation deck at this lodge is enormous and right on top of the kopje with the boulders having been incorporated into the design. Getting up to it on narrow stone steps between massive rocks is like entering Aladdin's Cave! The rooms are very pleasantly furnished and decorated. They all have a bathroom with hot water. Unfortunately, it costs US$38/49 for a single/double with breakfast except during April, May and June when there is a 50% discount. It *may* be possible to arrange to pay in shillings here (in which case it's an absolute bargain) but you must do this in Arusha before you set off. The lodge has a generator but they only switch it on between sunset and around midnight. Three course dinners are available and are good value. There are no guide books, maps, postcards or film for sale in the shop at the lodge.

North-east of Seronera village near the park border is the *Lobo Wildlife Lodge* (tel Arusha 3842). It is built into the faults and contours of a massive rock promontory overlooking the plains. It's very similar to the Seronera Lodge in terms of what it offers. It is somewhat cheaper though, at US$24/33 for a single/double with breakfast. There is a 50% discount during April, May and June.

MIKUMI NATIONAL PARK

Mikumi National Park covers an area of 3237 square km. It sits astride the main Dar es Salaam to Mbeya highway about 300 km from Dar es Salaam. Not many budget travellers seem to visit this park probably because of the lack of cheap accommodation but there is a lot of wildlife to be seen here. Elephant, lion, leopard, buffalo, zebra, impala, wildebeest and wart hog can be seen at any time of year. One of the principal features of Mikumi is the **Mkata River flood plain**, an area of lush vegetation, which attracts elephant and buffalo in particular.

Hippos can also be seen at **Hippo Pools** about five km from the park entrance gate.

For those on a budget, the only option for cheap accommodation is the camp site about four km from the park entrance gate. You need to bring all your own requirements except for water and firewood.

Other than this there is the *Mikumi Wildlife Lodge* (tel Dar es Salaam 23491) which is built around a watering hole and costs US$24/33 for a single/double. Also the *Mikumi Wildlife Camp* (tel Dar es Salaam 68631), a luxury tented camp, which costs slightly less than the lodge. You can only pay in foreign currency at both places but the lodge offers a 50% discount during April, May and June.

SELOUS GAME RESERVE

Little known but covering an area of 54,600 square km, Selous is probably the world's largest game reserve. It's the quintessential East African wilderness, largely untouched by humans. It is said to contain the world's largest concentration of elephant, buffalo, crocodile, hippo and wild dog as well as plenty of lion, rhino, antelope and thousands of dazzling bird species. The estimates are probably over optimistic because of poaching but there are supposedly some 100,000 elephants in this reserve. There is a good chance of seeing a herd several 100 strong.

Opened in 1905 it remained largely a trophy collectors' and big game hunters' preserve for many years. Only the northern tip of the reserve can be said to have been adequately explored. Most of it is trackless wilderness and almost impossible to traverse during the rainy season when floods and swollen rivers block access. The best time to visit is from July to March. In any case, the lodges and camp sites are closed from April to June.

One of the main features of the reserve is the huge Rufiji River which has the largest water catchment area in East

Africa. Massive amounts of silt are dumped annually during the wet season into the Indian Ocean opposite Mafia Island. For the rest of the year when the floods subside and the water level in the river drops, extensive banks of shimmering white and blonde sand are exposed.

In the northern end of the reserve where the Great Ruaha River flows into the Rufiji is **Stiegler's Gorge**. On average 100 metres deep and 100 metres wide, it is probably the most well known feature of the park. There's a cable car which spans the gorge for those who are game enough to go across. Most of the safari camps and the lodges are here. The gorge is named after the German explorer, Selous, who was killed here by an elephant in 1907.

Places to Stay

The only available camps and the lodge are expensive but if you have the money there are four camps: *Mbuyu Safari Camp* (tel Dar es Salaam 31957, 32671); *Stiegler's Gorge Safari Camp & Lodge* (tel Dar es Salaam 48221); *Beho Beho Safari Camp* (tel Dar es Salaam 68631/3), and *Rufiji River Camp* (tel Dar es Salaam 63546). They all cost around US$20/35 for a single/double with breakfast.

Getting There & Away

Visiting Selous Game Reserve isn't really feasible for budget travellers. In order to get there and drive around once inside, you need a strong 4WD vehicle. Hitching is out of the question. Also the lodge and the only available camps are expensive.

Without your own transport you will have to go through a tour company. Check with the following in Dar es Salaam: Rubada (tel 48221), PO Box 9230; Bushtrekker Safaris (tel 31957, 32671), PO Box 5350; Kearsley Travel & Tours (tel 20807), PO Box 801; Across Tanzania Safaris Ltd (tel 23121, 38748), PO Box 21996. You could also check out Ranger Safaris Ltd (tel 3074, 3023), PO Box 9, Arusha.

RUAHA NATIONAL PARK

Ruaha National Park was created in 1964 from half of the Rungwa Game Reserve and covers some 13,000 square km. Like the Selous, it's a wild, undeveloped area. Access is difficult but there's a lot of wildlife here as a result, particularly elephant, kudu, roan and sable antelope, hippo and crocodile. The Great Ruaha River which forms the eastern boundary of the park has spectacular gorges. The rest of the park though, is mostly undulating plateau averaging 1000 metres in height with occasional rocky outcrops.

Visiting the park is only feasible in the dry season from July to December. During the rest of the year the tracks are virtually impassable.

Places to Stay

If you do manage to get there, you can find accommodation in *rondavels* equipped with beds, showers and kitchen at *Msembe Camp*. Contact the Park Warden, Ruaha National Park, PO Box 369, Iringa.

Getting There & Away

As with the Selous, you need a strong, 4WD vehicle or to go on an organised tour. It's not really a possibility for budget travellers.

GOMBE STREAM NATIONAL PARK

This tiny park, which is primarily a chimpanzee sanctuary, is on the shores of Lake Tanganyika between Kigoma and the Burundi border. In recent years it has become very popular with travellers going north to or coming south from Burundi. The park is the site of Jane Goodall's research station which was set up in 1960. It's a beautiful place and the chimps are great fun. A group of them usually come down to the research station every day but if they don't the rangers generally know where to find them. You must have a guide with you whenever you are away from the station or the lake shore. This costs US$10 per party per day and the guides are mellow, interesting people.

Places to Stay

It's possible to camp on the lake shore. Firewood is available but bring your own utensils. There are also caged huts to stay in, each with six beds and a table and chairs. The huts are caged to keep the baboons out. A bed costs US$10 per night plus you will have to pay the standard park fee of US$15 per person – not a cheap visit these days!

You need to bring all your food with you though eggs and fish are sometimes available at the station. If you do run out of food you can get more at Mwangongo village about 10 km north. It has a market twice a week (enquire at the station as to the days). Be careful when walking between the cookhouse and the huts at the station, especially if you are carrying food. Baboons have jumped on quite a few people and robbed them of their food.

There's a well stocked library at the hostel.

Getting There & Away

There are no roads to Gombe Stream so the only way in is to take a small lake boat from either Ujiji or the first Tanzanian village over the border from Burundi. For details of these, see under Boat in the Getting There & Around section. The boats leave from the lake.

MAHALE MOUNTAINS NATIONAL PARK

This national park, like Gombe Stream, is mainly a chimpanzee sanctuary but you won't find it marked on most maps since it was created only on 14 June 1985. It's on the knuckle shaped area of land which protrudes into Lake Tanganyika about half way down the lake opposite the Zaïrois port of Kalemie. The highest peak in the park – Nkungwe – at 2460 metres ensures that moist air blowing in from the lake condenses there and falls as rain. This rain supports extensive montane forests, grasslands and alpine bamboo.

Numerous valleys intersect the mountains and some of them have permanent streams which flow into the lake. The eastern side of the mountains are considerably drier and support what is known as miombo woodlands. It's a very isolated area.

The animals which live in this park show closer affinities with western rather than eastern Africa. They include chimpanzee, brush-tailed porcupine, various species of colobus monkey including the Angolan black and white colobus, guinea fowl and mongoose. Scientists, mainly from Japan, have been studying the chimpanzees for 20 years and more than 100 of the animals have become habituated to human contact. Their population has dramatically increased since 1975 when local people were moved to villages outside the park which put a stop to poaching and field burning activities. This relocation has also led to the reappearance of leopard, lion and buffalo which were very rarely seen in the past.

Unlike other national parks in Tanzania, this is one which you can walk around – there are no roads in any case. Very few tourists come here because of the remoteness of the area but it's worth it if you have the time and initiative.

Places to Stay

Camping, at a cost of US$15 per day, is allowed in specific areas if you have equipment (there's none for hire). Otherwise a guesthouse is under construction at Kasiha village which should be complete by the time you read this. You need to bring all your food requirements with you from Kigoma since meals are not available here. It's a good idea to check with the park headquarters in Kigoma about current conditions, transport and accommodation before you set off. The park entry fee is the usual US$15 per head.

Getting There & Away

The only way to get to the park is by lake steamer from Kigoma using either the

MV *Liembe* or the MV *Mwongozo*. You have to get off at Mugambo (usually in the middle of the night) and take a small boat to the shore. From Mugambo you need to charter a small boat from either the local fishermen or merchants to Mahale (Kasiha

village) which should take about three hours. The schedule for the MV *Liembe* can be found in the Getting There & Around section. For the MV *Mwongozo* schedule you need to enquire in Kigoma.

Togo

Togo, like The Gambia further to the west, is an idiosyncratic legacy of 19th-century European colonialism. This narrow sliver of a country has brought together people from very different cultural and linguistic backgrounds without any discernible tribal rivalry. But there has been a good deal of political opposition to the military regime of Major-General Gnassingbé Eyadéma, which has ruled the country since 1967. Most of the opposition leaders live in exile in Paris. The Rassemblement du Peuple Togolais, founded by Eyadéma and the only legal political party in the country, for many years has actively sought out its opposition at a grass-roots level and brutally repressed former trade union radicals. As a result, many Togolese have sought political asylum abroad.

At the time of independence in 1960, it would have made a lot of sense to incorporate Togo into Ghana, especially as the border between them divides the Ewe heartland. A referendum in 1962 favoured integration, but it was blocked by the country's first president, Sylvanus Olympio. The opportunity to merge now seems to have passed.

Togo became a German colony in the 1894, but it wasn't until 1902 that pacification was complete. The Germans set about establishing plantations and building a communications network, until WW I intervened. After the war, the colony was divided between the British and French under a League of Nations mandate. The division of the Ewe people was not to their liking, and there emerged a nationalist movement centred around the unification of the territory. This was not to be. Not only were the French strongly opposed to it, but a plebiscite in the British part of the colony in 1956 led to its being incorporated into Ghana, which was about to be granted independence. The French part gained its independence in 1960 under the leadership of Olympio, and his party, the Comité de l'Unité Togolais.

Not long after independence, however, a major split developed between Olympio, a member of a powerful trading family and director of the British-financed United Africa Company, and the youth arm of his party, the Juvento. The Juvento had played an important part in the radicalisation of the nationalist movement and was not to be taken lightly. Nevertheless, Olympio tried to suppress it. He was overthrown in a military coup in 1963 and replaced by Nicolas Grunitzky, who had been brought back from exile in Paris. Grunitzky was overthrown by Eyadéma in a second military coup in 1967. Eyadéma has ruled ever since.

One of the ironies of Togo is that the north could produce sufficient millet, rice and yams to make the country self-sufficient in these foodstuffs. But it doesn't as a result of the long-term and seasonal migration of workers to Ghana. At any one time, an estimated 200,000 to 300,000 young Togolese men are working in Ghana.

Togo ran up some alarming debts when it was hit by a drought in the late 1970s at a time when its borders with Nigeria had been closed for several years. Servicing the debts began to consume so much of the country's budget that the IMF stepped in with standby loans.

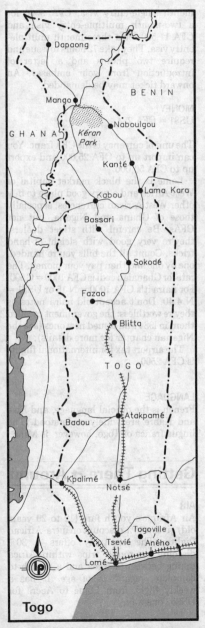

Togo

Facts

GEOGRAPHY & CLIMATE

Togo has a coastline of only 56 km, yet it stretches inland for some 540 km. The centre of the country is mountainous and forested with deciduous trees. The north and south are savannah. The main rainy season lasts from April to July, with a shorter rainy period from October to November.

PEOPLE

Togo is densely populated with around three million inhabitants. The largest tribal groups are the Ewe and Kabre.

VISAS

Visas are required by all, except nationals of Belgium, Britain, Canada, Denmark, France, West Germany, Italy, Luxemburg, the Netherlands, Norway, Sweden and the USA.

In Africa there are Togolese embassies in Accra (Ghana), Kinshasa (Zaïre), Lagos (Nigeria), Libreville (Gabon) and Tripoli (Libya). Where there is no Togolese embassy, visas can generally be obtained from the French embassy.

Visa extensions can be obtained from the Sûreté National in Lomé. They cost CFA 2500 for a month, with four photos and the *timbres fiscaux* purchased from the government building around the corner. They take three days to issue and the bureaucracy can be a headache.

Exit visas are no longer required, regardless of how long you stay.

Other Visas

There are many embassies in Lomé, among them are those of Egypt, France, Gabon, Ghana, Libya, Nigeria, Tunisia and Zaïre.

The French Consulate issues visas for Burkina Faso, CAR, Chad, Djibouti, Ivory Coast, Mauritania and Senegal. It's open from 8.30 to 11.30 am Monday to Friday. All visas cost CFA 3000, require two photos and take 48 hours to issue. They are usually good for a stay of three months. To get to the consulate (which is in a different building from the French Embassy) from Hotel Le Benin on Blvd de la République, go up Ave General de Gaulle for one block before taking the small road off to the right. The consulate is halfway up the block.

Benin There is no Benin embassy in Lomé. Travellers from Togo, however, can now get a visa at the Ouidah border on the Lomé to Cotonou road. A one-month visa costs CFA 1000 and is issued while you wait. This is the only border that issues Benin visas.

Gabon These cost CFA 4000 and take one month to issue as all applications are referred to Libreville.

Ghana The embassy is opposite the Hospitalier de Tokain (signposted) off Route de K'Palimé. It's about two to three km from the city centre and is open from 8 am to 2 pm Monday to Friday. Visas cost CFA 5750 for Commonwealth citizens and CFA 9000 for other nationals, require two photos and take three days to issue. Have the name of a good hotel in Accra handy when applying for a visa.

Mali While there is no Mali embassy in Lomé, embassy staff are supposed to visit the Air Mali office on Thursday, Friday and Saturday. Their hours are irregular, so it's a hit-and-miss affair. If you miss, you'll have to go elsewhere, like Accra or Ghana.

Nigeria The embassy is on Blvd Circulaire, Lomé. The cost of a visa depends on your nationality, but is usually CFA 1360. Two photos are required and the visa should be issued in 24 hours or less, though the bureaucracy can be a problem.

Zaïre The Zaïre Embassy is near the Nigerian Embassy on Blvd Circulaire, Lomé. Visas cost CFA 4500 for a one-

month single-entry visa, CFA 9000 for a two-month multiple-entry visa and CFA 11,500 for a three-month multiple-entry visa. They take 72 hours to issue and require two photos and a letter of introduction from your embassy. An onward ticket may be demanded.

MONEY
US$1 = CFA 284

The unit of currency is the CFA franc. You can import up to CFA 25,000 and export up to CFA 50,000.

Lomé is the black market capital of West Africa and a very good place to buy other West African currencies, especially those of Ghana and Nigeria, but not CFAs. Be careful with street dealers: they're very good with sleight-of-hand tricks. Count all the bills you're handed, one by one and then pay your money. The rate for Ghanaian cedi is CFA 1000 = C 500. For naira it's CFA 1000 = N 15 or US$1 = N 4.40. Don't accept old naira notes as they're worthless: the government recalled them in 1984 and issued new ones (see the Nigerian chapter for more details).

The airport tax for international flights is CFA 2500.

LANGUAGE
French is the official language, and Ewe and Kabre are widely understood. The lingua franca of Togo, however, is Mina.

Getting There & Around

AIR
Air Afrique's youth fare (12 to 29 years old) gives a 45% discount on intra-African flights. The company offers a 30% discount on round trips within Africa taking between a week and a month to complete, regardless of age. It has a weekly flight from Lomé to Accra for US$52 one way.

Nigerian Airways flies from Lomé to Nairobi, via Lagos, for CFA 110,000.

Air Afrique, Air Gabon and Air Zaïre all fly from Lomé to Libreville (Gabon), but the flights are expensive at around CFA 90,000. Air Zaïre is very liberal about excess baggage.

ROAD

Except in the extreme north, roads are very good, and sealed all the way to the Burkina Faso border. Hitching is fairly easy, but becomes progressively more difficult the further north you go as traffic thins.

Minibus & Taxi

There is an excellent network of minibuses, which cost about the same as pick-up trucks but are more comfortable and usually less crowded.

Taxis cost about CFA 1000 per 100 km. A backpack can cost up to CFA 125 extra, depending on the distance and your haggling ability.

Journey times depend a lot on how many police checkpoints there are. They used to occur every 30 km or so, but are now being phased out. There is no direct service between Sokodé and Dapaong.

Minibuses and taxis are available to Benin and Nigeria from Lomé. Extra is charged for baggage.

Some examples of minibus fares are:

To get to Ouagadougou (Burkina Faso), it's cheaper to travel in stages. To do this, rise early and take a minibus (CFA 3000) or Peugeot taxi (CFA 4000) to Dapaong. From there, take a taxi to Ouagadougou (CFA 3500). This leg takes eight to 11 hours, including three hours at the border. A direct taxi from Lomé to Ouagadougou costs CFA 12,500, plus baggage, and takes 24 hours.

If the border is closed between Togo and Ghana, which it often is, take a short detour from Dapaong to Burkina Faso before going to Bawku. If the border is open, there are direct buses from Dapaong to Bawku.

TRAIN

The main line runs north from Lomé to Blitta, via Atakpamé. There are branch lines from Lomé to K'Palimé, and Lomé to Aného. The train to Blitta leaves Lomé daily about 5.45 am and arrives between 1 and 1.30 pm. It then turns around and arrives back in Lomé about 9 pm. First class is comfortable. Second class is crowded and costs CFA 1150.

There are usually two trains daily to K'Palimé, leaving Lomé at 1.30 and 6.30 pm and beginning the return journey at 6.30 am and 2 pm. The journey takes about four hours and costs CFA 630 (2nd class). The train from Lomé to Aného costs CFA 250 (2nd class).

Carry food and water. Fruit can be bought at stations along the way.

	fare	time
Lomé to K'Palimé	CFA 590 plus CFA 200 a backpack	two to four hours
Lomé to Atakpamé	CFA 1000	2½ hours
Lomé to Dapaong	CFA 3000 plus CFA 500 a backpack	12 hours
Lomé to Sokodé	CFA 1685	five hours
Sokodé to Lama Kara	CFA 325	two hours
Lama Kara to Dapaong	CFA 1015	five hours

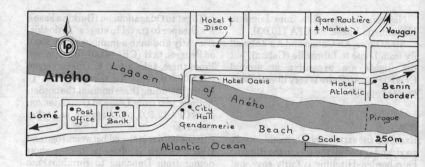

Around the Country

ANÉHO (formerly Anécho)
There's a lagoon here where you can go out with the fisherfolk for free or in exchange for a *petit cadeau* (small present).

Places to Stay & Eat
Most travellers stay at *Hotel Atlantic*, on the road heading towards the Benin border. A large double with fan costs CFA 3000. A smaller double without fan costs CFA 2000. The showers and toilets are clean and there's hot water. You can camp on a reserved site bordering the lagoon and use the hotel's facilities. The owner is a German woman, married to a Togolese. She is extremely helpful and speaks good French and English. The hotel has an excellent restaurant, which is very reasonably priced considering the enormous size of the dishes. Expect to pay around CFA 1900 for a meal.

If it's full, try *Hotel Oasis*, on the same road about 500 metres back towards town. Rooms all have bathrooms, and doubles cost CFA 3500/5000 without/with air-con. It's good value, but the food is expensive. Other hotels include *Hotel Royal Holiday* at CFA 3500 a double and *As des Picques* at CFA 2500 a double, which is good value.

There are street stalls near the railway station where you can eat cheaply.

ATAKPAMÉ
Places to Stay & Eat
A popular place to stay is *Relais des Plateaux*, 500 metres from the bus station. It is pleasant and has double rooms with shower and fan for CFA 4500. There are more expensive rooms with air-con. Good meals are available for between CFA 150 and CFA 2500. *Rock Hotel* is considerably more expensive.

Bar le Retour, just across from the Shell depot at the bus station, is popular and has double rooms from CFA 1500. Fans are an extra CFA 300 and there are bucket showers. The food is cheap.

Other travellers have recommended *Hotel Alafia* in Hiheatro, a village about two km from Atakpamé on the K'Palimé road. It's an excellent hotel with rooms for CFA 1500, plus a bar and restaurant. Cheap rooms can also be found at *Affaires Sociales*, close to the taxi park on the main road.

If you're not eating at Relais des Plateaux, try *Bar Solidarité*. It has similar prices and is patronised by Peace Corps volunteers.

Entertainment
On Saturday nights everyone heads for the *Rock Hotel* disco. There is a swimming pool at the *Sotoco* which you can use for CFA 1000.

BADOU

Badou is 80 km west of Atakpamé near the Ghana border. It is reached by mountain roads, twisting through some excellent scenery and fantastic tropical forest. The best **waterfall** in Togo is near the village of Akloa, 10 km from Badou. It's a 35-minute walk through open country and rainforest, and although the path is easy to find, a guide is included in the CFA 500 you pay to the Village Development Committee, which issues a receipt.

Places to Stay

Hotel Badou and *Hotel Abuta* are both expensive. Abuta costs CFA 3850/5150 a single/double, with a 15% discount for two or more nights. Both hotels allow camping, which costs CFA 1000 per person a night at the Abuta. It rains a lot here.

DAPAONG (formerly Dapango)

A must to visit in Dapaong is the **Parc National de la Fosse des Lions**, where large herds of elephant can be seen even in the wet season. For a small group a taxi to the park would cost around CFA 3500. The trip takes about four hours.

Places to Stay & Eat

The *Cercle de l'Amitié* has double rooms for CFA 3000/3500 without/with fan, as well as more expensive air-con rooms. A dormitory bed costs CFA 1500, or you can sleep on the roof for CFA 1000. It's a clean place. At *Affaires Sociales*, a double room costs CFA 2000/2500 without/with air-con and a dormitory bed costs CFA 800.

More expensive are *Hotel Lafia*, which has air-con doubles for CFA 4100, and *Le Campement*, where a double costs CFA 4300/6300 with fan/air-con.

Sometimes it's possible to find a bed at the *Peace Corps House* for CFA 500. But the place is difficult to find and a long way from the bus station.

Cheap meals are available from the restaurant on the road to Lomé, about one km from the town centre. In the evenings,

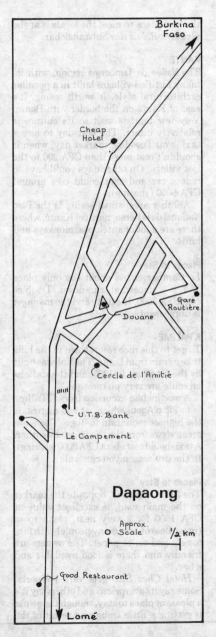

Dapaong

the best place to meet the locals is at the pleasant *Relais des Savannes* bar.

KANTÉ

The **Vallée de Tamberma** region, with its many fortified villages built in a peculiar architectural style, is worth seeing. It's east of Kanté on the border with Benin. Very few tourists visit so its culture is relatively intact. The best day to hire a taxi is on Tuesday, market day, when it shouldn't cost more than CFA 200 to the last village. On other days you'll have to rent a car and that could cost around CFA 6000 (sharing).

Another area worth seeing is the **Parc National de la Kéran**, north of Kanté, where there are a lot of antelopes, monkeys and birds.

Places to Stay

Le Campement is about the only place and it's somewhat run-down. Doubles cost CFA 3500. It's dirty and the manager is unpleasant.

K'PALIMÉ

To get to this nice resort town in the hills take a train from Lomé. The line was built by the Germans in 1905, and the stations en route are very picturesque.

A worthwhile excursion from K'Palimé is to **Pic d'Agou**, which, at 956 metres, is the highest mountain in Togo. There are great views from the top in good weather. A taxi should cost about CFA 3000 (sharing). In the dry season you can walk.

Places to Stay

The *Mini Brasserie*, opposite the market on the main road, is excellent value at CFA 1500 for a very neat, clean room (regardless of how many people) with fan, towels and toilet paper. The owners are friendly and there is food available and a bar.

Hotel Chez Solo gets varied reports. Some say its overpriced and others say it's a pleasant place to stay, though the owner is getting a little smug as a result of the

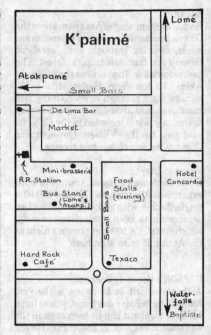

publicity. Rooms range from CFA 1500 without fan to CFA 1800 with fan. Primitive cold water showers are available and dinner costs CFA 450. There are 16 *rondavels* and more being built, so it's rarely full.

Closer to the centre, but still a little way out of town, is *Auberge Amoto* which has double rooms with fan for CFA 3250. It's clean and the people are friendly. Cheap meals are available. Also in this price range is *Hotel Concordia*, which costs CFA 2500/3600 a single/double with fans and showers.

Another place to stay is *Le Campement* at Kloto, about 12 km from K'Palimé.

Places to Eat

Good meals are available from the *Hard Rock Café*, which is a 15-minute walk from the city centre. It's popular with Peace Corps volunteers and other Europeans.

There is a good fufu (mashed yam served with a strong sauce and eaten with the fingers) restaurant at the bus station.

LAMA KARA
To visit the **Tamberma villages** in the area you can hire a car, driver and guide for CFA 15,000 (including petrol) for a tour of about five hours. Get together a group to share the costs then ask at your hotel where to hire transport.

The village of **Ketau** is worth visiting for its huge market on Wednesdays – the second largest market in Togo.

Travellers heading to Dapaong should see if there are any Sotoco trucks taking passengers.

Places to Stay
Hotel Sapaw is a nice place to stay and popular with travellers. It's about 1½ km from the truck park and not far from Hotel Kara, the town's best hotel. Just as good and perhaps a little cheaper is *Le Manguier*, next to the Mini-Rizerie. Many Peace Corps volunteers stay here. There's also *Le Campement*, which has rooms with showers for CFA 3000.

Places to Eat
Steak & chips costs CFA 800 at *Hotel Sapaw*. Just behind the hotel is *Le Jardin*, a good place to eat and drink. *Sous Les Mangues*, across from the post office, is a popular eating place with travellers and the Peace Corps. Another restaurant that has been recommended is *Wax Restaurant*, not far from the Sapaw Hotel (not to be confused with Hotel Sapaw).

Some six km east of Kara on the road to Ketao and Djougou is the village of Lassa, where the orphanage *Le Jardin des Enfants* is run by some French people. It offers excellent French cuisine in a very mellow environment for CFA 2000, including wine. It's a popular place with the Peace Corps from northern Togo and is open only at weekends. All the proceeds go to the orphanage.

Hotel Kara is a popular weekend watering hole with Peace Corps volunteers. It has a swimming pool (CFA 600 for visitors) and disco (CFA 500 entry and expensive drinks).

LOMÉ
Most travellers stay in Lomé only for a couple of days before heading east to the beaches, some 9½ km away. You are warned not to walk outside the beach camp sites at night as it is *extremely dangerous*. There have been robberies close by even in daylight hours (see accommodation section). A taxi to the beach camp sites will cost you CFA 400 to CFA 500. Route taxis are cheaper.

Four km from the centre in Quartier de Bé is **Le Marché-Bé**. It has all the normal wares plus a voodoo and fetish section – skins, bones, love potions, etc. It's worth a visit. Few tourists go there.

Information
Tourist Office & Maps The tourist office is next to Garage Renault, between Rue du Commerce and Blvd de la République, about a km east of the centre. Detailed maps of Lomé are available at Service Topographique et Cadastre, near the corner of Rue Maréchal Joffre and Ave Albert Sarraut, between the station and the sea.

Post The poste restante charges CFA 100 a letter. Letters are held for two months. The staff is friendly, but incompetent and letters are often misfiled.

Newspapers American newspapers and the *Economist* are available at Malidis, 400 metres north of the UTB building.

American Express American Express (tel 6190) is at STMP, 2 Rue de Commerce.

Moneychangers If you change money on the street, you're bound to be ripped off with a very fast sleight-of-hand trick (see the Money section). Ask around the main market for an American called Charlie

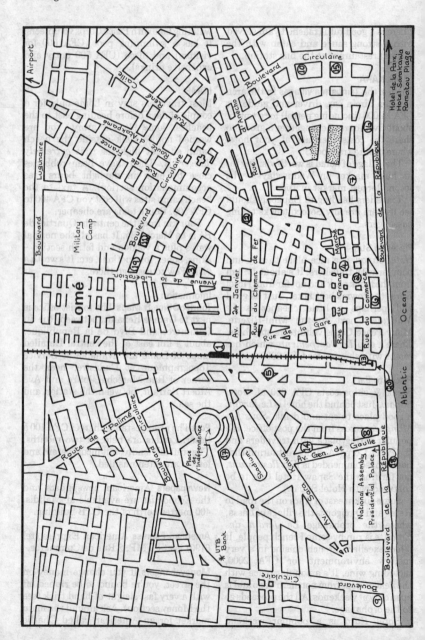

1	Railway Station	11	Mosque
2	Cathedral	12	Restaurant Senegalaise
3	GPO	13	Hotel Atlantique
4	Grand Marché	14	French Consulate
5	Sûrete National & Police	15	Zaïre Embassy
6	Air Afrique & UTA	16	Tourist Office
7	United States Embassy	17	Hotel 2 Février
8	French Embassy	18	Hotel Le Benin
9	British Embassy & Hotel de la Plage	19	BIAO Bank
10	Nigerian Embassy	20	BCCI Bank

Biddle. He's honest, gives a good rate and is usually found on the 3rd floor of the big unfinished building at the market. You can't miss it, it's the only three-storey building there. Alternatively, try kiosk No 7 on the south side of the commercial street, which runs east from the taxi drop-off point.

Airline Offices Most of the airlines have their offices on the Rue du Commerce, Rue du Grand Marché and Route d'Atakpamé.

Transport For vehicles heading north the station is some 10 km north of the city centre. Take a bus or taxi.

Taxis around town cost between CFA 175 and CFA 200 during the day and CFA 250 at night. A taxi to the airport costs CFA 1000.

Vaccinations These are given at Centre de Santé Publique and the Institute of Hygiene, one block east of Ave Sarakawa. The institute is open Monday to Friday from 7 am to noon and 2.30 to 5.30 pm. It has supplies of cholera vaccine (CFA 900), but you will have to bring other vaccines with you. The best place to get them is Pharmacie Pour Tous, near Café de Chine on Route de K'Palimé. Togopharma and Pharmacie de Boulevard usually don't stock vaccines. An injection costs CFA 450, without vaccine.

Places to Stay

There is numerous accommodation for the budget traveller. One of the best, but not cheapest, places is *Hotel California*. It costs CFA 3500/5000/6000 a single/double/ triple. It has air-con and hot showers. Similar is *Hotel Croix de Sud*, near the College Protestant on Route de K'Palimé. It is good value at CFA 4000 a double with air-con. It is on a major taxi run, and therefore easy and cheap to get to.

Sometimes a bed may be found for CFA 1000 at the French volunteers house, known as *Casse de Passage*. It's near Hotel Sara Kawa, which in turn is near Ablogamé Station.

Hotel de la Plage, on the seafront at the corner of Blvd Circulaire and Blvd de la République, has single rooms without fan for CFA 2500 and double rooms with fan and shower for CFA 4000. It also has more expensive rooms with air-con, shower and toilet. With its nice large rooms and sea views, it's good value. But there is a lot of theft because the showers adjoining the rooms are not completely enclosed and are easy to get through. Beware of walking on the beach at night as robberies occur frequently.

Three other hotels worth considering are *Hotel Boulevard* and *Hotel Ahoudikpé*, both on Blvd Circulaire, and *Hotel Mawuli*, next to the mosque behind the post office. The Boulevard costs CFA 2300/ 3300 a single/double with fan. The

Ahoudikpé is good value and quiet. It has double rooms from CFA 2500. The Mawuli is fairly clean and has double rooms for CFA 2300. Similar to these is *Hotel Paloma*, near the main market. It has doubles for CFA 2300, bucket showers and a bar. It can get noisy at times.

More expensive is *Hotel Continental* (tel 210178), 39 Route d'Atakpamé. It offers doubles for CFA 4000/4500 with fan/air-con. Twin rooms with air-con cost CFA 5500. Slightly more expensive are *Hotel Abri* and *Hotel Maxim*, both charging CFA 5000 to CFA 6000 a room. Another place that has been recommended is *Hotel Todman*, on Route de K'Palimé. It has pleasant doubles with fan, shared toilets and showers and a restaurant. *Foyer des Marins* has also been recommended.

If you're looking for something up-market try *Hotel Le Benin*. Meals can be served by the swimming pool. If you're staying in Lomé for two or three months, it's worth renting a house. In June, July, August and, to some extent, September, many European expatriates go home to Europe for their annual holidays. Many of them (the majority being French and German) look for house-sitters before they go. If you build up a few contacts with the expatriates, you may be able to get a house. Some ask for rent, while others let you stay rent-free so long as you pay for gas and electricity and leave a deposit to cover possible breakages.

A room in a private house near the city centre will cost around CFA 3500 a week, while one outside the city will cost around CFA 1200 a week.

Beach Accommodation The camp sites of *Robinson Plage*, *Campement Ramatou* and *Alice Place* are all close to one another about 9½ km from Lomé. Food prices are outrageous. For something costing CFA 1000 to CFA 1500 in Lomé, you will be charged CFA 2500 to CFA 3000.

Ramatou is about 100 metres from the sea. It has good toilets and showers and costs CFA 500 to camp or CFA 2000 to CFA 3000 for a *paillotte* (a wooden beach hut). There is a restaurant. Robinson Plage is on the beach under the palms. It is run by a friendly, easy-going French couple, and has a mellow terrace which gets good sea breezes. A *paillotte* sleeping four to eight people costs CFA 3600. It costs CFA 1000 to camp. The toilets and showers are good. Alice Place (which is actually called Chez Alice et Koffi) is 300 metres from the beach. It's popular with Swiss people. *Paillottes* cost the same as at the other two resorts but to camp is CFA 750.

There is nowhere cheap to eat in the vicinity of these camps, but you can at least cook your own food on a small fire at Ramatou. Beers and soft drinks are pricey at CFA 200 for a small bottle.

Theft is on the increase at these places. It is also *extremely dangerous* to walk out of the camp sites at night. Even during the day people have been robbed close to the camp sites. It is advisable to walk in groups.

Places to Eat
There are street stalls all over Lomé where you can buy rice, fufu, paté, etc.

One of the best deals in town for western food is *Marox*, a German fast-food outlet. A hamburger costs CFA 650, half a chicken CFA 800, and a half-litre of beer CFA 300. It serves good coffee and German specialities, such as sauerkraut. There is a small department store next door where you can buy sausage, cheese and the like.

L'Amitié and *Futa Djalon* both have inexpensive Senegalese food. Futa Djalon has beer.

In the evenings, at a street stall run by the 'chicken lady', you can eat salad for CFA 200 to CFA 300 and roast chicken for CFA 500. It's generally safe eating and good food. It's on Blvd Circulaire, near Hotel Ahoudikpé. Other good food stalls set up in the evenings near the Ghana border post. There are also cheap bars and expensive restaurants to be found. *Jungle Bar* has kebabs and cheap drinks, and you can get a good Greek sandwich from *Le Chawarma*.

More up-market are *Restaurant Lakshmi*, which offers French cuisine in a mellow atmosphere, *La Phonician* and *La Vogue*, which both serve Lebanese food. A meal at these restaurants will cost CFA 3000 to CFA 4000. Other places recommended for good food are *Relais de la Poste*, 50 metres from the post office; *Escale*, at the market on Blvd Circulaire; *Bopato*, in front of the BIAO bank; and *La Rabile*, at the corner of Route d'Atakpamé and Blvd Circulaire.

For an all-you-can-eat breakfast for CFA 1600 go to *Hotel Sarakawa*, one of Lomés most expensive hotels.

The supermarket *Goyi-Score* is the cheapest stockist of European products.

Entertainment

African Queen Nightclub, on Ave de la Libération about 2½ km from the central post office in Tokoin, has great African music. It's 100% African: you'll rarely see a white face. The toilets stink and the rusty chairs will ruin your clothes, but it raves until the small hours to a mixture of African and Brazilian reggae. Similar is *Ricardo's Bar*, near the Ghana border. *Don't walk alone at night.*

Café Santa Fé is the most popular expatriate watering hole. Draught beer costs CFA 125. Also popular is *Café des Arts*, on Blvd Circulaire near the corner of Ave de la Libération. It has a superb atmosphere and the clientele is a mixture of Africans, expatriates and travellers. Draught beer costs CFA 100. It serves cheap brochettes, omelettes and salads on the terrace.

Another good place for a beer is *Bar Panoramique*, on the 35th floor of Hotel du 2 Février. On a clear day the views are excellent. The drinks are normally quite pricey, but there's a half-price happy hour from 5 to 6.30 pm.

For a weekend treat of home-made German cakes and coffee, try *Foyer des Marins* – a club catering specifically for seafarers, but run by a German missionary who welcomes everyone. Sailors from all over the world frequent the club, which provides them with breakfast and a hot meal at night. It also has a bar, where the drinks are relatively cheap; a swimming pool; billiard, pool and table tennis tables; souvenir shop; and chapel, where regular services are held. As with in-port life anywhere in the world, the club has its share of seaminess. In complete contrast is *Maquina Loca* – a 'nightclub chic'.

The *American Cultural Centre* is in front of the US Embassy. It has a library and screens free movies on Friday evenings. The *French Cultural Centre*, on Ave 24 Janvier close to the main post office, has a library and shows movies daily. Both centres are worth visiting.

If you meet the British staff at the refinery, you may be invited to their private bar (snooker, darts, videos, BBC news, etc) in the evenings or their swimming pool in the day. You might meet them going to Lomé from Robinson Plage or Ramatou Plage between 7 and 8.30 am, in which case they'll probably give you a lift, whether you're hitching or not. They're extremely friendly and enjoy talking with travellers.

SOKODÉ

There are lots of cheap hotels in Sokodé. *Relais de la Cigale* has rooms for CFA 2000 or dormitory beds for CFA 500. It also has a good restaurant. Other good inexpensive restaurants are *Mama J'ai Faim* and the *buvette* at *Affaires Sociales*. If you're looking for company, try *Bar Sans Souci*, which is a Peace Corps hang-out.

TOGOVILLE

The north side of Lac (lake) Togo is the centre of the country's fetish cult. Some travellers say it is a tourist trap and not worth visiting. North of Togoville is **Vogan**. It holds one of the most important markets in the area on Fridays. Rarely will you see a tourist here.

Places to Stay

On the north side of the lake you'll be lucky to find anywhere to stay at a reasonable price. You might, however, be able to persuade the *Mission Catholique* to help out – it's an advantage if you're a Jesuit. On the south side most people stay at Agbodrafo. Again, cheap accommodation is nonexistent. The *Swiss Castle Club-Hotel* has closed and *Hotel du Lac* is very expensive. Its cheapest doubles are CFA 8000, and then they jump to CFA 11,000. The hotel has a swimming pool and facilities for sailing and windsurfing. To go to Togoville by canoe from Hotel du Lac costs CFA 500.

Two new hotels are being built by a Swiss partnership, so accommodation choices may improve.

Tunisia

Tunisia, the smallest of the three Maghreb states, has a rich cultural and social heritage stemming from the many empires that have come and gone in this part of the world. These empires range from the Phoenicians through to the Romans, Byzantines, Arabs, Ottoman Turks and the French.

Phoenician staging posts were established very early on along the Mediterranean, but remained relatively unimportant until the mother cities on the Syrian coast lost their independence in the 6th century BC and Greek colonies began to be planted in Cyrenaica (eastern Libya) from the 7th century BC. As a result, Carthage, a few km from Tunis, rapidly grew into the metropolis of the Phoenician world, recording a population of about half a million in its heyday.

The Phoenicians, who were principally maritime traders, had a profound effect on the native Berbers by teaching them advanced agricultural methods and urban living. The Jews, too, many of whom were involved in trade, helped spread the idea of a monotheistic religion among these pagan tribes.

Carthage eventually fell to the Romans, who literally ploughed the city into the ground. The Romans were quick, however, to appreciate the value of the settled Tunisian plains as a granary for their empire and began to build cities here. The remains of these cities are among the country's principal attractions, though Roman Carthage is somewhat disappointing as much of its stone was carted away by the Arabs to build their cities.

The most significant Roman contribution to this part of Africa, however, was largely incidental. It was the opening of North Africa to Christianity. In the centuries following the Roman conquest, Carthage became the greatest of Christian centres after Alexandria and produced one of its

greatest figures – St Augustine, a Libyan Berber educated in Carthage.

Roman rule was never popular. Opposition to it found expression in religious doctrinal differences and the adoption of Donatism, regarded by the orthodox Byzantine Church as a heresy. Persecutions launched by Byzantium as a result, alienated much of the population. But the many centuries of influence, first of Judaism and then of Christianity, paved the way for the rapid adoption of Islam, which had the advantage of not being associated with foreign rule.

The Arabs first arrived in 670 AD and established a base at Kairouan. But they lost their hold in a disastrous attempt to conquer the lands further west. They didn't regain control until the end of the century, after the Byzantine navy was defeated because it could not cut the Arab supply lines through Libya to Egypt. Even then, they had to contend with a confederacy of marauding tribes – led by a woman, Kahina – which swept down from the Aurès Mountains in eastern Algeria.

This sort of resistance from the Berber tribes was to continue for many centuries. Even after Islam, the dissidents found expression in the Kharijite schism, as they had in Donatism during the Christian era. (Kharijism was a puritanical form of Shi'ism that stemmed from disagreements as to who should succeed to the caliphate, the Prophet's companions or his relations.) After the political fragmentation of the Arab Empire, Tunisia became part of the

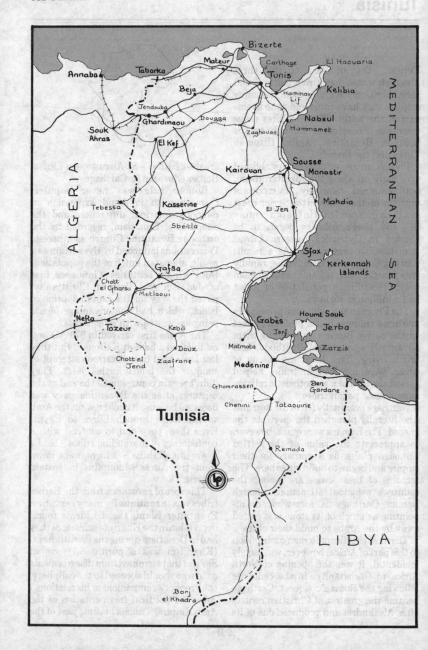

Moroccan Empire of the Almohades. It remained so until the dual threats of the Christian armies in Spain and the Bedouin in the central Maghreb forced the Moroccan rulers to divide their administration and appoint the Hafsid family as governors of the eastern half of the empire in Tunis.

The Hafsids were spectacularly successful in defeating the Bedouin, but in doing so intensified the destruction of the central Maghreb and effectively cut Tunisia from Morocco. In the years that followed, Tunisia became an island of stability and prosperity and in 1230 created the independent Hafsid monarchy, which began trading with Europe on its own account.

The Hafsids remained in power until 1574, when Tunisia was conquered by the Ottoman Turks. Ottoman rule, however, soon became merely nominal after the defeat of the Turkish fleet by the Christians at Lepanto. Power in Tunis, as in Algiers, came to reside in self-perpetuating cliques descended from the conquering Greek corsairs and Anatolian janissaries (the professional elite of the Ottoman armies, composed of forcibly recruited Christian youths rigorously trained in both warfare and the Muslim religion).

In time, the conquerors merged with the local people and by the 18th century had produced their own national monarchy, the Husainid beys. The Husainid beys revived the Hafsid practice of direct trading with Europe and the Sudan, despite remaining nominally part of the Ottoman Empire.

In the late 19th century, the Turks, frightened of losing their grip on even more of their North African lands, tried to reassert their authority over Algeria and Tunisia. They were stopped by the French navy, which annexed Algiers. Tunisia was spared colonisation until much later as the beys, aware of the growing power of industrialised European nations, had taken steps to outlaw piracy and westernise

their administration. Indeed, in 1857 they adopted their first constitution.

The continued extravagance of the beys – like that of Muhammed Ali in Egypt – led to more and more European interference until in 1883 the French declared a protectorate over Tunisia.

In the 1930s, the Néo-Destour movement for national liberation grew up under the leadership of Habib Bourguiba. It soon threatened French dominance and four years later Bourguiba was jailed and the movement banned. When Tunis was briefly occupied by the Germans during WW II, Bourguiba was released and the beys were allowed to appoint ministers from among the Néo-Destour.

This, however, came to an end with the Allied victories in North Africa and Bourguiba went into exile in Egypt. From there, he organised propaganda and commanded two years of guerrilla warfare against the French, eventually forcing Paris to grant autonomy to Tunisia in 1955. Bourguiba returned to head the new government. A year later, Tunisia was granted independence. In 1957 the bey was deposed and Tunisia became a republic with Bourguiba as president. In 1975 the National Assembly made him president for life.

In 1981 the first multiparty elections were called, through which Bourguiba consolidated his power. As the '80s progressed, however, he was increasingly seen to be losing touch with his people and the rest of the Arab world. In November 1987, the interior minister, Zine el-Abidine ben Ali, orchestrated his downfall in a peaceful and popular coup and had himself installed as president.

Since independence, Tunisia has been one of the most stable and moderate Arab countries. As such, its friendship has been cultivated by the USA and West Germany, which supply the bulk of its foreign aid. A union with Libya, negotiated hurriedly, collapsed almost as soon as it was announced, when Libya expelled thousands of Tunisian workers.

Tunisia strained its relations with France and Italy in the 1960s by expropriating European-owned farms. The tension eased with the offer of compensation.

Tunisia is rapidly becoming one of the major Mediterranean tourist attractions, drawing millions of northern Europeans to its shores every year. The result is it's now fairly expensive for the budget traveller.

Facts

GEOGRAPHY & CLIMATE

In the north the main feature is the Tunisian Dorsale, a continuation of the Atlas Mountains. To the north of this range is the Medjerda Valley, the country's main river system which flows into the Gulf of Tunis. South of the range a high plain falls away to a series of salt lakes (*chotts*) then to a sandy desert, known as the Grand Erg Oriental, on the edge of the Sahara.

Tunisia has mild wet winters and hot dry summers. In the south temperatures can reach over 45°C. Rainfall is very variable, but in the south averages about 150 mm annually while in the north it's around 1500 mm.

PEOPLE

Because of the thoroughness of the Arab invasions, the original Berber people now only make up 1% of the total population and are confined mainly to the dry and inhospitable south of the country. In this respect, Tunisia differs from the other Maghreb states of Algeria and Morocco with their substantial Berber populations. Also, in the past, there has been large immigration from Spain, Italy, Malta and Ottoman Turkey, and many Jews still live here.

The population is over seven million, the vast majority of whom are Muslims.

VISAS

Visas are required by all, except nationals of western European countries, Canada, Japan, South Korea and the USA, who can stay for three months.

Transit visas for a one-week stay are available on arrival at the border (cost TD 2.500). If you want to stay longer, get your visa beforehand as it's a very long process to obtain an extension on a transit visa.

Extensions are available only from the Tunis extension office at 30 Ave de la République – a nondescript wooden shed down by the old port. They cost TD 2.500, payable only in revenue stamps from the office at 22 Ave de la République, take up to 10 days to issue, and require two photos, bank receipts and a *facture* (receipt) from your hotel. You cannot apply for an extension until at least day five of your original one-week visa.

Other Visas

Algeria Visas are issued without fuss the same day if you apply before 10.30 am, cost TD 9.500 and require four photos. Dutch nationals are regularly refused visas here. The Algerian Consulate is at 136 Ave de la Liberté and is open for visas from 8.30 to 11.30 am Monday to Saturday. A taxi from the centre costs 500 millimes. Bus No 35, from Ave Bourguiba opposite the Africa Hotel, runs along the parallel Rue de Palestine.

Libya Before you apply for a visa, you must have your passport details translated into Arabic. They won't look at you otherwise. You can get this done at your embassy in Tunis, and sometimes at the passport office in your country. Visas cost TD 3 and take several days to issue. The Libyan Embassy is at 48 Rue 1 du Juin.

Nigeria Tunis is a very good place to get visas, in contrast to further south where they're a real hassle to obtain. Three-month visas are issued by the British

Embassy, at 5 Place de la Victoire, without fuss in 24 hours.

MONEY

US$ 1 = TD 0.840
UK£ 1 = TD 1.245

The unit of currency is the Tunisian dinar = 1000 millimes. The import and export of dinar is prohibited. You can re-exchange up to 30% or TD 100 by producing bank receipts to prove you changed the money in the first place. There is a black market, but you have to be Tunisian to find it. It's very unlikely anyone will offer this service.

To buy an international air ticket, you must produce a *bon de passage*. You get this from the bank by showing your bank receipts for money changed. If you need to apply for a visa extension, get the *bon de passage* first because the embassy does not return bank receipts.

ACCOMMODATION

There are few camp sites with good facilities, but you can pitch a tent anywhere if you have the permission of the owner of the land. There are purpose-built camp sites about 1½ km south of Hammam Plage, follow the signs to *Hotel Salwa* on the road to Hammam Lif; Nabeul, *Hotel Les Jasmins*; Hammamet, *L'Ideal Camping*; and Tozeur, *Camping Paradis* and *Belvedere*.

Where there is no camping ground it is often possible to camp at a youth hostel (*auberge de jeunesse*), which is the next cheapest place to stay. To stay at the hostels you need a Youth Hostel membership card. Most hostels are about as congenial as a prison and are located well away from town centres. Demand is high in summer. There are youth hostels or youth centres in Ain Draham, Beja, Bizerte, Gasfa, Kasserine, El Kef, Nabeul, Monastir, Radés (Tunis), Sousse and Zarzis.

For a little more money, you often do much better at a cheap hotel. These are usually reasonably clean and cost about TD 2 for a bed in a share room. Women and couples are often not welcome.

Going up the hotel scale, for about TD 6 you get a reasonable double with handbasin and often shower. These places are well maintained, the rooms are often cleaned daily and unless you're really scrimping, are the best places to stay, especially for women.

LANGUAGE

Arabic and French are the main languages. English, German and Italian are quite common in places.

You'll get a much better reception from the locals if you try to speak Arabic rather than French.

Getting There & Around

AIR

Reductions of 50% are available for under 24s on fares to Cairo from Tunis. Ask at Atou-tours in Tunis. The normal fare is TD 165. With so many charter flights from Europe and London landing in Tunis all year round, there may be a cheap seat going. You'll have to do the rounds of the tourist resorts (Nabeul, Sousse or Jerba) and speak to the company reps.

Tunis Air operates internal flights to Tozeur, Sfax, Monastir and Jerba.

ROAD
Hitching

Hitching is not too bad down the coast to the Libyan border and as far south as Tozeur, and you'll rarely have to pay. It is more difficult, but still possible, for two people. In the north it isn't quite as easy because the area is overrun with tourists. Don't expect quick lifts on minor roads as there is little traffic.

Bus

An excellent network of regular and fairly

cheap buses link all the major centres, and many minor ones, throughout the country.

The national bus company, SNTRI, has daily air-con buses from Tunis to Jerba, Medenine, Tataouine, Zarzis, Gabès, Matmata, Tozeur, Gafsa, Douz, Nefta, Le Kef, Kasserine, Sfax, Sousse, Kairouan, Bizerte, Tabarka and Jendouba. Advance booking is advisable, especially in summer.

SNTRI also runs buses to Algeria. They depart daily from Tunis to Annaba, and vice versa, and every second day from Tunis to Constantine. You must book as demand is high. Passengers are not picked up along the way.

Taxi

Large taxis (*louages*), usually Peugeot 404s that seat five passengers, ply the same routes as the buses. They are more expensive than the buses, but generally more comfortable and faster. They leave when full.

TRAIN

The rail network is not well developed. Trains are often slow and inconvenient. The exception is the coastal route from Tunis to Sfax and Gabès, where there is a frequent air-con express via Sousse. Fares cost a little more than the equivalent bus fare, plus you have to pay a supplement (usually less than TD 1) on the air-con services. Tunis to Sfax costs TD 4.650 2nd class.

There is a daily train from Tunis to Algiers, via Jendouba, Souk Ahras, Annaba and Constantine. It costs TD 6 and takes about 24 hours.

BOAT

Tunis is one of the gateways to Africa by ferry from Italy. There are hydrofoil connections between Trapani in Italy and Kelibia from June to September.

There are five ferries daily between Sfax and the Kerkennah Islands in summer and two in winter. The trip takes 1½ hours and costs 500 millimes a person

and TD 4.500 a vehicle. To take a vehicle across in summer, you need to queue early.

Ferries run regularly both day and night between Jorf and the island of Jerba. The fare is 50 millimes. Alternatively, you can drive to Jerba from Zarzis over the old Roman causeway.

TO/FROM ALGERIA

There are four main border crossings, and some minor ones. The most northerly border crossing is Tabarka to Annaba, via El Kala. There are few cars along this coastal route, so be prepared to walk a little if you're hitching.

In the mountains inland from Tabarka is the very quiet and fairly relaxed border post of Babouch. The daily buses from Tunis to Annaba cross here. They depart from the Southern Bus Station in Tunis and from Annaba at 6 am. The fare is TD 6 and advance bookings are necessary. The buses do not pick up passengers along the way. You must join them at either Tunis or Annaba.

Not the most scenic route, but a popular border crossing is Ghardimaou to Souk Ahras. Hitching can be difficult as there are few villages between the two places. To ensure you don't get stuck, take the daily Tunis to Algiers train from Jendouba to Annaba. There's nothing in the way of scenery to miss and you can get off at Souk Ahras, though there's nothing there.

The most scenic and interesting route is from Nefta to El Oued. This route passes the salt lakes of southern Tunisia and travels the edge of the Grand Erg Oriental. From Tunis you can go as far as Metlaoui by train. There's also a daily air-con bus from Tunis to Nefta. *Louages* run from Nefta to the border at Hazoua-Bou Aroua for 500 millimes, or there is a bus daily at 10 am. The border is about 40 km west of Nefta, and the border posts are four km apart. From the Algerian side there are taxis to and from El Oued.

TO/FROM LIBYA

The best route is the coast road from Gabès to Tripoli via Ben Gardane and Ras Agedir. The border, however, is closed at present. The only way you can enter Libya from Tunisia at present is by air.

Around the Country

AIN DRAHAM

This is Tunisia's hill station. At 1000 metres above sea level, in among the cork forests, the summer temperatures are a good deal more tolerable than on the coast and plains. In winter, it snows regularly, and a depth of up to one metre is not uncommon.

Other than walking, there is not much to do.

Places to Stay

There is a *Youth Hostel* at the top end of town on the road to Jendouba. The only hotel is the pleasant *Hotel Beauséjour*. Rooms cost TD 6/8 a single/double with bath and breakfast. It's popularity as a hunting lodge in colonial times is evidenced by the porcine trophies on the walls.

Seven km along the Jendouba road and in a cork forest is *Hotel Les Chênes*, another old hunting lodge well adorned with various stuffed things. Rooms cost TD 11/16 a single/double with breakfast. Camping in the grounds is usually allowed.

BIZERTE

Bizerte is the only place in Tunisia to have seen fighting after WW II. When independence was granted, the French wanted to retain their naval base here and it wasn't until after 1000 Tunisian soldiers had died in a short battle in 1963 that the French finally withdrew. The shipping canal connects the large Lake Bizerte with the Mediterranean, and is spanned by a new bridge that can be raised to let ships through.

Information

The helpful local tourist office is on the corner of Blvd Habib Bourguiba and Blvd Hassan en Nouri. There is transport information posted in the window when the office is closed. The post office is on Ave d'Algérie, and the telephone office is around the back. The banks are mostly grouped around the main square. One bank is rostered to be open on weekends (the tourist office has details).

The bus station is near the canal at the end of Ave d'Algérie. *Louages* for Tunis, Raf Raf and Ras Jebel leave from under the bridge. For Tabarka, they leave from a small square at the other end of Ave d'Algérie. The railway station is by the port, near the end of Rue de Belgique.

Things to See

The **medina** and new city meet around the heavily polluted **old port**. The medina is of little interest as is the Spanish fort on the hill.

There is a good beach at **Remel Plage**, a few km south-east on the Tunis road. Buses going to Raf Raf or Ras Jebel can drop you at the turn-off, one km distant. There is also a strip of beach to the north of town, accessed by the No 29 bus which leaves from near the tourist office. The best beach here is at **Les Grottes**, about two km to the right of the bus route, just before Cap Blanc, the northernmost tip of Africa.

The best beach in the country is at **Raf Raf**. It's a long streak of white sand that curves for a km or so and is backed by the pine-clad Cap Farina at its far end. It is popular in summer, especially at weekends, and you have to walk a bit to find some space. There are regular buses from Bizerte and Ras Jebel. The basic grass huts on the beach are primarily for day use, but you can stay overnight if you don't mind sleeping on sand. If they're a bit rough, there's *Hotel Dalia* for a steep TD 12 a double with breakfast.

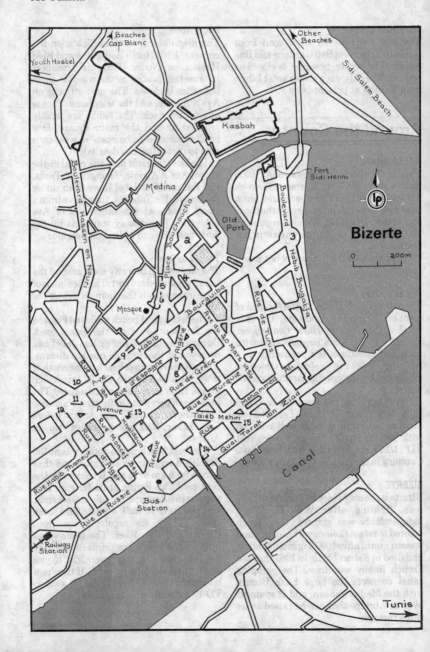

1	Artisanat
2	Market
3	Buses to northern beaches
4	Louages (Regional)
5	Hotel Africain
6	Hotel Zitouna
7	Hotel Continental
8	GPO
9	Regional Tourist Office
10	Tunis Air
11	Restaurant le Coq d'Or
12	Restaurant Jeunesse
13	Banks
14	Louages (Tunis)
15	National Tourist Office

Places to Stay & Eat

The *Youth Hostel* at the Remel Plage turn-off has very basic facilities and is a good place to camp. It costs TD 2 a bed and is handy to the beach.

In town, the best of the cheapies is *Hotel Continental* on Rue d'Espagne. It's basic and somewhat overpriced at TD 6 a double with cold showers only. Other places are *Hotel Africain* and *Hotel Zitouna* at TD 2 a person. They are both near the medina and a bit rough. For a splurge, try *Hotel Petit Mousse* on the beach to the north. It costs TD 10/15 a single/double with breakfast. It has a good outdoor restaurant.

On the next corner to Hotel Continental, *Restaurant Bar de la Liberté* does good food. The patisserie opposite the hotel is one of the best outside Tunis.

DOUGGA

Dougga is an excellent Roman ruin in a commanding position on the edge of the Tebersouk Mountains. It's worth seeing, but does require a bit of effort as there is no cheap accommodation close by and it's a three-km walk from the road to the site, unless you strike it lucky with a lift. The best place to stay is at El Kef, 60 km to the west. Buses or *louages* heading for Tunis will drop you in the village. The dirt road to the site starts behind the village.

There is a six-km surfaced road to the site from the village of Tebersouk, but there is very little traffic and hitching is difficult.

Things to See

Central to the ruins is the **Square of the Winds**. At its centre is an enormous circular inscription listing the names of the 12 winds. The **Capitol** is a huge monument dedicated to the gods Jupiter, Juno and Minerva. It has a fine frieze of the apotheosis of Antonius Pius on the portico. Fragments of the enormous statue of Jupiter are now housed in the Bardo in Tunis, as are the best mosaics from the site. On the southern edge of the site is **Trifolium House**, which was the town brothel. Next door, the **Cyclops Baths** are largely ruined except for the communal latrines just inside the entrance.

DOUZ

Douz is a quiet Saharan backwater, except during the Oasis Festival in December when it is absolutely packed. The festival is held in the best part of the *palmeraie*, past the Marhala and Sahara hotels. The town has a bank and post office, and there are regular *louages* to Kebili, a daily air-con bus to Tunis and the occasional bus to Tozeur.

Things to See

The **market** is in the centre of town and market day is Thursday. It's a good day to be in the area, but gets crowded with bus loads of tourists. The **animal market** is close by and doesn't get the crowds.

The oasis villages of **Zaafrane** and **El Faouar**, to the south, are worth exploring. There are daily buses along the surfaced road to El Faouar. The only accommodation is in Douz, although there is supposedly a hotel in El Faouar.

Places to Stay

The best place is *Hotel 20 Mars*. Avoid *Hotel du Calme*; and *Hotel l'Oasis* is not much better. All charge TD 2 a person.

Hotel Marhala, in the *palmeraie*, is not bad value at TD 6/9 a single/double with breakfast.

EL JEM

This small town is in the middle of the country's olive-growing region. It only takes a couple of hours to look around, so can be easily seen en route from Tunis to Sfax, or as a day trip from the relaxed coastal village of Mahdia to the east. *Louages* leave for Mahdia, Kairouan, Sfax and Sousse from outside the railway station.

Things to See

El Jem has a very well preserved **Roman amphitheatre** that sticks out like a sore thumb. It is the most impressive Roman monument in North Africa. The amphitheatre, which seated 30,000 people, was a legacy of the reign of Emperor Gordian who was installed here at the age of 80 in 232 AD. It suffered badly in the 17th century when one side was blown up to flush out some dissidents who had hidden inside.

About 500 metres south of the railway station on the main road to Sfax is a small **museum** housing mosaics and other artefacts found in the area.

Places to Stay

Hotel Julius, with its pleasant central courtyard, is near the railway station and costs TD 7 a double.

GABÈS

There is little reason to stay in this heavily industrialised town on the Gulf of Gabès. There is a *palmeraie*, but it's not much chop, although all the tour groups get trotted through it in *calèches* (horse carts).

The bus station is at the western end of Blvd Farhat Hached. *Louages* leave from outside the enormous post office on the same street. The railway station is just off Ave 1 Juin, not far from the centre.

Places to Stay & Eat

Hotel de la Poste, on Ave Bourguiba above a café of the same name, is good value at TD 3 a double with handbasin. *Hotel Marhaba*, opposite the bus station, has similar prices but is noisy. *Restaurant à la Bonne Table*, on Ave Bourguiba almost opposite Hotel de la Poste, has good food and does an excellent dish called chicken farçi.

GHARDIMAOU

Ghardimaou is deadly dull. It has one bank and the Algiers train stops here. Buses and *louages* leave from near the railway line at the entrance to the town. The only hotel is the unsignposted *Thubernic Hotel*, opposite the railway station. Rooms cost TD 5 a double.

HAMMAMET

This is real tourist territory and unless you have a burning desire to be among other foreigners, it is best avoided, especially in summer. Share taxis and buses leave from outside the over-restored kasbah. The railway station is one block from Ave Habib Bourguiba.

Places to Stay

Hotel Bennila is one of the cheapest and charges TD 4.500 a person with breakfast, rising to TD 10 in summer. *Ideal*

1	Market
2	Hotel Restaurant Ben Nejima
3	Bus Station
4	Medina Hotel
5	Bus to Chenini
6	Artisanat
7	GPO
8	Louage Station
9	Youth Hostel
10	Railway Station
11	Hotels Regina & Keilani
12	Hotel de la Poste
13	Atlantic Hotel
14	Restaurant à la Bonne Table
15	Tourist Office

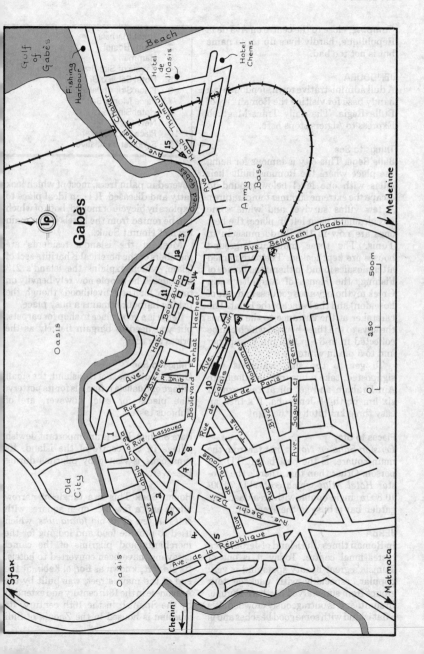

Camping, close to the centre on Ave de la République, hardly lives up to its name but is not too bad.

JENDOUBA

A dull administrative town, Jendouba is a handy base for visiting the Roman city of Bulla Regia. The daily Trans-Maghreb Express to Algiers stops here.

Things to See

Bulla Regia This city is famous for being the place where the Romans built their villas with one level below ground to escape the extreme summer temperatures. A few villas survive, and while some mosaics have been left in place, the best ones are now in the Bardo museum in Tunis. The three main underground houses are kept locked. They are named after mosaics found in them: the Palace of Fishing, the House of Amphitrite (in Greek mythology a sea goddess and wife of Poseidon) and the Palace of the Hunt. The caretaker at the entrance to the site has the keys to the three houses, which can be collected from 8 am to 8 pm in summer and to 5 pm in winter.

To get to the site, which is well signposted, take a bus from Jendouba to Ain Draham and get off at the turn-off six km north of Jendouba. It's then an easy three km hitch to the right.

Places to Stay

Pension Saha en Noum, not far from the main square, is the best bet at TD 2 a person. Other than that, there's the two-star *Hotel Atlas* which costs TD 7.800/10.800 a single/double with breakfast. The garden bar is busy in the evenings.

JERBA

In Roman times, the island of Jerba was a recreational centre. Today it is one of Tunisia's great beauty spots and is very popular, especially with package tour groups from sun-starved northern Europe. In summer it is outrageously crowded. It's a flat island with some good beaches and is

1	Hotel Marhala
2	Youth Hostel
3	Hamman
4	Zaouia of Sidi Brahim
5	Hotel Sable d'Or
6	Place Sidi Abdelkader
7	Place Mongi Bali
8	Hotel Sindbad
9	New Hotel
10	Place Hedi Chaker
11	Syndicat d'Initiative

covered in palm trees, most of which look tatty and diseased. It is an ideal place to explore by bicycle or moped, both of which can be rented from the hotels in the main town of Houmt Souk.

Most of the island's residents are members of the heretical Kharijite sect of Islam, which explains the island's 213 mosques. The people now rely heavily on tourism for their livelihood, though the fishing harbour remains a busy place.

Jerba is a good place to shop for carpets, but you need to bargain fiercely as the prices are high.

Things to See

On the south coast of the island, the small village of **Guellala** is famous for its pottery. The pieces for sale, however, are of dubious taste.

Hara Seghira This is an important Jewish village in the centre of the island. Its synagogue is visited by pilgrims during Passover.

Houmt Souk This is a tangle of narrow alleys and a few nice open squares with cafés. A few of its old *foundouks*, which used to provide food and lodging for the merchants and pilgrims of the camel caravans, have been converted to hotels. Its old fort, known as **Borj el Kebir**, at the end of the main street, was built by the Aragonese in the 13th century and extended by the Spanish in the 16th century. Its **museum** is housed in the Zaouia of Sidi

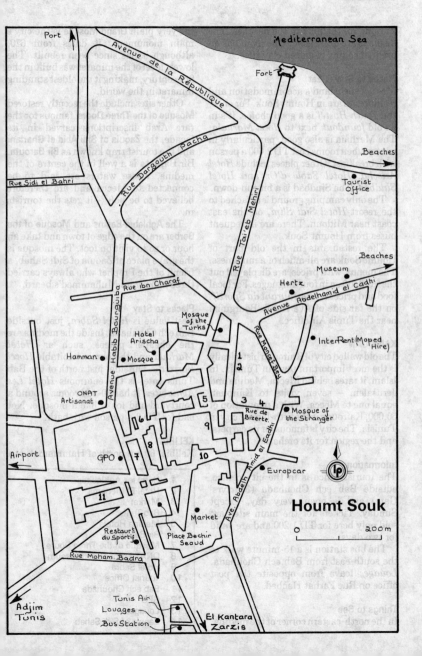

Houmt Souk

0   200m

Zitouni, on the road to the beaches. The displays are quite good. One room has an original ceiling of glazed clay tiles.

Places to Stay & Eat
Most of the island's accommodation and restaurants are in Houmt Souk. For once, the *Youth Hostel* is a good choice. It's in an old *foundouk* next to *Hotel Marhala*. The Marhala is also good, particularly in winter when rooms cost TD 2.600 a person with breakfast. Other places include *Hotel Arischa*, *Hotel Sable d'Or* and *Hotel Sindbad*. The Sindbad is a bit run-down.

The only camping ground is attached to the resort *Hotel Sidi Slim*, on the east coast near Midoun. There are infrequent buses from Houmt Souk.

The restaurants in the old part of Houmt Souk are all much of a muchness. The menus, with prices, are displayed out the front, often in four languages. For local food and prices try *Restaurant du Sportif*, on the far side of Ave Habib Bourguiba near the Tunis Air office.

KAIROUAN
The old walled city of Kairouan historically is the most important town in Tunisia. In Islam, it rates behind Mecca, Medina and Jerusalem – seven visits to Kairouan equal one to Mecca. With a population of 50,000, Kairouan is the fifth-largest city in Tunisia. The city is famous for its carpets, and the region for its orchards.

Information
The tourist office is in the city centre, outside Bab ech Chouhada (Martyrs' Gate) and is open every day, except Sunday. Tickets for the main sites are sold only here for TD 1.200 and are valid for two days.

The bus station is a 15-minute walk to the south-east from Bab ech Chouhada. *Louages* leave from opposite the post office on Rue Farhat Hached.

Things to See
In the north-eastern corner of the medina,

the very plain **Grand Mosque** is the city's main monument. It dates from 670, although it has since been rebuilt. The lowest level of the minaret was built in the 8th century, making it the oldest standing minaret in the world.

Other sites include the recently restored **Mosque of the Three Doors**, famous for the rare Arab inscriptions carved in its façade, the **Zaouia of Sidi Abid el Ghariani** and the tourist trap known as **Bir Barouta**. Bir Barouta is a well in the centre of the medina, whose waters are said to be connected to Mecca and are therefore believed to be holy – it gets the tourists in.

The **Aghlabid Basins** and **Mosque of the Berber** are on the edge of town and take an hour or so to visit on foot. The mosque is the grave place of Zaouia of Sidi Sahab, a friend of the Prophet who always carried three hairs from Muhammed's beard.

Places to Stay
Best value is *Hotel Sabra*, just outside Bab ech Chouhada. Inside the medina are the cheaper places, such as *Hotel Marhala* and the barely habitable *Hotel Barrouta*. Outside, just north of the Bab Tunis gate, is the enormous *Hotel Les Aghlabites*. It has 60-odd rooms around a courtyard and looks like a mosque. Not bad for TD 3 a person with bath.

KELIBIA
Kelibia, 60 km north of Hammamet, is a

1	Hotel les Aghlabites
2	Hotel El Menema
3	Market
4	Bab Tunis
5	Medina Hotels
6	Bir Barouta
7	Mosque of the Three Doors
8	ONAT Emporium/Museum
9	Hotel Sabra
10	Tourist Office
11	Bab ech Chouhada
12	GPO
13	Louages
14	Zaouia of Sidi Sahab

Kairouan

small fishing village on Cap Bon Peninsula, dominated by a 16th-century Spanish fort. Despite its backwater feeling, it has hydrofoil connections with Trapani in Italy from June to September. The bus and *louage* station is in the town centre.

Places to Stay

The hotels are on the beach down by the fort, two km from the town centre. They are serviced by regular shuttle taxis. *Hotel Florida* is the better of the two hotels and costs TD 8/14 a single/double with breakfast. The *Youth Hostel* is also on the beach, further around past the fishing harbour on the Mansourah road. It is the usual charmless cell block. You can camp in the grounds.

KERKENNAH ISLANDS

The Kerkennah Islands are a good place to wind down and do nothing for a few days. A far cry from a tropical island paradise, the two islands, joined by a causeway, are fairly dry and covered with palm trees, most of which look diseased. While there's been a bit of low-key resort development, the place basically is untouched.

The highest point on the islands is three metres above sea level, making bicycles the ideal mode of transport. They can be rented from Club des Iles. All ferries are met by a bus that travels the 25 km to the main town of Remla, on Ile Chergui. The islands' facilities are concentrated in Remla.

Places to Stay & Eat

The only conventional hotel is *Hotel el Jazira*, on the main road in Remla. It is basic and clean, and costs TD 2.500 a bed. It has the only bar on the islands and one of the few restaurants, making it the social hub. The resorts at *Sidi Fredj* on the north coast all charge upwards of TD 10 a person, although it may be possible to bargain a bit in winter.

Restaurant Le Sirene is down by the water in Remla. While the food is good, the opening hours are erratic.

EL KEF

El Kef, an agricultural town with a commanding position, has no specific attractions but on the whole is an interesting place. Its altitude makes it a welcome few degrees cooler than the surrounding plains. The bus and *louage* station is a 20-minute walk downhill from the town centre.

Things to See

The regional **museum**, not far from the presidential palace, has some excellent articles from the nomadic Bedouin. The **kasbah**, on top of the hill, is very run-down but gives some fine views over the plains. There is a small **museum** outside.

Places to Stay

The best bet is the new *Hotel Medina* at 18 Rue Farhat Hached. Good value at TD 5 a double. Other cheapies include *Hotel La Source* and *Hotel Auberge*. The La Source is barely fit for habitation and the Auberge has a sleazy bar.

MAHDIA

Mahdia, on the central coast, is a laid-back place with a history so far undiscovered by the tour groups. It was the capital of the early Fatimid rulers in the 10th century. After they moved to Cairo, it remained sufficiently important to be taken over by the Christians later that century, the Normans in the 12th century and the Spaniards in the 16th century.

The bus and train stations are about 500 metres from the town centre, past the fishing port.

Things to See

The main gate to the old medina, **Skifa el Kahla**, is all that remains of the 10-metre-thick wall that protected Mahdia on the headland. The unadorned **Grand Mosque** is a 20th-century replica of one built by the Mahdi in the 10th century. On the high point of the headland, the **Borj el Kebir** fort has been heavily restored and is not worth the effort of visiting.

Places to Stay & Eat

Hotel el Jazira in the medina is excellent. It is a bargain at TD 2 with hot showers. *Grand Hotel* and *Rand Hotel*, both a 15-minute walk from the main gate along the Sousse road, cost around TD 7 to TD 10 a double.

Restaurant El Moez, on the edge of the medina near the market, serves some of the best shakshuka in the country. By evening, its variety is limited.

MATMATA

Matmata, with its unusual troglodyte dwellings, is one of the main attractions of the south. The tour buses roll in and out every day, but none stay overnight, making the late afternoon and early morning the best times to wander around.

There are only a few buildings above ground, so your first impression will be that there is little here. The TV aerials and parked cars, however, give it away. The houses are all built along the same lines: a central courtyard, usually circular, is dug out of the soft sandstone and the rooms are then dug out from its perimeter. Entry is through a corridor to ground level. A quick wander around turns up dozens of these places. But, understandably, the residents are tired of being stared at like goldfish.

The village of **Haddej**, a few km to the north, is much less touristed and you can usually find someone to show you around.

Places to Stay

The hotels are all old converted underground houses. The best is *Hotel Marhala*; good value at TD 3.500/5.900 for spotlessly clean singles/doubles with breakfast. Half board (*demi pension*) is also good value at TD 5 a person, especially as there is little choice in restaurants in town. The other hotels, *Hotel Les Berbiers* and *Hotel Sidi Driss* are marginally cheaper but not quite as good.

The *Youth Hostel* is an above-ground building, lacking the atmosphere of its underground competition. It's OK at TD 1.500 a person.

MEDENINE

Medenine is in the *ksour* area (a *ksar* is an old fortified granary: its plural being *ksour*) of the country's south. The best *ksour* are further south, near Tataouine. There is a small *ksar* in Medenine itself, which has been restored to something of a tourist trap. The best *ksar* in the area is the one that dominates the village of **Metameur**, about six km north of town. Part of it has been converted to a cheap hotel.

The bus station is in the town centre, with the *louage* station almost opposite.

Places to Stay

Best of the cheapies is *Hotel Essaada*, a couple of minutes' walk from the bus station. It is basic but adequate at TD 2 a person. *Hotel Les Palmiers* is similar, but a bit further from the town centre. The converted *ksar* at Metameur is good value at TD 3 a person with breakfast, if a bit isolated.

NABEUL

Nabeul is Tunisia's major tourist trap, like Hammamet only more so. The same advise applies – give it a miss in summer. Out of season things are a bit more relaxed. The town is popular because of its beaches and Friday market, neither of which are anything special. The dozen or so resort hotels have a bit of a monopoly on the best beach, but it's not too difficult to stroll in and use the facilities.

The bus station for buses to Tunis and Hammamet is close to the centre on Ave Habib Thameur. For Kelibia and places on the Cap Bon Peninsula, buses and *louages* leave from a dusty lot at the eastern end of Ave Farhat Hached, the main street. The railway station is in the centre, a couple of blocks towards the beach from the main street.

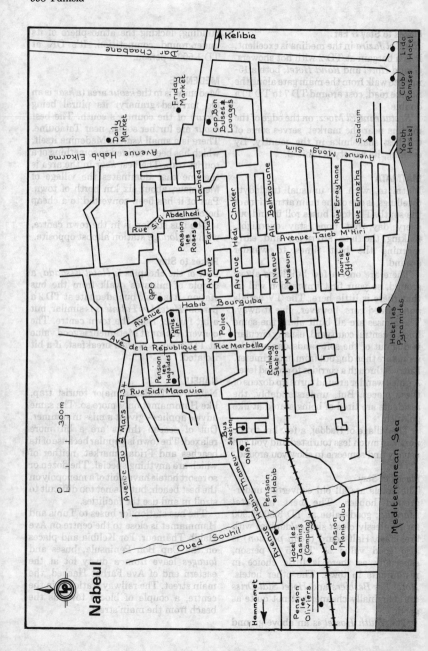

Nabeul

Kelibia

Dar Chaâbane

Friday Market

Daily Market

Cap Bon Buses Louages

Avenue Habib Elkorma

Rue Sidi Abdelhedi

Rue
Hached

Avenue Farhat Hached

Avenue Hédi Chaker

Avenue Ali Belhaouane

Avenue Mongi Slim

Avenue Taieb M'Hiri

Rue Errayhane

Rue Ennozha

Stadium

Youth Hostel

Club Ramses

Lido Hotel

Pension les Roses

QPO

Avenue Habib Bourguiba

Tunis Air

Police

Ave. de la République

Rue Marbella

Museum

Tourist Office

Avenue du 2 Mars 1934

Pension Hafsides

Rue Sidi Maaouia

Railway Station

Bus Station

ONAT

Avenue Habib Thameur

Pension el Habib

Oued Souhil

Hotel les Jasmins (Camping)

Pension Monia Club

Pension les Oliviers

Hammamet

Mediterranean Sea

Hotels les Pyramides

300m

0

N

Places to Stay

The *Youth Hostel* is on a beach about two km from the centre of town – a stinking hot walk in summer. It's clean, has cold showers and your gear is safe. In Nabeul, the two cheapest places to stay are *Pension Les Roses*, on Ave Farhat Hached, and *Pension el Habib*, on the Hammamet road. Both cost TD 4/6 a single/double in the off season. *Hotel Les Jasmins*, a couple of km towards Hammamet, has a good shady camping ground and is only a few minutes' walk from the beach.

NEFTA

Nefta, a beautiful oasis town, is the last town before the Algerian border, 23 km to the west. The new and old towns are divided by the *corbeille*, a deep, palm-lined gully which is the town's water source. The spring water comes out of the ground hot, and there are bathing pools for men and women. The *palmeraie* continues to the edge of the Chott el Jerid and contains a number of *marabouts* (tombs of holy men belonging to the mystical Islamic sect, the Sufis).

There is a daily bus to the Algerian border at 10 am. *Louages* make the journey at odd times during the day.

Places to Stay

The best place to stay is *Hotel Marhala*, on the western edge of town. Although the building is an old brick factory, it has been fitted out well and is good value at TD 3/6 a single/double with breakfast. *Hotel Mirage* and the enormous *Sahara Palace* are both expensive.

SFAX

Sfax, with its old, walled medina, is an interesting place as yet undiscovered by tour groups. This, however, is changing. The new town is of little interest, except as the departure point for ferries to the Kerkennah Islands.

The highlight of the medina is the **Museum of Popular Traditions**, housed in a beautiful 17th-century mansion. It's at 5 Rue Sidi Ali Nouri, a small side street to the right off the main street, Rue Mongi Slim, through the medina.

Information

There's a tourist office in the small green-roofed pavilion on a small square on Ave Habib Bourguiba. The post office is the large official-looking building on Ave Habib Bourguiba, near the railway station. There are plenty of banks, mostly along Ave Habib Bourguiba and Rue de la République.

The modern railway station is close to the centre at the eastern end of Ave Habib Bourguiba. The SNTRI office is almost directly opposite. The regional bus station is at the opposite end of Ave Habib Bourguiba. The ferry port is a 15-minute walk south of the main square.

Places to Stay

The cheapies are in the medina, to the right as you go through Bab Diwan. *Hotel Besbes* has reasonable rooms for TD 5 a double. *Hotel Essaada*, next door, is similar, as are a few places along the narrow Rue Mongi Slim. *Hotel Medina* at No 53 charges TD 6 a double.

Better is the friendly *Hotel de la Paix*. It's outside the medina on Rue Alexander Dumas, which runs south of Ave Habib Bourguiba, and charges TD 6 for a good-sized double with shower. The best place of all, if you can afford it, is *Hotel Les Oliviers*. It's an elegant older-style place on Ave Habib Thameur, two blocks south of Ave Habib Bourguiba. Rooms cost TD 12/18 a single/double with breakfast.

SOUSSE

Sousse is like Hammamet and Nabeul, except here you can stay in the interesting medina and leave the beach strip to the package tourists. Perhaps the most unusual feature of the town is that the main Tunis to Sfax railway line runs right down the centre of the main street. What is more amazing is that there are no

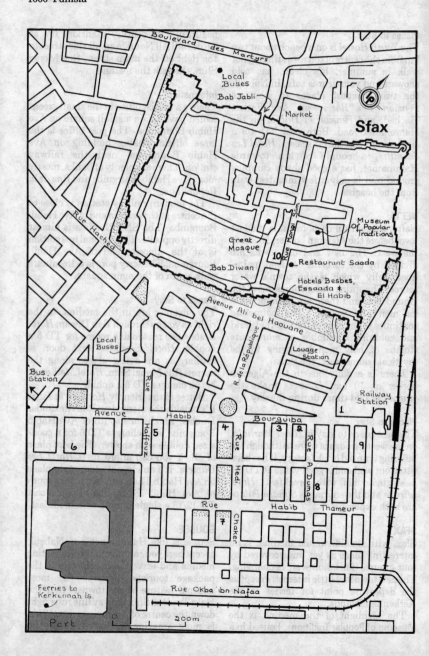

Sfax

1	GPO
2	French Consulate
3	Hotel Sfax Centre
4	Town Hall & Museum
5	Pizzeria Restaurant
6	Fish Market
7	Hotel Les Oliviers
8	Hotel de la Paix
9	SNTRI Buses
10	Hotel Medina

warning signals whatsoever, and you could easily adorn the front of an engine.

Information

The main tourist office is on the corner of the main street and Ave Habib Bourguiba. The local syndicat d'initiative is in a small white domed building across the road near the medina. Tickets to the Grand Mosque are sold here. The post office and railway station are close by.

Try to avoid arriving by SNTRI bus as the main station is a solid three km to the north from the centre. Regional buses to Monastir, Mahdia and Kairouan leave from Place Farhat Hached, near the port entrance. *Louages* leave from Bab Jedid station, not far from the eastern Bab Jedid gate.

Things to See

The main monuments of the medina are the **ribat**, a sort of fortified monastery, and the **Grand Mosque**. Both are in the north-eastern corner not far from Place Farhat Hached.

The ribat dates from the 9th century. Its primary purpose was that of a fort, but when the men weren't involved in hostilities they would pursue Islamic study in the small cells surrounding the courtyard. Its design was simple and functional. A narrow spiral staircase leads to the top of the tower, from where you get an excellent view of the medina and into the courtyard of the Grand Mosque below.

The Grand Mosque is also fairly simple.

Built in the 9th century, it was restored in both the 17th and 20th centuries. The courtyard is open to visitors daily, except Friday. Tickets must be bought in advance from the syndicat d'initiative.

The **kasbah** on top of the hill has a **museum** with some well-presented mosaics from the area. There is no access to the kasbah from the medina, so make sure you are outside the medina wall before climbing the hill.

Places to Stay & Eat

Hotel Zouhour, in the medina at 48 Rue de Paris, is the most presentable of the cheapies and charges TD 2 a person. There are no showers. The best rooms are on the top floors as the windows open outwards. Neither *Hotel Perles* nor *Hotel Baghdad* are up to much.

More expensive is *Hotel Amira*, inside the medina near Bab Jedid. It charges TD 10 a double with hot showers and breakfast served on the upstairs terrace – a good place. Next to the Grand Mosque is the more up-market *Hotel Medina*, which charges TD 9/13 a single/double with bath and breakfast. *Hotel Claridge*, on Ave Habib Bourguiba, is also good value at TD 7.700 a person.

The main street is lined with restaurants catering to tourists. The menus are in four languages, and often the waiters speak all of them. The seafood is excellent. Try the tuna steaks at *Restaurant le Bonheur*. It's a good restaurant and the prices are reasonable.

TABARKA

This pleasant little town on the north coast is becoming more popular as people start to appreciate its backwater atmosphere and beautiful setting on a small bay dominated by a Genoese fort.

There is a tourist office on the main street, as well as the usual banks and a post office. The SNTRI buses leave from one block inland of the main street. *Louages* go from near the entrance to Mimosas Hotel. It is also possible to get to

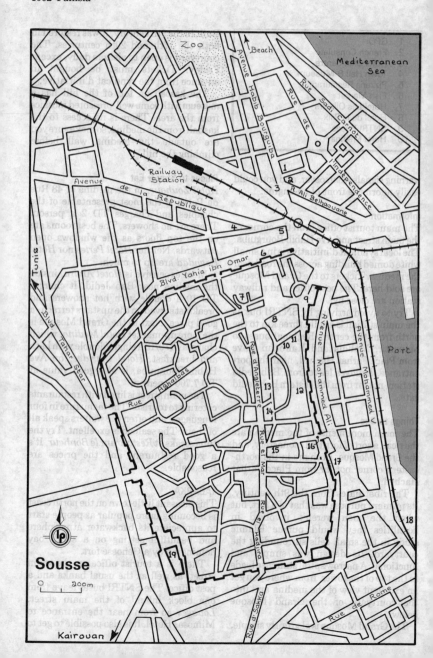

Sousse

0   200m

1	Juice Stall
2	Hotel Claridge
3	Tourist Office
4	GPO
5	Syndicat d'Initiative
6	Local Buses & Louages
7	Ribat
8	Grand Mosque
9	Restaurant Populaire
10	Hotel Medina
11	Hotel Baghdad
12	Hotel Amira
13	Hotel Gabès
14	Hotel Zouhour
15	Restaurant Medina
16	Bab Jedid
17	Bab Jedid Louage Station
18	Trains to Mahdia & Monastir
19	Kasbah & Museum

Algeria, either by hitching or taking a bus to the border.

Places to Stay & Eat

With only one budget hotel, accommodation is at a premium. At the height of summer if you arrive after midday you'll be lucky to get *any* hotel bed. *Hotel Corail* is the cheapest, and even here you pay TD 10 a double (perhaps negotiable out of season). *Hotel de France* charges TD 15 a double. Its restaurant is the best value in town, with a set menu costing TD 3.

Opposite Hotel France, *Restaurat Khemis* has good calamari and passable fish.

TATAOUINE

Tataouine is a friendly town, 50 km south of Medenine. It is a good base for visiting the surrounding Berber villages. The bus station is in the town centre, as is the *louage* station.

Things to See

The three-storey **Ksar Megabla** is about a one-hour walk from the centre. Despite it being semiderelict, the locals still use the solid rooms to pen their sheep and goats.

It's to the side of the hill on the right of the road to Remada.

Chenini This is a spectacular Berber village perched on the edge of an escarpment 18 km west of Tataouine. It is not served by public transport, so it's a matter of hitching (there's little traffic) or hiring a *louage*, which will cost TD 10 for the return trip with about an hour at the village. It is worth the effort, but because the place is on the Land Rover trail, it is best to get there either late or early in the day.

Ghoumrassen This village is surrounded by rocky cliffs and has numerous cave dwellings to explore, many of which are still filled with their former occupants' belongings. It is the largest of the Berber villages and the only one served by public transport.

Places to Stay & Eat

Hotel Ennour, about 500 metres from the centre along the road to Medenine, is the better of the two cheapies. Beds cost TD 1.500. *Hotel la Gazelle* offers comfort at TD 9/13 a single/double with breakfast, and considerably less in the off-season.

The best place to eat is *Restaurant B Moussa*, near the central town square with the statue.

TOZEUR

Tozeur is an oasis town very much on the tourist route. Still, it is very relaxed and enjoyable. The *palmeraie* is enormous and can be explored by camel (for hire outside Hotel Continental) if you can't handle walking. Quite a few souvenir shops have sprung up in the town centre. They all sell the colourful local rugs for which the area is famous. Bargain hard if you're buying.

The bus station is on Ave Farhat Hached, with the *louage* station almost opposite. There are regular buses between Tozeur and Kebili. Passenger rail services have been discontinued: the train only runs as far as Metlaoui.

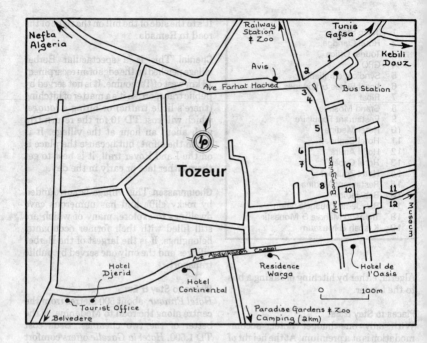

On the map:
Nefta
Algeria

Railway
Station
& Zoo

Tunis
Gafsa

Kebili
Douz

Avis

Bus Station

Ave Farhat Hached

Tozeur

Ave Bourguiba

Museum

Ave Abdulkacem Chebbi

Hotel
Djerid

Hotel
Continental

Residence
Warga

Hotel de
l'Oasis

0   100m

Tourist Office

Belvedere

Paradise Gardens & Zoo
Camping (2km)

Things to See

The **palmeraie** is best explored along the road signposted 'To Paradise Gardens and Zoo'. It's a two-km walk, but the luxuriant **garden** is worth the effort. The **zoo** is the usual collection of sorry specimens housed in depressingly small cages; the *fennecs* (desert foxes) are especially pathetic.

There is another **zoo** north of town near the railway station that claims to have 'performing' scorpions.

The road across the **Chott el Jerid** to Kebili should not be missed, especially on a clear sunny day when the mirages and other optical illusions are stunning.

Places to Stay & Eat

Hotel Essaada in the town centre charges TD 2 a person, plus 400 millimes for a hot shower. *Residence Warda* is another cheapie. There is camping at *Paradise Gardens* and *Belvedere*, three km from

town on the track past Hotel Continental. There's also a camping ground at Degache, 18 km from Tozeur on the road to Kebili.

Restaurant du Paradis, a few doors along from Hotel Essaada, is good value.

TUNIS

Tunis, the capital of Tunisia, is a major gateway to Africa and there's plenty to do and see.

Information

Tourist Office The tourist office is on Ave Habib Bourguiba at Place de l'Afrique in the city centre. It has some glossy brochures, but little else.

Banks The major banks are along Ave Habib Bourguiba. Some have extended trading hours: the one next to Africa Hotel stays open late and on Saturdays.

1	Louage Station
2	Bank
3	Fuel Station
4	Syndicat d'Initiative
5	Restaurant de la République
6	Restaurant du Paradis
7	Hotel Essaada
8	Souvenir Shops
9	Market
10	GPO
11	Hotel Splendid
12	Restaurant & Pool

Post & Telephone The post office is on Rue Charles de Gaulle, in the centre of the cheap hotel area south of Ave Habib Bourguiba. The telephone office is in the same building, accessed from Rue Jamel Abdelnasser. It is open 24 hours and you can dial direct to Europe.

Ferry The Tirrenia Line (tel 242 801), for ferry tickets to Italy, is at 122 Rue de Yougoslavie. The Compagnie Tunisienne de Navigation office (tel 242 999) is at 5 Ave Dag Hammerskjoeld.

Useful Addresses Some useful addresses are:

UK Embassy
    5 Place de la Victoire (tel 245 100)
Egyptian Embassy
    16 Rue Essayouti, El Menzeh (tel 230 004)
French Embassy
    Place de l'Indépendence, Ave Habib Bourguiba (tel 245 700)
Libyan Embassy
    48 Rue 1 Juin,
Moroccan Embassy
    39 Rue 1 Juin (tel 288 063)
USA Embassy
    144 Avenue de la Libertè (tel 282 566)
West German Embassy
    18 Ave Challaye (tel 281 246)
Algerian Consulate
    136 Rue de la Libertè
American Express
    Carthage Tours, 59 Ave Habib Bourguiba (tel 254 605)
Thomas Cook
    Wagons-Lits office, International Hotel, 49 Ave Habib Bourguiba (tel 347 622)

Things to See
It's worth wandering around the **medina** for half a day or more. It's certainly not the overcrowded tangle of Fés or Cairo, but interesting all the same. The main street into the medina from the new city, Rue Jemaa ez-Zitouna, is virtually one continuous line of souvenir shops. This street has possibly the highest prices in the country, but you can get a good idea of what is available.

One of the most interesting souks is **Souk des Chechias**, where they make the small red felt caps in real sweatshops. These caps are really only worn by the older men these days.

The **Dar Ben Abdallah Museum** is a bit hard to find, but worth the effort. It is off to the right of Rue des Tenturiers, along Rue Sidi Kacem, in the southern part of the medina. Once a Turkish palace, it now houses a collection of traditional costumes and everyday items. The building itself is probably of more interest than the actual exhibits.

The one thing in the new city not to be missed is the **Bardo Museum**. It houses a truly magnificent collection of Roman mosaics and marble statuary. It is three km from the city centre. To get there take the No 3 bus from opposite Africa Hotel on Ave Habib Bourguiba to its end; the museum, housed in an old palace set in a large garden, is on the right. It is open 9.30 am to 4.30 pm Tuesday to Saturday and entry costs TD 1.

The Punic and Roman ruins of **Carthage** are definitely one of the main attractions of Tunis. The ruins are scattered over a wide area and include Roman baths, houses, cisterns, basilica and old streets. The best way to see Carthage is to take the TGM rail from Ave Habib Bourguiba to Carthage Hannibal station, and wander from there. If time is short, visit the **National Museum**, on top of the hill next to the deconsecrated cathedral, and the **Byrsa Quarter**, in the grounds of the museum. The Romans did such a good job of destroying Carthage that this is about

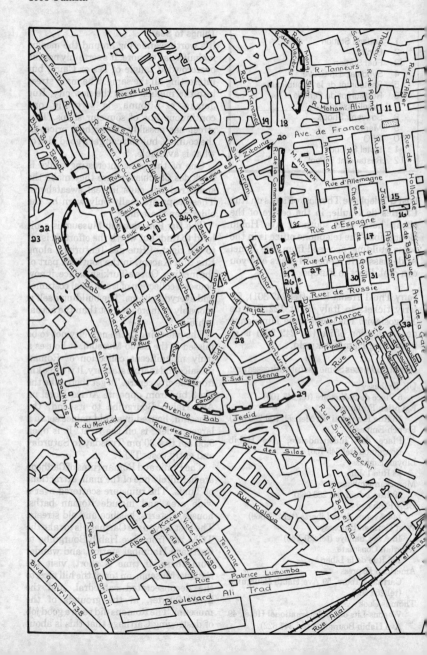

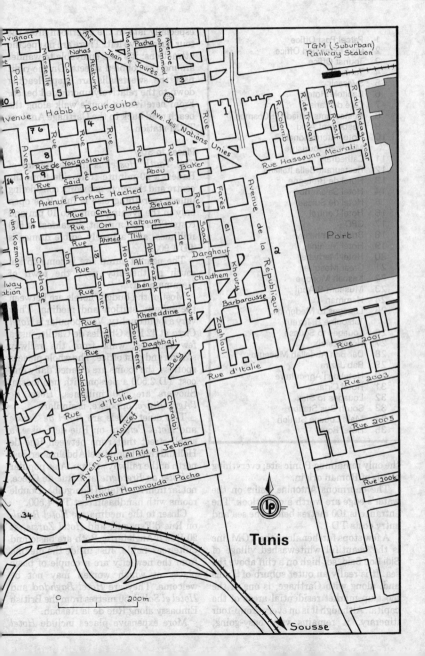

Tunis

0 ____ 200m

→ Sousse

1	Parcel Post Office
2	Visa Extension Office
3	Tourist Office
4	Tunis Air
5	Swissair
6	Capitole Hotel
7	Café de Paris
8	Restaurants Erriadh & Cosmos
9	Restaurant Abid
10	Hotel International Maghreb Tourisme
11	Cathedral
12	Restaurant Bella Italiana
13	Hotel de Bretagne
14	Hotel Salammbô
15	Hotel de Suisse
16	Hotel Central
17	GPO
18	British Embassy
19	Hotel Medina
20	Hotel Marhaba
21	Great Mosque
22	Kasbah Mosque
23	Museum 9 April
24	Hamman
25	Louages to Medenine, Tataouine & Tozeur
26	Louages to Sousse
27	Hotel Zarzis
28	Dar Ben Abdallah Museum
29	Bab Jazira
30	Hotel de l'Agriculture
31	Hotel Cirta
32	Louages to Sfax
33	South Bus Station
34	Main Louage Station
35	Hotel Royal

the only remaining Punic site; everything else is of Roman origin.

The enormous **Antonine Baths** on the water's edge are worth a quick look. The entrance is 100 metres before the sea and entry costs TD 1.

A few stops further along the TGM line is the beautiful whitewashed village of **Sidi Bou Said**, set high on a cliff above the sea. It is really an outer suburb of Tunis and, along with Carthage, is one of the most up-market residential areas of the capital. Although it is on every group-tour itinerary, it remains very easy-going,

especially late in the afternoon after the tour buses have left. There are no specific attractions; it's just enjoyable to wander around the cobbled streets. On the right past the sweetstalls are steps leading down to the relatively uncrowded beach. From here it's an hour's walk along the beach road back to the Carthage Amilcar TGM station.

Places to Stay

The *Youth Hostel* is in the suburb of Radés, a 20-minute train ride from the centre and therefore not worth considering unless everything else is full. It is open only in the evening from 7 to 10 pm and costs TD 1.500 a night. Breakfast is 500 millimes, and a barely edible dinner is TD 1.900.

The nearest camp site is some 15 km south of the city near the town of Hammam Lif.

Most of the budget hotels are between the railway station and medina. They vary a lot in quality. Very popular is *Hotel Cirta* at 42 Rue Charles de Gaulle, just a few minutes' walk from the railway station and post office. The whole place is spotless, the rooms are cleaned daily and cost TD 2.500 a person with handbasin. Showers are 500 millimes. *Hotel de l'Agriculture*, opposite, is similar.

Two quiet hotels are *Hotel de Suisse* and *Hotel Central* on Rue de Suisse, a small street that runs between Rue de Hollande and Rue Jamel Abdelnasser, just north of the railway station. Also popular is *Hotel de Bretagne* at 7 Rue de Grèce, not far from Ave Habib Bourguiba. Double rooms with handbasin cost TD 4.500.

Closer to the medina are *Hotel Royal*, on Rue d'Espagne, and *Hotel Zarsis*, at 20 Rue d'Angleterre. Both are basic and quite reasonable. Just inside the medina from the new city are a couple of basic places at which women may not be welcome. They are *Hotel Baghdad* and *Hotel el Soleil*, 50 metres from the British Embassy along Rue de la Kasbah.

More expensive places include *Hotel*

Bristol, in a small cobbled alley just south of Ave Habib Bourguiba behind Café de Paris, which charges TD 7 a double; *Hotel Salammbo*, at 6 Rue de Grèce, where a double with bath and breakfast costs TD 9; and the good-value *Hotel Transatlantique*, at 106 Rue de Yougoslavie.

Places to Eat

There are a couple of good local places that serve cheap appetising food. *Restaurant Carcassonne*, at 8 Ave de Carthage, just off Ave Habib Bourguiba near Café de Paris, has a good four-course *repas* (set menu) for TD 2, which is plenty for two when supplemented with the free bread.

Also good is *Restaurant Abid* on Rue de Yougoslavie, near the corner of Rue Ibn Khaldoun. Along Rue Ibn Khaldoun are some more good restaurants. *Restaurant Le Cosmos* at No 7 is one of the best in Tunis – the seafood is excellent, try the fish soup. Even though you are looking at around TD 10 to TD 15 for two people, the price includes a half-bottle of local red wine. Similar is *Restaurant l'Etoile* at No 3.

For cheaper snacks there are plenty of rotisseries serving chicken & chips to go,

or patisseries offering filling savouries, individual pizzas and, of course, cakes. The patisseries usually have a coffee bar out the back, making them a good place for croissant and coffee breakfasts. Some of the best patisseries are on Rue Charles de Gaulle, between Ave Habib Bourguiba and the post office.

Getting Around

If you arrive by air, the yellow city bus No 35 runs between the airport and city centre every half hour. For the return journey, it leaves from opposite Africa Hotel on Ave Habib Bourguiba.

Boats from Italy dock at La Goulette, on the far side of Lac de Tunis. The cheapest way to the city is by TGM suburban train from La Goulette. From the port, walk straight out to the kasbah, turn left and walk until you come to a railway crossing (about 500 metres); the TGM station is 100 metres to the right. The fare is 180 millimes. In the other direction this line goes to Carthage, Sidi Bou Said and the beach suburb of La Marsa. Tunis to La Marsa costs 320 millimes.

Uganda

From being Winston Churchill's 'Pearl of Africa' before independence in 1962, Uganda lay shattered and bankrupt in 1986. The once prosperous and fairly cohesive country had been broken on the rack of tribal animosity, nepotism, power-mad politicians and military tyranny. Though much of the blame can be laid squarely at the feet of the sordid and brutal military dictator Idi Amin, who was overthrown in 1979, others have much to answer for. Indeed, there was little to choose between any of Uganda's rulers until 1986. All appear to have been spawned from the same degenerative mould.

Despite the killings, the disappearances, the brutality, and the fear and destructiveness of those years, Ugandans appear to have weathered the storm remarkably well. They are not a sullen, bitter or cowed people, rather they are quick to smile and enthusiastic to carry on and rebuild the country after the nightmares of the past. Undoubtedly part of the reason for this positive approach is the new government of President Yoweri Museveni, which seems intent on making a clean sweep of the government, the civil service and army. Despite huge odds and an empty treasury, Museveni has made great efforts to get the country back on its feet. He has stamped on corruption, banned meetings of political parties to prevent a resurgence of intertribal rivalry and squabbling among powerbrokers and gone out of his way to reassure tribal elders that his administration will be a balanced one. Perhaps most important of all, his army is the best disciplined the country has ever had – despite what to western eyes is the astonishing sight of fatigue-clad teenagers, some as young as 14.

Gone are the days when every road was littered with checkpoints manned by drunken and surly soldiers intent on squeezing every last penny out of civilians and taking at gunpoint what they wanted from stores. While it's easy to be cynical, there's a distinct feeling that a genuine change has occurred. Even the Ugandans acknowledge it: and they'd be the last people to be naively optimistic.

Until the 19th century, very few outsiders came to Uganda. Despite its fertility and capacity to grow surplus crops, there were virtually no trading links with the coast. A number of indigenous kingdoms emerged from the 14th century onwards, among them the Buganda, Bunyoro, Toro, Ankole and Busoga, with Bunyoro initially being the most powerful. Over the following centuries, however, Buganda, whose people are Bagandas, eventually assumed the mantle of the dominant kingdom. The Baganda make up some 20% of Uganda's population and are ruled by a *kabaka* (king).

During the reign of Kabaka Mwanga in the mid-19th century, contacts were made with Arab traders from the coast and European explorers. The Christian missionaries that followed were very unpopular with the rulers of Buganda and Toro and there were wholesale massacres of their followers and those of Islam.

After the treaty of Berlin in 1890, which defined the various European countries' spheres of influence in Africa, Uganda was declared a British protectorate in 1894, along with Kenya and the islands of Zanzibar and Pemba. The colonial administrators adopted a policy of indirect

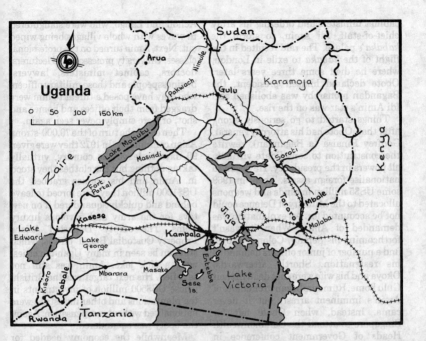

rule, giving the traditional kingdoms a considerable degree of local autonomy. But, at the same time, they favoured the Baganda in their recruitment for the civil service. The other tribes, faced with an inability to get administrative posts or make inroads on the Baganda-dominated commercial sector, were forced to seek other ways of joining the mainstream. The Acholi and Lango, for example, chose the army, and became the tribal majorities in the military. These monopolies on various professions eventually led to the intertribal conflicts that tore Uganda apart after independence.

Unlike Kenya, and to a lesser extent Tanzania, Uganda never experienced a large influx of European settlers and the accompanying expropriation of land. Instead, the tribes were encouraged to grow cash crops for export through their own cooperative organisations. As a result, nationalist organisations were late on the

scene, and when they did arrive it was on a tribal basis. So exclusive were some of these nationalist movements that when independence was being discussed the Baganda considered secession. By the mid-1950s, however, a Lango schoolteacher, Dr Milton Obote, managed to put together a loose coalition that led Uganda to independence in 1962 on the promise that the Baganda would have autonomy. The *kabaka* was the new nation's president and Milton Obote its prime minister.

It wasn't a particularly good time for Uganda to come to grips with independence. Civil wars were raging in neighbouring southern Sudan, Zaïre and Rwanda, and refugees were streaming into the country adding to its problems. Also, it soon became obvious that Obote had no intention of sharing power with the *kabaka*. A confrontation was inevitable. Obote moved fast, arresting a number of cabinet ministers and ordering his army chief-of-staff, Idi Amin, to storm the *kabaka's* palace. The raid resulted in the flight of the *kabaka* to exile in London, where he died some three years later. Obote declared himself president, the Bagandan monarchy was abolished and Idi Amin's star was on the rise.

Things started to go seriously wrong after that. Obote had his attorney general, Godfrey Binaisa (a Bagandan), rewrite the constitution to consolidate virtually all powers in the presidency. He began to nationalise foreign assets. Then, in 1969 some US$5 million in funds and weapons allocated to the Ministry of Defence could not be accounted for. An explanation was demanded of Amin. When it wasn't forthcoming his deputy, Colonel Okoya, and a number of junior officers demanded his resignation. Shortly afterwards, Okoya and his wife were shot dead in their Gulu home. Rumours began to circulate of Amin's imminent arrest, but it never came. Instead, when Obote left for Singapore to attend the Commonwealth Heads of Government conference in January 1971, Amin staged a coup. The British, who probably suffered most from Obote's nationalisation programme, were one of the first countries to recognise the new regime. Obote returned to exile in Tanzania.

So began Uganda's greatest reign of terror. All political activities were quickly suspended and the army was empowered to shoot on sight anyone suspected of opposing the regime. Over the next eight years an estimated 300,000 Ugandans were killed. Many of the victims lost their lives in a brutal manner – bludgeoned to death with sledgehammers and iron bars or tortured to death in prisons and police stations all over the country. Nile Mansions, next to the Conference Centre in Kampala, was particularly notorious. The screams of those being tortured or beaten to death there could often be heard round the clock for days on end. Prime targets of Amin's death squads were the

Acholi and Lango, who were slaughtered in waves with whole villages being wiped out. Next, Amin turned on the professional classes. University professors and lecturers, doctors, cabinet ministers, lawyers, businesspeople and those military officers who may have posed a threat to him were dragged from their offices and homes and shot, or were simply never seen again.

Then came the turn of the 70,000-strong Asian community. In 1972 they were given 90 days to leave the country, virtually taking nothing but the clothes they stood in. Amin and his cronies grabbed the US$1000 million they were forced to leave behind and quickly squandered it on new toys for the army and frivolous luxury items. The empty 'Departed Asians Property Custodial Board' offices, which still can be seen in many Ugandan cities, were a sick joke. Amin was still not satisfied. His next target was the British, whose US$500 million of investments in tea plantations and other industries were nationalised without compensation. Again, the booty was squandered.

Meanwhile the economy headed for bankruptcy, industrial activity ceased, hospitals and rural health clinics closed, roads and railways fell apart, the cities became garbage dumps and their utilities ceased to function. The prolific wildlife was machine-gunned down by soldiers for meat; ivory, skins and the tourist industry evaporated; and streams of refugees fled in all directions.

Faced with this chaos and an inflation rate that hit 1000%, Amin was forced to delegate more and more powers to the provincial governors, who in turn became virtual warlords in their own areas. Towards the end, the treasury was so bereft of funds that it was unable to pay the soldiers' wages. At the same time, international condemnation of the sordid regime was growing stronger by the day as more and more news of massacres, torture and summary executions leaked out of the country.

Libya, under the increasingly idiosyncratic leadership of Gaddafi, was just about Amin's only supporter. Libya bailed out the Ugandan economy supposedly in the name of Islamic brotherhood (Amin had conveniently become a Muslim) and began an intensive drive to equip the Ugandan forces with sophisticated weapons.

The rot, however, had spread too far and was way past the point where it could be arrested by a few million dollars worth of Libyan largesse. Faced with a restless army in which intertribal fighting had broken out, Amin was forced to seek a diversion. He chose a war with Tanzania, ostensibly to teach it a lesson for supporting anti-Amin dissidents. It was his last major act of insanity and in it were the seeds of his downfall.

On 30 October 1978, the Ugandan army rolled across north-west Tanzania virtually unopposed and annexed more than 1200 square km of territory. The air force, meanwhile, bombed the Lake Victoria ports of Bukoba and Musoma. Nyerere ordered a full-scale counter-attack but it took months to mobilise his ill-equipped and poorly-trained forces. By the following spring, however, he had managed to scrape together a 50,000-strong people's militia composed mainly of illiterate youths from the bush. With these and the many exiled Ugandan liberation groups, who were united only in their determination to rid Uganda of Amin, the two armies met. East Africa's supposedly best-equipped and best-trained army threw down its weapons and fled. The Tanzanians pushed on into the heart of Uganda. Kampala fell without a fight, and by the end of April organised resistance had effectively ceased. Amin fled to Libya, where he remained until Gaddafi threw him out after a shoot-out with Libyan soldiers. Amin was living in Jeddah on a Saudi Arabian pension until he was kicked out in December 1988. Amin tried to return to Uganda via Zaïre but in the process was picked up by Zaïre officials at the border for having a false passport.

The Tanzanian action was criticised, somewhat half-heartedly, by the Organisation for African Unity (OAU) and Tanzania was forced to foot the estimated US\$500 million war bill. This was a crushing blow for an already desperately poor country. No other country has ever come forward with a contribution.

The rejoicing in Uganda was short-lived. The 12,000 or so Tanzanian troops who stayed in the country supposedly to help in its rebuilding and to maintain law and order turned on the Ugandans as soon as their pay didn't come through. They took what they wanted from shops at gunpoint, hijacked trucks coming in from Kenya with international relief aid and slaughtered more wildlife.

Once again the country slid into chaos and gangs of armed bandits began to roam the cities, killing and looting. Food supplies ran out and hospitals could no longer function. Nevertheless, thousands of exiled Ugandans began to answer the new president's call to return home and help with reconstruction. Usefu Lule, a modest and unambitious man, had been installed as president with Nyerere's blessing. But when he began to adopt policies that displeased Nyerere, he was replaced by Godfrey Binaisa amid pro-Lule riots in Kampala. Obote, meanwhile, bided his time in Dar es Salaam.

Binaisa quickly came under pressure to set a date for general elections and a return to civilian rule. Though this was done, he found himself at odds with other powerful members of the provisional government on ideological, constitutional and personal grounds – particularly over his insistence that the pre-Amin political parties not be allowed to contest the elections. The strongest criticism came from two senior members of the army, Tito Okello and David Ojok, who were supporters of Obote. Fearing a coup, Binaisa tried to dismiss Ojok. Ojok refused to step down and instead placed Binaisa under house arrest. The government was taken over by a military commission that called elections for later that year. Obote returned from exile to an enthusiastic welcome in many parts of the country and swept to victory in elections blatantly rigged in his favour. Binaisa returned to exile in the USA.

The honeymoon with Obote proved to be relatively short. Like Amin, he favoured certain tribes. Large numbers of civil servants, army and police commanders belonging to southern tribes were replaced with Obote supporters from northern tribes. The State Research Bureau, a euphemism for the secret police, was re-established and the prisons began to fill up once more. Obote was about to complete the destruction that Amin initiated. More and more reports leaked out of atrocities and killings. Mass graves, which were unrelated to the Amin era, were unearthed. The press was muzzled and western journalists expelled. Obote again was in search of absolute power.

Intertribal tension was again on the rise. In mid-1985 Obote was overthrown in a coup staged by the army under the leadership of Okello.

Okello, however, was not the only opponent of Obote. Shortly after Obote was installed as president for the second time, a guerrilla army opposed to his tribally-biased government was formed in western Uganda. It was led by Yoweri Museveni, who had lived in exile in Tanzania during Amin's regime and who had served as defence minister during the chaotic administrations of 1979-80. From a group of 27 men, grew a guerrilla force of around 20,000, many of them orphaned teenagers.

In the early days few gave the guerrillas, known as the National Resistance Army, much chance. Government troops often made murderous sweeps across the notorious Luwero Triangle and artillery supplied by North Korea pounded areas where the guerrillas were thought to be hiding. Few outside Uganda even knew of the existence of the NRA, due to Obote's muzzling of the press and expulsion of journalists. At times it seemed Museveni might give up the fight – he spent several months in London at one point – but his dedicated young lieutenants never gave up.

The NRA was no bunch of drunken thugs like Amin's and Obote's soldiers. New recruits were indoctrinated in the bush by political commissars and taught that they had to be the servants, and not the oppressors, of the people. Discipline was tough. Museveni was determined that never again would the army disgrace Uganda.

By the time Obote was ousted and Okello had taken over, the NRA controlled a large slice of western Uganda and was a power to be reckoned with. Recognising this, Okello tried to arrange a truce based on the sharing of power. The peace talks were held in Nairobi. They failed. Wisely, Museveni didn't trust the man who had been one of Obote's closest military aides for more than 15 years or his prime minister, Paulo Mwanga, who was Obote's vice-president and minister of defence. Also, Okello's army was notorious for its lack of discipline and brutality. Besides, units of Amin's army had returned from exile in Zaïre and Sudan and thrown their lot in with Okello. What Museveni wanted was a clean sweep of the administration, army and police. He wanted corruption stamped out and the perpetrators of atrocities under Amin and Obote brought to trial. These demands were anathema to Okello, who himself was up to his neck in corruption and responsible for many atrocities.

The fighting continued in earnest and by late January 1986 it was obvious that Okello's days were numbered. The NRA launched an all-out offensive to take the capital in February. Okello's troops fled almost without a fight, though they somehow found the time to loot whatever remained. It was an entirely typical parting gesture, as was the gratuitous shooting-up of many of Kampala's high-rise offices.

Okello's inglorious rabble were finally

pushed over the border into Sudan. The civil war effectively was over, apart from the mopping-up here and there in the extreme north-west and Karamoja province. Despite Museveni's Marxist leanings (he studied political science at Dar es Salaam University in the early 1970s and trained with the anti-Portuguese guerrillas in Mozambique), he has proved to be very pragmatic since taking over from Okello. Quite a few civilians, who can not even vaguely be described as Marxist, have been appointed to his cabinet in an effort to reassure the country's influential Catholic community of his government's intentions. Newspapers have reappeared on the streets and a big drive has been launched to clean up Kampala and get its public utilities repaired and working again.

It seems things are getting better (they certainly couldn't get worse!), but only time will tell. Meanwhile, it's again safe to visit the country.

Facts

Most of Uganda is fairly flat, with a few mountains in the extreme east (Mt Elgon), extreme west (Ruwenzori) and close to the Rwanda border. The bulk of the country enjoys a tropical climate with daytime temperatures averaging around 26°C and falling to 16°C at night. The hottest months are December to February, when the daytime range is 27°C to 29°C. The rainy seasons are from March to May and October to November, the wettest month being April. During the wet seasons the average rainfall is 175 mm a month. Humidity is generally low, except in the wet seasons.

The population stands at 15½ million.

VISAS

Visas are required by all, except nationals of Commonwealth countries, Denmark, Finland, West Germany, Iceland, Ireland, Italy, Norway, Spain, Sweden and Turkey. They cost about US$20 and generally allow for a stay of two weeks, with extensions available. Some travellers have reported that six-day transit visas are available free of charge.

In Africa there are Ugandan embassies in Addis Ababa (Ethiopia), Cairo (Egypt), Khartoum (Sudan), Kigali (Rwanda), Kinshasa (Zaïre), Nairobi (Kenya) and Tripoli (Libya).

In Kigali the embassy is on Rue de Kalisimbi, opposite the post office. While it is open Monday to Friday from 8 am to 12 noon and 2 to 5 pm, it only deals with visa applications on Monday, Wednesday and Friday. A single or multiple-entry three-month visa costs RFr 1934, requires two photographs and is issued in 24 hours.

In Nairobi, the embassy is on the 5th floor, Baring Arcade, Phoenix House, Kenyatta Ave. It is open Monday to Friday from 9 am to 12.45 pm. A two-week single-entry visa costs KSh 330, requires two photographs and is issued while you wait.

If you haven't got a visa, you could try your luck by just turning up at the border (eg from Zaïre). They may let you in on payment of the usual visa fee, but don't blame us if they don't! Those who do not require a visa are given a free one-month (more if requested) Visitor's Pass at the border.

Visas can be renewed at any district commissioner's office free of charge. At the Kasese office, however, you'll be sent to the Uganda-Zaïre border post at Mpondwe. The trip shouldn't take you more than a day. *Matatus* are available.

Other Visas
The French Embassy in Embassy House on King George VI Way, issues visas for CAR, Chad and other former French colonies.

Burundi The embassy (tel 545840) is at 2 Katego Rd, near the Uganda Museum.

While it's open weekdays from 8.30 am to 12.30 pm and 2.30 to 5 pm, they only issue visas on Wednesday and Friday. Visas take 48 hours to issue so put your forms in on Monday or Wednesday. Two photos are required.

Egypt The embassy (tel 254525) is on the 5th floor, Standard Bank Building, 2 Nile Ave, on the corner of Pilkington Ave opposite Jubilee Park. It's open Monday to Friday from 10 am to 3 pm (ring the door bell if it looks closed). One photo is required and visas are issued in 24 hours (less if you get there early and ask them to hurry it up). There's no fuss and an onward ticket is not required.

Kenya The high commission (tel 31861) is at Plot No 60 Kira Rd, near the Uganda Museum. It's open Monday to Friday from 8.30 am to 12.30 pm and 2 to 4.30 pm. Visas are issued in 24 hours. No photographs are required.

Rwanda The embassy (tel 241105) is on the 2nd floor, Baumann House, Obote Ave (Parliament Ave). One-month, multiple-entry visas require two photographs and take 24 hours to issue.

Sudan The embassy (tel 243518) is on the 4th floor, Embassy House, King George VI Way, on the corner of Obote Ave. It's open Monday to Friday from 9 am to 3 pm and on Saturday from 10 am to 12 noon. A one-month visa costs US$9 (shillings are not accepted), requires two photos, a letter of introduction from your embassy and an onward ticket. It can take either 24 hours or three weeks to issue, depending on whether the application has to be referred to Khartoum, which largely depends on the war situation in the country's south.

Tanzania The high commission (tel 56755) is at 6 Kagera Rd and is open Monday to Friday from 9 am to 3 pm. Visas require two photographs and are generally issued the same day. There's no fuss and they don't want to know how much money you have (very different from Nairobi).

Zaïre The embassy (tel 233777) is at 20 Philip Rd, Kololo District. It's open Monday to Friday from 8 am to 3 pm. You must have a letter of introduction from your embassy and four photographs.

MONEY

US$1 = USh 59.75

Numerous strategies have been employed in the past few years in a bid to contain the continued and alarming depreciation of the Ugandan shilling. But none has been successful to any appreciable degree, because of the political and economic chaos that has engulfed Uganda. To be blunt, no-one wants Ugandan shillings and they are worthless outside the country.

By late 1986, Uganda seemed headed for the hyperinflation of countries such as Bolivia, Peru, Argentina and Mozambique. While you could still pay for food, budget accommodation and transport with local currency, beyond that no-one was interested in anything other than hard currency. The black market virtually dictated the economy. Its exchange rate was at least 15 times higher than the official bank rate.

Things haven't improved greatly except that to make life simpler the government knocked a few zeros off the shilling in April 1987 devaluing it by a factor of 100. One hundred old shillings were worth one new shilling. Inflation went berserk and by the end of the year US$1 on the black market bought USh 240 – almost five times the bank rate, and rising rapidly.

It's been impossible to keep up with the changes, so make enquiries on the travellers' grapevine before going there.

Unfortunately, this monetary chaos has made a mockery of the prices of transport, food and accommodation in this chapter. We've tried to pin things down in US dollars, but you'd be wise to use these as a guide only.

The government is well aware of this and because it desperately needs foreign currency, the tourist industry has become one of its targets. If you fly into Uganda you will be required to change US$150 on arrival, plus US$30 each day of your intended stay at the official rate. Re-exchange into hard currency is not permitted when you leave. Budget travellers, however, need not despair. If you enter overland things are much more flexible. There are no banks on Uganda's western borders with Zaïre and Rwanda. And while they may say you have to change US$30 a day of your intended stay when you do get to a bank, no mention is made of the compulsory US$150 change. The choice is yours.

I haven't heard of any traveller having problems leaving Uganda because they haven't changed US$30 a day at the official rates. But I cannot guarantee you such an easy passage through the Kenyan border.

That's not all. Since the government is so keen on acquiring hard currency, all the Ugandan Hotels Corporation hotels demand payment in foreign currency, as do all the other top-end hotels. Internal flights, likewise, have to be paid for in foreign currency and most embassies do not accept shillings for payment of visas. But entry and camping fees to the national parks can still be paid for in shillings, as can letters and telephone calls, making international calls very cheap.

Currency declaration forms are usually issued at the border on entry, but it's very unlikely you'll be asked to show the money you declare. But if you grossly underestimate your funds, it would be prudent to hide the excess. These forms are hardly ever collected or even looked at when you leave the country (this is certainly true on the Rwanda and Zaïre borders), so whether you change a minimal amount of money at a bank just to get a bank stamp on the currency form is up to you.

Don't be tempted to have a bank stamp made up at one of the many rubber stamp-making stalls around Kampala. Not only is it totally unnecessary, it's fraud. If you're caught, you'll probably be jailed. Remember, there's money to be made by informing on tourists who get up to these tricks.

On some borders they don't issue currency declaration forms (eg Katuna, between Uganda and Rwanda) and on others they run out of forms (even at the Malaba post between Uganda and Kenya). This makes nonsense of the whole operation. Not only that, but when entering Uganda at Malaba, the office where they deal with currency forms is across the road from customs and immigration. Often large trucks are parked between the two, so if you walk out of customs and immigration and onto a waiting minibus you could hardly be blamed for not knowing there was a currency form office there at all.

Banking hours are Monday to Friday from 8.30 am to 12.30 pm.

HEALTH

You must take precautions against malaria. Bilharzia is a serious risk in any of Uganda's lakes (Victoria, Kyoga, etc) and rivers. Avoid swimming and walking around barefoot, especially where there are a lot of reeds.

AIDS, known locally as 'slim', is a serious problem. A study of prostitutes in Rwanda showed that some 80% of them carried the AIDS antibody. No similar study has been done in Uganda, but if local sob stories about 'no social life anymore' are anything to go by you'd be wise to assume the worst. Blood transfusions could also be risky. If you will require any injections carry your own disposable syringe, unless you're absolutely certain the one being used hasn't been used before.

PHOTOGRAPHY

Carry everything you need. There's

almost nothing available in Uganda. There are no restrictions on photography. Indeed, most Ugandans like being photographed and want copies sent to them.

LANGUAGE
The official language is English and most people speak it. The other major languages are Luganda and Swahili. Swahili is not used much in Kampala.

Getting There & Around

AIR
Few travellers enter Uganda by air because most of the discounted tickets from Europe and North America use Nairobi as the gateway to East Africa. There is the further complication that if you fly into Uganda you will be hit for the US$150 compulsory change plus US$30 for each intended day of your stay. Only someone with no choice would fly into Uganda.

Unlike in Nairobi, there are no discounted international airline tickets available in Kampala.

If you're thinking of flying to Nairobi, book well in advance as demand is heavy from international aid workers, banking officials and government delegations.

ROAD
There's an excellent system of sealed roads between most major centres, though there are some bad sections where maintenance has been neglected or were destroyed in the civil wars. Work is going ahead on repairing and improving major routes. The main road between Uganda and Kenya – eg from Malaba to Kampala – is excellent.

Hitching
Hitching is possible, and in some situations, such as getting into national parks, virtually obligatory as there's no public transport. Most of the lifts you'll get will be with international aid agencies, missionaries, businesspeople and the occasional diplomat. You may have to wait a long time.

Minibus, Matatu & Bus
Uganda is the land of the minibus and *matatu*. There's never a shortage of them. Fares are fixed and they leave when full – 'full' usually meaning 'way beyond capacity'. Many drivers are speed maniacs and 'accidents' are frequent.

The regular buses that connect the major towns are cheaper than minibuses, but much slower. On the other hand, they're also much safer. They stop frequently to pick up and set down passengers. It is advisable to buy tickets in advance as demand is heavy.

Buses are more expensive than trains, even 1st-class specials, but quicker.

Most towns and cities have a bus station/*matatu* park, so just turn up and tell people where you want to go. On the open road just put out your hand. Examples of bus/*matatu* fares and journey times are:

Tororo to Kampala – *matatu* US$1.80, 3½ hours
Jinja to Kampala – *matatu* US$0.60, 1½ hours; bus US$0.40, two hours plus
Kampala to Entebbe – *matatu* US$0.20, 20 to 25 minutes; taxi (which private cars turn into on sighting white faces) US$0.40
Kampala to Mbarara – *matatu* US$2, 4½ to five hours
Kampala to Kasese – bus (Monday, Wednesday and Friday in the early evening) US$3.20, about 12 hours
Kasese to Fort Portal – *matatu* US$0.60, about 1½ hours
Kasese to Kabale – *matatu*; daily bus (leaves Kasese about 9 am) US$2, about 9½ hours (the last part of the journey south crosses a mountain pass giving spectacular views to the west of volcanoes along the Uganda-Rwanda border)

Kabale to Kisoro – *matatu*/pick-up truck US$1.60, six hours (leaving from outside the Capital Motel/post office – spectacular but rough in parts)

TRAIN

There are two main lines in Uganda. The first starts at Tororo and runs west to Kasese, via Jinja and Kampala. The other runs from Tororo north-west to Pakwach, via Mbale, Soroti, Lira and Gulu.

Travelling by train is a good way of getting around Uganda, except perhaps between Tororo and Kampala where the service is extremely slow. It's certainly preferable, cheaper, much safer and, obviously, much less crowded than by *matatu*.

There are three classes on most trains, and four on some. They are: 1st class special – new carriages with two-bunk compartments and handbasins that work and usually well-maintained communal toilets; 1st class – old carriages with two-bunk compartments that have seen better days, handbasins that generally don't work and communal toilets that often don't flush; upper class – old carriages with four to six-berth compartments; and economy – seats only and often crowded. While 1st class special is cheaper than the bus, ordinary 1st class is very acceptable. Sexes are separated in the first three classes, unless your group fills a compartment.

Booking two days in advance should be sufficient to secure a bunk class. To buy a ticket, first get a reservation (not necessary in economy) and then queue to pay. There's usually some semblance of order at the ticket offices.

Despite the massive 1987 devaluation, train fares have remained the same in dollar terms so they're an absolute bargain.

There are dining cars on some trains and food sellers at most stations. The food is usually very cheap.

The train schedules are as follows:

Tororo to Kampala via Jinja – departs Tororo 6 am, Kampala 9 am; about 9½ hours

Tororo to Pakwach via Mbale and Gulu – daily train departs both ends 5 pm

Kampala to Kasese – economy-class train departs Kampala and Kasese 4 pm, arriving 7 am the next day; upper-classes train departs Kampala 7 pm, arriving 10 am the next day (returning at 8.30 pm); often up to 2½ hours late at final destination. The fares are USh 100 (1st class), USh 57 (upper class) and USh 23 (economy).

BOAT

The ferry service across Lake Victoria from Jinja to Mwanza (Tanzania) has been improved. The boats are modern and, although primarily for freight and rail cars, have room for about 30 passengers. The fare is about US$5 and the journey takes some 16 hours. There is usually one ferry a week in either direction, but the schedules vary. Ask at the dock.

TO/FROM KENYA

The two main border posts with Kenya are Malaba and Busia, with Malaba being the most used. Busia is handy for direct travel from Kisumu to Jinja or Kampala, bypassing Tororo.

There are overnight trains from Nairobi to Malaba, via Nakuru and Eldoret. They leave on Tuesday, Friday and Saturday at 3 pm and arrive at 8.30 am the next day. In the opposite direction they leave Malaba on Wednesday, Saturday and Sunday at 4 pm and arrive at 9.30 am. The fares are KSh 336/145/63 in 1st/2nd/3rd class. They do not connect with the Ugandan rail system, so from Malaba to Tororo you must go by road before picking up the Tororo train to Jinja or Kampala.

There are several night buses travelling between Nairobi and Malaba. They depart from either end at around 7.30 pm and arrive at the other end about 5.30 am the next day. The fare is KSh 110.

Several buses do the run between Nairobi and Bungoma in daylight hours, departing about 8 am and arriving about 5 pm. The fare is KSh 90. There are plenty of *matatus* between Bungoma and Malaba, which cost KSh 15 and take about 45 minutes. At Malaba, the Kenyan and Ugandan border posts are about one km apart. You'll have to walk as no *matatus* ply the gap.

When leaving Kenya they'll want your currency declaration form and will ask if you have any Kenyan shillings (it's illegal to export them), but otherwise there's no fuss or baggage searches. When entering Uganda, go first to immigration (no fuss – office on the right hand side coming from Kenya) and then cross the road to the currency declaration form office. This office sometimes runs out of forms, but it's no problem as the process is little more than a formality. It's unlikely they'll want to see your money.

If leaving Uganda at Malaba they may ask for your currency form, but as they're often not issued at the borders with Zaïre, Rwanda and Sudan, you can safely tell them you weren't given one.

Ugandan customs and immigration usually closes for an hour at lunch.

There are plenty of moneychangers at both border posts, but rates are poor. Change only what you need to get to the nearest bank – at Bungoma on the Kenyan side and Tororo on the Ugandan side. There are no banks at Malaba on either side.

There are frequent *matatus* in either direction between Malaba and Tororo, they cost US$0.12 and take less than an hour. Between Tororo and Jinja or Kampala *matatus* run frequently until the late afternoon. There's also a train, but it's very slow.

If driving across the Malaba border, expect to be there for several hours as you'll be in a solid line of trucks from one border post to the other.

TO/FROM RWANDA

The two crossing points between Uganda and Rwanda are at Gatuna/Katuna, south of Kabale, and Cyanika, south of Kisoro. Both border posts on the Ugandan side are very easy-going. It's unlikely you'll be asked for a currency form if leaving, or issued with one if arriving. Entering or leaving Rwanda is much the same.

There are frequent daily *matatus* between Kabale and the Gatuna border post that cost US$0.40 and take about 30 minutes. They leave Kabale from in front of the Skyline Hotel. It's also possible to get a *matatu* here all the way to Kigali. From the Rwandan side there are frequent minibuses to Kigali until mid-afternoon for RFr 250. The trip takes about 2½ hours.

Remember the one hour time difference between the two countries. At 11 am Rwandan time, you'll find the Ugandan border closed, and they're slow to return from lunch.

Very little traffic uses the Cyanika crossing, about 12 km from Kisoro, so you may have to walk. From the border, however, there are several minibuses daily to Ruhengeri, which cost RFr 100 and take one hour.

TO/FROM SUDAN

The only point of entry into Sudan is via Nimule, north of Gulu, but it's closed at present because of the civil war in southern Sudan.

TO/FROM TANZANIA

The only practicable direct route between Uganda and Tanzania is the Lake Victoria ferry between Jinja and Mwanza. Attempting to go overland across the Kagera salient from Masaka to Bukoba, via Kyaka, will prove extremely frustrating. The road has been shocking ever since Tanzanian troops repelled Idi Amin's forces in 1979. Very few vehicles ever travel this route. But there are discussions going on between Uganda, Tanzania and

Rwanda to do something about improving the roads in this area. There's even talk of a railway between Tanzania and Rwanda, but that's a long time off.

TO/FROM ZAÏRE

The two main crossing points are south from Kasese to Rutshuru, via Ishasha, and north-west from Kasese to Beni, via Katwe and Kasindi. There are less-used border posts further north between Mahagi and Pakwach and between Aru and Arua. If you're thinking of using the quieter posts, you'd be wise to make enquiries about security before setting off. Rag-bag remnants of Idi Amin's, Obote's and Okello's troops may still be making a nuisance of themselves in the area. It's also possible to cross the border between Kisoro and Rutshuru (about 30 km), but the road is rough and there's very little traffic.

The Ishasha border is probably the most reliable in terms of transport. Still you may have to hitch between Ishasha and the Katunguru junction on the main Kasese to Mbarara road as there are no regular *matatus*. Friday is probably the best day to cross as there's a market at Ishasha and plenty of traffic. It's certainly the best day to cross from Zaïre because the trucks plying between Rutshuru and Ishasha leave around 5.30 am and return in the evening. There's a Saturday market at Isharo, about halfway between the two towns, making early Saturday morning a good time to travel.

If entering Uganda at Ishasha, you first pass through the customs hut, where there may be a cursory baggage check, before registering at the police hut down the road. The officials may not be aware that Commonwealth citizens do not require visas, so if you have problems ask them to check with the immigration officer in the third hut. Otherwise, there's no hassles.

A variation on this route involves a side trip to the Ugandan fishing village of Rwenshama, on the shores of Lake Idi Amin (formerly Lake Edward). There is a turn-off to the village about halfway between Ishasha and Katunguru, on the main Kasese to Mbarara road. There's a *Rest House*, with clean accommodation for US$0.20/0.30 a single/double. It provides soap and towels, has bucket showers and kerosene lanterns. You can find good food (fish and matoke) at the *Friend's Corner Hotel*. There are plenty of hippos wallowing just offshore, and the fishing boats put out around 4 pm and return around 6.30 am. You can change US dollars in the village, but at a very poor rate. Zaïres are more useful, as many locals go to the Ishasha market.

There are occasional vehicles direct to Kasese, but for a drive through a different part of the Ruwenzori National Park take a *matatu* from outside the rest house to Rukungiri. The trip costs about US$0.60 and takes roughly four hours. From Rukungiri take another *matatu* to Ishaka, for about the same price. From there, either take a bus or *matatu* for the three-hour trip to Kasese; again, about US$0.60.

It's also likely that you will have to do some hitching on the road from Kasese to Beni, via Katwe, Mpondwe and Kasindi. Again, depending on the day you go, you could be waiting for hours regardless of which of the two turn-offs you take going west. Make enquiries in Kasese before setting off on this road.

Around the Country

FORT PORTAL

Fort Portal is a small, quiet and pleasant town at the northern end of the Ruwenzori. While some travellers use it as a base from which to go mountain trekking, it's not as convenient as Kasese because it's much further from the jumping-off point of Ibanda.

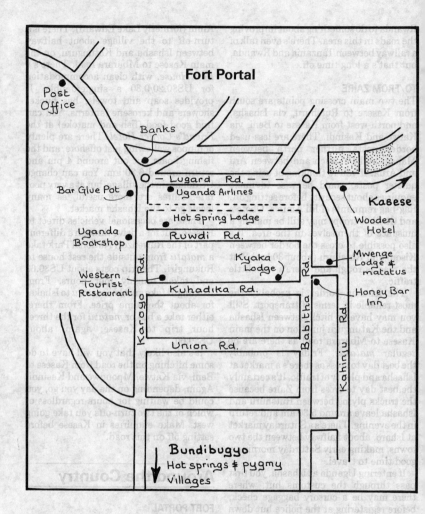

Fort Portal

Post Office

Banks

Bar Glue Pot

Uganda Airlines

Hot Spring Lodge

Uganda Bookshop

Ruwdi Rd.

Kyaka Lodge

Western Tourist Restaurant

Kuhadika Rd.

Union Rd.

Lugard Rd.

Kasese

Wooden Hotel

Mwenge Lodge & matatus

Honey Bar Inn

Babitha Rd.

Kahinju Rd.

Karoyo Rd.

Bundibugyo
Hot springs & pygmy villages

Things to See

There's nothing to see as such in Fort Portal, but nearby **Bundibugyo**, in the Semliki Valley on the other side of the Ruwenzori, is definitely worth a day trip. Organise a group to fill a *matatu*, because the ones running commercial trips between the two towns won't stop for sightseers. Tell the driver what you want to see and

that you want to stop along the way before you set out. The two main attractions are the **hot springs** near Sempaya and the pygmy tribes of the Semliki Valley forests. But the drive in itself is worth it as it offers magnificent views over the rainforest and savannah and into Zaïre. The pygmy tribes, unlike those in eastern Zaïre, are very uncommercialised because Uganda hasn't had any tourists for at least a decade.

Places to Stay
The best of the budget hotels and a popular one with travellers is *Wooden Hotel*, Lugard Rd. It has rooms for US$1/1.60 a single/double. There's a bar and good restaurant. Second choice would be *Hot Spring Lodge*, Ruwdi Rd, which offers rooms for US$0.60/0.80 a single/double. If the Hot Springs is full and you want an el cheapo place, try *Kyaka Lodge*, Kuhadika Rd. It's scruffy but has rooms for US$0.30/0.50 a single/double. Better is *Centenary Hotel*, run by the Church of Uganda Mothers' Union. It is friendly and cheap at US$1 a double. The last of the budget accommodation is at *Mwenge Lodge*, near the *matatu* park between Babitha Rd and Kahinju Rd. It has tiny singles for US$0.70, larger singles for US$1 and doubles for US$2. It's scruffy and poor value in comparison to what else is available.

Those wanting more commodious accommodation and services should go to *Mountains of the Moon Hotel*. It's expensive because it's part of the Ugandan Hotels Corporation chain which accepts only hard currency (unless there are so few guests it will do a deal in shillings).

Places to Eat
Good, cheap food is available at *Wooden Hotel*. For a change, try *Western Tourist Restaurant* on Kuhadika Rd.

Two good bars are *Bar Glue Pot* on Karoyo Rd, and *Honey Bar Inn* on Babitha Rd.

GULU
Gulu is the largest town in the country's north and is on the railway line between Tororo and Pakwach. It's a jumping-off point for a visit to **Paraa** on the Victoria Nile, which runs through the Kabalega National Park. At Patiko, 25 km north of Gulu, is **Baker's Fort**, built in the 1870s as a base from which to suppress the slave trade when Britain was active in the Sudan.

Places to Stay
A good, cheap place to stay is the *Church of Uganda Guest House* – excellent value at US$0.45 a double. Other places that have been recommended are *New Gulu Restaurant*, Pakwach Rd, and *Luxor Lodge*, opposite the truck park.

The top-range hotel is *Acholi Inn*. Again, it's one of the hard currency hotels in the Uganda Hotel Corporation chain.

JINJA
Jinja, on the shores of Lake Victoria, is the major marketing and industrial centre of southern Uganda. It's also close to the Owen Falls where the Victoria Nile leaves the lake. At the Owen Falls there is a hydroelectric station which produces the bulk of Uganda's electricity. Jinja once had a large Asian community, as evidenced by many of the street names around the market. The town escaped the worst horrors of the last civil war, so doesn't have the air of dereliction of other towns in the area that suffered greatly.

Things to See
The actual Owen Falls have disappeared under the lake created by the **Owen Falls Dam** at the source of the Victoria Nile. The dam, which is several km west of town on the road to Kampala, was inaugurated in 1954. The road to Kampala crosses its wall. Photography is prohibited.

Places to Stay
Two places that are equally good value are *Victoria View Hotel* and *Market View Hotel*, close to one another on Kutch Rd. The Market View is appropriately named, but the Victoria View is the result of wishful thinking. The Victoria View is very pleasant, clean and offers rooms for US$2 a double with bathroom. The Market View is equally pleasant, clean and offers rooms for US$1.55/1.75 a single/

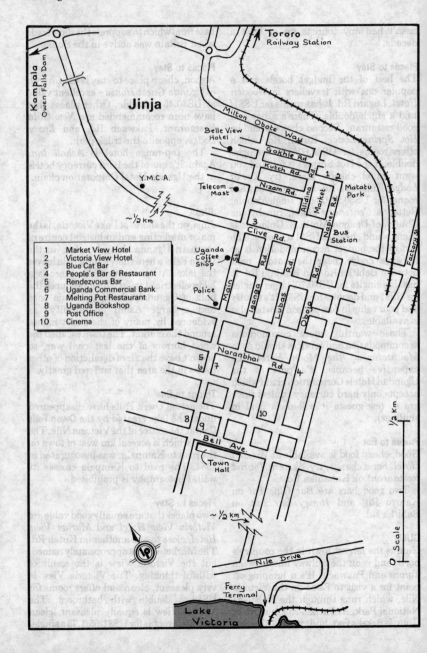

Jinja

Kampala
Owen Falls Dam

Tororo
Railway Station

Y.M.C.A.

~ ½ km

Belle View Hotel

Milton Obote Way

Gokhle Rd.

Kutch Rd.

Nizam Rd.

Telecom Mast

Market

Aldina Rd.

Napier Rd.

Matatu Park

Clive Rd.

Bus Station

Uganda Coffee Shop

Police

Main St.

Ganga Rd.

Lubas Rd.

Obote Rd.

Naranbhai Rd.

Bell Ave.

Town Hall

~ ½ km

Nile Drive

Ferry Terminal

Lake Victoria

Factory St.

½ km

0   Scale

1. Market View Hotel
2. Victoria View Hotel
3. Blue Cat Bar
4. People's Bar & Restaurant
5. Rendezvous Bar
6. Uganda Commercial Bank
7. Melting Pot Restaurant
8. Uganda Bookshop
9. Post Office
10. Cinema

double with shared bathroom. Both hotels have a restaurant.

For something cheaper, ask if there are spare rooms at *Blue Cat Bar* on Clive Rd.

More expensive, but good value nevertheless, is *Belle View Hotel* on Kutch Rd. It's very comfortable and spotlessly clean but there is no hot water. Rooms cost US$2.60 a single without bathroom and US$3 a double with bathroom. There's an excellent bar and restaurant downstairs.

Places to Eat

The liveliest restaurant is the *Mango Bar & Restaurant*, which has a bar, outdoor garden area with music and a good variety of food at lunchtime. Its prices are very reasonable. For a splurge try *Belle View Hotel*, where the food is excellent and the portions generous. Expect to pay US$0.80 for chicken and matoke and US$1.60 for meat and matoke.

Entertainment

Films are screened at the town hall every Sunday afternoon. Worth going along if you're in town.

KABALE

Kabale is in the Kigeza area, which the tourist literature often and rather inappropriately calls the 'Little Switzerland of Africa'. But there's no denying it's very beautiful with its intensively cultivated and terraced hills, forests and lakes and tea plantations extending all the way to Gatuna on the Rwandan border.

Kabale is Uganda's highest town at about 2000 metres. It gets cool at night.

Information

The Uganda Commercial Bank, next to the post office, will not change travellers' cheques. You will have to ask around the shops. Moneychangers hang around at Highlands Hotel and the petrol stations opposite Skyline Hotel.

Things to See

The Kigeza is superb hiking country. You can set off down any track and let it take you where it will. There's always good views over the surrounding countryside and the locals are keen to stop and chat.

But perhaps the best trip is to **Lake Bunyonyi**, a famous beauty spot over the ridge to the west of Kabale. It's a large and very irregularly shaped lake with many islands. Many of the villagers on the lake's shores have boats and so it shouldn't be difficult to arrange a trip on the water. The surrounding hillsides, as elsewhere in this region, are intensively cultivated. There are two ways of getting to the lake. You can either walk up and over the ridge from Kabale, taking about three hours if you pick the right tracks, or hitch to Kisoro and get off where the road touches the lake, about halfway. It's not always easy hitching, but one or two *matatus* go that way in the morning, leaving from outside the Capital Motel or post office.

Places to Stay

If you are camping there is a free site, with no facilities, close to White Horse Inn.

The cheapest place to stay and a popular place with travellers is *St Paul's Training Centre & Hostel*. It's very friendly and costs US$0.30 for a dormitory bed and US$0.60 a double. There are no showers. Similar in price but fairly noisy because of its bar is *Kabale Bar & Lodge*. It's a small place at the far end of the main street. It's very basic and has cold showers.

Perhaps the best value is *Capital Motel*, close to the post office. Rooms cost US$2 a double and although it's basic, it provides clean sheets, communal hot showers in the morning and evening and laundry facilities in the courtyard (clothes don't disappear off lines). There's a bar (usual prices) upstairs, but no restaurant. If you have a car, it can be locked in the compound at night.

Similar are *Rubanza Restaurant & Lodge*, which has a good, cheap restaurant,

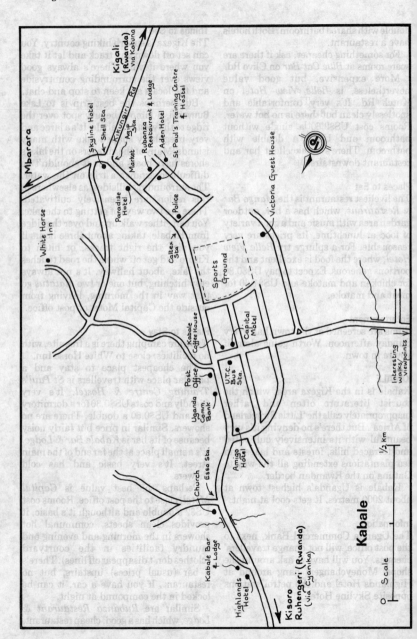

Kabale

and *Paradise Hotel*, on the main street. More expensive, but convenient for the morning *matatu* to Rwanda, is *Skyline Hotel*, opposite the Shell and Agip stations on the town's main intersection.

Going upmarket, there are two comfortable mid-range hotels. They are *Highlands Hotel*, at the far end of town, and *Victoria Guest House*, at the back of the sportsground. Both charge US$3 a double with bathroom and toilet. Hot water is available at the Highlands, (if there's no hot water in the taps, tell reception and they'll fill buckets for you). Both hotels have a bar and restaurant. The Highlands is much larger than the Victoria, and will almost certainly have vacancies. It's also popular with travellers.

Kabale's top-range hotel is *White Horse Inn*, on the hill overlooking the town. It's part of the Uganda Hotels Corporation hard-currency chain. Some travellers do manage to negotiate a deal in shillings, but it's not easy.

Places to Eat
You can get a good breakfast of omelette, bread, tea or coffee at *Twincos*, opposite the post office. They also serve cheap lunches and dinners. Many travellers have recommended *Rubanza Restaurant & Lodge* for good, cheap meals.

Given the street exchange rate, perhaps the best value is *Highlands Hotel*, with its starched white tableclothes and waiter service in the dining hall. The food is excellent and there's a choice of several main courses. It's open to nonresidents and often there's an open fire burning in the evenings. There's a large bar, where you can get the usual drinks as well as the house speciality – banapo, a banana wine said to be made by the hotel owner. It's worth trying and much cheaper than beer! Breakfasts, however, aren't such good value. There's also a pleasant bar at *White Horse Inn*.

KAMPALA
Kampala, the capital of Uganda, suffered a great deal in the six years or so of civil strife that began with Idi Amin's defeat in 1979 at the hands of the Tanzanian army and ended, hopefully, with the victory of Yoweri Museveni's NRA in early 1986. While the city is slowly getting back on its feet and services are gradually being restored, it still bears the scars of street fighting, the aftermath of the enforced departure of its Asian population, the looting and years of corruption that resulted in neglect of its infrastructure.

Information
The Ministry of Tourism & Wildlife (tel 32971) acts as a tourist office. It is on Obote Ave (Parliament Ave), opposite the British High Commission and American Embassy. The staff is very friendly and helpful. They have a free booklet about the country, *Uganda: the Pearl of Africa*; an excellent large-scale street map of Kampala; and a free leaflet on trekking in the Ruwenzori, *Guiding Notes to the Ruwenzori*, which is very much out of date.

Excellent large-scale maps of Uganda (Series 1301, Sheet NA-36), with much more detail than the usual East Africa offerings of Michelin and Bartholomews, are available from either of the two Ugandan Bookshops. If they have sold out, try the map sales office on the ground floor of the Department of Lands & Surveys, further up Obote Ave. It has a large selection of detailed maps.

The Ugandan Bookshops are the best places to go for English-language publications. One branch is on the corner of Colvile St and Kimathi Ave, and the another is on the corner of Buganda Rd and The Square (the small park in front of the High Court building). There is another bookshop on Kampala Rd, between Pilkington Rd and Colvile St.

Things to See
The **Uganda Museum** on Kira Rd is closed for renovations, but that doesn't mean you can't get in. It's worth turning up and

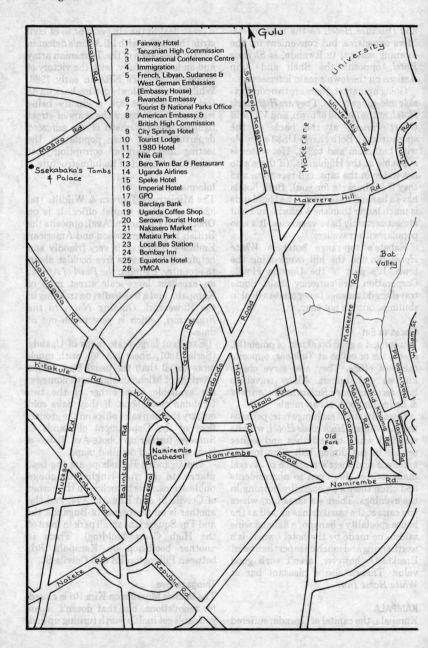

1	Fairway Hotel
2	Tanzanian High Commission
3	International Conference Centre
4	Immigration
5	French, Libyan, Sudanese & West German Embassies (Embassy House)
6	Rwandan Embassy
7	Tourist & National Parks Office
8	American Embassy & British High Commission
9	City Springs Hotel
10	Tourist Lodge
11	1980 Hotel
12	Nile Gill
13	Bero Twin Bar & Restaurant
14	Uganda Airlines
15	Speke Hotel
16	Imperial Hotel
17	GPO
18	Barclays Bank
19	Uganda Coffee Shop
20	Serown Tourist Hotel
21	Nakasero Market
22	Matatu Park
23	Local Bus Station
24	Bombay Inn
25	Equatoria Hotel
26	YMCA

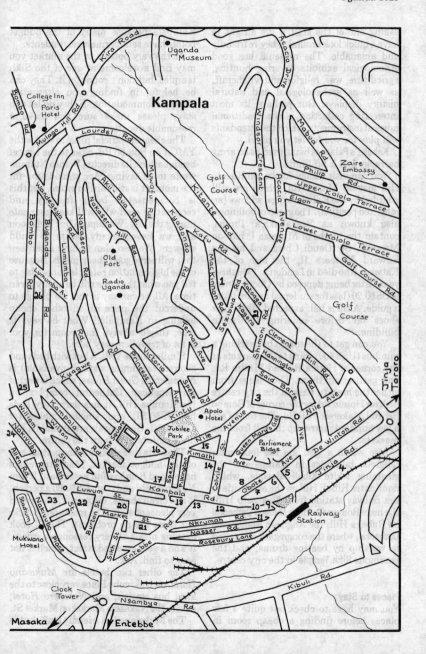

Kampala

asking one of the staff if it's alright to have a quick look around. They're friendly and amenable. The museum has good ethnological exhibits covering hunting, agriculture, war, religion and witchcraft, as well as archaeological and natural history displays. But perhaps its most interesting collection is the traditional musical instruments, which the attendants will play for you (or let you play).

Kabaka's Palace is being used as an army barracks and is off limits.

You can visit **Kasubi Tombs**, on Kasubi Hill just off Masiro Rd, which are still guarded by the Kabaka kings' widows (an inherited position). The group of buildings, also known as Ssekabaka's Tombs, contain the tombs of Muteesa I, his son Mwanga, Sir Daudi Chwa and his son Edward Muteesa II, the last of the Kabakas who died in London in 1969 three years after being deposed by Obote. Entry is US$0.20 (less for students) and includes a guide. A tip is half expected. Take your shoes off before entering the main building.

You can get to the tombs by catching a minibus (USh 400) going to the markets at the corner of Hoima Rd and Masiro Rd, and getting off there. They leave from either the *matatu* park in the city centre (ask for Hoima Rd) or the corner of Bombo Rd and Makerere Hill Rd. The tombs are a few hundred metres up the hill from the markets.

Also worth a visit are the four main religious buildings in Kampala – the gleaming white **Kibuli Mosque**, which dominates Kibuli Hill on the other side of the railway station from Nakasero Hill; the huge Roman Catholic **Rubaga Cathedral** on Rubaga Hill; the Anglican **Namirembe Cathedral**, where the congregation is called to worship by beating drums; and the enormous **Sikh Temple** in the city centre.

Places to Stay

You may have to check out quite a few places before finding a cheap room in Kampala because many of the budget hotels have semipermanent residents.

At the very bottom of the market you may find a welcome at one of the Sikh temples, but don't count on it. They can be helpful in finding you alternative cheap accommodation. If they do let you stay, please make sure you leave a reasonable donation.

The cheapest official place to stay is the *YMCA* on Bombo Rd, close to the Unicef headquarters. Its director, Franco Ntambi, wrote to us saying: 'Accommodation for the moment is still fairly austere, but this is compensated by a friendly and cooperative staff who will keep gear safe during the day. We hope to buy beds soon and we have already begun to build showers. We also plan to have a canteen that will serve good cheap meals. Because of the high inflation rate it is impossible to tell you what the price will be at any given time. All we can say is that we pledge to undercut the price of all other cheap lodging in Kampala.' What he says is true; they'll always find room for you. A lot of travellers stay here.

Similar to the YMCA but with beds and showers (assuming water is available) is *Namirembe Guest House*, which is part of the Anglican Cathedral complex on Namirembe Hill. It has dormitory beds for US$0.50, and singles/doubles for US$0.60/1. Good meals are available, but it's a *matatu* ride from the centre.

There are three hotels at the bottom end of the budget market. Many travellers have rated *Bombay Inn* as the best. It's on Nakivubo Rd and costs US$0.60 a person. It has clean sheets, electricity, water and very pleasant staff. The rooms don't lock, but there are no problems. They'll cook evening meals at very reasonable prices. It's on a very crowded street, which is not easy to find. Ask.

The other two hotels are *Mukwano Hotel*, on Nakivubo Place very close to the local bus station, and *Nakasero Hotel*, next to the Nakasero Market on Market St. The Mukwano has friendly staff, but is very scruffy with filthy toilets and no showers worth mentioning. It charges US$0.50 a dormitory bed, and US$1/1.50/1.80 a single/double/triple. It's in a rough area and often a bad smell from the garbage-strewn creek across the road pervades the place.

The Nakasero is mainly a brothel and often full or reserved. It charges locals US$1.10 a double, but as a traveller you're unlikely to get it at this price because they can make more money by renting it out several times a day.

Another budget hotel in terms of value for money is *1980 Hotel*, on Nkrumah Rd very close to the railway station. It costs US$2.30 a double without bathroom including a very simple breakfast (hygiene is very suspect in the kitchen). Maintenance on the communal cold water showers was abandoned years ago and the water pressure is very weak – start filling a bucket about 30 minutes before you want to shower. There's a bar on the 1st floor serving cold beers.

Better, though a *matatu* ride from the centre, is *Paris Hotel*. It's on Mulago Hill Rd close to the corner of Bombo Rd where there's a large roundabout and mosque. It charges travellers US$3 a double without bathroom. The showers, as elsewhere, depend on available water pressure. Snacks are served at the bar on the ground floor.

In the mid-range hotels, the first to try is *Serown Tourist Hotel*, opposite the Nakasero Market. It's huge and likely to have rooms when all the others are full. It's been a popular place to stay for years, but is badly in need of major renovation. The staff is friendly and gear left in the rooms is safe. It costs US$3/3.10 a single/double and US$3.70 a double with bathroom. Clean sheets are provided. In most cases the bathrooms are a joke because the plumbing fittings have been ripped out and you have to take your bucket onto the roof to draw water from the tanks, and there isn't much in them.

If it's full try *Tourist Lodge*, on Kampala (Jinja) Rd, just around the corner from the railway station. It's small, so is often full, but its facilities are better than those at the Serown. It costs US$3/4 a single/double with working bathroom. The rooms are clean and comfortable, though, as with most places, it has seen better days. There's a snack bar on the 1st floor, but it rarely seems to function. Like the Serown, it's popular with travellers.

Two doors down towards the railway station on the same street is *City Springs Hotel*, which costs US$4.50 a double with bathroom. There are no singles. This is the only hotel in this range that has hot water. It has a very good bar and restaurant on the 1st floor. The only trouble with the City Springs is that reception often doesn't know what's going on upstairs. An hour after telling you there is a room, they'll tell you they're full!

Another large hotel likely to have vacancies when everywhere else is full is *Equatoria Hotel* on Kyagwe Rd, between South St and William St. Rooms cost US$2.65/3.50 a single/double with bathroom. It's reasonable value, but like everywhere else, tatty. It has a bar and restaurant.

Lastly, there is *Rena Hotel* on Namirembe Rd for US$5 a night.

All the top-range hotels demand payment in hard currency – they won't even accept shillings backed up with a currency declaration form and bank stamps – so they're not worth considering unless you have money to throw away.

Places to Eat

There's a good choice of street stalls around the local bus station and *matatu* park and around the stadium on Nakivubo Place. What is available can be seen cooking in pots on charcoal – fish, meat, matoke, cabbage, beans, chapatis, rice, etc. This lunchtime trade is very popular with the locals.

Another cheap food outlet is *Sinbad Restaurant*, opposite the railway station. You can get a good, cheap, traditional lunch at *Nakasero Hotel*, next to the Nakasero Market. Similar is *Mascot Restaurant*, Speke Rd, round the corner from the post office. They offer excellent breakfasts.

Sooner or later, most travellers turn up at *Nile Grill*, on Kampala Rd opposite Obote Ave. It's the equivalent of the Thorn Tree Cafe in Nairobi, except that it's not part of a hotel. It's open daily from 9 am to 9 pm and is very popular as a meeting place and restaurant with local office workers and expatriates. It has a bar, restaurant and beer garden. The food is worth a splurge, even though the prices are relatively high in official exchange rate shillings. You don't have to eat: some people just use it as a coffee house and bar.

The *Bero Twin Bar & Restaurant* on Kampala Rd, at the corner of Entebbe Rd, is also worth a splurge. It serves excellent western-style food, but there are no tables outside. On Bombo Rd outside the town centre (just beyond the roundabout at the top of the hill) is *College Inn Restaurant & Hotel*. It has a very pleasant atmosphere, friendly staff and good food. It's considerably cheaper than the Nile Grill and Bero Twin.

One of the best places to go for Indian food is *Step In Restaurant*, on Kampala Rd opposite the Centre Cinema.

The fantastic buffets offered by the *Athena Club* are worth the money. Take a taxi from town.

A popular coffee spot is *Uganda Coffee Shop*, on Kampala Rd near the corner of Burton St and opposite the park in front of the High Court. It's on the 1st floor and has a balcony, from which you can watch the street. A lot of civil servants use this place. There's another café on a side street linking Kampala Rd with Nkrumah Rd, past the Nile Grill before you reach the Tourist Lodge.

Entertainment

The many years of strife and the dangers of going out at night just about killed Kampala's entertainment scene. It's slowly coming alive again, but, for the present, is restricted mainly to bars and restaurants.

A very lively bar, with cheap cold beer and African music, is *California Bar & Restaurant*, on Luwum St just round the corner from Serown Tourist Hotel. The clientele is very friendly and you won't get hassled if you're female.

A good place for a cold beer during the day is *Slow Boat Pub*, on the top side of Kampala Rd opposite the Bero Twin Restaurant. It's mainly a concrete beer garden, though there is a small indoors area. Beers are cheaper than at the Nile Grill.

There are lots of other bars on Kampala Rd, between The Square and Kyagwe Rd, but they're mainly pick-up joints.

Around Kampala

Outside Kampala at **Entebbe** are the **Botanical Gardens** which are well worth a half-day visit. They were laid out along the lake's shore in 1901, between the Sailing Club and town centre. There are some interesting and unusual trees and shrubs, and the grounds are well maintained. There's a **zoo** close by.

There's little else of interest in Entebbe, unless you want to see the airport where Israeli commandos stormed a hijacked jet and freed the hostages – much to the chagrin of Idi Amin.

Minibuses run frequently to Entebbe from the *matatu* park in central Kampala, they cost US$0.20 and take about 25 minutes. Get off before the end of the line. In Entebbe, try *Nakabugo Ajjuddo Restaurant*, on the main street close to the corner of Hill Lane. It offers good food at reasonable prices.

As one hard-bitten traveller put it, somewhat cynically: 'Uganda's main tourist attraction must be war – best destroyed villages between Sudan and Arua; best tank 18 km north of Kampala on the Masindi road; best plane shot down nine km north of Paraa, and the Luwero Triangle 62 km north of Kampala.'

Grotesque as it may seem, the notorious Luwero Triangle, which bore the brunt of horrendous intertribal atrocities and the second reign of Obote, has become a strange sort of tourist attraction. If you are at all interested in the horrors of war, it's all here and no-one is trying to disguise it. Mass graves of butchered villagers are everywhere: the locals will show you the unearthed skeletons and retell the unbelievable stories of brutality.

KASESE

Kasese is at the western railhead of Uganda and is the base for trips up the Ruwenzori or to the Ruwenzori National Park (Queen Elizabeth II National Park). It's a small, quiet town but economically very important because of the nearby copper mines at Kilembe (copper was Uganda's third biggest export in the 1970s).

Information

You will probably be met (if not at the railway station then in town) by Mr Singhi, who has made it his business to approach all tourists and travellers and tell them what there is to see and do in the area. He's very friendly and doesn't expect payment for his services. He's a mine of information about mountain climbing, copper mining, hot springs and pygmies.

Places to Stay

By far the best place to stay is *Saad Hotel* (tel 157/9), Ruwenzori Rd. The staff is very friendly and the rooms extremely pleasant and spotlessly clean. It has twin rooms with adjoining shower and toilet for US$3. They will let three people share one room. If hot water is not on tap, it will be brought to your room in buckets. Videos are sometimes shown in the lounge. Downstairs is a restaurant that is equally good value for breakfast, lunch or dinner. Lunch is a huge, set-menu meal which you will be unable to finish, though you can also order à la carte. Prices are very reasonable. The Saad is very popular with travellers and rightly so.

If it's full (unlikely), the next best is *Kaghesera Hotel*, Speke St. It's pleasant, very clean and has hot water. It costs US$1.10/1.54 a single/double with shower and toilet. It has a restaurant with set lunches and à la carte (slightly cheaper than the Saad).

For something cheaper, try *Highway Lodging*, Margherita Rd. It costs US$0.90 a single or double without bathroom. It's a bit scruffy, but clean sheets are provided and the manager is friendly. Two other similar places are *Paradise Bar & Lodging* and *Rwenzori Guest House*, both on Speke St. *Moonlight Lodgings*, Margherita Rd, is very poor value for money. It does, however, serve reasonable food in the restaurant.

Some three km out of town on the road towards the mountains is *Hotel Margherita*. It's part of the hard-currency Uganda Hotels Corporation chain. It's poor value next to the Saad.

Places to Eat

There are several inexpensive traditional restaurants around the *matatu* park and market, serving such staples as meat stews, matoke, beans and rice for less than US$0.20. Otherwise, try one of the set lunches or à la carte meals at either the *Saad Hotel* or *Kaghesera Hotel*. If you don't mind walking, you could try *Margherita Hotel*, which accepts shillings in payment for meals. Its lunches are as good as those offered at the Saad.

There are two good bars in Kasese. They are *Summit Club Bar* on Speke St and an unnamed place on Stanley St, opposite the Uganda Commercial Bank. The Saad Hotel does not serve beer as it's owned by Muslims.

At one time the Golf Club, on the other side of the golf course from the Magherita, had a bar and disco on Saturday nights. It was closed after being badly vandalised but it may be up and running again. It would be worth making enquiries.

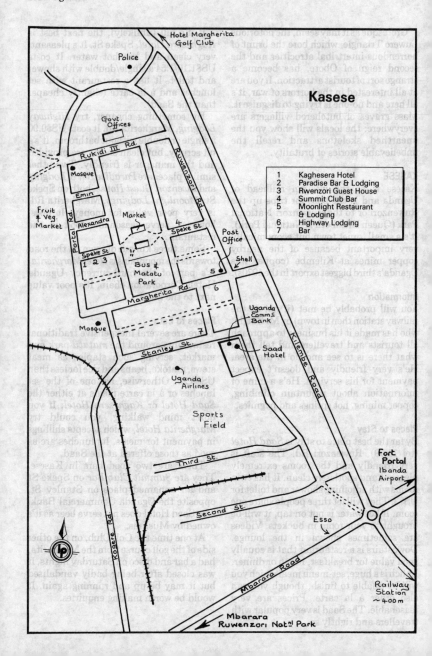

Kasese

Hotel Margherita
Golf Club

Police

Govt.
Offices

Rukidi III Rd.

Mosque

Emin

Fruit
& Veg.
Market

Alexandra

Speke St.

Market

Speke St.

Post
Office

Shell

Bus &
Matatu
Park

Mosque

Margherita Rd.

Uganda
Comm. Bank

Saad Hotel

Stanley St.

Uganda
Airlines

Sports
Field

Third St.

Second St.

Esso

Mbarara Road

Railway
Station
~ 400 m

Kogere Rd.

Mbarara
Ruwenzori Nat.ᵃˡ Park

Fort
Portal
Ibanda Airport

1	Kaghesera Hotel
2	Paradise Bar & Lodging
3	Rwenzori Guest House
4	Summit Club Bar
5	Moonlight Restaurant & Lodging
6	Highway Lodging
7	Bar

KISORO

Kisoro is at the extreme south-western tip of the country, on the Ugandan side of the Virunga mountains, across from Ruhengeri in neighbouring Rwanda. Many travellers prefer to enter Rwanda this way, rather than direct from Kabale. It's a beautiful area and the journey from Kabale is both spectacular and, at times, hair-raising. Kisoro is also the place to see mountain gorillas – but don't get your hopes up too high as few sightings have been made recently. It's cheaper to see the gorillas here than in Rwanda.

Things to See

To see the **mountain gorillas** the man to contact is Zacharia. He's been taking travellers up the mountains in search of gorillas for years. He lives in the village of Giterderi, which is a two-hour walk from Kisoro. Take the road to Rwanda and the first right turn past the Travellers' Rest. Carry on past Rafiki Hotel and then take the left fork to Giterderi. Zacharia charges US$0.40 a day for his services, which is excellent value but you can't be guaranteed a sighting. If you don't have a tent, he'll probably let you sleep on his floor the day before you set off. Another guide called Sahan Erizahari has started up in business. He lives at a village accessed by taking the right fork past Rafiki Hotel. Make enquiries about him before you leave Kisoro.

Places to Stay

One of the cheapest places to stay is *Centenary Hotel* at US$0.40/0.60 a single/double. There are only three singles available. It's popular with budget travellers. You can also find cheap rooms at *Rafiki Hotel*.

For something more upmarket try *Mubano Hotel*, where a double VIP suite (lounge and bedroom) costs US$2. The hotel has a restaurant that serves excellent food at reasonable prices.

Kisoro's top-range hotel is *Travellers' Rest*, part of the Uganda Hotels Corporation chain. Payment must be in hard currency. There's hot water on request, but no electricity.

Places to Eat

You can get a very good breakfast for US$0.30 at *Bufumbira's Bakery*. For lunch or dinner go to *Mubano Hotel*.

MASAKA

Masaka was virtually destroyed by the Tanzanian army in the closing stages of the war that ousted Idi Amin in 1979. Rebuilding is gradually taking place.

There's very little to do in Masaka, but it's from here that you visit the **Sese Islands** in Lake Victoria. Take a *matatu* to Bukakata on the lake's shore and then the weekday ferry to Bugala Island, on which stands the main town of **Kalangula**. The ferry generally leaves at about 8 am. If you miss it, you may have to stay overnight in Bukakata. There *may* be a bus from the ferry jetty on Bugala Island to Kalangula. If not, you can either hire a bicycle or walk. For accommodation, ask at the missions in Kalangula or take a room in one of the few simple lodges.

Places to Stay & Eat

A good place to stay in Masaka is *Masaka Safari Lodge*, about a three-minute walk from the bus station. It's very clean and costs US$0.70 a double. Similar is *Victoria End Rest Inn*, on the main street. The rooms have showers and toilets.

About 20 km east of Masaka is Lake Nabugabo, where you can stay at the *Church of Uganda Holiday & Conference Centre*. It has *bandas* for US$1.20 a night. The owners are very pleasant. There's a beautiful camp site as well.

MBARARA

There's little of interest in Mbarara, except the devastation left from the war. You may, however, find yourself staying overnight en route to or from Kampala.

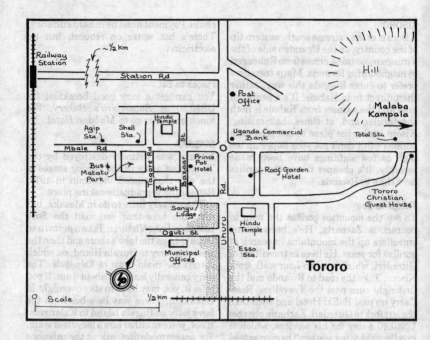

Places to Stay

Perhaps the best place to stay, and certainly one of the cheapest, is the *Church of Uganda Hostel*. It's next to the bus station and near the market and costs US$0.20 for a dormitory bed. For a private room, try *New Ankole Hotel* on the main road past the police station. It costs US$1.20 a double with bathroom and (usually) hot water. It's set in beautiful grounds and has a good restaurant.

TORORO

At the eastern railhead of Uganda, just over the border from Kenya, is Tororo. Once this town must have been particularly beautiful with its many flowering trees. It also must have had a substantial Asian community as its two large Hindu temples suggest. These days, however, it's semiderelict, with empty and boarded-up shops, shabby hotels, vacant lots and few

restaurants with precious little choice in food. It's only redeeming feature is the intriguing, forest-covered volcanic plug that rises up abruptly from an otherwise flat plain at the back of the town. The views from the top would be well worth the climb.

It's difficult to change money in Tororo after bank hours. This is one place where you will have to go looking for money-changers, rather then them finding you.

Places to Stay & Eat

The only accommodation worth considering is that offered at the *Tororo Christian Guest House*, diagonally opposite the Total petrol station on the Mbale Rd from Malaba. It's very clean and those who run it are very friendly. It costs US$0.90 for a dormitory bed, or US$1.30/1.55 a double/triple. The communal showers are clean and excellent meals are available at reasonable prices.

The other hotels are in an execrable state, even though their staff and management are often very friendly. The *Prince Pot Hotel* on Bazaar St is virtually derelict. But it somehow staggers on and even manages to provide clean sheets, though precious little else. The showers don't work and the toilet stinks unbelievably. The bar downstairs is noisy and stays open till late. Rooms cost US$1.20 a double. The locks on the doors are pure Heath Robinson, but gear left in the rooms appears to be safe. The restaurant downstairs serves passable meals and is popular with truck drivers. Further down the street, *Sanyu Lodge* offers accommodation of a similar standard. Slightly better is *Roof Garden Hotel*, which costs US$3.30 a double.

National Parks

KABALEGA NATIONAL PARK

Kabalega National Park used to contain some of the largest concentrations of game in Uganda. Unfortunately, the retreating troops of Idi Amin and then of Okello, both armed with automatic weapons, and the depravations of poachers during the years of civil war wiped out most of the animals in the big league. Now in this 3900 square km park, through which the Victoria Nile flows into Lake Mobutu Sese Seko (formerly Lake Albert), there are no lions, only a few rhino and one herd of elephant numbering around 20 individuals. Of the smaller game there remain plenty of Uganda kob, buffalo, hippo and crocodile. The game is recovering slowly from the onslaught but it will be a long time before it returns to its former numbers – if ever. Many of the park's lodges were vandalised at the same time.

Despite all this, it's still worth visiting Kabalega for the animals that are left and the **Murchison & Karuma falls**. Entry to the park costs the equivalent of US$10 in local currency.

There are now only two places to stay in the park and both are at Paraa, south of Pakwach. There is no regular transport to Paraa from Pakwach and hitching is extremely difficult. From the south, you should be able to find a *matatu* from Masindi to the lakeside town of Butiaba but that's about as far as 'regular' transport goes. The cheapest place to stay is the *Education Centre*, where you can get a dormitory bed for US$0.30 and have use of its cooking facilities. Then there's *Paraa Lodge*, which is essentially derelict.

Once you could stay at *Chobe Lodge*, on the east side of the park, but the last we heard it was closed. Things, however, may have changed, so ask. The turn-off to the lodge is a little over halfway between Masindi and Gulu, and then its about 16 km in. There's no regular transport to Chobe.

All the park launches were destroyed during the civil war so boat trips are no longer possible. Likewise, it's impossible to find vehicles to drive you around the park. Again, things may have changed so make enquiries.

RUWENZORI NATIONAL PARK

The Ruwenzori National Park used to be a magnificent place to visit with its great herds of elephant, buffalo, kob, waterbuck, hippo and topi and, in the south around Ishasha, its tree-climbing lions. But like Kabalega, much of the game was wiped out by the retreating troops of Amin and Okello and the Tanzanian army, which occupied the country after Amin's demise and also did their ivory and trophy-hunting best. There's now very little game in the park other than gazelle, buffalo, hippo and perhaps two small herds of elephant (certainly one). But it's worth visiting just for the hippos and birds – there are few places in Africa where you will be able to see so many hippos. The park, formerly called Queen Elizabeth II National Park, covers 2000 square km

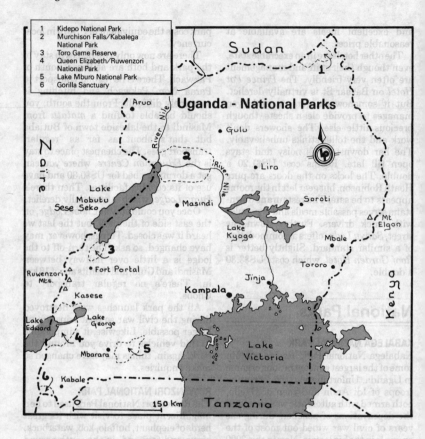

1	Kidepo National Park	
2	Murchison Falls/Kabalega National Park	
3	Toro Game Reserve	
4	Queen Elizabeth/Ruwenzori National Park	
5	Lake Mburo National Park	
6	Gorilla Sanctuary	

Uganda - National Parks

south of the Ruwenzori mountains and east of Lake Edward. Entry to the park costs the equivalent of US$10 in local currency, and considerably less for students.

Every visitor to the park takes a launch up the **Kazinga Channel** to see the hippos and pelicans. If you're lucky, you might catch sight of a rare herd of elephant and *very* occasionally a lion or leopard. The trips are worth it just to see the hippos – there are thousands of them! Unfortunately, the launch isn't always working, but when it is it costs US$10 so get a small group together to share the cost. If no-one else is

staying at the Student Hostel, ask around at the lodge. The best time to go is from dawn till 9 am and after 4 pm if you want to see anything other than hippos, pelicans and buffalo. The trip lasts about two hours.

There's a small **museum** next to the Lodge which contains skulls and a few other things. It's open weekdays from 3 to 6 pm and at weekends from 10 am to 12 noon.

Most people stay at *Mweya Safari Lodge*, which is on a raised peninsula between the Kazinga Channel and Lake Edward, south of Kasese. There is regular transport (*matatus* and buses) from Kasese to the park entrance turn-off, just before Katunguru on the Kazinga Channel. From there you will have to hitch and there's not much traffic on this the road to Katwe, Mpondwe, and Kasindi and Beni in Zaïre. There's even less traffic from the park gate to Mweya Lodge. Local people walk the last stretch (about seven km), but park officials are extremely reluctant to allow visitors to do this. Nevertheless, most travellers seem to make it in a morning or an afternoon.

The cheapest place to stay at Mweya is the *Student Hostel*, down the peninsula from the lodge. It costs US$0.60 a person for a bed in a four or six-berth concrete hut (couples are normally given a room to themselves). The mattresses are dirty and sheets are not provided, but there's no bed bugs and the rooms can be locked. There are cold showers and toilets. It's very good value. Otherwise, you can camp in front of the hostel and be entertained by the hippos grunting and browsing outside your tent at night – generally they don't regard tents as edible. For something a little more salubrious, try the *Institute of Ecology Hostel* nearer to the lodge which costs US$1.30 a person.

Mweya Safari Lodge is part of the hard-currency Uganda Hotels Corporation chain and, as such, expensive. You can, however, pay for meals and drinks in shillings, so there's little point in carrying food. The meals are quite good and there's a fair choice on the menu. It's wise to make reservations for all meals or else there may be no food – they bring in food to cater for those who book in advance at the lodge and Ecology Institute rather than for impromptu visitors. Prices are reasonable.

RUWENZORI MOUNTAINS

These fabled, mist-covered mountains on Uganda's western border with Zaïre are almost as popular as Kilimanjaro and Mt Kenya, but they are definitely harder to climb. They have a well-deserved reputation for being very wet at times –

best summed up by a comment on the wall of Bujuku hut: 'Jesus came here to learn how to walk on water. After five days, anyone could do it'. You need to be prepared and have warm, waterproof clothing.

The mountain range, which is not volcanic, stretches for about 100 km. At its centre there are a number of permanent snow and glacier-covered peaks – Mt Stanley, 5590 metres; Mt Speke, 5340 metres; Mt Baker, 5290 metres; Mt Gessi, 5156 metres; Mt Emui, 5240 metres; and Mt Luigi di Savoia, 5028 metres. The two highest peaks are Margherita (5590 metres) and Alexandra (5570 metres), both on Mt Stanley.

The climbing ranges from the easy ascent of Mt Speke, which requires only limited mountain experience, to the hard routes of Mt Stanley and Mt Baker, which should not be attempted unless you are of alpine standard. You don't, of course, have to go all the way to the top. The guides will be happy to take you around the lower reaches if you want. Five days would be the absolute minimum for a visit to the range, but seven to eight days would be more normal with one or two days at the top huts. The driest and therefore best times to go climbing are from late December to the end of February and mid-June to mid-August. But even then, the higher reaches are often enveloped in mist, though this normally clears for a short time each day.

If you're a serious climber get the *Guide to the Ruwenzori* by Osmaston & Pasteur (Mountain Club of Uganda, 1972) before arriving in Uganda. The only two places it's available are from the publishers, West Col Productions, 1 Meadow Close, Goring-on-Thames, Reading, Berks, UK, and at Stanfords Map Centre, Long Acre, Covent Garden, London WC2, UK. It costs £8.95, plus postage.

To organise a climb you must first contact John Matte (PO Box 276, Kilimbe, via Kasese, Uganda), the Mountain Club agent in charge of

No of days	1	2	3	4	5	6	7
cassava	1 kg	2 kg	3 kg	4 kg	5 kg	6 kg	7 kg
sugar	175 gm	250 gm	325 gm	500 gm	1 kg	1 kg	1½ kg
smoked fish	1 kg	2 kg	3 kg	4 kg	5 kg	6 kg	7 kg
ground nuts	500 gm	500 gm	500 gm	500 gm	500 gm	1 kg	1½ kg
tea	50 gm	50 gm	50 gm	50 gm	100 gm	100 gm	100 gm
salt	60 gm	60 gm	60 gm	60 gm	120 gm	120 gm	120 gm
powdered milk	600 ml	600 ml	600 ml	600 ml	600 ml	600 ml	600 ml
cooking oil	600 ml	600 ml	600 ml	600 ml	600 ml	600 ml	600 ml

arranging huts, guides and porters. If you want to start on a certain day, book at least one week in advance. If it's not busy, treks can usually be arranged with just a few days' notice.

Then you must get all the food, equipment and medicine for both your party and the guides and porters. You cannot do this at the starting point (Ibanda), as there's only a very limited quantity and extremely limited choice of local foodstuffs. Buy your supplies in either Kasese or Fort Portal. Current food requirements for each guide/porter are given at the top of the page.

You also need to supply a minimum of four cigarettes a day per guide/porter ('Sportsman' is the preferred brand), as well as a blanket and jumper. Blankets can be rented from John Matte for US$0.40 and jumpers for US$0.15. No footwear is necessary for guides/porters as far as Bujuku hut (4400 metres), but above this level those who wear their own boots are entitled to an additional daily allowance.

Suggested medicines are aspirin for headaches, insomnia and mountain sickness; adhesive plaster and bandages; an antiseptic lotion such as Dettol; and an effective drug for pneumonia – high altitude pneumonia (pulmonary oedema) is the most common disabling sickness at high altitudes.

Your own equipment should include plenty of warm and waterproof clothing, sleeping bags, strong boots (John Matte has some very old and very heavy boots for hire,

which are definitely not recommended), a compass, primus stove and lamps.

Guides and porters will not go onto glaciers without the proper clothing and footwear. So, if glaciers are part of your plan you will also have to provide ice axes, ropes and crampons (available from John Matte).

The take-off point for a climb is the Mountain Club at Ibanda, about 22 km from Kasese. Take the road to Fort Portal for about 10 km, before turning left towards the 'Rwenzori High School' and 'Bugoye Sub-Dispensary' (signposted). There's an electrical substation by the turn-off. There's plenty of transport as far as the turn-off, but the 12 km along a gravel road to Ibanda is little travelled. You may have to walk. People along this road are very friendly. The tailor at Bugoye sells warm beer (but no soft drinks). If you're carrying all the supplies for a trek, hire a matatu in Kasese.

The Mountain Club is a very grandiose title for what is little more than a filthy hovel, with even filthier beds full of bed bugs. If you can possibly bring a tent with you, do so, and camp next to the club. Mrs Matte will cook reasonable meals for visitors, depending on what's available. There's a river behind the club which is clean and good for bathing. Excess baggage can be locked up. There is electricity at Ibanda, but no telephones.

Most parties walk up the Mubuku and Bujuku valleys to the central peaks, staying overnight at the various huts. Some of the huts are in poor shape, the lower

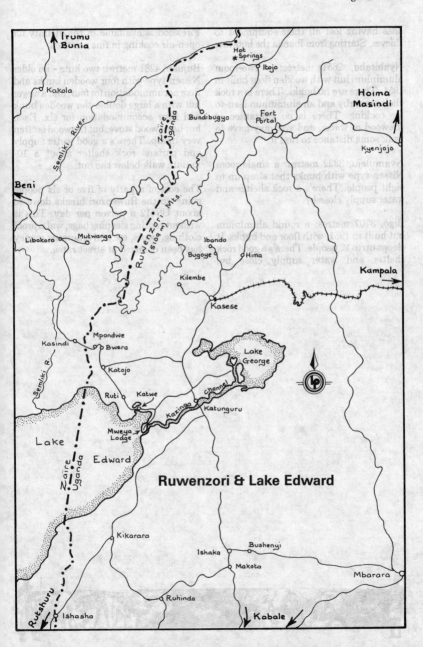

Ruwenzori & Lake Edward

ones having lost all their equipment to thieves. Starting from Ibanda the huts are:

Nyabitaba, 2651 metres: a two-room aluminium hut with wooden floor built in 1951. There are no bunks. There is a rock shelter nearby and an aluminium lean-to for cooking. There is no guarantee of firewood or water, and you may have to walk some distance to find it.

Nyamuleju, 3322 metres: a single-room Nissen-type with bunks that sleep up to eight people. There's a rock shelter and water supply close by.

Bigo, 3707 metres: a round aluminium hut built in 1951, with floor and bunks. It sleeps up to 12 people. There's a good rock shelter and water supply close by. Firewood is available in the vicinity for open-air cooking in fine weather.

Bujuku, 4281 metres: two huts – an older Nissen-type with four wooden bunks and floor accommodation for four, and a newer hut with a large double-tier wooden bunk and floor accommodation for six. Each hut has a wood stove, but firewood is often very damp. There's a good water supply and porters' rock shelter about a 10-minute walk below the hut.

The cost of a party of five or six people going up the Ruwenzori breaks down to about US$12 a person per day. This is without renting sleeping bags, waterproof clothing, boots, etc and assuming money has been changed at street rates.

Zaïre

The Amazonia of Africa, this vast country is the archetypal explorer's dream. In the heart of the tropics, Zaïre is covered with endless rainforests, enormous rivers, mountains, volcanoes and prolific wildlife. It also possesses one of the most diabolical transport systems in the world. In short, it has everything that adds up to genuine adventure.

Any traveller who has been to Zaïre will entertain you for hours with the most improbable stories you're ever likely to come across. There's certainly no rushing through this place – even if you wanted to – and whichever route you choose, it'll take a long time to reach the other side.

Politically, the country is a daunting one, as anyone with even a vague interest in armed conflict in Africa will know, but you're unlikely to come face to face with any of this and the village people are some of the friendliest in the world. Don't pass up one of the most memorable trips of your life because of impressions you may have formed about the country through reading newspapers reporting one armed conflict after another.

The earliest inhabitants of Zaïre were bands of hunters and gatherers who lived in the densely forested areas without a social structure or kinship system, much as the Pygmies of today still do. In time, however, settled communities sprang up along the rivers and at the edges of the forest as progressive waves of migrating Bantu and Nilotic tribes moved into the area from the north. They survived by fishing and primitive farming. As they gradually improved their agricultural techniques and grew into more complex societies these communities were able to increasingly dominate the Pygmies and extend their areas of control until, by the 14th century, the first great kingdoms had come into being.

Foremost among these was the kingdom of Kongo which, through a combination of conquest and matrimonial alliances as well as an elaborate political structure, controlled a large part of the coastal area around the mouth of the Zaïre River. Governors appointed to subject states over a wide area were responsible for collecting tribute in the form of ivory, cloth and slaves. Further south emerged a similar pattern of feudal states whose power was based on control over long-distance trade. The most important of these kingdoms were the Luba, Kuba and Lunda.

Into this scene came the Portuguese in 1482. Their arrival marked the beginning of new networks of exchange and trade, which gradually undermined the power of the Kongo kingdom. Above all else, it was the Portuguese demand for slaves which led to the eclipse of the kingdom. Before the arrival of the Europeans, slavery had constituted a small part of the wealth on which the Kongo based its power. By the 17th century the Portuguese demand for slaves for their Brazilian plantations far outstripped the numbers that could be supplied by traditional methods. In order to procure sufficient numbers, Portuguese raiding parties (and the kingdoms further south) quickly began to undermine the economy of the Kongo, and war was declared in 1660. The Kongo was resoundingly beaten by the superior fire power of the Portuguese, and the kingdom went into rapid decline.

The kingdoms of the interior, however, continued to grow by trading slaves and

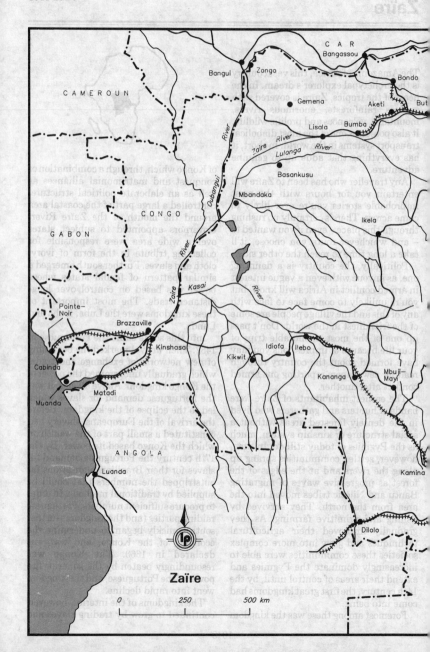

Zaïre

0   250   500 km

ivory for firearms, cloth and luxuries with the Portuguese. Their power was enhanced in the 19th century by the arrival of other slavers from Zanzibar – mostly Arabs – who used Bagamoyo (on the Tanzanian coast) and Ujiji (on Lake Tanganyika) as their main trading posts.

Despite the many centuries of trade with European powers, there was no direct penetration of the interior until the 19th century. One of the most famous people to explore this area was, of course, David Livingstone, whose chronicles inspired both Catholic and Protestant churches alike to dispatch missionaries by the thousand to Christianise and bring 'civilisation' to the poor benighted 'savages' of 'darkest Africa'.

As elsewhere in the world, however, the rush to save souls proved to be just a prelude to economic exploitation and colonisation. The era had arrived when Africa was being scoured for minerals and suitable land on which cash crops could be grown to fuel the expanding industrial economies of Europe and North America.

It was the American newspaper reporter, Stanley, who after originally going in search of Livingstone (whom he met at Ujiji) turned his attention to exploring the area himself, and finally paved the way for the colonisation of this part of Africa. After returning from one of his exploratory trips Stanley was met at Marseilles by representatives of King Leopold of the Belgians. As a result he became the king's personal representative.

Employing Stanley's knowledge of the area, Leopold laid claim to a vast region of central Africa and was successful in getting the other European powers to ratify his claims at the Berlin Conference in 1884-85. Leopold's personal empire became known as the Congo Free State, although as the indigenous people were soon to discover, Leopold's 'freedom' was to ride on the backs of their enslavement.

While Leopold remained the sole owner of this vast territory, its inhabitants were subjected to one of the most brutal and ruthless forms of colonisation ever to disgrace the face of the earth. When news of the worst atrocities leaked out Leopold was forced to hand over the territory to the Belgian government.

Colonial administration by the Belgian government, however, resulted in little real change. The old racist stereotypes remained intact, 'pacification' programmes were a regular feature of the colony right up to the start of WW II, and there was no attempt whatsoever to train Africans for positions of responsibility or leadership in the colonial administration. The Catholic Church retained a virtual monopoly over education, with the best schools reserved for the children of the white settlers, and higher education denied to all except those Africans prepared to enter the priesthood.

The years following the depression of the 1930s saw a phenomenal economic boom in the country, and this underwrote a large part of the war effort during WW II. It didn't, however, come hand in hand with political reform.

Only in the 1950s, with independence movements sweeping other African colonies, did the Belgian authorities deem it time to relax their paternalistic rule and allow a number of African political parties to emerge. However, the change came too suddenly and too late for any unity to be forged between the many disparate tribal and regional groups in this huge country. The only exception to this was Patrice Lumumba's Movement National Congolaise (MNC), which stood for a strong central government able to resist secessionist tendencies by more locally based parties. Riots in Kinshasa (then known as Leopoldville) in 1959 shook the colonial authorities so badly that independence was granted abruptly the following year.

The country was ill-prepared for independence, although Patrice Lumumba tried hard to maintain cooperation between the various parties. However, only days after independence was granted,

Moise Tshombe, the governor of what was then Katanga Province (now Shaba), declared the secession of his province. Lumumba appealed to the UN for assistance in bringing the rebels to heel, but on returning from New York was dismissed by the president, Joseph Kasavubu, with assistance from a powerful army commander, Mobutu. Lumumba was eventually delivered into the hands of his arch rival, Moise Tshombe, and murdered.

The Katangan secession was finally crushed only after massive UN intervention. The return of Katanga to the fold, however, was not to result in a solution to the country's problems. Kasavubu was soon faced with armed insurgency from many quarters including supporters of Lumumba, governors of the eastern provinces and plain would-be warlords in other parts of the country.

In an attempt to defuse the situation, Kasavubu invited Moise Tshombe back from exile to be prime minister. Tshombe was able to secure western financial and military assistance (including white mercenary troops) and use it to impose a crude kind of control over virtually all the Congo. Despite this neither he nor Kasavubu were capable of inspiring the necessary political confidence. So, when a revolt broke out among the Simba tribespeople of the north-east in 1965, both were swept from power in a coup led by General Mobutu. Tshombe went into exile for the second time, but in 1967 a chartered plane carrying him was forced to land in Algeria. There, two years later in an undisclosed prison, it was announced he had died of heart failure.

Mobutu has continued to rule since the coup of 1965, but his regime has been plagued by the same kind of economic and political upheavals which dogged his predecessors. With power increasingly concentrated in his own hands he has become more and more dependent on his western backers.

There have been many attempts to

popularise Mobutu's regime. Some of these have been merely cosmetic, such as the Africanisation of names (in 1971 the name of the country was changed from Congo to Zaïre, Katanga to Shaba; and Christian names were dropped, much to the anger of the Catholic Church). Others have been less cosmetic, like the announcement of 'amnesties' for dissident leaders in exile (many of whom were subsequently arrested and executed, or simply murdered on arrival). Yet none of these attempts have essentially changed the autocratic nature of Mobutu's regime.

The strongest challenge to his position came in 1977 after the price of copper had plummeted to almost half its former price, resulting in a foreign debt of US$300 million – the world's highest per capita at the time. In that year some 5000 guerrillas of the Front de Libération Nationale du Congo (FLNC) invaded Shaba province from Angola and got as far as the important mining town of Kolwezi. It quickly became obvious that Mobutu's soldiers were no match for the FLNC, which was only expelled with the aid of 1500 regular Moroccan troops, French transport planes and military advisers, Egyptian pilots and other military assistance from Belgium, Britain, West Germany and the USA, as well as food supplies from the People's Republic of China. A year later the same thing happened. Mobutu's troops were once again shown to be inadequate in dealing with the situation, and the insurgents were only repulsed with the aid of French and Belgian paratroopers.

By now Mobutu had become an embarrassment for his western backers in terms of international credibility. After the second defeat of the FLNC, some 250,000 civilians had fled to Angola. Pressure was put on Mobutu to liberalise his regime. One result of this was a rapprochement between Zaïre and Angola. Mobutu agreed to end assistance to anti-MPLA groups fighting to overthrow the Marxist government of President Neto in return for Neto's agreement to disarm the FLNC guerrillas and remove them from the border area with Shaba province. Since then a number of rivals and former dissidents – particularly Nguza Karl i Bond, who was condemned to death after the first Shaba war – have been reinstated in the government and efforts have been made to restore its diplomatic and economic credibility.

Nevertheless, with corruption widespread, continued low prices for copper and cobalt (two of Zaïre's major exports), a disintegrating transport system, massive smuggling and insufficient investment, Zaïre's external debt has continued to rise – by 1986 it had grown to around US$6 billion. Although the IMF and the World Bank had both successfully pressured Mobutu into announcing a programme of austerity in return for further loans, the rot continued and, in 1987, Mobutu reneged on these promises and threatened to limit debt repayment to 10% of export earnings. The gamble paid off and the country's debts were again rescheduled, but Mobutu's action has made foreign donors more reluctant to invest in Zaïre.

While the survival of Mobutu's regime depends to a large degree on its ability to secure further loans and rescheduling of its debts, of equal importance is the USA's political support for the regime. With the so-called Front Line States clamouring for economic and political sanctions against South Africa, and the negotiations for both the independence of Namibia and Cuban military withdrawal from Angola, Zaïre is regarded by the USA and Western Europe as one of the few moderate states in Africa capable of mediating between the different sides (Zaïre is one of South Africa's most important African trading partners). Neither Europe nor America is in a hurry to see Zaïre radicalised so, despite their demands for a restructuring of the economy, tighter fiscal control and greater efficiency, they have continued to underwrite Mobutu's regime.

There is no doubt that Zaïre does have

vast potential though its problems are equally vast. Two of the main ones are poor or nonexistent communications and transport, and lack of skilled personnel. Incredibly, in such a diverse country, Zaïre is not even self-sufficient in basic foodstuffs.

Facts

GEOGRAPHY & CLIMATE

The greater part of the country consists of a huge, flat basin through which the rivers Zaïre, Kasai and Oubangui flow to the Atlantic Ocean. Most of the region is covered by lush, tropical rainforest. Further south in Shaba province, the forest gives way to savannah. The country's eastern borders run the length of the Rift Valley, taking in lakes Mobutu Sese Seko, Kivu, Tanganyika and Mweru. Here the land rises into a string of mountains, some of which top 5000 metres in height, particularly in the Ruwenzori Range.

Temperatures vary between 20°C and 30°C in the central forest area and between 15°C and 25°C on the high plateau. Eastern Zaïre enjoys a Mediterranean climate. Humidity is high at all times. The best time to visit is from June to September south of the equator and from November to March north of the equator. These periods correspond to what might be called the 'dry' season.

PEOPLE

The population is about 31 million and consists of up to 200 different ethnic groupings, several of which straddle the borders with neighbouring countries. The main groups are the Bantu (around nine million) and the Nilotic and Hamitic tribes (two to three million). The Pygmies, who have spurned all attempts to integrate them into modern life, live mainly in the forests of the north-east.

There are about 100,000 expatriates, the majority from Belgium.

VISAS

Visas are required by all. They can be obtained from Zaïre's embassies in Abidjan (Ivory Coast), Accra (Ghana), Addis Ababa (Ethiopia), Algiers (Algeria), Bangui (Central African Republic), Brazzaville (Congo), Bujumbura (Burundi), Cairo (Egypt), Conakry (Guinea), Cotonou (Benin), Dakar (Senegal), Dar es Salaam (Tanzania), Harare (Zimbabwe), Kampala (Uganda), Khartoum (Sudan), Kigali (Rwanda), Lagos (Nigeria), Libreville (Gabon), Lome (Togo), Luanda (Angola), Lusaka (Zambia), Maputo (Mozambique), Monrovia (Liberia), Nairobi (Kenya), Nouakchott (Mauritania), N'Djamena (Chad), Rabat (Morocco), Tripoli (Libya), Tunis (Tunisia), Yaoundé (Cameroun) and from the Zaïre Consulate in Kigoma (Tanzania).

The cost of a visa depends on whether you want a one-month single-entry, a two-month multiple-entry or a three-month multiple-entry visa. If there's any chance you are going to need a multiple-entry visa get it at the start. You'll save a lot of hassle this way.

All visa applications must be accompanied by a letter of introduction from your embassy (except in Bangui and Harare). Some embassies issue these free, others charge for them. British embassies charge about US$7.50! You may also be asked for an onward ticket and vaccination certificates (cholera and yellow fever). On the visa application form it may say 'Entry through Kinshasa only', but this isn't stamped in your passport so it doesn't make any difference.

Some Zaïre embassies may be reluctant to issue multiple-entry visas. If so, tell them you will be going by road from Bukavu to Uvira. The best road between these two places loops through Rwanda so you need not only a Rwandan transit visa (bought at the border for US$7 to US$10), but also a multiple-entry visa for Zaïre in order to get back in again. In the past, some travellers without these were forced to buy a Rwandan transit visa and to pay a bribe on re-entry into Zaïre.

However, I made this trip on the bus from Bukavu without a valid Rwandan visa and with only a single-entry Zaïre visa. There were no questions and no hassles whatsoever and my passport wasn't stamped at any of the entry or exit posts. It may be, however, that this is a special concession for bus passengers and doesn't apply to people driving their own vehicles and their passengers (which includes hitchhikers). If you're hitching, it is a good idea to have that Rwandan visa and a multiple-entry visa for Zaïre. Rwandan visas can be bought on the border as a rule, but they cost Z 6400 for a two-week visa.

Alternatively, there's a road from Bukavu to Uvira via Nya Ngezi (beautiful views) which goes entirely through Zaïre. Many trucks go this way and the journey time is much the same.

In Dar es Salaam, (embassy on Malik Rd off Upanga Rd), visas cost TSh 300, require four photographs and a letter of introduction from your embassy and take 24 hours to issue. It's difficult to get anything other than a one-month single-entry visa. Avoid having to apply for your visa at the consulate in Kigoma (Tanzania) as they take *two weeks* to issue! It's open for applications on Monday, Wednesday and Friday from 9 am to 12.30 pm and 3 to 6.30 pm. Visas cost TSh 200, with four photographs. Kigoma is not a place to be stuck in for two weeks, though you could go and sit out the time at the Gombe Stream National Park.

In Harare a three-month multiple-entry visa costs Z$15 and is issued while you wait. No letter of introduction is necessary.

In Nairobi (embassy in Electricity House, Harambee Ave; tel 29771) one-month single-entry visas cost KSh 160, two-month multiple-entry visas cost KSh 280, and three-month multiple-entry

visas cost KSh 360. Four photographs, a letter of introduction and vaccination certificates are required, and they take 24 hours to issue. You may also be asked for an onward ticket, but it doesn't have to start in Zaïre. The staff are pleasant and the embassy is open Monday to Friday from 10 am to 12 noon.

In Lusaka visas cost Kw 100 for one month and Kw 250 for three months, and require two photos and a letter of introduction from your embassy. If you get there early in the morning you can collect your visa the same day.

There are no Zaïre consulates in either Gisenyi or Cyangugu (Rwanda) and no consulates in Uganda (other than the embassy in Kampala).

In the past travellers who wanted to go across the river on the ferry from Brazzaville (Congo) to Kinshasa had to have a *laissez-passer* issued by the Zaïre Embassy in Brazzaville in addition to a Zaïre visa. The embassy would only issue the *laissez-passer* if you had obtained your visa in another country. It was catch-22. Many travellers were caught out and forced to take an expensive flight between the two capitals.

It seems that this nonsense has now finished. Assuming you have a Zaïre visa, you can go either to the immigration office next to the Hotel de Ville (in Brazzaville) or to the same place on the riverfront, fill in two forms and get an exit stamp free of charge. Then take the ferry to Kinshasa. On arrival, you fill in one form, have your baggage checked, get an entry stamp, and off you go – no worries.

At the Zambia-Zaïre border the customs officials may demand to see your international vaccination card. If you haven't got one (or it's out of date) they'll charge you for the vaccine, stamp your certificate but won't vaccinate you!

Visa Extensions

The main cities where visa extensions can be obtained are Bukavu, Kinshasa, Kisangani and Lubumbashi. Bukavu is reported to be one of the easiest places to apply and you can get up to an additional three months. In Kisangani extensions cost Z 400 for one month and Z 1000 for three months, plus Z 100 'administrative fee', and are issued in 24 hours without hassle. Some travellers have reported the same for Kinshasa (issued in one day) but others have been made to wait four or five days.

In Lubumbashi extensions officially take eight to 10 days but with luck they can take as little as two days. The cost varies depending on who you are, where you come from and on how hard-pressed for cash the official who issues them is, but Z 400 per extra month is about average. Two photographs are usually required, but there's generally no fuss about onward tickets or sufficient funds.

Other Visas

Burundi In Kinshasa these cost Z 510, require two photos and an onward ticket and are issued in 24 hours. It's easier, however, to get your visa at the consulate in Bukavu since no onward ticket is required. A one-month visa costs the same as in Kinshasa, plus two extra photos, and is issued within 24 hours.

The consulate is in the Sinelac Building, 184 Ave du President Mobutu. Visas can be applied for in the afternoons only from Monday to Thursday from 3 to 5 pm. It's closed on Saturdays and Sundays.

Congo These cost Z 300 and require two photos and a letter of introduction from your embassy. French nationals must apply for a special permit, which costs Z 280. When applying for the visa, you must tell them which day you intend to cross the river. The people at the embassy are not at all friendly.

Rwanda The embassy (tel 30108) is at 50 Ave de la Justice, Gombe, Kinshasa. Visas cost US$12.50 (or the equivalent in zaïres), require two photos and are issued in 24 hours. They allow for a stay of one month. There are no Rwandan consulates in Bukavu or Goma (the main towns bordering Rwanda) so get your visa in Kinshasa if you are passing through there. If not, there are a number of options:

1 The most expensive way is to buy a transit visa, which allows for a stay of two weeks, on the border. This will cost between US$30 and US$45 depending on whether you pay in US dollars, zaïres or Rwandan francs (the last is the cheapest because of black market parities – if you have access to the black market).

2 Enlist the help of the Belgian Consulate in Goma (very helpful), pay RFr 1500 (about US$17 at official rates) and wait two weeks.

3 Go direct to Burundi via Uvira and get a normal visa at normal prices in Bujumbura, then go direct to Rwanda.

4 Go direct to Uganda from Zaïre and get a normal visa in Kampala (a long way round).

You also need to consider what is written earlier under Visas about the trip from Bukavu to Bujumbura via Uvira.

Zambia In Lubumbashi a double-entry transit visa valid for three months can be obtained the same day you apply. The frontier with Zaïre is open again.

Kenya, Tanzania & Uganda There are no consulates for these countries in eastern Zaïre. The nearest embassies are in Kigali (Rwanda) and Bujumbura (Burundi).

Kenyan visas cost Z 500, require one photo and a letter of introduction from your embassy. They're issued in 24 hours.

Ugandan visas cost Z 1500, require two photos and are issued in 24 hours. Both embassies are open from 8 am to 2 pm.

There are also embassies for Algeria, Angola, Benin, Cameroun, Central African Republic, Chad, Egypt, Ethiopia, Gabon, Guinea, Ivory Coast, Liberia, Libya, Mauritania, Morocco, Nigeria, Sudan, Togo and Tunisia in Kinshasa.

MONEY

US$1 = Z 120

The unit of currency is the zaïre = 100 makutas, though you're not likely to see anything smaller than 50 makuta these days. Both old and new bank notes are in circulation. They're all legal tender, but the design on them is different and the old notes are huge and usually decrepit. Most of them ought to carry a government health warning. Banks love giving them to you perhaps as a joke, but more probably because they're usually low denomination so it's easy to miss a few out here and there without you noticing (or being willing to count them all).

Zaïre devalued the currency by a massive 520% in 1983 and allowed it to float after that. It has been losing its value steadily by about 40% per year (the inflation rate) since then, though the government is considering putting a stop to this and giving the zaïre a fixed value. As a result, there is little difference between the bank rate and the street rate especially when the banks are closed. At most you can expect 5% to 10%.

Changing cash on the street market does, however, save a lot of time and, of course, you don't pay commission. You can even change travellers' cheques in certain stores at the same rate as the bank offers, but only when the banks are open. When they're closed, the rate can drop by 20%! It's not always easy to find someone who wants to change money (Asian and European shopkeepers are your best bet), but most people can be persuaded to change if you'll accept something nearer the bank rate.

If you only have travellers' cheques you need to shop around before changing money. Commission can vary from 1% to 20%! Some banks won't even change travellers' cheques (the Banque de Kinshasa in Goma and the Banque de Zaïre in Bukavu, for example). The Banque Commerciale Zaïroise is probably the best bet as their commission is only Z 38 per transaction. You can have your cheque cashed usually in half an hour, though this varies considerably from place to place, and in many banks it can take up to three hours.

Avoid the Union des Banques Zaïroises – some travellers have been charged 20% commission.

Banking hours are Monday to Friday from 8 am to 12 noon but if you're changing travellers' cheques be there before 11 am. They won't entertain you after that.

There are a lot of hilarious stories circulating about banks and travellers' cheques in eastern Zaïre. One traveller spent all day at a bank in Bukavu trying to change a travellers' cheque, but they wouldn't do it because it didn't have 'Specimen' printed across it like the bank's sample! We heard of another where the manager wouldn't change a US$100 cheque because his sample was a US$50 cheque. Others may refuse if your cheque is from a different company than the one from which the manager has a sample. You should not run into anything as silly as this at the Banque Commerciale Zaïroise in either Goma or Bukavu, but you cannot change travellers' cheques at the bank in Uvira.

Currency declaration forms were abolished in May 1986. The import or export of local currency is officially prohibited and you may be asked if you have any when leaving Zaïre. In most places – the airport at Kinshasa being the exception – it's unlikely that you will be searched. There will, however, be some occasions when you simply have to take zaïres into Zaïre (at weekends, for instance, if you have only travellers' cheques, or any day of the week if crossing to Uvira from Bujumbura where banks won't change cheques). You must hide them though.

There is one other place where you need to be wary regarding money and that is at the immigration office at the Onatra River pier in Kisangani. Here you may be strip-searched and your baggage pulled apart when you get off the boat. This happened to a lot of travellers in the past when currency declaration forms were issued. Any undeclared currency discovered on this search was invariably confiscated or else you handed the bulk of it across as a 'fine' or bribe. Since currency forms were abolished this may no longer apply, but they may ask for bank receipts. Just be careful and let us know if there are any hassles.

Corruption is endemic in Zaïre, though quite a few travellers get through without coming up against it. If you find yourself being hassled, act friendly, joke, make complimentary comments about the president, but steadfastly refuse to give them money. And carry your passport at all times. Soldiers at roadblocks outside of Kinshasa get more and more insistent about cigarettes and money as the night wears on, so avoid travelling at those times. At Kinshasa Airport, everyone – from the customs people to the bag rummagers, ticket collectors and police – will threaten and harass you for money. They go so far as to take things out of your baggage and tell you they will be keeping it. If you're leaving by way of Kinshasa Airport, don't attempt to take any zaïres with you. Once you've been through check-in they won't allow you back into the reception area, so you'll end up having them confiscated.

POST
When collecting mail from a poste restante there's a small charge for each letter.

FOOD
There are chronic food shortages in certain parts of the country so food prices vary widely, even over short distances. The state of the roads also affects food prices. To keep your costs down eat what grows locally.

FILM & PHOTOGRAPHY
Bring all your film requirements to Zaïre. There are few places to buy film and where this is possible it will be expensive and probably old.

When you enter, Zaïre customs may demand that you buy a 'photography permit' for each camera that you have. The usual charge is about US$3. It's probably bullshit, but there's not a lot you can do about it except waste half a day trying to get the price down.

Don't take photographs of anything vaguely connected with the military or of government buildings, banks, bridges, border posts, post offices or ports. If anyone sees you the chances are you'll lose your film. There is intense paranoia about spies in some places (Uvira is one of them) because Zaïre doesn't get on well with her neighbours Burundi, Rwanda and Tanzania. They also haven't forgotten the Katanga secession in the 1960s, the invasions from Angola in the 1970s and the more recent insurgencies from Tanzania.

If you don't want to run into problems, get a written OK to take pictures from the Sous-Regional Commissioner before going ahead. You may have to cross his palm to get it, but don't offer unless it's strongly indicated. Travellers have been arrested for taking pictures of such innocent scenes as markets.

LANGUAGE
French is the official government language, but Lingala is the official language of the armed forces. Other major languages spoken in certain areas are Swahili, Tshiluba and Kikongo. Little English is spoken. Here is a short vocabulary in Lingala.

hello	*mbote*
What's new?	*sangonini?*
nothing new	*sangote*
go	*nake*
depart	*kokende*
where?	*wapi?*
where are?	*okeyi wapi?*
why?	*ponanini?*
OK/thanks	*malam*
very far	*musika*
tomorrow	*lobi*

house	ndako
home	mboka
eat	kolia
drink	komela
things to eat	biloko yakolia
water	mai
manioc	songo
bananas	makemba
rice	loso
beans	madeso
salted fish	makaibo
fresh fish	mbisi
meat	niama
peanuts	injunga karanga
market	nazondo
strong	makasi
a lot	mingi

Getting There & Around

Getting around Zaïre is an exercise in initiative, patience and endurance. It also promises some of the most memorable adventures you're ever likely to have. To enjoy it to the full, you need to forget all about such fetishes as how long it takes to get from A to B, the sort of food you will be eating and the standard of accommodation you're likely to find. Nothing can be guaranteed, nothing runs on time, and in the wet season you could be stranded waiting for a lift for weeks. Not only that, apart from the river boats on the Zaïre and Kasai rivers and the railways in the east and south-east of the country, the only way of getting around the country is to hitch lifts on trucks. There are few public buses.

With rare exceptions, the roads are diabolical so you'll probably end up at your destination covered in mud, bruised, battered and thoroughly exhausted. Free lifts are the exception rather than the rule unless you meet the occasional Kenyan or Somali driver. The price of lifts often reflects the difficulty of getting there rather than the distance.

You don't have to go by truck, though. If the spirit of adventure runs in your veins you can get through this country in all manner of weird and wonderful ways. Some travellers have literally walked from Kisangani to the Rift Valley, staying in Pygmy villages along the way, and have encountered the most disarming hospitality at every stop. Others have haggled for a pirogue (dugout canoe) in Bangui, Central African Republic, got the price down to CFA 10,000 after three days of haggling, and sailed it down to Kwamouth at the junction of the Zaïre and Kasai rivers. After selling it there, they struck out down the Kasai River and eventually reached Lubumbashi. Whichever way you go it's going to be an adventure!

As far as reasonably predictable transport goes, there are certain routes for getting from one end of the country to the other. In the west the starting points are either Kinshasa, (to/from Congo) or Zongo (to/from Central African Republic). In the east there is Aba (to/from Sudan), Beni or Rutshuru (to/from Uganda), Goma and Bukavu (to/from Rwanda), Uvira (to/from Burundi) and Kalemie (to/from Tanzania). In the south the route is Lubumbashi to Chingola, Kitwe or Ndola (to/from Zambia). The border with Angola is effectively closed. The main crossroads of all these routes are Kisangani, Kabalo and Kamina.

Don't take any road marked on a map as anything other than a possibility. Sometimes it won't even exist. The Bartholomews maps commit some serious errors by confusing, for instance, the small eastern towns of Komande and Komanda along the borders with Uganda. The Michelin maps are better in this respect.

AIR

Air Zaïre offers 40% student discounts to those under 26 years old with an international student card and a letter from their embassy confirming this.

Flights are often cancelled at short notice for various reasons – one of them being that the planes have been requisitioned by the government.

OVERLAND THROUGH ZAÏRE

The most popular route is from Bangui to Zongo on the Central African Republic border, to Goma, Bukavu and Uvira on the border with Rwanda and Burundi.

The main reason this route is so popular is that it's one of the few feasible routes between the countries of West Africa and the game parks and mountains of East Africa. It also recommends itself because you're likely to meet other travellers en route. By exchanging information you can get a pretty good idea of the state and possibilities of the transport further along your intended route as well as a lot of other useful information. You can, of course, come from Lubumbashi (on the Zambia border) or Kalemie (from Tanzania across Lake Tanganyika).

On the main route, Kisangani on the banks of the Zaïre River is the principal 'bottleneck' where you can be sure of running into other travellers. Here you have to make a decision as to where to head for next.

If you're heading east from Kinshasa you have the choice of going along the Zaïre River to Kisangani and taking it from there, or heading south-east to Lubumbashi and into Zambia.

Depending on how much time you want to spend in Zaïre you can come up with a combination of these possibilities to suit your inclinations – Lubumbashi to Bangui and Zongo, or Goma to Lubumbashi, for example.

This section has been organised to treat Bangui to Zongo and Kisangani, and Kisangani to Goma, Bukavu and Uvira as the basic routes, then to deal with the alternative routes separately and to incorporate them (where appropriate) into the basic routes.

Bangui to Zongo to Kisangani

Bangui to Zongo The ferry across the Oubangui River from Bangui to Zongo costs CFA 100 plus CFA 50 to CFA 100 for a rucksack. It's not always in operation, in which case you'll have to take a motorboat or pirogue across the river. This might cost a little more since in those circumstances it's a seller's market.

To take your own vehicle across the river you will have to hire the whole ferry and if the engine is 'under repair' you'll have to hire a tug as well. The owner of each vehicle has to pay the full amount regardless of how many vehicles are on the ferry. Hire of the ferry costs CFA 3500; the tug, if needed, costs CFA 3850.

Don't cross the river on Saturday or Sunday as the customs people don't work at weekends and you'll just find yourself hanging around in Zongo till Monday morning. If the price is right, stock up on enough Zaïre currency in Bangui to get you through the first few days, but hide it well. If you only have travellers' cheques there are banks in Zongo, Gemena, Bumba and Lisala.

Zongo to Lisala From Zongo it's possible to get free lifts to Gemena or you can get a truck for Z 300. The road isn't too bad and the journey takes about nine hours. From Gemena a truck to Akula costs Z 150 to Z 200 and takes about seven hours. Akula is on the Mongala River which you can cross by ferry. It's free if there's a truck going across, otherwise there's a small charge. If the ferry is out of order there are pirogues available for the same price.

Akula to Lisala by truck costs Z 400 and takes about 10 hours but there's usually only one every two days or so.

Lisala to Kisangani From Lisala it's possible to get free lifts as far as Bumba and even Buta, but most travellers take the Zaïre River boat from Lisala to Kisangani. You can also take the boat from Bumba.

You must report to the authorities in Gemena, Bumba and Buta. Usually this is just a formality but, to be safe, it's best to assume they're going to give you a thorough search. There are often so-called 'administration fees' to pay when you report (Z 50 is average) and you may also be hassled for 'gifts'. If these are small and you don't want to waste time, it's probably best to pay them and get on your way.

It's definitely worth waiting for the Onatra boat at either Lisala or Bumba if you have the time, though it's rarely on schedule. Waiting for up to a week wouldn't be unusual. Bumba is a better place to wait than Lisala. This is the same steamer which comes upstream from Kinshasa (or downstream from Kisangani). The fare from Lisala to Kisangani is Z 870 (2nd class) and Z 594 (3rd class) including food. Fares between Kinshasa and Kisangani are Z 11,000 (deluxe class), Z 8000 (1st class), Z 2229 (2nd class) and Z 1679 (3rd class). You cannot buy a ticket which doesn't include food. The journey from Kinshasa to Kisangani takes 12 days on average. Lisala to Kisangani should take about three days but delays are normal, so expect four or five.

Student reductions of 50% are available on the fares (minus the cost of meals) at Kinshasa, Kisangani, Lisala or Bumba, but you need a *lettre d'attestation* from the local education officer at the last two. In Lisala his office is on the hillside above the port towards the post office. This man is not the same as the mission school headmaster as the port officials may tell you. In Kinshasa, a letter of confirmation from your embassy suffices. Once you have bought your ticket it has to be stamped by the immigration officials. There's the inevitable small 'fee' for this.

The boat consists of six barges lashed together with the power unit up at the front and each barge has a dining room and at least one bar. The food varies from barge to barge, but the kitchen staff are often friendly. First class is up at the front in the power unit and consists of two-bunk cabins with a small shower and toilet. Each barge has an upper deck 2nd class consisting of four-berth cabins, and a

lower deck 3rd class where you make do with deck space. Second class is quite acceptable but 3rd class is usually crowded and dirty. Second class has communal showers using river water pumped up by the power unit. If your group occupies a whole 2nd-class cabin you can lock it for the duration of the voyage, which isn't a bad idea as there are always thieves on board.

When buying 1st or 2nd-class tickets it's important to make sure the barge number is written on the ticket, otherwise it will be almost impossible to find an empty cabin. When the boat arrives, get on the appropriate barge and find the person who allocates cabins. If for any reason you end up in 3rd class with a 2nd-class ticket, kick up a polite but determined fuss. Even so, there's no absolute guarantee you'll get a cabin straight away, or that you won't end up in a cabin with more than four people. Organisation on these boats is Neanderthal and military personnel are allowed to occupy cabins without a ticket, so no-one knows just how much space will be available at each stop.

There is usually a nightly ticket check in each class and the boat often stops for two hours while a search for stowaways is conducted. There are hundreds of these, but rarely more than a few are caught.

In 1st class you get three substantial meals a day, which are basic but edible and are mainly western-style meat and vegetables. In 2nd and 3rd class there is only one meal per day and your ticket is stamped when you collect each meal. The food is filling and consists of heaps of rice with sauce and a good quantity of fish, chicken, goat, pork and even monkey, plus beans and sometimes manioc or spinach. It's not exactly cordon bleu but you won't starve. If you don't like the food, the boat calls at plenty of places where food is available or where you can buy fresh fish, meat and fruit. Local people come alongside the boat in their dugouts selling food. It's also possible to buy meals in the 1st-class dining room for Z 100. Water is taken from the river and is not filtered.

Despite whatever discomforts and hassles you may experience on these boats they are a classic African experience which should not be missed. Each barge rages 24 hours a day to loud music with people drinking (Zaïreans love their Primus beer!), smoking and dancing, and there can be up to 1500 people on board. The whole boat is like a travelling village with market stalls, smoked fish, live tortoises, dead and alive crocodiles (the latter with their jaws wired shut!), pots and pans and all manner of other paraphernalia both profane and sacred. Pigs and goats are slaughtered on board whenever the meat supply runs out for the kitchens. You certainly won't ever forget it!

Those seeking a relatively quiet spot to read, write, enjoy the river views or sleep outside the stuffy confines of the cabins should head for the barge roof.

If heading upriver watch out for the immigration officials on arrival in Kisangani. In the days when currency forms were issued they made a killing by thoroughly searching all foreigners and confiscating any undeclared cash. There's probably some new scheme for fleecing travellers.

If you're waiting for the ferry at either Lisala or Bumba, you can get an idea of how long it will be before the ferry arrives as the ticket officers there make a radio call daily to find out where the boat is.

If you don't fancy the boat, or if it isn't due for days, there's the possibility of persuading the captains of cargo barges to take you to Kisangani. The easiest way to get on is to buy them a few beers.

These cargo boats are usually a number of barges linked together and pulled by a tug. They're much slower than the normal boat (average time between Lisala and Kisangani is nine days, or between Bumba and Kisangani it's seven days), but they are infinitely more spacious than 3rd class on the boat and are cheaper than

the ferry. Bumba to Kisangani should cost around Z 450 per person. There are no canteens on board so you'll have to buy your food from dugouts which come out to the barges or, occasionally, on shore. Expect to spend a lot of time stranded on sand banks.

The alternative to river transport is to consider going overland through Buta and Isiro, then down to Nia Nia and Epulu (Station de Capture d'Epulu). The railway line between Bumba and Isiro is said to be 'out of order' indefinitely, but this may not be the case. Certainly there is no point in asking at the station in Buta because they haven't a clue what's going on. Instead, go to what is known as the 'Triangle' about three km out of town. Freight trains leave from here and you may be able to get on one of them. They certainly take local people but the guards are hesitant to take foreigners. Take along a few beers or a good line in Lingala.

By road from Bumba to Isiro can take a week – you can spend two to three days waiting for a vehicle. If you get stuck, try Sotexco between the centre and the Protestant Mission in Buta. They sometimes have trucks which go direct to Isiro although they won't be cheap. From Isiro you can often hitch free to Mungbere.

There's little point in going to Faradje because of the civil war in southern Sudan. The border is officially closed, though this is subject to interpretation depending on the risks you are prepared to take. If there is transport going there, however, you can head further east to Aba, then south to Aru and cross the Ugandan border to Arua. The villagers between Faradje and Aba (about 70 km) are friendly and you'll never be without food or a place to stay. There may still be a bus along this stretch called Tulla Tulla – aptly named since this means 'couldn't care less' in Lingala. Their schedule is about as reliable.

Kisangani to Goma, Bukavu & Uvira
The main route between Kisangani and

the eastern border with Uganda and Rwanda is along the Kisangani, Beni, Bunia road via Bafwasende, Nia Nia, Epulu, Mambasa and Komanda. Another possibility is the less used route between Bukavu and Kindu further south. There are no railways or river boats over this stretch so the only way to cover it is to hitch rides with trucks, walk or take a flight. There are flights from Kisangani to Goma.

In the past the road from Kisangani to Komanda was one of the worst in Africa with potholes large enough to swallow a truck. It can still get like that in the wet season, but for most of the year it's fairly well maintained and you can expect to get from Kisangani to one of the towns in eastern Zaïre in around three days. If you have punctures or engine trouble, or it's raining heavily, allow six days. Occasionally in the wet season it might take up to two weeks, but that would be exceptional.

The road from Kisangani to Komanda and Bunia has been repaired and is in excellent condition. The worst stretches are between Mambasa and Komanda and Butembo and Lubero. If you get word that the Butembo to Lubero road is bad, there are two parallel ones, but don't take the Butembo to Manguredjipa road as it's bad in all seasons.

There are fairly regular trucks between Kisangani and Komanda (and the other towns in eastern Zaïre). The average price is around Z 1200 (negotiable). The alternative is to try getting a ride with overland trucks at the Hotel Olympia in Kisangani. They normally charge Z 1 per km for lifts – about the same as trucks.

The roads running along the border area between Uvira and Bunia via Bukavu, Goma, Butembo and Beni pass through spectacular countryside, including the volcanoes of Nyiragongo and Nyamulgira and the fabled Ruwenzori Mountains. The sights more than compensate for the bruising and battering you have to put up with. There's also plenty of traffic in this part of the country because it's an

important coffee and tea growing area. Indeed, this is the only part of Zaïre where you will find regular buses.

To find lifts from Kisangani it's best to contact the Belgian man mentioned in the Kisangani information section. He can generally organise a truck all the way to Beni or even beyond. Otherwise you have to go out to Kibibi (Kibbi) about six km from the centre. The only trouble with hitching a ride from there is that by the time they get to Kibibi most trucks are full and you'll be waiting hours. If you want to chance it, take either the Air Zaïre shuttle bus from the Palace Hotel or find a ride at the market. The fare should be about Z 10. It's often possible to find lifts going all the way to Goma from Kibibi.

Some examples of journeys follow:

Kisangani to Komanda Expect to pay around Z 1200 for a truck between these two places. You may be able to do this journey in 2½ gruelling days but that would be exceptional; three days in the dry season is the norm but allow six in the wet season.

Komanda to Beni This costs Z 500 by truck and takes around 10 hours. Pick-ups are quicker and generally do the journey in about six hours.

Beni to Kasindi It costs Z 250 and takes about five hours. The best day to find a lift in Beni is Thursday as there's a market near the border. The road is OK in the dry season.

Kasindi is on the Zaïre-Uganda border and is a possible crossing point if you're headed for Kasese. The Ugandan customs post is three km down the road from Kasindi.

Beni to Butembo There are two possible routes. The most direct route is the main north-south road along which there are frequent pick-ups. Ask at the petrol station in Beni just down the Komanda road from the roundabout. The fare is

Z 300 to Z 350. There are also minibuses from the same place.

The second route is more circuitous and goes via Ishango on the shore of Lake Edward. It can take up to a week and you first need permission from immigration in Kasindi but those who have gone this way have recommended it.

From Kasindi you can go direct into Uganda. It's about three km to the Ugandan border post, which is closed from 12 noon to 2 pm.

Butembo to Goma A bus leaves on Monday and Thursday in the early morning. The fare is Z 1000 and the journey takes about 14 hours. Advance booking is advisable. Trucks generally cost less (around Z 500) and can be quicker (some travellers have done this leg in around nine hours). The Butembo to Lubero section is often impassable in the wet season.

Butembo to Kayna Bayonga Trucks should cost around Z 60 though they may start at Z 90. The journey should take about 13 hours.

Goma to Rutshuru There are pick-ups between these two places which cost Z 150 and take about two hours. The road is in bad shape.

Rutshuru to Inshasha This is another of the possible crossing points into Uganda, but there's hardly any traffic along the road, a lot of which has been dug up in an attempt to prevent coffee smuggling. You'll probably have to walk the whole way. There are plenty of cheap lodging houses in the first Ugandan village.

Goma to Bukavu The best way to do this trip by road is to take a pick-up for Z 500. The journey takes about 12 hours (assuming no stops) over a badly rutted road but there are spectacular views all the way. Take food because the expensive cafés en route usually only have tea and bread despite the variety of vegetables for sale everywhere. There's also a weekly bus from Goma on Fridays that costs Z 400. You need to book in advance.

The best and most comfortable way to do this journey, however, is to take one of the Goma to Bukavu ferries across Lake Kivu.

Lake Kivu Ferries There are two ferries between Goma and Bukavu on Lake Kivu: the *Matadi* and *Karisimbi*. The *Matadi* is a passenger boat though it will take motorcycles. The *Karisimbi* carries both passengers and cargo and takes longer. Neither of them call at Rwandan ports nor do the Rwandan ferries call at Zaïrean ports.

The *Matadi* sails from Goma on Wednesdays and Saturdays at 7.30 am and from Bukavu on Tuesdays and Fridays at 7.30 am. The fare is Z 260 plus Z 10 for 'validation' by immigration, and the journey takes six hours. All the seats are numbered. You need to be at the dock at least half an hour before departure. Breakfast is available for Z 100 (reasonable value) and Primus beer for Z 35.

The boat stops two or three times for 10 minutes en route to set down and pick up passengers and at these times fruit sellers in dugouts surround the boat and sell their wares. Be careful taking photographs of these people – they don't like it and will hurl fruit at you. Otherwise, it's a pleasant trip with incomparable views of the Virunga volcanoes across the lake.

The *Karisimbi* leaves Goma on Saturdays and Bukavu on Wednesdays. The fare is Z 85 plus Z 25 tax and it takes 10 to 12 hours.

Buying tickets for these boats is usually simple. Turn up at the ticket office (at the dock) the previous day before 9.30 am and join the queue, after having made your presence known (this is important otherwise you'll wait all day). It shouldn't take more than half an hour and you don't usually have to bribe anyone. Having bought your ticket it must be 'validated' by customs at the port gate. This is where the other Z 10 goes.

There are times when buying a ticket can be like getting a front seat at Bishop Tutu's enthronement. This is when there's a large government party going from one side to the other. At such times government officials, police, army personnel, other important people, their friends and friends of friends get priority. Chaos erupts and it can take all morning to get a ticket. Make sure you have your passport when you go to buy a ticket as they won't sell you one without it. An individual can buy several tickets as long as he/she has the passports for everyone who wants a ticket.

Bukavu to Kindu The alternative route between the Zaïre River and the eastern border (Bukavu-Kindu) takes somewhat more effort and initiative than the main Kisangani to Goma route. Between Bukavu and Kamituga there are two to three trucks everyday and most of them charge Z 300 to Z 350. The road is not too bad and basic commodities are available en route. The journey takes two or three days. West of here it's difficult to find bread, candles, soft drinks, beer and most fruit and vegetables until you get to Kampene. Between Kamituga and Kitutu the number of vehicles decreases to one every two to three days and you'll probably have to do a lot of walking. The villages en route are friendly and you can always find food and a bed for the night.

The direct road from Kama to Kampene isn't marked on the maps, but it is slightly quicker than going via Itabatshi and should take about two days to walk. When you get to Kampene, go to the Entriaco offices just outside town. They have several daily trucks to Kindu. Ask at the transport office and they'll give you a free pass. The journey takes one to two days and the roads get better all the time.

Bukavu to Uvira There are two possible routes between these places. The first – quicker and more comfortable – is the one which loops through Rwanda for part of the way. There is one bus daily in either direction which leaves when full (usually between 7.30 and 8 am). The fare is Z 250 and the journey takes about 5½ hours.

In theory, since you have to cross two borders on this route, you need a Rwandan transit visa and a re-entry visa for Zaïre. In practice it may not be necessary. (See the Visa section.) Ask around about this before leaving Bukavu if you don't want to be caught out.

The other route avoids Rwanda entirely and takes a more westerly route via Nya-Ngezi and Kamanyola. It's a spectacular route, but there are no buses so you need to find a lift with a truck. There are usually several of these daily though some only go as far as Nya-Ngezi and you may get stuck there. Bukavu to Uvira will cost about Z 400 and can take as little as four hours. Once as far as Kamanyola, however, you can find pick-ups to Uvira for around Z 100.

Both the buses via Rwanda and the trucks via Nya-Ngezi leave from the Place Major Vangu opposite the Hotel Nambu.

Uvira to Burundi Border Taxis to the Zaïre border post run all day until late afternoon, cost Z 50 and take about 10 minutes. The border is easy-going and there's no baggage search. From here to the Burundi border post it's a one-km walk although there are bicycle taxis available!

The Burundi border post is equally easy-going and there are moneychangers outside the office who will offer a reasonable rate of exchange from zaïres to Burundi francs. From the border post to Bujumbura there are occasional taxis (BFr 50) or you can hitch.

Kisangani to Lubumbashi & Kalemie
The first part of this journey involves getting to Kindu, from where there is a railway all the way to Lubumbashi. At Kabalo there is a branch line to Kalemie on Lake Tanganyika.

The train from Kisangani to Ubundu is supposed to run twice a week on Tuesday and Saturday, but it's often cancelled because of fuel shortages and derailments. You may have to wait up to 10 days. Even so, there's supposedly a choice between ordinary trains and *rapide*! The journey generally takes 16 to 20 hours but has been known to take 30! There are three classes but 3rd class is a test of endurance as it's always crammed to the gunwales with a writhing, perspiring mass of bodies. The fares on the ordinary train are Z 452 (1st class), Z 220 (2nd class) and Z 95 (3rd class). The *rapide* costs Z 290 ('luxe' class), Z 265 (1st class), Z 235 (2nd class) and Z 100 (3rd class).

Take food and water, though food can be bought at stops on the way – groundnuts, rice, corn, elephant meat, caterpillars and beer are available.

When you get to Ubundu you may be lucky and connect with the river boat down to Kindu. This only runs every so often so, again, you'll probably be waiting around. There are two kinds of boat – a barge, and an ordinary boat with three classes. Organisation is virtually nonexistent in 3rd and 2nd class, so if you want a bunk you'll have to move fast. Good food is available in the 1st-class dining room, but the boat stops frequently at wayside ports so you can usually buy rice, manioc, nuts, oranges and bananas. Fares on the boat are Z 1045 (1st class), Z 890 (2nd class) and Z 385 (3rd class). The journey takes four to six days.

It may still be possible to buy a combined rail/boat ticket for the Kisangani to Ubundu and Kindu to Kamina trains and the Ubundu-Kindu River boat, though this is going to limit your options if there are delays.

If something goes wrong with either the Ubundu train or the boats and you get sick of hanging around, you can attempt to get to Kindu by road, but it's not easy. There's little traffic after Lubutu, and the Lubutu to Punia stretch was recently described as 'the most desperate piece of road I've ever experienced' by one traveller who almost didn't make it. He

added, 'You get stuck in mud up to the wheel arches six or seven times a day. There are log bridges that need rebuilding before you can cross and a winch is essential. Spare parts (if you need them) would take weeks to get if they arrived at all.'

As you might imagine, there are few vehicles along this track. Many travellers who have attempted this road have had to walk the part from Lubutu to Punia (145 km). If you have to do this, it should take about five days. There are plenty of friendly villages along the way, but stay clear of the Yumbi police post. Once you get to Punia, however, you'll find plenty of transport going south to Kindu.

At Kindu there is a train all the way to Lubumbashi with a branch from Kabalo to Kalemie on Lake Tanganyika. It departs once a week on either Friday or Saturday, but is often delayed. The journey can take as little as 2½ days, but may take up to five. Student concessions of 50% are available if you have a student card and authorisation. Try not to travel on this train alone, especially if you are a single woman. We've had reports of gangs of thieves terrorising passengers with the connivance of the railway staff. There are also many drunks on it who can get violent, so keep a low profile. From Kamina there are trains to Lubumbashi for Z 456 (2nd class).

If heading for Kalemie (and Tanzania) the fares on the train from Kindu to Kalemie are Z 930 (1st class), Z 795 (2nd class) and Z 345 (3rd class) on the ordinary train; and Z 1175 ('luxe' class), Z 1035 (1st class), Z 880 (2nd class) and Z 380 (3rd class) on the *rapide*.

In the opposite direction the train leaves Lubumbashi on Friday afternoon and the fare to Kalemie is Z 2720 (2nd class). The journey takes three days. Food can be bought along the way or from the dining car. Expect hassles getting a ticket at Lubumbashi if you are white.

There are no regular boats across Lake Tanganyika from Kalemie to either Bujumbura (Burundi) or Kigoma (Tanzania) but there are irregular barges and cargo boats – at least one per week. If there is a passenger boat you may get across to Kigoma for Z 105. For the barges and cargo boats you'll have to bargain with the captain (Z 510 is about the current price) and before you can leave you will need a letter of authorisation from immigration. Most of the boats crossing the lake depart in the evenings and arrive the next morning.

Don't count on getting a boat; many people have been disappointed. If you draw a blank, go by road to Uvira, then Bujumbura and take the regular ferry (MV *Liemba*) from there.

Kinshasa to Kisangani

Other than flying, the only way to get between these two cities is to take the Onatra river steamer. It's a fantastic journey and a 'must' in this part of Africa. For details of the conditions on this boat, read the section on Lisala to Kisangani. The journey from Kinshasa to Kisangani is supposed to take 15 days (eight to nine days in the opposite direction) but there are often delays.

Tickets should be bought at the Gare Fluvial in Kinshasa where the staff are helpful. The cabin numbers on your ticket mean nothing.

Kinshasa to Lubumbashi

The first part of this trip involves getting to Ilebo. The direct way is to take the Onatra river steamer down the Kasai River from Kinshasa to Ilebo. It goes in either direction once every two weeks (sometimes only once per month), taking six days. The fares are Z 3642 (1st class – cabins with two beds and three meals per day), Z 1438 (2nd class – cabins with six beds and two meals per day), and Z 1017 (3rd class – dormitory beds and one meal per day).

If you don't want to take the steamer there are plenty of cargo barges, either in Kinshasa or Kwamouth, which go to

Mangai, about one day's ride by truck from Ilebo. In the opposite direction there are plenty of barges from Ilebo to Kinshasa and it's fairly easy to get a free ride on one.

The third possibility is to take a bus from Kinshasa to Kikwit with Compagnie Sotraz, which has a depot close to the GPO in Kinshasa. Their luxury buses leave daily between 7 am and noon and between 3 and 6 pm. The fare is Z 715 but at either end you must buy your ticket at the bus station at 4 am! The road is surfaced all the way to Kikwit.

From Kikwit, trucks and Land Rovers leave daily at around 6 am for Idiofa and should cost around Z 300. From Idiofa to Ilebo it is a further two days journey on a truck at a cost of around Z 400.

Between Kikwit and Ilebo there is a river to cross. A ferry crosses twice a day and the times are variable but the boat usually makes the crossing between 9 and 11 am and between 3 and 4 pm. If you're hitching, either wait at the river crossing or at the friendly, pleasant Hotel Los Palmos on the road down to the river. All trucks must pass this hotel. If buses don't appeal, there are trucks from Kinshasa to Ilebo virtually everyday, even in the rainy season. They can take just two days but often take longer. Expect to pay about Z 700.

From Ilebo you can go all the way to Lubumbashi by train. The ordinary train leaves on Tuesday and the *rapide* on either Saturday or Sunday. The former takes six days and the latter four. In the opposite direction, the ordinary train leaves Lubumbashi on Saturday and the *rapide* on Thursday. Fares are Z 2675 (1st class deluxe *rapide*), Z 2225 (1st class), Z 1965 (2nd class *rapide* – compartment with six bunks) and Z 1670 (2nd class ordinary). Third class has bench seats only. The fare from Kananga to Lubumbashi is Z 1632 (1st class). Student concessions of 50% are available if you have a student card and authorisation (a *lettre d'attestation*), either from the local government office or the railways office (see Ilebo for details).

This is a pretty rugged train trip – millions of screaming kids, pots, pans, vast amounts of luggage, dried fish, etc – and stops in the middle of nowhere are frequent so that ticket inspectors can eject ticketless passengers (there are always plenty of them). Travellers can also expect the usual litany of dumb and tedious questions from officialdom.

The *rapide* has a buffet car and bar where you can get a decent meal for Z 150. Otherwise there are plenty of hawkers selling food at the stations along the way. There is rarely any water on the train so take your own.

If you want to head north to Kisangani, or east to Lake Tanganyika, change trains at Kamina.

From Lubumbashi to the Zambian border you can go by truck, pick-up, taxi or train, but there are no through passenger trains to Zambia. The train goes only as far as Sakania, then only once a week at 9 am on Wednesday. All road transport from Lubumbashi leaves from the 'Zone Kenya'. Trucks from here to Chilabombwe (Zambia) cost Z 20 to Z 40. Otherwise, get a taxi (Z 35) or a pick-up (Z 25) from the Zone Kenya to Kasumbalesa, a minibus from there to Chilabombwe (Kw 1), a bus from there to Chingola (Kw 0.50), and finally another bus from there to Kitwe (Kw 1.80). From Kitwe there are trains south to Lusaka. If you take the train from Lubumbashi to Mokambo there is a bus direct from there to Chingola for Z 40.

Kinshasa to Matadi
A *rapide* leaves Kinshasa at 7.15 am on Monday, Wednesday and Friday and arrives at Matadi the same day at 2.30 pm. From Matadi to Kinshasa it leaves at 8.30 am on Monday, Thursday and Saturday. The fare is Z 213 (1st class) and Z 185 (2nd class). There are also ordinary trains (2nd and 3rd classes) but they take about twice as long. In addition, Sotraz buses run between the two places for Z 256.

Kinshasa to Zongo
When the river is high enough there are boats all the way from Kinshasa to Zongo. You can pick up boats from Brazzaville to Bangui at the same time.

Around the Country

ABA
There are no hotels or cafés in Aba but you may get accommodation at the *Mission Catholique* – don't count on it though.

AKETI
Two cheap places to stay are the *Hotel Bosingo* and the *Hotel Ma Campagne*, on each side of the market. Rooms at either cost Z 250. If they're full there's another place called the *Hotel Homowo*.

BENI
Beni is the starting point for climbing the Ruwenzori Mountains from the Zaïre side (you can also do this from the Ugandan side). Several of the hotels offer excess baggage storage facilities, though you can also leave gear at the park warden's office in Mutsora.

Places to Stay
One of the best and cheapest places is the *Hotel Walaba*, about 100 metres down the Kasindi road from the roundabout. It costs Z 58 for a double and has bucket showers. It's a good place to meet other travellers and the Somali owner, Mohammed, will change money if you're stuck. Both he and the predominantly Ugandan staff speak English. You can leave baggage safely while you climb the Ruwenzoris. They don't mind if you cook your own food and they also have a good cheap restaurant.

There's the friendly *Jumbo Hotel*, where a double costs Z 350. It also has an excess baggage store. To get there go down the main street to the roundabout, turn left and the hotel is 30 metres down on the left. A traveller recommended the *Basmie*

Hotel, good value at Z 150 a double. It's run by friendly Ugandan and Somali owners and cheap food is available. You can leave excess baggage safely while you climb the Ruwenzoris.

There is also the *Hotel Sina Makosa*, where a room costs Z 180, and the *Majestic Hotel*, by the roundabout, which costs Z 200 per room. Other travellers have recommended the *Hotel Virunga*, the *Hotel Busa Beni* and the *Hotel Bashu*. Give the *Hotel Beni* a miss if you're on a budget: it's expensive and geared for well-heeled tourists.

For a vague spot of luxury, try the spotless and friendly *Hotel Isale*. Rooms cost Z 400 a double.

Places to Eat

The restaurant at the *Hotel Walaba* offers rice and beans for Z 25, meat and rice for Z 45 and omelettes for Z 25 to Z 40. Their bread is baked on the premises. Good breakfasts are obtainable from the *Restaurant Ronde-Pointe* on the roundabout (omelettes, bread and tea for Z 70). The snacks from outside the Paradisio Club (a disco) are also recommended.

The *Restaurant Bismallah* on the roundabout at the northern end of the main street offers rice and meat meals. This is a good place to ask about lifts going south. The *Restaurant Sukisa* next door to the Hotel Sina Makosa offers good, cheap food as long as you don't mind sending it back to the kitchen a few times to make it *moto sana* (they don't speak English or French). For a splurge go to the *Hotel Beni* where a dinner costs Z 600.

Next to the Hotel Walaba is a small well-stocked market. There are a number of similar shops (mostly Greek-owned) in the centre of town, which are useful if you're organising a trek up the Ruwenzori.

The local intoxicant is made from sorghum and bananas and is cheap.

BINGA

This is a small but busy market town with several cheap hotels. To change money ask at the Mission Catholique. The large cooperative about two km from the village is a good place to ask for lifts.

BUKAVU

Built over several lush tongues of land jutting out into Lake Kivu, and sprawling back up the steep mountain side behind, Bukavu is a large but quite attractive city with a fairly cosmopolitan population.

The town is effectively divided into two parts following the lines of Ave des Martyrs de la Révolution, which heads south up a valley from the lake shore, and Ave du President Mobutu, which winds its way east above the lake shore. The two parts are separated by the grassy saddle of a hill. Most of the budget hotels and restaurants, the main market (Marché Maman Mobutu) and truck parks are along Ave des Martyrs de la Révolution, while the business centre, government offices, consulates, the huge cathedral and the ritzier parts of the city are along Ave du President Mobutu.

Information

National Parks Office This office (Institut Zaïrois pour la Conservation de la Nature) is at 185 Ave du President Mobutu and is open Monday to Friday from 8.30 am to 3 pm and on Saturday from 8.30 am to 12 noon. It's run by a friendly German director who speaks fluent French and English (the institute is actually a joint Zaïrean-German project). The director will tell you to make a booking here if you want to visit the plains gorillas in the Parc National de Kahuzi-Biega north of Bukavu. This isn't strictly necessary except on Sundays when there may be a lot of visitors. During the rest of the week it's unlikely you'll be turned down if you're at the take-off point by 9 am.

Consulates The Burundi Consulate is on the top floor of the Sinelac Building, 184 Ave du President Mobutu (look for the three flags of Burundi, Rwanda and Zaïre). See the Visas section for details.

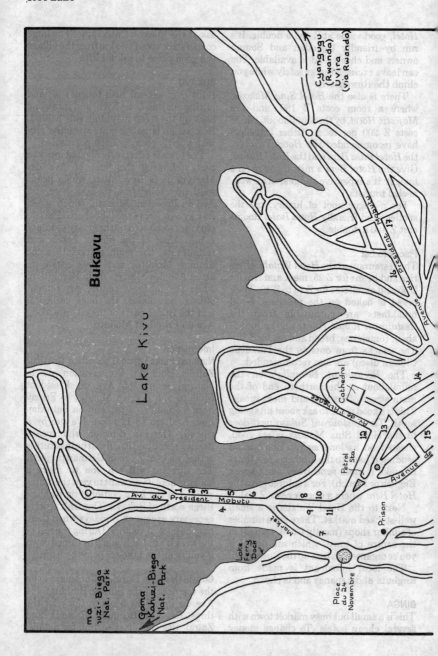

Bukavu

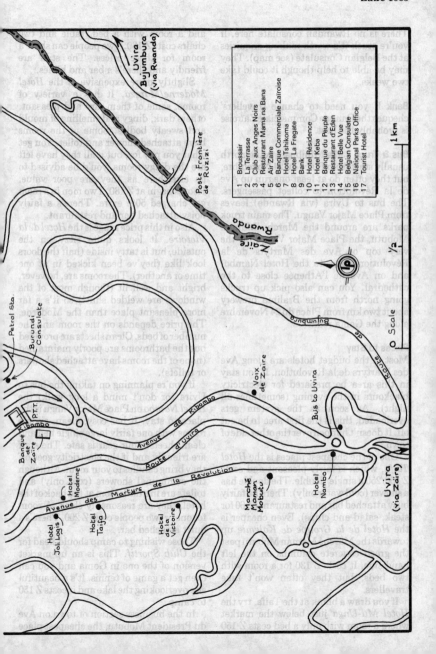

There is no Rwandan consulate here. If you're stuck it's worth making enquiries at the Belgian Consulate (see map). They may be able to help though it could take two weeks.

Bank If you need to change travellers' cheques the Banque Commerciale Zaïroise is probably the best.

Bus & Truck Parks Minibuses going north usually start from Place du 24 Novembre, but they often do at least one run up Ave de la Révolution to collect passengers. The bus to Uvira (via Rwanda) leaves from Place Major Vangu. The main truck parks are around the Marché Maman Mobutu, the Place Major Vangu (at the very top of Ave des Martyrs de la Révolution opposite the Hotel Nambo) and on Ave de l'Athenée close to the cathedral. You can also pick up trucks going north from the Bralima brewery about two km from Place du 24 Novembre along the Goma road.

Places to Stay
Most of the budget hotels are along Ave des Martyrs de la Révolution. If you stay in this area be prepared for electricity blackouts in the evening (sometimes all night). As soon as the system gets overloaded, this is the first area to be cut off. It doesn't happen over the other side of town.

One of the cheapest places is the *Hotel Taifa*, which is fairly pleasant and costs Z 150/250 a single/double. The double has a shower (cold water only). There's a fairly busy attached bar and restaurant (Z 60 for steak, salad and chips). Even cheaper is the *Hotel de la Groupe de Kalemie* up towards the Marché Maman Mobutu past the green concrete columns on the left hand side. It costs Z 130 for a room with two beds, but they often won't take travellers.

If you draw a blank at the Taifa, try the *Hotel Mu-Unga* just below the market where a room with only a bed costs Z 150

and a room with a bed, table and two chairs costs Z 180. Two people can share a room for these prices. The staff are friendly and there's a bar and bibles.

Slightly more expensive is the *Hotel Moderne/Mareza*. It has a variety of rooms, some of them airy and pleasant, others dark, dingy and smelling of mould and sweaty bodies. Some of the rooms have attached shower and toilet. You get what you pay for, but if all they have left are the dingy rooms, you'd be advised to go elsewhere as they are poor value. Rooms begin at Z 180. Two men in a room get charged 50% extra. There's a fairly noisy attached bar and restaurant.

Also in this price range is the *Hotel de la Victoire*. It looks quite ritzy on the outside, but is tatty inside (half the doors look like they've been kicked in at one time or another). The rooms are, however, bright and well lit (though most of the windows are welded shut!) so it's a far more pleasant place than the Moderne. The price depends on the room and the number of beds. Clean sheets are provided but the bathrooms are poorly maintained (none of the rooms have attached showers or toilets).

If you're planning on taking the bus to Uvira (or don't mind a long walk) the *Hotel Nambo* on Place Major Vangu is the place to stay. It has cosy, clean, simple rooms with one fairly large single bed and clean sheets. Your gear is safe. The staff are friendly and if the electricity goes off they bring candles to your room. Although the communal showers (cold only) and toilets are in a dark room at the back of the hotel, they are reasonably clean. A room for one or two people costs Z 200. There's a quiet attached bar.

Those wishing to camp should head for the *Club Sportif*. This is an up-market version of the one in Goma and you can even get a game of tennis. It's a beautiful site overlooking the lake and it costs Z 150 to camp.

In the business section of town on Ave du President Mobutu, the cheapest place is the *Hotel Keba* opposite the Hotel Residence. It's good value at Z 246 a double and Z 303 a double with bathroom. Two men sharing a room are charged more.

Other travellers have recommended the *Hotel Canadien* (also known as the Ruzivi Hotel), opposite the Burundi Consulate, which costs Z 315 a double with shower and toilet. Camping is also allowed for Z 50 per person. One of the most popular mid-range hotels is the *Hotel Joli Logis*. It is set in a compound with lawns and ample parking space and costs Z 357 a single and Z 497 a double, both with attached shower (hot water), toilet and clean sheets. The staff are friendly (some English spoken) and there's a bar attached to the office but separate from the rooms.

Those in need of relative luxury should try the second category rooms at the *Hotel La Fregate*, Ave du President Mobutu almost next door to the Hotel Residence. These cost Z 690 (one or two people) and they also have more expensive rooms. There's no restaurant at this hotel.

Avoid the *Hotel Tshikoma* near Place du 24 Novembre as it's decidedly overpriced for what it offers.

Places to Eat

There's a good choice of cheap, African-style restaurants. Two of the simplest are the *Unity Restaurant* and the *Café du Peuple*. Both are at the back of the small meat and vegetable market overlooking the lake ferry dock (Market on the street map). The Café du Peuple is highly recommended and popular with local people. Some travellers rate it as the best restaurant in Bukavu. The food is good and portions are large. Rice and roast beef in tomato and onion sauce costs Z 40. If you want potatoes with it then it's Z 45. A cup of milk coffee costs Z 7. The Unity isn't quite as good but offers rice and meat for Z 30 and rice and beans for Z 25.

Also good is the *ABC Restaurant* next to the entrance to the Hotel Joli Logis.

The food is tasty and the staff friendly. Rice and beans in sauce costs Z 35, meat, sauce and rice Z 55, and chicken, sauce and rice Z 65. Chips instead of rice costs Z 10 extra. A large pot of coffee or tea with milk costs Z 10. It's open from 8 am to 4 pm daily.

Further up the hill near Marché Maman Mobutu, the *Tua Tugaure Restaurant* is reasonably good. Rice and beans cost Z 20, meat and rice Z 25 and omelettes Z 30. The teahouse below this restaurant next to Chez Abou hairdressers offers excellent curd-type yogurt for Z 7 a glass.

In the centre of town, the *Mama Na Bana*, Ave du President Mobutu, is good value and friendly. It offers rice, ugali or fou-fou served with chicken, fish or beef as well as brochettes and omelettes. You can eat for Z 30 and up. Also recommended is the *Café de l'Avenue* on Ave du President Mobutu opposite the electricity office. They offer large, spicy brochettes (Z 25) as well as salads, rice and beef. It's a pleasant place to eat overlooking the valley.

There's an excellent patisserie selling yogurt and cheap breakfasts (omelette, bread, jam and tea/coffee) about 200 metres from the Mama Na Bana on the opposite side of the road.

Entertainment

There are hundreds of small bars in Bukavu and though most of them are just beer-swilling places or sperm palaces they can be great fun if you're in the mood. Some of them get pretty wild as the night wears on. There's usually African music playing. Other than these try the *Club aux Anges Noirs* on Ave du President Mobutu.

The *Club Sportif* has a pleasant bar overlooking the lake and you may meet someone who is prepared to take you out sailing.

BUMBA

This town has a good choice of hotels, but there are few restaurants. The best place

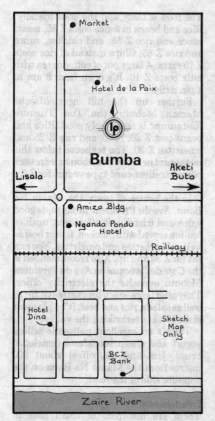

to stay is the *Hotel Dina* near the Onatra office. It costs Z 200 for a room with bathroom and verandah. They'll allow two people to stay in one room for that price if you plead poverty.

Another good place is the *Nganda Pondu Hotel*, which is basic but adequate and costs Z 300 per room. Bucket showers are available. The *Hotel de la Paix*, close to the market, has clean, basic rooms and good service, but costs Z 500 per room with bath, cold shower and electricity. There is a bar but no restaurant, though a local woman will cook for you if you advance the money. The price is negotiable.

BUNIA

Bunia is a large town in the hills above Lake Mobutu Sese Seko and is one of the starting points for the trip west to Kisangani via Komanda, Mambasa and Nia Nia. If you get this far it's worth making a side trip to the fishing village of **Tshoma** on the lake via the border post town of Kasenye. It's a lively village with bars open 24 hours a day to accommodate the fisherfolks' unsocial hours. Hospitality is excellent and fresh fish is very cheap. Unfortunately it's not safe to swim in the lake because of bilharzia.

Transport is fairly easy to find and there are regular trucks from the fisheries in Tshoma to Beni if you're heading south (the fare is about Z 300).

Places to Stay

One of the most popular places is the *Chez Tout Bunia Hotel* which has an attached restaurant. Further down the hill in the *cité* are plenty of other cheapies. The *Hotel Rubi*, on the main street, is one of the best. Another hotel which has been recommended is the *Butembo II*. It is friendly and has great food.

BUTA

Stay at the *Protestant Mission* about four km out of town. It's run by friendly Norwegians.

BUTEMBO

With a population of some 100,000, Butembo is a large town about half way between Goma and Bunia. There's a good market and excellent views of the surrounding countryside.

Trucks leave from 'Concorde' at the Goma end of town.

Places to Stay & Eat

Most of the cheapies are near the market. The *Lodgement Apollo II* costs Z 110 per room (one or two people), has electricity in the evenings and bucket showers. The *Semuliki Hotel* at the north end of town on the main road has doubles without shower or toilet but does have a good, attached restaurant.

Somewhat more expensive is the *Hotel Ambiance* which costs Z 300 a double. It's very pleasant, has electricity, running water, showers and washing facilities.

The *Oasis Hotel*, a colonial-style place with a delightful air of deteriorating elegance, used to be popular but when the Belgian owner died in 1987 the place fell apart – there's no water or electricity at present. A room costs Z 450 a double. The only part of the hotel which seems to function is the bar and disco. Renovations (of a sort) are being done so things may improve.

Other travellers have recommended staying at one or other of the three missions close to town.

Apart from the Semuliki Hotel, the *Restaurant Cafeteriat* near the market is recommended. Soup costs Z 20, meat, rice and potatoes Z 50 and coffee with milk Z 20.

DINGILA

A small town about 25 km north-east of Bambesa, Dingila is on the Michelin maps but not on the Bartholomews maps. The cheapest place to stay is the *Hotel Disco* where *rondavels* are for hire. Good food is available, otherwise there are few places to eat in town in the evening.

The *Hotel Bas-Vele* has also been recommended in the past.

EPULU (Station de Capture d'Epulu)

The **Pygmy villages** in this area have become touristy through overexposure to package tour overland trucks and you will be hassled for food, presents and other gifts as well as charged for photographs. The best thing to do is to go for a 'package deal' for Z 200. This includes a visit to a Pygmy village, a photo permit and seeing the okapis. Photographs of Pygmies will cost a few cigarettes or some sweets. Scented soap is also much sought after.

There are far better, relatively unspoilt, Pygmy villages between Mambasa and

Komanda, which hardly ever see white people. Trucks normally drive straight through this area so you'll miss them if hitching.

The **okapi** are worth seeing – this is the only area where they live in Africa – but you'll be charged Z 20 to see them (Z 15 for students) plus Z 60 per camera to photograph them.

Places to Stay

There are small hotels in the village where you can stay, otherwise camp at the *Station de Capture*. It is a beautiful spot and costs Z 100 plus Z 100 per tent for the first night, and Z 80 per person plus Z 80 per tent for each subsequent night. Some travellers have been offered a place on the verandah free.

FARADJE

The *Mission Catholique* will reluctantly put you up.

GEMENA

You must have your passport stamped for entry and exit to Gemena at the Seigneurie (Agence National de Documentation) near the post office. It's just a formality.

The Banque Commerciale Zaïroise will change travellers' cheques at 1% commission.

Places to Stay & Eat

The *Mission Catholique* is extremely reluctant to help out with accommodation, but there is another mission some three km out of town which isn't quite so unwelcoming. If you can't get in at either, try the soap factory which usually has floor space and may even fix you up with a lift.

Other than these places, there's a good choice of simple, cheap hotels to choose from. Two of the most convenient ones are next to each other and close to the central market and only some 50 metres from where the trucks leave for Zongo. The first is the *Hotel Papa Boualey* which costs Z 150 to Z 250 depending on the room. It has a good lively atmosphere and is used mainly as a whorehouse so if it's full, keep trying. There's electricity when the town generator is working and water is always available from the large storage tanks. Next door is the *Hotel Club la Cara*. It's noisy but clean and costs Z 150 to Z 250 depending on the room. Close by is the *Hotel de l'Ombre* which charges Z 70 per room, but it's not very clean and has water problems.

There are two good restaurants just off the central market offering rice and beans or fish for Z 30. The market itself is usually well stocked and offers fried plantain, manioc, rice rissoles, avocados, pineapples and snails. There are a number of stalls offering coffee and bread.

GOMA
Goma sits at the foot of the brooding Nyiragongo volcano at the northern end of Lake Kivu and is not far from the chain of volcanoes which make up the Parc National des Virungas on the border between Zaïre and Rwanda.

Like Bukavu, it is an important business, government and resort town with a fairly cosmopolitan population and there's quite a contrast between the ritzy landscaped villas down by the lake shore and the *cité* behind it. The President maintains a palatial villa, but stay away from it. Many travellers have got into trouble for inadvertently getting too close.

Nevertheless, it's a dusty, somewhat run-down town with a surprising number of unsurfaced roads. Goma also has the only international airport in this part of Zaïre.

Information
National Parks Office This is next door to the Banque Commerciale Zaïroise one street back from the main street (see map) but it's not easy to find. Look for two large corrugated-iron doors which take you through into a metalworker's yard. The office is a small concrete building on the

right hand side. It's open daily from 9 to 11 am (sometimes later). You must make advance bookings here to see the mountain gorillas at Djomba near Rutshuru. It's also possible to book at Rwindi at the radio shack, but you may have to wait a week for confirmation.

Bank If changing travellers' cheques the best bank is the Banque Commerciale Zaïroise. It shouldn't take longer than half an hour and commission is minimal.

Ferry Tickets for the Lake Kivu ferry to Bukavu have to be bought down at the dock the day before departure. Be there before 9.30 am and bring your passport (one person can buy several tickets so long as he/she has all the passports of the people who want to travel).

Places to Stay
Although many travellers prefer to stay in one of the budget hotels around the market area, the best place is the *Catholic Mission Guest House*, an unmarked yellow building close to the Hotel Tuneko. It's comfortable, spotlessly clean, sheets and towels are provided (and *boiled* (!) after use), there's hot water in the showers, a library, and it's totally secure. This little haven of peace and quiet costs just Z 180/350 a single/double including breakfast. All the rooms have a washbasin. It's popular with travellers. What puts some people off is the loud *mère* who runs the place, but you only see her at breakfast. There's also a 10 pm curfew.

Cheaper than the Catholic Guest House and recommended by many travellers is the *Chambres Aspro*. Despite the unusual name, it's not subsidised by a drug company, but is run by a friendly family who will let you use their stove to warm up water or to cook.

Similar and also friendly is the *Hotel Abki* next to the football field, where a room (one or two people) costs Z 150. There are bucket showers, but the water supply is erratic. You can leave excess

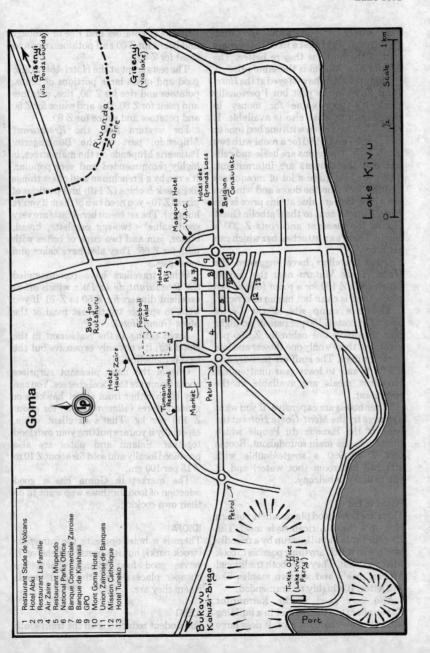

Goma

1 Restaurant Stade de Volcans
2 Hotel Abki
3 Restaurant La Famille
4 Air Zaïre
5 Restaurant Mupendo
6 National Parks Office
7 Banque Commerciale Zairoise
8 Banque de Kinshasa
9 GPO
10 Mont Goma Hotel
11 Union Zairoise de Banques
12 Mission Catholique
13 Hotel Tuneko

gear safely if you want to climb Nyiragongo. Try to get a room in the main part of the hotel as they're better. The *Macho Kwa Macho* is the same price.

Many travellers have stayed at the *Hotel Haut Zaïre* in the past but I personally think it's poor value for money in comparison to what else is available. It costs Z 225 for a room with one bed (one or two people) and Z 250 for a room with two single beds. The rooms are basic and cell-like and the showers are intermittent. There are also quite a lot of mosquitoes and the 'locks' on the doors and windows are a joke. Better value at this price is the *Hotel Tuneko* next to the Catholic Guest House. It's pleasant and costs Z 200 a single. There's an attached bar which can get noisy.

Other travellers have suggested the *Guest House Mutara* near the market which costs Z 180 for a room (one or two people) and is clean but has no electricity.

There's a camp site at the *Cercle Sportif*. It costs Z 150 per person per night plus they have one cabin for Z 250 per night, but there's only one shower and lots of mosquitoes. The staff are friendly and it's fairly safe to leave gear unattended. Excellent meals are available at the restaurant.

Other hotels are expensive. If you want a splurge try the *Mont-Goma Hotel* at the back of the Banque du Peuple which fronts onto the main roundabout. Rooms cost Z 490/990 a single/double with attached bathroom (hot water) and, if you're lucky, a balcony.

Places to Eat

There are three good places where you can pick up a cheap African-style meal. The *Restaurant la Famille* is run by a friendly family who will do anything possible to cook what you want. They offer both traditional African meals and western staples like omelettes. It's highly recommended.

Also very good is the *Restaurant Tumaini* next to the market in a building with a low overhanging roof. It does large portions of potatoes and rice or cabbage and beans for Z 30 and potatoes, rice and meat for Z 40.

The restaurant at the *Hotel Abki* is also good and offers large portions of beans, potatoes and rice for Z 30, rice, potatoes and meat for Z 80, rice and sauce for Z 50 and potatoes and sauce for Z 60.

For western food the *Restaurant Mupendo*, part of the Boulangerie/Patisserie Mupendo on the main street, is highly recommended and very popular. It's run by a Frenchman and offers things like steak & chips (Z 110) and portions of pizza (Z 70 – you need two of them if you're hungry). The set menu breakfasts are very good value – two-egg omelette, bread, butter, jam and two cups of coffee with milk for Z 65. They also have cakes and meat pies.

Other travellers have recommended the *Restaurant de la Paix* which offers excellent dinners for Z 50 to Z 70. If you want to splurge try the set meal at the *Mont-Goma Hotel*.

Avoid eating at the restaurant in the *Hotel Rif*. It's not only expensive but the food is diabolical.

One of the most pleasant surprises about Goma are the local cheeses. You can buy them either from street hawkers or general stores (*alimentations*) for about Z 150 per kg. That's excellent value, especially if you are putting your own food together. Salami and patés are also produced locally and sold for about Z 10 to Z 15 per 100 gm.

The market in Goma has a good selection of food for those who want to do their own cooking.

IDIOFA

There is a hotel opposite the *carrefour* (truck park), but it's pretty expensive. It serves good food though. There are cheaper places – ask the local people where they are.

ILEBO

For student reductions on the train south

to Kananga and Lubumbashi, you need to get a *lettre d'attestation* from the Sous-Division de l'Enseignement office near the BCZ. If this office is closed, go to the manager of the SNCZ (railways) and obtain a written authorisation. Then go to the *lycée* and ask the *directrice* (a pleasant woman) for a school transportation *lettre d'attestation* (Z 10). With this you can get 50% reductions on the rail fares.

Places to Stay

Free (ie, donation) accommodation is possible either at the *Noviciat* (a college for priests), which takes men only, or at the *Mission Catholique*. Ask for Père Eugene at the latter.

The *Hotel des Palmes* is a pleasant old colonial-style place and offers rooms for Z 300. The owner, Patrice, is a smart guy and is friendly and helpful. He runs the best nightclub in town – *La Kermesse*. You can also try the *Hotel Ngongo Ngoma* which has rooms for Z 200. Another recommended hotel is the *Hotel Frefima*.

INSHASHA

This is the Zaïre-Uganda border village. The Zaïre customs are fairly easy-going and the paperwork is completed quickly but the post is closed on Sundays. From the Zaïre customs post it is about 500 metres to the Ugandan post.

There is a hotel just south of the National Park Lodge which costs Z 165 a double with towels and soap provided. There's no electricity but kerosene lanterns are provided.

In the village there's a bakery/restaurant where you can buy omelettes (Z 25) and tea (Z 10) and they sometimes offer meat or fish with rice or potatoes. There's also a market if you are putting your own food together.

ISIRO

If you're staying more than 24 hours in Isiro, remember to register with immigration.

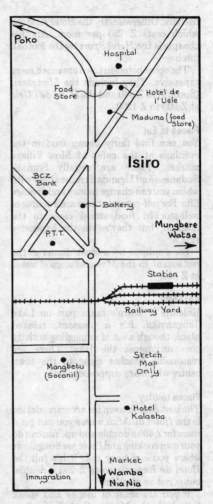

Places to Stay

Ask at the *Tennis Club* if you can either sleep on the verandah or camp in the grounds. It's guarded at night and they have a swimming pool as well as a relatively cheap bar, but no food. If you are alone the *Mission Catholique* will offer free food and accommodation, but they won't take groups. The people are friendly. Otherwise, try the *Hotel Kalasha* which costs Z 250 per room. Another cheapie is the *Hotel Sport* by the football pitch.

The other hotels in town are much more expensive. They include the *Mangbetu* (Soconil) at Z 840 and the *Hotel de l'Uele* at Z 900 to Z 1200.

Places to Eat
You can find fairly cheap food in the evenings at the cafés at Mon Village market. There are usually Somali, Sudanese and Ugandan traders here with whom you can change money and arrange lifts. For self-caterers there are a couple of well-stocked food stores close to the hospital, but they're on the expensive side.

For a splurge try a steak dinner at the restaurant in the *Mangbetu*, good value at Z 500.

KALEMIE
Kalemie is Zaïre's main port on Lake Tanganyika. It's a pleasant, relaxed place, though a lot of smuggling activity goes on across the lake. There are reasonable **beaches** close to the town centre which are supposedly safe.

Places to Stay
The best deal in town for accommodation is the *Hotel du Midi* where you can get a room for Z 400 a double and up. You can do your own cooking and there are bungalows where you can hang out. If it's full the *Hotel de Kalemie* costs Z 250 a double, but is not as pleasant.

If you are short of money and speak French try the *Mission Catholique*, they may let you stay free.

KAMINA
Kamina is the railway junction for the lines from Kindu to Lubumbashi and Ilebo to Lubumbashi. There's not a lot to do and you are strongly advised to avoid staying unless absolutely necessary. The reason is that some 20 km from the city is one of the largest army bases in the country and they like you to know about it. Expect rapacious immigration officials, suspicious police and aggressive whores.

Places to Stay
There are a few hotels in the Z 200 range though the cheapest place to stay is the *Kamina Hotel* at Z 150 per room.

For something to do in the evening, try either *La Cachette*, or *Le Mamba*, which is a disco joint with go-go girls and European music.

KANANGA
With a population well over half a million, this is one of Zaïre's largest cities. Some 20 km outside of town, however, is a large army camp so, as in Kamina, expect aggressive police, army patrols and lots of whores. Kananga has a good **museum** if you are interested in local craft work. There's a small entry fee.

Places to Stay
You can sometimes find accommodation with the *Protestant Missions* (there are two of them) or with the Peace Corps, but don't count on it. The cheapest hotel is the *Hotel Kamina*. Others include the *Hotel Palace* and the *Hotel Musube*.

KASINDI
From Kasindi it's a one-hour walk (mostly downhill) to the Ugandan border. From there, taxis are available to Kasese.

The *Hotel Kivu* is reasonable value at Z 100 per room with clean sheets and bucket showers, but no electricity (candles provided). Try to get a room in the main block during the wet season as the one with the thatched roof leaks. The hotel has a restaurant where you can get rice and meat for Z 40 and omelettes for Z 20. There are other hotels in town at Z 150 per room on average.

KAYNA-BAYONGA
This town is a truck-stop on the road between Goma and Butembo, especially

going south as drivers are not allowed to travel through the national park (Virunga) at night. As far as views are concerned, this is to your advantage, otherwise you would miss the Kabasha escarpment.

Trucks leave between 5.30 and 6 am, either from the Hotel Italie or from the market. After that you'll have to rely on transport passing through from elsewhere.

Places to Stay & Eat

Although there are a few small *logements* in the town centre, most truck drivers (and therefore travellers looking for a lift) stay at the *Hotel Italie* about three km north of the town. There is a variety of rooms ranging from singles at Z 100 to better double rooms at Z 275 to Z 400. There are clean, concrete toilets, bucket showers (cold water) and kerosene lamps (no electricity).

If you stay at the Italie you'll probably have to eat there too, though the food is relatively expensive (omelettes for Z 80, tea for Z 30). On the other hand, they don't mind cooking for those who arrive late (say, up to 10 pm).

If you stay in the town centre there are three places where you can pick up food. Two of them are on the main street, but one is really only a bar which has bread. The other offers the best value, with meat and rice for Z 60 and tea for Z 10, though the proprietor may try to charge a 'tourist price'.

The third restaurant is down an alley off the main street and has meat and rice for Z 80 and tea for Z 10. There's a good daily market if you are putting your own food together.

KIKWIT

For somewhere to stay try the *Hotel Mutashi* opposite the beer garden of the only large hotel on the main road to Ilebo. Otherwise you can find a room at the *Hotel des Vallées* for Z 330.

KINDU

One of the cheapest places to stay is the *Hotel Lusa*, two blocks from the main street, but be careful about people breaking into your room whilst you are sleeping. If you don't like this place try the *Hotel Maniema*, which costs Z 578 for a large, clean double room with shower and toilet. The *Hotel Relais* is similarly priced. Don't bother going to the Mission Catholique as they're very unfriendly.

KINSHASA

The rest of Zaïre may be pretty wild and untamed but Kinshasa, the capital, sprang from the jungle into the fast lane a long time ago. The main part of town resembles many other colonially planned African capitals and has wide, tree-lined boulevards, parks and all the usual shops, hotels and restaurants catering for office workers, government bureaucrats and expatriates. It might be just what you're looking for if you've just spent several weeks out in the sticks, but the most interesting and lively part of the city is the *cité* with its live bands, bars and clubs.

The city is full of live bands and if you're lucky you might get to see the most famous of them – Franco. Franco has virtually taken over the juke boxes, not only of Zaïre, but of just about the whole of East Africa. It's impossible to go into a bar anywhere along a broad corridor stretching from Kinshasa to Mombasa and not hear Franco.

Carry your passport at all times. If you get stopped at night without it, you'll probably be hauled before the army for questioning. Unless you're with friends who can go and find your passport, you may be hit with a large 'fine' – they won't allow you to go back to wherever you left it. Also, expect a visit from the security forces at your hotel between 3 and 4 am to check passports and baggage.

Information

Tourist Office & Maps The tourist office (tel 22417) is on Blvd du 30 Juin. There is a mapping agency at Service Géologique Nationale, BP 898.

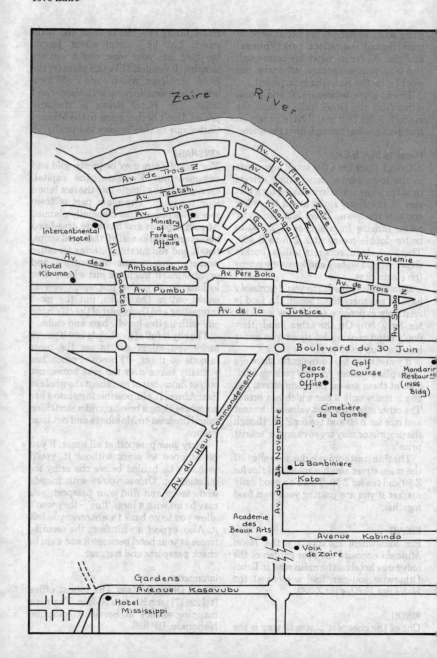

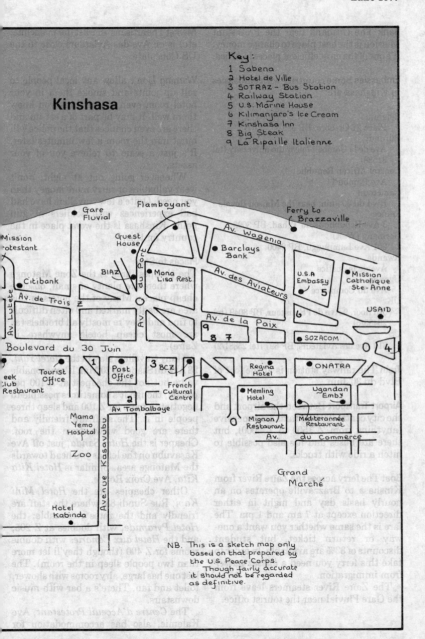

Kinshasa

Key:
1 Sabena
2 Hotel de Ville
3 SOTRAZ – Bus Station
4 Railway Station
5 U.S. Marine House
6 Kilimanjaro's Ice Cream
7 Kinshasa Inn
8 Big Steak
9 La Ripaille Italienne

Mission Protestant
Gare Fluvial
Flamboyant
Ferry to Brazzaville
Av. Wagenia
Guest House
Citibank
BIAZ
Av. du Port
Mona Lisa Rest.
Barclays Bank
Av. des Aviateurs
U.S.A Embassy
Mission Catholique Ste-Anne
Av. Lukete
Av. de Trois Z
Av. de la Paix
USAID
9 8 7
SOZACOM
Boulevard du 30 Juin
Greek Club Restaurant
Tourist Office
1
Post Office
3 BCZ
French Cultural Centre
Regina Hotel
ONATRA
4
2
Av. Tombalbaye
Memling Hotel
Ugandan Emby
Mama Yemo Hospital
Avenue Kasavubu
Mignon Restaurant
Méditerannée Restaurant
Av. du Commerce
Zoo
Grand Marché
Hotel Kabinda

NB. This is a sketch map only
based on that prepared by
the U.S. Peace Corps.
Though fairly accurate
it should not be regarded
as definitive.

Bank The Citibank near the Protestant Mission is the best place to change money. It's one of the most efficient places in Africa.

Embassies Some countries with embassies in Kinshasa are:

Belgium
   Place 27 Octobre, BP 899
Burundi
   Ave de la Gombe 17 near the university (tel 31588)
Central African Republic
   Ave Pumbu 11
Cameroun
   Blvd du 30 Juin, near the Maison Royale
France
   3 Ave République du Tchad, BP 3093
Germany (West)
   201 Ave Lumpungu, BP 8400
Rwanda
   Ave de la Justice
Uganda
   Ave du Commerce
UK
   5th floor, 9 Ave de l'Equateur, BP 8049 (tel 23483/6)
US
   310 Ave des Aviateurs, BP 697 (tel 25881/2)

Train The railway station is at the foot of Blvd du 30 Juin.

Airport Transport Between the airport and the city centre (29 km) taxis are expensive (anything from Z 1500 to Z 3000), but there are buses and it's also possible to hitch a ride with trucks.

Boat The ferry across the Zaïre River from Kinshasa to Brazzaville operates on an hourly basis day and night in either direction except at 7 am and 1 pm. The fare is the same whether you want a one-way or return ticket, but student discounts of 33% are available. In order to take this ferry you need a *laissez-passer* from immigration.

The Zaïre River steamers leave from the Gare Fluvial near the tourist office.

Market The artisans' market (for malachite, etc) is on Ave des Aviateurs close to the US Consulate.

Warning Don't allow any local people to roll up joints and smoke them in your hotel room even if you think you know them well. It may be part of a set-up and there are even chances that the police will burst into the room a few minutes later. It's just a scam to relieve you of your assets.

Whenever going out at night, don't wear valuables or carry more money than you need. Quite a few travellers have had bad experiences with soldiers at gun point. Kinshasa is the worst place in the country for this.

Places to Stay

The cheapest area is the Zone Matonge where there are plenty of small, obscure cheap places. Many of the hotels in this area are badly marked and often difficult to find and they're mostly all brothels (as are most cheap hotels anywhere in Zaïre).

Many travellers stay in the *Hotel Yaki*, 28 Ave du Stade du 20 Mai. It's reasonable value but not the cheapest at Z 100 per person, though it's sometimes possible to negotiate a room for Z 100 and sleep three people in it. The staff are friendly and there are good views from the roof. Cheaper is the *Hotel Sanda*, just off Ave Kasavubu on the left as you head towards the Matonge area. Similar is *Hotel Kita Kita*, Ave Croix Rouge.

Other cheapies are the *Hotel Mini Kapi*, Rue Sundi 88, where the staff are friendly and the rates reasonable; the *Hotel Pyramide*, with doubles at Z 205; and the *Hotel aux Canaries* with double rooms for Z 400 (though they'll let more than two people sleep in the room). The last one has large, airy rooms with shower, toilet and fan. There's a bar with music downstairs.

The *Centre d'Acceuil Protestant*, Ave Kalemie, also has accommodation for

Z 800/1600 a single/double but they will allow four people to sleep in a room. Your belongings are relatively safe. Latest reports, however, suggest they are beginning to discourage travellers.

In the centre of town, the best value is the *Hotel Regina*, Blvd du 30 Juin near the Sozacom Building. This is a brown coloured building and is the tallest in the city. There's no sign for this hotel so use the street map of Kinshasa as a guide. You can get a huge room with toilet and shower for Z 313 a double, but they'll let more than two people sleep in each room.

The *Hotel Guesthouse*, Ave du Flambeau, is in a quiet location and offers rooms for Z 750/1300 a single/double including air-con.

Places to Eat

There's plenty of good, cheap street food available in Kinshasa so if you are short of funds you won't have problems. A good place for bread with peanut butter and coffee in the morning is the small market next to the Hotel Yaki. For beans or fish and rice try the stalls by the roundabout opposite Big Steak, not far from the Yaki – an enormous bowl of beans and rice costs Z 15. Cheap breakfasts can be found in the Grand Marché.

The *Restaurant de l'Ocean* off Blvd du 30 Juin has also been recommended. Beans and rice cost Z 100 and beers Z 50. Similarly priced is the *Cafeteria Bravo*, opposite Air Zaïre and near the main post office, which offers good cheap food.

The *Greek Club*, Blvd du 30 Juin, has been recommended for inexpensive, but excellent Greek food. Another place worth trying is *Chez Babylon* in the Matonge district, which is basically a bar but has a good selection of Zaïrean delicacies in the evening – fish, eels, caterpillars, grasshoppers, prawns and termites, etc. Prices are reasonable at around Z 450 for four people.

Entertainment

A good place to escape from the sometimes oppressive atmosphere of Kinshasa with a few cold beers is the bar of the *L'Orange Brasserie*, Blvd du 30 Juin. There's a good rooftop nightclub/disco at *La Créche* in Matonge. They put on good live bands and there's no cover charge; beers are cheap too.

For something to do on a Friday evening try going along to the US Marines weekly party which is open to all. Ask at the US Embassy for directions. Great pizzas!

KISANGANI

Formerly Stanleyville, Kisangani is the main city on the middle reaches of the Zaïre River. It's a fairly pleasant city which offers many contrasts. There are a lot of Greek expatriates here as well as travellers on their way through Zaïre.

Information

There's a sort of 'Mr Fix-It' in Kisangani who's the person to see for all manner of things – changing money, arranging lifts, buying and selling cars. He's a Belgian man married to a Zaïre woman and both of them are reliable. A man called Eugene, who works for these people, used to be the usual contact, but mention in the last edition of this book has apparently gone to his head and it seems that he's resting on his laurels and doesn't have a lot of useful information these days other than what's obvious.

If you don't go through the Belgian man, be careful when arranging lifts. There are one or two rip-off merchants in this town who work hand-in-glove with the police. You may be told, for instance, that there is a truck going to Goma (or wherever) at 5 am. While you're being led to it, the police stop you, take your passports and refuse to hand them back unless you give them money. All this time, the man who is taking you to the truck is urging you to settle up or you'll miss the truck. After you've handed over money and finally got to where the truck is supposed to leave – bingo! – there's no truck.

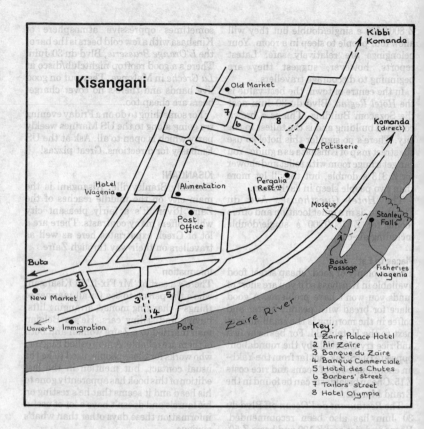

Kisangani

Key:
1 Zaïre Palace Hotel
2 Air Zaïre
3 Banque du Zaïre
4 Banque Commerciale
5 Hotel des Chutes
6 Barbers' street
7 Tailors' street
8 Hotel Olympia

Other places to try for lifts are the beer depots and warehouses.

The best bank for changing travellers' cheques is the Banque Commerciale Zaïroise near the port and the Hotel des Chutes. They charge about 1% commission and take about an hour.

Don't take photographs of the dock area as your film and camera will be confiscated.

Things to See

For something to do visit the **Wagenia Fisheries** at Stanley Falls. It's somewhat touristy but still alright. Get a group together and contact 'Frenzy' who is the son of the village chief. At the falls you'll see the fisherfolk dropping baskets into the falls to catch fish. Frenzy will organise all this plus pirogue trips along the river and smooth the way for photographs, all for Z 150 per person. Go on your own and those photographs alone will cost US$10.

Places to Stay

Most travellers stay at the *Hotel Olympia*, a Greek-owned place where you can camp for Z 50 per person (plus Z 50 if you have a car). Rooms vary in price, but start at Z 500 and go up to Z 1500 a double, the latter with bathroom. On the other hand, some travellers have managed to stay for much less, though, naturally, it didn't include a bed or bedding. Watch your gear as quite a bit of theft goes on. The food tends to be on the expensive side but it's good. A set lunch of soup, meat, chips and vegetables followed by fruit costs Z 200. The Olympia is a good place to meet overland trucks and to enquire about lifts further east.

In the Zone de Chopo, the *Hotel Baninga* has some cheap rooms, as does the *Hotel Kinshasa* at Z 120 a double. Another reasonably priced hotel is the *Hotel Kisangani* at Z 350 a double. You can also camp for a small charge.

If you're planning on getting one of the more expensive rooms at the Olympia, you might also consider the *Hotel des Chutes* near the river. It is a pleasant old colonial-style hotel with double rooms for Z 500 and it has a restaurant and bar. Similarly priced is the *Wagenia Hotel* though this place doesn't have a restaurant.

Those looking for comfort or a splurge should head for the *Zaïre Palace Hotel* above Air Zaïre. The hotel has a good bar and restaurant.

Places to Eat
Most of the restaurants are Greek-owned and the food is generally expensive, but one which is reasonable is the *Pergalia Restaurant* around the corner from the post office. Here you can get an excellent three-course lunch (soup, avocado vinaigrette, steak or beef rissole with chips and vegetables) for Z 150. They also have Greek yogurt, fresh bread and ice cream.

Both the *Ali Baba*, close to the Zaïre Palace Hotel, and the *Transit Café* are good and are cheaper than the Pergalia. You can pick up kebabs, salad and chips at either for around Z 50. The Transit has a blackboard listing the arrivals of planes, trains and boats, and is a good place to meet other travellers. It's about half way between the Olympia and Wagenia hotels.

Self-caterers can buy food from the new market just outside town and cook it in the garden of the Olympia.

KOMANDA
There are two cheap hotels (about Z 100 per room) near the roundabout and another (for Z 80) on the road to Beni.

Komanda has a small, adequate market and a bakery. There's also a restaurant on the roundabout, which offers rice and stringy beef for Z 50 and tea for Z 10.

LISALA
The Seigneurie and the river boat ticket office share the same room in the main port building. If you need to change money when the banks are closed try the Baptist Mission or the Portuguese merchants. There is electricity in Lisala between 6 and 10 pm daily.

Places to Stay
There are huts available at the old rice factory for Z 80 (sleep as many as you can get in). Cheap *rondavels* are available at the *Complexe Venus* overlooking the river some two to three km from the centre. They cost Z 150 and there's no running water but bucket showers are available. The more expensive *Motel Nsele* costs Z 550 per room and includes air-con when the electricity is on.

LUBUMBASHI
The capital of Shaba province, Lubumbashi is in the heart of the copper belt. Formerly called Elizabethville, it's a pleasant city with large numbers of Lebanese, Greek and Italian expatriates.

Places to Stay & Eat
Because there's quite a lot of money floating around in Lubumbashi, hotel prices tend to be expensive. The following places are all good.

The *Hotel Globe* in front of the railway station has excellent rooms with shower and toilet for Z 900 a double plus a few cheaper rooms with communal showers

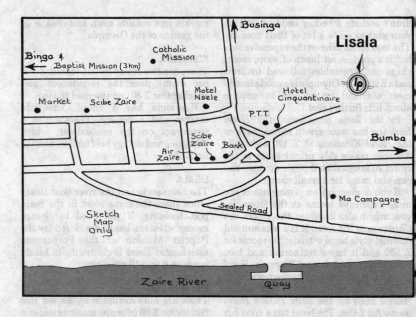

and toilets for Z 650 a double. The *Hotel du Shaba*, 486 Ave du Mama Yemo, has clean rooms for Z 1200 a double. It's owned by a friendly Belgian man and there is a restaurant.

The *Hotel Silver House*, near the SNCZ Hotel, has rooms for Z 700, and a mixed bar. Others in a similar price range include the *Hotel de la Paix*, near the hospital, the *Hotel Silver Star* and the *Hotel Macris*. The last of these is Greek-run and is close to the Silver Star. Another traveller recommended the *Hotel Kenya*, about two km from the centre, which is noisy but only costs Z 300.

For cheap food try the cafés opposite the market where you can get beans and meat. The food at the *Belle Vue* has been highly recommended.

MAHAGI

In this town north-east of Bunia you're unlikely to meet any other travellers.

The *Hotel Touristique* charges Z 100 per person and is a good place to stay. If you give one of the women Z 50 they'll cook you the best Zaïrean food you've ever tasted.

MAMBASA

The *Mission Catholique* on the road towards Beni may let you stay and use the showers, but leave a donation and bring your own food. The people are friendly and helpful.

MAPANGU

Ask for the *Maison de la Passage*, owned by PLZ (Plantations Lever Zaïre). It's a rest house for the use of PLZ employees but is rarely used by them.

MT HOYO

Mt Hoyo is about 13 km off the Beni to Bunia road close to Komanda. Mt Hoyo's attractions are the waterfalls known as the **Chutes de Venus**, the **grottoes** and the **Pygmy villages** nearby. It also used to be possible to climb Mt Hoyo (a two-day trek), but the track is now overgrown and there's no longer a hut at the top. This shouldn't deter those who are determined and guides can be found at the hotel.

The Chutes and grottoes are managed as an extension of Parc National des Virunga so you have to pay Z 600 for a seven-day permit plus Z 50 for a photography permit. This includes the services of a compulsory guide. The guide may say that you have to pay him direct but this isn't true: you must pay at the Auberge. The tour of the Chutes and grottoes lasts about two hours and takes you to three different cavern systems (illuminated with a kerosene lantern) and finally down to the base of the waterfall.

Visits to one of the Pygmy villages cost Z 200 per group but too many tourists have been and they're very commercialised. You'll be hassled to death and will have to pay for every photograph you take. If you have the time, it's better to spend a few days and gradually build up a relationship with the Pygmies by trading with them or buying food from them before going to visit their village.

Alternatively, find someone who is willing to guide you to one or other of the more remote Pygmy villages in the forest. Overland trucks don't get this far.

If you come to Mt Hoyo on the Eka Massambe bus from Butembo (Monday and Thursday from Butembo, about seven hours, Z 450) it will drop you at the Mt Hoyo turn-off at about 5 pm. This means you'll have to complete the 13-km walk to the hotel at night. It's possible to hire porters for this three-hour walk (the average charge is Z 150). Seven km down the road is a fruit plantation with pineapples, papayas, avocados and bananas for sale. Buy some while you have the chance because food at the hotel is expensive.

Places to Stay

The hotel, *Auberge de Mont Hoyo*, charges a minimum of Z 2500 for a chalet with three beds and you will literally have to beg for electricity. If you have a tent you can camp for Z 150 per person including the use of toilet and showers. If you don't have a tent and can't afford the hotel there's a small room to rent (sleeps up to four people on the floor) adjoining the toilet and bathroom. Meals are expensive which is why you're advised to buy food on the way in. The rest can be bought from Pygmies who come up to the hotel.

MUANDA

Muanda is a resort town for local and expatriate workers on the nearby oil rigs, and travellers who have been here have commented enthusiastically on the friendliness they found.

Places to Stay & Eat

Naturally, with oil money flowing through the place, there are a lot of expensive hotels. For budget travellers there is the *Mission Catholique* about six km from town, offering beds for Z 100 per person. If you stay you need to bring your own food. Hitching from the Mission to town is very easy.

In the town itself fresh fish can be bought very cheaply indeed (enough for two people for Z 30) from the fisherpeople. The market has a reasonable range of food but not much in the way of fruit and vegetables and it closes early in the afternoon.

Food bought at hotels is generally expensive though the *Hotel Mangrove* has been recommended. The best place to eat, however, is the extremely friendly *Restaurant Chez Kotatala* where the food is reasonably priced.

NIA NIA

If you're lucky you might be offered a room at the *Mission Catholique*, run by two Italians. The old *père* is somewhat eccentric.

RUTSHURU

Rutshuru is perhaps the most convenient take-off point for a visit to the mountain gorillas in the Parc National des Virunga where they are found on the slopes of Muside and Sabinyo volcanoes (which Zaïre shares with Rwanda and Uganda). You first have to make your way to Djomba (sometimes spelt Jomba). The turn-off for this place is about two km south of Rutshuru and is clearly signposted.

If you're coming from or going to Uganda you will probably also come through Rutshuru unless you are going to cross the border further north between Beni and Kasese via Kasindi.

Places to Stay & Eat

The best place is the *Mission Catholique*, which has a guesthouse where you can stay for Z 150 per person. There are showers and meals are available for Z 70. They may let you camp in the grounds of the mission without charge.

Cheaper is the unnamed lodging house about 50 metres north of the police station on the opposite side of the road. It has rooms for Z 100 (one or two people). There are bucket showers, an earth toilet and the owner is friendly. He may help you find transport.

The more expensive *Hotel Grefamu* is on the main road and costs Z 275 a double.

Other hotels recommended by travellers are the *Hotel du Parc* and the *Katata Hotel*. The Katata is clean and has hot water, but is more expensive than the others.

UBUNDU

The *Mission Catholique* might provide free accommodation. If not, there is a small, cheap hotel.

UVIRA

Uvira is on the north-west tip of Lake Tanganyika facing Bujumbura across the lake. It's not a particularly attractive or interesting place. While here try to avoid army personnel if possible and keep that camera out of sight – there's a lot of mercenary paranoia in the area.

The actual port area, Kalundu, is some

four km south of Uvira (taxis for Z 50). You'll be lucky to find a boat going south from here (most travellers have drawn a blank) and the road south may be unsafe to travel on – there was guerrilla activity around here a couple of years ago.

Places to Stay & Eat

One of the cheapest places is the *Hotel Babyo 'La Patience'*, Ave Bas-Zaïre near the mosque, with rooms for Z 150 a double. If it's full, the *Pole Pole* costs Z 150 a single. There's no running water but there's a bar and good brochettes for sale.

A good place is the *Tanganyika Restaurant*. It is just down the road from La Patience and is run by Ugandan refugees. The food is good, the staff are pleasant and English is spoken. For a splurge, try the *Hotel La Côte* which offers good three-course meals for around Z 300.

For nightlife try the *Lobe Disco* which gets crowded after 9.30 pm. The *Nyanda au Grand Lac* also has music sometimes.

ZONGO

Beware of immigration in Zongo. They often search travellers thoroughly (mainly for currency) and you'll get hassles if they find anything. They sometimes demand that you supply them with an itinerary after which they'll tell you the places where it's necessary to get your passport stamped. If you plan to return through Zongo, make sure you comply otherwise they may send you back for those stamps. If you're not coming back this way it obviously doesn't matter.

Places to Stay

There are a number of cheap places around the immigration office for Z 150 per room. One is the friendly *Hotel Nyaswa* between the bank and the river.

You cannot camp next to the police or immigration office. The only place you'll be allowed to camp is on the outskirts of town and you are certain to be robbed in the night. This has happened even to large groups so it's not worth it.

National Parks

If you are passing through Kinshasa and will subsequently be visiting the national parks on the eastern borders of Zaïre it is worth buying one of the special passes from the national parks office. These passes, available only in Kinshasa, cost Z 5000 and cover your entry fees to all the national parks.

PARC NATIONAL DE KAHUZI-BIEGA

Lying between Bukavu and Goma, this park was created in 1970 with an initial area of 600 square km, but was expanded to 6000 square km in 1975. The principal reason for its creation was to preserve the habitat of the plains gorilla (*gorilla gorilla graueri*) which was once found all the way from the right bank of the Zaïre River to the mountains on the borders with Uganda and Rwanda. These days, like the mountain gorillas living on the slopes of the volcanoes on the borders between Zaïre, Rwanda and Uganda, it is an endangered species.

Many other animals, of course, live in this park and these include chimpanzee, many other kinds of monkey, elephant, buffalo, antelope, leopard, genet, serval and mongoose. The park's bird life is also prolific.

The altitude varies between 900 and 3308 metres (Mt Kahuzi) and the average annual rainfall is fairly heavy at 1900 mm with the most falling in April and November. The dry season runs through the months of June, July and August. Most areas of the park have a temperate climate with a fairly constant average temperature of 15°C.

Because of the heavy rainfall and the varying altitude there's a wide variety of vegetation, ranging from the dense rainforests at the lower levels, through bamboo forests between 2400 and 2600 metres and finally heath and alpine meadows on the summits of the highest mountains.

Many of the animals live in the denser parts of the forest and so are often difficult to see. This is also true of the gorillas which are nowhere near as habituated to human contact as their cousins in Rwanda and so tend to flee as soon as they see or hear you.

Visiting the Gorillas

There are several groups of gorillas although usually you will only see one or other of the groups not used to humans. They can be visited any day of the year including public holidays. Children under 15 years of age are not allowed to visit the gorillas.

The national park office in Bukavu (Institut Zaïrois pour la Conservation de la Nature, 185 Ave du President Mobutu) will tell you that it's necessary to make a booking with them. This isn't really necessary, except on Sundays when demand can be high, but if you want to do so the office is open Monday to Friday from 8.30 am to 3 pm and on Saturday from 8.30 am to 12 noon. If you don't make a booking be at the Station Tshivanga (park entrance and take-off point) by 8 am on the day you want to go. If you have a booking you don't need to be there until 9 am.

The park entry fee is Z 3000 per person. This includes the compulsory guide and trackers (who chop the vegetation to make a track) though they all expect a tip at the end. The average tip is Z 25 to Z 30 for the guide and Z 20 for each tracker. As long as this fee holds, it is considerably cheaper to see gorillas in Zaïre than in Rwanda.

You must have appropriate footwear and clothing, preferably a pair of stout boots and waterproof clothes – this is not a picnic. It's often very muddy and hard going up steep slopes and you need to be careful what you grasp hold of to pull yourself up. Many vines and the like carry thorns or will sting, so a pair of gloves is an excellent idea. It can rain even in the dry season. The guides can generally locate a group of gorillas within two hours though it can be as much as five hours and as little as five minutes (unusual). If you don't see any the first day your fee covers you for another attempt the next. No refunds are possible if you can't make it the next day.

There is an additional fee of Z 50 for a camera. Officially, movie cameras and video cassette recorders are prohibited, but some people apparently manage to take the former as they report being charged Z 250 for them. You need the fastest film for taking photographs of the gorillas – ASA 800 to ASA 1600 would be the thing to go for. Anything less and you're going to be disappointed when you get home.

As the gorillas in Zäire are not really used to human presence (though this is gradually changing), when you finally find a troop of them, the trackers start hacking away at the bush to give you a better view. The troop retreats and the 'view' becomes a running hunt and retreat with the silverback male making mock charges to give the other members of his group time to retreat.

To get to the take-off point at Station Tshivanga you have a choice of bus and walk, or taxi. The taxi is really only feasible if there's a group of you as you're looking at Z 1700 to Z 2000. It does mean though, that you can probably set off from Bukavu in time to reach Tshivanga by 8 am, see the gorillas and be back in Bukavu by early or mid-afternoon.

If you have to use public transport you'll need a minimum of two days. The first day you take a bus (frequent) from Place du 24 Novembre in Bukavu to Miti along a surfaced road; the fare is about Z 50. From Miti it's seven km to Tshivanga and lifts are difficult to find. You may have to walk so it's best to plan on staying at Tshivanga for the night and

seeing the gorillas the next day. If you do this, bring everything with you (tent, food, drinks) although occasionally the people at Tshivanga have a tent for hire, but don't count on it. Food and drink should be bought in Bukavu, or in Miti which has an adequate fruit and vegetable market though canned food, etc is limited. Camping at the park entrance costs Z 40.

PARC NATIONAL DES VIRUNGA

This park covers a sizeable area of the Zaïre-Uganda and Zaïre-Rwanda borders, stretching all the way from Goma almost to Lake Mobutu Sese Seko via Lake Edward. Much of it is contiguous with national parks in Uganda and Rwanda.

Covering an area of 8000 square km, the Virunga was Zaïre's first national park and was created in 1925. For administrative purposes, the park has been divided into four sections. From the south they are: Nyiragongo, Nyamulgira and Karisimbi; Rwindi and Vitshumbi; Ishango; and, lastly, the Ruwenzori.

Entry to any part of the Virunga (except if passing straight through on transport between Rutshuru and Kayna-Bayonga) costs Z 600 for a seven-day permit plus Z 50 for a camera permit. You can go from one part of the park to another without paying twice as long as your first seven-day permit is still valid.

Nyiragongo, Nyamulgira & Karisimbi

This section of the park covers these three volcanoes as well as the gorilla sanctuary at Djomba on the slopes of Muside and Sabinyo volcanoes along the border with Rwanda.

The Djomba Gorilla Sanctuary The sanctuary is managed by the Institut Zaïrois pour la Conservation de la Nature (a joint Zaïro-German project). Before going to Djomba (the take-off point for visits) you must first make a booking at the IZCN office in Goma. It is open daily between 9 and 11 am and sometimes later. The office is not easy to find so refer to the Goma section for details. The fee is Z 3000 per person and there's a hut in Djomba where you can stay for Z 400 per person per night complete with stove, but you must take all your food or have the villagers cook for you. Camping costs Z 360 including the hire of a tent. The villagers also have a limited range of food, which they'll sell if you want to do your own cooking.

You can also make bookings at the Rwindi Lodge for the gorilla visit but *don't do it!*. Quite a few travellers have been caught out by doing this. Your booking will eventually get through but you will most likely arrive before it does, and that probably means you won't see them because the trips will be booked up for days ahead. If this happens, speak to Dr Conrad – he may be able to fix up a gorilla viewing at Rumangabo station nearer to Goma.

To see the gorillas you must be at the take-off point by 8 am. The fee includes a guide (compulsory) but he will expect a tip at the end. Even so, this makes it considerably cheaper to see the gorillas here than in Rwanda. The guides can usually find a group of gorillas within an hour or two. The maximum (human) group size is six visitors plus two guides.

Getting to Djomba, seven km from the Ugandan border, involves going first to Rutshuru. There is a daily bus between Goma and Rutshuru in either direction which costs Z 150 and takes about 2½ hours. It leaves Goma about 2 pm from a private house between the Hotel Haut Zaïre and the main north-south road. In the opposite direction it departs Rutshuru about 6.15 am. Get there early if you want a seat.

The turn-off for Djomba is about two km before Rutshuru and is clearly signposted. If you're using the Michelin map of this area it's not precise and it appears that the road goes off from the centre of town. This isn't the case; the turn-off you want branches from a roundabout with a petrol station on it

about four km from the actual centre of Rutshuru, but the signposts would have you believe that you are already in Rutshuru. The urban area, however, starts about two km from the roundabout and the centre is about four km from it. There's another right fork in the centre of town which takes you to Uganda via Ishasha. The bus from Goma takes you right into the centre unless you ask to be let off before then.

From the turn-off on the Goma to Rutshuru road it's about 26 km to Djomba over a rough road (4WD needed) and transport is sporadic. Finally, from Djomba it's a seven-km walk gradually uphill to the starting point and the hut that you can stay in overnight.

If you don't want to stay in the hut there's a *Mission Catholique* in Djomba where you can stay for Z 300 per bed including breakfast, and other meals are available for Z 250. It's excellent value. There's also an *American Baptist Mission* at Rwanguba, five km uphill from Djomba.

Recently another group of gorillas was discovered at Bukima, which is considerably closer to the Goma to Rutshuru road than Djomba, but they are harder to find as the project personnel have only had the last three years to habituate them to human contact. Few travellers have so far seen them.

To get to Bukima, find transport from Goma to Rutshuru, but get out at the park headquarters at Rumangabo about 45 km north of Goma. The turn-off is marked by a triangular stone monument at the side of the road. A park guard will accompany you to Bukima, a 2½ to three-hour walk from Rumangabo.

The evening before the visit you can either camp at Rumangabo and walk up to Bukima the next morning, or go direct to Bukima and camp there or stay in a simple local-style shelter overnight (usually free). Wooden cabins are planned for the future.

As with the gorillas at Djomba, you must make a reservation at the office in

Goma before coming. Groups are limited to three people plus guides at present but this will shortly be increased to six.

Nyiragongo Nyiragongo (3470 metres), which broods over Goma, used to be a spectacular sight several years ago when it was erupting but at present it's quiescent. It's still worth climbing to the top though, if only for the views. Since it only takes five hours up and three hours down it can be done in one day as long as you set off very early. This isn't recommended, however, as the summit is only clear of mist or cloud in the early morning and again, briefly, in the late afternoon. Make it a two-day event.

The take-off point is Kibati, about 12 km north of Goma on the Rutshuru road. Here you find the Camp des Guides which is a long white unmarked building set back above the road at the foot of the volcano. You can either hitch or walk to this place. Fees are paid at the camp (Z 1200 park entry plus Z 50 for a camera). If you plan to spend the night in the hut about 30 minutes walk from the crater rim, it will cost Z 40 extra per person. The huts are in bad shape but there is usually water there. Bring all the food and firewood/charcoal you need from Kibati. The park entry fee is supposed to cover the cost of a guide (compulsory) but most people have to pay another Z 100 'tip', though for this the guide will usually double as a porter.

It's possible to stay at the Camp des Guides the day before going up the mountain, but there's no regular accommodation as such. Many travellers buy the head guide a bottle of beer and end up sleeping on his floor. He's a friendly and interesting guy. Otherwise you could camp.

On the first day you need to start off before 1 pm as it's a three-hour walk to the base of the crater cone proper, then another hour to the huts. On the way up you pass some interesting vegetation and topographical features – tropical forest, hardened lava flows (recent, old and ancient) and giant lobelia.

On the second day you need to get up early so you can get off by 6.30 am. Wear warm clothes. It's a half-hour walk to the crater rim and the weather should be clear. Looking down into the base of the crater you'll probably still see wisps of steam and vapour coming from the walls, while the base itself is an uneven cooled mass of lava. Sulphur fumes hang in the air. The views of Goma, Lake Kivu and over into Rwanda are terrific. By about 9.30 am the mist will start closing in for the day and you lose the views. The descent takes about three hours.

Nyamulgira To climb Nyamulgira (3055 metres) you need a minimum of three days, but you shouldn't have to pay the park entry fee again as long as you haven't used up your original seven days. As on Nyiragongo, you'll have to tip the guides extra. Bring all your food requirements and, as there's nowhere to stay at the Nyamulgira base camp, you'll need a tent.

The trip starts at Kibati (as for the other volcano) and the first part involves a 45-km walk to the base camp through beautiful countryside. The next section is a six-hour climb through an incredibly varied landscape ranging from old and recent lava flows (some of them pocked with lava pools) to dense upland jungles. You may be lucky and catch sight of elephant, chimpanzee, buffalo and antelope, but you'll definitely see and hear hundreds of different birds.

The first night on the mountain is spent at a decaying, rambling hut (for which you pay extra), though it is possible to return to the base camp the same day as long as you set off early enough. Camping is an alternative. The guides generally cook their own food.

The next day you set off for the crater rim. It takes about one hour to reach the tree line, then another hour to get to the crater rim across recent lava flows (slippery when wet). As from Nyiragongo, the views from the summit are magnificent. You descend the mountain the same day.

Rwindi & Vitshumbi The main attraction in this part of the park is the game – lion, elephant, hippo, giraffe, antelope, hyena, buffalo and many others. The Ruwenzori National Park in neighbouring Uganda (contiguous with Virunga) used to be much the same, but was sadly depleted of wildlife in the various civil wars fought there since Idi Amin was ousted. If you come to this part of the Virunga you need to make enquiries beforehand to see if vehicles can be hired for a safari. If not, you're going to be reliant on tourist traffic and they're not always keen on picking up hitchers. Entry to Rwindi costs Z 2000.

The *lodge* at Rwindi is somewhat expensive at Z 3200 per room, or Z 4400 for a cottage, though if you wait until the bar closes it may be possible to bed down by the swimming pool. Camping is officially forbidden in or around the lodge. If you can't afford to stay at the lodge enquire about rooms in the drivers' quarters. You may be lucky, in which case it will cost Z 300 for a room with two beds though there are no bathroom facilities. There's also a small *Guest House* in the nearby village but they're not keen on taking tourists.

Whilst you're in this area you should pay a visit to the fishing village of **Vitshumbi** at the southern end of Lake Edward, but if you're not staying in this part of the park a visit to the fishing village of **Kiavinyonge** at the northern end of the lake near Kasindi is more interesting.

Ishango This is similar to the Rwindi-Vitshumbi part of the park except you don't find elephants here. Ishango is just a park camping area with a small airstrip and a derelict lodge, which you can use free of charge but it's usually filthy and smelly with bat shit. Camping is preferable, but you'll be charged Z 200 per tent for this. There are no fences so be careful at night. People who have camped have encountered hyenas and leopards too close to the camp for comfort.

Those who know the area well, say that it's possible to swim in either Lake Edward or in the Semliki River which flows into it here as there's apparently no danger of bilharzia, but they do warn strongly about hippos. If you do decide to go for a swim, watch closely for 10 to 15 minutes to make sure there are no hippos anywhere near you. One traveller who ignored this had a buttock bitten off a few years ago. He was lucky and survived because (after a long hassle) the Ugandans allowed him through to the nearest hospital; there are none close by in Zaïre. The wildlife, and particularly the bird life, is prolific where the Semliki flows into the lake.

To get to Ishango you need first to get to Kasindi either from Beni (Zaïre) or Kasese (Uganda). There are usually a fair number of trucks on the road between the two places and you can hitch. Wait at the turn-off in Kasindi for a lift into the park. If you get stuck it's three km to the park entrance and you can generally rent a bedroom in one of the buildings there. The average charge is Z 50 per night for two people. You will have to pay another Z 600 park entry fee if your seven-day permit has run out, but there is a way around this *if* you don't want to go to Ishango. If that's the case, tell them you are going to **Kiavinyonge** which is 10 km beyond Ishango and not strictly in the national park. No-one else pays to get there as the only road in is through Kasindi and Ishango. The trip involves a ferry crossing over a river literally swarming with hippos.

Kiavinyonge is a large fishing village and at about 6 am the boats all land their catches on the sandy beach in front of the restaurant and houses. The village suddenly becomes a sea of activity as the men sort out the nets and the women sort the fish, which gets smoked during the day. There are herds of hippo wallowing in the water close to the beach. Large marabou birds are seen everywhere. The village itself has a spectacular setting at the foot of a range of mountains leading down to the lake. Few tourists come to this village so you're in for a treat if you like to get off the beaten track.

In Kiavinyonge stay at the *Lodgement Special* at the west end of the village where they have rooms for Z 80 (one or two people). Don't be put off if they're not sure what to do with you when you turn up! There's a restaurant on the lake shore selling coffee, tea, bread and hot corned beef (!) from 6 am to 8 pm but the best thing to eat is fish and rice (about Z 50 per person). You're not going to find it fresher anywhere else!

When you want to leave Kiavinyonge enquire about trucks taking fish to Butembo. They leave around 8 am, cost about Z 250 and take four hours. It's an incredible journey up over the mountains on a dirt road with many hairpin bends and alpine scenery. This is not the normal Kasindi to Butembo road.

Ruwenzori This is the most northerly part of the Virunga and its major interest to travellers is, of course, the climb up the Ruwenzori mountains. This is also possible from the Ugandan side since the border between the two countries passes along the summits. Don't underestimate the difficulties of this trek from either side. It's much tougher than climbing Kilimanjaro. True, some people do make it in joggers and normal clothes but they suffer for it. You can almost freeze to death without adequate clothes and a warm sleeping bag anywhere above Hut 3 (about 4300 metres). Snow is not unusual either at or above this point. Prepare for it properly and it will be one of the most memorable trips in your life.

Before you even think about doing this trek get hold of the appropriate footwear and clothing and a good sleeping bag. Don't forget a beanie and gloves. Pots and pans are useful and will repay their cost

several times over, especially if you're trying to economise on weight by taking dried soups. You need to take *all* your own food including enough for your guide and porters. A stove for cooking on is also very useful, but not absolutely essential.

Many of the huts where you will stay are in poor shape. There is no glass in the windows for a start. Sheets of plastic or even just plastic bags work wonders for your well-being when pinned up across open windows with drawing pins. The guide and porters are partial to cigarettes at the end of a day. If you run out, they can get very unpleasant. Avoid bad relations by making sure you both know exactly what your and the guide's responsibilities are, who is paying for what, where you are going to go, how many days it's going to take – be firm but keep them sweet.

The best selection of food is in Beni but there are also fairly well-stocked shops and a reasonable market (meat, fruit, vegetables, beer, sodas, etc) in Mutwanga. This is where the guides and porters get their supplies.

The actual trek starts by turning up at the park headquarters in Mutsora, about four km from Mutwanga. Both of these places are about half way between Beni and Kasindi on the road to Uganda. There are trucks from close to the Hotel Walaba in Beni to the Mutsora-Mutwanga turn-off for about Z 150 (though they often start at Z 200). From there you walk though it is possible to get a lift all the way to Mutwanga. It's about 13 km from the turn-off on the Beni to Kasindi road to either Mutsora or Mutwanga.

At the park headquarters in Mutsora you pay the necessary fees and arrange guides and porters. Fees are Z 1200 (park entrance), Z 2000 (guide), Z 2000 (guide's porter), Z 2000 per porter for your own gear, Z 100 per person per night (hut fees) and Z 50 (per camera). You pay for all the food but the guide and porters provide their own equipment.

A large, clean, well-furnished room at the park headquarters costs Z 300 and they'll allow three people to sleep in one room. Camping costs the same plus there's a vehicle charge so you might as well stay in the lodge unless you particularly want to camp. Most budget travellers, however, go to Mutwanga, about four km away. Here you will find what has become a legend among the travelling cognoscenti – an abandoned hotel, variously called the *Hotel Ruwenzori* or the *Hotel Engles*, with three swimming pools but no windows or furniture.

No-one, including the Belgian owner or the caretaker, minds if you stay the night and it's completely free (but please leave a tip with the caretaker). You can also camp free of charge. It's a great place and anyone will tell you where it is. The caretaker will even chop wood for you (at a price) and sell you food. Don't forget that tip! When the revolution happened the authorities wouldn't talk sense about finance so the owner let it fall into disuse. The dispute is still going on.

As for going up the Ruwenzoris, the standard trek takes five days. The trip is: Mutsora (1700 metres) to Hut 1 (Kalongi; 2042 metres), about five hours; Hut 1 to Hut 2 (Mahungu; 3333 metres), about 5½ hours; Hut 2 to Hut 3 (Kyondo; 4303 metres), about 4½ hours; Hut 3 to the summit and back to Hut 1, about seven hours; Hut 1 to Mutsora, about four hours. It's possible to stay at Hut 3 if the weather is unfavourable for an assault on the summit.

There's also a fourth hut (Moraine; 4312 metres) on the edge of the moraine but you'll probably be charged an extra Z 100 for this and you have to sign an indemnity releasing the national parks from any responsibility for whatever might happen to you – part of the route is across bare rock with only a rope to hold on to. Properly equipped climbers can also make the ascent on the peaks of Mt Stanley.

There are beds (that have never seen cleaners – but what do you want!) at Huts 1 and 2, but none in the rest. Water is available at or near each of the huts except Hut 2 (where you have to walk two km to find it on occasion). Be warned, too, that the climb from Hut 1 to Hut 2 is the worst of the lot. It's all up hill and hard going between roots and vines. For much of the way the ground is very wet and rain can be frequent, even outside of the wet season.

There are variations on this route and scheduling, but you must arrange these before setting off.

Trekkers and climbers who would like more information on the various routes, as well as detailed notes on the natural history of the mountains, should get hold of a copy of the *Guide to the Ruwenzori* by Osmaston & Pasteur, last published in 1972. The only two places I know where you can still buy this book are West Col Productions, 1 Meadow Close, Goring-on-Thames, Reading, Berks, UK, and Stanfords Map Centre, Long Acre, Covent Garden, London WC2, UK. It costs UK£8.95 (plus postage).

Zambia

This strangely shaped country is one of Africa's most absurd legacies of colonialism. Its borders do not correspond to any single or complete tribal (or even linguistic) area, nor to the boundaries of any organised society which existed here prior to the arrival of the Europeans. As a result, regionalism constantly threatens to tear the country apart and this is deliberately exploited by politicians to further their own ends. It has made it all but impossible for the Zambian leadership to generate any sense of national identity.

This regionalism is one of the main reasons why the president, Kenneth Kaunda, declared a one-party state, though he has also conveniently used it to consolidate his supremacy over the political machinery of the country. Zambia certainly has an elected government but its powers are considerably limited. Kaunda is not only head of both the government and the party but is commander of the armed forces, and has the power to order the arrest and indefinite detention of anyone he regards as a threat.

Kaunda makes all the major policy decisions, and the function of his government is not so much to debate the merits of these decisions but merely how best to implement them. On the other hand, he has been a consistent supporter of African liberation movements and has always been willing to support genuine diplomatic initiatives to prevent bloodshed.

Known before independence as Northern Rhodesia, Zambia was largely the creation of Cecil Rhodes' British South Africa Company. The company laid claim to this part of Africa in the 1890s. Rhodes' purpose in coming here was to search for minerals and recruit cheap labour for South African and Rhodesian mines and plantations. The new colony was slow to develop, even though a railway had been pushed through the territory to the copper mines of Katanga by 1910, and a lead and zinc mine had opened up at Kabwe.

In the late 1920s, however, vast deposits of copper ore were discovered on the Katangan border and by 1940 the mines employed 30,000 workers. Migrant labour became a major feature of the country and, with the imposition of taxes and commercial farming by white settlers on land appropriated from the local people, it was almost obligatory for families in the centre and south of the colony.

The colony was put under direct British control in 1924. Not long after that the white settlers began to agitate for federation with Southern Rhodesia (now Zimbabwe) in order to consolidate their political control over the country.

The federation didn't come about until 1953. Federation was seen clearly by African nationalists for what it really was, and mass demonstrations followed. Considerable pressure was put on the British government to end federation and grant independence, but this took 11 years.

The colonial authorities and their supporters were not keen to see this happen. By the time of independence the British South Africa Company had extracted some US$160 million in royalties from 'ownership' of the mineral resources. The British Treasury had collected about US$80 million in taxes yet spent only US$10 million on the colony. At the same time, some US$200 million of wealth created by Northern Rhodesia had been

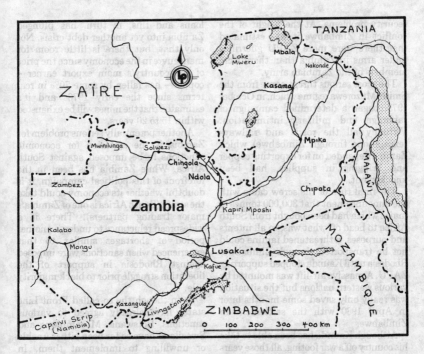

spent or invested in Southern Rhodesia in the 10 years of federation. Zambia still suffers from the effects of this staggering loss of capital and lack of investment.

Kaunda, however, refused to allow the country's poverty or total reliance on the transportation systems of Southern Rhodesia, South Africa and colonial Mozambique and Angola to compromise his commitment to the liberation of white-ruled territories. The Mozambique liberation front, Frelimo, was the first of such groups to be given bases and assistance. Others have included SWAPO (the Namibian liberation front) and both wings of the Zimbabwe Patriotic Front (ZAPU, led by Joshua Nkomo, and ZANU, led by Robert Mugabe).

At the same time, Kaunda kept – and has continued to keep – a close eye on the activities of these liberation fronts and has insisted on their cooperation whenever

diplomatic initiatives are launched. If they refused to cooperate, he has not been above withdrawing support or even deporting them.

Thus, in 1971, ZAPU militants opposed to Nkomo were deported back to Rhodesia (and the Smith regime's prisons), while in 1975 ZANU guerrillas opposed to any diplomatic settlement with Smith were rounded up and imprisoned and the organisation banned from the country (Mozambique subsequently became ZANU's operational base). The more radical members of SWAPO have been subjected to similar constraints and in 1975 Zambia actually intervened in Angola to aid the South African and USA-assisted forces of Jonas Savimbi's UNITA.

Zambia's support for these liberation movements has many times threatened it with financial ruin and near famine. On occasion it has also led to serious internal security problems. At the height of the conflict in Zimbabwe it was estimated that there were more ZAPU guerrillas under arms in Zambia than there were members of the Zambian army.

The most serious threat came from the Smith-Muzorewa regime which, in October 1978, began a determined campaign of sabotage and military intimidation. Virtually all the roads and railways (except one through Zimbabwe) which Zambia depended on for exporting copper and bringing in supplies, had been knocked out.

The final turn of the screw came with the announcement that 300,000 tonnes of maize which had been bought from South Africa to head off what was, to all intents and purposes, a threatened famine could not be transported through Zimbabwe-Rhodesia until Kaunda stopped supporting ZAPU. A massive air-lift was mounted by various western nations but the situation was really only saved some months later in April 1980 with the settlement in Zimbabwe.

Although Kaunda has been able to take his country off a war footing, all those years of sacrifice, fears of armed intervention, saboteurs and spies have left their mark. The economy teeters on the brink of collapse, foreign exchange reserves are almost exhausted, there are serious shortages of food, fuel and other basic commodities, and both the crime and unemployment rate have risen sharply.

In 1986 an attempt was made to diversify the economy and do something about the country's balance of payments by withdrawing basic food subsidies and fixing the kwacha's rate of exchange by holding a weekly auction. While the weekly auction has taken place, the food price rises led to serious country-wide riots in which many people lost their lives forcing Kaunda to restore subsidies.

To some degree, the restoration of prices has contained the social and political unrest but has led to a break with the IMF over nonrepayment of short-term loans and this, in turn, has plunged Zambia into yet another debt crisis. Not only that, but there is little room for manoeuvre in the economy since the price of the country's main export earner – copper – has fallen by some 70% in real terms since the early 1970s and it's estimated that the mines will be exhausted within 15 to 20 years.

Another potentially serious problem for Zambia is the agitation for economic sanctions to be imposed against South Africa. While Zambia has been in the forefront of this political campaign, it is doubtful whether its economy could take the strain (South Africa is one of Zambia's major trading partners). There is a widespread reluctance to undergo another period of shortages similar to that experienced when sanctions were imposed against Rhodesia in support of the liberation struggle prior to black majority rule.

Even though the so-called Front Line states have already agreed to various sanctions, Botswana, Mozambique and Swaziland have so far been either unable or unwilling to implement them. In addition, Zambia has failed to persuade either Malawi or Zaïre to reduce their trading activities with South Africa. Given these circumstances, it's clear that any sanctions imposed by Zambia would be relatively ineffective. Zambia has already been in Pretoria's firing line in the last few years due to the presence of the exiled ANC headquarters in Lusaka.

Facts

Zambia sits on a gently undulating plateau which is between 900 and 1500 metres high. This plateau is studded with lakes and is covered with a mixture of deciduous forest, savannah and marshland. Geographically, it's not spectacular except for one feature – the Victoria Falls. This, of course, is one of the natural wonders of the world and no-one within striking distance would want to miss such a sight.

There are three distinct seasons: cool and dry from May to August, hot and dry from September to October, and rainy from November to April. Average temperatures are 16°C in winter and 24°C in summer.

The population stands at around seven million.

WARNING

Because of the political and economic turmoil, many travellers have reported unpleasant experiences in this country, so you're advised to keep a low profile, especially with police and military personnel. Don't do anything which might even vaguely be regarded as suspicious. This kind of letter is not at all unusual:

Watch out for soldiers and policemen – some are incorruptible – but you can get into some real shit for peanuts. People are rough along the usual tourist-trail but very friendly once you go to the north.

Some advice: don't wear khaki clothes, baggy pants or anything that looks military; don't take pictures of post offices, railway stations, etc; and don't make any arrangements to meet people in front of a post office or railway station in the evening. You're arrested for nothing here. I was writing (in French) a postcard to a girlfriend when a soldier arrested me and took me to the police station. I was accused of spying. They told me I was to be shot and left me scared shitless but later let me go, though the police officer kept my postcard, saying, 'We're keeping this as evidence against you'.

It wasn't over yet. I went back to the station and found it locked. When I tried to open it to get on to the platform I heard someone calling behind me. When I turned round I had a gun in my belly and the same fucking soldier shouting, 'You filthy spy!' Back to the police station where they searched through my backpack. I had a close shave when they narrowly missed the hard currency I hadn't declared at the border. They let me out after two hours. I must say the South African stamp in my passport didn't help matters.

A friend of mine got a butt in the face, another one was beaten up and a third arrested when he took a picture of the sunset near a border post. I also had a friend who offered a cigarette to two soldiers; they arrested him because he was walking around in camouflage trousers near a post office. They beat him up and then left him on the pavement when they discovered his passport.

These sorts of letters are almost always about encounters with police and military personnel. Take care at all times when dealing with these personnel if you are white, and expect to be arrested at any time. Most travellers are at pains to point out that the ordinary people you meet are quite different and if you keep out of the way of police and soldiers you can have a really good time here.

Crime – particularly robbery with violence – is on the increase in Zambia, mainly because the economy is in such a mess and unemployment is high. We've had reports of hitch-hikers being held up at gunpoint by truck drivers. This isn't to say that you won't meet friendly people, but be careful.

VISAS

Visas are required by all except nationals of Commonwealth countries, the Irish Republic, Sweden, Romania and Yugoslavia. If you have South African stamps in your passport (even if you're one of those nationals who don't need a visa), this can cause problems and might even result in entry being refused The one border crossing point where this won't happen is Victoria Falls. There's so much traffic across this border – especially people on day trips from Zimbabwe – that officials don't check passports thoroughly.

In Africa, there are Zambian embassies and high commissions in Addis Ababa (Ethiopia), Cairo (Egypt), Dar es Salaam (Tanzania), Gaborone (Botswana), Harare (Zimbabwe), Kinshasa (Zaïre), Lagos (Nigeria), Lilongwe (Malawi), Luanda (Angola), Maputo (Mozambique) and Nairobi (Kenya). There is also a consulate in Lubumbashi (Zaïre).

Zambian visas can be a hassle to get, especially if you are a USA citizen. A normal tourist visa can take two to three weeks to issue, and up to six weeks in some cases. Few travellers can afford to wait this long so find out from a Zambian embassy if visas are available at the border. The embassy in Harare has been telling Americans they can do this for a long time, and it has been confirmed. What you'll get is a 21-day visa for Kw 2.25. If they tell you that visas are available at the border, ask for a letter stating this so you can show it at the border.

If you're coming in from Zaïre at Kasumbalesa or Mokambo, get your visa at the Zambian consulate in Lubumbashi. Ask for a transit visa which allows double entry, costs Z 15 and is issued on the spot. When you get to the border, the immigration official will ask how long you want to stay and is more than likely to stamp you in for two weeks despite what it says on the transit visa about you only having 48 hours! A tourist visa at the same consulate costs Z 60 and takes 24 hours to be issued.

Visa extensions are very easy to get at immigration on Cairo Rd, next to the post office in Lusaka.

Other Visas
Kenya These cost Kw 15, require two photos and are issued in 24 hours. The high commission is reported to be open every day.

Mozambique A visa costs US$3.50 and is issued while you wait.

Tanzania The high commission is in Ujaama House, United Nations Ave, Lusaka. A visa costs Kw 3, requires two photos and is issued the same day if you are early. Applications are only accepted in the morning (8 am to 12 noon). You will probably be refused a visa if there is any evidence in your passport that you have visited South Africa.

Zaïre One-month, single-entry visas cost Kw 100. Three-month, multiple-entry visas cost Kw 250. Both types of visa require two photos, a letter of introduction from your own embassy and they are issued the same day. The staff are pleasant.

MONEY
US$ 1 = Kw 8.00
UK£ 1 = Kw 10.25

The unit of currency is the kwacha = 100 ngwee. Import/export of local currency is allowed up to Kw 10. Change only the amount of money that you need into kwacha as they're virtually impossible to get rid of outside Zambia.

Zambia floated its currency in 1986 and the currency remains very unstable as each week the government puts up a limited amount for auction. Initially this virtually killed the black market for hard currency, however, the black market has raised its head again and you can expect up to Kw 13 for the US dollar. Be careful – the risks are high. Zimbabwean dollars can be hard to change – even on the Zambian side of the Victoria Falls.

Currency declaration forms are issued on arrival and will be thoroughly checked if you leave Zambia via the Nakonde border post (Zambia-Tanzania). Keep all your bank receipts if you want to avoid hassles.

It's worth shopping around before you change travellers' cheques at a bank. Some, such as Standard Chartered, charge high commission, but others, like Barclays, are more reasonable. It is definitely not safe to have money sent to a bank in Zambia. You must show currency declaration forms and bank receipts when buying airline tickets for domestic or international flights.

Airport departure tax is Kw 10 for domestic flights and Kw 20 for international flights.

ACCOMMODATION

Most of the hotels in Zambia are expensive and the more up-market ones demand payment in foreign currency. Somewhat cheaper are the government rest houses, of which there are a few although most are not in towns where you're likely to be staying. The ones of interest to travellers are at Chipata, Livingstone and Mbala.

In the national parks there are a series of 'catering' and 'noncatering' lodges. Some of these are open all year whereas others are only open during the dry season. They are not cheap, which is a great pity as Zambia has some very extensive national parks with plenty of wildlife.

Whatever else you do, don't attempt to sleep in a railway station unless you want to be woken up by the police or the army indiscriminately wielding rifle butts.

PHOTOGRAPHY

Police and army personnel have a phobia about spies. Keep cameras out of sight, except on game reserves, unless you're looking for trouble.

LANGUAGE

English is the official language. The tribal languages of Bemba, Lozi, Nyanja and Tonga are common in certain parts of the country.

Getting There & Around

AIR

If you want to avoid the numerous road blocks, domestic flights are cheap. A return fare from Ndola to Lusaka costs Kw 235.80.

ROAD

Except along the Lusaka-Lubumbashi road, hitching is relatively easy in Zambia and you shouldn't have much trouble finding lifts. Many of the truckies are

Somalis; some charge for lifts, others don't. There's only one drawback to hitching and that is drunkenness – drunk drivers are a real problem. The roads are littered with stoved-in trucks and cars. If you don't want to end up as one of the corpses at the side of the road, be very careful who you ride with.

Many travellers have warned that it's dangerous to hitch between Lusaka and Kapiri Mposhi because you may be robbed. Often the drivers are in on this racket even though at the time it may appear that they were robbed too.

The majority of roads are badly pot-holed and the breakdown rate is high for both government and private buses. The Lusaka-Chipata road is the exception as it an extremely good modern highway. There's a shortage of tyres for buses in Zambia and bus companies won't provide spares (the drivers apparently sell them). As a result, you can expect long delays due to flat tyres (which are common). When this happens the driver has to wait for their opposite number to come past and take a message to Lusaka requesting a spare. Now that takes some beating!

The most heavily used bus routes (those between Lusaka and the Zimbabwean, Zaïrois, Malawian and Tanzanian borders) are covered later.

One other route which is of importance is that to Mpulungu on Lake Tanganyika. There is a UBZ bus from Lusaka to Mbala on Tuesday and Friday at 5.30 pm. It returns from Mbala on Thursday and Sunday. The trip takes about 18 hours. From Mbala to Mpulungu you'll have to hitch or take a taxi.

There is a minor road between Mpulungu and Tunduma (Tanzania-Zambia border) via Mbala but there's only one or two trucks per week and none during the wet season. To get between the two it's more reliable to make a triangular loop via Kasama as there are buses and plenty of trucks going this way. Try not to get stuck for the night in Kasama as all accommodation is expensive.

If you prefer to take a bus from Lusaka to Kapiri Mposhi (for the TAZARA train to Dar es Salaam) instead of the train, there are daily UBZ buses on the hour from 8 am to 1 pm, and another at 5.30 pm, which cost Kw 7 and take three hours. They leave from the old (district) bus station in Lusaka on the corner of Freedom Way and Kalundwe Rd. Book in advance if you can or call 215911 for reservations. Other buses do this trip from the new bus station but they're said to be unreliable.

There are daily buses in either direction between Lusaka and Livingstone which depart between 5.30 and 6 am, cost Kw 24 and take about seven hours.

If you have problems finding seats on buses, try the 'post buses' which deliver mail but will also take prebooked passengers. Bookings should be made at a post office but get in early as there's heavy demand for seats.

TRAIN
There are two lines of interest to travellers. One is from Kitwe to Lusaka and Livingstone; the other is from Kapiri Mposhi to Dar es Salaam (known as the TAZARA railway).

TAZARA – Kapiri Mposhi to Dar es Salaam
This railway, which was built by the People's Republic of China in the 1960s. It used to run efficiently, and in fact was meant to, as part of its *raison d'être* was to relieve Zambia's total reliance on the railway systems of Zimbabwe and Zaïre for exports and imports.

These days, the line is in a sorry state and trains can be cancelled at short notice, though there are usually three trains a week in either direction. One is a so-called express and the other two are ordinary trains. On these ordinary trains you have to get out at the border, walk across to the Tanzanian side and take another train from there. This isn't necessary on the express train as customs

and immigration formalities are done on board.

The only sure way of knowing what time and on which day the trains depart is to be there with a ticket in your hand. Tuesday evening (for the express) and Monday evening and Friday morning (for the ordinary trains) are the usual departure days but don't count on it. The journey usually takes 36 to 48 hours but it can take 60 if there are problems.

Tickets should be booked in advance at the TAZARA office at Nsefu House near the GPO in Lusaka, or at the station in Kapiri Mposhi. Fares from Kapiri Mposhi to Dar es Salaam are Kw 268 (1st class), Kw 185 (2nd class) and Kw 84 (3rd class) on the express and Kw 254 (1st class), Kw 172 (2nd class) and Kw 70 (3rd class) on the ordinary trains. Student discounts of 50% are available for card holders, but they're sometimes hard to get and perseverance is frequently required.

First class consists of a two-bunk compartment, 2nd class is a six-bunk compartment and 3rd class is wooden benches. Only a masochist would travel any distance in 3rd class. It's not only very crowded and very uncomfortable, but there are thieves to contend with. The only real difference between 1st and 2nd class is the number of people to a compartment.

Meals are usually available and can be served in your compartment. Otherwise, there are plenty of food and drink vendors at stations en route.

Trains from Lusaka to Kapiri Mposhi do not connect with the TAZARA departures so you'll have to stay overnight in Kapiri. Buses from Kapiri Mposhi to the border are usually booked up far in advance so you might as well wait for the train. The trains from Lusaka to Kapiri Mposhi are the same as those from Lusaka to Kitwe (the schedule is given later).

The TAZARA railway crosses the border at Tunduma-Nakonde. This is one of the most notorious border crossings in Africa. Most travellers refer to it with unbridled abuse and you should be prepared for the worst. Very thorough searches right down to your underwear are common – women included – and the officials who do the searching would have no problems finding employment with the Mafia.

If they find anything which you shouldn't have, or you haven't got something which you should have, then you're in for a hard time. Fines and bribes are the order of the day. If they don't find anything which they can give you a hard time about then you may well be stood-over for 'presents'. What they're mainly looking for is money which you can't explain and drugs.

The trains from Kapiri Mposhi to Livingstone depart at 12 midnight and 7 am.

Livingstone to Lusaka & Kitwe

There are two trains per day in either direction. They depart Livingstone at 12 midnight and 7.30 am and take 12 to 15 hours to Lusaka. The trains then take a further 11 to 14 hours to Kitwe. In the opposite direction the express train departs Kitwe at 7 pm arriving in Lusaka around 5.40 am the next day. From Lusaka the trains depart for Livingstone at around 6 am and 2.30 pm.

The trains are often late by up to three hours and, on occasion, even six hours. This means that you must take arrival and departure times at Lusaka as a guide only. Similarly, arrival times at Livingstone and Kitwe (depending on which way you are going) will be affected.

The Lusaka to Kitwe line goes via Kapiri Mposhi so this is the train you take to connect with the TAZARA.

There are three classes: sleeper (two-bunk compartments – same sex or couples only), standard (Pullman-type seats), and economy (wooden benches). Economy is very crowded and not recommended for long journeys. The fares from Lusaka to Livingstone are Kw 47 (sleeper), Kw 34 (standard) and Kw 23.50 (economy); Lusaka to Kitwe costs Kw 41 (sleeper).

Reductions of 50% are available for holders of international student cards though some degree of persistence is sometimes needed to get them. Reservations should be made in Lusaka at the railways offices (tel 218648), Dedan Kimathi Rd. This is a different office from the TAZARA booking office.

BOAT
Lake Tanganyika Ferry

The main ferry on Lake Tanganyika is the historic MV *Liemba* which connects Zambia with Tanzania and Burundi. It's a legend amongst African travellers and first saw service in 1914 as the *Graf von Goetzn* during German colonial days in Tanzania. It was greased and scuttled during WW I to prevent the British getting their hands on it.

In 1927, however, the British colonial authorities raised the boat from the bottom, reconditioned it and put it back into service under its present name. It has been servicing the lake ever since, apart from occasional breakdowns.

There used to be another boat, the MV *Mwongozo*, which doubled up on the *Liemba's* schedule so that there was a twice-weekly service but the *Mwongozo* now only serves Tanzanian towns on the lake.

The *Liemba* runs on a regular weekly schedule though it can be delayed if there is engine trouble or if there is a lot of cargo to be loaded or off-loaded, but it's generally not more than a day late. Assuming there are no delays, it departs Mpulungu at 5 pm on Friday and arrives at Kigoma (Tanzania) at 10 am on Sunday via various other smaller Tanzanian ports. From Kigoma it departs later the same day and arrives at Bujumbura (Burundi) at 7.30 am on Monday. From Bujumbura it departs at 4 pm on Monday and arrives at Kigoma at 8 am on Tuesday. From Kigoma it sets sail later on

Tuesday and arrives at Mpulungu at 8 am on Thursday.

There are three classes: 1st class is a cabin with two bunks, 2nd class is a cabin with four bunks, and 3rd class is deck space on the lower deck. It's worth going 1st or 2nd class to be on the upper deck, but don't expect anything in the way of luxury – it's more quaint than luxurious. Third class is tolerable and rarely crowded between Bujumbura and Kigoma but very crowded between Kigoma and Mpulungu.

The *Liemba* is owned by the Tanzanian Railways Corporation so, if you board at a Tanzanian port you can pay the fare in Tanzanian shillings but you must pay in US dollars if you board at Mpulungu. That makes the journey expensive and, in the past, many travellers have attempted to get around this by paying for a ticket in hard currency from Mpulungu to the first Tanzanian port and then buying a ticket for the rest of the journey in Tanzanian shillings on the boat. This is no longer possible as the authorities are wise to the ruse. They will, however, sell you a ticket to Kipili (the third Tanzanian port) for US$12 and then you can buy another ticket for the rest of the journey in Tanzanian shillings on the boat.

Tickets bought in Mpulungu for the entire journey to Bujumbura cost US$68.50 (1st class), US$50 (2nd class) and US$30 (3rd class).

In Mpulungu tickets must be bought from Cosy Enterprises near the boat jetty; they don't allow you to buy them on the boat.

Meals, beer and soft drinks can be bought on the boat and must be paid for in Tanzanian shillings. Make sure you buy some before you board, otherwise you'll find things relatively expensive. Meals on board are reasonable value but nothing special. A large plate of rice and beef curry costs TSh 120, and a meal with dessert costs TSh 150; a large bottle of Primus beer costs TSh 120.

TO/FROM BOTSWANA

The first part of this journey involves taking a bus or train to Livingstone close to the Victoria Falls. From there a road branches off west to Kazungula (60 km). There's not much traffic along this road so it's better to arrange a lift beforehand at the large truck park in front of the customs building in Livingstone (on the road to Victoria Falls). You can often pick up a lift here as far as Gaborone and even Johannesburg. There's also a daily bus in either direction which leaves Livingstone in the early morning; the fare is Kw 5. The ferry across the Zambezi is free.

TO/FROM MALAWI

There are no longer any direct UBZ buses from Lusaka to Lilongwe via Chipata but there are private bus lines which do the run from the railway bus station in Lusaka. One of them goes on Tuesday at 4 pm and costs Kw 60. You need to book in advance as there's heavy demand for tickets. The journey takes about 18 hours.

It's almost as easy to do the Lusaka to Lilongwe journey in stages. There is a daily UBZ bus in either direction which departs Lusaka at 8 am and arrives in Chipata around 5 pm; the fare is Kw 58. You need to book in advance. Private bus lines also do this run from the Kamwala bus station near the railway station in Lusaka but they're very crowded. From Chipata, take a *matatu* to the Malawian border (Kw 5) and a bus from there to Lilongwe (several daily).

Coming south into Zambia from Tanzania, there's another popular route into Malawi from Nakonde to Chitipa. Buses of the Zambian National Bus Company (based in Nakonde) make the journey from Nakonde to Chitipa three times a week at 7 am on Monday, Wednesday and Friday, but this varies due to breakdowns, and tyre and petrol shortages. The trip takes three to four hours and costs Kw 2.90. Don't attempt this during the wet season as the buses are very unreliable and there will be precious little other traffic.

Sometimes the bus only goes as far as the Zambian border (Nyala) and you must walk the 10 km from there to Chitipa. Try not to walk this stretch alone as robberies have been reported. Buses to the border only cost Kw 1.50. If you have to take a taxi it will cost about Kw 5. The two border posts are about three km apart, and if there's no transport between the two, simply follow everybody else along the clearly marked path through the fields. From the Malawi border post there should be transport to Chitipa but you may have to walk (it's a further six km).

TO/FROM TANZANIA

The main border crossing is Nakonde-Tunduma. Most travellers cross on the TAZARA railway but you can also come by road using buses or hitching on trucks. There are direct buses between Tunduma and Lusaka which take about 24 hours and generally depart Tunduma around 8 am. If you don't want to go all the way to Lusaka, there are buses between Tunduma and Kapiri Mposhi which cost Kw 9.75 and take about 21 hours.

There is a less used border crossing north-east of Mbala near Mpulungu, but there's not much traffic.

You can also get into Tanzania via Mpulungu on the Lake Tanganyika ferry to Kigoma.

TO/FROM ZAÏRE

From Lusaka to Lubumbashi you have a choice of crossing the border either between Chilabombwe and Kasumbalesa or between Chingola and Mokambo. Most travellers take the train from Lusaka to Kitwe and then use a combination of taxis, buses and trucks to get from there to Lubumbashi. There are no direct trains, even though the two railway systems are linked, and Kitwe is the last station for passenger traffic coming from the south. Crossing either border is no problem but you should expect baggage and body searches in Zambia because there is a lot of diamond smuggling going on.

You're advised not to hitch on the road from Lusaka to Lubumbashi because of bandits – robberies are quite common. White drivers will simply speed up rather than risk stopping and getting robbed. It's also not a good idea to be in Chilabombwe at night. Again, robberies are common. Chingola is a safer place to stay for the night.

You'll be lucky to find a bank along the Zambia-Zaïre border area. It's easy to change kwacha into zaïres (and vice versa) on the street. Hotels in the border zone are expensive. You'll be lucky to find anything for less than Z 550, though there are cheaper dormitories in some places.

Kitwe to Chingola

Buses are available for Kw 1.80. If you're heading for Mokambo there is a bus from Chingola for Z 40 (or the equivalent). Between Mokambo and Lubumbashi there is a weekly passenger train (it departs Lubumbashi on Wednesday at 9 am).

If you don't want to go that way, an alternative is to take the bus from Chingola to Chilabombwe which costs Kw 2. It's sometimes possible to pick up trucks from here going all the way to Lubumbashi for around Z 20 to Z 40 (they terminate in the 'Zone Kenya' in Lubumbashi). Otherwise, take a minibus or a taxi for Kw 6 from Chilabombwe to Kasumbalesa, and from there either a taxi (Z 35) or a pickup (Z 25) to Lubumbashi. You can change spare kwacha into zaïres (and vice versa) very easily at Chilabombwe.

TO/FROM ZIMBABWE

For obvious reasons, most travellers go via Victoria Falls. To get there, take a bus or train from Lusaka to Livingstone. There are usually two buses per day in either direction. From Lusaka they leave at 6 am and 4.30 pm, cost Kw 26 and take about 10 hours. There is also a UTC express bus which departs Lusaka on Friday at 10 am and costs Kw 44.

There are direct UBZ buses between Lusaka (Freedom Way terminal) and Harare via Chirundu. They depart at 7 am on Monday, Wednesday and Friday, and at 6 pm on Tuesday, Thursday and Saturday. The fare is Z$46 (or the equivalent in kwacha). There's heavy demand for seats so you need to book in advance. Express Motorways (the Zimbabwean bus company) no longer cover this route.

Both the Zimbabwean and Zambian immigration officials make very thorough searches. To enter Zimbabwe you must have an onward ticket and/or sufficient funds.

Around the Country

CHIPATA

There are three rest houses you can try in town. The government rest house, *Luangwa House*, near the hospital; *Kapata Rest House*, Kapata Ave opposite the bus station; and another near the market.

Another accommodation possibility is the friendly seminary run by Irish priests along the 10-km stretch between the Zambian border post (in Chipata itself) and the Malawian border post. Otherwise there is the more expensive *Chipata Motel* which costs Kw 112 for a double.

CHIRUNDU

This town is on the Zambia-Zimbabwe border.

You can camp at the *Chirundu Hotel* and use their facilities. One traveller warned: 'Do *not* go walking, even down to the river, or you are liable to get eaten. Just sitting by the side of the road you see plenty of big game and every day elephants come to drink out of the swimming pool'.

KACHOLOLA

This is an overnight truckies' stop

between Lusaka and Lilongwe. If you don't want to sleep out, there is the *Comfortable Lodge* which costs Kw 50 a double including breakfast.

KAPIRI MPOSHI

A good place to stay is the *Unity Motel*, about one km from the railway station. It costs Kw 125/150 a single/double with shower and clean toilet. It's adequate but over-priced. You can also camp here for Kw 5 which includes the use of hot showers. The *Kapiri Motel* is more expensive.

The station for the TAZARA railway is about 1½ km from the centre of town.

KARIBA DAM

The Zimbabwean side of the Kariba Dam is the more popular area to stay for most people but you can also stay on the Zambian side. The self-catering *Eagle's Rest Chalets* (tel Siavonga 52 or Lusaka 250981) in Siavonga East has been highly recommended. Camping costs Kw 3 per person per night and there are chalets for Kw 11 per person for the first night, Kw 9.35 for the next three nights and Kw 7.25 for each night after that. The chalets are equipped with bedding, electricity, a refrigerator and a shower and toilet block with hot water. You must bring your own pots, pans and crockery. You can swim nearby in bilharzia-free water. To get to the chalets, take the Siavonga turn-off and follow the signs. It's about four km to the chalets from the main road.

Other than the chalets, there's a *Government Rest House* for Kw 11 per room. There is a bar and meals are served but the place lacks the views and tranquillity of the chalets. There's also a bar and restaurant at the *Lakeside Lodge* in Siavonga West, though rooms are expensive.

KITWE

The two hotels in the centre of town, the *Hotel Edinburgh* and the *Nkana Hotel*, are four-star and two-star respectively so expect corresponding prices. The *Buchi Hotel* is cheaper but it's about six km out of town. Otherwise, try the *Nkara Hotel* which charges Kw 100/150 a single/double but you must pay in foreign currency unless you have bank receipts.

LIVINGSTONE

Livingstone is the Zambian town nearest **Victoria Falls**. Lots of travellers pass through here to soak up some of the magic (and the spray!) of one of the world's most magnificent sights. The falls are about seven km away and there are frequent buses there for Kw 1.50 or taxis for Kw 17. The taxi/bus rank is near the post office. You can also hitch with ease.

In Livingstone itself, have a look at the **Livingstone Museum** adjacent to the tourist office. The museum has an interesting archaeological collection as well as Livingstone paraphernalia – letters, etc. There's also a collection of African maps dating back to 1690. Entry is Kw 0.50. Entry to the **Victoria Falls Museum** is Kw 0.50.

There are **dance performances** every Saturday and Sunday from 3 to 5 pm a few km from Livingstone towards the falls on the right. There is an entry fee of Kw 1.

Tours of the **Musi-O-Tunya National Park** (white rhino and antelope) can be arranged at the International Hotel for Kw 20 per person. You can also arrange boat rides down the Zambezi (to see hippos and elephants) from here.

Day trips across the border to the Zimbabwean side of the falls are subject to

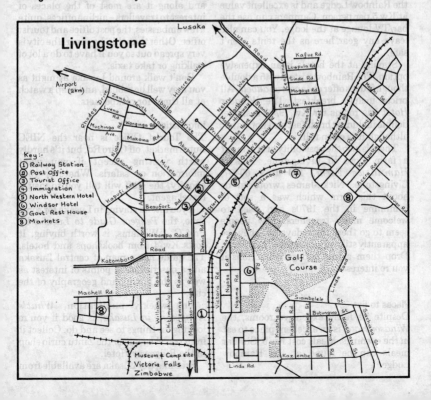

Livingstone

Key:-
1. Railway Station
2. Post Office
3. Tourist Office
4. Immigration
5. North Western Hotel
6. Windsor Hotel
7. Govt. Rest House
8. Markets

Airport (2km)

Lusaka

Golf Course

Museum & Camp site
Victoria Falls
Zimbabwe

normal entry requirements (onward ticket or a returnable deposit of US$1000).

Places to Stay

The cheapest place is the *Government Rest House* which costs Kw 3.50/6.40 a single/double although you may be able to sleep on the floor for less. It's often full but sometimes they pretend it's full when it isn't, so it's best to book first at the tourist office.

The *North Western Hotel* offers rooms for Kw 81/95 a single/double in the old wing and Kw 100/110 a single/double in the new wing.

For campers with their own tents there is a site between the Rainbow Lodge and the International Hotel near the small police post at the falls. It's managed by the Rainbow Lodge and is excellent value at Kw 5 per person. Campers can use the bar/TV lounge at the lodge. You can also leave any gear here as the tents aren't safe.

Staying at the hotels is an expensive option. The Rainbow costs Kw 45 a double though it does offer cheaper *rondavels*. All prices include breakfast. The *Windsor Hotel* has rooms for Kw 19/46 a single/ double including breakfast and hot water, although it is often full.

There is also the possibility of staying at a farm close to Livingstone. This is *Hamungwe Farm*, PO Box 60407, Livingstone. Nick James wrote to us about this farm which was a sort of commune in the 1970s and used to welcome many travellers. Few people seem to go there these days but they are apparently still very keen to see new faces. Drop them a line and get directions if you're interested.

Places to Eat

Despite its fairly expensive rooms, the *Windsor Hotel* is an excellent place to eat in the evenings. Meals cost Kw 9. Similar meals can be found at the Rainbow Lodge.

The *International Hotel* is a ritzy place to eat and drink but make sure you have kwacha – they won't take Zimbabwean dollars and are disdainfully reluctant to change money (cash or cheques) unless you are a guest. The weekend buffets cost Kw 15 and are very good value. A meal of steak and chips will cost Kw 25.

If you're looking for somewhere to go in the evening, try the bar in the *North Western Hotel*, which is an expatriate hang-out.

LUSAKA

Lusaka is a modern city with wide boulevards lined with flowering trees though there are far fewer high-rise blocks than in Harare. The main drag is Cairo Rd and along it are most of the places of interest to travellers – airline offices, quite a few embassies, the post office and tourist office. Other than this, however, the city is very spread out so you'll have to do a lot of walking or take taxis.

Don't walk around Lusaka at night as you may well be robbed, and keep a watch at all times for pickpockets.

Information

The Tourist Office is near the NIEC Supermarket, off Cairo Rd, but it's hardly worth visiting except if you want information on safaris. Whatever your enquiry, the staff will tell you to visit a travel agent.

If you intend staying in Lusaka for some time, the *Peugeot Guide to Lusaka* by Prof G J Williams, is worth buying. It costs Kw 4 from bookshops and hotels. The guide has a map of central Lusaka and a description of points of interest as well as the history and geography of the city.

The weekly publication, *What's Happening in Lusaka*, is good if you're looking for things to see and do. Collect it from travel agents or the Zintu curio shop in the Ridgeway Hotel.

Free maps of Lusaka are available from

KLM. For other maps of Zambia the best place is the Map Sales Office, Department of Lands, Mulungushi House, Independence Ave (opposite the British High Commission). This is the building near the red and white chequered water tower.

If you need a cycle shop try C S Cycles, Chachacha Rd. They don't have anything for lightweight bicycles and stock only Indian and Chinese models.

There is a duty-free shop opposite the post office on Cairo Rd at the junction with Chiparamba Rd. It sells imported cheeses, cigarettes, liquor, beer and many other things. Only hard currency, travellers' cheques and credit cards are accepted.

The airport is 14 km from the city centre.

Embassies Some embassies and high commissions in Lusaka include:

Australian High Commission
    Memaco House, South end Cairo Rd
Botswana High Commission
    2647 Haile Selassie Avenue (tel 25084)
British High Commission
    Independence Ave (tel 216770)
Kenya High Commission
    United Nations Ave (tel 212531)
Tanzania High Commission
    Ujaama House, United Nations Ave (tel 211422)
USA Embassy
    United Nations Ave (tel 214911)
Zimbabwe High Commission
    Memaco House, South end Cairo Rd

Things to See

About 18 km from Lusaka on the road to Kafue is the **Mundawanga Zoo & Botanical Gardens**. Catch a minibus that goes past the gardens from the roundabout at the south end of Cairo Rd. Entry to the the zoo costs Kw 2 and it has mainly Zambian animals. The gardens cost Kw 1 to enter and are very pleasant with lots of thick vegetation, quiet corners, lawns and ponds – good for a picnic or a quiet afternoon.

Places to Stay

There is no accommodation near the bus or train stations. The cheapest place is still the *Sikh Temple* just off our map of Lusaka on Kabile Rd above Katima Mulilo Rd and near the Irish ambassador's house. The old priest is very friendly and quite happy to have travellers. Accommodation is in double rooms or on the classroom floor if there are no beds left. You can't smoke, drink or cook meat and you should leave a donation. Lifts are easy from the temple into the centre but not in the opposite direction. A bus to the showground will take you near the place, otherwise take a taxi from town (Kw 10).

Similar is the *Salvation Army* in the centre of town where you can either sleep on the verandah or camp in the grounds free of charge. There's a high wall around the place and 24-hour security so it's a safe place to stay.

Another place worth trying is the *Hubert Young Hostel*, which caters mainly for teachers. It's very cheap and meals are available, but because of this it's often full. The hostel is next to the Ridgeway Hotel. If you're going there ask for the hotel as the hostel isn't well known.

The *Danish Volunteer Hostel* near Profund House is also worth a try as it welcomes travellers so long as there is no seminar in progress. A room with shower and kitchen costs just Kw 15.

The *YMCA* (tel 252726, 254751), Nationalist Rd, takes both men and women and costs Kw 25/33 a single/double, or you can sometimes sleep on the floor in the common room for less. Basic meals cost Kw 3.50 but you can also do your own cooking if you have the equipment. To get there, take a taxi to the University Teaching Hospital on Nationalist Rd. From there it's a 100-metre walk on the right hand side.

The *YWCA* is also on Nationalist Rd. Accommodation is available for Kw 80 per person including breakfast. Other meals cost Kw 15. There are only six beds and no dormitory so it's almost always full.

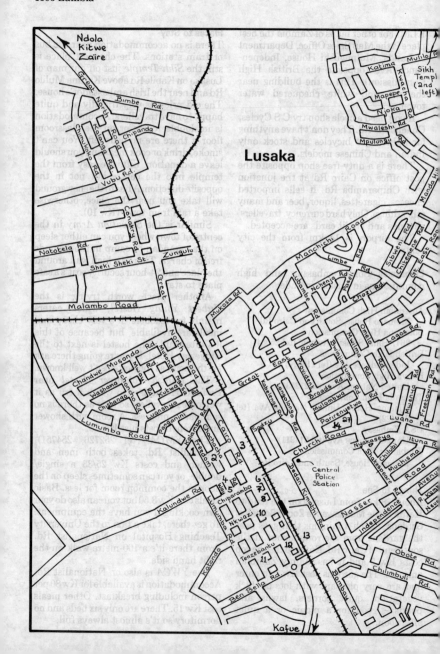

Ndola
Kitwe
Zaïre

Sikh
Templ
(2nd
left)

Lusaka

Central
Police
Station

Kafue

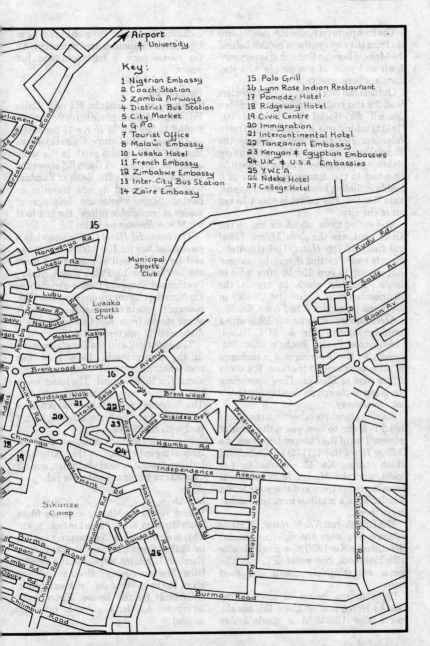

Airport
University

Key:
1 Nigerian Embassy
2 Coach Station
3 Zambia Airways
4 District Bus Station
5 City Market
6 G.P.O.
7 Tourist Office
8 Malawi Embassy
9 Lusaka Hotel
10 Lusaka Hotel
11 French Embassy
12 Zimbabwe Embassy
13 Inter-City Bus Station
14 Zaire Embassy
15 Polo Grill
16 Lynn Rose Indian Restaurant
17 Pamodzi Hotel
18 Ridgeway Hotel
19 Civic Centre
20 Immigration
21 Intercontinental Hotel
22 Tanzanian Embassy
23 Kenyan & Egyptian Embassies
24 U.K. & U.S.A. Embassies
25 Y.W.C.A.
26 Ndeke Hotel
27 College Hotel

Great East Road
Parliament Road
Addis Ababa Drive
Nangwenya Rd.
Lukasu Rd.
Lubu
Kayu Rd.
Nalubutu Rd.
Mushemi
Kasisi
Municipal Sports Club
Lusaka Sports Club
Kudu Rd.
Sable Av.
Chila Rd.
Roan Av.
Busuma Rd.
Brentwood Drive
Avenue
Birdcage Walk
Haile Selassie Avenue
Chikwa Rd.
Kenyatta Avenue
Chisidza Cres.
Brentwood Drive
Presidents Lane
Chimanga
Naumbo Rd.
Government Rd.
Independence Avenue
Manchenkela Rd.
Yotam Mulenga Rd.
Chitukuba Rd.
Sikanze Camp
Mopani Av.
Zimba Rd.
Obote Rd.
Chilumbulu Road
Burma Road
Jacaranda Rd.
Mbita Rd.
Paul Banda Rd.
Burma Road

The camp site on Kafue Rd, two to three km from the city centre, is hidden behind the Makeni Service Station. It is very run-down and most of the people who stay there are permanents.

Outside the city itself, a lot of travellers head for the hostel run by the Zambian Council for Social Development (tel 714412) which was known as the Dutch Volunteer Hostel or sometimes as the 'Dutch Farm'. It's run by Alex and is a very pleasant place to stay. The cost is Kw 6.50 for a bed in the dormitory and Kw 22 a double including breakfast. Lunch/dinner costs Kw 4/6. The hostel is about 10 km out of the city.

Also out of town, about six km on the Kitwe road, are the *Zani Muone Hotel* and the *Hill Top Hotel*. Unfortunately, the only way of getting there is by taxi and that's going to cost Kw 10 after a lot of hassle. Another place to try is the *Mennonite Guest House* (tel 253456) in the Roma township. A bed costs Kw 25.

Accommodation is also available with a farming family, Mr & Mrs Bland, Yieldingtree Farm, Botha's Rust Rd, Lusaka, for Kw 15 per night or in exchange for some work around the farm. It's about 10 km west of Lusaka. They appreciate you going to church on Sunday but that's not compulsory.

Staying anywhere other than the places listed is going to cost you quite a bit of money. Two of the cheaper hotels are the *College Hotel* (tel 217172) on Church Rd which charges Kw 43 a double for full board, and the *Masiye Motel* which is seven km out of town and charges Kw 59 a double. Take a minibus from the market to get there.

The British-run *Ndeke Hotel*, off Haile Selassie Ave near the Intercontinental Hotel, costs Kw 120/156 a single/double with bathroom, hot water, TV, etc. The meals are relatively cheap and good value.

Right in the centre of town is the *Lusaka Hotel*, just off Cairo Rd, but the rooms cost US$45/55 a single/double including breakfast. Payment must be in US dollars (or another hard currency). All the rooms have a bathroom and hot water.

Places to Eat

Zamby's, on Chachacha Rd near Cairo Rd, is a good cheap place to try for curries. Expect to pay Kw 10 to Kw 15 per meal. *Abe's Halal Food Centre*, Cairo Rd across from the GPO, is also good. In the same area, *The Garden*, on Cairo Rd above the shops and opposite the Bank of Zambia, was recommended by one traveller as having 'large wholesome helpings of stodge at reasonable prices'. For fast food try *Mister Rooster* on Cairo Rd.

The *Pamodzi Hotel Coffee Shop* has a good salad bar for Kw 3.50 plus 20% tax and service, as well as curries and roast chicken for Kw 10. *Pete's Steak House*, Northmead Shopping Centre about three km from the city centre on Great East Rd, is one of the main expatriate hang-outs. It offers steaks from Kw 10 and there's a disco after 11 pm (entry Kw 10).

The *Polo Grill* and the *Longhorn*, both in the showgrounds, have good but somewhat pricey food - expect to pay about Kw 15 for a meal. The latter has a bar which is popular with expatriates. The *Ridgeway Hotel* is a good spot for a beer (Kw 3) on the terrace overlooking a pool with crocodiles.

For fruit and vegetables and an interesting experience try the markets off Independence Ave near the bridge, and off Chachacha Rd near Luanshwa Rd.

MBALA

Whilst you're in Mbala, visit the **Moto Moto Museum**, about three km from town. This is a personal collection put together by Father Corbell during his 40 years in Zambia. It relates largely to the Bemba tribe. The fascinating collection has been given to the government with exhibition halls built by the Danes. Entry costs 50 ngwee. Ask for a guide to take you around.

Forty km from Mbala are the **Kalambo Falls**, the second highest in Africa, with a sheer drop of 212 metres. They're difficult to get to unless you team up with someone who has a vehicle and is prepared for a three-day hike, but they're well worth it.

Places to Stay

There's a good *Government Rest House* here. If it's full you can get a bed in a dormitory in a private rest house opposite the bus station.

Other than this there are two hotels – the *Arms Hotel* and the *Grasshopper Inn*. They both cost the same at Kw 25 a double but the latter is much better value.

Outside of Mbala is the *Outward Bound School* where you can camp for Kw 2 or rent a room (if one is available) for Kw 10. You can take food with you or eat in the canteen (dinner costs Kw 8). It's a great spot to stay and highly recommended as it overlooks Mpulungu and Lake Tanganyika. To get there, go 10 km down to the road to Mpulungu where there's a turn-off. From there it's a six-km walk if you can't get a lift.

MPULUNGU

Mpulungu is the Zambian terminal for the Lake Tanganyika ferry, the MV *Liemba*. Tickets for the ferry should be bought from Cosy Enterprises on the day of departure.

Places to Stay

The government rest house, known as the *Bwananyina*, is next to the old church and is a good place to stay but you are supposed to have a letter from the district superintendent in Mbala in order to do this. It's often full but, if that's the case, ask the caretaker if he can help out. The charge is Kw 2.75 per person. The bathroom is communal but has hot water. You can also camp in the grounds for 15 ngwee with use of toilet and bathroom, but watch out for thieves. The rest house is in a beautiful position overlooking Lake Tanganyika.

Also cheap is *Fisher's Inn*, a government-run hostel for fishermen which costs just Kw 1.50 for a bed. To stay here you first have to see the helpful district officer, Mr Kababwe, in his office near the harbour.

There's another *Rest House* by the market. It costs Kw 13.50 a double and is often full.

The best place in Mpulungu, however, is the *Nkupi Lodge* run by Kathy & Denish Budhia which caters especially for backpackers. It's a little way from the centre of town on the waterfront and offers *rondavels* and good wholesome cooking. It's very clean and is a great place to stay. Camping is also possible for a small fee. Many travellers recommend this place.

If everything is full, you could head off for the *Outward Bound School*, 30 km from Mpulungu on the road to Mbala (details under Mbala).

NAKONDE

This small town on the border between Zambia and Tanzania isn't exactly the world's most riveting spot. In fact, it's been described by more than one traveller as 'the arsehole of Africa'. Probably the only reason you'd stay here is if you want to go to Malawi and there doesn't happen to be any transport, or you're coming the other way and can't get across the border that evening.

A mobile bank comes to town once a week but you can also change money near the market and in the guesthouses.

Places to Stay

The *Government Rest House*, about 500 metres from the border on the main road, costs Kw 7.25 per bed but has been described as a 'dirty smelly building'.

The *Kalinda Rest House* costs Kw 6 a double plus 10% tax (you can put three people in a double). To reach the Kalinda, go about 100 metres from the border on the main road and then turn right, keeping on for another 50 metres.

The *Ikumbi Rest House*, about 50 metres from the border on the main road, costs Kw 8.50 a double. Water often runs out in the guesthouses.

National Parks

Zambia's national parks are nowhere near as easy to visit on a budget as those in Zimbabwe, South Africa and East Africa. This is mainly because of transport difficulties and the cost of accommodation once you actually get there.

In Zambia the emphasis seems to be on people with a lot of money to spend. This is a pity as there's plenty of game to see and some of the parks are quite extensive. In fact, there's precious little worth seeing in Zambia, apart from Victoria Falls and the national parks, so it really is time the government did something about catering for people on a budget.

Entry to the national parks costs Kw 2 per vehicle plus 75 ngwee per person. Further details are available from the tourist offices in Lusaka, Livingstone or Ndola.

Various travel agencies in Lusaka and Livingstone organise safaris to the national parks so if you want to visit them, get a group together and make enquiries. Zambian residents can pay for safaris in kwacha so if you know anyone, it's worth getting them to book for you, otherwise you must pay in hard currency. Booked through a resident, you should be paying around Kw 40 per night which includes the cost of *banda*, transport, a cook (excellent) but excluding food.

If you want to stand any chance of visiting **Kafue Gorge**, you must get permission first from ZESCO headquarters in Lusaka. This is because the hydroelectric power station there is a sensitive installation and the government is concerned about spies and saboteurs. If you just get permission from ZESCO in Kafue and from the Kafue police, you will be sent back.

The **botanical & zoological gardens** of Munda Wanga at Chilanga on the road to

Kafue are well worth a visit. The staff are helpful and there are not too many people during the week. Entrance is Kw 2 plus Kw 1.50 if you have a camera. It's only a short journey from Lusaka. Some of the animals and birds are free-range and these include antelope, baby elephants, camels, crested cranes and storks.

Places to Stay - Kafue National Park There are the two inexpensive, self-catering camps in Kafue National Park which are run by the Wildlife Conservation Society of Zambia (tel 254226), PO Box 30255, Lusaka, off Brentwood Drive near the Lusaka Central Sports Club. The *David Shepherd Lodge* on the edge of Lake Iteshi-teshi is open all year and costs Kw 15 per person per night and can be reached along a paved road from Lusaka. The other camp is *Kafwala Camp* north of Kafue National Park on the banks of the Kafue River. It's only open in the dry season and costs Kw 12.50 per person per night, and you need to bring your own food. Both these camps should be booked in advance.

In Kafue there are three non-catering camps: Chunga (10 beds, open all year), Kalala (six beds, open June to October), and Lufupa (six beds, open June to October).

Across the river from Chunga camp is the *Safari Village* which has a bar and restaurant so, if you're running low on food, you can eat there for Kw 30 per meal. The nearest place to Chunga camp where you can buy food (other than meals at the Safari Village) is Mumbwa, 125 km away. There are always plenty of baboons, impala, hippopotamuses and crocodiles at Chunga camp, and the manager, Crispin, offers game drives and boat rides for Kw 30 per person.

Other than these, there is a choice of self-catering and catering lodges in Kafue which are operated by the government, but they're not cheap.

Places to Stay – South Luangwa National Park

In South Luangwa there are three non-catering camps: Lion (six beds, open June to October), Big Lagoon (12 beds, open June to October), and Nsefu (12 beds, open June to October).

There are some self-catering and catering lodges which are operated by the government but they are not cheap.

THE COPPER BELT

It used to be possible to tour one or another of the mines in the copper belt along the Zaïre border but it is difficult to get permission these days. You must first make a written application to the Director of Public Relations, ZCCM Ltd, 74 Independence Ave, PO Box 30048, Lusaka.

When making an application, make sure that you stress some particular interest or experience, and give them at least three weeks notice. It's better to tell them that you will arrange your own transport and accommodation. If you want to take photos, make this clear in the letter because permission for anything, especially photography, has to come from the top in this country.

Zimbabwe

Zimbabwe has had a long history of civilisation, as the massive stone structures at Great Zimbabwe, Khami and Dhlo-Dhlo testify. The first of the major civilisations to establish themselves were the Mwene Mutapa (or Monomatapas as the Portuguese called them). By the mid-1440s, King Mutota had welded together an empire, which included almost all the Rhodesian plateau and large parts of what is today Mozambique. The empire's wealth was based on agriculture and small-scale industries like textiles, gold, copper and iron smelting. Trade was conducted with Arab and Swahili merchants along the coast and these people were regular residents of the empire's trading towns.

The arrival of the Portuguese in the early 16th century destroyed this trade and led to a series of wars with the Europeans, which gradually weakened the empire to the point where it was in rapid decline by the beginning of the 17th century. While this was going on, another empire, the Rozwi to the west of the Mwene Mutapa, was gradually expanding and taking advantage of the Mwene Mutapa decline to gain control of external trade. By 1690 they had driven the Portuguese off the plateau and taken over much of the land once controlled by the Mwene Mutapa. The next two centuries were peaceful and prosperous, and it was during this time that the centres of Great Zimbabwe, Khami and Dhlo-Dhlo reached their peak.

The Rozwi Empire met its end in the mid-19th century as a result of the turmoil in the Transvaal and Natal. Mzilikazi, one of the military commanders of the expansionist Zulu state, quarrelled with Shaka and, to get out of the reach of Shaka's vengeance, led his splinter group north over the Limpopo River and into Matabeleland. The Rozwi were no match for the Zulu and the empire was shattered.

Mzilikazi set up his capital near present-day Bulawayo and was succeeded in 1870 by his son, Lobengula. Because of increasing pressure from European settlers, Lobengula turned out to be the last of the Ndebele rulers.

In 1888 a treaty was signed with the British South Africa Company allowing them to mine gold in the kingdom. Having got a foot in the door, however, the company began to send in increasing numbers of settlers, and war broke out with the Ndebele in 1893. It was an unequal contest against superior arms and, following the defeat of the Ndebele, European immigration began in earnest. By 1904 there were some 12,000 settlers in the country, and double that number by 1911.

The conflict between Black and White came into sharp focus after the 1922 referendum in which the whites chose to become a self-governing colony rather than be included in the Union of South Africa. Although the colony's constitution was, in theory, nonracial, the franchise was based on financial considerations effectively excluding most blacks from the vote.

White supremacy was further enhanced in 1930 by a land act which excluded Africans from ownership of the best farming land and by a labour law in 1934 which prohibited them from entering skilled trades and professions. The effect of these measures was to force Africans to work on white farms, mines and factories at subsistence wages.

Zimbabwe

Abysmally poor wages and conditions led to the gradual radicalisation of the African labour force. By the time Southern Rhodesia, Northern Rhodesia and Nyasaland were federated in 1953, the mining and industrial concerns were in favour of a more racially mixed middle class as a counterweight to the more radical elements in the labour force.

White farmers, skilled workers and businesspeople, however, regarded this as a threat to their privileged position. When Garfield Todd, the Federation's prime minister, attempted to satisfy some of the more moderate African demands, he was thrown out. The same thing happened to his successor in 1962 following the approval of a new constitution which envisaged a vague African-European parity distant in the future. Even this was too much for the white farmers and workers.

African impatience with the prospects of constitutional change resulted in the formation of a number of political parties and sporadic acts of sabotage. Foremost among the parties was the Zimbabwe African People's Union (ZAPU) under the leadership of Joshua Nkomo. It was soon joined by the Zimbabwe African National

Union (ZANU), a breakaway group under the leadership of Ndabaningi Sithole which was dissatisfied with the pace of progress under Nkomo's leadership. In the aftermath of the Federation's break-up in 1963 – which paved the way for the independence of Northern Rhodesia (Zambia) and Nyasaland (Malawi) – both ZAPU and ZANU were banned and most of the leadership was imprisoned.

Meanwhile, in response to Britain's refusal to grant independence to South Rhodesia until an accommodation could be worked out between Black and White, Ian Smith had taken over leadership of the Rhodesian Front party and there was overwhelming White support for a unilateral declaration of independence (UDI). In the election of May 1965, Smith's party picked up every one of the 50 seats in the government and UDI was declared in December.

Britain reacted by declaring Smith's action illegal and imposed economic sanctions in an attempt to bring him to heel. The UN eventually voted to make these sanctions mandatory in 1968, but with South Africa openly assisting Smith, and with Mozambique still under colonial rule, the loopholes were enormous. The sanctions were ignored by most western countries, including certain British companies.

What was intended to bring Smith to the negotiating table within weeks was an almost complete failure. In fact, under laws passed to restrict the export of profits and impose strict import controls, the Rhodesian economy actually grew with the expansion of import substitution manufacturing. Under such circumstances Smith was in no mood to make any concessions and the various attempts by the British government to get him to revoke UDI and accept Black majority rule were futile.

Given such intransigence, both ZANU and ZAPU opted for guerrilla warfare. ZANU took the initiative in 1966, but it wasn't until Frelimo had liberated substantial areas of neighbouring Mozambique that they were able to set up bases there and escalate the conflict. In the meantime, ZAPU set up its bases in Zambia. The guerrilla raids, which gradually struck deeper and deeper into the country with ever-increasing ferocity, led to an alarming increase in White emigration from Rhodesia and the abandonment of many of their farms in the eastern part of the country.

The overthrow of the fascist regime in Portugal in 1974, which led to the independence of both Angola and Mozambique in the following year, was the single most important event to alter totally the balance of power in the area. It forced both the USA and South Africa to reappraise their attitude towards southern Africa, if they were to protect their economic and political interests.

Both countries began to pressure Smith into accommodating the nationalists. With assistance from Kaunda's Zambia, the various nationalist groups were persuaded to come together under the united front of Muzorewa's African National Congress, and Smith was persuaded to release from detention the most important leaders of the nationalist movement – Nkomo, Sithole and Mugabe among them.

As far as Smith was concerned, this was just an exercise in window-dressing and the talks broke down amid an atmosphere of recrimination between Smith and the nationalists on the one hand, and between the various nationalist leaders on the other. Mugabe, meanwhile, made his way to Mozambique where he replaced Sithole as the leader of ZANU.

Other attempts were made to bring the two sides together, notably at Geneva when ZAPU and ZANU were induced to form an alliance known as the Patriotic Front, while Sithole and Muzorewa led separate delegations. Again the talks were a failure, and though the Patriotic Front survived in name, the differences were as strong as ever.

Not long after the Geneva conference, Smith, faced with wholesale White emigration and a collapsing economy, was forced to try a new ploy: this was an 'internal settlement'. Both Sithole and Muzorewa were induced to join a so-called transitional government in which the whites were to be guaranteed 28 out of the 100 seats in the government plus a veto over all legislation for the next 10 years; a guarantee for all White property and pension rights; and White control of the armed forces, police, judiciary and civil service. An amnesty was also declared for Patriotic Front guerrillas. The effort was a dismal failure. Indeed, the only thing which happened was an intensification of the war. To salvage the settlement, Smith entered into secret negotiations with Nkomo, offering to ditch both Sithole and Muzorewa, but Nkomo proved intransigent.

Finally, with support for Smith waning among the White population and the destruction of the country's largest fuel depot by guerrillas of the Patriotic Front, Smith was forced to call a general election of both Black and White sections of the population and hand over leadership of the country to Muzorewa, but on much the same conditions as the previous transitional government. Diplomatic recognition of the new government of what was now called Zimbabwe-Rhodesia was withheld by all but a tiny handful of countries but that didn't prevent the Rhodesian armed forces from mounting devastating raids on suspected guerrilla and refugee camps in both Mozambique and Zambia.

The Commonwealth conference in Lusaka in 1979 eventually paved the way for a Black majority government when an agreement was reached between British Prime Minister Thatcher, Kaunda of Zambia and Julius Nyerere of Tanzania. A conference was to be held in London between the two leaders of the Patriotic Front – Nkomo and Mugabe – and the leaders of Zimbabwe-Rhodesia – Muzorewa and Smith. Kaunda and Nyerere were to lean on the Patriotic Front and Thatcher was to lean on Smith. After 14 weeks of talks an agreement was reached whereby 20 seats in the new government would be reserved specifically for whites and the remainder for blacks. In the carefully monitored elections which followed, Mugabe's ZANU picked up 57 seats, Nkomo's ZAPU 20 and Muzorewa's UANC only three. Thus Zimbabwe finally joined the ranks of Africa's independent nations in April 1980 under an internationally recognised Black majority government headed by Robert Mugabe.

Despite the long and bitter struggle, Mugabe, a committed Marxist thinker, displayed remarkable restraint in dealing not only with the White section of the population but Home Affairs (though Mugabe retained command of the armed forces), and whites were made Minister of Commerce & Industry and Minister of Agriculture.

It was a promising start, but the honeymoon quickly soured. There was a resurgence of the rivalry between ZANU and ZAPU and, after armed conflicts between supporters of the two parties, Mugabe ordered the arrest of five prominent Nkomo supporters in 1980 and demoted Nkomo in 1981. Another event which inflamed tension was the arrest of the Minister of Manpower Planning, Edgar Tekere, for the alleged murder of a white farmer, and though he was eventually found not guilty he was not offered another cabinet post.

More recently, Nkomo was accused of plotting to overthrow the government and there was a resurgence of guerrilla activity in Matabeleland, the area from which ZAPU draws the bulk of its support. In early 1983 Mugabe sent in the North Korean-trained Fifth Brigade to quell these disturbances, but it appears they went berserk. Over 1000 people were reported dead in an orgy of killing in which whole villages were gunned down and prominent members of ZAPU were systematically eliminated. The conflict was essentially a tribal one between the majority Shona (largely ZANU supporters) and the minority Matabele (largely ZAPU supporters). Nkomo meanwhile fled to England and was to remain there until Mugabe publicly guaranteed his safe return.

Taking a leaf from Kaunda's and Nyerere's books and from the revolutionary governments of Angola and Mozambique, Mugabe next embarked on transforming Zimbabwe into a one-party state. Although the process has some way to go it is well on the way to completion. What has accelerated the process is the abolition in mid-1988 of the 20 seats guaranteed to the whites in the government. There's little doubt that this event will induce further emigration of the more die-hard white settlers, but there's no reason why it should be any more catastrophic than what happened in Kenya following independence. Mugabe may be a Marxist, but he's also a pragmatist and is in no hurry to see a wholesale departure of whites.

Facts

GEOGRAPHY & CLIMATE

Zimbabwe sits on a high plateau between the Limpopo and Zambezi rivers, and has a range of mountains in the east along the border with Mozambique. It has an exceptionally healthy climate with temperatures ranging from 22°C on the plateau to 30°C in the Zambezi Valley during the summer, and from 13°C to 20°C in the winter.

PEOPLE

The two main ethnic groups are the Shona (about 75% of the population) in the centre and the east, and the Ndebele (about 18%) in the west. The population is around 8.3 million.

WARNING

There was a lot of anti-government ZAPU

guerrilla activity in the early 1980s between Bulawayo and Victoria Falls, and a group of western travellers in an overland tour truck were kidnapped there in 1982. They were never found, though graves purporting to contain their remains were reported to have been found in 1985.

Since 1985, however, the situation has calmed down and there's not likely to be a resurgence of this sort of activity following the accord between ZANU and ZAPU on the creation of a one-party state. Nevertheless, you are advised to keep an eye on the situation and avoid hitchhiking in north-west Zimbabwe – use public transport instead.

VISAS

Visas are required by all except nationals of Commonwealth countries, EC member countries, Denmark, Japan, Norway, Sweden, Switzerland and the USA.

Immigration officials are strict about onward tickets, though if you have one they rarely ask to see how much money you have. MCOs are not acceptable. The only way to get into Zimbabwe without an onward ticket is by rail from Botswana. However, immigration will still want to see your money and/or credit card (and they check the expiry date on the card).

At any other point of entry, if you don't have an onward ticket you have to either buy one on the spot, or leave a returnable deposit in cash or travellers' cheques. The deposit varies but is usually US\$1000 or the equivalent. If you do have to leave a deposit, don't count on getting it back in the currency you paid. Some people have been given Zimbabwe dollars just before they were due to leave – and that's bad news because you can't take out more than Z\$20!

Many travellers have been turned back at the Zambia-Zimbabwe border because they didn't have 'sufficient funds' or an onward ticket. The Chirundu post is particularly bad. Even travellers with a Eurocard and a letter from a bank manager or US$900 to show have been refused entry. Patient and friendly persuasion can sometimes overcome this, but don't count on it. An airline ticket with Johannesburg as the starting point is acceptable as an onward ticket. Also, if coming from South Africa, a return Johannesburg to Bulawayo and Harare bus ticket with Express Motorways is acceptable.

Credit cards and sometimes even a cheque book backed by a cheque card are acceptable as a substitute for cash or travellers' cheques.

To avoid red tape, don't write 'journalist' on your entry form otherwise they'll give you 24 hours to get a temporary employment permit. On the other hand, this could be quite useful. The 14-day visa/work permit is no trouble to get (takes about two hours), and you're issued a press card. Immigration is on the 7th floor, Liquende House, Baker Ave, Harare. They're efficient and pleasant people.

You can go into Zambia for the day at Victoria Falls without a visa. Zimbabwean customs will issue a permit (Z$2.50) for the day so that you don't have to go through exit formalities. If you are carrying more than Z$20, however, you must leave the excess with customs. A receipt will be issued and there are no problems about reclaiming it when you return. Zambian customs will stamp your passport, but it's purely a formality. There are no searches, awkward questions about where else you have been, etc.

Attempting to go in the opposite direction (Zambia to Zimbabwe) for the day at Victoria Falls, however, is usually subject to normal entry requirements – an onward ticket and/or sufficient funds. This doesn't happen to everyone but, to avoid disappointment, you might as well assume it is going to happen.

In Africa, there are Zimbabwean embassies in Addis Ababa (Ethiopia), Algiers (Algeria), Dakar (Senegal), Dar es Salaam (Tanzania), Gaborone (Botswana), Lagos (Nigeria), Lilongwe (Malawi), Lusaka (Zambia), Maputo (Mozambique) and Nairobi (Kenya),

Other Visas
Kenya The Kenyan High Commission (tel 790847) is at 95 Park Lane, Harare. Three or six-month visas cost Z$10, require two photographs and are issued while you wait.

Mozambique The Mozambique Embassy (tel 790837) is at 152 Rhodes Ave, Harare. Visa regulations change from time to time depending on the internal security situation but, assuming there are no problems, a transit visa costs Z$12, requires three photos and takes 24 hours to issue.

Tourist visas are harder to come by and may need persistence unless you are flying into Maputo. The embassy is open Monday to Friday from 8 am to 12 noon.

Nigeria The Nigerian High Commission (tel 790765) is at 36 Samora Machel Ave, Harare. Entry permits are free but you need one photo and they take three days to issue.

South Africa Visas are available from the South African Diplomatic & Trade Mission (tel 707901), Temple Bar House, 39 Baker Ave, Harare. It's very busy so arrive early in the morning. A visa takes three to five (or more) working days to issue and requires two photos. They will issue a loose-leaf visa if a brief letter giving reasons for such is included.

Tanzania The Tanzanian High Commission (tel 724713) is at Ujamaa House, 23 Baines Ave on the corner of Blakiston St, Harare. Visas cost Z$16, require two photos and are issued in three hours. You must use the visa within three months. Your passport will be thoroughly checked for South African stamps and you may be asked where your 'other' passport is!

Zaïre The Zaïre Embassy (tel 45827) is at 5 Pevensey Rd, off Enterprise Rd, about eight km from the centre. Three-month, multiple-entry visas cost Z$15, require two photos and are issued the same day – often within 15 minutes. The embassy is open Monday to Friday from 8 am to 3 pm.

Zambia The Zambian High Commission (tel 790851) is on the 6th floor, Zambia House, Union Ave near Julius Nyerere Way. USA passport holders have been having a hard time getting visas for Zambia and they can take two to three weeks to issue (four to six weeks in some cases!). You will be told at the embassy in Harare, however, that 21-day visas are obtainable at the border for Kw 2.25. Most have found this to be true but it might be a good idea to get a letter from them confirming it so that you don't run into problems later on.

Border Post Hours

Beitbridge

6 am to 8 pm daily

Plumtree, Victoria Falls, Kariba, Chirundu, Mutare, Nyamapanda, Kazungula

6 am to 6 pm Monday to Friday, and
8 am to 12 noon on Saturday

Working in Zimbabwe

It's still relatively easy to find work in Zimbabwe in certain trades. Employers will usually fix you up with work permits (up to two years). Teaching is one of the easiest jobs to get, especially in the sciences. The pay is entirely in Zimbabwean dollars and fairly low. Pay can be months in arrears.

Private colleges are a better bet as far as pay is concerned (usually about twice the government rates). Paid leave at both types of school is usually four months per year. The two best colleges in Harare are Speciss College, Rhodes Ave, and ILSA Independent College, Fife Ave. If you have a Higher School Certificate or 'A' levels you can teach to this level in government schools, but private colleges demand degrees.

Other than this, the private sector is always looking for computer and engineering staff. Try Central African Pharmaceuticals.

MONEY

US$ 1 = Z$1.80   (official rate)
UK£ 1 = Z$3.20   (official rate)

The unit of currency is the Zimbabwe dollar (Z$) = 100 cents. The import or export of local currency is limited to Z$20. If you only have travellers' cheques you won't be issued with a currency declaration form on arrival. If you're bringing in cash, however, insist that they issue you with one. Without this form you are only allowed to take out US$20 in foreign notes when you leave. Customs may ask to see bank receipts as well when you leave so don't throw these away. There may be body searches for currency at Harare Airport when you leave, but there are reportedly no such hassles when leaving by road from Bulawayo to Francistown (Botswana).

Banking hours are 8.30 am to 2 pm on Monday, Tuesday, Thursday and Friday, 8 am to 12 noon on Wednesday and 8.30 to 11 am on Saturday.

Although there is a black market, the transaction isn't as simple as elsewhere in Africa. If often involves using a resident's Zimbabwean dollars held in a bank account. You repay them in hard cash (US dollars or rand). On this basis it's possible to get up to Z$3.20 to the US dollar. The best rates are in Harare.

It used to be possible to bring in rands and sell them for 2½ to three times what you paid for them in South Africa (buy for R 500 in South Africa, sell for Z$1300 in Zimbabwe), but this is now officially illegal so you have to be careful who you approach if you're going to do it. Kenyan shillings are not accepted for exchange at the banks, but Barclays Bank will exchange US dollar travellers' cheques for

US dollars cash. However, they only cash up to US$20 and make an entry in your passport, so you can only do it once.

If you're travelling north from Botswana it's worth stopping in Tonota, a large village 35 km south of Francistown. Along the main road the ladies who operate the craft stalls under a large shady tree will gladly convert pula or rand to Zimbabwean dollars. The ladies are all Mazezuru, a religious group which dresses completely in white.

You must produce bank receipts when buying airline tickets (but not train tickets), even for Botswana or South Africa. You can reconvert up to Z$100 into hard currency when leaving the country if you have sufficient bank receipts to cover that amount.

There's an 18% sales tax on all commodities including airline tickets but excluding raw foodstuffs.

Bringing in cheap digital watches and selling them for a substantial profit used to be a way of topping up funds, but it's hardly worth it any longer as too many of them have been brought in from Botswana. Audio and video tapes, colour film and cameras are still in demand, however. Cameras usually fetch twice their original price. Whisky also fetches a good price. Duty-free allowances are five litres of alcoholic beverages, not more than two litres of which can be spirits.

Petrol costs Z$1.16 per litre but you cannot buy it on Sunday.

The airport departure tax for international flights is US$10 and must be paid for in foreign currency at the airport. You can, however, buy the stamp in advance at a bank with Zimbabwe dollars.

PHOTOGRAPHY

Colour negative film can be difficult to find in Zimbabwe and slide film is almost unobtainable. What you may come across in some photography shops in Harare is slide film made in East Germany but there's rarely anything other than ASA 100 available. A cartridge of 36 exposures goes for around Z$19.50.

Be very careful of taking any photos of army camps, road blocks, dams, police stations, post offices, etc.

LANGUAGE

English is the official language. African languages spoken are Ndebele and various Shona dialects.

English	Shona	Ndebele
good morning	*mangwanani*	*livuke njani*
good afternoon	*masikati*	*litshonile*
good evening	*manheru*	*litshone njani*
How are you?	*makadii?*	*linjani/kunjani?*
good/very well	*ndiripo zvangu*	*skhona/ngiyaphila/siyaphila*
bad	*handisi kunzwa zvakanaka*	*angiphilanga kuhle*
thank you	*ndatenda/mazvita*	*ngiyabonga/siyabonga kakulu*
please	*ndapota*	*uxolo*
goodbye	*chisarai zvakanaka*	*lisale sesihamba/lisale kuhle*
welcome	*titamberei*	*siyaalemukela*
danger	*ngozi*	*mingozi*
friend	*shamwari*	*mngane/umngane*
sorry	*ndine urombo*	*uxolo*
excuse me	*pamusoroi*	*uxolo/ngixolela*
man/men	*murume/varume*	*indoda/amadoda*
woman/women	*mukadzi/vakadze*	*umfazi/abafazi*

mr/sir	*changamire*	*umnimzana*
madam	*mudzimai/madzimai*	*inkosikazi/amankazan*
child/children	*mwana/vana*	*umtwana/abantwana*
boy/boys	*mukomana/vakomana*	*umfana/abafana*
girl/girls	*musikana/vasikana*	*inkazana/amankazana*
how much?	*i marii*	*yimalini*
expensive	*zvinodhura*	*kuyadula*
shop	*chitoro*	*isitolo*
money	*mari*	*imali*
where	*kupi*	*ngaphi*
why	*sei*	*ngani*
when	*rini*	*nini*
how	*sei/nei*	*njani*
beer	*doro/whawha*	*utshwala*
bread	*chingwa*	*isinkwa*
eggs	*mazai*	*amaqanda*
fish	*hove*	*inhlanzi*
fruit	*muchero/michero*	*izithelo*
meat	*nyama*	*inyama*
milk	*mukaka*	*ucago*
potatoes	*matapiri*	*amagwili*
rice (cooked)	*mupunga wakabikwa*	*irice ephikiweyo*
salt	*munyu*	*isaudo*
vegetables	*muriwo*	*umbhida/imbhida*
water	*mvura*	*amanzi*
ice/cold	*chando/hunotonhora*	*okuqandayo*
hot	*kupisa*	*kuyatshisha*
small/large	*diki/guru*	*okuncane/ncinyane*
another/more	*rimwe*	*futhi/okunye*
enough	*zvakwana*	*kwenele*
What time is it?	*dzava nguvai*	*yisikhati bani*
now	*zvino*	*khathesi*
morning	*mangwanani*	*ekuseni*
evening	*manheru*	*ntambama*
afternoon	*masikati*	*emini yantambama*
today	*nhasi*	*lamhia*
yesterday	*nezuro*	*izolo*
tomorrow	*mangwana*	*kusasa*
time/hour	*nguva*	*isikhati*
night	*usiku*	*ebusuku*
day	*kwakachena*	*emini*
Monday	*muvhuro*	*umvulo/ngumvulo*
Tuesday	*chipiri*	*ngolwesibili*
Wednesday	*chitatu*	*ngolwesithathu*
Thursday	*china*	*ngolwesine*
Friday	*chishanu*	*ngolwesihlanu*

Saturday	mugovera	ngesabatha
Sunday	svondo	ngesonto
1	potsi	okukodwa
2	piri	okubili
3	tatu	okuthathu
4	ina	okune
5	shanu	okuyisihlanu
6	tanhatu	okuyisithupha
7	nomwe	okuyisikhombisa
8	tsere	okuyisitshiyangalo mbili
9	pfumbamwe	okuyisitshiyangalo lunye
10	gumi	okuli tshumi

leopard	mbada	ingwe
rhinoceros	chipembere	ubhejane
buffalo	nyati	inyathi
lion	shumba	isilwane/ngwenyama
elephant	nzou	indhlovu
baboon/monkey	gudo/bveni	indwangu/inkawu
zebra	mbizi	idube
impala	mhara	impala
giraffe	swiza	intundla
hyena	bere	impisi
wart hog	njiri	ingulube yeganga
hippo	mvuu	imvubu

Getting There & Around

NAME CHANGES

Zimbabwe has been going through a process of Africanising its place and street names. This may be confusing if you're using old editions of maps. The following is a list of some old and new names:

new	old
Chegutu	Hartley
Chimanimani	Melsetter
Chinhoyi	Sinoia
Chipinge	Chipinga
Chivhu	Enkeldoorn
Dete	Dett
Esigodini	Essexvale
Guruwe	Sipolilo
Gweru	Gwelo
Harare	Salisbury
Hwange	Wankie

Marondera	Marandellas
Mashava	Mashaba
Masvingo	Fort Victoria
Mberengwa	Belingwe
Mhangura	Mangula
Murewa	Mrewa
Mutare	Umtali
Mutoko	Mtoko
Mutorashanga	Mtorashanga
Mvuma	Umvuma
Mvurwi	Umvukwes
Mwenezi	Nuanetsi
Nkayi	Nkai
Nyazura	Inyazura
Sango	Vila Salazar
Shurugwe	Selukwe
Somabhula	Somabula
Tsholotsho	Tjolotjo
Zvishavana	Shabani

AIR

From Africa

Ethiopian Airways flies Harare/Addis/

Bombay. Discounts are available. Air France flies Seychelles to Harare via Mauritius and Réunion.

To travel from Harare to Lilongwe and Blantyre Air Malawi are probably the best airline. You don't have to show currency forms.

For those with little time or who don't want to take the train from Harare to Victoria Falls (one full day and a night), Air Zimbabwe fly from Harare to Victoria Falls and vice versa twice daily. A day-return ticket costs Z$194 and a period return is Z$223. Combined transport and accommodation deals are available at certain times of the year for about the same price so it's worth making enquiries before buying a straight ticket from Air Zimbabwe.

From Australia

There is one flight per week by Qantas from Sydney to Harare via Perth. There is a direct connection to Johannesburg on this flight.

From Europe

From London to Harare there are six return flights per week, two by British Airways and four by Air Zimbabwe. Advance purchase flights from London to Bulawayo via Harare cost UK£629 return.

From Paris to Harare UTA has one return flight per week via Kinshasa. (You cannot get on this flight in Kinshasa.) From Frankfurt to Harare there are two return flights per week by Air Zimbabwe via Athens.

From Lisbon to Harare there is one return flight per week by TAP via Brazzaville. There is one flight per week by Swissair from Zürich to Harare via Geneva and Athens on the way out but direct on the return leg.

ROAD
Hitching

Hitching is easy in Zimbabwe and many travellers prefer it as a way of getting around, although it's not advisable to hitch at night. Make an effort to look like a tourist (hang a camera around your neck). All the whites have cars so they tend to be suspicious of others who are apparently so poor they can't afford one. They're friendly enough, however, once you tell them you're travelling.

Don't be hesitant to accept lifts from black drivers despite what you will be told to the contrary by whites, but ask if payment is expected before getting in. Many station wagons act as unofficial taxis.

Bus

There are two types of buses – express and local. The former are operated by Express Motorways Africa Ltd and they only run between the major cities. Their head office is at the corner of Hood and Highfield Rd, Southerton, Harare, and their booking office (tel 720392) is on Rezende St, behind the post office in Harare. In Bulawayo, book at Musgrove & Watson travel agents, and in Mutare at the Tourist Information Bureau. There's heavy demand for seats, so book in advance.

The Express Motorways bus departs Harare at 7.45 am on Monday, Wednesday, Friday and Saturday, and at 1 pm on Thursday and Sunday. In the opposite direction they depart Bulawayo at 7.45 am on Tuesday, Thursday and Saturday, and at 1 pm on Monday and Sunday. The fare is Z$28 one way and the journey takes 6¼ hours. The buses call at Chegutu, Kadoma, Kwekwe, Gweru and Insiza.

Another company called Ajayo's runs buses from Bulawayo to Harare at 7.30 am on Monday, Wednesday and Friday. The buses are of a similar quality but take 6½ hours. Some of the routes are:

Harare to Mutare – express bus costs Z$18 and the journey takes 3¾ hours
Bulawayo to Masvingo – express bus departs daily at 8 am, costs Z$14.10 and takes four hours
Kariba to Harare – express bus costs

Z$10.15 and takes six hours, leaves Kariba at 6 am

There are buses to just about everywhere. They're relatively slow and overcrowded, but they are cheap and you're much more likely to meet interesting people on them. They're also quite safe despite what you might hear to the contrary. The only problem about them is that they leave from the bus stations in the African townships and so can be difficult to find. There are also no timetables at these bus stations and people can be vague about departure times.

Give these buses a go – you'll undoubtedly raise a few eyebrows, but once the initial shock of seeing a foreigner using a local bus has worn off, you'll find the black people take it in their stride and quickly warm to you. Resident whites will most likely stare at such a spectacle in downright horror or simply not believe their eyes. Two bus companies which have been recommended are the Zimbabwe Omnibus Co and the Shu-Shine Bus Co.

In Harare, the long-distance 'African' buses depart from Mbare Market bus terminal in Harare Township. To get there from the centre of town, take the local bus with 'Harare' on the signboard (13 cents). Local buses labelled 'City' go to the bus terminal near the railway station. Some of the routes are:

Bulawayo to Masvingo This will take you to the Great Zimbabwe ruins. One bus daily (Z$7.50) departs at about 6 am from the corner of Lobengula St and Selbourne Ave, but get there early. Zimbabwe Omnibus Company also cover this route in both directions. Their bus terminus in Bulawayo (tel 74059) is on the corner of Lobengula St and 6th Ave, and the bus departs at 1.30 pm daily.

Bulawayo to Victoria Falls The 'Wankie Express' (operated by F Pullen & Co) departs from the bus station at the end of 6th Ave extension daily at around 9 am and arrives at 3.30 pm. In the opposite direction it departs from the African township in Victoria Falls at 10 am daily and arrives at 4.30 pm. The fare is Z$8.80 You can also pick up this bus opposite Barclays Bank in Victoria Falls.

Harare to Masvingo Local buses cost Z$10.50 and take about five hours. They depart from the Mbare bus station in Harare and from the Mucheke bus station in Masvingo.

Mutare to Inyanga A local bus costs Z$2.70 but avoid any buses marked 'via Banda' as they take a two hour detour over unsurfaced roads.

Cycling

Almost all the roads are surfaced and in excellent repair. In addition, the shoulders of the roads are often sealed and marked off from the rest of the road by a yellow line to separate them from vehicular traffic. This was done deliberately so they could be used as cycle lanes.

The predictable climate helps considerably, with winter being the most pleasant season. The winds are generally easterly and only rarely strong enough to make cycling difficult. Distances between towns and points of interest are long by European standards, though generally only a day's ride apart. There are plenty of small stores between towns where you can stop and have a drink and a chat. The people in these stores are friendly.

If you're bringing a lightweight bicycle, bear in mind that there is next to nothing available in terms of spares for these in most places, including Harare. You will certainly find no 27-inch tyres for sale anywhere. The local bicycles use either 26-inch or 28-inch wheels so you can get spares for these. Those who have done it suggest you bring with you all the tools and spare parts you think you may need. The two best cycle shops in Harare are Zacks on Kenneth Kaunda Ave directly opposite the railway station; and Manica Cycles, 2nd Ave, close to Zacks.

Driving

Hiring vehicles in Zimbabwe is expensive so you'll have to be part of a group to make it worthwhile or even possible. On the other hand, it's often the only feasible way to tour the national parks unless you have plenty of time and patience to wait around for lifts. There is also a severe shortage of rental vehicles so book cars well in advance.

Avis offers unlimited mileage with a minimum rental period of six days and allows pick-ups and drop-offs without charge at Bulawayo, Harare, Kariba and Victoria Falls. Hertz demands a minimum rental period of 10 days if you want unlimited mileage, and charge extra if you drop the car off somewhere else.

Both Avis and Europcar have approximately the same rates. The cheapest cars (Mazda 323, Ford Laser, VW Golf) cost Z$47 per day plus 58 cents per km, or Z$109 per day with unlimited km. In the next category (Nissan Sunny), costs Z$54 per day plus 65 cents per km, or Z$124 per day with unlimited km. Charges include insurance but not collision damage waiver. This is an extra Z$10 per day and,

if you don't take it, you'll have to leave an additional deposit. Discounts of 30% to 40% apply for weekend rentals (Friday afternoon to Monday morning). Petrol costs Z$1.16 per litre.

Foreign-registered vehicles can be imported temporarily free of charge and third party insurance is available at the border if you're not already covered.

A driving licence from your country is sufficient provided it is in English. Otherwise, you must have an authenticated translation plus a photograph.

TRAIN

Zimbabwe has a good network of railways which connect all the major cities. They're very cheap, especially in economy (3rd) class. Most trains have three classes, but certain express trains have only 1st and 2nd classes.

For internal journeys, bookings open 30 days ahead. For journeys on through-trains to Botswana and South Africa, bookings open 90 days ahead. You're advised to book as far ahead as possible. Bedding can be hired for Z$4.20 (plus Z$4.20 if you want a mattress) so long as you buy tokens at a booking office. Bedding hired on the train itself costs Z$5.

Harare to Mutare

station	daily	station	daily
Harare	9.30 pm	Mutare	9.00 pm
Marondera	11.50 pm	Nyazura	11.15 pm
Macheke	12.50 am	Rusapi	12.20 am
Rusapi	3.23 am	Macheke	2.49 am
Nyazura	4.01 am	Marondera	4.00 am
Mutare	6.00 am	Harare	6.00 am

The fares on this sector are Z$22.05 (1st class), Z$15.40 (2nd class) and Z$4.90 (economy).

There's also a daily train in either direction between Victoria Falls and Livingstone (Zambia) which departs at about 12 noon but it involves a lot of hassles and delays at both the Zimbabwean and Zambian customs so it's much easier to go by road.

Bulawayo to Harare

There is a choice of day and night trains on this route. The night trains have all classes Monday to Thursday, and on Saturday, and the schedule is as follows:

station	time	station	time
Bulawayo	9.00 pm	Harare	9.00 pm
Gweru	1.10 am	Kadoma	12.01 am
Kadoma	4.00 am	Gweru	3.00 am
Harare	7.00 am	Bulawayo	6.40 am

On Friday and Sunday, the night trains have only 1st and 2nd classes and the schedule is as follows:

station	time	station	time
Bulawayo	8.00 pm	Harare	8.00 pm
Gweru	12.23 am	Kadoma	10.43 pm
Kadoma	3.08 am	Gweru	1.55 am
Harare	6.00 am	Bulawayo	5.35 am

The day trains depart daily in either direction and have only 2nd and economy classes. The schedule is as follows:

station	time	station	time
Bulawayo	8.00 am	Harare	8.00 am
Gweru	11.30 am	Kadoma	10.24 am
Kadoma	1.46 pm	Gweru	1.07 pm
Harare	4.00 pm	Bulawayo	4.10 pm

The fares on this sector are Z$37.80 (1st class), Z$26.40 (2nd class) and Z$8.40 (economy).

Bulawayo to Gaborone, Mafikeng & Johannesburg

The international rail schedule to Botswana and South Africa is as follows:

station	daily	Tues	station	daily	Thur
Bulawayo	12.35 pm	11.30 am	Johannesburg	–	1.30 pm
Plumtree	3.53 pm	1.35 pm	Mafikeng	12.45 pm	9.00 pm
Francistown	6.26 pm	3.51 pm	Ramatlhabama	2.20 pm	9.30 pm
Gaborone	6.10 am	1.30 am	Gaborone	6.30 pm	1.04 am
Ramatlhabama	10.42 am	5.00 am	Francistown	6.00 am	9.56 am
Mafikeng	11.20 am	5.30 am	Plumtree	8.55 am	12.14 pm
Johannesburg		12.45 pm	Bulawayo	11.25 am	2.15 pm

The daily train in either direction has all classes and a buffet car service between Bulawayo and Ramatlhabama. The Tuesday service from Bulawayo and the Thursday train from Johannesburg has only 1st and 2nd classes and has a dining car attached between Gaborone and Bulawayo. For connections to the rest of South Africa on the daily trains you must change at Mafikeng.

Also, at present, because of political problems between Botswana and South Africa-Bophuthatswana, the daily train (but not the Tuesday and Thursday 1st and 2nd class train) does not cross the border, so passengers have to get out at Lobatse and make their own way to Mafikeng. A taxi from Lobatse to Ramatlhabama costs about P 2 and a taxi from there to Mafikeng about R 2.

Bulawayo to Victoria Falls

station	daily	station	daily
Bulawayo	7.00 pm	Victoria Falls	5.30 pm
Hwange	3.34 am	Thomson Junct	8.50 pm
Thomson Junct	4.35 am	Hwange	9.12 pm
Victoria Falls	7.30 am	Bulawayo	7.15 am

This journey is a classic experience on an old steam locomotive with mahogany-interior carriages. There are all classes on the train and a buffet car and bar facilities. The fares are Z$37.80 (1st class), Z$26.40 (2nd class) and Z$8.40 (economy).

BOAT

The Lake Kariba ferry sails in either direction between Kariba and Mlibizi (250 km east of Victoria Falls) once a week if there's sufficient passenger demand. The fare is Z$100 one-way in deck class including average meals, and the journey takes 24 hours. As far as seeing animals is concerned, the trip is better from Mlibizi to Kariba, as you are nearer the banks in the daylight hours. If heading for Victoria Falls, arrange a lift from Mlibizi whilst on the ferry.

TO/FROM BOTSWANA

There is an express bus twice weekly in both directions from Harare to Gaborone via Bulawayo and Francistown. It departs from Harare on Thursday and Sunday and from Gaborone on Tuesday and Saturday at 6 am. The journey takes 15 hours. There is also the train from Bulawayo (see the Train section for schedule).

From Victoria Falls to Kazungula there is little traffic, but there's the chance of getting a lift with a police truck which does the run every morning. The Botswana officials will fix you up with a lift to Kasane. It's easier to hitch a ride from Livingstone (Zambia) to Kazungula and Kasane.

TO/FROM MALAWI

You can travel to Malawi from Zimbabwe via Mozambique if you don't want to go via Zambia. The route is Nyamapanda to

Tete to Zobue. Nyamapanda is the border village.

Convoys of trucks (up to 60 per day) make the journey daily, except Saturdays, in either direction taking about 24 hours. Every convoy is accompanied by an army escort since there's a lot of MNR guerrilla activity in this area of Mozambique. If possible, arrange a lift beforehand in Harare by contacting trucking companies and asking if they are doing the run. Most are happy to help out. Try Mr Watson (tel Harare 64318). Lifts are often free, but you need to bring along enough food for two days. If you draw a blank in Harare then go to Nyamapanda and ask around there.

The trucks collect at Nyamapanda the night before, then move off between 6 and 8 am the next day. There's nothing much at this border village except a bar and disco (the latter is expensive). The majority of the truck drivers are keen to be near the front of the convoy so there's a lot of jockeying to overtake each other. This frequently leads to crashes since the road isn't really wide enough, and there are a lot of craters marking spots where land mines planted by the MNR have exploded.

At Tete, there's an enormous bridge over the Zambezi but it has been damaged so often by the MNR that only one truck at a time is allowed to cross.

This trip is not for the faint-hearted. It's rough and potentially dangerous. If the truck you are in runs out of spare tyres and you get left behind, there's a very real danger that you'll be shot or kidnapped by the MNR at night. To do this trip you will need a Mozambique transit visa (available from the embassy in Harare).

TO/FROM SOUTH AFRICA

The only direct crossing is by road or rail from Bulawayo or Harare to Pretoria and Johannesburg via Beitbridge. Most travellers take the train (via Botswana – there are no direct train connections via Beitbridge), but hitching from Bulawayo or Harare to Johannesburg is relatively easy. Expect a few waits here and there. The only trouble with hitching via Beitbridge is that South African immigration and customs officials don't like hitchhikers and can be very obnoxious. Everyone, including women, can expect a body search.

The best time to cross the border at Beitbridge is around 12.30 pm as that's when the shift changes and the officials often can't be bothered to go to too much trouble. At this time you can generally get through in under 15 minutes. Customs are very tight going either way. If you're coming from South Africa to Zimbabwe and intend to return, declare all photo equipment, radios, etc on the form provided, and make sure you state serial numbers.

TO/FROM ZAMBIA

For obvious reasons, almost everyone goes via Victoria Falls-Livingstone, but there are also border crossings at Kariba and Chirundu. The latter is the main Harare to Lusaka route and the road is in bad repair from the border to Lusaka.

The only direct buses between Harare and Lusaka are those operated by United Bus Company of Zambia (UBZ). Daily buses depart from the Mbare bus terminal in Harare at 8.30 am and arrive in Lusaka around 6 pm; the fare is Z$46. The buses go via Chirundu. There's heavy demand for seats so book in advance.

If you prefer to go via Victoria Falls, first take a train or bus to the town of Victoria Falls, then either walk or take a taxi from there to the Zambian customs (about three km) followed by a bus or taxi to Livingstone. From Livingstone there are trains and buses to Lusaka. There's also a daily train in either direction between Victoria Falls and Livingstone.

Around the Country

BULAWAYO

This is Zimbabwe's second largest city and one of the country's major commercial and industrial centres. It was founded in 1894 on the site of one of Lobengula's *kraals* (Lobengula was the last of the Matabele kings).

Cecil Rhodes used the place as a headquarters on a number of occasions and the *rondavel* which he constructed still stands in the gardens of Government House.

Information

The tourist office (tel 60867) is in City Hall, on Fife St between Selbourne Ave and 8th Ave. It's open Monday to Friday from 8.30 am to 4.45 pm and on Saturday from 8.30 am to 12 noon.

The Automobile Association (tel 70063) is in Fanum House on the corner of Selbourne Ave and Wilson St.

American Express (tel 62521) is in the Federal Centre on 10th Ave between Main and Fort Sts.

For local crafts, there is an import/export firm on Rhodes St between 9th and 10th Ave which offers some of the cheapest sandstone carvings you'll find anywhere. It looks more like a factory than a craft shop, so don't be put off by appearances.

Things to See

The **Natural History Museum** in Centenary Park on Selbourne Ave (open daily from 9 am to 5 pm) has been described as the finest in southern Africa. It has excellent

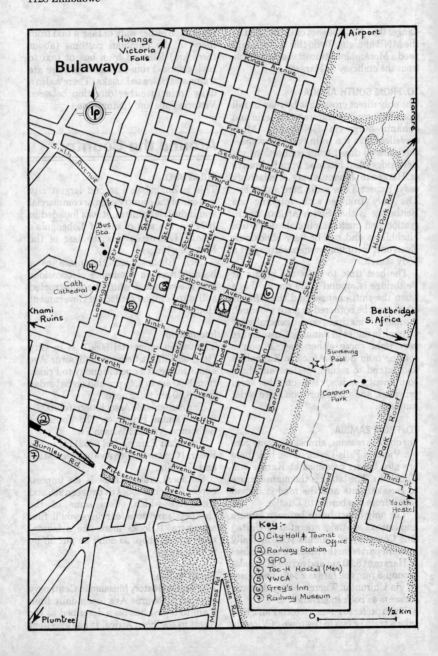

Bulawayo

↑ Airport

↑ Hwange
Victoria
Falls

Kings Avenue

First Avenue

Second Avenue

Third Avenue

Fourth Avenue

Fifth Avenue

Sixth Ave. Street

Selbourne Avenue

Eighth Avenue

Rhodes

Ninth Ave

Eleventh Avenue

Main

Abercorn

Fife

Grey

Wilson

Barrow

Twelfth Avenue

Thirteenth Avenue

Fourteenth Avenue

Fifteenth Avenue

Sixth Avenue Ext.

Lobengula Street

Jameson Street

Fort Street

Hume Park Rd.

Park Road

Oak Road

Third St.

→ Harare

→ Beitbridge
S. Africa

← Khami Ruins

← Plumtree

Burnley Rd

Matopos Rd

Hillside Rd

Bus Sta.

Cath. Cathedral

Swimming Pool

Caravan Park

Youth Hostel

Key :-
1. City Hall & Tourist Office
2. Railway Station
3. GPO
4. Toc-H Hostel (Men)
5. YWCA
6. Grey's Inn
7. Railway Museum

0   ½ km

tribal cultural displays, a stuffed mammal collection and a room full of Rhodes' memorabilia. You need to spend a whole day here if you want to take in everything.

The **Railway Museum** is a must for railway buffs. You'll see antique locos, rolling stock and even a 'museum on wheels' – a 1904 passenger coach with original fittings. Admission costs 20 cents and it's open Tuesday to Friday from 9.30 am to 12 noon and 2 to 4 pm, and on Sundays from 2 to 5 pm.

The stone ruins of **Khami**, one of the most important sites of the Rozwi empire, are 22 km west of the city. The remains date from the 17th century and were occupied until 1820. They consist of a series of terraces and passages supported by huge granite walls, some of which overlook the Khami Gorge. This is one of Zimbabwe's most important archaeological sites and is well worth a visit.

Bulawayo is the starting point for a visit to the **Rhodes Matopos National Park**, which begins 32 km south of the city (more details are in the National Parks section). There's also the smaller **Tshabalala Sanctuary** about 10 km from the city centre on the Matopos road, which contains a varied selection of wildlife including giraffe, kudu, zebra, impala, wildebeest and water birds. It's open daily from 6 am to 6 pm and you're permitted to walk.

The **Chipangali Wildlife Trust**, 25 km from Bulawayo on the main Johannesburg road, operates an orphanage for sick or abandoned young animals including lions, leopards, cheetahs, elephants and many species of antelope and wart hog. It's open Tuesday to Sunday from 10 am to 4.30 pm and is closed Mondays and public holidays; entry is Z\$2.

Places to Stay

The **Youth Hostel** (tel 76488) is on the corner of 3rd Ave and Townsend Rd, Suburbs, Bulawayo, two km east out of town along 12th Ave, which becomes 3rd Ave. It's clean, tidy and pleasant, is run by a friendly couple and costs Z\$3 for members and Z\$5 for nonmembers. There are cooking facilities, crockery and cutlery and (in theory) it's closed between 10 am and 5 pm.

If you prefer to camp, there's an excellent site in the middle of *Town Camping & Caravan Park* (tel 60185), a 10-minute walk from the centre. It's 'the best in Africa', said one traveller, and it costs Z\$3 per tent plus Z\$1.10 per person. The *YWCA Hostel* (tel 60185), on the corner of 9th Ave and Lobengula St, takes both women and men and costs Z\$15 per person.

For hotel accommodation the following places are recommended. *Grey's Inn* (tel 60121), 73 Grey St near the junction with Selbourne Ave. It costs Z\$18/31 a single/double without bath, or Z\$30/40 a single/double with bath. Prices include breakfast. Beware of the bar crowd – they tend to be ex-Rhodesian army types who don't take kindly to pro-Mugabe talk.

Hotel Cecil (tel 60295), on the corner of Fife St and 3rd Ave. It costs Z\$30/40 for a single/double with breakfast and bathroom.

Plaza Hotel (tel 64281), on the corner of 14th Ave and Abercorn St. Here singles/doubles cost Z\$30/45 including breakfast.

Other places you could try if these are full include the *Waverly Hotel* (tel 60033, 60036) at 133 Lobengula St (Z\$20/30 a single/double), the *Hotel Selbourne* on Selbourne Ave between Fife and Rhodes Sts opposite the Town Hall (Z\$40 a single with bath), and the *New Royal Hotel* (tel 65764) on the corner of 6th Ave and Rhodes St.

Places to Eat

If you're not eating at your hotel or putting your own food together, try *Buffalo Bill's Steak & Pizza Saloon* at the Selbourne Hotel, where they give generous portions of western food. You can eat a cheap bar lunch at the *Plaza Hotel* for Z\$3.

If you want pub-grub, try the *Wine Barrel*, which is part of the Bulawayo Sun Hotel. They have draught beer, house wine and things like ploughman's lunch and paté for around Z$1.50. Good, cheap snacks are available in the beer garden of the *Selborne Hotel*. Also try the *Grasshut* for good snacks, or the *Mexicana Takeaway* on Fife St. Good Chinese takeaways can be found at *Tunkus Chinese Takeaways* on Selbourne Ave between Rhodes and Grey Sts.

You can eat cheaply at a lot of Indian restaurants and African places. There are also many cheap cafés opposite the railway station.

For a splurge, try a garlic steak at the *Costa Brava Restaurant*, 103 Fife St between 10th and 11th Ave. Expect to pay around Z$9.

It's suggested you avoid the *White Horse Bar* unless you're really looking for trouble. The *Plaza Hotel* is just about the only place to find music and nightlife during the week, but it's often full of plain clothes police.

An excellent bakery is the *Haefeli Swiss Bakery* on the corner of Fife St and 10th Ave.

HARARE

The capital of Zimbabwe with a population of about half a million, Harare was founded in 1890 by the 'Pioneer Column' sent north from Bechuanaland (now Botswana) by Rhodes' British South Africa Company. It's a very pleasant city with wide boulevards and avenues planted out with flowering ornamental trees. Facilities are excellent and the central business district is more like the state capitals of Australia than Nairobi, although there's no doubt that this is an African capital.

There's naturally an adjustment in progress as the white settlers come to terms with full majority Black rule but it's unlikely you will come across the sort of entrenched conceit about notions of supposed superiority which is common further south. It's also a safe place to walk around, and the climate is very pleasant.

Information

Tourist Office There are two tourist offices in Harare. The Harare City Publicity Association (tel 705085) is in Cecil Square, on the corner of 2nd St and Stanley Ave. It caters to those looking for local information and is open weekdays from 8 am to 5 pm and on Saturdays from 8 am to 12 noon. They have the free publications, *This Month in Harare* and *Amazing Zimbabwe: A Comprehensive Guide*.

Nationwide information is best obtained from the Zimbabwe Tourist Board on Stanley Ave near the National Parks office on the corner of 4th St. It's open weekdays from 8 am to 1 pm and 2 to 4.30 pm. They're more helpful than the Publicity Association but don't expect a full range of literature.

The National Parks headquarters (tel 706077) is at 93B Stanley St (PO Box 8151, Causeway, Harare) and is open weekdays from 7.45 am to 4.15 pm. You can make bookings here for accommodation at the parks.

The Mountain Club of Zimbabwe run regular outings with rock climbing, bushwalks, occasional talks and film nights. They'll take you along on a share-cost basis.

Maps Excellent, detailed maps of most parts of Zimbabwe can be bought from the Surveyor General, Mapping Section, ground floor, Electra House, Samora Machel Ave, close to the junction with Nyerere Way. The most useful of these for the traveller are the 1:250,000 and 1:50,000 'tourist maps'. They cost a mere Z$2 to Z$3 each and no identification is needed. The office is open weekdays from 8 am to 1 pm and 2 to 4 pm.

Vaccinations You can get cholera and yellow fever shots for Z$2 each from the Central Hospitals Clinic, Mazoe St, between 1.30 and 3 pm on Tuesday and Friday. They also offer free typhoid shots on the same days. No appointment is necessary.

Bookshops There are quite a lot of book exchanges in Harare, though most of them aren't up to much. One worth visiting is the Booklovers' Paradise Book Exchange, 48 Angwa St between Baker and Union Aves. It charges only 40 cents per book on exchange. Otherwise, there are plenty of well-stocked bookshops in the central business district for new books.

Bus The bus to the airport departs from the rear of Air Zimbabwe every hour on the hour from 6 am to 11 pm, and also at 6.30 and 7.30 am, and costs Z\$2. A taxi will cost Z\$15.

Embassies Other than the embassies mentioned in the Visas section others include:

Angola
   Doncaster House, Speke Ave and Angwa St (tel 7906750)
Australia
   Throgmorton House, Julius Nyerere Way (tel 794591)
Botswana
   Southern Life Building, Stanley Ave (tel 729551)
Canada
   45 Baines Ave (tel 793801)
Denmark
   Pollack House, 30 Forbes Ave (tel 790398)
West Germany
   14 Samora Machel Ave (tel 702368)
Italy
   7 Bartholomew Close, Greendale (tel 47279)
Malawi
   42/44 Harare St (tel 705611)
Netherlands
   47 Enterprise Rd, Highlands (tel 793138)
Sweden
   Trustee House, Samora Machel Ave (tel 790651)
Switzerland
   9 Lanark Rd, Belgravia (tel 703997)
USA
   Arax House, 172 Rhodes Ave (tel 794521)

Things to See

The **Queen Victoria Museum** in the new Civic Centre complex near the gold-coloured Sheraton Hotel is worth a visit for its Mashonaland wildlife and anthropological displays. It's open every day from 9 am to 5 pm and entry costs 20 cents.

Also worth a visit is the **National Gallery of Zimbabwe** near the large Monomatapa Hotel on Kings Crescent near Park Lane. It has excellent displays of African artefacts, with masks and carvings from all over Africa. The paintings might not inspire you but they do show what Zimbabwean modern art is up to. Inexpensive baskets are for sale in the lobby. The gallery is open Tuesday to Sunday from 9 am to 5 pm and entry is 20 cents. In the garden behind the gallery there's a display of Shona stone sculpture.

The other museum in Harare is the **MacGregor Geological Museum**, Maufe Building, on the corner of Selous Ave and 4th St.

On Sundays there is a popular **arts & crafts market** with street musicians in the Harare Public Gardens between the Monomatapa Hotel and the US Embassy.

For a great view over Harare, walk to the summit of **The Kopje**, west of the city centre. Low bushes obscure the view at most points but there are places where you can see the whole city. It's safe to walk up there.

The **National Botanical Gardens** along 5th St beyond the golf course are well laid out with extensive lawns and a variety of African plants. At **Chapungu Kraal**, eight km from the centre, you can see a traditional Shona village and some five Shona stone sculptures. Traditional dances are performed at 3 pm on Saturday and 11 am and 3 pm on Sunday. Admission is Z\$4.

Outside Harare, about 20 km from the city on the Bulawayo road, there are the **Larvon Bird Gardens** where you can see about half of the species found in Zimbabwe. Admission costs Z\$2. It's well

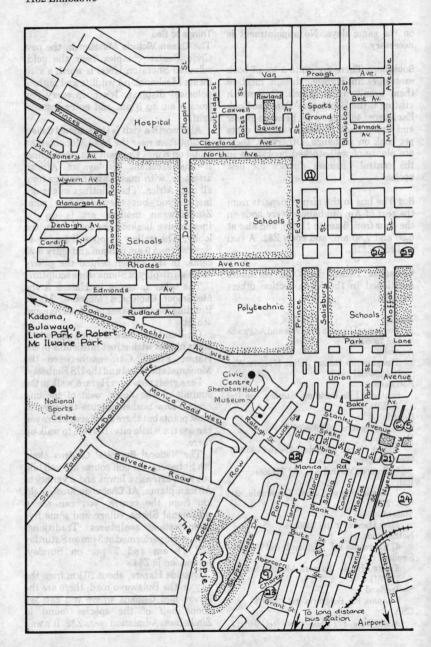

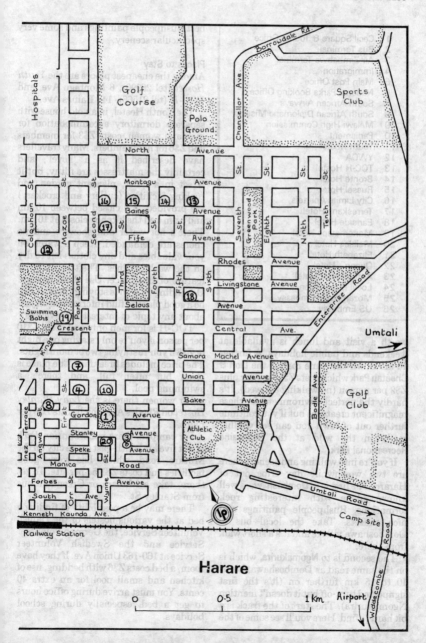

1	Cecil Square & Tourist Office
2	Bus Terminal
3	Air Zimbabwe Terminal
4	Immigration
5	Main Post Office
6	National Parks Booking Office
7	South African Airways
8	South African Diplomatic Mission
9	Malawi High Commission
10	Parliament
11	Youth Hostel
12	YWCA
13	TOC-H Hostel
14	Brontë Hotel
15	Russel Hotel
16	City Limits Apartels
17	Terreskane Hotel
18	Earlside Hotel
19	Monomatapa Hotel
20	Meikles Hotel
21	Elizabeth Hotel
22	Queen's Hotel
23	Ambassador Hotel
24	Local Bus Station
25	Mozambique Embassy
26	US Embassy

worth a visit and lunch is available at weekends and public holidays. A further 10 km down the same road is the **Lion & Cheetah Park** which costs Z$10 per car plus Z$2 per person (no walking allowed). It's hardly the perfect environment for these magnificent creatures but if you continue further out of town you can see wildlife really in the wild at the **McIlwaine Recreational Park**.

If you're into walking and scenery there are two worthwhile day trips out of Harare. The first is to **Domboshawa**, a well known place with interesting rock formations, Bushpeople paintings and nice sunsets. Take the local bus to Domboshawa village and it's a short walk from there.

The second is to **Ngomakurira**, which is on the same road as Domboshawa, but is 10 to 15 km further on (it's the first signposted turn-off but it doesn't mention Ngomakurira). The start of the track is a bit hard to find. Here you'll see some of the best Bushpeople paintings and some very spectacular scenery.

Places to Stay

Among the cheapest places are the *Youth Hostel* (tel 26990), 6 Montagu Ave, and *TOC-H* (tel 21566), 148 Baines Ave.

The Youth Hostel, in an old house with separate dormitory accommodation for men and women, costs Z$3 for members and Z$6 for nonmembers. Many travellers have described it as a 'hovel', and certainly the mattresses are filthy, but it is set in a quiet, pleasant garden and cooking facilities (cutlery and crockery) are provided. It's closed between 10 am and 5 pm and the kitchen closes at 10 pm. There's hot water and showers and no chores are demanded. Keep a watch on your valuables and any clothes left to dry on the washing lines. Theft is a regular feature of this place. Use those lockers! Depending on who is staying there, it can be a good place to find information on just about any topic of interest to travellers.

TOC-H is for men only and costs Z$10 per person if you're staying one night or Z$8 if you're staying two or more nights. The price includes breakfast. The place is clean but often full, and there's a swimming pool.

For women there is the *Lady Stanley Hostel* on Rhodes Ave which costs Z$8 per night.

For campers there is *Coronation Park* about five km south-east of the city on the Mutare road which has very good facilities and costs Z$1.50 per site. To get there, take a Manara or Greendale bus from Stanley St.

There may be a possibility of finding a bed at the various hostels of the Danish Volunteer Service, the German Volunteer Service and the Swedish Volunteer Service at 160-163 Union Ave. If they have room, a bed costs Z$6 with bedding, use of kitchen and small pool for an extra 40 cents. You must arrive during office hours to get a bed, especially during school holidays.

If you don't mind a little running around, there's an incredibly cheap place called *Carter House*. It is beside the Mbare bus station opposite the large market there and it costs just Z$1 for a dormitory bed. You must be out by 7 am each day but there's a baggage lock-up room where you can leave gear during the day. One traveller described it as 'all quite puritanical but has showers, toilets and cooking facilities. You'll probably be the only foreigner there'. To get to Carter House take a local bus from the corner of Angwa St and Manica Rd near the main post office. The bus will be signposted either Harare or Mbare.

Hotel accommodation tends to be expensive in Harare though facilities are usually good.

At the bottom end of the scale, the *Elizabeth Hotel* (tel 708591), on the corner of Julius Nyerere Way and Manica Rd, is a reasonable place to stay. It costs Z$20/30 a single/double without bath and Z$25/40 a single/double with bath. Prices do not include breakfast. There's a resident band and disco every night. Similar is the *Queen's Hotel* (tel 700876) on the corner of Manica Rd and Pioneer St, which has its own restaurant and features live bands and a disco bar seven days a week. It costs Z$30/45 a single/ double.

Also in this category is the *Terreskane Hotel* (tel 707031) 102 Fife St at 2nd St, which offers single rooms without bath for Z$25 and double rooms with bath for Z$60. Prices do not include breakfast. This hotel has its own restaurants, bars and swimming pool.

At the top end of this range is the *Earlside Hotel* (tel 21101) on the corner of 5th St and Selous Ave. This is a good place to stay if you want to be close to the centre. It's a fairly old place but is well maintained and popular. Rooms cost Z$25/35 a single/ double including breakfast. It's good value and the staff are friendly and sympathetic.

Other than these you are looking at fairly expensive accommodation if you want to be close to the centre. One place you will always find a room is the *Russel Hotel* on the corner of Baines Ave and 3rd St, which also has an annexe called the *City Limits Apartels*, also on Baines Ave at the junction of 2nd St. Rooms cost Z$30/40 a single/double with breakfast. Rates for dinner and breakfast are Z$35/ 50 a single/double. The rooms are very pleasant and are self-contained (fridge, TV, bathroom with constant hot water, balcony, etc, but without cooker). If you stay in the annexe, you must take breakfast (and other meals, if required) at the main hotel.

On the same street is the *Brontë Hotel* (tel 796631) 132 Baines Ave at the junction with 4th St. It's a large hotel with extensive gardens and it costs Z$50/70 for a single/double with bathroom and breakfast. The rooms are spacious, there's a swimming pool, bar and many other amenities but it's definitely a tired traveller's splurge. Similar is the *Courtney Hotel* (tel 706411) on the corner of Selous Ave and 8th St, which offers singles/ doubles with private bath, TV, etc, for Z$50/70 including breakfast. The hotel has its own restaurant and bar.

Others in this range are the *Executive Hotel* (tel 792803) on the corner of 4th St and Samora Machel Ave, which costs Z$50/65 a single/double including breakfast and bathroom, and the *Oasis Motel* (tel 704217) 124 Baker Ave, which costs Z$70/ 90 a single/double. All the rooms have their own bathroom, TV and telephone (free local calls) and there's a restaurant, swimming pool and coffee shop.

Away from the city centre, the *Kentucky Airport Hotel* (tel 506550) St Patrick's Rd, Hatfield, has been recommended. It costs Z$40/70 for a single/double including breakfast.

Two other places which might be worth checking out are the *Feathers Hotel* (tel 36611/2) Sherwood Drive, Mabelreigh, about eight km from the city centre, which has rooms from Z$35 a single, and the *Kamfinsa Park Hotel* (tel 48024) Acturis Rd, Greendale, also about eight km from the city centre, which offers singles for Z\$30 without bath and singles/ doubles for Z\$40/50 with bath including breakfast. Both hotels have their own restaurant, bar and swimming pool.

Places to Eat

If you're not eating at your hotel, try either the *Europa Restaurant*, on Julius Nyerere Way near Samora Machel Ave (a friendly place which offers good, cheap meals), or *Eddie's Takeaways* on Stanley St. Both have been popular with budget travellers for years.

Even better is *Natie's Grill*, on 1st St between Samora Machel Ave and Union Ave. It offers fantastic thick hamburgers with mushrooms, onions and real Cheddar cheese for Z\$6. Also on the menu are steaks with many exotic sauces, waffles covered with real whipped cream and honey for Z\$3.60 and excellent coffee with real cream for 80 cents. The grill is opposite the *Cottage Pie* which has similar fare. The *Lido* at 51 Union Ave is a popular, clean, bright snack bar with great burgers from Z\$4 to Z\$6.

Also good are the *Go Go Restaurant*, on Angwa St between Manica Rd and Speke Ave (chicken & chips for Z\$2.50), and *Fun City*, 1st St between Union and Baker Aves, which is open seven days a week until midnight. *Toff's Takeaways* on Baker Ave is cheap and has good bread.

In a similar category is *Barbours Terrace Restaurant & Cafeteria*, 1st St, which is part of a department store and offers good food at modest prices.

Good cheap takeaways can be found at *Big Lev's*, 2nd St between Samora Machel and Union Aves, and there's fish & chips at the *Sunflower*, Samora Machel Ave between Julius Nyerere Way and Moffat St.

Meals at the *Earlside Hotel* are cheap and very good value. Breakfast and dinner cost Z\$3 and lunch Z\$5.

For moderately priced Greek food try the licensed *Demis Taverna* on the corner of Speke Ave and Moffat St. You can make a meal out of just the appetisers (stuffed spinach leaves, moussaka) or order the marinated lamb chops – four of them – for around Z\$7. The *Homegrown*, on the opposite corner has some vegetarian meals and boasts the best salad bar in Harare. Their wholewheat bread is baked on the premises. There's live music most nights.

Da Guido's Trattoria in the shopping complex at the corner of Montagu St and Salisbury Ave close to the youth hostel has good pizza and other cheap Italian food. It is very popular.

Entertainment

Two of the best places for excellent live music are the *Queen's Hotel* on the corner of Manica Rd and Pioneer Ave, and the *Elizabeth Hotel* (the *'Liz'*). If you're lucky you'll see Thomas Mapfumo or Oliver Mutukindzi. It's unlikely you'll see more than the occasional white Zimbabwean here.

There are plenty of other places to go but they're not as lively. The *Playboy*, Union Ave near the Jameson Hotel, and the *Hangar*, on Moffat St, have been recommended.

During the day, the *Terreskane Hotel* is usually lively and has a good mix of black and white clientele. The *Wine Barrel* at the Monomatapa Hotel is a die-hard Rhodesian singles bar and you must have smart casual dress (no joggers).

Another place which has been recommended is *Job's Night Spot*, Julius Nyerere Way between Forbes and Kaunda Aves. The owner is Job Kakane, Bob Marley's friend who was responsible for bringing him to Zimbabwe for the independence celebrations in 1980.

The bar at *Meikle's Hotel* is a popular place for well-dressed black and white local residents, and although it's best described as elegant, the drinks and snacks are not too expensive (beers cost

Z$1.50). Similar is the bar at the *Jameson Hotel* on Samora Machel Ave.

Another interesting place to try is the *City Marketing Municipal Beer Garden*. If you're white, you'll be one of the few white visitors the drinkers here have seen. Just front-up and go in. Once the initial surprise has subsided, you're unlikely to leave without having made a lot of friends and drunk a lot of beer (they drink it out of buckets here!). Weekends are the best time to go.

Nonresidents can use the swimming pool at the *Monomatapa Hotel* for 40 cents per day.

INYANGA

This is the centre for exploring the **Inyanga National Park** and Mt Inyanga north of Mutare. It's a large area in the extreme north-east of Zimbabwe with red-leaved Msasa trees, rocky hills, waterfalls and prolific wildlife as well as the popular 'World's View' from which you can watch beautiful sunsets.

Mt Inyanga (2595 metres high), the highest point in Zimbabwe, can be climbed in about 1½ hours and offers incredible views over Mozambique and the escarpment, as it drops away precipitously. You can no longer camp at World's View (Troutbeck) despite what people will tell you.

Places to Stay

There is a camp site in the national park which costs Z$6 per site. Firewood, stoves and hot showers are provided but bring your own food and drink. Chalets are also available – details in the National Parks section.

Accommodation in the town is generally expensive but the *Holiday Hotel* (tel 336) isn't prohibitive at Z$30/40 a single/double with full board. The staff are friendly and the price of accommodation includes temporary membership of the Inyanga Club. Those who have stayed here describe it as good value. There is a swimming pool, tennis, billiards and other sports facilities but no bar, so bring your own or ask a waiter to get it for you.

KARIBA

The town of Kariba has grown up around the dam wall and the power station and, along with a number of resorts strung out down the lake, has become the local substitute for the sea shore.

It's a breeze to hitch here from Harare on Saturday mornings but is hopeless afterwards.

Places to Stay

Most of the hotels are too expensive for budget travellers but there are a couple of cheap possibilities if you want to stay here. One is the *Mophani Bay Caravan Park* close to the (very expensive) Cutty Sark Hotel – turn right 10 km after the Kariba turn-off heading for Makuti and Harare. A site costs Z$3 per person plus Z$2.75 (up to six people per site). Hot water is available. There's a small shop at the Cutty Sark where you can buy bread, milk, canned meat and the like.

Otherwise, try the *MOTH* camp site (tel 409; PO Box 67), near the Yacht Club, for Z$3 per person per night. They also have cottages for Z$10/16 a single/double. It's very clean, pleasant and there's a good swimming pool. Bring your own food with you and cook it on the barbeque. The site is 10 minutes' walk from the ferry.

Further to the south along the lake shore is a good camp site operated by the Department of Wildlife, Nyamanyama, which costs Z$6 per night.

If you don't have camping gear, try the *Most High Hotel* (formerly the Christian Centre) near the centre of town which costs Z$25 a double with toilet, hot shower, writing desk, carpeted floors, soap and towel. They offer meals but the club next door is slightly cheaper. The *Yacht Club* has shed-like cottages for Z$5 per night, plus Z$2 for one week's temporary membership (unless you can get signed in by a member as a guest).

The *Lake View Inn* has rooms for Z$50

per person with air-con, bathroom and toilet and a huge breakfast. The *Zambesi Valley Hotel* in Nyamhunga township is an African hotel but white travellers are made welcome. Singles/doubles cost Z$35/60 including breakfast. There's a disco in the evenings.

Other travellers have recommended the *Fothergill* and *Spurwing* island resorts. The latter costs Z$35 per night with full board and is excellent. It has thatched huts and really friendly staff. You can arrange game-viewing trips with them. The *Kariba Breeze Hotel* on the lake shore is worth trying in the off season, which runs from the end of the New Year holiday to the beginning of April.

One of the best places to eat is the *Cutty Sark Hotel*. For Z$15 you can have an all-you-can-eat barbeque lunch or dinner. The same thing can be found at the *Caribbea Bay*. The swimming pools at either hotel can be used free of charge if you eat there.

A day-cruise on the lake with lunch at Fothergill Island costs Z$25 and can be booked through most hotels.

If you're heading for the border, you can get a lift with the white manager of the Mophani Bay camp site. He lives in a house on the hill beside the site and leaves for work near the border daily at 7 am.

MASVINGO (Nyanda/Fort Victoria)

Masvingo is the urban centre nearest to the **Great Zimbabwe National Monument** – one of the most important and impressive archaeological sites in southern Africa. The ruins, 28 km south-east of Masvingo, date back as far as 1200 AD and are estimated to have once housed a population in excess of 10,000. By the time the Portuguese arrived, however, the city was already in decline.

Built of stone, the walls range from just over a metre to more than five metres thick and are as high as nine metres. They're certainly worth more than one visit. The site is open daily from 6 am to

6 pm and entry costs Z$1. There's a small museum on the site.

Buses to the Great Zimbabwe ruins leave from Masvingo township (Mucheke). Any bus marked 'Morgan Steiner Mission' or 'Zapo' will take you there. Ask them to drop you at the ruins and then walk the last two km. The last bus leaves Masvingo at 3.30 pm and from the ruins at 4.14 pm. A taxi costs Z$30. You can rent bicycles from the Great Zimbabwe Hotel for Z$2 an hour. Hitching is difficult because there are so few cars so allow plenty of time.

Places to Stay

Despite what you may be told, it's still possible to camp at the Great Zimbabwe ruins. You must buy a ticket (Z$2) from the office in the Curio Shop building. The site is next to the parking area and has toilets and cold showers. Watch out for the resident monkeys. Meals are available from the adjacent hotel and are quite cheap. The hotel may also be a good place to find a lift back to Masvingo.

Those without tents should ask the official who collects the fee for the ruins about renting a *rondavel* which cost just Z$1 per *rondavel*! They have no furniture and only cement floors but there are toilets, showers and a kitchen sink. They're in a pleasant location.

For hotel accommodation, there is the *Great Zimbabwe Hotel* (tel 2274; PO Box 9082, Masvingo) at the ruins. This is a two-star hotel and a room costs Z$139 a double including breakfast. The table d'hôte dinner costs Z$17.50. You can get pub-grub at the bar (eg, cheeseburgers & chips for Z$4).

In Masvingo itself, there's a good municipal camp site, signposted *Caravan Park*, 500 metres out of town on the Birchenough Bridge-Mutare road, which costs Z$3 per tent. The facilities are excellent and firewood is provided.

Hotels are generally very expensive. One of the cheapest is the *Mundondo Hotel*, near the bus station, which costs Z$25 for a room. The *Chevron Hotel* (tel

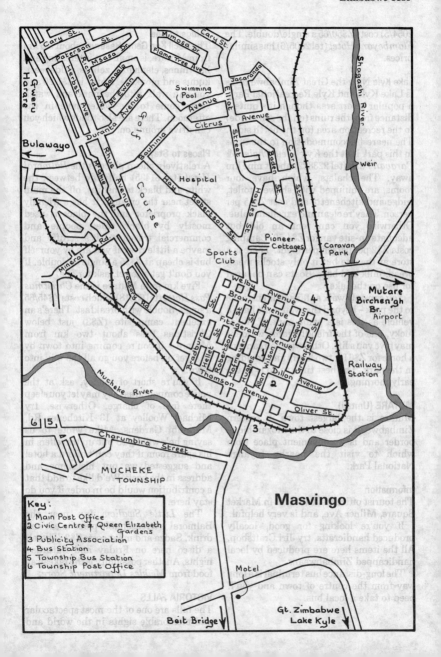

Masvingo

Key:
1 Main Post Office
2 Civic Centre & Queen Elizabeth Gardens
3 Publicity Association
4 Bus Station
5 Township Bus Station
6 Township Post Office

2054/5) costs Z$50/65 a single/double. The *Flamboyant Hotel* (tel 2005/6) has similar prices.

Lake Kyle Near the Great Zimbabwe ruins is Lake Kyle and Kyle Recreational Park, a popular resort area though it's quite a distance from the ruins (on the south side) to the recreation area (on the north side). The nearest accommodation to the ruins in this park is at the *Kyle View Chalets & Caravan Park* (tel 223822) about nine km away. The chalets, which have four rooms, are equipped with shower, toilet, fridge and kitchenette and cost Z$15 per person. They're clean and excellent value. Otherwise you can rent an old but adequate on-site van for Z$4.50. Camping costs Z$2 per person per night. There is a store at the site but it only stocks meat, bread, milk and beer. Boats can be hired for use on the lake.

You can only walk as far as the entrance to the park – beyond that you must have a vehicle as this is a game park. If you're lucky, one of the friendly game wardens may give you a lift. Otherwise you can rent a horse for Z$6 for two hours and go riding in the park. The best time to go is in the early morning.

MUTARE (Umtali)

Mutare is the largest town in eastern Zimbabwe. It is close to the Mozambique border and is a convenient place from which to visit the nearby Inyanga National Park.

Information

The tourist office (tel 64711) is in Market Square, Milner Ave, and is very helpful.

If you're looking for good, locally produced handicrafts, try Jiri Craftshop. All the items here are produced by local handicapped Zimbabweans.

The long-distance bus terminal is a long way from the centre of town and you'll need to take a local bus.

Things to See

The **Cecil Kop Game Reserve**, about 3½ km from Mutare, is small but interesting and has rhinos, elephants, zebras, wildebeest, kudus and monkeys. Entry is Z$1.20 and you can walk into the park and watch game come to the water hole in the afternoon. There are also roads which you can drive around on.

Places to Stay

A relatively cheap place is the *Balmoral Hotel* (tel 61435) half way between the white and black townships, off the main street near the cinema. It has a friendly black proprietor and the place is used mostly by black sales people and commercial travellers. It's scruffy and maybe a little risky if you are by yourself but is cheap at Z$25 a single or double. If you don't get a towel, ask for one.

Five km from Mutare is the *Christmas Pass Hotel* (tel 63818) which costs Z$45/65 a single/double with breakfast. There's an excellent camp site (Z$3) just below Christmas Pass about two km from Mutare – if you're coming into town by bus, get off before you go all the way into town.

If you're short of money, ask at the police compound as they may let you sleep there free of charge. Otherwise, try Michael Woolley at 13 Kitchener Rd, Murambi Gardens. Mike wrote to us saying he's willing to put up travellers in his spare room if they can't afford a hotel and suggested we put his name and address in the book. We'd like to add that a contribution would be in order if you do stay here.

The *Little Swallow Inn* near the Balmoral is a reasonable place to eat and drink. Sadza and meat costs Z$2. There's a disco here on Friday and Saturday nights. Another possibility is the takeaway food from *Meikles Department Store*.

VICTORIA FALLS

The falls are one of the most spectacular and memorable sights in the world and

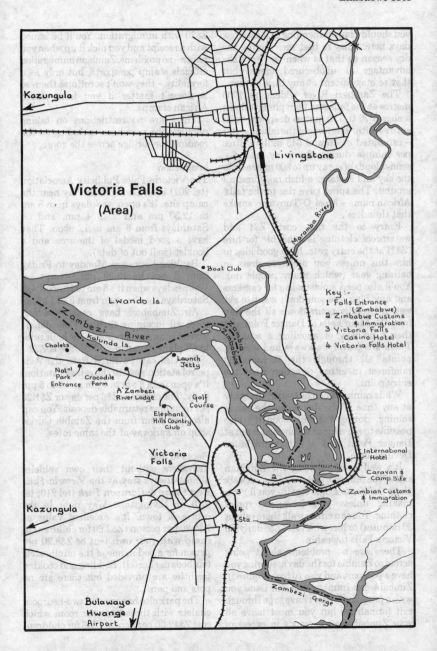

Victoria Falls

(Area)

Kazungula

Livingstone

Maramba River

Boat Club

Lwando Is.

Zambezi River

Kalunda Is.

Key :-
1 Falls Entrance (Zimbabwe)
2 Zimbabwe Customs & Immigration
3 Victoria Falls Casino Hotel
4 Victoria Falls Hotel

Zambia
Zimbabwe

Chalets

Launch Jetty

Nat'nl Park Entrance

Crocodile Farm

A'Zambezi River Lodge

Golf Course

Elephant Hills Country Club

Victoria Falls

Kazungula

International Hotel

Caravan & Camp Site

Zambian Customs & Immigration

1
2
3
4
Sta.

Bulawayo
Hwange
Airport

Zambezi Gorge

you should plan on spending at least a few days here. They're best seen during the dry season as that is when you have the advantage of unobscured views, but they're magnificent at any time of year.

The Zambezi River widens to 1700 metres at the falls and then plunges down a chasm 70 to 110 metres deep across its entire width. The force of the falling water – estimated at around 545 million litres per minute during the rainy season – sends clouds of spray up to 500 metres into the sky and sustains a lush rainforest all around. The spray gave rise to the falls' African name – Mosi-O-Tunya or 'smoke that thunders'.

Entry to the falls costs Z$1 and waterproof clothing is available for hire (Z$1) at the entry gate. It's a good idea to hire this unless you prefer to dress in bathing gear (which many people do). You'll also need a plastic bag for cameras and anything else you don't want to get wet. It literally pours down all the way from the Main Falls to Danger Point and there's no way of avoiding a soaking. There are gravel walkways and viewing points all through the surrounding rainforest in either direction from the entry point.

While rainbows can be seen in the spray at any time of the day when the sun is shining, during the full moon it's also possible to see a lunar rainbow at 9 pm at Danger Point and at 12 midnight at Devil's Gorge.

It's well worth visiting the Zambian side of the falls too, especially the catwalk along the Knife Edge. Again, you'll get a soaking unless you have waterproof clothing. You can either walk there (about 30 minutes) or hire a bicycle (Z$6 daily) in Victoria Falls township.

There are no problems about going across to Zambia for the day assuming you have a passport and visa (where required). Zimbabwean immigration will issue you with a pass so you don't have to go through exit formalities but you must leave all your Zimbabwean currency in excess of Z$20 with immigration. You'll be issued with a receipt and you pick it up when you return – no problems. Zambian immigration officials stamp passports, but only as a formality – they won't scrutinise them so it doesn't matter if you have South African stamps.

There are no restrictions on taking photographs anywhere, including on the road/railway bridge across the gorge.

Information

The Victoria Falls Publicity Association (tel 202) is on Livingstone Way near the camp site. It's open weekdays from 8 am to 12.30 pm and 2 to 4 pm, and on Saturdays from 8 am to 12 noon. They have a good model of the area and a booklet (well out of date).

Banking hours are Monday to Friday from 8 am to 12.30 pm, except on Wednesdays when it's 8 am to 12 noon. On Saturdays they're open from 8 to 11 am.

Air Zimbabwe have coaches which meet all incoming flights. They depart from the town centre about one hour prior to all plane departures. The fare is Z$2.

Bicycles can be hired from the Avis petrol station next to the railway station. It's open from 8 am to 1 pm and 2 to 5 pm daily. The charge is Z$6 per day or Z$1.20 per hour plus returnable deposit. You can also hire them from the Zambia Curios shop on Parkway at the same rates.

Places to Stay

Travellers without their own vehicles almost always stay at the *Victoria Falls Rest Camp & Caravan Park* (tel 210; tel 210) on Livingstone Way right in the centre of town. It's excellent value at Z$5.20 per person (Z$2.60 for children) to camp with your own tent or Z$8.20 per person for a bed in one of the minihostels (six beds per hostel). Bedding and cooking facilities are provided but there are no pots and pans.

The park also has one and two-bedroom chalets with three beds per room which cost Z$12.30 per person (Z$6 for children)

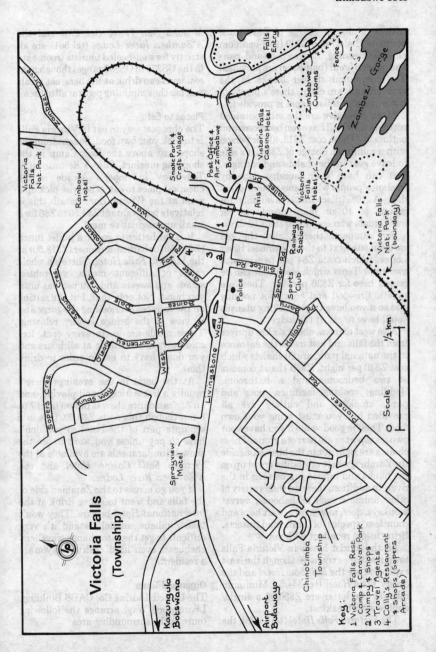

Victoria Falls
(Township)

Key:
1 Victoria Falls Rest
  Camp & Caravan Park
2 Wimpy & Shops
3 Travel Agents
4 Cally's Restaurant
  & Shops (Sopers
  Arcade)

with a minimum charge of Z$20 (one-bedroom chalet) and Z$30 (two-bedroom chalet). Bedding, fridge, pots and pans and outside *braai* (barbeque) are provided. The communal shower blocks in the caravan park are clean, there's plenty of hot water and toilet paper is provided.

More expensive are the self-contained cottages which all have two bedrooms and bathroom. These cost Z$15.40 per person with a minimum charge of Z$35. It's safe to leave gear in the chalets and cottages. You can have your laundry done by freelance people who come around every day. A 10% discount is available for groups of 10 or more people or for individuals who stay more than 10 days.

For campers, there's also the old caravan site next to the A'Zambezi River Lodge, which costs Z$4 per person with own tent. Tents which sleep four can be rented here for Z$30 per day. There are toilets, firewood and *braai* but nothing else so if you haven't got cooking utensils you'll have to eat at the lodge.

Also west of town, about six km upriver from the falls and just inside the entrance to the national park, are 20 chalets which cost Z$40 per night. Each chalet consists of two bedrooms and a bathroom. Bedding, cooking facilities, pots and pans, crockery and cutlery are all provided but you must bring your own food. They're good value if you have your own transport or are part of a group. These chalets are right out in the bush alongside the Zambezi where crocodiles crawl up on the banks and hippos can be seen in the river. In addition, there's a wide variety of other animals such as baboons, vervet monkeys, deer, mongooses, wart hogs and countless species of birds and insects. Bring insect repellent with you.

All the tourist hotels in Victoria Falls town itself are expensive though the least expensive are the *Rainbow Hotel* and the *Spray View Hotel* (tel 344/5). Minimum rates at the latter are Z$50/90 a single/double with breakfast.

The *Victoria Falls Hotel* (tel 344/5), the *Masaka Sun Hotel* (tel 275) and the *A'Zambezi River Lodge* (tel 561) are all strictly for well-heeled tourists (rooms are in the US$75 to US$90 range) though non-residents can drink at the bars, eat meals and use the swimming pools at all of them.

Places to Eat

The cheapest way to eat in Victoria Falls is to cook your own food, bought from the shops just above the Rest Camp in the shopping precinct. *Cally's Restaurant & Takeaway* in Soper's Arcade is the cheapest place to eat, otherwise pick up a meal at the *Wimpy Bar*, though this is relatively poor value at Z$4.50 to Z$6 for a small unimaginative meal.

It is far better to go for a buffet lunch (Z$16.50) or barbeque dinner (Z$18.50) at the *Victoria Falls Hotel*. There's a whole range of different meats, vegetables, salads and sweets and you can eat until you burst. Not only that, but the setting on the terraces overlooking the gorge and in view of the bridge is very relaxing. These meals are worth every cent. Ice-cold beers are available at all hours and you don't have to eat in order to drink there.

At the hotel in the evenings there's usually a live African band playing, and an African dance show is put on from 7 to 8 pm though this costs Z$9.50. (It's in a separate part of the hotel so you don't have to pay unless you want to see the show.) Similar meals are available at the *Victoria Falls Casino Hotel* and the *A'Zambezi River Lodge*.

If you go across to the Zambian side of the falls and want to eat or drink at the *International Hotel* beware. They won't take Zimbabwean dollars and it's very difficult to get them to change travellers' cheques or even 'hard' cash unless you are a resident.

Organised Tours

The United Touring Co, CABS Building, Livingstone Way, arrange the following tours in the surrounding area:

Flight of the Angels
  This is a 15-minute flight over the Falls which costs Z$52 and is 'worth every cent' according to everyone who has gone on it. Flights depart from 8 to 11.30 am and 2 to 3.30 pm daily.
Sprayview Air Safari
  This is a 30-minute flight over the falls and surrounding area which costs Z$104. Flights depart from 6.30 am to 3.30 pm daily.
Victoria Falls National Park Game Viewing
  A minibus tour of the national park. Tours depart daily (subject to weather) at 6.30 am and 3.30 pm. The cost is Z$25 per person. A minimum of four people is required.
Zambezi River Cruises
  These depart daily at 10.15 am and 2.15 pm and cost Z$25. A minimum of 18 people are required and there's free transport from town 30 minutes before departure.
Sundowner Cruise
  This cruise lasts about one hour and they depart from May to September at 5 pm and from October to April at 5.15 pm. The cost is Z$25 and there's a bar on board. This is generally known as the 'Booze Cruise' but there's no free beer anymore.

If you are interested in a canoeing safari either above or below the falls, contact Abercrombie & Kent (tel 725511, 721349), Southampton House, on the corner of 1st and Union Aves, Harare (PO Box 2997, Harare). These people are also agents for Sobek's Rafting Tours which take off down the Zambezi from below Victoria Falls. They're not cheap though! Expect to pay Z$115 per day (weekdays) and Z$144 (weekends).

National Parks

One of the best ways to see Zimbabwe is to use the national park lodges, caravan sites and camp sites. There are over 250 chalets, cottages and lodges within the various parks and they're all very reasonably priced. Facilities include basic furniture, refrigerators, bedding and lighting (kerosene pressure lamps, gas or electricity).

Camp sites in the national parks cost Z$5 per night per site (up to six people) and have excellent facilities. Firewood has to be purchased from the park authorities, usually at Z$3 a bundle.

Some of the lodges are only open at certain times of the year so you need to make enquiries about this. It's advisable to book in advance if possible, particularly during school holidays. You can do this at the National Parks Booking Office (tel 706077), 93B Stanley Ave, PO Box 8151, Causeway, Harare. You must report at the park office on arrival even if you have confirmed bookings. Entrance fees to the parks vary.

The only trouble with the national parks is getting to them as local transport is very limited. Local 'African' buses run to or near most parks, but there may be only one every two days or so, which means you really need your own vehicle. Also, you need to take most of your own food and drink. Renting a car isn't cheap so you have to get a group together to share the cost.

Recent reports suggest that it's fairly easy to hitch into most parks and that you seldom have to pay for lifts.

CHIMANIMANI NATIONAL PARK
Park HQ (tel Chimanimani 03322), Private Bag 2063, Chimanimani. This park is at the foot of the mountains 21 km from Chimanimani, south of Mutare near the border with Mozambique. Entry costs Z$1. Chalets and camping are available at the base camp, the latter for Z$6.

The park is a hikers' paradise and there are breathtaking views over Mozambique within easy walking distance of the base camp. Further into the park there are a number of caves which are suitable for sleeping in overnight (no charge). There's also an abandoned hut which can be used for the same purpose. Those without tents can stay at the *Outward Bound School* which is about three km from the base camp. The charge is Z$6 for two people on the concrete floor.

Without your own vehicle, you'll either have to hitch a ride or take the local bus from Chimanimani which goes to within six km of the base camp, but it doesn't go every day.

Places to Stay

In Chimanimani itself you can stay in a house owned by the Women's Institute for Z$3 per person which includes wood for a fire. The house has two beds only. Get the key from the *Chimanimani Hotel*. The latter also allows camping in the grounds for Z$1 per person plus Z$1 if you want a shower. A reasonable three-course meal can be bought at the hotel for Z$10 to Z$12. Excess baggage can safely be left at the hotel.

CHINHOYI (SINOIA) CAVES RECREATIONAL PARK

Park HQ (tel 2550), PO Box 193, Chinhoyi. These caves about eight km north of Chinhoyi are well worth a stopover on the way from Harare to Kariba. Another attraction here is the deep blue pool accessible via one of the caves or a tunnel through the limestone rock. Entry to the park is free.

Places to Stay

There's an enormous camp site here along the main road which costs Z$6 per site, and bungalows are also available.

HWANGE (WANKIE) NATIONAL PARK

Park HQ (tel Dett 64), Private Bag DT5776, Dete. This is Zimbabwe's largest game park, covering over 14,500 square km, and is the place to see animals large and small. Elephants, giraffes, lions, leopards, hippos, crocodiles, buffalo, cheetahs, jackals, zebras, wildebeest and impala are all here. The northern and eastern regions of the park are closed from December to April, as is Robins Camp. Entry to the park costs Z$3.

Guided foot safaris are available at Main Camp if you're not part of an organised tour group. Otherwise, a good thing to do here is to take the UTC bus from the Safari Lodge (it also passes by Main Camp at 6.30 am) and get off at the Nyama platform (toilet facilities and running water). Stay there when the bus leaves and get the evening bus back to Main Camp at around 5.30 pm. The fare is Z$11.50 return. In between you can spend the whole day watching the animals as they come down to drink at the water hole. The platform is usually deserted most of the day.

Roberto 'Beat' Accorsi of Shamwari Safaris (tel 61071/2), PO Box 2421, Bulawayo, has been recommended if you want to go on an organised safari in this park.

If you are part of a group and thinking of hiring a vehicle to tour the park, Hertz/ UTC keep their vehicles near the entrance to Main Camp. You can book a vehicle in Victoria Falls, Bulawayo or Harare and arrange to be met on the junction of the main Hwange-Bulawayo road (take the 'Wankie Express' to get there). This will save you a lot of mileage charges.

Places to Stay

There are three camps in all – Main Camp, Sinamatella and Robins – as well as a number of bush camps set up in remote areas for the use of those who go on foot safaris. All the camps offer chalet-type accommodation plus camp sites, and there's a safari lodge at Main Camp. Camping costs Z$3 per site and the chalets cost Z$10 which is excellent value as they have four beds, cooking facilities, spotless communal showers and toilets and there's an attendant who cleans the house, washes the dishes and makes fires.

To get to Main Camp, take the train from Bulawayo to Victoria Falls and get out at Dett Station. There's also a bus from Bulawayo to Victoria Falls on Monday, Wednesday and Friday which passes by Main Camp and the Safari Lodge.

KYLE RECREATIONAL PARK

Park HQ (tel 2913), Private Bag 9136, Masvingo. This is a popular resort area 32 km east of Masvingo and across the lake from the Great Zimbabwe ruins (it's 62 km around the lake to the ruins).

There are giraffes, white rhinos, wildebeest, kudus and impalas to be seen in the park. Horse rides are available for Z$4 for two hours together with a guide, but they tend to be heavily booked so it's useful to have your own transport.

Places to Stay

You can camp or rent self-contained thatched cottages which sleep three people for Z$10 per night.

MANA POOLS NATIONAL PARK

This park was described by one traveller as being the best game park in Africa after Ngorongoro Crater in Tanzania. Another person remarked that people drive all the way from South Africa to see it. One of the reasons is that you are free to walk anywhere your courage will take you, and the opportunities for animal photography are unique but you will not be allowed into the park in the first place unless you have transport.

The park is only open from 1 May to 31 October. You should book accommodation in advance through the National Parks office in Harare, though this isn't strictly necessary. There is no food for sale in the park or nearby, so you must bring all your own and/or catch fish (which is permitted).

Before entering the park you must check in at the office in Marongora on the main Chirundu-Harare road and get a permit. This is also a good place to wait for lifts. Try to avoid the school holiday period (August-September) as it can get quite crowded.

Places to Stay

The accommodation is mostly camping (officially Z$3 per night though you may get it for less). The main camping area is about 70 km from the park entrance through wild bush, so don't get dropped off before this if you are hitching. There are two lodges available for Z$20 per day which sleep up to eight people and have cooking facilities and a refrigerator. You'll come very close to game if camping - don't be surprised if you bump into elephants or lions when climbing out of your tent!

RHODES INYANGA NATIONAL PARK

Park HQ (tel Mutare 274), Private Bag T7901, Mutare. This is one of Zimbabwe's most popular parks and covers an area of 330 square km at altitudes ranging from 2000 to 2300 metres. It also encloses Mt Inyanga which, at 2592 metres, is Zimbabwe's highest mountain. Animals which you will come across are kudu, klipspringer, reedbuck, hyena, leopard and duiker. The park is open all year.

You can get as far as Inyanga village from Mutare by bus. There are beautiful views out over Mozambique. You can see most of the attractions on foot but it's also possible to rent horses for Z$4. Have warm clothes handy as it gets quite cold at night.

There is a daily local bus to this park from Mutare between 6.30 and 7 am; it returns sometime after 9 pm. The fare is Z$2.

Places to Stay

Lodges, chalets and camping are available. Chalets start at Z$7 per night. Camp site fees are Z$3 per night plus Z$1 if you want firewood. If you intend to camp, stock up on food in Mutare as the local store in Inyanga doesn't have much.

RHODES MATOPOS NATIONAL PARK

Park HQ (tel Matopos 0-1913), Private Bag K5142, Bulawayo. Some 32 km south of Bulawayo, the Matopo Hills consist of wind-sculpted granite hills and strange balancing rock formations alternating with cool, wooded valleys. They have been a place of retreat for centuries - first for the Bushpeople, who left a legacy of painted caves, and then for the Matabele, who fought a fierce rebellion here in the last years of the 19th century.

Game in the park is abundant and includes black and white rhino, giraffe, wart hog, leopard, eland, wildebeest and the world's largest concentration of black eagles. The park is open all year.

Also in the park is **Malindidzimu Hill**, otherwise known as **View of the World**, which is associated with local legends about benevolent spirits, and is the site of Cecil Rhodes' grave.

Horseback riding through the park is available at Z$4 per hour.

Places to Stay

There are four accommodation areas in all, with lodges, caravan and camp sites. The accommodation at Maleme Dam costs from Z$7 per night for lodges with four beds, kitchen and bathroom, to chalets without kitchen or bathroom for Z$4 per night.

LAKE MCILWAINE NATIONAL PARK

Park HQ (tel Norton 229), Private Bag 962, Norton. Forty km west of Harare on the Bulawayo road, this park (open year round) offers game viewing and boating. The game is mostly various species of antelope. Horses can be rented from the park officials.

Places to Stay

A lodge, chalets and camp sites are available. Cottages are for rent from Z$4.

VUMBA BOTANICAL RESERVE

Park HQ (tel Mutare 2127), Private Bag V7472, Mutare. This park is 32 km from Mutare along a steep, winding road in the middle of lush jungle and tea, coffee and banana plantations. It covers an area of 42 hectares of lush, virgin forest overlooking the Mozambique plains some 1000 metres below.

The reserve also includes the **Vumba Botanical Gardens** which consist of a landscaped area dissected by small streams which has been planted out with both indigenous and exotic plants from many parts of the world. The reserve is open all year and entry costs Z$1.

Places to Stay

The *Youth Hostel* has been closed but camping is available at Z$6 per site (up to six people). It's an excellent site with hot showers and a swimming pool and firewood is available for about Z$3. There's a vague possibility of staying at a boarding school at Vumba Heights, but don't count on it – ask for the warden.

For hotel accommodation you have the choice of the *Impala Arms* (tel Mutare 60722; PO Box 524), the *White Horse Inn* (tel 216612; PO Box 3193, Paulington) or the *Cotswold Cottage*. The last is the cheapest and is good value but they're all very popular with local Mutare residents so there's little chance of just turning up and finding a vacant room; book in advance by telephone. Hitching a ride with residents on their way there should be relatively easy. The Impala Arms costs Z$55 for bed and breakfast.

Index

MAPS

THANKS

Thanks to all the following people:

Peter Aawlak (Aus), Pete Abel & Debbie Ellen (UK), Chris Adam (D), Belle Adler (USA), Joe Adler & Marianne Allesso, Stewart Allen (F), Mickey Allen (Afr), Bill Allerey (UK), Waddi & Giffi Allertins-Kirkwood, Garreth Anderson (UK), Inger Andersson (Dk), Dave Andrew (UK), Karen Antrobus (C), Peter Arnold (UK), Kenneth Askey, Sylvie Askin (USA), Steve Askin (Zim), Tore Asmussen (Dk), Rob Atkins (UK), Brent Atkinson (USA), Thomas Austin (UK), M Ayland (UK), Helmut Bader (D), Rochelle Bagatell, Michael Ball (Aus), Sebastian Ballard (UK), Pete Bardoel (Nl), Richard Barker (UK), Bill & Delia Barkley, Shaun Baron (C), Rodney Bartlett (Aus), Bonnie Baskin (USA), Peter Beck (Aus), Bobbie C Bell (USA), Val Bell (Z), Gordon Benin, Bronwyn Benn (Aus), Garry Bennett (Sp), C Bennett, Martin Berkeley (UK), Jose Bernaerts (Nl), Thierry Berney (CH), Nancy Bernstein (USA), Karin Biemel (Aus), David & Anna Billington (Aus), Jan Birkemose (Dk), Robert Bisset (UK), Ruud Blacker (Nl), William Blatt (USA), Frans Blessing (Dk), Jane Bliss, Mr & Mrs Blomme (C), Anne Boardman (UK), Marie-Louise Boley, James Bonanno (Aus), Steve Bonosh (Aus), Susan Booy, Mike Brack (SA), Rachel Brand (USA), A Brandt (USA), Bernhard Braza (Aus), Francis Brendon (UK), Clarissa Bretherton (UK), Stuart Britton (UK), Carolyn Broadwell (USA), Julie Bromley (UK), David Brooks (USA), David Brown (UK), Joyce Brown (C), Celia Brown, Neil Bryan, Roelof Buffinga (Nl), Mick Bull, Glen Burgess (Aus), Dennis Burnham, Lynne Byrnes (Aus), Douglas Cairns (USA), Anita Calcraft (UK), Dean Callaway (C), Carol Camero (AFR), Graeme & Helena Campbell (Aus), Carol S Cancio, Piers Carey, Hans Carlsen (Sw), Timothy P Carlson (USA), John Carrier (Sw), Pete Carter (Aus), Sean-Cheryl Casey (USA), Sue Chamberlain (USA), Chris Chamberlain (USA), Trudy Chamberlain (UK), Michael Chambers (Aus), Delores Cheeks (C), Paul Chinnock (UK), John Cholod (USA), Glen Christian (Nl), Ben Churcher (Aus), Joseph Cislo, Kevin Clarke (USA), Palmore Clarke (USA), Margaret Coates (C), Hugh Cobbett (Afr), Trish Coffey (USA), Sonia Cogo (Aus), Gary Collinson (Aus), Scott Colmas (Isr), G P Cone (NZ), Tom Conklin (C), Kenneth Connolly (UK), Jacques Conrade, Paul Cook, Ted Cookson (USA), Tim & Lynn Corcoran (Aus), Ford Cottages (UK), Debra & John Courtney (UK), Andy Couturier (USA), Nigel Crawhall (C), Simon Criuick (UK), Les Cronk (USA), Charles Crouch (UK), Bonnie Cruse & Oliver Garus (C), Buster Culverwell, Steve Curney (C), Stephen Currie (Aus), Luca Daffara (I), Magnus Dahl (Sw), Torbjorn Dalasen (Sw), Tom & Helen Dale (Aus), Christo & Liz Danielsson (Sw), Diane Davey (Aus), B David (Sw), Jan G Davies (UK), Gill Davies (UK), Patrick Davis (Ire), Mark Davis & Kylie Griffin (USA), Bob Day (Aus), Andrew Dinwoodie (UK), G Dixon, Gisela Dobbeling (D), Michael Donkin (UK), Myra Donnelley (USA), Michael Doyle (Ire), Lisbeth Duehohn (Dk), Laurie Dunn (USA), Malcolm Dunn (C), Russell Eastough (UK), Michael Eddleston (UK), Anselm Eglseder (D), Bill Eldridge (UK), Dave Else (UK), Peter Engbers (Nl), Ernest Jr Eschenlohr, P D Everett (Aus), Laura Fanell, Bradley Farr, Simon Farrell (UK), Adam Faull (UK), Geoffrey Faust (USA), Grahame Ferguson (UK), Louise Ferguson, Kevin Flesher & Laura Farrell, Jes Ford & Alison Lescure (UK), Peter Forster (UK), Per Frederiksen (Dk), Anna Fredriksson (Sw), Hans Friederich, Eliese Friesenborg, Henrik Frost (Sw), Michael & Karen Fry (Aus), Regina Fugmann (Lux), Klaus Fuhrmann (D), Julie Galbraith, Tony Gallagher (Aus), James Gardner (UK), Anne & Geoff Gardner (Aus), Mark Garland (UK), Leah Garrett (USA), Renzo Garrone (I), Mark Gauthier (C), Gilles Gautier, Geoff Gedden (UK), M W Gegory (UK), Johan Gertsson (Sw), Fabrizio Giuffrida (I), Rob Glastra (Nl), Martin Gleave (NZ), Heather Glenn (USA), Lesliey Godferey (SA), G M Gooden, Edward Goss (USA), Till Gottbrath (D), Carl Goulding (UK), Nick Gowlland, Sylvie Goyet (F), Jonathon Green (UK), Rhonda Green (C), Eric Grist (UK), C D Groppa (USA), Michael Grossband (UK), Michael Grossbard (Aus), E Grossmith (C), Brenda Grove (USA), Duncan Guy (SA), David Gwinn (USA), Lee Hass, Bob Hackett (USA), David Haettenschwille (USA), Jessica Hahn (USA), S Hall (UK), Roger Hallhag (Sw), Jarmo Hamalainen (Fin), Frank Hamersley (UK), Mrs J Hamersley (Aus), Tilman Hamilton (USA), Sue Hancock (Aus), Leif Hange (USA), Bjarne Stig Hansen (Dk), Henrik Juhl Hansen & Claus Pederson (Dk), Jim Harding (UK), A Harrison (UK), Kate Harrison, David & Carol Hart (USA), Jack Hart (NZ), Carole Hartley (C), Frank Hartman (D), Donald Hatch (Nl), Soren V

Hausen (Dk), Richard Haycraft (UK), Eve Hebert (C), C Hedges (UK), Colin Henchan (Ire), Frans Hendriks (Nl), Brian Henriksen, Irene Hewwit (Ire), Pieter Van Der Heyde (Nl), Richard Hill (UK), Lydia Hill (USA), Angela Hill (Aus), Mark Hilton (UK), Horst Hocke (D), Michael Hoffman, Gerrit Holtland (Nl), Bob Holtzapple (USA), Kevin Hopkins, Nick Hopkinson, Adrian Horsman, Adrian Horsman (Ire), Mike Huffman, Damon Hurst, Richard Hyder (UK), Angela Hynes (USA), E & A Immelman (SA), Peter Iversen (Dk), Shahbab Jaabir, Rick & Debbie Jacob (C), Daniel Jacobs (UK), Tom Jager (Nl), Vincent Jansen (Nl), Rune Mark Jargensen (Dk), Kevin Jay (Aus), Gert-Owe Jehander (Sw), Jan Jennings (USA), Bernard Jennings, Hanne Jespersen (Dk), Mrs K G Jeynes (UK), Ken Jeynes (UK), Michael Johansson (Dk), Mark Jones (Aus), Bridgette Jones (UK), Jodie de Jonge (USA), Dan Judge (USA), Claus B Juhl (Dk), Per Jutterstrom (Sw), Safia Kabraji (UK), Kim Kanger (Sw), Pradeep Kapadiva (USA), Kas Vaneirsel (Nl), Judy Katz (USA), Mary KaVanagh (NZ), Wilfred Kearse Jr (USA), John Kelly (Aus), Chris Kelly & Daniel Selby (UK), Martin Kemp & Vanessa White, Oliver Kempe (Sw), Judy Kendall (UK), Judy & Neil Kennedy (NZ), Jeff Kennedy (USA), Susan Kennett (Aus), Michael Kerrisk, Timothy KeVane, Riaz Khan (UK), Edna King (Aus), Mayfield G H Kinzer, John Kleeman (UK), Roderick Knight (USA), Wolfgang Koeth (D), Ville Korkee (Fin), Christian Korsgaard (Dk), Susan Kotchonoski, Paul Kratzer, Karl-Christian Kristensen (Dk), J G M Krol (Nl), Jan Kucera (USA), Ditler Kudsk-Jorgensen (Dk), Joachim Kuelken (UK), Maureen Kujawski (USA), Glenn Russell (USA), Edna June Kurz, Elly Laanen (Nl), Janet Lack (UK), Ian Lackington (UK), Charles Henry Landon, I Larivers, Bob Lassen (NZ), Anthony Laude (UK), Mike Lees (UK), Henning Lege (D), Tony Leisner (USA), Charlie Leonard (USA), Markus Lethipou (F), Krista Lewis (SA), Stuart Liakin (UK), Charles Link, Naomi Linzer (USA), Marie Lippens (Bel), Brian Lloyd (NZ), Bill Lockhart, Wilko Lokhorst (Nl), Josephine Long (UK), G D Long (UK), Christopher Lorenzen, Erich Luckerbauer (A), Richard Luff (UK), Robert Lukesch (Aus), Jan Luoik (SA), Sharon Lyons (C), B Macrae (Aus), M Magnus (UK), Mary Mahon (UK), A R Marriot, Michelle Marshall (Aus), Nicola Mather (UK), Steve Matson (USA), A Matthews (UK), Chris Matuszek (UK), Castelli Maurizio (I), Con Maxwell (Ire), Louisa Mayock (USA), Ian McDonnell (C), Peter McFarlane (UK), Mike McGully (USA), C McInnes (UK), Rob McKenzie (C), Ricky N McLean (NZ), Richard Meares (UK), H T Meechan (UK), Sylvia Mercer (UK), Doug Michie (USA), Keith Miller, Dr Peter Mills (UK), Mike Milner (SA), Scott Milsom (C), Zahayron Mojhede (USA), Susanne Moller, Lothar Moltgen (F), Dan Monroe, Layton Montgomery (USA), Kate Morgan, Richard Morgan (UK), Philip Morrice (UK), Trevor Morrison (Aus), Karl-Heinz Mosthav, Peter Mouldey (C), Els Mourits (Nl), Michiel Van Overbek (Nl), B Munday (UK), Werner Murgg (Aus), Ilse Mwanza, Christian Naef (CH), Martin Neinhuis (Nl), Phil Nelson (UK), Albert Nesdale (UK), Martha Neuman (USA), Paul Neumann (CH), Bob Newman (USA), Per Munk Nielsen (Dk), Martin Nienhuis (Nl), Nick North, Kathleen Northrop (USA), Franco Ntambi, Mrs Ogiwie (Dk), Brian Ojay, Jim Oldham (Sp), Lise Olsen (USA), Anders Olsson (Sw), Dean Oman (USA), Eric Onstad, T Van Ooyen (Nl), Clive Oppenheimer (UK), Virginia Orr, Anne Ossig (D), Michael Van Overbeek (Nl), John Ovink (Nl), Richard Page (UK), Denzil Paine (UK), Piet Pals (Nl), C Parker (USA), David Parkinson (Aus), Charles Pascoe (Aus), Ronald Pater (Nl), Chris Paterson (USA), Roger Pawling (UK), Karen Peachey (UK), Robert Pearson (Aus), Peter Penczer (USA), Terry Peter (Aus), Paul Petercell (USA), Ulf M Petersen (Aus), Elaine Plaisance (USA), Ina Postma (Nl), Barbara & Jomasz Potkanski (Pol), Jenny Preston (UK), Ben Price (USA), Patrick Price, Rodney Prider (Aus), M Pritchard, Jean Putnam (USA), Cornelia Rapp & P Chirwa, Michel L Stella Ravelomanantsoa, Joshna Ray (UK), Monica Raymond (USA), Matti Remes (Fin), H Richards (UK), Colin T Richardson, Dr Neil Riley (UK), Christopher Ritter (USA), Paul Roberts (UK), Jonathan Roberts (UK), Jane Roberts (UK), Elizabeth Robinson (USA), Anne Robinson, Kerry Rollo (UK), Sonia Roschnik, Ian Rose (UK), Chris Rowe (Aus), Lucy Royle (UK), Janice Ruhl, Nick Rumney (Aus), C J Rushin-Bell, Anton Rysoyk (Nl), Gregory Salter (UK), Sam Bacon (UK), Paul Sargent (USA), Tom Sawyer (Aus), K Sayer, Thomas Schaumberger (A), Leonard Scheurkogel (Nl), Tim Schey (USA), Anya Schiffrin (UK), Keegan Schmidt (USA), Threes Schreurs (Nl), Anita Schwager & Hans Schwegler (CH), C M Senecal (C), Enzo Sentuti (I), Barry Sesnan, Katie Seward

(UK), Tahir Shah (UK), Penni Shambrook (UK), Peter Shannon (Aus), Barry Shanon (Isr), M M O Sharbal, Matthew Shaw (UK), Eric Sheffield (UK), Doug Shemin (USA), Simon Shepheard (UK), D Sherry (UK), Steve Sherwood (UK), Ilan Shimshoni (Isr), Christopher Shingleton (UK), Russel Shor (USA), Laura Silvani (Sp), Sam Simm (UK), Jane Simm (UK), Ruben Simm (UK), L Simwanda, John Skelly (USA), Gary Sladek (USA), Philip Slater, Renate Slot & Arend Mosterd (Nl), Brian Smart (USA), Nick Smedley (UK), Mark Smith (USA), Stuart & Liz Smith, Bev Smith (USA), Michael Smyth (UK), Martien Van Soestbergen (Nl), Christian Sommer (Dk), Julain Spicer (UK), Susan Starbird (USA), Marc Steegen (Bel), Tom Stephenson, G H Stonehurst (Aus), Lyn Strahm-Minich (USA), V Straight (NZ), Sandra Stuart (UK), Gerard Sturt (Aus), Val Surch, Scott Surgent (USA), Bob Swain (UK), Wombat Tahanga (Aus), Meile Tamminga (Nl), Rusling Tan (C), Gerhard Tanew (Aus), Barry Taylor & Tony Reavley (USA), Vincent Tempelman (USA), Craig Terrens (Aus), Philip Thimodo, David Thomas (UK), Caroline Thomas (UK), R & A Thompson (USA), Michael Thompson (UK), William Thomson (C), S Tissot (C), S Torneman & D Wagner, Peter Torres (USA), Finn Traff (Dk), Steve Trott (UK), Patrick Turkey (USA), Wendy Turnbull, Glyn Turner (USA), Hans Tversjell (Nl), Julie Urenn (UK), Michael Uzlman (USA), K D Vaitha, Jos Van Baal (Nl), M Van den Berg (Nl), Jos Van der Palen (Nl), J & V Van der Veur (Aus), Robert Van der Weij (Nl), Marja Van Dorp (Nl), Lode Vauderemenlen, Bill Veach (USA), J H Verschuur (Nl), Major D Viccous (UK), Massimo Viegi (I), J W Vink (Nl), Patrick Von Scheele (Sw), Markus Wagner (Aus), Nicole Walker (Aus), Nona Walker (UK), Kevin Wallace (Aus), Basil M A Waloff (UK), Thomas Walsh, Gretchen Walsh (USA), Lilian Wardell (Ire), Jenny & Col Warren (Aus), Gary Wawler, Eric Wear (UK), Nicolas Weir (UK), Eric A Wessman (USA), Jim Wetterer (USA), Ian Whatmore (UK), Paul Wheatley, Sharon Wheatley (UK), Jill Whitcomb (USA), John Whitney (Aus), John Wightman (SA), Robert Wilkinson, Andrew Wilkinson (C), Tom Wimber, James Wright (UK), Pat Yale (UK), Jose Yanes (Sp), Gary Zaret (USA), Claudia Zeilek (D), Karen Zischke (USA), Mike Zissler (Aus).

A – Austria, Aus – Australia, Bel – Belgium, C – Canada, Ch – Switzerland, D – West Germany, Dk – Denmark, Fin – Finland, Fr – France, I – Italy, Ire – Ireland, Isr – Israel, Lux – Luxemburg, Nl – Netherlands, NZ – New Zealand, SA – South Africa, Sp – Spain, Sw – Sweden, UK – United Kingdom, USA – United States of America, Zim – Zimbabwe

CURRENCY CHART

country	currency	abbreviation
Algeria	Algerian dinar	AD 10
Angola	kwanza	Kz 10
Benin	CFA franc	CFA 10
Botswana	pula	P 10
BIOT	pound sterling	UK£10
Burkina Faso	CFA franc	CFA 10
Burundi	Burundi franc	BFr 10
Cameroun	CFA franc	CFA 10
Cape Verde	escudo	Es 10
CAR	CFA franc	CFA 10
Chad	CFA franc	CFA 10
Comoros	Comoran franc	CFr 10
Congo	CFA franc	CFA 10
Djibouti	Djibouti franc	DFr 10
Egypt	Egyptian pound	E£10
Equatorial Guinea	CFA	CFA 10
Ethiopia	birr	Birr 10
Gabon	CFA franc	CFA 10
Gambia, The	dalasi	Da 10
Ghana	cedi	C 10
Guinea	Guinean franc	GFr 10
Guinea-Bissau	peso	P 10
Ivory Coast	CFA franc	CFA 10
Kenya	Kenyan shilling	KSh 10
Lesotho	maloti	Ml 10
Liberia	Liberian dollar	L$10
Libya	Libyan dinar	LD 10
Madagascar	Malagasay franc	MFr 10
Malawi	kwacha	Kw 10
Mali	CFA franc	CFA 10
Mauritania	ouguiya	UM 10
Mauritius	Mauritian rupee	MRs 10
Morocco	dirham	Dr 10
Mozambique	metical	Me 10
Namibia	rand (South Africa)	R 10
Niger	CFA franc	CFA 10
Nigeria	naira	N 10
Réunion	French franc	FFr 10
Rwanda	Rwandan franc	RFr 10
São Tomé & Principe	dobra	D 10
Senegal	CFA franc	CFA 10
Seychelles	Seychelles rupee	SRs 10
Sierra Leone	leone	Le 10
Somalia	Somali shilling	SSh 10
South Africa	rand	R 10
Spanish North Africa	peseta	Ptas 10
Sudan	Sudanese pound	S£10
Swaziland	emalangeni	E 10
Tanzania	Tanzanian shilling	TSh 10
Togo	CFA franc	CFA 10
Tunisia	Tunisian dinar	TD 10
Uganda	Ugandan shilling	USh 10
Zaïre	zaïre	Z 10
Zambia	kwacha	Kw 10
Zimbabwe	Zimbabwe dollar	Z$10

Temperature

To convert °C to °F multiply by 1.8 and add 32

To convert °F to °C subtract 32 and multiply by ·55

Length, Distance & Area

	multiply by
inches to centimetres	2.54
centimetres to inches	0.39
feet to metres	0.30
metres to feet	3.28
yards to metres	0.91
metres to yards	1.09
miles to kilometres	1.61
kilometres to miles	0.62
acres to hectares	0.40
hectares to acres	2.47

Weight

	multiply by
ounces to grams	28.35
grams to ounces	0.035
pounds to kilograms	0.45
kilograms to pounds	2.21
British tons to kilograms	1016
US tons to kilograms	907

A British ton is 2240 lbs, a US ton is 2000 lbs

Volume

	multiply by
Imperial gallons to litres	4.55
litres to imperial gallons	0.22
US gallons to litres	3.79
litres to US gallons	0.26

5 imperial gallons equals 6 US gallons
a litre is slightly more than a US quart, slightly less
than a British one

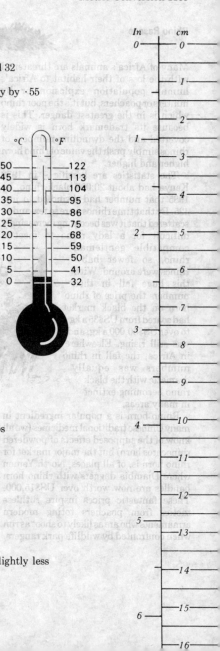

Rhino Rescue

Many of Africa's animals are threatened with the loss of their habitat to Africa's human population explosion or by hunters or poachers, but it's the poor rhino which is in the greatest danger. This is because its trademark horn is widely coverted and the dwindling numbers of rhinos simply push the value of rhino horn higher and higher.

The statistics are horrific – in 1970 Kenya had about 20,000 black rhino, by 1985 that number had dwindled to just 425. By that time rhinos were so few and so scattered that it was becoming increasingly difficult for a lady rhino to meet a compatible gentleman rhino, so fewer baby rhinos were around. With this huge fall in their numbers the price of rhino horn on the black market had soared from US$35 a kg to over US$30,000 a kg, and was still rising. Elsewhere in Africa, the fall in rhino numbers was equally dramatic with the black rhino becoming extinct in many areas.

Rhino horn is a popular ingredient in many Chinese traditional medicines (we all know of the supposed effects of powdered rhinoceros horn) but the major market for rhino horn is, of all places, North Yemen where Djambia daggers with rhino horn handles are now worth over US$15,000. These fantastic prices inspire ruthless tactics from poachers toting modern armaments who are as likely to shoot as run when confronted by wildlife park rangers.

The only viable way of saving rhinos seems to be establishing small parks where they can be carefully watched and protected. Rhino Rescue, an organisation set up in 1986 specifically to save the rhino, funded the first manageable rhino sanctuary at Nakuru National Park in Kenya. The 144 square km park is now protected by a 74 km electric fence with guard posts every 15 km. (The construction includes over 11,000 fence posts and 880 km of high tensile wire needing daily checking.) An initial group of 19 rhino was established and the park could eventually support 60 rhinos.

Additional sanctuaries are planned, but saving the rhino isn't going to come cheap. Donations can be sent to Rhino Rescue, PO Box 1, Saxmundham, Suffolk IP17 3JT, England.

Dear traveller

Prices go up, good places go bad, bad places go bankrupt...and every guidebook is inevitably outdated in places. Fortunately, many travellers write to us about their experiences, telling us when things have changed. If we reprint a book between editions, we try to include as much of this information as possible in a Stop Press section. Most of this information has not been verified by our own writers.

We really enjoy hearing from people out on the road, and apart from guaranteeing that others will benefit from your good and bad experiences, we're prepared to bribe you with the offer of a free book for sending us substantial useful information.

Thank you to everyone who has written and, to those who haven't, I hope you do find this book useful – and that you let us know when it isn't.

Tony Wheeler

Conservation is still a big issue in Africa. One of the biggest problems has been the poaching of the rapidly decreasing herds of elephants and rhinos, especially in Kenya and Tanzania. These two nations led the world in baning all trade in ivory. Now however, some leading conservationists like Richard Leakey and the nations concerned have realised that most countries can not sustain elephant herds beyond present levels due to lack of roaming and grazing land. Thus, the policy of a worldwide ban is coming up for review.

Travel is restricted in Ethiopia, Somalia, Angola, Mozambique, southern Sudan, Rwanda, Liberia, Mali, Western Sahara (occupied by Morocco) and across the Mauritania-Senegal border, due mostly to civil wars.

On the economic front things are not much better. Most countries have financial difficulties and rampant inflation which, apart from making the poor poorer, are also partly to blame for increased crime rates.

Recession is affecting the tourist industry worldwide and Africa is no exception. Less people are travelling and as a result airlines and hotels are offering plenty of good bargains.

In the last couple of years a few African nations have established or have been in the process of forming some type of democratic governments, mainly due to local popular pressure.

The following section was compiled using information sent to us by these travellers: Marina Abegolo (Aus), Robert J Abel (UK), Beth Blue (USA), Martin Bohnstedt (D), Andrew Borg (Aus), Ann Brooks (UK), Brierley (SA), Tim Brunsdon, Louise Burton (Aus), Mark Chipperfield (Aus), David Collins (UK), Steve Coyle (USA), Kathryn Cuvelier (F), C Danielsson (Sw), Mike Davis (UK), Lisa Doan (USA), Paul Ferguson (Aus), Alena Gomez (USA), Louise Hackney (USA), Kate Hannaford & Simon Walker (UK), J P Heida, Rob van Hobeemen (Nl), Paul Hodgson (UK), Jan Ippen (Nl), Jan Kucera (USA), Dr A Lane (UK), M Leong (UK), Cosmo Lush (UK), Fergus Mahon (UK), E J McDaid (SA), George Musser (USA), Marc Nathan & Ingola Conze (SA), Mike Naylor, Penny & Rachel (UK), J & A Pritchard (UK), C Rasch (Nl), Susie Rockwell (UK), Ole Saalmann (D), Nigel Sawyer (UK), Magnus Seger (Sw), P L Shinnie (C), Thomas Siffer (B), U & O Siljeholm (Sw), S Sleeman & S France (NZ), Malcolm Solamano & Samantha

Monk (Aus), Dan Spedding (Aus), Doug Strachan (NZ), Bob le Sueur, Len Sullivan (USA), Daniel Suther, Mrs H Thompson (UK), T K A Turner (UK), Lieve Youques (B), Petar Vuckovic (Ju), Cathy Zavis & Andrew Subin (USA).

Visas & Permits

Algeria All nationalities now require a visa. It takes two weeks to issue a visa in Rabat, Morocco, and it costs UK£5. British citizens can only obtain their visa in the UK. A single entry visa costs £35 and a multiple entry visa costs £60. It is necessary to pay upfront, and then after an interview a week later, you may get a visa. If you do not, the Algerians keep the money.

It is illegal to take Algerian currency out of the country. You can deposit any unused currency with the customs officers who will give you a receipt and, apparently, you'll get it back if you return to Algeria within the following 12 months.

Benin You can now only obtain 48-hour visas for Benin. It takes two days to get these visas in Niamey, Accra or Abidjan. Apparently, you can apply for an extension of up to one month at the immigration office in Cotonou.

White tourist cards are no longer necessary but exit visas are required by everyone. These are obtained from the immigration office. They are issued within 48 hours, free of charge, Monday to Friday.

Burkina Faso All nationalities now require visas for Burkina Faso. Visas are no longer issued at the French Embassy in Mali. They are now issued at the French Ambassador's residence. Take a taxi to the Hippodrome, turn left at the Belle Italia restaurant, take the 3rd dirt road on the right and you'll see the residence on the right-hand side. A three month entry visa costs CFA 6000 and is issued in two or three hours.

CAR Several travellers informed us that it is no longer possible to obtain CAR visas at the French Embassy in Lomé (Togo), Lagos (Nigeria) or Niamey (Niger), which is a problem considering that Cameroun will not issue visas without an ongoing visa!

They finally obtained their visas in Yaoundé by first going to the Consular Affairs Office in the Bastos district and obtaining the text of a telex requesting a visa. They took this telex to Intelcam (which is opposite the post office in town) and sent it to Bangui for CFA 950. A reply was received in less than 48 hours. They then paid CFA 200 to collect the reply and took it to the embassy in Yaoundé. They had to fill out one form, pay CFA 2500 and wait 24 hours. No photos were necessary.

Congo When leaving Congo by plane or ferry to Kinshasa an exit permit is required. You have to apply for it in the morning at immigration and you pick it up at 3 pm. It is free. You must show a receipt from a hotel stating that your lodging has been paid for. One traveller obtained the exit permit and then left Congo via M'Binda on the border with Gabon. No one asked to see her exit permit!

Egypt To extend your visa you must have US$180 in bank receipts. One way around this is to convert American Express travellers' cheques into cash dollars at the Nile Hilton.

Ghana Visas are now valid for a 30-day stay and cannot be renewed except in Accra. The Immigration Department is no longer in the Ministry of Interior building but in an office of its own just off Independence Ave and not far from the Canadian High Commission. There is a sign on the main road showing its location.

Foreigners must now register with immigration within 48 hours of arrival. The necessary forms are given out by immigration officers on arrival at the airport. You must also re-register in every district you travel through.

Guinea Visas are difficult to obtain. Apparently in some places, such as Dakar,

Senegal, they will not issue one for you. If you go to the embassy don't mention that you're a tourist as they don't like that. Either say you're visiting friends or studying. Normally, they'll give you a transit visa or a 15-day visa. If you are lucky, they'll give you a *certificat d' hébergement*, which allows you to stay with the Guinean friend who invited you.

Some travellers wrote and said that they were lucky to obtain a one month visa with the help of a German businessman and a GFr 100 tip for the Guinean Consul.

In Bissau, a visa for Guinea costs GFr 100. It is possible to extend your visa in Conakry, but you need plenty of money and a high-ranking official for a friend.

Lesotho A visitor's visa is no longer required for Lesotho. Lesotho now maintains its own diplomatic mission in Johannesburg. The address is 8th floor, 130 President St, Johannesburg.

Caledonspoort is a much easier border crossing point than Maseru Bridge to enter Lesotho. The South African authorities will not allow anyone into Lesotho via Sani Pass unless they are in 4WD vehicles.

Mali Photo permits are not required anymore. If the Mopti police ask you for a photo permit, they are only trying to make extra cash for themselves. You do need a permit to visit Mopti, Timbuktu and some other places. Apparently, they are available from the police office for CFA 1000.

Mozambique In South Africa you can get your visa for Mozambique from the Mozambique Labour Department (tel (011) 834 2119), 29 Market St, Johannesburg. The visa application form costs R 0.50. You need two photographs and photocopies of the first two pages of your passport. Presently, the only method of entering Mozambique safely from South Africa is to fly in. Your visa specifies the port of entry which will be Maputo International Airport.

Namibia Australians do need visas. Visa applications can be made to Miss van Rooy (tel 061 3989111, fax 223 817), Department of Civil Affairs, Windhoek, Namibia. You can fax passport details and state how long you wish to stay. Visas are issued for 14 days and can be extended in Windhoek for up to two months in three days. Crossing the border into Namibia is free of hassles.

Senegal According to the Senegalese Consulate in Rotterdam, it is advisable to obtain a visa for Senegal as travellers will have problems if they are not carrying one. The departure tax is CFA 4000.

Sierra Leone The Sierra Leone Consulate in Gambia has moved. Ask anyone to tell you where it is – it's easy to find. The consulate staff have taken it upon themselves to charge non-African Commonwealth citizens for their visas and permits. They are supposed to be free. Australians and New Zealanders have to pay Da 50 and British citizens have to pay Da 240! On challenging these charges, you will be shown a phoney receipt book and told that people have been paying for their visas since 1985. Everywhere else, visas for Sierra Leone are free for Commonwealth citizens.

South Africa South African visas take one day to obtain in Lilongwe, Malawi, while in Harare they can take two to three weeks.

Sudan Currency forms now exist, and penalties are very high for unofficial money changing. The Sudanese get hanged for it. Permits are available for the following routes: Halfa-Dongola- Karima-Atbara, Wad Medami-Karela-Bur Sudan, Kosti-El Fasker (transit only) and Nyala-Am Dafod (this is the route from Sudan to Central Africa via CAR). All other areas including Jebel Marra, are off limits, as they are very dangerous due to tribal wars and robberies at gunpoint.

Tanzania Those nationalities not requiring a visa do need a visitor's pass to enter Tanzania, but it is necessary to obtain one before arrival if you are flying in. This is necessary for groups and individuals alike, otherwise bribes will have to be paid. A visitor's pass obtained in London is issued free of charge in five days.

Togo For a visa extension you require three forms, four photographs and a tax stamp worth CFA 1000. This stamp can be obtained from a building next door to the Chamber of Commerce.

Tunisia Australian citizens are now able to obtain a one month visa on entry at the Tunisian border.

Uganda We have had a report that travellers with a vehicle had to pay US$80 cash to get across the border into Uganda. The customs officials didn't accept a Carnet de Passage.

Zimbabwe Currency declaration forms have now been introduced. They should be filled out and stamped whenever you're changing money, and given to the customs on departure.

Temporary work permits for six to 12 months are relatively easy to obtain in certain professions (geologists, teachers, engineers, computer analysts, etc) in Harare.

Zaïre Visas for Zaïre are very expensive in Cameroun, but much cheaper in CAR.

Health
Malaria is rampant in Malawi and Kenya, especially in Lamu. Many people get it even when taking their malaria tablets. It is recommended to use nets and repellants, as some people have died from malaria. Chloroquine and Paludrine seem to be ineffective against many new strains of malaria. Larium is a new malaria tablet that is effective against these strains. Only one tablet per week is recommended – the cost is quite high at US$94 for twelve months supply.

Fansidar should not be used as a prophylactic. It has many dangerous side effects and has been taken off the market in several countries. Fansidar should only be

used as a cure for malaria if Nivaquine (or its equivalent) does not work.

Bilharzia can be hard to recognise as in many cases it is not painful. In many people the symtons of bilharzia appear as an allergy and they get treated for their allergy rather than for bilharzia.

One traveller wrote and told us about some traditional cures for diarrhoea. Coca-cola apparently contains a good balance of water, salt and sugar. Let it stand for a while first so the gas escapes. Another cure is to swallow the kernels of a papaya fruit. Apparently, drinking broth is very good if you've been sweating a lot.

Dangers & Annoyances
Warning A 24 year old American woman, travelling through West Africa on her own in a 1976 Toyota Landcruiser, was murdered by a man from Kumasi, Ghana. The suspect was apprehended and he admitted to murdering the woman, stealing all her possessions and trying to withdraw US$10,000 from her bank account in England.

According to the woman's parents, the US Embassy in Burkina Faso was not interested in helping to find out what happened to their daughter, even though they knew of her disappearance.

Women travellers should beware if invited into the immigration office at Parmelap, on the Guinean side of the Sierra Leone border. We have heard that the officer working there uses proposal methods that are far from traditional! Also be cautious of Lebanese traders on the lookout for eligible foreign women to marry their sons.

We have received a report of a missionary stopping on a forested road in Kenya to see if the person lying in the middle of the road needed assistance. The missionary was attacked and beaten by a group of people, and his wife was killed. With violent crime increasing greatly in Nairobi, people driving in the countryside and to the national parks should be careful where and why they stop.

Fighting continues in northern Ethiopia. Asmara, Eritrea, Tigray and Gondar are out of bounds. It's also difficult to visit Lalibela, Dire Dawa and Harrar. You can travel in the country south of Addis Ababa.

There is also fighting in the Buba Mountains in Sudan. Many villages have been burned and people have been killed. Bandits from Chad sometimes raid villages at Jebel Marra, not far from the Chad-Sudanese border.

In Egypt, people caught with drugs will be jailed. There are several foreigners in Egyptian jails serving sentences for drug possession.

Early in 1991, rebels invaded Rwanda from Uganda and they are still in Ruhengeri and Parc National des Volcans. The situation is far from stable. It is recommended to check the situation out in Kigali before you proceed any further. The border with Uganda was also closed.

The road between Lilongwe (Malawi) and Lusaka (Zambia) via Chipata is still not safe due to attacks by Mozambique rebels along this road. Don't hitch or travel along these roads after dark.

Casamance, in southern Senegal, is not safe at the moment because of rebel attacks on the roads.

Travelling in the eastern highlands of Zimbabwe, especially in Chimanimani National Park, is still dangerous due to land mines that have been indiscriminately laid along the border areas.

Crime, especially thefts and muggings, are on the increase. Many travellers have notified us that places that used to be free of crime or were relatively safe have become quite dangerous, especially at night.

There have recently been a lot of violent attacks on and thefts from tourists all over Cameroun. In Yaoundé, the grounds of the Presbyterian Mission (Foyer International) are now extremely dangerous at night. If arriving at night take a taxi to the door.

In Ghana, there are lots of pickpockets working at the airport in Accra and at markets, slashing or snatching bags. The Senegalese capital, Dakar, is becoming increasingly unsafe day or night. Incidents of purse snatching, pick pocketing and armed robbery and violence appear to be increasing. Many of the hustlers and hawkers are obnoxious and threatening to tourists. Some travellers recommend even hiring a guide for the day if you plan to walk around the city.

Be very careful in Harare, Zimbabwe. Thefts and assaults on travellers by mobs are occurring every day in broad daylight.

No matter where you travel, you hear of travellers being ripped off. Luckily, many of them let us know straight away so that we can pass the news on to you. A few people have written to us regarding a scam in Nakuru, Kenya. Several people have lost hundreds of shillings by paying to have 'leaking brakes' repaired. Apparently, when they see a car driven by a foreigner, someone from the petrol station pours oil or some other substance on the ground under the vehicle, when it is stationary, and then points it out to the driver who often believes there really is a leak of some sort.

Recently we've had a few people complaining about having to pay bribes to government officials. One traveller claimed that the Cameroun police refused to let the ferry from Nigeria dock after 6 pm unless they were paid a large bribe. Everyone on the boat refused to pay and, consequently, had to spend the night in the mangrove swamp. Apparently, Nigerian and Cameroun police were asking for bribes on the ferry. Just pretend you don't have any naira or CFA and you will probably be ignored.

In Ghana, you are not allowed to drive a car with foreign number plates. They are quite strict about this law. The Ghanian police receive a low wage and so bribing is very common. They usually ask for C 50 to C 100.

In Mali, the border guards are always hunting for bribes and might try to find something wrong with your vaccination card. If necessary, you can bribe them with a couple of cigarettes.

One traveller said immigration officials

at the Zongo border point in Zaïre demanded a 'first entry fee' of CFA 5000. Unfortunately, they had to pay or they wouldn't have been allowed to enter the country.

The police and military in Guinea-Bissau are apparently asking travellers to change money with them instead of the bank; if you refuse they might even ask to see your money. It is advisable to carry as little cash across the border as possible.

In Niger it takes a long time of bargaining and dealing to sell a car. Be careful when dealing with prospective buyers, as some will try to sell you anything or ask for gifts, money or meals in a restaurant, and then they disappear before finalising a deal that they never planned to make – they only wanted to get as much out of you as they could.

A very common trick in Tanzania is to approach a traveller and claim to be a student trying to go to Europe to study and needing money. If the traveller parts with some money, he/she is approached by men claiming to be plain-clothes policemen and is asked to pay a fine because it is illegal to give money to local people. Another traveller informed us he was confronted with the same trick in Senegal.

We have heard many stories of travellers who have stayed at the *Saad Hotel* in Kasese, Uganda. The story is always the same. Travellers who stay at the hotel are threatened by the police with imprisonment to extort bribes.

ACROSS THE SAHARA

In early 1991, the only way to leave Algeria from its southern border was from Tamanrasset to In Guezzam/Assamaka and then to Arlit in Niger. The route from Algeria to Mali and Mauritania was closed. We have been informed by a traveller that it is possible to go from Morocco to Algeria by train.

CAMEROUN

A reservation on a train for a couchette is always necessary ahead of time. It is a different matter with 1st class tickets, as there isn't always a 1st class carriage available and

no one can tell for certain if one will be available. It is advisable to buy a 2nd class ticket instead of a 1st class one and if there is a 1st class carriage then pay the difference for 1st class on the train itself. Otherwise, you may buy a 1st class ticket only to find there is no 1st class car. Watch out for thieves who reach into the windows as trains are pulling away from stations.

EGYPT

Several travellers reported that upon arriving at Cairo Airport they were conned into paying for organised tours as they were incorrectly told that now Egypt was unsafe to travel in. This information is false as Egypt is safe to travel in, and you are best advised to avoid all people offering such services.

We've heard that getting on the ferry from Nuweiba to Aqaba is a long and complicated process. Anyone taking the ferry should not fall into the trap of joining the long queue of Egyptians lined up outside the port gate. You should head straight into the building inside the gate to the right. There you go through customs, then passport control, before waiting for ages until you are allowed to go to another building to purchase your ticket. At the ticket office, you'll probably be told to go to the nearest bank and change enough foreign currency to buy a ticket for E£35.50. You have to return to the ticket office with the money and a bank receipt. If you already have the cash insist on paying with that.

Travellers' Tips & Comments

If you want to have a camel ride to the oasis in Dahab, you need to pay the police E£ for registration papers. So when bargaining for the price of the ride, make sure the cost includes the police registration fee. The total cost will be around E£20.

Mark Milton – UK

Five of us paid E£110 for a two day and two night trip on a felucca from Aswan to Edfu. They tell you it will be three full days, but since they sail all night it is not even two full days. We left on a Monday at 2 pm and arrived on Wednesday morning at 9 am. We didn't want to sail through the night but either they wouldn't listen or didn't understand what we were saying. We met several other people who had the same experience.

Judith Wolford – USA

GAMBIA

There is now an air carrier called Gambia Air Shuttle which operates regular flights to Dakar and Ziguinchor in Senegal, Bissau in Guinea-Bissau, Sal in Cape Verde, Conakry in Guinea and Bamako in Mali. Prices start at Da 400.

The airport departure tax at Yumdum Airport has been increased to Da 70 per person and you have to pay in US dollars or UK pounds.

GUINEA-BISSAU

Prices in Bissau have tripled and inflation has risen accordingly. The price for petrol is about Fr 7, and it's hard to find.

KENYA

Encashment slips are issued when changing money. These are needed at time of departure if you require to convert your Kenyan shillings back into hard currency. Prices have risen considerably in Kenya. The airport departure tax is now US$20.

The ferries on Lake Victoria at the moment have discontinued their service between Kenya and Tanzania.

In Kenya crime also seems to be increasing. Many people are being robbed or mugged during all hours of the day and night in Nairobi. Even the local street hawkers and entertainers will warn you against going out at night. Apparently, the bus from Nairobi to Lamu now carries an armed guard due to past attacks by Somali bandits. Travellers should not walk alone at night in the streets or on the beaches in Kenya. We have had many reports of rapes and other attacks on the beach in Lamu.

The old GPO in Nairobi has closed and is being demolished. You'll have to buy stamps at the post office in Ronald Ngala St, or at the old parcel post office in Haile Selassie Ave. Post Restante mail can be collected at the old parcel post office.

Travellers' Tips & Comments

I would like to comment on what it can be like for two single women in Lamu. We are well seasoned travellers and are not easily intimidated, however, we found Lamu extremely discomforting. During the day, 90% of the people in the streets are men. In the evening, this rises to 99%. Due to the high unemployment rate, all the men are hanging around, many trying to make money by directing tourists to a particular dhow captain or guest house proprietor. It is very uncomfortable to be the only women in the street, especially as the streets are not lit at night, with men making plenty of comments as you pass by.

Beware of dhow captains, guest house proprietors and others who want payment in advance for services. We paid for a dhow ride that could never have occurred because of the tide. Of course, deposits are not refundable.

We hate to sound harsh, but basically everyone in Lamu was money hungry for tourist dollars.

A Mall & U Song – USA

LIBERIA

Liberia has suffered an extremely bloody civil war, which has practically turned the whole country upside down. The nation is still divided by two of the rebel groups that defeated Doe's regime and by the West African multinational peace keeping force. Liberia's economy is in tatters, and the nation is having difficulties forming a government because of differences between the two rebel groups. Travel into the country is not advisable due to the unstable situation.

MALI

The northern border to Mali was closed as a result of the conflicts the country was having with Tuareg in 1990. Check the latest information before visiting the area.

MAURITANIA

The Mauritanian Embassy in Dakar, Senegal, is closed because of tensions between the two countries. In 1990, due to the problems Mali was having with the Tuareg nomads along its northern border, and Mauritania's ongoing dispute with Senegal in the southern part of the country, it was difficult if not impossible to reach Mauritania by land. The flights between Dakar and Nouakchott have stopped as well. The only way of getting into Mauritania from Senegal was by travelling to Banjul, Gambia, and taking the plane from there.

It should also be noted that alcohol is prohibited in Mauritania.

MOZAMBIQUE

There is a large military presence in Maputo. You have to be very careful where you walk. Outside any military installation a yellow line is printed on the pavement, two metres from the wall. You must keep outside this line or you'll be arrested. Carry your identification papers at all times.

NAMIBIA

The recent UN-supervised elections in Namibia resulted in the victory of SWAPO – a leftist Black nationalist movement that fought a guerrilla war against South Africa for 23 years. An impressive 98% of eligible voters turned out for the election.

There has been a significant increase in prices since independence. The entrance fee for all national parks is R 5 per vehicle and R 5 per adult. Camping costs R 25 per night, for up to eight people. All the parks have bungalows or other facilities such as set-up tents or mobile homes. Reservations for all parks can be made in advance in Windhoek at the Nature Conservatory on Kaiser (Independence) St near the main post office.

It appears to be quite difficult to hitch in Namibia, as there is very little traffic on the roads. The only exception is around national parks, as long as it is possible to meet people with cars and arrange lifts with them to other parks or other tourist sights.

NIGERIA

Departure tax for international flights is N 50. It is forbidden to take niara out of the country. Beware of airport officials who try to extort bribes from you.

Prices have skyrocketed recently, and the naira has been devalued even further, making Nigeria a very cheap country to travel in. In Kano, the government Tourist Camp has a legal moneychanger on the premises, with the best rates for cash in the country.

SOMALIA

President Barre was defeated by several rebel groups from all over the country. The nation is facing a difficult task of forming a government with the different rebel groups, and reviving the faltering economy. Thus, the country might be slowly opening up for travelling.

SOUTH AFRICA

There are only five youth hostels in South Africa and very little alternative cheap accommodation except for campsites. Anyone not travelling with a tent is going to find life very expensive as you'll be lucky to find a hotel charging less than R 80 to R 100 per night.

TANZANIA

It is compulsory to change US$40 on arrival in Zanzibar, even if arriving from Dar es Salaam. Passports, declaration forms and vaccination certificates are also checked. In early 1991, there was only one boat that plied the route between Zanzibar and Mombassa, Kenya.

The exchange rate on the black market is double the official one. Be careful if you intend to use the black market as there are a lot of undercover police officers working with moneychangers. In Namanga, on the Kenya-Tanzania border, there is a common confidence trick. Frequently you will be approached and told that there is no bank in Namanga and will be offered Tanzanian shillings for Kenyan shillings. Don't change money with these people as you will be ripped off. There is a bank on the Tanzanian side of the border in Namanga.

A warning to anyone who is going to climb Mt Kilimanjaro. We have had a complaint that porters and guides demand their tips before the descent from the top of the mountain. If they don't receive the amount requested, they threaten not to carry anyone's backpacks down.

Travellers' Tips & Comments

In Zanzibar, it is difficult to find rooms in hotels, even if you turn up early. Poverty is such that you pay extra for most things. You will probably be told that buses or trains are full unless you pay extra.

Jake Evans – UK

THE ROAD TO MALAWI

There is still a seven km walk to the border from the junction where you get off if you come on the bus from Dar Es Salaam or the minibus from Kyela. Try not to cross the border late in the day or on a Sunday. There is hardly any traffic on a Sunday.

We received a letter from some Swedish travellers who took the bus from Mbeya to the border at Kyela. As everyone was fighting for seats, they decided to pay someone to get theirs. During the trip, things were stolen from the bags on the top of the bus. They complained that Tanzanian border officials took some of their money. Money was also confiscated from a Polish guy who was body searched. He lost US$100 because his currency declaration form was not in order. We've heard that the officials will always manage to find a fault with something in order to extract some money from you.

UGANDA

Declaration forms still have to be filled out at the border, although no checks are apparently made on the amount declared.

Ugandan customs officials wear plain clothes, so be respectful to the suspicious looking person who wants to rummage through your pack!

In Kampala it is now possible to change money in 'For-Ex Bureaux' for a better rate than in the banks, but not outside the capital. Consequently the banks in the countryside have no competition and their rates are not realistic. It is a similar case with black market rates, which decrease the further you go from Kampala. Only US dollars are accepted on the black market.

ZAÏRE

Travellers have told us that you need to show an onward ticket when entering Zaïre. We have had complaints about Kinshasa being an expensive and unpleasant city. Two English travellers said the police constantly tried to invent problems in order to bribe them. They (two women) would deal with the problem by calling local people over and asking them to explain exactly what the policeman was talking about. More often than not, the policeman would then disappear, seeing that he was only making problems for himself.

ZAMBIA

Generally, security is tight in Lusaka and there are many trigger-happy young soldiers, posted to rural areas, who spend their time making life difficult for foreigners. They can be dangerous if their authority is challenged. Always carry your passport with you. Never show interest in (or knowledge of) public installations, military tanks, etc. One traveller wrote that one unwritten rule is that you do not walk on the pavement in front of the main post office in Lusaka! Make sure you ask for permission before taking any photographs.

Lonely Planet Guidebooks

Lonely Planet guidebooks cover every accessible part of Asia as well as Australia, the Pacific, South America, Africa, the Middle East and parts of North America and Europe. There are four series: *travel survival kits*, covering a single country for a range of budgets; *shoestring guides* with compact information for low-budget travel in a major region; *walking guides*; and *phrasebooks*.

Mail Order

Lonely Planet guidebooks are distributed worldwide and are sold by good bookshops everywhere. They are also available by mail order from Lonely Planet, so if you have difficulty finding a title please write to us. US and Canadian residents should write to Embarcadero West, 112 Linden St, Oakland CA 94607, USA and residents of other countries to PO Box 617, Hawthorn, Victoria 3122, Australia.

The Lonely Planet Story

Lonely Planet published its first book in 1973 in response to the numerous 'How did you do it?' questions Maureen and Tony Wheeler were asked after driving, bussing, hitching, sailing and railing their way from England to Australia.

Written at a kitchen table and hand collated, trimmed and stapled, *Across Asia on the Cheap* became an instant local bestseller, inspiring thoughts of another book.

Eighteen months in South-East Asia resulted in their second guide, *South-East Asia on a shoestring*, which they put together in a backstreet Chinese hotel in Singapore in 1975. The 'yellow bible' as it quickly became known to backpackers around the world, soon became *the* guide to the region. It has sold well over ½ million copies and is now in its 6th edition, still retaining its familiar yellow cover.

Today there are over 80 Lonely Planet titles – books that have that same adventurous approach to travel as those early guides; books that 'assume you know how to get your luggage off the carousel' as one reviewer put it.

Although Lonely Planet initially specialised in guides to Asia, they now cover most regions of the world, including the Pacific, South America, Africa, the Middle East and Eastern Europe. The list of *walking guides* and *phrasebooks* (for 'unusual' languages such as Quechua, Swahili, Nepalese and Egyptian Arabic) is also growing rapidly.

The emphasis continues to be on travel for independent travellers. Tony and Maureen still travel for several months of each year and play an active part in the writing, updating and quality control of Lonely Planet's guides.

They have been joined by over 50 authors, 40 staff – mainly editors, cartographers, & designers – at our office in Melbourne, Australia, and another 10 at our US office in Oakland, California. Travellers themselves also make a valuable contribution to the guides through the feedback we receive in thousands of letters each year.

The people at Lonely Planet strongly believe that travellers can make a positive contribution to the countries they visit, both through their appreciation of the countries' culture, wildlife and natural features, and through the money they spend. In addition, the company makes a direct contribution to the countries and regions it covers. Since 1986 a percentage of the income from each book has been donated to ventures such as famine relief in Africa; aid projects in India; agricultural projects in Central America; Greenpeace's efforts to halt French nuclear testing in the Pacific and Amnesty International. In 1990 $60,000 was donated to these causes.

Lonely Planet's basic travel philosophy is summed up in Tony Wheeler's comment, 'Don't worry about whether your trip will work out. Just go!'